87%

of college students report that access to learning analytics can positively impact their learning experience.

75%

of students using adaptive technology report that it is "very helpful" or "extremely helpful" in aiding their ability to retain new concepts.

"I can honestly say that the first time I used SmartBook after reading a chapter I understood what I had just read better than I ever had in the past."
– Nathan Herrmann, Oklahoma State University

"I really enjoy how it has gotten me engaged in the course and it is a great study tool without having to carry around a heavy textbook."
– Madeline Uretsky, Simmons College

Professors spend:

Less time on administrative tasks

72%

90%

More time on active learning

"Connect keeps my students engaged and motivated. Requiring Connect assignments has improved student exam grades."
– Sophia Garcia, Tarrant County College

Mc Graw Hill Education

Because learning changes everything.™

To learn more about Connect History visit the McGraw-Hill Education American History page: www.mhhe.com/history

EXPERIENCE
HISTORY

INTERPRETING AMERICA'S PAST

NINTH EDITION

James West Davidson

Brian DeLay
UNIVERSITY OF CALIFORNIA, BERKELEY

Christine Leigh Heyrman
UNIVERSITY OF DELAWARE

Mark H. Lytle
BARD COLLEGE

Michael B. Stoff
UNIVERSITY OF TEXAS, AUSTIN

Mc
Graw
Hill
Education

EXPERIENCE HISTORY: INTERPRETING AMERICA'S PAST, NINTH EDITION

Published by McGraw-Hill Education, 2 Penn Plaza, New York, NY 10121. Copyright ©2019 by McGraw-Hill Education. All rights reserved. Printed in the United States of America. Previous editions ©2014, 2011, and 2008. No part of this publication may be reproduced or distributed in any form or by any means, or stored in a database or retrieval system, without the prior written consent of McGraw-Hill Education, including, but not limited to, in any network or other electronic storage or transmission, or broadcast for distance learning.

Some ancillaries, including electronic and print components, may not be available to customers outside the United States.

This book is printed on acid-free paper.

2 3 4 5 6 7 8 9 QVS 23 22 21 20 19

ISBN   978-1-259-54180-3 (bound edition)
MHID   1-259-54180-0 (bound edition)
ISBN   978-1-260-16451-0 (loose-leaf edition)
MHID   1-260-16451-9 (loose-leaf edition)

Senior Portfolio Manager: *Jason Seitz*
Lead Product Developer: *Dawn Groundwater*
Senior Product Developer: *Sara Gordus*
Marketing Manager: *Will Walter*
Content Project Managers: *Susan Trentacosti, Katie Reuter, Karen Jozefowicz*
Senior Buyer: *Laura Fuller*
Design: *Jessica Cuevas*
Senior Content Licensing Specialist: *Ann Marie Jannette*
Cover Image: *©McGraw-Hill Education*
Compositor: *Aptara®, Inc.*

All credits appearing on page or at the end of the book are considered to be an extension of the copyright page.

Library of Congress Cataloging-in-Publication Data

Names: Davidson, James West, author. | DeLay, Brian, 1971- author. | Heyrman,
    Christine Leigh, author. | Stoff, Michael B., author.
Title: Experience history : interpreting America's past / James West
    Davidson, Brian DeLay, University of California, Berkeley, Christine Leigh
    Heyrman, University of Delaware, Mark H. Lytle, Bard College, Michael B.
    Stoff, University of Texas, Austin.
Other titles: Interpreting America's past
Description: Ninth edition. | New York, NY : McGraw-Hill Education, [2019]
Identifiers: LCCN 2018026957| ISBN 9781259541803 (alk. paper) | ISBN
    1259541800 (alk. paper)
Subjects: LCSH: United States–History. | United States–History–Study and
    teaching.
Classification: LCC E178.1 .E94 2019 | DDC 973–dc23 LC record available at
https://lccn.loc.gov/2018026957

The Internet addresses listed in the text were accurate at the time of publication. The inclusion of a website does not indicate an endorsement by the authors or McGraw-Hill Education, and McGraw-Hill Education does not guarantee the accuracy of the information presented at these sites.

mheducation.com/highered

Brief Contents

Contents

AFTER THE FACT

9 THE EARLY REPUBLIC 1789–1824

AFTER THE FACT

10 THE OPENING OF AMERICA 1815–1850

11 THE RISE OF DEMOCRACY 1824–1840

12 AFIRE WITH FAITH 1820–1850

16 THE CIVIL WAR AND THE REPUBLIC 1861–1865

AFTER THE FACT

17 RECONSTRUCTING THE UNION 1865–1877

18 THE NEW SOUTH AND THE TRANS-MISSISSIPPI WEST 1870–1914

AFTER THE FACT

19 THE NEW INDUSTRIAL ORDER 1870–1914

20 THE RISE OF AN URBAN ORDER 1870–1914

21 REALIGNMENT AT HOME AND EMPIRE ABROAD 1877–1900

AFTER THE FACT

22 THE PROGRESSIVE ERA 1890–1920

23 THE UNITED STATES AND THE COLLAPSE OF THE OLD WORLD ORDER 1901–1920

24 THE NEW ERA 1920–1929

25 THE GREAT DEPRESSION AND THE NEW DEAL 1929–1939

26 AMERICA'S RISE TO GLOBALISM 1927–1945

AFTER THE FACT

27 COLD WAR AMERICA 1945–1954

28 THE SUBURBAN ERA 1945–1963

AFTER THE FACT

31 THE CONSERVATIVE CHALLENGE 1976–1992

32 THE UNITED STATES IN A GLOBAL COMMUNITY 1980–PRESENT

LIST OF
Maps and Charts

©Granger

How Do You Experience History?

The answer to that question requires an active verb. *Doing* history is not simply a matter of reading a narrative or memorizing a set of facts. That's because history is not merely "the past"; it's a reconstruction assembled from the past's raw materials. The history you make depends on how actively you've engaged with those materials.

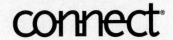

By nature, textbook programs strive to be comprehensive, smooth, and seamless. The narrative speaks with a single authoritative voice. But history doesn't consist of one voice; it has multiple voices, like our diverse nation. Historians must take into account the dialogues, disagreements, and diverse actors that all have been a part of American history.

In this text, we hope to show you those multiple voices. With our *After the Fact* essays, we reveal how historians grapple with the large themes that help make sense of the past. With our *Historian's Toolbox* feature, we explore how historians cross-examine all sorts of evidence, from diaries and newspapers to political cartoons and sheet music; from furniture and clothing to photographs and films. In short, this program is designed to let you *experience* history the way historians do.

Our narrative is further enriched by a comprehensive set of learning activities found in Connect History. By harnessing the power of Connect, your students will get the help they need, when and how they need it, so that your class time can be more rewarding for your students and you.

Primary Sources Help Students Think Critically about History

Primary sources help students think critically about history and expose them to contrasting perspectives of key events. The Ninth Edition of *Experience History* provides three different ways to use primary source documents in your course.

>> POWER OF PROCESS FOR PRIMARY SOURCES. Power of Process is a critical thinking tool for reading and writing about primary sources. As part of Connect History, McGraw-Hill Education's learning platform Power of Process contains a database of over 400 searchable primary sources in addition to the capability for instructors to upload their own sources. Instructors can then select a series of strategies for students to use to analyze and comment on a source. The Power of Process framework helps students develop essential academic skills such as understanding, analyzing, and synthesizing readings and visuals such as maps, leading students toward higher-order thinking and writing.

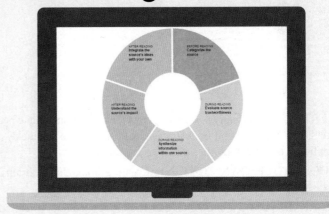

Power of Process for Primary Sources

Features that offer contrasting perspectives or showcase historical artifacts. Within the print or eBook, the Ninth Edition of *Experience History* offers the following features:

>> **MANY HISTORIES.** Two primary source documents offer contrasting perspectives on key events for analysis and discussion. Introductions and Thinking Critically questions frame the documents. For example, how did Spaniards and Aztecs differ in their account of first contact? Or, what were the arguments used to justify the internment of Japanese Americans during WWII, and how did they compare to the experiences of those imprisoned?

Many HISTORIES

WHO WAS TO BLAME FOR THE BOSTON MASSACRE?
Following the shootings in King Street, Captain Thomas Preston and six of his men stood trial for murder. Two radical patriot lawyers, Josiah Quincy Jr. and future President John Adams, served as defense council. Convinced that Boston must prove itself fair and faithful to the rule of law, both lawyers performed brilliantly. The jury acquitted Preston and four of the soldiers, and convicted two others of manslaughter. The depositions from the trial provide some of our best evidence for how soldiers and Bostonians viewed the standoff differently.

DOCUMENT 1
Deposition of Captain Thomas Preston, March 12, 1770

The mob still increased and were more outrageous, striking their clubs or bludgeons one against another, and calling out, come on you rascals, you bloody backs, you lobster scoundrels, fire if you dare, G-d damn you, fire and be damned, we know you dare not, and much more such language was used. At this time I was between the soldiers and the mob, parleying with, and endeavouring all in my power to persuade them to retire peaceably, but to no purpose. They advanced to the points of the bayonets, struck some of them and even the muzzles of the pieces, and seemed to be endeavouring to close with the soldiers. On which some well-behaved persons asked me if the guns were charged. I replied yes. They then asked me if I intended to order the men to fire. I answered no, by no means, observing to them that I was advanced before the muzzles of the men's pieces, and must fall a sacrifice if they fired; that the soldiers were upon the half cock and charged bayonets, and my giving the word fire under those circumstances would prove me to be no officer. While I was thus speaking, one of the soldiers having received a severe blow with a stick, stepped a little on one side and instantly fired, on which turning to and asking him why he fired without orders, I was struck with a club on my arm, which for some time deprived me of the use of it, which blow had it been placed on my head, most probably would have destroyed me. On this a general attack was made on the men by a great number of heavy clubs and snowballs being thrown at them, by which all our lives were in imminent danger, some persons at the same time from behind calling out, damn your bloods—why don't you fire. Instantly three or four of the soldiers fired, one after another, and directly after three more in the same confusion and hurry. The mob then ran away, except three unhappy men who instantly expired, in which number was Mr. Gray at whose rope-walk the prior quarrels took place; one more is since dead, three others are dangerously, and four slightly wounded. The whole of this melancholy affair was transacted in almost 20 minutes. On my asking the soldiers why they fired without orders, they said they heard the word fire and supposed it came from me. This might be the case as many of the mob called out fire, but I assured the men that I gave no such order; that my words were, don't fire, stop your firing. In short, it was scarcely possible for the soldiers to know who said fire, or don't fire, or stop your firing.

Source: www.famous-trials.com/massacre/270-evidence

DOCUMENT 2
Deposition of Robert Goddard

The Soldiers came up to the Centinel and the Officer told them to place themselves and they formed a half moon. The Captain told the Boys to go home least there should be murder done. They were throwing Snow balls. Did not go off but threw more Snow balls. The Capt. was behind the Soldiers. The Captain told them to fire. One Gun went off. A Sailor or Townsman struck the Captain. He thereupon said damn your bloods fire think I'll be treated in this manner. This Man that struck the Captain came from among the People who were 7 feet off and were round on one wing. I saw no person speak to him. I was so near I should have seen it. After the Capt. said Damn your bloods fire they all fired one after another about 7 or 8 in all, and then the officer bid Prime and load again. He stood behind all the time. Mr. Lee went up to the officer and called the officer by name Capt. Preston. I saw him coming down from the Guard behind the Party. I went to Gaol the next day being sworn for the Grand Jury to see the Captain. Then said pointing to him that's the person who gave the word to fire. He said if you swear that you will ruin me everlastingly. I was so near the officer when he gave the word fire that I could touch him. His face was towards me. He stood in the middle behind the Men. I looked him in the face. He then stood within the circle. When he told 'em to fire he turned about to me. I looked him in the face.

Source: www.bostonmassacre/hesteltrial/6goddard.htm.

THINKING CRITICALLY

Preston and Goddard come to different conclusions about the shootings but describe similar details (the snowballs, the man who struck Preston). Can details from these two accounts be reconciled? Do they simply have different perspectives on the same event, or do you think one of the depositions must be misleading? Given the tensions these accounts relate, do you think that a violent confrontation between soldiers and Bostonians was inevitable?

Historian's TOOLBOX

An Ancient Calendar

©Charles Walker/TopFoto/The Image Works

During summer solstice, the spiral is bisected by a single shaft of light. At the winter solstice, as shown here, sunlight shines at the outside edges of the spiral.

Why might the Chacoans have used a spiral rather than another image?

On a blazing hot summer day in 1977, Anna Sofaer climbed up to the top of Fajada Butte in Chaco Canyon, New Mexico, spotted three sandstone slabs resting carefully against a wall, and walked over to investigate. What she saw against the wall astounded her: a spiral glyph, bisected by a pure shaft of light. An artist and amateur archaeologist, Sofaer had keen interest in how indigenous American cultures harnessed light and shadow in their architecture. Knowing that it was nearly the summer solstice, she recognized instantly that she'd discovered an ancient Ancestral Puebloan calendar. Later research revealed that the device also marked the winter solstice, the summer and winter equinoxes, and the extremes of the moon's 18- to 19-year cycle (the major and minor standstills). These discoveries prompted still more research, and scholars now believe that there are structures throughout Chaco Canyon aligned to solar and lunar events.

THINKING CRITICALLY

What practical reasons might there have been to build these sorts of sun and moon calendars? Might there have been cultural, religious, or social purposes to track accurately the movements of the sun and moon?

>> **HISTORIAN'S TOOLBOX.** In each chapter, these feature boxes showcase historical images and artifacts, asking students to focus on visual evidence and examine material culture. Introductions and Thinking Critically questions frame the images.

>> **CREATE.** **Select primary source documents that meet the unique needs of your course.** No two history courses are the same. Using McGraw-Hill Education's Create allows you to quickly and easily create custom course materials with cross-disciplinary content and other third-party sources.

- **CHOOSE YOUR OWN CONTENT:** Create a book that contains only the chapters you want, in the order you want. Create will even renumber the pages for you!

- **ADD READINGS:** Use our American History Collections to include primary sources, or Taking Sides: Annual Editions. Add your own original content, such as syllabus or History major requirements!

- **CHOOSE YOUR FORMAT:** Print or eBook? Softcover, spiral-bound, or loose-leaf? Black-and-white or color? Perforated, three-hole punched, or regular paper?

- **CUSTOMIZE YOUR COVER:** Pick your own cover image and include your name and course information right on the cover. Students will know they're purchasing the right book—and using everything they purchase!

- **REVIEW YOUR CREATION:** When you are all done, you'll receive a free PDF review copy in just minutes! To get started, go to create.mheducation.com and register today.

MAP TOOLS TO PROMOTE STUDENT LEARNING

>> MAPPING THE PAST. This feature provides students with a map's historical context along with questions designed to develop map-reading skills as well as to launch an interpretive analysis of the map.

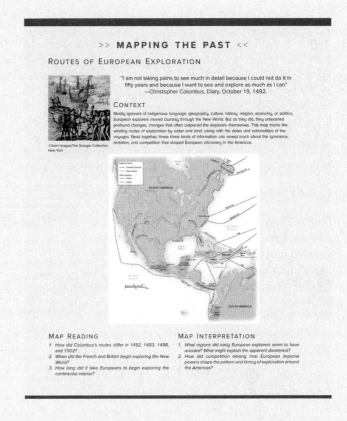

Using Connect History and more than 100 maps, students can learn the course material more deeply and study more effectively than ever before.

>> INTERACTIVE MAPS. Interactive maps give students a hands-on understanding of geography. *Experience History* offers over 30 interactive maps that support geographical as well as historical thinking. These maps appear in both the eBook and Connect History exercises. For some interactive maps, students click on the boxes in the map legend to see changing boundaries, visualize migration routes, or analyze war battles and election results. With others, students manipulate a slider to help them better understand change over time. New interactive maps feature advanced navigation features, including zoom, as well as audio and textual animation.

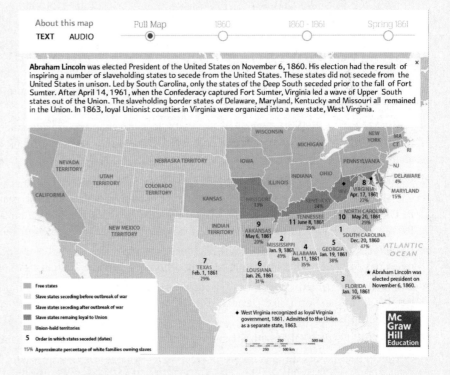

A complete list of maps can be found in a separate section of the frontmatter.

SmartBook 2.0 Tailors Content to the Individual Student

Available within Connect History, SmartBook has been updated with improved learning objectives to ensure that students gain foundational knowledge while also learning to make connections to help them formulate a broader understanding of historical events. SmartBook 2.0 personalizes learning to individual student needs, continually adapting to pinpoint knowledge gaps and focus learning on topics that need the most attention. Study time is more productive and, as a result, students are better prepared for class and coursework. For instructors, SmartBook 2.0 tracks student progress and provides insights that can help guide teaching strategies.

Contextualize History

Help students experience history in a whole new way with our new **Podcast Assignments**. We've gathered some of the most interesting and popular history podcasts currently available and built assignable questions around them. These assignments allow instructors to bring greater context and nuance to their courses while engaging students through the storytelling power of podcasts.

New Content in *Experience History*, 9e

>> A THEMATIC TIMELINE at the beginning of each chapter is a new feature that previews key events and the themes connecting them.

>> NEW MAP EXERCISES, "Mapping the Past," in most chapters provide students with a map's historical context and then take them through a series of questions designed to develop map-reading skills as well as to launch an interpretive analysis of the map.

>> CHAPTER BIBLIOGRAPHIES have been updated to reflect new scholarship.

>> CHAPTERS have been revised to reflect new trends in scholarship. For example, CHAPTER 7, THE AMERICAN PEOPLE AND THE AMERICAN REVOLUTION, includes a new section about the varied roles of women in the Revolutionary War, and the discussion of the contribution of the French in the war has been expanded.

>> CHAPTER 9, THE EARLY REPUBLIC, looks beyond America's shores to consider the significance of Caribbean slave rebellions to the early republic and the connection between the Haitian Revolution and the Louisiana Purchase.

>> CHAPTER 12, AFIRE WITH FAITH, includes expanded coverage of abolitionism reflecting the pivotal role played by free blacks in the North, like David Walker, in radicalizing the antislavery movement after 1830. The influence of British abolitionism is also discussed.

>> CHAPTER 13, THE OLD SOUTH, has added material on the Upper South and the domestic slave trade, reflecting new scholarship.

>> CHAPTER 18, THE NEW SOUTH AND THE TRANS-MISSISSIPPI WEST, features a new Historian's Toolbox, "Custer's Defeat, Indian Style," that analyzes the colored pencil-and-ink drawings of the battle by Red Horse, a Lakota Sioux Indian. The chapter has also added material clarifying the Dawes Severalty Act of 1887.

>> CHAPTER 19, THE NEW INDUSTRIAL ORDER, includes expanded coverage of the environmental costs of industrialization as well as additional material on the Homestead Steel Strike of 1892.

>> CHAPTER 20, THE RISE OF AN URBAN ORDER, adds new material on the gender transition from prim "young ladies" to more liberated "school girls," in the section on "Public Education in an Urban Industrial World."

>> CHAPTER 25, THE GREAT DEPRESSION AND THE NEW DEAL, provides a new Historian's Toolbox, "Wonder Woman, Women's Rights, and Birth Control," exploring the connections between Margaret Sanger and Wonder Woman's creator.

>> CHAPTER 30, THE VIETNAM ERA, expands coverage of the adverse environmental effects of the American escalation in Vietnam, changing riverine ecologies and cultural traditions.

>> CHAPTER 31, THE CONSERVATIVE CHALLENGE, features a new chapter introduction, "Born Again," profiling the rise of Jerry Falwell and his campaign to move evangelicals away from political quietism to support for Ronald Reagan.

>> CHAPTER 32, THE UNITED STATES IN A GLOBAL COMMUNITY, adds a new document to the chapter's Many Histories feature, "Our Changing Climate," from *The National Climate Assessment,* issued by the U.S. Global Change Research Program. This chapter also includes a new section, "A Divided Nation," on the election of 2016 and Donald Trump's economic, ethnic, and racial nationalism, put forward during his first years in office. There is discussion of the Paris Agreement on global warming; the attack on Obamacare; the passage of a new tax cut; and the controversy over Russian meddling in the election, Trump's firing of James Comey, and the appointment of Robert Mueller.

LIST OF
Author-Selected Primary Source Documents in Power of Process

Power of Process for Primary Sources is a critical thinking tool for reading and writing about primary sources. As part of Connect History, McGraw-Hill Education's learning platform, Power of Process contains a database of over 400 searchable primary sources in addition to the capability for instructors to upload their own sources. Instructors can then select a series of strategies for students to use to analyze and comment on a source. The Power of Process framework helps students develop essential academic skills such as understanding, analyzing, and synthesizing readings and visuals such as maps, leading students toward higher-order thinking and writing.

The following primary source documents, carefully selected by the authors to coordinate with this chapter, are available in the Power of Process assignment type within Connect History at http://connect.mheducation.com.

Chapter 1

1. Thoughts on Creation, from Native Peoples of New Netherlands
2. A Traveler from Virginia Viewing Indian Ruins in the Ohio Valley

Chapter 2

3. Excerpt from a Short Account of the Destruction of the Indies by Bartolomé de las Casas, 1542
4. A Spanish Conquistador Visits the Aztec Marketplace in Tenochtitlán

Chapter 3

5. A Virginia Settler Describes the Indian War of 1622 in England
6. An Act for the Apprehension and Suppression of Runaways, Negroes, and Slaves, Virginia, September 1672

Chapter 4

7. Mary Rowlandson's Narrative of Being Taken Captive by the Indians
8. A Puritan Wrestles with Her Faith

Chapter 5

9. George Whitefield Sermonizes on "The Eternity of Hell-Torments"
10. Franklin Attends Whitefield's Sermon

Chapter 6

11. Thomas Hutchinson Recounts the Destruction of His Home during the Stamp Act Riots
12. Thomas Paine Attacks Monarchy

Chapter 7

13. Abigail Adams Reports on the Fighting around Boston
14. A North Carolina Soldier Witnesses the Partisan War in the Southern Backcountry

Chapter 8

15. The Confederation Congress Passes the Northwest Ordinance
16. "An Aged Matron of Connecticut" Urges Women's Education

Chapter 9

17. George Washington Takes His Farewell
18. Tecumseh Responds to William Henry Harrison

Chapter 10

19. Moving On by Basil Hall
20. Lowell's Female Factory Workers Voicing Their Protests

Chapter 11

21. Margaret Bayard Smith on Andrew Jackson's Inauguration in 1828
22. Chief Justice Marshall Delivers the Supreme Court's Opinion in *The Cherokee Nation v. Georgia*

Chapter 12

23. Lyman Beecher Warns Against Roman Catholicism
24. Women Issue a "Declaration of Sentiments" from Seneca Falls

Chapter 13

25. A Southern Master Describes Disciplining His Slaves and Their Resistance
26. Nat Turner Explains His Motives

Chapter 14

27. The United States Promises to Save Mexico from Indian Raiders
28. Disappointment in the Gold Diggings

Acknowledgments

We would like to express our deep appreciation to the following individuals who contributed to the development of our U.S. history programs:

Melissa Anyiwo,
Curry College

Jeremiah Bauer,
Metropolitan Community College

Mark Ehlers,
United States Military Academy

Robert Galler,
St. Cloud University

Joshua Hammack,
Santiago Canyon College

Lisa Johnson,
Paris Junior College

Richard D. Kitchen,
New Mexico Military Insititute

Mary Lyons-Carmona,
Metro Community College

Walton P. Sellers III,
Louisiana State University, Eunice

Daniel Spegel,
Metropolitan Community College

Joanne Sundell,
Erie Community College

Melissa Weinbrenner,
Northeast Texas Community College

About the Authors

JAMES WEST DAVIDSON

RECEIVED HIS PH.D. FROM YALE UNIVERSITY. A historian who has pursued a full-time writing career, his works include *After the Fact: The Art of Historical Detection* (with Mark H. Lytle), *The Logic of Millennial Thought: Eighteenth-Century New England*, and *Great Heart: The History of a Labrador Adventure* (with John Rugge). He is co-editor with Michael Stoff of the *Oxford New Narratives in American History*, which includes his study *'They Say': Ida B. Wells and the Reconstruction of Race*. Most recently he wrote *A Little History of the United States*.

BRIAN DELAY

RECEIVED HIS PH.D. FROM HARVARD and is an Associate Professor of History at the University of California, Berkeley. He is a frequent guest speaker at teacher workshops across the country and has won several prizes for his book *War of a Thousand Deserts: Indian Raids and the U.S.-Mexican War*. His current book project, *Shoot the State*, explores the connection between guns, freedom, and domination around the Western Hemisphere, from the American Revolution through World War II.

CHRISTINE LEIGH HEYRMAN

IS THE ROBERT W. AND SHIRLEY P. GRIMBLE Professor of American History at the University of Delaware. She received her Ph.D. in American Studies from Yale University. The author of *Commerce and Culture: The Maritime Communities of Colonial Massachusetts, 1690-1750*, she received the Bancroft Prize for her second book, *Southern Cross: The Beginnings of the Bible Belt,* and the Parkman Prize for her third, *American Apostles: When Evangelicals Entered the World of Islam*. Her latest book,

forthcoming, is *Doomed Romance: A Story of Broken Hearts, Lost Souls and Sexual Politics in Nineteenth-Century America.*

MARK H. LYTLE

A PH.D. FROM YALE UNIVERSITY, is the Lyford Paterson and Mary Gray Edwards Professor of History Emeritus at Bard College. He served two years as Mary Ball Washington Professor of American History at University College Dublin, in Ireland. His publications include *The Origins of the Iranian-American Alliance, 1941-1953, After the Fact: The Art of Historical Detection* (with James West Davidson), *America's Uncivil Wars: The Sixties Era from Elvis to the Fall of Richard Nixon*, and most recently, *The Gentle Subversive: Rachel Carson, Silent Spring, and the Rise of the Environmental Movement*. His forthcoming book, *The All-Consuming Nation*, considers the tension between the post–World War II consumer democracy and its environmental costs.

MICHAEL B. STOFF

IS ASSOCIATE PROFESSOR OF HISTORY and University Distinguished Teaching Associate Professor at the University of Texas at Austin. The recipient of a Ph.D. from Yale University, he has been honored many times for his teaching, most recently with the University of Texas systemwide Regents Outstanding Teaching Award. In 2008, he was named an Organization of American Historians Distinguished Lecturer. He is the author of *Oil, War, and American Security: The Search for a National Policy on Foreign Oil, 1941-1947*, co-editor (with Jonathan Fanton and R. Hal Williams) of *The Manhattan Project: A Documentary Introduction to the Atomic Age*, and series co-editor (with James West Davidson) of the *Oxford New Narratives in American History*. He is currently working on a narrative of the bombing of Nagasaki.

An artist's reconstruction of the city of Cahokia, ca. 1100 CE, whose population may have reached 30,000. More than 100 flat-topped pyramidal mounds dominated the settlement. Note how tiny the human figures are in comparison to the temples built atop the mounds. The two tall poles at the center of the open plaza were where the important game of chunkey was played, as an illustration later in this chapter explains.

Courtesy of Cahokia Mounds State Historic Site, Collinsville, Illinois. Painting by William R. Iseminger

>> An American Story

THE POWER OF A HIDDEN PAST

Stories told about the past have power over both the present and the future. Until recently, most students were taught that American history began several centuries ago—with the "discovery" of America by Columbus, or with the English colonization of Jamestown and Plymouth. History books ignored or trivialized the continent's precontact history. But the reminders of that hidden past are everywhere. Scattered across the United States are thousands of ancient archaeological sites and hundreds of examples of monumental architecture, still imposing even after centuries of erosion, looting, and destruction.

Man-made earthen mounds, some nearly 5,000 years old, exist throughout eastern North America in a bewildering variety of shapes and sizes. Many are easily mistaken for modest

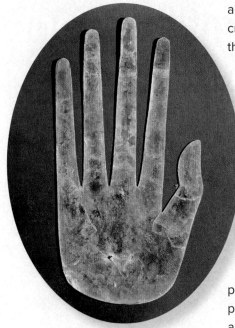

©Werner Forman/Universal Images Group/Getty Images

| *The skilled craftspeople of the Hopewell tradition worked most often with copper but made exquisite objects from a variety of materials. This image of a human hand, discovered in a Hopewell mound, was cut from a single sheet of mica.*

hills, but others evoke wonder. In present-day Louisiana an ancient town with earthworks took laborers an estimated 5 million work hours to construct. In Ohio a massive serpent effigy snakes for a quarter-mile across the countryside, its head aligned to the summer solstice. In Illinois a vast, earthen structure covers 16 acres at its base and once reached as high as a 10-story building.

Observers in the colonial and revolutionary eras looked on such sites as curiosities and marvels. George Washington, Thomas Jefferson, and other prominent Americans collected ancient artifacts, took a keen interest in the excavation of mounds, and speculated about the Indian civilizations that created them. Travelers explored these strange mounds, trying to imagine in their mind's eye the peoples who had built them. In 1795 the Reverend James Smith traced the boundaries of a mound wall that was strategically placed to protect a neck of land along a looping river bend in the Ohio valley. "The wall at present is so mouldered down that a man could easily ride over it. It is however about 10 feet, as near as I can judge, in perpendicular height. . . . In one place I observe a breach in the wall about 60 feet wide, where I suppose the gate formerly stood through which the people passed in and out of this stronghold." Smith was astonished by the size of the project. "Compared with this," he exclaimed, "what feeble and insignificant works are those of Fort Hamilton or Fort Washington! They are no more in comparison to it than a rail fence is to a brick wall."

But in the 1830s and 1840s, as Americans sought to drive Indians west of the Mississippi and then confine them on smaller and smaller reservations, many observers began thinking differently about the continent's ancient sites. Surely the simple and "savage" people just then being expelled from American life could not have constructed such inspiring monuments. Politicians, writers, and even some influential scientists instead attributed the mounds to peoples of Europe, Africa, or Asia—Hindus, perhaps, or Israelites, Egyptians, or Japanese. Many nineteenth-century Americans found special comfort in a tale about King Madoc from Wales who, supposedly shipwrecked in the Americas in the twelfth century, had left behind a small but ingenious population of Welsh pioneers who built the mysterious mounds before being overrun by Indians. Some observers even thought Indian skin boats resembled Welsh coracles, designs brought over by King Madoc. The Welsh hypothesis seemed to offer poetic justice, because it implied that nineteenth-century Indians were only receiving a fitting punishment for what their ancestors had done to the remarkable mound builders from Wales.

These fanciful tales were discredited in the late nineteenth and twentieth centuries. In recent decades archaeologists working across the Americas have discovered in more detail how native peoples built the hemisphere's ancient architecture. They have also helped to make clear the degree to which prejudice and politics have blinded European Americans to the complexity, wonder, and significance of America's history before 1492. At least 15,000 years of human habitation in North America allowed a broad range of cultures to develop, based on agriculture as well as hunting and gathering. In North America a population in the millions spoke hundreds of languages. Cities evolved as well as towns and farms, exhibiting great diversity in their cultural, political, economic, and religious organization. <<

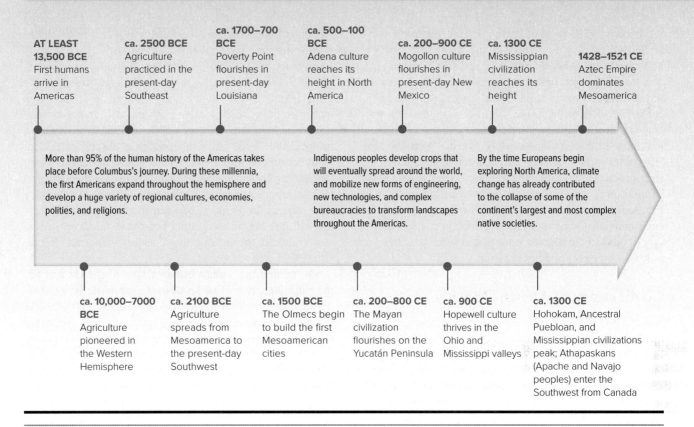

AT LEAST 13,500 BCE
First humans arrive in Americas

ca. 2500 BCE
Agriculture practiced in the present-day Southeast

ca. 1700–700 BCE
Poverty Point flourishes in present-day Louisiana

ca. 500–100 BCE
Adena culture reaches its height in North America

ca. 200–900 CE
Mogollon culture flourishes in present-day New Mexico

ca. 1300 CE
Mississippian civilization reaches its height

1428–1521 CE
Aztec Empire dominates Mesoamerica

More than 95% of the human history of the Americas takes place before Columbus's journey. During these millennia, the first Americans expand throughout the hemisphere and develop a huge variety of regional cultures, economies, polities, and religions.

Indigenous peoples develop crops that will eventually spread around the world, and mobilize new forms of engineering, new technologies, and complex bureaucracies to transform landscapes throughout the Americas.

By the time Europeans begin exploring North America, climate change has already contributed to the collapse of some of the continent's largest and most complex native societies.

ca. 10,000–7000 BCE
Agriculture pioneered in the Western Hemisphere

ca. 2100 BCE
Agriculture spreads from Mesoamerica to the present-day Southwest

ca. 1500 BCE
The Olmecs begin to build the first Mesoamerican cities

ca. 200–800 CE
The Mayan civilization flourishes on the Yucatán Peninsula

ca. 900 CE
Hopewell culture thrives in the Ohio and Mississippi valleys

ca. 1300 CE
Hohokam, Ancestral Puebloan, and Mississippian civilizations peak; Athapaskans (Apache and Navajo peoples) enter the Southwest from Canada

A CONTINENT OF CULTURES

IMMIGRANTS FROM ASIA ARCHAEOLOGICAL AND GENETIC EVIDENCE indicate that the first inhabitants of the Americas arrived from Siberia at least 15,500 years ago BP.* New evidence suggests that the first arrivals could even have come tens of thousands of years earlier than that. (For more details, see the After the Fact essay "Tracking the First Americans," at the end of the chapter). Gradually these **nomads** filtered southward, some likely following the Pacific coastline in small boats, others making their way down a narrow, glacier-free corridor along the eastern base of the Rocky Mountains and onto the northern Great Plains. There they found and hunted a stunning array of huge mammals, so-called megafauna. These animals included mammoths that were twice as heavy as elephants, giant bison, sloths that were taller than giraffes, several kinds of camels, and terrifying, 8-foot-long lions. Within a few thousand years the descendants of these Siberians, people whom Columbus would wishfully dub "Indians," had spread throughout the length and breadth of the Americas.

This first colonization of the Americas coincided with, and perhaps accelerated, profound changes in the natural world. The last Ice Age literally melted away as warmer global temperatures freed the great reservoirs of water once locked in glaciers. A rise in sea levels inundated the Bering Strait, submerging the land bridge, and creating new lakes and river systems. The emergence of new **ecosystems**—climates, waterways, and land environments in which humans interacted with other animals and plants—made for ever-greater diversity. The first human inhabitants of the Americas had fed, clothed, warmed, and armed themselves in part by hunting megafauna, and some combination of overhunting and climate change resulted in the extinction of most of these giants by the end of the Ice Age. As glaciers receded and human populations increased, the first Americans had to adapt to changing conditions. They adjusted by hunting smaller animals with new, more specialized kinds of stone tools and by learning to exploit particular places more efficiently.

*Before the Present, used most commonly by archaeologists when the time spans are in multiple thousands of years. This text will also use CE for Common Era, equivalent to the Christian Era or AD; BCE is Before the Common Era, equivalent to BC.

DIVERSIFIED SOCIETIES So it was that between 10,000 and 2,500 years ago distinctive regional cultures developed among the peoples of the Americas. Those who remained in the Great Plains turned to hunting the much smaller descendants of the now-extinct giant bison; those in the deserts of the Great Basin survived on small game, seeds, and edible plants; those in the Pacific Northwest relied mainly on fishing; and those east of the Mississippi, besides fishing and gathering, tracked deer and bear and trapped smaller game animals and birds. Over these same centuries, what seems to have been one original, common language evolved into regional dialects and eventually into a multitude of distinct languages. Linguistic diversity paralleled other sorts of divergences, in social organizations, kinship practices, politics, and religion. Technological and cultural unity gave way to striking regional diversity as the first Americans learned how to best exploit their particular environments. Glimpses of these profound changes may be found today in burials, stone tools, and some precious sites of long-term or repeated occupation.

Civilizations of Ancient Mexico

AGRICULTURAL REVOLUTION To the south, pioneers in **Mesoamerica** began domesticating squash 10,000 years ago. Over the next several thousand years farmers added other crops including beans, tomatoes, and especially corn to an agricultural revolution that would transform life through much of the Americas. Because many crops could be dried and stored, agriculture allowed these first farmers to settle in one place.

By about 1500 BCE, farming villages began giving way to larger societies, to richer and more complex cultures. As the abundant food supply steadily expanded their populations, people began specializing in certain kinds of work. While most continued to labor on the land, others became craftworkers and merchants, architects and artists, warriors and priests. Their built environment reflected this social change as humble villages expanded into skillfully planned urban sites that were centers of trade, government, artistic display, and religious ceremony.

OLMEC CITY-BUILDERS The Olmecs, the first city-builders in the Americas, constructed large plazas and pyramidal buildings, and sculpted enormous heads chiseled from basalt. The Olmec cultural influence gradually spread throughout Mesoamerica, perhaps as a result of their trade with neighboring peoples. By about 100 BCE, the Olmecs' example had inspired the flowering of Teotihuacán from a small town

©Adalberto Rios Szalay/Sexto Sol/Getty Images

in central Mexico into a metropolis of towering pyramids. The city had bustling marketplaces, palaces decorated with mural paintings that housed an elite of warriors and priests, schools for their children, and sprawling suburbs for commoners. At its height, around 650 CE, Teotihuacán spanned 15 square miles and had a population of nearly 200,000—making it the sixth-largest city in the world.

MAYAN CIVILIZATION More impressive still were the achievements of the Mayas, who benefited from their contacts with both the Olmecs and Teotihuacán. In the lowland jungles of Mesoamerica they built cities filled with palaces, bridges, aqueducts, baths, astronomical observatories, and pyramids topped with temples. Their priests developed a written language, their mathematicians discovered the zero, and their astronomers devised a calendar more accurate than any then existing. In its glory, between the third and ninth century CE, the Mayan civilization boasted some 50 urban centers scattered throughout the Yucatán Peninsula, Belize, Guatemala, and Honduras.

But neither the earliest urban centers of the Olmecs nor the glittering city-state of Teotihuacán survived. Even the enduring kingdom of the Mayas had collapsed by 900 CE. Like the ancient civilizations of Greece and Rome, they thrived for centuries and then declined. Scholars still debate the reasons for their collapse. Military attack may have brought about their ruin, or perhaps their large populations exhausted local resources.

AZTEC EMPIRE Mayan grandeur was eventually rivaled in the Valley of Mexico. In the middle of the thirteenth century the Aztecs, a people who had originally lived on Mesoamerica's northern frontiers, swept south and settled in central Mexico. By the end of the fifteenth century they ruled over a vast empire from their capital at Tenochtitlán, an island metropolis of perhaps a quarter of a million people. At its center lay a large plaza bordered by sumptuous palaces and the Great Temple of the Sun. Beyond stood three broad causeways connecting the island to the mainland; many other tall temples were adorned with brightly painted carved images of the gods, zoological and botanical gardens, and well-stocked marketplaces. Through Tenochtitlán's canals flowed gold, silver, exotic feathers and jewels, cocoa, and millions of pounds of maize—all trade goods and tribute from the several million other peoples in the region subjugated by the Aztecs.

Unsurpassed in power and wealth, in technological and artistic attainments, theirs was also a highly stratified society. The Aztec ruler, or Chief Speaker, shared

©Werner Forman/HIP/The Image Works

Aztec merchants, or pochtecas, *spoke many languages and traveled on foot great distances throughout Mesoamerica and parts of North America. Pictured at left is Yacatecuhtli, Lord Nose, the patron god of merchants. He carries a symbol of the crossroads, with bare footprints. The merchant on the right carries a cargo of quetzal birds.*

governing power with the aristocrats, who monopolized all positions of religious, military, and political leadership, while the commoners—merchants, farmers, and craftworkers—performed all manual labor. There were slaves as well, some captives taken in war, others from the ranks of commoners forced by poverty to sell themselves or their children.

Farmers, Potters, and Builders of the Southwest

MOGOLLON AND HOHOKAM PEOPLES Mesoamerican crops and farming techniques began making their way north to the American Southwest by 1000 BCE. At first the most successful farmers in the region were the Mogollon and the Hohokam peoples, two cultures that flourished in New Mexico and southern Arizona during the first millennium CE. Both tended to cluster their dwellings near streams, relying on either floodplain irrigation or a system of floodgates and canals to sustain their crops. The Mogollon came to be the master potters of the Southwest. The Hohokam pioneered vast and complex irrigation systems in arid southern Arizona that allowed them to support one of the largest populations in precontact North America.

THE ANCESTRAL PUEBLO Their neighbors to the north in what is now known as the Four Corners Region of Arizona, Colorado, New Mexico, and Utah, commonly referred to by the term Anasazi, are today more properly known as the Ancestral Pueblo peoples. The Ancestral Pueblo peoples adapted corn, beans, and squash to the relatively high altitude of the Colorado Plateau and soon parlayed their growing surplus and prosperity into societies of considerable complexity. Their most stunning achievements were villages of exquisitely executed

masonry buildings—apartment-like structures up to four stories high and containing hundreds of rooms at such places as Mesa Verde (Colorado) and Canyon de Chelly (Arizona). Villages in Chaco Canyon (New Mexico), the largest center of Ancestral Puebloan settlement, were linked to the wider region by hundreds of miles of wide, straight roads.

Besides their impressive dwellings, the Ancestral Pueblo people filled their towns with religious shrines, astronomical observatories, and stations for sending signals to other villages. Their craftworkers fashioned delicate woven baskets, beautiful feather and hide sashes, decorated pottery, and turquoise jewelry that they traded throughout the region and beyond. For more than a thousand years, this civilization prospered, reaching a zenith between about 900 and 1100 CE. During those three centuries, the population grew to approximately 30,000 spread over 50,000 square miles, a total area larger than present-day California.

Chiefdoms of the Eastern Woodlands

East of the Mississippi, Indian societies prospered in valleys near great rivers (Mississippi, Ohio, Tennessee, and

©George H. H. Huey/Alamy

The remains of Pueblo Bonito, one of the nine Great Houses built by Ancestral Puebloans in Chaco Canyon. By the end of the eleventh century, Pueblo Bonito stood four stories high at the rear and contained 800 rooms as well as many towers, terraces, a large central plaza, and several round "kivas" for religious and ceremonial purposes.

©Mary Evans Picture Library/The Image Works

| *Chunkey was the name of a small clay donut-like disk about the width of a human hand, the centerpiece of a game first made popular at Cahokia. The figurine, about 8 inches high, shows a player holding the chunkey in his right hand. It was rolled across a playing field while contestants chased it, taking aim with sticks. Over 600 years later the game was still being played by many Indian peoples, including the Mandan, who were depicted by artist George Catlin. The chunkey appears at lower right.*

©National Geographic Creative/Alamy

Cumberland), the shores of the Great Lakes, and the coast of the Atlantic. Everywhere the earliest inhabitants depended on a combination of fishing, gathering, and hunting—mainly deer but also bear, raccoon, and a variety of birds. Around 2000 BCE some groups in the temperate, fertile Southeast began growing the gourds and pumpkins first cultivated by Mesoamerican farmers, and later they also adopted the cultivation of maize. But unlike the ancient peoples of the Southwest, most Eastern Woodland peoples continued to subsist largely on animals, fish, and nuts, all of which were abundant enough to meet their needs and even to expand their numbers.

ADENA AND HOPEWELL   Indeed, many of the mysterious earthen mounds that would so fascinate Europeans were built by peoples who did not farm. About 1000 BCE, residents of a place now known as Poverty Point in northeastern Louisiana fashioned spectacular earthworks—six semicircular rings that rose 9 feet in height and covered more than half a mile in diameter. Although these structures might have been sites for studying the planets and stars, hundreds of other mounds—built about 2,000 years ago by the Adena and the Hopewell cultures of the Ohio and Mississippi valleys—served as the burial places of their leading men and women. Alongside the corpses mourners heaped their richest goods—headdresses of antlers, necklaces of copper, troves of shells and pearls—rare and precious items imported from as far north as Canada, as far west as Wyoming, and as far east as Florida. All these mounds attest powerfully not only to the skill and sheer numbers of their builders but also to the complexity of these ancient societies, their elaborate religious practices, and the wide scope of their trading networks.

MISSISSIPPIAN CULTURE   Even so, the most magnificent culture of the ancient Eastern Woodlands, the Mississippian, owed much of its prominence to farming. By the twelfth century CE these peoples had emerged as the premier city-builders of North America, and their towns radiated for hundreds of miles in every direction from the hub of their trading network at Cahokia, a port city of perhaps 30,000 located directly across from present-day St. Louis at the confluence of the Missouri and Mississippi Rivers. Cahokia's many broad plazas teemed with farmers hawking their corn, squash, and beans and with craftworkers and merchants displaying their wares. But what commanded every eye were the structures surrounding the plazas—more than 100 flat-topped pyramidal mounds crowned by religious temples and the palaces of rulers.

Life on the Great Plains

MIGRATORY PEOPLES   Cahokia's size and power depended on consistent agricultural surpluses. Outside the Southwest and the river valleys of the East, agriculture played a smaller role in shaping North American societies. On the Great Plains, for example, some people did cultivate corn, beans, squash, and sunflowers, near reliable rivers and streams. But more typically plains communities relied on hunting and foraging, migrating to exploit seasonally variable resources. Plains hunters pursued game on foot; the horses that had once roamed the Americas became extinct after the last Ice Age. Sometimes large groups of people worked together to drive the buffaloes over cliffs or to trap them in corrals. The aridity of the plains made it a dynamic and unpredictable place to live. During times of reliable rainfall, bison populations boomed, hunters flocked to the region, and agricultural communities blossomed along major rivers. But sometimes centuries passed with lower-than-average precipitation, and families abandoned the plains for eastern valleys or the foothills of the Rocky Mountains.

Survival in the Great Basin

Some peoples west of the Great Plains also kept to older ways of subsistence. Among them were the Numic-speaking peoples of the Great Basin, which includes present-day Nevada and Utah, eastern California, and western Wyoming and Colorado. Small family groups scoured their stark, arid landscape for the limited supplies of food it yielded, moving with each passing season to make the most of their environment. Men tracked elk and antelope and trapped smaller animals, birds, even toads, rattlesnakes, and insects. But the staples of their diet were edible seeds, nuts, and plants, which women gathered and stored in woven baskets to consume in times of scarcity. Several families occasionally hunted together or wintered in common quarters, but because the desert heat and soil defied farming, these bands usually numbered no more than about 50 people.

The Plenty of the Pacific Northwest

The rugged stretch of coast from the southern banks of present-day British Columbia to northern California has always been an extraordinarily rich natural environment. Its mild climate and abundant rainfall yield forests lush with plants and game; its bays and rivers teem with salmon and halibut, its oceans with whales and porpoises, and its rocky beaches with seals, otters, abalone, mussels, and clams. Agriculture was unnecessary in such a bountiful place. From their villages on the banks of rivers, the shores of bays, and the beaches of low-lying offshore islands, the ancestors of the Nootkans, Makahs, Tlingits, Tshimshians, and Kwakiutls speared or netted salmon, trapped sea mammals, gathered shellfish, and launched canoes. The largest of these craft, from which they harpooned whales, measured 45 feet bow to stern and nearly 6 feet wide.

SOCIAL AND CEREMONIAL DISTINCTIONS By the fifteenth century these fecund lands supported a population of perhaps 130,000. They also permitted a culture with the leisure time needed to create works of art as well as an elaborate social and ceremonial life. The peoples of the Northwest built houses and canoes from red cedar; carved bowls and dishes from red alder; crafted paddles and harpoon shafts, bows, and clubs from Pacific yew; and wove

This ornately carved and painted house post once supported the main beams of a dwelling belonging to a Kwakiutl whaler in the Pacific Northwest. Depicting a man of wealth and high rank, the figure has a whale painted on his chest and copper ornaments on his arms. Two smaller figures, in shadow by the whaler's knees, each support one end of a plank seat. These were his household slaves, most likely children captured in an attack on rival tribes.
©The Granger Collection, New York

baskets from bark and blankets from mountain goat wool. They evolved a society with sharp distinctions among nobles, commoners, and slaves, the latter being mainly women and children captured in raids on other villages. Those who were free devoted their lives to accumulating and then redistributing their wealth among other villagers in elaborate potlatch ceremonies in order to confirm or enhance their social prestige.

The Frozen North

Most of present-day Canada and Alaska were equally inhospitable to agriculture. In the farthest northern reaches—a treeless belt of Arctic tundra—temperatures fell below freezing for most of the year. The Subarctic, although densely forested, had only about 100 frost-free days each year. As a result, the peoples of both regions survived by fishing and hunting. The Inuit, or Eskimos, of northern Alaska harvested whales from their umiaks, boats made by stretching walrus skin over a driftwood frame and that could bear more than a ton of weight. In the central Arctic, they tracked seals. The inhabitants of the Subarctic, both Algonquian-speaking peoples in the East and Athapaskan speakers of

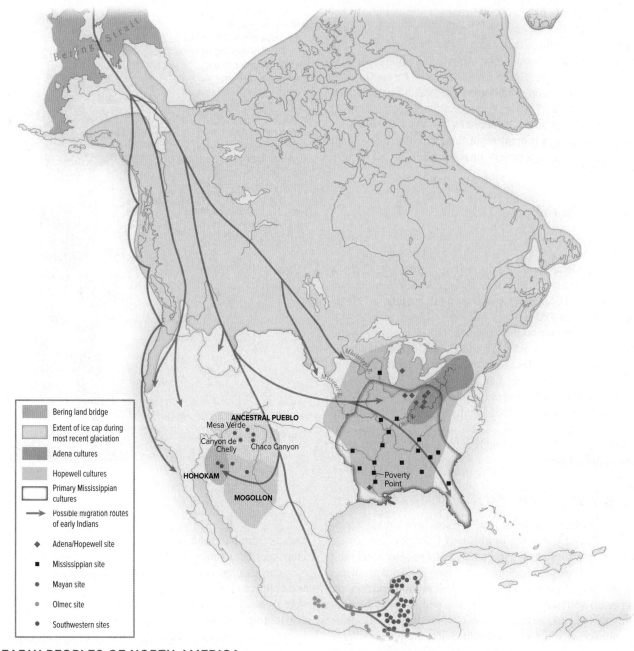

EARLY PEOPLES OF NORTH AMERICA

Migration routes across the Bering Strait from Asia were taken by peoples whose descendants created the major civilizations of ancient America. The influence of Mesoamerica is most striking among the cultures of the Southwest and the Mississippians. **Based on the information in After the Fact, "Tracking the First Americans" (at the end of the chapter), which migration route on this map is being more closely considered due to recent archaeological discoveries?**

the West, moved from their summer fishing camps to berry patches in the fall to moose and caribou hunting grounds in the winter.

REVIEW

How did native cultures differ from region to region, and what accounts for these differences?

INNOVATIONS AND LIMITATIONS

THE FIRST AMERICANS THEREFORE EXPRESSED, governed, and supported themselves in a broad variety of ways. And yet they shared certain core characteristics, including the desire and ability to reshape their world. Whether they lived in forests, coastal regions, jungles, or prairies, whether they inhabited high mountains or low deserts, native communities experimented constantly with the resources around them. Over the course of millennia, nearly all the hemisphere's peoples found ways to change the natural world in order to improve and enrich their lives.

America's Agricultural Gifts

RISE OF AGRICULTURE No innovation proved more crucial to human history than native manipulation of individual plants. Like all first farmers, agricultural pioneers in the Americas began experimenting accidentally. Modern-day species of corn, for example, probably derive from a Mesoamerican grass known as teosinte. It seems that ancient peoples gathered teosinte to collect its small grains. By selecting the grains that best suited them and bringing them back to their settlements, and by returning the grains to the soil through spillage or waste disposal, they unintentionally began the process of domestic cultivation. Soon these first farmers began deliberately saving seeds from the best plants

©vainillaychile/Shutterstock

| *Teosinte, a Mesoamerican grass. Selective harvesting by native peoples helped transform teosinte into maize (corn).*

and sowing them in gardens. In this way, over hundreds of generations, American farmers transformed the modest teosinte grass into a staple crop that would give rise to the hemisphere's mightiest civilizations.

WORLDWIDE SPREAD OF AMERICAN CROPS Indeed, ever since contact with Europe, the great breakthroughs in Native American farming have sustained peoples around the world. In addition to corn, the first Americans gave humanity scores of varieties of squash, potatoes, beans, and other basic foods. Today, plants domesticated by indigenous Americans account for three-fifths of the world's crops, including many that have revolutionized the global diet. For good or ill, a handful of corn species occupies the center of the contemporary American diet. In addition to its traditional forms, corn is consumed in chips, breads, and breakfast cereals; corn syrup sweeteners are added to many of our processed foods and nearly all soft drinks; and corn is fed to almost all animals grown to be consumed, even farmed fish.

Other Native American crops have become integral to diets all over the world. Potatoes revolutionized northern European life in the centuries after contact, helping to avert famine and boost populations in several countries. Ireland's population tripled in the century after the introduction of potatoes. Beans and peanuts became prized for their protein content in Asia. And in Africa, corn, manioc, and other New World crops so improved diets and overall health that the resulting rise in population may have offset the population lost to the Atlantic slave trade.

Landscapers

Plant domestication requires the smallest of changes, changes farmers slowly encourage at the genetic level. But native peoples in the precontact Americas transformed their world on grand scales as well. In the Andes, Peruvian engineers put people to work by the tens of thousands creating an astonishing patchwork of terraces, dikes, and canals designed to maximize agricultural productivity. Similar public-works projects transformed large parts of central Mexico and the Yucatán. Even today, after several centuries of disuse, overgrowth, and even deliberate destruction, human-shaped landscapes dating from the precontact period still cover thousands of square miles of the Americas.

CULTIVATED TREES OF THE AMAZON Over the past generation, scholars have begun to find evidence of incredible manipulation of landscapes and environments in the least likely of places. The vast Amazon rain forest has long been seen by Westerners as an imposing symbol of untouched nature. But it now seems that much of the Amazon was in fact made by people. Whereas farmers elsewhere in the world domesticated plants for their gardens and fields, farmers in the Amazon cultivated food-bearing trees for thousands of years, cutting down less useful species and replacing them with ones that better suited human needs. All told there are more than 70 different species of domesticated trees throughout

Theodore de Bry, Florida Indians Planting Maize. *Both men and women were portrayed as involved in agriculture. Except for the digging stick at the center rear, however, the farming implements drawn by the artist are European in origin.*

©Service Historique de la Marine, Vincennes, France/Bridgeman Images

©Emmanuel Lattes/Alamy

In both North and South America native peoples used techniques to shape their physical environment, from burning prairies and forests (to harvest/hunt animals) to creating irrigation systems (to control floodwaters for agriculture). This photograph from present-day Peru shows the exquisite terracing Incas employed to maximize agricultural yields amid hills, valleys, and mountains. Some researchers think these circular terraces were used for agronomic experiments.

the Amazon. At least one-eighth of the nonflooded rain forest was directly or indirectly created by humans. Likewise, native peoples laboriously improved the soil across as much as a tenth of the Amazon, mixing it with charcoal and a variety of organic materials. These managed soils are more than 10 times as productive as untreated soils in the Amazon. Today, farmers in the region still eagerly search for the places where precontact peoples enriched the earth.

Native North Americans likewise transformed their local environments. Sometimes they moved forests. Ancestral Puebloans cut down and transported more than 200,000 trees to construct the floors and roofs of the monumental buildings in Chaco Canyon. Sometimes they moved rivers. By taming the waters of the Salt and Gila Rivers in present-day Arizona with the most extensive system of irrigation canals anywhere in precontact North America, the Hohokam were able to support large populations in a desert environment. And sometimes they moved the land itself. Twenty-two million cubic feet of earth were moved to construct just one building in the Mississippian city of Cahokia.

FIRE AS A TOOL Indians also employed fire to systematically reshape landscapes across the continent. Throughout North America's great eastern and western forests, native peoples periodically set low fires to consume undergrowth and fallen trees. In this way the continent's first inhabitants managed forests and also animals. Burning enriched the soil and encouraged the growth of grasses and bushes prized by game animals such as deer, elk, beaver, rabbit, grouse, and turkey. The systematic use of fire to reshape forests helped hunters in multiple ways: it increased the overall food supply for grazing animals, it attracted those animal species hunters valued most, and, by clearing forests of ground debris, fire made it easier to track, kill, and transport game. Deliberate burns transformed forests in eastern North America to such an extent that bison migrated from their original ranges on the plains and thrived far to the east. Thus, when native hunters from New York to Georgia brought down a buffalo, they were harvesting a resource that they themselves had helped to cultivate.

The Shape of a Problem

No matter how great their ingenuity, the first Americans were constrained by certain natural realities. One of the most important is so basic that it is easy to overlook. Unlike Eurasia, which stretches across the Northern Hemisphere along an east-west axis, the Americas fall along a north-south axis, stretching nearly pole to pole. Consequently, the Americas are broken up by tremendous geographic and climactic diversity, making communication and technology transfer far more difficult than it was in the Old World.

Consider the agricultural revolution in Eurasia. Once plants and animals were first domesticated in the Fertile Crescent around 10,000 years ago, they quickly began spreading east and west. Within 1,500 years these innovations had been adopted in Greece and India. A thousand years later the domesticated plants and animals of the Fertile Crescent had reached central Europe, and, from there, it took perhaps 200 years for them to be embraced in present-day Spain. Eurasia's east-west axis facilitated these transfers. Locations at roughly the same latitude share the same seasonal variation, have days of the same length, and often have similar habitats and rates of precipitation, making it relatively easy for plants and animals to move from one place to the next.

In contrast, the north-south orientation of the Americas erected natural barriers to plant and animal transfer. Mesoamerica and South America, for example, are about as far apart as the Balkans and Mesopotamia. It took roughly 2,000 years for plants and animals domesticated in Mesopotamia to reach the Balkans. But because Mesoamerica and South America are separated by tropical, equatorial lowlands, it took domesticated plants such as corn several thousand years to jump between the two regions. Sometimes the transfer never happened at all before European contact. South American potatoes would have thrived in central Mexico, but the tropics stopped their northward migration. Equatorial jungles also denied Mesoamerican societies the llama and the alpaca, domesticated more than 5,000 years ago in the Andes. One wonders what even greater heights the Olmec, Toltec, Mayan, and Aztec civilizations would have achieved if they had had access to these large creatures as draft animals and reliable sources of protein.

TRANSFER OF TECHNOLOGY, AGRICULTURE, AND ANIMALS Dramatic variations in climate likewise delayed the transfer of agriculture from Mexico to regions north of the Rio Grande. Archaeologists have discovered evidence of 10,000-year-old domesticated squash in a cave in southern Mexico, an indication that agriculture began in the Americas nearly as early as anywhere else in the world. Yet squash and corn were not cultivated in the present-day American Southwest for another 7,000 years, and the region's peoples did not embrace a fully sedentary, agricultural lifestyle until the start of the Common Era. Major differences in the length of days, the growing season, average temperatures, and rainfall between the Southwest and central Mexico meant that farmers north of the Rio Grande had to experiment for scores of generations before they perfected crops suited to their particular environments. Corn took even longer to become a staple crop in eastern North America, which is why major urban centers did not arise there until approximately 1000 CE.

By erecting barriers to communication and the spread of technology, then, the predominantly north-south orientation of the Americas made it more difficult for the hemisphere's inhabitants to build on one another's

| *Fewer large mammal species were available for domestication in the Americas, perhaps because the first wave of humans on the continent contributed to mass extinctions. Native Americans did domesticate dogs, shown here in a watercolor-and-ink sketch of a Mandan dog sled painted by Karl Bodmer in 1834.*

An Ancient Calendar

©Charles Walker/TopFoto/The Image Works

During summer solstice, the spiral is bisected by a single shaft of light. At the winter solstice, as shown here, sunlight shines at the outside edges of the spiral.

Why might the Chacoans have used a spiral rather than another image?

On a blazing hot summer day in 1977, Anna Sofaer climbed up to the top of Fajada Butte in Chaco Canyon, New Mexico, spotted three sandstone slabs resting carefully against a wall, and walked over to investigate. What she saw against the wall astounded her: a spiral glyph, bisected by a pure shaft of light. An artist and amateur archaeologist, Sofaer had keen interest in how indigenous American cultures harnessed light and shadow in their architecture. Knowing that it was nearly the summer solstice, she recognized instantly that she'd discovered an ancient Ancestral Puebloan calendar. Later research revealed that the device also marked the winter solstice, the summer and winter equinoxes, and the extremes of the moon's 18- to 19-year cycle (the major and minor standstills). These discoveries prompted still more research, and scholars now believe that there are structures throughout Chaco Canyon aligned to solar and lunar events.

THINKING CRITICALLY

What practical reasons might there have been to build these sorts of sun and moon calendars? Might there have been cultural, religious, or social purposes to track accurately the movements of the sun and moon?

successes. Had American innovations spread as quickly as innovations in Eurasia, the peoples of the Western Hemisphere would likely have been healthier, more numerous, and more powerful than they were when Europeans first encountered them in 1492.

Animals and Illness

One other profound difference between the Eurasian world and the Americas concerned animals and disease.

Most diseases affecting humans originated from domesticated animals, which came naturally into frequent and close contact with the humans who raised them. As people across Eurasia embraced agriculture and started living with one another and with domesticated animals in crowded villages, towns, and cities, they created ideal environments for the evolution and transmission of infectious disease. For example, measles, tuberculosis, and smallpox all seem to have derived from diseases afflicting cattle.

Place and Timing of Pioneering Plant and Animal Domestications

PLACE	PLANT	ANIMAL	APPROX. DATE
Southwest Asia	Wheat, pea, olive	Sheep, goat	8500 BCE
China	Rice, millet	Pig, silkworm	By 7500 BCE
New Guinea	Sugarcane, banana	None	ca. 7000 BCE?
Sahel	Sorghum, African rice	Guinea fowl	By 5000 BCE
Mesoamerica	Corn, beans, squash	Turkey	By 3500 BCE
Andes & Amazonia	Potato, manioc	Llama, guinea pig	By 3500 BCE
Tropical West Africa	African yams, oil palm	None	By 3000 BCE
Eastern North America	Sunflower, goosefoot	None	2500 BCE
Ethiopia	Coffee, teff	None	?

Source: Jared M. Diamond, *Guns, Germs, and Steel: The Fates of Human Societies*, 20th ann. ed. New York, NY: W. W. Norton, 2017).

EURASIA'S DEADLY ADVANTAGE Eurasians therefore paid a heavy price for living closely with animals. Yet in the long run, the continent's terrible illnesses hardened its population. Victims who survived into adulthood enjoyed acquired immunity to the most common diseases: that is, if they had already encountered a particular illness as children, their immune systems would recognize and combat the disease more effectively in the event of reinfection. By the fifteenth century, then, Eurasian bodies had learned to live with a host of deadly communicable diseases.

But Native American bodies had not. With a few important exceptions, including tuberculosis, pneumonia, and possibly herpes and syphilis, human populations in the Western Hemisphere seem to have been relatively free from major communicable pathogens. Insofar as most major diseases emerge from domesticated animals, it is easy enough to see why. Indigenous Americans domesticated turkeys, dogs, Muscovy ducks, and guinea pigs but raised only one large mammal—the llama or alpaca (breeds of the same species).

This scarcity of domestic animals had more to do with available supply than with the interest or ability of their would-be breeders. The extinction of most species of megafauna soon after humans arrived in the Americas deprived the hemisphere of 80 percent of its large mammals. Those that remained, including modern-day bison, elk, deer, and moose, were more or less immune to domestication because of peculiarities in their dispositions, diets, rates of growth, mating habits, and social characteristics. In fact, of the world's 148 species of large mammals, only 14 were successfully domesticated before the twentieth century. Of those 14, only one—the ancestor to the llama/alpaca—remained in the Americas following the mass extinctions. Eurasia, in contrast, was home to 13—including the five most common and adaptable domestic mammals: sheep, goats, horses, cows, and pigs.

With virtually no large mammals to domesticate, Native Americans were spared the nightmarish effects of most of the world's major communicable diseases—until 1492. After that date, European colonizers discovered the grim advantage of their millennia-long dance with disease. Old World infections that most colonizers had experienced as children raged through indigenous communities, usually doing the greatest damage to adults whose robust immune systems reacted violently to the novel pathogens. Often native communities came under attack from multiple diseases at the same time. Combined with the wars that attended colonization and the malnutrition, dislocation, and despair that attend wars, disease would kill native peoples by the millions while European colonizers increased and spread over the land. Despite their ingenuity and genius at reshaping plants and environments to their advantage, native peoples in the Americas labored under crucial disadvantages compared to Europe—disadvantages that would contribute to disaster after contact.

REVIEW

How did the native inhabitants of the Americas transform their environments, and what natural constraints put them at a disadvantage relative to Europeans?

CRISIS AND TRANSFORMATION

SUDDEN DECLINES With its coastal plains, arid deserts, broad forests, and vast grasslands, North America has always been a place of tremendous diversity and constant change. Indeed, many of the continent's most dramatic changes took place in the few centuries before European contact. Because of a complex and still poorly understood combination of ecological and social factors, the continent's most impressive civilizations collapsed as suddenly and mysteriously as had those of the Olmecs and the Mayas of Mesoamerica. In the Southwest, the Mogollon culture went into eclipse around the twelfth century, the Hohokam and the Ancestral Puebloans by about the fourteenth. In the Eastern Woodlands, the story was strikingly similar. Most of the great Mississippian population centers, including the magnificent city of Cahokia, had faded by the fourteenth century.

Enduring Peoples

TRADING CITY OF PAQUIME The survivors of these crises struggled to construct new communities, societies, and political systems. In the Southwest, descendants of the Hohokam withdrew to small farming villages that relied on simpler modes of irrigation. Refugees embarked on a massive, coordinated exodus from the Four Corners region and established new, permanent villages in Arizona and New Mexico that the Spaniards would collectively call the Pueblos. The Mogollon have a more mysterious legacy, but some of their number may have helped establish the remarkable trading city of Paquime in present-day Chihuahua. Built around 1300, Paquime contained more than 2,000 rooms and had a sophisticated water and sewage system unlike any other in the Americas. The city included 18 large mounds, all shaped differently from one another, and three ball courts reminiscent of those found elsewhere in Mexico. Until its demise sometime in the fifteenth century Paquime was the center of a massive trading network, breeding macaws and turkeys for export and channeling prized feathers, turquoise, seashells, and worked copper throughout a huge region.

©Danny Lehman/Getty Images

| *The rooms of Paquime, divided by adobe mud walls, help archaeologists estimate population.*

The dramatic transformations remaking the Southwest involved tremendous suffering. Southwesterners had to rebuild in unfamiliar and oftentimes less productive places. Although some of their new settlements endure even to this day, many failed. Skeletal analysis from an abandoned pueblo on the Rio Grande, for example, indicates that the average life expectancy was only 16.5 years. Moreover, drought and migrations increased conflict over scarce resources. The most successful new settlements were large, containing several hundred people, and constructed in doorless, defensible blocks, or else set on high mesas to ward off enemy attacks. These changes were only compounded by the arrival of Athapaskan-speaking peoples (known to the Spanish as Apaches and Navajos) in the century or two before contact with Europeans. These hunters and foragers from western Canada and Alaska moved in small bands, were sometimes friendly, sometimes hostile toward different Pueblos, and eventually became key figures in the postcontact Southwest.

MUSKOGEAN PEOPLES In the Eastern Woodlands, the great Mississippian chieftainships never again attained the glory of Cahokia, but key traditions endured in the Southeast. In the lower Mississippi valley, the Natchez maintained both the temple mound–building tradition and the rigid social distinctions of Mississippian civilization. Below the chief, or "Great Sun," of the Natchez stood a hereditary nobility of lesser "Suns," who demanded respect from the lowly "Stinkards," the common people. Other Muskogean-speakers rejected this rigid and hierarchical social model and gradually embraced a new, more flexible system of independent and relatively **egalitarian** villages that forged confederacies to better cope with outsiders. These groupings would eventually mature into three of the great southeastern Indian confederacies: Creek, Choctaw, and Chickasaw.

IROQUOIANS To the North lived speakers of Iroquoian languages, roughly divided into a southern faction including Cherokees and Tuscaroras, and a northern faction including the powerful Iroquois and Hurons. Like Muskogeans to the South, these Iroquoian communities mixed farming with a hunting/gathering economy and lived in semipermanent towns. The distinctive feature of Iroquois and Huron architecture was not the temple mound but rather the longhouse (some stretching up to 100 feet in length). Each sheltered as many as 10 families.

ALGONQUINS The Algonquins were the third major group of Eastern Woodlands people. They lived along the Atlantic Seaboard and the Great Lakes in communities smaller than those of either the Muskogeans or the Iroquois. By the fifteenth century, the coastal communities from southern New England to Virginia had adopted agriculture to supplement their diets, but those in the colder

A Continent of Cultures

	NATURAL ENVIRONMENT	BUILT ENVIRONMENT	PRIMARY SUSTENANCE
Olmecs	Tropical lowlands of south central Mexico	First city-builders: large plazas, pyramidal structures, sculptured heads	Beans, squash, maize (corn)
Mayas	Lowland jungles of the Yucatán Peninsula	Cities contain palaces, bridges, aqueducts, baths, pyramids topped with temples	Beans, squash, maize
Aztecs	Valley of Mexico	Tenochtitlán—an island metropolis with canals, marketplaces, palaces, temples	Beans, squash, maize
Mogollon	Southern New Mexico	Exquisite pottery	
Hohokam	Southern Arizona	Canals, ball courts	Beans, squash, maize
Ancestral Pueblo	Colorado plateau	Masonry buildings	
Eastern Woodlands	Centered in valleys of great rivers, Great Lakes, and Atlantic coast	Mound building, sometimes figurative and monumental	Primarily animals, fish, and nuts; gourds and pumpkins in the southeast; and later maize
Great Plains	Semiarid long- and short-grass plains; rainfall varied and unpredictable	Hide shelters on poles	Primarily hunting and foraging, buffalo stampedes, but some maize, squash, beans, and sunflowers
Great Basin	Plateau between Rocky Mountains and the Sierras	Bands usually numbered less than 50; simple shelters	Elk, antelope trapped; also a wide variety of small game as available; seeds, nuts, and plants
Pacific Northwest	Coastal areas from British Columbia to northern California; abundant rainfall, mild climate	Large and long houses of cedar beams and hand-split boards; complex works of art	Lush forests provide plants and game; rivers and ocean, abundant fish and shellfish
Subarctic and Arctic Peoples	Open boreal forest and tundra stretch across Canada; usually fewer than 100 frost-free days a year	Skin tents and igloos in the arctic winters	Hunting and fishing (including whales, seals, muskrats); moose and caribou

Photos: (left) ©The Granger Collection, New York; *(right)* ©Service Historique de la Marine, Vincennes, France/Bridgeman Images

northern climates with shorter growing seasons depended entirely on hunting, fishing, and gathering plants such as wild rice.

CARIBBEAN CULTURES Cultures of equal and even greater resources persisted and flourished during the fifteenth century in the Caribbean, particularly on the Greater Antilles—the islands of present-day Cuba, Haiti and the Dominican Republic, Jamaica, and Puerto Rico. Although the earliest inhabitants of the ancient Caribbean, the Ciboneys, may have come from the Florida peninsula, it was the Tainos, later emigrants from northern South America, who expanded throughout the Greater Antilles and the Bahamas. Taino chiefs, known as caciques, along with a small

Many HISTORIES

HOW MANY PEOPLE LIVED ON HISPANIOLA IN 1492?

Estimates of the precontact population of the Americas are necessarily speculative. Historians disagree sharply over these estimates, partly because they have used different data and methods and partly because of the moral or political implications that many people associate with high or low figures. The greater the initial population, so the argument goes, the greater the crime of its destruction. The range of estimates is particularly striking for the island of Hispaniola (present-day Haiti and the Dominican Republic), site of Europe's first American colony and of the hemisphere's first demographic catastrophe. Historians Sherburne Cook and Woodrow Borah, relying especially on population estimates in the primary sources, have argued that several million people lived on the island in 1492. The historical demographer Massimo Livi-Bacci, using other methods to estimate the island's precontact population, doubts that it could have exceeded 400,000. These short excerpts cannot capture the complexity of the arguments, but they illustrate some of the differences.

DOCUMENT 1
Sherburne Cook and Woodrow Borah

It is now more than four centuries since [Bartolomé de] las Casas insisted that when Columbus first sighted Hispaniola, the island had 3 to 4 million native inhabitants and perhaps more. This estimate has been denied vigorously. Yet if we accept as substantially correct the count for tribute carried out by Bartolomé Columbus in 1496, and we have seen that there is good evidence for it, we have to concede the reliability of Las Casas. We have set forth previously the reasons for estimating that in 1496 the entire island was inhabited by 3,770,000

souls. There must have been more than this number in 1492, particularly if in 1496 somewhere near 40 percent of the natives were dying annually. . . . The most probable number may be put at 7 to 8 million. This is the order of magnitude obtained if we assume that the Columbus' count was relatively accurate. . . . [This figure] would give an average population density for Hispaniola of approximately double the density we found for central Mexico just before the coming of the Europeans. . . . The American Indians in general had available to them food plants

of far greater yield per hectare than any cultivated at that time in the Old World except the yams of sub-Saharan Africa and the rice of southeast Asia. The Indians of Hispaniola, relative to the Indians of central Mexico, had cassava, which yields more per hectare than maize and has remarkable storage qualities; they had also the more favorable agricultural conditions of Hispaniola.

Source: Cook, Sherburne F. and Borah, Woodrow, *Essays in Population History, 3 Volumes,* Vol. 1. Berkeley and Los Angeles, CA: University of California Press, 1971–1979, 405–408.

DOCUMENT 2
Massimo Livi-Bacci

There are many reasons to believe that the contact population could not have exceeded a few hundred thousand people. . . . The crown and the colonists were eager for gold. . . . Forcing the indios to work in the mines was a far more efficient way to obtain gold, and gold production reached a peak of 1,000 kg per year in the first years of Ovando's rule. Under the conservative hypothesis that annual individual productivity was 100 g, and that one third of adult males worked in the mines (about 8 percent of the total population), 10,000 laborers would have been needed to produce 1,000 kg, drawn from a total population of 120,000. This figure during Ovando's rule would be consistent with a population twice as large, or more, at the time of contact ten years before, as stipulated by Arranz.

[Another] approach is demographic in nature. It is during [Governor Nicolás de] Ovando's times (1502–1508) that the decline of the native population must have accelerated its pace—the logical

consequence of the wars of "pacification," the Spanish occupation of the whole island, the growing number of colonists, and the increased demand for construction, agriculture, and mining labor. At the end of Ovando's rule in 1508, the native population was said to be 60,000: how many could they have been 14 years earlier? A contact population of 400,000—reduced to 200,000 after the high mortality of 1494–1496 and suffering three other major epidemic outbreaks, each one wiping out one third of the total population— would have been reduced to the estimated 60,000 of 1508. Although this is not impossible, epidemics are not mentioned in the abundant available literature prior to the smallpox epidemic of 1518– 1519. The repartimiento of 1514 shows an age structure and a children to-women ratio consistent with rates of decline approaching 5 percent a year. This rate, if carried backward to 1492, would yield a population of about 80,000. . . .

These independent methods restrict the plausible range into which the initial contact population could fall. . . . The most likely figure [lies] between 200,000 and 300,000, with levels below 100,000 and above 400,000 both unlikely.

Source: Livi-Bacci, Massimo, "Return to Hispaniola: Reassessing a Demographic Catastrophe," *Hispanic American Historical Review,* vol. 83, no. 1, February 2003, 3–51.

THINKING CRITICALLY

What evidence do Cook and Borah use to produce their population estimate? What evidence does Livi-Bacci employ? Why do you think their approaches produced such dramatically different figures? Do you think that the moral implications of Hispaniola's demographic collapse are different if the original population was 400,000, as opposed to 8 million? Why or why not?

>> MAPPING THE PAST <<

Indians of North America, C. 1500

Courtesy of Cahokia Mounds State Historic Site, Collinsville, Illinois. Painting by William R. Iseminger

"A populous nation of people, and so extensive that those who give detailed reports of them do not know where it ends."—Don Antonio Balcarcel, Bishop of Guadalajara, 1676, on the Caddo Indians of Texas

Context

We need maps to orient our understanding of the past, but we should remember their limitations. No one has yet produced an adequate map of Native North Americans in the colonial period. Tribal names obscure complex, multifaceted identities. Labels like "Blackfeet," "Creek," or "Erie" falsely imply political stability, while the fixed position of these labels in one place masks the migrations, displacements, expansions, and contractions that kept the native world in constant motion.

Map Reading

1. What are the three subsistence modes represented on this map?
2. What names do you recognize?
3. Do rivers seem to correspond to the location of native communities? Which ones?

Map Interpretation

1. Based on this basic map, can you identify regions of denser and sparser population? What might account for the difference?
2. Try to locate a native group that seems out of place, based on what you already know about American history. How might you explain the geographic shift over time?
3. Choose a native group unfamiliar to you and briefly research it on the Internet. Are there any obvious reasons why the group is less familiar to you than others?

number of noble families, ruled island tribes, controlling the production and distribution of food and tools and exacting tribute from the great mass of commoners, farmers, and fisherfolk. Attending to these elites were the poorest Taino peoples—servants who bedecked their masters and mistresses in brilliant diadems of feathers, fine woven textiles, and gold nose and ear pieces and then shouldered the litters on which the rulers sat and paraded their finery.

North America on the Eve of Contact

By the end of the fifteenth century, North America's peoples numbered between 5 and 10 million—with perhaps another million living on the islands of the Caribbean—and they were spread among more than 350 societies speaking nearly as many distinct languages. (The total precontact population for all of the Americas is estimated at between 57 and 112 million.)

DIVERSE LIFEWAYS These millions lived in remarkably diverse ways. Some peoples relied entirely on farming; others on hunting, fishing, and gathering; still others on a combination of the two. Some, like the Natchez and the Iroquois, practiced matrilineal forms of kinship, in which women owned land, tools, and even children. Among others, such as the Algonquins, patrilineal kinship prevailed, and all property and prestige descended in the male line. Some societies, such as those of the Great Plains and the Great Basin in the West, the Inuit in the Arctic, and the Iroquois and Algonquins in the East, were roughly egalitarian, whereas others, like many in the Caribbean and the Pacific Northwest, were rigidly divided into nobles and commoners and servants or slaves. Some, such as the Natchez and the Tainos, were ruled by powerful chiefs; others, such as the Algonquins and the Pueblo peoples, by councils of village elders or heads of family clans; still others in the Great Basin, the Great Plains, and the far North by the most skillful hunter or the most powerful shaman in their band. Those people who relied on hunting practiced religions that celebrated their kinship with animals and solicited their aid as guardian spirits, whereas predominantly agricultural peoples sought the assistance of their gods to make the rain fall and the crops ripen.

When Europeans first arrived in North America, the continent north of present-day Mexico boasted an ancient, rich, and dynamic history marked by cities, towns, and prosperous farms. At contact it was a land occupied by several million men, women, and children speaking hundreds of languages and characterized by tremendous political, cultural, economic, and religious diversity.

> ✓ REVIEW
> What was life like in the Americas on the eve of European contact?

PUTTING HISTORY IN GLOBAL CONTEXT

MEDIEVAL SCANDINAVIANS SAILED as far west as Greenland. Then in 1001 a party of men and women under Leif Ericsson established an encampment known as Vinland on the northern tip of Newfoundland. That European outpost in North America may have endured several seasons or even decades, but eventually it was extinguished or abandoned. In contrast, the contact between Eastern and Western Hemispheres that began in 1492 was permanent, and the effects rising out of it were far-reaching. Epidemic diseases and the traumas of colonization would kill millions of Native Americans; animals and vegetables from both hemispheres would transform lives across the globe. And the newcomers from Europe, Africa, and Asia embarked on a series of encounters that reshaped North and South America.

So it is important to grasp the extent of American cultures before 1492, because for most of our nation's short history we have not wanted to remember the Americas as a populous, diverse, and civilized hemisphere when Christopher Columbus first dropped anchor in the Bahamas. In 1830, for example, President Andrew Jackson tried to answer the many critics of his Indian-removal policies. Although "humanity has often wept over the fate of the aborigines of this country," Jackson said, the Indians' fate was as natural and inevitable "as the extinction of one generation to make room for another." Pointing to the mysterious mounds that had so captivated the founding fathers, he proclaimed, "we behold the memorials of a once powerful race, which was exterminated, or has disappeared, to make room for the existing savage tribes." Just as the architects of the mounds supposedly met their end at the hands of these "savage tribes," the president concluded, so, too, must Indians pass away before the descendants of Europe. "What good man would prefer a country covered with forests and ranged by a few thousand savages, to our extensive republic, studded with cities, towns, and prosperous farms . . . and filled with all the blessings of liberty, civilization, and religion!"

Jackson and many others of his era preferred a national history that contained only a few thousand ranging "savages" to one shaped by millions of indigenous hunters, farmers, builders, and inventors. Yet what seems clear from modern research is the rich diversity of American cultures on the eve of contact between the peoples of Eurasia, Africa, and the Americas. We are still struggling to find stories big enough to encompass not only Indians but all those who have forged this complex, tragic, and marvelous nation of nations.

CHAPTER SUMMARY

Thousands of years after Siberian hunters migrated across the Bering Strait to Alaska, their descendants created civilizations that rivaled those of ancient Europe, Asia, and Africa.

- Around 1500 BCE Mesoamerica emerged as the hearth of civilization in the Western Hemisphere, a process started by the Olmecs and brought to its height by the Mayas. Their built cities are remarkable for their art, architecture, and trade.

- The adoption of agriculture gave peoples in the Southwest and the Eastern Woodlands the resource security necessary to develop sedentary cultures of increasing complexity.

- Inhabitants of the Great Plains, the Great Basin, the Arctic, and the Subarctic relied on fishing, hunting, and gathering.

- Peoples of the Pacific Northwest boasted large populations and prosperous economies as well as an elaborate social, ceremonial, and artistic life.

- The first Americans shaped their environments, pioneering crops and transforming landscapes.

- Nonetheless, the continent's north-south orientation inhibited the spread of agriculture and technology, and a lack of domesticatable animals compared to Europe would leave Native Americans with little protection against Old World diseases.

- North America's most impressive early civilizations had collapsed by the end of the fifteenth century. In their wake a diverse array of cultures evolved.

  - ▶ In the Southwest, Pueblo Indians were joined by Athapaskan-speakers eventually known as Apaches and Navajos.

  - ▶ In much of eastern North America, stratified chiefdoms of the Mississippian era gave way to more egalitarian confederacies of independent villages.

Digging Deeper

Scholars in several fields are transforming our understanding of the Americas prior to European contact. The magazine *Archaeology* offers clear explanations of the latest discoveries for nonscientific audiences. For an excellent overview, attentive to controversies among researchers, see Charles C. Mann, *1491: New Revelations of the Americas before Columbus* (2005). For North America specifically, see Alice Beck Kehoe, *North America before the European Invasions* (2nd ed., 2016). For the Southwest, see Linda S. Cordell and Maxine E. McBrinn, *Archaeology of the Southwest* (3rd ed., 2012). For the Eastern Woodlands, see George R. Milner, *The Moundbuilders: Ancient Peoples of Eastern North America* (2005); and Timothy Pauketat, ed., *Cahokia* (2010). Roger G. Kennedy, *Hidden Cities: The Discovery and Loss of Ancient North American Civilization* (1994), gives a fascinating account of how white Americans responded to the ruins of ancient American cultures. For the consequences of axis alignment and of domesticated animals, see the captivating work by Jared Diamond, *Guns, Germs, and Steel: The Fates of Human Societies* (20th ann. ed., 2017).

For the cultures of precontact Mexico, see Michael D. Coe and Rex Koontz, *Mexico: From the Olmecs to the Aztecs* (7th ed., 2013). For exhaustive surveys of all regional cultures in North America, see William C. Sturtevant, general editor, *Handbook of North American Indians*, 15 volumes to date (1978–2008).

After the Fact

Tracking the First Americans

What methods do historians use to discover the history of a past thousands of years before any humans knew how to write? Archaeological research is key; and by carefully unearthing layer after layer of soil, analyzing artifacts and their relation to these layers, scientists and historians have been able to discover a remarkable amount of information about the first immigrants to the Americas over 15,000 years ago.

But the deductions and inferences made about a past lacking historical documents are often contested. Like millions of other Americans who look to religious texts more than to evolutionary biology or archaeology for their deep history, many Indian people today reject what Western science has to say about their origins. Rather, they insist that their people are truly indigenous to America—that they didn't migrate here but *emerged* here from other planes of existence. A Navajo origin story, for example, explains how their ancestors came into this world, "the changeable world," after a harrowing journey through the Four Dark Worlds. For some these stories are profound metaphors; for others they describe actual events in ancient times. But adherents of either perspective often share an understandable skepticism about scientific "truth" that over the past two centuries has taken so little interest in their oral traditions, has gone through so many massive revisions, and has so often been used to justify native dispossession. After all, Andrew Jackson and other supporters of Indian removal insisted they had "science" on their side.

Archaeologists rarely question the basis of scientific knowledge, but they have continually argued with one another over the scant evidence discovered about early migrations. And progress often depends on accidental finds, such as the one made by an African American cowboy, George McJunkin. McJunkin, a former slave, was a talented rancher, not to mention a capable fiddler, amateur astronomer, and surveyor. Old fossils also fascinated him, and he happened upon one of the most important of the twentieth century.

THE CLOVIS DISCOVERIES

ON HORSEBACK ONE DAY IN 1908 near Folsom, New Mexico, McJunkin spotted some very old bison bones eroding from a slope. Bringing some home, he soon realized that they were far too large—that they must have belonged to an extinct bison species. Professional archaeologists ignored McJunkin's discovery, and only in 1926 after his death did New Mexican locals manage to convince scholars from the University of Colorado to investigate the original site. In doing so, they uncovered an exquisitely crafted stone spear-point embedded in the bison's ribs.

The discovery rocked the scientific community, which had long declared confidently that Indians had first arrived in the Americas only about 4,000 BP. Eleven years later another shock followed when archaeologists digging near Clovis, New Mexico, found a different sort of

©Brian_Brockman/Getty Images

Stone artifacts known as Clovis points have been found with skeletons of mammoths, mastodon, and bison.

projectile point near butchered mammoth bones. Finally, in 1949, scientists confirmed the great antiquity of both finds by using radiocarbon dating, a method for measuring decay rates of the radioactive isotope of carbon, which exists in organic matter such as bone and starts to break down immediately after an organism dies. Tests revealed that the Folsom site dated to 10,800 BP and that Clovis was nearly a thousand years older still. Soon archaeologists around the continent discovered other sites of comparable antiquity containing stone tools with the same Clovis characteristics. A new consensus emerged: Asian migrants first came to North America around 13,000 BP. These migrants brought with them a common stone-working technology, of the sort found at Clovis. The Clovis people fanned out across the Western Hemisphere, and, within one or two millennia, their culture gave way to regionally specific cultural and stone-working traditions, like Folsom.

EVIDENCE OF MIGRATION FROM SIBERIA TO NORTH AMERICA

BUT HOW DID ASIANS GET to North America? According to the long-standing consensus, they walked to Alaska—a region now separated from Siberia by 50 miles of ocean known as the Bering Strait. During the last Ice Age, with much of the world's water locked up in continent-straddling glaciers, ocean levels were far lower. Consequently, between around 25,000 BP and 15,000 BP, a now-submerged landmass called "Beringia" linked Alaska and Siberia. Following game onto and across Beringia, the first Americans gradually occupied this land and, over the course of many generations, some eventually moved east into what is now Alaska. For centuries massive glaciers blocked the way farther south. But geologists have argued that around 15,000 BP an ice-free corridor opened up along what is now the McKenzie River, east of the Canadian Rockies. Game animals and the people hunting them (with Clovis-point tools) eventually began to filter south, gradually emerging into the warmer and totally uninhabited lands of the present-day United States. This scenario enjoyed support for several decades, not only from geologists but also from some geneticists, who found that modern-day Native Americans diverged from Siberians perhaps 15,000 years ago.

Still, several provocative archaeological finds in Tennessee, Pennsylvania, Florida, and elsewhere suggested that humans had been living in the Americas longer—perhaps far longer. For example, a mastodon bone discovered in Washington State, some 800 years older than any Clovis site, had what seemed to be another bone embedded in it—perhaps from a projectile thrown by a human hunter. In the late 1970s researchers from Vanderbilt University discovered an ancient campsite dating to 14,600 BP at Monte Verde, Chile—a full millennium earlier than the oldest known Clovis tools. But the Monte Verde site was thousands of miles to the south and difficult to visit, dating techniques were open to multiple interpretations, and most archaeologists rejected these pre-Clovis claims. The standard story had endured for decades, and it would take incontrovertible evidence of earlier occupation to overthrow it.

©Album/Prisma/Newscom

THE NEW CONSENSUS

FOR MOST ARCHAEOLO-
GISTS, THAT INCONTRO-
VERTIBLE evidence has
finally arrived. A 2008
study demonstrated that
fossilized human feces excavated from a cave in Oregon
were more than 14,000 years
old. In 2011, archaeologist
Michael R. Waters (himself
once a staunch "Clovis-
firster") led a team that con-
firmed the antiquity of the mastodon bone from Washington State. They found that the
invasive bone chip was indeed from another animal and had almost certainly been fashioned
into a weapon by an ancient hunter. Most significantly, in 2011 Waters published yet another
analysis of a site he excavated on Buttermilk Creek, outside of Austin, Texas. It revealed a
typical collection of Clovis tools. But digging deeper into a layer of clay sediments, Waters and
his colleagues found dozens of stone tools made with a strikingly different technique. Lacking
the organic material necessary for radiocarbon dating, the team instead employed a newer
dating technology called optically-stimulated luminescence that can determine when stone was
last exposed to the sun by measuring light energy trapped in minerals. The results were
remarkable: the oldest tools at the site dated to 15,500 BP.

Most specialists now acknowledge that humans arrived in the present-day United States at
least 15,000–16,000 years ago, and that the Clovis stone-working tradition emerged here, long
after they arrived. The "shattering" of the Clovis barrier has reinvigorated the study of ancient
America, but there now seem to be more questions than ever. Previously excavated sites are
being reopened and tested anew in light of the revised theories. A number of archaeologists
insist that the earliest migrations took place 20,000 or even 40,000 years ago. Even these
claims could soon be overthrown; astonishing new discoveries in Southern California suggest
humans have been in North America for more than 130,000 years. Though many scholars still
reject these very early dates, they now do so more tentatively, mindful of the way in which
dogmatic loyalty to Clovis-first blinded the field to compelling evidence. And the controversy
over dates has reopened the question of the routes Siberians first took into North America.
Depending on the date of the first migration, immense glaciers may have made an overland
route virtually impossible. For this reason archaeologists have become more interested in the
possibility that the first arrivals came in small boats, gradually working their way down the
Pacific coast.

Some of the most exciting developments in the study of ancient America are emerging from
linguistics and genetics. Previous genetic research on the peopling of the Americas had compared present-day Native Americans and present-day Siberians by examining small regions of
their respective genomes, usually Y chromosomes or mitochondrial DNA. These studies

confirmed Siberia as the origin of the first migrants and suggested that all native peoples in the Americas descend from a single, ancestral migration. But today new technologies enable the sequencing of entire genomes, making research of this kind far more revealing and complete. In the summer of 2012, researchers unveiled a major new study demonstrating that there were in fact three totally separate migrations from Siberia to the Americas, an idea put forward long ago by linguist Joseph Greenberg but widely dismissed at the time. The first migration, at least 15,000 years ago, populated the entire hemisphere. The vast majority of today's Native Americans are descendants of this first founding group. Millennia later another migration brought the ancestors of the Eskimos and Aleutians who colonized the Arctic, and still another brought the Athapaskans of western Canada and the American Southwest (today's Apaches and Navajos).

It was the most ambitious study of Native American genetics ever undertaken, but the origins debate is hardly settled. Skeptics of the study note that a large majority of the hemisphere's native peoples perished in epidemics and wars in the centuries after contact, making any present-day genetic sample unrepresentative in critical respects. And many indigenous peoples remain deeply distrustful of the motivations behind such studies. They know all too well that stories told about the past have power over both the present and the future. The Genographic Project of the National Geographic Society asked all federally recognized tribes in the United States for genetic samples, in order to run an ambitious study on native origins. Out of 565 tribes, only 2 agreed.

San Diego Natural History Museum Paleontologist Don Swanson pointing at rock fragment near a large horizontal mastodon tusk fragment.

1400–1600

With sails bellying in a gale, the Dutch ship in this painting has furled the rest of its canvas. Sailors from western Europe risked much as they crossed the Atlantic in search of fish, silver, gold, and other commodities of trade.

©Rafael Valls Gallery, London, UK/Bridgeman Images

>> An American Story

FISHING NETS AND FAR HORIZONS

All the world lay before them. Or so it seemed to mariners from England's seafaring coasts, pushing westward toward unknown lands in the far Atlantic.

The scent of the new land came first—not the sight of it, but the smells: the scent of fir trees wafted from beyond the horizon; or the sight of shorebirds wheeling about the masts. Straight-away the captain would call for a lead to be thrown overboard to sound the depths. At its end was a hollowed-out socket with a bit of tallow in it, so that some of the sea bottom would stick when the lead was hauled up. Even out of sight of land, a good sailing master could tell where he was by what came up—"oosy sand" or perhaps "soft worms" or "popplestones as big as beans."

Through much of the fifteenth century the search for cod had drawn West Country sailors north and west, toward Iceland. In the 1480s and 1490s a few English tried their luck farther west, looking for the mythical *Hy-Brasil*—Gaelic for "Isle of the Blessed"—somewhere west of Ireland. These western ventures returned with little to show for their daring until an Italian named Giovanni Caboto, called John Cabot by the English, obtained the blessing of King Henry VII to hunt for unknown lands. From the port of Bristol his lone ship sailed west in the spring of 1497. This time the return voyage brought news of a "newfound" island where the trees were tall enough to make fine masts and the codfish were plentiful. Cabot returned to England to inform His Majesty of his success, received 10 pounds as his reward, and with the proceeds dressed himself in dashing silks. Then he returned to Bristol to undertake a more ambitious search for a northwest passage to Asia. In 1498 his five ships disappeared over the horizon and were never heard from again.

By the 1550s Cabot's island, now known as Newfoundland, attracted 400 vessels annually, fishermen not only from England but also from France, Portugal, and Spain. The harbor of present-day St. John's, Newfoundland, served as the informal hub of the North Atlantic fishery. Sailors dropped anchor to take on supplies in the spring, trade with native peoples, or to prepare for the homeward voyage in autumn. There was a good deal of swapping tales, for these seafarers knew as much as anyone else—if not more—about the new world of wonders that was opening to Europeans. They were acquainted with names like Cristoforo Colombo,

the Italian from Genoa whom Cabot might have known as a boy. They listened to Portuguese tales of sailing around the Horn of Africa in pursuit of spices and to stories of Indian empires to the south, rich in gold and silver that Spanish treasure ships were bringing home.

Indeed, Newfoundland was one of the few places in the world where so many ordinary folk of different nations could gather and talk, crammed aboard dank ships moored in St. John's harbor, huddled before blazing fires on its beaches, or crowded into smoky makeshift taverns. When the ships sailed home in autumn, the tales went with them, repeated in the tiniest coastal villages by those pleased to have cheated the sea and death one more time. Eager to fish, talk, trade, and take profits, West Country mariners were almost giddy at the prospect of Europe's expanding horizons.

Though most seafarers who fished the waters of Newfoundland remain unknown today, it is well to begin with these ordinary folk, for the European discovery of the Americas cannot be looked on simply as the voyages of a few bold explorers. Adventurers such as Columbus and Cabot were only the tip of a much larger expansion of European peoples and culture that began in the 1450s. That expansion arose out of a series of gradual but telling changes in the fabric of European society. Some of these changes were technological, arising out of advances in the arts of navigating and shipbuilding and the use of gunpowder. Some were

©The Morgan Library & Museum/Art Resource, NY

During the sixteenth century, West Country fisherfolk from England sailed from harbors such as Plymouth, shown here in a painting from the 1480s. Can you spot the primitive lighthouse?

economic, involving the development of trade networks like those linking Bristol with ports in Iceland and Spain. Some were **demographic**, bringing about a rise in Europe's population after a devastating century of plague. Other changes were religious, adding a dimension of belief to the political rivalries that fueled discoveries in the Americas. Yet others were political, making it possible for kingdoms to centralize and extend their influence across the ocean. Portugal, Spain, France, and England—all possessing coasts along the Atlantic—led the way in exploration, spurred on by Italian "admirals" such as Caboto and Colombo, Spanish *conquistadores*—"conquerors"—such as Hernán Cortés and Francisco Pizarro, and English sea dogs such as Humphrey Gilbert and Walter Raleigh. Ordinary folk rode these currents, too. The great and the small alike were propelled by forces that were remolding the face of Europe—and were beginning to remold the face of the world. <<

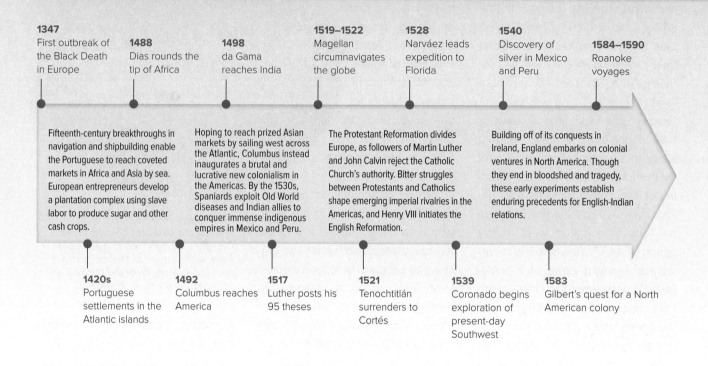

1347
First outbreak of the Black Death in Europe

1488
Dias rounds the tip of Africa

1498
da Gama reaches India

1519–1522
Magellan circumnavigates the globe

1528
Narváez leads expedition to Florida

1540
Discovery of silver in Mexico and Peru

1584–1590
Roanoke voyages

Fifteenth-century breakthroughs in navigation and shipbuilding enable the Portuguese to reach coveted markets in Africa and Asia by sea. European entrepreneurs develop a plantation complex using slave labor to produce sugar and other cash crops.

Hoping to reach prized Asian markets by sailing west across the Atlantic, Columbus instead inaugurates a brutal and lucrative new colonialism in the Americas. By the 1530s, Spaniards exploit Old World diseases and Indian allies to conquer immense indigenous empires in Mexico and Peru.

The Protestant Reformation divides Europe, as followers of Martin Luther and John Calvin reject the Catholic Church's authority. Bitter struggles between Protestants and Catholics shape emerging imperial rivalries in the Americas, and Henry VIII initiates the English Reformation.

Building off of its conquests in Ireland, England embarks on colonial ventures in North America. Though they end in bloodshed and tragedy, these early experiments establish enduring precedents for English-Indian relations.

1420s
Portuguese settlements in the Atlantic islands

1492
Columbus reaches America

1517
Luther posts his 95 theses

1521
Tenochtitlán surrenders to Cortés

1539
Coronado begins exploration of present-day Southwest

1583
Gilbert's quest for a North American colony

EURASIA AND AFRICA IN THE FIFTEENTH CENTURY

CHINA'S GLORY IN 1450, HOWEVER, THE WESTERN European kingdoms that would one day dominate much of the world still sat at the fringe of an international economy that revolved around China. By a variety of measures Ming China was the richest, most powerful, and most advanced society in the world. All Eurasia sought Chinese goods, especially spices, ceramics, and silks, and Chinese ships sped these goods to faraway ports. Seven times between 1405 and 1433, China's "treasure fleet"—300 ships manned by 28,000 sailors and commanded by Zheng He (pronounced "Jung Huh")—unfurled its red silk sails off the south China coast and traveled as far as the kingdoms of eastern Africa. The treasure fleet's largest craft were nine-masted junks measuring 400 feet long. They boasted multiple decks and luxury cabins with balconies. (By comparison, Columbus's largest ship in 1492 was a mere 85 feet long, and the crew aboard all three of his ships totaled just 90 men.) Chinese leaders soon grounded their trading fleet and put a stop to the long-distance voyages that might eventually have made Zheng He a forerunner to Columbus. But Chinese luxuries, most transported overland, continued to be Eurasia's most sought-after commodities.

ISLAMIC KINGDOMS The next mightiest powers in the Old World were not European kingdoms but rather huge Islamic empires, especially the Ottomans in the eastern Mediterranean. The Ottomans rose to prominence during the fourteenth and fifteenth centuries and expanded aggressively in every direction. Muslim rulers gained control of critical trade routes and centers of commerce between Asia and Europe. The Ottomans' greatest triumph came in 1453, when the sultan Mehmet II conquered Constantinople (now Istanbul), the ancient and supposedly impregnable Christian city that straddled Europe and Asia and was one of the world's premier trading hubs. Mehmet's stunning victory sounded alarms throughout Europe.

Europe's Place in the World

Europe's rulers had good reason for alarm. Distant from Asia's profitable trade and threatened both economically and militarily by the Ottomans, most of the continent remained fractious and vulnerable. During the fourteenth and fifteenth centuries, 90 percent of Europe's people, widely dispersed in small villages, made their living from the land. But warfare, poor transportation, and low grain yields all created food shortages, and undernourishment produced a population prone to disease. Under these circumstances life was nasty, brutish, and usually short. One-quarter of all children died in the first year of life. People who reached the age of 40 counted themselves fortunate.

It was also a world of sharp inequalities, where nobles and aristocrats enjoyed several hundred times the income of peasants or craftworkers. It was a world with no strong, centralized political authority, where kings were weak and warrior lords held sway over small towns and tiny fiefdoms. It was a world of violence and sudden death, where homicide, robbery, and rape occurred with brutal frequency. It was a world where security and order of any kind seemed so fragile that many people clung to tradition, and more than a few used witchcraft in an attempt to master the chaotic and unpredictable world around them.

THE BLACK DEATH   But Europe was changing, in part because of a great calamity. Between the late 1340s and the early 1350s, bubonic plague—known as the Black Death—swept away one-quarter of Europe's population. Some urban areas lost 70 percent of their people to the disease. The Black Death disrupted both agriculture and commerce, and provoked a spiritual crisis that resulted in violent, unsanctioned religious movements, scapegoating of marginal groups, even massacres of Jews. Although Europeans seem to have met recurrent outbreaks of the disease with less panic, the sickness continued to disrupt social and economic life nonetheless.

©Walters Art Museum, Baltimore, USA/Bridgeman Images

| *The spread of bubonic plague left Europeans dismayed and desperate. While a priest reads prayers over the bodies being buried in a common grave, a man suddenly taken by the plague writhes in agony. In the background, a cart collects more corpses. And in heaven (upper left) St. Sebastian, a Christian martyr, intercedes with God to end the suffering.*

Yet the sudden drop in population relieved pressure on scarce resources. Survivors of the Black Death found that the relative scarcity of workers and consumers made for better wages, lower prices, and more land. These changes intersected in an overall expansion of trade. In earlier centuries Italian merchants had begun building wealth by encouraging commerce across Europe and by tapping into trade from Africa, the Middle East, and, when able, from Asia. By the late fifteenth century, Europe's merchants and bankers had devised more efficient ways of transferring the money generated from manufacturing and trade and had established credit in order to support commerce across longer distances. Wealth flowed into the coffers of fifteenth-century traders, financiers, and landlords, creating a pool of capital that those investors could plow into new technologies, trading ventures, and, eventually, colonial enterprises.

MONARCHS FORGE NATION-STATES   The direction of Europe's political development also laid the groundwork for overseas colonization. After 1450 strong monarchs in Europe steadily enlarged the sphere of royal power at the expense of warrior lords. Henry VII, the founder of England's Tudor dynasty, Francis I of France, and Ferdinand and Isabella of Spain began the trend, forging modern nation-states by extending their political control over more territory, people, and resources. Such larger, more centrally organized states were able to marshal the resources necessary to support colonial outposts and to sustain the professional armies and navies capable of creating and protecting overseas empires. By the mid-fourteenth century western Europe had commercial networks, private fortunes, strong kingdoms, and ambitions that would lead to a transformative period of expansion.

Africa and the Portuguese Wave

IMPROVED NAVIGATION AND SAILING TECHNIQUES
European expansion began with Africa. For centuries, African spices, ivory, and gold had entered the Eurasian market either westward, through ports on the Indian Ocean, or northward, through the Sahara Desert and into the Mediterranean Sea. Powerful African kingdoms controlled the routes through which these prized commodities moved, and prices ballooned by the time the goods reached cities in Europe. Islamic expansion in the fifteenth century made competition all the more intense. Merchants throughout the continent yearned to access West African markets directly, by ship. But navigational and shipbuilding technology was not yet up to the challenge of the Atlantic's prevailing currents, which sped ships south along Africa's coast but made the return voyage virtually impossible.

Portugal was the first to solve this problem and tap directly into West African markets, thanks in large part to the vision and tenacity of one man. Prince Henry "the Navigator," as he became known, was a passionate advocate for Portugal's maritime interests, an ardent Catholic, and a man who dreamed of turning back Islam's rising tide. He understood

A Witch Bottle

Known as a "Bellarmine jar." Why? (Do a little web research!)

Pins and needles. Why might these have been deliberately bent?

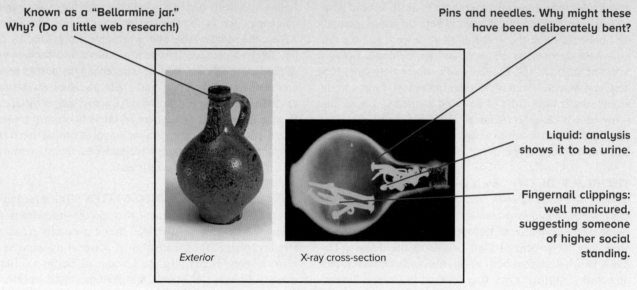

Exterior   X-ray cross-section

Liquid: analysis shows it to be urine.

Fingernail clippings: well manicured, suggesting someone of higher social standing.

(left) ©Geffrye Museum, London, UK/Bridgeman Images; (right) ©A.G. Massey. Used by permission

Historians often find clues about a culture from material artifacts discarded long ago. A Bellarmine jar was dug up in a cellar in England in 2004. Archaeologists recognized it as a "witch bottle," so called because some English folk used such items to defend against spells cast by supposed witches. The idea was to "put something intimate to the bewitched person in the bottle," explained historian Owen Davies, along with objects such as bent pins, intended to cause harm to the suspected witch.

When shaken, this bottle splashed and rattled. An X ray showed the objects inside, whose contents were examined in a laboratory. Among other items, the bottle included hair, navel fluff, and a heart-shaped piece of leather with a nail through it. The liquid also contained traces of sulphur (popularly called brimstone in the seventeenth century). An estimated 40,000–60,000 witches were hanged and burned in early modern Europe, demonstrating that despite the Reformation's disdain for "Popish superstitions," supernaturalism and magic remained potent religious strains.

THINKING CRITICALLY

Why might brimstone have been added to the witch bottle? What social factors help explain why fifteenth-century Europeans saw witchcraft as a significant part of the way the world worked? Would illnesses such as the plague contribute to attitudes about witchcraft?

Source: Geddes, Linda, "London's Magical History Uncorked from 'Witch Bottle'," *New Scientist*, June 4, 2009.

that direct commerce with West Africa would allow his kingdom to circumvent the costly trans-Sahara trade. To forward his vision, Henry funded exploratory voyages, established a maritime school, and challenged sailors and engineers to conquer the problem of the current. His advocacy helped the Portuguese develop the caravel, a lighter, more maneuverable ship that could sail better against contrary winds and in rough seas. More seaworthy than the lumbering galleys of the Middle Ages, caravels combined longer, narrower hulls—a shape built for speed—with triangular lateen sails, which allowed for more flexible steering. The caravel allowed the Portuguese to regularly do what few Europeans had ever done: sail down Africa's west coast and return home. Other advances, including a sturdier

version of the Islamic world's astrolabe, enabled Portugal's vessels to calculate their position at sea with unprecedented accuracy.

The farther south the Portuguese extended their influence along the Atlantic rim of sub-Saharan Africa, the more likely they were to meet with peoples who had had no earlier encounters with Europeans and, indeed, had no knowledge of the existence of other continents. On catching their first sight of a Portuguese expedition in 1455, the inhabitants of one village on the Senegal River marveled at the strangers' clothing and their white skin. As an Italian member of that expedition recounted, some Africans "rubbed me with their spittle to discover whether my whiteness was dye or flesh."

WEST AFRICAN STATES But the Portuguese were wrong to mistake such acts of innocence for economic or political naïveté. As they made their way south in stages, the newcomers found mature commercial networks and formidible African states, states eager to trade but intent on protecting their interests. Portugal could not simply take what it wanted from West Africa. With few exceptions, it proved impossible for European powers to colonize territory in West Africa before the nineteenth century because the region's people were too many and too organized. Furthermore, its disease environment was too dangerous. Malaria would kill between one-fourth and one-half of all Portuguese unwise and unlucky enough to try to stay. Hence the newcomers had to seek partners, to forge trading relationships with coastal elites. The Portuguese established forts and trading houses on the coast. They gave tribute or taxes to local powers in return for trading privileges and exchanged textiles, especially, but also raw and worked metal goods, currency (in the form of cowry shells), and beads for prized commodities such as gold, ivory, and malaguetta pepper. Portuguese traders also expressed interest in another commodity, one that would reshape the wider Atlantic world: slaves.

©SSPL/Science Museum/Art Resource, NY

| Astrolabe

Sugar and the Origins of the Atlantic Slave Trade

Unfree labor has existed in nearly all human societies. Although the norms, characteristics, and economic importance of slavery have varied widely over time and place, men, women, and children have been held as slaves from before recorded history to the present. (U.S. and international organizations estimate that today there are as many as 27 million people held in some form of labor bondage and that nearly 1 million unfree people are sold across international borders every year.)

By the Middle Ages, elites in Europe had largely abandoned the slave culture of the Roman Empire and relied instead on serfs or peasants for labor. Slaves became more important as status symbols than as workers, and most were young white women. Indeed, the word "slave" comes originally from "Slav"; Slavic girls and women from the Balkans and the coasts of the Black Sea were frequent targets of slave raids.

CHANGES IN EUROPEAN SLAVERY

But European slavery began to change again following the Crusades. In 1099 Christian forces captured Jerusalem from the Seljuk Turks (forerunners to the Ottomans). In the Holy Land the crusaders discovered sugar plantations that the Turks had cultivated. At that time some sugar was being produced by Moors in North Africa and Iberia, yet it remained an expensive luxury item coveted by merchants and elites as a medicine and preservative. Crusaders recognized sugar's economic potential, but because it was so labor-intensive they found it a difficult commodity to produce. It required intense work during planting and close tending during the growing season. On maturity the crop had to be harvested and processed 24 hours a day to avoid being spoiled. In short, sugar demanded cheap, pliable labor. The newly arrived crusaders relied in part on slave labor to make their plantations turn a profit.

| This African fortune-teller reads the palm of her white client in this seventeenth-century painting by a Franco-Flemish artist, Nicolas Regnier. In early modern Europe, class and religion were more important than color and ethnicity in defining social divisions. Slaves, servants, and free workers of all races often worked and socialized together.

©Erich Lessing/Art Resource, NY

SPREAD OF SUGAR Once Islamic forces under the famed leader Saladin reconquered Jerusalem in the twelfth century, European investors established new plantations on eastern Mediterranean islands. In addition to being labor-intensive, though, sugar was a crop that quickly exhausted soils and forced planters to move operations regularly. Plantations spread to new islands, and by the early 1400s sugar was even being grown in Portugal. As production expanded, planters had to work harder than ever to obtain the necessary labor because of the Black Death and because Ottoman conquests restricted European access to the traditional slaving grounds of the eastern Mediterranean and the Balkans.

Thus by the fifteenth century the Portuguese were already producing sugar on slave-run plantations, but they were seeking new cropland and new sources of slaves. Once again Prince Henry's vision enhanced his kingdom's economic interests. While Portugal's merchants were establishing trading posts along the west coast of Africa, Iberian mariners were discovering or rediscovering islands in the eastern Atlantic: the Canaries, Madeira, and the Azores, islands with rich, volcanic soils ideally suited to sugarcane. By the late fifteenth century sugar plantations were booming on the Atlantic islands, staffed by West African slaves. By the middle of the sixteenth century people of African descent accounted for 10 percent of the population of Lisbon, Portugal's capital city.

DIAS AND DA GAMA Portugal was growing great in wealth and in ambition. Convinced that they could reach coveted Asian markets by sea, bold mariners sailed their caravels farther and farther south. In 1488 Bartolomeu Dias rounded the Cape of Good Hope on the southern tip of Africa, sailing far enough up that continent's eastern coast to claim discovery of a sea route to India. Ten years later Vasco da Gama reached India itself, and Portugal's interests ultimately extended to Indochina and China.

Portuguese geographers had long felt certain that travel around Africa was the shortest route to the Orient, but an Italian sailor disagreed. Cristoforo Colombo was 25 years old when he shipwrecked on the Portuguese coast in 1476. The ambitious young man spent the next 10 years learning from the world's master mariners. He also threw himself into research, devouring Lisbon's books on geography and cartography. Columbus (the Latinized version of his name) became convinced that the fastest route from Portugal to China lay west, across the uncharted Atlantic Ocean. He appealed to Portugal's king to support an exploratory voyage, but royal geographers scoffed at the idea. They agreed that the world was round but insisted (correctly, as it turns out) that the globe was far larger than Columbus had calculated; hence the proposed westward route was too distant to be practical. Almost a decade of rejection had grayed Columbus's red hair, but—undaunted—he packed up in 1485 and took his audacious idea to Spain.

> **✓ REVIEW**
> Why did Europeans begin to develop commercial networks in the Atlantic, and how did the Portuguese operate in Africa?

SPAIN IN THE AMERICAS

BUT COLUMBUS ARRIVED A FEW years too early. Spain's monarchs, Ferdinand and Isabella, were then engaged in a campaign to drive the Muslims out of their last stronghold on the Iberian Peninsula, the Moorish kingdom of Granada. At first the monarchs rejected Columbus's offer, leading him to make other (failed) overtures to the kings of England, France, and even Portugal again. Then in 1492 Ferdinand and Isabella took Granada and completed their reconquest of Spain, or *reconquista*. Flush with victory and ready to expand their horizons, the pair granted Columbus another audience. The mariner insisted that a westward route to Asia would allow Spain to compete with Portugal and generate sufficient revenue to continue the reconquest, even into the Holy Land itself. Ignoring the advice of their geographers, the monarchs agreed to his proposal.

COLUMBUS REACHES AMERICA Columbus's first voyage across the Atlantic could only have confirmed his conviction that he was destiny's darling. His three ships, no bigger than fishing vessels that sailed to Newfoundland, plied their course over placid seas, south from Seville to the Canary Islands and then due west. On October 11, a little more than two months after leaving Spain, branches, leaves, and flowers floated by their hulls, signals that land lay near. Just after midnight, a sailor spied cliffs shining white in the moonlight. On the morning of October 12, the *Niña,* the *Pinta,* and the *Santa Maria* set anchor in a shallow sapphire bay, and their crews knelt on the white coral beach. Columbus christened the place San Salvador (Holy Savior).

The Spanish Beachhead in the Caribbean

Like many men of destiny, Columbus mistook his true destination. At first he confused his actual location, the Bahamas, with an island off the coast of Japan. He coasted along Cuba and Hispaniola (today's Haiti and Dominican Republic), expecting at any moment to catch sight of gold-roofed Japanese temples or fleets of Chinese junks. He encountered instead a gentle, generous people who knew nothing of the Great Khan but who welcomed the newcomers profusely. Columbus's journals note that these people wore little clothing, but they did wear jewelry—tiny pendants of gold suspended from the nose. He dubbed the Taino people "Indians"—inhabitants of the Indies.

Columbus would long insist that he had indeed reached the Indies, and it would take some years before other mariners and geographers understood clearly that these newfound islands and the landmasses beyond them lay between Europe and Asia. One of the earliest geographers to do so was the Florentine Amerigo Vespucci, who first described Columbus's Indies as *Mundus Novus,* a "New World." Rather than dub the new lands "Columbia," a German mapmaker called them "America" in Vespucci's honor. The German's maps proved wildly successful, and the name stuck.

WEST AFRICA AND THE CARIBBEAN COMPARED Whether Columbus had found Asian isles or a new world, Europeans seemed to agree that the simple societies he encountered were better suited to be ruled than partnered with. Unlike the kingdoms of West Africa, the Taino chiefdoms lacked the military power to resist European aggression. Moreover, although the newfound islands would eventually present their own threats to European health, they seemed a good deal more inviting than the deadly coast of West Africa. Hints of gold, a seemingly weak and docile population, and a relatively healthy climate all ensured that Columbus's second voyage would be one of colonization rather than commerce. During the 1490s and early 1500s Spanish colonizers imposed a terrifically brutal regime on the Tainos, slaughtering native leaders and forcing survivors to toil in mines and fields.

Only a few Spaniards spoke out against the exploitation. Among them was Bartolomé de Las Casas, a man who spent several years in the Caribbean, participating in conquests and profiting from native labor. Eventually, Las Casas had an epiphany, renounced his role in the conquest, and, as a Dominican friar, became a tireless foe of Spanish cruelties toward Indians. He railed against the "unjust, cruel, and tyrannical warfare" waged on Indians, war waged in order to disrupt native societies and force their people into "the hardest, harshest, and most heinous bondage to which men or beasts might ever be bound into." Las Casas's writings, translated throughout Europe and illustrated with gruesome drawings, helped give rise to the "Black Legend" of Spanish oppression in the Americas.

NATIVE DEPOPULATION The warnings had some effect, but not for decades. Within a generation of Columbus's landfall, the Taino population had nearly collapsed from war, overwork, malnutrition, despair, and strange new Eurasian diseases. Ambitious Spaniards began scouring the Caribbean basin, discovering new lands and searching for new populations of Indians to subjugate or enslave in place of the vanishing Tainos. Soon the Bahamas were depopulated by Spanish slavers, and conquests had done to present-day Cuba, Jamaica, and Puerto Rico what they had done to Hispaniola.

Conquest of the Aztecs

Would-be conquistadors turned their eyes to the mainland. Spanish sailors surveyed the Yucatán Peninsula and clashed with the formidable Mayas. In 1519 an expedition led by the impetuous Hernán Cortés made contact with native peoples on Mexico's gulf coast. They spoke of an oppressive imperial people who ccupied a fantastic city to the west. These were the Aztecs.

SPANISH AND AZTEC SOCIETIES Aztecs had much in common with Spaniards. Both societies were predominantly rural, with most inhabitants living in small villages and engaging in agriculture. In both places, merchants and specialized craftworkers clustered in cities, organized themselves into guilds, and clamored for protection from the government. Aztec noble and priestly classes, like those in Europe, took the lead in politics and religion, demanding tribute from the common people.

©Terry Harris/Alamy

This modern re-creation of a sixteenth-century Taino Indian village is located in Holguin province, Cuba. Taino chiefdoms lacked the military power to resist European aggression, and Spanish colonists began subjecting them to a brutal regimen of war and slave labor that virtually wiped out the indigenous population.

Source: Library of Congress, Prints and Photographs Division [LC-USZ62-43530]

Much like the Aztecs, Spaniards tried to make sense of the alien in terms of the familiar. Here a European artist depicts Moctezuma in the style of a Greco-Roman Warrior.

>> MAPPING THE PAST <<

ROUTES OF EUROPEAN EXPLORATION

©Sarin Images/The Granger Collection, New York

> "I am not taking pains to see much in detail because I could not do it in fifty years and because I want to see and explore as much as I can"
> —Christopher Columbus, Diary, October 19, 1492.

CONTEXT

Mostly ignorant of indigenous language, geography, culture, history, religion, economy, or politics, European explorers moved clumsily through the New World. But as they did, they unleashed profound changes, changes that often outpaced the explorers themselves. This map tracks the winding routes of exploration by water and land, along with the dates and nationalities of the voyages. Read together, these three kinds of information can reveal much about the ignorance, ambition, and competition that shaped European discovery in the Americas.

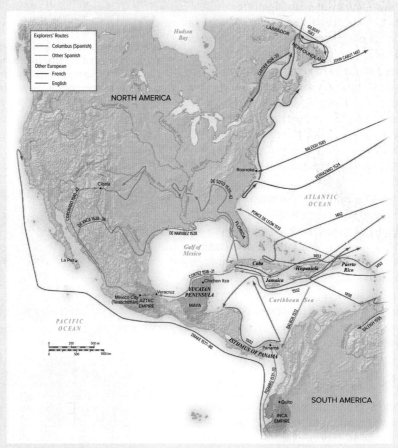

MAP READING

1. How did Columbus's routes differ in 1492, 1493, 1498, and 1502?
2. When did the French and British begin exploring the New World?
3. How long did it take Europeans to begin exploring the continental interior?

MAP INTERPRETATION

1. What regions did early European explorers seem to have avoided? What might explain the apparent disinterest?
2. How did competition among rival European imperial powers shape the pattern and timing of exploration around the Americas?

Finally, both societies were robustly expansionist, bent on bringing new lands and peoples under their control.

Yet critical differences between these two peoples shaped the outcome of their meeting. The Aztecs lacked the knowledge of ocean navigation, metal tools and weaponry, and firearms. Equally important, the relatively young Aztec Empire had not yet established total control over central Mexico. Formidable peoples remained outside Aztec domination, and conquered city-states within the empire bitterly resented Aztec rule. It was a weakness that Cortés exploited ably. Massing an army of disgruntled native warriors, Cortés and his men marched inland to the mighty Aztec capital Tenochtitlán, home to more people (roughly a quarter million) than any city then existing in Europe. When the emperor Moctezuma's ambassadors met Cortés on the road and attempted to appease him with gold ornaments and other gifts, an Indian witness noted that "the Spaniards . . . picked up the gold and fingered it like monkeys. . . . Their bodies swelled with greed." The newcomers were welcomed into the city as honored guests but soon seized Moctezuma and took him captive. For months Cortés ruled the empire indirectly, but the Aztecs drove the Spanish out after Moctezuma's death.

DISEASE AND DEFEAT In the midst of this victory the city encountered another foe—smallpox. Geographically isolated from Eurasia and its complex disease environment, the Aztecs and all other native peoples in the Americas lacked the acquired immunity that gave Europeans a degree of protection against Old World pathogens. The resulting **virgin soil epidemics**—so called because the victims had no prior exposure—took a nightmarish toll. Smallpox claimed millions in central Mexico between 1520 and 1521. This too presented Cortés with opportunities. Supported by a massive Indian force, he put Tenochtitlán to siege, killing tens of thousands before the ragged, starving survivors surrendered in August of 1521. The feared Aztec Empire lay in ruins. Conquistadors fanned out from central Mexico, overwhelming new populations and eventually learning of another mighty kingdom to the south. Again relying on political faction, disease, technological advantages, and luck, by 1532 Spaniards under Francisco Pizarro and his brothers had conquered the Inca Empire in South America, which in certain regards rivaled even the Aztecs.

The Columbian Exchange

Virgin soil epidemics, which contributed to the devastation of the Indian populations, were only one aspect of a complex web of interactions between the flora and fauna of the Americas on the one hand and that of Eurasia and Africa on the other. Just as germs migrated along with humans, so did plants and animals. These transfers, begun in the decades after Columbus first landed in the Caribbean, are known by historians as the **Columbian exchange,** and they had far-reaching effects on either side of the Atlantic. Europeans brought a host of American crops home with them, as seen in Chapter 1. They also most likely brought syphilis, an American disease that broke out across Europe in more virulent form than ever before. Europeans brought to the Americas

the horses and large dogs that intimidated the Aztecs; they brought oranges, lemons, figs, and bananas from Africa and the Canary Islands. Escaped hogs multiplied so rapidly that they overran some Caribbean islands, as did European rats.

ONGOING EXCHANGES The Columbian exchange was not a short-lived event. In a host of different ways it continued to reshape the globe over the next half millennium as travel, exploration, and colonization brought cultures ever closer. Instead of smallpox, today H1N1 influenza or the West Nile virus threatens populations worldwide. But the exchanges of the sixteenth century were often more extreme, unpredictable, and far-reaching because of the previous isolation of the two hemispheres.

The Crown Steps In

The proud conquistadors did not long enjoy their mastery in the Americas. Spain's monarchs, who had just tamed an aristocracy at home, were not about to allow a colonial nobility to arise across the Atlantic. The Crown bribed the conquistadors into retirement—or was saved the expense when men such as Francisco Pizarro were assassinated by their own followers. The task of governing Spain's new colonies passed from the conquistadors to a small army of officials, soldiers, lawyers, and Catholic bishops, all appointed by the Crown, reporting to the Crown, and loyal to the Crown. Headquartered in urban centers such as Mexico City (formerly Tenochtitlán), an elaborate, centralized bureaucracy administered the Spanish Empire, regulating nearly every aspect of economic and social life.

SPANISH AND INDIAN POPULATIONS Few Spaniards besides imperial officials settled in the Americas. By 1600 only about 5 percent of the colonial population was of Spanish descent, the other 95 percent being either Indian or African. Even by 1800 only 300,000 Spanish immigrants had come to Central and South America. Indians often remained on the lands that they had farmed under the Aztecs and the Incas, now paying Spanish overlords their taxes and producing livestock for export. More importantly, Indians paid for the new order through their labor, sometimes as slaves but more often through an evolving administrative system channeling native workers to public and private enterprises throughout New Spain. The Spanish also established sugar plantations in the West Indies; these were worked by black slaves who by 1520 were being imported from Africa in large numbers.

SILVER BONANZA Spain's colonies returned even more spectacular profits to the mother country by the 1540s—the result of silver discoveries of epic proportions in both Mexico and South America. Silver mining developed into a large-scale capitalist enterprise requiring substantial investment. European investors and Spanish immigrants who had profited from cattle raising and sugar planting poured their capital into equipment and supplies that would mine the silver deposits more efficiently: stamp mills, water-powered crushing equipment, pumps, and mercury. Whole villages of

HOW DID SPANIARDS AND AZTECS REMEMBER FIRST CONTACT?

The first encounter between the Spaniards under Hernán Cortés and ambassadors of the emperor Moctezuma in 1519 represents a fateful turning point in history. While we have no full contemporary account of that meeting, two remarkable sources present Spanish and Mexican memories of the event written years later. The first selection below was written in the 1560s by one of Cortés's lieutenants, the conquistador Bernal Díaz. The second section comes from a work compiled in the 1540s by the missionary Bernardino de Sahagún, in which indigenous informants recalled Aztec culture, religion, society, and history up to and through the conquest.

DOCUMENT 1
Bernal Díaz

Seeing the big ship with the standards flying they knew that it was there that they must go to speak with the captain; so they went direct to the flagship and going on board asked who was the Tatuan [Tlatoan] which in their language means the chief. Doña Marina who understood the language well, pointed him out. Then the Indians paid many marks of respect to Cortés, according to their usage, and bade him welcome, and said that their lord, a servant of the great Montezuma, had sent them to ask what kind of men we were and of what

we were in search. . . . [Cortés] told them that we came to see them and to trade with them and that our arrival in their country should cause them no uneasiness but be looked on by them as fortunate. . . .

[Several days later, one of Montezuma's emissaries] brought with him some clever painters such as they had in Mexico and ordered them to make pictures true to nature of the face and body of Cortés and all his captains, and of the soldiers, ships, sails, and horses, and of Doña Marina and Aguilar, even of the two greyhounds, and the cannon

and cannon balls, and all of the army we had brought with us, and he carried the pictures to his master. Cortés ordered our gunners to load the lombards with a great charge of powder so that they should make a great noise when they were fired off. . . . [The emissary] went with all haste and narrated everything to his prince, and showed him the pictures which had been painted.

Source: Díaz, Bernal, *The True History of the Conquest of New Spain,* excerpted in Schwartz, Stuart B., ed., *Victors and Vanquished: Spanish and Nahua Views of the Conquest of Mexico,* 2000, 85–91.

DOCUMENT 2
Fray (Friar) Bernardino de Sahagún

When they had gotten up into [Cortés's] boat, each of them made the earth-eating gesture before the Captain. Then they addressed him, saying, "May the god attend: his agent Moteucçoma who is in charge in Mexico for him addresses him and says, 'The god is doubly welcome.'"

Then they dressed up the Captain. They put on him the turquoise serpent mask attached to the quetzal-feather head fan, to which were fixed, from which hung the green-stone serpent earplugs. And they put the sleeveless jacket on him, and around his neck they put the plaited green-stone neckband with the golden disk in the middle. On his lower back they tied the back mirror, and also they tied behind him the cloak called a *tzitzilli.* And on his legs they placed the green-stone bands with the golden bells. And they gave him, placing it on his arm, the shield with gold and shells crossing, on whose edge were spread quetzal feathers, with a quetzal banner. And they laid the obsidian sandals before him. . . .

Then the Captain ordered that they be tied up: they put irons on their feet and necks. When this had been done they shot off the cannon. And at this point the messengers truly fainted and swooned; one after another they swayed and fell, losing consciousness. . . . Then [Cortés] let them go.

[Upon returning to Tenochtitlán and reporting to Moteucçoma, he replied] "I will not hear it here. I will hear it at the Coacalco; let them go there." And he gave orders, saying, "Let some captives be covered in chalk [for sacrifice]."

Then the messengers went to the Coacalco, and so did Moteucçoma. There upon the captives died in their presence; they cut open their chests and sprinkled their blood on the messengers. (The reason they did it was that they had gone to very dangerous places and had seen, gazed on the countenances of, and spoken to the gods.) . . .

When this was done, they talked to Moteucçoma, telling him what they had beheld, and they showed him what [the Spaniards'] food was like.

And when he heard what the messengers reported, he was greatly afraid and taken aback, and he was amazed at their food. It especially made him faint when he heard how the guns went off at [the Spaniards'] command, sounding like thunder, causing people to actually swoon, blocking the ears. And when it went off, something like a ball came out from inside, and fire went showering and spitting out. And the smoke that came out had a very foul stench, striking one in the face. And if they shot at a

hill, it seemed to crumble and come apart. . . . Their war gear was all iron. They clothed their bodies in iron, they put iron on their heads, their swords were iron, their bows were iron, and their shields were iron.

And the deer that carried them were as tall as the roof. And they wrapped their bodies all over; only their faces could be seen, very white. . . .

And their dogs were huge creatures, with their ears folded over and their jowls dragging. They had burning eyes, eyes like coals, yellow and fiery. . . .

When Moteucçoma heard it, he was greatly afraid; he seemed to faint away, he grew concerned and disturbed.

Source: de Sahagún, Fray Bernardino, *The Florentine Codex,* excerpted in Schwartz, Stuart B., ed., *Victors and Vanquished: Spanish and Nahua Views of the Conquest of Mexico,* 2000, 91–99.

THINKING CRITICALLY

How did the Aztecs and the Spaniards communicate? Why does Díaz pay so little attention to the gifts the emissaries brought Cortés? Why might the painters be absent from Document 2? What principles of critical thinking should be kept in mind when reading such documents?

Indians were pressed into service in the mines, joining black slaves and free white workers employed there.

In the last decades of the sixteenth century the economies of Mexico and Peru revolved around the mines. By 1570 the town of Potosí, the site of a veritable mountain of silver, had become larger than any city in either Spain or its American empire, with a population of 120,000. Local farmers who supplied mining centers with food and Spanish merchants in Seville who exported European goods to Potosí profited handsomely. So, too, did the Spanish Crown, which claimed one-fifth of all extracted silver. During the sixteenth century some 16,000 tons of the precious metal were exported from Spanish America to Europe.

The Search for North America's Indian Empires

Riches and glory radicalized Spanish expectations. Would-be conquistadors embarked on an urgent race to discover and topple the next Aztec or Inca Empire, a race to become the

©The Morgan Library & Museum/Art Resource, NY

Fabulous gold and silver discoveries in their New World empire led Spaniards to force Indians and Africans to labor in the mines under dangerous and brutal conditions. This late-sixteenth-century illustration portrays Africans mining for a Spaniard in Panama, but it seems almost pastoral, compared to the dangers of earthen collapses in the mining pits and tunnels or the risks of suffocation or black lung disease from the dust underground.

next Cortés or Pizarro. The prevailing mood was captured by the portrait of a Spanish soldier that adorns the frontispiece of his book about the West Indies. He stands with one hand on his sword and the other holding a pair of compasses on top of a globe. Beneath is inscribed the motto "By compasses and the sword/More and more and more and more."

PONCE DE LEÓN   Some of the most ambitious adventurers felt certain that more lands and riches would be found in the North. Spanish slavers had been the first to skirt the North American mainland, going as far north as present-day South Carolina. These voyages likely inspired Juan Ponce de León, conquerer of Puerto Rico, to make the first official expedition to the mainland, which he named Florida to mark the day of his landfall, *Pascua Florida* (Easter). Everywhere he went he met armed resistance from Florida's native inhabitants, people who had come to know and despise Spaniards as slave raiders. Ponce de León sailed back to Puerto Rico and then returned for some years to Spain, until Cortés's early exploits in Mexico rekindled his ambitions. Filled with visions of glory, he returned to Florida in 1521 only to be mortally wounded in a battle with Calusa Indians.

PÁNFILO DE NARVÁEZ AND CABEZA DE VACA   Ponce de León died miserably, yet his countrymen still believed that wealthy Indian empires remained undiscovered in the North. In 1526 Spain established a settlement in present-day Georgia, but the endeavor soon collapsed. Two years later Pánfilo de Narváez, a red-bearded veteran from the conquest of Cuba, led a major expedition back to Florida. Ignoring advice from his second-in-command, Álvar Núñez Cabeza de Vaca, Narváez separated from his main force near Tampa Bay and led 300 men on a harrowing march in search of riches. For months the force plundered its way through Florida, while the men fell ill or fell victim to Indian archers, whose longbows could bury an arrow six inches into a tree. Disillusioned and desperate, 242 survivors lashed together makeshift rafts and tried to sail along the Gulf Coast to Mexico. Weeks later proud Narváez and most of his men had disappeared at sea, whereas Cabeza de Vaca and a handful of survivors washed up on islands off the Texas coast.

Local Indian groups then turned the tables and made slaves of the Spaniards. Cabeza de Vaca later recalled that his captors were appalled to learn that the starving castaways had eaten their dead. After years as prisoners, Cabeza de Vaca and three others, including a black slave named Esteban, escaped to make an extraordinary trek across Texas and northern Mexico. Somewhere in present-day Chihuahua they passed through what had been the trading hinterland of Paquime, and Cabeza de Vaca noted an enduring regional commerce in feathers and "green stones"—turquoise. Finally, in July 1536 a shocked party of Spanish slavers stumbled across the four ragtag castaways and brought them to Mexico City.

HERNÁN DE SOTO   The stories the four men told of their trek inspired two more massive expeditions to discover and conquer North America's elusive Indian empires. The first was led by Hernán de Soto, who had grown wealthy helping to conquer

Peru. Confident that Florida held similar riches, de Soto scoured the Southeast's agricultural villages searching for gold and taking whatever he wanted: food, clothing, luxury goods, even young women whom he and his men "desired both as servants and for their foul uses." As they raped, stole, and killed their way through the Southeast, de Soto and his men unwittingly had the honor of being the first and last Europeans to glimpse several declining Mississippian chiefdoms, echoes of Cahokia's ancient majesty. Some native communities resisted, inflicting huge losses on de Soto's men. Others shrewdly feigned friendship and insisted that gold and glory could be found in this or that nearby village, thus ridding themselves of a great danger and directing it at enemies instead. De Soto's men ravaged Indian societies through parts of present-day Florida, Georgia, North and South Carolina, Tennessee, Alabama, Mississippi, Arkansas, Louisiana, and Texas. The expedition never found the treasures it sought, but it did hasten the transformation of the southeastern chiefdoms into decentralized confederacies.

VÁZQUEZ DE CORONADO   Spanish ambition met a similar fate in the West. In 1539, 29-year-old Francisco Vázquez de Coronado led 300 Spaniards and 1,000 Mexican Indian warriors north into the present-day American Southwest. Emboldened by tales of cities more wondrous even than Tenochtitlán, Coronado's brash confidence began to fail him when instead he found only

©Dorling Kindersley/Getty Images

| As Hernán de Soto traveled through North America, he brought a herd of pigs much like this razorback hog. At times the herd numbered more than 700. The animals were an efficient way of providing protein to the expedition. More than 80 percent of a carcass could be consumed, compared with only 50 percent of a cow or sheep. Hogs could be herded on the march as well, foraging for food as they went. But some anthropologists and historians believe that the hogs were also carriers of disease that migrated to humans. The diseases may have sparked the deaths of thousands of Indians, who lacked the immunity built up by Europeans over centuries of exposure to Eurasian illnesses.

SPANISH AMERICA, CA. 1600

By 1600 Spain was extracting large amounts of gold and silver from Mexico and South America, as well as profits from sugar plantations in the Caribbean. Each year Spanish treasure ships ferried bullion from mines such as the one at Potosí to the Isthmus of Panama, where it was transported by land to the Caribbean coast, and from there to Spain. An expedition from Acapulco sailed annually to the Philippines as well, returning with Asian spices and other trade goods. For an English "sea dog" (read: pirate) looking to capture Spanish treasure, which geographic location would be the best place to pick off Spanish treasure ships?

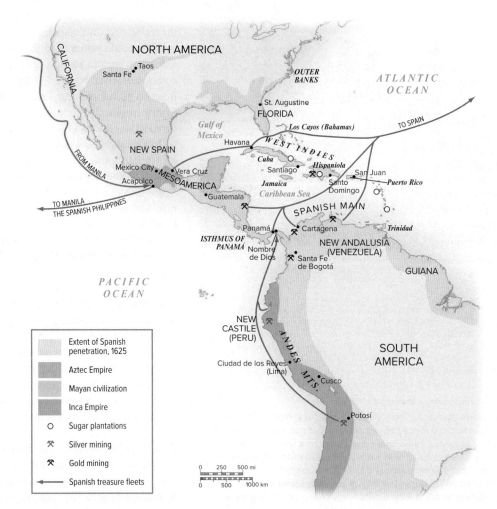

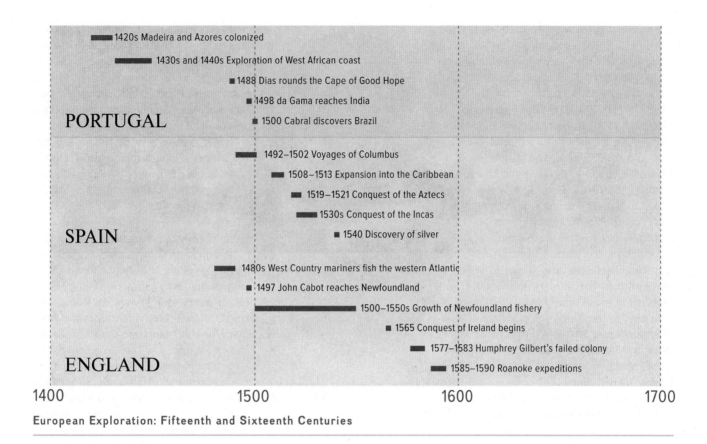

PORTUGAL

■■■ 1420s Madeira and Azores colonized

■■■■ 1430s and 1440s Exploration of West African coast

■ 1488 Dias rounds the Cape of Good Hope

■ 1498 da Gama reaches India

■ 1500 Cabral discovers Brazil

SPAIN

■■■ 1492–1502 Voyages of Columbus

■■ 1508–1513 Expansion into the Caribbean

■■ 1519–1521 Conquest of the Aztecs

■■■ 1530s Conquest of the Incas

■ 1540 Discovery of silver

■■■ 1480s West Country mariners fish the western Atlantic

■ 1497 John Cabot reaches Newfoundland

■■■■■■ 1500–1550s Growth of Newfoundland fishery

■ 1565 Conquest of Ireland begins

■■■ 1577–1583 Humphrey Gilbert's failed colony

ENGLAND

■■ 1585–1590 Roanoke expeditions

1400   1500   1600   1700

European Exploration: Fifteenth and Sixteenth Centuries

mud and straw pueblos inhabited by modest farmers. Determined to turn his hugely expensive expedition to advantage, Coronado sent men in all directions. Some went west, until they ran into the vastness of the Grand Canyon and had to turn back. Others traveled east, taking up temporary residence among the Pueblo peoples of the upper Rio Grande. The increasingly abusive visitors soon provoked battles with their hosts, forcing them to abandon 13 villages, which the Spaniards then destroyed. Desperate to redeem his reputation and investment, Coronado followed an Indian he dubbed the Turk out onto the Great Plains in search of a rumored kingdom called Quivira. Perhaps the Turk had in mind one of the easternmost Mississippian chiefdoms, but the frustrated conquistador became convinced he had been deceived. He had the Turk strangled somewhere in present-day Kansas and in 1542 returned to Mexico, where Crown authorities brought him to trial for inflicting "great cruelties" on Indians.

SPAIN'S DOMINANCE IN THE AMERICAS Conquistadors such as Coronado might be ruined by their unfulfilled ambitions, but Spain could afford its failed North American excursions. It had taken vast wealth from the Americas, conquered the hemisphere's mightiest peoples, and laid claim to most of the New World. Spaniards warily expected competition, and yet for most of the sixteenth century rival European powers took little interest in the Americas. England's fishermen continued to explore the North Sea, Labrador, and Newfoundland. Portugal discovered and laid claim to Brazil. France sent expeditions to explore North America's eastern shoreline (Giovanni da Verrazano, 1524) and the St. Lawrence River

valley (Jacques Cartier, 1534, 1535, and 1541). These efforts proved important in the long run, but for most of the century Spain could treat the Americas as their own. They owed that luxury, in part, to religious upheaval in Europe. During the second decade of the sixteenth century—the same decade in which Cortés laid siege to Tenochtitlán—religious changes of enormous significance began spreading through Europe. That revolution in Christianity, known as the Protestant Reformation, occupied European attentions and eventually figured as a crucial force in shaping the history of the Americas.

✓ **REVIEW**

How did the Spanish respond to the discovery of a "new world"?

RELIGIOUS REFORM DIVIDES EUROPE

DURING THE MIDDLE AGES, THE Roman Catholic church defined what it meant to be a Christian in western Europe. Like other institutions of medieval society, the Catholic Church was a hierarchy. At the top was the pope in Rome, and under him were the descending ranks of other church officials—cardinals, archbishops, bishops. At the bottom of the Catholic hierarchy were parish priests, each serving his own village, as well as monks and nuns living in monasteries and convents.

But medieval popes were weak, and their power was felt little in the lives of most Europeans. Like political units of the era, religious institutions of the Middle Ages were local and decentralized.

RISE OF THE PAPACY   Between about 1100 and 1500, however, as the monarchs of Europe grew more powerful so, too, did the popes. The Catholic Church acquired land throughout Europe, and its swelling bureaucracy added to church income from tithing (taxes contributed by church members) and from fees paid by those appointed to church offices. In the thirteenth century church officials also began to sell "indulgences." For ordinary believers who expected to spend time after death purging their sins in purgatory, the purchase of an indulgence promised to shorten that punishment by drawing on a "treasury of merit" amassed by the good works of Christ and the saints.

By the fifteenth century the Catholic Church and the papacy had become enormously powerful but increasingly indifferent to popular religious concerns. Church officials meddled in secular politics. Popes and bishops flaunted their wealth, while poorly educated parish priests neglected their pastoral duties. At the same time, popular demands for religious assurance grew increasingly intense.

The Teachings of Martin Luther

Into this climate of heightened spirituality stepped Martin Luther, who abandoned studying the law to enter a monastery. Like many of his contemporaries, Luther was consumed by fears over his eternal fate. He was convinced that he was damned, and he could not find any consolation in the Catholic Church. Catholic doctrine taught that a person could be saved by faith in God and by his or her own good works—by leading a virtuous life, observing the sacraments (such as baptism, the Mass, and penance), making pilgrimages to holy places, and praying to Christ and the saints. Because Luther believed that human nature was innately evil, he despaired of being able to lead a life that "merited" salvation. If men and women are so bad, he reasoned, how could they ever win their way to heaven with good works?

JUSTIFICATION BY FAITH ALONE   Luther finally broke through his despair with the Bible. It convinced him that God did not require fallen humankind to earn salvation. Salvation, he concluded, came by faith alone, the "free gift" of God to undeserving sinners. The ability to live a good life could not be the *cause* of salvation but its *consequence:* once men and women believed that they had saving faith, moral behavior was possible. Luther elaborated that idea, known as "justification by faith alone," between 1513 and 1517.

©Pixtal/agefotostock

| Martin Luther argued that salvation came by faith alone, a free gift of God to undeserving sinners.

Luther was ordained a priest and then assigned to teach at a university in Wittenberg, Germany. He became increasingly critical, however, of the Catholic Church as an institution. In 1517 he posted on the door of a local church 95 theses attacking the Catholic hierarchy for selling salvation in the form of indulgences.

The novelty of this attack was not Luther's open break with Catholic teaching. Challenges to the church had cropped up throughout the Middle Ages. What was new were the passion and force behind Luther's protest. Using the blunt, earthy Germanic tongue, he expressed the anxieties of many devout laypeople and their outrage at the church hierarchy's neglect. The "gross, ignorant asses and knaves at Rome," he warned, should keep their distance from Germany, or else "jump into the Rhine or the nearest river, and take . . . a cold bath."

The pope and his representatives in Germany at first tried to silence Martin Luther, then excommunicated him. But opposition only pushed Luther toward more radical positions. He asserted that the church and its officials were not infallible; only the Scriptures were without error. Every person, he said, should read and interpret the Bible for himself or herself. In an even more direct assault on church authority, he advanced an idea known as "the priesthood of all believers." Catholic doctrine held that salvation came only through the church and its clergy, a privileged group that possessed special access to God. Luther asserted that every person had the power claimed by priests.

Although Luther had not intended to start a schism within Catholicism, independent Lutheran churches were forming in Germany by the 1520s. And, during the 1530s, Luther's ideas spread throughout Europe, where they were eagerly taken up by other reformers.

The Contribution of John Calvin

The most influential of Luther's successors was John Calvin, a French lawyer turned theologian. Calvin agreed with Luther that men and women could not merit their salvation. But, whereas Luther's God was a loving deity who extended his mercy to sinful humankind, Calvin conceived of God as awesome, all-knowing and all-powerful—the controlling force in human history that would ultimately triumph over Satan. To bring about that final victory, to usher in his heavenly kingdom, God had selected certain people as his agents, Calvin believed. These people—"the saints," or "the **elect**"—had been "predestined" by God for eternal salvation in heaven.

THE "ELECT"   Calvin's emphasis on predestination led him to another distinctively Protestant notion—the doctrine of calling. How could a person learn whether he or she belonged to the elect who were saved? Calvin answered: strive to behave like a saint. God expected his elect to serve the good of society by unrelenting work in a "calling," or occupation, in the world. In place of the Catholic belief in the importance of good works, Calvin emphasized the goodness of work itself. Success in attaining discipline and self-control, in bringing order into one's own life and the entire society, revealed that a person might be among the elect.

Calvin fashioned a religion to change the world. Whereas Luther believed that Christians should accept the existing social order, Calvin called on Christians to become activists, reshaping society and government to conform with God's laws laid down in the Bible. He wanted all Europe to become like Geneva, the Swiss city that he had converted into a holy commonwealth in which the elect regulated the behavior and morals of everyone else. And unlike Luther, who wrote primarily for a German audience, Calvin addressed his most important book, *The Institutes of the Christian Religion* (1536), to Christians throughout Europe. Reformers from every country flocked to Geneva to learn more about Calvin's ideas.

The Birth of Spanish Florida and French Huguenots

The Protestant Reformation shattered the unity of Christendom in western Europe. Spain, Portugal, Ireland, and Italy remained firmly Catholic. England, Scotland, the Netherlands, Switzerland, and France developed either dominant or substantial Calvinist constituencies. Much of Germany and Scandinavia opted for Lutheranism. As religious groups competed for political power and the loyalties of believers, brutal wars swept sixteenth-century Europe, and France experienced some of the worst violence. An influential group of Huguenots (Calvin's French followers) saw in North America a potential refuge from religious persecution. Under the leadership of Jean Ribault, 150 Huguenots from Normandy in 1562 established a simple village on Parris Island off present-day South Carolina. That experiment ended in desperation and cannibalism, but two years later Ribault led another, larger group to a site south of present-day Jacksonville, Florida. Here the Huguenots constructed a settlement they named Fort Caroline and nurtured a cordial relationship with the local Timucua Indians. It seemed a promising start.

HUGUENOTS AS A THREAT TO SPAIN But Spanish authorities in the Caribbean took the Huguenots for a triple threat. First, French pirates had long sought to siphon silver from the Americas by waylaying Spanish galleons. Silver shipments rode the Gulf Stream past the Bahamas and up the southeastern coast of North America before turning east toward Spain. In only four years, from 1556 to 1560, French ships preying on this vulnerable route had helped cut Spain's colonial revenues in half. With good reason, Spanish administrators feared that Fort Caroline would entrench the threat of piracy. Second, Spain had to worry that France would plant successful colonies and take a broader interest in the Americas, perhaps eventually making claims on all of North America. Finally, many Spanish Catholics saw Protestantism as a loathsome contagion, to be expunged from Europe and barred from the Americas.

These interlocking concerns prompted Spain to found a permanent colony in Florida. To do so the Crown turned to a focused and unforgiving man named Pedro Menéndez de Avilés. In 1565 Menéndez established a settlement on the coast called St. Augustine (still the United States' oldest continuously occupied, non-Indian settlement) and immediately marched north to destroy Fort Caroline. He and 500 soldiers slogged through the rain and marsh until they found the simple fort. In battle and through later executions, the attackers killed Ribault and about 500 of his Huguenots. Flush with victory, Menéndez established several more outposts on Florida's Atlantic and Gulf coasts, and in 1570 even encouraged a short-lived Jesuit mission just miles from where English colonists would establish Jamestown a generation later. As for the Huguenots, the calamity at Fort Caroline dashed hope that the New World would be their haven. Most had to resign themselves to intensifying persecution in France.

The English Reformation

While the Reformation wracked northern Europe, King Henry VIII of England labored at a goal more worldly than those of Luther and Calvin. He wanted a son, a male heir to continue the Tudor dynasty. When his wife, Catherine of Aragon, gave birth to a daughter, Mary, Henry petitioned the pope to have his marriage annulled in the hope that a new wife would give him a son. This move enraged the king of Spain, who also happened to be Catherine's nephew. He persuaded the pope to refuse Henry's request. Defiantly, England's king proceeded with the divorce nonetheless and quickly married Anne Boleyn. He then went further, making himself, not the pope, the head of the Church of England. Henry was an audacious but practical man, and he had little interest in promoting reformist doctrine. Apart from discarding the pope, the Church of England remained essentially Catholic in its teachings and rituals.

ENGLISH PURITANS   England's Protestants gained ground during the six-year reign of Henry's son Edward VI but then found themselves persecuted when Edward's Catholic half-sister Mary became queen in 1553. Five years later the situation turned again, when Elizabeth I (Anne Boleyn's daughter) took the throne, proclaiming herself the defender of Protestantism. Elizabeth was no radical Calvinist, however. A vocal minority of her subjects were reformers of that stripe, calling for the English church to purge itself of bishops, elaborate ceremonies, and other Catholic "impurities." Because of the austerity and zeal of such Calvinist radicals, their opponents proclaimed them "**Puritans**."

ELIZABETH'S FEARS   Radical Protestants might annoy Elizabeth as she pursued her careful, moderate policies, but radical Catholics frightened her. She had reason to worry that Spain might try to employ English Catholics to undermine her rule. More ominously, Elizabeth's advisors cautioned that Catholic Ireland to the west would be an ideal base from which Spain or France could launch an invasion of England. Beginning in 1565 the queen encouraged a number of her elite subjects to sponsor private ventures for subduing the native Irish and settling loyal English Protestants on their land. As events fell out, this Irish venture proved to be a prelude to England's bolder attempt to found colonies across the Atlantic.

REVIEW

How did religious reform divide Europe in the sixteenth century?

ENGLAND'S ENTRY INTO AMERICA

AMONG THE GENTLEMEN EAGER TO win fame and fortune were Humphrey Gilbert and Walter Raleigh, two adventurers with conquistador appetites for more and more. The pair were like most of the English who went to Ireland, ardent Protestants who viewed the native Catholic inhabitants as superstitious, pagan savages: "They blaspheme, they murder, commit whoredome," complained one Englishman, "hold no wedlocke, ravish, steal and commit all abomination without scruple." Thus the English found it easy enough to justify their conquest. They proclaimed it their duty to teach the Irish the discipline of hard work, the rule of law, and the truth of Protestant Christianity. And, while the Irish were learning these civilized, English ways, they would not be allowed to buy land or hold office or serve on juries or give testimony in courts or learn a trade or bear arms.

When the Irish rebelled at that program of "liberation," the English ruthlessly repressed them, slaughtering not only combatants but civilians as well. Most English in Ireland, like most Spaniards in America, believed that native peoples who resisted civilization and proper Christianity should be subdued at any cost. No scruples stopped Gilbert, in an insurgent country, from planting the path to his camp with the severed heads of Irish rebels.

THE IRISH EXPERIENCE AS A MODEL   The struggle to colonize and subdue Ireland would serve as a rough model for later English efforts at expansion. The approach was essentially military, like that of the conquistadors. It also set the ominous precedent that Englishmen could treat "savage" peoples with a level of brutal cruelty that would have been inappropriate in wars between "civilized" Europeans. But the campaigns in Ireland seemed to leave the queen's men with little more than lessons. "Neither reputation, or profytt is to be wonne" in Ireland, concluded Gilbert. He, Raleigh, and many other West Country gentry wanted to take their ambition and their Irish education to North America.

The Ambitions of Gilbert, Raleigh, and Wingina

GILBERT'S UTOPIAN DREAMS   In 1578 Gilbert was the first to get his chance for glory when Elizabeth granted him a royal patent—the first English colonial **charter**—to explore, occupy, and govern any territory in America "not actually possessed of any Christian prince or people." The vague, wildly unrealistic charter matched Gilbert's vast ego. It ignored the Indian possession of North America and made him lord and proprietor of all the land lying between Florida and Labrador. In many ways his dreams looked backward. Gilbert hoped to set up a kind of medieval kingdom of his own, where loyal tenant farmers would work the lands of manors, paying rent to feudal lords. Yet his vision also looked forward to a utopian society. He planned to encourage England's poor to emigrate by providing them free land and a government "to be chosen by consent of the people." Elizabeth had high hopes for her haughty champion, but a fierce storm got the better of his ship, and the Atlantic swallowed him before he could ever plant a settlement.

WALTER RALEIGH   Meanwhile, Gilbert's stepbrother Raleigh had been working more industriously to lay the groundwork for a British American empire. Raleigh enlisted the talents of Richard Hakluyt, a clergyman with a passion for spreading knowledge of overseas discoveries. At Raleigh's bidding, Hakluyt wrote an eloquent plea to Elizabeth for the English settlement of America, titled *A Discourse Concerning Westerne Planting* (1584). The temperate and fertile lands of North America, Hakluyt argued, would prove ideal for growing tropical commodities and would be an excellent base from which to harry the Spanish, search for a northwest passage to the Orient, and extend the influence of Protestantism. He also stressed the advantages of colonies as potential markets for English goods and as havens for the poor and unemployed. Finally, Hakluyt predicted that because the "Spaniardes have executed most outragious and more then

Turkishe cruelties in all the west Indies," Indians would greet Englishmen as liberators.

FIRST ROANOKE SETTLEMENT

Raleigh's chance to test the prediction finally came in 1584, when Elizabeth granted him a patent nearly identical to Gilbert's. By the summer Raleigh had dispatched an exploratory voyage to the Outer Banks of present-day North Carolina. Expedition leaders reported making friendly contact with a people known as the Roanoke and ruled by a "weroance," or chief, named Wingina. The enthusiastic Hakluyt envisioned a colony that would become the Mexico of England, full of plantations producing sugar and silk and mountains yielding gold. Elizabeth knighted Raleigh and allowed him to name the new land "Virginia," after his virgin queen.

WINGINA'S PLANS But Raleigh was not the only one with grand plans. Almost certainly Wingina had encountered or at least heard of Europeans before 1584. Like most coastal groups in the region, his people would have obtained prized European tools and commodities through indirect trade or by scouring wrecked ships. Preoccupied with the political geography of his own region and eager to fortify his own and his people's power, Wingina recognized that friendly relations with the English would give him privileged access to their trade and influence. Perhaps he believed he would act as patron to the newcomers. After all, they knew little of the region, spoke no Indian languages, and even lacked the basic skills necessary to survive in the area without native assistance. In short, Wingina seems to have welcomed the English and encouraged their return because he believed that they could be useful and that they could be controlled. It was a tragic if understandable miscalculation—one that Indian leaders would make again and again in colonial America.

Raleigh apparently aimed to establish on Roanoke a mining camp and a military garrison. In a stroke of genius, he included in the company of 108 men a scientist, Thomas Hariot, to study the country's natural resources and an artist, John White, to make drawings of the Virginia Indians. *A Briefe and True Reporte of the New Found Land of Virginia* (1588), written by Hariot and illustrated by White, served as one of the principal sources about North America and its Indian inhabitants for more than a century. Far less inspired was Raleigh's choice to lead the expedition—two veterans of the Irish campaigns, Sir Richard Grenville and Ralph Lane. Even his fellow conquistadors in Ireland considered Lane proud and greedy. As for Grenville, he was given to breaking wineglasses between his teeth and then swallowing the shards to show that he could stand the sight of blood, even his own.

The bullying ways of both men quickly alienated the natives of Roanoke. Wingina found the newcomers disrespectful,

haughty, and cruel: when a local stole a cup, the English tried to teach everyone a lesson by torching his village and destroying its corn stores. As winter arrived and supplies ran low, the hungry colonists made greater and greater demands. The Roanokes' resentment fueled English anxiety that a revolt was brewing, and these anxieties led only to more brutality and more resentment. The following summer Wingina made a final attempt to regain control of the situation. He had agreed to parlay with Lane about improving relations. But the meeting was a ruse. Lane's men opened fire at the Indian envoys, killed Wingina, and hacked the head from his body. All that averted a massive counterattack was the arrival of England's preeminent privateer, Sir Francis Drake, fresh from freebooting up and down the Caribbean. The settlement's 102 survivors piled onto Drake's ships and put an ocean between themselves and the avenging Roanokes.

A Second Roanoke—and Croatoan

Undaunted, Raleigh organized a second expedition to plant a colony farther north, in Chesapeake Bay. He now projected an agricultural community of manors, much like those in England. He recruited 119 men, women, and children, members of the English middle class, and granted each person an estate of 500 acres. He also appointed as governor the artist John White, who brought along a suit of armor for ceremonial occasions.

White deplored Lane's treachery toward Wingina and hated the brazen, senseless violence that had characterized the entire endeavor. The artist had spent his time on Roanoke closely observing native peoples, their material cultures, and their customs. His sensitive watercolors, especially those featuring women and children, indicate a genuine respect and affection. White felt strongly that under prudent, moral leaders an English colony could indeed coexist peacefully with American Indians.

Despite his best intentions, everything went wrong. In July of 1587 the expedition's pilot, Simon Ferdinando, insisted on leaving the colonists at Roanoke Island rather than along Chesapeake Bay. Understandably, the Roanokes took no pleasure in seeing the English return, and even before Ferdinando weighed anchor the settlers began skirmishing with Indians. Sensing that the situation on Roanoke could quickly become desperate, the colonists prevailed on White to sail back with Ferdinando and bring reinforcements.

©Private Collection/Bridgeman Images

| *John White's sensitive watercolor* Indian Elder or Chief *may well be of Wingina. The portrayal includes the copper ornament worn hanging from his neck, indicating high social status and the presence of an active trade network, since copper is not found on the island. Just as Raleigh had to gauge his strategy in dealing with the Indians, Wingina had to decide how to treat the strange newcomers from across the Atlantic.*

But White returned home in 1588 just as the massive Spanish navy, the Armada, was marshaling for an assault on England. Elizabeth enlisted every seaworthy ship and able-bodied sailor in her realm to stave off invasion. The Armada was defeated, but Raleigh left the Roanoke colonists to fend for themselves. When White finally returned to Roanoke Island in 1590, he found only an empty fort and a few cottages in a clearing. The sole clue to the colony's fate was carved on a post: CROATOAN. It was the name of a nearby island off Cape Hatteras, between the Outer Banks and the mainland.

Had the Roanoke colonists fled to Croatoan for safety? Had they moved to the mainland and joined Indian communities? Had they been killed by Wingina's people? The fate of the "lost colony" remains a mystery, though later rumors suggest that the missing colonists merged with native societies in the interior. His dream of a tolerant, cooperative colony dashed, White sailed back to England, leaving behind the lit-

tle cluster of cottages, which would soon be overgrown with vines, and his suit of armor, which was already "almost eaten through with rust."

> **REVIEW**
>
> Why did Elizabeth agree to charter a colony in America, and how successful were the first attempts?

PUTTING HISTORY IN GLOBAL CONTEXT

ALL THE WORLD LAY BEFORE THEM. Or so it had seemed to the young men from England's West Country who dreamed of gold and glory, conquest and colonization. True, they lived on the fringe of the civilized world in the fifteenth and sixteenth centuries. China remained the distant, exotic kingdom of power and wealth, supplying silks and spices and other luxurious goods. Islamic empires stood astride the land routes from Europe to the east. Nations on the western edge of Europe thus took to the seas. Portugal sent slave and gold traders to Africa, as well as merchants to trade with the civilizations of the Indies. Spanish conquerors such as Cortés toppled Indian empires and brought home mountains of silver. But England's West Country sea dogs—would-be conquistadors—met only with frustration. In 1600, more than a century after Columbus's first crossing, not a single English settlement existed in the Americas. The Atlantic had devoured Humphrey Gilbert before he could establish an outpost; Raleigh's Roanoke ventures lay in ruins.

What was left of the freebooting world of West Country adventurers? Raleigh, his ambition unquenchable, sailed to South America in quest of a rich city named El Dorado. In 1603, however, Elizabeth's death brought to the English throne her cousin James I, the founder of the Stuart dynasty. The new king arrested the old queen's favorite for treason and imprisoned him for 15 years in the Tower of London. Set free in 1618 at the age of 64, Raleigh returned to South America, his lust for El Dorado undiminished. Along the way he plundered some Spanish silver ships, defying King James's orders. It was a fatal mistake, because England had made peace with Spain. Raleigh lost his head.

James I did not want to harass the king of Spain; he wanted to imitate him. The Stuarts were even more determined than the Tudors had been to enlarge the sphere of royal power. There would be no room in America for a warrior nobility of conquistadors, no room for a feudal fiefdom ruled by the likes of Raleigh or Gilbert. Instead, there would be English colonies in America like the new outpost of Jamestown, planted on the Chesapeake Bay in Virginia in 1607. There would be profitable plantations and other bold enterprises, enriching English royalty and managed by loyal, efficient bureaucrats. Colonizing America would strengthen English monarchs, paving their path to greater power, just as the dominions of Mexico and Peru had enlarged the authority of the Spanish Crown. America would be the making of kings and queens.

Or would it? For some Europeans, weary of freebooting conquistadors and sea rovers, the order and security that Crown rule and centralized states promoted in western Europe would be enough. But others, men and women who were often desperate and sometimes idealistic, would cast their eyes west across the Atlantic and want more.

CHAPTER SUMMARY

During the late fifteenth century, Europeans and Africans made their first contact with the Americas.

- Western Europeans had lived on the fringes of an international economy drawn together by Chinese goods.

- Technological advances, the rise of new trade networks and techniques, and increased political centralization made Europe's expansion overseas possible.

- Led by Portugal, European expansion pushed south along the West African coast. Sugar plantations and a slave trade in Africans became critical to this expansive commerce.

- Spain led in exploring and colonizing the Americas, consolidating a vast and profitable empire. Divisions within Indian empires and the devastating effects of European diseases made Spanish conquest possible.

- The early conquistadors were replaced by a centralized royal bureaucracy. The discovery of vast silver deposits provided Spain with immense wealth, while leading to sharply increased mortality among the native population.

- Conquistadors also explored much of the present-day southeastern and southwestern United States. The native peoples they encountered thwarted their efforts.

- Martin Luther and later John Calvin spearheaded the Protestant Reformation, which spread to England, Scotland, the Netherlands, and the Huguenots in France.

- England did not turn to exploration and colonization until the 1570s and 1580s. By that time, European rivalries were heightened by splits arising out of the Protestant Reformation.

- England's merchants and gentry supported colonizing ventures, although early efforts, such as those at Roanoke, failed.

Digging Deeper

For ordinary folk in the era of exploration, see Kenneth R. Andrews, *Trade, Plunder, and Settlement* (1985). For Portugal's initial expansion, see Malyn Newitt, *A History of Portuguese Overseas Expansion, 1400–1668* (2004). David Northrup's *Africa's Discovery of Europe, 1450–1850* (2008) explores West Africa's encounter with Europeans. For sugar and expansion, see Philip D. Curtin, *The Rise and Fall of the Plantation Complex* (2nd ed., 1998). The demographic catastrophe that followed contact is explored in Massimo Livi-Bacci, *Conquest: The Destruction of the American Indios* (2008). For telling comparisons between Iberian and English colonialism in the New World, see John Elliott's magisterial *Empires of the Atlantic World: Britain and Spain in America, 1492–1830* (2007). Charles C. Mann's *1493: Uncovering the New World Columbus Created* (2011) deftly integrates insights from multiple disciplines about the consequences of contact. Jace Weaver considers native engagement with the Atlantic World generally in *The Red Atlantic* (2014). For Spain in the Caribbean, see David Abulafia, *The Discovery of Mankind* (2008). Miguel Leon-Portilla and Lysander Kemp give us a fascinating glimpse into how Aztecs viewed the Spanish conquest in *The Broken Spears* (2006). For an indispensable narrative of Spain's activities in North America, see David J. Weber, *The Spanish Frontier in North America* (1992). Coronado's sojourn is the subject of the exacting work by Richard Flint, *No Settlement, No Conquest* (2008). For the Southeast, see Daniel S. Murphree, *Constructing Floridians* (2006). For a good introduction to the Reformation in England, see Eamon Duffy, *The Stripping of the Altars* (2nd ed., 2005). For early English attempts at colonization, in both Ireland and the Americas, consult the works of Nicholas Canny, as well as Michael Leroy Oberg, *The Head in Edward Nugent's Hand* (2007).

3

Colonization and Conflict in the South

1600–1750

This Native American drawing on a canyon wall in present-day Arizona represents the progress of the Spanish into the Southwest. Indians would soon put horses, prominently featured here, to their own uses.

©Medioimages/Photodisc/Getty Images

>> An American Story

OUTLANDISH STRANGERS

In the year 1617, European time, on a bay Europeans called the Chesapeake, in a land they named Virginia, the mighty weroance Powhatan surveyed his domain with satisfaction. While in his prime, the tall, robust man had drawn some 30 villages along the Virginia coast into a powerful confederacy. As tribute for his protection and leadership, Powhatan collected food, furs, and skins. He forged alliances with communities too distant or too powerful for him to dominate. He married the daughters of prominent men, dozens in all, to solidify his network of patronage and power. His confederacy numbered perhaps 20,000 souls. Some coastal villages had fiercely resisted Powhatan's efforts to incorporate them; some peoples to the west still threatened the security of his confederacy.

After 1607 Powhatan was forced to take into account yet another group. The English, as this new people called themselves, came by sea, crammed into three ships. They were 100 men and 4 boys, all clad in heavy, outlandish clothing, many dressed in gaudy colors. The ships followed a river deep into Powhatan's territory and built a fort on a swampy, mosquito-infested site that they called Jamestown.

Powhatan knew of these strangers from across the waters, who had larger boats and louder, more deadly weapons. But the Indians quickly learned how to use guns, and they vastly outnumbered the English, a clumsy and unprepared people who seemed unlikely to live long and prosper in Powhatan's land. Even amid the bounty of the Chesapeake they failed to feed themselves. With bows and arrows, spears and nets, Indian men brought in an abundance of meat and fish. Fields tended by Indian women yielded generous crops of corn, beans, squash, and melon, and edible nuts and fruits grew wild. Still, for several years the English starved. Powhatan could understand why the English refused to grow food. Cultivating crops was women's work—like building houses; or making clothing, pottery, and baskets; or caring for children. And the English settlement included no women until two arrived in the fall of 1608. Yet even after more women came, the English still starved, and they expected—no, they demanded—that Powhatan's people feed them.

Worse, these hapless folk put on such airs. They boasted about the power of their god—they had only one—and denounced the Indians' "devil-worship" of "false gods." They crowed endlessly about the power of their king, James I, who expected Powhatan to become his vassal. The English had even planned a "coronation" to crown Powhatan as a "subject king." He was unimpressed. "If your king has sent me presents," he responded, "I also am a king, and this is my land. . . . Your father is to come to me, not I to him." In the end the English did come to Powhatan, only to find what "a fowle trouble there was to make him kneele to receave his crowne. . . . [He] indured so many perswasions, examples and instructions as tired them all. At last by leaning hard on his shoulders, he a little stooped, and . . . put the Crowne on his head."

Inconceivable to Powhatan— that he should bow before this King James, the ruler of so small and savage a people! When the Indians made war, they killed the male warriors of rival communities but adopted their women and children. But when Powhatan's people defended their land from these invaders, the English retaliated by murdering Indian women and children. Worse, the English could not even keep order among themselves. Too many of them wanted to lead, and they squabbled constantly among themselves.

Only one man, a brash fellow called Captain John Smith, had

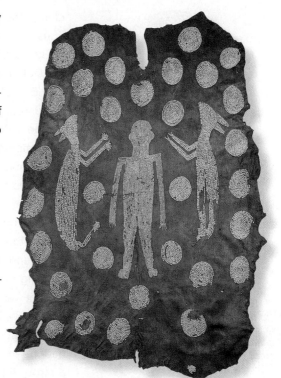

©Ashmolean Museum, University of Oxford, UK/ Bridgeman Images

| *When the English attempted to crown Powhatan as a subject king, he may have sent King James I this cloak as a reciprocal present. Made from four tanned deerskins, the mantle is decorated with many small marine shells sewn into designs. In addition to human and animal figures, the cloak has 34 roundlets that may represent the Indian districts under Powhatan's control.*

briefly brought order to the English settlement. Powhatan granted him a grudging respect, though Smith bragged endlessly of his earlier exploits across the ocean, where he had fought as a soldier of fortune. He told fanciful tales of his irresistible appeal to beautiful women who had rescued him from harrowing perils. A rough man, he bullied the Indians for food and would have enslaved them if it had been in his power. Even so, Smith took a genuine interest in Indian ways. But the fellow returned to England in 1609 after being

©National Portrait Gallery, Smithsonian Institution/ Art Resource, NY

| *No stranger to self-promotion, Captain John Smith included this portrait of himself and verses celebrating his ennobling exploits at the beginning of his* Description of New England *(1616).*

injured when some English gunpowder blew up by mistake. Thereafter the newcomers returned to squabbling and starving.

The temptation to wipe out the helpless, troublesome, arrogant tribe of English—or simply to let them starve to death—was almost overwhelming. But Powhatan had allowed the English to survive. Like Wingina before him, he decided that even these barbaric people had their uses. English labor, English trading goods, and, most important, English guns would help subdue his Indian rivals, within and beyond his confederacy. In 1614 Powhatan cemented his claim on the English and their weapons with the marriage between his favorite

child, Pocahontas, and an ambitious Englishman, John Rolfe.

By 1617 events had vindicated Powhatan's strategy of tolerating the English. His chiefdom flourished, ready to be passed on to his brother. Powhatan's people still outnumbered the English, who seldom starved outright now but continued to fight among themselves and sicken and die. Only one thing had changed in the Chesapeake by 1617: the English were clearing woodland along the rivers and planting tobacco.

That was the doing of Powhatan's son-in-law, Rolfe, a man as strange as the rest of the newcomers. Rolfe had been obsessed with finding a crop that could be grown in Virginia and then sold for gain across the sea. When he succeeded by growing tobacco, other English followed his lead. Odder still, not women but men tended the tobacco fields. Here was more evidence of English inferiority. Men wasted long hours laboring when they might supply their needs with far less effort.

In 1617 Powhatan, ruler of the Pamunkeys, surveyed his domain, and sometime in that year, he looked no longer. He had lived long enough to see the tobacco fields lining the riverbanks, straddling the charred stumps of felled trees. But perhaps he went to his grave believing that he had done what Wingina had failed to do: bend the English to his purposes. He died before those stinking tobacco weeds spread over the length of his

land and sent his hard-won dominion up in smoke.

Wingina and Powhatan were not the only native leaders that dreamed of turning Europeans to their advantage. Across North America, the fleeting if destructive encounters of the sixteenth century gave way to sustained colonialism in the seventeenth. As Europeans began to settle the edges of North America in earnest, Indian peoples struggled not only to survive and adapt to new realities but also, when possible, to profit from the rapid changes swirling around them.

Those often dramatic changes reflected upheavals under way all across the globe. The tobacco John Rolfe had begun to cultivate was only one of several plantation **monocultures** that Europeans began to establish in their far-flung colonies. Sugar, already flourishing in the Atlantic islands off the coast of West Africa, was gaining a foothold in the islands of the Caribbean. Rice, long a staple in Asia and grown also in Africa, made its way into South Carolina toward the end of the seventeenth century. Because these crops were grown most efficiently on plantations and required intensive labor, African slavery spread during these years, fueled by an expanding international slave trade. Whites, blacks, and Indians were all, in different ways, caught up in the wrenching transformations. <<

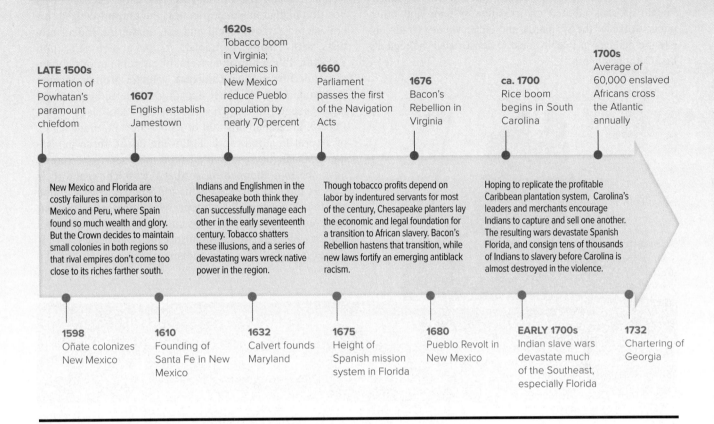

LATE 1500s
Formation of Powhatan's paramount chiefdom

New Mexico and Florida are costly failures in comparison to Mexico and Peru, where Spain found so much wealth and glory. But the Crown decides to maintain small colonies in both regions so that rival empires don't come too close to its riches farther south.

1598
Oñate colonizes New Mexico

1607
English establish Jamestown

1610
Founding of Santa Fe in New Mexico

1620s
Tobacco boom in Virginia; epidemics in New Mexico reduce Pueblo population by nearly 70 percent

Indians and Englishmen in the Chesapeake both think they can successfully manage each other in the early seventeenth century. Tobacco shatters these illusions, and a series of devastating wars wreck native power in the region.

1632
Calvert founds Maryland

1660
Parliament passes the first of the Navigation Acts

1675
Height of Spanish mission system in Florida

Though tobacco profits depend on labor by indentured servants for most of the century, Chesapeake planters lay the economic and legal foundation for a transition to African slavery. Bacon's Rebellion hastens that transition, while new laws fortify an emerging antiblack racism.

1676
Bacon's Rebellion in Virginia

1680
Pueblo Revolt in New Mexico

ca. 1700
Rice boom begins in South Carolina

1700s
Average of 60,000 enslaved Africans cross the Atlantic annually

Hoping to replicate the profitable Caribbean plantation system, Carolina's leaders and merchants encourage Indians to capture and sell one another. The resulting wars devastate Spanish Florida, and consign tens of thousands of Indians to slavery before Carolina is almost destroyed in the violence.

EARLY 1700s
Indian slave wars devastate much of the Southeast, especially Florida

1732
Chartering of Georgia

Spain's North American Colonies

Long before Powhatan made his fateful choices, Spain had already established lasting colonies north of Mexico. But while France and especially England would eventually colonize territory ideally suited to European-style agriculture, territory capable of sustaining large colonial populations, Spain confined its North American ventures to the ecologically challenging regions of the upper Rio Grande and coastal Florida. Because economic opportunities and quality farmland existed in abundance elsewhere in Spanish America, relatively few Spaniards chose to eke out an existence in distant and difficult northern outposts. Nonetheless, Spain's colonial endeavors would have tremendous implications for North America's native peoples and for the geopolitics of the continent as a whole.

The Founding of a "New" Mexico

By the 1590s Coronado's dismal expedition a half century earlier had been all but forgotten. Again, rumors were circulating in Mexico about great riches in the North. New Spain's viceroy began casting about for a champion of means to establish a "new" Mexico, one perhaps as magnificent and profitable as its namesake. He chose Juan de Oñate, son of one of New Spain's richest miners and husband to Isabel de Tolosa Cortés Moctezuma, granddaughter of Hernán Cortés and great-granddaughter of Moctezuma. Oñate needed wealthy connections. Colonizing New Mexico would eventually cost him and his backers more than half a million pesos. But the would-be conquistador expected to recoup the investment with ease. Ignorant of North America's geography and overestimating New Mexico's riches, Oñate even requested and received permission to sail ships up the Pacific to Pueblo country so that twice a year he could resupply his would-be colony and export its expected treasures.

CAUTIOUS RELATIONS The magnitude of his mistaken assumptions began coming into focus in 1598, when he led 500 colonists, soldiers, and slaves to the upper Rio Grande and, like Coronado before him, found modest villages, no ocean, and no evidence of significant mineral wealth. But, whatever the disappointments, Oñate had come with women and children, with livestock and tools, with artisans and tradesmen, with seeds and books and Bibles. He had come to stay. Eager to avoid the violence of earlier encounters, and perhaps hopeful of a mutually beneficial relationship, Tewa-speaking Pueblos evacuated a village for the newcomers to use. Many native leaders pledged Oñate their allegiance, Pueblo artisans labored on irrigation systems and other public works for the Spaniards, and Indian women (traditionally the builders in Pueblo society) constructed the region's first Catholic church.

THE ACOMA SIEGE The colonizers mistook this cautious courtesy for subservience. Oñate's oldest nephew, Juan de Zaldívar, was bolder and cruder than most. At Acoma Pueblo, known today as "Sky City" because of its position high atop a majestic mesa, he brazenly seized several sacred turkeys to kill and eat, answering Indian protests with insults. Outraged, Acoma's men fell upon Zaldívar, killing him and several of his companions. Oñate responded by putting Zaldívar's younger brother Vicente in command of a punitive expedition. Fueled by grief and rage, Vicente de Zaldívar and his men laid siege to the Pueblo, killed perhaps 800 of its people, and made slaves of several hundred more. Following up on these punishments, Oñate decreed that all adult male survivors were to have one foot chopped off so that they might spend their lives as limping advertisements for Spanish power. Scholars now doubt that this sentence was actually carried out, but even today, many Pueblos still consider Oñate's harsh edict as emblematic of Spanish cruelty. Whether or not Oñate executed his cruel judgment, the savagery of the

(top) ©ZUMA Press Inc/Alamy; (bottom) ©Kevin Fleming/Corbis/VCG/Getty Images

| *Like many other Pueblo peoples, the founders of Acoma built their village atop a sandstone mesa to gain protection from enemies. As punishment for resisting his troops, Juan de Oñate ordered that every surviving Acoma male have one foot cut off. Four hundred years later, when this statue of Oñate was erected, vandals attacked the statue with a saw. "We took the liberty of removing Oñate's right foot on behalf of our brothers and sisters of Acoma Pueblo," they announced. Monuments to and celebrations of the "distant past" often provoke passionate disagreements in the present. What other monuments or commemorations have provoked disagreements?*

Acoma siege and the brutal repression of other acts of defiance educated all of the region's native communities about the risks of resistance.

IMPOVERISHED NEW MEXICO But it was easier to instill terror than grow rich. Desperate to salvage their enterprise and turn their investments to account, Oñate and key followers toiled on long, fruitless expeditions in search of gold, silver, and cities, and a place to dock those biannual ships. Some more-practical entrepreneurs decided to exploit the resources they could see. The younger Zaldívar, head-strong conquerer of Acoma, spent time with Apache hunters and decided it would be more efficient to domesticate bison than search for them on the plains. He and his men labored for three days to build a sprawling cottonwood corral, only to discover that bison were "stubborn animals, brave beyond praise," dangerous to catch, and virtually impossible to hold. With varying degrees of enthusiasm, most Spaniards had to turn to more mundane and less hazardous pursuits, to farming and husbandry, in order to support themselves and their families. Others despaired of even securing a living in arid New Mexico, let alone getting rich. The Spanish Crown had promised to make minor nobles of those who stayed at least five years, but many spurned even this incentive and fled back into New Spain.

They were not the only ones losing confidence. In 1606 royal authorities removed Oñate from his position, brought him up on charges of mismanagement, and, as they had with Coronado, accused him of abusing Indians. Ruined, the would-be conquerer spent the rest of his days struggling to rebuild his fortune and clear his name. Meanwhile, a new viceroy decided that the colonization of "worthless" New Mexico had been an expensive mistake and began planning for its evacuation. The colony would have been abandoned but for the Franciscan religious order. Arguing that it would be a crime and a sin to forsake the many thousands of Indians they claimed to have baptized since 1598, the Franciscans convinced a skeptical King Philip III to continue supporting his outpost on the upper Rio Grande.

The Growth of Spanish Florida

FRANCISCANS RENEW SPAIN'S EFFORTS Franciscans would become key actors in Spanish North America. Members of a medieval religious order founded by St. Francis of Assisi, Franciscan monks foreswore property, remained **celibate**, and survived by begging for alms or accepting donations from wealthy patrons. Like their peers and occasional rivals the Jesuits, Franciscans wore only sandals, simple robes, and a rope belt and took it as their charge to live with and minister to the poor. Contact with the Americas reinvigorated their mission. Franciscans accompanied Columbus on his second voyage, and they began ministering to the Indians of central Mexico soon after Tenochtitlán fell. By the 1570s Spanish authorities started secularizing central Mexico's missions, transforming them into self-supporting parishes, and the friars looked to the frontiers for new fields of conversion. Jesuits established several missions in present-day Arizona, and Franciscans went on to become powerful figures in colonial New Mexico.

FLORIDA'S STRATEGIC IMPORTANCE The Crown needed them, nowhere more so than in Florida. Seventeenth-century New Mexico was a Catholic obligation for Spain's

| Artist Jacques Le Moyne recorded this scene of Florida Indians holding council in the 1560s. Observers from Jean Ribaut's French expedition can be seen in the foreground.

©Service Historique de la Marine, Vincennes, France/Bridgeman Images monarchs, but a small worry compared with the strategic importance of Florida. As long as pirates or rival colonies on the Atlantic Seaboard threatened Spanish shipping, the king had to control Florida. Pedro Menéndez de Avilés did much to secure the peninsula in the 1560s when he destroyed France's Fort Caroline and established several Spanish posts on the coast (Chapter 2). By the 1580s, however, the energetic Menéndez was dead and nearly all his coastal establishments destroyed by Indians or privateers. Only St. Augustine endured, with a population of perhaps 500 in 1600. Spanish Florida needed something more than a beachhead along the coast if it was to survive.

FRANCISCAN FLORIDA The king turned to the Franciscans, as part of a two-stage policy to consolidate his influence over Florida's interior. First, royal administrators enticed or menaced the peninsula's many native peoples into alliances. In return for trade privileges and regular diplomatic presents, native leaders promised to trade with no other European power, support the Spanish in war, and tax their people on behalf of the Spaniards. Second, allied Indian communities were made to accept Franciscan missions and a few resident soldiers, a policy that would be critical to molding and monitoring native villages. Franciscans set about their work with characteristic determination. By 1675, 40 missions were ministering to as many as 26,000 baptized Indians. That same year, the bishop of Cuba toured Florida and spoke enthusiastically of converts who embraced "with devotion the mysteries of our holy faith."

Spain's plan for Florida seemed to be working, barely. St. Augustine had grown to a settlement of 1,500 by the time of the bishop's tour. Still, Florida's mission system and network of Indian alliances convinced Spanish authorities that they could maintain their grip on this crucial peninsula.

Popé and the Pueblo Revolt

As the seventeenth century progressed, Spain's colony in New Mexico also seemed to stabilize. Although more than a few desperate colonists fled south, enough remained to establish a separate Spanish town, El Villa Real de Santa Fe, in 1610. Santa Fe (the second-oldest European town in the United States after St. Augustine) became the hub of Spanish life in New Mexico. The demands of agriculture and stock raising forced many families to settle elsewhere on the Rio Grande, on well-watered lands near Pueblo villages. Economic and political life revolved around a dozen prominent families. By 1675 New Mexico had a colonial population of perhaps 2,500. It was a diverse community, including Spaniards, Africans, Mexican Indians, mestizos (persons of mixed Spanish-Indian heritage), and mulattoes (of Spanish-African heritage).

INDIAN CAPTIVES This population of 2,500 also included large numbers of Indian captives. Occasionally captives came to Spanish households through war, as

after the siege of Acoma. In addition, Spaniards purchased enslaved women and children from other Indians and regularly launched slave raids against so-called enemy Indians such as Utes, Apaches, and Navajos. By 1680 half of all New Mexican households included at least one Indian captive, someone who, depending on age, gender, and the master's disposition, could be treated as a low-status family member or terrorized and abused as disposable human property.

The colonists also extracted labor from Pueblo Indians. Officially Pueblo households had to surrender three bushels of corn and one processed hide or large cotton blanket each year. Pueblos were also sometimes made to labor on public works, and elite Spaniards often exploited their privileges by insisting on more tribute and labor than legally allowed. Still, the populous Pueblos would have been able to satisfy Spanish demands with little difficulty but for other changes in their world. First and most importantly, colonialism meant epidemics. Smallpox arrived in the early 1620s. In less than a generation the Pueblo population plumeted by 70 percent, to about 30,000. Whereas New Mexico had approximately 100 native villages at contact, by 1680 only 30 remained inhabited. Infestations of locusts, severe droughts, and crop failures compounded the crisis. By 1667 a distraught Franciscan reported widespread famine, with native men, women, and children "lying dead along the roads, in the ravines, and in their hovels." Mounted Utes, Apaches, and Navajos, embittered by New Mexican slaving and barred from their customary trade in the pueblos, launched punishing raids against the most vulnerable Pueblo villages.

PUEBLO SUFFERING In their deepening misery Pueblos turned to religion—their own. Since 1598 the Franciscans had worked tirelessly to supress the dances, idols, and ceremonies that long mediated Pueblo relationships with the divine. By the 1670s Pueblo elders could argue convincingly that the calamities of the past decades could be reversed only by a rejection of Christianity and a return to the old faith. Such revivalist sentiments threw the friars into a panic. Franciscans and civil authorities scrambled to extinguish the movement, arresting key Pueblo leaders, executing two and whipping 43 others in front of large crowds.

One of the 43, a prominent Tewa man known to history as Popé, nursed his wounds in Taos and laid the groundwork for a general uprising against the Spaniards. Appealing to headmen throughout the Pueblo world, Popé called for a war to purify the land. Many individuals and some entire villages refused to participate. But on August 10, 1680, Indians from across New Mexico rose up and began killing Spaniards. Astonished survivors fled to Santa Fe, followed by Popé and his army, who put the town to siege. Weeks later the desperate Spanish governor, wounded by an arrow in the face and a gunshot to the chest, gathered the remainder of the colonial population and fled south out of New Mexico. The most successful pan-Indian uprising in North American history,

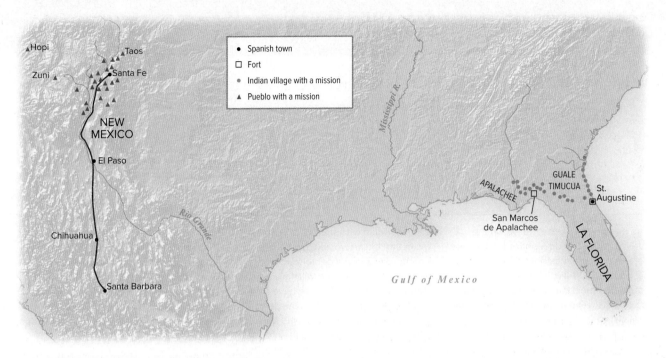

SPANISH MISSIONS IN NORTH AMERICA, CA. 1675

From St. Augustine, Spanish missionaries spread north into Guale Indian villages in present-day Georgia and westward among the Indians of Timucua Province and Apalachee Province. In New Mexico, missions radiated outward from the Rio Grande, as distant as Hopi Pueblos in the west.

the Pueblo Revolt sent shock waves throughout Spanish America, and left the Catholic devout agonizing over what they might have done to provoke God's wrath.

 REVIEW
Where and why did Spain establish colonies in North America, and how did native peoples resist colonization?

ENGLISH SOCIETY ON THE CHESAPEAKE

BY 1700, THEN, SPAIN VIEWED its situation in the Americas from a very different perspective than it had 100 years earlier. The Pueblo Revolt had checked its power at the northern reach of its American possessions. Equally disturbing was the progress of Spain's European rivals in the Americas during the seventeenth century. During the sixteenth, both France and England had envied the wealth Spain reaped from its American conquests. But neither nation did much to check Spain's power, beyond preying on Spanish ships and fishing for cod. During the seventeenth century, this would change.

MERCANTILISM In fact, by 1600 other European kingdoms were beginning to view overseas colonies as essential to a nation's power and prosperity. They did so in part because of an economic model known as **mercantilism**, which guided

Europe's commercial expansion for 200 years. (The theory was so named by the eighteenth-century economist Adam Smith.) Mercantilists called for the state to regulate and protect industry and commerce. Their primary objective was to enrich the nation by fostering a favorable balance of trade. Once the value of exports exceeded the cost of imports, they theorized, gold and silver would flow into home ports.

If a nation could make do without any imports from other countries, so much the better. It was here that the idea of colonies entered the mercantilist scheme. Colonial producers would supply raw materials that the mother country could not produce, while colonial consumers swelled demand for the finished goods and financial services that the mother country could provide. Convinced that colonies would enhance national self-sufficiency, mercantilists urged states to sponsor overseas settlements.

Mercantilist notions appealed to Europe's monarchs. A thriving trade meant that more taxes and customs duties would fill royal coffers, increasing royal power. That logic led England's King James I to approve a private venture to colonize the Chesapeake Bay, a sprawling inlet of the Atlantic Ocean fed by over 100 rivers and streams.

The Virginia Company

In 1606 the king granted a charter to a number of English merchants, gentlemen, and aristocrats, incorporating them as the Virginia Company of London. The members

WHAT CAUSED THE PUEBLO REVOLT?

In the chaotic days following the outbreak of the Pueblo Revolt, shocked Spanish authorities detained several Indians and interrogated them about the rebels' motives. The first informant, Pedro García, was a Spanish-speaking Indian who had been raised in a Spaniard's household. Don Pedro Nanboa, the second informant, was captured by the Spanish and gave his testimony through an interpreter. The final declaration comes from Juan, detained and interrogated more than a year after the rebellion.

DOCUMENT 1
Pedro García

The deponent said that he was in the service of Captain Joseph Nieto, because he was born and has been brought up in his house. . . . While weeding part of a corn field on his master's estancia, which is something like a league from the pueblo of Galisteo, [he] saw coming to the place where he was an Indian named Bartolomé, the cantor mayor of the Pueblo of Galisteo. He came up weeping and said to him, "What are you doing here? The Indians want to kill the custodian, the fathers, and the Spaniards, and have said that the Indian who shall kill a Spaniard will get an Indian woman for a wife, and he who kills four will get four women, and he who kills ten or more will have a like number of women; and they have said that they are going to kill all the servants of the Spaniards and those who know how to speak Castilian, and they have also ordered that rosaries be taken away from everyone and burned. Hurry! Go! Perhaps you will be lucky enough to reach the place where the Spaniards are and will escape with your wife and an orphan girl that you have." Asked why they were plotting such treason and rebellion, he said that the said cantor told him that they were tired of the work they had to do for the Spaniards and the religious, because they did not allow them to plant or do other things for their own needs; and that, being weary, they had rebelled.

Source: "Declaration of Pedro García, an Indian of the Tagno Nation, a native of Las Salinas, August 25, 1680," in Hackett, Charles Wilson, ed., Revolt of the Pueblo Indians of New Mexico and Otermín's Attempted Reconquest, 1680–1682. Albuquerque, NM: University of New Mexico Press, 1942, 23–26.

DOCUMENT 2
Don Pedro Nanboa

Having been asked his name and of what place he is a native, his condition, and age, he said that his name is Don Pedro Nanboa, that he is a native of the pueblo of Alameda, a widower, and somewhat more than 80 years of age. Asked for what reason the Indians of this Kingdom have rebelled, forsaking their obedience to his Majesty and failing in their obligation as Christians, he said that for a long time, because the Spaniards punished sorcerers and idolaters, the nations of the Teguas, Taos, Pecuríes, Pecos, and Jemez had been plotting to rebel and kill the Spaniards and religious, and that they have been planning constantly to carry it out, down to the present occasion. . . . He declared that the resentment which all the Indians have in their hearts has been so strong, from the time this kingdom was discovered, because the religious and the Spaniards took away their idols and forbade their sorceries and idolatries; that they have inherited successively from their old men the things pertaining to their ancient customs; and that he has heard this resentment spoken of since he was of an age to understand. What he has said is the truth and what he knows, under the oath taken, and he ratifies it.

Source: "Declaration of One of the Rebellious Christian Indians Who Was Captured on the Road, September 6, 1680," in Hackett, Charles Wilson, ed., Revolt of the Pueblo Indians of New Mexico and Otermín's Attempted Reconquest, 1680–1682. Albuquerque, NM: University of New Mexico Press, 1942, 60–62.

DOCUMENT 3
Juan, of the Tegua Nation

Asked for what reasons and causes all the Indians of the Kingdom in general rebelled . . . he said that what he knows concerning this question is that not all of them joined the said rebellion willingly; that the chief mover of it is an Indian who is a native of the Pueblo of San Juan, named El Popé, and that from fear of this Indian all of them joined in the plot that he made. Thus he replied. Asked why they held the said Popé in such fear and obeyed him, and whether he was the chief man of the pueblo, or a good Christian, or a sorcerer, he said that the common report that circulated and still is current among all the natives is that the said Indian Popé talks with the devil, and for this reason all held him in terror, obeying his commands although they were contrary to the señores governors, the prelate and the religious, and the Spaniards, he giving them to understand that the word which he spoke was better than that of all the rest; and he states that it was a matter of common knowledge that the Indian Popé, talking with the devil, killed in his own house a son-in-law of his named Nicolás Bua, the governor of the pueblo of San Juan. On being asked why he killed him, he said that it was so that he might not warn the Spaniards of the rebellion, as he intended to do.

Source: "Declaration of the Indian, Juan, December 18, 1681," in Hackett, Charles Wilson, ed., Revolt of the Pueblo Indians of New Mexico and Otermín's Attempted Reconquest, 1680–1682. Albuquerque, NM: University of New Mexico Press, 1942, 60–62.

THINKING CRITICALLY

Why does Pedro García say the Indians rebelled? Don Pedro Nanboa? Juan, the Tegua Indian? Can modern historians take these documents at face value? Why or why not? How might the circumstances of each informant have shaped his testimony?

of the new **joint stock company** sold stock in their venture to English investors, as well as awarding a share to those willing to settle in Virginia at their own expense. With the proceeds from the sale of stock, the company planned to send to Virginia hundreds of poor and unemployed people as well as scores of skilled craftworkers. These laborers were to serve the company for seven years in return for their passage, pooling their efforts to produce any commodities that would return a profit to stockholders. If gold and silver could not be found, perhaps North America would yield other valuable commodities—furs, pitch, tar, or lumber. In the spring of 1607—nearly a decade after Oñate had launched Spain's colonies in New Mexico—the first expedition dispatched by the Virginia Company founded Jamestown.

JAMESTOWN'S PROBLEMS Making the first of many mistakes, Jamestown's 104 colonists pitched their fort on an inland peninsula in order to prevent a surprise attack from the Spanish. Unfortunately, the marshy, thickly wooded site served as an ideal breeding ground for mosquitoes. The settlers, as well as those who followed them, were weakened by bouts of dysentery, typhoid, and yellow fever. They died by the scores. During the summers, Indians familiar with the region's environment scattered beyond the estuary waters of the Chesapeake to find food. The English newcomers, by contrast, remained close to their fort, where the brackish waters became even more salty in the hot summer months. Salt poisoning in the wells left many colonists listless and apathetic.

Even before sickness took its toll, few of Jamestown's colonists had much taste for labor. The gentlemen of the expedition expected to lead rather than to work, and most of the other early settlers were gentlemen's servants and craftworkers who knew nothing about growing crops. As did the colonists on Roanoke, Jamestown's settlers resorted to bullying native people for food. Many colonists suffered from malnutrition, which heightened their susceptibility to disease. Though more colonists had arrived since 1607, only 60 inhabitants lived through the winter of 1609–1610, known as the "starving time." Some desperate colonists unearthed and ate corpses; one settler even butchered his wife. De facto martial law failed to turn the situation around, and skirmishes with the Indians became more brutal and frequent as rows of tobacco plants steadily invaded tribal lands.

Reform and a Boom in Tobacco

KEY REFORMS Determined to salvage their investment, Virginia Company managers in 1618 set in place sweeping reforms. To attract more capital and colonists, the company established a "headright" system for granting land to individuals. Those already settled in the colony received 100 acres apiece. New settlers each received 50 acres, and anyone who paid the passage of other immigrants to Virginia—either family members or servants—received 50 acres per "head."

The company also abolished martial law, allowing the planters to elect a representative assembly. Along with a governor and an advisory council appointed by the company, the House of Burgesses had the authority to make laws for the colony. It met for the first time in 1619, beginning what would become a strong tradition of representative government in the English colonies.

The new measures met with immediate success. The free and unfree laborers who poured into Virginia during the 1620s made up the first wave of an English migration to the Chesapeake that numbered between 130,000 and 150,000 over the seventeenth century. Drawn from the ranks of ordinary English working people, the immigrants were largely men, outnumbering women by six to one. Most were young, ranging in age from 15 to 24. Because of their youth, most lacked skills or wealth. Some of those who came to the Chesapeake as free immigrants prospered as Virginia's tobacco economy took off. When in the 1620s demand soared and prices peaked in European markets, colonists with an eye for profit planted every inch of their farms in tobacco and reaped windfalls.

INDENTURED SERVANTS Indentured servants accounted for three-quarters of all immigrants to Virginia. For most of them, the crossing was simply the last of many moves made in the hope of finding work. Although England's population had been rising since the middle of the fifteenth century, the demand for farm laborers was falling because many landowners were converting croplands into pastures for sheep. The search for work pushed young men and women out of their villages, sending them through the countryside and then into the cities. Down and out in London, Bristol, or Liverpool, some decided to make their next move across the Atlantic and signed **indentures**. Pamphlets promoting immigration promised abundant land and quick riches once servants had finished their terms of four to seven years.

Even the most skeptical immigrants were shocked at what they found. The death rate in Virginia during the 1620s was higher than that of England during times of epidemic disease. The life expectancy for Chesapeake men who reached the age of 20 was a mere 48 years; for women it was lower still. Servants fared worst of all, because malnutrition, overwork, and abuse made them vulnerable to disease. As masters scrambled to make quick profits, they extracted the maximum amount of work before death carried off their laborers. An estimated 40 percent of servants did not survive to the end of their indentured terms.

WAR WITH THE CONFEDERACY The expanding cultivation of tobacco also claimed many lives by putting unbearable pressure on Indian land. After Powhatan's death in 1617 leadership of the confederacy passed to Opechancanough, who watched, year after year, as the tobacco mania grew. In March 1622 he coordinated a sweeping attack on white settlements that killed about a quarter of Virginia's colonial population. English retaliation over the next decade cut

©Linda Davidson/The Washington Post/Getty Images

| This facial reconstruction gives an idea of what one of the few girls at Jamestown might have looked like before the "starving time" winter of 1609–1610. The reconstruction is based on a skull found at Jamestown by archaeologists, which exhibits cuts and sawing marks around the cranium and facial areas. The evidence suggests that she was killed for food by another desperate colonist.

down an entire generation of young Indian men, drove the remaining Powhatans to the west, and won the colonists hundreds of thousands more acres for tobacco.

News of the ongoing Indian war jolted English investors into determining the true state of their Virginia venture. It came to light that, despite the tobacco boom, the Virginia Company was plunging toward bankruptcy. Nor was that the worst news. Stockholders discovered that more than 3,000 immigrants had succumbed to the brutal conditions of Chesapeake life. An investigation by James I revealed the grisly truth, causing the king to dissolve the Virginia Company and take control of the colony himself in 1624. Henceforth Virginia would be governed as a royal colony.

DECLINE IN MORTALITY RATES As the tobacco boom broke in the 1630s and 1640s, Virginians began producing more corn and cattle. Nutrition and overall health improved as a result. More and more poor men began surviving their indenture and establishing modest farms of their own. For women who survived servitude, prospects were even better. Given the ongoing gender imbalance in the colony, women stood a good chance of improving their status by marriage. Even so, high mortality rates still fractured families: one out of every four children born in the Chesapeake did not survive to maturity, and among those children who reached their 18th birthday, one-third had lost both parents to death.

By 1650 Virginia could boast about 15,000 colonists, although much of that increase resulted from servants and free immigrants arriving in the colony every year. But Virginians looking to expand into more northerly bays of the Chesapeake found their way blocked by a newer English colony.

The Founding of Maryland and the Renewal of Indian Wars

Unlike Virginia, established by a private corporation and later converted into a royal colony, Maryland was founded in 1632 by a single aristocratic family, the Calverts. They held absolute authority to dispose of 10 million acres of land, administer justice, and establish a civil government. All these powers they exercised, granting estates, or "manors," to their friends and dividing other holdings into smaller farms for ordinary immigrants. From all these "tenants"—that is, every settler in the colony—the family collected "quitrents" every year, fees for use of the land. The Calverts appointed a governor and a council to oversee their own interests while allowing the largest landowners to dispense local justice in manorial courts and make laws for the entire colony in a representative assembly.

Virginians liked nothing about Maryland. To begin with, the Calvert family was Catholic and had extended complete religious freedom to all Christians, making Maryland a haven for Catholics. Worse still, the Marylanders were a source of economic competition. Two thousand inhabitants had settled on Calvert holdings by 1640, virtually all of them planting tobacco on land coveted by the Virginians.

Another obstacle to Virginia's expansion was the remnant of the Powhatan confederacy. Hounded for corn and supplies (most colonial fields grew tobacco rather than food), and constantly pressured by the expanding plantation economy, Virginia's native peoples became desperate and angry enough to risk yet another war. Aged Opechancanough led a new generation of Indians into battle in 1644 against the encroaching Virginia planters. Though his warriors killed several hundred English and brought the frontier to a standstill, Opechancanough was eventually captured and summarily shot through the head. The Powhatan confederacy died with him. Virginia's Indians would never again be in a position to resist the colony militarily. Over the next decades and centuries, many Indians fled the region altogether. But whole communities remained, quietly determined to continue their lives and traditions in their homeland.

Changes in English Policy in the Chesapeake

Throughout the 1630s and 1640s colonial affairs drew little concern from royal officials. England itself had become engulfed first by a political crisis and then by a civil war.

THE ENGLISH CIVIL WAR Outraged at the contempt that King Charles I had shown toward Parliament, disaffected **elites** and radical Puritans overthrew the king and executed him in 1649. When the "republic" of Oliver Cromwell turned out to be something closer to a military dictatorship, most English were happy to see their throne restored in 1660 to Charles II, the son of the beheaded king. The new monarch was determined to ensure that not only his subjects at home

COLONIES OF THE CHESAPEAKE, 1700–1750

Settlements in Virginia and Maryland spread out along the many bays of the Chesapeake, where tobacco could easily be loaded from plantation wharves. The "fall line" on rivers, dividing Tidewater and Piedmont regions, determined the extent of commercial agriculture, since ships could not pick up exports beyond that point.

but also his American colonies abroad contributed to England's prosperity. His colonial policy was reflected in a series of regulations known as the Navigation Acts.

NAVIGATION ACTS   The first, passed by Parliament in 1660, gave England and English colonial merchants a monopoly on the shipping and marketing of all colonial goods. It also ordered that the colonies could export certain "enumerated commodities" only to England or other British ports. These goods included sugar, tobacco, cotton, ginger, indigo (a blue dye), and

eventually rice. In 1663 Parliament added another regulation, giving British merchants a virtual monopoly on the sale of European manufactured goods to Americans by requiring that most imports going to the colonies pass through England. In 1673 a third Navigation Act placed duties on the coastal trade of the American colonies and provided for customs officials to collect tariffs and enforce commercial regulations.

These acts were mercantilistic, insofar as they were designed to ensure that England—and no foreign nations or their merchants—would profit from colonial production and trade. Chesapeake planters chafed under the Navigation Acts. They were used to conducting their affairs as they pleased—and they were often pleased to trade with the Dutch. What was worse, the new restrictions came at the same time as a downturn in tobacco prices. In the effort to consolidate its empire, England had unintentionally worsened the economic and social difficulties of Chesapeake society.

✔ **REVIEW**

How did the Chesapeake colonies support the aims of British mercantilism?

CHESAPEAKE SOCIETY IN CRISIS

BY THE 1660S OVERPRODUCTION WAS depressing tobacco prices, and wealthy planters reacted by putting even more prime coastal land into production. Newly freed servants had either to become tenants or try to establish farms to the west in Indian country. Meanwhile, export duties on tobacco paid under the Navigation Acts helped plunge many small planters into crushing debt, and some were forced back into servitude. By 1676 one-quarter of Virginia's free white men remained landless and frustrated.

DIMINISHING OPPORTUNITIES Diminishing opportunities in the 1660s and 1670s provided the tinder for unrest in Virginia. As the discontent of the poor mounted, so did the worries of big planters. The assembly of the colony lengthened terms of servitude, hoping to limit the number of servants entering the free population. It curbed the political rights of landless men, hoping to stifle opposition by depriving them of the vote. But these measures only set off a spate of mutinies among servants and protests over rising taxes among small planters.

Bacon's Rebellion and Coode's Rebellion

NATHANIEL BACON Those tensions came to a head in 1676. The rebellion was renewed fighting between desperate Indians and the expanding colonial population. Virginia's royal governor, William Berkeley, favored building forts to guard against Indians, but frontier farmers opposed his plan as an expensive and ineffective way to defend their scattered plantations. As they clamored for an expedition to punish the Indians, Nathaniel Bacon stepped forward to lead it.

©Virginia Historical Society/Courtesy Xanterra Corporation

| *This ceramic pipe from the 1670s was probably used by an indentured servant or tenant farmer living near Jamestown. Its design, featuring an animal carved around the pipe bowl, combined features typical of pipes made by English colonists, Indians, and African Americans. Virginia during this period experienced unstable relations between the expanding English population, the declining Indian population (due to wars and enslavement), and the growing number of enslaved Africans taking a larger role in the colony.*

Wealthy and well connected, Bacon had arrived recently from England, expecting to receive every favor from the governor—including permission to trade with the Indians from his frontier plantation. But Berkeley and a few select friends already held a monopoly on the Indian trade. When they declined to include Bacon, he took up the cause of his poorer frontier neighbors against their common enemy, the governor. Other recent, well-to-do immigrants who resented being excluded from Berkeley's circle of power and patronage also joined Bacon.

In the summer of 1676 Bacon marched into Jamestown with a body of armed men and bullied the assembly into approving his expedition to kill Indians. While Bacon carried out that grisly business, slaughtering friendly as well as hostile Indians, Berkeley rallied his supporters and declared Bacon a rebel. Bacon retaliated by turning his forces against those led by the governor. Both sides sought allies by offering freedom to servants and slaves willing to join their ranks. Many were willing: for months the followers of Bacon and Berkeley plundered one another's plantations. In September 1676 Bacon reduced Jamestown to a mound of ashes. It was only his death from dysentery a month later that snuffed out the rebellion.

Political upheaval also shook Maryland, where colonists had long resented the sway of the Calvert family. As proprietors, the Calverts and their favorites monopolized olitical offices, just as Berkeley's circle had in Virginia. Well-to-do planters wanted a share of the Calverts' power. Smaller farmers, like those in Virginia, wanted a less expensive and more representative government. Compounding the tensions were religious differences: the Calverts and their friends were Catholic, but other colonists, including Maryland's most successful planters, were Protestant.

The unrest among Maryland's discontented planters peaked in July 1689. A former member of the assembly, John Coode, gathered an army, captured the proprietary governor, and then took grievances to authorities in England. There Coode received a sympathetic hearing. The Calverts' charter was revoked and not restored until 1715, by which time the family had become Protestant.

GROWING STABILITY After 1690 rich planters in both Chesapeake colonies fought among themselves less and cooperated more. In Virginia older leaders and newer arrivals divided the spoils of political office. In Maryland Protestants and Catholics shared power and privilege. Those arrangements ensured that no future Bacon or Coode would mobilize restless gentlemen against the government. By acting together in legislative assemblies, the planter elite managed to curb the power of royal and proprietary governors for decades.

But the greater unity among the Chesapeake's leading families did little to ease that region's most fundamental problem—the sharp inequality of white society. The gulf between rich and poor planters, which had been etched ever more deeply by the troubled tobacco economy, persisted long after the rebellions of Bacon and Coode. All that saved white society in the Chesapeake from renewed crisis and conflict was the growth of black slavery.

From Servitude to Slavery

Like the tobacco plants that spread across Powhatan's land, a labor system based on African slavery was an on-the-ground innovation. Both early promoters and planters preferred paying for English servants to importing alien African slaves. Black slaves, because they served for life, were more expensive than white workers, who served only for several years. Because neither white nor black newcomers lived long, cheaper servant labor was the logical choice. The black population of the Chesapeake remained small for most of the seventeenth century, constituting just 5 percent of all inhabitants in 1675.

THE LIVES OF SERVANTS AND SLAVES Africans had arrived in Virginia by 1619, most likely via the Dutch, who dominated the slave trade until the middle of the eighteenth century. The lives of those newcomers resembled the lot of white servants, with whom they shared harsh work routines and living conditions. White and black bound laborers socialized with one another and formed sexual liaisons. They conspired to steal from their masters and ran away together; if caught, they endured similar punishments. There was more common ground: many of the first black settlers did not arrive directly from Africa but came from the Caribbean, where some had learned English and had adopted Christian beliefs. And not all were slaves: some were indentured servants. A handful were free.

A number of changes after 1680 caused planters to invest more heavily in slaves than in servants. First, as death rates in the Chesapeake began to drop, slaves became a more profitable investment. Although they were more expensive to buy than servants, planters could now expect to get many years of work from their bondspeople. Equally important, masters would have title to the children that slaves were now living long enough to have. At the same time, the influx of white servants was falling off just as the pool of available black labor was expanding. When the Royal African Company lost its monopoly on the English slave trade in 1698, other merchants entered the market. The number of Africans sold by British dealers swelled to 20,000 annually.

Africa and the Atlantic Slave Trade

From 1492 to 1820, enslaved Africans arriving in the Americas outnumbered European migrants by nearly five to one. Put differently, before the twentieth century, African workers did most of the heavy lifting in the economies of the Americas.

DIMENSIONS OF THE SLAVE TRADE For a century after Columbus's arrival, the traffic in slaves to the Americas had numbered a few thousand annually. But as sugar cultivation steadily prospered after 1600, slave imports rose to 19,000 a year during the seventeenth century and mushroomed to 60,000 a year in the eighteenth century. All told, as many as 21 million people were captured in West Africa between 1700 and 1850: some 9 million among them entered the Americas as slaves, but millions died before or during the Atlantic crossing, and as many as 7 million remained slaves in Africa. Although slavery became indispensable to its economy,

British North America played a relatively small role in the Atlantic slave trade. Nine-tenths of all Africans brought to the New World landed in Brazil or the Caribbean islands.

TRANSFORMATION OF WEST AFRICAN SOCIETY The rapid growth of the trade transformed not only the Americas but also Africa. Slavery became more widespread within African society, and slave trading more central to its domestic and international commerce. Most important, the African merchants and political leaders most deeply invested in the slave trade used their profits for political advantage—to build new chiefdoms and states such as Dahomey, Asante, and the Lunda Empire. Their ambitions and the greed of European slave dealers drew an increasingly large number of Africans, particularly people living in the interior, into slavery's web. By the late seventeenth century, Africans being sold into slavery were no longer only those who had put themselves at risk by committing crimes, running into debt, or voicing unpopular political and religious views. The larger number were instead captives taken by soldiers or kidnappers in raids launched specifically to acquire prisoners for the slave trade, or else desperate refugees captured while fleeing war, famine, and disease. During the decades after 1680, captives coming directly from Africa made up more than 80 percent of all new slaves entering the Chesapeake and the rest of mainland North America. Many were shipped from the coast of Africa that Portuguese explorers had first probed, between the Senegal and Niger Rivers. Most of the rest came from Angola, farther south.

Seized by other Africans, captives were yoked together at the neck and marched hundreds of miles through the interior to coastal forts or other outposts along the Atlantic. There, they were penned in hundreds of prisons, in lots of anywhere from 20 or 30 to more than 1,000. They might be forced to wait for slaving vessels in French *captiveries* below the fine houses of traders on the island of Gorée, or herded into "out-factories" on the Banana Islands upstream on the Sierra Leone River, or perhaps marched into the dank underground slave-holds at the English fort at Cape Coast. Farther south, captives were held in marshy, fever-ridden lowlands along the Bight of Benin, waiting for a slaver to drop anchor. One African, Ottobah Cugoano, recalled finally being taken aboard ship:

> There was nothing to be heard but the rattling of chains, smacking of whips, and the groans and cries of our fellow-men. Some would not stir from the ground, when they were lashed and beat in the most horrible manner. . . . And when we found ourselves at last taken away, death was more preferable than life, and a plan was concerted amongst us that we might burn and blow up the ship and to perish altogether in the flames.

THE MIDDLE PASSAGE Worse than the imprisonment was the voyage itself: the so-called Middle Passage, a nightmarish journey across the Atlantic that could take anywhere between three weeks and three months, depending on currents, weather, and where ships disembarked and landed. Often several hundred black men, women, and children were packed below-decks, squeezed

AFRICAN TRANSATLANTIC SLAVE TRADE, 1450–1760

Toward the end of the seventeenth century, Chesapeake and Carolina planters began importing increasing numbers of slaves. In Africa the center of that trade lay along a mountainous region known as the Gold Coast, where more than a hundred European trading posts and forts funneled the trade. Unlike most of the rest of West Africa's shoreline, the Gold Coast had very little dense rain forest. Despite the heavy trade, only about 4 percent of the total transatlantic slave trade went to North America.

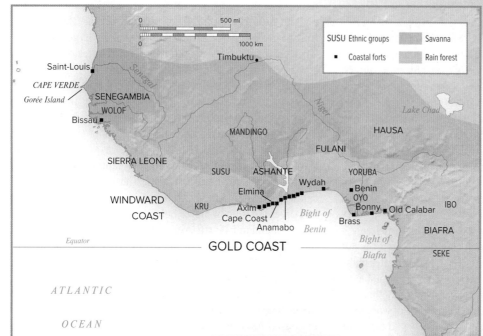

©Scala/Ministero per i Beni e le Attività culturali/Art Resource, NY

| Katharina, sketched by Albrecht Dürer in 1521, was a servant of a Portuguese diplomat living in Antwerp. She was probably one of the increasing number of Africans being brought to Europe owing to the growing slave trade along the West African coast.

| Slaves captured in the African interior were marched out in slave "coffles," a forced march in which captives were linked either by chains or by wooden yoke restraints linking two slaves together as they walked.

©Sarin Images/The Granger Collection, New York

| Africans found themselves in a variety of conditions in the Americas. Most toiled on plantations. Some, however, like these "watermen" along the James River in Virginia (lower right), claimed more independence. Still others ran away to Maroon communities in the interior. This armed Maroon (a runaway slave; lower left) is from Dutch Guiana, where conditions on the plantations were particularly harsh.

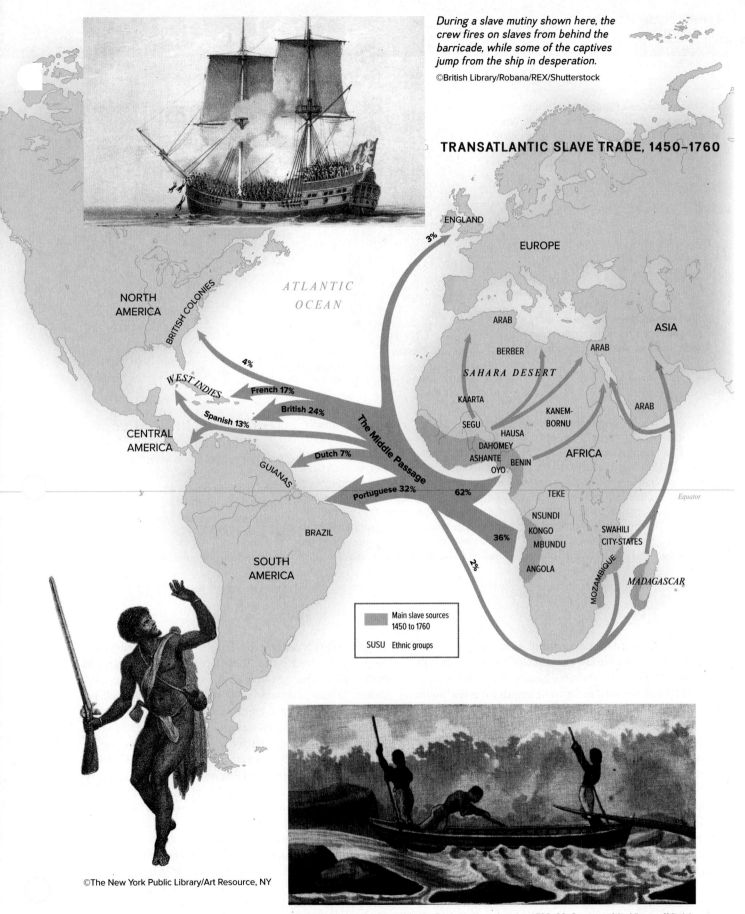

During a slave mutiny shown here, the crew fires on slaves from behind the barricade, while some of the captives jump from the ship in desperation.

©British Library/Robana/REX/Shutterstock

TRANSATLANTIC SLAVE TRADE, 1450–1760

ENGLAND

3%

EUROPE

ATLANTIC OCEAN

NORTH AMERICA

BRITISH COLONIES

ARAB

ASIA

BERBER

ARAB

SAHARA DESERT

4%

WEST INDIES

French 17%

KAARTA

ARAB

British 24%

KANEM-BORNU

Spanish 13%

SEGU

HAUSA

CENTRAL AMERICA

DAHOMEY

AFRICA

Dutch 7%

ASHANTE

BENIN

The Middle Passage

OYO

GUIANAS

Portuguese 32%

62%

TEKE

Equator

NSUNDI

KONGO

SWAHILI CITY-STATES

BRAZIL

MBUNDU

36%

SOUTH AMERICA

2%

ANGOLA

MOZAMBIQUE

MADAGASCAR

| | Main slave sources 1450 to 1760 |
| SUSU | Ethnic groups |

©The New York Public Library/Art Resource, NY

Blacks working on the James River by Benjamin Henry Latrobe, 1798–99. Courtesy of the Library of Virginia

Pendant Mask from Benin

These images of mudfish alternate with those of Portuguese merchants. What might the mudfish be meant to symbolize? (Use a few key terms to find answers on the web.)

These pieces of inlaid iron represent medicine-filled incisions that were said to have given Idia metaphysical powers.

Object is hollow at the back; may have been used as a receptacle for medicines, as well as a pendant.

Source: The Michael C. Rockefeller Memorial Collection, Gift of Nelson A. Rockefeller, 1972/The Metropolitan Museum of Art

This exquisite sixteenth-century ivory mask, now in New York's Metropolitan Museum of Art, graced the neck of Benin's king during ceremonial occasions. Its subtlety and precision suggest that it was produced by Benin's famed guild of royal ivory carvers, specifically for royalty. The object communicates a tremendous amount of visual information. The face itself is a portrait of Idia, mother of Benin's great early-sixteenth-century leader Esigie. A powerful political figure in her own right, Idia helped secure the throne for her son and remained an influential advisor throughout his reign. On her head and around her neck are miniature faces of Portuguese merchants who brought great wealth to Benin and enriched and empowered its leaders through the slave trade.

THINKING CRITICALLY

Why pair the mudfish and the Portuguese? Do you think that the artist conceived of the Portuguese merchants as equals? Would you expect Benin's artistic sophistication to shape how the Portuguese regarded the kingdom?

Source: Metropolitan Museum of Art.

onto platforms built in tiers spaced so close that sitting upright was impossible. It was difficult to know whether the days or the nights were more hellish. Slaves were taken out and forced to exercise for their health for a few hours each day; the rest of the day, the sun beat down and the heat below the decks was "so excessive," one voyager recalled, that the doctors who went below to examine slaves "would faint away, and the candles would not burn." At night, the slaves "were often heard making a howling melancholy kind of noise, something expressive of extreme anguish," noted a doctor aboard another ship. When he made inquiries, he discovered it was because the slaves, in sleeping, had dreamed "they were back in their own country again, amongst their families and friends" and "when they woke up to find themselves in reality on a slave ship they began to bay and shriek." Historians estimate that for every 85 enslaved Africans that set foot in the Americas, 15 died during the middle passage.

"SEASONING" After the numb, exhausted survivors reached American ports, they faced more challenges to staying alive. The first year in the colonies was the most deadly for new, "unseasoned" slaves. The sickle-cell genetic trait gave them a greater immunity to malaria than Europeans, but Africans were highly susceptible to respiratory infections. One-quarter of all Africans died during their first year in the Chesapeake, and among Carolina and Caribbean slaves, mortality rates were far higher. In addition to the new disease environment, Africans had to adapt to lives without freedom in a wholly unfamiliar country and culture.

Exchanging a labor system based on servitude for one based on slavery transformed the character of Chesapeake society. Most obviously, the number of Afro-Virginians rose sharply. By 1740, 40 percent of all Virginians were black, and most of those were African-born. Unlike many African men and women who had arrived earlier from the

Caribbean, these new inhabitants had little familiarity with English language and culture. This larger, more distinctively African community was also locked into a slave system that was becoming ever more rigid and demeaning. By the late decades of the seventeenth century, new laws made it more difficult for masters to free slaves. Other legislation systematically separated the races by prohibiting free black settlers from having white servants and outlawing interracial marriages and sexual relationships. The legal code encouraged white contempt for black Virginians in a variety of other ways. While masters were prohibited from whipping their white servants on the bare back, slaves had no such protection. And "any Negro that shall presume to strike any white" was to receive 30 lashes for that rash act.

GROWING RACISM   The new laws both reflected and encouraged **racism** among white colonists of all classes. Deepening racial hatred, in turn, made it unlikely that poor white planters, tenants, and servants would ever join with poor black slaves to challenge the privilege of great planters. Instead of identifying with the plight of the slaves, the Chesapeake's poorer white residents considered black Virginians their natural inferiors. They could pride themselves on sharing with wealthy white gentlemen the same skin color and on being their equals in the eyes of the law.

OPPORTUNITIES FOR WHITE SETTLERS   The leaders of the Chesapeake colonies cultivated unity among white inhabitants by improving economic prospects for freed servants and lesser planters. The Virginia assembly made provisions for freed servants to get a better start as independent farmers. It lowered taxes, allowing small planters to keep more of their earnings. New laws also gave most white male Virginians a vote in elections, allowing them an outlet to express their grievances. Economic trends toward the end of the seventeenth century contributed to the greater prosperity of small planters, because tobacco prices rose slightly and then stabilized. As a result of Bacon's savage campaign against the Virginia Indians, new land on the frontier became available. Even the domestic lives of ordinary people became more secure as mortality rates declined and the numbers of men and women in the white population evened out. As a result, virtually all men were now able to marry, and families were fragmented less often by the premature deaths of spouses and parents.

After 1700 the Chesapeake evolved into a more stable society. Gone were the bands of wild, landless, young bachelors one step ahead of the law, the small body of struggling lesser planters one step ahead of ruin, and the great mass of exploited servants one step away from rebellion. Virginia and Maryland became colonies of farming families, most of them small planters who owned between 50 and 200 acres. These families held no slaves, or at most two or three. And they accepted, usually without question,

Source: Library of Congress, Geography and Map Division [74693166]

| *Tobacco planters at a Virginia wharf where tobacco is being prepared for shipment in barrels. By the time this scene was drawn, in 1751, a labor system of slavery was firmly in place, replacing the socially unstable supply of white-servant laborers in place a century earlier.*

the social and political leadership of their acknowledged "superiors," great planters who styled themselves the "gentry."

The gentry's fortunes rested in part on the cultivation of tobacco on thousands of acres by hundreds of slaves. But the leading planters made even more money by marketing the tobacco of their humbler neighbors, selling them manufactured goods, supplying them with medical and legal services, lending money, and hiring out slaves. Unlike the rough-hewn barons of the early tobacco boom, the gentry did not owe their wealth to wringing work from poor whites. Instead, they amassed great estates by wringing work from black slaves while converting their white "inferiors" into modestly prosperous small planters and paying clients. But the gentry wanted more than money: they wanted the respect of lesser whites. And they received it. On court days, gentlemen served as justices of the peace, bedecked in wigs and robes and seated on raised benches. On Sundays, worshipers filed into the Anglican chapel in order of social rank, with gentlemen heading the procession. When the local militia trained, it did so at the head of gentlemen officers. The courthouse, the church, and the training field all served as theaters in which the new Chesapeake gentry dramatized their superiority and lesser men deferred.

 REVIEW

Why did slavery replace servitude as the dominant labor system in Virginia and Maryland?

FROM THE CARIBBEAN TO THE CAROLINAS

TRANSFORMATION OF THE CARIBBEAN   DURING THE SAME DECADE THAT the English invaded Powhatan's land, they began to colonize the Caribbean, whose islands extended north and west, like beads on a string, from the Lesser Antilles toward the more substantial lands of Puerto Rico, Hispaniola, Jamaica, and Cuba (Mapping the Past).

>> MAPPING THE PAST <<

CAROLINAS AND THE CARIBBEAN

"People no longer come to Barbados, many having departed to Carolina . . ."
—Sir Jonathan Atkins, Governor of Barbados, 1680

Source: Library of Congress, Prints and Photographs Division [LC-USZ62-124469]

CONTEXT

This map underscores the geographic link between West Indian and Carolina colonies. Immigrants from Barbados dominated politics in early South Carolina, while Carolinians provided foodstuffs, grain, and cattle to the West Indies. As South Carolinians began growing rice, Caribbean slave ships found it an easy sail north and west to unload their cargoes in Charles Town.

MAP READING

1. What other islands did Britain control, circa 1750?
2. What native peoples did colonists in Carolina have to contend with?
3. What explains the pattern of intensive rice cultivation represented on this map?

MAP INTERPRETATION

1. What does this map tell you about the different empires competing for advantage in the circum-Caribbean? How do you think inter-imperial competition shaped British colonial expansion in the region?
2. Can this map help explain why some British colonists decided to seek their fortunes in Carolina?

At their long journey's end English sailors found what seemed a paradise: shores rimmed with white sand beaches that rose sharply to coral terraces, then to broad plateaus or mountain peaks shrouded in rain forests. The earliest arrivals came intending not to colonize but to steal from the Spanish. Even after 1604, when some English settled on the islands, few intended to stay.

Yet the English did establish permanent plantation colonies in the West Indies. Beyond that, their Caribbean settlements became the jumping-off points for a new colony on the North American mainland—South Carolina. Because of the strong West Indian influence, South Carolina developed a social order in some ways distinct from that of the Chesapeake colonies. In other ways, however, the development paralleled Virginia and Maryland's path. In both regions, extreme violence, high mortality, and uncertainty gave way to relative stability only over the course of many decades.

Paradise Lost

The English had traded and battled with the Spanish in the Caribbean since the 1560s. From those island bases English buccaneers conducted an illegal trade with Spanish settlements, sacked the coastal towns, and plundered silver ships bound for Seville. Weakened by decades of warfare, Spain could not hold the West Indies. The Dutch drove a wedge into Caribbean trade routes, and the French and the English began to colonize the islands.

In the 40 years after 1604, some 30,000 immigrants from the British Isles planted crude frontier outposts on St. Kitts, Barbados, Nevis, Montserrat, and Antigua. The settlers— some free, many others indentured servants, and almost all young men—devoted themselves to working as little as possible, drinking as much as possible, and returning to England as soon as possible. They cultivated for export a poor quality of tobacco, which returned just enough profit to maintain straggling settlements of small farms.

CARIBBEAN SUGAR Then, nearly overnight, sugar cultivation transformed the Caribbean. In the 1640s Barbados planters learned from the Dutch how to process sugarcane. The Dutch also supplied African slaves to work the cane fields and marketed the sugar for high prices in the Netherlands. Sugar plantations and slave labor rapidly spread to other English and French islands as Europeans developed an insatiable sweet tooth for the once-scarce commodity. Caribbean sugar made more money for England than the total volume of commodities exported by all the mainland American colonies.

Even though its great planters became the richest people in English America, they could not have confused the West Indies with paradise. Throughout the seventeenth century, disease took a fearful toll, and island populations grew only because of immigration. In the scramble for land, small farmers were pushed onto tiny plots that barely allowed them to survive.

SLAVERY IN THE CARIBBEAN The desperation of bound laborers posed another threat. After the Caribbean's conversion to cultivating sugar, African slaves gradually replaced indentured servants in the cane fields. By the beginning of the eighteenth century, resident Africans outnumbered English by four to one. Fear of servant mutinies and slave rebellions frayed the nerves of island masters. They tried to contain the danger by imposing harsh slave codes and inflicting brutal punishments on all laborers. But planters lived under a constant state of siege. One visitor to Barbados observed that whites fortified their homes with parapets from which they could pour scalding water on attacking servants and slaves. During the first century of settlement, seven major slave uprisings shook the English islands.

As more people, both white and black, squeezed onto the islands, some settlers looked for a way out. With all the land in use, the Caribbean no longer offered opportunity to freed servants or even planters' sons. It was then that the West Indies started to shape the history of the American South.

The Founding of the Carolinas

The colonization of the Carolinas began with the schemes of Virginia's royal governor, William Berkeley, and Sir John Colleton, a supporter of Charles I who had been exiled to the Caribbean at the end of England's civil war. Colleton saw that the Caribbean had a surplus of white settlers, and Berkeley knew that Virginians needed room to expand as well. Together the two men set their sights on the area south of Virginia. Along with a number of other aristocrats, they convinced Charles II to make them joint proprietors in 1663 of a place they called the Carolinas, in honor of the king.

NORTH CAROLINA A few hardy souls from Virginia had already squatted around Albemarle Sound in the northern part of the Carolina grant. The proprietors provided them with a governor and a representative assembly. About 40 years later, in 1701, they set off North Carolina as a separate colony. The desolate region quickly proved a disappointment. Lacking good harbors and navigable rivers, the colony had no convenient way of marketing its produce. North Carolina remained a poor colony, its sparse population engaged in general farming and the production of masts, pitch, tar, and turpentine.

SOUTH CAROLINA The southern portion of the Carolina grant held far more promise, especially in the eyes of one of its proprietors, Sir Anthony Ashley Cooper, Earl of Shaftesbury. In 1669 he sponsored an expedition of a few hundred English and Barbadian immigrants, who planted the first permanent settlement in South Carolina. By 1680 the colonists had established the center of economic, social, and political life at the confluence of the Ashley and Cooper Rivers, naming the site Charles Town (later Charleston) after the king. Like others before him, Cooper hoped to create an ideal society in America. His utopia was a place where a few landed

With large majorities of their populations enslaved, the sugar-producing islands of the Caribbean were anxious, fearful places of brutal labor and gruesome discipline. But they were also sites of rich social life and cultural development, as this slave dance on the island of St. Vincent suggests.

©Christie's Images/Bridgeman Images

aristocrats and gentlemen would rule with the consent of many smaller property holders. With his personal secretary, the renowned philosopher John Locke, Cooper drew up an intricate scheme of government, the Fundamental Constitutions. The design provided Carolina with a proprietary governor and a hereditary nobility who, as a Council of Lords, would recommend all laws to a Parliament elected by lesser landowners.

The Fundamental Constitutions met the same fate as other lordly dreams for America. Instead of peacefully observing its provisions, most of the Carolinians, immigrants from Barbados, plunged into the economic and political wrangling that had plagued Maryland's first government. They challenged proprietary rule, protested or ignored laws and regulations imposed on them, and rejected the proprietors' relatively benevolent vision of Indian relations. Instead of forging genuine alliances with regional Indians, Carolina's colonists fomented a series of Indian slave wars that would nearly destroy the colony altogether.

Carolina, Florida, and the Southeastern Slave Wars

Taking wealthy Barbados as the model, the colonists intended from the start to grow Carolina's economy around cash crops tended by African slaves. But before they could afford to establish such a regime, the newcomers needed to raise capital through trade with Indians. Colonists gave textiles, metal goods, guns, and alcohol in exchange for hundreds of thousands of deerskins, which they then exported.

GROWTH OF THE INDIAN SLAVE TRADE But the trade soon came to revolve around a commodity dearer still. As did most peoples throughout history, southeastern Indians sometimes made slaves of their enemies. Carolina's traders vastly expanded this existing slave culture by turning captives into prized commodities. Convinced that local Indians were physically weaker than Africans and more likely to rebel or flee, colonial traders bought slaves from Indian allies and then exported them to other mainland colonies or to the Caribbean. They found eager native partners in this business. Contact with Europe had unleashed phenomenal changes in interior North America; epidemics ruined one people and gave advantage to another, new commercial opportunities sparked fierce wars over hunting and trading territories, and many thousands of Indian families became displaced and had to rebuild their lives somewhere new. The chaos, conflict, and movement gave enterprising Indians ample opportunity to enslave weak neighbors and stock Carolina's slave pens.

RAIDS INTO SPANISH FLORIDA To ensure a steady supply of slaves and maximize profits, Carolinian merchants courted a variety of Indian allies during the late seventeenth and early eighteenth centuries and encouraged them to raid mission Indians in Spanish Florida. By 1700 Florida's Indian peoples were in sharp decline, and Charles Town's slave traders turned to the large and powerful Creek, Choctaw, Chickasaw, and Cherokee confederacies of the interior, encouraging them to raid one another. Before long the slave wars had a momentum all their own, extending as far west as the Mississippi River. Even native peoples who deplored the violence and despised the English felt compelled to participate, lest they, too, become victims. One small Indian community elected an elder representative to travel to Charles Town and discover what his people needed to do to stay safe. The town's traders seized the man and sold him into slavery. The trade had become central to Carolina's growing economy, and colonists high and low sought to profit from it. In 1702 Governor James Moore, one of the colony's chief slave traders, launched an audacious raid against Spanish St. Augustine and Florida's missions, returning with hundreds of Indian captives. His campaign inspired still more raids, and over the next few years Creeks, Yamasees, and Englishmen laid waste to 29 Spanish missions, shattering thousands of lives and destroying Spain's precarious system of Indian alliances in Florida. By 1706 Spanish authority was once again confined to St. Augustine and its immediate vicinity, and within another 10 years most of Florida had been depopulated of Indians.

It seemed a double victory from Charles Town's perspective. The English had bested a European rival for the Crown and had reaped enormous profits besides. The fragmentary evidence suggests that Carolinians had purchased or captured between 30,000 and 50,000 Indian slaves before 1715. Indeed, before that date South Carolina was a net exporter of slaves: it exported more slaves than it imported from Africa or the Caribbean. But in 1715 Carolina's merchants finally paid a price for the wars that they had cynically fomented for over 40 years.

YAMASEE WAR With Florida virtually exhausted of slaves, the Yamasees grew nervous. Convinced that Carolina would soon turn on them as it had on other one-time allies, the Yamasees struck first. They attacked traders, posts, and plantations on the outskirts of Charles Town, killing hundreds of colonists and dragging scores more to Florida to sell as slaves in St. Augustine. Panicked authorities turned to other Indian peoples in the region but found most had either joined the Yamasee or were too hostile and suspicious to help. Though Carolina narrowly survived the Yamasee War, it took decades

to recover. The destructive regional slave trade virtually came to an end, and animal skins again dominated regional commerce. The powerful southern confederacies grew wary of aligning too closely with any single European power and henceforth sought to play colonies and empires off each other. It was a strategy that would bring them relative peace and prosperity for generations.

White, Red, and Black: The Search for Order

Postwar Carolina invested more and more of its resources in African slaves and in the cultivation of rice, a crop that eventually made South Carolina's planters the richest social group in mainland North America. Unfortunately, South Carolina's swampy coast, so perfectly suited to growing rice, was less suited for human habitation. Weakened by chronic malaria, settlers died in epic numbers from yellow fever, smallpox, and respiratory infections. The white population grew slowly, through immigration rather than natural increase, and numbered only 10,000 by 1730.

Early South Carolinians had little in common but the harsh conditions of frontier existence. Most colonists lived on isolated plantations; early deaths fragmented families and neighborhoods. Immigration after 1700 further intensified the colony's ethnic and religious diversity, adding Swiss and German Lutherans, Scots-Irish Presbyterians, Welsh Baptists, and Spanish Jews. The colony's only courts were in Charles Town; churches and clergy of any denomination were scarce. On those rare occasions when early Carolinians came together, they gathered at Charles Town to escape the pestilential air of their plantations, to sue one another for debt and haggle over prices, or to fight over religious differences and proprietary politics.

Finally, in 1729, the Crown formally established royal government; by 1730 economic recovery had done much to ease the strife. Even more important in bringing greater political stability, the white colonists of South Carolina came to realize that they must unite if they were to counter the Spanish in Florida and the French and their Indian allies on the Gulf Coast.

| Mulberry Plantation in South Carolina was first carved from coastal swamps in 1714. This painting, done half a century later, shows the Great House visible in the distance, flanked by slave quarters. African slaves skilled in rice cultivation oversaw the arduous task of properly planting and irrigating the crop.

"View of Mulberry, House and Street, 1805" by Thomas Coram (American, 1756-1811), Oil on paper. Image ©Gibbes Museum of Art/Carolina Art Association, 1968.18.01

Southern Colonies

COLONY	FOUNDING/SETTLEMENT	CHARACTER AND DEVELOPMENT	APPROXIMATE COLONIAL POPULATION
New Mexico	Oñate expedition 1598; Santa Fe 1610	Arid; few Spanish colonists; agriculture, stock raising, trade with Indians	2,500, including Indian slaves, in 1675
Florida	St. Augustine 1565	Spain uses as a buffer against English settlements to the north	40 Franciscan missions to c. 26,000 baptized Indians by 1675. 1,500 Spaniards in Florida by 1700.
Virginia	Jamestown 1607	Tobacco boom 1620s; population of young, single, indentured servants; Bacon's Rebellion 1676; slavery replaces servitude as the prevailing labor system, 1680s	72,000, including 56,000 white, 16,000 black, in 1700
Maryland	Founded by the Calverts as proprietors, 1632	Religious freedom for Christians; tobacco economy; Coode's Rebellion 1689	30,000, including 27,000 white, 3,000 black, in 1700
West Indies (British)	English settlements after 1604: islands of Barbados, Antigua, St. Kitts, Nevis, and Montserrat	Tobacco gives way to sugar boom, 1640s; African slaves become majority population on sugar islands	65,000, including 15,000 white, 50,000 black, in 1700
Carolinas	Charles Town established by colonists from England and Barbados, 1669	Trade in hides and Indian slaves; increased stability as rice cultivation established; made royal colony in 1729; North Carolina becomes separate colony in 1701	South Carolina: 6,000—3,500 white, 2,500 black; North Carolina: 10,700—10,300 white, 400 black, in 1700
Georgia	Chartered in 1732	Refuge for debtors; slavery not allowed until shortly before it becomes a royal colony in 1752	5,000, including 4,000 white, 1,000 black, in 1752

SLAVERY IN SOUTH CAROLINA The growing black population gave white Carolinians another reason to maintain a united front. During the first decades of settlement, frontier conditions and the scarcity of labor had forced masters to allow enslaved Africans greater freedom within bondage. White and black laborers shared chores on small farms. On stock-raising plantations, called "cowpens," black cowboys ranged freely over the countryside. African contributions to the defense of the colony also reinforced racial interdependence and muted white domination. Whenever threats arose—during the Yamasee War, for example—black Carolinians were enlisted in the militia.

White Carolinians depended on black labor even more after turning to rice as their cash crop. In fact, planters began to import slaves in larger numbers partly because of West African skill in rice cultivation. But whites harbored deepening fears of the black workers whose labor built planter fortunes. As early as 1708 black men and women had become a majority in the colony, and by 1730 they outnumbered white settlers by two to one. As their colony recovered and began to prosper, white Carolinians put into effect strict slave codes like those in the Caribbean that converted their colony into an armed camp and snuffed out the marginal freedoms that African settlers once enjoyed.

The Founding of Georgia

After 1730 white South Carolinians could take comfort not only in newfound prosperity and new political harmony but also in the founding of a new colony on their southern border. South Carolinians liked Georgia a great deal more than the Virginians had liked Maryland, because the colony formed a buffer between British North America and Spanish Florida in much the same way that Yamasees had, before the war.

JAMES OGLETHORPE Enhancing the military security of South Carolina was only one reason for the founding of Georgia. More important to General James Oglethorpe and other idealistic English gentlemen was the aim of aiding the "worthy poor" by providing them with land, employment, and a new start. They envisioned a colony of hardworking small farmers who would produce silk and wine, sparing England the need to import those commodities. That dream seemed within reach when George II made Oglethorpe and his friends the trustees of the new colony in 1732, granting them a charter for 21 years. At the end of that time Georgia would revert to royal control.

The trustees did not, as legend has it, empty England's debtors' prisons to populate Georgia. They freed few debtors but recruited from every country in Europe paupers who seemed willing to work hard—and who professed Protestantism. Trustees paid the paupers' passage and provided each with 50 acres of land, tools, and a year's worth of supplies. Settlers who could pay their own way were encouraged to come by being granted larger tracts of land. Much to the trustees' dismay, that generous offer was taken up not only by many hoped-for Protestants but also by several hundred Ashkenazim

(German Jews) and Sephardim (Spanish and Portuguese Jews), who established a thriving community in early Savannah.

The trustees were determined to ensure that Georgia became a small farmers' utopia. Rather than selling land, the trustees gave it away, but none of the colony's settlers could own more than 500 acres. The trustees also outlawed slavery and hard liquor in order to cultivate habits of industry and sustain equality among whites. This design for a virtuous and egalitarian utopia was greeted with little enthusiasm by Georgians. They pressed for a free market in land and argued that the colony could never prosper until the trustees revoked their ban on slavery. Because the trustees had provided for no elective assembly, settlers could express their discontent only by moving to South Carolina—which many did during the early decades.

As mounting opposition threatened to depopulate the colony, the trustees caved in. They revoked their restrictions on land, slavery, and liquor a few years before the king assumed control of the colony in 1752. Under royal control, Georgia continued to develop an ethnically and religiously diverse society, akin to that of South Carolina. Similarly, its economy was based on rice cultivation and the Indian trade.

REVIEW

How was the colonization of Carolina both distinct from and parallel to that of the Chesapeake?

PUTTING HISTORY IN GLOBAL CONTEXT

EMPIRE . . . UTOPIA . . . INDEPENDENCE . . . For more than a century after the founding of Oñate's colony on the upper Rio Grande in 1598, those dreams inspired newcomers to New Mexico, Florida, the Chesapeake, the English Caribbean, the Carolinas, and Georgia.

Although South Carolina and the English West Indies were more opulent and unstable societies than Virginia and Maryland, the colonies stretching from the Chesapeake to the Caribbean had much in common. So did the South American sugar and coffee plantations of the Guianas and the sugar plantations of Brazil. As Europeans put down colonies throughout the Americas, Indian farmers and hunters were enslaved or expelled. Planters depended on a single staple crop, which brought wealth and political power to those commanding the most land and the most labor. And the biggest planters relied for their success on the very people whom they most feared—enslaved African Americans. That fear was reflected in the development of repressive slave codes and the spread of racism throughout all classes of white society.

The dream of an expanding empire faltered for the Spanish, who discovered few riches in the Southwest and eventually found rebellion. The dream of empire failed, too, when James I and Charles I of England found their power checked by Parliament. And the dream foundered fatally for many Indians, unable to resist Old World diseases and land-hungry colonists.

English lords dreamed of establishing feudal utopias in America. But proprietors in Maryland and the Carolinas were hounded by frontier planters and farmers looking for their own economic and political power. Georgia's trustees failed to erect their utopia for the poor. And Indian resistance dimmed the utopian dreams of Spanish Catholic missionaries in the American Southwest.

The dream of independence proved most deceptive, especially for English colonists. Almost half of white-servant emigrants to the Chesapeake died from disease or were worn down by tobacco barons. And real independence eluded even English planters. The poorer ones depended on richer settlers for land and leadership, while even the richest needed English and Scottish merchants to supply credit and market their crops.

And everywhere in the American Southeast and Southwest, the dreams of Europeans depended on the labor of the least free members of colonial America. That stubborn reality would haunt Americans of all colors who continued to chase after freedom and independence.

CHAPTER SUMMARY

During the seventeenth century, Spain and England moved to colonize critical regions of southern North America.

- Native peoples everywhere in the American South resisted colonization, despite losses from warfare, disease, and enslavement.

- Spanish colonies in New Mexico and Florida grew slowly and faced a variety of threats. By the late seventeenth century, Spanish New Mexico had been lost to the Pueblo Revolt and Florida's delicate mission system was under siege from English Carolina and its Indian allies.

- Thriving monocultures were established in all of England's southern colonies—tobacco in the Chesapeake, rice in the Carolinas, and sugar in the Caribbean.

- Despite a period of intense enslavement of native peoples, African slavery emerged as the dominant labor system throughout these regions.

- Instability and conflict characterized both Spanish and English colonies in the South for most of the first century of their existence.

Digging Deeper

David J. Weber's *Spanish Frontier in North America* (1992) remains indispensable. Andrés Reséndez's *The Other Slavery* (2015) brilliantly excavates the history of Indian servitude in Spanish North America, and James F. Brooks's *Mesa of Sorrows* (2015) uses a single traumatic event to explore violence, identity, and memory in the Southwest. For Spain in the Southeast, see Paul E. Hoffman's *Florida's Frontiers* (2002); and Daniel S. Murphree's *Constructing Floridians* (2006).

For enduring treatments of early Virginia, see Edmund S. Morgan, *American Slavery, American Freedom* (1975); and Kathleen Brown, *Good Wives, Nasty Wenches, and Anxious Patriarchs* (1996). James D. Rice's *Tales from a Revolution* (2012) explores the multiple perspectives of Indians to Bacon's Rebellion. For Indians in the colonial Southeast, see Gregory A. Waselkov, Peter Wood, and Tom Hatley, eds., *Powhatan's Mantle* (2006). For native Virginia, see also Helen C. Rountree, *Pocahontas, Powhatan, Opechancanough* (2005). Bernard Bailyn's *The Barbarous Years* (2012) paints an unforgivingly brutal portrait of English colonization in North America.

Recent years have seen a surge in scholarship on African slavery in the New World. David Brion Davis provides a magisterial overview in *Inhuman Bondage* (2006). For British North America, see Ira Berlin, *Many Thousands Gone* (1998); and Philip D. Morgan, *Slave Counterpoint* (1998). The classic account of the British Caribbean remains Richard S. Dunn's *Sugar and Slaves* ([1972] 2000). Vincent Brown's *Reaper's Garden* (2008) examines the brutalities of the Jamaican slave system. Stephanie E. Smallwood's *Saltwater Slavery* (2007) provides a haunting portrait of the Middle Passage.

The best overview of South Carolina's development remains Robert M. Weir, *Colonial South Carolina* (1982). The complexities of Carolina's slave wars are explored in Alan Gallay, *The Indian Slave Trade* (2002). For the topic more broadly, see Christina Snyder, *Slavery in Indian Country* (2010).

4

Colonization and Conflict in the North

1600–1700

By 1664, when this map of New Amsterdam was engraved, the town had grown considerably from its origins as a fort and fur-trading outpost. Behind the houses in the foreground, a palisade fence remains as a wall protecting against Indian attacks. A gallows stands in the foreground and a windmill in the distance. The English renamed the city New York when they pushed out the Dutch, in this year.

©Collection of the New-York Historical Society, USA/Bridgeman Images

>> An American Story

BEARS ON FLOATING ISLANDS

They came to her one night while she slept. Into her dreams drifted a small island, and on the island were tall trees and living creatures, one of them wearing the fur of a white rabbit. When she told of her vision, no one took her seriously, not even the wise men among her people, shamans and conjurers whose business it was to interpret dreams. No one, that is, until two days later, when the island appeared to all, floating toward shore. On the island, as she had seen, were tall trees, and on their branches—bears. Or creatures that looked so much like bears that the men grabbed their weapons and raced to the beach, eager for the good hunt sent by the gods. They were disappointed. The island was not an island at all but a strange wooden ship planted with the trunks of trees. And the bears were not bears at all but a strange sort of men whose bodies were covered with hair. Strangest among them, as she had somehow known, was a man dressed all in white. He commanded great respect among the bearlike men as their "shaman," or priest.

In that way, foretold by the dreams of a young woman, the Micmac Indians in 1869 recounted their people's first encounter with Europeans more than two centuries earlier. Uncannily, the traditions of other northern tribes record similar dreams predicting the European arrival: "large canoes with great white wings like those of a giant bird," filled with pale bearded men bearing "long black tubes." Perhaps the dreamers gave shape in their sleep to stories heard from other peoples who had actually seen white strangers and ships. Or perhaps, long before they ever encountered the newcomers, these Indians imagined them, just as Europeans fantasized about a new world.

However Micmacs and other northern Indians first imagined and idealized Europeans, they quickly came to see them as fully human. Traders might bring seemingly wondrous goods, goods that could transform the way labor, commerce, politics, and war functioned in native communities. And yet the

Source: Library and Archives Canada, Accession No. 1989-491-5, C-037056

| *Micmacs*

traders themselves hardly seemed magical. They could be by turns generous and miserly, brave and frightful, confident and confused, kind and cruel. Moreover, it soon became clear that these newcomers hailed from different nations, spoke different languages, and often seemed to have different goals. English colonists, it seemed, were every day more numerous and wanted nothing so much as land. The French, in contrast, were relatively few and seemed to care for nothing so much as trade—unless it was their Christian God they brought with them from across the waters. Strange to say, the Europeans argued over their deity as they did over so many other things. The English, the French, and the Dutch were all rivals, and

the Micmacs and others who encountered these new peoples studied them closely and began to make alliances.

As northern Indians became more and more aware of Europeans and their ways, they came also to realize that whatever their attitudes and intentions, the newcomers provoked dramatic changes everywhere they went. Thousands of English migrants coming into the land founded villages and towns that multiplied throughout the seventeenth century. They not only took up land but also brought animals and plants that changed the way Indians lived. The Dutch, Europe's most powerful commercial nation, established no more than a handful of trading settlements up and down the Hudson River, but they encouraged the Iroquois confederacy to push into rival Indian territories in a quest for furs to trade. Even the French, who styled themselves loyal allies to many Indian peoples and claimed to want little more than beaver pelts, brought with them profound, sometimes cataclysmic changes—changes that would upend the world that natives knew when Frenchmen were but bears on floating islands. <<

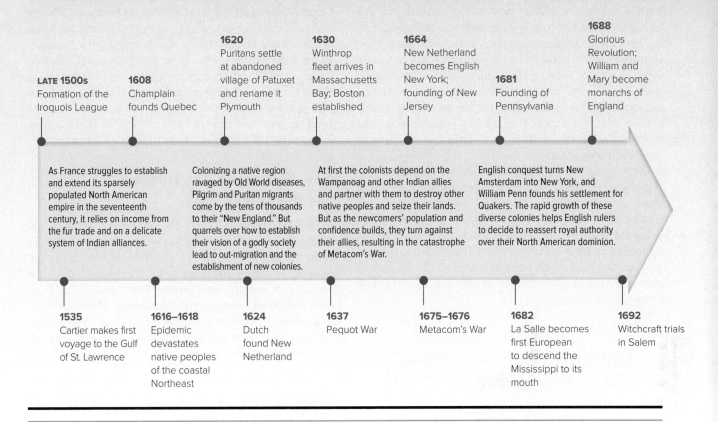

LATE 1500s
Formation of the Iroquois League

1608
Champlain founds Quebec

1620
Puritans settle at abandoned village of Patuxet and rename it Plymouth

1630
Winthrop fleet arrives in Massachusetts Bay; Boston established

1664
New Netherland becomes English New York; founding of New Jersey

1681
Founding of Pennsylvania

1688
Glorious Revolution; William and Mary become monarchs of England

As France struggles to establish and extend its sparsely populated North American empire in the seventeenth century, it relies on income from the fur trade and on a delicate system of Indian alliances.

Colonizing a native region ravaged by Old World diseases, Pilgrim and Puritan migrants come by the tens of thousands to their "New England." But quarrels over how to establish their vision of a godly society lead to out-migration and the establishment of new colonies.

At first the colonists depend on the Wampanoag and other Indian allies and partner with them to destroy other native peoples and seize their lands. But as the newcomers' population and confidence builds, they turn against their allies, resulting in the catastrophe of Metacom's War.

English conquest turns New Amsterdam into New York, and William Penn founds his settlement for Quakers. The rapid growth of these diverse colonies helps English rulers to decide to reassert royal authority over their North American dominion.

1535
Cartier makes first voyage to the Gulf of St. Lawrence

1616–1618
Epidemic devastates native peoples of the coastal Northeast

1624
Dutch found New Netherland

1637
Pequot War

1675–1676
Metacom's War

1682
La Salle becomes first European to descend the Mississippi to its mouth

1692
Witchcraft trials in Salem

FRANCE IN NORTH AMERICA

CARTIER AND CHAMPLAIN THE FIRST OFFICIAL EXPEDITION TO the land the French would call Canada took place in 1535, when Jacques Cartier sailed through the Gulf of St. Lawrence. But not until 1605 did the French plant a permanent colony, at Port Royal in Acadia (Nova Scotia). Three years later, Samuel de Champlain established Quebec farther up the St. Lawrence valley, where he could pursue the fur trade with less competition from rival Europeans. Champlain soon aligned himself with local Montagnais, Algonquins, and, especially, the mighty Hurons—a confederacy of farmers 20,000 strong whose towns near the Georgian Bay straddled a vast trading network.

The Origins of New France

The Hurons, Montagnais, and Algonquins had reason to embrace Champlain. Like Europeans elsewhere in North America, the Frenchman came with wondrous textiles, glass, copper, and ironware. At first the Indians treated such things as exotic commodities rather than utilitarian items. But before long, metal tools began transforming native life. The new knives made it far easier to butcher animals; trees could be felled and buildings put up far more easily with iron axes than with stone; cooking was more efficient with brass kettles that could be placed directly on the fire; flint strike-a-lights eliminated the need to carry hot coals in bounded shells; beads, cloth, needles, and thread allowed for a new level of creative and visual expression. Finally, because they traveled farther and truer than stone, metal arrowheads made hunters and warriors more deadly than ever.

FRENCH-INDIAN ALLIANCES For native peoples, all exchanges of goods were bound up in complex social relations. Thus the Montagnais, Algonquins, and Hurons insisted Champlain be a friend as well as a merchant. Champlain proved his worth in 1609 when he and his native companions confronted two hundred Mohawk warriors in what is now upstate New York. The Frenchman strode to the front as the battle was about to begin, raised his musket, and shot dead two Mohawk chiefs. Champlain's allies let out a joyous cry, for few if any of the warriors had ever seen a gun fired in combat. They drove the remaining Mohawks from the field. It was not the last time European newcomers would alter the balance of power in North America.

THE FUR TRADE The Montagnais, Algonquins, and Hurons became eager trading partners over the next generation. In return for European goods, they provided tens of thousands of beaver pelts. The pelts were the source of the world's best felt for making hats: sturdy, rain-resistant, and lush. Europeans had long ago trapped their continent's beaver populations to near extinction, so for generations most consumers had to make due with inferior wool hats. Once a steady stream of beaver pelts began coming in from North America, "beavers," as the newly available hats were known, became all the rage. Aristocrats, the merchant elite, military officers, and anyone else with money and social ambition had to have one. As early as the 1610s a beaver sold for ten times as much as a wool hat.

Although some imperial rivals derided New France as nothing more than a *comptoir,* a storehouse for the skins of dead animals, revenue from the pelt trade sustained Champlain's colonial dreams, barely. He struggled to bring more permanent settlers to Canada, and, above all, he looked to bind his native allies firmly to the colonial project. To that end Champlain recruited certain French men and boys to live with Indian families, to learn their language and customs.

JESUIT MISSIONS Along with these *coureurs de bois,* or "runners in the woods," French authorities engaged Jesuits, members of the Society of Jesus, to establish missions among the Indians. The Jesuits were fired with the passions of the **Counter-Reformation** in Europe, a movement by devout Catholics to correct those abuses that had prompted the Protestant Reformation. At first France's Indian allies tolerated Jesuit missionaries but listened to them little. By the 1630s, however, Champlain began insisting that trading partners allow Jesuits to live among them. Conversions increased, cultural changes became more apparent, and internal divisions began to erupt within native communities. These pressures gradually left the Huron confederacy, in particular, fragmented and vulnerable to enemies.

New Netherland, the Iroquois, and the Beaver Wars

THE DUTCH STRENGTH IN TRADE If Canada was merely a *comptoir,* it was a profitable one. Potential revenues from the fur trade drew the attention of rival European powers, including the Dutch. By the beginning of the seventeenth century the Calvinist Dutch had finally freed their homeland from Spanish domination. Having won independence, they were equally determined to compete with Spanish merchants and to contain the spread of Spanish Catholicism. Along the Amazon River and the African

©Vandeville Eric/ABACA/Newscom

| *The brief life of Kateri Tekakwitha, a Mohawk woman, reflected the chaotic circumstances set in motion by European fur traders. Her mother was an Algonquin captured by Mohawk raiders, seeking to fill losses brought about by war and disease. Tekakwitha, her Indian name, meant "She who bumps into things," perhaps given to her because at the age of four a smallpox epidemic left her with impaired vision. In the midst of continued conflict, Tekakwitha converted to Christianity after contact with French Jesuit missionaries. They named her Kateri, in honor of St. Catherine of Sienna. She died at the age of 24 and in 2012 was canonized by Pope Benedict XVI.*

©Sarin Images/The Granger Collection, New York

| *This undated French engraving depicts something often overlooked or trivialized by European observers: native women's work. Two Iroquois women grind corn into meal while a swaddled infant rests in a backboard.*

coast, forts and trading posts of the Dutch West India Company protected and promoted Dutch commerce while harrying Spanish competitors.

Furthermore, by the early seventeenth century the Netherlands had the greatest manufacturing capacity in the world and had become the key economic power in Europe. Intent especially on trade, the Dutch had little desire to plant permanent colonies abroad because they enjoyed prosperity and religious freedom at home. But they did want to tap directly into the wealth flowing out of North America and therefore explored and laid claim to a number of sites around the Connecticut, Delaware, and Hudson Rivers (the last named for the Englishman Henry Hudson, who first explored it for the Dutch in 1609). Most of New Netherland's few settlers would cluster in the village of New Amsterdam on Manhattan Island at the mouth of the Hudson.

COLLAPSE OF THE BEAVER POPULATION More important for the geopolitics of the continent, the Dutch West India Company also established a trading outpost 150 miles upriver known as Fort Orange (present-day Albany). Initially the traders at Fort Orange hoped to obtain cheap furs by fostering competition among rival Indian customers. But by 1630 the powerful Mohawks had displaced their competitors and come to dominate the fort's commerce. Ever since their encounter with Champlain's musket, the Mohawks and the other four members of the **Iroquois League** (the Oneidas, Onondagas, Cayugas, and Senecas) had suffered from their lack of direct access to European goods. With Mohawk ascendancy around Fort Orange, the Iroquois finally had reliable access to the tools and weapons necessary to go on the offensive against their northern enemies. They felt compelled to do so because the beaver population, always fragile, had collapsed within their own territory. To maintain their trading position, Iroquois warriors began preying on Huron convoys on their way to Quebec and then selling the plundered pelts to the Dutch.

SMALLPOX EPIDEMIC Just as this old rivalry revived, and soon after the aging Champlain died of a stroke, two things happened to help plunge the region into catastrophe. First, waves of disease afflicted the settlements in the Northeast in the 1630s and took a nightmarish toll on nearly all the region's native peoples, especially agricultural communities in their densely populated towns. Between 1634 and 1640 smallpox killed more than 10,000 Hurons, reducing their total population by half and precipitating a spate of conversions to Christianity that divided the community all the more. The Iroquois likewise suffered greatly, but, unlike the Hurons, they reacted by waging war in an effort to obtain captives that could formally replace dead kin. The second transformative event was a dramatic expansion in the regional arms trade. Initially reluctant to deal in guns, by the late 1630s the Dutch at Fort Orange relaxed their policy in order to obtain more furs. Before long the Iroquois had many times more muskets than the Hurons, whom the French had traditionally refused to arm so long as they remained unconverted.

©Corbis/Getty Images

| *The Hurons, who became infected with smallpox in the 1630s, would have experienced fevers, aches, and vomiting before the telltale spots emerged on their skin. Agonizing pustules would have soon covered them from head to toe, as in the more recent photograph here, and sometimes the pustules merged into oozing sheets that caused large sections of the victims' skin to peel away from their bodies. This horrible disease claimed millions of lives in the Americas after 1492.*

Reeling from disease and internal division, the Hurons saw their world collapsing. In 1648 well-armed Iroquois warriors destroyed three Huron towns. The attacks continued into the next year. At one town under siege the Jesuit Paul Ragueneau saw desperate Hurons seek baptism and Christian consolation. "Never was their faith more alive, nor their love for their good fathers and pastors more keenly felt." The Hurons made the wrenching decision to burn their remaining towns and abandon their lands for good. As many as 2,000 became Iroquois, as either war captives or humble refugees. Others merged with neighboring peoples, while thousands more fled in desperation and starved to death or died of exposure in the harsh winter of 1649–1650.

So began the Beaver Wars, a series of conflicts at least as profoundly transformative for the colonial north as the Indian slave wars were for the south. Seeking new hunting grounds and new captives to replenish their diminishing population, Iroquois raiders attacked peoples near and far. After the Hurons, they struck and scattered the nearby Petuns, Eries, and Neutrals—peoples who, like the Hurons, were all Iroquoian speakers and could thus be integrated into Iroquois communities with relative ease. Iroquois warriors next moved against non-Iroquoian groups, including Delawares and Shawnees in the Ohio valley, and even extended their raids south to the Carolinas. To the north they attacked Algonquins in the Canadian Shield, and Abenakis and others in New England.

A French Map

Information on Pawnee Indians on the Great Plains suggests the scope of French exploration—or at least French interests—by the late seventeenth century.

Mapmaker included population estimates for some native groups.

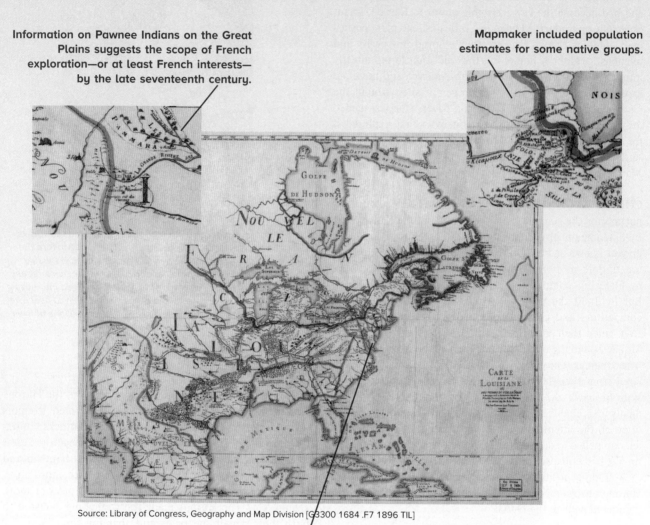

Source: Library of Congress, Geography and Map Division [G3300 1684 .F7 1896 TIL]

"There are a number of unknown savages and villages whose names are unknown," says the mapmaker. Why don't we see similar notations elsewhere?

Carte de Louisiane, by Jean Baptiste Louis Franquelin (1684)

Maps are and always have been far more than simple representations of physical or political space. Maps should also be seen as arguments. Consider the choices made by the cartographer who made the map above. Through the inclusion of certain physical, demographic, and geopolitical details, and through the exclusion of other information, this mapmaker sought to shape perceptions about North America. Choices about where to put boundaries, the relative size and boldness of the words used to identify different regions, the names applied to natural landmarks, and whether to even mention a given place or group all had political implications. The decisions Franquelin made along these lines would surely have been contested by mapmakers from rival empires and would likely have seemed bizarre and mostly useless to the continent's native peoples, who had their own methods for representing space through images.

THINKING CRITICALLY

Locate New Spain, New France, and Louisiana. Which English colonies does the map indicate? Could maps be used as tools in interimperial rivalries? Would Spain have agreed with France about the boundaries around Texas? Would England have agreed with France about the boundaries of New England or Virginia? What might native peoples have thought about any of these claims?

The Lure of the Mississippi

The Beaver Wars continued in fits and starts for the rest of the seventeenth century, bringing dozens of Indian nations to grief and provoking a massive refugee crisis as families fled their traditional territories and tried to rebuild their lives in peace. The wars also very nearly led to the ruin of New France. About 300 Frenchmen were killed or captured in the wars, cutting the colony's meager population in half by 1666. The survivors saw Champlain's carefully managed trading system thrown into disarray. French authorities scrambled to find reliable new partners in the fur trade and henceforth were less reluctant to trade guns to Indian allies. More broadly, the scope of the conflict and the far-flung movement of refugees compelled the French to take a more expansive view of the continent and their place in it.

By the 1660s, French traders, priests, and officers were making inroads among diverse refugee villages in the Western Great Lakes, a region the French referred to as the *pays d'en haut*. These peoples sought trade, assistance against the Iroquois, and mediation of their own disputes. While the French set about building alliances in the *pays d'en haut,* they became aware of and began exploring the greatest watercourse in North America.

LA SALLE DESCENDS THE MISSISSIPPI The Mississippi River travels nearly 2,500 miles from its source in present-day Minnesota to the Gulf of Mexico, carrying water from several other major rivers and dominating a drainage area larger than the Indian subcontinent in Asia. As the French began exploring the river in earnest in the 1670s, it dawned on them that the Mississippi valley could be the strategic key to success in North America. French officials set out courting Indian peoples along the river and its tributaries, employing their hard-won insights into native diplomatic culture along the way. The region's peoples—the Illinois, Shawnees, Quapaws, and others—expressed keen interest in French trade, as well as fear and hatred of their common Iroquois enemies. When René Robert Cavelier, Sieur de La Salle, became the first European to descend the river to the Gulf in 1682, he encountered the Natchez, Chickasaws, and others who had not seen Europeans since de Soto and his maniacal march nearly a century and a half before. Other Frenchmen went further, erecting trading posts and simple missions, and even making contact and tentative alliances with Osages, Arkansas, Ottos, Pawnees, and others west of the great river.

By the early eighteenth century New France had helped broker an uneasy peace between the Iroquois and Indian nations to the west, extended its influence over a vast area, and fortified its colonial core along the St. Lawrence. In 1700 the colony had scores of simple missions and three modest towns—Quebec, Montreal, and Trois-Rivières—containing a population of approximately 15,000. Most emigrants to New France eventually returned to Europe, and shortsighted French monarchs insisted that Canada be a Catholic colony, off limits to France's most obvious immigrants, the Protestant Huguenots. But even with its small colonial population, New France emerged as a powerful player in North America, given its strategic and economic alliances with native peoples. The French had reason to hope that their native allies could help contain the Spanish to the west and limit English expansion from the east.

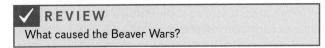

REVIEW
What caused the Beaver Wars?

THE FOUNDING OF NEW ENGLAND

AT FIRST THE ENGLISH REGARDED the northern part of North America as a place in which only the "mad" French could see possibility. English fisherfolk who strayed from Newfoundland to the coast of Acadia and New England carried home descriptions of the long, lonely coast, rockbound and rugged. Long winters of numbing cold melted into short summers of steamy heat. There were no minerals to mine, no crops suitable for export, no large native population available for enslaving. The Chesapeake, with its temperate climate and long growing season, seemed a much likelier spot.

But by 1620 worsening conditions at home had instilled in some English men and women the mixture of desperation and idealism needed to settle an uninviting, unknown world. Religious differences among English Protestants became a matter of sharper controversy during the seventeenth century. Along with the religious crisis came mounting political tensions and continuing problems of unemployment and recession. Times were bad—so bad that the anticipation of worse times to come swept English men and women to the shores of New England.

The Puritan Movement

The colonization of New England started with a king who chose his enemies unwisely. James I, shortly after succeeding Elizabeth I in 1603, vowed to purge England of all radical Protestant reformers. The radicals James had in mind were the Puritans, most of whom were either Presbyterians or Congregationalists. Although both groups of Puritan reformers embraced Calvin's ideas, they differed on the best form of church organization. Individual **Presbyterian** churches (or congregations) were guided by higher governing bodies of ministers and laypersons. Those in the **Congregationalist** churches, in contrast, believed that each congregation should conduct its own affairs independently, answering to no other authority.

Like all Christians, Protestant and Catholic, the Puritans believed that God was all-knowing and all-powerful. And, like all Calvinists, the Puritans emphasized that idea of divine sovereignty known as **predestination**. At the center of their thinking was the belief that God had ordained the outcome of history, including the eternal fate of every human being. The Puritans found comfort in their belief in predestination because it provided their lives with meaning and purpose. They felt assured that a sovereign God was directing the fate of individuals, nations, and all of creation. The Puritans strove to play their parts in that divine drama of history and to discover in their performances some signs of personal salvation.

The divine plan, as the Puritans understood it, called for reforming both church and society along the lines laid down by John Calvin. It seemed to the Puritans that England's government hampered rather than promoted religious purity and social order. It tolerated drunkenness, theatergoing, gambling, extravagance, public swearing, and Sabbath-breaking. It permitted popular recreations rooted in pagan custom and superstition—sports such as bear baiting and maypole dancing and festivals such as the celebration of Christmas and saints' days.

PURITAN CALLS FOR REFORM

Even worse, the state had not done enough to purify the English church of the "corruptions" of Roman Catholicism. The Church of England counted as its members everyone in the nation, saint and sinner alike. To the Puritans, belonging to a church was no birthright. They wished to limit membership and the privileges of baptism and communion to godly men and women. The Puritans also deplored the hierarchy of bishops and archbishops in the Church of England, as well as its elaborate ceremonies in which priests wore ornate vestments. Too many Anglican clergy were "dumb dogges" in Puritan eyes, too poorly educated to instruct churchgoers in the truths of Scripture or to deliver a decent sermon. In reformer John Foxe's vision of good and evil, Anglican priests on the right side of the drawing are shown in vestments and headdresses worshiping Satan before an altar. Anglican worshipers (bottom right) superstitiously count rosary beads and follow a priestly procession like so many dumb sheep. In contrast, Puritan worshipers (bottom left) conspicuously hold their Bibles and attend only to the word of God.

Because English monarchs had refused to take stronger measures to reform church and society, the Puritans

became their outspoken critics. Elizabeth I had tolerated this opposition, but James I would not endure it and intended to rid England of these radicals. With some of the Puritans, known as the Separatists, he seemed to succeed.

The Pilgrim Settlement at Plymouth Colony

The Separatists were devout Congregationalists who concluded that the Church of England was too corrupt to be reformed. They abandoned Anglican worship and met secretly

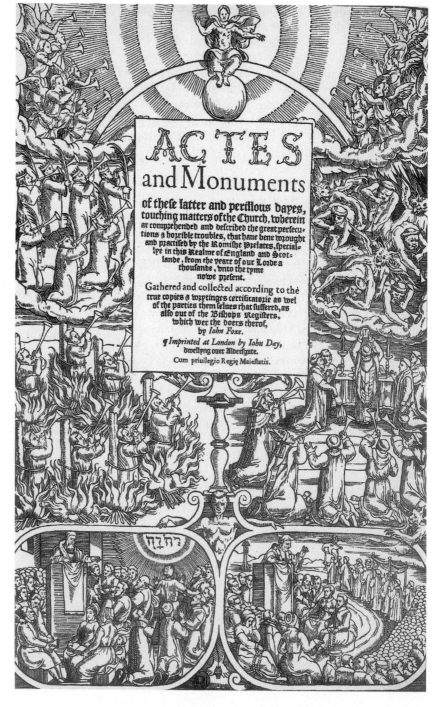

| John Foxe's Actes and Monuments (1563), a book revered by the Puritan founders of New England, arrayed the forces of righteousness (left side of page) against a host of devils, priests, and their sheeplike followers within the Church of England at right. Under the Catholic Queen Mary, Protestants were regarded as heretics and some were burned at the stake (middle left).

©Universal History Archive/UIG/Bridgeman Images

EARLY NEW ENGLAND

Source: Library of Congress, Prints and Photographs Division [LC-USZC4-4311]

"We must be knit together, in this work, as one man."
—John Winthrop, 1630

CONTEXT

Winthrop's colony would not stay "knit together" for long. While most of the Protestant immigrants to New England were relatively homogenous, they quarreled enough over doctrine, politics, and resources to fragment into several distinct settlements. This map represents streams of European migration, as well as the internal migrations within New England that led to new colonial communities.

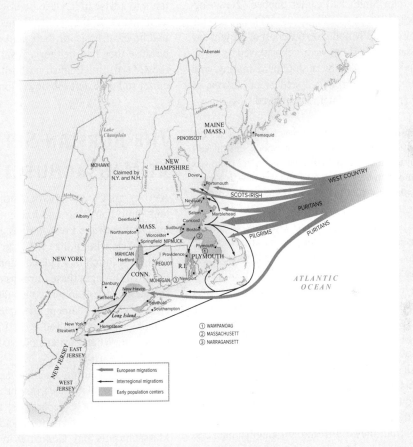

MAP READING

1. What were the main groups of colonists to early New England, and where did they establish themselves?
2. What native peoples did colonists in New England have to contend with?
3. What river proved attractive to colonial settlers?
4. What regions attracted interregional migration in New England?

MAP INTERPRETATION

1. Consider those places outside Massachusetts Bay where colonists established new settlements. Why these places? Do you see common features or advantages that help explain the pattern?
2. Did different groups of European migrants sort themselves into different subregions of New England? If so, which ones?

in small congregations. From their first appearance in England during the 1570s, the Separatists suffered persecution from the government—fines, imprisonment, and, in a few cases, execution. Always a tiny minority within the Puritan movement, the Separatists were people from humble backgrounds: craftworkers and farmers without influence to challenge the state. By 1608 some had become so discouraged that they migrated to Holland, where the Dutch government permitted complete freedom of religion. But when their children began to adopt Dutch customs and other religions, some Separatists decided to move again, this time to Virginia.

EARLY DIFFICULTIES   It can only be imagined what fate would have befallen the unworldly Separatists had they actually settled in the Chesapeake during the tobacco boom. But a series of mistakes—including an error in charting the course of their ship, the *Mayflower*—brought the little band far to the North, to a region Captain John Smith had earlier dubbed "New England." In November 1620 some 88 Separatist "Pilgrims" set anchor at a place they called Plymouth on the coast of present-day southeastern Massachusetts. They were sick with scurvy, weak from malnutrition, and shaken by a shipboard mutiny, and neither the site nor the season invited settlement. As one of their leaders, William Bradford, later remembered:

> For summer being done, all things stand upon them with a weather beaten face, and the whole country, full of woods and thickets represented a savage hue. If they looked behind them, there was the mighty ocean which they had passed and was now as a main bar and gulf to separate them from all the civil parts of the world.

For some, the shock was too great. Dorothy Bradford, William's wife, is said to have fallen overboard from the *Mayflower* as it lay anchored off Plymouth. It is more likely that she jumped to her death.

Few Pilgrims could have foreseen founding the first permanent European settlement in New England, and many did not live long enough to enjoy the distinction. They had arrived too late to plant crops and had failed to bring an adequate supply of food. By the spring of 1621 half the immigrants had died. English merchants who had financed the *Mayflower* voyage failed to send supplies to the struggling settlement. Plymouth might have become another doomed colony had the Pilgrims not received better treatment from native inhabitants than they did from their English backers.

EFFECT OF EPIDEMIC DISEASE   Though they understood it only dimly, the Pilgrims were, in one historian's memorable phrase, the "beneficiaries of catastrophe." Only four years before their arrival, coastal New England had been devastated by a massive epidemic, possibly the plague. Losses varied locally, but overall the native coastal population may have been reduced by as much as 90 percent. Abandoned villages lay in ruins up and down the coast, including the village of Patuxet, where the Pilgrims established Plymouth. Years later visitors would still marvel at heaps of unburied human remains dating from the epidemic.

The Wampanoags dominated the lands around Plymouth. Still reeling from loss in 1620 and eager to obtain trade goods and assistance against native enemies, Massasoit, their chief, agreed to help the starving colonists. Initially, the peoples communicated through a remarkable Wampanoag named Squanto, who had been kidnapped by English sailors before the epidemic. Taken to Europe, Squanto learned English and eventually returned to America in time to play a crucial intermediary role between Massasoit and the newcomers. The Pilgrims accepted Wampanoag hospitality and instruction and invited native leaders to a feast in honor of their first successful harvest in 1621 (the genesis of the "First Thanksgiving" story).

THE MAYFLOWER COMPACT   The Pilgrims set up a government for their colony, the framework of which was the Mayflower Compact, drawn up on board ship before landing. That agreement provided for a governor and several assistants to advise him, all to be elected annually by Plymouth's adult males. In the eyes of English law the Plymouth settlers had no clear basis for their land claims or their government, because they had neither a royal charter nor approval from the Crown. But English authorities, distracted by problems closer to home, left the tiny colony of farmers alone.

THE PURITAN SETTLEMENT AT MASSACHUSETTS BAY

AMONG THE CROWN'S DISTRACTIONS WERE two groups of Puritans more numerous and influential than the Pilgrims. They included both the Presbyterians and the majority of Congregationalists who, unlike the Pilgrim Separatists, still considered the Church of England capable of being reformed. But the 1620s brought these Puritans only fresh discouragements. In 1625 Charles I inherited his father's throne and all his enemies. When Parliament attempted to limit the king's power, Charles simply dissolved it, in 1629, and proceeded to rule without it. When Puritans pressed for reform, the king began to move against them.

This persecution swelled a second wave of Puritan migration that also drew from the ranks of Congregationalists. Unlike the humble Separatists, these immigrants included merchants, landed gentlemen, and lawyers who organized the Massachusetts Bay Company in 1629. Those able Puritan leaders aimed to build a better society in America, an example to the rest of the world. Unlike the Separatists, they had a strong sense of mission and destiny. They were not abandoning the English church, they insisted, but merely regrouping across the Atlantic for another assault on corruption.

Despite the company's Puritan leanings, it somehow obtained a royal charter confirming its title to most of present-day Massachusetts and New Hampshire. Advance parties in 1629 established the town of Salem on the coast well north of Plymouth. In 1630 the company's first governor, a tough-minded and visionary lawyer named John Winthrop, sailed from England with a dozen other company stockholders and

SUDBURY, MASSACHUSETTS

Everyday life in New England centered in small towns such as Sudbury, west of Boston. Families lived in houses clustered around the meetinghouse, in contrast to the decentralized plantations of the South. The privately held farm lots were mixed together as well so that neighbors worked and lived in close contact with one another. **How does the pattern of settlement in Sudbury differ from the pattern of settlement in the Chesapeake region?**

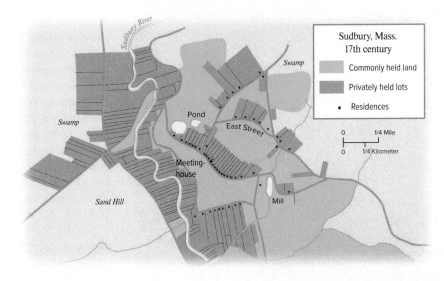

a fleet of men and women to establish the town of Boston. The newcomers intended to build a godly "city on a hill" that would serve as an example to the world.

ESTABLISHING THE COLONY'S GOVERNMENT

Once established in the Bay Colony, Winthrop and the other stockholders transformed the charter for their trading company into the framework of government for a colony. The company's governor became the colony's chief executive, and the company's other officers became the governor's assistants. The charter provided for annual elections of the governor and his assistants by company stockholders, known as the freemen. But to create a broad base of support for the new government, Winthrop and his assistants expanded the freemanship in 1631 to include every adult male church member.

The governor, his assistants, and the freemen together made up the General Court of the colony, which passed all laws, levied taxes, established courts, and made war and peace. In 1634 the whole body of the freemen stopped meeting, and instead each town elected representatives or deputies to the General Court. Ten years later, the deputies formed themselves into the lower house of the Bay Colony legislature, and the assistants formed the upper house. By refashioning a company charter into a civil constitution, Massachusetts Bay Puritans were well on the way to shaping society, church, and state to their liking.

Contrary to expectations, New England proved more hospitable to the English than did the Chesapeake. The character of the migration itself gave New England settlers an advantage, for most arrived in family groups—not as young, single, indentured servants of the sort whose discontents unsettled Virginia society. The heads of New England's first households were typically freemen—farmers, artisans, and merchants. Most were skilled and literate. Since husbands usually migrated with their wives and children, the ratio of men to women within the population was fairly evenly balanced.

THE "GREAT MIGRATION"

Most of the immigrants, some 21,000, came in a cluster between 1630 and 1642. Thereafter new arrivals tapered off because of the outbreak of the English Civil War. This relatively rapid colonization fostered solidarity because immigrants shared a common past of persecution and a strong desire to create an ordered society modeled on Scripture.

> ✓ **REVIEW**
> Who settled the earliest New England colonies?

STABILITY AND ORDER IN EARLY NEW ENGLAND

LONG-LIVED NEW ENGLANDERS PURITAN IMMIGRANTS AND THEIR descendants thrived in New England's bracing but healthy climate. The first generation of colonists lived to an average age of 70, nearly twice as long as Virginians and 10 years longer than men and women living in England. With 90 percent of all children reaching adulthood, the typical family consisted of seven or eight children who came to maturity. Because of low death rates and high birthrates, the number of New Englanders doubled about every 27 years—while the populations of Europe and the Chesapeake barely reproduced themselves. By 1700 New England and the Chesapeake would both have populations of approximately 100,000. But, New England's population expanded primarily through natural increase, in contrast to the southern colonies, which relied on the arrival of indentured servants and convicts from Europe. (Slaves from Africa wouldn't become the key driver of southern population growth until the eighteenth century.)

As emigrants arrived in the Bay Colony after 1630, they carved out an arc of villages around Massachusetts Bay. Within a decade settlers pressed into Connecticut, Rhode Island, and New Hampshire. Connecticut and Rhode Island received separate charters from Charles II in the 1660s, guaranteeing their residents the rights to land and government. New Hampshire, to which Massachusetts laid claim in the 1640s, did not become a separate colony until 1679. The handful of hardy souls settled along the coast of present-day Maine had also accepted the Massachusetts Bay Colony's authority.

Source: Library of Congress, Prints and Photographs Division [HABS MASS, 12-HING,5-26]

The Old Ship Meetinghouse, built in Hingham, Massachusetts, in 1681, expresses the importance of hierarchy among New England Puritans. Wealthy families enjoyed the enclosed wooden pews on the ground floor, whereas poorer folk sat on benches in the second-floor gallery. The raised pulpit (front) bespeaks the congregation's respect for the authority and learning of the clergy.

PATTERNS OF SETTLEMENT Early New Englanders established most of their settlements with an eye to stability and order. Unlike the Virginians, who scattered across the Chesapeake to isolated plantations, most New Englanders established tight-knit communities like those they had left behind in England. Each family received a lot for a house along with about 150 acres of land in nearby fields. Farmers left many of their acres uncultivated as a legacy for future generations, for most had only the labor of their own families to work their land. While the Chesapeake abounded with servants, tenant farmers, and slaves, almost every adult male in rural New England owned property. With little hope of prospering through commercial agriculture, New England farmers also had no incentive to import large numbers of servants and slaves or to create large plantations.

Strong family institutions contributed to New England's order and stability. Although the early deaths of parents regularly splintered Chesapeake families, two adult generations were often on hand to encourage order within New England households. Husbands and fathers exacted submission from wives and strict obedience from children. Land gave New England's long-lived fathers great authority over even their grown children; sons and daughters relied on paternal legacies of farms in order to marry and establish their own families.

CHURCH MEMBERSHIP Whereas churches were few and far between in seventeenth-century Virginia, they constituted the center of community life in colonial New England. Individual congregations ran their own affairs and regulated their own membership. Those wishing to join had to convince ministers and church members that they had experienced a genuine spiritual rebirth or "conversion." Most New Englanders sought and won membership. As majority institutions supported by public taxes, churches had the reach and the resources to oversee public morality, often censuring or expelling wayward neighbors. Still, ministers enjoyed less public power in New England than in the old country. New England's ministers did not serve as officers in the civil government, and the Congregational churches owned no property. In contrast, Catholic and Anglican church officials wielded real temporal power in European states, and the churches held extensive tracts of land.

Finally, New Englanders governed themselves more democratically than did their counterparts in England.

HIERARCHY OF LEADERSHIP Communities throughout the region held regular town meetings of all resident white men. The town fathers generally set the meeting's agenda and offered advice, but the unanimous consent of townsmen determined all decisions. Colony governments in early New England also evolved into representative and responsive institutions. Typically the central government of each colony, such as the General Court of Massachusetts Bay, consisted of a governor and a bicameral legislature, including an upper house, or council, and a lower house, or assembly. All officials were elected annually by the freemen—white adult men entitled to vote in colony elections. Voting qualifications varied, but the number of men enfranchised made up a much broader segment of society than that in seventeenth-century England.

Communities in Conflict

Although most New Englanders called themselves Puritans and Congregationalists, the very fervency of their convictions often led them to disagree about how best to carry out the teachings of the Bible and the ideas of John Calvin. During the first decades of colonization, such disagreements led to the founding of breakaway colonies. In 1636 Thomas Hooker, the minister of Cambridge, Massachusetts, led part of his congregation to Connecticut, where they established the first English settlement. Somewhat more liberal than other Bay Puritans, Hooker favored more lenient standards for church membership. He also opposed the Bay's policy of limiting voting in colony elections to church members. In contrast, New Haven (a separate colony until it became part of Connecticut in 1662) was begun in 1638 by strict Congregationalists who found Massachusetts too liberal.

ROGER WILLIAMS While Connecticut and New Haven emerged from voluntary migration, enforced exile filled Rhode Island with men and women whose radical ideas unsettled the rest of Massachusetts. Roger Williams, Rhode Island's founder, had come to New England in 1631, serving as a respected minister of Salem. But soon Williams announced that he was a Separatist, like the Pilgrims of Plymouth. He encouraged the Bay Colony to break all ties to the corrupt Church of England. He also urged a more complete **separation of church and state** than most New Englanders were prepared to accept, and later in his career he endorsed full religious toleration. Finally, Williams denounced the Bay's charter—the legal document that justified Massachusetts's existence—on the grounds that the king had no right to grant land that he had not purchased from the Indians. When Williams boldly suggested that Massachusetts actually inform the king of his mistake, angry authorities prepared to deport him. Instead, Williams fled the colony in the dead of winter to live with the Indians. In 1636 he became the founder and first citizen of Providence, later to be part of Rhode Island.

ANNE HUTCHINSON Another charismatic heretic from Massachusetts arrived soon after. Anne Hutchinson, a skilled midwife and the spouse of a wealthy merchant, came to Boston in 1634. Enthusiasm for her minister, John Cotton, started her on a course of explaining his sermons to gatherings of her neighbors—and then to elaborating ideas of her own. The fact that a woman would do such things made the authorities uneasy; but they became alarmed when they learned that Hutchinson embraced controversial positions on doctrine. Soon a majority of the Bay's ministers accused the troublesomely popular Hutchinson of holding heretical views. She in turn denounced her detractors, and the controversy escalated. In 1638 the Bay Colony government expelled Hutchinson and her followers for sedition. She settled briefly in Rhode Island before moving on to Long Island, where she died in an Indian attack.

Goodwives and Witches

If Anne Hutchinson had been a man, her ideas would still have been deemed heretical. However, if she had been a man, she might have found other ways to express her intelligence and magnetism. But life in colonial New England offered women, especially married women, little scope for their talents.

Most adult women were hardworking farm wives who cared for large households of children. Between marriage and middle age, most New England wives were pregnant except when breast-feeding. When they were not nursing or minding children, mothers were producing and preparing much of what was consumed and worn by their families. They planted vegetable gardens and pruned fruit trees, salted beef and pork and pressed cider, milked cows and churned butter, kept bees and tended poultry, cooked and baked, washed and ironed, spun, wove, and sewed. While husbands and sons engaged in farmwork that changed with the seasons, took trips to taverns and mills, and went off to hunt or fish, housebound wives and daughters kept busy with a dizzying array of tasks.

WITCHCRAFT Communities sometimes responded to assertive women with accusations of witchcraft. Like most early modern Europeans, New Englanders believed in wizards and witches, men and women who were said to acquire supernatural powers by signing a compact with Satan. A total of 344 New Englanders were charged with witchcraft during the first colonial century, with the Salem Village episode of 1692 producing the largest outpouring of accusations and 20 executions. More than three-quarters of all accused witches were women, usually middle-aged and older, and most of those accused were regarded as unduly independent. Before they were charged with witchcraft, many had been suspected of heretical religious beliefs, others of sexual impropriety. Still others had inherited or stood to inherit property.

The People in the Way

SIMILARITIES BETWEEN PURITANS AND INDIANS Whatever their political battles, doctrinal disputes, and inequalities, New Englanders were all participants in a colonial project that depended on taking land from other people. Perhaps 100,000 Algonquin men and women lived in the area reaching from the Kennebec River in Maine to Cape Cod at contact. Like the Puritans, they relied on fishing in spring and summer, hunting year-round, and cultivating and harvesting corn and other crops in spring and fall. And, to an even greater degree than among the colonists, Indian political authority was local. Within each village, a single leader known as the "sachem" or "sagamore" directed economic life, administered justice, and negotiated with other tribes and English settlers. As with New England's town fathers, a sachem's power was contingent on keeping the trust and consent of his people.

Thus the newcomers had more in common with their hosts than they cared to admit. But English expansion in the region had to come at someone's expense, and colonists obtained Indian lands in one of three ways. Sometimes they purchased it. Sales varied—they might be free and fair, fraudulent, subtly coerced, or forced through intimidation and violence. Second, colonists eagerly expanded into lands emptied by epidemics. The English often saw God's hand in such events. Following a terrible smallpox epidemic in 1633–1634, for example, one observer exclaimed that "without this remarkable and terrible stroke of God upon the natives, [we] would with much more difficulty have found room, and at far greater charge have obtained and purchased land."

Third and finally, colonists commonly encouraged and participated in regional wars to obtain native lands. This proved easy enough to do, because, like Europeans, the Indians of New England quarreled frequently with neighboring nations. The antagonism among the English, Spanish, Dutch, and French was matched by the hostilities among the Abenakis, Pawtuckets, Massachusetts, Narragansetts, and Wampanoags of the north Atlantic coast. Epidemics often intensified existing rivalries. Affecting some villages and nations more than others, outbreaks of Old World disease opened up new opportunities for stronger neighbors to press the advantage. New England settlers, like those in the Chesapeake, studied Indian feuds to better exploit them.

The English began by aligning with Massasoit and his Wampanoags against other coastal peoples in New England. In 1637 colonial forces joined the Narragansetts in a campaign against the formidable Pequots, who controlled coveted territory in present-day Connecticut. The colonists shocked even their Indian allies

ACCUSATIONS AND DEFENSES IN THE SALEM WITCHCRAFT TRIALS

The Salem witchcraft trials of 1692 set neighbor against neighbor and resulted in the execution of 20 women and men. One of the accused was tavern owner John Proctor, on whom Arthur Miller loosely based the main protagonist in his famous play The Crucible. *The documents below include testimony of three witnesses against Proctor and his own remarkable response.*

DOCUMENT 1
The Accusations

Sarah Bibber

The Deposition of Sarah Bibber agged about 36 years who testifieth and saith that on the 3 june 1692. Jno: proctor. sen'r came to me and did most greviously torment me by pinching pricking and almost presing me to death urging me to drink: drink as Red as blood which I refusing he did tortor me with variety of tortors and immediatly he vanished away also on the same day I saw Jno: proctor most greviously tortor Susannah Shelden by claping his hands on hir throat and almost choaking hir. also severall times sence Jno: proctor sen'r has most greviously tortored me a grat many times with a variety of tortors

Sara vibber ownid this har testimony to be the truth on har oath before the Juriars of Inqwest this: 30. of June 1692.
   Jurat in Curia
   (Reverse) Sarah Bibber

Ann Putnam

The Deposistion of Ann putnam Jun'r who testifieth and saith I have often seen the Apperishtion of Jno procktor senr. amongst the wicthes but he did not doe me much hurt tell a little before his examination which was on the 11th of April 1692 and then he sett upon me most greviously and did tortor me most dreadfully also in the time of his examination he afflected me very much: and severall times sence the Apperishtion of John procktor senr, has most greviously tortored me by pinching and allmost choaking me urging me vehemently to writ in his book also on the day of his examination I saw the Apperishtion of Jno: proctor senr goe and affect and most greviously tortor the bodys of Mistris pope mary walcott Mircy lewes. Abigail williams and Jno: Indian. and he and his wife and Sarah Cloys keept Elizabeth Hubburd speachless all the time of their examination

(mark) Ann Putnam

Ann Putman owned what is above written upon oath before and unto the Grand inquest on the 30'th Day of June 1692
   (Reverse) Ann puttnam ag't John procter

Mary Warren

The deposition of mary warrin aged 20 y'rs ho testifieth I have seen the apparition of John procter sen'r among the wiches and he hath often tortored me by penching me and biting me and Choakeing me and presing me one my Stomack tell the blood came out of my mouth and all so I saw him tortor Mes poap and marcey lues and John Indian a pon the day of his examination and he hath allso temted me to right in his book and to eat bread which he brought to me which I Refuseing to doe: Jno proctor did most greviously tortor me with variety of torturs all most Redy to kill me.

Mary Warren owned the above written upon her oath before & unto the Grand inquest on the 30'th Day of June 1692

Source: http://etext.virginia.edu/etcbin/salembrowse?id=684.

DOCUMENT 2
The Defense

SALEM-PRISON, July 23, 1692. *Mr. Mather, Mr. Allen, Mr. Moody, Mr. Willard, and Mr. Bailey.*
Reverend Gentlemen.

The innocency of our Case with the Enmity of our Accusers and our Judges, and Jury, whom nothing but our Innocent Blood will serve their turn, having Condemned us already before our Tryals, being so much incensed and engaged against us by the Devil, makes us bold to Beg and Implore your Favourable Assistance of this our Humble Petition to his Excellency, That if it be possible our Innocent Blood may be spared, which undoubtedly otherwise will be shed, if the Lord doth not mercifully step in. The Magistrates, Ministers, Jewries, and all the People in general, being so much inraged and incensed against us by the Delusion of the Devil, which we can term no other, by reason we know in our own Consciences, we are all Innocent Persons. Here are five Persons who have lately confessed themselves to be Witches, and do accuse

some of us, of being along with them at a Sacrament, since we were committed into close Prison, which we know to be Lies. Two of the 5 are (Carriers Sons) Youngmen, who would not confess any thing till they tyed them Neck and Heels till the Blood was ready to come out of their Noses, and 'tis credibly believed and reported this was the occasion of making them confess that they never did, by reason they said one had been a Witch a Month, and another five Weeks, and that their Mother had made them so, who has been confined here this nine Weeks. My son William Procter, when he was examin'd, because he would not confess that he was Guilty, when he was Innocent, they tyed him Neck and Heels till the Blood gushed out at his Nose, and would have kept him so 24 Hours, if one more Merciful than the rest, had not taken pity on him, and caused him to be unbound. These actions are very like the Popish Cruelties. They have already undone us in our Estates, and that will not serve their turns, without our Innocent Bloods. If it

cannot be granted that we can have our Trials at Boston, we humbly beg that you would endeavour to have these Magistrates changed, and others in their rooms, begging also and beseeching you would be pleased to be here, if not all, some of you at our Trials, hoping thereby you may be the means of saving the sheeding our Innocent Bloods, desiring your Prayers to the Lord in our behalf, we rest your Poor Afflicted Servants,

JOHN PROCTER, etc.

Source: http://etext.virginia.edu/etcbin/salembrowse?id=684

THINKING CRITICALLY

What patterns do you see in the accusations? What does the language in all four pieces tell you about how members of this community conceived of Satan? How does Proctor try to defend himself? What do you think he was trying to accomplish by comparing the interrogations his son and others faced to "Popish Cruelties"?

when they set fire to the main Pequot village, killing hundreds of men, women, and children. Plymouth's William Bradford recalled that "it was a fearful sight to see them thus frying in the fire, and the streams of blood quenching the same, and horrible was the stink and scent thereof; but the victory seemed a sweet sacrifice, and they gave the praise thereof to God, who had wrought so wonderfully for them." Several years later the colonists turned against their former allies, joining forces with the Mohegans to intimidate the Narragansetts into ceding much of their territory. Only a few colonists objected to those ruthless policies, among them Roger Williams. "God Land," he warned one Connecticut leader, "will be (as it now is) as great a God with us English as God Gold was with the Spainards."

Though no images of Metacom survive from his time, in later years artists frequently portrayed him. This image is based on an engraving by Paul Revere.

Source: Library of Congress, Prints and Photographs Division [LC-USZ62-96234]

> ✓ **REVIEW**
> What were the sources of stability and conflict in early New England?

Metacom's War

Throughout these wars, the colonists more or less nurtured their original alliance with Massasoit and his Wampanoags. As long as regional enemies bore the brunt of English expansion, Massasoit and his people could live in relative safety. Indeed, certain colonists tried to bring the two societies closer together. While the impulse to convert was not nearly as strong in New England as in New Spain or New France, a few Englishmen worked tirelessly to bring the word of their God to Indians.

MISSIONS TO THE INDIANS Most famously, Puritan minister John Eliot began preaching in Algonquian in the 1640s. Over the next two decades he oversaw a project to publish the scriptures in Algonquian using the Latin alphabet. He also trained scores of native ministers (many of whom became literate) and established seven villages or "praying towns" exclusively for Christian Indians. Eliot was not alone. According to its charter of 1650, for example, Harvard College defined its mission as "the education of English & Indian youth of this Country in knowledge and godliness." In 1655 Harvard established an Indian college and dormitory on campus specifically to instruct Wampanoag youth in the English language and in Protestantism. None of these efforts embodied respect for Indian culture or religion. But some in New England, at least, wanted to assimilate Indians rather than drive them away.

And yet the colony always grasped for more land. By the time Massasoit died and was succeeded by his son in the 1660s, the partnership had become a relationship of subordination and suspicion. Colonial authorities reacted to rumors of pending native rebellion with humiliating interrogations and increasingly severe rules and restrictions. The colonists' cows and pigs invaded and destroyed Indian fields, provoking innumerable conflicts as white pressures on Indian lands increased. When Indians tried to adapt by raising their own cows and pigs, colonial authorities barred them from using common pasture or selling meat in Boston. At the same time, as many as half the dwindling Wampanoags had followed Eliot into the praying towns, threatening tribal unity in a time of mounting crisis.

By 1675 these and other pressures convinced Massasoit's son, Metacom, whom the English called King Philip, that his nation could be preserved only by chancing war. Complaining that the English were plotting to kill him and other sachems and replace them with Christian Indians more willing to sell land, Metacom organized for war. He rallied many of southern New England's remaining native nations, peoples who had likewise suffered from colonization, and together they laid waste to more than two dozen towns in Plymouth Colony. By the spring of 1676, indigenous fighting men from across the region were raiding settlements within 20 miles of Boston. The offensive threatened New England's very existence.

But the momentum could not be sustained. Faced with shortages of food and ammunition, Metacom tried and failed to secure alliances with former enemies, including the Mohegans and the Mohawks. These powerful peoples instead aligned themselves with the English. By early 1676 the tide had turned. Metacom was killed that summer. Colonial forces dismembered his body and brought his severed head to Boston and his hands to Plymouth as trophies. The Indian offensive collapsed but not before threatening New England's very existence. In proportion to population, "King Philip's War" inflicted twice the casualties on New England that the United States as a whole would suffer in the American Civil War. And Metacom's desperate gamble exhausted native military power in southern New England, virtually destroyed the Wampanoags as a coherent people, and consigned the region's surviving Indians, Christian or not, to quiet and often desperate lives on the margins of colonial life.

THE MID-ATLANTIC COLONIES

THE INHABITANTS OF THE MID-ATLANTIC colonies—New York, New Jersey, Pennsylvania, and Delaware—enjoyed more secure lives than most southern colonials. But they lacked the common bonds that lent stability to early New England. Instead, throughout the mid-Atlantic region a variety of ethnic and religious groups vied for wealth from farming and the fur trade and contended bitterly against governments that commanded little popular support.

English Rule in New York

By the 1660s the Dutch experiment on the mid-Atlantic coast was faltering. While Fort Orange continued to secure furs for the Dutch West India Company, the colonial population remained small and fractious. The company made matters worse by appointing corrupt, dictatorial governors who ruled without an elective assembly. It also provided little protection for outlying Dutch settlements; when it did attack neighboring Indian nations, it did so savagely, triggering terrible retaliations. By the time the company went bankrupt in 1654, it had virtually abandoned its American colony.

Taking advantage of the disarray in New Netherland, Charles II ignored Dutch claims in North America and granted his brother, James, the Duke of York, a proprietary charter there. The charter granted James all of New Netherland to Delaware Bay as well as Maine, Martha's Vineyard, and Nantucket Island. In 1664 James sent an invading fleet, whose mere arrival caused the Dutch to surrender.

ETHNIC AND RELIGIOUS DIVERSITY   New York's dizzying diversity would make it difficult to govern. The Duke inherited 9,000 or so colonists: Dutch, Belgians, French, English, Portuguese, Swedes, Finns, and Africans—some enslaved, others free. The colony's ethnic diversity ensured a variety of religions. Although the Dutch Reformed Church predominated, other early New Netherlanders included Lutherans, Quakers, and Catholics. There were Jews as well, refugees from Portuguese Brazil, who were required by law to live in a ghetto in New Amsterdam. The Dutch resented English rule, and only

©Lebrecht Music and Arts Photo Library/Alamy

| *Asser Levy and his wife were among the earliest Jewish immigrants to New Netherland. Here, they perform the blessing of the new moon, marking the beginning of a new month. Levy pushed successfully for Jews to be integrated into Dutch society.*

after a generation of intermarriage and acculturation did that resentment fade. James also failed to win friends among New Englanders who had come to Long Island seeking autonomy and cheap land during the 1640s. He grudgingly gave in to their demand for an elective assembly in 1683 but rejected its first act, the Charter of Liberties, which would have guaranteed basic political rights. The chronic political strife discouraged prospective settlers. By 1698 the colony numbered only 18,000 inhabitants, and New York City, the former New Amsterdam, was an overgrown village of a few thousand.

The Founding of New Jersey

Confusion attended New Jersey's beginnings. The lands lying west of the Hudson and east of the Delaware River had been part of the Duke of York's proprietary grant. But in 1664 he gave about 5 million of these acres to Lord Berkeley and Sir George Carteret, two of his favorites who were already involved in the proprietary colonies of the Carolinas. New Jersey's new owners guaranteed settlers land, religious freedom, and a representative assembly in exchange for a small quitrent, an annual fee for the use of the land. The proprietors' terms promptly drew Puritan settlers from New Haven, Connecticut. At the same time, unaware that James had already given New Jersey to Berkeley and Carteret, New York's Governor Richard Nicolls granted Long Island Puritans land there.

More complications ensued when Berkeley and Carteret decided to divide New Jersey into east and west and sell both halves to **Quaker** investors—a prospect that outraged New Jersey's Puritans. Although some English Quakers migrated to West Jersey, the investors quickly decided that two Jerseys were less desirable than one Pennsylvania and resold both East and West Jersey to speculators. In the end the Jerseys became a patchwork of religious and ethnic groups. Settlers who shared a common religion or national origin formed communities and established small family farms. When the Crown finally reunited East and West as a single royal colony in 1702, New Jersey was overshadowed by settlements not only to the north but now, also, to the south and west.

Quaker Odysseys

Religious and political idealism similar to that of the Puritans inspired the colonization of Pennsylvania, making it an oddity among the mid-Atlantic colonies. The oddity began with an improbable founder, William Penn. Young Penn devoted his early years to disappointing his distinguished father, Sir William Penn, an admiral in the Royal Navy. Several years after being expelled from college, young Penn finally chose a career that may have made the admiral yearn for mere disappointment: he undertook a lifelong commitment to put into practice Quaker teachings. By the 1670s he had emerged as an acknowledged leader of the Society of Friends, as the Quakers formally called themselves.

QUAKER BELIEFS   The Quakers behaved in ways and believed in ideas that most people regarded as odd. They dressed

| The artist who sketched this Quaker meeting called attention to one of that sect's most controversial practices by placing a woman at the center of his composition. Women were allowed to speak in Quaker worship services and to preach and proselytize at public gatherings of non-Quakers. The Puritans roundly condemned this liberty as contrary to the teachings of St. Paul.

©De Luan/Alamy

in a deliberately plain and severe manner. They withheld from their social superiors the customary marks of respect, such as bowing, kneeling, and removing their hats. They refused to swear oaths or to make war. They allowed women public roles of religious leadership. That pattern of behavior reflected their egalitarian ideals, the belief that all men and women shared equally in the "Light Within." Some 40,000 English merchants, artisans, and farmers embraced Quakerism by 1660, and many suffered fines, imprisonment, and corporal punishment.

PENNSYLVANIA ESTABLISHED Since the English upper class has always prized eccentricity among its members, it is not surprising that Penn, despite his Quakerism, remained a favorite of Charles II. More surprising is that the king's favor took the extravagant form of presenting Penn in 1681 with all the land between New Jersey and Maryland. Perhaps the king was repaying Penn for the large sum that his father had lent the Stuarts. Or perhaps the king was hoping to export England's Quakers to an American colony governed by his trusted personal friend.

Penn envisioned that his proprietary colony would provide a refuge for Quakers while producing quitrents for himself. To publicize his colony, he distributed pamphlets praising its attractions throughout the British Isles and Europe. The response was overwhelming: by 1700 its population stood at 21,000. The only early migration of equal magnitude was the Puritan colonization of New England.

Patterns of Growth

Perhaps half of Pennsylvania's settlers arrived as indentured servants; the families of free farmers and artisans made up the rest. The majority were Quakers from Britain, Holland, and Germany, but the colonists also included Catholics, Lutherans, Baptists, Anglicans, and Presbyterians. In 1682, when Penn purchased and annexed the Three Lower Counties (later the colony of Delaware), his colony included the 1,000 or so Dutch, Swedes, and Finns living there.

Quakers from other colonies—West Jersey, Maryland, and New England—also flocked to the new homeland. Those experienced settlers brought skills and connections that contributed to Pennsylvania's rapid economic growth. Farmers sowed their rich lands into a sea of wheat, which merchants exported to the Caribbean. The center of the colony's trade was Philadelphia, a superb natural harbor situated at the confluence of the Delaware and Schuylkill Rivers.

In contrast to New England's landscape of villages, the Pennsylvania countryside beyond Philadelphia was dotted with dispersed farmsteads. Commercial agriculture required larger farms, which kept settlers at greater distances from one another. As a result, the county rather than the town became the basic unit of local government in Pennsylvania.

QUAKERS AND INDIANS Another reason that farmers did not need to cluster their homes within a central village was that they were at peace with the coastal Indians, the Lenni Lenapes (also called Delawares by the English). Thanks to two Quaker beliefs—their commitment to pacifism and their conviction that the Indians rightfully owned their land—peace prevailed between native inhabitants and newcomers. Before Penn sold any land to colonists, he purchased it from the Indians. He also prohibited the sale of alcohol to the tribe, strictly regulated the fur trade, and learned the language of the Lenni Lenapes. "Not a language spoken in Europe," he remarked, "hath words of more sweetness in Accent and Emphasis than theirs."

"Our Wildernesse flourishes as a Garden," Penn declared late in 1683, and in fact, his colony lived up to its promises.

New arrivals readily acquired good land on liberal terms, while Penn's Frame of Government instituted a representative assembly and guaranteed all inhabitants the basic English civil liberties and complete freedom of worship.

Quakers and Politics

Even so, Penn's colony suffered constant political strife. Rich investors whom he had rewarded with large tracts of land and trade monopolies dominated the council, which held the sole power to initiate legislation. That power and Penn's own claims as proprietor set the stage for controversy. Members of the representative assembly battled for the right to initiate legislation. Farmers opposed Penn's efforts to collect quitrents. The Three Lower Counties agitated for separation, their inhabitants feeling no loyalty to Penn or Quakerism.

PENN'S COMPROMISES Penn finally bought peace at the price of approving a complete revision of his original Frame of Government. In 1701 the Charter of Privileges, Pennsylvania's new constitution, stripped the council of its legislative power, leaving it only the role of advising the governor. The charter also limited Penn's privileges as proprietor to the ownership of ungranted land and the power to veto legislation. Thereafter an elective unicameral assembly, the only single-house legislature in the colonies, dominated Pennsylvania's government.

As Pennsylvania prospered, Philadelphia became the commercial and cultural center of England's North American empire. Gradually the interior of Pennsylvania filled with immigrants—mainly Germans and Scots-Irish—who harbored no "odd" ideas about Indian rights, and the Lenni Lenapes and other native peoples were bullied into moving farther west.

Northern Colonies

COLONY	FOUNDING/ SETTLEMENT	CHARACTER AND DEVELOPMENT	APPROXIMATE POPULATION (1700)
New France	1605 Port Royal (Acadia); 1608 Quebec	Fur-traders and Jesuit missionaries; small number of farmers in 1660s; French into western Great Lakes in 1670s; Mississippi valley in 1680s	15,000
Massachusetts (including Maine)	Plymouth 1620; Massachusetts Bay 1629	Separatist and Puritan settlements; most colonists arrive in family groups; village-centered agricultural settlements	56,000
Connecticut	Thomas Hooker leads congregation to Connecticut 1636	New Haven, a separate, stricter settlement, joins Connecticut in 1662	26,000
Rhode Island	Roger Williams 1636	Williams champions separation of church and state, respect for Indian land claims	6,000
New Hampshire	Portsmouth 1631	Allied with Massachusetts for several decades; becomes royal colony 1680	5,000
New Netherland/ New York	Dutch settle 1624; England takes possession 1664	Dutch at Fort Orange (later Albany) ally with Iroquois to vie for furs; Dutch arms trade helps fuel Beaver Wars	9,000 by 1664 under Dutch; 18,000 in 1700
New Jersey	Duke of York grants lands out of New York holdings 1664	Patchwork of ethnic groups; small family farms; becomes royal colony 1702	14,000
Pennsylvania/Delaware (separates in 1703)	Penn receives lands in 1681 from Charles II; Philadelphia principal town	Penn recruits colonists from across Britain and Europe; dispersed farms the norm rather than village settlements; Penn pledges to deal fairly with Indians	20,000

As for William Penn, he returned to England and spent time in a debtors' prison after being defrauded by his unscrupulous colonial agents. He died in 1718, an ocean away from his American utopia.

✓ **REVIEW**
In what ways were the mid-Atlantic colonies more diverse than the other colonies of the period?

ADJUSTMENT TO EMPIRE

WHATEVER HIS PERSONAL DISAPPOINTMENTS, PENN'S colony had enjoyed spectacular growth—as indeed had British North America more generally. And yet by the 1680s England's king had reason to complain. Although North America now abounded in places named in honor of English monarchs, the colonies themselves lacked any strong ties to the English state. Until Parliament passed the first of the Navigation Acts in 1651, England had not even set in place a coherent policy for regulating colonial trade. And the acts had not produced the desired sense of patriotism in the colonies. While Chesapeake planters grumbled over the customs duties levied on tobacco, New Englanders, the worst of the lot, ignored the Navigation Acts altogether and traded openly with the Dutch. Royally appointed proprietors increasingly met defiance in New York, New Jersey, the Carolinas, and Pennsylvania. If England were to prosper from colonies as Spain's monarchs had, the Crown needed to take matters in hand.

The Dominion of New England

And the Crown did so in 1686. At the urging of the new King James II (formerly the Duke of York), the Lords of Trade consolidated the colonies of Connecticut, Plymouth, Massachusetts Bay, Rhode Island, and New Hampshire into a single entity to be ruled by a royal governor and a royally appointed council. By 1688 James had added New York and New Jersey to that domain, now called the Dominion of New England. Showing the typical Stuart distaste for representative government, James also abolished all northern colonial assemblies. The king's aim to centralize authority over such a large territory made the Dominion not only a royal dream but also a radical experiment in English colonial administration.

The experiment proved to be short-lived. In England James II had revealed himself to be yet another Stuart who tried to dispense with Parliament and who had embraced Catholicism besides. Parliament dispensed with the king just as it had with Charles I during the English Civil War of the 1640s. In a quick, bloodless coup d'état known as the Glorious Revolution, Parliament forced James into exile in 1688. In his place it elevated to the throne his daughter, Mary, and her Dutch husband, William of Orange. Mary was a distinctly better sort of Stuart—a staunch Protestant—and she agreed to rule with Parliament.

| *The tidy, productive farmsteads of the Pennsylvania countryside were the basis of that colony's prosperity during the eighteenth century. Their produce fueled the growth of Philadelphia and sustained the expansion of sugar plantations on England's Caribbean islands.*

©The New York Public Library/Art Resource, NY

THE GLORIOUS REVOLUTION William and Mary officially dismembered the Dominion of New England and reinstated representative assemblies everywhere in the northern colonies. Connecticut and Rhode Island were restored their old charters, but Massachusetts received a new charter in 1691. Under its terms Massachusetts, Plymouth, and present-day Maine were combined into a single royal colony headed by a governor appointed by the Crown rather than elected by the people. The charter also imposed religious toleration and made property ownership rather than church membership the basis of voting rights.

Royal Authority in America in 1700

CLOSER REGULATION OF TRADE William and Mary were more politic than James II but no less interested in revenue. In 1696 Parliament enlarged the number of customs officials stationed in each colony to enforce the Navigation Acts. To help prosecute smugglers, Parliament established colonial vice-admiralty courts, tribunals without juries presided over by royally appointed justices. To keep current on all colonial matters, the king appointed a new Board of Trade to replace the old Lords of Trade. The new enforcement procedures generally succeeded in discouraging smuggling and channeling colonial trade through England.

| *England, in an effort to regulate colonial trade, required all ships bound from America to pass through British ports and pay customs duties. Places such as Plymouth, Liverpool, and Bristol (shown here) thrived as a result. Contrast this large, bustling commercial center with the modest size of Plymouth 200 years earlier (illustration in Chapter 1).*

©Bristol Museum and Art Gallery, UK/Bridgeman Images

These changes were enough for England and its monarchs for half a century thereafter. English kings and queens gave up any dreams of imposing the kind of centralized administration of colonial life represented by the Dominion of New England. Clearly, royal control had increased over the previous half century. By 1700 royal governments had been established in Virginia, New York, Massachusetts, and New Hampshire. New Jersey, the Carolinas, and Georgia would shortly be added to the list. Royal rule meant that the monarch appointed governors and (everywhere except Massachusetts) also appointed their councils. Royally appointed councils could veto any law passed by a colony's representative assembly, royally appointed governors could veto any law passed by both houses, and the Crown could veto any law passed by both houses and approved by the governor.

THE LIMITS OF ROYAL POWER Nonetheless, the sway of royal power remained more apparent than real after 1700. The Glorious Revolution asserted once and for all that Parliament's authority—rule by the legislative branch of government—would be supreme in the governing of England. In the colonies members of representative assemblies grew more skilled at dealing with royal governors and more protective of their rights. They guarded most jealously their strongest lever of power—the right of the lower houses to levy taxes.

The political reality of the assemblies' power reflected a social reality as well. No longer mere outposts along the Atlantic, the colonies of 1700 were becoming more firmly rooted societies. Their laws and traditions were based not only on what they had brought from England but also on the conditions of life in America. That social reality had already

blocked Stuart ambitions to shape the future of North America, just as it had thwarted the designs of lordly proprietors and the dreams of religious reformers.

> ✓ **REVIEW**
> How did William and Mary try to increase colonial revenues?

PUTTING HISTORY IN GLOBAL CONTEXT

THE DREAM OF EMPIRE would revive among England's rulers in the middle of the eighteenth century—in part because the rulers of France had never abandoned their own imperial visions. France had long been Europe's largest kingdom in terms of land and overall population. By the 1660s, bureaucratic, financial, and political reforms had left the French with the mightiest military as well. Determined to have more territory, France's ambitious king, Louis XIV, unleashed this titanic war machine against his neighbors on four different occasions between 1667 and 1714.

Even after 1714, France, England, and, to a lesser extent, Spain waged a kind of cold war for a quarter of a century, jockeying for position and influence. Western European monarchs had come to realize that confrontations in North America's vast and distant interior could influence the outcome of their feuds closer to home. In this global chess game, the British had the advantage of numbers: nearly 400,000 subjects in the colonies in 1720, compared with only about 25,000 French spread along a thin line of fishing stations and fur-trading posts, and a meager 5,000 or so Spaniards in New Mexico, Texas, and Florida combined. But by a considerable margin, native peoples still represented the majority population in North America. Moreover, they still controlled more than 90 percent of its territory. If events in North America could affect the balance of power in Europe, then French and Spanish administrators could still believe and hope that their Indian alliances might yet help them prevail against each other, especially against Britain's booming colonies.

CHAPTER SUMMARY

While the French colonized Canada, the Protestant Reformation in England spurred the colonization of New England and Pennsylvania.

- During the seventeenth century, the French slowly established a fur trade, agricultural communities, and religious institutions in Canada while building Indian alliances throughout the Mississippi drainage.

- Competition over the fur trade in New France and New Netherland contributed to a devastating series of wars between Iroquois, Hurons, and dozens of other Indian groups.

- Over the same period, English Puritans planted more populous settlements between Maine and Long Island.

- The migration of family groups and a rough equality of wealth lent stability to early New England society, reinforced by the settlers' shared commitment to Puritanism and a strong tradition of self-government.

- The mid-Atlantic colonies also enjoyed a rapid growth of people and wealth, but political wrangling as well as ethnic and religious diversity made for a higher level of social conflict.

- Whereas New Englanders attempted to subdue native peoples, colonists in the mid-Atlantic enjoyed more harmonious relations with the region's original inhabitants.

- The efforts of the later Stuart kings to centralize England's empire ended with the Glorious Revolution in 1688, which greatly reduced tensions between the colonies and the parent country.

Digging Deeper

For penetrating studies of French and Indian relations, see Allan Greer, *Mohawk Saint* (2005); and Brett Rushforth, *Bonds of Alliance* (2013). Colin G. Calloway's *One Vast Winter Count* (2003) masterfully synthesizes the history of natives and Europeans in early North America west of the Appalachians; and Daniel K. Richter does the same for eastern North America in *Before the Revolution* (2011). For a history of Dutch America, see Jaap Jacobs, *New Netherland* (2005). *Vermeer's Hat* (2008) by Timothy Brook is a marvelous exploration of the ways furs and other commodities bound together the seventeenth-century world. For important work on Indians in the colonial Northeast, see Jenny Hale Pulsipher, *Subjects unto the Same King* (2008); and Andrew Lipman, *The Saltwater Frontier* (2015). The best and most recent introduction to Puritanism is John Coffey and Paul C. H. Lim, *The Cambridge Companion to Puritanism* (2008). For Puritanism in New England, read Stephen Foster, *The Long Argument* (1991); and Mark A. Peterson, *The Price of Redemption* (1997). And to learn more about the diversity of religious and supernatural views in New England, consult Philip Gura, *A Glimpse of Sion's Glory* (1984); and David D. Hall, *Worlds of Wonder, Days of Judgment* (1989).

For the everyday lives of northern colonists in New England and New York, rely on Virginia DeJohn Anderson's *New England's Generation* (1991) and Joyce D. Goodfriend's *Before the Melting Pot* (1991). For African slavery in New England, see Wendy Warren, *New England Bound* (2016). For a geographical perspective on British America (including the West Indies and Canada), see Stephen J. Hornsby, *British Atlantic, American Frontier* (2005). For the complex interplay among English colonialism, environmental change, and Indian power in the Northeast, see William Cronon's classic *Changes in the Land* (rev. ed., 2003). The event and memory of "King Philip's War" are the subjects of Jill Lepore's *The Name of War* (1998).

5 The Mosaic of Eighteenth-Century America

1689–1768

In this detail from a remarkable painting, Don Pedro de Villasur lies dead, hands extended in the air as he is being dragged by his arms and legs outside his blue tent. Just below, the Spanish (wearing hats) form a circle to fend off the attack of Pawnee warriors. Jean L'Archevêque stands bareheaded on the right side of the circle, wearing blue clothing. The full painting is shown in the story.

Segesser II. Courtesy Palace of the Governors (NMHM/DCA) 149803

>> An American Story

THE TALE OF A TATTOOED TRAVELER

August 13, 1720: morning sunlight breaks over the confluence of the Platte and Loup Rivers in what today is Nebraska. Jean L'Archevêque rises stiffly from where he slept and looks about camp. A few dozen Spanish soldiers huddle in the early light, donning their long, leather vests and their wide-brimmed hats. At another end of the encampment the Pueblo Indian men who have accompanied the expedition speak softly to one another, making less noise than the soldiers, though double their number. A friar in his habit passes among the tents. Don Pedro de Villasur, lieutenant governor of New Mexico and leader of the party, threads his arms through a bright, red officer's coat and orders the soldiers to bring in their horses.

Segesser II. Courtesy Palace of the Governors (NMHM/DCA) 149803

| *17 feet long by 4½ feet high, this painting on bison or elk hide was likely made by a mission-trained Indian, after Villasur's downfall.*

Most of these men had known L'Archevêque for years—had come to appreciate his sly humor and grown accustomed to his thick French accent. But on this morning, as they set about the king's business some 600 miles from their homes and families, there must have been something unnerving about the dark, swirling tattoos that covered the Frenchman's face. They had been put there years earlier by Indians who had captured L'Archevêque in the aftermath of a Texas expedition that had ended in calamity. One had only to look at those tattoos to be reminded that things sometimes go badly for both kings and their servants.

Born in 1672 in Bayonne, France, L'Archevêque was only a boy when he boarded ship to the French Caribbean, fleeing his family's financial troubles. Then in 1684 he joined an expedition led by the French explorer René Robert Cavelier, Sieur de La Salle. Three years earlier La Salle had been the first to navigate the immense Mississippi River from the Great Lakes to the Gulf of Mexico. He was famous and respected. Now he was

set to plant a permanent settlement near the Mississippi's mouth, as a strategic foothold for France. Yet try as he might, La Salle could not find the mouth of the Mississippi when he approached this time from the Gulf of Mexico. Instead, he landed on the coast of present-day Texas and threw up some ramshackle buildings. As months stretched into years, the expedition lost its ships, while the nearly 300 colonists sickened, starved, and died. The survivors blamed their leader and hatched a plan to be rid of him. Young L'Archevêque played a part, distracting the great explorer while an accomplice blew his head apart with a musket shot.

As the colony spiraled into ruin, L'Archevêque and a few desperate companions eventually found themselves unhappy guests among Caddo Indians in east Texas. These were the people who tattooed the young man's face, carefully inserting a dye made from walnuts into countless tiny cuts. Spanish explorers, determined to root out La Salle's French colony, stumbled across L'Archevêque in 1690, ransomed him from the Caddos, and imprisoned him—first in Mexico City and then for two and a half years in Spain. Finally he was freed and returned to Mexico City.

Meanwhile, news of La Salle's stillborn colony convinced Spanish officials to take more energetic measures to secure their claims on the North American West. A permanent French settlement could be used all too easily as a base to threaten New Spain and its famous silver mines. Crucially, Spain had to reconquer New Mexico, from which it had been driven out by Popé's Pueblo Revolt of 1680 (Chapter 3). When Spanish colonists returned in earnest in 1692, they met only fragmented resistance from the Pueblo villages.

It was in reconquered New Mexico that Jean L'Archevêque found his first real home since boyhood. Sent north perhaps because of his facility with not only French but also Indian languages, L'Archevêque quickly became a fixture in Santa Fe, prospering, marrying well, and gaining the trust of his neighbors. The Spanish had not long returned to New Mexico before they began hearing complaints from the plains Apaches about Pawnee raiders armed with French guns and mocking the Spanish, calling them "women." In 1720, with Spain and France at war in Europe, New Mexico's governor ordered his lieutenant Villasur to take L'Archevêque and a group of Indian and Spanish fighters to confront the French—hence the long trek to the Platte River, where the men awoke at daybreak on August 13 to do the king's business.

But, again, things sometimes go badly for kings and their servants. Moments after ordering his men to bring in their horses, Villasur heard wild screams and saw dozens of painted Pawnee warriors rush the camp. The lieutenant governor was one of the first to die, killed with mouth agape just outside his tent; L'Archevêque fell soon after, his death demonstrating how unsettled the North American continent had become in the eighteenth century. The young Frenchman from Bayonne had been shipwrecked, recruited to murder, and tattooed in Texas, imprisoned in Mexico and Spain, married and made respectable on the upper Rio Grande, and finally shot dead and buried alongside Spanish and Indian companions somewhere in Nebraska. It was a remarkable and turbulent odyssey. <<

THEMATIC TIMELINE

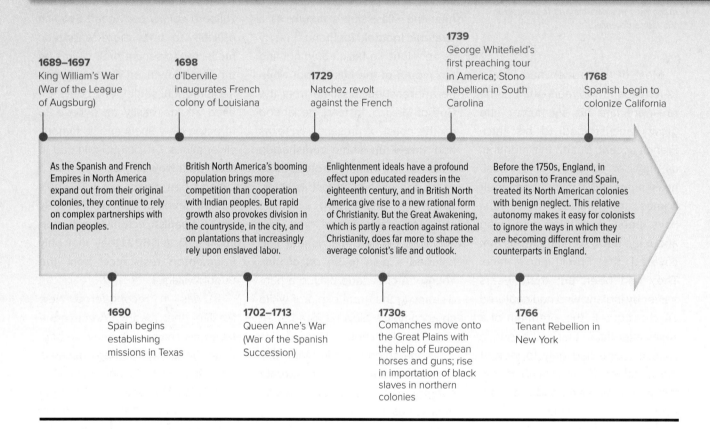

1689–1697
King William's War (War of the League of Augsburg)

As the Spanish and French Empires in North America expand out from their original colonies, they continue to rely on complex partnerships with Indian peoples.

1690
Spain begins establishing missions in Texas

1698
d'Iberville inaugurates French colony of Louisiana

British North America's booming population brings more competition than cooperation with Indian peoples. But rapid growth also provokes division in the countryside, in the city, and on plantations that increasingly rely upon enslaved labor.

1702–1713
Queen Anne's War (War of the Spanish Succession)

1729
Natchez revolt against the French

Enlightenment ideals have a profound effect upon educated readers in the eighteenth century, and in British North America give rise to a new rational form of Christianity. But the Great Awakening, which is partly a reaction against rational Christianity, does far more to shape the average colonist's life and outlook.

1730s
Comanches move onto the Great Plains with the help of European horses and guns; rise in importation of black slaves in northern colonies

1739
George Whitefield's first preaching tour in America; Stono Rebellion in South Carolina

1768
Spanish begin to colonize California

Before the 1750s, England, in comparison to France and Spain, treated its North American colonies with benign neglect. This relative autonomy makes it easy for colonists to ignore the ways in which they are becoming different from their counterparts in England.

1766
Tenant Rebellion in New York

CRISIS AND TRANSFORMATION IN NORTHERN NEW SPAIN

JEAN L'ARCHEVÊQUE'S LIFE TESTIFIES IN a very personal way to the unpredictable changes unleashed by contact between European and American civilizations. As Europeans established colonies and began competing with one another across the far reaches of the continent, individuals throughout North America, especially native peoples, found life changing at astonishing speed. Europeans, with their animals, plants, technologies, diseases, and designs, drove the existing dynamism in the Americas to a fever pitch of transformation. But Europeans could not predict and did not control the process. Despite their grand ambitions, colonial newcomers often found their own plans upended and their lives reordered by the same forces reworking native life.

Defensive Expansion into Texas

As European rivals laid claim to more and more of North America, nervous Spanish officials stared at their maps. Around the region that had been the Aztec Empire, Spain controlled enormous cities, booming towns, and agricultural

>> MAPPING THE PAST <<

EUROPEAN TERRITORIAL CLAIMS

> "From the accounts which the Moaches give, it is believed that the sea is not very far away."
> —Tomás Vélez Cachupín, Governor of New Mexico, 1750.

Source: Library of Congress, Prints and Photographs Division [LC-USZ62-98768]

CONTEXT

Europeans still had a very imperfect understanding of North American geography in 1750, after more than two centuries of colonization and exploration. Native peoples continued to dominate the vast majority of the continent. But competition between empires led European statesmen to make sweeping and often unrealistic territorial claims in treaties and on maps. This map represents some of those competing claims. The British dominated most of the eastern seaboard and its hinterland, and through their bases around Hudson's Bay had influence (but little territorial control) throughout northern Canada. France claimed most of the midcontinent, and depended on Indian allies to sustain that claim. Spain's pockets of settlements and missions in the West were still relatively untroubled by imperial rivals in the mid-eighteenth century. But mounting interimperial competition created zones of contested French, British, and Spanish claims throughout eastern North America.

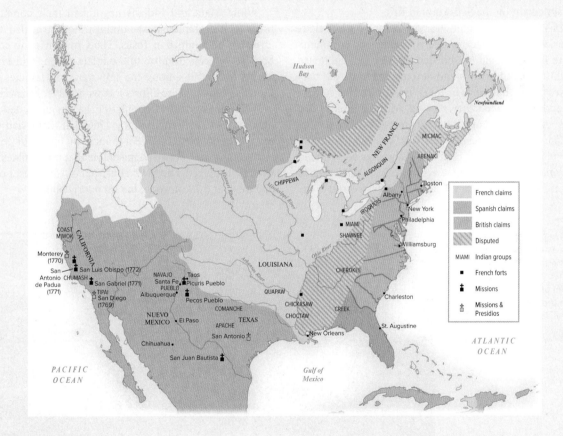

MAP READING

1. How do waterways and harbors figure into the imperial claims you see here?
2. Do prominent geographic features influence the patterns of claims?
3. Where don't Europeans claim continental territory?

MAP INTERPRETATION

1. Consider the pattern of imperial territorial claims. Using the history you've already learned, can you explain the pattern you see?
2. Why do you think Europeans made claims on territories that they could not control?

villages—a region still populated by millions despite waves of epidemic disease. Though drier and home to far fewer people, the lands hundreds of miles north of Mexico City were of special concern because of their remarkable silver mines. To protect these lands from French designs, Spain had to start paying more attention to the blank spaces still farther north on their maps—spaces entirely controlled by Indians.

TEXAS AS A BUFFER AGAINST THE FRENCH Nowhere did the French seem more menacing than in Texas, one of the most important blank spots on Spanish maps. La Salle's catastrophic adventure could have turned out differently: before his grisly death, the Frenchman pledged to invade northern New Spain with an army of thousands of Indians, who, he believed, had "a deadly hatred of the Spaniards." Fearful that another French expedition might actually acquire such an army, in 1690 Spain began establishing missions among the native peoples of Texas. The project started haltingly, but by the early 1720s the Spanish had fortified their claim on Texas with 10 Franciscan missions, 4 presidios (military garrisons), and the beginnings of a civilian settlement on the San Antonio River.

Still, missions disappointed Franciscans and natives alike. Missionaries hoped to create orderly, regimented communities where Indians could be shielded from outside influence and taught to be industrious and devout. The friars did baptize natives by the thousands in Texas. But Indians insisted on coming and going when they pleased. Many nonsedentary peoples sought the food and sanctuary missions offered, only to leave periodically to rendezvous with kin, hunt, and harvest wild plant foods. Their comings and goings confounded the missionaries. Matters were even worse for Franciscans in east Texas, where sedentary Caddos barely tolerated the missions. Farmers themselves, and relatively secure in their fixed villages of beehive-shaped homes, Caddos had no need for the missionaries' crops or protection. Just as important, they could and did trade with Frenchmen from Louisiana, who offered more manufactured goods at better prices than Spaniards did.

INDIANS AND MISSIONS However successful they were at retaining autonomy, Indians throughout Texas paid a steep price for any benefits they wrung from missions. Those compelled inside by hunger and insecurity often endured harsh discipline and corporal punishment for disobeying orders. Even worse, missions proved ideal vectors for epidemic disease. In the 1730s alone, smallpox killed more than 1,000 mission Indians near San Antonio. Other illnesses became commonplace as nomadic peoples with sanitary practices suitable for life on the move crowded together in filthy, cramped buildings. Children were especially vulnerable to the new regime. In eighteenth-century Mission San Antonio, for example, only one in three newborns survived to his or her third birthday.

While friars and Indians negotiated their complex and tragic relationship, Spanish administrators struggled to foster civilian communities in Texas. The Crown tried to convince Spanish subjects to move to the infant colony and even sent agents to recruit among the impoverished families on the Canary Islands. These efforts met with only token success. In 1731 Texas's nonnative population barely amounted to 500 men, women, and children; by 1760 that figure had slightly more than doubled. In 1778 a Franciscan inspector described San Antonio as "a town so miserable that it resembles a most wretched village." The town consisted of "59 houses of stone and mud, and 79 of wood, but all poorly built."

| These two Franciscans were regarded as hero-martyrs by their fellow missionaries after Comanches and Wichitas killed them during a 1758 attack on the San Saba mission in Texas.

©DeAgostini/Getty Images

Crisis and Rebirth in New Mexico

Spain had pushed into the blank space on the map that was Texas, but after generations into the project it still controlled only an archipelago of missions, presidios, and a few towns—surrounded on all sides by unconquered Indians, whose power in the region was, if anything, expanding. At first Apaches posed the greatest threat to Spain's ambitions in Texas. Their raids thinned Spanish herds, prevented ranching and farming communities from expanding outward, and threatened missions with destruction. Spaniards responded with slave raids on Apache camps, and the violence escalated.

COMANCHE NEWCOMERS By the 1730s, however, a new force emerged to eclipse even Apaches. They called themselves Numunuu, "the People." Their enemies came to call them Comanches. Emerging from the foothills of the Rockies in the late sixteenth century, Comanches integrated European horses into their lives, moved permanently onto the plains, and quickly became some of the most formidable equestrian warriors in history. They allied with Indians who could provide them French guns and ammunition from Louisiana and embarked on a program of territorial expansion. By the mid-eighteenth century Comanches drove most Apaches from the plains and took over their rich bison-hunting territories in what is today southern Colorado, eastern New Mexico, and west Texas. Without bison, Apaches turned more and more to stealing Spanish animals to survive. Spaniards from Santa Fe to San Antonio soon found themselves at war with Apaches and Comanches both; New Mexico often came into conflict with Navajos and Utes as well. Much of northern New Spain became a theater of desolation; abandoned villages up and down the Rio Grande testified to the limits of Spanish power.

Spaniards accused the "barbarians" of animalistic savagery, but all sides inflicted horrors on their enemies. Outside the little besieged town of Tucson, for example, Lieutenant Colonel Pedro de Allende boasted that he had decapitated a fallen Apache in front of the dead man's comrades and "charged the Apache line single-handed, with the head stuck on his lance." Away from the din of battle, a prominent Spaniard noted that his people accuse the Indians of cruelty but added, "I do not know what opinion they would have of us."

A BROKERED PEACE By the 1780s nearly everyone had had enough of war. A farsighted Comanche leader named Ecueracapa helped broker peace with Spanish authorities in 1786, after which the new allies cooperated to entice or threaten Utes, Navajos, and Apaches into peace as well. Northern New Spain entered a period of relative calm, expansion, and economic growth. Changes were most dramatic in New Mexico, where Spanish subjects opened up new farms and ranches, enlarged their flocks and herds, and devoted new energy to local manufacturing. As New Mexico's non-Indian population grew (20,000 by the close of the eighteenth century), new

roads funded by the Crown helped ease the province's isolation. Finally, peace meant that *nuevo mexicanos* could accumulate wealth by trading more with their Indian neighbors and with merchants in Chihuahua, Durango, and Mexico City. Trade and supply caravans began setting out from Santa Fe for Chihuahua once or even twice a year.

DISTINCTIVE NEW MEXICAN CULTURE Some of the New Mexicans who profited most from the newfound opportunities began to patronize artists and skilled craftsmen. By the late eighteenth century a distinctive New Mexican culture started to emerge, one marked by new traditions in such crafts as woodworking and weaving, as well as in religious art and practice. A master craftsman known only as the Laguna Santero helped define this movement by training local apprentices in his workshop and making pieces for wealthy patrons. The Laguna Santero, his apprentices, and others he inspired began making exquisite portraits of saints on pine boards (*retablos*), hide paintings, elaborate altar screens for churches, and wooden statues of saints (*bultos*)—all art forms still associated with New Mexican folk culture today.

Spanish California

Spanish California was the empire's last major colonial project in North America. Like the colonies in Texas and Florida, settlement was sparked by a fear of foreign competition, this time from Russians moving south from Alaska. Though Spaniards first explored the California coast in 1542, not until 1768 did the Crown authorize permanent colonization. A joint expedition of military men and Franciscans led by the pragmatic Gaspar de Portolá and the iron-willed Fray (Friar) Junípero Serra, braved shipwrecks, scurvy, and earthquakes to establish ramshackle **presidios** (military garrisons) and missions at San Diego and Monterey.

©Private Collection/Bridgeman Images

| *The Ukrainian Louis Choris visited Mission Dolores in 1822 and captured this scene of Ohlone Indians playing games of chance. But the artist's overall impression of Ohlone life at the mission was one of sorrow and despair. "I have never seen one laugh. I have never seen one look one in the face. They look as though they were interested in nothing."*

THE FOUNDERS OF SPANISH CALIFORNIA

Historians often turn to census data for insights into people's lives that are difficult to come by in other records. Often scholars analyze masses of historic census data with the help of computers. But these censuses from early colonial California survey households in what were then the tiny villages of Los Angeles and San José, making it relatively easy for us to look for patterns. For example, these documents reveal the striking heterogeneity of the "Spanish" colonization of California. Preoccupied with blood and birthright, officials throughout Spanish America routinely labeled people according to their supposed heritage. Mestizo/a referred to a child of a Spaniard and an Indian; mulato/a to a child of a Spaniard and an African; coyote to a child of a mestizo/a and an Indian; chino/a to a child of a Spaniard and a salta-atras (a person with African features born of white parents); and pardo/a (a child of an African and an Indian). The second census, from San José, includes occupation and birthplace information for the head of house.

Census of Los Angeles, 1781

NAME	AGE		NAME	AGE
(1) Lara, Josef de; español	50		(6) Vanegas, Josef; indio	28
Maria Antonio Campos, india sabina	23		Maria Maxima Aguilar; India	20
Josef Julian	4		Cosme Damien	1
Juana de Jesus	6			
Maria Faustina	2		(7) Rosas, Alejandro; indio	19
			Juana Rodriguez; coyote india	20
(2) Navarro, Josef Antonio; mestizo	42			
Maria Rufina Dorotea; mulata	47		(8) Rodriguez, Pablo; indio	25
Josef Maria	10		Maria Rosalia Noriega; india	26
Josef Clemente	9		Maria Antonia	1
Maria Josefa	4			
			(9) Camero, Manuel; mulatto	30
(3) Rosas, Basillio; indio	67		Maria Tomasa; mulata	24
Maria Manuela Calixtra; mulata	43			
Jose Maximo	15		(10) Quintero, Luis; negro	55
Carlos	12		Maria Petra Rubio; Mulata	40
Antonio Rosalino	7		Josef Clemente	3
Josef Marcelino	4		Maria Gertrudis	16
Juan Esteban	2		Maria Concepcion	9
Maria Josefa	8		Tomasa	7
			Rafaela	6
(4) Mesa, Antonio; negro	38			
Ana Gertrudis Lopez; mulata	27		(11) Moreno, Jose; mulato	22
Antonio Maria	8		Maria Guadalupe Gertrudis	19
Maria Paula	10			
			(12) Rodriguez, Antonio Miranda; chino	50
(5) Villavicencio, Antonio; español	30		Juana Maria	11
Maria de los Santos Seferina; india	26			
Maria Antonio Josefa	8			

Source: Weber, David, *Foreigners in Their Native Land: Historical Roots of the Mexican Americans*, 30th Anniversary ed. Albuquerque, NM: University of New Mexico Press, 2003, 33.

Census of San José, 1790

NAME	AGE		NAME	AGE
(1) Romero, Antonio, farmworker, pardo, from Guadalajara	40		(2) Archuleta, Ignacio; farmworker, Spaniard, from Horcasitas [Sonora]	36
Petra Aceves; parda	28		Gertrudis Pacheco; Spaniard	36
[Antonio]	14		[Petra]	9

NAME	AGE	NAME	AGE
[Miguel]	11	(10) Lugo, Serafino; farmworker, español, from Villa Sinaloa	50
[Gregorio]	8	Gertrudis Pacheco, española	50
[Florentino]	6	[Juan]	19
[Juan José]	5	[Nicolas]	13
(3) Alvírez, Claudio; farmworker, coyote, from Tetuache [Sonora]	48	[Rafael]	11
Ana María Gonzales; india	30	(11) Castro, Joaquín; farmworker, español, from Villa Sinaloa	50
[José]	8	Martina Botiller, española	50
[Brígida]	5	[Francisco María]	18
[Juan]	2	[Carlos]	15
[Jacoba]	baby	[unnamed orphan]	?
(4) Gonzales, Manuel; farmworker, indio, from San Bartolomé [Chihuahua]	70	[unnamed orphan]	?
Gertrudis Aceves; parda	20	(12) Alegre, Antonio; farmworker, español, from Genoa [Italy]	50
[Francisco]	18	Catarina; India	28
[Romualdo]	13	[Vicenta Anastacia]	6
(5) Rosales, Bernardo; farmworker, mulato, from Terrenate [Sonora]	?	(13) Bojórquez, Pedro; cowboy, español, from Villa Sinaloa	36
Mónica; india, from Mission San Antonio	28	Angela Trejo; española	43
[Josefa]	14	[Hermenegildo Ignacio]	12
[Cornelio]	12	[Bartolomé Francisco]	10
[Petra]	10	[Juan José]	6
[María Antonia]	7	(14) Aceves, Antonio; farmworker, mulato, from San Bartolomé [Chihuahua]	50
(6) Amézquita, Manuel; farmworker, mulato, from Terrenate [Sonora]	?	Feliciana Cortés, mestiza	50
Graciana Arroyo, mulata	26	[José Antonio]	18
[Gabriel]	14	[José Maria]	11
[Serafín]	10	(15) Sáez, Nazario; cowboy, español, from San Bartolomé [Chihuahua]	48
[Ventura]	6	Micaela Sotelo, españa	40
[Augustina]	4	[Juana]	16
[Salvador]	2	[Juan María]	12
(7) Vásquez, Tiburcio; farmworker, mestizo, from Ahualulco [Jalisco]	35	[María Benita]	10
María Bojórquez, española	30	[María Felipa]	8
[Francisco]	12	(16) Cagüelas, Pedro; cowboy, indio, from San Luis Obispo	20
[Felipe]	10	Secundina, India	18
[Resurección]	8	(17) Osuna, Miguel; tailor, español, from Real de San Francisco [Sonora], single	52
[Hermenegildo]	6	(18) Nervo, Pedro Ruiz; español, from San Blas [Nayarit], single	21
[Rosalía]	4		
[Faustino]	2		
[Féliz]	1		
(8) Avila, Francisco; farmworker, español, from El Fuerte [Sinaloa], widower	46		
Francisco Xavier	16		
(9) Mesa, Valerio; farmworker, español, from San Juan Bautista [Sonora]	60		
Leonor Borboa, española	50		
[Juan]	19		
[Nicolas]	13		
[Rafael]	11		

Source: Mason, William M., *The Census of 1790: A Demographic History of Colonial California*, Ballena Press Anthropological Papers No. 45. Menlo Park, CA: Ballena Press, 1998, 98–100.

THINKING CRITICALLY

Other than individual ethnic heritage, what sorts of information or patterns can you find in these censuses? Can you spot any familial connections? What can these documents tell us about family size, marriage age, naming customs, or prevailing norms regarding interethnic unions? What sorts of cautions do historians need to keep in mind when working with documents such as these?

Officials found it difficult to recruit colonists for California and even turned to orphanages and prisons in New Spain, with little success. Moreover, it seemed nearly impossible to get colonists to California alive. The sea route along the Pacific coast proved costly and often deadly, and the back-breaking overland route from northwestern New Spain had to be abandoned after 1781, when an uprising of Yuma Indians shut down the crossing at the Colorado River. Still, the colony enjoyed steady if modest growth. By 1800 California had two more presidios (at San Francisco and Santa Barbara), three Spanish towns (San José, Los Angeles, and Branciforte, near present-day Santa Cruz), and a total of 18 Franciscan missions, ministering to 13,000 Indian converts.

THE CHANGING CALIFORNIA ENVIRONMENT Like their colleagues in Texas and Florida, Franciscans tried to entice Indians into missions with promises of food, shelter, instruction, and protection. As time went on, missions became self-sufficient and more effective at both attracting Indians and policing those who came in. All the while, Indians saw the world changing around them. In Monterey, for example, imported pigs, sheep, mules, horses, and cows multiplied at astonishing speed. These animals radiated out from the mission and presidio, overgrazing and annihilating native plants. Soon weeds and plants that Spaniards had unwittingly brought with them began to spread throughout the region, outcompeting the disturbed native vegetation.

By 1800 the lands around Monterey had been thoroughly transformed. Pollen analysis of the vegetable matter in adobe from the early nineteenth century indicates that by the time the bricks were made, alien weeds had all but displaced native plants. With their lands transformed by overgrazing and invasive plant species, and their populations diminished by epidemics, native families around Monterey abandoned their villages and either fled to the interior or surrendered to the discipline and danger of mission life.

California's three colonial towns depended on missions for food and labor. Given the difficulties of immigrating to California, the colonial population grew mainly through natural increase. By 1800 California was home to only 1,800 Hispanic residents. Despite their relative poverty and isolation, these men, women, and children maintained distinctive traditions. An English visitor to Monterey savored local parties, bullfights, and hunts in the countryside. Most of all, he marveled at the "exhilarating" fandango, a dance that "requires no little elasticity of limbs as well as nimbleness of capers & gestures." The whirling men and women moved "with such wanton attitudes & motions, such leering looks, sparkling eyes and trembling limbs, as would decompose the gravity of a stoic."

Like most English-speaking visitors to California, this excitable traveler found Hispanic women both alluring and improper. Proper women knew their place, and, while delightful to watch, fandango seemed a good deal too joyous and suggestive to be proper. Had the Englishman probed deeper, he would have learned of other, far more consequential differences between Spanish and English women than the former's love of bold and beautiful dance.

Women and the Law in New Spain and British North America

Women in California and throughout the Spanish world had a host of important legal rights denied to women in English-speaking realms. For comparison's sake, consider a few critical moments in the lives of two imaginary women: Soledad Martínez, of Los Angeles, California; and Constance Snowling, of Albany, New York.

SPANISH LEGAL ADVANTAGES FOR WOMEN When Soledad's parents passed away, Spanish law ensured that she would inherit their property on an equal footing with her brothers. English law, in contrast, allowed fathers to craft wills however they wished. Constance could theoretically receive nothing upon her parents' deaths. If, as was usually the case, Constance's father died without a will, by law his eldest son inherited all his land and any buildings on it. Constance and any other sisters or brothers would receive only a share of the remaining personal property (money, tools, furniture, clothing, and so on).

The legal advantages enjoyed by women in the Spanish Empire become even more apparent in marriage. Suppose that both Soledad and Constance were fortunate enough to come into their marriages with some personal property of their own and with modest dowries—sums of money meant to help the young couple get established. After her wedding, Soledad retained complete legal control over her personal property and could dispose of it however she wished (with or without her husband's blessing). Moreover, although her husband had the right to manage the dowry and invest it as he

Source: A84.2.1 *Untitled* (Portrait of a Spanish Woman). ca. 1856. Photographer unknown. Ambrotype. Collection of Oakland Museum of California. Gift of Dr. Stanley B. Burns.

| *This lovingly framed and preserved photograph is an ambrotype of a California woman taken sometime in the 1850s. We don't know her name. But her wedding ring and her elegant clothing tell us that she was a married woman of means. The California of her youth was being transformed by the Gold Rush.*

saw fit, it still belonged to Soledad. Once death or divorce ended the marriage, he was legally obliged to return its full value to her or her family. Finally, as a married woman Soledad retained the right to buy and sell land in her own name and could legally represent herself in court. Wives in the English-speaking world had no such rights in the colonial era. Upon marriage, Constance surrendered her dowry and even her personal property to her new husband, who could dispose of all of it however he wished. As a married woman, Constance had virtually no control over property of any kind, could not write a will, and could initiate no legal actions without her husband's consent.

Finally, if our two imaginary colonial women had outlived their husbands, they would have experienced widowhood very differently. In addition to the full value of her dowry, Soledad was legally entitled to at least one-half of all property she and her deceased husband had accumulated in marriage. Upon Soledad's death, this property would pass to her own children or to her other family members. Constance had no claim on her dowry following her husband's death. She would have entered widowhood with her personal "paraphernalia" (clothes, jewelry, and similar items), any land she had been fortunate enough to inherit during marriage, and control over a third of her dead husband's property. Crucially, however, Constance could use this property only to support herself in life. Upon her death, it would pass into the hands of her husband's family.

Not all Spanish and English women would have felt these legal differences as keenly as Soledad and Constance. Poor women who inherited little, came into marriages with paltry dowries, and lived hand to mouth as adults endured poverty whether they lived under English or Spanish law. But for those who did have some property or wealth, it mattered a great deal whether they lived in New Spain or British North America.

WOMEN'S LEGAL RIGHTS IN NEW FRANCE   France's legal traditions descended from the same Roman sources as Spain's, so women in New France enjoyed legal protections similar to women in Florida, Texas, New Mexico, and California. And France's and Spain's colonies in North America had other, less happy things in common. Like northern New Spain, New France generally cost the Crown more money than it brought in. Like their Spanish counterparts, French administrators found it all but impossible to convince or compel large numbers of their fellow subjects to move to the colonies. As in Florida, Texas, New Mexico, and California, the colonial population of New France struck many well-heeled observers as degraded, insolent, lazy, and ignorant. And, as with all Spanish colonies north of the Rio Grande, New France remained dependent on Indians generations after its founding.

REVIEW
Why did Spain establish colonies in Texas and California, and what role did missions play in establishing the Spanish presence?

EIGHTEENTH-CENTURY NEW FRANCE

LIKE THE SPRAWLING VASTNESS OF Spain's territorial claims in North America, France's imperial reach was nothing if not ambitious. French colonial maps laid claim to the heart of the continent, a massive imperial wedge stretching from Newfoundland southwest to the Mississippi delta, then northwest across the Great Plains and into the cold north woods, and east again through Upper Canada to the North Atlantic. Of course it was one thing to draw an empire on a map, another to make the empire a reality.

Colonial Compromises

Despite their grand claims, most eighteenth-century French Americans continued to live along the St. Lawrence River. Most dwelt in farming communities up and down the river valley between the small cities of Montreal and Quebec, capital of New France. Jesuit missions also lined the river, ministering to native converts. The Crown had given the valley a boost with an energetic colonization program in the 1660s and 1670s, but thereafter the French population grew almost totally through natural increase. Fortunately for France, the colonists excelled at natural increase—nurturing large, thriving families and basically doubling their own population every generation.

GROWTH ALONG THE ST. LAWRENCE RIVER   Those determined enough to endure darkness, isolation, and numbing cold in winter, then heat, humidity, and swarming mosquitoes in summer, found life in Canada considerably easier than life in France. Colonists were healthier and lived longer, were much more likely to own their own land, and enjoyed significantly more autonomy over their lives than rural peasants across the Atlantic. By 1760 the valley was home to around 75,000 French colonists, soldiers, and priests. Many Canadian households also included Indian slaves: women and children, mostly, who had been captured by other Indians in places as faraway as the Arkansas valley and sold into trade networks that eventually brought them to New France. Though modest by Anglo-American standards, by the mid-eighteenth century the colonial project along the St. Lawrence River had nonetheless put an unmistakable French stamp upon the land.

FRENCH AND INDIANS IN THE *PAYS D'EN HAUT*   To the west and north in the country known as the *pays d'en haut* ("upper country"), France's eighteenth-century venture took on a very different look. Around the Great Lakes, north around Lakes Manitoba and Winnipeg, and south along the Mississippi River basin, forts and missions rather than farms or towns anchored French ambition. More exactly, the goodwill of Indian peoples provided the anchor. Though as quick as other Europeans to use violence to get what they wanted, the French in North America recognized that they were too few to secure their interests through force alone. France gained an edge over its rivals in the interior by being useful to Indians, primarily the Algonquian-speaking nations that spread across eastern Canada and the upper Mississippi. French merchants brought coveted European presents and trade goods, while military men, administrators, and Jesuits often mediated in conflicts between native groups. Vastly outnumbered by Indians throughout most of the territory that it claimed in North America, France remained deeply dependent on native peoples.

Dependence meant compromise. Cultural differences between the French and their Indian allies often seemed vast and irreconcilable. The two peoples had radically divergent expectations about warfare, trade, marriage, child rearing, religion, food, beauty, and many other areas of life. Few cultural differences seemed as difficult to bridge as those concerning law. In 1706, for example, men associated with a prominent Ottawa leader known as Le Pesant killed a priest and a French

soldier outside of Fort Detroit. Enraged French authorities demanded that Le Pesant be delivered to them so that he could be tried and, once found guilty, executed for murder. Ottawa leaders countered by offering to replace the dead Frenchmen with Indian slaves. "Raising" the dead this way was a common Ottawa remedy in cases of murder between allies, because it helped avoid a potentially disastrous cycle of blood revenge. Moreover, Le Pesant was a powerful man. His execution would have political consequences dangerous to the broader French alliance.

Neither side surrendered to the other. Instead, they crafted a novel solution that exemplified the pattern of creative, mutual compromises typical of what one scholar has called the "middle ground" characterizing French-Indian relations in the *pays d'en haut.* On a snowy morning, grim Ottawa leaders turned over Le Pesant to the French commander at Fort Detroit who then quickly condemned the man to death. But

Algonquin and French Views Regarding Trade and Justice

	ALGONQUIN VALUES	FRENCH VALUES
Trade	Trade embedded in personal relationships. Expectation that exchanges will be relatively uniform and consistent season to season. Negative changes in trade terms attributed to decay of personal relationship.	Trade structured mostly by markets, and only marginally by personal relationships. Trade terms will naturally change as market conditions change. Nothing inherently personal about fluctuations in prices or trade terms.
Justice	Upon a murder, most urgent question was "To what group did the killer belong?" Response to the murder would be determined and pursued by family of the victim. Families could (a) seek another death in revenge—especially if the killer belonged to an enemy people; (b) accept presents to "cover" the death; or (c) take an Indian slave in compensation and thereby "raise" the victim.	Upon a murder, most urgent question was "Who was the killer?" Response to the murder would be determined and pursued by state authorities. State authorities held that the only legitimate remedy for a murder was the apprehension, trial, and execution of the killer.

Source: Library of Congress, Prints and Photographs Division [LC-USZ62-45595]

before the execution could be carried out, Le Pesant escaped to freedom. It is exceedingly difficult to believe that French authorities would have been careless enough to allow this most wanted of men to slip away. Moreover, Le Pesant was elderly and obese—hardly a nimble escape artist. Clearly the French and their Ottawa allies came to an understanding. Le Pesant would be surrendered and, once condemned, quietly allowed to escape. This new compromise more or less satisfied both sides and became a model solution to later French-Indian murder cases.

Necessary and inevitable, such compromises nonetheless rankled authorities in Paris. In 1731 one such official bemoaned the fact that after more than a century, colonial administrators in New France had failed to make the "savages" obedient to the Crown. The colony's governor-general dashed off a terse reply: "If this has not been done, it is because we have found the task to be an impossible one. Kindly apprise me of any means you should conceive of for securing such obedience."

France on the Gulf Coast

Forced into uncomfortable compromises in the north, authorities in Paris hoped to establish a colony on the Gulf Coast that could be more profitable and more French. When shipwreck on the Texas coast sealed La Salle's doom, it fell to Pierre Le Moyne d'Iberville to establish French Louisiana. A veteran sailor and soldier, d'Iberville spent much of the 1690s destroying British settlements in Newfoundland and the North Atlantic. Sent to the Gulf in 1698, he inaugurated the new colony of Louisiana with a post at Biloxi Bay. D'Iberville's successors established settlements at Mobile Bay and, in 1718, the town of New Orleans. Crown officers and entrepreneurs envisioned an agricultural bonanza, expecting Louisiana to have far more in common with the Caribbean's lucrative sugar islands than with the maddening *pays d'en haut*.

Nothing went according to plan. Here, too, Indians forced the French into painful concessions. While disease and aggression devastated the smaller Indian communities along the coast, more powerful peoples in the interior endured and protected their interests. Louisiana came into conflict with the mighty Chickasaws, and in 1729 the Natchez Indians rose up against French encroachment, killing or capturing some 500 colonists. Underfunded and usually neglected by the Crown, Louisiana's officials became notoriously corrupt and arbitrary. The colony was, according to one observer, a place "without religion, without justice, without discipline, without order, and without police."

DIFFICULTIES IN FRENCH LOUISIANA More to the point, the Gulf Coast was without many French colonists. The region quickly acquired a reputation among would-be French migrants as unattractive and unhealthy. When colonists were not fighting Indians, they contended with heat, humidity, hurricanes, droughts and crop failures, with never-ending battles to turn swamps and forests into farmland, and with the scourges of malaria and yellow fever. One despairing official lamented that "death and disease are disrupting and suspending all operations . . . the best workers are dead." By 1731, two-thirds of the French who had chanced the journey to Louisiana had died or fled. Still, like New Mexico, Canada, California, and Texas, colonial Louisiana persevered to become more populous and more prosperous. Nearly 4,000 French men, women, and children called the colony home by 1746. Their fortunes had in large part come to depend on another, even-larger group of newcomers: French Louisiana's African slaves.

Slavery and Colonial Society in French Louisiana

When the first colonists founded New Orleans in 1718, they immediately clamored for bound laborers. Their goal was to create prosperous plantations in the surrounding Mississippi delta. A year later the Company of the Indies, which managed France's slave trade, brought nearly 6,000 slaves, overwhelmingly men, directly from Africa to Louisiana. Unfortunately for white planters, Louisiana tobacco and, later, indigo proved inferior to the varieties exported from Britain's colonies. Instead of providing the formula for economic success, the sudden influx of Africans challenged French control. In 1729 some newly arrived slaves joined forces with the Natchez Indians in their rebellion. The alliance sent waves of panic through the colony, whose population by then had more slaves than free French. The French retaliated in a devastating counterattack, enlisting both the Choctaw Indians, rivals of the Natchez, and other enslaved blacks, who were promised freedom in return for their support.

The planters' costly victory persuaded French authorities to stop importing slaves into Louisiana. Thus the colony did not develop a plantation economy until the end of

Louisiana's socially mixed society is evident from this market scene: the buyers and sellers include Indians as well as colonials of French, Spanish, and African descent.
Source: The Maryland Historical Society, XIV.17

the eighteenth century, when the cotton boom transformed its culture. In the meantime, blacks continued to make up a majority of all Louisianans, and by the middle of the eighteenth century, nearly all were native-born. The vast majority were slaves, but their work routines—tending cattle, cutting timber, producing naval stores, manning boats—allowed them greater freedom of movement than most slaves enjoyed elsewhere in the American South. They were also encouraged to market the produce of their gardens, hunts, and handicrafts, which became the basis of a thriving trade with both white settlers and the dwindling numbers of coastal Native Americans. But the greatest prize—freedom—was awarded those black men who served in the French militia, defending the colony from the English and Indians as well as capturing slave runaways. The descendants of these black militiamen would become the core of Louisiana's free black community.

Male subjects throughout French America stood ready to perform militia duty, formally or informally. They had to. While the French struggled to sustain peaceful relations with key Indian allies, they turned to violent coercion when they thought it would work. Though not as devastating as the Beaver Wars (Chapter 3), conflicts with Indians proved to be common enough to require a ready defense.

IMPERIAL RIVALRIES More fundamentally, France found itself in conflict with the English in the backcountry beyond the Appalachian Mountains. The rivalries had their beginnings in Europe and flared regularly throughout the late seventeenth century and into the eighteenth. In 1689 England joined the Netherlands and the League of Augsburg (several German-speaking states) in a war against France. While the main struggle raged in Europe, French and English colonials, joined by their Indian allies, skirmished in what was known as King William's War. Peace returned in 1697, but only until the Anglo-French struggle resumed with Queen Anne's War, from 1702 to 1713.

For a quarter of a century thereafter, the two nations waged a kind of cold war, competing for advantage. At stake was not so much control over people or even territory as control over trade. In North America, France and England vied for access to the sugar islands of the Caribbean, a monopoly on supplying manufactured goods to Spanish America, and dominance of the fur trade. The British had the advantage of numbers: nearly 400,000 subjects in the colonies in 1720, the year of L'Archevêque's death, compared with only about 25,000 French. But this is precisely where France's many compromises paid dividends. So long as the French maintained their network of alliances with powerful native peoples, British colonies had little chance of expanding west of the Appalachian Mountains.

REVIEW
How did Louisiana differ from French Canada?

FORCES OF DIVISION IN BRITISH NORTH AMERICA

BRITISH COLONIALS FROM MAINE TO the Carolinas distrusted the French and resented their empire of fish and furs. But the English were preoccupied with their own affairs and, by and large, uninterested in uniting against New France. Indeed, a traveler during the first half of the eighteenth century would have been struck by how hopelessly divided and disunited England's mainland colonies were, split by ethnicity, race, region, wealth, and religion. The British colonies were a diverse and fragmented lot.

Population Growth

One of the largest new groups—250,000 men, women, and children—had come to the colonies from Africa in chains. White arrivals included many English immigrants but also a quarter of a million Scots-Irish, the descendants of seventeenth-century Scots who had regretted settling in northern Ireland; perhaps 135,000 Germans; and a sprinkling of Swiss, Swedes, Highland Scots, and Spanish Jews. Most non-English white immigrants were fleeing lives torn by famine, warfare, and religious persecution. All the voyagers, English and non-English, risked the hazardous Atlantic crossing. Many had paid for passage by signing indentures to work as servants in America. The immigrants and slaves who arrived in the colonies between 1700 and 1775 swelled an American population that was already growing dramatically from natural increase. The birthrate in eighteenth-century America was triple what it is today. Most women bore between five and eight children, and most children survived to maturity.

NORTH AMERICA LEADS A GLOBAL RISE IN POPULATION This astonishing population explosion was quite possibly the fastest in the world at the time. Even so, the surge was merely one part of a more general global acceleration of population in the second half of the eighteenth century. China's population of 150 million in 1700 had doubled to more than 313 million by century's end. Europe's total rose from about 118 million to 187 million over the same period. The unprecedented global population explosion had several causes. Europe's climate, for one, had become warmer and drier, allowing for generally better harvests. Health and nutrition improved globally with the worldwide spread of Native American crops. Irish farmers discovered that a single acre planted with the American potato could support an entire family. The tomato added crucial vitamins to the Mediterranean diet, and in China the American sweet potato thrived in hilly regions where rice would not grow.

Dramatic population increase in the British colonies, fed by the importation of slaves, immigration, and natural increase, made it hard for colonials to share any common identity. Far from fostering political unity, almost every aspect of social development set Americans at odds with one another. And that process of division and disunity was reflected in the outpouring of new settlers into the backcountry.

Moving into the Backcountry

To immigrants from Europe weary of war or worn by want, the seaboard's established communities must have seemed havens of order and stability. But by the beginning of the eighteenth century, Anglo-America's colonists had to look farther and farther west to obtain farmland. With older rural communities offering bleak prospects to either native-born or newly arrived families, both groups turned westward in search of new opportunities. The founding of frontier communities in New England was left mainly to the descendants of old Yankee families. Immigrants from Europe had more luck obtaining land south of New York. By the 1720s German and Scots-Irish immigrants as well as native-born colonists were pouring into western Pennsylvania. Some settled permanently, but others streamed southward into the backcountry of Virginia and the Carolinas, where they encountered native-born southerners pressing westward.

ISOLATION OF THE BACKCOUNTRY Living in the West could be profoundly isolating. From many farmsteads it was a day's ride to the nearest courthouse, tavern, or church. Often lacking decent roads or navigable rivers, frontier families had no means of sending crops to market and aimed for self-sufficiency instead. Distance inhibited the formation of strong social bonds, as did the rapid turnover in western communities. Many families pulled up stakes three or four times before settling permanently. Most backcountry inhabitants could not afford to invest in a slave or even a servant. Those conditions made the frontier, more than anywhere else in America, a society of equals. Most families crowded into one-room shacks walled with mud, turf, or crude logs. And everyone worked hard.

FRONTIER WOMEN Hard work dominated the lives of backcountry settlers. Besides doing the usual chores of farm women, western wives and daughters joined male family members in the fields. One traveler from the East expressed his astonishment at seeing German women in western Pennsylvania "at work abroad on the Farm mowing, Hoeing Loading Dung into a Cart." Perhaps even more difficult to endure than the hard labor was the loneliness of many women's lives. The reactions of women to being resettled on the frontier can be imagined from the promise that one Scottish husband offered his wife: "We would get all these trees cut down . . . [so] that we would see from house to house."

Social Conflict on the Frontier

Despite the discomforts of frontier life, cheap land lured many families to the West. Benjamin Franklin, Pennsylvania's most successful entrepreneur, inventor, and politician, had observed the hordes of Scots-Irish and German immigrants lingering in Philadelphia just long enough to scrape together the purchase price of a frontier farm. From Franklin's point of view, the backcountry performed a valuable service by siphoning off surplus people from congested eastern settlements. But he knew, too, that the opened frontier unleashed discord, especially between the Eastern Seaboard and the backcountry.

Ethnic differences heightened sectional tensions between East and West. People of English descent predominated along the Atlantic coast, whereas Germans, Scots-Irish, and other white minorities were concentrated in the interior. Many English colonials regarded these new immigrants as culturally inferior and politically subversive. Charles Woodmason, an Anglican missionary in the Carolina backcountry, lamented the arrival of "5 or 6,000 Ignorant, mean, worthless, beggarly Irish Presbyterians, the Scum of the Earth, the Refuse of Mankind," who "delighted in a low, lazy, sluttish, heathenish, hellish life."

German immigrants were generally credited with steadier work habits, as well as higher standards of sexual morality and personal hygiene. But like the clannish Scots-Irish, the Germans preferred to live, trade, and worship among themselves. By 1751 Franklin was warning that the Germans would retain their separate language and customs: the Pennsylvania English would be overrun by "the Palatine Boors."

Ethnic prejudices only aggravated clashes between wealthy landlords and backcountry tenants. In eastern New Jersey, landed proprietors insisted that squatters pay rent on land

Courtesy, North Carolina Division of Archives and History

| *This log cabin, built in the North Carolina backcountry in 1782, would have been dark inside, given its lack of windows. The spaces between the logs in such cabins were usually chinked with thin stones or wedges of wood and then daubed with mortar.*

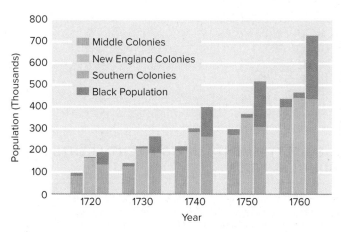

ESTIMATED POPULATION BY REGION, 1720–1760

(Chart legend: Middle Colonies, New England Colonies, Southern Colonies, Black Population; y-axis: Population (Thousands) 0–800; x-axis: Year 1720, 1730, 1740, 1750, 1760)

that had become increasingly valuable. When the squatters, many of them migrants from New England, refused to pay rents, the proprietors began evictions, touching off riots in the 1740s. Tenant unrest also raged in New York's Hudson River valley, where about 30 manors around New York City and Albany dominated the region. The estates encompassed some 2 million acres and were worked by several thousand tenants. Newcomers from New England, however, demanded to own land and preached their ideas to Dutch and German tenants. Armed insurrection exploded in 1757 and again, more violently, in 1766. Tenants refused to pay rents, formed mobs, and stormed the homes of landlords.

Eighteenth-Century Seaports

While most Americans on the move flocked to the frontier, others swelled the populations of colonial cities. By present-day standards such cities were small, harboring from 8,000 to 22,000 citizens by 1750. The scale of seaports remained intimate, too: all of New York City was clustered at the southern tip of Manhattan island, and the length of Boston or Charleston could be walked in less than half an hour.

All major colonial cities were seaports, their waterfronts fringed with wharves and shipyards. A jumble of shops, taverns, and homes crowded their streets; the spires of churches studded their skylines. By the 1750s the grandest and most populous was Philadelphia, which boasted straight, neatly paved streets, flagstone sidewalks, and three-story brick buildings. Older cities such as Boston and New York had a medieval aspect: most of their dwellings and shops were wooden structures with tiny windows and low ceilings, rising no higher than two stories to steeply pitched roofs. The narrow cobblestone streets of Boston and New York City also challenged pedestrians, who competed for space with livestock being driven to the butcher, roaming herds of swine and packs of dogs, clattering carts, carriages, and horses.

THE COMMERCIAL CLASSES Commerce, the lifeblood of seaport economies, was managed by merchants who tapped the wealth of surrounding regions. Traders in New York City and Philadelphia shipped the Hudson and Delaware valleys' surplus of grain and livestock to the West Indies. Boston's merchants sent fish to the Caribbean and Catholic Europe, masts to England, and rum to West Africa. Charlestonians exported indigo to English dyemakers and rice to southern Europe. Other merchants specialized in the import trade, selling luxuries and manufactured goods produced in England—fine fabrics, ceramics, tea, and farming implements.

No large-scale domestic industry produced goods for a mass market: instead, craft shops filled orders for specific items placed by individual purchasers. Some **artisans** specialized in the maritime trades as shipbuilders, blacksmiths, and sailmakers. Others, such as butchers, millers, and distillers, processed and packed raw materials for export. Still others served the basic needs of city dwellers—the men and, occasionally, women who baked bread, mended shoes, combed and powdered wigs, and tended shops and taverns.

On the lowest rung of a seaport's social hierarchy were free and bound workers. Free laborers were mainly young

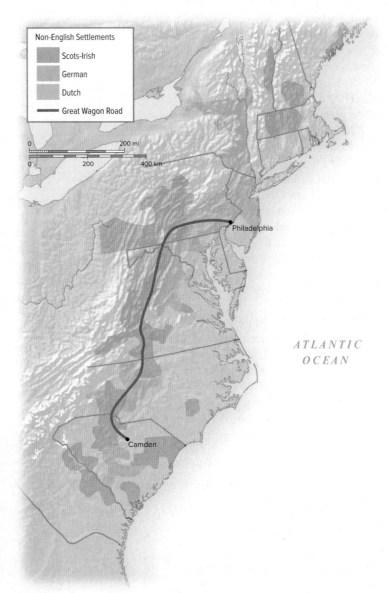

NON-ENGLISH SETTLEMENTS IN EIGHTEENTH-CENTURY BRITISH NORTH AMERICA

Many non-English settlers spilled into the backcountry: the Scots-Irish and Germans followed the Great Wagon Road through the western parts of the middle colonies and southern colonies; the Dutch and other Germans moved up the Hudson River valley. In what ways did the concentration of non-English immigrants in the backcountry influence the development of that region?

white men and women—journeyman artisans, sailors, fishermen, domestic workers, seamstresses, and prostitutes. The ranks of unfree workers included apprentices and indentured servants doing menial labor in shops and on the docks.

INCREASE OF AFRICANS IN NORTHERN SEAPORTS
Black men and women also made up a substantial part of the bound labor force of colonial seaports, but the character of slavery in northern seaports changed decisively during the mid-eighteenth century. When wars raging in Europe reduced the supply of white indentured servants, colonial cities imported a larger number of Africans. In the two decades after 1730, one-third of all people arriving in New York harbor were black; by 1760 blacks constituted more than three-quarters of all bound laborers in Philadelphia.

High death rates and a preference for importing African males inhibited the growth of slave families. Even so, city-dwelling African Americans forged an urban black culture exhibiting a new awareness of a common West African past. The influence of African traditions appeared most vividly in an annual event known as "Negro election day," celebrated in northern seaports. During the festival, similar to ones held in West Africa, some black men and women paraded in their masters' clothes or mounted on their horses. An election followed to choose black kings, governors, and judges who then held court and settled minor disputes among black and white members of the community. Negro election day did not challenge the established racial order with its temporary reversal of roles. But it did allow the black communities of seaports to honor their own leaders.

WOMEN IN CITIES
Working women found a number of opportunities in port cities. Young single women from poor families worked in wealthier households as maids, cooks, laundresses, seamstresses, or nurses. The highest-paying occupations for women were midwifery and dressmaking, and both required long apprenticeships and expert skills.

The wives of artisans and traders sometimes assisted their husbands and, as widows, often continued to manage groceries, taverns, and print shops. But less than 10 percent of women in seaports worked outside their own homes. Most women spent their workday caring for households: seeing to the needs of husbands and children, tending to gardens and domestic animals, and engaged in spinning and weaving—activities crucial to the household economy.

URBAN DIVERSIONS AND HAZARDS
All seaport dwellers—perhaps 1 out of every 20 Americans—enjoyed a more stimulating environment than other colonials did. Plays, balls, and concerts for the wealthiest; taverns, clubs, celebrations, and church services for everyone. Men of every class found diversion in drink and cockfighting. Crowds of men, women, and children swarmed to tavern exhibitions of trained dogs and horses or the spectacular waxworks of one John Dyer, featuring "a lively Representation of Margaret, Countess of Herrinburg, who had 365 Children at one Birth."

Then as now, cities were also places of economic insecurity. In seaports throughout British North America, poverty became increasingly apparent as the eighteenth century wore on. Although the major seaports established workhouses to employ the able-bodied poor, city governments continued to aid most of the dependent with small subsidies of money, food, and firewood. Furthermore, epidemics and catastrophic fires occurred with greater frequency and produced higher mortality rates in congested seaports than in the countryside.

Social Tension in Seaports

The swelling of seaport populations, like the westward movement of whites, often churned up trouble. English, Scots-Irish, Germans, Swiss, Dutch, French, and Spanish jostled uneasily against one another in the close quarters of Philadelphia and New York City. To make matters worse,

In the mid-eighteenth century, Philadelphia became the largest city in the colonies and the second largest in all the British Empire. Its busy harbor served not only as a commercial hub but also as the disembarkation point for thousands of people.

©Sarin Images/The Granger Collection, New York

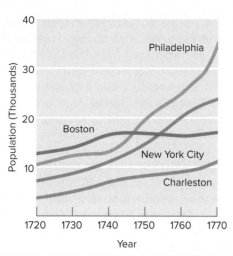

ESTIMATED POPULATION OF COLONIAL CITIES, 1720–1770

Although Boston's population remained stable after 1740, it was surpassed owing to the sharp growth of New York City and, especially, Philadelphia.

religious differences heightened ethnic divisions. Jewish funerals in New York City, for example, drew crowds of hostile and curious Protestants, who heckled mourners.

Class resentment also stirred unrest. Some merchant families flaunted their wealth, building imposing town mansions and dressing in the finest imported fashions. During hard times, symbols of merchant wealth such as expensive coaches and full warehouses became targets of mob vandalism. Crowds also gathered to intimidate and punish other groups who provoked popular hostility—politicians, prostitutes, and "press gangs." Impressment, attempts to force colonials to serve in the British navy, triggered some of the most violent urban riots.

 REVIEW
What kinds of divisions led to social tensions and conflicts in British North America?

SLAVE SOCIETIES IN THE EIGHTEENTH-CENTURY SOUTH

INEQUALITIES AND DIVISIONS BETWEEN SLAVE and free in the South dwarfed those between seaport dwellers. By 1775 one out of every five Americans was of African ancestry, and more than 90 percent of all black Americans lived in the South, most along the seaboard. Here, on tobacco and rice plantations, slaves fashioned a distinctive African American society and culture. But they were able to build stable families and communities only late in the eighteenth century and against enormous odds.

THE CHESAPEAKE AND THE LOWER SOUTH The character of a slave's life depended to a great extent on whether he or she lived in the Chesapeake or the Lower South. Slaves in the low country of South Carolina and

Georgia lived on large plantations with as many as 50 other black workers, about half African-born. They had infrequent contact with whites. "They are as 'twere, a Nation within a Nation," observed Francis LeJau, an Anglican priest in the low country. And their work was arduous, because rice required constant cultivation. Black laborers tended young plants and hoed fields in the sweltering summer heat of the mosquito-infested lowlands. During the winter and early spring, they built dams and canals to regulate the flow of water into the rice fields. But the use of the **task system** rather than gang labor widened the window of freedom within slavery. When a slave had completed his assigned task for the day, one planter explained, "his master feels no right to call upon him."

Most Africans and African Americans in the Chesapeake lived on plantations with fewer than 20 fellow slaves. Less densely concentrated than in the low country, Chesapeake slaves also had more contact with whites. Unlike Carolina's absentee owners, who left white overseers and black drivers to run their plantations, Chesapeake masters actively managed their estates and subjected their slaves to closer scrutiny.

The Slave Family and Community

The four decades following 1700 marked the heaviest years of slave importation into the Chesapeake and Carolina regions. Those Africans had survived the trauma of captivity, the Middle Passage, and sale at slave auctions only to be thrust into a bewildering new world: a sea of unfamiliar faces, a clamor of different languages, a host of demands and threats from men and women who called themselves masters.

AFRICAN SLAVES VS. AMERICAN-BORN SLAVES The newcomers also had to adjust to their fellow slaves. The "new Negroes" hailed from a number of diverse West African peoples, each with a separate language or dialect and distinctive cultures and kinship systems. Often, they had little in common with one another and even less in common with the American-born black minority. Native-born African Americans enjoyed better health, command of English, and experience in dealing with whites. They were also more likely to enjoy a family life, because their advantages probably made the men the preferred partners of black women, who were outnumbered two to one by black men. And, since African-born women waited two or three years before marrying, some African-born men died before they could find a wife. Competition for wives often bred conflict.

After the middle of the eighteenth century, a number of changes fostered the growth of black families and the vitality of slave communities. At the same time that slave importations began to taper off, the rate of natural reproduction among blacks started to climb. Gender ratios became more equal. These changes, along with the rise of larger plantations throughout the South, made it easier for black men and women to find partners and start families. Elaborate kinship networks gradually developed, often extending over several plantations in a single neighborhood. And, as the African-born generations were replaced by native-born offspring, earlier sources of tension and division within the slave community disappeared.

The Hadley Chest

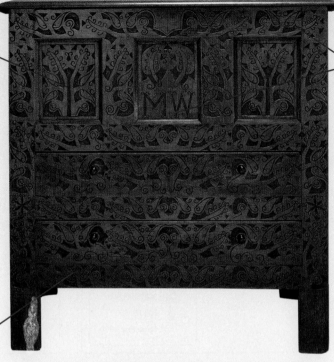

Later owners stripped and refinished this chest, removing the original painted surface that probably featured brilliant blues and reds.

The initials "MW" identify the original owner, while the carvings of tulips and oak leaves, a decorative motif fashionable in early America, covered its facade.

What sorts of possessions do you think Martha Williams might have kept in these drawers?

Unidentified maker, *Hadley Chest*, 1700–1725. 44 7/8 x 45 1/2 x 20 3/8 in. Oak and pine. Collection of Shelburne Museum, museum purchase, acquired from John Kenneth Byard, 1957. 3.4-35

Objects can help historians appreciate complex connections. For example, the first owner of this exuberantly designed cupboard of white oak and pine, Martha Williams, lived in western Massachusetts during the decades around 1700, a time of chronic warfare between the English and their French and Indian allies. Most likely she received the chest as part of her dowry when she married Edward Partridge in 1707, its very solidity assuring this young couple of stability and continuity in a violent and insecure world. Items of similar design have turned up elsewhere in New England, and their first collector dubbed them "Hadley chests," a distinct local craft tradition. This chest and the textiles it probably contained open a window into the sorts of property Anglo-American women retained in marriage and passed down to their descendants. According to historian Laurel Thatcher Ulrich, an artifact such as the Hadley chest "teaches us that material objects were not only markers of wealth but devices for building relationships and lineages over time, and it helps us to understand the cultural framework within which ordinary women became creators as well as custodians of household goods."

THINKING CRITICALLY

Why did Martha Williams have her maiden name emblazoned on the cupboard? Might it have something to do with the restrictive English laws about what women could own in marriage? Do you think women in New Spain or New France would have done the same? What might objects such as these tell us about how women viewed property and identity in British North America?

Even so, black families remained vulnerable. If a planter fell on hard times, members of black families might be sold off to different buyers to meet his debts. When an owner died, black spouses, parents, and children might be divided among surviving heirs. Even under the best circumstances, fathers might be hired out to other planters for long periods or sent to work in distant quarters. The migration of slaveholders from the coast to the interior also disrupted black efforts to fashion domestic and communal bonds.

Between 1755 and 1782, masters on the move resettled fully one-third of all adult African Americans living in Tidewater, Virginia. Most slaves forced to journey west were men and women in their teens and early 20s, who had to begin again the long process of establishing families and neighborhood networks far from kin and friends.

Black families struggling with terrible uncertainties were sustained by the distinctive African American culture evolving in the slave community. The high percentage of native Africans

DISTRIBUTION OF THE AMERICAN POPULATION, 1775

The African American population expanded dramatically during the eighteenth century, especially in the southern colonies. The high volume of slave imports accounts for most of the growth in the first half of the century, but natural increase was responsible for the rising black population during later decades.

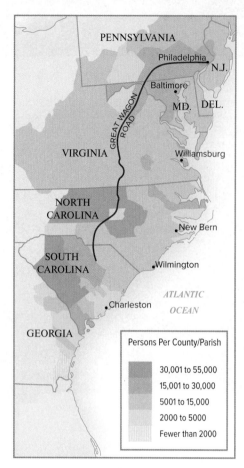

Persons Per County/Parish

- 30,001 to 55,000
- 15,001 to 30,000
- 5001 to 15,000
- 2000 to 5000
- Fewer than 2000

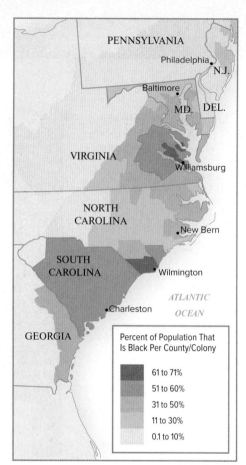

Percent of Population That Is Black Per County/Colony

- 61 to 71%
- 51 to 60%
- 31 to 50%
- 11 to 30%
- 0.1 to 10%

among the eighteenth-century American black population made it easier for slaves to retain the ways of their lost homeland. Christianity won few converts, in part because white masters feared that baptizing slaves might make them more rebellious but also because African Americans preferred their traditional religions. African influence appeared as well in the slaves' agricultural skills and practices, folktales, music, and dances.

Slave Resistance in Eighteenth-Century British North America

British North America had no shortage of African Americans who both resisted captivity and developed strategies for survival. Collective attempts at escape were most common among recently arrived Africans. Groups of slaves, often made up of newcomers from the same region, fled inland and formed **"Maroon" communities** of runaways. These efforts were rarely successful, because the Maroon settlements were too large to go undetected for long.

More-acculturated blacks turned to subtler subversions, employing what one scholar has called "weapons of the weak." Domestics and field hands alike faked illness, feigned stupidity and laziness, broke tools, pilfered from storehouses, hid in the woods for weeks at a time, or simply took off to visit other plantations. Other slaves, usually escaping bondage as solitary individuals, found a new life as craftworkers, dock laborers, or sailors in the relative anonymity of colonial seaports.

THE STONO REBELLION Sometimes slaves rebelled openly. Whites in communities with large numbers of blacks lived in gnawing dread of arson, poisoning, and insurrection. Four slave conspiracies were reported in Virginia during the first half of the eighteenth century. In South Carolina more than two decades of abortive uprisings and insurrection scares culminated in the Stono Rebellion of 1739, the largest slave revolt of the colonial period. Nearly 100 Africans, led by a slave named Jemmy, seized arms from a store in the coastal district of Stono and killed several white neighbors before they were caught and killed by the colonial militia. But throughout the eighteenth century, slave rebellions occurred far less frequently on the mainland of North America than in the Caribbean or Brazil. Whites outnumbered blacks in all of Britain's mainland colonies except South Carolina, and only there did rebels have a haven for a quick escape—Spanish Florida. Faced with those odds, most slaves reasoned that the risks of rebellion outweighed the prospects for success—and most sought opportunities for greater personal freedom within the slave system itself.

 REVIEW

How did African American culture evolve in the slave community, and what form did resistance to captivity take?

I The Old Plantation *affords a rare glimpse of life in the slave quarters. At this festive gathering, both men and women dance to the music of a molo (a stringed instrument similar to a banjo) and drums, depicted* (far right) *in the painting.*

(detail) ©The Colonial Williamsburg Foundation. Gift of Abby Aldrich Rockefeller. (#1935.301.3)

Eighteenth-Century North America: A Mosaic

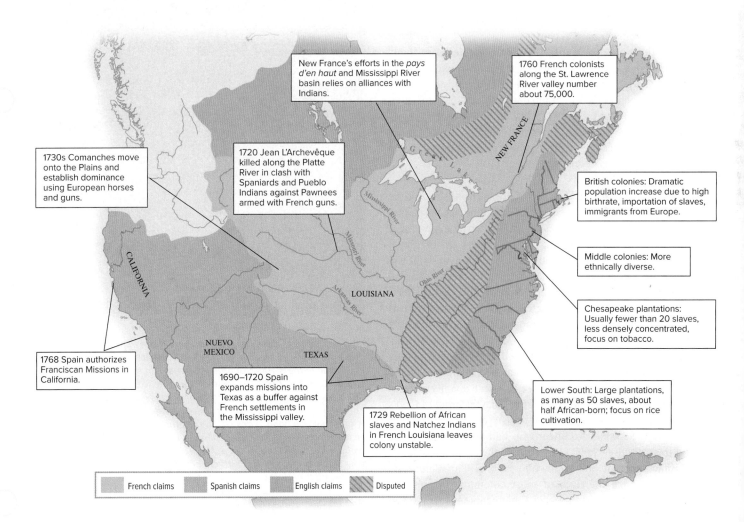

New France's efforts in the *pays d'en haut* and Mississippi River basin relies on alliances with Indians.

1760 French colonists along the St. Lawrence River valley number about 75,000.

1730s Comanches move onto the Plains and establish dominance using European horses and guns.

1720 Jean L'Archevêque killed along the Platte River in clash with Spaniards and Pueblo Indians against Pawnees armed with French guns.

British colonies: Dramatic population increase due to high birthrate, importation of slaves, immigrants from Europe.

Middle colonies: More ethnically diverse.

Chesapeake plantations: Usually fewer than 20 slaves, less densely concentrated, focus on tobacco.

1768 Spain authorizes Franciscan Missions in California.

1690–1720 Spain expands missions into Texas as a buffer against French settlements in the Mississippi valley.

1729 Rebellion of African slaves and Natchez Indians in French Louisiana leaves colony unstable.

Lower South: Large plantations, as many as 50 slaves, about half African-born; focus on rice cultivation.

French claims · Spanish claims · English claims · Disputed

ENLIGHTENMENT AND AWAKENING IN AMERICA

WHERE COLONISTS LIVED, HOW WELL they lived, whether they were male or female, native-born or immigrant, slave or free—all these variables fostered distinctive worldviews, differing attitudes and assumptions about the individual's relationship to nature, society, and God. The diversity of colonials' inner lives became even more pronounced during the eighteenth century because of the **Enlightenment**, an intellectual movement that started in Europe during the seventeenth century.

The Enlightenment in America

The leading figures of the Enlightenment, the *philosophes,* stressed the power of human reason to promote progress by revealing the laws that governed both nature and society. Like many devotees of the Enlightenment, Benjamin Franklin of Philadelphia was most impressed by its emphasis on useful knowledge and experimentation. He pondered air currents and then invented a stove that heated houses more efficiently. He toyed with electricity and then invented lightning rods to protect buildings in thunderstorms. Other amateur colonial scientists constructed simple telescopes, classified animal species native to North America, and sought to explain epidemics in terms of natural causes.

American colleges helped promote Enlightenment thinking. Although institutions such as Harvard (founded 1636) and Yale (1701) initially focused on training ministers, by the eighteenth century their graduates included lawyers, merchants, doctors, and scientists. Most offered courses in mathematics and the natural sciences that taught students algebra and such advanced theories as Copernican astronomy and Newtonian physics.

RATIONAL VS. TRADITIONAL CHRISTIANITY By the middle of the eighteenth century, Enlightenment ideals had given rise to "rational Christianity," which commanded a small but influential following among Anglicans or liberal **Congregationalists** in the colonies. Their God was not the Calvinists' awesome deity but a benevolent creator who offered salvation not to a small, predestined elite, but to everyone. They believed that God's greatest gift to humankind was reason, which enabled all human beings to follow the moral teachings of Jesus. They muted the Calvinist emphasis on human sinfulness and the need for a soul-shattering conversion. An even-smaller number of Americans steeped in the Enlightenment embraced deism, which rejected the divinity of Jesus and looked to nature rather than the Bible for proof of God's existence. In the magnificent design of creation, deists detected a Supreme Architect who had wrought the world and then withdrew to let events unfold through natural law.

Enlightenment philosophy and rational Christianity did little to change the lives of most colonials. French and Spanish authorities suppressed Enlightenment literature in their colonies. Likewise, innovations in Protestant doctrine were meaningless in New Spain and New France, where Catholicism was the only European religion tolerated. Eighteenth-century British North Americans suffered from fewer restrictions, and more than half of all white men (and a smaller percentage of white women) could read. But few colonial readers had the interest or the background necessary to tackle the learned writings of Enlightenment *philosophes.* The great majority still looked for ultimate truth in biblical revelation rather than human reason and explained the workings of the world in terms of divine providence rather than natural law.

Widespread attachment to traditional Christian beliefs was strengthened by the hundreds of new churches built during the first half of the eighteenth century. Church attendance ran highest in the northern colonies, where some 80 percent of the population turned out for public worship on the Sabbath. In the South, because of the greater distances involved and the shortage of clergy, about half of all colonials regularly attended Sunday services.

Despite the prevalence of traditional religious beliefs, many ministers grew alarmed over the dangerous influence

©Private Collection/The Stapleton Collection/Bridgeman Images

| *A sharp critic of the evangelical revivals that swept both sides of the Atlantic, the English artist William Hogarth satirized preaching in the style of George Whitefield. In this detail from an engraving of 1762 titled* Credulity, Superstition, and Fanaticism, *the minister wears a clown's jacket under his gown and plays upon the superstitious beliefs of his congregation by dangling a witch from one hand, a devil from the other. The page before him reads, "I speak as a fool"; the ribbon to his right shows a scale of "vociferation" that runs from a "Natural Tone" of speaking all the way up to "Bull Roar." Hogarth did not think critical thinking was incompatible with biblical teachings, for below the engraving he included a bit of scripture: "Believe not every Spirit, but try the Spirits whether they are of God: because many false Prophets are gone out into the World."*

of rational Christianity. They also worried that the lack of churches might tempt many frontier families to abandon Christianity altogether. Exaggerated as these fears may have been, they gave rise to a major religious revival that swept the colonies during the middle decades of the eighteenth century.

The First Great Awakening

The **Great Awakening**, as the revival came to be called, first appeared in the 1730s among Presbyterians and Congregationalists in the middle colonies and New England. Many ministers in these churches preached an "evangelical" message, emphasizing the need for individuals to experience "a new birth" through religious conversion. Among them was Jonathan Edwards, the pastor of a Congregational church in Northampton, Massachusetts. Edwards's Calvinist preaching combined moving descriptions of God's grace with terrifying portrayals of eternal damnation. "The God that holds you over the pit of hell, much as one holds a spider or some loathsome insect over the fire, abhors you and is dreadfully provoked," he declaimed to one congregation. "There is no other reason to be given, why you have not dropped into hell since you arise in the morning, but that God's hand has held you up."

These local revivals of the 1730s were mere tremors compared to the earthquake of religious enthusiasm that shook the colonies with the arrival in the fall of 1739 of George Whitefield. This handsome (though cross-eyed) "boy preacher" from England electrified crowds from Georgia to New Hampshire during his two-year tour of the colonies. He and his many imitators among colonial ministers turned the church into a theater, enlivening sermons with dramatic gestures, flowing tears, and gruesome depictions of hell. The drama of such performances appealed to people of all classes, ethnic groups, and races. By the time Whitefield sailed back to England in 1741, thousands of awakened souls were joining older churches or forming new ones.

The Aftermath of the Great Awakening

Whitefield also left behind a raging storm of controversy. Many "awakened" church members now openly criticized their ministers as cold, unconverted, and uninspiring. To supply the missing fire, some laymen—"and even Women and Common Negroes"—took to "exhorting" any audience willing to listen. The most popular ministers became **itinerants**, traveling as Whitefield did from one town to another.

RELIGIOUS DIVISIONS Although Americans had been fighting over religion well before the Great Awakening, the new revivals left colonials even more divided along religious lines. The largest single group of churchgoers in the northern colonies remained within the Congregational and Presbyterian denominations. But both of these groups split into factions over the revivals. Quakers and Anglicans shunned them. In contrast, the most radical converts joined forces with the warmest champions of the Awakening, the Baptists.

While northern churches splintered and bickered, the fires of revivalism spread to the South and its backcountry. From the mid-1740s until the 1770s scores of new Presbyterian and Baptist churches formed, sparking controversy. Ardent Presbyterians disrupted Anglican worship by loosing packs of dogs in local chapels. County officials, prodded by resentful Anglican parsons, harassed, fined, and imprisoned Baptist ministers.

And so a diverse lot of Americans found themselves continually at odds with one another: arguing over religion and the Enlightenment, conflicted over racial and ethnic tensions, and divided between coastal and backcountry cultures. Benjamin Franklin, a man who made it his business to know, surely understood the depth of those divisions. Even he had brooded over the boatloads of non-English newcomers. He had lived in two booming seaports and felt the explosive force of the frontier. He personified the Enlightenment—and yet looked on in admiration at a George Whitefield sermon on the steps of the Philadelphia courthouse.

Franklin recognized these divisions. Yet oddly enough, even though he knew how little held colonials together, he still harbored hopes for their political unity. After all, most were English. That much they had in common.

 REVIEW

Describe the different outlooks of Enlightenment and evangelical Christians.

ANGLO-AMERICAN WORLDS OF THE EIGHTEENTH CENTURY

MOST COLONISTS IN BRITISH NORTH America prided themselves on being English. Colonial towns bore English names; colonial governments drew on English precedents; colonial diets, dress, architecture, furniture, and literature all followed English models. And yet there were important differences. Some differences made colonials feel inferior, ashamed of their simplicity when compared with London's sophistication. But they also came to appreciate the greater equality of their society and the more representative character of their governments. If it was good to be English, it was better still to be English in America.

English Economic and Social Development

The differences between England and America began with their economies. Large financial institutions such as the Bank of England and influential corporations such as the East India Company were driving England's commercial development. A growing number of textile factories and mines were deepening its industrial development. Although most English men and women worked at agriculture, it, too, had become a business. Gentry rented their estates to tenants, the rural middle class. In turn, these tenants hired men and women from the swollen ranks of England's landless to perform the farm labor. In contrast, most colonial farmers owned their land, and most family farms were a few hundred acres. The scale of commerce and manufacturing was equally modest, limited by the preference of colonials to farm instead.

England's more developed economy fostered the growth of cities, especially London, a teeming colossus of 675,000 in 1750. In contrast, 90 percent of all eighteenth-century colonials lived in towns of fewer than 2,000.

The Consumer Revolution

But in another respect, England's more advanced economy drew the colonies and the parent country together. Americans were so eager to acquire British-made commodities that their per capita consumption of imported manufactures rose 120 percent between 1750 and 1773. People of all classes demanded and indulged in small luxuries such as a tin of tea, a pair of gloves, and a bar of Irish soap. In both England and its colonies, the spare and simple material life of earlier centuries was giving way to a new order in which even people of ordinary means owned a wider variety of things.

John Stuart, the third Earl of Bute (1713–1792), in the ceremonial robes of the House of Lords. The lavish style epitomizes the opulence of Britain's ruling class in the eighteenth century.

Inequality in England and America

Then there were people of no means. In England they were legion. London seethed with filth, crime, and desperate poverty. The poor and the unemployed as well as pickpockets and prostitutes crowded into its gin-soaked slums, taverns, and brothels. The contrast between the luxuries enjoyed by a wealthy few Londoners and the misery of the many disquieted colonial observers. Ebenezer Hazard, an American Quaker visiting London, knew for certain he was in "a Sink of Sin."

CLASS DISTINCTIONS New wealth and the inherited privileges of England's landed aristocracy made for deepening class divisions. Two percent of England's population owned 70 percent of its land. By right of birth, English aristocrats claimed membership in the House of Lords; by custom, certain powerful gentry families dominated the other branch of Parliament, the House of Commons.

The colonies had their own prominent families, but no titled ruling class holding political privilege by hereditary right. And even the wealthiest colonial families lived far more humbly than their English counterparts. Probably the finest mansion in eighteenth-century America, William Byrd's plantation at Westover, Virginia, was scarcely a tenth the size of the Marquis of Rockingham's country house, a sprawling edifice longer than two football fields.

If England's upper classes lived more splendidly, its lower classes were larger and worse off than those in the colonies. Less than a third of England's inhabitants belonged to the "middling sort" of traders, professionals, artisans, and tenant farmers. More than two-thirds struggled for survival at the bottom of society. In contrast, the colonial middle class counted for nearly three-quarters of the white population. With land cheap, labor scarce, and wages for both urban and rural workers 100 percent higher in America than in England, it was much easier for colonials to accumulate savings and farms of their own.

Colonials were both fascinated and repelled by English society. Benjamin Rush, a Philadelphia physician, felt in the House of Lords as if he "walked on sacred ground." He begged his guide for permission to sit on the throne therein and then sat "for a considerable time." Other colonials gushed over the grandeur of aristocratic estates and imported suits of livery for their servants, tea services for their wives, and wallpaper for their drawing rooms.

But colonials recognized that England's ruling classes purchased their luxury and leisure at the cost of the rest of the nation. In his autobiography, Benjamin Franklin painted a devastating portrait of the degraded lives of his fellow workers in a London print shop, who drowned their disappointments by drinking throughout the workday, even more excessively on the Sabbath, and then faithfully observing the holiday of "St. Monday" to nurse their hangovers. Like Franklin, many colonials regarded the idle among England's rich and poor alike as ominous signs of a degenerate nation.

Politics in England and America

ENGLAND'S BALANCED CONSTITUTION Colonials were also of two minds about England's government. While they praised the English constitution as the basis of all liberties, they were alarmed by the actual workings of English politics. In theory, England's **balanced constitution** gave every order of society a voice in government. Whereas the Crown represented the monarchy and the House of Lords the aristocracy, the House of Commons represented the democracy, the people of England.

In fact, webs of patronage and outright bribery compromised the whole system. The monarch and his ministers had the power to appoint legions of bureaucrats to administer the growing state and empire. By the middle of the eighteenth century, almost half of all members of Parliament held such Crown offices or government contracts. Many had won their seats in corrupt elections, where the small electorate (perhaps a quarter of all adult males) were bought off with money or liquor.

COLONIAL GOVERNMENTS Americans liked to think that their colonial governments mirrored the ideal English constitution. Most colonies had a royal governor who represented the monarch in America and a bicameral (two-house) legislature made up of a lower house (the assembly) and an upper house (or council). The democratically elected assemblies, like the House of Commons, stood for popular interests, whereas the councils, some of which were elected and others appointed, more roughly approximated the House of Lords.

But these formal similarities masked real differences between English and colonial governments. On the face of it, royal governors had much more power than the English Crown. Unlike kings and queens, royal governors could veto laws passed by assemblies; they could dissolve those bodies at will; they could create courts and dismiss judges. However, governors who asserted their full powers quickly met opposition from their assemblies, who objected that such overwhelming authority endangered popular liberty. In any showdown with their assemblies, most royal governors had to give way, because they lacked the government offices and contracts that bought loyalty. The colonial legislatures possessed additional leverage, since all of them retained the sole authority to levy taxes.

At the same time, widespread ownership of land meant that more than half of the colonies' white adult male population could vote. The larger electorate made it more difficult to buy votes. The colonial electorate was also more watchful. Representatives had to reside in the districts that they served, and a few even received binding instructions from their constituents about how to vote.

Coffeehouses such as this establishment in London were favorite gathering places for eighteenth-century Americans visiting Britain. Here merchants and mariners, ministers and students, lobbyists and tourists warmed themselves, read newspapers, and exchanged gossip about commerce, politics, and social life.

Most Americans were as pleased with their inexpensive and representative colonial governments as they were horrified by the conduct of politics in England. John Dickinson, a young Pennsylvanian training as a lawyer in London, was scandalized by a parliamentary election he witnessed in 1754. The king and his ministers had spent over 100,000 pounds sterling to buy support for their candidates, he wrote his father, and "if a man cannot be brought to vote as he is desired, he is made dead drunk and kept in that state, never heard of by his family and friends, till all is over and he can do no harm."

Courtesy of the Bostonian Society

| This tea caddy, owned by a Massachusetts colonial, was a new consumer luxury, as was the tea it held.

The Imperial System before 1760

Few Britons gave the colonists as much thought as the colonists gave them. It would be hard to overstate just how insignificant North America was in the English scheme of things. Those few Britons who thought about America at all believed that colonials resembled the "savage" Indians more than the "civilized" English. As a London acquaintance remarked to the Boston merchant Thomas Hancock, it was a pity Mrs. Hancock had to remain in Boston when he could "take her to England and make her happy with Christians."

The same indifference contributed to England's haphazard administration of its colonies. Aside from passing an occasional law to regulate trade, restrict manufacturing, or direct monetary policy, Parliament made no effort to assert its authority in America. Its members assumed that Parliament's sovereignty extended over the entire empire, and nothing had occurred to make them think otherwise.

BENEFITS OF BENIGN NEGLECT

For the colonies, this chaotic and inefficient system of colonial administration left them a great deal of freedom. Even England's regulation of trade rested lightly on the shoulders of most Americans. Southern planters were obliged to send their rice, indigo, and tobacco to Britain only, but they enjoyed favorable credit terms and knowledgeable marketing from English merchants. Colonials were prohibited from finishing iron products and exporting hats and textiles, but they had scant interest in developing domestic industries. Americans were required to import all manufactured goods through England, but by doing so, they acquired high-quality goods at low prices. At little sacrifice, most Americans obeyed imperial regulations. Only sugar, molasses, and tea were routinely smuggled.

Following this policy of **benign neglect**, the British Empire muddled on to the satisfaction of most people on both sides of the Atlantic. Economic growth and political **autonomy** allowed most Americans to like being English, despite their misgivings about their parent nation. The beauty of it was that Americans could be English in America, enjoying greater economic opportunity and political equality. If imperial arrangements had remained as they were in 1754, the empire might have muddled on indefinitely.

> ✓ **REVIEW**
> What were the similarities, differences, and connections between England and America?

OVERSEAS TRADE NETWORKS

Commercial ties to Spain and Portugal, Africa, and the Caribbean sustained the growth of both seaports and commercial farming regions on the British North American mainland and enabled colonials to purchase an increasing volume of finished goods from England. The proceeds from exports in foodstuffs and lumber to the West Indies and trade in fish to Spain and Portugal enabled northern merchants and farmers to buy hardware and clothing from the mother country. Southern planters financed their consumption of English imports and their investment in African slaves with the profits from the sale of tobacco, rice, and indigo abroad.

Putting History in Global Context

By the 1750s North America was changing, both within the British world and in relation to the international order. For decades, Europe's imperial wars found their way to America almost as an afterthought. Colonial officials, traders, land speculators, and would-be pioneers regularly seized on news of the latest European conflict as an excuse to attack their Spanish or French or British counterparts in the North American borderlands. The interests of kings and queens had to be served, of course. And yet it was easier to exploit war for local or personal purposes out on the far margins of Europe's empires. Eastern North America's native peoples likewise sought advantage in these interimperial flare-ups. But for them the stakes were higher. When chiefs joined in a fight for profit or revenge, or to please one or another colonial ally, they also put their own people at risk.

However the various players positioned themselves, they often found that the outcome of their struggles could be determined by men they would never see: well-heeled diplomats sipping drinks around mahogany tables in European capitals. Victories, defeats, territories won or lost—all this could be and often was undone in Paris, Madrid, or London, where negotiators casually agreed to ignore territorial gains and losses in the colonies and return everything as it was before the fighting broke out. The message was clear: great imperial struggles began in Europe and ended in Europe. America followed.

Though few recognized it in 1754, this older model was about to be swept away. That year marked the beginning of yet another imperial war, one begun not in Europe but in the American borderlands. Rather than following events, this time Indians proved decisive to the war's origins, course, and outcome. And rather than the conflict ending with a return to the status quo, this time war would produce changes greater than anyone could have anticipated. In waging the war and managing its aftermath, London would pursue policies that made it difficult—and ultimately impossible—for its American subjects to remain within the empire.

Chapter Summary

During the eighteenth century, Spain, France, and Great Britain competed for power and influence in North America. Native peoples, too, played off these shifting alliances. British North Americans grew increasingly diverse, which made the prospect of any future colonial political union appear remote.

- Spain established mission systems in Texas and California, largely to preempt the expansion of European rivals.

- Low immigration compelled New France to seek sustainable alliances with Indian peoples throughout the Far North and the Mississippi drainage. French Louisiana grew very slowly and failed to develop into a booming plantation colony.

- Differences became more pronounced among whites because of the immigration of larger numbers of non-English settlers, the spread of settlement to the backcountry, and the growth of major seaports.

- The South became more embattled, too, as a result of the massive importation of slaves directly from Africa.

- Religious conflict among colonials was intensified by Enlightenment ideas and the first Great Awakening.

- Still, a majority of white colonials took pride in their common English ancestry.

Digging Deeper

For early Texas and New Mexico, see Juliana Barr, *Peace Came in the Form of a Woman* (2007); Ross H. Frank, *From Settler to Citizen* (2000); and Omar S. Valerio-Jiménez, *River of Hope* (2013). On mission-era California, look to Steven W. Hackel's *Children of Coyote, Missionaries of Saint Francis* (2005); and Lisbeth Haas, *Saints and Citizens* (2013). For France in America, see *The People of New France* by Allan Greer (2000); and Michael Witgen, *An Infinity of Nations* (2012). Alan Taylor's *American Colonies* (2001) takes a sweeping, continental perspective on North American history during this era. For women's property rights, see Deborah A. Rosen, "Women and Property across Colonial America: A Comparison of Legal Systems in New Mexico and New York," *William and Mary Quarterly* 60, no. 2 (2003): 355–382.

For the demographics of European colonization in British North America, see Bernard Bailyn, *Voyagers to the West* (1986). On the tensions and transformations that came with diverse societies, see John Smolenski, *Friends and Strangers* (2010); and Peter Silver, *Our Savage Neighbors* (2007). Philip Morgan's *Slave Counterpoint* (1998) contrasts slave cultures in the early South. For tensions in American seaports, consult Jill Lepore, *New York Burning* (2005); and Gary Nash's *Urban Crucible* (1979). Thomas S. Kidd's *The Great Awakening* (2007) is a comprehensive history of the religious transformation.

Nancy Shoemaker, *A Strange Likeness* (2004); and James H. Merrell, *Into the American Woods* (1999), are two compelling accounts of perceived differences between Indians and colonists. For a rich synthesis of native and colonial history in eastern North America, see Daniel K. Richter, *Before the Revolution* (2011). Caroline Winterer's *American Enlightenments* (2016) brilliantly reveals the diversity of the movement. On religion, see Patricia U. Bonomi, *Under the Cope of Heaven* (1986); and George M. Marsden, *Jonathan Edwards* (2003).

6

Imperial Triumph, Imperial Crisis

When the taxes from Parliament's Stamp Act were repealed in 1766, Paul Revere constructed an obelisk to stand under Boston's Liberty Tree. The large monument was framed in wood and covered with drawings executed on oiled, semi-transparent paper. Inside was space for 300 lanterns to illuminate the drawings at night. On the far left panel, a threatened Indian represents America being menaced by British officials, including the evil Lord Bute, portrayed as a flying devil. In the second panel, the Indian points to his retreating foes, as the Goddess of Liberty blows her trumpet. Alas, the oiled paper caught fire, and the obelisk burned down shortly after its construction.

Source: Library of Congress, Prints and Photographs Division [LC-DIG-ppmsca-05479]

>> An American Story

GEORGE WASHINGTON AND THE HALF KING

Everyone seemed to want something from the Ohio Country. And when so many rivals—assertive, anxious, and aggressive—assembled in one location, it was a situation made for disaster. Young George Washington, deep in the forests of the Ohio Country, learned this lesson in the spring of 1754.

The region north of the Ohio River had been a no-man's-land for decades following the Beaver Wars (Chapter 4). Though the mighty Iroquois had no interest in occupying the territory, they claimed sovereignty over it into the 1750s by right of conquest. By then, however, Delawares, Shawnees, Mingos, and other native peoples had established villages in the territory. If they looked to the Iroquois it was for advice, not orders. Who, then, could claim dominion over the Ohio Country?

European rivalries compounded these uncertainties. By the 1750s both Britain and France saw the lands as vital to their strategic interests. Pennsylvania traders had wandered the territory for years, their reports drawing the interest of land speculators. The Ohio Country boasted forests of white oak, plentiful game, and grassy meadows, ideally suited for farming. Chunks of black coal thrust from the ground, hinting at mineral riches. Wealthy Virginians and Pennsylvanians envisioned colonies in the Ohio Country—schemes London happily encouraged in hopes of weakening New France. In 1745 the Virginia House of Burgesses granted 300,000 acres of land to a newly formed enterprise called the Ohio Company. For their part, the French in Quebec relied on the Ohio lands as a buffer between their own relatively small settlements and the populous British settlements to the east. Anxious, the French built new forts and shored up their Indian alliances.

The British countered. In 1754 Virginia's governor (a major investor in the Ohio Company) ordered 200 militiamen under 22-year-old Lieutenant Colonel George Washington (another investor) to assert British interests in the Ohio Country. Washington's militia marched west with the help of several Indians under the "Half King" Tanaghrisson, the Iroquois representative for the Ohio Country. Tanaghrisson had grown up near the important forks of the Ohio River (present-day Pittsburgh) and advised the British to build a "strong house" at this key position. He had even laid down the fort's first log in a ceremony. Washington, who was intelligent, able,

and disciplined but inexperienced and badly out of his depth, soon discovered how little control he had over the circumstances—or even over his own expedition.

To begin with, the French had beaten the Virginians to the forks of the Ohio, where they erected Fort Duquesne. On hearing of the approaching British militia, the French commander there dispatched 35 men under an ensign

©The Granger Collection, New York

| *Indians and Europeans negotiate in the Ohio Country, an area coveted by the English, French, Delawares, Shawnees, and Mingos.*

named Jumonville to advise Washington to withdraw. The Virginians learned of the approaching party and marched to intercept it, following Tanaghrisson's lead, "in a heavy rain and a night as dark as pitch," as Washington recalled. At dawn, just as the French were crawling out from under their bark lean-tos to make breakfast, the British and their Indian companions opened fire. Badly wounded along with nearly half of his men, the ensign cried out to stop shooting, that he had come only to talk. Once Washington had gotten control of his force, Jumonville handed him a letter from the French commander. But it was in French, which Washington did not read. He turned to fetch his translator. Just then Tanaghrisson stepped in front of the wounded Jumonville. The grave Iroquois representative was older and far more experienced than Washington, and he had his own agenda. Unhappy with the emboldened French posture in the region and convinced that Iroquois interests would be best served if the French and British were at each other's throats, he did something neither

Washington nor his French counterpart could have possibly expected. "You're not dead yet, my father," he told Jumonville; and then sank a hatchet into the officer's head, ripped his skull apart, and pulled out his brains. Washington staggered back dumbstruck as Tanaghrisson's Indians set about killing the other wounded soldiers.

This was not how it was supposed to happen. Washington hastily retreated some way, threw up a makeshift structure, aptly named "Fort Necessity," and waited for reinforcements from Virginia. About a month later a formidable French force (led by Jumonville's grieving brother) laid siege and quickly compelled Washington's surrender. The Virginians returned home in defeat, bearing the news that the Shawnees, Delawares, and Mingos had either sided with the French or refused to fight at all. "The chief part" of his men, Washington wrote in dismay, "are almost naked, and scarcely a man has either Shoes, Stockings or Hat." It was an ignominious beginning to a long, exhausting war that would eventually spread across the entire globe. <<

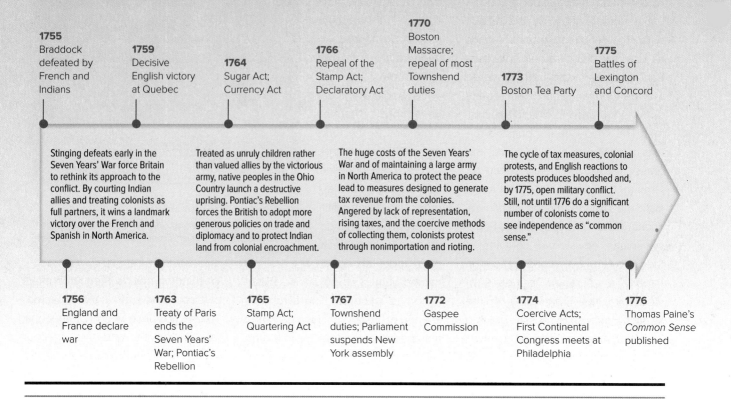

1755 Braddock defeated by French and Indians

1759 Decisive English victory at Quebec

1764 Sugar Act; Currency Act

1766 Repeal of the Stamp Act; Declaratory Act

1770 Boston Massacre; repeal of most Townshend duties

1773 Boston Tea Party

1775 Battles of Lexington and Concord

Stinging defeats early in the Seven Years' War force Britain to rethink its approach to the conflict. By courting Indian allies and treating colonists as full partners, it wins a landmark victory over the French and Spanish in North America.

Treated as unruly children rather than valued allies by the victorious army, native peoples in the Ohio Country launch a destructive uprising. Pontiac's Rebellion forces the British to adopt more generous policies on trade and diplomacy and to protect Indian land from colonial encroachment.

The huge costs of the Seven Years' War and of maintaining a large army in North America to protect the peace lead to measures designed to generate tax revenue from the colonies. Angered by lack of representation, rising taxes, and the coercive methods of collecting them, colonists protest through nonimportation and rioting.

The cycle of tax measures, colonial protests, and English reactions to protests produces bloodshed and, by 1775, open military conflict. Still, not until 1776 do a significant number of colonists come to see independence as "common sense."

1756 England and France declare war

1763 Treaty of Paris ends the Seven Years' War; Pontiac's Rebellion

1765 Stamp Act; Quartering Act

1767 Townshend duties; Parliament suspends New York assembly

1772 Gaspee Commission

1774 Coercive Acts; First Continental Congress meets at Philadelphia

1776 Thomas Paine's *Common Sense* published

THE SEVEN YEARS' WAR

THE SEVEN YEARS' WAR, WHICH actually lasted nine years, pitted Britain and its ally, Prussia, against France, in league with Austria and Spain. The conflict raged from 1754 until 1763 and deserves to be called the first global war. Because the contending powers had colonial possessions and economic interests around the world, the fight spanned the continent of Europe, the coast of West Africa, India, the Philippines, the Caribbean, and North America. The spark that started this worldwide conflagration came from the Ohio Country.

Britain and France had come to blows in the backcountry before. And Indian peoples had long sought to profit from their interimperial rivalry and turn it to their own ends. But for the first time, bloodshed in the forests of North America would lead Europe into war, rather than the other way around. And Washington's misadventure at Fort Necessity set the pattern for the early years of the conflict more broadly, years marked by British missteps and British defeats.

Years of Defeat

Washington's surrender only stiffened Britain's resolve to assert its claims to the Ohio Country: hence its decision to send two divisions under General Edward Braddock to wrest the region from France. France responded by sending the equivalent of eight divisions to Canada. There was therefore great anticipation surrounding Braddock's campaign. Unfortunately for the English, General Braddock had all but sealed his doom before even marching into the backcountry. Ignoring American advisors who insisted that Indian alliances would be key to victory, Braddock alienated native leaders and refused to acknowledge their claims to land. "The English should inhabit and inherit the land . . . no savage should inherit the land," he insisted. In 1755 Braddock's divisions pushed into the Ohio Country with fewer than 10 Indians along. After five weeks of agonizing progress through dense woods and over rough terrain, the troops were ambushed by French and Indian sharpshooters firing into the British column from the cover of trees. As his men fell around him, Braddock calmly rode back and forth on horseback and ordered the troops to remain or get back in formation and return fire as they had been trained. But none had been trained for this kind of fighting, and gathering together only made them easier to shoot. The smoke and gunfire, the screams of dying men and horses, and—perhaps most memorably—the haunting cries of the attacking Indians gradually overcame British discipline. Three hours into the battle Braddock still sat atop his horse, as brave as he was unimaginative, yelling at his men to fight as if they were on a European battlefield. Finally, the general lurched up in his saddle and collapsed, a musket ball buried deep in his back. The British troops still able to walk or run fled the scene.

The monumental defeat sent shock waves throughout the empire, emboldened the French, and convinced many wavering Indian peoples that the French were the people to back. Raiding parties began striking backcountry settlements from New York to Virginia, and terrified refugees fled east.

ALBANY PLAN OF UNION Britain's war went from bad to worse in North America. British colonists generally saw the French and their Indian allies as a common threat but found cooperation among colonies elusive. At the start of the war, representatives from throughout the colonies came to the so-called Albany Congress, designed in part to repair the "Covenant Chain," the long-standing alliance between Britain and the Iroquois that had been badly damaged by British

missteps and French victories in the Ohio Country. More broadly, Benjamin Franklin presented the other colonial delegates with a plan for colonial cooperation, in which a federal council made up of representatives from each colony would assume responsibility for a united colonial defense. The Albany delegates were alarmed enough by the wavering Iroquois and the threatening French to accept the idea. But when they brought the proposal home to their respective legislatures, not a single one approved the Albany Plan of Union. "Everyone cries, a union is necessary," Franklin complained, "but when they come to the manner and form of the union, their weak noodles are perfectly distracted."

London did little to encourage collective self-sacrifice. When England and France formally declared war in May

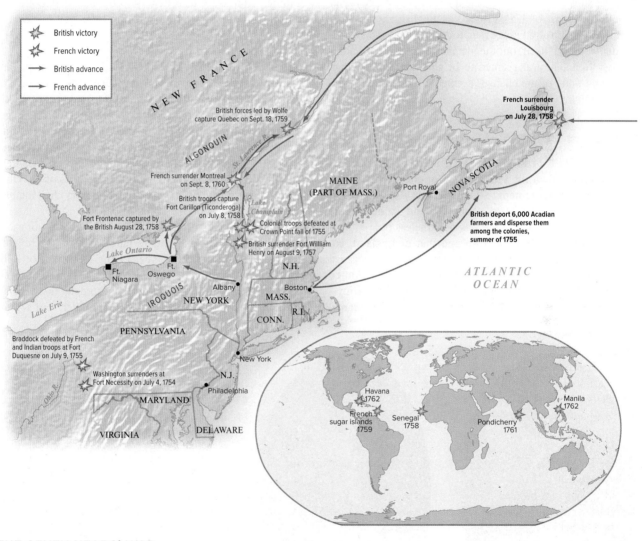

THE SEVEN YEARS' WAR

After Washington's surrender and Braddock's defeat in the Pennsylvania backcountry, the British and French waged their final contest for supremacy in North America in northern New York and Canada. But the rivalry for empire between France and Britain was worldwide, with naval superiority providing the needed edge to Britain. The British navy isolated French forces in India, winning a victory at Pondicherry, while English offensives captured the French sugar islands in the Caribbean and French trading posts along the West African coast. When Spain entered the war on the side of France, British fleets captured both Havana and the strategic port of Manila in the Philippines. **Which victory sealed the British triumph over New France? Why was the win geographically important?**

1756, John Campbell, the Earl of Loudoun, took command of the North American theater. American soldiers and colonial assemblies alike despised Lord Loudoun. They balked at his efforts to take command over colonial troops and dragged their heels at his high-handed demands for men and supplies. Meanwhile, the French appointed an effective new commanding general of their forces in Canada, Louis Joseph, the marquis de Montcalm. Montcalm drove southward, capturing key British forts and threatening the security of both New York and New England.

THE WAR WIDENS   France decided to press its advantage in Europe as well. In addition to threatening England itself, French ships began attacking British holdings throughout the Mediterranean. Meanwhile, the complex system of alliances that was supposed to keep continental Europe at peace began to fail. In August of 1756 Prussia, an English ally, invaded Austria, a French ally. France went to Austria's aid and Prussia suddenly found itself on the defensive, begging London for salvation. The war seemed to be spreading in all directions, and none of the changes seemed to bode well for the British Empire.

A Shift in Policy

WILLIAM PITT TURNS THE TIDE   British fortunes rebounded only when the veteran English politician William Pitt came out of retirement to direct the war. Pitt was an odd character. Subject to bouts of depression and loathed for his opportunism and egotism, he was nonetheless buoyed by a strong sense of destiny—his own and that of England. He believed Great Britain must seize the world's trade, because trade meant wealth and wealth meant power. France seemed to him the greatest obstacle to this British destiny—and Pitt returned to the political fray charged with energy.

"I know that I can save this country," he declared with typical confidence, "and that no one else can."

Pitt's strategy was bold. He would leave the fighting in Europe to the Prussians but support them with massive infusions of cash with which they could buy supplies and recruit men. France was strongest in Europe, he reasoned, so Britain ought to focus its military energies elsewhere. Better to attack France around the world—in the Caribbean, in West Africa, and in the Indian Ocean. Most especially, Pitt would attack them in North America. He audaciously pledged to drive France out of the continent altogether. To do so he would have to convince the colonists who had been alienated by Braddock's arrogance and Loudoun's harsh policies that they would be treated as equals. Pitt recalled Loudoun, put limits on the powers enjoyed by his successor, pledged to respect the officers in colonial militias, and, crucially, promised that London—not the colonies—would bear the financial burden of the war.

INDIANS AND THE WAR EFFORT   Last but certainly not least, the new government acknowledged the centrality of Indians to the war effort. The officers Pitt sent to execute the new approach listened to colonial Indian agents and go-betweens, authorized new, high-level conferences, and approved the distribution of presents to key leaders. These conciliatory gestures and more accommodating policies were well timed, because by then, the Indian peoples of the Ohio Country and the *pays d'en haut* (upper country) had increasingly come to question the French alliance.

Though French authorities often took Indians more seriously than their English counterparts, they, too, struggled to reconcile cultural difference. In the aftermath of joint victories, for example, French officers sometimes felt obliged by European military protocol to deny their Indian allies customary war spoils—captives, plunder, and scalps.

| John Campbell

| William Pitt

Hated and Loved

John Campbell (left), the Earl of Loudoun, was a Scottish military man and an aristocrat who expected that colonial soldiers would obey his commands. But colonials and their legislatures resisted his efforts to organize and fund the military campaign. "They have assumed to themselves, what they call Rights and Priviledges, totaly unknown in the Mother Country," he complained. William Pitt (right) was no less arrogant ("I know that I can save this country," he declared, "and that no one else can."). But Pitt was willing to treat the colonists as equals and pay handsomely for their services. For Americans' opinion of Pitt, see the porcelain figure in Historian's Toolbox, later in this chapter.

(*left*); ©Christie's Images/Bridgeman Images, (*right*); Source: Library of Congress, Prints and Photographs Division [LC-DIG-pga-03847]

Disgruntled native warriors generally took them anyway and often refused to fight for France again. More critical than even such cultural differences, the economic toll of the war damaged French-Indian alliances. By 1757 Britain's unsurpassed navy had instituted a formidable blockade on the St. Lawrence that cut off supplies to Canada. Without arms, ammunition, and metal goods, French authorities found it increasingly difficult to maintain their Indian alliances. More and more withdrew from the conflict or sided with Britain.

Years of Victory

The reforms galvanized the colonies. Most British North Americans were proud to be part of the empire and welcomed the chance to help fight for it so long as they would be treated as equals. With Pitt's reforms in place, the tide of the war finally began to turn. In July of 1758 the British gained control of the St. Lawrence River when the French fortress at Louisbourg fell before the combined force of the Royal Navy and British and colonial troops. In August a force of New Englanders strangled France's frontier defenses by capturing Fort Frontenac, thereby isolating French forts lining the Great Lakes and the Ohio valley. More and more Indians, seeing the French routed from the interior, switched their allegiance to the English.

Source: Library of Congress, Prints and Photographs Division [LC-DIG-pga-03470]

| *"The Death of General Wolfe"* depicts the dying moment of the English general on the battlefield at Quebec. A painting by Benjamin West, the actual scene bore no resemblance to this composition. But in an era with no film, television, or newspaper photographs, such paintings conveyed history through a visual narrative. The painting's message was spread further when engravings of it, such as this one, were made and sold. At far left, a courier brings news of the British victory, conveyed to Wolfe by the two men gesturing toward the messenger. One is a Scot and the other an American ranger, to signify that the victory has been achieved by the British Empire, not merely England. Finally, a Mohawk warrior—whose people also fought with the British—is placed prominently in the foreground, contemplating the scene.

WOLFE AND MONTCALM BATTLE FOR QUEBEC The British succeeded even more brilliantly in 1759. In Canada, Brigadier General James Wolfe gambled on a daring stratagem and won Quebec from Montcalm. Under the cover of darkness, naval squadrons landed Wolfe's men beneath the city's steep bluffs, where they scaled the heights to a plateau known as the Plains of Abraham. Montcalm might have won by holding out behind the walls of his fortress and awaiting reinforcements. Instead, he matched Wolfe's recklessness and offered battle. Five days later both Wolfe and Montcalm lay dead, along with 1,400 French soldiers and 600 British and American troops. Quebec had fallen to the British. A year later the French surrender of Montreal ended the imperial war in North America, although it continued elsewhere around the world for another two years.

TREATY OF PARIS The Treaty of Paris, signed in February 1763, ended the French presence on the continent of North America. The terms confirmed British title to all French territory east of the Mississippi. Spain had foolishly entered the war on France's side in 1762 and quickly lost Havana to British warships. The treaty restored Cuba to Spain, but at a high price: the Spanish relinquished Florida to Britain. With France driven from the continent, something had to be done with the vast and ill-defined territory of Louisiana, west of the Mississippi. Spain did not want the trouble and expense of administering this sprawling region, but it did not want Britain to have it. Somewhat reluctantly, then, Spain accepted nominal dominion over all land west of the great river, as well as the port of New Orleans, in the separate Treaty of San Ildefonso. In addition to its North America spoils, Britain won several Caribbean islands in the war, as well as Senegal in West Africa.

After generations of inconclusive imperial wars, British North Americans found the victory almost impossibly grand. Towns up and down the Atlantic coast glowed bright with celebratory bonfires and rang with the sounds of clanking tankards and jolly song. How good it was to be British!

Postwar Expectations

Grand expectations came hot on the heels of joyful celebration. The end of the war, Americans felt sure, meant the end of high taxes. The terms of the peace, they were confident, meant that the fertile lands of the Ohio valley would be thrown open to English settlement. The prosperity of the war years alone made for a mood of optimism. British military spending and William Pitt's subsidies had made money for farmers, merchants, artisans, and anyone else who had anything to do with supplying the army or navy. Colonials also took pride in their contributions of troops and money to the winning of the war. In view of that support, Americans expected to be given more consideration within the British Empire. Now, as one anonymous pamphleteer put it, Americans would "not be thought presumptuous, if they consider[ed] themselves upon an equal footing" with English in the parent country.

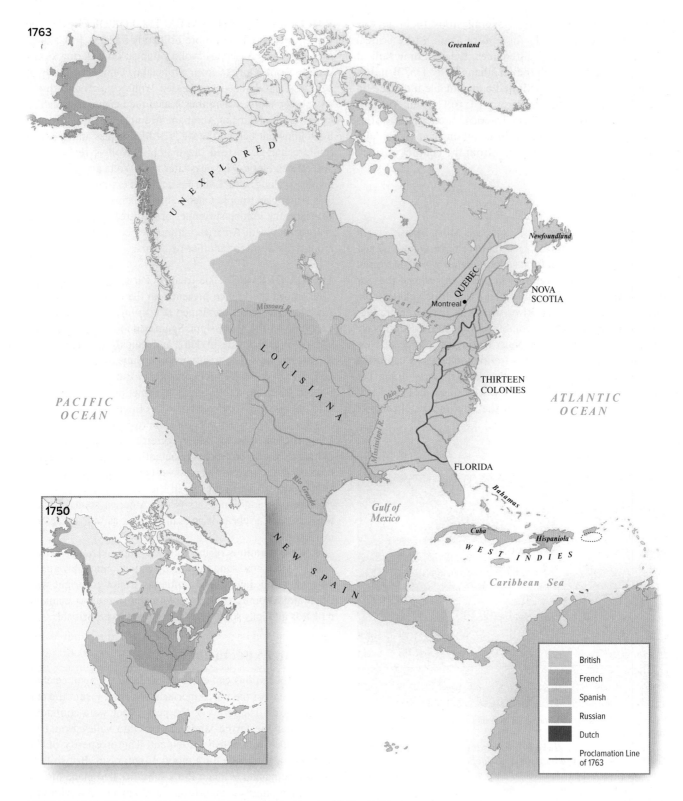

EUROPEAN CLAIMS IN NORTH AMERICA, 1750 AND 1763

The British victory in the Seven Years' War secured Great Britain's title to a large portion of present-day United States and Canada. Colonials hoped to settle the newly won territory, but politicians in London intended to restrict westward movement with the Proclamation of 1763.

ENGLISH RESENTMENTS But most imperial officials in America thought that if Americans took pride in being English, they had done a poor job of showing it. British statesmen grumbled that colonial assemblies had been tightfisted when it came to supplying the army. British commanders charged that colonial troops had been lily-livered when it came to fighting the French. Such accusations were unjust, but they stuck in the minds of many Britons at home. The nation had accumulated a huge debt that would saddle it with high taxes for years to come. To make matters worse, some Britons suspected that, with the French removed from North America, the colonies would move toward independence. As early as 1755 Josiah Tucker, a respected English economist, had warned that "to drive the French out of all North America would be the most fatal step we could take."

Americans in 1763 were not, in truth, revolutionaries in the making. They were loyal British subjects in the flush of postwar patriotism. Americans in 1763, deeply divided, were not even "Americans." But most postwar English colonials did expect to enjoy a more equal status in the empire. And most Britons had no inclination to accord them that equality. The differing expectations of the colonies' place in the empire poised the postwar generation for crisis.

> ### REVIEW
> What started the Seven Years' War, and how did Britain emerge victorious?

THE IMPERIAL CRISIS

IT WAS COMMON SENSE. Great Britain had waged a costly war to secure its empire in America; now it needed to consolidate those gains. The empire's North American territory needed to be protected, its administration tightened, and its colonies made as profitable as possible to the parent nation. In other words, the empire needed to be centralized. That conclusion dictated Britain's decision to leave a standing army of several thousand troops in America after the Seven Years' War. And, of course, armies needed to be paid for; that would mean taxes. That the colonists, who benefited most from the great victory, ought to pull out their purses for king and country—well, Britain's political leaders thought that, too, was common sense.

Pontiac's Rebellion

British authorities justified the army's continued presence in part by pointing to the various foreign peoples that the Crown now had to administer. The army must be prepared to police French colonists in Canada, Spaniards in Florida, and, especially, dozens of native peoples west of the Appalachians. General Jeffery Amherst, the top British officer in North America, believed Indian troubles could be avoided if military and civil authorities simply projected strength.

Now that French power had been expelled, Amherst thought, Britain need not purchase Indian friendship with presents, and subsidize trade, and sponsor tiresome diplomatic ceremonies. All this was to cease. Knowledgeable colonists saw too much of Edward Braddock in all of this. When they insisted that presents, favorable trade, and diplomacy were the indispensable elements of Indian relations, Amherst would have none of it. "When men of what race soever behave ill," the general insisted, "they must be punished but not bribed." Indians had to learn that the English now were masters of the land.

NEOLIN Britain's new attitude of triumph provoked great anxiety within Indian communities that had troubles enough to contend with. Many had lost men in the war, crops had been destroyed or had failed, and whole villages and towns had been put to the torch. British traders, now untroubled by French competition, bartered eagerly but charged far more for their goods than previously. Finally, the end of the war brought a surge of speculators and colonists eager to claim land beyond the mountains. These interlocked crises prompted calls for a return to tradition—for a revival that would empower resistance movements across tribal lines. Such was the message of a Delaware holy man named Neolin, who told followers he spoke for God, or the Master of Life. The Master of Life commanded his Indian children to "drive [the British] out, make war on them. I do not love them at all; they know me not, and are my enemies. Send them back to the lands I have created for them and let them stay there."

Pontiac, a charismatic and tactically gifted Ottawa chief, embraced Neolin's message of renaissance and rebellion. In the summer of 1763 he organized attacks against British forts. Shawnees, Mingos, Potawatomis, Wyandots, and other Indian peoples in the Ohio Country, or the *pays d'en haut,* working with Pontiac or independently, captured every British fort west of Detroit by early July. Colonial settlements in the backcountry came under attack from Pennsylvania to Virginia, leaving hundreds of colonists dead and hundreds more fleeing east. Enraged and determined to assert British rule, Amherst organized troops to march west and attack Indian forces and native villages. He also authorized the commander at Fort Pitt to give Indians blankets from the forts' infirmary, where several men had been stricken with smallpox.

THE PAXTON BOYS Hatreds mounted on all sides. In western Pennsylvania, where Indian raids had taken an especially grim toll, a number of Scots-Irishmen calling themselves the "Paxton Boys" set out to purge the colony of Indians altogether. In December of 1763 they burst into a small village of Christian Indians, killed the six people they found there, and burned it to the ground. Fourteen others who had been absent fled to the town of Lancaster. Learning that Lancaster's officials had put the survivors into protective custody, the Paxton Boys organized a mob,

>> MAPPING THE PAST <<

THE APPALACHIAN FRONTIER

Source: Library of Congress, Prints and Photographs Division [HABS WVA,20-CHAR,5–3 (CT)]

"As to those who come to trouble your lands,—drive them out, make war upon them. I do not love them at all."—The Master of Life, as reported by the Delaware prophet Neolin, 1761

CONTEXT

Emboldened by the presence of British forts and soldiers, land-hungry colonials spilled into the West through the Cumberland Gap, a notch in the chain of mountains stretching the length of the North American interior. Only Indians and some white hunters knew of the Cumberland Gap before it was scouted in 1750 by Dr. Thomas Walker and a party of Virginians on behalf of a company of land speculators. The threat of settler invasion in the Ohio country energized the region's Indians. Inspired by Neolin and Pontiac, native warriors seized eight British forts before troops under Colonel Henry Bouquet stopped the offensive at Bushy Run, Pennsylvania about twenty-five miles east of Fort Pitt. The Proclamation Line of 1763 slowed settler expansion, but only for a time. In 1775, Daniel Boone took the first large party of pioneers through the Cumberland Gap and established a fort at Boonesborough in present-day Kentucky.

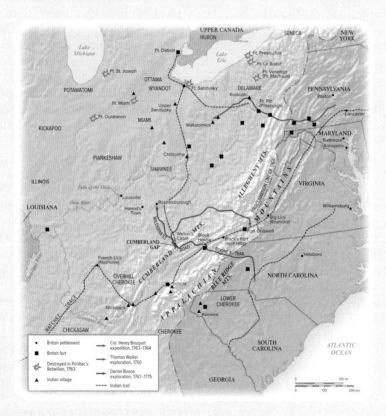

MAP READING

1. Which three smaller mountain ranges are a part of the larger Appalachian Mountains?
2. Which river has the most British forts established along it?
3. What town in Pennsylvania can be reached along the Indian trail that was known as the Natchez Trace?
4. Who established the so-called Wilderness Road?

MAP INTERPRETATION

1. Why was the Cumberland Gap so important?
2. What can this map tell us about the military priorities in Pontiac's War?
3. What does this map reveal about the importance of rivers?

forced their way into the safe house, and massacred all 14 men, women, and children with broadswords. Colonists and natives alike were increasingly willing to simplify difference and see all "Indians" or all "whites" as despicable enemies.

When officials in London learned of Pontiac's Rebellion and all the violence it occasioned, they attributed it to bad leadership and immediately replaced Amherst. More important, the Crown issued the Proclamation of 1763, which transformed colonial policy in critical ways. Presents and respectful diplomacy were to resume, and the Crown put two Indian superintendents in place (one in South Carolina and one in New York) to help oversee good relations. Most critical, colonial settlement west of the Appalachians was to cease immediately. The so-called proclamation line designated all western territories as Indian territory and strictly off limits to colonization. (Quebec and Florida were the exceptions, divided into eastern and western halves, for colonials and Indians.) Restricting westward movement might ease Indian fears, the British hoped, and so stave off future conflicts.

THE PROCLAMATION VS. THE ENVIRONMENT ON THE GROUND In drawing their proclamation line, British officials in London adopted what they thought would be a commonsense boundary rooted in the environment on the ground. The Appalachian Mountains, after all, provided a natural barrier, and the line forbidding settlement could be defined in reference to physical features: "any lands beyond the heads or sources of any of the rivers which fall into the Atlantic Ocean from the west or northwest." Yet the real environment was more ambiguous and diverse. Rivers (and their valleys) often acted as pathways into the interior, beckoning Indians and white settlers alike to breach mountain "barriers." In some areas, Indians remained powerful to the east of the Appalachians (the Creeks and Cherokees to the south, the Iroquois to the north). In other areas west of the mountains, the chaos of the Seven Years' War had left lands largely unoccupied, into which white settlers had entered. Although the proclamation line did not ignore the environment on the ground, actual conditions were infinitely more complicated, and the British Indian commissioners almost immediately began redrawing the line in an effort to keep up with the realities.

Amherst's recall and the conciliatory measures helped defuse the conflict, and the violence had more or less subsided by the fall of 1764. Insofar as it helped push Britain to change its Indian policy, Pontiac's Rebellion helped the Indians who launched it. But the war's animosities endured. And however sensible and just the proclamation line might have seemed from the perspective of the Ohio Country or London, few British colonists would see it as anything but betrayal by their own government. Many of them wondered why they had fought and sacrificed in the war against France, if all the territory they helped win was to be set aside for Indians.

George Grenville's New Measures

If Pontiac's Rebellion and the Proclamation of 1763 had been the only postwar disappointments colonists faced, that would have been trouble enough. But George Grenville, the first lord of the treasury, had yet to confront the dismal financial consequences of the Seven Years' War.

Britain's national debt had doubled in the decade after 1754. Adding to that burden was the drain of supporting troops in the colonies. As matters stood, heavy taxes were already triggering protests among hard-pressed Britons. Americans, in contrast, paid comparatively low taxes to their colonial governments and little in trade duties to the empire. Indeed, Grenville discovered that the colonial customs service paid out four times more in salaries to its collectors than it gathered in duties and was thereby operating at a net loss. Rampant bribery and tax evasion allowed merchants to avoid existing duties on foreign molasses, for example, which New England merchants imported in order to make rum.

SUGAR ACT George Grenville reasoned that if Americans could pay out a little under the table to protect an illegal trade, they would willingly pay a little more to go legitimate. Parliament agreed. In April 1764 it passed the Revenue Act, commonly called the Sugar Act. This **tariff** actually lowered the duty on foreign molasses from six to three pence a gallon. This time, however, the tax would be scrupulously collected, ships would be tightly monitored for compliance, and violators would be tried in admiralty courts, far harsher than typical colonial courts.

CURRENCY AND QUARTERING ACTS Grenville made other, similar proposals, all approved by Parliament. There was the Currency Act of 1764, which prohibited the colonies from making their paper money legal tender. That prevented Americans from paying their debts to British traders in currency that had fallen to less than its face value. There was the Quartering Act of 1765, which obliged any colony in which troops were stationed to provide them with suitable accommodations. That contributed to the cost of keeping British forces in America. Finally, in March of 1765, Parliament passed the Stamp Act.

STAMP ACT The Stamp Act placed **taxes** on legal documents, customs papers, newspapers, almanacs, college diplomas, playing cards, and dice. After November 1, 1765, all these items had to bear a stamp signifying that their possessor had paid the tax. Violators of the Stamp Act, like those disobeying the Sugar Act, were to be tried without juries in admiralty courts. The English had been paying a similar tax for nearly a century, so it seemed to Grenville and Parliament that colonials could have no objections.

Every packet boat from London that brought news of Parliament's passing another of Grenville's measures dampened postwar optimism. For all the differences between the colonies and England, Americans still held

(detail) "A View of the Year of 1765", by Paul Revere, 1765. MHS Neg.#1448. Courtesy of the Massachusetts Historical Society

| *Visual imagery brought home the urgency of resistance to Americans who could not read political pamphlets or radical newspapers. This detail from an engraving by Paul Revere includes a liberty tree, from which is hung an effigy of the Boston stamp distributor, and a beast busily destroying the Magna Carta while trampling American colonials. The date on the tree, August 14, 1765, marked the first Stamp Act riot in Boston.*

much in common with the English. Those shared ideas included firm beliefs about why the British constitution, British customs, and British history all served to protect liberty and the rights of the empire's freeborn citizens. For that reason the new measures, which seemed like common sense to Grenville and Parliament, did not make sense to Americans.

The Beginning of Colonial Resistance

LOCKE ON PROPERTY AND LIBERTY Like other Britons, colonials in America accepted a maxim laid down by the English philosopher John Locke: property guaranteed liberty. Property, in this view, was not merely real estate, or wealth, or material possessions. It was the source of strength for every individual, providing the freedom to think and act independently. Protecting the individual's right to own property was the main responsibility of government, because if personal property was not sacred, then neither was personal liberty.

It followed from this close connection between property, power, and liberty that no people should be taxed without consenting—either personally or through elected representatives. The power to tax was the power to destroy by depriving a person of property. Yet both the Sugar Act and the Stamp Act were taxes passed by members of Parliament, none of whom had been elected by colonials.

Like the English, colonials also prized the right of trial by jury as one of their basic constitutional liberties. Yet both the Sugar Act and the Stamp Act would prosecute offenders in the admiralty courts, not in local courts, thus depriving colonials of the freedom claimed by all other English men and women.

The concern for protecting individual liberties was only one of the convictions shaping the colonies' response to Britain's new policies. Equally important was their deep suspicion of power itself, a preoccupation that colonials shared with a minority of radical English thinkers. These radicals were known by a variety of names: the Country Party, the Commonwealthmen, and the **Opposition**. They drew their inspiration from the ancient tradition of classical **republicanism**, which held that representative government safeguarded liberty more reliably than either monarchy or oligarchy did. Underlying that judgment was the belief that human beings were driven by passion and insatiable ambition. One person (a monarch), or even a few people (an oligarchy), could not be entrusted with governing, because they would inevitably become corrupted by power and turn into despots. Even in representative governments, the people were obliged to watch those in power at all times. The price of liberty was eternal vigilance.

The Opposition believed that the people of England were not watching their rulers closely enough. During the first half of the eighteenth century, they argued, the entire executive branch of England's government—monarchs and their ministers—had been corrupted by their appetite for power. Proof of their ambition was the executive bureaucracy of civil officials and standing armies that steadily grew larger, interfered more with citizens' lives, and drained increasing amounts of money from taxpayers. Even more alarming, in the Opposition's view, the executive branch's bribery of members of Parliament was corrupting the representative branch of England's government. They warned that a sinister conspiracy originating in the executive branch of government threatened English liberty.

Opposition thinkers commanded little attention in England, where they were dismissed as a discontented radical fringe. But they were revered by political leaders in the American colonies. The Opposition's view of politics confirmed colonial anxieties about England, doubts that ran deeper after 1763. Parliament's attempt to tax the colonies and the quartering of a standing army on the frontier confirmed all too well the Opposition's description of how powerful rulers turned themselves into tyrants and reduced the people whom they ruled to slaves. In sum, Grenville's new measures led some colonials to suspect that ambitious men ruling England might be conspiring against American liberties.

IMPACT OF POSTWAR RECESSION Britain's attempt to raise revenue after 1763 was a disaster of timing, not just psychologically but also economically. By then, the colonies were in the throes of a recession. The boom produced in America by government spending during the war had collapsed once subsidies were withdrawn. Colonial merchants were left with stocks full of imported goods gathering dust on their shelves. Farmers lost the brisk and profitable market of the army.

Colonial response to the Sugar Act reflected the painful postwar readjustments. New England merchants led the opposition, objecting to the Sugar Act principally on economic grounds. But with the passage of the Stamp Act, the terms of the imperial debate widened. The Stamp Act hit all colonials, not just New England merchants. It took money from the pockets of anyone who made a will, filed a deed, traded out of a colonial port, bought a newspaper, consulted an almanac, graduated from college, took a chance at dice, or played cards. More important, the Stamp Act served notice that Parliament claimed the authority to tax the colonies directly and for the sole purpose of raising revenue.

Riots and Resolves

That unprecedented assertion provoked an unprecedented development: the first display of colonial unity. During the spring and summer of 1765 American assemblies passed resolves denying that Parliament could tax the colonies. The right to tax Americans belonged to colonial assemblies alone, they argued, by the law of nature and by the liberties guaranteed in colonial charters and in the British constitution.

PATRICK HENRY'S RESOLVES Virginia's assembly, the House of Burgesses, took the lead in protesting the Stamp Act, prodded by Patrick Henry. Just 29 years old in 1765, Henry had tried his hand at planting in western Virginia before recognizing his real talent—demagoguery. Blessed with the eloquence of an evangelical preacher, the dashing charm of a southern gentleman, and a mind uncluttered by much learning, Henry parlayed his popularity as a smooth-talking lawyer into a place among the Burgesses. He took his seat just 10 days before introducing the Virginia Resolves against the Stamp Act.

The Burgesses passed Henry's resolutions upholding their exclusive right to tax Virginians. They stopped short of adopting those resolves that called for outright resistance. When news of Virginia's stand spread to the rest of the colonies, other assemblies followed suit, affirming that the sole right to tax Americans resided in

(detail) ©The Colonial Williamsburg Foundation. Museum Purchase (#1958-3)

| *This idealized likeness of Patrick Henry, by the American artist Thomas Sully, conveys the subject's intensity. Henry's eloquence and passion as an orator made a vivid impression on his contemporaries.*

their elected representatives. But some colonial newspapers deliberately printed a different story—that the Burgesses had approved all of Henry's resolves, including one that sanctioned disobedience to any parliamentary tax. That prompted a few assemblies to endorse resistance. In October 1765, delegates from nine colonies convened in New York, where they prepared a joint statement of the American position and petitioned the king and Parliament to repeal both the Sugar Act and the Stamp Act.

Meanwhile, colonial leaders turned to the press to arouse popular opposition to the Stamp Act. Disposed by the writings of the English Opposition to think of politics in conspiratorial terms, they warned that Grenville and the king's other ministers schemed to deprive the colonies of their liberties by unlawfully taxing their property. The Stamp Act was only the first step in a sinister plan to enslave Americans.

Whether or not fears of a dark conspiracy haunted most colonials in 1765, many resisted the Stamp Act. The merchants of Boston, New York City, and Philadelphia agreed to stop importing English goods in order to pressure British traders to lobby for repeal. In every colony, organizations emerged to ensure that the Stamp Act, if not repealed, would never be enforced.

SONS OF LIBERTY The new resistance groups, which styled themselves the "Sons of Liberty," consisted of traders, lawyers, and prosperous artisans. With great success, they organized the lower classes of seaports in opposition to the Stamp Act. The sailors, dockworkers, poor artisans, apprentices, and servants who poured into the streets resembled mobs that had been organized from time to time earlier in the century. Previous riots against houses of prostitution, merchants who hoarded goods, or supporters of smallpox inoculation had not been spontaneous, uncontrolled outbursts. Crowds chose their targets and their tactics carefully and then carried out the communal will with little violence.

In every colonial city, the mobs of 1765 burnt the stamp distributors in effigy, insulted them on the streets, demolished their offices, and attacked their homes. One hot night in August 1765 a mob went further than the Sons of Liberty had planned. They all but leveled the stately mansion of Thomas Hutchinson, the unpopular lieutenant governor of Massachusetts and the brother-in-law of the colony's stamp distributor. The destruction stunned Bostonians, especially the Sons of Liberty, who resisted Britain in the name of protecting private property. Thereafter they took care to keep crowds under tighter control. By the first of November, the day that the Stamp Act took effect, most of the stamp distributors had resigned.

Lord Chatham and America

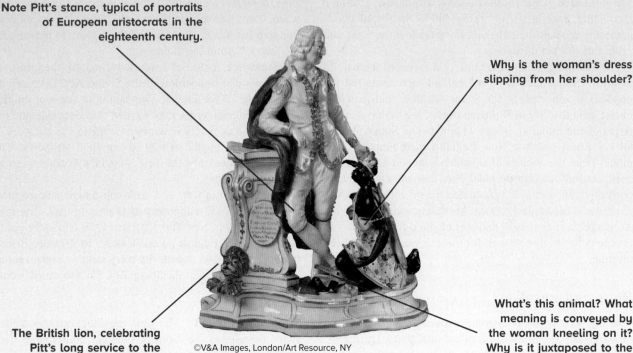

Note Pitt's stance, typical of portraits of European aristocrats in the eighteenth century.

Why is the woman's dress slipping from her shoulder?

The British lion, celebrating Pitt's long service to the British Empire

©V&A Images, London/Art Resource, NY

What's this animal? What meaning is conveyed by the woman kneeling on it? Why is it juxtaposed to the book next to Pitt?

This 1766 porcelain attests to the great popularity of William Pitt, the Earl of Chatham, among Americans who resisted the Stamp Act. Almost alone among British politicians, Pitt had grasped and approved the colonists' objections to taxation. During Parliament's debate over the repeal of the Stamp Act, Grenville asked sarcastically: "Tell me when the colonies were emancipated?" Pitt shot back, "I desire to know when they were made slaves." The porcelain's representation of "America" as an enslaved African American woman kneeling before him, her face raised in gratitude, references Pitt's celebrated remark and echoes the colonists' association of taxation with slavery

THINKING CRITICALLY

What is the significance of the feather headdress worn by the "America" figure? Why choose a black woman to represent "America"? What do those choices suggest about the ways in which colonials disaffected with Britain regarded themselves and their place within the British Empire? Why is Pitt represented extending his hand to the kneeling woman but not meeting her gaze?

Repeal of the Stamp Act

Meanwhile, the repeal of the Stamp Act was already in the works back in England. The man who came—unintentionally—to America's relief was George III. The young king was a good man, industrious and devoted to the empire, but he was also immature and not particularly bright. Insecurity made him an irksome master, and he ran through ministers rapidly. By the end of 1765 George had replaced Grenville with a new first minister, the Marquis of Rockingham. Rockingham had opposed the Stamp Act from the outset, and he had no desire to enforce it. He received support from London merchants, who were beginning to feel the pinch of the American nonimportation campaign, and secured repeal of the Stamp Act in March 1766.

VIRTUAL VS. ACTUAL The Stamp Act controversy demonstrated to colonials how similar in political outlook they were to one another and how different they were from the British. Americans found that they shared the same assumptions about the meaning of representation. To counter colonial objections to the Stamp Act, Grenville and his supporters had claimed that Americans *were* represented in Parliament, even though they had elected none of its members.

Americans were virtually represented, Grenville insisted, for each member of Parliament stood for the interests of the whole empire, not just those of the particular constituency that had elected him.

Colonials could see no virtue in the theory of **virtual representation**. After all, the circumstances and interests of colonials, living an ocean away, were significantly different from those of Britons. The newly recognized consensus among Americans was that colonials could be truly represented only by those whom they had elected. Their view, known as **actual representation**, emphasized that elected officials were directly accountable to their constituents.

Americans also had discovered that they agreed about the extent of Parliament's authority over the colonies: it did not include the right to tax. Colonials conceded Parliament's right to legislate and to regulate trade for the good of the whole empire. But taxation, in their view, was the free gift of the people through their representatives—who were not sitting in Parliament.

DECLARATORY ACT Members of Parliament brushed aside colonial petitions and resolves, all but ignoring these constitutional arguments. To make its own authority clear, Parliament accompanied the repeal of the Stamp Act with a Declaratory Act, asserting that it had the power to make laws for the colonies "in all cases whatsoever." In fact, the Declaratory Act clarified nothing. Did Parliament understand the power of legislation to include the power of taxation?

The Townshend Acts

In the summer of 1766 George III—again inadvertently—gave the colonies what should have been an advantage by changing ministers again. The king replaced Rockingham with William Pitt, who enjoyed great favor among colonials for his leadership during the Seven Years' War and for his opposition to the Stamp Act. If the man who believed that Americans were "the sons not the bastards of England" had been well enough to govern, matters between Great Britain and the colonies might have turned out differently. But almost immediately after Pitt took office, his health collapsed, and power passed into the hands of Charles Townshend, the chancellor of the exchequer, who wished only to raise more revenue. In 1767 he persuaded Parliament to tax the lead, paint, paper, glass, and tea that Americans imported from Britain.

In addition, Townshend was determined to curb the power of the upstart American assemblies. To set a bold example, he singled out for punishment the New York legislature, which was refusing to comply with provisions of the Quartering Act of 1765. The troops that were left on the western frontier after the Seven

Source: Library of Congress, Prints and Photographs Division [LC-USZ62-21637]

Years' War had been pulled back into colonial seaports in 1766. In part their movement was meant to economize on costs, but royal officials also hoped the troops' presence would help quiet agitation over the Stamp Act. When the largest contingent came to New York, that colony's assembly protested, claiming that the cost of quartering the troops constituted a form of indirect taxation. But Townshend held firm, and Parliament backed him, suspending the New York assembly in 1767 until it agreed to obey the Quartering Act.

Townshend also dipped into the revenue from his new tariffs in order to make royal officials less dependent on the assemblies. Governors and other officers such as customs collectors and judges had previously received their salaries from colonial legislatures. The assemblies lost that crucial leverage when Townshend used the revenues to pay those bureaucrats directly. Finally, in order to ensure more effective enforcement of all the duties on imports, Townshend created an American Board of Customs Commissioners, who appointed a small army of new customs collectors. He also established three new vice-admiralty courts in Boston, New York City, and Charleston to bring smugglers to justice.

The Resistance Organizes

JOHN DICKINSON AND SAMUEL ADAMS In Townshend's efforts to centralize the administration of the empire, Americans saw new evidence that they were not being treated like the English. A host of newspapers and pamphlets took up the cry against taxation. The most widely read publication, "A Letter from a Farmer in Pennsylvania," was the work of John Dickinson—who was, in fact, a Philadelphia lawyer. He urged Americans to protest the Townshend duties by consuming fewer imported English luxuries. The virtues of hard work, thrift, and home manufacturing, Dickinson argued, would bring about repeal.

As Dickinson's star rose over Philadelphia, the Townshend Acts also shaped the destiny of another man, farther north. By the 1760s Samuel Adams was a leader in the Massachusetts assembly. In some ways his rise had been unlikely. Adams's earlier ventures as a merchant ended in bankruptcy; his stint as a tax collector left all of Boston in the red. But he proved a consummate political organizer and agitator. First his enemies and later his friends claimed that Adams had decided on independence for America as early as 1768. In that year he persuaded the assembly to send to other colonial legislatures a circular letter condemning the Townshend Acts and calling for a united American resistance.

As John Dickinson and Samuel Adams whipped up public outrage, the Sons of Liberty again organized the opposition in the streets. Customs officials, like the stamp distributors before them, became targets of popular hatred. But the customs collectors gave as good as they got. Using the flimsiest excuses, they seized American vessels for violating royal regulations. With cold insolence they shook down American merchants for what amounted to protection money. The racketeering in the customs service brought tensions in Boston to a flash point in June 1768 after officials seized and condemned the *Liberty,* a sloop belonging to one of the city's biggest merchants, John Hancock. Several thousand Bostonians vented their anger in a night of rioting, searching out and roughing up customs officials.

The new secretary of state for the colonies, Lord Hillsborough, responded to the *Liberty* riot by sending two regiments of troops to Boston. In the fall of 1768 the redcoats, like a conquering army, paraded into town under the cover of warships lying off the harbor. In the months that followed, citizens bristled when challenged on the streets by armed soldiers. Even more disturbing to Bostonians was the execution of British military justice on the Common, an open field on the outskirts of the city. British soldiers were whipped savagely for breaking military discipline, and desertion was punished by execution.

The *Liberty* riot and the arrival of British troops in Boston pushed colonial assemblies to coordinate their resistance more closely. Most legislatures endorsed the Massachusetts circular letter sent to them by Samuel Adams. They promptly adopted agreements not to import or to consume British goods. The reluctance among some merchants to revive nonimportation in 1767 gave way to greater enthusiasm by 1768, and by early 1769 such agreements were in effect throughout the colonies.

The Stamp Act crisis had also called forth intercolonial cooperation and tactics such as nonimportation. But the protests against the Townshend Acts raised the stakes by creating new institutions to carry forward the resistance. Subscribers to the nonimportation agreements established "committees of inspection" to enforce the ban on trade with Britain. The committees publicly denounced merchants who continued to import, vandalized their warehouses, forced them to stand under the gallows, and sometimes resorted to tar and feathers.

After 1768 the resistance also brought a broader range of colonials into the politics of protest. Artisans, who recognized that nonimportation would spur domestic manufacturing, began to organize as independent political groups. In many towns, women took an active part in opposing the Townshend duties. The "Daughters of Liberty" took to heart John Dickinson's advice: they wore homespun clothing instead of English finery, served coffee instead of tea, and boycotted shops selling British goods.

Liberty's Other Sons

The resistance after 1768 grew broader in another sense as well. Many of its supporters in the colonies felt a new sense of kinship with freedom fighters throughout Europe. Eagerly they read about the doings of men such as Charles Lucas, an Irish newspaper editor and member of the Irish Parliament, and John Wilkes, a London journalist and a leading politician of the Opposition. Both men charged the king's ministers with corrupting the political life of the British Isles. The doings of political rebels even in distant Poland and Turkey engaged colonial sympathies, too. But perhaps the international cause that proved dearest to American lovers of liberty was the fate of Corsica.

COLONIALS FOLLOW PAOLI'S STRUGGLE For years, this tiny island off the coast of Italy had fought for its independence, first from the Italian state of Genoa and then from France, which bought the island in 1768. The leader of the Corsican rebellion, Pascal Paoli, led what one New York newspaper touted as a "glorious struggle." Many in the British Empire hoped that England would rally to defend Corsica's freedom, if only to keep France from seizing this strategic point in the Mediterranean. But British statesmen had no intention of going to war with France over mere Corsica, and when French troops routed his rebel army, Paoli fled to exile in England in 1769. Adding insult to injury, this "greatest man of earth," as he was lionized, began to hobnob with

Source: Harris Brisbane Dick Fund, 1932/The Metropolitan Museum of Art

| *John Wilkes, an English journalist and member of the Opposition.*

British nobles. He even accepted a pension of 1,000 pounds sterling a year from George III. The moral of the sad story, according to more than one colonial newspaper, was that British corruption pervaded not only the empire but all of Europe as well. Paoli had been "bought"—and if the Corsican sons of liberty could not survive, would their American counterparts manage to remain virtuous for very long?

The Boston Massacre

Meanwhile, the situation in Boston deteriorated steadily. British troops found themselves regularly cursed by citizens and occasionally pelted with stones, dirt, and human excrement. The British regulars were particularly unpopular among Boston's laboring classes because they competed with them for jobs. Off-duty soldiers moonlighted as maritime laborers, and they sold their services at rates cheaper than the wages paid to locals. By 1769 brawls between British regulars and waterfront workers broke out frequently.

With some 4,000 redcoats enduring daily contact with some 15,000 Bostonians under the sway of Samuel Adams, what happened on the night of March 5, 1770, was nearly inevitable. A crowd gathered around the customshouse for the sport of heckling the 10 soldiers who guarded it. The redcoats panicked and fended off insults and snowballs with live fire, hitting 11 rioters and killing 5. Adams and other propagandists seized on the incident. Labeling the bloodshed "the Boston Massacre," they publicized that "atrocity" throughout the colonies. The radical *Boston Gazette* framed its account in an eye-catching black-bordered edition headed with a drawing of five coffins.

While Townshend's policies spurred the resistance in America, the obvious finally dawned on Parliament. It recognized that Townshend's duties on imported English goods only discouraged sales to colonials and encouraged them to manufacture at home. The argument for repeal was overwhelming, and the way had been cleared by the unexpected death of Townshend. In 1770 his successor, Lord North, convinced Parliament to repeal all the Townshend duties except the one on tea, allowing that tax to stand as a source of revenue and as a symbol of Parliament's authority.

Resistance Revived

Repeal of the Townshend duties took the wind from the sails of American resistance for more than two years. But the controversy between England and the colonies had not been resolved.

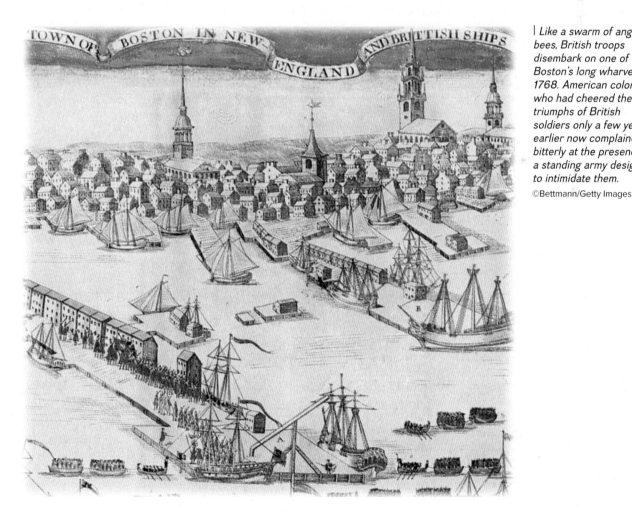

Like a swarm of angry bees, British troops disembark on one of Boston's long wharves in 1768. American colonials who had cheered the triumphs of British soldiers only a few years earlier now complained bitterly at the presence of a standing army designed to intimidate them.

©Bettmann/Getty Images

WHO WAS TO BLAME FOR THE BOSTON MASSACRE?

Following the shootings in King Street, Captain Thomas Preston and six of his men stood trial for murder. Two radical patriot lawyers, Josiah Quincy Jr. and future President John Adams, served as defense council. Convinced that Boston must prove itself fair and faithful to the rule of law, both lawyers performed brilliantly. The jury acquitted Preston and four of the soldiers, and convicted two others of manslaughter. The depositions from the trial provide some of our best evidence for how soldiers and Bostonians viewed the standoff differently.

DOCUMENT 1
Deposition of Captain Thomas Preston, March 12, 1770

The mob still increased and were more outrageous, striking their clubs or bludgeons one against another, and calling out, come on you rascals, you bloody backs, you lobster scoundrels, fire if you dare, G-d damn you, fire and be damned, we know you dare not, and much more such language was used. At this time I was between the soldiers and the mob, parleying with, and endeavouring all in my power to persuade them to retire peaceably, but to no purpose. They advanced to the points of the bayonets, struck some of them and even the muzzles of the pieces, and seemed to be endeavouring to close with the soldiers. On which some well-behaved persons asked me if the guns were charged. I replied yes. They then asked me if I intended to order the men to fire. I answered no, by no means, observing to them that I was advanced before the muzzles of the men's pieces, and must fall a sacrifice if they fired; that the soldiers were upon the half cock and charged bayonets, and my giving the word fire under those circumstances would prove me to be no officer. While I was thus speaking, one of the soldiers having received a severe blow with a stick, stepped a little on one side and instantly fired, on which turning to and asking him why he fired without orders, I was struck with a club on my arm, which for some time deprived me of the use of it, which blow had it been placed on my head, most probably would have destroyed me. On this a general attack was made on the men by a great number of heavy clubs and snowballs being thrown at them, by which all our lives were in imminent danger, some persons at the same time from behind calling out, damn your bloods—why don't you fire. Instantly three or four of the soldiers fired, one after another, and directly after three more in the same confusion and hurry. The mob then ran away, except three unhappy men who instantly expired, in which number was Mr. Gray at whose rope-walk the prior quarrels took place; one more is since dead, three others are dangerously, and four slightly wounded. The whole of this melancholy affair was transacted in almost 20 minutes. On my asking the soldiers why they fired without orders, they said they heard the word fire and supposed it came from me. This might be the case as many of the mob called out fire, fire, but I assured the men that I gave no such order; that my words were, don't fire, stop your firing. In short, it was scarcely possible for the soldiers to know who said fire, or don't fire, or stop your firing.

Source: www.famous-trials.com/massacre/210-evidence.

DOCUMENT 2
Deposition of Robert Goddard

The Soldiers came up to the Centinel and the Officer told them to place themselves and they formed a half moon. The Captain told the Boys to go home least there should be murder done. They were throwing Snow balls. Did not go off but threw more Snow balls. The Capt. was behind the Soldiers. The Captain told them to fire. One Gun went off. A Sailor or Townsman struck the Captain. He thereupon said damn your bloods fire think I'll be treated in this manner. This Man that struck the Captain came from among the People who were 7 feet off and were round on one wing. I saw no person speak to him. I was so near I should have seen it. After the Capt. said Damn your bloods fire they all fired one after another about 7 or 8 in all, and then the officer bid Prime and load again. He stood behind all the time. Mr. Lee went up to the officer and called the officer by name Capt. Preston. I saw him coming down from the Guard behind the Party. I went to Gaol the next day being sworn for the Grand Jury to see the Captain. Then said pointing to him that's the person who gave the word to fire. He said if you swear that you will ruin me everlastingly. I was so near the officer when he gave the word fire that I could touch him. His face was towards me. He stood in the middle behind the Men. I looked him in the face. He then stood within the circle. When he told 'em to fire he turned about to me. I looked him in the face.

Source: www.bostonmassacre/net/trial/d-goddard.htm.

THINKING CRITICALLY

Preston and Goddard come to different conclusions about the shootings but describe similar details (the snowballs, the man who struck Preston). Can details from these two accounts be reconciled? Do they simply have different perspectives on the same event, or do you think one of the depositions must be misleading? Given the tensions these accounts relate, do you think that a violent confrontation between soldiers and Bostonians was inevitable?

Colonials still paid taxes on molasses and tea, taxes to which they had not consented. They were still subject to trial in admiralty courts, which operated without juries. They still lived with a standing army in their midst. Beneath the banked fires of protest smoldered the live embers of Americans' political inequality. Any shift in the wind could fan those embers into flames.

The wind did shift, quite literally, on Narragansett Bay in 1772, running aground the *Gaspee,* a British naval schooner in hot pursuit of Rhode Island smugglers. Residents of nearby Providence quickly celebrated the *Gaspee*'s misfortune by burning it down to the waterline. Outraged British officials sent a special commission to look into the matter, intending once again to bypass the established colonial court system. The arrival of the Gaspee Commission re-ignited the imperial crisis, and in America, once again, resistance flared.

COMMITTEES OF CORRESPONDENCE It did so through an ingenious mechanism, the **committees of correspondence**. Established in all the colonies by their assemblies, the committees drew up statements of American rights and grievances, distributed those documents within and among the colonies, and solicited responses from towns and counties. The brainchild of Samuel Adams, the committee structure formed a new communications network, one that fostered an intercolonial agreement on resistance to British measures. The strategy succeeded, and not only among colonies. The committees spread the scope of the resistance from colonial seaports into rural areas, engaging farmers and other country folk in the opposition to Britain.

The committees had much to talk about when Parliament passed the Tea Act in 1773. The law was an effort to bail out the bankrupt East India Company by granting that corporation a monopoly on the tea trade to Americans. Because the company could use agents to sell its product directly, cutting out the middlemen, it could offer a lower price than that charged by colonial merchants. Thus, although the Tea Act would hurt American merchants, it promised to make tea cheaper for ordinary Americans. Still, many colonials saw the act as Parliament's attempt to trick them into accepting its authority to tax the colonies. They set out to deny that power once and for all.

In the early winter of 1773 popular leaders in Boston called for the tea cargoes to be returned immediately to England. On the evening of December 16, thousands of Bostonians, as well as farmers from the surrounding countryside, packed into the Old South Meetinghouse. Some members of the audience knew what Samuel Adams had on the evening's agenda, and they awaited their cue. It came when Adams told the meeting that they could do nothing more to save their country. War whoops rang through the meetinghouse, the crowd spilled onto the streets and out to the waterfront, and the Boston Tea Party commenced. From the throng emerged 50 men dressed as Indians to disguise their identities. The party boarded three vessels docked off Griffin's Wharf, broke open casks containing 90,000 pounds of tea, and brewed a beverage worth 10,000 pounds sterling in Boston harbor.

The Empire Strikes Back

COERCIVE ACTS The Boston Tea Party proved to British satisfaction that the colonies aimed at independence. Lord North's assessment was grim: "We are now to dispute whether we have, or have not, any authority in that country." To reassert its authority, Parliament passed the Coercive Acts, dubbed in the colonies the "Intolerable Acts." The first of these came in March 1774, two months after hearing of the Tea Party, when Parliament passed the Boston Port Bill, closing that harbor to all oceangoing traffic until such time as the king saw fit to reopen it. And George, Parliament announced, would not see fit until colonials paid the East India Company for its losses.

During the next three months, Parliament approved three other "intolerable" laws designed to punish Massachusetts. The Massachusetts Government Act handed over the colony's government to royal officials. Even convening town meetings would require royal permission. The Impartial Administration of Justice Act permitted any royal official accused of a crime in Massachusetts to be tried in England or in another colony. The Quartering Act allowed the housing of British troops in uninhabited private homes, outlying buildings, and barns—not only in Massachusetts but in all the other colonies as well.

| *While the new political activism of some American women merely amused male leaders of the resistance, it inspired the scorn of some partisans of British authority. When the women of Edenton, North Carolina, renounced imported tea, this British cartoon mocked them. Can you find at least five details in the painting used by the artist to insult the Americans?*

FEAR OF CONSPIRACY Many colonials saw the Coercive Acts as proof of a plot to enslave the colonies. In truth, the taxes and duties, laws and regulations of the past decade *were* part of a deliberate design—a plan to centralize the administration of the British Empire that seemed only common sense to British officials. But those efforts by the king's ministers and Parliament to run the colonies more efficiently and profitably were viewed by more and more Americans as a sinister conspiracy against their liberties.

For colonials, the study of history confirmed that interpretation, especially their reading of the histories written by the English Opposition. The Opposition's favorite historical subject was the downfall of republics, whether those of ancient Greece and Rome or more recent republican governments in Venice and Denmark. The lesson of their histories was always the same: power overwhelmed liberty, unless the people remained vigilant. The pattern, argued radicals, had been repeated in America over the previous dozen years: costly wars waged; oppressive taxes levied to pay for them; standing armies sent to overawe citizens; corrupt governors, customs collectors, and judges appointed to enrich themselves by enforcing the measures. Everything seemed to fit.

QUEBEC ACT Week after week in the spring of 1774, reports of legislative outrages came across the waters. Shortly after approving the Coercive Acts, Parliament passed the Quebec Act, which established a permanent government in what had been French Canada. Ominously, it included no representative assembly. Equally ominous to Protestant colonials, the Quebec Act officially recognized the Roman Catholic church and extended the bounds of the province to include all land between the Mississippi and Ohio Rivers. Suddenly New York, Pennsylvania, and Virginia found themselves bordering a British colony whose subjects had no voice in their own government.

With the passage of the Coercive Acts, many more colonials came to believe not only that ambitious men plotted to enslave the colonies but also that those conspirators included almost all British political leaders. At the time of the Stamp Act and again during the agitation against the Townshend Acts, most colonials had confined their suspicions to the king's ministers. By 1774 members of Parliament were also implicated in that conspiracy—and a few radicals were wondering aloud about George III.

FIRST CONTINENTAL CONGRESS CALLED As alarm deepened in the wake of the Coercive Acts, one colony after another called for an intercolonial congress—like the one that had met during the Stamp Act crisis—to determine the best way to

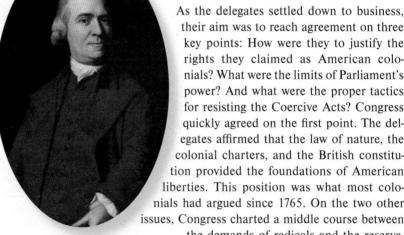

©Collection of the New-York Historical Society, USA/Bridgeman Images

| *Samuel Adams, a radical who master-minded colonial resistance tactics.*

defend their freedom. But many also remained unsettled about where the logic of their actions seemed to be taking them: toward a denial that they were any longer English.

✓ **REVIEW**

How did British colonial policy change after the Seven Years' War, and what was the colonial response?

TOWARD THE REVOLUTION

BY THE BEGINNING OF SEPTEMBER 1774, when 55 delegates to the First Continental Congress gathered in Philadelphia, the news from Massachusetts was grim. The colony verged on anarchy, it was reported, as its inhabitants resisted the enforcement of the Massachusetts Government Act.

In the midst of this atmosphere of crisis, the members of Congress also had to take one another's measure. Many of the delegates had not traveled outside their own colonies. (All but Georgia sent representatives.) Although the delegates encountered a great deal of diversity, they quickly discovered that they esteemed the same traits of character, attributes that they called "civic virtue." These traits included simplicity—and self-reliance, industry and thrift, and above all, an unselfish commitment to the public good. Most members of the Congress also shared a common mistrust of England, associating the mother country with vice, extravagance, and corruption.

Still, the delegates had some misgivings about those from other colonies. Massachusetts in particular brought with it a reputation—well deserved, considering that Samuel Adams was along—for radical action and a willingness to use force to accomplish its ends.

The First Continental Congress

As the delegates settled down to business, their aim was to reach agreement on three key points: How were they to justify the rights they claimed as American colonials? What were the limits of Parliament's power? And what were the proper tactics for resisting the Coercive Acts? Congress quickly agreed on the first point. The delegates affirmed that the law of nature, the colonial charters, and the British constitution provided the foundations of American liberties. This position was what most colonials had argued since 1765. On the two other issues, Congress charted a middle course between the demands of radicals and the reservations of conservatives.

Since the time of the Stamp Act, most colonials had insisted that Parliament had no authority to tax the colonies. But later events had demonstrated that Parliament could undermine colonial liberties by legislation as well as by taxation. The suspension of the New York legislature, the Gaspee Commission, and the Coercive Acts all fell into this category. Given those experiences, the delegates adopted a Declaration of Rights and Grievances on October 14, 1774, asserting the right of the colonies to tax and legislate for themselves. The Declaration of Rights thus limited Parliament's power over Americans more strictly than colonials had a decade earlier.

JOSEPH GALLOWAY'S PLAN By denying Parliament's power to make laws for the colonies, the Continental Congress blocked efforts of the most conservative delegates to reach an accommodation with England. Their leading advocate, Joseph Galloway of Pennsylvania, proposed a plan of union with Britain similar to the one set forth by the Albany Congress in 1754. Under it, a grand council of the colonies would handle all common concerns, with any laws it passed subject to review and veto by Parliament. For its part, Parliament would have to submit for the grand council's approval any acts it passed affecting America. A majority of delegates judged that Galloway's proposal left Parliament too much leeway in legislating for colonials, and they rejected his plan.

Although the Congress denied Parliament the right to impose taxes or to make laws, delegates stopped short of declaring that it had no authority at all in the colonies. They approved Parliament's regulation of trade, but only because of the interdependent economy of the empire. And although some radical pamphleteers were attacking the king for plotting against American liberties, Congress acknowledged the continuing allegiance of the colonies to George III. In other words, the delegates called for a return to the situation that had existed in the empire before 1763, with Parliament regulating trade and the colonies exercising all powers of taxation and legislation.

THE ASSOCIATION On the question of resistance, the Congress satisfied the desires of its most radical delegates by drawing up the Continental Association, an agreement to cease all trade with Britain until the Coercive Acts were repealed. They agreed that their fellow citizens would immediately stop drinking East India Company tea and that by December 1, 1774, merchants would no longer import goods of any sort from Britain. A ban on the export of American produce to Britain and the West Indies would go into effect a year later, during September 1775—the lag being a concession to southern rice and tobacco planters, who wanted to market crops already planted.

REVERE AND THE SUFFOLK RESOLVES The Association provided for the total cessation of trade, but Samuel Adams and other radicals wanted bolder action. They received help from Paul Revere, a Boston silversmith who had long provided newspapers with many lurid engravings showing British abuses. On September 16, Revere galloped into Philadelphia bearing a copy of resolves drawn up by Bostonians and other residents of Suffolk County. The Suffolk Resolves, as they were called, branded the Coercive Acts as unconstitutional and called for civil disobedience to protest them. Congress endorsed the resolves, as Adams had hoped. But it would not approve another part of the radicals' agenda—preparing for war by authorizing proposals to strengthen and arm colonial militias.

Thus the First Continental Congress steered a middle course. Although determined to bring about repeal of the Coercive Acts, it held firm in resisting any revolutionary course of action. If British officials had responded to its recommendations and restored the status quo of 1763, the war for independence might have been postponed—perhaps indefinitely. However, even though the Congress did not go to the extremes urged by the radicals, its decisions drew colonials farther down the road to independence.

The Last Days of the British Empire in America

Most colonials applauded the achievements of the First Continental Congress. They expected that the Association would bring about a speedy repeal of the Coercive Acts. But fear that the colonies were moving toward a break with Britain led others to denounce the doings of the Congress. Conservatives were convinced that if independence were declared, chaos would ensue. Colonials, they argued, would quarrel over land claims and sectional tensions and religious differences, as they had so often in the recent past. Without Britain to referee such disputes, they feared, the result would be civil war, followed by anarchy.

THOMAS GAGE IN BOSTON The man in America with the least liking for the Continental Congress sat in the hottest seat in the colonies, that of the governor of Massachusetts. General Thomas Gage now watched as royal authority crumbled in Massachusetts and the rebellion spread to other colonies. In June 1774 a desperate Gage dissolved the Massachusetts legislature, only to see it re-form, on its own, into a Provincial Congress. That new body assumed the government of the colony in October and began arming the militia. Gage then started to fortify Boston and pleaded for more troops—only to find his fortifications damaged by saboteurs and his requests for reinforcements ignored by Britain.

©Philadelphia History Museum at the Atwater Kent/Courtesy of Historical Society of Pennsylvania Collection/Bridgeman Images

| *A British grenadier.*

Parliament and the Road to Revolution

DATE	ACT	DETAILS	REACTION
1764	Sugar Act	Decreased existing tax on molasses but increased policing and punishment for violation	Angry protests by New England merchants
1764	Currency Act	Prohibited colonies making paper bills legal tender	
1765	Quartering Act	Compelled colonies to house army troops	New York refuses to comply
1765	Stamp Act	Taxed legal documents, various paper products, and dice	Assemblies deny Parliament's right to tax colonies; nonimportation campaign; mobs intimidate stamp distributors
1766	Declaratory Act	Though Stamp Act repealed, Parliament insists on power to tax colonies	Patriot writing flourishes; crowds attack customs agents; nonimportation more sophisticated
1767	Townshend Acts	Taxed lead, paper, paint, glass, and tea	Riots; propaganda; Townshend duties repealed except for tea
1770	Boston Massacre	5 men shot dead by British troops in Boston	Refusal to let the tea shipments land; destruction of tea in Boston Harbor and elsewhere
1773	Tea Act	Allowed East India Company to sell tea in colonies at discount, but tea would still be taxed	First Continental Congress meets in Philadelphia
1774	Coercive Acts	Closed Boston's port; placed Massachusetts government under royal control	

(top) Source: Library of Congress, Prints and Photographs Division [LC-USZ62-21637]; (bottom) Source: Library of Congress, Prints and Photographs Division [LC-USZC4-523]

COLLAPSE OF ROYAL AUTHORITY Outside Boston, royal authority fared no better. Farmers in western Massachusetts forcibly closed the county courts, turning out royally appointed justices and establishing their own tribunals. Popularly elected committees of inspection charged with enforcing the Association took over towns everywhere in Massachusetts, not only restricting trade but also regulating every aspect of local life. The committees called on townspeople to display civic virtue by renouncing "effeminate" English luxuries such as tea and fine clothing and "corrupt" leisure activities such as dancing, gambling, and racing. The committees also assigned spies to report on any citizen unfriendly to the resistance. "Enemies of American liberty"

risked being roundly condemned in public or beaten and pelted with mud and dung by hooting, raucous mobs.

Throughout the other colonies a similar process was under way. During the winter and early spring of 1775 provincial congresses, county conventions, and local committees of inspection were emerging as revolutionary governments, replacing royal authority at every level. As the spectacle unfolded before General Gage, he concluded that only force could subdue the colonies. It would take more than he had at his command, but reinforcements might be on the way. In February of 1775 Parliament had approved an address to the king declaring that the colonies were in rebellion.

The Fighting Begins

As spring came to Boston, the city waited. A band of artisans, organized as spies and express riders by Paul Revere, watched General Gage and waited for him to act. On April 14 word from Lord North finally arrived: Gage was to seize the leaders of the Provincial Congress, an action that would behead the rebellion, North said. Gage knew better than to believe North—but he also knew that he had to do something.

LEXINGTON AND CONCORD   On the night of April 18 the sexton of Boston's Christ Church hung two lamps from its steeple. It was a signal that British troops had moved out of Boston and were marching toward the arms and ammunition stored by the Provincial Congress in Concord. As the lamps flashed the signal, Revere and a comrade, William Dawes, rode out to arouse the countryside.

When the news of a British march reached Lexington, its Minuteman militia of about 70 farmers, chilled and sleepy, mustered on the Green at the center of the small rural town. Lexington Green lay directly on the road to Concord. About four in the morning 700 British troops massed on the Green, and their commander, Major John Pitcairn, ordered the Lexington militia to disperse. The townsmen, outnumbered and overawed, began to obey. Then a shot rang out—whether the British or the Americans fired first is unknown—and then two volleys burst from the

©DEA Picture Library/Getty Images

| *Thomas Paine, the author of* Common Sense

ranks of the redcoats. With a cheer the British set off for Concord, 5 miles distant, leaving eight Americans dead on Lexington Green.

By dawn, hundreds of Minutemen from nearby towns were surging into Concord. The British entered at about seven in the morning and moved, unopposed, toward their target, a house lying across the bridge that spanned the Concord River. While three companies of British soldiers searched for American guns and ammunition, three others, posted on the bridge itself, had the misfortune to find those American arms—borne by the rebels and being fired with deadly accuracy. By noon, the British were retreating to Boston.

The narrow road from Concord to Boston's outskirts became a corridor of carnage. Pursuing Americans fired on the column of fleeing redcoats from the cover of fences and forests. By the end of April 19, the British had sustained 273 casualties; the Americans, 95. It was only the beginning. By evening of the next day, some 20,000 New England militia had converged on Boston for a long siege.

Common Sense

The bloodshed at Lexington Green and Concord's North Bridge committed colonials to a course of rebellion—and independence. That was the conclusion drawn by Thomas Paine, who urged other Americans to join the rebels.

| *The Irish artist John Dixon created this mezzotint,* The Oracle, *in 1774. In it, Father Time puts on a magic-lantern show for an audience of women who represent Britain, Scotland, Ireland, and America. The image projected on the wall conjures up a brilliant future for the British Empire, in which protest and discord give way to freedom and unity—wishful thinking, since little more than a year later colonists and redcoats were shooting at each other at Lexington. Note that America, who sits in the shadows apart from the three other women, is a tawny Indian princess, her face hidden, a weapon at her side. What does this representation suggest about the ways that Britons viewed Americans?*

©The New York Public Library, USA/Bridgeman Images

Paine himself was hardly an American at all. He was born in England, first apprenticed as a corsetmaker, appointed later a tax collector, and fated finally to become midwife to the age of republican revolutions. Paine came to Philadelphia late in 1774, set up as a journalist, and made the American cause his own. "Where liberty is, there is my country," he declared. In January 1776 he wrote a pamphlet to inform colonials of their identity as a distinct people and their destiny as a nation. *Common Sense* enjoyed tremendous popularity and wide circulation, selling 120,000 copies.

After Lexington and Concord, Paine wrote, as the imperial crisis passed "from argument to arms, a new era for politics is struck—a new method of thinking has arisen." That new era of politics for Paine was the age of republicanism. He denounced monarchy as a foolish and dangerous form of government, one that violated the dictates of reason as well as the word of the Bible. By ridicule and remorseless argument, he severed the ties of colonial allegiance to the king. *Common Sense* scorned George III as "the Royal Brute of Britain," who had enslaved the chosen people of the new age—the Americans.

Nor did Paine stop there. He rejected the idea that colonials were or should want to be English. The colonies occupied a huge continent an ocean away from the tiny British Isles—clear proof that nature itself had fashioned America for independence. England lay locked in Europe, doomed to the corruption of an Old World. America had been discovered anew to become an "asylum of liberty."

 REVIEW

What had happened by the mid-1770s to transform nonimportation and political protest into organized rebellion?

Putting History in Global Context

MANY AMERICANS HAD LIKED being English, but being English hadn't worked. Perhaps that is another way of saying that over the course of nearly two centuries, colonial society and politics had evolved in such a way that for Americans an English identity no longer fit.

The radicals in America viewed this change in identity in terms of age-old conspiracies that repeated themselves throughout history. First, the people of a republic were impoverished by costly wars—as the colonists could well appreciate after the Seven Years' War. Then the government burdened the people with taxes to pay for those wars—as in the case of the Sugar Act or the Stamp Act or the Townshend duties. Next, those in power stationed a standing army in the country, pretending to protect the people but actually lending military force to their rulers. The rhetoric of the Opposition about ministerial conspiracies gave such talk a fervid quality that, to some modern ears, may seem an exaggeration.

Take away the rhetoric, however, and the argument makes uncomfortable sense. The British administration began its "backwoods" war with France, intending to limit it to the interior of North America. But the war aims of William Pitt—the leader Americans counted as their friend—grew with every victory, and he urged war with Spain even as France was looking for peace. Britain had already taken its war in Europe farther afield, driving France out of India. When it declared war against Spain, British naval forces in India sailed farther east, in a surprise attack on Spain's colony in the Philippines. At the same time, another fleet raced toward Spanish Cuba. Peace came only once Britain and the major powers had bankrupted their treasuries. Conspiracy may not have been at the heart of the plan. But wars must be paid for. And the prevailing assumptions in a monarchy about who should pay led to the effort to regulate and bring order to Britain's "ungrateful" colonies.

In America, colonists were ungrateful precisely because they had established political institutions that made the rights of "freeborn Britons" more available to ordinary citizens than they were in the nation that had created those liberties. Perhaps, in other words, most Americans had succeeded *too* well at becoming English, regarding themselves as political equals entitled to basic constitutional freedoms. In the space of less than a generation, the logic of events made clear that despite all that the English and Americans shared, in the distribution of political power they were fundamentally at odds. And the call to arms at Lexington and Concord made retreat impossible.

On that point Paine was clear. It was the destiny of Americans to be republicans, not monarchists. It was the destiny of Americans to be independent, not subject to British dominion. It was the destiny of Americans to be American, not English. That, according to Thomas Paine, was common sense.

Chapter Summary

Britain's stunning victory in the Seven Years' War prompted it to embrace policies designed to administer new territories and boost revenue. These policies provoked a backlash in the colonies that would ultimately lead to the Revolutionary War.

- French and Indian forces inflicted major defeats on the British during the mid-1750s, in large part thanks to British policies that had alienated colonists and Indians alike.

- Starting in 1757, William Pitt's reforms galvanized the colonies, secured Indian allies, and salvaged the war. By 1760 the French had been defeated throughout the continent.

- Partly thanks to Pontiac's Rebellion, the British prohibited colonial settlement west of the Appalachians.

- The acts by Parliament in the early 1760s—the Proclamation of 1763, the Sugar Act, the Stamp Act, the Currency Act, and the Quartering Act—were all designed to generate revenue and bind the colonies to the empire.

- These new measures violated what Americans understood to be their constitutional and political liberties.

- Although Parliament repealed the Stamp Act in the face of colonial protests, it reasserted its authority to tax Americans by passing the Townshend Acts in 1767.

- With the passage of the Coercive Acts in 1774, many Americans concluded that all British actions in the past decade were part of a deliberate plot to enslave Americans by depriving them of property and liberty.

- The First Continental Congress denied Parliament any authority in the colonies except regulating trade; it also prohibited trade with Britain until the Coercive Acts were repealed.

- When in April 1775 British troops tried to seize arms at Concord, the first battle of the Revolution took place.

Digging Deeper

Fred Anderson, *Crucible of War* (2000), offers a magisterial account of the Seven Years' War; and Colin G. Calloway, *The Scratch of a Pen* (2006), explores the implications of British victory for American Indians, while Paul Mapp's *The Elusive West* (2011) brilliantly explains the significance of the Far West to interimperial competition. *The Stamp Act Crisis* (1953) by Edmund S. Morgan and Helen M. Morgan remains the clearest and most vivid portrayal of that defining moment. For American resistance after the Stamp Act, see Pauline Maier, *From Resistance to Revolution* (1972); and to understand that struggle as lived and recalled by a Boston artisan, read Alfred F. Young's engaging book *The Shoemaker and the Tea Party* (1999). Two key interpretations of the logic of revolutionary resistance in Massachusetts and Virginia are Robert A. Gross, *The Minutemen and Their World* (1976); and Timothy H. Breen, *Tobacco Culture* (1985).

Bernard Bailyn, *The Ideological Origins of the American Revolution* (1967), remains the classic study of the English Opposition and republican political thought in America. For a more recent exploration, stressing the long-standing nature of republican thinking in America, see Thomas P. Slaughter, *Independence* (2014). T. H. Breen's *The Marketplace of Revolution* (2004) takes a very different perspective, emphasizing the importance of economics and consumer sentiment. For biographies of eighteenth-century Americans who led—or opposed—the resistance to Britain, see Pauline Maier, *The Old Revolutionaries* (1980); Bailyn's *The Ordeal of Thomas Hutchinson* (1974); and two biographies of Thomas Paine (both published in 2006): *Thomas Paine and the Promise of America* by Harvey J. Kaye; and *Thomas Paine: Enlightenment, Revolution, and the Birth of Modern Nations* (2006) by Craig Nelson.

7

The American People and the American Revolution

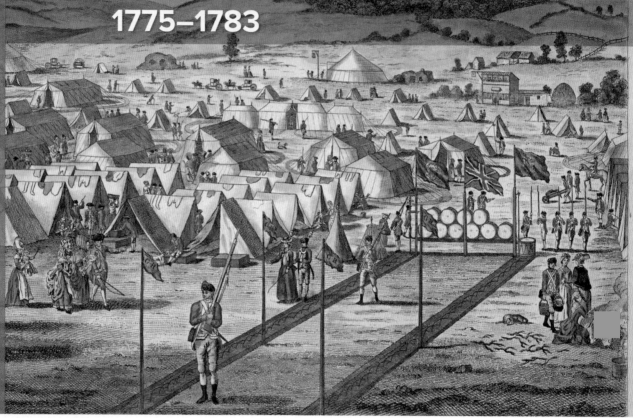

1775–1783

This British military encampment, drawn in 1780, illustrates some less noticed aspects of a wartime existence, not only for men, but for women as well. More than 20 women appear in this depiction; some are visitors, but both the British and American armies depended on thousands of women who cooked and washed for the men, nursed the wounded, buried the dead, and scavenged the field for clothing and equipment. Note that a great many of the tents have laundry spread out to dry across their ridgelines.

©Anne S.K. Brown Military Collection, Brown University Library

>> An American Story

"WILL HE FIGHT?"

From a high place somewhere in the city—Beacon Hill, perhaps, or Copse Hill—General Thomas Gage looked down on Boston. Through a spyglass his gaze traveled over the church belfries and steeples, the roofs of brick and white frame houses. Finally he fixed his sights on a figure far in the distance across the Charles River. The man was perched atop a crude fortification on Breed's Hill, an elevation lying just below Bunker Hill on the Charlestown peninsula. Gage took the measure of his enemy: an older man, past middle age, a sword swinging beneath his homespun coat, a broad-brimmed hat shading his eyes. As he passed the spyglass to his ally, an American loyalist, Gage asked Abijah Willard if he knew the man on the fort. Willard peered across the Charles and identified his own brother-in-law, Colonel William Prescott. A veteran of the Seven Years' War, Prescott was now a leader in the rebel army laying siege to Boston.

"Will he fight?" Gage wondered aloud.

"I cannot answer for his men," Willard replied, "but Prescott will fight you to the gates of hell."

Fight they did on June 17, 1775, both William Prescott and his men. The evening before, three regiments had followed the colonel from Cambridge to Breed's Hill—soldiers drawn from the thousands of militia who had swarmed to surround British-occupied Boston after the bloodshed at Lexington and Concord. All through the night, they dug deep trenches and built up high earthen walls atop the hill. At the first light of day, a British warship spotted the new rebel outpost and opened fire. By noon barges were ferrying British troops under Major General William Howe across the half mile of river that separated Boston from Charlestown. The 1,600 raw rebel troops tensed at the sight of scarlet-coated soldiers streaming ashore, glittering bayonets grasped at the ready. The rebels were farmers and artisans, not professional soldiers, and they were frightened out of their wits.

But Prescott and his men held their ground. The British charged Breed's Hill twice, and Howe watched in horror as streams of fire felled his troops. Finally, during the third British frontal assault, the rebels ran out of ammunition and were forced to withdraw. Redcoats poured into the rebel fort, bayoneting its handful of remaining defenders. By nightfall the British had taken Breed's Hill and the rest of the Charlestown peninsula. They had bought a dark triumph at

©ART Collection/Alamy

| *Bookstore owner, voracious reader, and occasional street fighter, burly Henry Knox superintended the patriot artillery during the Battle of Bunker Hill.*

the cost of 228 dead and 800 wounded.

The cost came high in loyalties as well. The fighting on Breed's Hill fed the hatred of Britain that had been building since April. Throughout America, preparations for war intensified: militia in every colony mustered; communities stockpiled arms and ammunition. Around Charlestown civilians fled the countryside, abandoning homes and shops set afire by the British shelling of Breed's Hill. "The roads filled with frightened women and children, some in carts with their tattered furniture, others on foot fleeing into the woods," recalled Hannah Winthrop, one of their number.

The bloody, indecisive fight on the Charlestown peninsula known as the Battle of Bunker Hill actually took place on Breed's Hill. And the exchange between Thomas Gage and Abijah Willard that is said to have preceded the battle may not have taken place. But the story has persisted in the folklore of the

American Revolution. Whether it really happened or not, the conversation between Gage and Willard raised the question that both sides wanted answered. Were Americans willing to fight for independence from British rule? It was one thing, after all, to oppose the British ministry's policy of taxation. It was another to support a rebellion for which the ultimate price of failure was hanging for treason. And it was another matter entirely for men to wait nervously atop a hill as the seasoned troops of their own "mother country" marched toward them with the intent to kill.

Indeed, the question "Will they fight?" was revolutionary shorthand for a host of other questions concerning how ordinary Americans would react to the tug of loyalties between long-established colonial governments and a long-revered parent nation and monarch. For slaves, the question revolved around their allegiance to masters who spoke of liberty or to their masters' enemies who promised liberation. For those who led the rebels, it was a question of strengthening the resolve of the undecided, coordinating resistance, instilling discipline—translating the *will* to fight into the *ability* to do so. And for those who believed the rebellion was a madness whipped up by artful politicians, it was a question of whether to remain silent or risk speaking out, whether to take up arms for the king or flee. All these questions were raised, of necessity, by the act of revolution. But the barrel of a rifle shortened them to a single, pointed question: Will you fight? <<

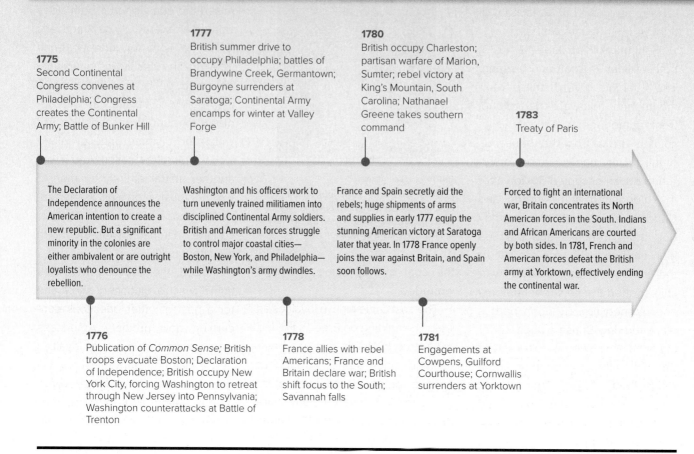

1775
Second Continental Congress convenes at Philadelphia; Congress creates the Continental Army; Battle of Bunker Hill

1777
British summer drive to occupy Philadelphia; battles of Brandywine Creek, Germantown; Burgoyne surrenders at Saratoga; Continental Army encamps for winter at Valley Forge

1780
British occupy Charleston; partisan warfare of Marion, Sumter; rebel victory at King's Mountain, South Carolina; Nathanael Greene takes southern command

1783
Treaty of Paris

The Declaration of Independence announces the American intention to create a new republic. But a significant minority in the colonies are either ambivalent or are outright loyalists who denounce the rebellion.

Washington and his officers work to turn unevenly trained militiamen into disciplined Continental Army soldiers. British and American forces struggle to control major coastal cities—Boston, New York, and Philadelphia—while Washington's army dwindles.

France and Spain secretly aid the rebels; huge shipments of arms and supplies in early 1777 equip the stunning American victory at Saratoga later that year. In 1778 France openly joins the war against Britain, and Spain soon follows.

Forced to fight an international war, Britain concentrates its North American forces in the South. Indians and African Americans are courted by both sides. In 1781, French and American forces defeat the British army at Yorktown, effectively ending the continental war.

1776
Publication of *Common Sense;* British troops evacuate Boston; Declaration of Independence; British occupy New York City, forcing Washington to retreat through New Jersey into Pennsylvania; Washington counterattacks at Battle of Trenton

1778
France allies with rebel Americans; France and Britain declare war; British shift focus to the South; Savannah falls

1781
Engagements at Cowpens, Guilford Courthouse; Cornwallis surrenders at Yorktown

THE DECISION FOR INDEPENDENCE

THE DELEGATES TO THE SECOND Continental Congress gathered at Philadelphia on May 10, 1775, just one month after the battles at Lexington and Concord. They had to determine whether independence or reconciliation offered the best way to protect the liberties of their colonies.

For a brash, ambitious lawyer from Braintree, Massachusetts, British abuses dictated only one course. "The Cancer [of official corruption] is too deeply rooted," wrote John Adams, "and too far spread to be cured by anything short of cutting it out entire." Yet, during the spring and summer of 1775, even strong advocates of independence did not openly seek a separation from Britain. If the radicals' objective of independence was ever to be achieved, greater agreement among Americans had to be attained. Moderates and conservatives harbored deep misgivings about independence: they had to be brought along slowly.

The Second Continental Congress

To bring them along, Congress adopted the "Olive Branch Petition" in July 1775. Drawn up by Pennsylvania's John Dickinson, the document affirmed American loyalty to George III and asked the king to disavow the policies of his principal ministers. At the same time, Congress issued a declaration denying that the colonies aimed at independence. Yet, less than a month earlier, Congress had authorized the creation of a rebel military force, the **Continental Army**, and had issued paper money to pay for the troops.

AGGRESSIVE BRITISH RESPONSE A Congress that sued for peace while preparing for war was a puzzle that British politicians—least of all, Lord George Germain—did not even try to understand. A tough-minded statesman now charged with overseeing colonial affairs, Germain was determined to subdue the rebellion by force. George III proved just as stubborn: he refused to receive the Olive Branch Petition. By the end of that year, Parliament had shut down all trade with the colonies and had ordered the Royal Navy to seize colonial merchant ships on the high seas. In November 1775 Virginia's royal governor, Lord Dunmore, offered freedom to any slaves who would join the British. During January of the next year, he ordered the shelling of Norfolk, Virginia, reducing that town to smoldering rubble.

British belligerence withered the cause of reconciliation within Congress and the colonies. Support for independence gained more momentum from the overwhelming reception of Paine's *Common Sense* in January 1776. Radicals in Congress realized that the future was theirs and were ready to act. In April 1776 the delegates opened American trade to every nation in the world except Great Britain; a month later Congress advised the colonies to establish new state governments. And on June 7 Virginia's Richard Henry Lee offered the motion "that these United Colonies are, and of right ought to be, free and independent States . . . and that all political connection between them and the State of Great Britain is, and ought to be, totally dissolved."

The Declaration

Congress postponed a final vote on Lee's motion until July. Some opposition still lingered among delegates from the middle colonies, and a committee appointed to write a declaration of independence needed time to complete its work. That committee included some of the leading delegates in Congress: John Adams, Benjamin Franklin, Connecticut's Roger Sherman, and New York's Robert Livingston. But the man who did most of the drafting was a young planter and lawyer from western Virginia.

THOMAS JEFFERSON Thomas Jefferson was just 33 years old in the summer of 1776 when he withdrew to his lodgings on the outskirts of Philadelphia, pulled a portable writing desk onto his lap, and wrote the statement that would explain American independence to a "candid world." In the document's brief opening section, Jefferson set forth a general justification of revolution that invoked the "self-evident truths" of human equality and "unalienable rights" to "life, liberty, and the pursuit of happiness." These natural rights had been "endowed" to all persons "by their Creator," the Declaration pointed out; thus there was no need to appeal to the narrower claim of the "rights of Englishmen."

BLAMING GEORGE III While the first part of the Declaration served notice that Americans no longer considered themselves English, its second and longer section denied England any authority in the colonies. In its detailed history of American grievances against the British Empire, the Declaration referred only once to Parliament. Instead, it blamed George III for a "long train of abuses and usurpations" designed to achieve "absolute despotism." Unlike *Common Sense,* the Declaration denounced only the reigning king of England; it did not attack the institution of monarchy itself. But like *Common Sense,* the Declaration affirmed that government originated in the consent of the governed and upheld the right of the people to overthrow oppressive rule.

Later generations have debated what Jefferson meant by the "pursuit of happiness" and whether he had either women or black Americans in mind when he wrote the famous phrase "all men are created equal." His own contemporaries in Congress did not pause to consider those questions and surely would have found themselves divided if they had. No matter. By firmly grounding the Declaration on the natural rights due all people, Jefferson placed equality at the center of the new nation's identity, setting the framework for a debate that would continue over the next two centuries. Congress adopted the Declaration of Independence on July 4, 1776.

THE BRITISH PERSPECTIVE The colonies thus followed the course set by common sense into the storms of independence. To those Britons who took a wide view of their empire, it made no sense whatsoever, and their perplexity is understandable. Since the end of the Seven Years' War, Britain had added to its overseas dominion a vast and diverse number of subjects formerly under French rule—Native Americans, French Catholic Canadians, peoples of African descent in the Caribbean. And then there was India, part Hindu, part Muslim, most of it ruled by the East India Company. What better, more efficient way to regulate this sprawling empire than to bring all of its parts under the rule of a sovereign Parliament? What other way could the empire endure and prosper—and fend off future challenges from Catholic, monarchical France? Of course, it was impossible to grant colonials the same rights as Britons: it would require an empire firmly based on hierarchy to hold chaos at bay. Most colonial

| *Rough draft of the Declaration of Independence*
©CORBIS/Corbis via Getty Images

elites assented to the logic of that position—East India Company officials, Bengal nabobs, Canadian traders and landlords. Only the leading men in Britain's original 13 colonies would not go along.

American Loyalists

But the sentiment for independence was not universal. Americans who would not back the rebellion, supporters of the king and Parliament, numbered perhaps one-fifth of the population in 1775. While they proclaimed themselves **loyalists**, their rebel opponents dubbed them "tories"—"a thing whose head is in England, whose body is in America, and whose neck ought to be stretched." That division made the Revolution a conflict pitting Americans against one another as well as the British. In truth, the war for independence was the first American civil war.

SOURCES OF LOYALIST SUPPORT Predictably, the king and Parliament commanded the strongest support in colonies that had been wracked by internal strife earlier in the eighteenth century. In New York, New Jersey, Pennsylvania, and the Carolinas, not only did memories of old struggles sharpen worries of future upheaval, but old enemies often took different sides in the Revolution. The Carolina backcountry emerged as a stronghold of loyalist sentiment because of influential local men who cast their lot with Britain. To win support against Carolina's rebels, whose ranks included most wealthy coastal planters, western loyalist leaders played on ordinary settlers' resentments of privileged easterners. Decades-old grievances also influenced the revolutionary allegiances of former land rioters of New York and New Jersey. If their old landlord opponents opted for the rebel cause, the tenants took up loyalism.

Other influences also fostered allegiance to Britain. Government officials who owed their jobs to the empire, major city merchants who depended on British trade, and Anglicans living outside the South retained strong ties to the parent country. Loyalists were also disproportionately represented among recent immigrants from the British Isles. The inhabitants of Georgia, the newest colony, inclined toward the king, as did the Highland Scots, many of whom had arrived in the colonies as soldiers during the Seven Years' War or had worked for a short time in the southern backcountry as tobacco merchants and Indian traders.

Although a substantial minority, loyalists never became numerous enough anywhere to pose a serious menace to the Revolution. A more formidable threat was posed by the British army. And the greatest threat of all was posed by those very Americans who claimed that they wanted independence. For the question remained: Would they fight?

✔ **REVIEW**

What were the arguments for and against independence, and how did the advocates for independence prevail?

| This detail from a painting, commemorating the signing of the Declaration of Independence, shows Benjamin Franklin (seated center) weighing the consequences of the decisions he and his colleagues are about to undertake. John Hancock, the president of the Congress, is reported to have remarked, "We must be unanimous; there must be no pulling different ways; we must all hang together." Franklin is said to have rejoined, "Yes, we must indeed all hang together, or most assuredly, we shall all hang separately."

©Philadelphia History Museum at the Atwater Kent/Courtesy of Historical Society of Pennsylvania Collection/Bridgeman Images

ABIGAIL AND JOHN ADAMS SPAR ON WOMEN'S RIGHTS AND THE AMERICAN REVOLUTION

While she managed the family farm in Braintree, Massachusetts, he served as a delegate to the Continental Congress at Philadelphia, running the war and framing a new national government. She had concerns about the war and advice about the future government:

DOCUMENT 1
Abigail Adams to John Adams, March 31, 1776

I wish you would ever write me a Letter half as long as I write you; and tell me if you may where your Fleet are gone? What sort of Defence Virginia can make against our common Enemy . . . ? Whether it is so situated as to make an able Defence? Are not the Gentery Lords and the common people vassals . . . ?

I have sometimes been ready to think that the passion for Liberty cannot be Eaquelly Strong in the Breasts of those who have been accustomed to deprive their fellow Creatures of theirs. . . .

I long to hear that you have declared an independency—and by the way in the new Code of Laws which I suppose it will be necessary for you to make I desire you would Remember the Ladies, and be more generous and favourable to them than your ancestors. Do not put such unlimited power into the hands of the Husbands. Remember all Men would be tyrants if they could. If perticular care and attention is not paid to the Ladies we are determined to foment a Rebelion, and will not hold ourselves bound by any Laws in which we have no voice, or Representation.

That our Sex are Naturally Tyrannical is a Truth so thoroughly established as to admit of no dispute, but such of you as wish to be happy willingly give up the harsh title of Master for the more tender and endearing one of Friend. Why then, not put it out of the power of the vicious and the Lawless to use us with cruelty and indignity with impunity. Men of Sense in all Ages abhor those customs which treat us only as the vassals of your Sex. Regard us then as Beings placed by providence under your protection and in imitation of the Supreem Being make use of the power only for our happiness.

Source: Adams Family Papers, Massachusetts Historical Society.

DOCUMENT 2
John Adams to Abigail Adams, April 14, 1776

You justly complain of my short Letters, but the critical State of Things and the Multiplicity of Avocations must plead my Excuse. . . . You ask what Sort of Defence Virginia can make. I believe they will make an able Defence. Their Militia and minute Men have been some time employed in training themselves. . . . Their neighbouring Sister or rather Daughter Colony of North Carolina, which is a warlike Colony, and has several Battallions at the Continental Expence, as well as a pretty good Militia, are ready to assist them. . . . The Gentry are very rich, and the common People very poor.

This Inequality of Property, gives an Aristocratical Turn to all their Proceedings, and occasions a strong Aversion in their Patricians, to Common Sense. But the Spirit of these Barons, is coming down, and it must submit. . . .

As to your extraordinary Code of Laws, I cannot but laugh. We have been told that our Struggle has loosened the bands of Government every where. That Children and Apprentices were disobedient—that schools and Colledges were grown turbulent—that Indians slighted their Guardians and Negroes grew insolent to their Masters. But your Letter was the first Intimation that another Tribe more numerous and powerfull than the rest were grown discontented. —This is rather too coarse a Complement but you are so saucy I wont blot it out.

Depend upon it, We know better than to repeal our Masculine systems. Altho they are in full Force, you know they are little more than Theory. We dare not exert our Power in its full Latitude. We are obliged to go fair, and softly, and in Practice you know We are the subjects. We have only the Name of Masters, and rather than give up this, which would completely subject Us to the Despotism of the Peticoat, I hope General Washington, and all our brave Heroes would fight.

Source: Adams Family Papers, Massachusetts Historical Society.

DOCUMENT 3
Abigail Adams to John Adams, May 7, 1776

I can not say that I think you very generous to the Ladies, for whilst you are proclaiming peace and good will to Men, Emancipating all Nations, you insist on retaining an absolute power over Wives, But you must remember that Arbitrary power is like most other things which are very hard, very liable to be broken—and notwithstanding all your wise Laws and Maxims we have it in our power not only to free ourselves but to subdue our Masters, and without violence throw both your natural and legal authority at our feet

> Charm by accepting, by submitting sway
> Yet have our Humour most when we obey.

Source: Adams Family Papers, Massachusetts Historical Society.

THINKING CRITICALLY

What rights for women did Abigail Adams advocate? What rights receive no mention in her March 31st letter? What did John Adams mean by "another tribe"? How did he respond to his wife's advice? Both Adamses were keenly aware of class and racial inequalities. How did that awareness shape their respective views of gender inequality?

THE FIGHTING IN THE NORTH

IN THE SUMMER OF 1775 Americans who wished to remain neutral probably outnumbered either loyalists or rebels. From the standpoint of mere survival, staying neutral made more sense than fighting for independence. Even the most ardent advocates of American rights had reason to harbor doubts, given the odds against the rebel colonists defeating the armed forces of the British Empire.

GEORGE WASHINGTON, GENERAL Perhaps no friend of American liberty saw more clearly how slim the chances of a rebel victory were than George Washington. But Washington's principles, and his sense of honor, prevailed. June of 1775 found him, then 43 years old, attending the deliberations of the Second Continental Congress and dressed—a bit conspicuously—in his officer's uniform. The other delegates listened closely to his opinions on military matters, because Washington was the most celebrated American veteran of the Seven Years' War who remained young enough to lead a campaign. Better still, as a southerner he could bring his region into what thus far had remained mostly New England's fight. Congress readily appointed him commander-in-chief of a newly created Continental Army.

The Two Armies at Bay

Thus did Washington find himself, only a month later, looking to bring some order to the rebel forces massing around Boston. He knew he faced a formidable foe.

Highly trained, ably led, and efficiently equipped, the king's troops were seasoned professionals. Rigorous drills and often severe discipline welded rank-and-file soldiers, men drawn mostly from the bottom of British society, into a savage fighting machine. At the height of the campaign in America, reinforcements brought the number of British troops to 50,000, strengthened by some 30,000 **Hessian** mercenaries from Germany and the support of half the ships in the British navy, the largest in the world.

"REGULARS" VS. THE MILITIA Washington was more modest about the army under his command, and he had much to be modest about. At first Congress recruited his fighting force of 16,600 rebel "regulars," the Continental Army, from the ranks of local New England militia bands. Although enlistments swelled briefly during the patriotic enthusiasm of 1775, for the rest of the war Washington's Continentals suffered chronic shortages of men and supplies. Even strong supporters of the Revolution hesitated to join the regular army, with its low pay and strict discipline and the constant threat of disease and danger. Most men preferred to fight instead as members of local **militia** units, the "irregular" troops who turned out to support the regular army whenever British forces came close to their neighborhoods.

The general reluctance to join the Continental Army created a host of difficulties for its commander and for Congress. Washington wanted and needed an army whose size and military capability could be counted on in long campaigns. He could not create an effective fighting force out of militias that mustered occasionally or men who enlisted for short stints in the Continental Army. In contrast, most republican leaders feared standing armies and idealized "citizen-soldiers"—men of civic virtue who volunteered whenever needed—as the backbone of the common defense. "Oh, that I was a soldier," chubby John Adams fantasized in 1775. "Everyone must and will and shall be a soldier."

But everyone did not become a soldier, and the dwindling number of volunteers gradually overcame republican fears of standing armies. In September 1776 Congress set terms in the Continental Army at a minimum of three years or for the duration of the war and assigned each state to raise a certain number of troops. They offered every man who enlisted in the army a cash bounty and a yearly clothing issue; enlistees for the duration were offered 100 acres of land as well. Still the problem of recruitment persisted. Less than a year later, Congress recommended that the states adopt a draft, but Congress had no authority to compel the states to meet their troop quotas.

Even in the summer of 1775, before enlistments fell off, Washington was worried. As his inexperienced Continentals laid siege to British-occupied Boston, most officers provided no real leadership, and the men under their command shirked their duties. They slipped away from camp at night; they left sentry duty before being relieved; they took potshots at the British; they tolerated filthy conditions in their camps.

Meanwhile, the war began to take a toll on civilians. Refugees on foot and in hastily packed carts filled the roads, fled advancing armies. Those who remained to protect their homes and property might be caught in the crossfire of contending forces or cut off from supplies of food and firewood. Loyalists who remained in areas occupied by rebel troops faced harassment, imprisonment, or the confiscation of their property. Rebel sympathizers met similar fates in regions held by the British. The demands of war also disrupted family economies throughout the northern countryside. The seasons of intense fighting drew men off into military service just when their labor was most needed on family farms.

WOMEN AND THE WAR While Washington strove to impose discipline on his Continentals, he also attempted, without success, to rid himself of "the Women of the Army." Thousands of poor women, as many as 1 for every 15 soldiers, drifted after the troops. In return for half-rations, they cooked and washed for the men, nursed the wounded, buried the dead, and scavenged the field for clothing and equipment. Necessity mattered more than patriotism, and a great many women attached themselves to the better-supplied British camps. Nonetheless, these women provided indispensable (if often underappreciated) work for Washington's forces, not least by reducing the desertion rate of their male companions.

Other colonial women played more direct roles in the Revolution. Some dressed as men in order to enlist and fight alongside their brothers or husbands. Deborah Sampson of

>> MAPPING THE PAST <<

PATTERNS OF ALLEGIANCE

©Archive Photos/Stringer/Getty Images

"Rebellion is the foulest of all crimes."—New Jersey Loyalist James Moody, 1761

CONTEXT

History shaped the geography of rebellion in British North America. Rebels enjoyed strong support throughout most of the colonies, but perhaps one out of five colonists remained loyal to the crown. As you can see in this map, loyalism was concentrated in the mid-Atlantic (particularly parts of New York, New Jersey, and Maryland) and in the South (the Carolinas, Georgia, and the Gulf Coast). In these places, the Revolution could take on the character of a civil war, one fueled by long-standing grievances over class, ethnicity, and local politics.

Legend:
- Strongly loyalist
- Loyalist or neutral Indians
- Strongly neutralist
- Strong support for rebels
- Other British territory

MAP READING

1. Where in the thirteen colonies was neutrality the norm?
2. What coastal regions did loyalists control?
3. To what degree did allegiance map onto colonial borders?

MAP INTERPRETATION

1. Imagine you are a British war planner looking at this map in 1776. How would the geographic pattern of rebellion, neutrality, and loyalism shape your war strategy?
2. Might the war have ended differently if loyalists had been geographically concentrated instead of spread out among several colonies?

Massachusetts served for nearly a year and a half, protecting her secret even after being shot in battle. Another female soldier, Sally St. Clair, had her gender revealed only when she was killed fighting the British. Still other women achieved fame through their heroic service—women like the daring spy Lydia Darragh, the wartime messenger Deborah Champion, and 25-year-old Margaret Corbin, who was gravely wounded while "manning" cannon after her artillerist husband was shot dead.

Notwithstanding such remarkable stories, the prevailing gender norms of the day meant that the vast majority of colonial women spent the war at the home front. Those with fathers or husbands in the army had to assume responsibility for running farms and businesses, raising children, and protecting their households in wartime. In addition, thousands of women helped to supply the troops by sewing clothing, making blankets, and saving rags and lead weights for bandages and bullets. Others organized relief for the widows and orphans of soldiers, and led protests against merchants who hoarded scarce commodities. Wives and daughters were left to assume the work of husbands and sons while coping with loneliness, anxiety, and grief. Often enough the disruptions, flight, and loss of family members left lasting scars. Two years after she fled British campaigns into upstate New York, Ann Eliza Bleecker confessed to a friend, "I muse so long on the dead until I am unfit for the company of the living."

Laying Strategies

At the same time that he tried to discipline the Continentals, Washington designed a defensive strategy to compensate for their weakness. To avoid exposing raw rebel troops on "open ground against their Superiors in number and Discipline," he planned to fight the British from strong fortifications. With that aim in mind, in March 1776, Washington barricaded his army on Dorchester Heights, an elevation commanding Boston Harbor from the south. That maneuver, which allowed American artillery to fire on enemy warships, confirmed a decision already made by the British to evacuate their entire army from Boston and sail for Halifax, Nova Scotia.

THE BRITISH CHOOSE CONVENTIONAL WAR Britain had hoped to reclaim its colonies with a strategy of strangling the resistance in Massachusetts. But by the spring of 1776 it saw clearly that more was required than a show of force against New England. Instead, Britain's leaders chose to wage a conventional war in America, capturing major cities and crushing the Continental forces in a decisive battle. Military victory, the British believed, would enable them to restore political control and reestablish imperial authority.

The first target was New York City. General William Howe and Lord George Germain, the British officials now charged with overseeing the war, chose that seaport for its central location and—they hoped—its large loyalist population. Howe's army intended to move from New York City up the Hudson River, meeting with British troops under General Sir Guy Carleton coming south from Canada. Either the British

drive would lure Washington into a major engagement, crushing the Continentals, or, if unopposed, the British offensive would cut America in two, smothering resistance to the south by isolating New England.

HOWE BROTHERS The strategy was sounder than the men placed in charge of executing it. Concern for preserving troops addicted General Howe to caution, when daring more would have carried the day. Howe's brother, Admiral Lord Richard Howe, the head of naval operations in America, also stopped short of pressing the British advantage, owing to his personal desire for reconciliation. The reluctance of the Howe brothers to fight became the formula for British frustration in the two years that followed.

THE CAMPAIGNS IN NEW YORK AND NEW JERSEY By mid-August, 32,000 British troops, including 8,000 Hessians, the largest expeditionary force of the eighteenth century, faced Washington's army of 23,000, which had marched down from Boston to take up positions on Long Island. At dawn on August 22 the Howe brothers launched their offense, easily pushing the rebel army back across the East River to Manhattan. After lingering on Long Island for a month, the Howes again lurched into action, ferrying their

©Archive Photos/Stringer/Getty Images

| *At the Battle of Princeton, British troops bayoneted the rebel general Hugh Mercer, an assault later memorialized in this drawing. It focuses attention not only on Mercer's courage but also on the savagery of the redcoats, both of which helped the rebels gain civilian support.*

forces to Kip's Bay, just a few miles south of Harlem. When the British landed, the handful of rebel defenders at Kip's Bay fled—straight into the towering wrath of Washington, who happened on the scene during the rout. For once the general lost his habitual self-restraint, flogged both officers and men with his riding crop, and came close to being captured himself. But the Howes remained reluctant to hit hard, letting Washington's army escape from Manhattan to West-chester County.

BRITISH CAPTURE NEW YORK CITY   Throughout the fall of 1776 General Howe's forces followed as Washington's fled southward across New Jersey. On December 7, with the

British nipping at their heels, the rebels crossed the Delaware River into Pennsylvania. There Howe stopped, pulling back most of his army to winter in New York City and leaving the Hessians to hold the British line of advance along the New Jersey side of the Delaware River.

REBEL VICTORIES AT TRENTON AND PRINCETON
Although the retreat had shriveled rebel strength to only 3,000 men, Washington decided that the campaign of 1776 was not over. On a snowy Christmas night, the Continentals floated back across the Delaware, picked their way over roads iced with sleet, and finally slid into Hessian-held Trenton at eight in the morning. One thousand German soldiers, still

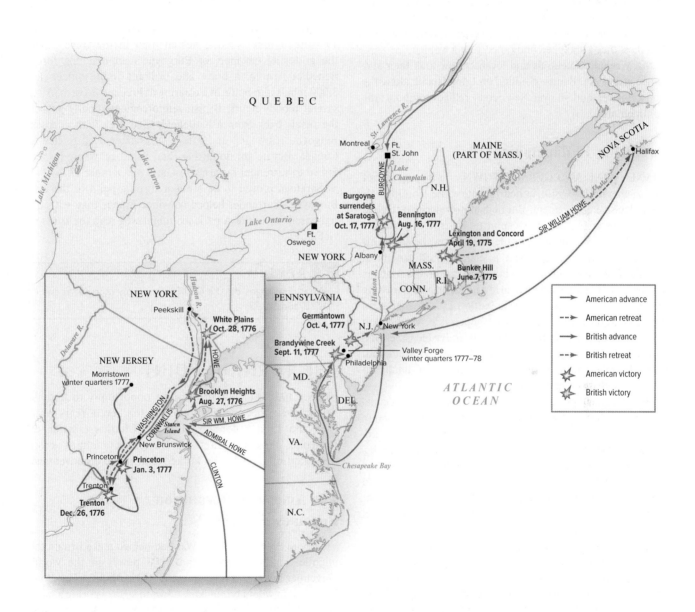

THE FIGHTING IN THE NORTH, 1775–1777

After the British withdrew from Boston in 1775, they launched an attack on New York City the following year. Washington was forced to retreat northward, then across the Hudson and south into New Jersey and Pennsylvania, before surprising the British at Trenton and Princeton. Burgoyne's surrender at Saratoga in 1777 marked a turning point in the war. If General Howe had moved forces toward Albany, could he and General Burgoyne have split rebel New England from the rest of the former colonies? If so, how?

recovering from their spirited Christmas celebration and caught completely by surprise, quickly surrendered. Washington's luck held when, on January 3, 1777, the Continentals defeated British troops on the outskirts of Princeton, New Jersey.

During the winter of 1776–1777 the British lost more than battles: they alienated the very civilians whose loyalties they had hoped to maintain. In New York City the presence of the main body of the British army brought shortages of food and housing and caused constant friction between soldiers and city dwellers. In the New Jersey countryside still held by the Hessians, the situation was more desperate. Forced to live off the land, the Germans aroused resentment among local farmers by seizing "hay, oats, Indian corn, cattle, and horses, which were never or but very seldom paid for," as one loyalist admitted. The Hessians ransacked and destroyed homes and churches; they kidnapped and raped young women.

Many repulsed neutrals and loyalists now took their allegiance elsewhere. Bands of militia on Long Island, along the Hudson River, and all over New Jersey rallied to support the Continentals.

Capturing Philadelphia

BRANDYWINE AND GERMANTOWN   In the summer of 1777 General Howe still hoped to entice the Continentals into a decisive engagement. But he had now decided to goad the Americans into battle by capturing Philadelphia. Rather than risk a march through hostile New Jersey, he sailed his army to Maryland and began a march to Philadelphia, 50 miles away. Washington had hoped to stay on the strategic defensive, holding his smaller army together and harassing the enemy but avoiding full-scale battles. Howe's march on the new nation's capital made that impossible. Washington engaged Howe twice—in September at Brandywine Creek and in October in an early dawn attack at Germantown—but both times the rebels were beaten back. He had been unable to prevent the British occupation of Philadelphia.

But in Philadelphia, as in New York City, British occupation created hostile feelings, as the flood of troops drove up the price of food, fuel, and housing. While inflation hit hardest at the poor, the wealthy resented British officers who became their uninvited house guests. Philadelphians complained of redcoats looting their shops, trampling their gardens, and harassing them on the streets. Elizabeth Drinker, the wife of a Quaker merchant, confided in her diary that "I often feel afraid to go to bed."

Even worse, the British march through Maryland and Pennsylvania had outraged civilians, who fled before the army and then returned to find their homes and barns bare, their crops and livestock gone. Everywhere Howe's men went in the mid-Atlantic, they left in their wake Americans with compelling reasons to support the rebels. Worst of all, just days after Howe marched his occupying army into Philadelphia in the fall of 1777, another British commander in North America was surrendering his entire army to rebel forces at Saratoga, New York.

Disaster for the British at Saratoga

The calamity that befell the British at Saratoga was the doing of a glory-mongering general, John "Gentleman Johnny" Burgoyne. After his superior officer, Sir Guy Carleton, bungled a drive into New York in 1776, Burgoyne won approval to command another attack from Canada. The following summer he set out from Quebec with a force of 9,500 redcoats, 2,000 women and children, and a baggage train that included the commander's silver dining service, his dress uniforms, and numerous cases of his favorite champagne. As Burgoyne's bloated entourage lumbered southward, General Horatio Gates waited for it several miles below Saratoga at Bemis Heights, with an army more than 12,000 men strong.

BURGOYNE SURRENDERS AT SARATOGA   On September 19 Gates's rebel scouts, nested high in the trees, spied the glittering bayonets of Burgoyne's approaching force. Benedict Arnold, a brave and brilliant young officer, led 3,000 rebels into battle at a clearing at Freeman's Farm. After several bloody hours, British reinforcements finally pushed the rebels back from a battlefield piled high with corpses. Burgoyne regrouped and a few weeks later tried to flee to Canada. But he got no farther than Saratoga, where he was forced to surrender his army to Gates on October 17.

Saratoga proved to be a major turning point in the war. Burgoyne's surrender helped convince France that, with the right assistance, the Americans might well reap the fruits of victory.

> ✔ **REVIEW**
> What challenges did the Continental Army face between 1775 and 1777?

THE TURNING POINT

FRANCE HAD BEEN WAITING for an opportunity to humble Britain ever since being throttled in the Seven Years' War. Now the French foreign minister, Charles Gravier de Vergennes, took great interest in the drama unfolding across the Atlantic, and patiently worked to turn it to his advantage.

The American Revolution Becomes a Global War

Victory in the Seven Years' War had helped make Britain the mightiest military and commercial power in the world. Vergennes saw that if it lost most of its North American colonies, Britain would be cut back down to size, restoring a more favorable balance of power. Though France was building ships at a furious pace, in 1775 it didn't yet have a navy big enough for outright war. If Vergennes was going to help the rebels, he first had to do so quietly.

Initially, French authorities helped by simply looking the other way when rebel smugglers tried to buy guns and ammunition in their ports. The North Americans had no arms industry to speak of, so the rebellion totally depended on foreign imports. Painfully aware of this fact, the Continental Congress dispatched representatives to Europe, led by the resourceful Benjamin Franklin, in order to make arms deals and woo potential allies. Before long Vergennes convinced Spain to cooperate in a massive, covert supply program, jointly providing the Americans huge cash loans, desperately needed supplies, hundreds of tons of gunpowder, and tens of thousands of muskets. The victory at Saratoga was won with French muskets, and, with the navy nearly rebuilt, it helped Vergennes convince his cautious young king that the time had come for a formal alliance with the rebels against Britain.

France signed treaties of commerce, friendship, and alliance with America in early 1778; Congress eagerly approved them in May. Less than a year later Spain joined France, and by 1780 friendless Britain was at war with the Dutch, too.

Winding Down the War in the North

So it was that the Revolution widened into a global war after 1778. Preparing to fight France, Spain, and eventually Holland forced the British to divert resources and men from North America in order to fend off challenges all over the world. In May, Sir Henry Clinton replaced William Howe as commander-in-chief and received orders to withdraw from Philadelphia to New York City.

Only 18 miles outside Philadelphia, at Valley Forge, Washington and his Continentals were assessing their own situation. Some 11,000 rebel soldiers had passed a harrowing winter in that isolated spot, starving for want of food, freezing for lack of clothing, huddling in miserable huts, and hating the British who lay so close and yet so comfortably in Philadelphia. Both officers and rank-and-file cursed their fellow citizens, blaming their suffering on congressional disorganization and civilian indifference. Congress lacked both money to pay and maintain the army and an efficient system for dispensing provisions to the troops. Most farmers and merchants preferred to supply the British, who could pay handsomely, than to do business with a financially strapped Congress. What little did reach the army often was food too rancid to eat or clothing too rotten to wear. Perhaps 2,500 perished at Valley Forge, the victims of cold, hunger, and disease.

Why did civilians who supported the rebel cause allow the army to suffer? Probably because by the winter of 1777, the Continentals came mainly from social classes that received little consideration at any time. The respectable, propertied farmers and artisans who had laid siege to Boston in 1775 had stopped enlisting. Serving in their stead were single men in their teens and early 20s, some who joined the army out of desperation, others who were drafted, still others who were hired as substitutes for the more affluent. The landless sons of farmers, unemployed laborers, drifters, petty criminals, vagrants, indentured servants, slaves, even captured British and Hessian soldiers—all men with no other means and no other choice—were swept into the Continental Army. The social composition of the rebel rank-and-file had come to resemble that of the British army. It is the great irony of the Revolution: a war to protect liberty-and-property was waged by those Americans who were poorest and least free.

| A member of the Continental Congress (center) *refuses to look at the sufferings of cold, poorly clad white soldiers and a wounded African American fallen to the ground. Why would the British have published such a cartoon in 1778? What messages are conveyed?*

Source: Library of Congress, Prints and Photographs Division [LC-USZ62-46659]

The beginning of spring in 1778 brought a reprieve. Supplies arrived at Valley Forge, and so did a fellow calling himself Baron von Steuben, a penniless Prussian soldier of fortune. Although Washington's men had shown spirit and resilience ever since Trenton, they still lacked discipline and training. Those defects and more von Steuben began to remedy. Barking orders and spewing curses in German and French, the baron (and his translators) drilled the rebel regiments to march in formation and to handle their bayonets like proper Prussian soldiers. By the summer of 1778 morale had rebounded.

Spoiling for action after their long winter, Washington's army, now numbering nearly 13,500, harassed Clinton's army as it marched overland from Philadelphia to New York City. On June 28 at Monmouth Courthouse a long, confused battle ended in a draw. After both armies retired for the night, Clinton's forces slipped away to safety in New York City. Washington pursued, but he lacked the numbers to launch an all-out assault on New York City.

ARMY UPRISINGS During the two hard winters that followed, resentments mounted among the rank-and-file over spoiled food, inadequate clothing, and arrears in pay. The army retaliated with mutinies. Between 1779 and 1780, officers managed to quell uprisings in three New England regiments. But in January 1781 both the Pennsylvania and New Jersey lines in an outright **mutiny** marched on Philadelphia, where Congress had reconvened. Order returned only after Congress promised back pay and provisions and Washington put two ringleaders in front of a firing squad.

War in the West

The battles between Washington's Continentals and the British made the war in the West seem, by comparison, a sideshow of attacks and counterattacks that settled little. American fighters such as George Rogers Clark, with great daring, captured outposts such as Kaskaskia and Vincennes, without materially affecting the outcome of the war. Yet the conflict sparked a tremendous upheaval in the West, both from the dislocations of war and from the disease that spread in war's wake.

INDIANS CAUGHT IN A CROSSFIRE The disruptions were so widespread because the "War for Independence" had also become a war involving the imperial powers of Britain, France, and Spain. The same jockeying for advantage went on in the West as had occurred in previous imperial wars. The United States as well as the European powers pressed Indian tribes to become allies and attacked them when they did not. Caught in the crossfire, some Indian nations were pushed to the brink of their own civil war, splitting into pro-American or pro-British factions. None suffered more than the mighty Iroquois. When days of impassioned speeches failed to secure

Source: Library of Congress, Prints and Photographs Division [LC-DIG-ppmsca-19864]

While both sides in the Revolution sought Indian allies, the American rebels spread sensationalized stories of British and Indian cruelties. This London cartoon shows the prime minister, Lord North, joining with Indians to feast on a child, an act of cannibalism that revolts even a dog. The archbishop of York promises to walk in God's ways, but is followed by his porter, who professes that "we are hellish good Christians" and carries boxes of scalping knives, tomahawks, and crucifixes. Such propaganda fueled Americans' hatred of Indians as they pushed westward.

a unified Iroquois policy regarding the Revolution, the six confederated tribes went their own ways. Most Tuscaroras and Oneidas remained neutral or joined the Americans, whereas Mohawk, Onondaga, Seneca, and Cayuga warriors aided the British by attacking frontier settlements. This pro-British faction rallied around the remarkable Mohawk leader Joseph Brant. Bilingual, literate, and formidable in war, Brant helped lead devastating raids across the frontiers of New York and Pennsylvania. In response Washington dispatched troops into Iroquois country, where they put the torch to 40 towns and destroyed fields and orchards everywhere they went. Many Iroquois perished the following winter—whichever side they had supported in the war—and the confederacy emerged from the Revolution with but a shadow of its former power.

Other native peoples switched allegiances more than once. Near St. Louis, a young Kaskaskia chief, Jean Baptiste de Coigne, allied first with the French, then joined the British and briefly threw in his lot with the Spanish, before finally joining the Virginians. Indians understood well that the pressures of war always threatened to deprive them of their homelands. "You are drawing so close to us that we can almost hear the noise of your axes felling our Trees," one Shawnee told the Americans. Another group of Indians concluded in 1784 that the Revolutionary War had been "the greatest blow that could have been dealt us, unless it had been our total destruction." Thousands fled the raids and counter-raids, while whole villages relocated. Hundreds made their way even beyond the Mississippi, to seek shelter in territory claimed by Spain. The aftershocks

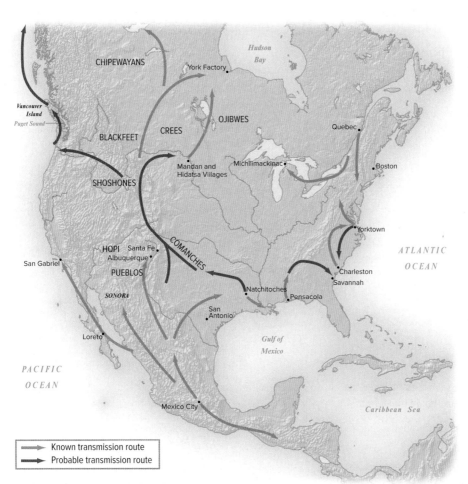

Smallpox spread across North America beginning late in 1775 as American forces launched an unsuccessful attack on the city of Quebec in Canada. The routes of transmission give only a rough idea of the disease's spread and impact, as it moved down the Eastern Seaboard and around the Gulf of Mexico, and then penetrated the interior, where the scattered surviving data make the pandemic's progress much harder to track. But the ravages of smallpox, combined with the disruptions sparked by the western raids of the Revolutionary War, placed severe stress on Indian peoples all across the continent. The disruption continued through the end of the eighteenth century.

Known transmission route
Probable transmission route

and dislocations continued for the next two decades; an entire generation of Native Americans grew up with war as a constant companion.

SMALLPOX PANDEMIC The political instability was vastly compounded by a smallpox epidemic that broke out first among American troops besieging Quebec in 1775. The disease soon spread to Continentals in New England, and Washington was obliged to inoculate them—secretly, for the vaccination left many soldiers temporarily weakened. From New England, the pox spread south along the coast, eventually reached New Orleans and next leapt to Mexico City by the autumn of 1779. From New Orleans it spread via fur-traders up the Mississippi River and across the central plains, and from New Spain northward as well. By the time the pandemic burned out in 1782, it had felled over 130,000. By contrast, the Revolutionary War caused the deaths of some 8,000 soldiers while fighting in battle and another 13,000 from disease, including the mortality from smallpox.

> ✓ **REVIEW**
>
> How did the Revolution become a global war, and what were conditions like for both soldiers and civilians?

THE STRUGGLE IN THE SOUTH

DESPITE THEIR ARMED PRESENCE IN the North, the British had come to believe by the autumn of 1778 that their most vital aim was to regain their colonies in the mainland South. The Chesapeake and the Carolinas were more profitable to the empire and more strategically important, being so much closer to rich British sugar islands in the West Indies. Inspired by this new "southern strategy," Clinton dispatched forces to the Caribbean and Florida. In addition, the British laid plans for a new offensive drive into the Carolinas and Virginia.

BRITAIN'S SOUTHERN STRATEGY English politicians and generals believed that the war could be won in the South. Loyalists were numerous, they believed, especially in the backcountry, where resentment of the patriot seaboard would encourage frontier folk to take up arms for the king at the first show of British force. And southern rebels—especially the vulnerable planters along the coast—could not afford to turn their guns away from their slaves. So, at least, the British theorized. All that was needed, they concluded, was that the British army establish a beachhead in the South and then, in league with loyalists, drive northward, up the coast.

British and American Forces in the Revolutionary War Compared

	IN THEORY	ON THE GROUND
British	Advantage: superior army	Advantage: training paid off in winning many major battles and controlling cities
		Disadvantage: but formal training left British forces vulnerable to guerrilla attacks
	Advantage: superior navy	Advantage neutralized by French navy at Cornwallis's surrender
		Disadvantage: entry of France into the war in 1778 obliged the British to divide their forces
		Disadvantage: British troops alienated rather than conciliated civilians
American	Disadvantage: badly trained, supplied, and equipped	Disadvantage: took years for the Continentals to gain training, discipline, and experience
	Advantage: militias turned out to defend home territories	Disadvantage: militias tended to disappear when the immediate threat passed
	Advantage: French alliance	Disadvantage: took Franklin's diplomacy nearly 3 years to secure alliance
	Disadvantage: slaves running for freedom undermined rebel resolve	Disadvantage neutralized: except for Dunmore, British were reluctant to enlist African Americans

The Siege of Charleston

The southern strategy worked well for a short time in a small place. In November 1778 Clinton sent 3,500 troops to Savannah, Georgia. The resistance in the tiny colony quickly collapsed, and a large number of loyalists turned out to help the British. Encouraged, the army moved on to South Carolina.

During the last days of 1779 an expedition under Clinton himself set sail from New York City. Landing off the Georgia coast, his troops mucked through malarial swamps to the peninsula lying between the Ashley and Cooper Rivers. At the tip of that neck of land stood Charleston, and the British began to lay siege. By then, an unseasonably warm spring had set in, making the area a heaven for mosquitoes and a hell for human beings. Sweltering and swatting, redcoats weighted down in their woolen uniforms inched their siege works toward the city. By early May Clinton's army had closed in, and British shelling was setting fire to houses within the city. On May 12 Charleston surrendered.

Clinton sailed back to New York at the end of June 1780, leaving behind 8,300 redcoats to carry the British offensive northward to Virginia. The man charged with leading that campaign was his ambitious and able subordinate, Charles, Lord Cornwallis.

The Partisan Struggle in the South

Cornwallis's task in the Carolinas was complicated by the bitter animosity between rebels and loyalists there. Many Carolinians had taken sides years before Clinton's conquest of Charleston. In the summer and fall of 1775 the supporters of Congress and the new South Carolina revolutionary government mobbed, tortured, and imprisoned supporters of the king in the backcountry. These attacks only hardened loyalist resolve: roving bands seized ammunition, broke their leaders out of jail, and besieged rebel outposts. But within a matter of months, a combined force of rebel militias from the coast and the frontier managed to defeat loyalist forces in the backcountry.

REBELS AND LOYALISTS BATTLE FOR THE BACKCOUNTRY With the fall of Charleston in 1780, the loyalist movement on the frontier returned to life. Out of loyalist vengefulness and rebel desperation issued the brutal civil war that seared the southern backcountry after 1780. Neighbors and even families fought and killed each other as members of roaming rebel and tory militias. The intensity of **partisan warfare** in the backcountry produced unprecedented destruction. Loyalist militia plundered plantations and assaulted local women; rebel militias whipped suspected British supporters and burned their farms; both sides committed brutal assassinations and tortured prisoners. All of society, observed one minister, "seems to be at an end. Every person keeps close on his own plantation. Robberies and murders are often committed on the public roads. . . . Poverty, want, and hardship appear in almost every countenance."

Cornwallis, when confronted with the chaos, erred fatally. He did nothing to stop his loyalist allies or his own troops from mistreating civilians. A Carolina loyalist admitted that "the lower sort of People, who were in many parts originally attached to the British Government, have suffered so severely . . . that Great Britain has now a hundred enemies, where it had one before." Although rebels and loyalists alike plundered and terrorized the backcountry, Cornwallis's forces bore more of the blame and suffered the consequences.

A growing number of civilians outraged by the behavior of the king's troops cast their lot with the rebels. That upsurge of popular support enabled Francis Marion, the "Swamp Fox," and his band of white and black raiders to cut British lines of communication between Charleston and the interior. It swelled another rebel militia led by "the Gamecock," Thomas Sumter, who bloodied loyalist forces throughout the central part of South Carolina. It mobilized the "over-the-mountain men," a rebel militia in western Carolina who claimed victory at the Battle of Kings Mountain in October 1780. By the end of 1780 these successes had persuaded most civilians that only the rebels could restore order.

BRITISH VICTORY AT CAMDEN If rebel fortunes prospered in the partisan struggle, they faltered in the conventional warfare being waged at the same time in the South. In August of 1780 the Continentals commanded by Horatio Gates lost a major engagement to the British force at Camden, South Carolina. In the fall of 1780 Congress

©DEA/Bulloz/Getty Images
| *General Nathanael Greene*

replaced Gates with Washington's candidate for the southern command, Nathanael Greene, an energetic 38-year-old Rhode Islander and a veteran of the northern campaigns.

Greene Takes Command

Greene bore out Washington's confidence by grasping the military situation in the South. He understood the needs of his 1,400 hungry, ragged, and demoralized troops and instructed von Steuben to lobby Virginia for food and clothing. He understood the importance of the rebel militias and sent Lieutenant Colonel Henry "Light Horse Harry" Lee to assist Marion's raids. He understood the weariness of southern civilians and prevented his men from plundering the countryside.

Above all, Greene understood that his forces could never hold the field against the whole British army, a decision that led him to break the first rule of conventional warfare: he divided his army. In December 1780 he dispatched to western South Carolina a detachment of 600 men under the command of Brigadier General Daniel Morgan of Virginia.

COWPENS Back at the British camp, Cornwallis worried that Morgan and his rebels, if left unchecked, might rally the entire backcountry against the British. However, Cornwallis reckoned that he could not commit his entire army to the pursuit of Morgan's men, because then Greene and his troops might retake Charleston. The only solution, unconventional to be sure, was that Cornwallis divide *his* army. That he did, sending Lieutenant Colonel Banastre Tarleton and 1,100 men west after Morgan. Cornwallis had played right into Greene's hands: the rebel troops might be able to defeat a British army split into two pieces. For two weeks Morgan led Tarleton's troops on a breakneck chase across the Carolina countryside.

In January 1781 at an open meadow called Cowpens, Morgan routed Tarleton's force.

Now Cornwallis took up the chase. Morgan and Greene joined forces and kept going north until the British army wore out. Cornwallis finally stopped at Hillsboro, North Carolina, but few local loyalists responded to his call for reinforcements. Greene decided to make a show of force near the tiny village of Guilford Courthouse. On a brisk March day the two sides joined battle, each sustaining severe casualties before Greene was forced to retreat. But the high cost of victory convinced Cornwallis that he could not put down the rebellion in the Carolinas. "I am quite tired of marching about the country in quest of adventures," he informed Clinton.

VALUE OF THE MILITIA Although Nathanael Greene's command provided the Continentals with effective leadership in

THE FIGHTING IN THE SOUTH, 1780–1781

In December 1780 Nathanael Greene made the crucial decision to split his army, sending Daniel Morgan west, where he defeated the pursuing Banastre Tarleton at Cowpens. Meanwhile, Greene regrouped and replenished at Cheraw, keeping Cornwallis off balance with a raid (dotted line) toward Charleston and the coast. Then, with Cornwallis in hot pursuit, Greene and Morgan rejoined at Salisbury, retreating into Virginia. Cornwallis was worn down in this vain pursuit and lost three-quarters of the troops he began with before finally abandoning the Carolina campaign.

the South, it was the resilience of rebel militia that thwarted the British offensive in the Carolinas. Many Continental Army officers complained about the militia's lack of discipline, its habit of melting away when homesickness set in or harvest approached, and its cowardice under fire in conventional engagements. But when set the task of ambushing supply trains, harrying bands of local loyalists, or raiding isolated British outposts, the militia came through. Many southern civilians refused to join the British or to provide the redcoats with food and information, because they knew that once the British army left their neighborhoods, the rebel militia would be back. The Continental Army in the South lost many conventional battles, but the militia kept the British from restoring political control over the backcountry.

| *In 1845 painter William Ranney re-created a traditional retelling or account of the Battle of Cowpens recorded in John Marshall's biography of George Washington. According to Marshall, "a waiter, too small to wield a sword," saved the life of a relative of George Washington during the battle. Just as Lieutenant Colonel William Washington, leader of the patriot cavalry, was about to be cut down by a sword, the black man "saved him by wounding the officer with a ball from a pistol." Ranney depicts the unnamed man as a bugler astride a horse, as Morgan and Washington battle three British soldiers.*
©MPI/Archive Photos/Getty Images

What is implied by the tallying of children ["girls" and "boys"] with slave women?

Runaways

What is the significance of the list specifying occupations for some of the slave men?

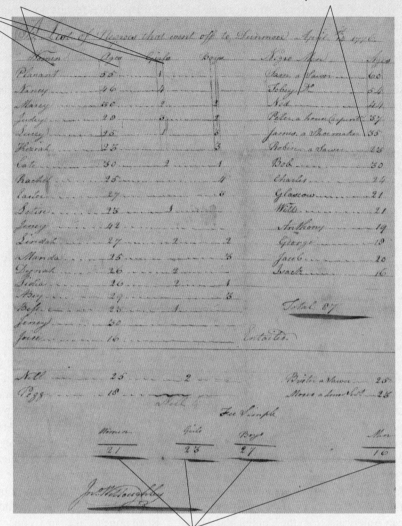

How does the number of female runaways compare with that of males? Children with adults?

Source: Virginia General Assembly, Legislative petitions of the General Assembly, "A List of Negroes that Went off to Dunmore, April 14, 1776". State government records collection, Courtesy of the Library of Virginia, Richmond, Va. 23219

"A List of Negroes That Went Off to Dunmore," dated April 14, 1776, Library of Virginia, Richmond.

Americans in earlier centuries were inveterate listmakers, providing present-day historians with a rich trove of evidence. College students recorded the titles of books they read; ministers noted the Bible passages on which they preached; clerks kept count of church members; tax assessors enumerated household members and the rates owed and paid; probate court officers inventoried the possessions of the dead, often down to chipped crockery and broken tools.

But the roster of slaves shown above is an extraordinary list, drawn up not on account of their master's death but because these 87 men, women, and children had fled their Virginia plantation, emboldened by Lord Dunmore's promise of freedom. It is impossible to know whether they ran away in small groups, stealing off over a period of several months between 1775 and 1776, or whether they ran away in larger companies within the space of a few days. But we do know that throughout

Virginia, as on this plantation, women and children made up a significant percentage of the runaways.

THINKING CRITICALLY

For what purposes might the Virginia master have composed this list? Why are slave artisans so well represented among the men on this list? Why were slave women and their children willing to risk escape in such large numbers?

African Americans in the Age of Revolution

The British also lost in the Carolinas because they did not seek greater support from those southerners who would have fought for liberty *with* the British—African American slaves.

Black Americans, virtually all in bondage, made up one-third of the population between Delaware and Georgia. Since the beginning of the resistance to Britain, white southerners had worried that the watchwords of *liberty* and *equality* would spread to the slave quarters. Gripped by the fear of slave rebellion, southern revolutionaries began to take precautions. Marylanders disarmed black inhabitants and issued extra guns to the white militia. Charlestonians hanged and then burned the body of Thomas Jeremiah, a free black who was convicted of spreading the word to others that the British "were come to help the poor Negroes."

WHITE FEARS OF REBELLION Southern whites fully expected the British to turn slave rebelliousness to their strategic advantage. As early as 1775 Virginia's royal governor, Lord Dunmore, confirmed white fears by offering to free any slave who joined the British. When Clinton invaded the South in 1779 he renewed that offer. One North Carolina planter heard that loyalists were "promising every Negro that would murder his master and family he should have his Master's plantation" and that "the Negroes have got it amongst them and believe it to be true."

But in Britain there was overwhelming opposition to organizing support among African Americans. British leaders dismissed Dunmore's ambitious scheme to raise a black army of 10,000 and another plan to create a sanctuary for black loyalists on the southeastern coast. Turning slaves against masters, they recognized, was not the way to conciliate southern whites.

Even so, southern fears of insurrection made the rebels reluctant to enlist black Americans as soldiers. At first, Congress barred African Americans from the Continental Army. But as the rebels became more desperate for manpower, policy changed. Northern states actively encouraged black enlistments, and in the Upper South, some states allowed free men of color to join the army or permitted slaves to substitute for their masters.

AFRICAN AMERICAN QUESTS FOR LIBERTY Slaves themselves sought freedom from whichever side seemed most likely to grant it. Perhaps 10,000 slaves took up Dunmore's offer in 1775 and deserted their masters, and thousands more flocked to Clinton's forces after the fall of Charleston. For many runaways the hope of liberation proved an illusion. Although some served the British army as laborers, spies, and soldiers, many died of disease in army camps (upward of 27,000 by one estimate) or were sold back into slavery in the West Indies. About 5,000 black soldiers served in the revolutionary army in the hope of gaining freedom. In addition, the number of runaways to the North soared during the Revolution. In total, perhaps 100,000 men and women—nearly a fifth

of the total slave population—attempted to escape bondage. Their odysseys to freedom took some to far-flung destinations: loyalist communities in Nova Scotia, a settlement established by the British in Sierra Leone on the West African coast, even the Botany Bay penal colony in Australia.

The slave revolts so dreaded by southern whites never materialized. Possibly the boldest slaves were drawn off into the armies; possibly greater white precautions discouraged schemes for black rebellions. In South Carolina, where the potential for revolt was greatest, most slaves chose to remain on plantations rather than risk a collective resistance and escape in the midst of the fierce partisan warfare.

 REVIEW

Why did the British fail to achieve their military and political goals in the South?

THE WORLD TURNED UPSIDE DOWN

DESPITE HIS LOSSES IN THE Carolinas, Cornwallis still believed that he could score a decisive victory against the Continental Army. The theater he chose for that showdown was the Chesapeake. During the spring of 1781 he had marched his army to the Virginia coast and joined forces with the hero of Saratoga and newly turned loyalist, Benedict Arnold. Embarrassed by debt and disgusted by Congress's shabby treatment of the Continental Army, Arnold had started exchanging rebel secrets for British money in 1779 before defecting outright in the fall of 1780. By June of 1781 Arnold and Cornwallis were fortifying a site on the tip of the peninsula formed by the York and James Rivers, a place called Yorktown.

Meanwhile, Washington and his French ally, the comte de Rochambeau, met in Connecticut to plan a major attack. Rochambeau urged a coordinated land-sea assault on the Virginia coast. Washington insisted instead on a full-scale offensive against New York City. Just when the rebel commander was about to have his way, word arrived that a French fleet under the comte de Grasse was sailing for the Chesapeake to blockade Cornwallis by sea. Washington's Continentals headed south.

Surrender at Yorktown

By the end of September, 7,800 Frenchmen, 5,700 Continentals, and 3,200 militia had sandwiched Yorktown between the devil of an allied army and the deep blue sea of French warships. "If you cannot relieve me very soon," Cornwallis wrote to Clinton, "you must expect to hear the worst." The British navy did arrive—but seven days after Cornwallis surrendered to the rebels on October 19, 1781. When Germain carried the news from Yorktown to the king's first minister, Lord North replied, "Oh, God, it is over." Then North resigned, Germain

©Fotosearch/Stringer/Getty Images

| On September 30, 1780, a wagon bearing this two-faced effigy was drawn through the streets of Philadelphia. The effigy represents Benedict Arnold, who sits between a gallows and the devil. Note the similarities between this piece of street theater and the demonstrations mounted on Pope's Day several decades earlier, shown in Chapter 3.

resigned, and even George III murmured something about abdicating.

It need not have ended at Yorktown, but timing made all the difference. At the end of 1781 and early in 1782, the British army received setbacks in the other theaters of the war: India, the West Indies, and Florida. The French and the Spanish were everywhere in Europe as well, gathering in the English Channel, planning a major offensive against Gibraltar. The cost of the fighting was already enormous. British leaders recognized that the rest of the empire was at stake and set about cutting their losses in America.

The Treaty of Paris, signed on September 3, 1783, was a diplomatic triumph for the American negotiators: Benjamin Franklin, John Adams, and John Jay. They dangled before Britain the possibility that a generous settlement might weaken American ties to France. The British jumped at the bait. They recognized the independence of the United States and agreed to ample boundaries for the new nation: the Mississippi River on the west, the 31st parallel on the south, and the present border of Canada on the north. American negotiators then persuaded a skeptical France to approve the treaty by arguing that, as allies, they were bound to present a united front to the British. Spain, the third member of the alliance, settled for retaining Florida and Minorca, an island in the Mediterranean.

If the Treaty of Paris marked both the end of a war and the recognition of a new nation, the surrender at Yorktown captured the significance of a revolution. Those present at Yorktown on that clear autumn afternoon in 1781 watched as the British second in command to Cornwallis (who had sent word that he was "indisposed") surrendered his superior's sword. He offered the sword first, in a face-saving gesture, to

the French commander, Rochambeau, who politely refused and pointed to Washington. But the American commander-in-chief, out of a mixture of military protocol, nationalistic pride, and perhaps even wit, pointed to *his* second in command, Benjamin Lincoln.

Some witnesses recalled that British musicians arrayed on the Yorktown green played "The World Turned Upside Down." Their recollections may have been faulty, but the story has persisted as part of the folklore of the American Revolution—and for good reasons. The world had, it seemed, turned upside down with the coming of American independence.

 REVIEW

How did the United States manage to prevail in the war and in the treaty negotiations?

PUTTING HISTORY IN GLOBAL CONTEXT

THE COLONIAL REBELS SHOCKED the British with their answer to the question "Would they fight?" The answer had been yes—but on their own terms. By 1777 most propertied Americans avoided fighting in the Continental Army. Yet whenever the war reached their homes, farms, and businesses, many Americans gave their allegiance to the new nation by turning out with rifles or supplying homespun clothing, food, or ammunition. They rallied around Washington in New Jersey,

Gates in upstate New York, Greene in the Carolinas. Middle-class American men fought, some from idealism, others out of self-interest, but always on their own terms, as members of the militia. These citizen-soldiers turned the world upside down by defeating professional armies.

Of course, the militia did not bear the brunt of the fighting. That responsibility fell to the Continental Army, which by 1777 drew its strength from the poorest ranks of American society. Yet even the Continentals, for all their desperation, managed to fight on their own terms. Some asserted their rights by raising mutinies, until Congress redressed their grievances. All of them, as the Baron von Steuben observed, behaved differently than European soldiers did. Americans followed orders only if the logic of commands was explained to them. The Continentals, held in contempt by most Americans, turned the world upside down by sensing their power and asserting their measure of personal independence.

Americans of African descent dared as much and more in their quests for liberty. Whether they chose to escape slavery by fighting for the British or the Continentals or by striking out on their own as runaways, their defiance, too, turned the world upside down. Among the tens of thousands of slaves who would not be mastered was one Henry Washington, a native of Africa who became the slave of George Washington in 1763. But Henry Washington made his own declaration of independence in 1776, slipping behind British lines and serving as a corporal in a black unit. Thereafter, like thousands of former slaves, he sought to build a new life elsewhere in the Atlantic world, settling first in Nova Scotia and finally in Sierra Leone. By 1800 he headed a community of former slaves who were exiled to the outskirts of that colony for their determined efforts to win republican self-government from Sierra Leone's white British rulers. Like Thomas Paine, Henry Washington believed that freedom was his only country.

In all those ways, a revolutionary generation turned the world upside down. They were a diverse lot—descended from Indians, Europeans, and Africans, driven by desperation or idealism or greed—but joined, even if they did not recognize it, by their common struggle to break free from the rule of monarchs or masters. What now awaited them in the world of the new United States?

CHAPTER SUMMARY

The American Revolution brought independence to Britain's former colonies after an armed struggle that began in 1775 and concluded with the Treaty of Paris in 1783.

- When the Second Continental Congress first convened, many delegates still hoped for reconciliation—even as they created the Continental Army.

- The Second Continental Congress adopted the Declaration of Independence on July 4, 1776.

- British victories in the North throughout 1776 and 1777 secured both New York City and Philadelphia. But harsh tactics alienated much of the populace.

- The British suffered a disastrous defeat at the Battle of Saratoga in early 1778, which prompted France to openly ally with the American rebels soon thereafter.

- By 1780 Britain aimed to win the war by claiming the South, and captured both Savannah, Georgia, and Charleston, South Carolina.

- Although the war in the West contributed little to the outcome of the Revolution, the competition for Indian allies among the United States, Britain, France, and Spain sparked two decades of dislocation and conflict across the continent, a situation made worse by a smallpox pandemic.

- The Continental Army in the South, led by Nathanael Greene and aided by guerrilla fighters in the partisan struggle, foiled the British strategy, and Cornwallis surrendered at the Battle of Yorktown in 1781.

- Except during the first year of fighting, the rank-and-file of the Continental Army were drawn from the poorest Americans, whose needs for food, clothing, and shelter were neglected by the Continental Congress.

Digging Deeper

The outstanding military histories of the American Revolution include Don Higginbotham, *The War of American Independence* (1971); and Robert Middlekauff, *The Glorious Cause, 1763 to 1789* (1982). Both provide a wealth of detail about battles, contending armies, and the role of militias and civilian populations in the fighting. For a compelling treatment of the lives of soldiers in the Continental Army, read Caroline Cox, *A Proper Sense of Honor* (2004); and to become better acquainted with their commander-in-chief, turn to *Washington's Revolution* (2015) by Robert Middlekauff. For rich new work on the West and the South during the Revolutionary era, see Claudio Saunt, *West of the Revolution* (2014); and Kathleen DuVal, *Independence Lost* (2015). Colin G. Calloway's *The American Revolution in Indian Country* (1995) explores how native people shaped and were shaped by the Revolution.

Jonathan R. Dull's *A Diplomatic History of the American Revolution* (1985) remains the standard work on the topic. The international alliance with France and Spain come in for lively chronicling by Larrie D. Ferreiro in *Brothers at Arms* (2016). Impressive interpretations of the war's impact on American society include Charles Royster, *A Revolutionary People at War* (1979); and John Shy, *A People Numerous and Armed* (rev. ed., 1990). Douglas R. Egerton, *Death or Liberty* (2009), offers a thoughtful history of African Americans during this era; and Cassandra Pybus, *Epic Journeys of Freedom* (2006), recounts the experiences of runaway slaves who seized on the wartime crisis to gain liberty. For the varied roles that women played in the Revolutionary era, see Carol Berkin, *Revolutionary Mothers* (2005); and Ellen Hartigan-O'Connor, *The Ties That Buy* (2009).

8 Crisis and Constitution

1776–1789

South Carolina's low country supplies the background for this portrait of a wealthy Charleston couple, John Purves and his wife, Anne Pritchard Purves. John saw military service in both the state militia and the Continental Army; Anne, with her classically draped dress, evokes the goddess of Liberty. What do you make of the expressions on their faces?

Courtesy, Winterthur Museum, Portrait by Henry Benbridge: Captain John Purves and His Wife, Eliza Anne Pritchard, 1775–1777, Charleston, SC, Oil paint on canvas, Bequest of Henry Francis du Pont, 1960.582

>> An American Story

"*THESE* UNITED STATES"

"I am not a Virginian, but an American," Patrick Henry declared in the Virginia House of Burgesses. Most likely he was lying. Certainly no one listening took him seriously, for the newly independent colonists did not identify themselves as members of a nation. They would have said, as did Thomas Jefferson, "Virginia, Sir, is my country." Or as John Adams wrote to another native son, "Massachusetts is our country." Jefferson and Adams were men of wide political vision and experience: both were leaders in the Continental Congress and more inclined than

©Collection of the New-York Historical Society, USA/Bridgeman Images

| *The Revolution provided many humble folk a new sense of pride and potential. These men, who manufactured pewter mugs and teapots, gave their support to the new Constitution: a "Federal Plan most solid and secure."*

most to think nationally. But like other members of the revolutionary generation, they identified deeply with their home states and even more deeply with their home counties and towns.

It followed that allegiance to the states, not the Union, determined the shape of the first republican political experiments. For a decade after independence, the revolutionaries were less committed to creating an American nation than to organizing 13 separate state republics. The Declaration of Independence referred explicitly not to *the* United States but to *these* United States. It envisioned not one republic so much as a federation of 13.

Only when peace was restored during the decade of the 1780s were Americans forced to face some unanswered questions raised by their revolution. The Declaration proclaimed that these "free and independent states" had "full power to levy war, conclude peace, contract alliances, establish commerce." Did that mean that New Jersey, as a free and independent state, could sign a trade agreement with France, excluding the other states? If the United States were to be more than a loose federation, how could it assert power on a national scale? Similarly, American borderlands to the west presented problems. If these territories were settled by Americans, would they eventually join the United States? Go their own ways as independent nations? Become new colonies of Spain or England?

Such problems were more than political; they were rooted in social realities. For a political union to succeed, the inhabitants of 13 separate states had to start thinking of themselves as Americans. When it came right down to it, what united a Vermont farmer working his rocky fields and a South Carolina gentleman presiding over a vast rice plantation? What bonds existed between a Kentuckian rafting the Ohio River and a Salem merchant sailing to China for porcelain?

And in a society in which all citizens were said to be "created equal," the inevitable social inequalities had to be confronted. How could women participate in the Revolution's bid for freedom if they were not free to vote or to hold property? How would free or enslaved African Americans live in a republic based on equality? As the British began leaving Yorktown, Charleston, and other ports, they transferred thousands of slaves who had been in their charge to New York City. Southern slaveholders followed, looking to reclaim their bondspeople. "The dreadful rumor" that slave masters were searching for their property "filled us all with inexpressible anguish and horror," reported Boston King, an escaped slave who had fought for the British; ". . . for some days we lost our appetite for food and sleep from our eyes." Repossessing such slaves could be perilous. One master was murdered by "about 12 or 15 of the Ward's blacks" when he came looking. How could black Americans feel a bond with white Americans when so often the only existing bonds had been forged with chains?

To such questions there were no final answers in 1781. There was ferment, excitement, and experimentation as 13 states each sought to create their governments anew; as Americans—or rather, Virginians and New Yorkers and Georgians and citizens of other countries—began to imagine how the revolutionary virtue of equality might transform their societies. But as the decade progressed, the sense of crisis deepened. <<

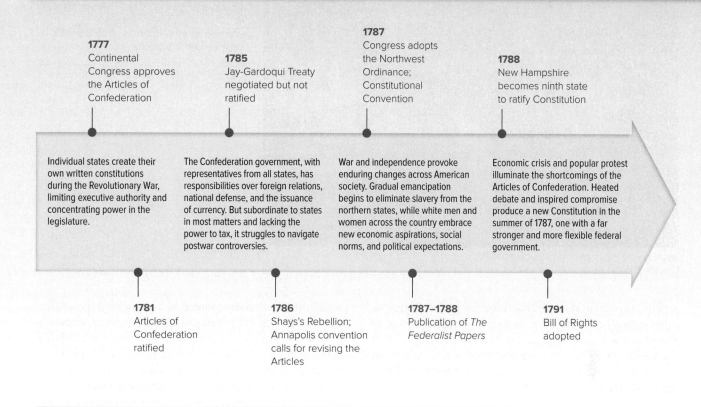

1777 Continental Congress approves the Articles of Confederation

1785 Jay-Gardoqui Treaty negotiated but not ratified

1787 Congress adopts the Northwest Ordinance; Constitutional Convention

1788 New Hampshire becomes ninth state to ratify Constitution

Individual states create their own written constitutions during the Revolutionary War, limiting executive authority and concentrating power in the legislature.

The Confederation government, with representatives from all states, has responsibilities over foreign relations, national defense, and the issuance of currency. But subordinate to states in most matters and lacking the power to tax, it struggles to navigate postwar controversies.

War and independence provoke enduring changes across American society. Gradual emancipation begins to eliminate slavery from the northern states, while white men and women across the country embrace new economic aspirations, social norms, and political expectations.

Economic crisis and popular protest illuminate the shortcomings of the Articles of Confederation. Heated debate and inspired compromise produce a new Constitution in the summer of 1787, one with a far stronger and more flexible federal government.

1781 Articles of Confederation ratified

1786 Shays's Rebellion; Annapolis convention calls for revising the Articles

1787–1788 Publication of *The Federalist Papers*

1791 Bill of Rights adopted

REPUBLICAN EXPERIMENTS

AFTER INDEPENDENCE WAS DECLARED IN July 1776, many of America's best political minds turned to drawing up **constitutions** for their individual states. Thomas Jefferson deserted the Continental Congress, leaving the conduct of the war and national affairs to other men, for the more important business of creating Virginia's new government.

BELIEF IN THE NEED FOR SMALL REPUBLICS In truth, the state constitutions were crucial republican experiments, the first efforts at establishing a government of and by the people. All the revolutionaries agreed that the people—not a king or a few privileged aristocrats—should rule. Yet they were equally certain that republican governments were best suited to small territories. They believed that the new United States was too sprawling and its people too diverse to be safely consolidated into a single national republic. They feared, too, that the government of a large republic would inevitably grow indifferent to popular concerns, being distant from many of its citizens. Without being under the watchful eye of the people, representatives would become less

accountable to the electorate and turn tyrannical. A federation of small state republics, they reasoned, would stand a far better chance of enduring.

The State Constitutions

The new state constitutions retained the basic form of their old colonial governments, all except Georgia and Pennsylvania providing for a governor and a bicameral legislature. But although most states did not alter the basic structure of their governments, they changed dramatically the balance of power among the different branches of government.

CURBING EXECUTIVE POWER From the republican perspective in 1776, the greatest problem of any government lay in curbing executive power. What had driven Americans into rebellion was the abuse of authority by the king and his appointed officials. To ensure that the executive could never again threaten popular liberty, the new states either accorded almost no power to their governors or abolished that office entirely. The governors had no authority to convene or dissolve the legislatures. They could not veto the legislatures' laws, grant land, or erect courts. Most important from the

| Americans responded to independence with rituals of "killing the king," like the one enacted by this New York City crowd in 1776 as it pulls down a statue of George III. Americans also expressed their mistrust of monarchs and their ministers by establishing new state governments with weak executive branches.

Source: The Miriam and Ira D. Wallach Division of Art, Prints and Photographs: Print Collection/New York Public Library

republican point of view, governors had few powers to appoint other state officials. All these limits were designed to deprive the executive of any patronage or other form of influence over the legislature. By reducing the governors' power, Americans hoped to preserve their states from the corruption that they deplored in British political life.

STRENGTHENING LEGISLATIVE POWERS What the state governors lost, the legislatures gained. Sam Adams, the Boston rebel leader, expressed the political consensus when he declared that "every legislature of every colony ought to be the sovereign and uncontrollable Power within its own limits of territory." To ensure that those powerful legislatures truly represented the will of the people, the new state constitutions called for annual elections and required candidates for the legislature to live in the districts they represented. Many states even asserted the right of voters to instruct the men elected to office about how to vote on specific issues. Although no state granted universal manhood suffrage, most reduced the amount of property required of qualified voters. Finally, state supreme courts were also either elected by the legislatures or appointed by elected governors.

By investing all power in popular assemblies, Americans abandoned the British system of mixed government. In one sense, that change was fairly democratic. A majority of voters within a state could do whatever they wanted, unchecked by governors or courts. On the other hand, the arrangement opened the door for legislatures to turn as tyrannical as governors. The revolutionaries brushed that prospect aside: republican theory assured them that the people possessed a generous share of civic virtue, the capacity for selfless pursuit of the general welfare.

WRITTEN CONSTITUTIONS In an equally momentous change, the revolutionaries insisted on written state constitutions. Whenever government appeared to exceed the limits of its authority, Americans wanted to have at hand the written contract between rulers and ruled. When eighteenth-century Britons used the word *constitution,* they meant the existing arrangement of government—not an actual document but a collection of parliamentary laws, customs, and precedents. But Americans believed that a constitution should be a written code that stood apart from and above government, a yardstick against which the people measured the performance of their rulers. After all, they reasoned, if Britain's constitution had been written down, available for all to consult, would American rights have been violated?

From Congress to Confederation

While Americans lavished attention on their state constitutions, the national government nearly languished during the decade after 1776. With the coming of independence, the Second Continental Congress conducted the common business of the federated states. It created and maintained the Continental Army, issued currency, and negotiated with foreign powers.

But while Congress acted as a central government by common consent, it lacked any legal basis for its authority. To redress that need, in July 1776 Congress appointed a committee to draft a constitution for a national government. The urgent business of waging the war made for delay, but Congress approved the first national constitution in November 1777. It took four more years—until February 1781—for all the states to ratify these Articles of Confederation.

ARTICLES OF CONFEDERATION The Articles of Confederation provided for a government by a national legislature—essentially a continuation of the Second Continental Congress. That body had the authority to declare war and make peace, conduct diplomacy, regulate Indian affairs, appoint military and naval officers, and requisition men from the states. In affairs of

Source: National Archives (596742)

First Seal of the United States

finance it could coin money and issue paper currency. Extensive as these responsibilities were, Congress could not levy taxes or even regulate trade. The crucial power of the purse rested entirely with the states, as did the final power to make and execute laws. Even worse, the national government had no distinct executive branch. Congressional committees, constantly changing in their membership, not only had to make laws but had to administer and enforce them as well. With no executive to carry out the policies of finance, war, and foreign policy, the federal government's influence was extremely limited.

Those weaknesses appear more evident in hindsight. For Congress in 1777 it was no easy task to frame a new government in the midst of a war. And most American leaders of the 1770s had given little thought to federalism, the means by which political power could be divided among the states and the national government. In any case, to have given significant powers to the national government would have aroused only opposition among the states, each jealous of its independence. Creating a strong national government would also have antagonized many Americans, who after all had just rebelled against the distant, centralized authority of Britain's king and Parliament.

Guided by republican political theory and by their colonial experience, American revolutionaries created a loose confederation of 13 independent state republics under a nearly powerless national government. They succeeded so well that the United States almost failed to survive the first decade of its independence. The problem was that republican theory and lessons from the colonial past were not always useful guides to postwar realities. Only when events forced Americans to think nationally did they begin to consider the possibility of reinventing "these United States"—this time under the yoke of a truly federal republic.

> **REVIEW**
>
> What political concerns shaped the first constitutions?

THE TEMPTATIONS OF PEACE

THE SURRENDER OF CORNWALLIS AT Yorktown in 1781 marked the end of military crisis in America. But as the threat from Britain receded, so did the source of American unity. The many differences among Americans, most of which lay submerged during the struggle for independence, surfaced in full force. Those domestic divisions, combined with challenges to the new nation from Britain and Spain, created conflicts that neither the states nor the national government proved equal to handling.

The Temptations of the West

The greatest opportunities and the greatest problems for postwar Americans awaited in the rapidly expanding West. With the boundary of the new United States now set at the Mississippi River, more whites spilled across the Appalachians, planting farmsteads and raw frontier towns throughout Ohio, Kentucky, and Tennessee. By 1790 places that had been almost uninhabited by whites in 1760 held more than 2.25 million, one-third of the nation's population.

After the Revolution, as before, western settlement fostered intense conflict. American claims that its territory stretched all the way to the Mississippi were by no means taken for granted by European and Indian powers. The West also confronted Americans with questions about their own national identity: Would the newly settled territories enter the nation as states on an equal footing with the original 13 states? Would they be ruled as dependent colonies? Could the federal government reconcile conflicting interests, cultures, and traditions over so great an area? The fate of the West, in other words, constituted a crucial test of whether "these" United States could grow and still remain united.

Rivalries flared along the southwestern frontier of the United States as Spain vied to win the allegiance of Indians by supplying them with British trade goods. The Indians welcomed such goods (note the plow, center, and European clothing worn by some of the Indians). Here a white man, probably the American Indian agent Benjamin Hawkins, visits an Indian village during the 1790s.

©The Granger Collection, New York

Foreign Intrigues

Both the British from their base in Canada and the Spanish in Florida and Louisiana hoped to chisel away at American borders. Their considerable success in the 1780s exposed the weakness of Confederation diplomacy.

Before the ink was dry on the Treaty of Paris, Britain's ministers were secretly instructing Canadians to maintain their forts and trading posts inside the United States' northwestern frontier. They reckoned—correctly—that with the Continental Army disbanded, the Confederation could not force the British to withdraw.

The British also made mischief along the Confederation's northern borders, mainly with Vermont. For decades, Ethan Allen and his Green Mountain Boys had waged a war of nerves with neighboring New York, which claimed Vermont as part of its territory. After the Revolution the Vermonters petitioned Congress for statehood, demanding independence from both New York and New Hampshire. When Congress dragged its feet, the British tried to woo Vermont into their empire as a province of Canada. That flirtation with the British pressured Congress into granting Vermont statehood in 1791.

SPANISH DESIGNS ON THE SOUTHWEST The loyalty of the southwestern frontier was even less certain. By 1790 more than 100,000 settlers had poured through the Cumberland Gap to reach Kentucky and Tennessee. Along with the farmers came speculators, who bought up large tracts of land from the Indians. But the commercial possibilities of the region depended entirely on access to the Mississippi and the port of New Orleans, since it was far too costly to ship southwestern produce over the rough trails east across the Appalachians. And the Mississippi route was still dominated by the Spanish, who controlled Louisiana as well as forts along western Mississippi shores as far north as St. Louis. The Spanish, seeing their opportunity, closed the Mississippi to American navigation in 1784. That action prompted serious talk among southwesterners about seceding from the United States and joining Spain's empire.

The Spanish also tried to strengthen their hold on North America by making common cause with the Indians. Of particular concern to both groups was protecting Spanish Florida from the encroachment of American settlers filtering south from Georgia—backwoods folk, Florida's governor complained, who were "nomadic like Arabs and . . . distinguished from savages only in their color, language, and the superiority of their depraved cunning and untrustworthiness." So Spanish colonial officials responded eagerly to the overtures of Alexander McGillivray, a young Indian leader whose mother was of French-Creek descent and whose father was a Scots trader. His efforts brought about a treaty of alliance between the Creeks and the Spanish in 1784, quickly followed by similar alliances with the Choctaws and the Chickasaws. What cemented such treaties were the trade goods that the Spanish agreed to supply the tribes, for, as McGillivray explained, "Indians will attach themselves to and serve them best who supply their necessities." Securing European gunpowder and guns had become essential to southeastern Indians, because their entire economies now revolved around hunting and selling deerskins to white traders. So eager were the Spanish to "serve" the Indians in that matter that they even permitted British merchants, who could command a steady supply of manufactured goods, to monopolize the Indian trade.

*The Confederation's settlement
of conflicting western land
claims was an achievement
essential to the consolidation
of political union. Some states
asserted that their original
charters extended their western
borders to the Mississippi River.
A few states, such as Virginia,
claimed western borders on the
Pacific Ocean. Which states
claimed western lands that they
eventually ceded to the
Confederation?*

The largest dealers developed a trading network that reached all
the way to the Mississippi by the 1790s. This flood of British
merchandise sustained the alliance between the Spanish and the
Indians, while British guns enabled the Creeks to defend their
hunting territory from American invaders.

Disputes among the States

LANDED VS. LANDLESS STATES   As if foreign intrigues
were not divisive enough, the states continued to argue among
themselves over western land claims. The old royal charters
for some colonies had extended their boundaries all the way
to the Mississippi and beyond. But the charters were often
vague, granting both Massachusetts and Virginia, for example, undisputed possession of present-day Wisconsin. In contrast, other charters limited state boundaries to within a few
hundred miles of the Atlantic coast. **Landed states** such as
Virginia wanted to secure control over the large territory
granted them by their charters. **Landless states** (which
included Maryland, Delaware, Pennsylvania, Rhode Island,
and New Jersey) called on Congress to restrict the boundaries of landed states and to convert western lands into a
domain administered by the Confederation.

The landless states argued that the landed states enjoyed
an unfair advantage from the money they could raise selling
their western claims. That revenue would allow landed
states to reduce taxes, and lower taxes would lure settlers
from the landless states. Meanwhile, landless states would
have to raise taxes to make up for the departed taxpayers,
causing even more residents to leave. Speculators were also
eager to see Congress control the western lands. Before
the Revolution, many prominent citizens of landless
Pennsylvania, Maryland, and New Jersey had purchased
tracts in the West from Indians. These speculators now also
lobbied for congressional ownership of all western lands—
except those tracts that they had already purchased from
the Indians.

The landless states lost the opening round in the contest
over ownership of the West. The Articles of Confederation
acknowledged the old charter claims of the landed states.
Then Maryland, one of the smallest landless states, retaliated
by refusing to ratify the Articles. Since every state had to
approve the Articles before they were formally accepted, the
fate of the United States hung in the balance. One by one the
landed states relented, Virginia being the last. Only then did
Maryland ratify the Articles, in February 1781.

This sketch of a new cleared farm idealizes many aspects of life on the late-eighteenth-century frontier. Although western farmers first sought to "improve" their acreage by felling trees, as the stumps dotting the landscape indicate, their dwellings were far less substantial than those depicted in the background above. And although Indians sometimes guided parties of white surveyors and settlers into the West, as shown in the foreground, Indians more often resisted white encroachment. For that reason, dogs, here perched placidly in a canoe, were trained to alert their white masters to the approach of Indians.

©Everett Collection Historical/Alamy

The More Democratic West

An even-greater bone of contention concerned the sort of men westerners elected to political office. The state legislatures of the 1780s were both larger and more democratic in their membership than the old colonial assemblies. Before the Revolution no more than a fifth of the men serving in the assemblies were middle-class farmers or artisans. Government was almost exclusively the domain of the wealthiest merchants, lawyers, and planters. After the Revolution twice as many state legislators were men of moderate wealth. The shift was more marked in the North, where middle-class men predominated among representatives. But in every state, some men of modest means, humble background, and little formal education attained political power.

CHANGING COMPOSITION OF STATE LEGISLATURES State legislatures became more democratic in their membership mainly because as backcountry districts grew, so too did the number of their representatives. Since western districts tended to be less developed economically and culturally, their leading men were less rich and cultivated than the Eastern Seaboard elite. But many of these eastern republican gentlemen, while endorsing government by popular consent, doubted whether ordinary people were fit to rule. The problem, they contended, was that the new western legislators concerned themselves only with the narrow interests of their constituents, not with the good of the whole state. As Ezra Stiles, the president of Yale College, observed, the new breed of politicians was those with "the all-prevailing popular talent of coaxing and flattering," who "whenever a bill is read in the legislature . . . instantly thinks how it will affect his constituents." And if state legislatures could not rise above narrow self-interest, how long would it be before a concern for the general welfare simply withered away?

The Northwest Territory

Such fears of "democratic excess" also influenced policy when Congress finally came to decide what to do with the **Northwest Territory**. Carved out of the land ceded by the states to the national government, the Northwest Territory comprised the present-day states of Ohio, Indiana, Illinois, Michigan, and Wisconsin, as well as part of Minnesota. With so many white settlers moving into these lands, Congress was faced with a crucial test of its federal system. If an orderly way could not be devised to expand the confederation of states beyond the original 13 colonies, the new territories might well become independent countries or even colonies of Spain or Britain. Congress dealt with the issue of expansion by adopting three ordinances.

JEFFERSON'S PLAN FOR THE NORTHWEST The first ordinance, drafted by Thomas Jefferson in 1784, divided the Northwest Territory into 10 states, each to be admitted to the Union on equal terms as soon as its population equaled that in any of the existing states. In the meantime, Jefferson provided for democratic self-government of the territory by all free adult males. A second ordinance of 1785 set up an efficient mechanism for dividing and selling public lands. The Northwest Territory was surveyed into townships 6 miles square. Each township was then divided into 36 lots of 1 square mile, or 640 acres.

Congress waited in vain for buyers to flock to the land offices it established. The cost of even a single lot—$640—was too steep for most farmers. Disappointed by the shortage of buyers and desperate for money, Congress finally accepted a proposition submitted by a private company of land speculators who offered to buy some 6 million acres in present-day southeastern Ohio. That several members of Congress numbered among the company's stockholders no doubt added to enthusiasm for the deal.

>> MAPPING THE PAST <<

THE ORDINANCE OF 1785

Source: Library of Congress, Prints and Photographs Division [LC-USZC2-1749]

"The land Speculators already Smell a rat and expect fine picking."
–Pennsylvania delegate Joseph Gardner, 1785

CONTEXT

Surveyors entered the Northwest Territory in September of 1785. They came to begin imposing on the land regular grids of 6 square miles to define new townships, as shown on this range map of a portion of Ohio. Farmers purchased blocks of land within townships, each 1 mile square. This pattern was followed in mapping and colonizing public lands all the way to the Pacific coast. Settler colonists would either buy directly from the federal government, or from land speculators. As Joseph Gardner predicted, speculators learned quickly how to work the system.

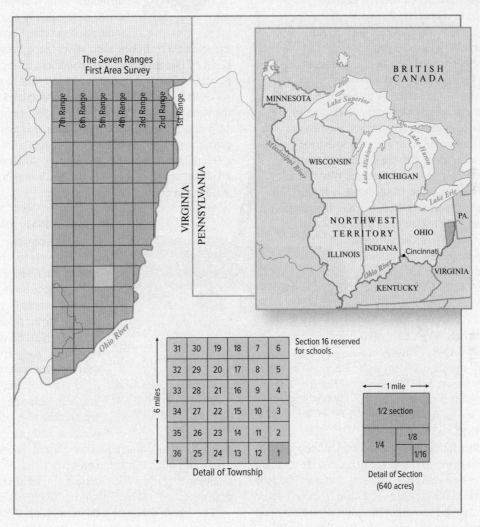

Detail of Township

Section 16 reserved for schools.

Detail of Section (640 acres)

MAP READING

1. What is the relationship between a range, a township, and a section in this plan?
2. How would sections be divided?
3. How many acres were set aside for schools?

MAP INTERPRETATION

1. Rivers, lakes, and landforms aren't arranged in tidy grids. What challenges might surveyors and landowners have experienced trying to work with Jefferson's system?
2. Why was it useful or important to set aside land for public schools? What might have been the long-term implications of doing so?

NORTHWEST ORDINANCE The transaction concluded, Congress calmed the speculators' worries that incoming settlers might enjoy too much self-government by scrapping Jefferson's democratic design and substituting the Northwest Ordinance of 1787. That ordinance provided for a period in which Congress held sway in the territory through its appointees—a governor, a secretary, and three judges. When the population reached 5,000 free adult males, a legislature was to be established, although its laws required the governor's approval. A representative could sit in Congress but had no vote. When the population reached 60,000, the inhabitants might apply for statehood, and the whole Northwest Territory was to be divided into not less than three or more than five states. The ordinance also guaranteed basic rights—freedom of religion and trial by jury—and provided for the support of public education. Equally significant, it also outlawed slavery throughout the territory.

With the Northwest Ordinance in place, Congress had succeeded in extending republican government to the West and incorporating the frontier into the new nation. The Republic now had an orderly way to expand its federation of states in a way that minimized the tensions between the genteel East and the democratic West that had plagued the colonies and the Confederation throughout much of the eighteenth century. Yet ironically, the new ordinance served to heighten tensions in a different way. By limiting the spread of slavery in the northern states, Congress deepened the critical social and economic differences between the North and the South, evident already in the 1780s.

THE TERRITORIAL SYSTEM AND NATIVE AMERICANS The consequences of the new territorial system were also significant for hundreds of thousands of the continent's other inhabitants. In the short term, the ordinance ignored completely the rights of the Shawnee, Chippewa, and other Indian peoples who lived in the region. In the long term, the system "laid the blue print," as one historian noted, for bringing new lands into the United States. The ordinance thus accelerated the pressures on Indian lands and aggravated the social and geographic dislocations already set in motion by disease and the western conflicts of the Revolutionary War.

Slavery and Sectionalism

When white Americans declared their independence, they owned nearly half a million black Americans. African Americans of the revolutionary generation, most of them enslaved, constituted 20 percent of the total population of the colonies in 1775, and nearly 90 percent of them lived in the

(top) ©Wilberforce House, Hull City Museums and Art Galleries, UK/Bridgeman Images; (bottom) ©Wilberforce House, Hull City Museums and Art Galleries, UK/Bridgeman Images

| Branding irons like these were sometimes used to burn a slaveholder's initials into the skin of his property to make running away more difficult.

South. Yet few political leaders directly confronted the issue of whether slavery should be permitted to exist in a truly republican society.

REPUBLICANISM AND SLAVERY When political discussion did stray toward the subject of slavery, southerners—especially ardent republicans—bristled defensively. Theirs was a difficult position, riddled with contradictions. On the one hand, they had condemned parliamentary taxation as tantamount to political "slavery" and had rebelled, declaring that all men were "created equal." On the other hand, enslaved African Americans formed the basis of the South's plantation economy. To surrender slavery, southerners believed, would be to usher in economic ruin.

Some planters in the Upper South resolved the dilemma by freeing their slaves. Such decisions were made easier by changing economic conditions in the Chesapeake. As planters shifted from tobacco toward wheat, a crop demanding a good deal less labor, Virginia and Maryland liberalized their manumission statutes, laws providing for freeing slaves. Between 1776 and 1789, most southern states also joined the North in prohibiting the importation of slaves, and a few antislavery societies appeared in the Upper South. But no southern state legally abolished slavery. Masters defended their right to hold human property in the name of republicanism.

REPUBLICANISM AND PROPERTY Eighteenth-century republicans regarded property as crucial, for it provided a man and his family with security, status, and wealth. More important, it provided a measure of independence: to be able to act freely, without fear or favor of others. People without property were dangerous, republicans believed, because the poor could never be politically independent. Southern defenders of slavery thus argued that free, propertyless black people would pose a political threat to the liberty of propertied white citizens. Subordinating the human rights of blacks to the property rights of whites, southern republicans reached the paradoxical conclusion that their freedom depended on keeping African Americans in bondage.

The North followed a different course. Because its economy depended far less on slave labor, black emancipation did not run counter to powerful economic interests. Antislavery societies, the first founded by the Quakers in 1775, spread throughout the northern states during the next quarter century. Over the same period the legislatures of most northern states provided for the immediate or gradual abolition of slavery. Freedom for most northern African Americans came slowly, but by 1830 there were fewer than 3,000 slaves out of a total northern black population of 125,000.

The Revolution, which had been fought for liberty and equality, did little to change the status of most black Americans. By 1800 more enslaved African Americans lived in the United States than had lived there in 1776. Slavery continued to grow in the Lower South as the rice culture of the Carolinas and Georgia expanded and as the new cotton culture spread westward.

Still, a larger number of slaves than ever before became free during the war and in the following decades, whether through military service, successful escape, manumission, or gradual emancipation. All these developments fostered the growth of free black communities, especially in the Upper South and in northern cities. By 1810 free African Americans made up 10 percent of the total population of Maryland and Virginia.

GROWTH OF THE FREE BLACK COMMUNITY The composition of the postwar free community changed as well. Before independence most free blacks had been either mulattoes—the offspring of interracial unions—or former slaves too sick or aged to have value as laborers. In contrast, a larger proportion of the free population of the 1780s were darker skinned, younger, and healthier. This group injected new vitality into black communal life, organizing independent schools, churches, and mutual benefit societies for the growing number of "free people of color." Richard Allen and Absalom Jones led the way in these efforts after being ejected from their pews in the midst of prayers one Sunday at St. George **Methodist** Episcopal Church in Philadelphia. Both men ended up founding independent black churches.

After the Revolution, slavery ceased to be a national institution. It became the **peculiar institution** of a single region, the American South. The isolation of slavery in one section set North and South on radically different courses of social development, sharpening economic and political divisions.

Wartime Economic Disruption

With the outbreak of the Revolution, Americans had suffered an immediate economic loss. Formerly, Britain had supplied manufactured goods, markets for American exports, and credit that enabled commerce to flourish. No longer. Hardest hit were southern planters, who had to seek new customers for their tobacco, cotton, and rice as well as find new sources of capital to finance production. Northerners too faced difficulties, for their major seaports were occupied for a time by British troops, whose presence disrupted commercial activity.

©Vintage collection 216/Alamy

In 1787 in Philadelphia, the year delegates to the Constitutional Convention met, Richard Allen and Absalom Jones founded Bethel African Methodist Episcopal Church. The first church was a former blacksmith's shop that the members hauled to a site they purchased on Sixth Street. By the time this illustration was created in 1829, a more spacious building had replaced the first church.

PUBLIC AND PRIVATE DEBT Matters did not improve with the coming of peace. France and Britain flooded the new states with their manufactures, and postwar Americans, eager for luxuries, indulged in a most unrepublican spending spree. The flurry of buying left some American merchants and consumers as deeply in debt as their governments. When loans from private citizens and foreign creditors like France proved insufficient to finance the fighting, both Congress and the states printed paper money—a whopping total of $400 million. The paper currency was backed only by the government's promise to redeem the bills with money from future taxes, because legislatures balked at the unpopular alternative of levying taxes during the war. For the bills to be redeemed, the United States had to survive, so by the end of 1776, when Continental forces sustained a series of defeats, paper money started to depreciate dramatically. By 1781 it was virtually without value, and Americans coined the expression "not worth a Continental."

POSTWAR INFLATION The printing of paper money, combined with a wartime shortage of goods, triggered an inflationary spiral. As goods became scarcer and scarcer, they cost more and more worthless dollars. In this spiral, creditors were gouged by debtors, who paid them back with depreciated currency. At the same time, soaring prices for food and manufactured goods eroded the buying power of wage earners and small farmers. And the end of the war brought on demands for prompt repayment from the new nation's foreign creditors as well as from soldiers seeking back pay and pensions.

Congress could do nothing. With no power to regulate trade, it could neither dam the stream of imported goods rushing into the states nor stanch the flow of gold and silver to Europe to pay for these items. With no power to prohibit the states from issuing paper money, it could not halt depreciation. With no power to regulate wages or prices, it could not curb inflation. With no power to tax, it could not reduce the public debt. Efforts to grant Congress greater powers met with determined resistance from the states. They refused Congress any revenue of its own, fearing the first steps toward "arbitrary" government.

POLITICAL DIVISIONS OVER ECONOMIC POLICY

Within states, too, economic problems aroused discord. Some major merchants and large commercial farmers had profited handsomely during the war by selling supplies to the American, British, and French armies at high prices. Eager to protect their windfall, they lobbied state legislatures for an end to inflationary monetary policies. They pushed for the passage of high taxes to pay wartime debts, a paper currency that was backed by gold and silver, and an active policy to encourage foreign trade.

Less affluent men fought back, pressing legislatures for programs that met their needs. Western farmers, often in debt, urged the states to print more paper money and to pass laws lowering taxes and postponing the foreclosure of mortgages. Artisans opposed merchants by calling for protection from low-priced foreign imports that competed with the goods they produced. They set themselves against farmers as well by demanding price regulation of the farm products they consumed. In the continuing struggle, the state legislatures became the battleground of competing economic factions, each bent on gaining its own particular advantage.

As the 1780s wore on, conflicts mounted. As long as the individual states remained sovereign, the Confederation was crippled—unable to conduct foreign affairs effectively, unable to set coherent economic policy, unable to deal with discontent in the West. Equally dismaying was the discovery that many Americans, instead of being selflessly concerned for the public good, selfishly pursued their private interests.

> **✔ REVIEW**
> What challenges did the West pose for the new republic?

REPUBLICAN SOCIETY

THE WAR FOR INDEPENDENCE TRANSFORMED not only America's government and economy but also its society and culture. Inspired by the Declaration's ideal of equality, some Americans rejected the subordinate position assigned to them under the old colonial order. Westerners, newly wealthy entrepreneurs, urban artisans, and women all claimed greater freedom, power, and recognition. The authority of the tradi-

tional leaders of government, society, and the family came under a new scrutiny; the impulse to defer to social superiors became less automatic. The new assertiveness demonstrated how deeply egalitarian assumptions were taking root in American culture.

The New Men of the Revolution

The Revolution gave rise to a new sense of social identity and a new set of ambitions among several groups of men who had once accepted a humbler status. The more democratic society of the frontier emboldened westerners to believe themselves the equals of easterners. One Kentuckian explained that the western migrants "must make a very different mass from one which is composed of men born and raised on the same spot. . . . They see none about them to whom or to whose families they have been accustomed to think themselves inferior."

The war also offered opportunities to aspiring entrepreneurs everywhere, and often they were not the same men who had prospered before the war. At a stroke, independence swept away the political prominence of loyalists, whose ranks included an especially high number of government officials, large landowners, and major merchants. And while loyalists found their properties confiscated by revolutionary governments, other Americans grew rich. Many northern merchants gained newfound wealth from military contracts or from privateering (sending privately owned, armed vessels to attack enemy shipping). Commercial farmers in the mid-Atlantic states prospered from the high food prices caused by wartime scarcity and army demand.

| *Gilbert Stuart's* The Skater *captures one American gentleman's characteristic sense of mastery over himself, nature, and society. But the Revolution gave other republican men a sense of power, too, including western backcountry farmers, aspiring entrepreneurs, and urban artisans such as the pewterers.*

Source: National Gallery of Art, Washington

URBAN ARTISANS The Revolution effected no dramatic redistribution of wealth. Indeed, the gap between rich and poor increased during the 1780s. But the republican ideal of equality emboldened city artisans to demand a more prominent role in politics. Calls for men of their own kind to represent them in government came as a rude shock to such gentlemen as South Carolina's William Henry Drayton, who balked at sharing power with men "who were never in a way to study" anything except "how to cut up a beast in the market to best advantage, to cobble an old shoe in the neatest manner, or to build a necessary house." The journeymen who worked for master craftsmen also exhibited a new sense of independence, forming new organizations to secure higher wages.

TRANSFORMING THE FRONTIER But the greatest gains accrued to those men newly enriched by the war and by the opportunities of independence. Representative of this aspiring group was William Cooper, a Pennsylvania Quaker who did not support the Revolution but in its aftermath strove to transform himself from a wheel wright into a gentleman. He hoped to become a gentleman by transforming thousands of acres of hilly, heavily forested land around Otsego Lake in upstate New York into wheat-producing farms clustered around a market village called Cooperstown. Yankee emigrants fleeing the shrinking farms of long-settled New England made Cooper's vision a reality and made him the leading land developer of the 1790s. But the influx of white settlement radically altered the environment of what had once been part of Iroquois country. Farmers killed off panthers, bears, and wolves to protect their livestock. Grains farming leeched nutrients from the thin topsoil, forcing farmers to clear more trees, and as the forest barrier fell, weeds and insects invaded. By the beginning of the nineteenth century, the children of many small farmers were migrating even farther west, to western New York and northern Ohio.

Similar scenarios played out on frontiers throughout the new United States. And everywhere, too, men like William Cooper demanded and received social recognition and political influence. Even though some, like Cooper, never lost the crude manners that betrayed humble origins, they styled themselves as the "aristocracy of merit" enshrined by republican ideals.

The New Women of the Revolution

Not long after the fighting with Britain had broken out, Margaret Livingston of New York wrote to her sister Catherine, "You know that our Sex are doomed to be obedient in every stage of life so that we shant be great gainers by this contest." By war's end, however, Eliza Wilkinson from rural South Carolina was complaining boldly to a woman friend: "The men say we have no business with political matters . . . it's not our sphere. . . . [But] I won't have it thought that because we are the weaker Sex (as to bodily strength my dear) we are Capable of nothing more, than minding the Dairy . . . surely we may have enough sense to give our Opinions."

What separated Margaret Livingston's resignation from Eliza Wilkinson's assertion of personal worth and independence was the Revolution. Eliza Wilkinson had managed her parents' plantation during the war and defended it from British marauders. Other women discovered similar reserves of skill and resourcefulness. When soldiers returned home, some were surprised to find their wives and daughters, who had been running family farms and businesses, less submissive and more self-confident.

EXCLUSION OF WOMEN FROM POLITICS But American men had not fought a revolution for the equality of American women. In fact, male revolutionaries gave no thought whatsoever to the role of women in the new nation, assuming that those of the "weaker sex" were incapable of making informed and independent political decisions. Most women of the revolutionary generation agreed that the proper female domain was the home, not the public arena of politics. Still, the currents of the Revolution occasionally left gaps that allowed women to display their keen political interests. When a loosely worded provision in the New Jersey state constitution gave the vote to "all free inhabitants" owning a specified amount of property, white widows and single women went to the polls. Only in 1807 did the state legislature close the loophole.

Courtesy, Winterthur Museum, Portrait by James Earl of Rebecca Mills (Mrs. William Mills) and Her Daughter Eliza Shrewsbury, 1794–1796, Charleston, SC, Oil paint on Canvas, Bequest of Henry Francis du Pont, 1960.554

A devoted mother with her daughter from the 1790s: but note the generation gap. While the mother holds fancy needlework in her lap, her daughter looks up from an opened book. Many women—especially younger women—in the decades around 1800 chose to include books in their portraits, indicating that literacy and education were becoming essential to their identity and self-esteem.

A Woman's Compass

A woman drinking spirits as her baby tumbles from her lap.

A woman crying, pointing to letters on a table. Was she jilted by a lover? Other possibilities?

Courtesy, Winterthur Museum, Engraving, Keep Within Compass, 1785–1805, England, Ink on laid paper, Gift of Henry Francis du Pont, 1954.93.1

A woman at hard labor in prison.

A woman being apprehended by the authorities. For prostitution? Drunkenness? Debt?

Keep Within Compass, *illustration, ca. 1785–1805, Winterthur Museum.*

Could there be any more eloquent testimony to the anxieties aroused by the newly confident (and sometimes outspoken) women of postrevolutionary America? Much like jokes, idealized images (for example, the smiling woman within the compass) can point historians toward areas of tension and conflict in the past. In this illustration, the four scenes displayed outside the compass send even clearer signals. Published sometime between 1785 and 1805 and titled *Keep Within Compass,* the illustration celebrates domesticity and wifely devotion while also warning women tempted to stray from that straight and narrow path. It promises a contented and prosperous life—lovely home, thriving garden, swishy silk dress, killer hat, and even a pet squirrel—to the woman "whose bosom no passion knows." But woe betide her erring sisters who strayed from the path of virtue, disgracing themselves as well as the men in their lives! Those twin themes proved equally popular in American novels published during the decades after the American Revolution.

THINKING CRITICALLY

Is the kind of virtue promoted by the illustration similar to or different from the republican understanding of virtue? What accounts for the concern about the virtue of women in the decades after the American Revolution? Why did the virtue of women loom so large, since they had few legal or political rights?

Mary Wollstonecraft's *Vindication*

In the wake of the Revolution there also appeared in England a book that would become a classic text of modern feminism, Mary Wollstonecraft's *A Vindication of the Rights of Woman* (1792). Attracting a wide, if not widely approving, readership in America as well, it called not only for laws to guarantee women civil and political equality but also for educational reforms to ensure their social and economic equality.

EDUCATION AS A ROUTE TO EQUALITY Like many young, single English women with more wit than fortune, Wollstonecraft started her working life as a governess and a school's headmistress. Then she turned to writing for her livelihood, producing book reviews, translations, a novel, and a treatise on women's education before dashing off *Vindication* in only six months. She charged that men deliberately conspired to keep women in "a state of perpetual childhood" by giving them inferior, frivolous educations. That encouraged young girls to fixate on fashion and flirtation and made them "only anxious to inspire love, when they ought to cherish a nobler ambition, and by their abilities and virtues exact respect." Girls, she proposed, should receive the same education as boys, including training that would prepare them for careers in medicine, politics, and business. No woman should have to pin her hopes for financial security on making a good marriage, Wollstonecraft argued. On the contrary, well-educated and resourceful women capable of supporting themselves would make the best wives and mothers, assets to the family and the nation.

Vindication might have been written in gunpowder rather than ink, given the reaction it aroused on both sides of the Atlantic. At first, Wollstonecraft won more than a few defenders among both men and women. This favorable reception ended abruptly after her death in childbirth in 1797, when a memoir written by her husband revealed that she had lived out of wedlock with him—and before him, with another lover. Even so, some of her readers continued to admire her views. The Philadelphia Quaker Elizabeth Drinker confided to her diary that "in very many of her sentiments, [Wollstonecraft] . . . *speaks my mind.*"

Republican Motherhood and Education

Wollstonecraft's ideas also lent support to the leading educational reformers in the revolutionary generation. Her sentiments echo in the writings of Judith Sargent Murray, a New Englander who urged the cultivation of women's minds to encourage self-respect and celebrated "excellency in our sex." Her fellow reformer, the Philadelphian Benjamin Rush, agreed that only educated and independent-minded women could raise the informed and self-reliant citizens that a republican government required.

The Revolution also prompted some states to reform their marriage laws, making divorce somewhat easier, although it remained extremely rare. But while women won greater freedom to divorce, courts became less concerned with enforcing a widow's traditional legal claim to one-third of her spouse's real estate. And married women still

(*left*) ©Tate Gallery, London/Art Resource, NY; (*right*) ©Interfoto/Sammlung Rauch/The Granger Collection, New York

Contrast the portrait of Mary Wollstonecraft rendered just before her death in 1797 (left) *with a strikingly masculinized rendering in a book published in the United States in 1809* (right), *which placed her in the company of "actresses, adventurers, authoresses, fortunetellers, gipsies, dwarfs, swindlers, and vagrants."*

could not sue or be sued, make wills or contracts, or buy and sell property. Any wages that they earned went to their husbands; so did all personal property that wives brought into a marriage; so did the rents and profits of any real estate they owned. Despite the high ideals of **republican motherhood**, most women remained confined to the domestic sphere of the home and deprived of the most basic legal and political rights.

The Attack on Aristocracy

Why wasn't the American Revolution more revolutionary? Independence secured the full political equality of white men who owned property, but women were still deprived of political rights, African Americans of human rights. Why did the revolutionaries stop short of extending equality to the most unequal groups in American society—and with so little sense that they were being inconsistent?

REPUBLICAN VIEW OF EQUALITY In part, the lack of concern was rooted in republican ideas themselves. Republican ideology viewed property as the key to independence and power. Lacking property, women and black Americans were easily consigned to the custody of husbands and masters. Then, too, prejudice played its part: the perception of women and blacks as naturally inferior beings.

But revolutionary leaders also failed to press for greater equality because they conceived their crusade in terms of eliminating the evils of a European past dominated by kings and aristocrats. They believed that the great obstacle to equality was monarchy—kings and queens who bestowed hereditary honors and political office on favored individuals and granted legal privileges and monopolies to favored churches and businesses. These artificial inequalities posed the real threat to liberty, most republicans concluded. In other words, the men of the Revolution were intent on attaining equality by leveling off the top of society. It did not occur to most republicans that the cause of equality could also be served by raising up the bottom—by attacking the laws and prejudices that kept African Americans enslaved and women dependent.

DISESTABLISHMENT OF STATE-SUPPORTED CHURCHES The most significant reform of the republican campaign against artificial privilege was the dismantling of state-supported churches. Most states had a religious establishment. In New York and the South, it was the Anglican church; in New England, the Congregational church. Since the 1740s, dissenters who did not worship at state churches had protested laws that taxed all citizens to support the clergy of established denominations. After the Revolution, as more dissenters became voters, state legislators gradually abolished state support for Anglican and Congregational churches.

SOCIETY OF CINCINNATI In the same anti-aristocratic spirit, reformers attacked the Society of Cincinnati, a group organized by former officers of the Continental Army in 1783. The society, which was merely a social club for veterans, was forced to disband for its policy of passing on its membership rights to eldest sons. In this way, critics charged, the Cincinnati was creating artificial distinctions and perpetuating a hereditary warrior nobility.

Today, many of the republican efforts at reform seem misdirected. While only a handful of revolutionaries worked for the education of women and the emancipation of slaves, enormous zeal went into fighting threats from a monarchical past that had never existed in America. Yet the threat from kings and aristocrats was real to the revolutionaries—and indeed remained real in many parts of Europe. Their determination to sweep away every shred of formal privilege ensured that these forms of inequality never took root in America. And if eighteenth-century Americans did not extend equality to women and racial minorities, it was a failure they shared with later revolutionary movements that promised more.

> **✓ REVIEW**
> How did the Revolution alter American society?

FROM CONFEDERATION TO CONSTITUTION

WHILE AMERICANS IN MANY WALKS of life sought to realize the republican commitment to equality, Congress wrestled with the problem of preserving the nation itself. With the new republic slowly rending itself to pieces, some political leaders concluded that neither the Confederation nor the state legislatures were able to remedy the basic difficulties facing the nation. But how could the states be convinced to surrender their sovereign powers? The answer came in the wake of two events—one foreign, one domestic—that lent momentum to the cause of strengthening the central government.

The Jay-Gardoqui Treaty

The international episode was a debate over a proposed treaty with Spain. In 1785 southwesterners still could not legally navigate the Mississippi and still were threatening to secede from the union and annex their territory to Spain's American empire. To shore up southwestern loyalties, Congress instructed its secretary of foreign affairs, John Jay, to negotiate an agreement with Spain preserving American rights to navigate the Mississippi River. But the Spanish emissary, Don Diego de Gardoqui, sweet-talked Jay into accepting a treaty by which the United States would give up all rights to the Mississippi for 25 years. In

Shays: ©Hi-Story/Alamy; *Bowdoin:* Source: Bowdoin College Museum of Art, Brunswick, Maine

| *These portraits provide a sharp contrast between opponents during Shays's Rebellion. A crude woodcut from a popular almanac represents Daniel Shays. The son of two Irish immigrants, Shays worked as a hired farmhand growing up. An officer in the Continental Army during the Revolution, he was presented with a ceremonial sword by General Lafayette, which he was forced to sell to make ends meet after the war. Governor of Massachusetts James Bowdoin was a merchant who pushed to collect unpaid taxes. His portrait, unlike Shays's, was painted by a respected artist, and the sheen of his satin clothing reflects his inability to sympathize with the poor farmers led by Shays.*

return, Spain agreed to grant trading privileges to American merchants.

Jay, a New Yorker, knew more than a few northern merchants who were eager to open new markets. But when the proposed treaty became public knowledge, southwesterners denounced it as nothing short of betrayal. The treaty was never ratified, but the hostility stirred up during the debate revealed the strength of sectional feelings. Only a decade later, when the Senate ratified a treaty negotiated with Spain by Thomas Pinckney in 1796, did Americans gain full access to the Mississippi.

Shays's Rebellion

On the heels of this humiliation by Spain came an internal conflict that challenged the notion that individual states could maintain order in their own territories. The trouble erupted in western Massachusetts, where many small farmers were close to ruin. By 1786 farm wages and prices had fallen sharply and farmers were selling little produce. Yet they still had to pay mortgages on their farms and other debts. In 1786 the lower house of the Massachusetts legislature obliged the farmers with a package of relief measures. But creditors in eastern Massachusetts, determined to safeguard their own investments, persuaded the upper house to defeat the measures.

In the summer of 1786 western farmers responded, demanding that the upper house of the legislature be abolished and that the relief measures go into effect. That

autumn 2,000 farmers rose in armed rebellion, led by Captain Daniel Shays, a veteran of the Revolution. They closed the county courts to halt creditors from foreclosing on their farms and marched on the federal arsenal at Springfield. The state militia quelled the uprising by February 1787, but the insurrection left many in Massachusetts and the rest of the country thoroughly shaken.

RESPONSE TO AGRARIAN UNREST Alarmed conservatives saw Shays's Rebellion as the consequence of radical democracy. "The natural effects of pure democracy are already produced among us," lamented one republican gentleman; "it is a war against virtue, talents, and property carried on by the dregs and scum of mankind." He was wrong. The rebels with Daniel Shays were no impoverished rabble. They were reputable members of western communities who wanted their property protected and believed that government existed to provide that protection. The Massachusetts state legislature had been unable to safeguard the property of farmers from the inroads of recession or to protect the property of creditors from the armed debtors who closed the courts. It had failed, in other words, to fulfill the most basic aim of republican government.

What if such violent tactics spread? Other states with discontented debtors feared what the example of western Massachusetts might mean for the future of the Confederation itself. But by 1786 Shays's Rebellion supplied only the sharpest jolt to a movement for reform that was already under way. Even before the rebellion, a group of Virginians had proposed a meeting of the states to adopt a uniform system of commercial regulations. Once assembled at Annapolis in September 1786, the delegates from five states agreed to a more ambitious undertaking. They called for a second, broader meeting in Philadelphia, which Congress approved, for the "express purpose of revising the Articles of Confederation."

Framing a Federal Constitution

SOCIAL PROFILE OF THE DELEGATES It was the wettest spring anyone could remember. The 55 men who traveled over muddy roads to Philadelphia in May 1787 arrived drenched and bespattered. Fortunately, most of the travelers were men in their 30s and 40s, young enough to survive a good soaking. Since most were gentlemen of some means—planters, merchants, and lawyers with powdered wigs and prosperous paunches—they could recover from the rigors of their journey in the best accommodations offered by America's largest city.

The delegates came from all the states except Rhode Island. The rest of New England supplied shrewd backroom politicians—Roger Sherman and Oliver Ellsworth from Connecticut and Rufus King and Elbridge Gerry, Massachusetts men who had learned a trick or two from

Crises of the 1780s—and Consequences

INTERNATIONAL CRISES

British efforts to annex Vermont to Canada

Spanish efforts to ally with Indians in the Southeast and with white settlers in the Ohio valley

↓

Culminated in debate over the Jay-Gardoqui Treaty (1785)

DOMESTIC CRISES

Postwar inflationary spiral

Debtor vs. creditor interests producing political divisions and deadlock in state legislatures

↓

Culminated in Shays's Rebellion (1786)

EXPOSED

Weakness of Confederation diplomacy; consequences of having no national army

Weakness of Confederation diplomacy and Indian policy; consequences of having no national army

Simmering tensions between East and West, North and South; potential of sectional conflict to threaten national union

EXPOSED

Confederation Congress's lack of power to set national economic policy, tax, regulate trade

Inability of sovereign states to solve economic conflicts

Potential for future agrarian violence; failure of state governments to protect property

(*left*) ©Brand X Pictures/PunchStock; (*right*) ©Hulton Archive/Getty Images

Sam Adams. The middle states marshaled much of the intellectual might: two Philadelphia lawyers, John Dickinson and James Wilson; one Philadelphia financier, Robert Morris; and the aristocratic Gouverneur Morris. From New York there was Alexander Hamilton, the mercurial and ambitious young protégé of Washington. South Carolina provided fiery orators Charles Pinckney and John Rutledge.

It was "an assembly of the demi-gods," gushed Thomas Jefferson, who, along with John Adams, was serving as a diplomat in Europe when the convention met. In fact, the only delegate who looked even remotely divine was the convention's presiding deity. Towering a full half foot taller than most of his colleagues, George Washington displayed his usual self-possession from a chair elevated on the speaker's platform in the Pennsylvania State House, where the delegates met. At first glance, the delegate of least commanding presence was Washington's fellow Virginian, James Madison. Short and slightly built, the 36-year-old Madison had no profession except hypochondria; he read a great deal and dressed in black. But he was an astute politician and a brilliant political thinker who, more than anyone else, shaped the framing of the federal Constitution.

The delegates from 12 different states had two things in common. They were all men of considerable political experience, and they all recognized the need for a stronger national union. So, when the Virginia delegation introduced Madison's outline for a new central government, the convention was ready to listen.

The Virginia and New Jersey Plans

What Madison had in mind was a truly national republic, not a confederation of independent states. His "Virginia Plan" proposed a central government with three branches: legislative, executive, and judicial. Furthermore, the legislative branch, Congress, would possess the power to veto all state legislation. In place of the Confederation's single assembly, Madison substituted a bicameral legislature, with a lower house elected directly by the people and an upper house chosen by the lower, from nominations made by state legislatures. Representatives to both houses would be apportioned according to population—a change from practice under the Articles, in which each state had a single vote in Congress. Madison also revised the structure of government that had existed under the Articles by adding an executive, who would be elected by Congress, and an independent federal judiciary.

PATERSON'S NEW JERSEY PLAN   After two weeks of debate over the Virginia Plan, William Paterson, a lawyer from New Jersey, presented a less radical counterproposal. Although his "New Jersey Plan" increased Congress's power to tax and to regulate trade, it kept the national government as a unicameral assembly, with each state receiving one vote in Congress under the policy of equal representation. The delegates took just four days to reject Paterson's plan. Most endorsed Madison's design for a stronger central government.

Even so, the issue of apportioning representation continued to divide the delegates. While smaller states pressed for each state's having an equal vote in Congress, larger states backed Madison's provision for basing representation on population. Underlying the dispute over representation was an even deeper rivalry between southern and northern states. While northern and southern populations were nearly equal in the 1780s, and the South's population was growing more rapidly, the northern states were more numerous. Giving the states equal votes would put the South at a disadvantage. Southerners feared being outvoted in Congress by the northern states and felt that only proportional representation would protect the interests of their section.

That division turned into a deadlock as the wet spring burned off into a blazing summer. Delegates suffered the daily torture of staring at a large sun painted on the speaker's chair occupied by Washington. The stifling heat was made even worse because the windows remained shut to keep any news of the proceedings from drifting out into the Philadelphia streets.

The Deadlock Broken

COMPROMISE OVER REPRESENTATION   Finally, as the heat wave broke, so did the political stalemate. On July 2 a committee headed by Benjamin Franklin suggested a compromise. States would be equally represented in the upper house of Congress, each state legislature appointing two

©Private Collection/Peter Newark American Pictures/Bridgeman Images

| *James Madison, the scholar and statesman whose ideas and political skill shaped the Constitution.*

senators to six-year terms. That satisfied the smaller states. In the lower house of Congress, which alone could initiate money bills, representation was to be apportioned according to population. Every 30,000 inhabitants would elect one representative for a two-year term. A slave was to count as three-fifths of a free person in the calculation of population, and the slave trade was to continue until 1808. That satisfied the larger states and the South.

ELECTORAL COLLEGE   By the end of August the convention was prepared to approve the final draft of the Constitution. The delegates agreed that the executive, now called the president, would be chosen every four years. Direct election seemed out of the question— after all, how could citizens in South Carolina know anything about a presidential candidate who happened to live in distant Massachusetts, or vice versa? But if voters instead chose presidential electors, those eminent men would likely have been involved in national politics, have known the candidates personally, and be prepared to vote wisely. Thus the Electoral College was established, with each state's total number of senators and representatives determining its share of electoral votes.

SEPARATION OF POWERS   An array of other powers ensured that the executive would remain independent and strong. He would have command over the armed forces, authority to conduct diplomatic relations, responsibility to nominate judges and officials in the executive branch, and the power to veto congressional legislation. Just as the executive branch was made independent, so too the federal judiciary was separated from the other two branches of government. Madison believed that this clear **separation of powers** was essential to a balanced republican government.

AMENDING THE CONSTITUTION   Madison's only real defeat came when the convention refused to give Congress veto power over state legislation. Still, the new bicameral national legislature enjoyed much broader authority than Congress had under the Confederation, including the power to tax and to regulate commerce. The Constitution also limited the powers of state legislatures, prohibiting them from levying duties on trade, coining money or issuing paper currency, and conducting foreign relations. The Constitution and the acts passed by Congress were declared the supreme law of the land, taking precedence over any legislation passed by the states. And changing the Constitution would not be easy. Amendments could be proposed only by a two-thirds vote of both houses of Congress or in a convention requested by two-thirds of the state legislatures. Ratification of amendments required approval by three-quarters of the states.

A REPUBLIC OF THE PEOPLE, NOT A CONFEDERATION OF STATES On September 17, 1787, 39 of the 42 delegates remaining in Philadelphia signed the Constitution. It was fortunate that the signatories included so many lawyers, because the summer's proceedings had been of such dubious legality that many skilled attorneys would be needed to make them seem otherwise. Charged only to revise the Articles, the delegates had instead written a completely new frame of government. And to speed up ratification, the convention decided that the Constitution would go into effect after only nine states had approved it, overlooking the fact that even a revision of the Articles would have required the assent of all state legislatures. They further declared that the people themselves—not the state legislatures—would pass judgment on the Constitution in special ratifying conventions. To serve final notice that the new central government was a republic of the people and not merely another confederation of states, Gouverneur Morris of Pennsylvania hit on a happy turn of phrase to introduce the Constitution. "We the People," the document begins, "in Order to form a more perfect Union . . ."

Ratification

THE ANTI-FEDERALISTS With grave misgivings on the part of many, the states called for conventions to decide whether to ratify the new Constitution. Those Americans with the gravest misgivings—the Anti-Federalists as they came to be called—voiced familiar republican fears. Older and less cosmopolitan than their **Federalist** opponents, the Anti-Federalists drew on their memories of the struggle with England to frame their criticisms of the Constitution. Expanding the power of the central government at the expense of the states, they warned, would lead to corrupt and arbitrary rule by new aristocrats. Extending a republic over a large territory, they cautioned, would separate national legislators from the interests and close oversight of their constituents.

THE FEDERALIST PAPERS Madison responded to these objections in *The Federalist Papers,* a series of 85 essays written with Alexander Hamilton and John Jay during the winter of 1787–1788. He countered Anti-Federalist concerns over the centralization of power by pointing out that each separate branch of the national government would keep the others within the limits of their legal authority. That mechanism of **checks and balances** would prevent the executive from oppressing the people while preventing the people from oppressing themselves.

To answer Anti-Federalist objections to a national republic, Madison drew on the ideas of an English philosopher, David Hume. In his famous tenth essay in *The Federalist Papers,* Madison argued that in a great republic, "the Society becomes broken into a greater variety of

RATIFICATION OF THE CONSTITUTION

State	Date	Vote For	Vote Against
Delaware	December 8, 1787	30	9
Pennsylvania	December 12, 1787	46	23
New Jersey	December 18, 1787	38	0
Georgia	January 3, 1788	26	0
Connecticut	January 9, 1788	128	40
Massachusetts	February 6, 1788	187	168
Maryland	April 26, 1788	63	11
South Carolina	May 23, 1788	149	73
New Hampshire	June 21, 1788	57	47
Virginia	June 25, 1788	89	79
New York	July 26, 1788	30	27
North Carolina	November 21, 1788	194	77
Rhode Island	May 29, 1790	34	32

REPUBLICAN REMEDY?

James Madison and "Brutus"—perhaps the Anti-Federalist judge Robert Yates—debated the proposed Constitution in the New York newspapers during 1787. One of the most contentious issues was whether a republic could effectively govern a territory as extensive as the United States.

DOCUMENT 1
James Madison

The two great points of difference between a democracy and a republic are: first, the delegation of the government in the latter, to a small number of citizens elected by the rest; secondly, the great number of citizens and greater sphere of country over which the latter may be extended.

The effect of the first difference is, on the one hand, to refine and enlarge the public views by passing them through the medium of a chosen body of citizens, whose wisdom may best discern the true interest of their country and whose patriotism and love of justice will be least likely to sacrifice it to temporary or partial considerations. Under such a regulation it may well happen that the public voice, pronounced by the representatives of the people, will be more consonant to the public good than if pronounced by the people themselves, convened for the purpose. On the other hand . . . men of factious tempers, of local prejudices, or of sinister designs, may, by intrigue, by corruption, or by other means, first obtain the suffrages, and then betray the interests of the people. The question resulting is, whether small or extensive republics are more favorable to the election of proper guardians of the public weal; and it is clearly decided in favor of the latter by two obvious considerations.

In the first place . . . if the proportion of fit characters be not less in the large than in the small republic, the former will present a greater option, and consequently a greater probability of a fit choice.

In the next place, as each representative will be chosen by a greater number of citizens in the large than in the small republic, it will be more difficult for unworthy candidates to practice with success the vicious arts by which elections are too often carried. . . .

The other point of difference is the greater number of citizen and extent of territory which may be brought within the compass of republican than democratic government; and it is this circumstance principally which render factious combinations less to be dreaded in the former than in the latter. The smaller the society, the fewer probably will be the distinct parties and interests composing it; the fewer the distinct parties and interests, the more frequently will a majority be found of the same party; and the smaller the number of individuals compassing a majority . . . the more easily will they concert and execute their plans of oppression. Extend the sphere and you take in a greater variety of parties and interests; you make it less probable that a majority of the whole will have a common motive to invade the rights of other citizens; or if such a common motive exists, it will be more difficult for all who feel it to discover their own strength and to act in unison with each other.

The influence of factious leaders may kindle a flame within their particular States but will be unable to spread a general conflagration through the other States. A religious sect may degenerate into a political faction in a part of the Confederacy; but the variety of sects dispersed over the entire face of it must secure the national councils against any danger from that source. A rage for paper money, for an abolition of debts, for an equal division of property, or for any other improper or wicked project, will be less apt to pervade the whole body of the Union than a particular member of it. . . .

In the extent and proper structure of the Union, therefore, we behold a republican remedy for diseases most incident to republican government.

Source: Madison, James, "Federalist No. 10," The Federalist: A Collection of Essays, Written in Favour of the New Constitution. New York, 1788.

DOCUMENT 2
"Brutus"

A free republic cannot succeed over a country of such immense extent, containing such a number of inhabitants, and these increasing in such rapid progression as that of the whole United States. . . .

Now, in a large extended country, it is impossible to have a representation, possessing the sentiments and of integrity, to declare the minds of the people, without having it so numerous and unwieldly, as to be subject in great measure to the inconveniency of a democratic government. . . .

In a republic, the manners, sentiments, and interest of the people should be similar. If this be not the case . . . [it] will retard the operations of government, and prevent such conclusions as will promote the public good. . . .

The productions of the different parts of the union are very variant, and their interests, of consequence, diverse. Their manners and habits differ as much as their climates and production; and their sentiments are by no means coincident.

The confidence which people have in their rulers, in a free republic, arises from their knowing them, from their being responsible to them for their conduct, and from the power they have of displacing them when they misbehave: but in a republic of the extent of this continent, the people in general would be acquainted with few of their rulers. . . . The consequence will be, they will have no confidence in their legislature, suspect them of ambitious views, be jealous of every measure they adopt, and will not support the laws they pass . . . no way will be left to render it otherwise, but by establishing an armed force to execute laws at the point of a bayonet.

Source: "Brutus" in the New York Journal, October 18, 1787.

THINKING CRITICALLY

How did Madison define the differences between a democracy and a republic? What did he regard as the chief advantage of a large republic? On what grounds did "Brutus" argue against large republics? Has our republican form of government been successful in avoiding the kinds of oppression and "improper projects" that Madison describes?

interests, of pursuits, of passions, which check each other." The larger the territory, the more likely it was to contain multiple political interests and parties so that no single faction could dominate. Instead, each would cancel out the others.

BILL OF RIGHTS The one Anti-Federalist criticism Madison could not get around was the absence of a national bill of rights. Opponents insisted on an explicit statement of rights to secure the freedoms of individuals and minorities from being violated by the federal government. Madison finally promised to place a bill of rights before Congress immediately after the Constitution was ratified.

Throughout the early months of 1788, Anti-Federalists continued their opposition. But they lacked the articulate and influential leadership that rallied behind the Constitution and commanded greater access to the public press. In the end, too, Anti-Federalist fears of centralized power proved less compelling than Federalist prophecies of the chaos that would follow if the Constitution were not adopted.

BILL OF RIGHTS RATIFIED By the end of July 1788 all but two states had voted in favor of ratification. The last holdout—Rhode Island, to no one's surprise—finally came aboard in May 1790, after Madison had carried through on his pledge to submit a bill of rights to the new Congress. Indeed, these 10 amendments—ratified by enough states to become part of the Constitution by the end of 1791—proved to be the Anti-Federalists' most impressive legacy. The bill of rights set the most basic terms for defining personal liberty in the United States. Among the rights guaranteed were freedom of religion, the press, and speech, as well as the right to assemble and petition and the right to bear arms. The amendments also established clear procedural safeguards, including the right to a trial by jury and protection against illegal searches and seizures. They prohibited excessive bail, cruel and unusual punishment, and the quartering of troops in private homes.

 REVIEW

What short-term crises precipitated the Constitutional Convention, and what were the main points of debate at that meeting?

PUTTING HISTORY IN GLOBAL CONTEXT

WITHIN THE SPAN OF A SINGLE generation, Americans had declared their independence twice. In many ways the political freedom claimed from Britain in 1776 was less remarkable than the intellectual freedom from the Old World that Americans achieved by agreeing to the Constitution. The Constitution represented a triumph of the imagination—a challenge to many beliefs long cherished by western Europe's republican thinkers.

Revolutionary ideals had been deeply influenced by the conflicts of British politics, in particular the Opposition's warnings about the dangers of executive power. Those concerns at first committed the revolutionaries to making legislatures supreme. In the end, though, Americans ratified a constitution that provided for an independent executive and a balanced government. The Opposition's fears of distant, centralized power had at first prompted the revolutionaries to embrace state sovereignty. But in the Constitution, Americans established a national government with authority independent of the states. Finally, the common sense among all of western Europe's republican theorists—that large national republics were an impossibility—was rejected by Americans, making the United States an impossibility that still endures.

What, then, became of the last tenet of the old republican creed—the belief that civic virtue would sustain popular liberty? The hard lessons of the war and the crises of the 1780s withered confidence in the capacity of Americans to sacrifice their private interests for the public welfare. The Constitution reflected the view that interest rather than virtue shaped the behavior of most people most of the time and that the clash of diverse interest groups would remain a constant of public life.

Yet Madison and many other Federalists did not believe that the competition between private interests would always foster the public welfare. That goal would be met instead by the new national government acting as "a disinterested and dispassionate umpire in disputes between different passions and interests in the State." A large republic, Federalists believed, with its millions of citizens, would yield more of that scarce resource—disinterested gentlemen dedicated to serving the public good. Such gentlemen, in Madison's words, "whose enlightened views and virtuous sentiments render them superior to local prejudices," would fill the small number of national offices.

Not all the old revolutionaries agreed. Anti-Federalists drawn from the ranks of ordinary Americans still believed that the national government should be composed of representations from every social class and occupational group, not dominated by "enlightened" gentlemen. "These lawyers and men of learning, and moneyed men, that talk so finely," complained one Anti-Federalist, would "get all the power and all of the money into their own hands, and then they will swallow up all us little folks."

That fear made Patrick Henry so ardent an Anti-Federalist that he refused to attend the Constitutional Convention in 1787, saying that he "smelt a rat." "I am not a Virginian, but an American," Henry had once declared. Most likely he was lying. Or perhaps Patrick Henry, a southerner and a slaveholder, could see himself as an "American" only so long as sovereignty remained firmly in the hands of the individual states. Henry's convictions, 70 years later, would rise again to haunt the Union.

CHAPTER SUMMARY

Leading Americans gave more thought to federalism, the organization of a United States, as events in the 1780s revealed the weaknesses of the state and national governments.

- For a decade after independence, the revolutionaries were less committed to creating a single national republic than to organizing 13 separate state republics, each dominated by popularly elected legislatures.

- The Articles of Confederation's national legislature left the crucial power of the purse, as well as all final power to make and execute laws, entirely to the states.

- Many conflicts in the new republic were occasioned by westward expansion, which created both international difficulties with Britain and Spain and internal tensions over the democratization of state legislatures.

- After the Revolution, Americans struggled to define republican society; workers began to organize, and some women claimed a right to greater political, legal, and educational opportunities.

- The Revolution's egalitarian principles sparked a debate over slavery that increased the split between northern and southern states. Antislavery societies appeared in the North; some planters in the Upper South freed their slaves, but no southern state abolished slavery.

- In the mid-1780s the political crisis of the Confederation came to a head, prompted by the controversy over the Jay-Gardoqui Treaty and Shays's Rebellion.

- The Constitutional Convention of 1787 produced an entirely new frame of government that established a truly national republic and provided for a separation of powers among a judiciary, a bicameral legislature, and a strong executive.

- The Anti-Federalists, opponents of the Constitution, pushed for a bill of rights, which was incorporated into the Constitution by 1791.

Digging Deeper

The work of Gordon S. Wood is indispensable for understanding the transformation of American politics and culture during the 1780s and thereafter; see especially *The Creation of the American Republic, 1776–1787* (1969) and *The Radicalism of the American Revolution* (1992). Woody Holton's *Unruly Americans* (2007) emphasizes struggles over economic policy and democracy. For a marvelous synthesis of current research on the Revolution and early republic, see the essays in Andrew Shankman, ed., *The World of the American Revolutionary Republic* (2014). For arguments over the Constitution, in and out of Congress, see Max M. Edling, *A Revolution in Favor of Government* (2008); Pauline Maier, *Ratification: The People Debate the Constitution* (2011); and Michael J. Klarman, *The Framers' Coup* (2016). To appreciate the Anti-Federalist argument, read Saul Cornell, *The Other Founders* (1999); and the classic writings of Cecelia Kenyon, collected in *Men of Little Faith* (2003).

Carroll Smith-Rosenberg's *This Violent Empire* (2010) argues that exclusion of "others" (especially Indians, African Americans, women, and the poor) was indispensable to early American nationalism. To explore the meaning of republicanism for American women, see two fine studies by Linda K. Kerber, *Women of the Republic* (1980) and *No Constitutional Right to Be Ladies* (1998); as well as Rosemarie Zagarri's superb biography of Mercy Otis Warren, *A Woman's Dilemma* (2nd ed., 2014). For a vivid sense of how the 1780s transformed local society and politics in one Massachusetts county, read John L. Brooke, *The Heart of the Commonwealth* (1991); and for a fascinating tale of how the Revolution made one ordinary man's life extraordinary, enjoy Alan Taylor, *William Cooper's Town* (1995). The best accounts of how the Revolution's legacy affected the lives of African Americans in the North include Shane White, *Somewhat More Independent* (1991); and Joanne Pope Melish, *Disowning Slavery* (1998).

After the Fact

| Historians Reconstruct the Past |

White and Black Southerners Worshiping Together

Religious beliefs, gatherings, and rituals reflect some of the deepest human emotions. Often they also lay bare some of society's deepest divisions. For both these reasons and more, historians often study religious institutions and practices to understand how a society functions.

During the 50 years before 1800, **evangelicals** introduced southerners to new ways of being religious. Those attending their worship services were drawn into the earliest southern Baptist, Methodist, and Presbyterian churches by the First Great Awakening and other revivals that followed. Some of these early services were held in private homes, others in crudely constructed churches, and still others in open fields. As evangelical preachers stressed the importance of being "reborn" by faith in Jesus Christ, some southerners wept, confessed their sins, and encouraged one another with hopeful words and warm embraces. Those who came to such gatherings engaged in the most intimate kind of sharing and self-revelation.

What made the services even more extraordinary is that some participants were white and some black. These reli-

Source: Herrnhut, Archiv der Brüder-Unität

gious fellowships were truly biracial and remained so until after the Civil War. That remarkable fact has intrigued historians. In a society increasingly shaped by the institution of slavery, evangelical churches were one of the few southern institutions that brought blacks and whites together rather than keeping them apart. How did members behave toward one another daily? Were born-again converts from both races treated equally? How was authority within such churches distributed among black and white members?

The questions are tantalizing, but the answers by no means easy to come by. Some letters and diaries survive from the last half of the eighteenth century, among them the daily journals and correspondence of ministers. A few preachers even published autobiographies of their experiences. But even more valuable information can be gathered from what might seem at first a rather drab source. There are scores of church records dating from this period, most kept by Virginia Baptists. The members of each Baptist church elected a clerk, always a white male "brother," whose duty it was to record all the business transacted at their monthly meetings, often in a ledger-sized bound volume called the "church book." Church books provide an insight into relations between whites and blacks in part because their clerks are not consciously trying to write about race relations. They are simply recording the everyday business of churches, week in, week out.

DECODING THE CHURCH BOOKS

SOMETIMES PRACTICAL CONCERNS DOMINATED THE meeting. Should the church building be repaired? Who among the brethren will be permitted to preach? (Many Baptist churches boasted several preachers besides the pastor.) On other occasions, members debated what, according to the Bible, was the holiest way to govern their churches. But at most meetings, members fixed their attention on admitting new converts to their fellowship and "disciplining" older members suspected of sexual misconduct or theft, slander or swearing, drinking or fighting. Church clerks duly noted all those accepted as new members, as well as the names of wayward brothers and sisters—and whether they were merely scolded for their faults or expelled.

Such records offer the most direct and vivid sense of African Americans' presence and participation in early evangelical churches. First, historians can start by doing a little counting. How many members are white and how many black? The records show that blacks made up a substantial minority—perhaps one-fifth to one-quarter—of the members in most churches. In a few, they constituted a majority. Many churches, too, authorized at least one African American brother to preach, sometimes permitting him that "liberty" only among other blacks but in other instances allowing him to address racially mixed gatherings. There were even a few predominantly white churches in early Virginia that black preachers served as pastors.

What about voting? In some churches, too, black men and, more rarely, black women were permitted to vote in meetings. In all, African American members could participate in deliberations and give testimony in discipline cases. Indeed, there are several instances of masters being disciplined after slave members complained of being abused. Black members, too, were sometimes charged with wrongdoing, but white men were far more likely than any other group of members to be hauled before the church for reported misdeeds. In short, evangelical churches like these Baptist fellowships were among the most racially egalitarian institutions in early southern society. They offered African Americans unusual opportunities to hold positions of authority, to voice their opinions, and to gain leverage over their masters.

LIMITS OF RACIAL EQUALITY

YET THESE SAME CHURCH RECORDS also reveal the limits of racial equality among early evangelicals. Like all evidence mined by historians, the sources yield data that are sometimes complex and contradictory.

Records of those meetings at which members discussed the mundane matter of church repair reveal, for example, that the Baptists segregated seating at public worship. African Americans were consigned to the least choice spots at the back of the church or in "sheds" attached to the side. Moreover, when white members filled every available seat, black members

Source: Free Library of Philadelphia, Print and Picture Collection

"Uncle Jack," shown in this 1849 engraving, preaches informally to a white congregation. He began his career as a minister in the 1790s and continued until 1832.

were ordered outdoors to listen from underneath open windows. The attitude that such practices convey—that whites regarded African Americans as "second-class" members—is also suggested by the manner in which many clerks recorded new church members. They always entered the full names of white converts; however, new African American members were usually listed last and often collectively as "several Negroes."

Church discussions about who might preach also show a growing concern on the part of white members to restrict the activities of black preachers. Increasingly after 1750, those allowed that "liberty" were given ever-stricter instructions about whom they might preach to, at which times, and from what texts of the Bible. At meetings in which the rules of conducting church business were discussed, white members also began to express concern about whether African American members should be allowed to vote. Most churches revoked that right before the end of the eighteenth century. Tracing how churches dealt with black members accused of misbehavior suggests a similar anxiety among white members, which increased over time. Although African Americans continued to make up only a tiny minority of church members suspected of misbehavior, those convicted of wrongdoing were far more likely than white members to be expelled rather than to receive a milder punishment.

In other words, a closer inspection of church records suggests that white evangelicals drifted toward more racially restrictive policies over the latter half of the eighteenth century. Why? The numbers in the church books are suggestive. After the Revolution, increasing numbers of African Americans were entering Baptist (and other evangelical) churches. As the percentage of black members rose, white evangelicals feared that the "freedoms" given to black worshipers might detract from the church's ability to win converts among slaveholders.

SEEKING A SEPARATE WAY

CLEARLY, EVANGELICALS WERE WINNING CONVERTS among African Americans. Yet other evidence suggests that black members were left unsatisfied by their treatment in white churches. The diaries and letters of white evangelicals reveal that many black members of biracial churches had also begun conducting their own separate devotions. Even by the 1790s,

©Paul Fearn/Alamy

A detail from John Antrobus's painting Plantation Burial *(1860).*

African American Christians were meeting nightly in the slave quarters to pray, sing, and hear the sermons of black preachers. Such "shadow churches" served as the crucible of Afro-Christianity, a melding of evangelical Protestant and West African religious traditions. John Antrobus's painting *Plantation Burial* (in a detail shown above) reflects the situation that prevailed by the mid-nineteenth century. Although blacks attended white services in greater numbers, their most vital worship often took place elsewhere. White masters and preachers were like the shadowy couple Antrobus painted on the right: virtually hidden between the two trees and divorced from the Christian worship of their slaves.

9 The Early Republic

1789–1824

Citizens staged Fourth of July parades as one way to define the identity of their young republic. This New York City parade in 1812 was led by the Tammany Society, whose members rejected the aristocratic inclinations of the Federalist Party. The society was named to honor a Delaware Indian chief; its members often marched wearing Indian-style garb, as seen here. But by 1812 the patriotic associations of Indian dress (recall the Boston Tea Party disguises) were less popular due to increased clashes with Indians on the frontier.

©Collection of the New-York Historical Society, USA/Bridgeman Images

>> An American Story

"I FELT MY BLOOD BOIL"

One spring evening in 1794 General John Neville rode home from Pittsburgh with his wife and granddaughter. As they went up a hill, his wife's saddle started to slip, so Neville dismounted. As he adjusted the strap, a rider galloped up and in a gruff voice asked, "Are you Neville the excise officer?"

"Yes," Neville replied, without turning around.

"Then I must give you a whipping!" cried the rider and leapt from his horse. He grabbed Neville by the hair and lunged at his throat. Breaking free, Neville finally managed to knock the man down, after which he fled. But Neville could not help but be shaken as he resumed his journey. The general was not accustomed to such treatment. As one of the wealthiest men in the area, he expected respect from those of lower social rank. And he had received it—until

This will make the 'Squire : ne our Bill of grog.

come friend burn I'll take thee to thy master.

to these art our old friend the long nosed gentlemen.

AN EXCISEMAN.

©Sarin Images/The Granger Collection, New York

| A tax collector in league with the devil.

becoming embroiled in a controversy over the new "whiskey tax" on distilled spirits. In a frontier district like western Pennsylvania, farmers regularly distilled their grain into whiskey for barter and sale. Not surprisingly, the **excise tax**, passed by Congress in 1791, was notoriously unpopular. Still, Neville had accepted an appointment to be one of the tax's regional inspectors. For three years he had endured the occasional threat, but this roadside assault showed that popular hostility was rising.

As spring turned to summer the grain ripened, and so did the people's anger. In mid-July a federal marshal arrived to serve summonses to a number of farmer-distillers who had not paid taxes. One, William Miller, squinted at the paper and was amazed to find the government ordering him to appear in court—hundreds of miles away in Philadelphia—in little more than a month. Worse, the papers claimed he owed $250.

And there, next to this unknown federal marshal, stood John Neville. "I thought $250 would ruin me," recalled Miller; "and I felt my blood boil at seeing General Neville along to pilot the sheriff to my very door." Within minutes 30 or 40 laborers had swarmed from a nearby field. Armed with muskets and pitchforks, they forced Neville and the marshal to beat a hasty retreat. Next morning, the local militia company marched to Neville's estate. A battle ensued, and the general, aided by his slaves, beat back the attackers. A larger group, numbering 500 to 700, returned the following day to find Neville fled and his home garrisoned by a group of soldiers from nearby Fort Pitt. The mob burned down most of the outbuildings and, after the soldiers surrendered, torched Neville's elegantly furnished home.

That summer, marauding bands roamed the countryside, burning homes and attacking tax collectors. Western Pennsylvania experienced the greatest unrest, but farmers in the western districts of several other states also defied federal officials, thus launching a full-scale "Whiskey Rebellion" in the summer of 1794.

Alexander Hamilton, a principal architect of the strong federal government established by the Constitution, knew a challenge to authority when he saw one: "Shall there be a government, or no government?" So did an alarmed George Washington, now president and commander-in-chief of the new republic, who led an army of 13,000 men—larger than that he had commanded at Yorktown against the British—into the Pennsylvania countryside. That show of force cowed the Pennsylvania protesters, snuffing out the Whiskey Rebellion.

Federalists such as Washington and Hamilton—supporters of a powerful national government—had high hopes for their newly created republic. But the riots and rebellion deepened fears for its future. The nation's founders recognized all too well how risky it was to unite such a vast territory. Yankee merchants living along Boston wharves had economic interests and cultural traditions distinct from those of backcountry farmers who raised hogs, tended a few acres of corn, and distilled whiskey. Even among farmers there was a world of difference between a South Carolina planter who shipped tons of rice to European markets and a New Hampshire family whose stony fields yielded barely enough to survive. Could the new government established by the Constitution provide a framework strong enough to unite such a patchwork of peoples, cultures, and classes? These newly united states were a fragile creation, buffeted by changes beyond their borders and struggling to create a stable government at home. During the nation's first three decades, the republic's survival depended on balancing the interests of a socially and economically diverse population. <<

189

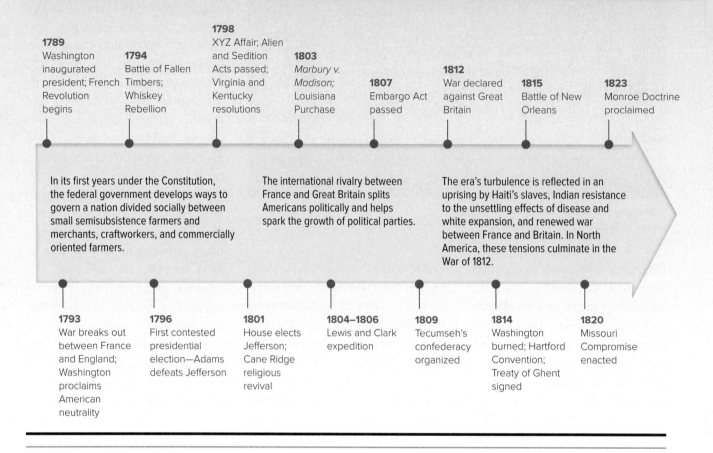

1789 Washington inaugurated president; French Revolution begins

1794 Battle of Fallen Timbers; Whiskey Rebellion

1798 XYZ Affair; Alien and Sedition Acts passed; Virginia and Kentucky resolutions

1803 *Marbury v. Madison;* Louisiana Purchase

1807 Embargo Act passed

1812 War declared against Great Britain

1815 Battle of New Orleans

1823 Monroe Doctrine proclaimed

In its first years under the Constitution, the federal government develops ways to govern a nation divided socially between small semisubsistence farmers and merchants, craftworkers, and commercially oriented farmers.

The international rivalry between France and Great Britain splits Americans politically and helps spark the growth of political parties.

The era's turbulence is reflected in an uprising by Haiti's slaves, Indian resistance to the unsettling effects of disease and white expansion, and renewed war between France and Britain. In North America, these tensions culminate in the War of 1812.

1793 War breaks out between France and England; Washington proclaims American neutrality

1796 First contested presidential election—Adams defeats Jefferson

1801 House elects Jefferson; Cane Ridge religious revival

1804–1806 Lewis and Clark expedition

1809 Tecumseh's confederacy organized

1814 Washington burned; Hartford Convention; Treaty of Ghent signed

1820 Missouri Compromise enacted

A SOCIAL AND POLITICAL PORTRAIT OF THE NEW REPUBLIC

WHEN THE CONSTITUTION WENT INTO effect, the United States stretched from the Atlantic Ocean to the Mississippi River. Comprising some 840,000 square miles in 1789, it was approximately four times the size of France, five times the size of Spain, ten times the size of Great Britain. The first federal census, compiled in 1790, counted approximately 4 million people, divided about evenly between the northern and southern states. Only about 100,000 settlers lived beyond the Appalachians in the Tennessee and Kentucky territories, which were soon to become states.

Within the Republic's boundaries were two major groups that lacked effective political influence: African Americans and Indians. In 1790 black Americans numbered 750,000, almost one-fifth the total population. More than 90 percent lived in the southern states from Maryland to Georgia; most were slaves who worked on tobacco and rice plantations, but there were free blacks as well. The census did not count the number of Indians living east of the Mississippi. North of the Ohio, the powerful Miami Confederacy discouraged settlement, while to the south, five strong, well-organized tribes—the Creeks, Cherokees, Chickasaws, Choctaws, and Seminoles—dominated the region from the Appalachians to the Mississippi River.

POPULATION GROWTH That composition would change as the white population continued to double about every 22 years. Immigration contributed only a small part to this astonishing growth. On average, fewer than 10,000 Europeans arrived annually between 1790 and 1820. The primary cause was natural increase, since, on average, American white women gave birth to nearly eight children each. As a result, the United States had an unusually youthful population: in 1790 almost half of all white Americans were under 16 years old. The age at first marriage was about 25 for men, 24 for women—and three or four years younger in newly settled areas—which contributed to the high birthrate.

This youthful, growing population remained overwhelmingly rural. Only 24 towns and cities boasted 2,500 or more

The population of the newly formed United States continued to double about every 22 years, the great majority of its growth due to high fertility rates. Artist Charles Willson Peale painted this portrait of his family, though it was only part of it. Peale married three times and over the years was the father of 18 children. Seven died before reaching the age of 18.

©Collection of the New-York Historical Society, USA/Bridgeman Images

residents, and 19 out of 20 Americans lived outside them. In fact, more than 80 percent of American families in 1800 were engaged in agriculture. In such a rural environment the movement of people, goods, and information was slow. Few individuals used the expensive postal system, and most roads were still little more than dirt paths hacked through the forest. In 1790 the country had 92 newspapers, but they were published mostly in towns and cities along major avenues of transportation.

Life in isolated regions contrasted markedly with that in bustling urban centers like New York City and Philadelphia. But the most basic division in American society was not between the cities and the countryside, important as that was. What would divide Americans most broadly over the coming decades was the contrast between semisubsistence and commercial ways of life. Semisubsistence farmers lived on the produce of their own land and labor. Americans in the commercial economy were tied more closely to the larger markets of a far-flung world.

Semisubsistence and Commercial Economies

Most rural white Americans in the interior of the northern states and the backcountry of the South lived off the produce of their own land. Wealth in those areas, although not distributed equally, was spread fairly broadly. And subsistence remained the goal of most white families. "The great effort was for every farmer to produce anything he required within his own family," one European visitor noted. In such an economy women played a key role. Wives and daughters had to be skilled in making articles such as candles, soap, clothing, and hats, since the cost of buying such items was steep.

With labor scarce and expensive, farmers also depended on their neighbors to help clear fields, build homes, and harvest crops. If a farm family produced a small surplus, it usually exchanged it locally rather than selling it for cash in a distant market. In this barter economy, money was seldom seen and was used primarily to pay taxes and purchase imported goods.

INDIAN ECONOMIES Indian economies were also based primarily on subsistence. In the division of labor women raised crops, while men fished or hunted—not only for meat but also for skins to make clothing. Because Indians followed game more seasonally than did white settlers, they moved their villages to several different locations over the course of a year. But both whites and Indians in a **semisubsistence economy** moved periodically to new fields after they had exhausted the old ones. Indians exhausted agricultural lands less quickly because they planted beans, corn, and squash in the same field, a technique that better conserved soil nutrients.

Despite the image of both the independent "noble savage" and the self-reliant yeoman farmer, virtually no one in the backcountry operated within a truly self-sufficient economy. Although farmers tried to grow most of the food their families ate, they normally bought salt, sugar, and coffee, and they often traded with their neighbors for food and other items. In addition, necessities such as iron, glass, lead, and gunpowder had to be purchased, and many farmers hired artisans to make shoes and weave cloth. Similarly, Indians were enmeshed in the wider world of European commerce, exchanging furs for iron tools or clothing and ornamental materials.

Outside the backcountry, Americans were tied much more closely to a **commercial economy**. Here, merchants, artisans, and even farmers did not subsist on what they produced but

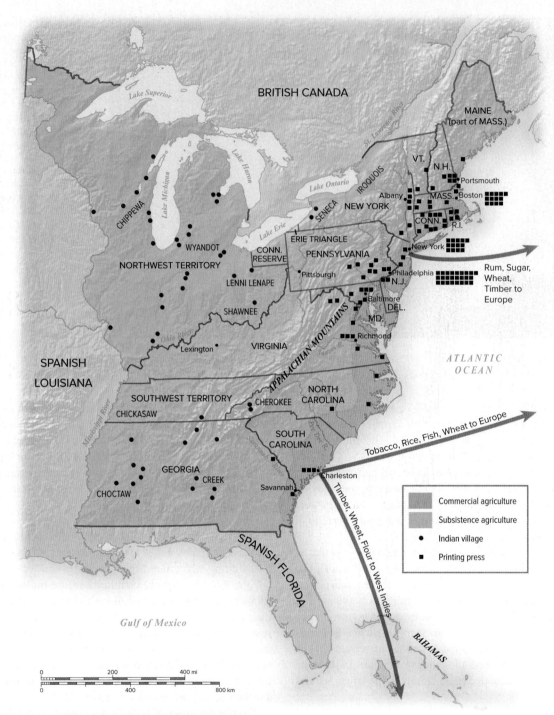

SEMISUBSISTENCE AND COMMERCIAL AMERICA, 1790

*To prosper, a commercial economy demanded relatively cheap transportation to move goods. Thus in 1790 American commerce was confined largely to settled areas along the coast and to navigable rivers below the fall line. Because commerce depended on an efficient flow of information and goods, newspapers flourished in these areas. **Did the split between commercial and semisubsistence ways of life reflect a division more between east and west or north and south? Why?***

instead sold goods or services in a wider market and lived on their earnings. Cities and towns, of course, played a key part in the commercial economy. But so did the agricultural regions near the coast and along navigable rivers.

For commerce to flourish, goods had to move from producers to market cheaply enough to reap profits. Water

offered the only cost-effective transportation over any distance; indeed, it cost as much to ship goods a mere 30 miles over primitive roads as to ship by boat 3,000 miles across the Atlantic to London. Cost-effective transportation was available to the planters of the Tidewater South, and city merchants used their access to the sea to establish trading ties to the West Indies and Europe. But urban artisans and workers were also linked to this market economy, as were many farm families in the Hudson valley, southeastern Pennsylvania, and southern New England.

In commercial economies wealth was less equally distributed. By 1790 the richest 10 percent of Americans living in cities and in the plantation districts of the Tidewater South owned about 50 percent of the wealth. In the backcountry the top 10 percent was likely to own 25 to 35 percent of the wealth.

The Constitution and Commerce

In many ways the fight over ratification of the Constitution represented a struggle between the commercial and the subsistence-oriented elements of American society. Urban merchants and workers as well as commercial farmers and planters generally rallied behind the Constitution. They took a broader, more cosmopolitan view of the nation's future, and they had a more favorable view of government power than did subsistence farmers.

Americans who remained a part of the semisubsistence **barter economy** tended to oppose the Constitution. More provincial in outlook, they feared concentrated power, were suspicious of cities and commercial institutions, opposed aristocracy and special privilege, and in general just wanted to be left alone.

And so in 1789 the United States embarked on its new national course, with two rival visions of the direction that the fledgling Republic should take. Which vision would prevail—a question that was as much social as it was political—increasingly divided the generation of revolutionary leaders in the early republic.

Washington Organizes the Government

Whatever the Republic was to become, Americans agreed that George Washington personified it. When the first Electoral College cast its votes, Washington was unanimously elected, the only president in history so honored. John Adams became vice president. Loyalty to the new republic, with its untried form of government and diversity of peoples and interests, rested to a great degree on the trust and respect Americans gave Washington.

George Washington realized that as the first occupant of the executive office, everything he did was fraught with significance. "I walk on untrodden ground," he commented. "There is scarcely any part of my conduct which may not hereafter be drawn into precedent."

THE CABINET The Constitution made no mention of a cabinet. Yet the drafters of the Constitution, aware of the experience of the Continental Congress under the Articles of Confederation, clearly assumed that the president would have some system of advisers. Congress authorized the creation of four departments—War, Treasury, State, and Attorney General—whose heads were to be appointed with the consent

of the Senate. Washington's most important choices were Alexander Hamilton as secretary of the Treasury and Thomas Jefferson to head the State Department. Washington gradually excluded Adams from cabinet discussions, and any meaningful role for the vice president, whose duties were largely undefined by the Constitution, soon disappeared.

The Constitution created a federal Supreme Court but beyond that was silent about the court system. The Judiciary Act of 1789 set the size of the Supreme Court at 6 members; it also established 13 federal district courts and 3 circuit courts of appeal. Supreme Court justices spent much of their time serving on these circuit courts, a distasteful duty whose long hours "riding the circuit" caused one justice to grumble that Congress had made him a "traveling postboy." The Judiciary Act made it clear that federal courts had the right to review decisions of the state courts and specified cases over which the Supreme Court would have original jurisdiction. Washington appointed John Jay of New York, a staunch Federalist, as the first chief justice.

Hamilton's Financial Program

HAMILTON'S TWO GOALS When Congress called on Alexander Hamilton to prepare a report on the nation's finances, the new secretary of the Treasury undertook the assignment eagerly. A brilliant thinker and an ambitious politician, he did not intend to be a minor figure in the new administration. Convinced that human nature was fundamentally selfish, Hamilton was determined to link the interests of the wealthy with those of the new government. He also intended to use federal power to encourage manufacturing and commerce in order to make the United States economically strong and independent of Europe.

FUNDING AND ASSUMPTION Neither goal could be achieved until the federal government solved its two most pressing financial problems: revenue and credit. Without revenue it could not be effective. Without credit—the faith of merchants and other nations that the government would repay its debts—it would lack the ability to borrow. Hamilton proposed that all $52 million of the federal debt, much of it generated by the Revolutionary War, be paid in full (or funded). He also recommended that the federal government assume responsibility for the remaining $25 million in debts that individual states owed—a policy of "assumption." He intended with these twin policies to put the new federal government on a sound financial footing and enhance its power by increasing its need for revenue and making the wealthy look to the national government, not the states. Hamilton also proposed a series of excise taxes, including a controversial 25 percent levy on whiskey, to help meet government expenses.

BANK OF THE UNITED STATES After heated debate, Congress deadlocked over funding and assumption. Finally, at a dinner with Hamilton, Jefferson and James Madison of Virginia agreed to support his proposal if, after 10 years in Philadelphia, the permanent seat of government would be

| Philadelphia was the largest and most prosperous city in the country in 1789. In this scene, young men wolf down fresh oysters after enjoying a play at Philadelphia's Chestnut Theater (background).

Source: Rogers Fund, 1942/The Metropolitan Museum of Art

located in the South, on the Potomac River between Virginia and Maryland. Aided by this understanding, funding and assumption passed Congress. In 1791 Congress also approved a 20-year charter for the first Bank of the United States. The bank would hold government deposits and issue banknotes that would be received in payment of all debts owed the federal government. Congress proved less receptive to the rest of Hamilton's program, although a limited tariff to encourage manufacturing and several excise taxes, including the one on whiskey, won approval.

The passage of Hamilton's program caused a permanent rupture among supporters of the Constitution. Madison, who had collaborated closely with Hamilton in the 1780s, broke with his former ally over funding and assumption. Jefferson finally went over to the opposition when Hamilton announced plans for a national bank. Eventually the two warring factions organized themselves into political parties: the Republicans, led by Jefferson and Madison, and the Federalists, led by Hamilton and Adams.* But the division emerged slowly over several years.

---

*The Republican Party of the 1790s, sometimes referred to as the Jeffersonian Republicans, is not to be confused with the modern-day Republican Party, which originated in the 1850s.

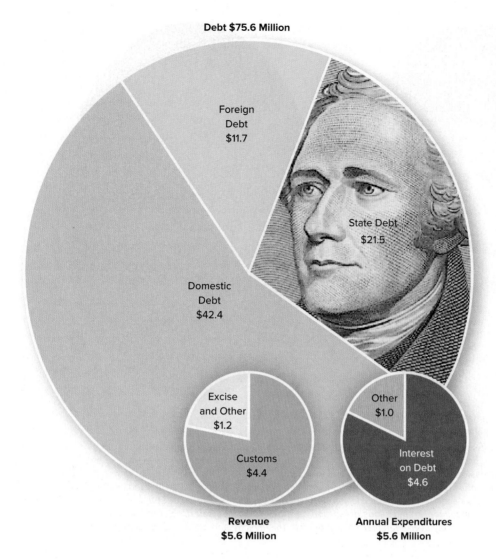

Debt $75.6 Million

Foreign
Debt
$11.7

State Debt
$21.5

Domestic
Debt
$42.4

Excise
and Other
$1.2

Customs
$4.4

Other
$1.0

Interest
on Debt
$4.6

Revenue
$5.6 Million

Annual Expenditures
$5.6 Million

Under Hamilton's financial system, more than 80 percent of federal revenues went to pay the interest on the national debt. Note that most of the revenue came from tariff duties (customs).
©McGraw-Hill Education/Ken Cavanagh

FEARS OF A FINANCIAL ARISTOCRACY Hamilton's program promoted the commercial sector at the expense of semisubsistence farmers. Thus it rekindled many of the concerns that had surfaced during the struggle over ratification of the Constitution. The ideology of the Revolution had stressed that republics inevitably contained groups who sought power in order to destroy popular liberties and overthrow the republic. To some Americans, Hamilton's program seemed a clear threat to establish a privileged and powerful financial aristocracy—perhaps even a monarchy.

SYSTEMS OF CORRUPTION Who, after all, would benefit from the funding proposal? During and after the Revolution, the value of notes issued by the Continental Congress dropped sharply. Speculators had bought up most of these notes for a fraction of their face value from small farmers and workers. If the government finally paid back the debt, speculators would profit accordingly. Equally disturbing, members of Congress had been purchasing the notes before the adoption of Hamilton's program. Nearly half the members of the House of Representatives owned U.S. securities, a dangerous

mimicking of Britain, where the Bank of England's loans to many members of Parliament gave it great political influence.

Fears were heightened because Americans had little experience with banks: only three existed in the country when the Bank of the United States was chartered. One member of Congress expressed a common attitude when he said that he would no more be caught entering a bank than a house of prostitution. Then, too, banks and commerce were a part of the urban environment that rural Americans so distrusted. Although Hamilton's opponents admitted that a certain amount of commerce was necessary, they believed that it should remain subordinate. Hamilton's program, in contrast, encouraged manufacturing and urbanization, developments that history suggested were incompatible with liberty and equality.

STRICT CONSTRUCTION OF THE CONSTITUTION After Congress approved the bank bill, Washington hesitated to sign it. When he consulted his cabinet, Jefferson stressed that the Constitution did not specifically authorize Congress to charter a bank. Both he and Madison upheld the idea of strict construction—that the Constitution should be

(*left*) Source: Thomas Jefferson, from life, c. 1791–1792, by Charles Willson Peale. Independence National Historical Park; (*right*) Source: National Gallery of Art, Washington

| *A study in contrasts, Jefferson and Hamilton increasingly came into conflict in Washington's administration. Despite his aristocratic upbringing, Jefferson* (left) *was awkward, loose-jointed, reserved, and ill at ease in public. Testifying before a congressional committee, he casually lounged in a chair and spoke in a rambling, nonstop manner. "Yet he scattered information wherever he went," conceded Senator William Maclay of Pennsylvania, "and some even brilliant sentiments sparkled from him." Hamilton* (right), *though short of stature, cut a dashing figure with his erect bearing, strutting manner, meticulous dress, and carefully powdered hair. Declared the wife of the British ambassador: "I have scarcely ever been more charmed with the vivacity and conversation of any man."*

interpreted narrowly and the federal government restricted to powers expressly delegated to it. Otherwise, the federal government would be the judge of its own powers, and there would be no safeguard against the abuse of power.

Hamilton countered that the Constitution contained implied as well as enumerated powers. He particularly emphasized the clause that permitted Congress to make all laws "necessary and proper" to carry out its duties. A bank would be useful in carrying out the enumerated powers of regulating commerce and maintaining the public credit; Congress thus had a right to decide whether to establish one. In the end Washington accepted Hamilton's arguments and signed the bill.

Economically Hamilton's program was a success. The government's credit was restored, and the national bank ended the inflation of the previous two decades and created a sound currency. In addition, Hamilton's theory of implied powers and broad construction gave the nation the flexibility necessary to respond to unanticipated crises.

> ✓ **REVIEW**
>
> Analyze the relationship between economic interests and politics in the 1790s.

THE EMERGENCE OF POLITICAL PARTIES

MEMBERS OF THE REVOLUTIONARY GENERATION fervently hoped that political parties would not take root in the United States. "If I could not go to heaven but with a party, I would not go at all," remarked Jefferson. Influenced by radical English republican thought, American critics condemned parties as narrow interest groups that placed selfishness and party loyalty above a concern for the public good. Despite Americans' distrust of such institutions, however, the United States became the first nation to establish truly popular parties.

SOCIAL CONDITIONS ENCOURAGING POLITICAL PARTIES Social conditions encouraged the rise of political parties. Because property ownership was widespread, the nation had a broad **suffrage**. During the American Revolution, legislatures lowered property requirements in many states, increasing the number of voters still further. If party members hoped to hold office, they had to offer a program attractive to the broader voting public. When parties acted as representatives of economic and social interest groups, they became one means by which a large electorate could make its feelings known. In addition, the United States had the highest literacy rate in the world and the largest number of newspapers, further encouraging political interest and participation. Finally, the fact that well-known patriots of the Revolution headed both the Federalists and the Republicans helped defuse the charge that either party was hostile to the Revolution or the Constitution.

Americans and the French Revolution

Although domestic issues first split the supporters of the Constitution, it was a crisis in Europe that pushed the nation toward political parties. Americans had hoped that their revolution would spark similar movements for liberty on the European continent, and in fact the American Revolution was only one of a series of revolutions in the late eighteenth century that shook the Western world, the most important of which began in France in 1789. There a rising population and the collapse of government finances sparked a challenge to royal authority that became a mass revolution. The French revolutionary ideals of "liberty, equality, and fraternity" eventually spilled across Europe.

DIFFERING VIEWS OF THE FRENCH REVOLUTION

Americans first hailed the French Revolution. Many rejoiced to learn that the Bastille prison had been stormed and that a new National Assembly had abolished feudal privileges and adopted the Declaration of the Rights of Man. But by 1793, American enthusiasm for the Revolution had cooled after radical elements instituted a reign of terror, executing the king and queen and many of the nobility. The French Republic even outlawed Christianity and substituted the worship of Reason. Finally, in 1793 republican France and monarchical England went to war. Americans were deeply divided over whether the United States should continue its old alliance with France or support Great Britain.

Hamilton and his allies viewed the French Revolution as sheer anarchy. French radicals seemed to be destroying the very institutions that held civilization together: the church, social classes, property, law and order. The United States, Hamilton argued, should renounce the 1778 treaty of alliance with France and side with Britain. By contrast, Jefferson and his followers supported the treaty and regarded France as a sister republic. They believed that despite deplorable excesses, its revolution was spreading the doctrine of liberty.

Washington's Neutral Course

Washington had compassion for refugees fleeing the French Revolution, and extended limited financial aid. But he believed the United States had to remain independent of European quarrels and wars. Thus he issued a proclamation of American neutrality and tempered Jefferson's efforts to support France.

©Private Collection/Archives Charmet/Bridgeman Images

| *The execution of King Louis XVI by guillotine left Americans divided over the French Revolution.*

NEUTRAL RIGHTS Under international law, neutrals could trade with belligerents—nations at war—as long as the trade had existed before the outbreak of hostilities and did not involve war supplies. But both France and Great Britain refused to respect the rights of neutrals in the midst of their desperate struggle. They began intercepting American ships and confiscating cargoes. In addition, Britain, which badly needed manpower to maintain its powerful navy, impressed into service American sailors it suspected of being British subjects. Britain also continued to maintain the western forts it had promised to evacuate in 1783, and it closed the West Indies, a traditional source of trade, to American ships.

JAY'S TREATY Recognizing that the United States was not strong enough to challenge Britain militarily, Washington sent Chief Justice John Jay to negotiate the differences between the two countries. Although Jay did persuade the British to withdraw their troops from the Northwest, he could gain no other concessions. Disappointed, Washington nonetheless submitted Jay's Treaty to the Senate. After a bitter debate, the Senate narrowly ratified it in June of 1795.

The Federalists and the Republicans Organize

Thus events in Europe contributed directly to the rise of parties in the United States by stimulating fears over the course of American development. By the mid-1790s both sides were organizing on a national basis. Hamilton took the lead in coordinating the Federalist party, which grew out of the voting bloc in Congress that had enacted his economic program. Increasingly, Washington drew closer to Federalist advisors and policies and became the symbol of the party, although he clung to the vision of a nonpartisan administration.

REPUBLICANS IN OPPOSITION   The guiding genius of the opposition movement was Hamilton's onetime colleague James Madison. Jefferson, who resigned as secretary of state at the end of 1793, became the symbolic head of the party, much as Washington reluctantly headed the Federalists. But it was Madison who orchestrated the Republican strategy and lined up their voting bloc in the House. The disputes over Jay's Treaty and over the whiskey tax in 1794 and 1795 gave the Republicans popular issues, and they began organizing on the state and local levels. Republican leaders had to be careful to distinguish between opposing the administration and opposing the Constitution. And they had to overcome the ingrained idea that an opposition party was seditious.

As more and more members of Congress allied themselves with one faction or the other, voting became increasingly partisan. By 1796 even minor matters were decided by partisan votes. Gradually, party organization filtered downward to local communities.

The 1796 Election

As long as Washington remained head of the Federalists, they enjoyed a huge advantage. But in 1796 the weary president, stung by the abuse heaped on him by the opposition press, announced that he would not accept a third term. In doing so, he set a two-term precedent that future presidents followed until Franklin Roosevelt. In his Farewell Address, Washington warned against the dangers of parties and urged a return to the earlier nonpartisan system. That vision, however, had become obsolete: parties were an effective way of expressing the interests of different social and economic groups within the nation. When the Republicans chose Thomas Jefferson to oppose John Adams, the possibility of a constitutional system without parties ended.

The framers of the Constitution did not anticipate that political parties would run competing candidates for both the presidency and the vice presidency. Thus they provided that, of the candidates running for president, the one with the most electoral votes would win and the one with the second highest number would become vice president. But Hamilton strongly disliked both Adams and Jefferson. Ever the intriguer, he tried to manipulate the electoral vote so that the Federalist vice presidential candidate, Thomas Pinckney of South Carolina, would be elected president. In the ensuing confusion, Adams won with 71 electoral votes, and his rival, Jefferson, gained the vice presidency with 68 votes.

Source: National Gallery of Art, Washington

| *John Adams*

Federalist and Republican Ideologies

The fault line between Federalists and Republicans reflected basic divisions in American life. Geographically, the Federalists were strongest in New England, with its commercial ties to Great Britain and its powerful tradition of hierarchy and order. Moving farther south, the party became progressively weaker. Of the southernmost states, the Federalists enjoyed significant strength only in aristocratic South Carolina. The Republicans won solid support in semisubsistence areas such as the West, where farmers were only weakly involved with commerce. The middle states were closely contested, although the most cosmopolitan and commercially oriented elements remained the core of Federalist strength.

In other ways, each party looked both forward and backward: toward certain traditions of the past as well as toward newer social currents that would shape America in the nineteenth century.

FEDERALIST IDEAS   Most Federalists viewed themselves as a kind of natural aristocracy making a last desperate stand against the excesses of democracy. They clung to the notion that the upper class should rule over its social and economic inferiors. In supporting the established social order, most Federalists opposed unbridled individualism. In their view, government should regulate individual behavior for the good of society and protect property from the violent and unruly.

Yet the Federalists were remarkably forward-looking in their economic ideas. They sensed that the United States would become a major economic and military power only by government encouragement of economic development.

REPUBLICAN IDEAS   The Republicans, in contrast, looked backward to the traditional Revolutionary fear that government power threatened liberty. The Treasury, they warned, was corrupting Congress, the army would enslave the people, and interpreting the Constitution broadly would make the federal government all-powerful. Nor did Republican economic ideals anticipate future American development. For the followers of Madison and Jefferson, agriculture—not commerce or manufacturing—was the foundation of American liberty and virtue. Republicans also failed to appreciate the role of financial institutions in promoting economic growth, condemning speculators, bank directors, and holders of the public debt.

Yet the Jeffersonians were more farsighted in matters of equality and personal liberty. Their faith in white men, regardless of station or status, put them in tune with the emerging egalitarian temper of society. They embraced the virtues of individualism, hoping to reduce government to the bare essentials. And they looked to the West— the land of small farms and a more equal society—as the means to preserve opportunity and American values.

The Presidency of John Adams

As president, John Adams became the head of the Federalists, although in many ways he was out of step with his party. Unlike Hamilton, Adams felt no pressing need to aid the wealthy, nor was he fully committed to Hamilton's commercial-industrial vision. As a revolutionary leader who in the 1780s had served as American minister to England, Adams also opposed any alliance with Britain.

Increasingly, Adams and Hamilton clashed over policies and party leadership. Part of the problem stemmed from personalities. Adams was so thin-skinned that it was difficult for anyone to get along with him, and Hamilton's intrigues in the 1796 election had not improved relations between the two men. Although Hamilton had resigned from the Treasury Department in 1795, key members of Adams's cabinet regularly turned to the former secretary for advice. Indeed, they opposed Adams so often that the frustrated president sometimes dealt with them, according to Jefferson, "by dashing and trampling his wig on the floor."

NAVAL WAR WITH FRANCE Adams began his term trying to balance relations with both Great Britain and France. Because the terms of Jay's Treaty were so favorable to the British, the French in retaliation set their navy and privateers to raiding American shipping. To resolve the conflict, Adams dispatched three envoys to France in 1797, but the French foreign minister demanded a bribe before negotiations could even begin. The American representatives refused, and when news of these discussions became public, the situation became known as the XYZ Affair.

In the public's outrage over French bribery, Federalist leaders saw a chance to retain power by going to war. In 1798 Congress repudiated the French alliance of 1778 and enlarged the army and navy.

But Adams feared he would become a scapegoat if his policies failed, and he distrusted standing armies. So an unofficial naval war broke out between the United States and France as ships in each navy raided the fleets of the other, while Britain continued to impress American sailors and seize ships suspected of trading with France.

Suppression at Home

ALIEN AND SEDITION ACTS Meanwhile, Federalist leaders attempted to suppress disloyalty at home. In the summer of 1798 Congress passed several measures known together as the Alien and Sedition Acts. The Alien Act authorized the president to arrest and deport aliens suspected of "treasonable" leanings. Although never used, the act directly threatened immigrants who had not yet become citizens, many of whom were prominent Jeffersonians. To limit the number of immigrant voters—again, most of them Republicans—Congress increased the period of residence required to become a **naturalized** citizen from 5 to 14 years. But the most controversial law was the Sedition Act, which established heavy fines and even imprisonment for writing, speaking, or publishing anything of "a false, scandalous and malicious" nature against the government or any officer of the government.

Because of the partisan way it was enforced, the Sedition Act quickly became a symbol of tyranny. Federalists convicted and imprisoned a number of prominent Republican editors, and several Republican papers ceased publication. In all, 25 people were arrested under the law and 10 convicted and imprisoned.

The crisis over the Sedition Act forced Republicans to develop a broader conception of freedom of the press. Previously, most Americans had agreed that newspapers should not be restrained before publication but that they could be punished afterward for sedition. Jefferson and others now argued that the American government was uniquely based on the free expression of public opinion, and thus criticism of the government was not a sign of criminal intent. Only overtly seditious acts, not opinions, should be subject to prosecution. The courts eventually endorsed this view, adopting a new, more absolute view of freedom of speech guaranteed by the First Amendment.

VIRGINIA AND KENTUCKY RESOLUTIONS The Republican-controlled legislatures of Virginia and Kentucky each responded to the crisis of 1798 by passing a set of resolutions. Madison secretly wrote those for Virginia, and Jefferson those for Kentucky. These resolutions proclaimed that the Constitution was a compact among sovereign states that delegated strictly limited powers to the federal government. When the government exceeded those limits and threatened the liberties of citizens, states had the right to interpose their authority. In the 1830s the two resolutions would serve as the precedent for state efforts to nullify federal laws.

But Jefferson and Madison were not ready to rend a union that had so recently been forged. The two men intended for the Virginia and Kentucky resolutions only to rally public opinion to the Republican cause. They opposed any effort to resist federal authority by force.

The Election of 1800

With a naval war raging on the high seas and the Alien and Sedition Acts sparking debate at home, Adams shocked his party by negotiating a peace treaty with France. It was a courageous act, for Adams not only split his party in two but also ruined his own chances for reelection by driving Hamilton's pro-British wing of the party into open opposition. But the nation benefited, as peace returned.

With the Federalist Party split, Republican prospects in 1800 were bright. Again the party chose Jefferson to run against Adams, along with Aaron Burr for vice president. Sweeping to victory, the Republicans won the presidency, as well as control of both houses of Congress for the first time. Yet for almost a week the election remained deadlocked. Jefferson and Burr received an equal number of votes, and Burr refused to concede until the Federalists decided that Jefferson represented the lesser of two evils. They allowed his

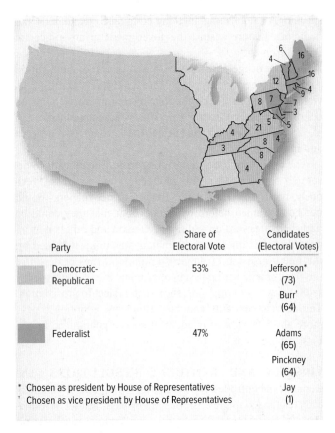

Party	Share of Electoral Vote	Candidates (Electoral Votes)
Democratic-Republican	53%	Jefferson* (73)
		Burr' (64)
Federalist	47%	Adams (65)
		Pinckney (64)
* Chosen as president by House of Representatives		Jay (1)
' Chosen as vice president by House of Representatives		

ELECTION OF 1800

election on the 36th ballot. In 1804 the Twelfth Amendment corrected the problem, specifying that electors were to vote separately for president and vice president.

John Marshall and Judicial Review

Having lost both the presidency and control of Congress in 1800, the Federalists expanded the size of the federal court system, the one branch of the federal government that they still controlled. The Judiciary Act of 1801 created 6 circuit courts and 16 new judgeships. Federalists justified these "midnight appointments" on the grounds that the expanding nation required a larger judiciary.

MARBURY V. MADISON   Among Adams's last-minute appointments was that of William Marbury as justice of the peace for the District of Columbia (the zone set aside for the new national capital). When James Madison assumed the office of secretary of state under the new administration, he found a batch of undelivered commissions, including Marbury's. Wishing to appoint loyal Republicans to these posts, Jefferson instructed Madison not to hand over the commissions, whereupon Marbury sued. The case of *Marbury v. Madison* went directly to the Supreme Court in 1803.

Chief Justice John Marshall, a Federalist and one of Adams's late-term appointments, actually ruled in favor of Madison—but in a way that strengthened the power of the

federal courts. Marshall affirmed the right of the Supreme Court to review statutes and interpret the meaning of the Constitution. "It is emphatically the province of and duty of the judicial department to say what the law is," he wrote in upholding the doctrine of **judicial review**. In Marshall's view, the Court "must of necessity expound and interpret" the Constitution and the laws when one statute conflicted with another or when a law violated the framework of the Constitution.

Marshall and his colleagues later asserted the power of the Court to review the constitutionality not only of federal but also of state laws. In fact, during his long tenure as chief justice (over 30 years), John Marshall extended judicial review to all acts of government.

FEDERALIST ACHIEVEMENTS AND DISAPPOINT-MENTS   As John Adams left office, he looked back with mixed feelings on the 12 years that the Federalist Party had held power. Under Washington's firm leadership and his own, his party had made the Constitution a workable instrument of government. The Federalists had proved that a republican form of government was compatible with stability and order. They had established economic policies that brought a return of prosperity. Washington had established the principle of American neutrality in foreign affairs, which became an accepted ideal by both parties for decades to come.

But most Federalists took no solace in such reflections, because the forces of history seemed to be running against them. Power had fallen into the hands of the ignorant rabble, led by that demagogue Thomas Jefferson.

The Political Culture of the Early Republic

Neither Federalists nor Republicans could accept the novel idea that political parties might peacefully resolve differences among competing social, geographic, and economic interests. Instead, each party regarded its opponents as a dangerous faction of ambitious men striving to increase their wealth and power at the expense of republican liberty.

What resulted was a **political culture** marked by verbal and, at times, physical violence. Republicans accused Washington and Hamilton of being British agents and monarchists; Federalists denounced Jefferson as an atheist and his partisans as a pack of "blood-drinking cannibals." The leading Republican newspaper editor in Philadelphia plunged into a street brawl with his Federalist rival; two members of Congress slugged it out on the floor of the House of Representatives. Mobs threatened the leaders of both parties, and at the height of the crisis of 1798–1799, Adams smuggled guns into his home for protection.

The deepening divisions among national leaders also encouraged ordinary Americans to take an interest in politics. Beginning in the 1790s and for decades thereafter, activists in cities and villages everywhere in the new republic organized grand festivals to celebrate American

patriotism and the glories of the Republicans or the Federalists. That grassroots movement democratized the conduct of politics by educating men and women, white and black, voters and nonvoters alike, about the issues of the day. In doing so, such activities encouraged strong partisan loyalties.

PARADES AND CELEBRATIONS Holidays such as the Fourth of July and Washington's Birthday became prime occasions for local party leaders to rally their fellow citizens. They hosted celebrations that began with parades in which marchers, hoisting banners to identify their particular trade, militia company, or social club, processed through the main street to a church, meeting hall, or public square. There the assembled throng of marchers and onlookers sang patriotic songs, recited prayers, and listened to the reading of the Declaration of Independence, all capped by a rousing sermon or political oration. Then the party started: in the North, taverns and hotels hosted community banquets; in the South, the crowds flocked to outdoor barbecues. Everywhere the feasts ended with many toasts to the glories of republican liberty and, of course, to the superiority of Federalists or Republicans.

These local celebrations not only made an impact on those who were able to attend the festivities but also reached a wider audience through newspaper accounts. During the 1790s and beyond, the number of local or regional newspapers in the new republic mushroomed, but their coverage was far from objective. Most editors were either staunch Federalists or ardent Republicans who could be counted on to publish glowing accounts of the festivities sponsored by their party and to instruct a much wider audience about party policies and values.

African American Celebrations

African Americans, too, were drawn to political festivals, but they discovered that party organizers were determined to keep them away. In the years after 1800, bullies often drove black men and women from Fourth of July celebrations with taunts, threats, and assaults. James Forten, a leading citizen of Philadelphia's African American community, complained that because of the hostility of drunken whites, "black people, upon certain days of public jubilee, dare not to be seen" on the streets after noon.

The growing free black population of northern cities countered such opposition by organizing celebrations to express their own political convictions. They established annual holidays to celebrate the abolition of the slave trade in Britain and the United States as well as the successful slave revolt in the Caribbean that resulted in the founding of Haiti in 1804. Those acts of defiance—the spectacle of blacks marching down the main streets with banners flying and bands of music playing, and of black audiences cheering orators who publicly condemned slavery—only inflamed racial hatred and opposition among many whites.

CALLING FOR FULL CITIZENSHIP But African Americans continued to press for full citizenship by persuading sympathetic white printers to publish poetry, slave narratives, and pamphlets composed by black authors. The strategy of those writings was to refute racist notions by drawing attention to the intelligence, virtue, and patriotism of black American women and men, both free and enslaved. Typical was the autobiography of Venture Smith, the first slave narrative published in the United States (1798), which followed his captivity as a young boy in West Africa through his lifelong struggle in New England to purchase his own freedom and that of his wife and children.

CAN THIS MARRIAGE BE SAVED?

Proponents of providing women with greater educational opportunities—here identified as "The Female Advocate"—often held ideals of marriage that differed dramatically from those embraced by more conservative Americans such as Samuel Jennings, a Methodist minister and the founder of a medical college in Baltimore.

DOCUMENT 1
"The Female Advocate" on the Virtues of an Educated Wife

How greatly doth a man of science [knowledge] misjudge in choosing a companion for life, if he selects one from the class of ignorant and untaught, that he may, by this mean, the more securely retain his favorite supremacy. Is it not a total blindness to the ideas of refined happiness, arising from a reciprocity of sentiments and the exchange of rational felicity, as well as an illiberal prejudice, thus to conduct? Shall a woman be kept ignorant, to render her more docile in the management of domestic concerns? How illy capable is such a person of being a companion for a man of refinement? How miserably capable of augmenting his social joys, or managing prudently the concerns of a family, or educating his children? Is it not of the utmost consequence, that the tender mind of the youth receive an early direction for future usefulness? And is it not

equally true, that the first direction of a child necessarily becomes the immediate and peculiar province of the woman? And may I not add, is not a woman of capacious and well stored mind, a better wife, a better widow, a better mother, and a better neighbor; and shall I add, a better friend in every respect. . . .

When women, no longer the humble dependent, or the obsequious slave, but the companion and friend, is party to an attachment founded on mutual esteem, then, and not till then, does man assume his intended rank in the scale of creation. . . .

Suppose one who has from her youth been indoctrinated and habituated to sentiments of female inferiority, one who has never been suffered to have an opinion of her own, but on the reverse, has been taught, and accustomed to rely, and implicitly believe, right or wrong, on

her parents, guardians, or husband. What will be the consequence of this, in a situation when deprived of the counsel of either or all of them, she is necessitated to act for herself, or be exposed to the fraudulence of an unfriendly world? Perhaps she is left a widow with a large property and a flock of small dependent children? But where have they to look for protection, or on whom to rely, but on their insufficient, helpless mother? How poorly capable is she to fill the vacancy, and act to her tender babes and orphans, in their bereaved situation, as is absolutely necessary, both father and mother? How incapable also is she of assisting in the settlement and adjustment of the estate; how liable to fraud, and how probable to be injured by unreal or exaggerated debts.

Source: The Female Advocate, Written by a Lady. New Haven, CT, 1801.

DOCUMENT 2
Samuel K. Jennings on the Virtues of a Submissive Wife

As it is your great wish and interest, to enjoy much of your husband's company and conversation, it will be important to acquaint yourself with his temper, his inclination, and his manner, that you may render your house, your person, and your disposition quite agreeable to him. . . .

Your choice in forming the connexion [marriage], was at best a passive one. Could you have acted the part of a courtier and made choice of a man whose disposition might have corresponded precisely with yours, there would have been less to do afterwards. But under present circumstances, it is your interest to adapt yourself to your husband, whatever may be his peculiarities. Again, nature has made man the stronger, the consent of mankind has given him superiority over his wife, his

inclination is, to claim his natural and acquired rights. He of course expects from you a degree of condescension, and he feels himself the more confident of the propriety of his claim, when he is formed, that St. Paul adds to his authority its support. "Wives submit to your own husbands, as unto the Lord, for the husband is the head of his wife."

In obedience then to this precept of the gospel, to the laws of custom and of nature, you ought to cultivate a cheerful and happy submission. . . .

Do not suppose, that my plan implies that the husband has nothing to do. So far from this he is bound "To love and cherish his wife, as his own flesh." But I repeat, this obligation seems, in a great degree, to rest on the condition of a loving and cheerful submission on the part of the wife. Here again perhaps you

object and say, "Why not the husband, first shew a little condescension as well as the wife?" I answer for these plain reasons. It is not his disposition; it is not the custom but with the henpecked; it is not his duty; it is not implied in the marriage contract; it is not required by law or the gospel.

Source: Jennings, Samuel K., The Married Lady's Companion or Poor Man's Friend, revised 2nd ed., New York, 1808.

THINKING CRITICALLY

How did "The Female Advocate" advise men to choose their wives? How to behave as husbands? Why did she believe that her advice served the best interests of men? On what grounds did Samuel Jennings argue that women should submit to their husbands?

The story of Venture Smith, hardworking and thrifty, resourceful and determined to better himself and his family, invited white readers to conclude that he was as true a republican and a self-made man as Benjamin Franklin.

Women's Education and Civic Participation

The new republic's political festivals and partisan newspapers aimed to woo the loyalty of white adult males who held enough property to vote. But they also sought the support of white women, some of whom joined in the crowds and even took part in the parades. In one New Jersey village the folks lining the parade route cheered as "16 young ladies uniformed in white with garlands in their hats" marched past, playing a patriotic anthem on their flutes. Federalists and Republicans alike encouraged women's involvement on those occasions, hoping that displays of approval from "the American Fair" would encourage husbands and male admirers to support their parties.

Many women seized on such opportunities for greater civic involvement. True, the law excluded most from taking direct part in voting and governing, but those prohibitions did not prevent women from taking an active interest in politics and voicing their opinions. When a female guest in a best-selling novel of the 1790s (the first by an American woman) "simpered" that their sex should not meddle with politics, her hostess shot back, "Why then should the love of our country be a masculine passion only? Why should government, which involves the peace and order of society, of which we are a part, be wholly excluded from our observation?"

WOMEN'S ACADEMIES What contributed to women's interest in the wider world was the formal education that increasing numbers of elite and middle-class girls received. By the 1790s the number of seminaries and academies for female students was skyrocketing, encouraged by a new ideal of republican motherhood (see Chapter 8). Although the curricula of those schools still included "ornamental" training in dancing, needlework, penmanship, and music, their offerings increasingly emphasized history, geography, geometry, algebra, chemistry, botany, and geology—even Greek and Latin. In the course of this solid academic training, students also spoke at school exhibitions and published school newspapers. Such activities encouraged young women to imagine themselves as independent citizens—not simply as republican mothers. And, after graduation, many women continued to cultivate their intellects in reading circles, literary societies, and mutual improvement associations. Those experiences habituated women to presenting their views before an audience in an articulate and self-possessed manner.

RISING FEMALE LITERACY Even young women unable to attend the new academies benefited from access to an increasing number of books and magazines, many of them aimed at a female audience. The new importance of reading to the identity of women appears in a striking number of

Miniature Panorama: Scenes from a Seminary for Young Ladies, c.1810–20; American; watercolor and ink on silk; Saint Louis Art Museum, Museum Purchase and funds given by the Decorative Arts Society (89:1976)

| *The artist used watercolor and ink to draw this scene on silk cloth. Young women were no longer being educated merely in the polite arts of dancing, sewing, and embroidery. An increasing number were taking such academic subjects as algebra, history, and geography (note the young woman making measurements on the globe).*

portraits depicting young girls, middle-aged matrons, and elderly dowagers with books in hand. By 1850, for the first time in American history, there were as many literate women as there were literate men.

✓ REVIEW

What fostered the intense political loyalties of the 1790s?

THE REPUBLICANS IN POWER

THE GROWING POLITICAL ENGAGEMENT OF ordinary white Americans played an important role in electing Thomas Jefferson to the presidency. He later referred to his election as "the Revolution of 1800," asserting that it "was as real a revolution in the principles of our government as that of 1776 was in its form." That claim exaggerates: Jefferson's presidency did little to enhance political rights or social opportunities of white women or African Americans. Even so, during the following two decades Republicans did set the United States on a more democratic course. And in their dealings with Britain and France, as well as with the Indian tribes of the West, Republican administrations defined, for better and worse, a fuller sense of American nationality.

The New Capital City

Thomas Jefferson was the first president to be inaugurated in the new capital, Washington, D.C. In 1791 George Washington had commissioned Pierre Charles L'Enfant, a French architect and engineer who had served in the American Revolution, to draw up plans for the new seat of government. L'Enfant designed a city with broad avenues, statues and fountains, parks and plazas, and a central mall. Because the Federalists believed that government was the paramount power in a nation, they had intended that the city would be a new Rome—a cultural, intellectual, and commercial center of the Republic.

The new city fell far short of this grandiose dream. It was located in a swampy river bottom near the head of the Potomac, and the surrounding hills rendered the spot oppressively hot and muggy during the summer. The streets were filled with tree stumps and became seas of mud after a rain. Much of the District of Columbia was wooded, and virtually all of it remained unoccupied. When the government moved to its new residence in 1800, the Senate chamber, where Jefferson took the oath of office, was the only part of the Capitol that had been completed.

This isolated and unimpressive capital reflected the new president's attitude toward government. Distrustful of centralized power of any kind, Jefferson deliberately set out to remake the national government into one of limited scope that touched few people's daily lives. The states rather than the federal government were "the most competent administrators for our domestic concerns," he asserted in his inaugural address. Ever the individualist, he recommended a government that left people "free to regulate their own pursuits of industry and improvement."

Jefferson's Philosophy

Jefferson was a product of the Enlightenment, with its faith in the power of human reason to improve society and decipher the universe. He considered "the will of the majority" to be "the only sure guardian of the rights of man," which he defined as "life, liberty, and the pursuit of happiness." Although he conceded that the masses might err, he was confident they would soon return to correct principles. His faith in human virtue exceeded that of most of the founding generation, yet in good republican fashion, he feared those in power, even if they had been elected by the people. Government seemed to Jefferson a necessary evil at best.

AGRARIAN VALUES   To Jefferson, agriculture was a morally superior way of life. "Those who labour in the earth are the chosen people of God, if ever he had a chosen people," he wrote in *Notes on the State of Virginia* (1787). Jefferson praised rural life for nourishing the honesty, independence, and virtue so essential in a republic.

Although Jefferson asserted that "the tree of liberty must be refreshed from time to time by the blood of patriots and tyrants," his reputation as a radical was undeserved. While he wanted to extend the suffrage to a greater number of Americans, he clung to the traditional republican idea that voters should own property and thus be economically independent. One of the largest slaveholders in the country, he increasingly

muffled his once-bold condemnation of slavery, and in the last years of his life he reproached critics of the institution who sought to prevent it from expanding westward.

Slaveholding aristocrat and apostle of democracy, lofty theorist and pragmatic politician, Jefferson was a complex, at times contradictory, personality. But like most politicians, he was flexible in his approach to problems and tried to balance means and ends. And like most leaders, he quickly discovered that he confronted very different problems in power than he had in opposition.

Jefferson's Economic Policies

The new president quickly proceeded to cut spending and to reduce the size of the government. He also abolished the internal taxes enacted by the Federalists, including the controversial excise on whiskey, and thus was able to get rid of all tax collectors and inspectors. Land sales and the tariff duties would supply the funds needed to run the scaled-down government.

The most serious spending cuts were made in the military branches. Jefferson slashed the army budget in half, decreasing the army to 3,000 men. In a national emergency, he reasoned, the militia could defend the country. Jefferson reduced the navy even more, halting work on powerful frigates authorized during the naval war with France.

COMING TO ACCEPT HAMILTON'S POLICIES   By such steps, Jefferson made significant progress toward paying off Hamilton's national debt. Still, he did not entirely dismantle the Federalists' economic program. Funding and assumption could not be reversed—the nation's honor was pledged to paying these debts, and Jefferson understood the importance of maintaining the nation's credit. More surprising, Jefferson argued that the national bank should be left to run its course until 1811, when its charter would expire. In reality, he expanded the bank's operations and, in words reminiscent of Hamilton, advocated tying banks and members of the business class to the government by rewarding those who supported the Republican Party. In effect, practical politics had triumphed over agrarian economics.

The Miami Confederacy Resists

For all his pragmatism, Jefferson still viewed the lands stretching from the Appalachians to the Pacific through the perspective of his agrarian ideals. America's vast spaces provided enough land to last for a thousand generations, he predicted in his inaugural address, enough to transform the United States into "an empire of liberty."

That optimistic vision contrasted sharply with the views of most Federalists, who feared the West as a threat to social order and stability. In the 1790s they had good reason to fear. British troops refused to leave their forts in the Northwest, and Indian nations still controlled most of the region. Recognizing that fact, the United States conceded that Indian nations had the right to negotiate as sovereign powers. North of

Federalists and Republicans

FEDERALIST POSITIONS

Rejection of political parties

Encouragement of commerce, manufacturing, urbanization

Importance of funding the national debt

Condemnation of the French Revolution as anarchy; support for British ties

Importance of order, hierarchy, curbing democratic excess and unbridled individualism

FEDERALIST ACHIEVEMENTS

Restored credit of national government

Ended postwar inflation and created sound currency

Instituted policy of neutrality (Washington)

Negotiated peace with France (Adams)

Established Supreme Court's right of judicial review (Marshall)

Proved republican government compatible with stability and order; peaceful transition to Republican power in 1800

DUBIOUS ACHIEVEMENTS

Alien and Sedition Acts

Forcible efforts to push Indian nations from the Ohio valley

REPUBLICAN POSITIONS

Rejection of political parties

Encouragement of agriculture as the basis of liberty and virtue

Suspicion of banks, speculators, public debt, taxation, government spending

Celebration of France as a fellow republic; suspicion of Britain as former foe

Support for the values of individualism, egalitarianism, limited government

REPUBLICAN ACHIEVEMENTS

Endorsed a broad conception of freedom of the press in response to Alien and Sedition Acts

Made significant progress in paying off the national debt; expanded the national bank

Dispatched Louis and Clark expedition (Jefferson)

Negotiated the Louisiana Purchase (Jefferson)

Proclaimed the Monroe Doctrine

Proved republican government compatible with stability and order; peaceful transition to power in 1800

DUBIOUS ACHIEVEMENTS

Virginia and Kentucky Resolutions

Forced cessions of Indians lands in the Ohio valley and the South

Embargo of 1807

Missouri Compromise

(*top*) Source: Library of Congress, Prints and Photographs Division [LC-USZ62-70508]; (*bottom*) ©Daniel Borzynski/Alamy

the Ohio, leaders of the Miami Confederacy, composed of eight tribes, stoutly refused to sell their homelands without "the united voice of the confederacy."

VICTORIES OF LITTLE TURTLE AND BLUE JACKET
In response the Washington administration sent 1,500 soldiers in 1790 under General Josiah Harmar to force the Indians to leave by burning their homes and fields. The Miami Confederacy, led by Blue Jacket and Little Turtle, roundly defeated the whites. Harmar was court-martialed, the nation embarrassed, and a second expedition organized the following

year under General Arthur St. Clair. This force of over 2,000 was again routed by Little Turtle, whose warriors killed 600 and wounded another 300. The defeat was the worst in the history of Indian wars undertaken by the United States. (In contrast, Custer's defeat in 1876 counted 264 fatalities.)

TREATY OF GREENVILLE President Washington dispatched yet another army of 2,000 to the Ohio valley, commanded by "Mad Anthony" Wayne, an accomplished general. At the Battle of Fallen Timbers in August 1794, Wayne won a decisive victory, breaking the Indians' hold on the Northwest.

In the Treaty of Greenville (1795), the tribes **ceded** the southern two-thirds of the area between Lake Erie and the Ohio River, opening it up to white families. Federalists were still not eager to see the land settled. Although they allowed the sale of federal land, they kept the price high, with a required purchase of at least 640 acres—more than four times the size of most American farms.

Once in power, Jefferson and the Republicans encouraged settlement by reducing the minimum tract that buyers could purchase (to 320 acres) and by offering land on credit. Sales boomed. By 1820 more than 2 million whites lived in a region they had first entered only 50 years earlier. From Jefferson's perspective, western expansion was a blessing economically, socially, and even politically, because most of the new westerners were Republican.

Napoleon, Haiti, and Louisiana

Jefferson's "empire of liberty" for whites required more than dispossessing Indian families of their lands; it required delicate diplomacy with the European powers in North America. This task was greatly complicated in 1802 when, under pressure from revolutionary France's audacious leader Napoleon Bonaparte, Spain surrendered the sprawling Louisiana territory to the French. Knowing better than anyone that the agricultural produce of the western United States had to travel down the Mississippi River to reach world markets, Jefferson was sobered when he heard the news. "There is on the globe one single spot, the possessor of which is our natural and habitual enemy," he told his envoy in France. "It is New Orleans."

LOUVERTURE LEADS AN UPRISING IN HAITI   Napoleon dreamed of re-creating France's North American empire by reoccupying Louisiana and eventually reconquering Canada. But first he had to subdue rebellious Saint-Domingue and recapture the immense profits from plantation sugar and coffee. Since the stunning slave rebellion in 1791, insurgents on the island had fought a complex series of wars and gained de facto independence from France under a brilliant leader, the former slave Toussaint Louverture.

Napoleon sent a massive, veteran army to re-conquer the colony and re-enslave its people. He captured Louverture and shipped him off to die in a frigid prison. But the campaign turned into a nightmare for Napoleon's men. Yellow fever and black men with guns devastated the French forces, who in turn resorted to mass killings and other atrocities. By 1804 the French withdrew, leaving the victorious rebels to declare their independent Republic of Haiti. By that time Napoleon was long sick of his rash adventure. "Damn sugar, damn coffee, damn colonies!" he exclaimed angrily.

THE LOUISIANA PURCHASE   Jefferson feared and despised the Haitian rebels, but ironically his goals depended on their success. Napoleon realized that without Saint-Domingue, his vision of a North American empire was

unworkable. So in April 1803 he offered to sell the entire Louisiana territory to the United States. James Monroe and Robert Livingston, the stunned U.S. envoys who had traveled to France in hopes of buying just the city of New Orleans, debated whether to exceed their instructions. Pressed for an immediate answer, the pair took a deep breath and agreed to buy Louisiana for about $15 million. In one fell swoop the American negotiators had doubled the country's nominal size by adding some 830,000 square miles.

LEWIS AND CLARK EXPEDITION   Even before the Louisiana Purchase was completed, Congress secretly funded an expedition up the Missouri River to the Pacific. Leading that party were Meriwether Lewis, who was Jefferson's personal secretary, and William Clark, a younger brother of George Rogers Clark. Jefferson instructed them to make detailed observations of the territory's geography, climate, and wildlife. They were also to investigate the practicability of an overland route to the Pacific, and engage in diplomacy with the Indians along the way. By pushing onward to the Pacific, Lewis and Clark would strengthen the American title to Oregon, which several nations claimed but none effectively occupied.

In the spring of 1804 the "Corps of Discovery" left St. Louis and headed up the Missouri River with 48 men. They laboriously hauled their boats upstream to present-day North Dakota, where they spent the winter with the Mandan Indians. The next spring, the expedition pushed on through the rugged mountains and then floated down first the Snake and then the Columbia River to the Pacific.

The country Lewis and Clark traversed had been shaken by momentous change over the previous decades. Trade goods circulated in greater quantities than ever before, across the plains and through the mountains. Horses and guns in particular upset older Indian ways, making tribes more mobile and more dangerous. Lewis and Clark spotted Spanish horse gear from Mexico in villages along the upper Missouri River, guns from French traders to the northeast, and British teapots along the Columbia River. Most disruptive, smallpox had made its way along the same trade routes ever since the pandemic of the 1780s (see Chapter 7). Indian populations plummeted, forcing many tribes to resettle.

After a bleak winter in Oregon, the expedition returned home over the Rockies in 1806. It brought back thousands of plant and animal specimens and produced a remarkably accurate map of its journey. Lewis and Clark had crossed a continent disrupted by change. In the century to come those changes would only accelerate.

Pressure on Indian Lands and Culture

East of the Mississippi, white settlers continued to flood into the backcountry. Jefferson endorsed the policy that Indian tribes either would have to assimilate into American culture by becoming farmers and abandoning their seminomadic

EXPLORATION AND EXPANSION: THE LOUISIANA PURCHASE

Source: Library of Congress, Prints and Photographs Division [LC-DIG-highsm-39302]

"The object of your mission is to explore . . . the most direct and practicable water communication across this continent for the purposes of commerce."
—Thomas Jefferson's instructions to Meriwether Lewis, 1803

CONTEXT

The vast, mostly uncharted Louisiana Purchase lay well beyond the most densely populated areas of the United States. The Lewis and Clark expedition dashed Jefferson's hope (long-held by Europeans and colonists) that there was a river system connecting the Pacific to the Atlantic. Just as geographic misperception shaped the Lewis and Clark expedition and its goals, political misperception shaped Lieutenant Zebulon Montgomery Pike's expedition to the West. Captured near Santa Fe as a trespassing foreign agent, Spanish authorities escorted him and his men south for a lengthy interrogation in New Spain before allowing them to leave. Pike later wrote a popular book about the experience, greatly enhancing American knowledge about New Spain.

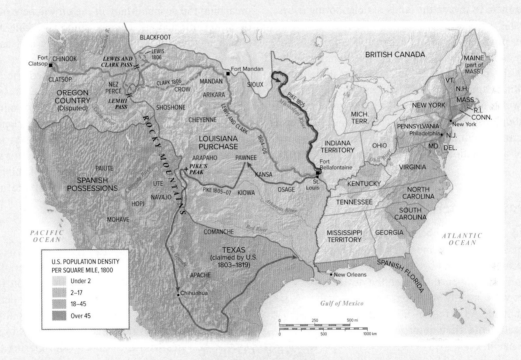

MAP READING

1. What were the three principal rivers Lewis and Clark followed?
2. Locate the place where Lewis and Clark wintered over on the first year of their expedition.
3. Why mark Lemhi Pass and Lewis and Clark Pass on the map?
4. What Indian groups did Lewis and Clark encounter on their expedition?

MAP INTERPRETATION

1. How did rivers shape U.S. exploration in the early nineteenth century?
2. If you were organizing exploration of the Louisiana Purchase in 1803, what routes would you suggest? What parts of the continent would you want to explore first? Why?
3. On the web, look up a map of U.S. population density for 2010. What is the range of densities there, compared with the range on this map?
4. Indians had been familiar with Pike's Peak for millennia, and Spaniards had known about it for nearly a century. What does it say about U.S. history that this majestic peak was named after a trespassing explorer?

hunting or would have to move west. Jefferson defended these alternatives as in the best interests of the Indians, because he believed that otherwise they faced extermination. But he also recognized that by becoming farmers they would need less land. He encouraged the policy of selling goods on credit in order to lure Indians into debt. "When these debts get beyond what the individuals can pay," the president observed, "they become willing to lop them off by a cession of lands."

Between 1800 and 1810, whites pressed Indians into ceding more than 100 million acres in the Ohio River valley. The loss of so much land devastated Indian cultures and transformed their environment by reducing hunting grounds and making game and food scarce. "Stop your people from killing our game," the Shawnees complained in 1802 to federal Indian agents. "They would be angry if we were to kill a cow or hog of theirs, the little game that remains is very dear to us." Tribes also became dependent on white trade to obtain blankets, guns, metal utensils, alcohol, and decorative beads. To pay for these goods with furs, Indians often overtrapped, which forced them to invade the lands of neighboring tribes, provoking wars.

The strain produced by white expansion led to alcoholism, growing violence among tribe members, family disintegration, and the collapse of the clan system designed to regulate relations among different villages. The question of how to deal with white culture became a matter of anguished debate. Although some Native Americans attempted to take up farming and accommodate to white ways, for most the course of assimilation proved unappealing and fraught with risk.

White Frontier Society

Whites faced their own problems on the frontier. In the first wave of settlement came backwoods families who cleared a few acres of forest by girdling the trees, removing the brush, and planting corn between the dead trunks. Such settlers were mostly squatters without legal title to their land. As a region filled up, these pioneers usually sold their improvements and headed west again.

Taking their place, typically, were young single men from the East, who married and started families. These pioneers, too, engaged in semisubsistence agriculture, save for the lucky few whose prime locations allowed them to transport their crops down the Ohio and Mississippi Rivers to New Orleans for shipment to distant markets. But many frontier families struggled, moving several times but never managing to rise from the ranks of squatters or tenant farmers to become independent landowners. Fledgling western communities lacked schools, churches, and courts, and inhabitants often lived miles distant from even their nearest neighbors.

©The Granger Collection, New York

| *The Prophet*

The Beginnings of the Second Great Awakening

This hardscrabble frontier proved the perfect tinder for sparking a series of dramatic religious revivals in the decades surrounding 1800. What lit the fire were missionary efforts by major Protestant churches—particularly the Baptists and the Methodists—who sent their ministers to travel the countryside on horseback and to preach wherever they could gather a crowd. Often those religious meetings took place outdoors and drew eager hearers from as far as 100 miles away, who camped for several days in makeshift tents to listen to sermons and to share in praying and singing hymns.

CANE RIDGE   Thus was born a new form of Protestant worship, the camp meeting, which drew national notice after a mammoth gathering at Cane Ridge, Kentucky, in August of 1801. At a time when the largest city in the state had only 2,000 people, more than 10,000 men, women, and children, white and black, flocked there to hear dozens of ministers preaching the gospel. Many in the crowd were overwhelmed by powerful religious feelings, some shrieking and shaking over guilt for their sins, others laughing and dancing from their high hopes of eternal salvation.

Some Protestant ministers denounced the "revival" at Cane Ridge and elsewhere as yet another instance of the ignorance and savagery of westerners. Other ministers were more optimistic: they saw frontier camp meetings as the first sign of a Protestant Christian renewal that would sweep the new republic. Their hopes set the stage for what would come to be called the Second Great Awakening, a wave of religious revivals that swept throughout the nation after 1800 (see Chapter 12).

The Prophet, Tecumseh, and the Pan-Indian Movement

Native peoples also turned to religion to meet the challenges of the early national frontier. Indeed, in traditional Indian religions, they found the resource to revitalize their cultures by severing all ties with the white world. During the 1790s a revival led by Handsome Lake took hold among the Iroquois, following the loss of most of the Iroquois lands and the collapse of their military power in western New York. Later, Lalawethika, also known as the Prophet, sparked a religious renewal among the Shawnees. The Prophet's early life was bleak: he was a poor hunter and as a child accidentally blinded himself in the right eye with an arrow; the ridicule of his fellow tribe members drove him to alcoholism. Suddenly, in April 1805 he lapsed into a trance so deep that he was given up for dead. When he revived he spoke of being reborn. From this vision and others he outlined a new creed for the Shawnees.

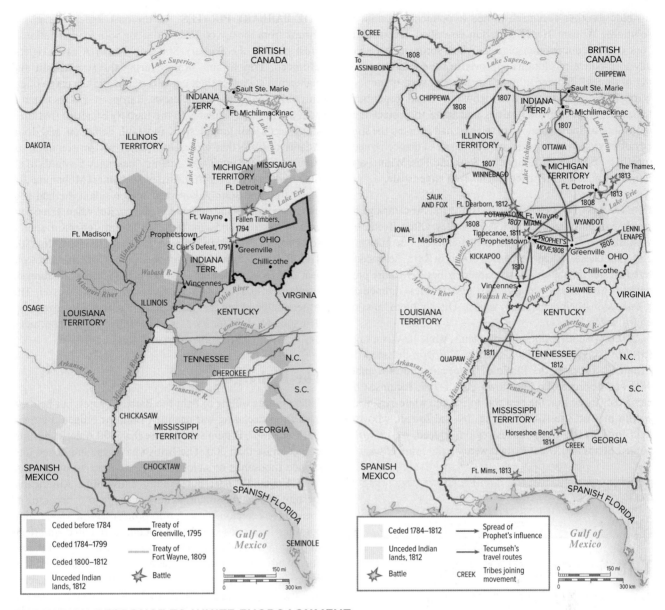

THE INDIAN RESPONSE TO WHITE ENCROACHMENT

*With land cessions and white western migration placing increased pressure on Indian cultures after 1790, news of the Prophet's revival fell on eager ears. It spread especially quickly northward along the shores of Lake Michigan and westward along Lake Superior and the interior of Wisconsin. Following the Battle of Tippecanoe, Tecumseh eclipsed the Prophet as the major leader of Indian resistance, but his trips south to forge political alliances met with less success. **How far south did Tecumseh travel in his attempt to unite Indian resistance?***

INDEPENDENCE FROM WHITE SOCIETY Taking a new name—Tenskwatawa (Open Door)—the Prophet urged the Shawnees to renounce whiskey and white goods and return to their old ways of hunting with bows and arrows, eating customary foods such as corn and beans, and wearing traditional garb. The Shawnees could revitalize their culture, he insisted, by condemning intertribal violence, embracing monogamous marriage, and rejecting the idea of private instead of communal property. Except for guns, which could be used in self-defense, his followers were to discard all items made by whites. Intermarriage with white settlers was forbidden.

Setting up headquarters in 1808 at the newly built village of Prophetstown in Indiana, Tenskwatawa led a wider revival among the tribes of the Northwest. Just as thousands of white settlers traveled to Methodist or Baptist camp meetings in the woods, where preachers denounced the evils of liquor and called for a return to a purer way of life, so thousands of Indians from northern tribes traveled to the Prophet's village for inspiration. Many were concerned about the threatened loss of Indian lands.

TECUMSEH'S POLITICAL STRATEGY Whereas Tenskwatawa's strategy of revitalization was primarily religious, his older brother Tecumseh turned to political and military solutions. William Henry Harrison described Tecumseh as "one of those uncommon geniuses which spring up occasionally to produce revolutions and overturn the established order of things." Tall and athletic, an accomplished hunter and warrior, Tecumseh traveled throughout the Northwest, urging tribes to forget ancient rivalries and unite to protect their lands. Just as Indian nations in the past had adopted the strategy of uniting in a confederacy, Tecumseh's alliance brought together the Wyandot, Chippewa, Sauk and Fox, Winnebago, Potawatomi, and other tribes on an even larger scale.

OBSTACLES TO A CONFEDERACY But the campaign for pan-Indian unity ran into serious obstacles. Often, Tecumseh was asking tribes to unite with their traditional enemies in a common cause. When he headed south in 1811, he encountered greater resistance. Most southern tribes were more prosperous, were more acculturated, and felt less immediate pressure on their land from whites. His southern mission ended largely in failure.

To compound Tecumseh's problems, while he was away a force of Americans under Governor Harrison defeated the Prophet's forces at the Battle of Tippecanoe in November 1811 and destroyed Prophetstown. As a result, Tecumseh became convinced that the best way to contain white expansion was to play off the Americans against the British, who still held forts in the Great Lakes region. Indeed, by 1811, the United States and Great Britain were on the brink of war.

REVIEW

How did Jefferson's presidency shape the settlement of the West?

THE SECOND WAR FOR AMERICAN INDEPENDENCE

As TECUMSEH WORKED TO ACHIEVE a pan-Indian alliance, Jefferson encountered his own difficulties in trying to achieve American political unity. The president hoped to woo all but the most extreme Federalists into the Republican camp. His reelection in 1804 showed how much progress he had made, as he defeated Federalist Charles Cotesworth Pinckney and carried 15 of 17 states. With the Republicans controlling three-quarters of the seats in Congress, one-party rule seemed at hand.

WAR BETWEEN BRITAIN AND FRANCE But events across the Atlantic complicated the efforts to unite Americans. Only two weeks after Napoleon agreed to sell Louisiana to the United States, war broke out between France and Great Britain. As in the 1790s the United States found itself caught between the world's two greatest powers. Jefferson insisted that the nation should remain neutral in a European war. But the policies he proposed to maintain neutrality sparked sharp divisions in American society and momentarily revived the two-party system.

THE BARBARY PIRATES In the past, Jefferson had not shrunk from the use of force in dealing with foreign nations—most notably the Barbary States of North Africa—Algiers, Morocco, Tripoli, and Tunis. During the seventeenth and eighteenth centuries their corsairs plundered the cargo of enemy ships and enslaved the crews. European nations found it convenient to pay tributes to the Barbary States so that their ships could sail unmolested. But both Jefferson and John Adams disliked that idea. The "policy of Christendom" of paying tribute, complained Adams, "has made Cowards of all their Sailors before the Standard of Mahomet [Mohammed]."

By the time John Adams became president, he had subdued his outrage and agreed to tributes. But when Tripoli increased its demands in 1801, President Jefferson sent a squadron of American ships to force a settlement. In 1803 Tripoli captured the U.S.S. *Philadelphia*. Only the following year did Lieutenant Stephen Decatur repair the situation by sneaking into Tripoli's harbor and burning the vessel. The American blockade that followed forced Tripoli to give up its demands for tribute. Even so, the United States continued paying tribute to the other Barbary states until 1816.

The Embargo

Jefferson was willing to fight the Barbary States, but he drew back from declaring war against Britain or France. Between 1803 and 1807, Britain seized more than 500 American ships; France more than 300. The British navy also impressed into service thousands of sailors, some of whom were deserters from England's fleet but others, native-born Americans. Despite such harassment, Jefferson pursued a program of "peaceable coercion" designed to protect neutral rights without war. His proposed **embargo** not only prohibited American ships from trading with foreign ports but also stopped the export of all American goods. The president was confident that American exports were so essential to the two belligerents that they would quickly agree to respect American neutral rights. In December 1807 Congress passed the Embargo Act.

Jefferson had seriously miscalculated. France did not depend on American trade and so managed well enough, while British ships quickly took over the carrying trade as American vessels lay idle. Under the embargo, both American imports and exports plunged. As the center of American shipping, New England port cities protested the loudest, and their merchants smuggled behind officials' backs.

Madison and the Young Republicans

Following Washington's example, Jefferson did not seek a third term. A caucus of Republican members of Congress selected James Madison to run against Federalist Charles Cotesworth Pinckney. Madison triumphed easily, although in discontented New England, the Federalists picked up 24 seats in Congress.

MADISON'S CHARACTER Few men have assumed the presidency with more experience than James Madison, yet

THE UNITED STATES AND THE BARBARY STATES, 1801–1815

The young United States, like many European powers, found its trading vessels challenged by the Barbary states of Morocco, Algiers, Tunisia, and Tripoli. When the pasha of Tripoli declared war on the United States in 1801, Jefferson dispatched a force that blockaded Tripoli to bring the war to an end in 1805. Tribute paid to the other Barbary states continued until 1816, after a new naval force, led by Commodore Stephen Decatur, forced the ruler of Algiers to end the practice.

his tenure as president proved disappointing. Despite his intellectual brilliance, he lacked the force of leadership and the inner strength to impose his will on less capable men.

WAR HAWKS With a president reluctant to fight for what he wanted, leadership passed to Congress. The elections of 1810 swept in a new generation of Republicans, led by the magnetic 34-year-old Henry Clay of Kentucky, who gained the rare distinction of being elected Speaker of the House in his first term. These younger Republicans were more nationalistic than the generation led by Jefferson and Madison. They sought an ambitious program of economic development and were aggressive expansionists, especially those from frontier districts. Their willingness to go to war earned them the name of War Hawks. Though they numbered fewer than 30 in Congress, they quickly became the driving force in the Republican Party.

The Decision for War

REPEAL OF THE EMBARGO During Jefferson's final week in office in early 1809, Congress repealed the Embargo Act. The following year Congress authorized trade with France and England but decreed that if one of the two belligerents agreed to stop interfering with American shipping, trade with the other would be prohibited.

Given these circumstances, Napoleon outmaneuvered the British by announcing that he would put aside the French trade regulations. Madison took the French emperor at his word and reimposed a ban on trade with England. French raiders continued to seize American ships, but American anger focused on the British, who then seized many more ships and continued to impress American sailors. Finally, on June 16, 1812, the British ministry suspended the searches and seizures of American ships.

The concession came too late. Two days earlier, unaware of the change in policy, Congress granted Madison's request for a declaration of war against Britain. The vote was mostly along party lines, with every Federalist voting against war. By contrast, members of Congress from the South and the West clamored most strongly for war. Their constituents were consumed with a desire to seize additional territory in Canada or in Florida (owned by Britain's ally Spain). In addition, they accused the British of stirring up hostility among the Indian tribes.

Perhaps most important, the War Hawks were convinced that Britain had never truly accepted the verdict of the American Revolution. To them, American independence—and with it republicanism—hung in the balance. For Americans hungering to be accepted in the community of nations, nothing rankled more than still being treated by the British as colonials.

THE WAR OF 1812

After the American victory on Lake Erie and the defeat of the western Indians at the Battle of the Thames, the British adopted a three-pronged strategy to invade the United States, climaxing with an attempt on New Orleans. But they met their match in Andrew Jackson, whose troops marched to New Orleans after fighting a series of battles against the Creeks and forcing them to cede a massive tract of land.

With Britain preoccupied by Napoleon, the War Hawks expected an easy victory. In truth, the United States was totally unprepared for war. Crippled by Jefferson's cutbacks, the navy was unable to lift the British blockade of the American coast, which bottled up the country's merchant marine and most of its navy. As for the U.S. Army, it was small and poorly led. When Congress moved to increase its size to 75,000, even the most hawkish states failed to meet their quotas. Congress was also reluctant to levy taxes to finance the war.

BATTLE OF LAKE ERIE   A three-pronged American invasion of Canada from Detroit, Niagara, and Lake Champlain failed dismally in 1812. Americans fared better the following

year, as both sides raced to build a navy on the strategically located Lake Erie. Led by Commander Oliver Hazard Perry, American forces won a decisive victory at Put-in-Bay in 1813.

As the United States struggled to organize its forces, Tecumseh sensed that his long-awaited opportunity had come to drive Americans out of the western territories. "Here is a chance . . . such as will never occur again," he told a war council, "for us Indians of North America to form ourselves into one great combination." Allying with the British, Tecumseh traveled south in the fall to talk again with his Creek allies. To coordinate an Indian offensive for the following summer, he left a bundle of red sticks with eager Creek soldiers. They were to remove one stick each day from the bundle and attack when the sticks had run out.

JACKSON DEFEATS THE CREEK INDIANS Some of the older Creeks were more acculturated and preferred an American alliance. But about 2,000 younger "Red Stick" Creeks launched a series of attacks, climaxed by the destruction of Fort Mims along the Alabama River in August 1813. Once again, the Indians' lack of unity was a serious handicap, as warriors from the Cherokee, Choctaw, and Chickasaw tribes, traditional Creek enemies, allied with the Americans. At the Battle of Horseshoe Bend in March 1814, General Andrew Jackson and his Tennessee militia soundly defeated the Red Stick Creeks. Jackson promptly dictated a peace treaty under which the Creeks ceded 22 million acres of land in the Mississippi Territory. They and the other southern tribes still retained significant landholdings, but Indian military power had been broken in the South, east of the Mississippi.

DEATH OF TECUMSEH Farther north, in October 1813, American forces under General William Henry Harrison defeated the British and their Indian allies at the Battle of the Thames. In the midst of heavy fighting Tecumseh was killed. With him died any hope of a pan-Indian movement.

The British Invasion

As long as the war against Napoleon continued, the British were unwilling to divert army units to North America. But in 1814 Napoleon was at last defeated. Free to concentrate on America, the British devised a coordinated strategy to invade the United States in the northern, central, and southern parts of the country. The main army headed south from Montreal but was checked when Americans destroyed the British fleet on Lake Champlain.

Meanwhile, a smaller British force captured Washington and burned several public buildings, including the Capitol and the president's home. To cover the scars of this destruction, the executive mansion was painted with whitewash and became known as the White House. The burning of the capital was a humiliating event: President Madison and his wife, Dolley, were forced to flee. But the defeat had little military significance. The principal British objective was Baltimore, where for 25 hours their fleet bombarded Fort McHenry in the city's harbor. When Francis Scott Key saw the American flag still flying above the fort at dawn, he hurriedly composed the verses of "The Star Spangled Banner," which was eventually adopted as the national anthem.

| *After Andrew Jackson's victory at New Orleans, the Hartford Convention looked to many like a traitorous leap into the arms of the British king.*

Remembering Lafayette

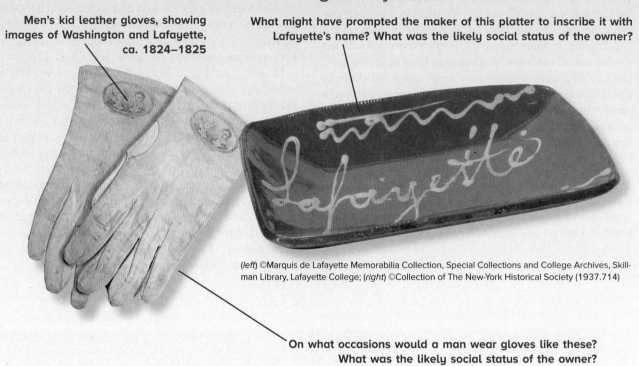

Men's kid leather gloves, showing images of Washington and Lafayette, ca. 1824–1825

What might have prompted the maker of this platter to inscribe it with Lafayette's name? What was the likely social status of the owner?

(*left*) ©Marquis de Lafayette Memorabilia Collection, Special Collections and College Archives, Skillman Library, Lafayette College; (*right*) ©Collection of The New-York Historical Society (1937.714)

On what occasions would a man wear gloves like these? What was the likely social status of the owner?

Events that were commemorated even as they unfolded hold a special fascination for historians. Just as the celebration of Franklin's arrival in Paris tells us much about the French in the 1770s, the hoopla in the United States over the return of the Marquis de Lafayette reveals a great deal about early national Americans. A major general in the Continental Army, a comrade-in-arms of Washington, and a lifelong defender of liberal values and human rights, Lafayette made his second voyage from France to the United States in 1824 at the invitation of President James Monroe. A triumphal 13-month tour of all 24 states followed, the Marquis traveling by stagecoach and steamboat and drawing crowds that numbered in the tens of thousands. While only a lucky few Americans basked in the 67-year-old hero's presence at dinners and balls, nearly all could afford to purchase one of the souvenirs produced by artisans of both humble and fine crafts.

THINKING CRITICALLY

Consider the challenges confronting President Monroe's administration. What might he have hoped to accomplish by inviting Lafayette to the United States? What do the two objects suggest about Lafayette's popularity as a public figure?

The third British target was New Orleans, where a formidable army of 7,500 British troops was opposed by a hastily assembled force commanded by Major General Andrew Jackson. The Americans included regular soldiers; frontiersmen from Kentucky and Tennessee; citizens of New Orleans, including several companies of free African Americans; Choctaw Indians; and a group of pirates. Jackson's outnumbered and ill-equipped forces won a stunning victory, which made the general an overnight hero.

HARTFORD CONVENTION   In December 1814, while Jackson was organizing the defense of New Orleans, New England Federalists met in Hartford to map strategy against the war. Angry as they were, the delegates still rejected calls for secession. Instead, they proposed a series of amendments to the Constitution that showed their displeasure with the government's economic policies and their resentment of the South's national political power.

JACKSON'S VICTORY AT NEW ORLEANS   To the convention's dismay, its representatives arrived in Washington to present their demands just as news of Andrew Jackson's victory was being trumpeted on the streets. The celebrations badly undercut the Hartford Convention, as did news from across the Atlantic that American negotiators in Ghent, Belgium, had signed a treaty ending the war. Hostilities had ceased, technically, on Christmas Eve 1814, two weeks before the Battle of New Orleans. Both sides were relieved to end the conflict, even though the Treaty of Ghent left unresolved the issues of impressment, neutral rights, and trade.

COLLAPSE OF THE FEDERALIST PARTY   The return of peace hard on the heels of Jackson's victory sparked a new confidence in many Americans. The new nationalism sounded the death knell of the Federalist Party, for even talk of secession at the Hartford Convention had tainted the party with disunion and treason. In the 1816 election Madison's secretary of state, James Monroe, resoundingly defeated Federalist Rufus King of New York. Four years later Monroe ran for reelection unopposed.

Monroe's Presidency

The major domestic challenge that Monroe faced was the renewal of sectional rivalries in 1819, when the Missouri Territory applied for admission as a slave state. Before the controversy over Missouri erupted, slavery had not been a major issue in American politics. Congress had debated the institution when it prohibited the African slave trade in 1808, the earliest year this step could be taken under the Constitution. But lacking any specific federal legislation to stop it, slavery had crossed the Mississippi River into the Louisiana Purchase. Louisiana entered the Union in 1812 as a slave state, and in 1818 Missouri, which had about 10,000 slaves in its population, asked permission to come in, too.

In 1818 the Union contained 11 free and 11 slave states. As the federal government became stronger and more active, both the North and the South worried about maintaining their political power. The North's greater population gave it a majority in the House of Representatives, 105 to 81. The Senate, of course, was evenly balanced, because each state had two senators regardless of population. But Maine, which previously had been part of Massachusetts, requested admission as a free state. That would upset the balance unless Missouri came in as a slave state.

MISSOURI COMPROMISE   Representative James Tallmadge of New York disturbed this delicate state of affairs when in 1819 he introduced an amendment that would establish a program of gradual emancipation in Missouri. For the first time Congress directly debated the morality of slavery, often bitterly. The House approved the Tallmadge amendment, but the Senate refused to accept it, and the two houses deadlocked.

When Congress reconvened in 1820, Henry Clay of Kentucky promoted what came to be known as the Missouri Compromise. Under its terms Missouri was admitted as a slave state and Maine as a free state. In addition, slavery was forever prohibited in the remainder of the Louisiana Purchase north of 36°30′ (the southern boundary of Missouri). Clay's proposal, the first of several sectional compromises he would engineer in his long career, won congressional approval and Monroe signed the measure, ending the crisis. But southern fears for the security of slavery and northern fears about its spread remained.

Monroe's greatest achievements were diplomatic, accomplished largely by his talented secretary of state, John Quincy Adams, the son of President John Adams. An experienced diplomat, Adams thought of the Republic in continental terms and was intent on promoting expansion to the Pacific. Such a vision required dealing with Spain, which had never recognized the legality of the Louisiana Purchase. In addition, between 1810 and 1813 the United States had occupied and unilaterally annexed Spanish West Florida.

But Spain was preoccupied with events farther south in the Americas. In the first quarter of the nineteenth century, its colonies one after another revolted and established themselves as independent nations. These revolutions

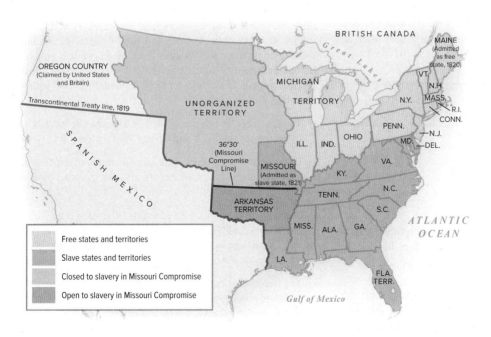

THE MISSOURI COMPROMISE AND THE UNION'S BOUNDARIES IN 1820

increased the pressure on the Spanish minister to America, Luis de Onís, to come to terms with the United States. So, too, did Andrew Jackson, who marched into East Florida and captured several Spanish forts in 1818. Jackson had exceeded his instructions, but Adams understood the additional pressure this aggression put on Onís and refused to disavow it.

TRANSCONTINENTAL TREATY Fearful that the United States might next invade Texas or other Spanish territory, Spain agreed to the Transcontinental Treaty in February 1819. Its terms set the boundary between American and Spanish territory all the way to the Pacific. Spain not only gave up its claims to the Pacific Northwest but also ceded Florida. To obtain the line to the Pacific, the United States abandoned its contention that Texas was part of the Louisiana Purchase.

More importantly, the United States also came to terms with Great Britain. Following the War of 1812, the British abandoned their connections with the western Indian tribes and no longer attempted to block American expansion to the Rocky Mountains. In a growing spirit of cooperation, the countries agreed in 1818 to the 49th parallel as the northern boundary of the Louisiana Purchase and also to joint control of the Oregon Territory for 10 years, subject to renewal.

MONROE DOCTRINE In his annual message to Congress, on December 2, 1823, Monroe also announced that the United States would not interfere with already established European colonies in the Western Hemisphere. But any intervention in the new republics of Latin America, he warned, would be considered a hostile act: "The American continents . . . are henceforth not to be considered as subjects for future colonization by any European powers." The essence of this policy was the concept of two worlds, one old and one new, each refraining from interfering in the other's affairs. American public opinion hailed Monroe's statement and then promptly forgot it. Only years later would it be referred to as the Monroe Doctrine.

 REVIEW
What were the causes of the War of 1812?

PUTTING HISTORY IN GLOBAL CONTEXT

THE THREE DECADES AFTER 1789 demonstrated how profoundly events in the wider world could affect life within the United States, shaping its politics, its boundaries, its economy—its future.

The French Revolution contributed to splintering the once-united leaders of the American Revolution into two rival parties. The wars that followed, between France and England, deepened the divisions between Federalists and Republicans and prompted both parties to mobilize the political loyalties of ordinary white American men and women. Napoleon's ambitions to conquer Europe handed Jefferson the Louisiana Territory, while British efforts to reclaim its American empire tempted some New Englanders to secede from the Union and encouraged Tecumseh's hopes of mounting a pan-Indian resistance on the frontier. The Haitian Revolution in the Caribbean prompted free blacks in northern cities to protest racial inequalities and slavery within the United States.

But by the 1820s most white Americans paid less attention to events abroad than to expanding across the vast North American continent. Jefferson had dreamed of an "empire of liberty," delighting in expansion as the means to preserve a nation of small farmers. But younger, more nationalistic Republicans had a different vision of expansion. They spoke of internal improvements, protective tariffs to foster American industries, roads and canals to link farmers with towns, cities, and wider markets. These new Republicans were not aristocratic, like the Federalists of old. Still, their dream of a national, commercial republic resembled Franklin's and Hamilton's more than Jefferson's. They had seen how handsomely American merchants and commercial farmers profited when European wars swelled demand for American wheat and cotton. They looked to profit from speculation in land, the growth of commercial agriculture, and new methods of industrial manufacturing. If they represented the rising generation, what would be the fate of semisubsistence farm communities? The answer was not yet clear.

CHAPTER SUMMARY

Basic social divisions between the commercial and semisubsistence regions shaped the politics of the new United States. Between 1789 and the 1820s the first parties emerged and, along with them, a more popular and participatory political culture. Over the same decades, Indian confederacies mounted a sustained resistance to westward expansion, while events in Europe deepened divisions among Federalists and Republicans and threatened the very existence of the fledgling American republic.

- The first party to organize in the 1790s was the Federalists, led by Alexander Hamilton and George Washington.

- Divisions over Hamilton's policies as secretary of the Treasury led to the formation of the Republicans, led by James Madison and Thomas Jefferson.

- The commercially minded Federalists believed in order and hierarchy, supported loose construction of the Constitution, and wanted a powerful central government to promote economic growth.

- The Republican Party, with its sympathy for agrarian ideals, endorsed strict construction of the Constitution, wanted a less active federal government, and harbored a strong fear of aristocracy.

- The French Revolution, the XYZ Affair, the naval war, and the Alien and Sedition Acts also deepened the partisan division between Federalists and Republicans during the 1790s. The Federalists demonstrated that the new government could be a more active force in American society, but their controversial domestic and foreign policies, internal divisions, and open hostility to the masses led to their downfall.

- Before becoming president, Jefferson advocated the principles of agrarianism, limited government, and strict construction of the Constitution. But once in power, he failed to dismantle Hamilton's economic program and promoted western expansion by acquiring Louisiana from France.

- Chief Justice John Marshall proclaimed that the courts were to interpret the meaning of the Constitution (judicial review), a move that helped the judiciary emerge as an equal branch of government.

- Lewis and Clark produced the first reliable information and maps of the Louisiana territory. The lands they passed through had been transformed over the previous 25 years by disease, dislocation, and the arrival of horses and guns.

- The Shawnee prophet Tenskwatawa and his brother Tecumseh organized the most important Indian resistance to the expansion of the new republic, but the movement collapsed with the death of Tecumseh during the War of 1812.

- France and Britain both interfered with neutral rights, and the United States went to war against Britain in 1812.

- In the years after 1815 there was a surge in American nationalism, reinforced by Britain's recognition of American sovereignty and the Monroe Doctrine's prohibition of European intervention in the Western Hemisphere. But the crisis over Missouri was an early indication of growing sectional rivalries.

Digging Deeper

Two good overviews of early national politics are Stanley Elkins and Eric McKitrick's *The Age of Federalism* (1993); and James Roger Sharp, *American Politics in the Early Republic* (1993). Another approach to understanding the politics of this period is to read about the lives of leading political figures: among the best are Joseph J. Ellis's biographies of John Adams (*Passionate Sage,* 1993) and Thomas Jefferson (*American Sphinx,* rev. ed., 1998); and two biographies of Alexander Hamilton, one by Ron Chernow (the basis for the musical, *Hamilton*) and one by Gerald Stourzh. For excellent work on the early republic in international context, see David Armitage, *The Declaration of Independence: A Global History* (2007); Eliga H. Gould, *Among the Powers of the Earth* (2012); and Janet Polasky, *Revolutions without Borders* (2015). For Haiti and the early American republic, see Ashli White, *Encountering Revolution* (2010); and James Alexander Dun, *Dangerous Neighbors* (2016).

To become better acquainted with the popular political culture of the early republic, consult *Beyond the Founders* (2004), a superb collection of essays edited by Jeffrey L. Pasley, Andrew W. Robertson, and David Waldstreicher. For an engaging narrative about the political influence exerted by white women, see Catherine Allgor, *Parlor Politics* (2000); and for rich descriptions of the social and political interactions among whites, African Americans, and Indians in the new republic, see Joshua D. Rothman, *Notorious in the Neighborhood* (2003); and John Wood Sweet, *Bodies Politic* (2003). To gain a fuller understanding of the lives of Indians, slaves, and whites in the West, rely on Leonard J. Sadosky, *Revolutionary Negotiations* (2009); Stephen Aron, *American Confluence* (2006); and Adam Rothman, *Slave Country* (2005).

After the Fact
| Historians Reconstruct the Past |

Sally Hemings and Thomas Jefferson

So much goes into the weighing of historical evidence: not only the application of logic and reason, and the use of large theories and small inferences, but also the influence of emotion and a culture's prevailing myths. The distortions created by the latter pair come into play especially when topics like race and sex are involved—as can be seen by following the trail of a story first made public more than two centuries ago.

SOME RUMORS—AND SOME FACTS

THE RUMORS BEGAN IN ALBEMARLE County, Virginia, more than 200 years ago; they came to the notice of a contemporary journalist by the name of James Callender. A writer for hire, Callender had once lent his pen to the Republicans but turned from friend into foe when the party failed to reward him with a political appointment. When his story splashed onto the pages of the *Recorder,* a Richmond newspaper, the trickle of rumor turned into a torrent of scandal. Callender alleged that Thomas Jefferson, during his years in Paris as the American minister, had contracted a liaison with one of his own slaves. The woman was the president's mistress even now, he insisted, in 1802. She was kept at Monticello, Jefferson's plantation, and Jefferson had fathered children with her. Her name was Sally Hemings.

Solid information about Sally Hemings is scarce. She was one of six children, we know, born to Betty Hemings and her white master, John Wayles, a Virginia planter whose white daughter, Martha Wayles Skelton, married Jefferson in 1772. We know that Betty Hemings was the child of an African woman and an English sailor, which means Betty's children with Wayles, Sally among them, were quadroons—light-skinned and one-quarter African. We know that Sally accompanied one of Jefferson's daughters to Paris as her maid in 1787 and that, on returning to Virginia a few years later, she performed domestic work at Monticello. We know that she had six children and that the four who survived to adulthood escaped from slavery into freedom: Jefferson assisted her two eldest children, Beverly and Harriet, in leaving Monticello in 1822, and her two youngest children, Madison and Eston, were freed by Jefferson's will in 1827. We know that shortly after Jefferson's death, his daughter, Martha Jefferson Randolph, freed Sally Hemings and that she lived with her two sons in Charlottesville until her death in 1835.

©Art Collection 2/Alamy

This view of Monticello was painted shortly after Jefferson's death. It portrays his white descendants surrounded by a serene landscape.

DUELING ORAL TRADITIONS

WE KNOW, TOO, THAT JEFFERSON'S white descendants stoutly denied (and, to this day, some still deny) any familial connection with the descendants of Sally Hemings. Even though Callender's scandal quickly subsided, doing Jefferson no lasting political damage, Jefferson's white grandchildren were still explaining away the accusations half a century later. In the 1850s Jefferson's granddaughter, Ellen Coolidge Randolph, claimed that her brother, Thomas Jefferson Randolph, had told her that one of Jefferson's nephews, Samuel Carr, fathered Hemings's children. In the 1860s Henry Randall, an early biographer of Jefferson, recalled a conversation with Thomas Jefferson Randolph in the 1850s in which he attributed paternity to another nephew, Samuel's brother Peter Carr.

Until the end of the twentieth century most scholars resolved the discrepancy of this dual claim by suggesting that one of the Carr nephews had fathered Sally Hemings's children. And all of Jefferson's most eminent twentieth-century biographers—Douglass Adair, Dumas Malone, John Chester Miller, and Joseph J. Ellis—contended that a man of Jefferson's character and convictions could not have engaged in a liaison with a slave woman. After all, Jefferson was a Virginia gentleman and an American *philosophe* who believed that reason should rule over passion; he was also an eloquent apostle of equality and democracy and an outspoken critic of the tyrannical power of masters over slaves. And, despite his opposition to slavery, Jefferson argued in his *Notes on the State of Virginia* (1785) for the likelihood that peoples of African descent were inferior intellectually and artistically to those of European descent. Because of that conviction he warned of the dire consequences that would attend the mixing of the races.

The official version of events did not go unchallenged. Madison Hemings, a skilled carpenter, in 1873 told an Ohio newspaper reporter of an oral tradition, long repeated among his family, that his mother had been Thomas Jefferson's "concubine" and that Jefferson had fathered all her children. Even so, nearly a century passed before Madison Hemings's claims won wider attention. In 1968 the historian Winthrop Jordan noted that Sally Hemings's pregnancies coincided with Jefferson's stays at Monticello. In 1975 Fawn Brodie's best-selling "intimate history" of Jefferson portrayed his relationship with Sally Hemings as an enduring love affair; four years later, Barbara Chase-Riboud set Brodie's findings to fiction.

OVERTURNING CULTURAL ASSUMPTIONS

AN EVEN MORE POWERFUL CASE for Jefferson's paternity of all of Hemings's children was made in 1997 by Annette Gordon-Reed. She drew on her legal training to subject the handling of the evidence by Jefferson's biographers to a close and telling cross-examination. Although they had dismissed Madison Hemings's recollections as mere family lore and wishful thinking, Gordon-Reed argued that such oral testimony was, in fact, no more or less reliable than the oral testimony of Jefferson's white Randolph descendants.

One year later Gordon-Reed's arguments crested on a tidal wave of new revelations: a team of DNA research scientists headed by Eugene A. Foster discovered an exact match on the Y-chromosome markers between Thomas Jefferson's line and the descendants of Eston Hemings. (Eston was Sally's youngest child and the only one who left male-line descendants whose DNA could be tested.) Since the chance of such a match occurring randomly was less than 1 in 1,000, the DNA evidence made it highly probable that Thomas Jefferson fathered at least one of Sally Hemings's children. In addition, Foster's team found no DNA match between the Hemings line and the Carr family, thus discrediting the assertions of Jefferson's white descendants. Intrigued by these findings, historian Fraser D. Neiman undertook a sophisticated statistical analysis of Hemings's conceptions and Jefferson's returns to Monticello (where he spent about half his time), which established a 99 percent probability that he had fathered all of Hemings's children.

This new evidence has persuaded most historians that Thomas Jefferson conducted a monogamous liaison with Sally Hemings over 38 years and that their union produced at least one and most likely all six of her children. As a result, the debate among historians has moved on to explore questions left unresolved by the new scientific findings.

UNRESOLVED QUESTIONS

ONE SUCH QUESTION BEARS ON how historians should assess the credibility of their sources. Specifically, how reliable are the oral traditions passed down through families? Both the DNA and the statistical evidence bear out Madison Hemings's recollections. Surely that outcome, as Annette Gordon-Reed has urged, should prompt future historians to scrutinize the oral testimonies of white masters such as the Jeffersons and the Randolphs as closely as they do the narratives of slaves and the oral traditions of their descendants. But does it follow that historians should regard the recollections of nonliterate peoples as possessing a superior claim to being accurate recoveries of the past? Gordon-Reed and a host of other historians warn against that conclusion, arguing that all oral testimony must be tested against the findings yielded by the documentary record and scientific research. Their caution is warranted by the fact that the DNA findings to date have failed to show a match between the Jefferson line and that of Thomas Woodson, another Monticello slave whose African American descendants have long cited their own family's oral tradition as evidence of a biological connection to Jefferson.

An equally intriguing question concerns the character of the relationship between Sally Hemings and Thomas Jefferson. Was it forced and exploitative or consensual and even affectionate? On the

Jefferson, Thomas. *Farm Book*, 1774-1824, page 145. Original manuscript from the Coolidge Collection of Thomas Jefferson manuscripts. Courtesy of the Massachusetts Historical Society

The names of Sally Hemings and her sons appear on this list of Thomas Jefferson's slaves.

one hand, the long duration of their liaison suggests that it may have been based on a shared emotional intimacy. (If Jefferson fathered all of Hemings's children, their involvement began in Paris during the late 1780s and endured at least until the birth of Eston Hemings in 1808.) As Annette Gordon-Reed points out, even stronger support for this interpretation is that Sally Hemings and all her children were the only nuclear slave family at Monticello who finally attained their freedom. Furthermore, biographers have never doubted Jefferson's affection for his first wife, Martha Wayles Skelton, before she died in 1782. Is it not likely that Jefferson felt similarly toward Sally, who was in fact Martha's unacknowledged half-sister?

©Howard University/Moorland-Spingarn Research Center

This bell once belonged to Martha Wayles Jefferson, the wife of Thomas Jefferson. According to Hemings family tradition, she gave the bell to Sally Hemings, who was her half-sister.

On the other hand, the sexual exploitation of black women was common among white masters in the Chesapeake, the Carolinas, and the Caribbean. Like them, Jefferson may have availed himself of the privileges of ownership to compel sexual favors over many years from a slave whom he fancied. Or perhaps Sally Hemings submitted to Jefferson's sexual demands because she hoped to win better treatment—and, in the end, freedom—for herself and her children. Many bondswomen (among them, possibly, Sally's mother, Betty Hemings, and her grandmother) used that strategy to protect their children from the ravages of slavery. What lends added support to either of those interpretations is the testimony of Madison Hemings, who recalled that although Jefferson was affectionate with his white Randolph grandchildren, he was "not in the habit of showing partiality or fatherly affection" to his children with Sally Hemings.

In the last analysis, the significance of Sally Hemings's relationship with Thomas Jefferson may reside in its power to reveal the complexity of southern plantation societies between the American Revolution and the Civil War. In that place and time the American South was not starkly divided into whites and blacks; instead, it was a culture in which the races had been mingling for generations, yielding many people of mixed ancestry, such as Sally Hemings. Israel Jefferson, who passed part of his life in slavery at Monticello, remembered her as being "mighty near white," with "long straight hair down her back." Because of their shared bonds of blood, such light-skinned slaves sometimes enjoyed greater privileges and freedoms from their masters, but they also had to negotiate more complicated relationships with them and with less favored members of the slave community.

VIRGINIAN LUXURIES

(detail) ©The Colonial Williamsburg Foundation. Museum Purchase (#1993.100.1)

This painting was discovered on the reverse side of a portrait of a Virginia gentleman. Experts believe that it dates from the early republic, and the artist, still unknown, evidently shared Jefferson's criticisms of slavery.

The decades following the War of 1812 saw the rise of a national market economy that sparked changes for millions of ordinary Americans. As factories began turning out products assisted by machines, they replaced small shops where handmade goods were made by craftworkers. Shoemakers, who fashioned each pair of shoes from start to finish, increasingly found themselves out of a job.

Source: Library of Congress, Prints and Photographs Division [LC-DIG-ppmsca-51946]

>> An American Story

FROM BOOM TO BUST WITH ONE-DAY CLOCKS

In the years before the Civil War, the name of Chauncey Jerome could be found traced in neat, sharp letters in a thousand different places across the globe: everywhere from the fireplace mantels of southern planters to the log cabins of Illinois prairie farmers and even in Chinese trading houses in Canton. Chauncey Jerome was a New England clock-maker whose clever, inexpensive, and addictive machines had conquered the markets of the world.

Jerome, the son of a Connecticut blacksmith, at first barely made a living peddling his clocks from farmhouse to farmhouse.

Then in 1824 his career took off thanks to a "very showy" bronze looking-glass clock. Between 1827 and 1837 Jerome's factory produced more clocks than any other in the country. But when the Panic of 1837 struck, the entrepreneur had to scramble to avoid financial ruin.

Looking for a new opportunity, he set out to produce an inexpensive brass "one-day" clock—so called because its winding mechanism kept it running that long. Traditionally, the works of these clocks were made of wood, and the wheels and teeth had to be painstakingly cut by hand. Furthermore, wooden clocks could not be exported overseas because the humidity on board ship swelled the wood and ruined them. Jerome's brass version proved more accurate as well as cheaper. Costs came down further when he began to use interchangeable parts and combined his operations for making cases and movements within a single factory in New Haven, Connecticut. By organizing the production process, Jerome brought the price of a good clock within the reach of ordinary people. So popular were the new models that desperate competitors began attaching Jerome labels to their own inferior imitations.

Disaster struck again in 1855, when Jerome went into partnership with several unreliable associates. Within a few years his business faltered, then failed. At the age of 62, the once-prominent business leader found himself working again in a clock factory as an ordinary mechanic. He lived his last years in poverty.

Jerome rose higher than most Americans of his generation, and he fell farther. Yet his fellow citizens shared his dreams of success, just as they were haunted by the fear of losing everything. For Jerome, it wasn't only material comforts that vanished; so did respect. "One of the most trying things to me now," he confessed in his autobiography, "is to see how I am looked upon by the community since I lost my property. I never was any better when I owned it than I am now, and never behaved any better. But how different is the feeling towards you, when your neighbors can make nothing more out of you. . . . You are passed by without notice."

As the **boom-and-bust economy** swirled around him, Jerome sensed that society had taken on a different tone—that the marketplace and its ethos had become dominant. "It is all money and business, business and money which make the man now-a-days," he complained. "Success is every thing, and it makes very little difference how, or what means he uses to obtain it." The United States, according to one foreign traveler, had become "one gigantic workshop, over the entrance of which there is the blazing inscription *'No admission here except on business.'*"

During the life of Chauncey Jerome, the United States became a commercial republic dominated by a national market. Americans from different regions tied themselves to one another eagerly, even aggressively, through the mechanism of the free market. They sold cotton or wheat and bought manufactured cloth or brass one-day clocks. They borrowed money not merely to buy a house or farm but also to speculate and profit. They relied, even in many rural villages, on cash and paper money instead of bartering for goods and services. Manufacturing changed as well, shifting from the master-apprentice system of production set in urban and rural workshops toward mechanization and the rise of the factory system.

Those economic developments reshaped the lives and values of many Americans. They moved from face-to-face dealings with neighbors to impersonal transactions with distant buyers and sellers. They shifted from performing mechanically simple tasks to tackling the more technologically complex, and growing numbers moved from sparsely settled rural areas to densely populated cities and towns. Equally important, they came to regard free market capitalism, upward mobility, and conspicuous consumption as integral to the emerging American national identity.

Such were the changes Chauncey Jerome witnessed—indeed, changes he helped to bring about himself, with his clocks that divided the working days of Americans into more disciplined, orderly segments. <<

Source: Library of Congress, Prints and Photographs Division [LC-USZC4-4161]

Like this peddler, young Chauncey Jerome sold his clocks from farmhouse to farmhouse.

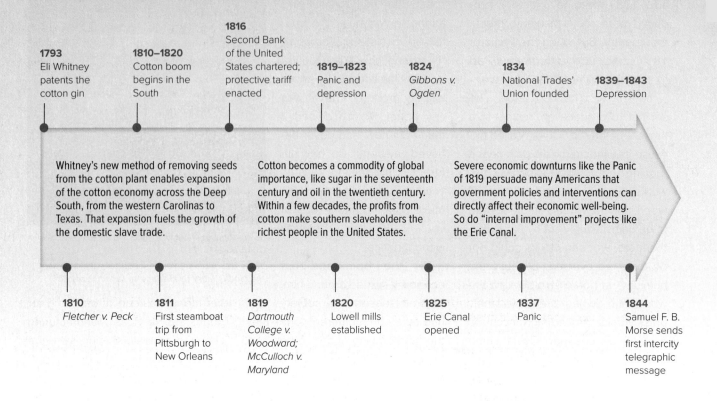

1793
Eli Whitney patents the cotton gin

1810–1820
Cotton boom begins in the South

1816
Second Bank of the United States chartered; protective tariff enacted

1819–1823
Panic and depression

1824
Gibbons v. Ogden

1834
National Trades' Union founded

1839–1843
Depression

Whitney's new method of removing seeds from the cotton plant enables expansion of the cotton economy across the Deep South, from the western Carolinas to Texas. That expansion fuels the growth of the domestic slave trade.

Cotton becomes a commodity of global importance, like sugar in the seventeenth century and oil in the twentieth century. Within a few decades, the profits from cotton make southern slaveholders the richest people in the United States.

Severe economic downturns like the Panic of 1819 persuade many Americans that government policies and interventions can directly affect their economic well-being. So do "internal improvement" projects like the Erie Canal.

1810
Fletcher v. Peck

1811
First steamboat trip from Pittsburgh to New Orleans

1819
Dartmouth College v. Woodward; McCulloch v. Maryland

1820
Lowell mills established

1825
Erie Canal opened

1837
Panic

1844
Samuel F. B. Morse sends first intercity telegraphic message

THE NATIONAL MARKET ECONOMY

IN 1844 JOHN BURROWS HEARD that potatoes were selling for $2 a bushel in New Orleans. Potatoes fetched less than 50 cents a bushel in Davenport in the Iowa Territory where Burrows was a small merchant, so he loaded 2,500 bushels on a flatboat and started down the Mississippi River. Along the way he learned that other merchants, acting on the same information, had done the same and that the market in New Orleans was now glutted with potatoes. When he reached his destination 6 weeks later, he could not sell his load. Desperate, he finally swapped his potatoes at 8 cents a bushel, taking a load of coffee in return. He made nothing on the transaction, since it had cost him that much to ship the load to New Orleans.

Burrows's experience demonstrated that a national market economy required not just the efficient movement of goods but also rapid communications. Looking back many years later on the amazing transformation that had occurred in his lifetime, Burrows commented, "No one can realize the difficulties of doing a produce business in those days."

A truly national system of markets began to grow following the War of 1812, when the United States entered a period of unprecedented economic expansion. As it grew, the economy became varied enough to sustain and even accelerate its growth. Before the war it had been tied largely to international trade. The United States exported staples such as cotton, wheat, tobacco, and timber; if the nations that bought these commodities suddenly stopped doing so, the domestic economy suffered. That happened during the European wars of the 1790s and again after 1803. Because so many Americans remained rural and primarily self-sufficient, they could not absorb any increase in goods produced by American manufacturers.

GROWTH OF A DOMESTIC MARKET But the War of 1812 marked the turning point in the creation and expansion of a domestic market. First the embargo and then the war itself stimulated the growth of manufacturing, particularly in textiles. In 1808 the United States had 8,000 spindles spinning cotton thread; by the end of the war the number had jumped to around 130,000. In addition, war had also bottled up capital in Europe. When peace was restored, this capital flowed into the United States, seeking investments. Finally, the war experience led the federal government to adopt policies designed to spur economic expansion.

The New Nationalism

After the war with Britain, leadership passed to a new generation of the Republic—younger men such as Henry Clay, John C. Calhoun, and John Quincy Adams. All were ardent nationalists eager to use federal power to promote rapid development of the nation. Increasingly dominant within the Republican Party, they advocated the "New Nationalism," a set of economic policies designed to foster the prosperity of all regions of the country and bind the nation more tightly together.

NATIONAL BANK Even James Madison saw the need for increased federal activity, given the problems the government experienced during the war. The national bank had closed its doors in 1811 when its charter expired. Without it the country had fallen into financial chaos. Madison had opposed Hamilton's national bank in 1791, but now, with his approval, Congress in 1816 chartered the Second Bank of the United States for a period of 20 years. Madison also agreed to a mildly protective tariff to aid budding American industries by raising the price of competing foreign goods. Passed in 1816, it set an average duty of 20 percent on imported woolen and cotton cloth, iron, and sugar. The measure enjoyed wide support in the North and the West, but a number of southern representatives voted against it because most of its benefits went to northern manufacturers.

Madison also recommended that the government promote internal improvements such as roads, canals, and bridges. The war had demonstrated how cumbersome it was to move troops or supplies overland. Although Madison did not believe that federal funds could be used merely for local projects, he was willing to support projects broader in scope. His successor, James Monroe, approved additional ones.

The Cotton Trade

WHITNEY'S COTTON GIN Cotton proved to be the key to American economic development after 1815. By the end of the eighteenth century, southern planters had discovered that short-fiber cotton would grow in the lower part of the South. But the cotton contained sticky green seeds that could not be easily separated from the lint by hand. The needed breakthrough came in 1793 when Eli Whitney invented the cotton gin, a mechanical device that removed the seeds from the lint. The gin allowed a laborer to clean 50 pounds of cotton a day, compared with only 1 pound by hand. With prices high on the world market, cotton production in the Lower South soared. By 1840 the South produced more

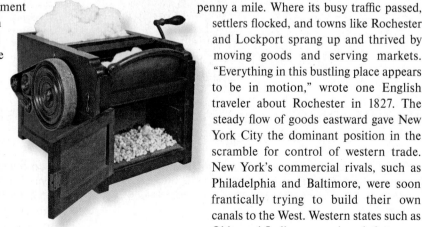

©Bettmann/Getty Images
| *Whitney's cotton gin*

than 60 percent of the world supply, which accounted for almost two-thirds of all American exports.

The cotton trade was the major expansive force in the economy until the depression of 1839. Northern factories increasingly made money by turning raw cotton into cloth, while northern merchants reaped profits from shipping the cotton and then reshipping the textiles. Planters used the income they earned to purchase foodstuffs from the West and goods and services from the Northeast.

The Transportation Revolution

To become truly national, a market economy needed an efficient transportation network linking various regions of the nation. The economy had not become self-sustaining earlier partly because the only means of transporting goods cheaply was by water. That limited trade largely to coastal and international markets, because even on rivers, bulky goods moved easily in only one direction—downstream.

But dramatic change came after 1815, drawing new regions into the market. From 1825 to 1855—the span of a single generation—the cost of transportation on land fell 95 percent while its speed increased five-fold.

THE CANAL AGE Canals attracted considerable investment capital, especially after the success of the wondrous Erie Canal. Built between 1818 and 1825 the canal stretched 364 miles from Albany on the Hudson River to Buffalo on Lake Erie. Its construction by the state was an act of faith; in 1816 the United States had only 100 miles of canals, none longer than 28 miles. Then, too, the proposed route ran through forests, disease-ridden swamps, and unsettled wilderness. The canal's engineers lacked experience, but they made up for that by sheer ingenuity. Improving on European tools, they devised a cable and screw that allowed one man to pull down even the largest trees and a stump-puller that removed up to 40 stumps a day.

The project paid for itself within a few years. The Erie Canal reduced the cost of shipping a ton of goods from Buffalo to New York City from more than 19 cents a mile to less than 3 cents a mile. By 1860 the cost had fallen to less than a penny a mile. Where its busy traffic passed, settlers flocked, and towns like Rochester and Lockport sprang up and thrived by moving goods and serving markets. "Everything in this bustling place appears to be in motion," wrote one English traveler about Rochester in 1827. The steady flow of goods eastward gave New York City the dominant position in the scramble for control of western trade. New York's commercial rivals, such as Philadelphia and Baltimore, were soon frantically trying to build their own canals to the West. Western states such as Ohio and Indiana, convinced that prosperity depended on cheap transportation,

THE TRANSPORTATION NETWORK OF A MARKET ECONOMY, 1840

Source: Library of Congress, Prints and Photographs Division [LC-USZC2-3436]

"... a steamboat now makes the journey [from New Orleans to Pittsburg] in fifteen or twenty days, stopping also at all the immediate places of importance ... Distance is no longer thought of in this region—it is almost annihilated by steam!"—Robert Baird, *View of the Valley of the Mississippi; or, The Emigrant's and Traveller's Guide to the West* (1832)

CONTEXT

Canals played their most important role in the Northeast, where they linked eastern cities to western rivers and the Great Lakes. On the Erie Canal, a system of locks raised and lowered boats in a series of steps along the route. Steamboats were most crucial in the extensive river systems in the South and West.

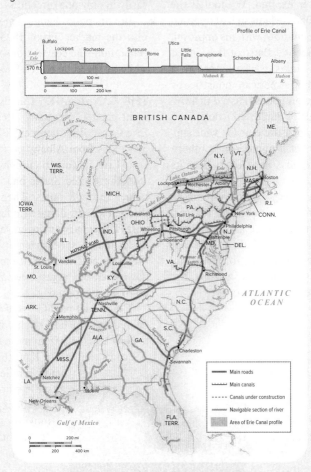

MAP READING

1. *What section of the country boasted the largest concentration of canals?*
2. *Which two sections of the country did the new roads and canals most efficiently interlink?*
3. *What waterway connected the Great Lakes to the Hudson River?*

MAP INTERPRETATION

1. *What accounts for the concentration of canals in one region of the United States?*
2. *What do transportation networks reveal about evolving economic relationships between different sections of the United States?*
3. *What resulted from the linkage of the Great Lakes to the Hudson River?*

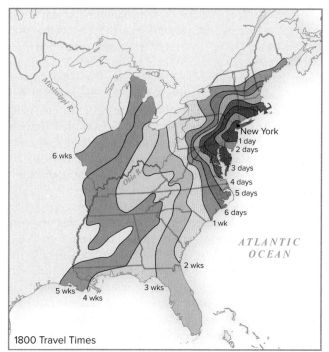

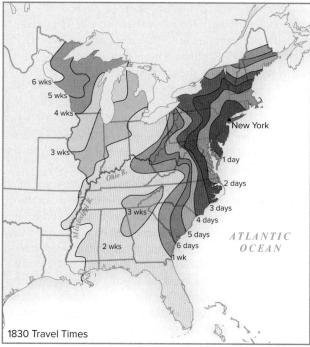

TRAVEL TIMES, 1800 AND 1830

constructed canals to link interior regions with the Great Lakes. By 1840 the nation had completed more than 3,300 miles of canals—a length greater than the distance from New York City to Seattle—at a cost of about $125 million. Almost half that amount came from state governments.

By 1850 the canal era was over. The depression of 1839 caused several states to halt or slow their construction, especially since many poorly planned canals lost money. Still, whether profitable or not, canals sharply reduced transportation costs and stimulated economic development in a broad belt along their routes.

STEAMBOATS AND RAILROADS Because of its vast expanse, the United States was particularly dependent on river transportation. But shipping goods downstream from Pittsburgh to New Orleans took 6 weeks, and the return journey required 17 weeks or more. Steamboats reduced the time of a trip from New Orleans to Louisville from 90 to 8 days while cutting upstream costs by 90 percent.

Robert Fulton demonstrated the commercial possibilities of propelling a boat with steam when his ship, the *Clermont,* traveled in 1807 from New York City to Albany on the Hudson River. But steamboats had the greatest effect on transportation on

Source: Library of Congress, Prints and Photographs Division [LC-USZ62-103288]

| *A far cry from the sleek trains of today, the earliest railroad cars looked more like horse-drawn conveyances.*

western rivers, where the flat-bottomed boats could haul heavy loads even when the water level was low. The number of steamboats operating in those waters jumped from 17 in 1817 to 727 in 1855. Since steamboats could make many more voyages annually, the carrying capacity on western rivers increased 100-fold between 1820 and 1860. Although railroads would end the steamboat's dominance by 1860, the steamboat was the major form of western transportation during the years in which the national market economy grew up, and it proved the most important factor in the rise of manufacturing in the Ohio and upper Mississippi valleys.

In 1830 the nation had only 13 miles of railroad track, and most of the lines constructed in the following decade served as feeder lines to canals. But soon enough, cities and towns saw that their economic future depended on having good rail links, so that by 1840 railroad and canal mileage were almost exactly equal (3,325 miles). By 1850 the nation had a total of 8,879 miles of track. Railroad rates were usually higher than canal or steamboat charges, but the new iron roads operated year-round, offered more direct routes, and moved goods about twice as fast. Even so, not until the 1850s did they come to dominate the transportation system.

The Communications Revolution

What rail and steam engines did for transportation, Samuel F. B. Morse's telegraph did for communications. Morse patented a device that sent electrical pulses over a wire in 1837, and before long, telegraph lines fanned out in all directions, linking various parts of the country instantaneously. By 1860 more than 50,000 miles of telegraph lines had been laid. The new telegraph sped business information, helped link the transportation network, and allowed newspapers to provide readers with up-to-date news.

The invention of the telegraph and the perfection of a power press (1847) by Robert Hoe and his son Richard revolutionized journalism. The mechanical press greatly increased the speed with which sheets could be printed over the old hand method. Mass-produced newspapers, often selling for only a penny, gained huge circulations, since ordinary families could afford them. Hoe's press had a similar impact on book publishing, since thousands of copies could be printed at affordable prices.

POSTAL SYSTEMS COMPARED The development of a national market economy depended on mass communications that transmitted commercial information and connected producers and sellers separated by great distances. Although postage was relatively expensive, the American postal system subsidized the distribution of newspapers and spread other information widely. Indeed, in the years before the Civil War, the postal system had more employees than any other enterprise in the country. Although the postal system's primary purpose was to promote commerce, it made a profound social impact by accustoming people to long-range and even impersonal communication. By 1840 the post office was handling almost 41 million letters and 39 million newspapers a year.

Alexis de Tocqueville, a French political philosopher on a visit to the United States, was amazed at the scope of the postal system by the 1830s. "There is an astonishing circulation of letters and newspapers among these savage woods," he reported from the Michigan frontier. There was hardly a village or town in the country, no matter how remote, that was not connected with the rest of the country through the postal system. While the British and French post offices handled a greater volume of mail, he noted, the United States throughout these years had a much more extensive postal system. In 1828 there were almost twice as many post offices in the United States as in Great Britain, and over five times as many as in France.

In the Americas, the Canadian postal system was so limited that merchants and even government officials routinely used the United States postal system to get mail to other provinces, and by midcentury Mexico had no regularized mail service for the whole country. In China the government maintained a very efficient military-courier system for official communications, but foreigners developed the first private postal system, mainly for business correspondence. Most countries had no true postal system in these years, since literacy was so limited.

The Transformation of Agriculture

The new forms of transportation and communication had a remarkable effect on farm families: they became linked ever more tightly to a national market system. Before the canal era, wheat could be shipped at a profit no farther than 50 miles. But given cheap transportation, farmers eagerly grew more grain and sold the surplus in distant markets.

COMMERCIAL AGRICULTURE In this shift toward commercial agriculture, farmers began cultivating more acres, working longer hours, and adopting scientific farming methods, including crop rotation and the use of manures as fertilizer. Instead of bartering goods with friends and neighbors, they more often paid cash or depended on banks to extend them credit. Instead of taking the crops to market themselves, they began to rely on regional merchants, intermediaries in a far-flung distribution system. Like southern planters, western wheat farmers increasingly sold in a world market. Banks and distributors advanced credit to farmers, who more and more competed in a market controlled by impersonal forces centered in distant locations.

As transportation and market networks connected more areas of the nation, they encouraged regional specialization. The South increasingly concentrated on staple crops for export, and the West grew foodstuffs, particularly grain. By 1850 Wisconsin and Illinois were major wheat-producing states. Eastern farmers, unable to compete with wheat yields from fertile western farms, shifted to grazing sheep or producing fruits, vegetables, and dairy products for rapidly growing urban areas. Although foreign commerce expanded, too, the dramatic growth in domestic markets far outstripped the volume of trade abroad. The cities of the East looked primarily to southern and western markets.

John Marshall and the Promotion of Enterprise

For a national market system to flourish, a climate favorable to investment had to exist. Under the leadership of Chief Justice John Marshall, the Supreme Court became the branch of the federal government most aggressive in protecting the new forms of business central to the growing market economy.

Marshall, who presided over the Court from 1801 to 1835, at first glance seemed an unlikely leader. Informal in manners and almost sloppy in dress, he was nonetheless a commanding figure, combining a forceful intellect with a genial ability to persuade. Time after time he convinced his colleagues to uphold the sanctity of private property and the power of the federal government to promote economic growth.

CONSTITUTIONALITY OF THE NATIONAL BANK

In the case of *McCulloch v. Maryland* (1819), the Court upheld the constitutionality of the Second Bank of the United States. Just as Alexander Hamilton had argued in the debate over the first national bank, Marshall emphasized that the Constitution gave Congress the power to make all "necessary and proper" laws to carry out its delegated powers. If Congress believed that a bank would help it meet its responsibilities, such as maintaining the public credit and regulating the currency, then it was constitutional. The bank had to be only useful, not essential. "Let the end be legitimate," Marshall wrote, "let it be within the scope of the Constitution, and all means which are appropriate, which are plainly adapted to that end, which are not prohibited . . . are constitutional." By upholding Hamilton's doctrine of implied powers, Marshall enlarged federal power to an extraordinary degree.

INTERSTATE COMMERCE

Marshall also encouraged a more freewheeling commerce in *Gibbons v. Ogden* (1824).

(*Inset*): ©Hulton Archive/Getty Images; Source: Library of Congress, Prints and Photographs Division [LC-USZC2-3031]

| *Supreme Court Chief Justice John Marshall wrote the opinion striking down a steamboat monopoly granted by the state of New York. In doing so, Marshall gave the federal government the right to regulate interstate commerce "to its utmost extent."*

The case gave Marshall a chance to define the greatest power of the federal government in peacetime: the right to regulate interstate commerce. In striking down a steamboat monopoly granted by the state of New York, the chief justice gave the term *commerce* the broadest possible definition, declaring that it covered all commercial dealings and that Congress's power over interstate commerce could be "exercised to its utmost extent." The result was increased business competition throughout society.

PROTECTION OF CONTRACTS

In the case of *Fletcher v. Peck* (1810), Marshall took an active role in defining contract law, then in its infancy, and showed how far he was willing to go to protect private property. The Supreme Court unanimously struck down a Georgia law taking back a land grant that a group of speculators had obtained by bribing members of the legislature. A grant was a contract, Marshall declared, and because the Constitution forbade states to impair "the obligation of contracts," the legislature could not interfere with the grant once it had been made. Although the framers of the Constitution probably meant contracts to refer only to agreements between private parties, Marshall made no distinction between public and private agreements, thereby greatly expanding the meaning of the contract clause.

Marshall's most celebrated decision on the contract clause came in *Dartmouth College v. Woodward*, decided in 1819. The case arose out of the attempt by New Hampshire to alter the college's charter granted by George III in 1769. The Court overturned the state law on the grounds that state charters were also contracts and could not be altered by later legislatures. By this ruling Marshall intended to protect **corporations**, which conducted business under charters granted by individual states. Thus the Marshall Court encouraged economic risk taking. Its decisions protected property and contracts, limited state interference in business affairs, and created a climate of confidence.

IMPORTANCE OF CORPORATIONS

State laws also fostered economic development by encouraging banks, insurance companies, railroads, and manufacturing firms to form as corporations. By pooling investors' resources, corporations provided a way to raise capital for large-scale undertakings while limiting the financial liability of individual investors. Originally, state legislatures were required to approve a special charter for each new corporation, but in the 1830s states began to adopt general incorporation laws that automatically granted a charter to any applicant who met certain minimum qualifications. That change further stimulated organization of the national market.

 REVIEW

In what ways were the transportation and communication revolutions essential to a national market economy? How did the Marshall Court's decisions encourage the new markets?

A PEOPLE IN MOTION

"EATING ON THE FIRST OF MAY," commented one New York City resident, "is entirely out of the question." That day was "moving day," when all the leases in the city expired. On that date nearly everyone, it seemed, moved to a new residence or place of business. Bedlam prevailed as furniture and personal belongings cluttered the sidewalks and people, movers, and horses crowded the streets. Whereas in Europe millions of ordinary folk had never ventured beyond their local village, a Boston paper commented in 1828, "here, the whole population is in motion."

This restless mobility affected nearly every aspect of American life. Americans ate so quickly that one disgusted European visitor described food being "pitchforked down" by his fellow diners. Steamboat captains risked boiler explosions for the honor of having the fastest boat on the river. Unlike Europe's trains, lightweight and hastily built railroads in the United States offered little safety or comfort of passengers. Even so, Americans quickly embraced this new mode of transportation because of its speed. Eighteen-year-old Caroline Fitch of Boston likened her first ride on a railroad to a "lightning flash": "It was 'whew!' and we were there, and 'whew!' and we were back again." Even within railroad cars Americans were too fidgety to adapt to the European system of individual passenger compartments. Instead, American cars had a center aisle, allowing passengers to wander the length of the train.

Horatio Greenough, a sculptor who returned to the United States in 1836 after an extended stay abroad, was amazed and a bit frightened by the pace he witnessed. "Go ahead! is the order of the day," he observed. "The whole continent presents a scene of scrambling and roars with greedy hurry." Not only the growth of a national market but also population growth, geographic mobility, and urbanization increased the sense of perpetual motion in a high-speed society.

Population Growth

The American population continued to double about every 22 years—more than twice the birthrate of Great Britain. The number of Americans—fewer than 4 million in 1790—surpassed 23 million in 1850. During the 1840s, as urban areas grew rapidly, the birthrate dipped about 10 percent, the first significant decrease in American history. In cities, families were smaller, in part because the labor of children was not as critical to the family's economic welfare. Life expectancy did not improve significantly during the first half of the nineteenth century, the population remained quite young, and early marriage remained the norm, especially in rural areas.

IMMIGRATION RISES AFTER 1830 From 1790 to 1820 natural increase accounted for virtually all the country's population growth. But immigration, which had been disrupted by the Napoleonic Wars in Europe, revived after 1815. By 1820, 20 percent of New York City's inhabitants were foreign-born; by the 1830s some 600,000 immigrants had arrived in the United States, more than double the number in the quarter century after 1790. Those newcomers were a harbinger of the flood of immigrants that reached America beginning in the late 1840s: by 1850 half of all New Yorkers had been born outside the United States.

Geographic Mobility

The vast areas of land available for settlement absorbed much of the growing population. By 1850 almost half of all Americans lived outside the original 13 states. Well over 2 million lived beyond the Mississippi River. As settlers streamed west, speculation in western lands reached frenzied proportions. In the single year of 1818, at the peak of land-buying fever, the United States sold 3.5 million acres

| Europeans were shocked that Americans bolted their food or gorged themselves on anything within reach, as this English drawing indicates. Such habits reflected both the indifferent preparation of food and the frenetic tempo of American life.

©Fotosearch/Getty Images

of its public domain. (In contrast, the government sold only 68,000 acres in 1800.) And by the 1820s, Congress had reduced the minimum tract offered for sale to 80 acres, which meant that an ordinary farm could be purchased for $100.

SPECULATORS HELP SETTLE WESTERN LANDS

Even so, speculators purchased most of the public lands sold, since the law put no limit on how many acres an individual or a land company could buy. These land speculators played a leading role in settlement of the West. To hasten sales, they usually sold land partially on credit—a vital aid to poorer farmers. They also provided loans to purchase needed tools and supplies, since the cost of establishing a farm was beyond the means of many young men. Many farmers became speculators themselves, buying up property in the neighborhood and selling it to latecomers at a tidy profit. "Speculation in real estate has been the ruling idea and occupation of the Western mind," one Englishman reported in the 1840s. "Clerks, labourers, farmers, storekeepers merely followed their callings for a living while they were speculating for their fortunes."

ON THE ROAD AGAIN Given such rapid settlement, geographic mobility became one of the most striking characteristics of the American people. The 1850 census revealed that nearly half of all native-born free Americans lived outside the state where they had been born. Often, too, the influence of the market uprooted Americans. In 1851 a new railroad line bypassed the village of Auburn, Illinois, on the way to Springfield. "It seemed a pity," wrote one resident, "that so pretty a site as that of the old town should be abandoned for so unpromising a one . . . much of it mere swamp—but railroad corporations possess no bowels of compassion, the practical more than the beautiful being their object." After residents quickly moved to the new town that sprang up around the depot, a neighboring farmer purchased the site and plowed up the streets, and Auburn reverted to a cornfield.

Urbanization

Although the United States remained a rural nation, the four decades after 1820 witnessed the fastest rate of urbanization in American history. In 1820 there were only 12 cities with a population of more than 5,000; by 1850 there were nearly 150. The 1820 census showed that only about 9 percent of the population lived in towns with a population of 2,500 or more. Forty years later the number had risen to 20 percent. As a result, the ratio of farmers to city dwellers steadily dropped from 15-to-1 in 1800 to 5.5-to-1 in 1850. Improved transportation and the productivity of midwestern farms made it possible to feed urban populations being swelled by the beginnings of industrialization and migration from both rural areas of the United States and Europe.

URBAN CENTERS, OLD AND NEW The most heavily urbanized area of the country was the Northeast.* The nation's largest city was New York, with more than half a million people, and older cities such as Philadelphia, Boston, Baltimore, and New Orleans continued to be major urban centers. In the West, strategically located cities such as Albany and Rochester in New York, Erie and Pittsburgh in Pennsylvania, Cincinnati and Cleveland in Ohio, and St. Louis, Missouri, sprang up primarily to provide provisions and transportation for migrants settling newly opened land. By the century's midpoint, 40 percent of the nation's total urban population resided in such interior cities. The South, with only 10 percent of its people living in cities, was the least urbanized region.

Cities grew far more rapidly than did the ability of local authorities to make them clean, healthy, and safe. A haze always hung in their air from the combined pollution of fires for cooking and heating, tobacco smoke from pipes and stogies, and the steam and coal dust belched by factories. Deadlier still was the water, which city dwellers drank from backyard wells dug next to outhouses—privies that often overflowed in rainy weather. Horse manure piled up in the streets, and when garbage choked the alleys, city fathers attacked the problem by sending geese and hogs to eat whatever the dogs, rats, and vultures had left. Small wonder, then, that city-bred boys were not as tall and strapping as farm boys, that the life expectancy of city-born babies was six years less than that of newborn southern slaves, and that the urban death rate was higher than the birthrate.

CRIME AND URBAN POVERTY Crime, too, posed a daily risk. Theft and assault were the most common, and gangs frequently launched attacks against their political and ethnic rivals, rioted to intimidate African Americans, and raped working-class women of both races. Small, ineffective police forces could do little to curb the disorder, and fire companies arriving at the scene of a blaze were more likely to fight one another than to contain the flames.

Desperate poverty posed an abiding—and worsening—problem. By the 1830s New York City had thousands of prostitutes, because the sex trade was one of the few well-paying occupations for women. In the 1850s nearly 2,000 vagrant children roamed Philadelphia's streets. Winter was the worst season for those living on the margins: the newspaper editor Horace Greeley commented that as Manhattan's rivers and canals froze up and the cost of food and fuel mounted, "mechanics and laborers lived awhile on the scanty savings of the preceding Summer and Autumn; then on such credit as they could wring from grocers and landlords, till milder weather brought them work again."

Yet migration into antebellum cities did not slacken. Indeed, the influx of foreign-born and rural migrants was all that kept

---

*The Northeast included New England and the mid-Atlantic states (New York, Pennsylvania, and New Jersey). The South comprised the slave states plus the District of Columbia.

Source: Library of Congress, Prints and Photographs Division [LC-USZC4-3168]

| *St. Louis, a major urban center that developed in the West, depended on the steamboat to sustain its commerce, as this 1859 illustration makes clear.*

city populations rising. Even young men without skills readily found work in the commercial, maritime, and construction businesses. Once employed, they earned higher wages doing less arduous labor than farmworkers. And then there was the lure of theaters, taverns, shops, public markets, and the endless variety of the passing scene. Far more beckoning, for many, than the sleepy farming villages that they had left behind.

 REVIEW

What motives led Americans to move about so frequently, and how did that mobility affect cities?

THE RISE OF FACTORIES

IT WAS AN ISOLATED LIFE, growing up in rural, hilly Vermont. But stories of the textile factories that had sprung up in Lowell and other towns in Massachusetts reached even small villages such as Barnard. Fifteen-year-old Mary Paul was working there as a domestic servant when she asked her father for permission to move to Lowell. "I am in need of clothes which I cannot get about here," she explained. In 1845 two friends from Barnard helped her find a job at the Lowell mills, from which she earned $128 in 11 months. After four years she

returned home but now found "countryfied" life too confining. This time she left her rural hometown for good. She moved about and supported herself at several occupations before finally marrying and settling down in nearby Lynn.

The market economy fundamentally transformed Mary Paul's life—and the lives of thousands of other rural Americans. The new factories and industries needed more than technological innovation to run smoothly: they also reorganized the labor employed in manufacturing.

Technological Advances

SMALL-SCALE MANUFACTURING Before 1815 the main setting for manufacturing had been the workshops of skilled artisans, where masters taught their trades to apprentices and **journeymen**. And in rural areas, some men engaged in part-time manufacturing in farm workshops, turning out articles such as tools, chairs, and wagons, while farm women and children worked in their homes during the winter months, fashioning items such as brooms and fans. By the beginning of the nineteenth century, New England merchants had devised a way to tap the labor of these rural workers; it was known as the putting-out system. Supplied with tools and materials by the merchants, farm families spun wool into thread or stitched the parts of shoes requiring the least skilled labor. These older forms of manufacturing persisted and even dominated production until the Civil War. But after 1815, factories with machinery tended by unskilled or semiskilled laborers were becoming increasingly important in many industries.

From England came many of the earliest technological innovations, machines that Americans often improved or adapted to more extensive uses. "Everything new is quickly introduced here," one European visitor commented in 1820. "There is no clinging to old ways; the moment an American hears the word 'invention' he pricks up his ears." From 1790 to 1860 the United States Patent Office granted more patents than England and France combined.

To protect their economic advantage, the British forbade the export of any textile machinery or emigration of anyone trained in their construction. But in 1790 a mill worker named Samuel Slater slipped past English authorities and built the first textile mill in America. Two decades later, the Boston merchant Francis Cabot Lowell imitated British designs for a power loom and then improved on them.

INTERCHANGEABLE PARTS The hearth of this early national culture of invention was southern New England. Home manufacturing in countless farm workshops had honed the mechanical skills of many Yankees who, thanks to the region's strong system of public education, also enjoyed almost universal literacy. One of the sharpest minds among these tinkerers belonged to Connecticut's Eli Whitney. Having won a contract to produce 10,000 muskets for the government, Whitney developed machinery that would mass-produce parts that were interchangeable from one gun to another. Once the process was perfected, a worker could assemble a musket quickly with only a few tools. Chauncey Jerome applied the same principle to the production of clocks.

But the production of cloth became the first manufacturing process to make significant use of machines on a large scale, both in England and in the United States. Eventually all the processes of manufacturing cloth took place in a single location, from opening the cotton bales to weaving the cloth, and machines did virtually all the work.

Textile Factories

LOWELL The factory system originated in the Northeast, where capital, water power, and transportation facilities were available. In 1820 a group of wealthy Boston merchants known as the Boston Associates set up operations at Lowell, Massachusetts. Intended as a model community, Lowell soon became the nation's most famous center of textile manufacturing. Its founders sought to avoid the exploitation and misery that characterized the factory system in England by combining **paternalism** with high profits. Instead of relying primarily on child labor or a permanent working class, the Lowell mills employed daughters of New England farm families, who became the first factory workers in the United States. They lived in company boardinghouses under the watchful eye of a matron. To its many visitors Lowell presented an impressive sight: huge factories, well-kept houses,

bustling shops. Their employers encouraged women workers to attend lectures and to use the library. The mill employees even published their own magazine, the *Lowell Offering*.

HARD WORK IN THE MILLS But factory life involved strict rules and long hours of tedious, repetitive work. At Lowell work typically began at 7 a.m. (earlier in the summer) and continued until 7 at night, six days a week. With only 30 minutes for the noon meal, many workers had to run to the boardinghouse and back to avoid being late. Winter was the "lighting up" season, when work began before daylight and ended after dark. The only light after sunset came from whale oil lamps that filled the long rooms with smoke.

Employers also closely monitored the behavior of their labor force. Mill workers paid fines for lateness or misconduct, including talking on the job, and rules also forbade alcohol, cards, and gambling in the shop or yard. Boardinghouse matrons strictly guarded women's morals, supervised male visitors, and enforced a 10 p.m. curfew.

Although the labor was hard, the female operators earned from $2.40 to $3.20 a week, wages that were considered good at the time. (Domestic servants and seamstresses, two of the most common jobs women held, earned less than a dollar a week.) The average "mill girl," as they were called, was between 16 and 30 years old. Most were not working to support their families back home on the farm; instead, they wanted to save some money for perhaps the first time in their lives and sample some of life's pleasures. "I must . . . have something of my own before many more years have passed,"

| *Mill workers, Lowell*

Sally Rice wrote in rejecting her parents' request that she return home to Somerset, Vermont. "And where is that something coming from if I go home and earn nothing?"

The sense of sisterhood that united women in the boardinghouses made it easier for farm daughters to adjust to the stress and regimen the factory imposed on them. So did their view of the situation as temporary rather than permanent, because most women worked in the mills no more than five years before getting married.

But in the 1830s, as competition in the textile industry intensified, factory managers sought ways to raise productivity by increasing workloads and speeding up the machinery. When even those changes failed to maintain previous profits, factories cut wages. The ever-quickening pace of work finally provoked resistance among the mill workers, sparking several strikes in which some workers walked out. Management retaliated by firing strike leaders, hiring new workers, and blacklisting women who refused to return. In the 1840s workers' protests focused on the demand for a 10-hour day.

TRANSFORMATION OF LOWELL   The quest for profits also undercut the owners' paternalism. As the mills expanded, a smaller proportion of the workers lived in company boardinghouses, and moral regulations were relaxed. But the greatest change was a shift in the workforce from native-born women to Irish immigrants, including men and children. In 1845 the Irish made up only 8 percent of the Lowell workforce; by 1860 they amounted to almost half. Because these new workers were poor and desperate for work, wages went into an even-steeper decline, and a permanent working class began to take shape.

Lowell and the Environment

Lowell was a city built on water power. Early settlers had used the power of the Merrimack River to run mills, but never on the scale used by the new textile factories. As the market spread, Americans came to link progress with the fullest use of the natural resources of the environment. Just as they had done in Lowell itself, the Boston Associates sought to impose a sense of order and regularity on the surrounding physical

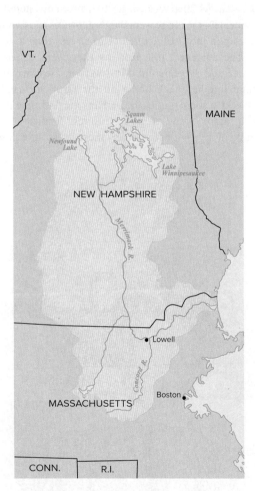

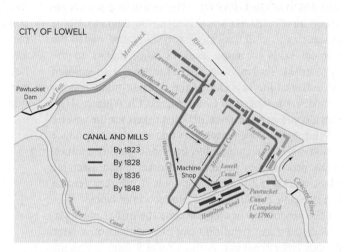

DEVELOPMENT OF THE LOWELL MILLS

As more mills were built at Lowell, the demand increased for water to power them. By 1859 the mills drew water from lakes 80 to 100 miles upstream, including Winnipesaukee, Squam, and Newfound. The map at left shows the affected watersheds. In the city of Lowell, a system of canals was enlarged over several decades. The photograph shows Pawtucket Canal as it has been preserved at Lowell National Historical Park.

Source: National Park Service/Lowell National Historical Park

environment in order to efficiently use its natural resources. In the process, they fundamentally reshaped the area's waterscape.

RESHAPING THE AREA'S WATERSCAPE

As more and more mills were built, the Boston Associates sought to harness water for energy. By 1836 Lowell had seven canals, with a supporting network of locks and dams, to govern the Merrimack's flow and distribute water to the city's 26 mills. At Lawrence they constructed the largest dam in the world at the time, a 32-foot-high granite structure that spanned 1,600 feet across the river. But, even dammed, the Merrimack's waters proved insufficient. So the Associates gained control of a series of lakes in New Hampshire covering more than 100 square miles that fed into the river system. By damming these lakes, they could provide a regular flow of water down the river, especially in the drier summer months. In the course of establishing this elaborate water-control system, they came to see water as a form of property, divorced from the ownership of land along the river. Water became a commodity that was measured in terms of its power to operate a certain number of spindles and looms.

By regulating the river's waters, the Boston Associates made the Merrimack valley the greatest industrial center in the country in the first half of the nineteenth century. But not all who lived in the valley benefited. By raising water levels, the dams flooded farmlands, blocked the transportation of logs downstream, and damaged mills upstream by reducing the current that powered waterwheels. The dams also devastated the fish population by preventing upstream spawning, and factories routinely dumped their wastes into the river. These wastes, combined with sewage from the growing population, eventually contaminated water supplies. Epidemics of typhoid, cholera, and dysentery broke out with increasing frequency.

In the end, the factory system fundamentally transformed the environment. Far from existing in harmony with its rural surroundings, Lowell, with its clattering machines and dammed rivers, presented a glaring contrast to rural life. The founding vision of Lowell had disappeared.

Industrial Work

ARTISAN SYSTEM

Most workers did not easily adapt to the disciplined work routine of the factory. Master artisans had worked in shops within their homes, treating journeymen and apprentices as members of the family. Journeymen took pride in their work, knowing that if they perfected their skill, they could become respected master artisans with their own shops. Apprentices not only learned a trade but also received some education and moral supervision from their masters. And in artisans' shops, all employees worked not by the clock, at a steady pace, but rather in bursts of intense labor alternating with more leisurely time.

TRANSFORMATION OF WORK

The factory changed that. Its discipline required workers to discard old habits, because industrialism demanded a worker who was sober, dependable, and self-disciplined. The machines, whirring and clacking away, set a strict schedule that had to be followed. Absenteeism, lateness, and drunkenness hurt productivity and disrupted the regular factory routine. Thus industrialization not only changed the way work was organized but also made work alienating rather than fulfilling.

The factory regimen was dehumanizing. One mill worker who finally quit complained of "obedience to the ding-dong of the bell—just as though we are so many living machines." And factory work was debasing: whereas the master-apprentice relationship was a close, personal bond, factories sharply separated workers from management. Few workers rose through the ranks to supervisory positions, and even fewer could achieve the artisan's dream of setting up one's own business. Even well-paid workers sensed their decline in status.

THE DECLINE OF THE CRAFTS

The craft of manufacturing goods declined as well. Factory-produced goods were not as finished or elegant as those done by hand, and the

Source: Museum Associates/LACMA

Set in a carpenter's shop, this painting titled The Young Mechanic *celebrates American ingenuity and skill by drawing the eye to the barefoot boy who is whittling a mast for the wooden boat held by its owner on the other side of the counter. Are there other ways of interpreting this scene?*

demands of productivity eroded both skills and pride in craftsmanship.

The career of Micajah Pratt, a shoemaker from Lynn, Massachusetts, illustrates the process. Pratt's father, also a skilled cobbler, knew how to judge the quality of leather, to cut out the various parts of a shoe, and to stitch and glue the parts together. He then sold the shoes in the shop where he and his apprentices made them. Following in his father's footsteps, Micajah began selling shoes in 1812 to customers in New England, but he discovered that there were ready markets in the South and the West for cheaply made shoes. So he hired workers to produce shoes in larger and larger central shops. Pratt cut costs further by using new production techniques, such as standardized patterns and sole-cutting machines. He eventually employed as many as 500 men and women.

So great was the national market that other shoe manufacturers in Lynn could not keep pace with demand. Increasingly they hired nearby farmers, fishermen, and their families to do part-time work at home. Women and girls sewed the upper parts of a shoe, men and boys attached the bottoms. This use of the putting-out system allowed wages to be reduced still further. A few highly paid workers performed such skilled tasks as cutting leather, but most work was done either in large central shops or in homes. With workers no longer able to make an entire shoe, in little more than a generation shoemaking ceased to be a craft. Though still not organized in a factory setting, shoe manufacture had become essentially an assembly-line process.

ECONOMIC SPECIALIZATION Similarly, for those industries now conducted within factories, the division of labor broke down the manufacture of an item into smaller,

more specialized (and less skilled) tasks. Although large factories were the exception rather than the rule during the first half of the nineteenth century, the tendency in manufacturing was toward more technology, greater efficiency, and increasing specialization. The division of labor accompanying early industrialization was only one way in which the national market economy promoted economic specialization. Just as the new transportation and communication networks allowed factories to focus on making a single item such as cloth or shoes, they also permitted farmers to concentrate on producing certain crops.

The Labor Movement

In this newly emerging economic order, workers sometimes organized to protect their rights. Craftworkers, such as carpenters, printers, and tailors, formed unions, and in 1834 individual unions came together in the National Trades' Union.

Union leaders argued that labor was degraded in America: workers endured long hours, low pay, and low status. Unlike most American social thinkers of the day, a number of labor leaders accepted the idea of conflict between different classes. They did not believe that the interests of workers and employers could be reconciled, and they blamed the plight of labor on monopolies, especially banking and paper money, and on machines and the factory system.

EMERGENCE OF UNIONS If the unions' rhetoric sounded radical, the solutions they proposed were moderate. Reformers agitated for public education and abolition of imprisonment for debt to provide better opportunities for workers.

©Bettmann/Getty Images

| *Waterfalls at mill towns, like this one in Pawtucket, Rhode Island, were places to swim, fish, and relax, as the people do in the foreground. Jumpers like Sam Patch leaped off the Pawtucket bridge and also off the roof of a nearby building into the foamy froth.*

Leaders saw effective unions and political action as the means to restore labor to its former honored position. Proclaiming the republican virtues of freedom and equality, they attacked special privilege and decried workers' loss of independence.

The labor movement gathered some momentum in the decade before the Panic of 1837, but in the depression that followed, its strength collapsed. During hard times, few workers were willing to strike or engage in collective action. Nor did skilled artisans, who spearheaded the union movement, feel a particularly strong bond with semiskilled factory workers and unskilled laborers. More than a decade of agitation did finally gain the 10-hour day for some workers by the 1850s, and the courts also recognized workers' right to strike, but these gains had little immediate impact.

Workers were united in resenting the industrial system and their loss of status. But they found themselves divided by a host of other factors: ethnic and racial antagonisms, gender, conflicting religious perspectives, occupational differences, party loyalties, and disagreements over tactics. For most workers, the factory and industrialism were not agents of opportunity but reminders of their loss of independence and a measure of control over their lives.

Sam Patch and a Worker's "Art"

Some workers fought against the loss of independence in unusual ways. The waterfalls that attracted capitalists looking to build mills also attracted workers in their off-hours, coming to picnic, swim, or fish. For those with nerve, the falls provided also a place to show off their skills as waterfall jumpers. Sam Patch was such a young man, known for his daring leaps into the Passaic River at the mills around Paterson, New Jersey.

In 1827 Patch became disgusted by a sawmill owner who was set to open a private park, "Forest Gardens," close to Passaic Falls. The owner said he would charge admission in order to keep out "the lazy, idle, rascally, drunken vagabonds" who might spoil the pleasure of more refined folk come to enjoy the view. Workers who resented this fencing out rejoiced when Patch vowed to spoil Forest Garden's opening-day party. As gentlefolk gathered, thousands of ordinary laborers crowded along the opposite bank and cheered as Patch leapt 70 feet straight into the foaming water.

Sam Patch's fame led him eventually to the biggest challenge of all: Niagara Falls. Twice he jumped more than 80 feet into the cascade's churning waters. But he drowned a month later when he dared the Genesee Falls in another mill town along the Erie Canal—Rochester, New York. Still, his fame persisted for decades. Leaping waterfalls was "an art which I have knowledge of and courage to perform," he had insisted. In a market economy in which skilled "arts" were being replaced by machine labor, Patch's acts were a defiant protest against the changing times.

> ✓ **REVIEW**
> How did the rise of factories affect the making of clothing? habits of work? the lives of farm girls? the waterscape of Lowell? handcrafted labor?

The Phases of Early Industrialization in the North

	LOCATION OF MANUFACTURE	LABOR FORCE	GOALS OF MANUFACTURE
Before 1815	Shops, private homes, family farms	Master craftsman supervising the education and behavior of journeymen and apprentices; some rural women and children employed part-time in the putting-out system	Filling orders for individual customers, pride in craftsmanship; for putting-out system, doing piecework consigned by merchants
1815–1830	First factories	Young women from New England farm families, most employed no longer than 5 years	Successful competition with British manufacturers, recruiting a stable workforce
1830s–1860	Factories with steadily increasing workloads, speeded-up machinery, greater regimentation to encourage sobriety, punctuality, efficiency	Steadily growing numbers of Irish immigrants—men, women, and children; declining status of workers; sharp separation of workers and management; beginnings of the labor movement	Highest possible rate of mass production

(*top*) Source: National Park Service; (*bottom left and right*) ©North Wind Picture Archives/Alamy

SOCIAL STRUCTURES OF THE MARKET SOCIETY

THE NEW DOMINATION OF THE market had a profound impact on American society as a whole. It greatly diminished the importance of women's contributions to household production, while placing a greater emphasis on the acquisition of material goods. It also restructured American society, widening the gulf between rich and poor and contributing to the growth of a middle class. It even changed the way Americans thought about time.

Household Production and Consumption

The average eighteenth-century American woman produced thread, cloth, clothing, and candles in the home for family use. But with the growth of factories, household manufacturing all but disappeared. As a result, women lost many of the economic functions they had once performed at home. Again, textiles are a striking example. Between 1815 and 1860 the price of cotton cloth fell from 18 to 2 cents a yard. Because manufactured cloth was also smoother and more brightly colored than homespun, most women purchased cloth rather than making it themselves. The new ready-made men's clothing also reduced the amount of sewing women did, especially in cities, where more men purchased clothing from retail stores.

Farm wives and daughters still contributed to the income of their households by stitching shoes or covering buttons, crafting straw bonnets and palm-leaf hats, or selling their produce of butter, eggs, and chickens. Working-class women in cities, both whites and blacks, also earned money through the putting-out system, doing piecework for the garment industry, while others boarded lodgers, took in laundry, and worked as domestic servants. But the new ideal for middle-class women was to restrict their labor to performing unpaid duties in their homes—what was now called "housework." For women of middling means or better and their families, households had become places of consumption rather than production.

MATERIALISM Even as household production diminished, Americans' demand for consumer goods skyrocketed. Europeans who visited the United States during these years remarked on how hard Americans worked and how preoccupied they were with material goods and achievements. The new generation did not invent materialism, but the spread of the market after 1815 made it much more evident. And in 1836 the American writer Washington Irving coined the classic phrase that captured the spirit of the age when he spoke, in one of his stories, of "the almighty dollar, that great object of universal devotion throughout the land."

WEALTH AND STATUS In a nation that had no legally recognized aristocracy and class lines that were only informally drawn, wealth and its trappings became the most obvious symbols of status. Dismissing birth as "a mere idea," one magazine explained, "Wealth is something substantial. Everybody knows that and feels it." Materialism reflected more than a desire for goods and physical comfort. It represented a quest for respect and recognition. "Americans boast of their skill in money making," one contemporary observed, "and as it is the only standard of dignity and nobility and worth, they endeavor to obtain it by every possible means." Families were rated by the size, not the source, of their fortunes. Americans also emphasized practicality over theory. The esteem of the founding generation for intellectual achievement sank from sight in the scramble for wealth that consumed the new generation.

The Emerging Middle Class

SEPARATION OF MIDDLE CLASS FROM MANUAL LABORERS In the years after 1815 a new middle class took shape in American society. A small class of shopkeepers, professionals, and master artisans had existed earlier, but the creation of a national market economy greatly expanded its size and influence. The growing number of mercantile firms, brokerage houses, insurance businesses, and banks created thousands of new positions for clerks, bookkeepers, and traveling salesmen (known as "drummers"). New factories needed managers and accountants, and the burgeoning railroad industry required superintendents, station agents, and conductors. These new occupations offered the salaries and steady employment that boosted many white men, typically native-born, into the emerging middle class.

Since their office work and selling increasingly took place away from where goods were actually produced, these middle-class men were all the more inclined to think of themselves as a distinct social group. "In America it is customary to denominate as 'clerk' all young men engaged in commercial pursuits," wrote one observer at midcentury. "Of course, the term is not applied to those engaged in mechanical trades." Members of the growing middle class had access to more education and enjoyed greater **social mobility**. They were paid not only more but differently as well. A manual worker might earn $300 a year, paid as wages computed on an hourly basis. White-collar employees received a yearly salary and might make $1,000 a year or more.

Middle-class neighborhoods, segregated along income and occupational lines, began to develop in towns and cities. And in large urban areas, the separation of work from place of residence combined with improvements in transportation made it possible for many middle-class residents to live in surrounding suburbs and travel to work. Leisure also became segregated as separate working-class and middle-class social organizations and institutions emerged.

MATERIAL GOODS AS EMBLEMS OF SUCCESS During these years, a distinct middle-class way of life evolved based in part on levels of consumption. Greater wealth meant the ability to consume more. Someone like Joseph Engles, a Philadelphia publishing agent, might boast a house furnished with not one but two sofas, a looking glass, thirteen chairs, five yards of carpet on the floors, and even a piano. Material

THE MARKET AND EQUALITY: SHE SAID, HE SAID

Frances Wright, a Scotswoman who would later make her career in America as an advocate of slaves, workers, and women, made her first trip in 1819 at the age of 23 and found much to celebrate. Alexis de Tocqueville, 25 when he arrived in the United States in 1831, agreed that white Americans were the freest people in the world, but he described their pursuit of equality as elusive and paradoxical.

DOCUMENT 1
Equality Secures Liberty: Frances Wright

The universal spread of useful and practical knowledge, the exercise of great political rights, the ease and, comparatively, the equality of condition give to this people [Americans] a quality peculiar to themselves. Every hand is occupied, and every head is thinking, not only of the active business of human life (which usually sits lighter upon this people than many others), but of matters touching the general weal of a vast empire. Each man being one of a sovereign people is not only a politician but a legislator—a partner, in short, in the grand concern of the state . . . one engaged in narrowly inspecting its operations, balancing its accounts, guarding its authority, and judging of its interests. A people so engaged are not those with

whom a lounger might find it agreeable to associate: he seeks amusement, and he finds business. . . .

It is not very apparent that public virtue is peculiarly requisite for the preservation of political equality; envy might suffice for this: You shall not be greater than I. Political equality is, perhaps, yet more indispensable to preserve public virtue than public virtue to preserve it; wherever an exclusive principle is admitted, baleful passions are excited. Divide a community into classes, and insolence is entailed upon the higher, servility or envy, and often both united, upon the lower. . . .

In all republics, ancient or modern, there has been a leaven of aristocracy.

America fortunately had, in her first youth, virtue sufficient to repel the introduction of hereditary honors. . . .

Liberty is here secure, because it is equally the portion of all. The state is liable to no convulsions, because there is nowhere any usurpations to maintain, while every individual has an equal sovereignty to lose.* No king will voluntarily lay down his scepter, and in a democracy all men are kings.

---

*"A grievous exception to this rule is found in the black slavery of the commonwealths of the South . . ."

Source: Wright, Frances, *Views of Society and Manners in America.* London, UK: 1821.

DOCUMENT 2
Equality Promotes Anxiety: Alexis de Tocqueville

In America I saw the freest and most enlightened men, placed in the happiest circumstances which the world affords; it seemed to me as if a cloud habitually hung upon their brow, and I thought them serious and almost sad even in their pleasures.

It is strange to see with what feverish ardor the Americans pursue their own welfare; and to watch the vague dread that constantly torments them lest they should not have chosen the shortest path which may lead to it.

A native of the United States clings to this world's goods as if he were certain never to die; and he is so hasty in grasping at all within his reach, that one would suppose he was constantly afraid of not living long enough to enjoy them. He clutches everything, he holds nothing fast, but soon loosens his grasp to pursue fresh gratifications.

In the United States a man builds a house to spend his latter years in it, and he sells it before the roof is on; he plants a garden, and lets it [rents it] just as the trees are coming into bearing; he brings a field into tillage, and leaves other men to gather the crops; he embraces a profession, and gives it up; he settles in a place, which he soon afterward leaves, to carry his changeable longings elsewhere. If his private affairs leave him any

leisure, he instantly plunges into the vortex of politics; and if at the end of a year of unremitting labor he finds he has a few days' vacation, his eager curiosity whirls him over the vast extent of the United States, and he will travel fifteen hundred miles in a few days, to shake off his happiness. Death at length overtakes him, but it is before he is weary of his bootless chase of that complete felicity which is for ever on the wing.

At first sight there is something surprising in this strange unrest of so many happy men, restless in the midst of abundance. The spectacle itself is, however, as old as the world; the novelty is to see a whole people furnish an exemplification of it. . . .

The equality of conditions leads by a still straighter road to several of the effects which I have here described. When all the privileges of birth and fortune are abolished, when all professions are accessible to all, and a man's own energies may place him at the top of any one of them, an easy and unbounded career seems open to his ambition, and he will readily persuade himself that he is born to no vulgar destinies. But this is an erroneous notion, which is corrected by daily experience. The same equality which allows every citizen to conceive these lofty hopes, renders all the citizens less able

to realize them; it circumscribes their powers on every side, while it gives freer scope to their desires. Not only are they themselves powerless, but they are met at every step by immense obstacles, which they did not at first perceive. They have swept away the privileges of some of their fellow-creatures which stood in their way; but they have opened the door to universal competition. . . .

Among democratic nations men easily attain a certain equality of conditions; they can never attain the equality they desire. It perpetually retires from before them, yet without hiding itself from their sight, and in retiring draws them on. At every moment they think they are about to grasp it; it escapes at every moment from their hold.

Source: de Tocqueville, Alexis, *Democracy in America.* 1835, 1840.

THINKING CRITICALLY

What did Frances Wright admire about Americans? How does she think political equality will help preserve public virtue? How did Alexis de Tocqueville account for the restless ambition of Americans? According to Tocqueville, what was the paradox of pursuing equality?

Source: Library of Congress, Prints and Photographs Division [LC-DIG-pga-03406]

| This traffic jam in New York City conveys the rapid pace and impatient quality of American life in the first half of the nineteenth century. "In the streets all is hurry and bustle," one European visitor to the city reported. "Carts, instead of being drawn by horses at a walking pace, are often met at a gallop, and always in a brisk trot. . . . The whole population seen in the streets seem to enjoy this bustle and add to it by their own rapid pace, as if they were all going to some place of appointment, and were hurrying on under the apprehension of being too late."

goods became emblems of success and status—as clockmaker Chauncey Jerome sadly discovered when his business failed and his wealth vanished. This materialistic ethos was most apparent in the middle class, as they strove to set themselves apart from other groups in society.

The rise of a middle class would soon launch far-reaching changes in American society. The middle class came to embrace a new concept of marriage, the family, and the home. Along with occupation and income, moral outlook also marked class boundaries during this period, as described in Chapter 12.

The Distribution of Wealth

As American society became more specialized and differentiated, greater extremes of wealth appeared. The concentration of wealth was greatest in large eastern cities and in the cotton kingdom of the South, but everywhere the tendency was for the rich to get richer. In New York City, Brooklyn, Boston, and Philadelphia, the top 1 percent of the wealth holders owned a quarter of the total wealth in 1825; by 1850 they owned half. By 1860, 5 percent of American families owned more than 50 percent of the nation's wealth. Not surprisingly, it was around 1840 that the term "millionaire" first appeared.

In contrast, those at the bottom of society held a smaller percentage of a community's wealth. In Connecticut towns between 1831 and 1851, the number of inhabitants listed as having no property increased by 33 percent. In Cincinnati the lower half of the city's taxpayers held 10 percent of the wealth in 1817; in 1860 their share had dropped to less than 3 percent.

In a market society, the rich were able to build up their assets, because those with capital were in a position to increase it dramatically by taking advantage of new investment opportunities. Although a few men, such as Cornelius Vanderbilt and John Jacob Astor, vaulted from the bottom ranks of society to the top, most of the nation's richest individuals came from wealthy families.

Social Mobility

The existence of great fortunes is not necessarily inconsistent with opportunities for social mobility or property accumulation. Although the gap between the rich and the poor widened after 1820, even the incomes of most poor Americans rose, because the total amount of wealth produced in America had become much larger. From about 1825 to 1860 the average per capita income almost doubled to $300. Voicing the

The Clock's Two Faces

A table clock made in Wilmington, Delaware, ca. 1790–1805. What is being shown below the clock face?

This dial of an 8-day tall clock shows the phases of the moon. Is the moon waxing or waning?

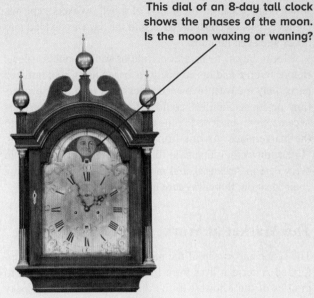

Which of these two clocks would be more helpful if you were wondering whether to travel at night?

(*left*) ©Randy Duchaine/Alamy; (*right*) Source: Gift of Dr. and Mrs. Brooks H. Marsh, 1976/ The Metropolitan Museum of Art

Clocks such as those crafted by Chauncey Jerome became fixtures in private homes, offices, factories, and schoolhouses throughout the United States during the first half of the nineteenth century. And their widespread adoption seems to hold a single, unmistakable meaning: everyday life in the new republic was becoming more regimented. But is the significance of clocks that simple? True, men and women increasingly regulated their lives by machines that ticked and chimed. Some clocks even showed the day of the month and the phases of the moon (the better to plan for travel at night). But historians who take an interest in material culture (the study of objects, buildings, and landscapes) believe that the popularity of clocks had two faces—one looking toward a fast-paced, industrialized future but another gazing nostalgically backward at a past that prized leisure and gentility. The clocks that a steadily growing number of Americans coveted and purchased for their halls, walls, shelves, tables, and mantels often featured faces adorned with flowers, fruit, and images of gracious homes or cozy cottages set in idyllic rural landscapes. (Washington's Mount Vernon was a patriotic favorite.) Even if a clock's owner could not yet afford a bountiful country estate, the painted scene proclaimed that he had at least taken a first step to fulfilling his aspirations by investing in that genteel possession, a timepiece.

THINKING CRITICALLY

A paradox?—Why would Americans decorate objects intended to encourage punctuality, efficiency, and diligence at work with tranquil images of the natural world and domesticity? How are clocks looking forward, reflecting new developments in American society? How do they provide reminders of older traditions?

---

popular belief, a New York judge proclaimed, "In this favored land of liberty, the road to advancement is open to all."

LIMITS OF SOCIAL MOBILITY   True, social mobility existed in these years—but not as much as contemporaries boasted. Most laborers—or more often their sons—did manage to move up the social ladder, but only a rung or two.

Few unskilled workers rose higher than to a semiskilled occupation. Even the children of skilled workers normally did not escape the laboring classes and enter the middle-class ranks of clerks, managers, or lawyers. For most workers, improved status came in the form of a savings account or homeownership, which gave them some security during economic downswings and in old age.

A New Sensitivity to Time

It was no accident that Chauncey Jerome's clocks spread throughout the nation along with the market economy. The new methods of doing business involved a new and stricter sense of time. Factory life required a regimented schedule in which work began at the sound of a bell, workers kept machines going at a constant pace, and the day was divided into hours and even minutes.

Clocks began to invade private as well as public space. Before Jerome and his competitors began using standardized parts, only the wealthy owned clocks, but with mass production ordinary families could afford them. Even farmers became more sensitive to time as they became integrated into the marketplace. As one frontier traveler reported in 1844, "In Kentucky, in Indiana, in Illinois, in Missouri, and here in every dale in Arkansas, and in cabins where there was not a chair to sit on, there was sure to be a Connecticut clock."

The Market at Work: Three Examples

The scope and sweep of the national market economy transformed American lives from the towns of the East Coast to prairies of the Midwest to the distant frontier of the Rocky Mountains.

THE MARKET TRANSFORMS KINGSTON, NEW YORK

In 1820 Kingston, New York, was a rural community of only 1,000 people, located along the Hudson River. But in 1828 the Delaware and Hudson Canal linked Kingston with the Pennsylvania coalfields, jolting the town's economy. The coal trade stimulated commerce and greatly increased the number of banks and the variety of businesses. Life in Kingston now focused on the docks, stores, and canal boats rather than on planting and harvest. By 1850 Kingston had a population of 10,000.

Its landscape had changed, too. In 1820 most storekeepers and artisans conducted business from their homes. By 1850 a commercial district boasted specialized stores, some handling china and glassware, others dry goods, clothing, or jewelry and watches. Separated from both the commercial center and the manufacturing facilities, which now hugged the city's outskirts, residential neighborhoods had become segregated along class lines. By midcentury, street signs and gas lamps were going up. Kingston had become a city.

SUGAR CREEK, ILLINOIS   A thousand miles west lay the small prairie settlement of Sugar Creek, Illinois. The first white settlers had moved to Sugar Creek in 1817, and their primary concern was simply surviving. The land they plowed was on the edge of the forest, where girdled trees often remained standing among the crops until they could be cleared. The roads to larger towns such as Springfield were mere cart paths, winding among the trees.

But by the 1840s and 1850s the market economy had made inroads at Sugar Creek. True, a farmer like Eddin Lewis might still keep an account book noting that James Wilson came by for "six days work planting corn [$]3.00." That was the traditional barter system in action, for no cash actually changed hands. Lewis was simply keeping tabs, noting also when he helped Wilson, so that eventually the account could be balanced. But Lewis had begun to drive hogs to St. Louis, where he received cash in return. By 1848 he was shipping

| Indians and fur-traders mixed at Fort Laramie, Wyoming, maintained by the government as a way station for the burgeoning fur trade of the 1830s. The scene looks exotic, but the fur trade was a serious and extensive business that stretched from the Rocky Mountains to eastern cities and to Europe beyond.

©Walters Art Museum, Baltimore, USA/ Bridgeman Images

south 6,000 pounds of barreled pork, as well as lard and 350 bushels of corn. Sugar Creek, in other words, was becoming more specialized, more stratified in its wealth, and more tied into regional and national markets.

MOUNTAIN MEN AND THE FUR TRADE Another thousand miles west a different sort of American roamed, who might at first seem unconnected to the bustle of urban markets. These were the legendary mountain men. Traveling across the Great Plains, along upland streams, and over the passes of the Rockies, hard-bitten outdoorsmen such as Jim Bridger, Jedediah Smith, and James Walker wore buckskin hunting shirts, let their unkempt hair grow to their shoulders, and stuck pistols and tomahawks in their belts. In good times they feasted on raw buffalo liver and roasted hump; when game was scarce, some were not above holding their hands "in an anthill until they were covered with ants, then greedily [licking] them off," as one trapper recalled. Wild and exotic, the mountain men quickly became romantic symbols of the American quest for individual freedom.

Yet these wanderers were tied to the market. During their heyday, from the mid-1820s to the early 1840s, they trapped beaver, whose pelts were shipped east and turned into fancy hats for gentlemen. The fur trade was not a sporting pursuit but a business, dominated by organizations such as John Jacob Astor's American Fur Company, and the trapper was part of a vast economic structure that stretched from the mountains to the eastern cities and on to Europe. The majority of these men went into the wilderness not to flee civilization but to make money. Of those who survived the fur trade, most returned from the wild and took up new careers. They, like farmers, were expectant capitalists for whom the West was a land of opportunity.

 REVIEW

Why did the middle class become larger and more distinct during the first half of the nineteenth century?

PROSPERITY AND ANXIETY

AS AMERICANS SAW THEIR NATION'S frontiers expand and its market economy grow, many began to view history in terms of an inevitable and continuous improvement. But the path of commerce was not steadily upward. Instead, it advanced in a series of wrenching boom-and-bust cycles: accelerating growth and overheated expansion, followed by a crash and then depression.

BOOM-AND-BUST CYCLES The country remained extraordinarily prosperous from 1815 until 1819, only to sink into a depression that lasted from 1819 to 1823. During the next cycle, slow economic expansion in the 1820s gave way to almost frenzied speculation and investment in the 1830s. Then came the inevitable contraction in 1837, and the country suffered an even more severe depression from 1839 to 1843. The third cycle followed the same pattern: growth during the 1840s, frantic expansion in the 1850s, and a third depression that began in 1857 and lasted until the Civil War. In each "panic," thousands of workers lost their jobs, overextended farmers lost their farms, and many businesses closed their doors.

In such an environment, prosperity and personal success seemed all too fleeting. Because Americans believed that the good times would not last—that the bubble would burst and another "panic" would set in—their optimism was often tinged by insecurity and anxiety. They knew too many individuals like Chauncey Jerome, who had been rich and then lost all their wealth in a downturn.

The Panic of 1819

The initial shock of this boom-and-bust psychology came with the Panic of 1819, the first major depression in the nation's history. From 1815 to 1818 cotton had commanded fabulous prices on the Liverpool market, reaching 32.5 cents a pound in 1818. In this heady prosperity, the federal government extended liberal credit for land purchases, and the new

| *This mock banknote illustrates the anxieties often felt in times of "bust," when the value of currencies plummeted and it was difficult to tell whether the banks that issued paper money were solvent.*

Source: Library of Congress, Prints and Photographs Division [LC-USZ62-89594]

national bank encouraged merchants and farmers to expand their operations by borrowing in order to catch the rising tide.

NATIONAL DEPRESSION But in 1819 the price of cotton collapsed and took the rest of the economy with it. Once the inflationary bubble burst, land values, which had been driven to new heights by the speculative fever, plummeted 50 to 75 percent almost overnight. As the economy went slack, so did the demand for western foodstuffs and eastern manufactured goods and services, pushing the nation into a severe depression. Because the market economy had spread to new areas, the downturn affected not only city folk but rural Americans as well. Especially hard hit were the new cotton planters in the Southwest, who were most vulnerable to the ups and downs of the world market.

PUTTING HISTORY IN GLOBAL CONTEXT

AS DEPRESSION SPREAD in the years following 1819, most Americans could not guess that the ups and downs of the boom-and-bust cycle would continue through the next three decades, their swings made sharper by the growing networks of the market economy. But the interconnections between buyers and sellers did feed both prosperity and panic. Farmers and factories specialized in order to sell goods to distant buyers. Canals and railroads widened the network, speeding products, information, and profits.

As markets tied distant lands more tightly together, international events contributed to the business cycles. It was the Liverpool market in England that bid the price of American cotton to its high at over 32 cents a pound; then in 1816 and 1817 English textile manufacturers, looking for cheaper cotton, began to import more of it from India, sending the price of cotton in New Orleans plummeting to 14 cents a pound. Broader changes also hurt American markets. The French and the British had been at war with one another for decades—more than 100 years, if the imperial wars of the seventeenth and eighteenth centuries were counted. In 1814 and 1815 the major powers of Europe hammered out a peace at the Congress of Vienna, one that lasted, with only minor interruptions, until the coming of World War I in 1914. When Europe had been at war, American farmers found a ready market abroad. With thousands of European soldiers returning to their usual work as farmers, demand for American goods dropped.

The stresses of the Panic of 1819 shook the political system at home, too. As the depression deepened and hardship spread, Americans viewed government policies as at least partly to blame. The postwar nationalism, after all, had been based on the belief that government should stimulate economic development through a national bank and protective tariff, by improving transportation, and by opening up new lands. As Americans struggled to make sense of their new economic order, they looked to take more direct control of the government that was so actively shaping their lives. During the 1820s the popular response to the market and the Panic of 1819 produced a strikingly new kind of politics in the United States.

CHAPTER SUMMARY

By uniting the country in a single market, the market revolution transformed the United States during the quarter century after 1815.

- The federal government promoted the creation of a market through a protective tariff, a national bank, and internal improvements.

- The development of new forms of transportation, including canals, steamboats, and eventually railroads, allowed goods to be transported cheaply on land.

- The Supreme Court adopted a pro-business stance that encouraged investment and risk taking.

- Economic expansion generated greater national wealth, but it also brought social and intellectual change.

Digging Deeper

The outstanding synthesis of American development during the first half of the nineteenth century is Daniel Walker Howe, *What Hath God Wrought* (2007). Also worth consulting is Christopher Clark, *Social Change in America* (2006). The most provocative analysis of economic development and its impact remains Charles Sellers, *The Market Revolution* (1991). Essential for understanding the sources and impact of economic instability is Jessica M. Lepler, *The Many Panics of 1837* (2013). One of the best books on the transportation revolution is John Lauritz Larson, *Internal Improvement* (2001); and for a fascinating study of the role played by the postal system in linking Americans, see Richard R. John, *Spreading the News* (1995). There are many fine studies of urban social classes during the first half of the nineteenth century, and among the best are Sean Wilentz, *Chants Democratic* (1984), which traces the formation of New York City's working class; and Stuart M. Blumin, *The Emergence of the Middle Class* (1989). To understand the market economy's effect on rural society, read John Mack Faragher's vivid account of the transformation of a farming community in frontier Illinois, *Sugar Creek* (1986); and Robert E. Shalhope, *A Tale of New England* (2003), which traces the fortunes of a Vermont farmer and his family.

There is also no shortage of excellent books exploring the relationship between the market revolution and antebellum American culture. Begin with Karen Halttunen's classic study of middle-class culture, *Confidence Men and Painted Women* (1982); and a more recent study, Thomas Augst, *The Clerk's Tale* (2003); and then turn to Paul E. Johnson's lively exploration of working-class culture, *Sam Patch, the Famous Jumper* (2003). To celebrate any occasion, treat yourself to Stephen Nissenbaum, *The Battle for Christmas* (1996). And to console yourself in between celebrations, turn to Scott A. Sandage, *Born Losers: A History of Failure in America* (2005).

11 The Rise of Democracy

1824–1840

Artist George Caleb Bingham captured one aspect of political campaigns in his *Canvassing for a Vote*. How does clothing distinguish the social classes of these men? It may not have been an accident that Bingham, who was skeptical of the smooth talk of many politicians of his day, painted the back side of a horse next to this campaigner. Why?

Source: Yale University Art Gallery

>> **An American Story**

"WANTED: CURLING TONGS, COLOGNE, AND SILK STOCKINGS . . ."

The notice, printed in a local paper, made the rounds in the rural Pearl River district of Mississippi. A traveler, the advertisement announced, had lost a suitcase while fording the Tallahala River. The contents included "6 ruffled shirts, 6 cambric handkerchiefs, 1 hair-brush, 1 tooth-brush, 1 nail-brush, . . ." And as the list went on, the popular reaction inevitably shifted from amusement to disdain: "1 pair curling tongs, . . . 1 bottle Cologne, 1 [bottle] rose-water, 4 pairs silk stockings, and 2 pairs kid gloves." The howls of laughter that filled the air could only have increased on learning that

ELECTIONEERING IN MISSISSIPPI.

Source: Cornell University Library, Making of America Digital Collection

| *Franklin Plummer campaigning*

anyone finding said trunk was begged to contact the owner—Mr. Powhatan Ellis of Natchez.

Powhatan Ellis was no ordinary backcountry traveler. Born into a genteel Virginia family, Ellis had moved to the raw Southwest to increase his fortune. With his cultivated tastes and careful dress, he upheld the tradition of the gentleman politician. In Virginia he would have commanded respect: indeed, in Mississippi he had been appointed district judge and U.S. senator. But for the voters along the Pearl River, the advertisement for his trunk of ruffled shirts, hair oils, and fancy "skunk-water" proved to be the political kiss of death. His opponents branded him an aristocrat and a dandy, and his support among the piney-woods farmers evaporated faster than a morning mist along Old Muddy.

No one was happier with this outcome than the resourceful Franklin E. Plummer, one of Ellis's political enemies. In truth, although Judge Ellis *had* lost a trunk, he had never placed the advertisement trying to locate it. That was Plummer's doing, a man who well understood the new playing field of politics in the 1820s. If Powhatan Ellis typified the passing political world of the Revolutionary era, Plummer was a product of the raucous democratic system emerging in its place. A New Englander, Plummer had worked his way south to bustling New Orleans, and then inland to Mississippi, where he hung out his shingle as an attorney. His shrewdness made up for any lack of legal training, and he was quickly elected to the legislature.

In 1830 Plummer ran for Congress against a wealthy Natchez merchant, military hero, and member of the state's political elite. The uncouth candidate seemed overmatched at first, but Plummer portrayed himself as the champion of the people battling against the aristocrats of Natchez. Contrasting his humble background with that of his wealthy opponent, Plummer proclaimed: "We are taught that the highway to office, distinction and honor, is as free to the *meritorious poor* man, as to the *rich*." Taking as his slogan "Plummer for the People, and the People for Plummer," he was easily elected.

On the campaign trail he knew how to affect the common touch. Once, while canvassing the district with his opponent, the pair stopped at a farmhouse. When his opponent, seeking the farmer's vote, kissed the daughter, Plummer lifted up a toddling boy and began picking

red bugs off him, telling the enchanted mother: "They are powerful bad, and mighty hard on babies." On another occasion, while his opponent slept, Plummer rose at dawn to help milk the family's cow—and won another vote. He was a master at secretly planting false stories attacking himself in the press, and then bringing out the sworn personal testimonials of well-known men defending his character and denouncing the charges against him.

As long as Plummer maintained this democratic style, he remained invincible. But running for Senate in 1835, his touch deserted him. Borrowing money from a Natchez bank, he purchased a stylish coach, put his servant in a uniform, and campaigned across the state. Aghast at such pretensions, his followers promptly abandoned him. He died in 1852 in obscurity and poverty. Ah, Plummer! Even the boldest of nature's noblemen may stumble, prey to the temptations of power and commerce!

The forces transforming American society after 1815 pulled Franklin Plummer in two ways. On the one hand, the growth of new markets opened up opportunities for more and more Americans. Through his connections with bankers and the well-to-do, Plummer saw the chance to gain status, wealth, and respect. Yet as new markets were producing a more **stratified**, unequal society, the nation's politics were becoming more democratic. These politics involved more voters than ever before" and created a new class of politicians. And the system's central feature—a byword on everyone's lips—was equality. But the relation between the new equalities of politics and the new opportunities of the market was a most uneasy one. <<

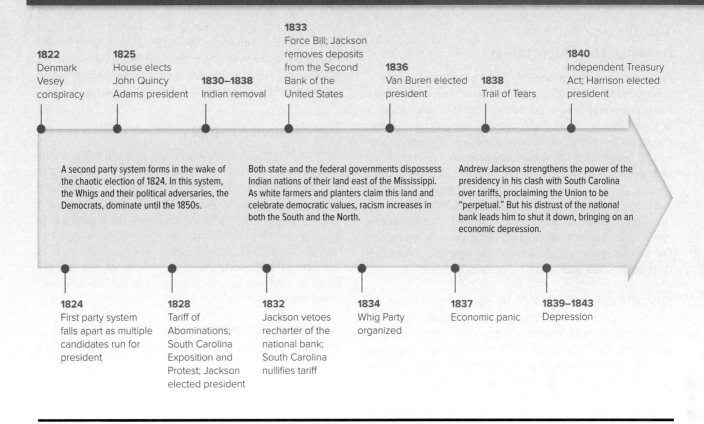

1822
Denmark Vesey conspiracy

1825
House elects John Quincy Adams president

1830–1838
Indian removal

1833
Force Bill; Jackson removes deposits from the Second Bank of the United States

1836
Van Buren elected president

1838
Trail of Tears

1840
Independent Treasury Act; Harrison elected president

A second party system forms in the wake of the chaotic election of 1824. In this system, the Whigs and their political adversaries, the Democrats, dominate until the 1850s.

Both state and the federal governments dispossess Indian nations of their land east of the Mississippi. As white farmers and planters claim this land and celebrate democratic values, racism increases in both the South and the North.

Andrew Jackson strengthens the power of the presidency in his clash with South Carolina over tariffs, proclaiming the Union to be "perpetual." But his distrust of the national bank leads him to shut it down, bringing on an economic depression.

1824
First party system falls apart as multiple candidates run for president

1828
Tariff of Abominations; South Carolina Exposition and Protest; Jackson elected president

1832
Jackson vetoes recharter of the national bank; South Carolina nullifies tariff

1834
Whig Party organized

1837
Economic panic

1839–1843
Depression

EQUALITY, OPPORTUNITY, AND THE NEW POLITICAL CULTURE OF DEMOCRACY

COMING FROM THE MORE STRATIFIED society of Europe, middle- and upper-class European visitors to the United States were struck by the "democratic spirit" that had become "infused into all the national habits and all the customs of society" during the 1820s and 1830s.

To begin with, they discovered that only one class of seats was available on stagecoaches and railcars. These were filled according to the rough-and-ready rule of first come, first served. In steamboat dining rooms or at country taverns, everyone ate at a common table, sharing food from the same serving plates. As one upper-class gentleman complained: "The rich and the poor, the educated and the ignorant, the polite and the vulgar, all herd on the cabin floor, feed at the same table, sit in each others laps, as it were." Being ushered to bed at an inn, visitors found themselves lodged 10 to 12 people a room, often with several bodies occupying a single bed. Fastidious Europeans were horrified at the thought of sleeping with unwashed representatives of American democracy.

Indeed, the democratic "manners" of Americans seemed positively shocking. In Europe social inferiors would speak only if spoken to. But Americans felt free to strike up a conversation with anyone, including total strangers. The British author Frances Trollope was offended by the "coarse familiarity of address" between classes, while another visitor complained that in a nation where every citizen felt free to shake the hand of another, it was impossible to know anyone's social station. This informality—a forward, even *rude* attitude—was not limited to shaking hands. At theaters, it was hard to get patrons to remove their hats so that those behind them could see. Still worse, men chewed tobacco and spit everywhere: in the national Capitol, in taverns, courts, and hospitals, even in private homes. Fanny Kemble, an English actress, reported that on an American steamboat "it was a perfect shower of saliva all the time."

Americans were self-consciously proud of such democratic behavior, which they viewed as a valued heritage of the Revolution. The keelboaters who carried the future King Louis-Philippe of France on a trip down the Mississippi made their republican feelings plain when the keelboat ran aground. "You kings down there!" bellowed the captain. "Show yourselves and do a man's work, and help us three-spots pull off this bar!" The ideology of the Revolution made it clear that, in the American deck of cards, "three-spots" counted as much as jacks, kings, and queens. Kings were not allowed to forget that—and neither was Franklin Plummer.

The Tension between Equality and Opportunity

Although Americans praised both opportunity and equality, a fundamental tension existed between the two values. Inevitably, widespread opportunity would produce inequality of wealth. In the 1790s less pronounced inequalities of wealth and status had prevailed because of the lack of access to markets. Shoemakers in Lynn, Massachusetts, with no way to ship large quantities of shoes across the country, could not become wealthy. Without steamboats or canals, farmers could not market surplus grain for profit. But by the 1820s and 1830s, as the opportunities of the market expanded, wealth became much more unevenly distributed. Thus the new generation had to confront contradictions in the American creed that their parents had been able to conveniently ignore.

MEANING OF EQUALITY By equality, Americans did not mean equality of wealth or property. "I know of no country where profounder contempt is expressed for the theory of permanent equality of property," Alexis de Tocqueville wrote. Nor did equality mean that all citizens had equal talent or capacity. Americans realized that individuals possessed widely differing abilities, which inevitably produced differences in wealth. "Distinctions in society will always exist under every just government," Andrew Jackson declared. "Equality of talents, or education, or of wealth cannot be produced by human institutions."

In the end, Americans embraced the equality of opportunity, not equality of condition. "True republicanism requires that every man shall have an equal chance—that every man shall be free to become as unequal as he can," one American commented. In an economy that could go bust as well as boom, Americans agreed that one primary objective of government was to safeguard opportunity. Thus the new politics of democracy walked hand in hand with the new opportunities of the market.

The New Political Culture of Democracy

DEATH OF THE CAUCUS SYSTEM The stately James Monroe, with his powdered hair and buckled shoes and breeches, was not part of the new politics. In 1824 as he neared the end of his second term, a host of new leaders in the Republican Party looked to succeed him. Traditionally, a congressional caucus selected the party's presidential nominee, and the Republican caucus finally settled on Secretary of Treasury William H. Crawford of Georgia. Condemning "King Caucus" as undemocratic, three other Republicans, all ardent nationalists, refused to withdraw from the race: Secretary of State John Quincy Adams; John C. Calhoun, Monroe's secretary of war; and Henry Clay, the Speaker of the House.

None of these men bargained on the sudden rise of another Republican candidate, Andrew Jackson, the hero of the Battle of New Orleans. Because of his limited political experience, no one took Jackson's candidacy seriously at first, including Jackson himself. But soon the general's supporters and rivals began receiving reports of his unusual popularity. From Cincinnati an observer wrote: "Strange! Wild! Infatuated! All for Jackson!" Savvy politicians flocked to his standard, but it was the people who first made Jackson a serious candidate.

The Election of 1824

Calhoun dropped out of the race, but that still left four candidates, none of whom received a majority of the popular vote. Jackson led the field and finished first in the Electoral College with 99 votes. Adams had 84, Crawford 41, and Clay 37. Under the Twelfth Amendment, the House was to select a president from the top three candidates. Clay, though himself eliminated, held enough influence as Speaker of the House to name the winner. After he met privately with Adams, he rallied the votes in the House needed to put Adams over the top.

CORRUPT BARGAIN? Two days later Adams announced that Clay would be his new secretary of state, the usual

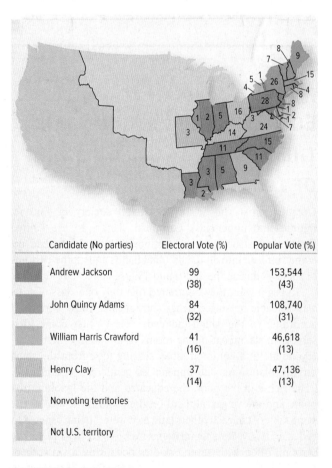

Candidate (No parties)	Electoral Vote (%)	Popular Vote (%)
Andrew Jackson	99 (38)	153,544 (43)
John Quincy Adams	84 (32)	108,740 (31)
William Harris Crawford	41 (16)	46,618 (13)
Henry Clay	37 (14)	47,136 (13)
Nonvoting territories		
Not U.S. territory		

ELECTION OF 1824

stepping-stone to the presidency. Jackson and his supporters promptly charged that there had been a "corrupt bargain" between Adams and Clay. Before Adams had even assumed office, the 1828 race was under way.

The election of 1824 shattered the old party system. Henry Clay and John Quincy Adams began to organize a new party, known as the National Republicans, to distinguish it from Jefferson's old party. Jackson's disappointed supporters eventually called themselves Democrats. By the mid-1830s, the National Republicans had given way to the Whigs, a political party that also drew members from another party that flourished briefly, the Anti-Masons. (The Anti-Masons had led a campaign against the Freemasons, or Masons, a fraternal order whose members—including George Washington and Benjamin Franklin—shared the Enlightenment belief in the power of reason but whose secret meetings and rituals seemed aristocratic and undemocratic to many Americans.) The Democrats, as the other major party, came together under the leadership of Andrew Jackson. Once established, this second American party system dominated the nation's politics until the 1850s.

Social Sources of the New Politics

NEW ATTITUDES TOWARD GOVERNMENT Why was it that a new **political culture** emerged in the 1820s? Both the revolution in markets and the Panic of 1819 played key roles. The ensuing depression convinced many Americans that government policy had aggravated, if not actually produced, hard times. As a result, they decided that the government had a responsibility to relieve distress and promote prosperity.

For the first time, large numbers of Americans saw politics as relevant to their daily lives. Agitation mounted, especially at the state level, for government to enact relief for those in debt and provide other forms of assistance. Elections soon became the means through which the majority expressed its policy preferences by voting for candidates pledged to specific programs. The older idea that representatives should be independent and vote according to their best judgment gave way to the notion that representatives were to carry out the will of the people, as expressed in the outcomes of elections.

DEMOCRATIC REFORMS With more citizens championing the "will of the people," pressure mounted to open up the political process. Most states eliminated property qualifications for voting in favor of white manhood suffrage, under which all adult white males were allowed to vote. Similarly, property requirements for officeholders were reduced or dropped.

Presidential elections became more democratic as well. By 1832 South Carolina was the only state in which the legislature rather than the voters still chose presidential electors. The Anti-Masons pioneered the convention as a more democratic method of nominating party candidates and approving a platform, and the other parties soon followed suit. Furthermore, because a presidential candidate had to carry a number of states in different sections of the country, the backing of a national party, with effective state and local organizations, became essential.

MALE SUFFRAGE IN EUROPE AND LATIN AMERICA These democratic winds of change affected European societies and eventually other areas of the world, but in no other major country were such reforms achieved as early, and with as little resistance, as in the United States. Suffrage provides a good example. In Britain, in response to growing demonstrations and the cautionary example of the French monarchy's overthrow in 1830, Parliament approved the Reform Bill of 1832, which enfranchised a number of property holders and gave Britain the broadest electorate in Europe. Yet in fact, only about 15 percent of the adult males in Britain enjoyed the right of suffrage after the bill's passage. In France the figure was less than 1 percent.

The democratic revolutions of 1848 championed universal male suffrage in France and Prussia. Yet this ideal soon suffered setbacks. By 1852 the French Republic had been replaced by a monarchy under the emperor Louis Napoléon. And in Prussia, the new constitution essentially negated universal male suffrage by dividing the electorate into three classes according to wealth, a formula that enabled 5 percent of the voters to elect one-third of parliament. Belgium, which had the most liberal constitution in Europe, did not approximate manhood suffrage until 1848. Even the second Reform Act (1867) in Britain enfranchised only about one-third of the adult males.

Likewise, the Latin American republics established in the 1820s and 1830s imposed property requirements on voting or, as Uruguay did, excluded certain occupational groups such as servants and peasants from the suffrage. One exception was Mexico, where a number of states adopted an extremely broad suffrage, but even there a new constitution in 1836 established a much more centralized state and sharply limited voting rights. The most restricted suffrage existed in the Republic of Haiti, where only army officers and a few other privileged individuals enjoyed the franchise. When the Revolution of 1843 brought a new constitution with mass-based suffrage, it met widespread resistance among elites, and the government quickly failed.

VOTER TURNOUT As the new reforms in the United States went into effect, voter turnout soared. Whereas in the 1824 presidential election only 27 percent of eligible voters bothered to go to the polls, four years later the proportion had more than doubled to 56 percent. In 1840, 78 percent of eligible voters cast ballots, probably the highest turnout in American history.

The Acceptance of Parties

RISE OF THE PROFESSIONAL POLITICIAN All these developments worked to favor the rise of a new type of politician: one whose life was devoted to party service and who often depended for his living on public office. As the number of state-sponsored internal improvement projects increased during the 1820s, so did the number of government jobs that could support party workers. No longer was politics primarily the province of the wealthy, who spent only part of their time on public affairs. Instead, political leaders were more likely to come from the middle ranks of society, especially those outside the South. Many became economically established after entering politics, but as Franklin Plummer demonstrated, large sums of money were not required to conduct a campaign. Indeed, successful politicians now had to mingle with the masses and voice their feelings—requirements that put the wealthy elite at a disadvantage.

VAN BUREN In many ways, Martin Van Buren epitomized the new breed of politician. The son of a New York tavern keeper, Van Buren lacked great oratorical skills or a magnetic personality. But he was a master organizer and tactician, highly skilled at using the new party system. His abilities eventually carried him to the White House. Unlike the Revolutionary generation, who had regarded political parties as dangerous and destructive, Van Buren argued that they were not only "inseparable from free governments" but "in many and material respects . . . highly useful to the country." While conceding that political parties were subject to abuse, he stressed that competing parties would watch one another and check abuses at the same time that they kept the masses informed.

The Politics of the Common Man

NEW STYLE OF POLITICS Andrew Jackson was one of the first political leaders to grasp the new politics in which the ordinary citizen was celebrated as never before. "Never for a moment believe that the great body of the citizens . . . can deliberately intend to do wrong," he proclaimed. Party leaders everywhere avoided aristocratic airs when on the stump. "I have always dressed chiefly in Home spun when among the people," one North Carolina member of Congress explained. "If a Candidate be dressed Farmerlike he is well received and kindly remembered by the inmates of the Log Cabin, and there is no sensation among the children or the chickens."

Politics became mass entertainment, in which campaign hoopla often overshadowed the issues. Parties used parades, glee clubs, massive rallies, and barbecues to rouse voters, and treating to drinks became an almost universal campaign tactic. ("The way to men's hearts is down their throats," quipped one Kentucky vote-getter.) Although politicians often talked about principles, political parties were pragmatic organizations, intent on gaining and holding power.

LIMITATIONS OF THE DEMOCRATIC POLITICAL SYSTEM The Jacksonian era has been called the Age of the Common Man, but such democratic tendencies had distinct limits. Women and slaves were not allowed to vote, nor could free African Americans (except in a few states, primarily in the Northeast) and Indians. Nor did the parties always deal effectively with (or even address) basic problems in society. Still, Van Buren's insight was perceptive. Popular

political parties provided an essential mechanism for peacefully resolving differences among competing interest groups, regions, and social classes.

 REVIEW
In what ways did the political culture of the 1820s and 1830s differ from that of the 1780s and 1790s?

JACKSON'S RISE TO POWER

THE NEW DEMOCRATIC STYLE OF politics first appeared on the state and local levels: Van Buren deftly working behind the scenes in New York; Amos Kendall of Kentucky campaigning in favor of debtor relief; Davy Crockett of Tennessee carefully dressed in frontier garb and offering voters a drink from a jug of whiskey and a chew from a large plug of tobacco. The national implications of these changes were not immediately clear.

John Quincy Adams's Presidency

When he assumed the presidency in 1825, John Quincy Adams might have worked to create a mass-based party. But Adams, a talented diplomat and a great secretary of state, possessed hardly a political bone in his body. Cold and tactless, he could build no popular support for the ambitious and

©Art Collection 3/Alamy

Oyster houses were the sports bars of antebellum America, and the preferred sport was politics. Newspapers expressed strong party loyalties, inspiring the man at the right to harangue his friend, who seems unpersuaded.

often farsighted programs he proposed. His plans for the federal government to promote not only manufacturing and agriculture, but also the arts, literature, and science, left his opponents aghast.

Nor would Adams take any steps to gain reelection, though he earnestly desired it. Despite urgent pleas from Henry Clay and other advisors, he declined to remove from federal office men who actively opposed him. Since Adams refused to be a party leader, Clay undertook to organize the National Republicans. But with a reluctant candidate at the top of the ticket, Clay labored under serious handicaps. The new style of politics came into its own nationally only when Andrew Jackson swept to power at the head of a new party, the Democrats.

JACKSON'S ELECTION   Building a new party was a tricky business. Because Jackson's coalition was made up of conflicting interests, "Old Hickory" remained vague about his own position on many issues. Thus the campaign of 1828

soon degenerated into a series of personal attacks, splattering mud on all involved. Aided by enormous majorities in the South, Jackson won handily.

In one sense the significance of the election was clear. It marked the beginning of politics as Americans have practiced it ever since, with two disciplined national parties actively competing for votes, an emphasis on personalities over issues, and the resort to mass electioneering techniques. Yet in terms of public policy, the meaning of the election was anything but clear. The people had voted for Jackson as a national hero without any real sense of what he would do with his newly won power.

President of the People

Certainly the people looked for change. "I never saw such a crowd here before," Senator Daniel Webster of Massachusetts wrote as inauguration day approached. "Persons have come 500 miles to see General Jackson, and they really seem to

©ART Collection/Alamy

| *"The Will of the People the Supreme Law"* reads the banner at this county election. One of the few occasions when most of the men would assemble at the village, Election Day remained an all-male event as well as a time of excitement, heated debate, and boisterous celebration. As citizens give their oath to an election judge, diligent party workers dispense free drinks, solicit support, offer party tickets, and keep a careful tally of who has voted. Liquor and drinking are prominently featured: one elector enjoys another round, a prospective voter who is too drunk to stand is held up by a faithful party member, and on the right a groggy partisan sports a bandage as a result of a political brawl.

think that the country is rescued from some dreadful danger!" Some 15,000 supporters cheered wildly after Jackson was sworn in.

At the White House reception, pandemonium reigned as thousands of ordinary citizens pushed inside to catch a glimpse of their idol. The new president had to flee after being nearly crushed to death by well-wishers. The crowd trampled on the furniture, broke glass, smashed mirrors, and ruined carpets and draperies. "It was a proud day for the people," boasted Amos Kendall, one of the new president's advisors. Supreme Court Justice Joseph Story was less thrilled: "I never saw such a mixture. The reign of King Mob seemed triumphant."

JACKSON'S CHARACTER   Whether loved as a man of the people or hated as a demagogue leading the mob, Jackson was the representative of the new democracy. The first president from west of the Appalachians, he moved as a young lawyer to the Tennessee frontier. He had a quick mind but limited schooling and little use for learning; after his death a family friend acknowledged that the general had never believed that the Earth was round. A man of action, his decisiveness served him well as a soldier and also in the booming economy around Nashville, where he established himself as a large landowner and slaveholder. Tall and wiry, with flowing white hair, Jackson carried himself with a soldier's bearing. His troops had nicknamed him Old Hickory out of respect for his toughness, but that strength sometimes became arrogance, and he could be vindictive and a bully. He was not a man to provoke, as his reputation for dueling demonstrated.

For all these flaws, Jackson was a shrewd politician. He knew how to manipulate men and could be affable or abusive as the occasion demanded. He would sometimes burst into a rage to get his way with a hostile delegation, only to chuckle afterward, "They thought I was mad." He also displayed a keen sense of public opinion, skillfully reading the shifting national mood.

SPOILS SYSTEM   As the nation's chief executive, Jackson defended the **spoils system**, under which public offices were awarded to political supporters, as a democratic reform.

©The Granger Collection, New York

Democratic reforms of the 1820s and 1830s brought a new sort of politician to prominence, one whose life was devoted to party service and whose living often depended on public office. This cartoon from 1834 shows the downside of the new situation. Andrew Jackson sports the wings, horns, and tail of a devil as he dangles the rewards of various political offices above a clamoring group of eager job-seekers.

Rotation in office, he declared, would guard against insensitive bureaucrats who presumed that they held their positions by right. The cabinet, he believed, existed more to carry out his will than to offer counsel, and throughout his term he remained a strong executive who insisted on his way—and usually got it.

The Political Agenda in the Market Economy

Jackson took office at a time when the market economy was spreading through America and the nation's borders were expanding geographically. The three major problems his administration faced were directly caused by the resulting growing pains.

First, the demand for new lands put continuing pressure on Indians, whose valuable cornfields and hunting grounds could produce marketable commodities like cotton and wheat. Second, as the economies of the North, South, and West became more specialized, their rival interests forced a confrontation over the tariff and whether South Carolina could nullify that federal law. And finally, the booming economy focused attention on the role of credit and banking in society and on the new commercial attitudes that were a central part of the developing market economy. The president attacked all three issues in his characteristically combative style.

 REVIEW

What were the most pressing problems faced by President Andrew Jackson?

DEMOCRACY AND RACE

AS A PLANTER, JACKSON BENEFITED from the international demand for cotton that was drawing new lands into the market. He had gone off to the Tennessee frontier in 1788, a rowdy, ambitious young man who could afford to purchase only one slave. Caught up in the get-rich-quick mania of the frontier, he became a prominent land speculator, established himself as a planter, and by the time he became president owned nearly 100 slaves. His popularity derived not only from defeating the British but also from opening extensive tracts of valuable Indian lands to white settlement. Through military fighting and treaty negotiating, he was personally responsible for obtaining about a third of Tennessee for the United States, three-quarters of Florida and Alabama, a fifth of Georgia and Mississippi, and a tenth of Kentucky and North Carolina.

Even so, in 1820 an estimated 125,000 Indians remained east of the Mississippi River. In the Southwest the Choctaws, Creeks, Cherokees, Chickasaws, and Seminoles retained millions of acres of prime agricultural land in the heart of the cotton kingdom. Led by Georgia, southern states demanded that the federal government clear these titles. In response Monroe in 1824 proposed to Congress that the remaining eastern tribes be relocated west of the Mississippi River.

NEW ATTITUDES TOWARD RACE   As white pressure for removal intensified, a shift in the attitude toward Indians and race increasingly occurred. Previously most whites had attributed cultural differences among whites, blacks, and Indians to the environment. After 1815 the dominant white culture stressed "innate" racial differences that could never be erased. A growing number of Americans began to argue that Indians were by nature inferior savages, obstacles to progress because they were incapable of adopting white ways.

Accommodate or Resist?

That argument placed Indians and other minorities in the Old Southwest in a difficult position. During the seventeenth and eighteenth centuries the region reflected a multiracial character, because Indians, Spanish, French, and Africans had all settled there. The intermixture of cultures could be seen in the garb of the Creek Indian chief William McIntosh, who adopted a style of dress that reflected both his Indian and white heritage. McIntosh's father was a Scot, his mother a Creek, his wife a Cherokee—and McIntosh himself had allied his people with Andrew Jackson's forces during the War of 1812. But not long after he signed a treaty for the cession of Creek lands in 1825, Creeks who believed that McIntosh had betrayed the tribe's interest murdered him. As southern whites increased their clamor for Indian removal, similar tensions among various tribal factions increased.

Among the Seminoles, mixed-bloods (those with white as well as Indian ancestry) took the lead in urging military resistance to any attempt to expel them. By contrast, mixed-bloods in the Cherokee Nation, led by John Ross, advocated a program of accommodation by adopting white ways to prevent removal. After a bitter struggle Ross prevailed, and in 1827 the Cherokees adopted a written constitution modeled after that of the United States. They also enacted the death penalty for any member who sold tribal lands to whites without consent of the governing general council. Developing their own alphabet, they published a bilingual newspaper, the *Cherokee Phoenix*. Similarly, the neighboring Creeks moved to centralize authority by strengthening the power of the governing council at the expense of local towns. They, too, made it illegal for individual chiefs to sell any more land to whites.

CHANGING NATURE OF CHEROKEE SOCIETY   The division between traditionalists and those favoring accommodation reflected the fact that Indians, too, had been drawn into a web of market relationships. As more Cherokee families began to sell their surplus crops, they ceased to share property communally as in the past. Cherokee society became more stratified and unequal, just as white society had, and economic elites dominated the tribal government. Women's traditional economic role was transformed as well, as men now took over farming operations, previously a female responsibility. As the cotton boom spread, some Cherokees became substantial planters who owned large numbers of black slaves and thousands of acres of cotton land. Largely of mixed ancestry, slaveholders were wealthier, had investments in other enterprises such as gristmills and ferries, raised crops for market, were more likely to read English, and were the driving force behind acculturation.

As cotton cultivation expanded among the Cherokees, slavery became harsher and a primary means of determining status, just as in southern white society. The general council passed several laws forbidding intermarriage with African Americans and excluding African Americans and mulattoes from voting or holding office. Ironically, at the same time that white racial attitudes toward Indians were deteriorating, the Cherokees' racial attitudes toward blacks were also hardening, paralleling the increased racism among white Americans.

Trail of Tears

PRESSURE FOR INDIAN REMOVAL   As western land fever increased and racial attitudes sharpened, Jackson prodded Congress to provide funds for Indian removal. He watched sympathetically as the Georgia legislature overturned the Cherokee constitution, declared Cherokee laws null and void, and decreed that tribal members would be tried in state courts. In 1830 Congress finally passed a removal bill.

But the Cherokees brought suit in federal court against Georgia's actions. In 1832 in the case of *Worcester v. Georgia,* the Supreme Court sided with the Cherokees. Indian tribes had full authority over their lands, wrote Chief Justice John Marshall in the opinion. Thus Georgia had no right to extend its laws over Cherokee territory. Pronouncing Marshall's decision "stillborn," Jackson ignored the Court's edict and went ahead with plans for removal.

Although Jackson assured Indians that they could be removed only voluntarily, he paid no heed when state governments harassed tribes into surrendering lands. Under the threat of coercion, the Choctaws, Chickasaws, and Creeks reluctantly agreed to move to tracts in present-day Oklahoma. In the process, land-hungry schemers cheated tribal members out of as much as 90 percent of their land.

REMOVAL OF THE CHEROKEES   The Cherokees held out longest, but to no avail. To deal with more-pliant leaders of the tribe, Georgia authorities kidnapped Chief John Ross, who led the resistance to relocation, and threw him into jail. Ross was finally released but not allowed to negotiate the 1835 treaty, which stipulated that the Cherokees leave their lands no later than 1838. When that time came, most refused

| A southern belle whose father owned a cotton plantation? Perhaps, but this was a Chickasaw Indian girl. Her elegant hair and fashionable dress suggest the complexity of cultural relations in the Old Southwest, where some Indians had acculturated to white ways, owned plantations and even slaves. This young woman was among the thousands of Indians removed to territory west of the Mississippi during the first half of the nineteenth century.

©National Museum of the American Indian, Smithsonian Institution (P00452)

to go. In response, President Martin Van Buren had the U.S. Army round up resistant members and force them, at bayonet point, to join the westward march. Of the 15,000 who traveled this Trail of Tears, approximately one-quarter died along the way of exposure, disease, and exhaustion, including Ross's wife. As for the western tracts awaiting the survivors, they were smaller and generally inferior to the rich lands that had been taken from the Cherokees.

MILITARY RESISTANCE   Some Indians chose resistance. In the Old Northwest a group of the Sauk and Fox led by Black Hawk recrossed the Mississippi into Illinois in 1832, only to be crushed by federal troops and the militia. More successful was the military resistance of a minority of Seminoles led by Osceola. Despite his death, they held out until 1842 in the Florida Everglades before being subdued and removed. In the end only a small number of southern tribe members were able to escape removal.

In his Farewell Address in 1837 Jackson defended his policy by piously asserting that the eastern tribes had been finally "placed beyond the reach of injury or oppression, and that [the] paternal care of the General Government will hereafter watch over them and protect them." But Indians knew the bitter truth of the matter. Without effective political power, they found themselves at the mercy of the pressures of the marketplace and the hardening racial attitudes of white Americans.

Removal and Epidemics in the West

As the Indian nations east of the Mississippi battled racism and removal, disease stalked those in the West. Smallpox, measles, cholera, and influenza followed in the wake of white traders and settlers, triggering at least 27 epidemics—more recorded than in any preceding century of contact—among Indians living west of the Mississippi. One such scourge came on the heels of removal in 1837, when an American Fur Company steamer unwittingly carried smallpox to trading posts along the upper Missouri. It spread like wildfire across the Great Plains, and within a year the epidemic had leapt the Rockies and headed south to Texas. All told, 50–95 percent of those infected lost their lives, shattering families, disrupting native economies, and demoralizing cultures during the same years that eastern nations were being forced into the

>> MAPPING THE PAST <<

INDIAN REMOVAL

Source: Library of Congress, Prints and Photographs Division [LC-DIG-pga-07580]

"I have heard a great many talks from our great father, and they all begun and ended the same. *Brothers!* When he made us a talk on a former occasion, he said, "Get a little farther; go beyond the Oconee and the Oakmulgee [rivers in Georgia]: there is a pleasant country." He also said, "It shall be yours forever." Now he says, "The Land you live on is not yours; go beyond the Mississippi . . . . *Brothers!* Will not our great father come there also?" —Speckled Snake, addressing the Cherokees, 1830

CONTEXT

During Jackson's presidency, the federal government concluded nearly 70 treaties with Indian tribes, in the Old Northwest as well as the South. Under their terms, the United States acquired approximately 100 million acres of Indian land.

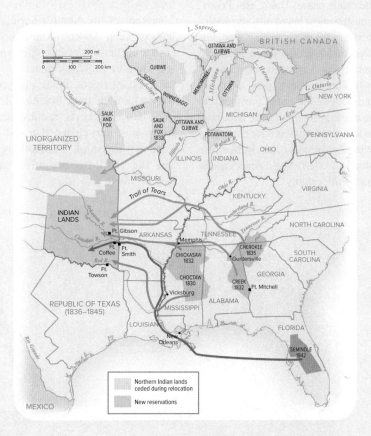

MAP READING

1. In what southern states did Indian nations cede their land?
2. Where did Black Hawk's Sauk and Fox Indians resist white encroachment?
3. What was the Trail of Tears?
4. What Indian nation was last to be removed to western lands and why?

MAP INTERPRETATION

1. What economic interest prompted southern planters to press for Indian removal? What commodity did they hope to cultivate on ceded lands?
2. What was the interest of white settlers and federal and state governments in removing Indian Nations from the Old Northwest?
3. What was the objective in removing Indian nations to the west of the Mississippi River?
4. Which Indian nations lived west of the Mississippi River, and how did they regard the removal?

West. Indeed, the massive forced migration of eastern Indians had profound consequences for plains peoples, who suddenly faced increased competition for resources and often came to blows with Cheyennes, Creeks, Chickasaws, Choctaws, and other formable newcomers.

The region's challenges and misfortunes did not affect native peoples equally. Some found their communities all but destroyed. Around 2,000 sedentary Mandans lived on the upper Missouri when smallpox arrived in 1837; before year's end fewer than 150 remained alive. Other agriculturalists such as the Wichitas, Omahas, and Pawnees endured their bouts with disease but increasingly found themselves hemmed in and weakened by immigrating peoples from the east and by the expansionist Sioux.

Still others reacted to the threats of the 1830s through creative diplomacy. Most important, in the summer of 1840 the Comanches and Kiowas of the southern plains and the Southern Cheyennes and Arapahoes of the central plains laid aside a longstanding and bloody feud and made peace. The "Great Peace" initiated a close trading relationship and allowed all four peoples to safely pursue economic opportunities in a changing West. For Cheyennes and Arapahos this meant unhampered access to buffalo-rich territory in present-day Colorado, increasingly important as they sold hides at Fort Bent to supply American markets. For Comanches and Kiowas the peace provided the security necessary for their men to embark on long-distance raiding expeditions deep into Mexico, expeditions at once dangerous and profitable. Despite a series of calamities, then, Indian peoples continued to be the masters of western North America well into the second half of the nineteenth century.

Free Blacks in the North

Unlike Indian removal, the rising discrimination against free African Americans during this period did not depend directly on presidential action. Still, Jackson's Democratic Party, which was in the vanguard of promoting white equality, was also the most strongly proslavery and the most hostile to black rights. The intensifying racism that accompanied the emergence of democracy in American life bore down with particular force on free African Americans. "The policy and power of the national and state governments are against them," commented one northerner. "The popular feeling is against them—the interests of our citizens are against them."

DISCRIMINATION Before the Civil War the free black population remained small: only about 171,000 in the North in 1840, about a quarter of whom were mulattoes. Although those numbers amounted to less than 2 percent of the North's population, most states enacted laws to keep African Americans in an inferior position. (For a discussion of free African Americans in the South, see Chapter 13.) Most black northerners lacked meaningful political rights. Black men could vote on equal terms with whites in only five New England states. New York imposed a property requirement only on black voters, which disenfranchised the vast majority. In New Jersey, Pennsylvania, and Connecticut, African American men lost the right to vote after having previously enjoyed that privilege.

| Smallpox epidemics decimated many Indian peoples, particularly the Mandans. This religious shrine, erected near a Mandan burial ground, was used for praying and fasting. It includes both animal and human skulls.

©The Stapleton Collection/ Bridgeman Images

OFFER DER MANDAN INDIANER. | OFFRANDE DES INDIENS MANDANS.
OFFERING OF THE MANDAN INDIANS

Black northerners also lacked the basic civil rights that whites enjoyed. Five states prohibited them from testifying against whites, and either law or custom excluded African Americans from juries everywhere except Massachusetts. In addition, several western states passed black exclusion laws prohibiting free African Americans from emigrating to their state. Though seldom enforced, these laws allowed for harassing the African American population in times of social stress.

The free states also practiced segregation, or the physical separation of the races. African Americans sat in separate sections on public transportation. They could not go into most hotels and restaurants, and, if permitted to enter theaters and lecture halls, they squeezed into the corners and balconies. White churches assigned blacks separate pews and arranged for them to take communion after white members. Virtually every community excluded black children from the public schools or forced them to attend overcrowded and poorly funded separate schools. One English visitor commented that "we see, in effect, two nations—one white and another black—growing up together . . . but never mingling on a principle of equality."

BLACK POVERTY Discrimination pushed African American males into the lowest-paying and most unskilled jobs: servants, sailors, waiters, and common laborers. In Philadelphia in 1838, 80 percent of employed black males were unskilled laborers, and three of five black families had less than $60 total wealth. African American women normally continued working after marriage, mostly as servants, cooks, laundresses, and seamstresses, because their wages were critical to the family's economic survival. Blacks were willing strikebreakers, because white workers, fearing economic competition and loss of status, were overtly hostile and excluded them from trade unions. A number of anti-black riots erupted in northern cities during these years. Driven into abject poverty, free blacks in the North suffered from an inadequate diet, were more susceptible to disease, and in 1850 had a life expectancy 8 to 10 years less than that of whites.

THE SPREAD OF WHITE MANHOOD SUFFRAGE

White manhood suffrage became the norm during the Jacksonian era, but in a number of states free black males who had been voting by law or by custom lost the right to vote. After 1821 a $250 property requirement disenfranchised about 90 percent of adult black males in New York. **What prompted the disenfranchisement of free blacks?**

AFRICAN COLONIZATION: HOPING FOR THE BEST AND SUSPECTING THE WORST

Henry Clay owned 50 slaves who worked his Kentucky plantation, but he was a lifelong advocate of gradual emancipation and a founder of the American Colonization Society in 1816. He explained his support in 1827. David Walker, a militant leader of the northern free black community, singled out Clay and other colonizationists for sharp criticism.

DOCUMENT 1
In Favor of Colonization: Henry Clay

Numbers of the free African race among us are willing to go to Africa. . . . Why should they not go! Here they are in the lowest state of social gradation; aliens—political, moral, social aliens—strangers though natives. There they would be in the midst of their friends, and their kindred, at home, though born in a foreign land, and elevated above the natives of the country, as much as they are degraded here below the other classes of the community. . . .

What is the true nature of the evil of the existence of a portion of the African race in our population? It is not that there are some, but that there are so many among us of a different caste, of a different physical, if not moral, constitution, who never can amalgate with the great body of our population. Here . . . the African part of our population bears so large a proportion to the residue, of European origin, as to create the most lively apprehension, especially in some quarters of the Union. Any project, therefore, by which, in a material degree, the dangerous element in the general mass can be diminished or rendered stationary, deserves deliberate consideration.

The Colonization Society has never imagined it to be practicable . . . to transport the whole of the African race within the limits of the United States. Nor is that necessary to accomplish the desirable objects of domestic tranquility, and render us one homogeneous people. Let us suppose . . . that the whole population at present of the United States, is twelve millions of which ten

may be estimated of the Anglo-Saxon and two of the African race. If there could be annually transported from the United States an amount of the African portion equal to the annual increase of the whole of that caste, while the European race should be left to multiply, we should find at the termination of the period . . . that the relative proportion would be as twenty to two. And if the process were continued, during the second term of duplication, the proportion would be forty to two—one which would eradicate every cause of alarm or solicitude from the breasts of the most timid.

Source: Clay, Henry, Speech at the Annual Meeting of the American Colonization Society, Washington, January 30, 1827 in Colton, Calvin, ed., *The Works of Henry Clay.* New York, 1904.

DOCUMENT 2
Against Colonization: David Walker

Here is demonstrative proof, of a plan got up, by a gang of slaveholders to select the free people of colour from among the slaves, that our more miserable brethren may be the better secured in ignorance and wretchedness, to work their farms and dig their mines, and thus go on enriching the Christians with their blood and groans. What our brethren could have been thinking about, who have left their native land and home and gone away to Africa, I am unable to say. This country is as much ours as it is the whites, whether they will admit it or not they will see and believe it by and by. They tell us about prejudice—what have we to do with it? Their prejudices will be obliged to fall like lightning to the ground, in succeeding generations; not, however, with the will and consent of all the whites, for some will be obliged to hold on to the old adage, viz: the blacks are not men, but were made to be an inheritance to us and our children for ever!!!!!! I hope the residue of the coloured people, will stand still and see the salvation of God and the miracle

which he will work for our delivery from wretchedness under the Christians!!!!!! . . .

I shall give an extract from the letter of that truly Reverend Divine, (Bishop [Richard] Allen) of Philadelphia, respecting this trick . . . he says, "Dear Sir, I have been for several years trying to reconcile my mind to the Colonizing of Africans in Liberia, but there have always been and there still remain great and insurmountable objections against the scheme. . . . Can we not discern the project of sending the free people of colour away from their country? Is it not for the interest of the slaveholders to select the free people of colour out of the different states, and send them to Liberia? Will it not make their slaves uneasy to see free men of colour enjoying liberty? It is against the law in some of the Southern States, that a person of colour should receive an education, under a severe penalty. . . . See the thousands of foreigners emigrating to America every year: and if there be ground sufficient for them to cultivate, and bread for them to eat, why would they wish to send the *first tillers* of the land away? Africans have made fortunes for

thousands, who are yet unwilling to part with their services; but the free must be sent away, and those who remain must be *slaves.* I have no doubt that there are many good men who do not see as I do, and who are for sending us to Liberia; but they have not duly considered the subject—they are not men of colour. This land which we have watered with our *tears* and *our blood* is now our *mother country,* and we are well satisfied to stay where wisdom abounds and the gospel is free."

Source: Walker, David, *Appeal to the Coloured Citizens of the World,* 1829.

THINKING CRITICALLY

What were Henry Clay's concerns about free African Americans? Why did he regard colonization as a viable solution to the problems he believed African Americans posed to the United States? What did David Walker and Richard Allen believe to be the true intentions of the colonizationists? Do you believe that they accurately assessed those motives?

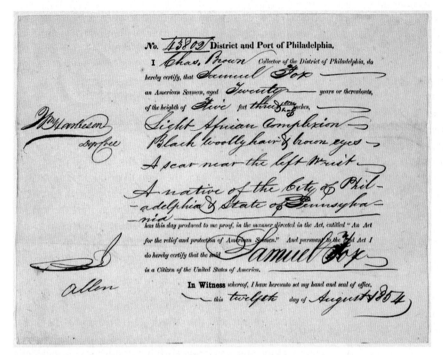

Source: Library of Congress, Manuscript Division, Black History Collection

| A Protection Certificate for Samuel Fox, a free black sailor, provides proof, while sailing abroad, that he is a U.S. citizen and a resident of Philadelphia.

The African American Community

AFRICAN COLONIZATION Free blacks had long suffered from such oppression and injustice. Between the Revolution and the War of 1812 they had responded by founding schools, churches, and mutual-aid societies to sustain their communities. Some, such as Paul Cuffe, sought to escape white prejudice entirely by establishing settlements of free blacks in West Africa. The Quaker son of a West African father and a Wampanoag Indian mother, Cuffe became a sea captain, and in 1816 his merchant ship brought 38 free black New Englanders to settle in West Africa. Cuffe's venture drew white sympathizers who formed the American Colonization Society (ACS) and founded Liberia in West Africa in 1821–1822. Several state legislatures in the North and the Upper South as well as all the major Protestant churches endorsed ACS plans to encourage free black emigration, but its members were an unlikely and unstable coalition. Some opposed slavery and hoped that colonization would encourage manumissions and gradual emancipation, while others believed that ridding the nation of free blacks would make it easier for slavery to flourish.

RISE OF BLACK MILITANCY Even as white support for colonization swelled during the 1820s, black enthusiasm for emigration diminished. Many African American leaders in the North were turning to more confrontational tactics: they advocated resistance to slavery and condemned racism and inequality. Among the most outspoken of this new, more militant generation was David Walker, whose *Appeal to the Coloured Citizens of the World* (1829) denounced colonization and urged slaves to use violence to end bondage.

Racism Strikes a Deeper Root

What prompted greater militancy among African Americans after 1820s was also the growth of an increasingly virulent racism among whites. Ironically, the success of efforts to promote education, religious piety, and temperance within the free black community threatened many lower-class whites and intensified their resentment of African Americans. That animosity found vent in race riots, which erupted in Pittsburgh, Boston, Cincinnati, and New Haven.

APPEAL OF MINSTRELSY The racist attitudes of the day were very much reflected in popular culture, nowhere more than in minstrel shows, the most popular form of entertainment in Jacksonian America. Originating in the 1830s and 1840s, minstrel shows featured white actors performing in blackface. Although popular throughout the country, minstrelsy's primary audience was in northern cities. Its basic message was that African Americans could not cope with freedom and therefore did not belong in the North. Enslaved African Americans were portrayed as happy and contented, whereas free black Americans were caricatured either as strutting dandies or as helpless ignoramuses. Drawing its patrons from laborers, Irish immigrants, and other poor whites, minstrelsy assured these white champions of democracy that they remained superior.

Source: J. Paul Getty Museum, Los Angeles, 84.XT.441.3

| The confident air of this African American man, displayed in a daguerreotype (an early photographic process), suggests the dignity free blacks maintained in the face of unrelenting hostility and discrimination.

DEEPENING RACISM   The unsettling economic, social, and political changes of the Jacksonian era heightened white Americans' fear of failure, which stimulated racism. The popular yet unrealistic expectation was that any white man might become rich. Yet in fact, 20 percent or more of white adult males of this era never accumulated any property. Their lack of success encouraged them to relieve personal tensions through increased hostility to their black neighbors. Subjecting black Americans to legal disabilities ensured that even the poorest whites would enjoy an advantage in the race for wealth and status. "The prejudice of race appears to be stronger in the states that have abolished slavery than in those where it still exists," Tocqueville noted. The power of racism in Jacksonian America stemmed, at least in part, from the fact that equality remained part of the nation's creed while it steadily receded as a social reality.

> ✓ **REVIEW**
>
> In what ways did Indians and free African Americans attempt to protect their communities in Jacksonian America?

THE NULLIFICATION CRISIS

REMOVAL AND RACISM PROVIDED ONE answer to the question of who would be given equality of opportunity in America's new democracy. Indians and African Americans would not. The issue of nullification raised a different, equally pressing question. As the market revolution propelled the economies of the North, South, and West toward increased specialization, how would various regions or interest groups accommodate their differences?

The Growing Crisis in South Carolina

The depression of 1819 struck hard at South Carolina. And even when prosperity returned to the rest of the nation, many of the state's cotton planters still suffered. With lands exhausted from years of cultivation, they could not compete with the fabulous yields of frontier planters in Alabama and Mississippi.

Increasingly, South Carolinians viewed federal tariffs as the cause of their miseries. When Congress raised the duty rates in 1824, they assailed the tariff as an unfair tax that raised the prices of goods they imported while benefiting other regions of the nation. Other southern states opposed the 1824 tariff as well, though none so vehemently as South Carolina.

DENMARK VESEY ACCUSED   The one state in which black inhabitants outnumbered whites, South Carolina had been growing more sensitive about the institution of slavery. In Charleston white anxieties fixed on Denmark Vesey, a literate, well-traveled, free black carpenter. On the flimsiest

evidence, much of it extracted by torture, whites accused Vesey and slaves from neighboring plantations of plotting to seize and then burn down the city. Although the accused denied the charges, authorities hanged Vesey and 34 other black men and banished 37 others from the state.

But white South Carolinians worried that other undetected conspirators lurked in their midst. As an additional measure of security, the state's leaders pushed for stronger constitutional protection of slavery. After all, supporters of high tariffs had already claimed that the "implied powers" of the Constitution gave them the right to promote manufacturing. What was to stop this same broad interpretation from being used to end slavery? "In contending against the tariff, I have always felt that we were combatting against the symptom instead of the disease," argued Chancellor William Harper of South Carolina. "Tomorrow may witness [an attempt] to relieve . . . your slaves."

When Congress raised the duty rates still higher in 1828 with the so-called Tariff of Abominations, South Carolina's legislature published the *South Carolina Exposition and Protest,* which outlined for the first time the theory of nullification. Only later was it revealed that its author was Jackson's own vice president, John C. Calhoun.

Calhoun's Theory of Nullification

Educated at Yale and at a distinguished law school, John C. Calhoun was the most impressive intellect of his political generation. During the 1820s the South Carolina leader made a steady journey away from nationalism toward an extreme states' rights position that advocated states having more power than the federal government. When he was elected Jackson's vice president, South Carolinians assumed that tariff reform would soon be enacted. But Jackson and Calhoun quarreled, and Calhoun lost all influence in the administration.

MINORITY RIGHTS VS. MAJORITY RULE   In his theory of nullification Calhoun addressed the problem of how to protect the rights of a minority in a political system based on the rule of the majority. The Union, he argued, was a compact among sovereign states. Thus the people of each state, acting in special popular conventions, had the right to nullify any federal law that exceeded the powers granted to Congress under the Constitution. The law would then become null and void in that state. In response, Congress could either repeal the law or propose a constitutional amendment expressly giving it the power in question. If the amendment was ratified, the nullifying state could either accept the decision or exercise its ultimate right as a sovereign state and secede from the Union.

NATIONALISTS' THEORY   When Senator Robert Hayne of South Carolina outlined Calhoun's theory in the Senate in 1830, Senator Daniel Webster of Massachusetts replied sharply that the Union was not a compact of sovereign states. The people and not the states, he argued, had created the

Constitution. "It is the people's constitution, the people's government, made for the people, made by the people, and answerable to the people." Webster also insisted that the federal government did not merely act as the agent of the states but had sovereign powers in those areas in which it had been delegated responsibility. Finally, Webster endorsed the doctrine of judicial review, which gave the Supreme Court authority to determine the meaning of the Constitution.

The Nullifiers Nullified

When Congress passed another tariff in 1832 that failed to give the state any relief, South Carolina's legislature called for the election of delegates to a popular convention, which overwhelmingly adopted an ordinance in November that declared the tariffs of 1828 and 1832 "null, void, and no law, nor binding upon this state, its officers or citizens" after February 1, 1833.

IDEA OF A PERPETUAL UNION Jackson, who had spent much of his life defending the nation, was not about to tolerate any defiance of his authority or the federal government's. In his Proclamation on Nullification, issued in December 1832, he insisted that the Union was perpetual. Under the Constitution, there was no right of secession. To reinforce Jackson's announced determination to enforce the tariff laws, Congress passed the Force Bill, reaffirming the president's military powers.

COMPROMISE OF 1833 Yet Jackson was also a skillful politician. At the same time that he threatened South Carolina, he urged Congress to reduce the tariff rates. With no other state willing to follow South Carolina's lead, Calhoun

reluctantly agreed to a compromise tariff, which Jackson signed on March 1, 1833, the same day he signed the Force Bill. South Carolina's convention repealed the nullifying ordinance, and the crisis passed.

Calhoun's doctrine had proved too radical for the rest of the South. Yet the controversy convinced many southerners that they were becoming a permanent minority. "It is useless and impracticable to disguise the fact," concluded nullifier William Harper, "that we are divided into slave-holding and non-slaveholding states, and this is the broad and marked distinction that must separate us at last." As that feeling of isolation grew, it was not nullification but the threat of secession that ultimately became the South's primary weapon.

✓ **REVIEW**

What were the issues being contested in the debate over nullification?

THE BANK WAR

JACKSON UNDERSTOOD WELL THE POLITICAL ties that bound the nation. He grasped much less firmly the economic and financial connections that linked different regions of the country through banks and national markets. In particular the president was suspicious of the national bank and the power it possessed. His clash with the Second Bank of the United States brought on the greatest crisis of his presidency.

The National Bank and the Panic of 1819

"MONSTER BANK" Chartered by Congress in 1816 for a 20-year period, the Second Bank of the United States at first suffered from woeful mismanagement. During the frenzy of speculation between 1816 and 1818, it recklessly overexpanded its operations. Then it turned about-face and sharply contracted credit by calling in loans when the depression hit in 1819. Senator Thomas Hart Benton of Missouri charged that the national bank foreclosed on so much property that it owned entire towns. To many Americans the Bank had already become a monster.

The psychological effects of the Panic of 1819 were almost as momentous as the economic. To many uneasy farmers and workers the hard times seemed like punishment for losing sight of the old virtues of simplicity, frugality, and hard work. For them banks became a symbol of the commercialization of American society and the passing of a simpler way of life.

Biddle's Bank

FUNCTION AS A CENTRAL BANK In 1823 Nicholas Biddle, a rich 37-year-old Philadelphia businessman, became president of the national bank. Biddle was intelligent and thoroughly familiar with the banking system, but he was also impossibly arrogant. Seeking to restore the Bank's reputation, he set out to provide the nation with a sound currency by regulating the amount of credit available in the economy.

©The Granger Collection, New York

As Daniel Webster outlines his nationalist theory of the Constitution and the Union, Senator Robert Hayne of South Carolina sits (front, left) with his hands together. Most of the seats in the Senate gallery are occupied by women, evidence of the widespread interest in politics.

Government revenues were paid largely in banknotes (paper money) issued by state-chartered banks. Because the Treasury Department regularly deposited U.S. funds in the national bank, the notes of state banks from all across the Union came into its possession. If Biddle believed that a state bank was overextended and had issued more notes than was safe, he presented them to that bank and demanded they be redeemed in **specie** (gold or silver). Because banks did not have enough specie reserves to back all the paper money they issued, the only way a state bank could continue to redeem its notes was to call in its loans and reduce the amount of its notes in circulation. This action had the effect of lessening the amount of credit in the economy.

But if Biddle felt that a bank's credit policies were reasonable, he simply returned the state banknotes to circulation without presenting them for redemption. Being the government's official depository gave Biddle's bank enormous power over state banks and over the economy. Under Biddle's direction the Bank became a financial colossus: it had 29 branches and made 20 percent of the country's loans, issued one-fifth of the total banknotes, and held fully a third of all deposits and specie. Yet for the most part, Biddle used the Bank's enormous power responsibly to provide the United States a sound paper currency, which the expanding economy needed.

OPPOSITION TO PAPER Although the Bank had strong support in the business community, workers complained that they were often paid in **depreciated** state banknotes. Such notes could be redeemed for only a portion of their face value, a practice that in effect cheated workers out of part of their wages. Those workers called for a "hard money" currency of only gold and silver. Hard-money advocates viewed bankers and financiers as profiteers who manipulated the paper money system to enrich themselves at the expense of honest, hardworking farmers and laborers.

The Clash between Jackson and Biddle

Jackson's own experiences left him with a deep distrust of banks and paper money. In 1804 his Tennessee land speculations had brought him to the brink of bankruptcy, from which it took years of painful struggle to free himself. Reflecting on his personal situation, he became convinced that banks and paper money threatened to corrupt the Republic.

As president, Jackson called for reform of the banking system from time to time, but Biddle refused even to consider curbing the Bank's powers. Already distracted by the nullification controversy, Jackson warned Biddle not to inject the bank issue into the 1832 campaign. When Biddle went ahead and applied for a renewal of the Bank's charter in 1832, four years early, Jackson was furious. "The Bank is trying to kill me," he stormed to Van Buren, "but I will kill it."

JACKSON'S VETO Despite the president's opposition, Congress passed a recharter bill in the summer of 1832. Immediately Jackson vetoed it as unconstitutional, rejecting

Chief Justice Marshall's ruling in *McCulloch v. Maryland* (1819) that Congress had the right to establish the Bank. Condemning the Bank as an agent of special privilege, the president pledged to protect "the humble members of society–the farmer, mechanics, and laborers." The message completely ignored the Bank's vital services in the economy.

The Bank Destroyed

When Congress failed to override Jackson's veto, the recharter of the Bank became a central issue of the 1832 campaign. Jackson's opponent was Henry Clay, a National Republican who eagerly accepted the financial support of Biddle and the national bank. Clay went down to defeat, and once reelected, Jackson was determined to destroy the Bank. A private corporation should not possess the power to influence government policy and the economy, he believed. And he was justly incensed over the Bank's heavy-handed attempt to influence the election.

REMOVAL OF THE DEPOSITS To cripple the Bank, the president simply ordered all the government's federal deposits withdrawn. Because such an act clearly violated federal law, Jackson was forced to transfer one secretary of the Treasury and fire another before he finally found in Roger Taney someone willing to take the job and carry out the edict. Taney (pronounced "Taw-ney") began drawing against the government's funds to pay its debts while depositing new revenues in selected state banks.

Biddle fought back by deliberately precipitating a brief financial panic in 1833. "Go to Biddle," Jackson snapped to businesspeople seeking relief. "I never will restore the deposits. I never will recharter the United States Bank, or sign a charter for any other bank." Eventually Biddle had to relent, and Jackson's victory was complete. When the Bank's charter expired in 1836, no national banking system replaced it. Instead, Jackson continued depositing federal revenues in selected state banks. Democrats controlled a large majority of these "pet banks."

Jackson's Impact on the Presidency

STRENGTHENING OF PRESIDENTIAL POWERS Jackson approached the end of his administration in triumph. He had seen Indian removal nearly to completion; he had confounded the nullifiers; and he had destroyed "Monster Bank." In the process, Jackson immeasurably enlarged the power of the presidency. "The President is the direct representative of the American people," he lectured the Senate when it opposed him. "He was elected by the people, and is responsible to them." With this declaration, Jackson redefined the character of the presidential office and its relationship to the people.

Jackson also converted the veto into an effective presidential power. During his two terms in office he vetoed 12 bills, compared with only 9 for all previous presidents combined. And whereas his predecessors had vetoed bills only on strict constitutional grounds, Jackson felt free to block laws simply

Biddle and Jackson Take the Gloves Off

Daniel Webster and Henry Clay, allies of Biddle, stand in his corner.

Can you identify this future president? What does he mean, "hit him in the breadbasket, it will make him throw up his deposits"?

This frontiersman bears the name of "Joe Tammany." The members of the original Tammany Society of New York rejected the aristocratic philosophy of the Federalist Party.

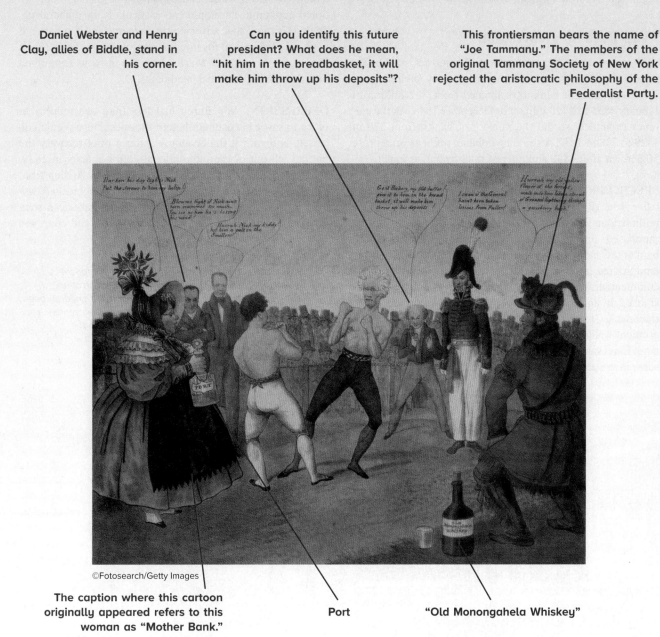

©Fotosearch/Getty Images

The caption where this cartoon originally appeared refers to this woman as "Mother Bank."

Port

"Old Monongahela Whiskey"

By their nature cartoons deal in visual symbols; to be accessible to their readers, the symbols cannot be subtle. For present-day viewers, however, some decoding is needed; and historians draw on their knowledge of the period to make sense of the symbols. This 1834 cartoon pits President Andrew Jackson (in black tights) against Nicholas Biddle in a bare-knuckled boxing match. Both the woman holding the bottle of port and the frontiersman (a cat on his hat, no less!) look ridiculous. But the cartoon definitely favors one of the fighters. Can you suggest several details that are tip-offs to the artist's point of view?

THINKING CRITICALLY

One key detail revolves around what the supporters are drinking. Why would it matter whether one drank port or whiskey? Why draw Jackson facing the audience and Biddle with his back to us? What are the larger cultural values at the center of the cartoon's message?

because he thought them bad policy. The threat of such action became an effective way to shape legislation to his liking, which fundamentally strengthened the power of the president over Congress. The development of the modern presidency began with Andrew Jackson.

"Van Ruin's" Depression

With the controls of the national bank removed, state banks rapidly expanded the amount of paper money in circulation. The total value of banknotes jumped from $82 million in January 1835 to $120 million in December 1836. As the currency expanded, so did the number of banks: from 329 in 1829 to 788 in 1837. A spiraling **inflation** set in as prices rose 50 percent after 1830 and interest rates by half as much.

SPECIE CIRCULAR As prices rose sharply, so did speculative fever. By 1836 land sales, which had been only $2.6 million four years earlier, approached $25 million. Buyers purchased almost all these lands entirely on credit with banknotes, many of which had little value. Settlers seeking land poured into the Southwest, and as one observer wryly commented, "under this stimulating process prices rose like smoke." In an attempt to slow the economy, Jackson issued the Specie Circular in July 1836, which decreed that the government would accept only specie for the purchase of public land. Land sales drastically declined, but the speculative pressures in the economy were already too great.

WHIG PARTY During Jackson's second term, his opponents had come together in a new party, the Whigs. Led by Henry Clay they charged that "King Andrew I" had dangerously concentrated power in the presidency. The Whigs also embraced Clay's "American System," designed to spur national economic development, particularly manufacturing. To do this the Whigs advocated a protective tariff, a national bank, and federal aid for internal improvements. In 1836 the Democrats nominated Martin Van Buren, who triumphed over three Whig sectional candidates.

DEPRESSION Van Buren had less than two months in office to savor his triumph before the speculative mania collapsed, and with it the economy. After a brief recovery the bottom fell out of the international cotton market in 1839, and the country entered a serious depression. Arising from causes that were worldwide, the depression demonstrated how deeply the market economy had penetrated American society. Thousands of workers were unemployed, and countless

| This Whig cartoon blames the Democratic Party for the depression that began during Van Buren's administration. Barefoot workers go unemployed, and women and children beg and sleep in the streets. Depositors clamor for their money from a bank that has suspended specie payments, while the pawnbroker and liquor store do a thriving business and the sheriff rounds up debtors.

businesses failed. Nationally wages fell 30 to 50 percent. "Business of all kinds is completely at a stand," wrote one business leader in 1840, "and the whole body politic sick and infirm, and calling aloud for a remedy."

The Whigs' Triumph

FIRST MODERN PRESIDENTIAL CAMPAIGN With the nation stuck in the worst depression of the century, the Whigs approached the election of 1840 in high spirits. To oppose Van Buren, they turned to William Henry Harrison, the military leader who had won fame defeating the Shawnee Indians at Tippecanoe. Using the democratic electioneering techniques that Jackson's supporters had first perfected, they portrayed Harrison as a man of the people while painting Van Buren as an aristocrat who wore a corset, ate off gold plates with silver spoons, and used cologne. Shades of Franklin Plummer!

Whig rallies featured hard cider and log cabins to reinforce Harrison's image as a man of the people. Born into one of Virginia's most aristocratic families, he lived in a 16-room mansion in Ohio. But the Whig campaign, by portraying the election as a contest between aristocracy and democracy, was perfectly attuned to the prevailing national spirit.

ELECTION OF 1840

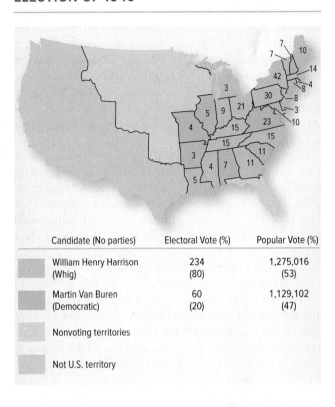

Candidate (No parties)	Electoral Vote (%)	Popular Vote (%)
William Henry Harrison (Whig)	234 (80)	1,275,016 (53)
Martin Van Buren (Democratic)	60 (20)	1,129,102 (47)
Nonvoting territories		
Not U.S. territory		

Winners and Losers in Jacksonian America

WINNERS	WHY	LOSERS	WHY
Ordinary white men	Expanding franchise; direct election of presidents		
Martin Van Buren	Epitomized the new professional politician; won the presidency	John Quincy Adams	Estranged from the new political culture and refused to become a party leader; lost the presidency to Jackson
Southern speculators and farmers	Removal opened up land once owned by the Indians	Native Americans east of the Mississippi	Jackson's support for removal forced them off their lands.
Southern masters, northern whites	Democrats' support for slavery, hostility to black rights	Free blacks and slaves	Democrats' support for slavery, hostility to black rights, growing racism in white society
Federal officeholders	Democrats' support for the spoils system	Southern supporters of nullification	Jackson's opposition to nullification and his compromise tariff
Workers who advocated a "hard money" currency and opposed the Second Bank of the United States	Before the Second Bank was abolished, workers often received their pay in depreciated state bank notes.	Nicholas Biddle, Henry Clay, and businessmen who supported the Second Bank of the United States	Jackson's determination to destroy the Bank

(top) Source: Library of Congress, Prints and Photographs Division [LC-USZC4-6691];
(bottom) Source: Library of Congress, Prints and Photographs Division [LC-USZC4-6691]

WOMEN AND THE CAMPAIGN Both parties used parades, barbecues, liberty pole raisings, party songs, and mass meetings to stir up enthusiasm. Deeming themselves the party of morality, Whigs appealed directly to women for support, urging them to become politically informed in order to instruct their husbands. Women attended Whig rallies, conducted meetings, made speeches, and wrote campaign pamphlets, many activities that before had been solely the duties of men. Democrats had no choice but to eventually follow suit.

Just as the Panic of 1819 had roused the voters to action, the depression and the two parties' response to it sparked mass interest. The result was a record turnout, as some 900,000 new voters were mobilized between 1836 and 1840 and nearly four-fifths of the eligible voters went to the polls. Although the popular vote was fairly close (Harrison led by about 150,000 votes out of 2.4 million cast), in the Electoral College Harrison won an easy victory, 234 to 60.

The "log cabin" campaign marked the final transition from the deferential politics of the Federalist era to the egalitarian politics that had emerged in the wake of the Panic of 1819. As the *Democratic Review* conceded after the Whigs' victory in 1840, "We have taught them how to conquer us."

 REVIEW

Why did Jackson oppose the Second Bank of the United States?

THE JACKSONIAN PARTY SYSTEM

THE SOCIAL AND ECONOMIC STRAINS of an expanding nation directly shaped the new political system. Whigs and Democrats held different attitudes toward the changes brought about by the market, banks, and commerce.

Democrats, Whigs, and the Market

DEMOCRATIC IDEOLOGY The Democrats tended to view society as a continuing conflict between "the people"—farmers, planters, and workers—and a set of greedy aristocrats. The last group was not Europe's landed aristocrats, of course, but a "paper money aristocracy" of bankers and investors, who manipulated the banking system for profit. For Democrats, the Bank War became a battle to restore the old Jeffersonian republic with its values of simplicity, frugality, hard work, and independence.

Jackson understood the dangers that private banks posed to a democratic society. Yet Democrats, in effect, wanted the rewards of the market without sacrificing the features of a simple agrarian republic. They wanted the wealth and goods that the market offered without the competitive, changing society, the complex dealings, the dominance of urban centers, and the loss of independence that came with it.

WHIG IDEOLOGY Whigs were more comfortable with the market. They envisioned no conflict between farmers and mechanics on the one hand and businesspeople and bankers on the other. Economic growth would benefit everyone by creating jobs, stimulating demand for agricultural products, and expanding opportunity. The government's responsibility was to provide a well-regulated economy that guaranteed opportunity for citizens of ability. In such an economy, banks and corporations were not only useful but necessary as well. Whigs and Democrats also disagreed over how active government should be. Despite Andrew Jackson's inclination to be a strong president, Democrats as a rule believed in limited government. Government's role in the economy was to promote competition by destroying monopolies and special privileges.

In *Charles River Bridge v. Warren Bridge* (1837) the Supreme Court strengthened the vision of an expanding capitalistic society undergirded by free competition. At issue was whether in authorizing construction of a free bridge Massachusetts violated the rights of the owners of a nearby toll bridge. Declaring that the public interest was the overriding concern, Chief Justice Roger Taney, whom Jackson had appointed to succeed John Marshall, struck down the idea of implied monopolies. The Court thus sought to promote equality of opportunity and economic progress.

In keeping with this philosophy of limited government, Democrats also rejected the idea that moral beliefs were the proper sphere of government action. Religion and politics, they believed, should be kept clearly separate, and they generally opposed humanitarian legislation as an interference with personal freedom. But they supported debtor relief, which in their view curbed the wealthy aristocrats who tyrannized the common worker.

WHIG BELIEF IN ACTIVE GOVERNMENT By contrast, the Whigs viewed government power positively. They believed that it should be used to protect individual rights and public liberty and that it had a special role when individual effort was ineffective. By regulating the economy and competition, the government could ensure equal opportunity. Indeed, for Whigs the concept that the government would promote the general welfare went beyond the economy. Northern Whigs in particular also believed that government power should be used to foster the moral welfare of the country. They were much more likely to favor temperance or anti-slavery legislation and aid to education. Whigs portrayed themselves not only as the party of prosperity but also as the party of respectability and proper behavior.

The Social Bases of the Two Parties

In some ways the social makeup of the two parties was similar. To be competitive Whigs and Democrats both had to have significant support among farmers, the largest group in society, and workers. Neither party could carry an election by appealing exclusively to the rich or the poor.

ATTITUDES TOWARD THE MARKET ECONOMY But the Whigs enjoyed disproportionate strength among the business and commercial classes, especially following the Bank War. Whigs appealed to planters who needed credit to finance their cotton and rice trade in the world market, to farmers who were eager to sell their surpluses, and to workers who wished to improve their social position. Democrats attracted farmers isolated from the market or uncomfortable with it, workers alienated from the emerging industrial system, and rising entrepreneurs who wanted to break monopolies and open the economy to newcomers like them. The Whigs were strongest in the towns, cities, and rural areas that were fully integrated into the market economy, whereas Democrats dominated areas of semi-subsistence farming that were more isolated and languishing economically. Attitude toward the market, rather than economic position, was more important in determining party affiliation.

RELIGIOUS AND ETHNIC FACTORS Religion and ethnic identities also shaped partisanship. As the self-proclaimed "party of respectability," Whigs attracted the support of high-status native-born church groups, including the Congregationalists and the Unitarians in New England and Presbyterians and Episcopalians elsewhere. The party also attracted immigrant groups that most easily merged into the dominant Anglo-Protestant culture, such as the English, Welsh, and Scots. Democrats, in contrast, recruited more Germans and Irish, whose more lenient observance of the Sabbath and (among Catholics) use of parochial schools generated native-born hostility. Democrats appealed to the lower-status Baptists and Methodists, particularly in states where they earlier had been subjected to legal disadvantages. Both parties also attracted freethinkers and the unchurched, but the Democrats had the advantage, because they resisted demands for temperance and sabbatarian laws, such as the prohibition of Sunday travel. In states where they could vote, African Americans were solidly Whig in reaction to the Democratic Party's strong racism and hostility to black rights.

Source: Library of Congress, Prints and Photographs Division [LC-USZ62-109977]

| *Whigs drew strongly from the business and commercial classes who were eager to improve themselves. This daguerreotype is said to be of the merchant Cyrus Field, a Whig with a strong commercial vision who partnered with other entrepreneurs to lay a telegraph cable across the Atlantic.*

 REVIEW

What were the major differences between the Whigs and the Democrats?

PUTTING HISTORY IN GLOBAL CONTEXT

IN THE AMERICAS AND in Europe the rise of democratic governance and the spread of market economies developed in similar ways over the same half century. Andrew Jackson's triumph, with the common people trampling the White House furniture, was only the latest in a series of upheavals stretching back to the American and French Revolutions of the eighteenth century. Latin America, too, experienced democratic revolutions. From 1808 to 1821 Spain's American provinces declared their independence one by one, taking inspiration from the writings of Jefferson and Thomas Paine as well as the French *Declaration of the Rights of Man*. Democracy did not always root itself in the aftermath of these revolutions, but democratic ideology remained a powerful social catalyst.

In the United States, the parallel growth of national markets and democratic institutions combined similar ups and downs. If Jackson championed the cause of the "common people," he also led the movement to remove Indians from their lands. The poorest white American might vote for "Old Hickory" and yet reassure himself that African Americans could never rise as high as he did in an increasingly racist society. And the advance of the market created social strains, including the increasing gap between the richest and the poorest.

Still, Americans were evolving a system of democratic politics to deal with the conflicts of the new order. The new national parties, like the new markets, became essential structures uniting the American nation. They advanced an ideology of equality and opportunity, competed vigorously with one another, and involved large numbers of ordinary Americans in the political process. Along with the market, democracy became an integral part of American life.

CHAPTER SUMMARY

Beginning in the 1820s the United States experienced a democratic revolution that was identified with Andrew Jackson.

- The rise of democracy was stimulated by the Panic of 1819, which caused Americans to look toward both politicians and the government to address their needs.

- The new political culture of democracy included the use of conventions to make nominations, the adoption of white manhood suffrage, and the acceptance of political parties as essential for the working of the constitutional system.

- The new politics had distinct limits, however. Women were not given the vote, and racism intensified.

  ► The eastern Indian tribes were forced to move to new lands west of the Mississippi River.

  ► Free African Americans were subject to increasingly harsh discrimination and exclusion.

- Andrew Jackson came to personify the new democratic culture. Through his forceful leadership, he expanded the powers of the presidency.

  ► Jackson threatened to use force against South Carolina when it tried to nullify the federal tariff.

  ► In response to John C. Calhoun's theory of nullification, nationalists advanced the idea of the perpetual Union.

  ► Jackson vetoed a bill to recharter the Second Bank of the United States and destroyed the Bank by removing its federal deposits.

- Under President Martin Van Buren, the nation entered a severe depression.

- Capitalizing on hard times and employing the democratic techniques pioneered by the Democrats, the Whigs gained national power in 1840.

- By 1840 the two parties had developed different ideologies.

  ► The Whigs were more comfortable with the mechanisms of the market and linked commerce with progress.

  ► The Democrats were uneasy about the market and favored limited government.

Digging Deeper

The most comprehensive reinterpretation of antebellum political history from Jackson to Lincoln is Sean Wilentz, *The Rise of American Democracy* (2005). A contrasting interpretation of the period, more sympathetic to the Whigs, can be found in Daniel Walker Howe, *What Hath God Wrought* (2007). For a broader perspective on the evolution of American political culture throughout the nineteenth century, see Glenn C. Altschuler and Stuart M. Blumin, *Rude Republic* (2000). A good interpretation of Jacksonian politics is Harry L. Watson, *Liberty and Power* (1990), and important discussions of party ideologies include Marvin Meyers, *The Jacksonian Persuasion* (1957); Daniel Walker Howe, *The Political Culture of the American Whigs* (1979); and Lawrence Frederick Kohl, *The Politics of Individualism* (1988). For the history of the Whig Party, the book to read is Michael F. Holt, *The Rise and Fall of the American Whig Party* (1999). Two important books treat broader themes: Brian Balogh's *A Government Out of Sight* (2005) explores the ways in which citizens experienced the authority of the national government, while Ronald P. Formisano's *For the People* (2012) traces the rise of populist movements.

The best account of the nullification crisis is still William W. Freehling, *Prelude to Civil War* (1966); and Robert V. Remini offers a succinct analysis of the banking controversy in *Andrew Jackson and the Bank War* (1967). Paul Goodman, *Towards a Christian Republic* (1988), is the most valuable study of Anti-Masonry. A useful overview of the free black community in the North is James Oliver Horton and Lois E. Horton, *In Hope of Liberty* (1997). For the hardening of racist attitudes among whites, see Bruce Dain, *A Hideous Monster of the Mind* (2003); and for a full treatment of white and black involvement in the colonization movement, see Richard S. Newman, *The Transformation of American Abolitionism* (2002). On Indian removal in the South, see John Ehle, *Trail of Tears* (1997); and Robert V. Remini, *Andrew Jackson and His Indian Wars* (2001).

12 Afire with Faith

1820–1850

Bursting with energy and enthusiasm, Methodists head toward a camp meeting in 1819. At a time when the nation had lurched into an economic "panic," the bonds of unity created by this revival and others like it brought a sense of stability and peace amid widespread change. Such revivals also motivated believers to create a better world around them.

Source: Library of Congress, Prints and Photographs Division [LC-USZC4-3264]

>> **An American Story**

THE BEECHERS AND THE KINGDOM OF GOD

In 1826 the Reverend Lyman Beecher was probably the most celebrated minister of the Republic, and the pulpit of Hanover Street Church was his to command. Beecher looked and spoke like a pious farmer, but every Sunday he was transformed when he mounted the pulpit of Boston's most imposing church. From there he would blaze forth denunciations of dancing, drinking, dueling, and "infidelity," all the while punctuating his sermon with pump-handle strokes of the right hand.

©Historical/Corbis/Getty Images

| *Lyman Beecher* (center) *with his family in 1855. Catharine and Isabella hold his hand; Harriet and Henry are at far right.*

Nor were Beecher's ambitions small. His goal was nothing less than to bring the kingdom of Christ to the nation and the world. Like many ministers, Beecher had studied the intriguing final book of the New Testament, the Revelation to John. The Revelation foretold in the latter days of Earth a glorious **millennium**—a thousand years of peace and triumph—when the saints would rule and evil would be banished from the world. Beecher was convinced that the long-awaited millennium might well begin in the United States.

Beecher's boundless energy went into more than devout preaching. He also raised a family of 11 children, every one of whom he prayed would lead in bringing the kingdom of God to America. He loved to wrestle on the floor with his sons, climb the highest trees, or go "berrying" with his daughters.

Still, the religious dimension of their lives was constant. The family attended two services on Sunday, a weekly prayer meeting, and a monthly "concert of prayer," where the devout met to pray for the conversion of the world. To usher in that kingdom, Beecher joined other Protestant ministers in supporting a host of religious reforms and missionary efforts. By 1820 voluntary organizations were blanketing the United States with tracts and Bibles, sending missionaries to every corner of the globe, promoting Sunday schools for children, ministering to sailors and the poor, reforming drunkards, and stopping business on the Sabbath. To Beecher, the organizations constituting this loosely united "Benevolent Empire" were signs of the coming kingdom.

As the new pastor at Hanover Street, Beecher also directed his artillery on a host of social evils. With scorn he attacked Unitarians, whose liberal, rational creed rejected the divinity of Jesus. In Boston Unitarians were mainly upper class and cultured. But Beecher also highlighted the "sinful" pastimes of the lower class: playing cards, gambling, and drinking. And he denounced Roman Catholic priests and nuns as superstitious, devious agents of "Antichrist."

These efforts at "moral reform" antagonized many immigrants and other working folk who enjoyed their lotteries or liquor. In disdain they referred to Hanover Street Church, with its imposing stone tower, as Beecher's "Stone Jug"— where its pastor drank most deeply of his religious spirits. In 1830 a blaze broke out in the basement and spread upward. Along with a mob, firefighters rushed to the scene—but did little more than watch the blaze and make jokes about "Old Beecher" and "hell-fire." If the reverend had little respect for their ways, they had little respect for his. The fiery heat cracked the stone tower top to bottom, and the church burned into ruins. Beecher put a brave face on matters. "Well, my jug's broke; just been to see it," he reported cheerfully the morning after. But the setback was sobering. Beecher was only beginning to learn that spiritual fires, as much as real ones, could spread in unpredictable ways. What did it mean, after all, to make a heaven on earth? Even the devout found it hard to agree. <<

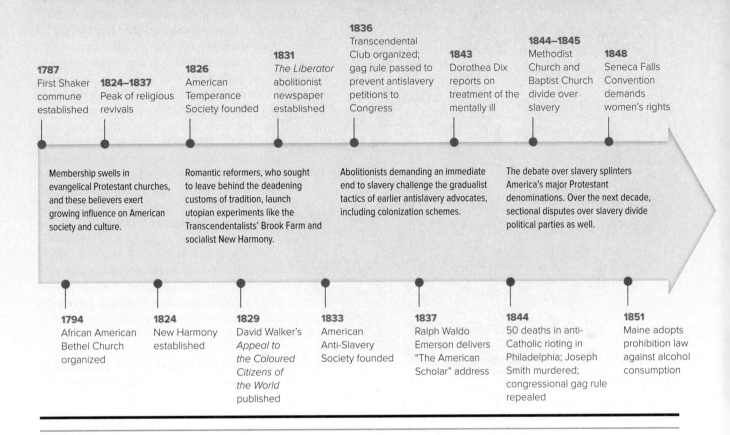

1787
First Shaker commune established

1824–1837
Peak of religious revivals

1826
American Temperance Society founded

1831
The Liberator abolitionist newspaper established

1836
Transcendental Club organized; gag rule passed to prevent antislavery petitions to Congress

1843
Dorothea Dix reports on treatment of the mentally ill

1844–1845
Methodist Church and Baptist Church divide over slavery

1848
Seneca Falls Convention demands women's rights

Membership swells in evangelical Protestant churches, and these believers exert growing influence on American society and culture.

Romantic reformers, who sought to leave behind the deadening customs of tradition, launch utopian experiments like the Transcendentalists' Brook Farm and socialist New Harmony.

Abolitionists demanding an immediate end to slavery challenge the gradualist tactics of earlier antislavery advocates, including colonization schemes.

The debate over slavery splinters America's major Protestant denominations. Over the next decade, sectional disputes over slavery divide political parties as well.

1794
African American Bethel Church organized

1824
New Harmony established

1829
David Walker's *Appeal to the Coloured Citizens of the World* published

1833
American Anti-Slavery Society founded

1837
Ralph Waldo Emerson delivers "The American Scholar" address

1844
50 deaths in anti-Catholic rioting in Philadelphia; Joseph Smith murdered; congressional gag rule repealed

1851
Maine adopts prohibition law against alcohol consumption

THE TRANSFORMATION OF AMERICAN EVANGELICALISM

LYMAN BEECHER EMBODIED THE SPIRIT of antebellum evangelical Protestantism. At the core of evangelicalism was the conviction that divine grace brought about a new birth, one that enabled belief in Jesus Christ. That conviction also committed the individual convert to reforming his or her own vices as well as the faults of others. But evangelicalism changed over the course of Beecher's long life. As it did, so did its influence on Christian believers. Early-nineteenth-century evangelical leaders such as Beecher sought to convert individuals through revivals and then to turn their energies toward reforming others through the voluntary associations of the Benevolent Empire. Their conservative aim, as he expressed it, was to restore America to "the moral government of God."

But the next generation of evangelical leaders, Beecher's children among them, sought not merely to convert individuals to Christianity but also to reform the most fundamental institutions structuring American society—slavery, the family, and the political and legal subordination of women. By the

1840s they were joined by many other believers in faiths both secular and religious—Unitarians and Transcendentalists, Shakers and socialists, Oneidans and Mormons. All were afire with the faith that they could radically remake the United States.

Before about 1800 most American evangelicals embraced the doctrines of Calvinism. Calvinists believed that God had determined which individuals were destined to be damned or saved and that no human effort could alter those eternal fates. They believed that individuals could do nothing to bring about their own salvation.

But such propositions seemed increasingly unreasonable to the proud American heirs of a revolution that celebrated human equality, free will, and reason. By the beginning of the nineteenth century a growing number of evangelicals moved toward a new outlook. It did not deny the sinfulness of human nature and the necessity of divine grace for salvation. But it did grant more power to free will and human effort. That more democratic belief—that all men and women might choose and win salvation, that each individual should take an active responsibility for redemption—came to characterize the religious views of most evangelicals among the ranks of Congregationalists, Presbyterians, Baptists, and

Source: Library of Congress, Prints and Photographs Division [LC-USZC4-2671]

| *In* The Way of Good and Evil, *devout Christians are all helped on the path to millennial perfection* (right) *by the virtues of family, religion, education, and hard work. Sinners on the left, however, take the path of disobedience, intemperance, and lying—straight to hell.*

FINNEY'S NEW MEASURES Like George Whitefield before him, Finney had an entrancing voice that carried great distances. His power over an audience was such that when he described the descent of a sinner into hell, those in the back of the hall rose to witness the final plunge. His success also resulted from his use of special techniques—"the new measures."

These methods of encouraging conversion had been developed during the frontier revivals of the Second Great Awakening. Finney's contribution was to popularize the techniques and use them systematically. He held "protracted meetings" night after night to build up excitement. Speaking boldly and bluntly, he prayed for sinners by name, encouraged women to testify in public gatherings, and placed those struggling with conversion on the "anxious bench" at the front of the church. Whereas the leaders of the first Great Awakening had looked on revivals as god-sent outpourings of grace, Finney viewed them as the consequence of human agency. "A revival is not a miracle," he coolly declared, "it is a purely scientific result of the right use of constituted means."

Like other evangelical revivalists of his day, Finney looked to help individuals undergo an emotionally wrenching conversion experience and be reborn. In doing so, he left little role for the deity in the drama of human deliverance. He endorsed free will and preached that all men and women who wanted to could be saved. To those anxious about their salvation, he thundered, "Do it!"

With salvation within reach of every individual, what might be in store for society at large? "If the church would do her duty," Finney confidently predicted, "the millennium may come in this country in three years."

Methodists. Over the course of the Second Great Awakening, their more optimistic view of human potential fostered revivals and sparked ambitious programs for reforming individuals and society.

Charles Grandison Finney and Modern Revivalism

The man who embodied this transformed evangelicalism was Charles Grandison Finney, the founder of modern revivalism. In 1821, as a young man, Finney experienced a soul-shattering conversion that led him to give up his law practice to become an itinerant minister. Eventually he was ordained in the Presbyterian Church, although he lacked any formal theological training. He first attracted national attention when in the mid-1820s and early 1830s he conducted a series of spectacular revivals in the booming port cities along the new Erie Canal.

©Encyclopaedia Britannica/UIG/REX/Shutterstock

| *Charles Grandison Finney*

The Appeal of Evangelicalism

The revivals of the Second Great Awakening drew converts from every segment of American society. Men, women and children, whites, African Americans and Indians, northerners and southerners, slave and free—all joined evangelical churches in unprecedented numbers during the opening decades of the nineteenth century. Evangelicalism proved a potent and protean faith, one that could be adapted to answer both the spiritual strivings and needs and the worldly anxieties and sufferings of diverse groups.

MEN AND THE MARKET In the North, middle-class white men under intense pressure from the

CENTRAL PART OF BUFFALO STREET, ROCHESTER, N. Y.

The view shows the central part of the city, near the junction of State and Exchange streets, with Buffalo street. The spire of the Court House is seen on the right; part of the Methodist church, and other public buildings, on the left.

©Sarin Images/The Granger Collection, New York

| In the winter of 1830–1831, Charles Finney preached frequently in Rochester, the nation's first inland boomtown.

market economy—lawyers, merchants, and manufacturers—found in evangelicalism's celebration of human ability the assurance that they could contend with the uncertainties in their lives. The emerging urban working class, struggling to stay afloat in the face of industrialization, found in evangelicalism's moral code a discipline that called for self-control and self-improvement. Rural southerners—planters and farmers alike—found their mastery over wives, children, and blacks confirmed by evangelical teachings. And white men of all classes, in North and South, found that church membership and the reputation it conferred for sobriety, honesty, and respectability often helped them to get ahead in a rootless, competitive society.

AFRICAN AMERICAN CHURCHES Blacks, both free and enslaved, joined antebellum churches in impressive numbers, even as they continued to forge a distinctive and liberating faith by infusing evangelicalism with African religious traditions. Sharpening racial tensions led to the formation of black Methodist and Baptist churches in a number of northern and southern cities. The most important was the African Methodist Episcopal (AME) Church, organized at Philadelphia in 1816. Richard Allen, a former Delaware slave who had bought his freedom, became that denomination's first bishop. Growing fears for the

security of slavery caused southern white communities, especially in the Deep South, to suppress independent black churches after 1820. But black evangelical churches continued to grow in the North and to serve as organizing centers for the swelling African American opposition to slavery. By 1856 the AME Church boasted some 20,000 members.

Despite the prominence of men as both clerical and lay leaders in the Second Great Awakening, it was women—black and white, northern and southern—whose presence dominated antebellum revivals and churches. In most revivals, female converts outnumbered males by about three to two. Usually the first convert in a family was a woman, and many men who converted were related to women who had come forward earlier.

WOMEN, MARRIAGE, AND CONVERSION Women played an important role in the Awakening partly because of changes in their own social universe. Instead of parents arranging the marriages of their children, couples were beginning to wed more often on the basis of affection. Under such conditions, a woman's prospects for marriage became less certain, and in older areas such as New England and the coastal South, the migration of so many young men to the West compounded this uncertainty. Yet marriage was deemed

PLEAS FOR AND AGAINST FOREIGN MISSIONS

Gardiner Spring, a New York Presbyterian minister, endorsed missions in 1820 with an urgency that appealed to many Americans. But not everyone was persuaded by evangelical ambitions, and among the doubters was the anonymous author of an essay published the same year in Philadelphia.

DOCUMENT 1
For Foreign Missions: Gardiner Spring

Men are not apt enough to lay out their plans for extended action. In this respect, how much wiser are the men of the world, in their generation, than the children of light? How magnificent the plans, how unwearied the watchfulness, how persevering the efforts after worldly aggrandizement? How ardent the hopes, how inspirited, how confident the expectation of men in the eager pursuit of the meat that perisheth, and the crown that fadeth away? Ah, what a weight of reproach falls upon the head of that Christian who can quietly see the interests of his Master's kingdom languish for the want of determined exertion? "EXPECT GREAT THINGS—ATTEMPT GREAT THINGS" should be the sacred and unalterable motto of men in every department of active labour, who have consecrated themselves to Jesus Christ. . . .

There is mighty work yet to be accomplished for the redemption of fallen men. Though a few sections of the globe have been delivered from their galling manacles, whole kingdoms are to the present hour in the bonds of iniquity. "Darkness covereth the earth, and gross darkness the people." According to the most judicious calculations, the population of the earth may be computed at eight hundred millions. . . . The proportion of these who bear the Christian name, has been judged to be,

In Asia	2,000,000
Africa	3,000,000
Europe	177,000,000
America	18,000,000
In all	200,000,000,

leaving six hundred millions who are destitute of the gospel. Let any man whom "the day spring from on high hath visited," survey these regions of darkness and earth without emotion, if he can. Eighteen hundred years have passed away since the blood of propitiation was shed for the sins of the world, and three-fourths of the world are at the present hour ignorant of the stupendous sacrifice [of Jesus Christ]. The single empire of China contains more immortal beings, than there are expectants of a happy immortality on the face of the whole earth. . . .

One would think there were enough in the contemplation of pagan pollution and wretchedness, to prove an effectual excitement to missionary exertion. . . .

If the world we inhabit is not under the obscure dominion of chance, but the direction of a wise and holy Governor, a new era is one day to open upon the earth. Moralists have taught, and poets have sung, that this iron age is to pass away, and notwithstanding this dreadful perspective, that the golden age of light and love is yet to stretch its splendours from pole to pole. . . . Nor is it difficult to see that these predictions are in a train of accomplishment. Long as the event has been delayed, long as the prince of darkness has reigned almost without molestation; the kingdom of Christ even now begins to extend its authority, and the glories of that kingdom to look toward their consummation. Within these last eight and twenty years, God has been bringing into view, more distinctly than ever, his own omnipotent hand, in governing the world for the sake of the church. . . .

Is it not high time for every rational man to say, I lay it down as a maxim of my life, and will hereafter regard it as one of the principles of my conduct, that the world is to be converted to Christ?

Source: Spring, Gardiner, *Memoirs of the Rev. Samuel Mills...* New York, NY: Evangelical Missionary Society, 1820, 242–247. Available online.

DOCUMENT 2
Against Foreign Missions (Anonymous)

What advantage would it be to the heathen, if they were all to take upon them such a religion as now prevails in those called Christian lands? Is it probable they would be any better? Is there any less integrity or uprightness among them, than among ourselves? Let us look at home; and let those who account themselves spiritual physicians, heal their own maladies, and correct the disorders in their own borders, before they undertake to cure others in distant lands, and set them right.

Are not many of those sent to propagate christianity among the heathen, mere men of the world, who differ as greatly from the apostles in their pride, as they do in the expense with which they undertake to propagate it? The apostles were humble men; and instead of being borne about on the shoulders of their fellow beings in splendid *palanquins,* like some of our modern missionaries to the east, they went about on foot. Thousands of money were not furnished them to preach among the heathen. . . .

People, in general, come into these missionary undertakings much in the same manner as they come into the fashions of the time; and in order to keep up one's popularity, and to be esteemed of some account it is necessary to take an active part in, or to applaud them. I feel no pleasure in making these remarks—I know they must give offence, and endanger the publication in which they may be inserted, but I am sensible that something ought to be said on the subject with all plainness. . . . Indeed, I seriously fear that the spirit and the way in which the missionary and other great undertakings, now going forward in christendom, are carried on, is very little better, or will accomplish very little more in behalf of true Christianity in the end, than the Croisades [Crusades] or holy wars of former times.

Source: Anonymous, "A Candid Address to Christians in General," *Reformer,* January 1, 1820, 6ff. Available through American Periodical Series Online.

THINKING CRITICALLY

What arguments and emotional appeals did Spring use to instill in his readers a devotion to the cause of missions? In what ways did he try to persuade them that the conversion of the world to Christianity was an achievable goal? Why did the anonymous author oppose foreign missions? What did he imply by suggesting that those missions could produce the same negative outcome as the Crusades of the Middle Ages?

important for a woman's happiness, and it remained essential for her economic security.

The unpredictability of these social circumstances drew young women toward religion. Women between the ages of 12 and 25 were especially susceptible to conversion. Joining a church heightened a young woman's feeling of initiative and gave her a sense of purpose. By establishing respectability and widening her social circle of friends, church membership also enhanced her chances of marriage. And before and after marriage, it opened opportunities to participate in benevolent and reform associations that took women outside the domestic circle and into a realm of public activism.

The Significance of the Second Great Awakening

As a result of the Second Great Awakening, the dominant form of Christianity in America became evangelical Protestantism. Membership in the major Protestant churches—Congregational, Presbyterian, Baptist, and Methodist—soared during the first half of the nineteenth century. By 1840 an estimated half of the adult population was connected to some church, with the Methodists emerging as the largest Protestant denomination in both the North and the South. Observers such as Alexis de Tocqueville noted the striking contrast with Europe, where adherence to Christianity declined sharply over the same decades.

INSTITUTIONAL INFLUENCE Not only their sheer numbers but also their institutional presence made evangelicals a formidable force. Their organizations to distribute tracts and Bibles, organize Sunday schools and staff missions, encourage temperance and promote Sabbath observance all operated at a national level. The only other institutions able to make such a claim were the Second Bank of the United States and the Post Office. Evangelical publications dominated the markets for both religious periodicals and books.

Few were more aware of the scope of evangelicalism's sway than Lyman Beecher. Earlier in his career, he had lamented the collapse of state-supported Congregationalist religious establishments throughout New England. But looking back in later years, he realized that the churches did not need government support to figure as powerful forces in the United States. To his delight, Beecher concluded that evangelicals had, in fact, gained "deeper influence" since disestablishment "by voluntary efforts, societies, missions, and revivals."

> ✓ **REVIEW**
>
> How did evangelical Protestants change their doctrines to appeal to new social conditions in the early decades of the nineteenth century?

REVIVALISM AND THE SOCIAL ORDER

HOW RIGHT BEECHER WAS. The revivals of the Second Great Awakening had profound and lasting consequences. Its effects went well beyond the churching of hundreds of thousands of American men, women, and children and the spectacular growth of evangelical Protestant denominations. Religious commitment fundamentally reshaped antebellum society because, to keep the fervor afire, Beecher, Finney, and their fellow revivalists channeled the energies of their converts into an array of benevolent and reform societies. But zealous evangelicals did a great deal more than teach Sunday school at home and dispatch missionaries abroad. As early as the 1820s and 1830s their activism had already significantly affected three aspects of American culture: drinking habits, ideals of women and the family, and Protestant attitudes toward a growing population of Roman Catholics.

The Temperance Movement

The temperance campaign, a reform dear to the heart of Lyman Beecher and other evangelical clergy, effected a sweeping change in the personal habits of many Americans.

Until the mid-eighteenth century most colonials (and Europeans) considered spirits an essential supplement to their diet. Liquor flowed freely at ministerial ordinations in New England towns, court days in the South, house-raisings, corn-huskings, and quilting bees on the frontier, not to mention weddings, elections, and militia musters everywhere. Colonial Americans did not condone public drunkenness, but they saw nothing amiss in the regular use of alcohol or even in occasional intoxication.

But alcohol consumption soared after the Revolution, so that by 1825 the average American over the age of 15 consumed over five gallons of distilled liquors a year, the highest level in American history and nearly triple present-day levels. Anne Royall, whose travels took her cross-country by stage, reported, "When I was in Virginia, it was too much whiskey—in Ohio, too much whiskey—in Tennessee, it is too, too much whiskey!"

SOCIAL COSTS OF DRINKING The social costs for such habits were high: broken families, abused and neglected wives and children, sickness and disability, poverty, and crime. The temperance movement undertook to eliminate these problems by curbing drinking.

Led largely by clergy, the movement at first focused on drunkenness and did not oppose moderate drinking. But in 1826 the American Temperance Society was founded, taking voluntary abstinence as its goal. During the next decade approximately 5,000 local temperance societies were founded. As the movement gained momentum, annual per capita consumption of alcohol dropped sharply. By 1845 it had fallen below two gallons a year.

Consumption of spirits in gallons

Annual Consumption of Distilled Spirits, per Capita, 1710–1920

Beginning in 1790, per capita levels of drinking steadily rose, until 1830, when the temperance movement produced a sharp decline over the next two decades.
©McGraw-Hill Education

The temperance movement lasted longer and attracted many more supporters than other reforms did. It appealed to young and old, to urban and rural residents, to workers and businesspeople. Moreover, it was one of the few reform movements with significant support in the South. Its success came partly for social reasons. Democracy necessitated sober voters; factories required sober workers. In addition, temperance attracted the upwardly mobile—professionals, small businesspeople, and skilled artisans anxious to improve their social standing. Finally, temperance advocates stressed the suffering that men inflicted on women and children, and thus the movement appealed to women as a means to defend the home and carry out their domestic mission.

Ideals of Women and the Family

Evangelicals also contributed substantially to a new ideal of womanhood, one being elaborated by the clergy and female authors in sermons, advice manuals, magazine articles, and novels during the first half of the nineteenth century. Called the "cult of **domesticity**" or "true womanhood" or "evangelical womanhood," that ideal cast wives and mothers as the "angels" of their households, the sex ideally suited to serve as dispensers of love, comfort, and moral instruction to husbands and children. The premise of that new ideal was that men and women, by their very nature, inhabited separate spheres. The rough-and-tumble world of business and

politics was the proper province of husbands and fathers, while women ruled the domestic sphere of home and family. "Love is our life our reality, business yours," Mollie Clark told one suitor.

This new ideal also held that women were by nature morally stronger and more religious than men. That view reversed the negative medieval and early modern views of women as the sinful daughters of the temptress Eve, more passionate by nature and thus less morally restrained and spiritually inclined than men. But the new ideal also held antebellum women to a higher standard of sexual purity. A man's sexual infidelity, although hardly condoned, brought no lasting shame. But a woman who engaged in sexual relations before marriage or was unfaithful afterward was threatened with everlasting disgrace. Under this new double standard, women were to be pure, passionless, and passive: they were to submerge their identities in those of their husbands.

©Stock Montage

As business affairs grew increasingly separate from the family in the nineteenth century, the middle-class home became a female domain. A woman's role as a wife and mother was to dispense love and moral guidance to her husband and her children. As this domestic scene makes clear, she was at the very center of the world of the family.

SEPARATION OF THE WORKPLACE AND HOME

Advocates of the new ideal of womanhood and the notion of separate spheres beamed their message mainly at elite and middle-class women. And that message found an impressionable audience among wives and daughters in the urbanizing Northeast. There the separation of the workplace from the home was most complete. As a result of industrialization, many men worked outside the home, while the rise of factories also led to a decline in part-time work such as spinning, which women had once performed to supplement family income. Home manufacturing was no longer essential, for, except on the frontier, families could easily purchase those articles that women previously had made, such as cloth, soap, and candles. "The transition from mother-and-daughter power to water-and-steam power," one New England minister noted, produced "a complete revolution of domestic life." This growing separation of the household from the workplace in the Northeast made it that much easier for the home to be idealized as a place of "domesticity," a haven away from the competitive, workaday world, with the mother firmly at its center.

DOMESTICITY IN EUROPE   The celebration of domesticity was not unique to the United States. The middle class became increasingly important in Europe, so that after 1850 it was culturally dominant. Employment opportunities expanded for women as industrialization accelerated, yet the social expectation among the middle class was that women would not be employed outside the home. This redefinition of women's roles was more sweeping in Europe because previously, middle-class women had left the task of child-raising largely to hired nurses and governesses. By midcentury these mothers devoted much more time to domestic duties, including rearing the children. Family size also declined, both in France and in England. The middle class was most numerous in England; indeed, the importance of the middle class in Britain during Queen Victoria's reign (1837–1901) gave these ideals the label **Victorianism**.

The Middle-Class Family in Transition

THE RISE OF PRIVACY AND SMALLER FAMILIES

As elite and middle-class homes came to be seen as havens of moral virtue, those domestic settings developed a new structure and new set of attitudes closer in spirit to those of the modern family. One basic change was the rise of privacy. The family was increasingly seen as a sheltered retreat from the outside world. In addition, the pressures to achieve success led middle-class young adults to delay marriage, since a husband was expected to have the financial means to support his wife. Smaller family size resulted, since wives, especially those among the urban middle class, began to use birth control to space children farther apart and to minimize the risks of pregnancy. In addition, it has been estimated that before 1860 one abortion was performed for every five or six live births.

With smaller families, parents could tend more carefully to their children's success. Increasingly, middle-class families took on the expense of additional education to prepare their sons for a career in business. They also frequently equalized inheritances rather than favoring the eldest son or favoring sons over daughters.

Most women in the United States did not have time to make domesticity the center of their lives. Farmers' wives and enslaved women had to work constantly, whereas lower-class families could not get by without the wages of female members. Still, some elite and middle-class women tried to live up to the new ideals, though many found the effort confining. "The great trial is that I have nothing to do," one complained. "Here I am with abundant leisure and capable, I believe, of accomplishing some good, and yet with no object on which to expend my energies."

In response to those frustrations, Lyman Beecher's eldest daughter, Catharine (who never married), made a career out of assuring women that the proper care of household and children was their sex's crucial responsibility. Like the earlier advocates of "republican motherhood" (see Chapter 8), Catharine Beecher supported women's education and argued that women exercised power as moral guardians of the nation's future. She also wrote several books on efficient home management. "There is no one thing more necessary to a housekeeper in performing her varied duties, than a habit of system and order," she told readers. "For all the time afforded us, we must give account to God."

EXPANDING PUBLIC ROLES FOR WOMEN   But many women yearned to exert moral authority outside the confines of their households, and, ironically, the new host of benevolent and reform societies allowed them that unprecedented opportunity. Devout wives and daughters, particularly those from middle-class families, flocked to these voluntary associations,

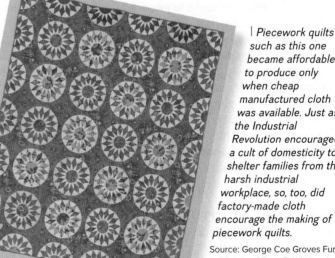

| Piecework quilts such as this one became affordable to produce only when cheap manufactured cloth was available. Just as the Industrial Revolution encouraged a cult of domesticity to shelter families from the harsh industrial workplace, so, too, did factory-made cloth encourage the making of piecework quilts.

Source: George Coe Groves Fund and Estate of Flora E. Whiting, by exchange, 2016/The Metropolitan Museum of Art

many of which had separate women's chapters. By serving in such organizations, they gained the practical experience of holding office on governing boards, conducting meetings, drafting policy statements, organizing reform programs, and raising money. Evangelicalism thus enabled women to enter public life and to make their voices heard in ways that were socially acceptable. After all, evangelical teachings affirmed that they were the superior sex in piety and morality, a point often repeated by those very women who devoted much of their time to benevolence and reform. They justified such public activism as merely the logical extension of their private responsibility to act as spiritual guides to their families.

Protestants and Catholics

Women's piety and their spiritual influence was surely on the mind of Isaac Bird one Saturday morning in the autumn of 1819. A devout evangelical preparing for the ministry, he had wandered into a Roman Catholic church in Boston and now watched with rapt attention a ritual, conducted entirely in Latin, in which two women "took the veil" and became nuns. Bird often visited Boston on his vacations to proselytize its poorest inhabitants. Many were Catholics, as he noted, some of them recent Irish and German emigrants and others African American, including a man who asked him many intelligent questions about religion and "treated me respectfully but seemed to feel that Protestants were all making a trade of preaching and praying." It troubled Bird, this gathering presence of devout Catholics.

Protestants had a long history of hostility toward Roman Catholics, especially in New England. Every November, colonial Bostonians had celebrated "Pope's Day" with boys decked out as the devil's imps parading through the streets with a cart carrying an effigy of the pope. The uproar over the Quebec Act in 1774 also bore loud witness to anti-Catholic sentiments. But before the beginning of the nineteenth century the number of Catholics had been small: in 1815, there were only 150,000 scattered throughout the United States, and they often had little access to priests or public worship.

That had begun to change by 1820. French Canadian Catholic emigrants were filtering into New England in growing numbers, an incoming tide that would rise sharply during the 1840s and 1850s, with a new wave of Catholic immigrants from the British Isles and German-speaking countries. By 1830 the Catholic population had jumped to 300,000, and by 1850 Catholics accounted for 8 percent of the U.S. population—the same proportion as Presbyterians. As these newcomers settled in eastern cities and on western frontiers, there were an increasing number of priests, nuns, and churches to minister to their spiritual needs.

CATHOLICISM AND PROTESTANTISM COMPARED
The differences between Roman Catholicism and Protestantism—especially evangelicalism—were substantial. Whereas evangelicals stressed the inward transformation of conversion, Catholics emphasized the importance of outward religious observances, such as faithfully attending mass and receiving the sacraments, as essential to salvation. Whereas evangelicals insisted that individuals read the Bible to discover God's will, Catholics urged their faithful to heed church teachings and traditions. Whereas Catholics believed that human suffering could be a penance paving the way toward redemption, evangelicals regarded it as an evil to be alleviated. Whereas evangelicals looked toward an imminent millennium, Catholics harbored no such expectation and played almost no role in antebellum benevolence and reform movements.

To Protestants, many elements of Catholicism seemed superstitious and even subversive. They rejected the Catholic doctrine of transubstantiation, which held that the bread and wine consecrated by the priest during mass literally turned into the body and blood of Jesus Christ. They condemned as idolatry the Catholic veneration of the Virgin Mary and the saints. They regarded Catholic nuns and convents as threats to the new ideals of womanhood and domesticity. They found it amiss that Catholic laymen had no role in governing their own parishes and dioceses, entrusting that responsibility entirely to priests and bishops.

But the worst fears of Protestants fastened on what they saw as the political dangers posed by Catholics, especially immigrants. Alarmed as Irish and German settlers poured into the West, Lyman Beecher warned that "the world has never witnessed such a rush of dark-minded population from one country to another, as is now leaving Europe and dashing upon our shores." Beecher foresaw a sinister plot hatched by the pope to snuff out American liberty. For what else would follow in a nation overwhelmed by Catholicism, "a religion which never prospered but in alliance with despotic government, has always been and still is the inflexible enemy of liberty of conscience and free enquiry, and at this moment is the mainstay of the battle against republican institutions?"

Evangelical missionaries dispatched abroad also fueled anti-Catholic sentiment at home. Their reports from the mission field, widely circulated in religious magazines, regaled readers with accounts of clashes with Catholic missionaries and ridiculed Catholic beliefs and rituals. Among them was Isaac Bird, who became a missionary in present-day Lebanon: he charged Catholic missionaries there with scheming to get him in trouble with local authorities and to prevent him from distributing Bibles. And he blamed the Catholic laypeople in the Middle East for discouraging the conversion of Jews and Muslims by practicing so "corrupt" a form of Christianity.

It was all the more appalling to evangelicals, then, that some Protestants found Catholic teachings appealing. So attractive that some 57,000 converted to Catholicism in the thirty years after 1830. In response to those defections, many Protestants, believing that converts were drawn by the artistic beauties of Catholic worship, began to include in their own churches recognizably Catholic elements, such as the symbol of the cross, the use of candles and flowers, organ and choir music, stained glass windows, and Gothic architecture. One such church was none other than Lyman Beecher's "Stone Jug," the Hanover Street Congregational Church in Boston.

A Bible Society Certificate

Holy Bible

Printing press

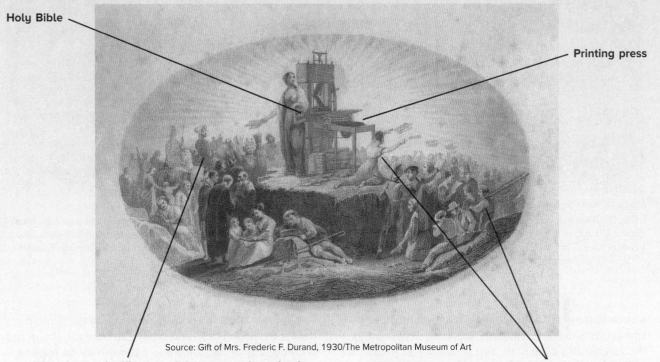

Source: Gift of Mrs. Frederic F. Durand, 1930/The Metropolitan Museum of Art

What is the significance of the man on horseback wearing a turban?

What is the significance of two women—rather than men—dispensing the Bibles? The man carrying a net?

The American Bible Society, one of the many evangelical Protestant voluntary associations founded in the early nineteenth century, celebrated its mission with this illustration. A rendering of the power of print to convert the world, it shows two female figures dispensing Bibles to a large and diverse crowd of people, some of whom are intently bent over the pages of their books. Another voluntary association, the American Tract Society, produced millions of small booklets narrating experiences of religious conversion or inculcating moral lessons. By the 1850s, millions of copies of both tracts and Bibles had flown off religious presses, along with millions more translated into several languages and dispatched throughout the world. Evangelical leaders believed that distributing this literature would encourage literacy and that the spread of literacy would produce, in turn, more evangelical Protestants both at home and abroad.

THINKING CRITICALLY

What indicates that Bible distribution played an important role in foreign missions? How would you describe those in the crowd who are reading Bibles with the most interest? What message does the artist convey by positioning children in the foreground of this picture? What is the significance of the classical dress worn by the two women distributing Bibles?

ATTACKS ON CATHOLICS Other Protestants attacked Catholicism directly. Writing under the name "Maria Monk," a team of evangelical ministers produced a lurid account of life in a convent, replete with sex orgies involving priests and nuns and a cellar planted with dead babies. Published in 1836, it outsold every other book except *Uncle Tom's Cabin* in the years before the Civil War. And with anti-Catholic sentiment running so high, predictably, there was violence. In 1834 a mob in Charlestown, Massachusetts, burned a convent to the ground.

The sisters and their students escaped injury, but during the summer of 1844 in Philadelphia, two separate outbreaks of anti-Catholic violence left 14 people dead, as well as two churches and three dozen homes in smoldering ruins.

Most antebellum Protestants condoned neither violence against Catholics nor the later nativist movement of the 1850s. But even liberal Protestants mistrusted the religion of Rome: in 1821 the Unitarian John Adams asked Thomas Jefferson whether "a free government [can] possibly exist

Source: Library of Congress, Prints and Photographs Division [LC-DIG-ppmsca-07575]

| This 1852 nativist cartoon warns Americans of the supposed dangers posed by the arrival of immigrants from Germany and Ireland. On the left, native Americans proclaim the virtues of "Constitution and Laws," while a horde of newcomers illustrates the threats. One banner reads "We are bound to carry out the pious intentions of his holiness the Pope." Why is another banner proclaiming "Fradom of Spache and Action!" spelled the way it is?

with a Roman Catholic religion." Anti-Catholicism had emerged as a defining feature of American Protestant identity, and the alienation of the two groups ran deep, enduring far into the twentieth century.

> ✓ **REVIEW**
>
> Name at least two ways in which evangelical activists influenced American culture during the 1830s and 1840s.

VISIONARIES

INCREASINGLY HOSTILE TO ROMAN CATHOLICS, evangelicals also stood at odds with other groups in antebellum America who envisioned new ways of improving individuals and society. Although often expressing optimism about the prospects for human betterment, these other reformers—Unitarians and Transcendentalists, socialists and communitarians—had little else in common with evangelicals.

The Unitarian Contribution

During the opening decades of the nineteenth century the religious division among Americans that produced the fiercest debates pitted evangelicals against deists, Unitarians, and other rational Christians.

Source: Library of Congress, Prints and Photographs Division [LC-USZ62-9797]

| Dorothea Dix

A majority only in eastern Massachusetts, Unitarians denied the divinity of Jesus while affirming the ability and responsibility of humankind to follow his moral teachings. Disdainful of the emotionalism of revivals, they were also inclined to interpret the Bible broadly rather than literally. To most Americans, such views were so suspect that the presidents who adhered to Unitarianism—John Adams, Thomas Jefferson, and John Quincy Adams—did not wish to publicize their beliefs.

Despite their many differences, Unitarians shared with evangelicals an esteem for the power of human agency and a commitment to the goal of social betterment. Small though their numbers were, Unitarians made large contributions to the cause of reform. Among their ranks were Dorothea Dix, a Boston schoolteacher who took the lead in creating state-supported asylums to treat the mentally ill; Samuel Gridley Howe, who promoted education for the blind and the deaf; and Horace Mann, who strove to give greater access to public schooling to children of poor and working-class families.

Unitarians made an equally important contribution to American literature; from their ranks came many of the Transcendentalists—novelists and poets, critics and philosophers—who led the artistic movement that later came to be known as the American Renaissance.

From Unitarianism to Transcendentalism

EMERSON'S DIVINITY SCHOOL ADDRESS What sparked Transcendentalism was an address delivered by a disenchanted Unitarian minister named Ralph Waldo Emerson to the students of Harvard Divinity School on a warm summer evening in July 1838. Outside, nature's world was alive and vibrant, he told his young audience: "The grass grows, the buds burst, the meadow is spotted with fire and gold in the tint of flowers." But from the pulpits of too many congregations came lifeless preaching. "In how many churches, by how many prophets, tell me," Emerson demanded, "is man made sensible that he is an infinite Soul?" Leaving the shocked audience to ponder his message, Emerson and his wife drove home beneath a night sky illuminated by the northern lights. Emerson's Divinity School Address glowed much like that July aurora and, in its own bold way, reflected the influence of Romanticism on American thinkers.

Romanticism began in Europe as a reaction against the Enlightenment. The Enlightenment had placed reason at the center of human achievement; Romanticism instead emphasized the importance of emotion and intuition as sources of truth. It gloried in the unlimited potential of the individual, who might soar if freed from the restraints of institutions. It extolled humanitarianism and sympathized with the oppressed. It elevated inner feelings and heartfelt convictions. Philosophically, its influence was strongest among intellectuals who took part in the Transcendentalist movement.

Transcendentalism is difficult to define, because it produced individualists who resisted being lumped together. It blossomed in the mid-1830s, when a number of Unitarian clergy such as George Ripley and Ralph Waldo Emerson resigned their pulpits, loudly protesting the church's teachings. The new "Transcendentalist Club" attracted a small following among other discontented Boston intellectuals, including Margaret Fuller, Bronson Alcott, and Orestes Brownson.

Like European Romantics, American Transcendentalists emphasized feeling over reason, seeking a spiritual communion with nature. By transcend they meant to go beyond or to rise above—specifically above reason and beyond the material world. As part of creation, every human being contained a spark of divinity, Emerson avowed. Transcendentalists also shared in Romanticism's glorification of the individual. "Trust thyself. Every heart vibrates to that iron string," Emerson advised. If freed from the constraints of traditional authority, the individual had infinite potential. Like the devout at Finney's revivals, who sought to improve themselves and society, listeners who flocked to Emerson's lectures were infused with the spirit of optimistic reform.

The American Renaissance

As the currents of Romanticism percolated through American society, the country's literature came of age. In 1820 educated Americans still tended to ape the fashions of Europe and to read British books. But as the population grew, education increased and the country's literary market expanded; American writers looked with greater interest at the customs and character of their own society. Emerson's address "The American Scholar" (1837) constituted a declaration of literary independence. "Our long dependence, our long apprenticeship to the learning of other lands draws to a close," he proclaimed. "Events, actions arise, that must be sung, that will sing themselves."

NATURE AND CIVILIZATION CLASH Many writers of the American Renaissance betrayed a concern that the advance of civilization, with its smoke-belching factories and crowded urban centers, might destroy both the natural simplicity of the land and the liberty of the individual. A compelling commentator on those themes was Henry David Thoreau, who became part of Emerson's circle. In 1845 he built a cabin on the edge of Walden Pond near Concord, Massachusetts, living there in relative solitude for 16 months to demonstrate the advantages of self-reliance. In *Walden* (1854) Thoreau argued that only in nature could one find true independence. By living simply, one could master oneself and the world. He denounced Americans' frantic competition for material goods and wealth: "Money is not required to buy one necessity of the soul," Thoreau maintained. Trapped by property, possessions, and the market, "the mass of men lead lives of quiet desperation."

Thoreau's individualism was so extreme that he rejected any institution that contradicted his personal sense of right. "The only obligation which I have a right to assume, is to do at any time what I think right," he wrote in his essay "On Civil Disobedience." Voicing the anti-institutional impulse of Romanticism, he took individualism to its antisocial extreme.

WHITMAN'S SELF-RELIANT SONGS In contrast to Thoreau's exclusiveness, Walt Whitman was all-inclusive, embracing American society in its infinite variety. A journalist and laborer in the New York City area, Whitman was inspired by the common people, whose "manners, speech, dress, friendships . . . are unrhymed poetry." In taking their measure in *Leaves of Grass* (1855), he pioneered a new, modern form of poetry, unconcerned with meter and rhyme and filled with frank imagery and sexual references.

Conceiving himself the representative of all Americans, Whitman exuberantly titled his first major poem "Song of Myself."

> I am your voice—It was tied in you—In me it began to talk.
> I celebrate myself to celebrate every man and woman alive.

DARKER SOULS Whitman, like the Transcendentalists, exalted the emotions, nature, and the individual, endowing these ideas with a joyous, democratic spirit. More brooding souls were Nathaniel Hawthorne and Herman Melville, two authors who did not share the Transcendentalists' sunny optimism. Hawthorne wrote of the power of the past to shape future generations. In *The Scarlet Letter* (1850), set in New England's Puritan era, Hawthorne probed the sufferings of a woman who bore an illegitimate child as well as the hypocrisy of the Puritan neighbors who condemned her. Herman Melville's dark masterpiece, *Moby-Dick* (1851), drew on his

Courtesy Concord Free Public Library

In the summer of 1858, members of the cultural Saturday Club of Boston made an excursion to the Adirondacks to observe nature. In Philosopher's Camp, *painted by William J. Stillman, who organized the expedition, a group on the left dissects a fish under the supervision of the famous scientist Louis Agassiz, while on the right others practice firing rifles. Symbolically, Ralph Waldo Emerson stands alone in the center of the painting in a contemplative mood.*

youthful experiences aboard a whaling ship. The novel's Captain Ahab relentlessly drives his ship in pursuit of the great white whale Moby-Dick. In Melville's telling, Ahab becomes a powerful symbol of American character: the prototype of the ruthless businessman despoiling nature's resources in his pursuit of success. Ahab is Emerson's self-reliant man, but in him, self-reliance is transformed into a monomania that eventually destroys his ship, its crew, and him.

But with so many opportunities opening before them, most Americans were not attuned to searching criticism. They preferred to celebrate, with Emerson, the glories of democracy and the quest for self-improvement.

Secular Utopian Communities

Both evangelicals and Unitarians focused their early reform efforts on improving individuals. But some antebellum believers, followers of both secular and religious faiths, sought to remake society at large by forming communities intended as examples to the rest of the world.

BROOK FARM Even some Transcendentalists attempted a utopian venture.

Source: Library of Congress, Prints and Photographs Division [LC-USZ62-82784]

Walt Whitman, poet of democracy

During the early 1840s Emerson's friend George Ripley organized Brook Farm, a community near Boston where members could live "a more wholesome and simple life than can be led amidst the pressure of our competitive institutions." Margaret Fuller and, even more surprisingly, Nathaniel Hawthorne, lived and labored there for a time, but, predictably, these Romantic individualists could not sustain the group cooperation essential for success.

SOCIALIST COMMUNITIES Some secular thinkers shared the Transcendentalists' view that competition, inequality, and acquisitiveness were corrupting American society. Among those critics were socialists, and their goal was to defend the interests of American workers from the ravages of industrialization. The most radical voice raised in their behalf belonged to Thomas Skidmore: in 1829 he published *The Rights of Man to Property,* which compared workers laboring for a daily wage to slaves and demanded that the government confiscate private property and redistribute it equally.

More influential was Robert Owen, the unlikely founder of America's first socialist community. A Welsh industrialist who had made a fortune manufacturing textiles,

Owen then turned to realizing his vision of a just society—one in which property was held in common and work equally shared. Such a benign social environment, he believed, would foster tolerant, rational human beings capable of self-government. What better place than America to make this dream come true?

NEW HARMONY Initially, Owen received a warm reception. John Quincy Adams not only attended both lectures that Owen delivered at the Capitol but also displayed a model of his proposed community in the White House. A few months later about 900 volunteers flocked to Owen's community at New Harmony, Indiana. Alas, most lacked the skills and commitment to make it a success, and bitter factions soon split the settlement. Owen made matters worse by announcing that he rejected both the authenticity of the Bible and the institution of marriage. New Harmony dissolved in 1827, but Owen's principles inspired nearly 20 other short-lived experiments.

©Apic/Getty Images
| *Herman Melville*

Owen's followers coined the term "socialism," but it was Charles Fourier, a French theorist, whose ideas interested even more Americans in collectivist communities during the 1840s. His disciples in the United States, most notably, Albert Brisbane, founded nearly 30 planned communities devoted to the principle that work should be satisfying and socially useful. But again, schisms ensured that none survived for more than a dozen years.

The United States proved to be a poor proving-ground for socialist experiments. Wages were too high and land too cheap for such communities to interest most Americans. And individualism was too strong to create a commitment to cooperative action. Communities founded by believers in religious rather than secular faiths proved far more enduring. Their common spiritual convictions muted individualism, and their charismatic leaders held divisions at bay.

Source: Jerome Robbins Dance Division/The New York Public Library

| *Dancing was an integral part of the Shakers' religion, as this picture of a service at Lebanon, New York, indicates. In worshiping, men and women formed separate lines with their hands held out and moved back and forth in rhythm while singing religious songs. One Shaker hymn proclaimed, "With ev'ry gift I will unite,/And join in sweet devotion/To worship God is my delight,/With hands and feet in motion." Note the presence of African Americans in the community.*

Religious Utopian Communities

THE SHAKERS   Among the most successful of these religiously based communal groups were the Shakers. Ann Lee, the illiterate daughter of an English blacksmith, believed that God had a dual nature, part male and part female, and that her own life would reveal the feminine side of the divinity, just as Christ had revealed the masculine. In 1774 she led a small band of disciples to America. Her followers sometimes shook in the fervent public demonstration of their faith—hence the name Shakers.

As the Second Great Awakening crested, recruits from revivals swelled Shaker ranks, and their new adherents founded about 20 villages. Members held the community's property in common, worked hard, and lived simply.

Convinced that the end of the world was at hand so there was no need to perpetuate the human race, Shakers practiced celibacy. Men and women normally worked apart, ate at separate tables in silence, entered separate doorways, and had separate living quarters. Shakers also accorded women unusual authority and equality. Elders typically assigned tasks by gender, with women performing household chores and men laboring in the fields, but leadership of the church was split equally between men and women. By the mid-nineteenth century a majority of members were female. Lacking any natural increase, membership began to decline after 1850, from a peak of about 6,000 members.

John Humphrey Noyes, a revival convert of Charles Finney, also set out to alter the relationship between the sexes, though in a markedly different way. While many evangelicals believed that men and women should strive for moral perfection, Noyes announced that he had actually reached this blessed state. Settling in Putney, Vermont, and, after 1848, in Oneida, New York, Noyes set out to create a community organized on his religious ideals.

COMPLEX MARRIAGE AT ONEIDA   In pursuit of greater freedom, Noyes preached the doctrine of "complex marriage." Commune members could have sexual relations with one another but only with the approval of the community and after a searching examination of the couple's motives. Noyes eventually undertook experiments in planned reproduction by selecting "scientific" combinations of parents to produce morally perfect children.

Under his charismatic leadership the Oneida Community grew to more than 200 members in 1851. But in 1879 an internal dispute drove him from power, and without his guiding hand the community fell apart. In 1881 its members reorganized as a business enterprise.

The Mormon Experience

The most spectacularly successful antebellum religious community—one that mushroomed into a denomination whose followers now number in the millions around the world—is the Church of Jesus Christ of Latter-Day Saints. The Mormons, as they are generally known, took their rise

©Lowell Georgia/Getty Images

The Mormon temple at Nauvoo, Illinois, was adorned with this sun stone and other celestial carvings drawn from a dream vision by Joseph Smith.

from the visions of a young man named Joseph Smith in Palmyra, in western New York, where the religious fires of revivalism often flared. The son of a poor farmer, Smith was robust, charming, almost hypnotic in his appeal. In 1827, at the age of only 22, he announced that he had discovered and translated a set of golden tablets on which was written the Book of Mormon. The tablets told the story of a band of Hebrews who in biblical times journeyed to America, splitting into two groups, the Nephites and the Lamanites. The Nephites established a Christian civilization, only to be exterminated by the Lamanites, whose descendants were said to be the Indians of the Americas. Seeking to reestablish the true church, Smith gathered a group of devoted followers.

Like nineteenth-century evangelicalism, Mormonism proclaimed that salvation was available to all. Mormon culture also upheld the middle-class values of hard work, thrift, and self-control. It partook of the optimistic, materialist attitudes of American society. And by teaching that Christ would return to rule the earth, it shared in the hope of a coming millennial kingdom.

MOVEMENT TO RESTORE THE ANCIENT CHURCH
Yet Mormonism was less an outgrowth of evangelicalism than of the primitive gospel movement, which sought to reestablish the ancient church. In restoring what Smith called "the ancient order of things," he created a **theocracy** uniting church and state, reestablished biblical priesthoods and titles, and adopted temple rituals.

Like Roman Catholics, the Mormons drew bitter opposition—and armed attacks. Smith's unorthodox teachings provoked persecution wherever he and his followers went, first to Ohio and then to Missouri. Mob violence finally hounded him out of Missouri in 1839. Smith then established a new holy city, which he named Nauvoo, located on the Mississippi River in Illinois.

Reinforced by a steady stream of converts from Britain, Nauvoo became the largest city in Illinois, with a population of 10,000 by the mid-1840s. There, Smith introduced the most distinctive features of Mormon theology, including baptism for the dead, eternal marriage, and polygamy, or plural marriage. As a result, Mormonism increasingly diverged from traditional Christianity and became a distinct new religion. To bolster his authority as a prophet, Smith established a theocratic political order under which church leaders controlled political offices and governed the community, with Smith as mayor.

Neighboring residents, alarmed by the Mormons' growing political power and reports that church leaders were practicing polygamy, demanded that Nauvoo's charter be revoked and the church suppressed. In 1844, while in jail for destroying the printing press of dissident Mormons in Nauvoo, Smith was murdered by an anti-Mormon mob. In 1846 the Mormons abandoned Nauvoo, and the following year Brigham Young, Smith's successor, led them westward to Utah.

> ✓ **REVIEW**
>
> In what ways did Transcendentalism shape the themes of writers of the American Renaissance? Who were the major communitarian reformers of the era?

RADICAL REFORM

AMONG THE MOST TRANSFORMATIVE events of American history was the rise of a militant antislavery movement known as abolitionism. Beginning in the 1830s, growing numbers of white Americans came to believe that the end of slavery should come immediately. Some who took that radical stance also joined in the first organized agitation for women's rights. What pushed antislavery advocates to reject the gradualism and colonization more common during earlier decades? And what inspired some of those abolitionist radicals to take up the cause of women?

The Beginnings of the Abolitionist Movement

First was the example of Britain, once the world's leading purchaser and transporter of slaves. Parliament had outlawed the slave trade in 1808 and pressed other European nations to do the same. Thereafter a growing number of activists called for an immediate end to slavery in all of Britain's Caribbean colonies. In 1833, bowing to overwhelming public pressure, Parliament emancipated nearly 800,000 slaves. American reformers

Source: Library of Congress, Prints and Photographs Division [LC-USZ62-49809]

| *Theodore Dwight Weld campaigned for immediatism, as William Lloyd Garrison did. But while Garrison ended up rejecting organized religion in the struggle against slavery, Weld preferred to work through the evangelical churches and cooperate with the clergy.*

had followed the British campaign closely, and it inspired some of them to call for an immediate end to slavery.

DAVID WALKER'S APPEAL Even more important was the activism of African Americans. A turning point in their agitation against slavery came in 1829 when a free black named David Walker published *An Appeal to the Coloured Citizens of the World.* Walker had moved to Boston from North Carolina a few years earlier, running a small used-clothing business, working as a community activist and also as an agent for the first black newspaper in the United States, *Freedom's Journal.* Walker's impassioned argument that America belonged as much to blacks as to whites ended what little support colonization still commanded in the free black community. Going beyond earlier calls for "uplift" through education, he urged both free and enslaved African Americans to unite and combat white oppression. And woe unto white Americans, Walker warned, if blacks had to fight in order to attain freedom and equality. Whites should instead "throw away your fears and prejudices" and "treat us like men." (See Many Histories, Chapter 11.)

Walker's militancy contrasted sharply with the more conservative strategies of earlier antislavery advocates. But shortly after Walker's death, a white New Englander, William Lloyd Garrison, took up his message. In 1829 Garrison was beginning his career as a reformer, working in Baltimore with Benjamin Lundy, the Quaker editor of an antislavery newspaper calling for a gradual end to slavery through colonization. But the more Garrison got to know Baltimore's free blacks, the more he realized that most African Americans regarded colonization as a southern strategy to secure slavery's future and promote racism.

GARRISON'S IMMEDIATISM Under their influence, Garrison soon developed views far more radical than Lundy's. Returning to Boson and enlisting help from the free black community there, he published the first issue of *The Liberator* on January 1, 1831. Both black and female writers found their contributions welcomed in its pages. Like Walker's *Appeal,* Garrison's *Liberator* rejected gradual emancipation, embraced immediatism, and denounced colonization. Like Walker, too, Garrison upheld the principle of racial equality and—going further than British abolitionists— opposed compensating slaveholders if they would free their laborers. Southerners ought to be convinced by "moral suasion," Garrison claimed, to renounce slavery as a sin. He diverged from Walker only in embracing a thoroughgoing pacifism.

Garrison attracted the most attention, but other abolitionists spoke with equal conviction. Wendell Phillips, from a socially prominent Boston family, held listeners spellbound with his speeches.

Lewis Tappan and his brother Arthur, two New York City silk merchants, boldly placed their wealth behind a number of humanitarian causes, including abolitionism. James G. Birney, an Alabama slaveholder, converted to abolitionism after wrestling with his conscience, and Angelina and Sarah Grimké, the daughters of a South Carolina planter, left their native state to speak against the institution. And there was Angelina's future husband, Theodore Weld, a scruffy, restless reformer who led a walkout of fellow students at Lane Seminary in Cincinnati when the college's president refused to support a campaign for immediate abolition. The president was none other than Lyman Beecher, who had left Boston to spread Christianity in the west.

To abolitionists, slavery was a moral, not an economic, question. The institution seemed a contradiction of the principle of the American Revolution that all human beings had been created with natural rights. Then, too, it went against the Romantic spirit of the age, which celebrated the individual's freedom and self-reliance. Abolitionists condemned slavery because of the breakup of marriages and families by sale, the harsh punishment of the lash, slaves' lack of access to education, and the sexual abuse of black women. Most of all, they denounced slavery as outrageously contrary to Christian teaching. As one Ohio antislavery paper declared: "We believe slavery to be a sin, always, everywhere, and only, sin—sin, in itself." So persistent were abolitionists in their religious objections that they forced the churches to face the question of slavery head-on. In the 1840s the Methodist and Baptist churches each split into northern and southern organizations over the issue.

The Spread of Abolitionism

ABOLITIONISTS' PROFILE   After helping organize the New England Anti-Slavery Society in 1832, Garrison joined with Lewis Tappan and Theodore Weld the following year to establish a national organization, the American Anti-Slavery Society. It coordinated a loosely affiliated network of state and local groups. During the years before the Civil War, perhaps 200,000 northerners belonged to an abolitionist society.

Abolitionists were concentrated in the East, especially New England, and in areas that had been settled by New Englanders, such as western New York and northern Ohio. The movement was not strong in cities or among businesspeople and workers. Most abolitionists were young, being generally in their 20s and 30s when the movement began, and had grown up in rural areas and small towns in middle-class families. Intensely religious, many had been profoundly affected by the revivals of the Second Great Awakening. More and more they came to feel that slavery was the fundamental cause of the Republic's degraded condition.

BLACK ABOLITIONISTS   Free African Americans, who made up the majority of subscribers to Garrison's *Liberator*, provided important support and leadership for the abolitionist movement. Frederick Douglass assumed the greatest prominence. Having escaped from slavery in Maryland, he became an eloquent critic of its evils. Initially a follower of Garrison, Douglass eventually broke with him and started his own newspaper in Rochester. Other important black abolitionists included Martin Delany, William Wells Brown, William Still, and Sojourner Truth. Aided by many other African Americans, these men and women battled against racial discrimination in the North as well as slavery in the South.

UNDERGROUND RAILROAD   A network of antislavery sympathizers also developed in the North to convey runaway slaves to Canada and freedom. Although not as extensive or as tightly organized as contemporaries claimed, the

| Black abolitionist Frederick Douglass (second from left at the podium) was only one of nearly 50 runaway slaves who appeared at an abolitionist convention held in August 1850 in Cazenovia, New York. Other runaways included Emily and Mary Edmonson (both in plaid dresses). When the Edmonsons' attempt at escape failed, Henry Ward Beecher (Lyman Beecher's son) rallied his congregation in Brooklyn to raise the money to purchase the girls' freedom.

©The Granger Collection, New York

Underground Railroad hid fugitives and transported them northward from one station to the next. Free African Americans, who were more readily trusted by wary slaves, played a leading role in the Underground Railroad. One of its most famous conductors was Harriet Tubman, an escaped slave who repeatedly returned to the South and eventually escorted to freedom more than 200 slaves.

Opponents and Divisions

The drive for immediate abolition faced massive obstacles within American society. With slavery increasingly important to the South's economy, southerners forced opponents of slavery to flee the region. In the North, where racism was equally entrenched, abolitionism provoked bitter resistance. Even abolitionists such as Garrison treated blacks paternalistically, contending that they should occupy a subordinate place in the antislavery movement.

On occasion, northern resistance turned violent. A hostile Boston mob seized Garrison in 1835 and paraded him with a rope around his body before he was finally rescued. Another anti-abolitionist mob burned down the headquarters of the American Anti-Slavery Society in Philadelphia. And in 1837 in Alton, Illinois, Elijah Lovejoy was murdered when he tried to protect his printing press from an angry crowd. The leaders of these mobs were not from the bottom of society but, as one of their victims noted, were "gentlemen of property and standing." Prominent leaders in the community, they reacted vigorously to the threat that abolitionists posed to their power and prosperity and to the established order.

DIVISIONS AMONG REFORMERS But abolitionists were also hindered by divisions among reformers. Lyman Beecher conceived of sin in terms of individual immorality, not unjust social institutions. But to the abolitionists, America could never become a godly nation until slavery was abolished. Among them was Beecher's daughter, Harriet Beecher Stowe, who in the 1850s wrote the most successful piece of antislavery literature in the nation's history, *Uncle Tom's Cabin*. Even the abolitionists themselves splintered, shaken by the opposition they encountered and unable to agree on the most effective response. More-conservative reformers wanted to work within established institutions, using the churches and political action to end slavery. But for Garrison and his followers, the mob violence demonstrated that slavery was only part of a deeper national disease, whose cure required the overthrow of American institutions and values.

By the end of the decade Garrison had worked out a program for the total reform of society. He embraced perfectionism—the belief that human beings could lead sinless lives—and denounced the clergy urged members to leave the churches, and called for an end to all government. Condemning the Constitution as proslavery—"a covenant with death and an agreement with hell"—he publicly burned a copy one July 4th. No person of conscience, he argued, could vote or otherwise participate in the corrupt political system. This platform was radical enough on all counts, but the final straw for Garrison's opponents was his endorsement of women's rights as an inseparable part of abolitionism.

The Women's Rights Movement

Women faced many disadvantages in American society. They were kept out of most jobs, denied political rights, and given only limited access to education beyond the elementary grades. When a woman married, her husband became the legal representative of the marriage and gained complete control of her property. If a marriage ended in divorce, the husband was awarded custody of the children. Any unmarried woman was made the ward of a male relative.

When abolitionists divided over the issue of female participation, women found it easy to identify with the situation of slaves, since both were victims of male tyranny. Sarah and Angelina Grimké took up the cause of women's rights after they were criticized for speaking to audiences that included men as well as women. Sarah responded with *Letters on the Condition of Women and the Equality of the Sexes* (1838), arguing that women deserved the same rights as men. Abby Kelly, another abolitionist, remarked that women "have good cause to be grateful to the slave," for in "striving to strike his irons off, we found most surely, that we were manacled ourselves."

SENECA FALLS CONVENTION Two abolitionists, Elizabeth Cady Stanton and Lucretia Mott, launched the women's rights movement after they were forced to sit behind a curtain at a world antislavery convention in London. In

| *Elizabeth Cady Stanton, one of the instigators and guiding spirits at the Seneca Falls Convention, photographed with one of her children.*

Varieties of Antebellum Reform

BENEVOLENCE AND MORAL REFORM	HUMANITARIAN REFORM	RADICAL REFORM
Circulation of Bibles, tracts	Asylum care for the insane	Socialist rejection of private property
Christian missions to the Indians, foreign nations	Improvement of public education, high schools	Women's rights and suffrage
Campaign to end business on the Sabbath, to found Sunday schools	Education for the blind and deaf	Complex marriage at Oneida; plural marriage among Mormons
Temperance	Prison reform	Prohibition
Missions to sailors, the poor	Antislavery, colonization	Abolitionism

(*left*) Source: ©Ingram Publishing/agefotostock;
(*right*) Source: Library of Congress, Prints and Photographs Division [LC-USZC4-5321]

1848 Stanton and Mott organized a conference in Seneca Falls, New York, that attracted about a hundred supporters. The meeting issued a Declaration of Sentiments, modeled after the Declaration of Independence, that began: "All men and women are created equal."

The Seneca Falls Convention called for educational and professional opportunities for women, laws giving them control of their property, recognition of legal equality, and repeal of laws awarding the father custody of the children in divorce. The most controversial proposal, and the only resolution that did not pass unanimously, was one demanding the right to vote. The Seneca Falls Convention established the arguments and the program for the women's rights movement for the remainder of the century.

In response several states gave women greater control over their property, and a few made divorce easier or granted women the right to sue in courts. But disappointments and defeats outweighed these early victories. Still, many of the important leaders in the crusade for women's rights that emerged after the Civil War had already taken their places at the forefront of the movement. They included Stanton, Susan B. Anthony, Lucy Stone, and—as Lyman Beecher by now must have expected, one of his daughters—Isabella Beecher Hooker.

The Schism of 1840

It was Garrison's position on women's rights that finally split antislavery ranks already divided over other aspects of his growing radicalism. The showdown came in 1840 at the national convention of the American Anti-Slavery Society, when delegates debated whether women could hold office in the organization. Some of Garrison's opponents favored women's rights but opposed linking the question to the slavery issue, insisting that it would drive off potential supporters. By packing the convention, Garrison carried the day. His opponents, led by Lewis

Tappan, resigned to found the rival American and Foreign Anti-Slavery Society.

The schism of 1840 lessened the influence of abolitionism as a reform movement. Although abolitionism heightened moral concern about slavery, it failed to convert the North to its program, and its supporters remained a tiny minority. Despite the considerable courage of its leaders, the movement lacked a realistic, long-range plan for eliminating such a deeply entrenched institution. Abolitionism demonstrated the limits of voluntary persuasion and individual conversions as a solution to deeply rooted social problems.

> ✓ **REVIEW**
>
> What helped spark the growth of an abolitionist movement? What factors caused the movement to splinter?

REFORM SHAKES THE PARTY SYSTEM

"WHAT A FOG-BANK WE ARE in politically. Do you see any head-land or light—or can you get an observation—or soundings?" The words came from a puzzled Whig politician writing a friend after the Massachusetts state elections of 1853. He was in such a confused state because reformers were increasingly entering the political arena to achieve results.

The Turn toward Politics

The crusading idealism of revivalists and reformers inevitably collided with the hard reality that society could not be perfected by converting individuals. Several movements, including those to establish public schools and erect asylums, had operated within the political system from the beginning. But a growing number of other frustrated reformers were abandoning the principle of voluntary persuasion and looking to government coercion to achieve their goals.

Politicians did not particularly welcome the new interest. Because the Whig and Democratic parties both drew on evangelical and nonevangelical voters, heated moral debates over the harmful effects of drink or the evils of slavery threatened to detach regular party members from their old loyalties and disrupt each party's unity. The strong opposition of German and Irish emigrants to temperance stimulated antiforeign sentiment among reformers and further divided both party coalitions, particularly the Democrats. "The temperance question is playing havock in the old party lines," commented one Indiana politician. The issue of abolition seemed even more disruptive.

WOMEN AND THE RIGHT TO VOTE Because women could not vote, they felt excluded when the temperance and abolitionist movements turned to electoral action to accomplish their goals. By the 1840s female reformers increasingly demanded the right to vote as the means to change society.

Nor were men blind to what was at stake: one reason they so strongly resisted female suffrage was because would give women real power.

The Maine Law

The political parties could resist the women's suffrage movement because most of its advocates lacked the right to vote. Less easily put off were temperance reformers. Although drinking had significantly declined in American society by 1840, it had hardly been eliminated. After 1845 the arrival of large numbers of German and Irish emigrants, who were accustomed to consuming alcohol, made voluntary prohibition even more remote. In response temperance advocates proposed state laws that would outlaw the manufacture and sale of alcoholic beverages.

Party leaders tried to dodge the question of prohibition, since large numbers of Whigs and Democrats were found on both sides of the issue. Temperance advocates countered by seeking pledges from candidates to support a prohibitory law. To win additional recruits, temperance

Source: Library of Congress, Prints and Photographs Division [LC-USZ62-10370]

By the 1850s a new antislavery party, the Republicans, was running John Frémont (far right) for president. This cartoon manages to tie just about every reform movement of the era to the Republicans—and in so doing, exhibits the usual stereotypical caricatures. Can you link each of Frémont's petitioners with one of the movements discussed in this chapter? How are the stereotypes being conveyed visually?

leaders adopted techniques used in political campaigns, including house-to-house canvasses, parades and processions, bands and singing, banners, picnics, and mass rallies.

The movement's first major triumph came in 1851. The Maine Law, as it was known, authorized search and seizure of private property in that state and provided stiff penalties for selling liquor. In the next few years a number of states enacted similar laws, although most were struck down by the courts or later repealed. Prohibition remained a controversial political issue throughout the century.

TEMPERANCE DISRUPTS THE PARTIES Although prohibition was temporarily defeated, the issue badly disrupted the Whig and Democratic Parties. It greatly increased party switching and brought to the polls a large number of new voters, including many "wets" who now looked to Democrats to preserve their right to drink. By dissolving the ties between so many voters and their parties, the temperance issue played a major role in the eventual collapse of the Jacksonian party system in the 1850s.

Abolitionism and the Party System

Slavery proved even more divisive. In 1835 abolitionists distributed more than a million pamphlets, mostly in the South, through the Post Office. A wave of excitement swept the South when the first batches arrived addressed to white southerners. Former senator Robert Hayne led a Charleston, South Carolina, mob that burned sacks of U.S. mail containing abolitionist literature, and postmasters in other southern cities refused to deliver the material. The Jackson administration allowed southern states to censor the mail, leading abolitionists to protest that their civil rights had been violated. In reaction, the number of antislavery societies in the North nearly tripled.

With access to the mails impaired, abolitionists began flooding Congress with petitions against slavery. Asserting that Congress had no power over the institution, angry southern representatives demanded action, and the House in response adopted the so-called gag rule in 1836. It automatically tabled without consideration any petition dealing with slavery. But southern leaders had made a tactical blunder. The gag rule allowed abolitionists not only to attack slavery but also to speak out as defenders of white civil liberties. The appeal of the antislavery movement was broadened, and in 1844 the House finally repealed the controversial rule.

Many abolitionists outside Garrison's extreme circle began to feel that an antislavery third party offered a more effective means of attacking slavery. In 1840 these political abolitionists founded the Liberty Party and nominated for president James Birney, a former slaveholder who had converted to abolitionism. Birney received only 7,000 votes, but the Liberty Party was the seed from which a stronger antislavery political movement would grow. From 1840 onward, abolitionism's importance would be in the political arena rather than as a voluntary reform organization.

✓ REVIEW
How did reform movements create instability in the political system?

PUTTING HISTORY IN GLOBAL CONTEXT

THE FERMENT OF REFORM during the decades from 1820 to 1850 reflected a multitude of attempts to deal with transformations working through not just the United States but also Europe. Americans crowded the docks of New York City eagerly awaiting the latest installment of Charles Dickens's novels from England, tales often set amid urban slums and dingy factories. European middle classes embraced the home as a domestic refuge, as did their counterparts in America. The "benevolent empire" of American reform organizations drew inspiration from similar British campaigns. Robert Owen launched his utopian reforms in New Lanark, Scotland, before his ideas were tried out at New Harmony, Indiana, and disciples of the French socialist Charles Fourier founded communities in the United States.

Abolition was potentially the most dangerous of these transatlantic reforms because slavery was so deeply and profitably intertwined with the industrial system. Slave labor produced cotton for the textile factories of New England, Great Britain, and Europe; plantation economies supplied the sugar, rice, tea, and coffee that were a part of European and American diets. Revolutionary France had abolished slavery in 1794, but Napoleon reinstated it, along with the slave trade. Great Britain outlawed the trade in 1808 (as did the United States) and then freed nearly 800,000 slaves in its colonies in 1834.

Any move for emancipation in the United States seemed out of the question, and as late as 1840 abolition lacked the power to threaten the political system. Birney's small vote, coupled with the disputes between the two national antislavery societies, encouraged political leaders to believe that the party system had turned back this latest threat of sectionalism. But the growing northern concern about slavery highlighted differences between the two sections. Despite the strength of evangelicalism in the South, the reform impulse spawned by the revivals found little support there, since reform movements were discredited by their association with abolitionism. The party system confronted the difficult challenge of holding together sections that, although sharing much, were also diverging in important ways. To the residents of both sections, the South increasingly appeared to be a unique society with its own distinctive way of life.

Chapter Summary

The jacksonian era produced the greatest number of significant reform movements in American history.

- The Second Great Awakening, which preached the doctrine of salvation available to all and the coming of the millennium, encouraged revivals and reform.

  - Revivals drew converts from every segment of American society and spoke to their spiritual needs.

  - Women were most prominent among revival converts.

  - The Second Great Awakening made evangelicals the dominant religious subculture in the United States.

  - Benevolence and reform societies decisively changed drinking habits and the ideals of womanhood and the family.

  - Evangelical religious fervor also fueled anti-Catholicism, although many Protestants adopted elements of Catholic art and rituals into their services and church architecture.

- Unitarianism and Transcendentalism, which emphasized the unlimited potential of each individual, also strengthened reform.

- Utopian communities sought to establish a model society for the rest of the world to follow.

- Mormons developed the most significant following among utopian communities but also drew persecution.

- Temperance, abolitionism, and women's rights movements each turned to political action to accomplish their goals.

  - Abolitionism precipitated both strong support and violent opposition, and the movement split in 1840.

  - Although it survived, the party system was seriously weakened by these reform movements.

Digging Deeper

Good introductions to antebellum evangelical religion and reform include Robert H. Abzug, *Cosmos Crumbling* (1994); Charles E. Hambrick-Stowe, *Charles G. Finney and the Spirit of American Evangelicalism* (1996); and Bertram Wyatt-Brown, *Lewis Tappan and the Evangelical War Against Slavery* (1971). For suggestive analyses of the relationship between antebellum evangelicalism and the sweeping changes in economic and political life, consult Richard Carwardine, *Evangelicals and Politics in Antebellum America* (1997); Candy Gunther Brown, *The Word in the World* (2004); and Paul E. Johnson and Sean Wilentz, *The Kingdom of Matthias* (1994). On antislavery activism, consult Patrick Rael, *Eighty-Eight Years* (2015); Manisha Sinha, *The Slave's Cause* 2016); and Eric Foner, *Gateway to Freedom* (2015). The best studies of the role of women in evangelical churches and reform societies are Anne Boylan, *The Origins of Women's Activism* (1988); Lori Ginzberg, *Women and the Work of Benevolence* (1990); and Nancy Hewitt, *Women's Activism and Social Change* (1984). To understand the link between reformist activism and the early women's rights movement, begin with Lori Ginzberg's *Untidy Origins* (2005) and Nancy Isenberg's *Sex and Citizenship in the United States* (1998).

Despite the dominant influence of evangelical Protestants, both Roman Catholics and Mormons attracted a growing number of adherents during the antebellum period. For a fascinating account of the origins and rise of Mormonism, see John L. Brooke, *The Refiner's Fire* (1996); and for a compelling account of how American Protestants responded to the growth of Roman Catholicism after the 1830s, see Ryan K. Smith, *Gothic Arches, Latin Crosses* (2006). To explore the reasons why a small but influential minority of nineteenth-century Americans rejected all forms of Christianity in favor of agnosticism or atheism, rely on James Turner, *Without God, Without Creed* (1985). On Transcendentalism, explore David S. Reynolds, *Beneath the American Renaissance* (1988); and Megan Marshall's biography, *Margaret Fuller: A New American Life* (2013).

13 The Old South

1820–1860

A nurse and child, about 1850. Because it took minutes to expose a daguerreotype print, the nurse is holding the child's hand still. Although the South encompassed a wide variety of subregions, classes of people, crops, and climates, its "peculiar institution," slavery, came to deeply shape its identity in the decades before the Civil War. As this portrait indicates, relations between the free and enslaved were closely, and often ambiguously, intertwined. What ambiguities are suggested by the daguerreotype?

>> **An American Story**

WHERE IS THE REAL SOUTH?

The impeccably dressed Colonel Daniel Jordan, master of 261 slaves at Laurel Hill, strolls down his oak-lined lawn to the dock along the Waccamaw River, a day's journey north of Charleston, South Carolina, to board the steamship *Nina.* On Fridays, it is Colonel Jordan's custom to visit the exclusive Hot and Hot Fish Club, founded by his fellow low-country planters, to play a game of lawn bowling or billiards and be waited on by black servants in livery as he sips a mint julep in the refined atmosphere that for him is the South.

Several hundred miles west another steamboat, the *Fashion,* makes its way along the Alabama River. One of the passengers is upset by the boat's slow pace. A very different sort of planter, he has been away from his lands in the Red River country of Texas and can't wait to get back. "Time's money, time's money!" he mutters. "Time's worth more'n money to me now; a hundred percent more, 'cause I left my niggers all alone; not a damn white man within four mile on 'em." When asked what they are doing, since the cotton crop has already been picked, he says, "I set 'em to clairin', but they ain't doin' a damn thing. . . . I know that as well as you do. . . . But I'll make it up, I'll make it up when I get thar, now you'd better believe." For this Red River planter, time is money and cotton is his world—indeed, cotton is what the South is all about. "I am a cotton man, I am, and I don't care who knows it," he proclaims. "I know cotton, I do. I'm dam' if I know anythin' but cotton."

At the other end of the South, the slave Sam Williams works in the intense heat of Buffalo Forge, an iron-making factory in the Shenandoah Valley. As a refiner, Williams heats pig iron in the white-hot coals, then slings the ball of glowing metal on an anvil, where he pounds it with huge, water-powered hammers to remove the impurities. Ambitious and hardworking, he earns extra money (at the same rate paid to whites) for any iron he produces beyond his weekly quota. In some years his extra income is more than $100. His wife, Nancy, in charge of the dairy, earns extra money as well, and the additional income allows them to buy extra food and items for themselves and their daughters. More important, it helps keep their family intact in an unstable environment. Their owner is very unlikely to sell slaves who work so hard. For Sam and Nancy Williams, family ties, worship at the local Baptist church, and socializing with their fellow slaves are what make life meaningful.

In the swampy bayous of the Deep South, only a few miles from the Mississippi delta, Octave Johnson hears the dogs coming. For a year Johnson has been a runaway slave. He fled from a Louisiana plantation when the work bell rang before daybreak and the overseer threatened to whip him for staying in bed. To survive, he hides in the swamps 4 miles behind the plantation—stealing turkeys, chickens, and pigs and trading with other slaves. Nearly 30 other slaves have joined him over the past year. The howling

Source: Library and Archives Canada/Henry Wentworth Acland/Sir Henry Wentworth Acland fonds/MIKAN 2859705

| *Selling snacks at the Richmond rail station*

dogs warn Johnson and his companions that the hound master Eugene Jardeau is out again. This time when the pack bursts upon them, the slaves do not flee but kill as many dogs as possible. Then they plunge into the bayou, and as the hounds follow, alligators make short work of another six. For Octave Johnson the real South is a matter of weighing one's prospects between the uncertainties of alligators and the overseer's whip—and deciding when to say no.

Ferdinand Steel and his family are not slaves, forced by an overseer to get up at five in the morning. They rise because the land demands it. Steel, a white southerner in his 20s, owns 170 acres of land in Carroll County, Mississippi. Unmarried, he moved there from Tennessee with his widowed mother, sister, and brother, only a few years after the Choctaws had been forced to give up the region

and march west. His life is one of continuous hard work, caring for the animals and tending the crops. His mother and sister have plenty to keep them busy: making soap, fashioning dippers out of gourds, and sewing. The Steel family grows cotton, too, but their total crop amounts to only five or six bales—never enough profit to consider buying even one slave. But the five bales at least mean cash, and cash means that when he goes to market, he can buy sugar and coffee, gunpowder and lead, a yard or two of calico, and quinine to treat the malaria that is common in those parts. Though fiercely independent, Steel and his scattered neighbors help one another to raise houses, clear fields, shuck corn, and quilt. They are bound together by blood, religion, obligation, and honor. For small farmers such as Ferdinand Steel, these ties constitute the real South. <<

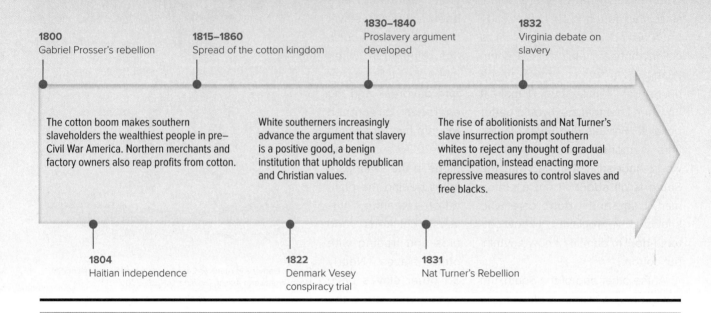

1800
Gabriel Prosser's rebellion

1815–1860
Spread of the cotton kingdom

1830–1840
Proslavery argument developed

1832
Virginia debate on slavery

The cotton boom makes southern slaveholders the wealthiest people in pre–Civil War America. Northern merchants and factory owners also reap profits from cotton.

White southerners increasingly advance the argument that slavery is a positive good, a benign institution that upholds republican and Christian values.

The rise of abolitionists and Nat Turner's slave insurrection prompt southern whites to reject any thought of gradual emancipation, instead enacting more repressive measures to control slaves and free blacks.

1804
Haitian independence

1822
Denmark Vesey conspiracy trial

1831
Nat Turner's Rebellion

THE SOCIAL STRUCTURE OF THE COTTON KINGDOM

THE PORTRAITS COULD GO ON and on. Different people, different Souths, all real. Such contrasts show how difficult it can be to define a regional identity. In 1860 the South included 15 slave states plus the District of Columbia, the South was a land of great geographic diversity. It extended from the Tidewater coastal plain along the Atlantic Seaboard to the prairies of Texas, from the Kentucky bluegrass region to the Gulf coast, from the mountains of western Virginia to the semitropical swamps of the Mississippi delta. Yet despite its many differences, the South was bound together by ties so strong, they eventually outpulled those of the nation itself. At the heart of this unity was an agricultural system made possible by the region's warm climate and long growing season. Within the United States, cotton, rice, and sugar could be grown only in the South. Most important, this rural agricultural economy was based on the institution of slavery, which affected all aspects of southern society. It shaped not only the culture of the slaves but also the lives of their masters and mistresses, and even the ways of farm families and herders in the hills who saw few slaves from day to day.

Of all the South's crops, cotton was the most important. Its spread through the region stimulated the nation's remarkable economic growth after the War of 1812. Demand

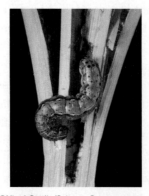

©Nigel Cattlin/Science Source

An army worm on a cotton boll

spurred by the textile industry sent the price of cotton soaring on the international market, and white southerners scrambled into the unplanted lands of the Southwest to reap the profits to be made in the cotton sweepstakes.

THE COTTON ENVIRONMENT This new cultivation dramatically transformed the South's landscape, turning countless acres of vines, brush, and trees into open fields. Cotton also imposed a demanding work discipline on slaves, who cultivated hundreds of acres, and white farming families, who tended many fewer. Typically they planted the newly cleared land in corn for a year, just long enough for tree stumps to decompose. In the next spring season, a heavy plow pulled by oxen or mules cleaved the fields into deep furrows, followed by workers who pitched cottonseed between the ridges. Then began the battle to protect the tender, newly sprouted plants. In the spring it was crucial to thin the excess cotton shoots and to yank out weeds throughout the summer. In years of heavy rains, when such competing vegetation flourished, masters put even their house slaves into the fields. Otherwise, a fungus might rot the cotton boll in wet weather, or beetles like the boll weevil attack the cotton buds, or—worst of all—the dreaded army worm invade, stripping field after field of its cotton.

Paradoxically, the more planters succeeded in opening new lands, the easier it was for the worm (and its parent moth) to spread across an entire region. During a summer in the 1850s, slaves on one plantation dug a deep trench between the cotton

COTTON AND OTHER CROPS OF THE SOUTH

By 1860 the cotton kingdom extended across the Lower South into the Texas prairie and up the Mississippi River valley. Tobacco and hemp were the staple crops of the Upper South, where they competed with corn and wheat. Rice production was concentrated in the swampy coastal region of South Carolina and Georgia as well as the lower tip of Louisiana. The sugar district was in southern Louisiana. Why was rice growing concentrated in coastal regions? Which staple crop predominates in the South, according to the map? Why is the answer different in the nineteenth century than it is in the eighteenth?

fields on a neighboring operation, in a desperate attempt to halt the army worms' progress. Into it they tumbled—"in untold millions," one observer reported, until the trench's bottom "for nearly a mile in extent, was a foot or two deep in [a] living mass of animal life." Then the slaves hitched a team of oxen to a heavy log and, as they pulled it through the ditch, "it seemed to float on a crushed mass" of worms.

The Boom Country Economy

COTTON PUSHES WESTWARD But the difficulties of cultivation did little to discourage white southerners' enthusiasm for cotton. Letters, newspapers, and word of mouth all brought tales of the Black Belt region of Alabama, where the dark soil was particularly suited to growing cotton, and of the tremendous yields from the soils along the Mississippi River's broad reaches. "The *Alabama Feaver* rages here with great violence and has *carried off* vast numbers of our Citizens," a North Carolinian wrote in 1817. A generation later, as the removal of the southern Indian tribes opened vast tracts of land to white settlement, immigrants were still "pouring in with a ceaseless tide," one observer reported, "including 'Land Sharks' ready to swallow up the home of the redmen, or the white, as oportunity might offer." By the 1840s planters even began to leave Mississippi and Alabama to head for the new cotton frontier along the Red River and up into Texas. Amazingly, by the eve of the Civil War nearly a third of the total cotton crop came from *west* of the Mississippi River.

THE UPPER SOUTH AND THE DOMESTIC SLAVE TRADE As cotton transformed the boom country of the Deep South, agriculture in the Upper South also adjusted. Scientific agricultural practices reversed the decline in tobacco, which had begun in the 1790s. More important, farmers in the Upper South made wheat and corn their major crops. Because the new crops required less labor, slaveholders in the Upper South sold 2 million black men, women, and children to planters in the Deep South. That domestic slave trade separated one-fifth of husbands and wives in the Upper South and one-third of all children from their parents. From their slaves' misery, masters reaped windfall profits. Eager buyers in cotton country paid as much as $1,500 in the late 1850s for a prime field hand, and the planters of that region could afford that investment in human property. As Senator James Henry Hammond of South Carolina boasted in 1858, cotton was king in the Old South: its primary export and the major source of southern wealth.

SOUTHERN PROSPERITY By 1860 the United States produced three-fourths of the world's supply of cotton. This boom fueled the southern economy so strongly that following the depression of 1839–1843, the southern economy grew faster than that in the North. Even so, per capita income in the South remained below that of the free states, and wealth was not as evenly distributed in the plantation South as in northern agricultural areas.

Prosperity masked other basic problems in the economy—problems that would become more apparent after the Civil War. Much of the South's new wealth resulted from migration of its population to more productive western lands. Once that prime agricultural land was settled, the South could not sustain its rate of expansion. Nor did the shift in population alter the structure of the southern economy, stimulate technological change, improve the way goods were produced and marketed, or generate internal markets.

ENVIRONMENTAL IMPACT OF SINGLE-CROP AGRICULTURE   The single-crop agriculture practiced by southern farmers rapidly wore out the soil. Tobacco was a particularly exhaustive crop, and corn also rapidly drained nutrients. To restore their soils, planters and farmers in the **Upper South** increasingly shifted to wheat production, but because they now plowed their fields rather than using a hoe, this shift intensified soil erosion. Destruction of the forests where commercial agriculture now took hold had the same effect, and many streams quickly silted up and were no longer navigable. Row-crop agriculture made floods and droughts more common. In addition, reliance on a single crop increased toxins and parasites in the soil, making southern agriculture more vulnerable to destruction than varied agriculture was.

Only the South's low population density lessened the impact on the environment. More-remote areas remained heavily forested, wetlands were still common, and as late as 1860, 80 percent of the region was uncultivated (cattle and hogs, however, ranged over much of this acreage). Throughout much of the South, farmers fired the woods in the spring to destroy insects, burn off brush, and increase grass for their browsing stock.

Perhaps the most striking environmental consequence of the expansion of southern society was the increase in disease, especially in the **Deep South**. Epidemic diseases such as malaria, yellow fever, and cholera were brought to the area by Europeans. The clearing of land—which increased runoff, precipitated floods, and produced pools of stagnant water—facilitated the spread of these diseases. In notoriously unhealthy areas, such as the coastal swamps of South Carolina's rice district, wealthy whites fled during the sickly summer months.

The Rural South

LACK OF MANUFACTURING   The Old South was dynamic, expanding, and booming economically. But the region remained overwhelmingly rural, with 84 percent of its labor force engaged in farming in 1860, compared with 40 percent in the North. Conversely, the South lagged in manufacturing, producing only 9 percent of the nation's manufactured goods. During the 1850s some southern propagandists urged greater investment in industry to diversify the South's economy. But as long as high profits from cotton continued, these advocates made little headway. With so little industry, few cities developed in the South. New Orleans, with a population of 169,000 in 1860, was the only truly southern city of significant size. Only 1 in 10 southerners lived in cities and towns in 1860, compared with 1 out of 3 persons in the North.

LACK OF EDUCATION   As a rural society the South showed far less interest in education. Southern colleges were inferior to those in the North, and public secondary schools were virtually nonexistent. Wealthy planters, who hired tutors or sent their children to private academies, generally opposed a state-supported school system. Thus free public schools were rare, especially in the rural districts that made up most of the South. Georgia in 1860 had only one county with a free school system, and Mississippi had no public schools outside its few cities. On average, southern white children spent only

| In this romanticized Currier and Ives print of a cotton plantation, field hands are waist-deep in cotton while other slaves haul the picked cotton to be ginned and then pressed into bales. Mounted on a horse, an overseer rides through the field supervising the work while the owner and his wife look on. Picking began as early as August and continued in some areas until late January. Because the bolls ripened at different times, a field had to be picked several times.

©Private Collection/Bridgeman Images

one-fifth as much time in school as did their northern counterparts.

The net result was high illiteracy rates. Among native-born white citizens, the 1850 census showed that 20 percent were unable to read and write. The comparable figure was 3 percent in the middle states and 0.4 percent in New England. In some areas of the South, more than a third of all white residents were illiterate.

Distribution of Slavery

Even more than agrarian ways, slavery set the South apart. Whereas in 1776 slavery had been a national institution, by 1820 slavery was confined to the states south of Pennsylvania and the Ohio River. The South's "peculiar institution" bound white and black southerners together in a multitude of ways.

Slaves were not evenly distributed throughout the region. More than half lived in the Deep South, where African Americans outnumbered white southerners in both South Carolina and Mississippi by the 1850s. Elsewhere in the Deep South the black population exceeded 40 percent in all states except Texas. In the Upper South, however, whites greatly outnumbered blacks. Only in Virginia and North Carolina did the slave population top 30 percent.

The distribution of slaves showed striking geographic variations within individual states as well. In areas of fertile soil, flat or rolling countryside, and good transportation, slavery and the plantation system dominated. In the pine barrens, areas isolated by lack of transportation, and hilly and mountainous regions, small family farms and few slaves were the rule.

SLAVE OCCUPATIONS Almost all enslaved African Americans, male and female, worked in agricultural pursuits, with only about 10 percent living in cities and towns. On large plantations, a few slaves were domestic servants and others were skilled artisans—blacksmiths, carpenters, or bricklayers—but most toiled in the fields.

Slavery as a Labor System

Slavery was, first and foremost, a system to manage and control labor. The plantation system, with its extensive estates and large labor forces, could never have developed without slavery, nor could it have met the world demand for cotton and other staples. Slaves represented an enormous capital investment, worth more than all the land in the Old South.

PROFITABILITY OF SLAVERY Furthermore, slavery remained a highly profitable investment. The average slaveowner spent perhaps $30 to $35 a year to support an adult slave. Allowing for the cost of land, equipment, and other expenses, a planter could expect one of his slaves to produce more than $78 worth of cotton—which meant that about 60 percent of the wealth produced by a slave's labor was clear profit. For those who drove slaves harder, the gains were even greater.

SLAVERY AND ARISTOCRATIC VALUES By concentrating wealth and power in the hands of the planter class, slavery shaped the tone of southern society. Planters were not aristocrats in the European sense of having special legal privileges or formal titles of rank. Still, the system encouraged southern planters to think of themselves as a landed gentry upholding the aristocratic values of pride, honor, family, and hospitality.

Whereas slavery had existed throughout most of the Americas at the beginning of the century, by the 1850s the United States, Cuba, and Brazil were the only slaveholding nations left in the region. Public opinion in Europe and in the

>> MAPPING THE PAST <<

THE SPREAD OF SLAVERY, 1820–1860

Source: Library of Congress, Prints and Photographs Division [LC-USZC4-2528]

"Cotton has enriched all through whose hands it has passed."—A New York City merchant and financier, 1835

CONTEXT

Between 1820 and 1860, the slave population of the South shifted southward and westward, concentrating especially heavily in coastal South Carolina and Georgia, in the Black Belt region of central Alabama and Mississippi (so named because of its rich soil), and in the Mississippi valley. Those regions stood at the epicenter of the South's booming cotton economy. Small farms with few slaves predominated only in those regions that lacked good transportation, such as northern Georgia, and in regions with poor soil, such as the piney woods of southern Mississippi.

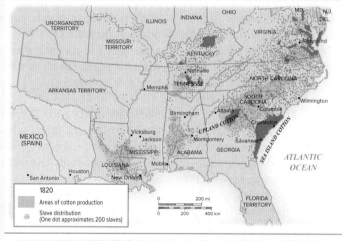

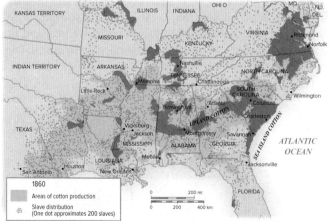

MAP READING

1. *Trace the spread of the cotton economy between 1820 and 1860.*
2. *Trace the expansion of slavery between 1820 and 1860.*
3. *Which parts of the South held the fewest slaves by 1860? Which held the greatest number of slaves?*

MAP INTERPRETATION

1. *Compare this map with the one in this chapter titled "Cotton and Other Crops of the South." Which staple crops demanded the most slave labor?*
2. *What factors besides their staple crops contributed to the relatively smaller slave populations in most of the Upper South by 1860?*
3. *What political concerns might the diminishing number of slaves in the Upper South have occasioned among planters in the Deep South?*
4. *Why were planters in the Deep South willing to risk filling the region with large concentrations of slaves?*

North had grown more and more hostile to the peculiar institution, causing white southerners to feel increasingly like an embattled minority. Yet they clung tenaciously to slavery, for it was the base on which the South's economic growth and way of life rested. The same drive for profit brought tens of thousands of enslaved Africans every year to work Cuba's sugar fields and Brazil's coffee plantations. Despite mounting opposition among some in the West, slavery was far from a dying institution in the Americas.

REVIEW

How did the cotton economy shape the South's environment and labor system?

CLASS STRUCTURE OF THE WHITE SOUTH

ONCE A YEAR AROUND CHRISTMASTIME, James Henry Hammond gave a dinner for his neighbors at his South Carolina plantation, Silver Bluff. The richest man for miles around as well as an ambitious politician, the aristocratic Hammond used these dinners to put his neighbors under personal obligation to him as well as receive the honor and respect he believed his due. Indeed, Hammond's social and political ambitions caused him to cultivate his neighbors, despite his low opinion of them, by hiring them to perform various tasks and by providing them a variety of services such as ginning their cotton and allowing them to use his gristmill. These services enhanced his ethic of paternalism, but his less affluent neighbors also displayed a strong personal pride. After he complained about the inconvenience of providing these services, only three of his neighbors came to his Christmas dinner that year, a snub that enraged him. As Hammond's experience demonstrated, class relations among whites in the Old South were a complex blend of privilege, patronage, and equality.

The Slaveowners

In 1860 the region's 15 states had a population of 12 million, of which roughly two-thirds were white, one-third were black slaves, and about 2 percent were free African Americans. Because of the institution of slavery, the social structure of the antebellum South differed in important ways from that of the North. Even so, southern society was remarkably fluid, and as a result, class lines were not rigid.

Of the 8 million white southerners in 1860, only about 2 million (one-quarter) either owned slaves or were members of slaveowning families. And most slaveowners owned only a few slaves. Censuses defined a planter as a person who owned 20 or more slaves; by that measure only about 1 out of every 30 white southerners belonged to families of the planter class.

A planter of consequence needed to own at least 50 slaves, and there were only about 10,000 such families—less than 1 percent of the white population. This privileged group made up the aristocracy at the top of the southern class structure. Owners of large numbers of slaves were rare; only about 2,000 southerners, such as Colonel Daniel Jordan, owned 100 or more slaves. Although limited in size, the planter class nevertheless owned more than half of all slaves and controlled more than 90 percent of the region's total wealth.

PLANTATION ADMINISTRATION The typical plantation had 20 to 50 slaves and 800 to 1,000 acres of land. On an estate larger than that, slaves would have to walk more than an hour to reach the farthest fields, losing valuable work time. Thus larger slaveowners usually owned several plantations, with an overseer to manage the slaves on each while the owner attended to business matters. The slaves were divided into field hands, skilled workers, and house servants, with one or more slaves serving as "drivers" to assist the overseer. Plantations remained labor-intensive operations. Only the production of sugar, among the southern staples, was heavily mechanized.

Tidewater and Frontier

Southern planters shared a commitment to preserve slavery as the source of their wealth and stature. Yet in other ways they were a diverse group. On the one hand, the tobacco and rice planters of the Atlantic Tidewater were part of a settled region and a culture that reached back 150 to 200 years. In contrast, such states as Mississippi and Arkansas were at or just emerging from the frontier stage, since most residents had arrived after 1815.

TIDEWATER SOCIETY It was along the Tidewater, especially the bays of the Chesapeake and the South Carolina coast, that the legendary "Old South" was born. Here, masters erected substantial homes, some of them—especially between Charleston and Columbia—the classic white-pillared mansions in the Greek revival style.

The ideal of the Tidewater South was the English country gentleman. As in England, in the Tidewater South the local gentry often served as justices of the peace, and the Episcopal Church remained the socially accepted road to heaven. Here, too, family names continued to be important in politics.

SOCIETY IN THE COTTON KINGDOM While the newer regions of the South boasted of planters with cultivated manners, as a group the cotton lords were a different breed. Whatever their background, whether planters, farmers, overseers, or businessmen, these entrepreneurs had moved west for the same reason so many other white Americans had: to make their fortunes. By and large, the cotton gentry were self-made men who through hard work, aggressive business tactics, and good luck had risen from ordinary backgrounds. For them,

Source: Library of Congress, Prints and Photographs Division [LC-DIG-cwpb-03718]

| *John Botts, a reasonably well-to-do planter with his family from Culpepper, Virginia. A good many southern planters lacked white-pillared stately homes like this one; though even here, the columns appear to need painting and a glass pane above the door is missing.*

the cotton boom and the exploitation of enslaved men and women offered the opportunity to move up in a new society that lacked an entrenched elite.

SLAVEHOLDERS' VALUES That business orientation was especially apparent in the cotton kingdom, where planters sought to maximize their profits and constantly reinvested their returns in land and slaves. As one visitor said of Mississippi slaveholders: "To sell cotton in order to buy negroes—to make more cotton to buy more negroes, 'ad infinitum,' is the aim and direct tendency of all the operations of the thoroughgoing cotton planter." And indeed there was money to be made. The combined annual income of the richest thousand families of the cotton kingdom approached $50 million,

while the wealth of the remaining 666,000 families amounted to only about $60 million.

Although most planters ranked among the richest citizens in America, their homes were often simple one- or two-story unpainted wooden frame houses, and some were log cabins. A visitor to one Georgia plantation reported that the house did not have a pane of glass in the windows, a door between the rooms, or a ceiling other than the roof. Practical men, few of the new cotton lords had absorbed the culture and learning of the traditional country gentleman.

The Master at Home

Whether supervising a Tidewater plantation or creating a cotton estate on the Texas frontier, the master had to coordinate a complex agricultural operation. He gave daily instructions concerning the work to be done, settled disputes between slaves and the overseer, and generally handed out rewards and penalties. In addition, the owner made the critical decisions concerning the planting, harvesting, and marketing of the crops. Planters also watched investments and expenditures, and they often sought to expand their production by clearing additional fields, buying more land or slaves, or investing in machinery such as cotton gins. As in any business these decisions required a sound understanding of the domestic and international market.

PATERNALISM In performing his duties the plantation owner was supposed to be the "master" of his crops, his family, and his slaves. Defenders of slavery held up this paternalistic ideal—the care and guidance of dependent "children"— maintaining that slavery promoted a genuine affection between caring master and loyal slaves. Yet in real life a concern for money and profits undermined this paternalistic ideal. Some of the most brutal forms of slavery existed on rice plantations in the Tidewater South, where the absenteeism of many owners combined with the sheer numbers of slaves

Southern Population, 1860

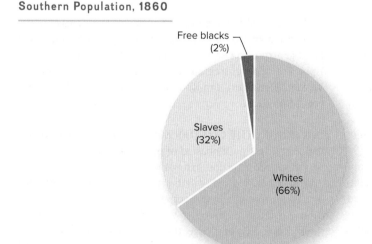

Total Population

White Population

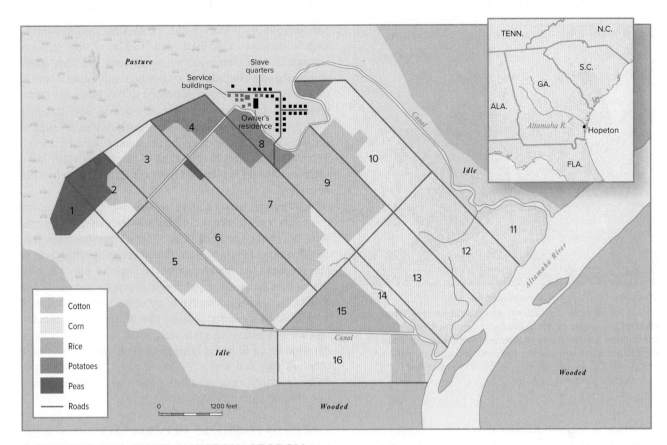

A PLANTATION LAYOUT, HOPETON, GEORGIA

Often covering a thousand acres or more, a plantation was laid out like a small village and contained several fields and usually extensive uncleared woods. Somewhere near the master's "big house" were the quarters—slave cabins clustered along one or more streets. Service buildings might include a smokehouse, stables, a gin house (for cotton) or a rice mill, and an overseer's dwelling. Like most large plantations, Hopeton produced a considerable amount of foodstuffs, but it grew both rice and cotton as staples. Most plantations concentrated on a single cash crop.

made close personal ties impossible. Owners of large plantations had little contact with their slaves, except for a few domestic servants. Nor could paternalism mask the reality that slavery everywhere rested on violence, racism, and exploitation.

The Plantation Mistress

Upper-class southern white women, like those in the North, grew up with the ideal of domesticity, reinforced by the notion of a paternalistic master who was lord of the plantation. But the plantation mistress soon discovered that, given the demands placed on her, the ideal was hard to fulfill.

MISTRESS'S DUTIES In her youth a genteel lady enjoyed a certain amount of leisure. But once she married and became a plantation mistress, a southern woman was often shocked by the size of her responsibilities. Nursing the sick, making clothing, tending the garden, caring for the poultry, and overseeing every aspect of food preparation were all her domain. She also had to supervise and plan the work of the domestic servants and distribute clothing. After taking care of breakfast, one harried Carolina mistress recounted that she "had

the [sewing] work cut out, gave orders about dinner, had the horse feed fixed in hot water, had the box filled with cork: went to see the carpenters working on the negro houses . . . now I have to cut out the flannel jackets." Sarah Williams, the New York bride of a North Carolina planter, admitted that her mother-in-law "works harder than any Northern farmer's wife I know."

Unlike female reformers in the North, upper-class southern women did not openly challenge their role, but some found their sphere confining, especially the never-ending task of managing slaves. Yet without the labor of slaves, the lifestyle of these women was impossible.

Some women drew a parallel between their situation and that of the slaves. Both were subject to male dominance, and independent-minded women found the subordination of marriage difficult. Susan Dabney Smedes, in her recollection of growing up on an Alabama plantation, recalled that "it was a saying that the mistress of a plantation was the most complete slave on it."

MISCEGENATION Many women were deeply discontented, too, with the widespread double standard for sexual behavior and with the daily reminders of **miscegenation** some

©The Historic New Orleans Collection/Bridgeman Images

Sarah Pierce Vick, the mistress of a plantation near Vicksburg, Mississippi, pauses to speak to one of her slaves, who may be holding feed for her horse. A plantation mistress had many duties and, while enjoying the comforts brought by wealth and status, often found her life more difficult than she had anticipated before marriage.

had to face. A man who fathered illegitimate children by slave women suffered no social or legal penalties, even in the case of rape (southern law did not recognize such a crime against slave women). In contrast, a white woman guilty of adultery lost all social respectability.

Mary Chesnut, the wife of a South Carolina planter, knew the reality of miscegenation firsthand from her father-in-law's liaisons with slave women. She sneered in her diary at the assumptions of male superiority. "Like the patriarchs of old, our men live all in one house with their wives and concubines; and the mulattoes one sees in every family partly resemble the white children. Any lady is ready to tell you who is the father of all the mulattoes one sees in everybody's household but her own. Those, she seems to think, drop from the clouds. My disgust sometimes is boiling over."

Still, only a small minority of women questioned either their place in southern society or the corrosive influence of slavery. Racism was so pervasive within American society that the few white southern women who privately criticized the institution displayed little empathy for the plight of slaves themselves, including black women.

Yeoman Farmers

FARMERS AND HERDERS   In terms of numbers, yeoman farm families were the backbone of southern society, accounting for more than half the southern white population. They owned no slaves and farmed the traditional 80 to 160 acres, like northern farmers. About 80 percent owned their own land, and the rest were tenant farmers who hoped one day to acquire a homestead. They settled almost everywhere in the South, except in the rice and sugar districts and valuable river

bottomlands of the Deep South, which were monopolized by large slaveowners. Like Ferdinand Steel, most were semisubsistence farmers who raised primarily corn and hogs, along with perhaps a few bales of cotton or some tobacco, which they sold to obtain the cash needed to buy items like sugar, coffee, and salt. Some were not so much farmers as herdsmen, who set large herds of scrawny cattle or pigs to forage in the woods until it was time for the annual drive to market. Yeoman farmers lacked the wealth of planters, but they had a pride and dignity that earned them the respect of their richer neighbors.

Southern farmers led more isolated lives than their northern counterparts. Yet the social activities of these people were not much different from those of northern farmers. Religion played an important role at camp meetings held in late summer after the crops were laid by and before harvest time. As in the North, neighbors also met to exchange labor and tools, always managing to combine work with fun. A Tennessee plains farmer recalled that his neighbors "seem to take delight in helping each other sutch as lay[ing] railings, cornshucking and house raising[.] [T]hey tried to help each other all they could and dancet all night." Court sessions, militia musters, political rallies—these too were occasions that brought rural folk together.

LIMITS TO ECONOMIC OPPORTUNITY   Because yeoman farmers lacked cheap slave labor, good transportation, and access to credit, they could not compete with planters in the production of staples. When it came to selling their corn and wheat, small farmers conducted only limited business with planters, who usually grew as many of their own foodstuffs as possible. In the North, urban centers became a market for small farmers, but in the South the lack of towns limited this internal market.

Thus, while southern yeoman farmers were not poor, they suffered from a chronic lack of money and the absence of conveniences that northern farm families enjoyed, such as cast-iron stoves, sewing machines, specialized tools, and good furniture. A few chafed at the absence of public schools and greater opportunities. Josiah Hinds, who hacked a farm out of the isolated woods of northern Mississippi, worried that his children were growing up "wild." He complained that "education is but little prized by my neighbours," who were satisfied "if the corn and cotton grows to perfection . . . [and] brings a fare price, and hog meat is at hand to boil with the greens."

ABSENCE OF CLASS CONFLICT   In some ways, then, the worlds of yeoman farmers and upper-class planters were not only different but also in conflict. Still, a hostility between the two classes did not emerge. Yeoman farmers admired planters and hoped that one day they would join the gentry themselves. And even white southerners who owned no slaves accepted slavery as a means of controlling African Americans as members of an inferior social caste based on race. "Now suppose they was free," one poor farmer told Frederick Law Olmsted, a traveler from the North, "You see they'd all think

MISTRESSES AND HOUSE SERVANTS

Mary Boykin Chesnut was a plantation mistress in South Carolina for many years. Her husband served in the U.S. Senate and later as an aide to Confederate President Jefferson Davis. In this diary excerpt (Document 1), Chesnut compares the conduct of antislavery advocates with that of her mother, grandmother, and mother-in-law. In the second document, an excerpt from a slave narrative, Harriet Ann Jacobs describes the mistress of the plantation where she had been enslaved.

DOCUMENT 1
A Plantation Mistress's View of Living with Slaves

November 27, 1861. "Ye who listen with credulity to the whispers of fancy," pause and look on this picture and that.

On one side Mrs. Stowe, Greeley, Thoreau, Emerson, Sumner* in nice New England homes—clean, clear, sweet-smelling—shut up in libraries, writing books which ease their hearts of their bitterness to us, or editing newspapers—all [of] which pays better than anything else in the world. . . .

What self-denial do they practice? It is the cheapest philanthropy trade in the world—easy. Easy as setting John Brown to come down here [in his 1859 raid on Harpers Ferry] and cut our throats in Christ's name.

Now, what I have seen of my mother's life, my grandmother's, my mother-in-law's:

These people were educated at Northern schools mostly—read the same as their Northern contemners, the same daily newspapers, the same Bible—have the same ideas of right and wrong—are highbred, lovely, good, pious—doing their duty as they

conceive it. They live in negro villages. They do not preach and teach hate as a gospel and the sacred duty of murder and insurrection, but they strive to ameliorate the condition of these Africans in every particular. They set them the example of a perfect life—life of utter self-abnegation. Think of these holy New Englanders, forced to have a negro village walk through their houses whenever they saw fit—dirty, slatternly, idle. . . . These women are more troubled by their duty to negroes, have less chance to live their own lives in peace than if they were African missionaries. They have a swarm of blacks about them as children under their care—not as Mrs. Stowe's fancy paints them, but the hard, unpleasant, unromantic, undeveloped savage Africans. And they hate slavery worse than Mrs. Stowe. . . .

I do not do anything whatever but get out of [the way of my slaves]. When I come home, I see the negroes themselves. They look as comfortable as possible and I hear

all they have to say. Then I see the overseer and the Methodist parson. *None* of these complain of each other. And I am satisfied. My husband supported his plantation by his law practice. Now it is running him in debt. We are bad managers. Our people have never earned their own bread. . . .

I say we are no better than our judges in the North—*and no worse.* . . . The slave-owners, when they are good men and women, are the martyrs. And as far as I have seen, the people here are quite as good as anywhere else. I hate slavery. I even hate the harsh authority I see parents think it their duty to exercise *toward their children.*

There now!! What good does it do to write all that?

---

*Harriet Beecher Stowe, author of *Uncle Tom's Cabin;* Horace Greeley, editor of the New York *Tribune;* Henry David Thoreau, Ralph Waldo Emerson, and Senator Charles Sumner of Massachusetts.

Source: Mary Chestnut's Civil War, edited by C. Vann Woodward. New Haven, CT: Yale University Press, 1981, 245–246.

DOCUMENT 2
A Slave's Experience of Living with a Plantation Mistress

Mrs. Flint, like many southern women, was totally deficient in energy. She had not strength to superintend her household affairs; but her nerves were so strong, that she could sit in her easy chair and see a woman whipped, till the blood trickled from every stroke of the lash. She was a member of the church; but partaking of the Lord's supper did not seem to put her in a Christian frame of mind. If dinner was not served at the exact time on that particular Sunday, she would station herself in the kitchen, and wait till it was dished, and then spit in all the kettles and pans that had been used for cooking. She did this to prevent the cook and her children from eking out their meager fare with the remains of the gravy and other scrapings. The slaves could get nothing to eat except what she chose to give them. Provisions were weighed out by the pound and ounce, three times a day. I can assure you she gave them no chance to eat wheat bread from her flour barrel. She knew how many biscuits a quart of flour would make, and exactly what size they ought to be.

Dr. Flint was an epicure. The cook never sent a dinner to his table without fear and trembling; for if there happened to be a dish not to his liking, he would either order her to be whipped, or compel her to eat every mouthful of it in his presence. The poor, hungry creature might not have objected to eating it; but she did object to having her master cram it down her throat till she choked. . . .

From others than the master persecution also comes in [cases of miscegenation]. I once saw a young slave girl dying soon after the birth of a child nearly white. In her agony she cried out, "O Lord, come and take me!" Her mistress stood by, and mocked at her like an incarnate fiend. "You suffer, do you?" she exclaimed. "I am glad of it. You deserve it all, and more too."

The girl's mother said, "The baby is dead, thank God; and I hope my poor child will soon be in heaven, too."

"Heaven!" retorted the mistress. "There is no such place for the like of her and her bastard."

The poor mother turned away, sobbing. Her dying daughter called her, feebly, and as she bent over her, I heard her say, "Don't grieve so, mother; God knows all about it; and HE will have mercy upon me."

Her sufferings, afterwards, became so intense, that her mistress felt unable to stay; but when she left the room, the scornful smile was still on her lips.

Source: Jacobs, Harriet Ann, Incidents in the Life of a Slave Girl. Written by Herself, edited by Lydia Maria Child. Boston, MA: Thayer & Eldridge, 1861, 22–24.

THINKING CRITICALLY

What does Chesnut mean when she says that most plantation mistresses set for their slaves "the example of a perfect life—life of utter self-abnegation"? Why might a mistress have such a cruel reaction to the dying slave girl in Harriet Jacobs's account? How should historians deal with the argument that one or the other account is not representative?

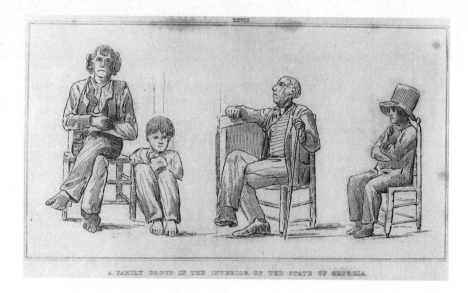

A majority of white southerners were members of non-slaveholding yeoman farm families. Ruggedly independent, these families depended on their own labor and lived under more primitive conditions than large plantation owners or small farmers in the North. Basil Hall, an Englishman traveling through the South in 1827 and 1828, sketched members of this Georgia family with the aid of a camera lucida, an optical device that projected an image from real life onto paper, where it could be traced with accuracy.

©William L. Clements Library, University of Michigan

A FAMILY GROUP IN THE INTERIOR OF THE STATE OF GEORGIA.

themselves as good as we." Racism and fear of black people were sufficient to keep non-slaveholders loyal to southern institutions.

Poor Whites

LIVES OF POOR WHITES The poorest white southerners were confined to land that no one else wanted: the wiregrass region of southeastern Georgia, the sand hills of central South Carolina, the pine barrens of the coastal plains from Virginia to southeastern Mississippi. These southerners lived in rough, unchinked, windowless log cabins located in the remotest areas and were often squatters without title to the land they were on. The men spent their time hunting and fishing, while women did the domestic work and what farming they could manage. Largely illiterate, they suffered from malnutrition stemming from a monotonous diet of corn, pork, and whiskey, and they were afflicted with malaria and hookworm, diseases that sapped their energy. Other white southerners scornfully referred to poor whites as crackers, white trash, sand-hillers, and clay-eaters. Numbers are hard to come by, but perhaps 5 percent of the white population comprised these poor folk.

RELATIONS WITH PLANTERS Because poor whites traded with slaves, exchanging whiskey for stolen goods, contemptuous planters often bought them out simply to rid the neighborhood of them. For their part, poor whites keenly resented planters, but their hostility toward African Americans was even stronger. Poor whites refused to work alongside slaves or perform any work commonly done by them and vehemently opposed ending slavery. Emancipation would remove one of the few symbols of their status—that they were, at least, free.

> **REVIEW**
> What was the relationship between the South's great planters and yeoman farmers?

THE PECULIAR INSTITUTION

SLAVES WERE NOT FREE. THAT overwhelming fact must be understood before anything is said about the kindness or the cruelty that individual slaves experienced; before any consideration of healthy or unhealthy living conditions; before any discussion of how slave families coped with hardship, rejoiced in shared pleasures, or worshiped in prayer. The lives of slaves were affected day in and day out, in big ways and small, by the basic reality that slaves were not their own masters. If a slave's workload was reasonable, it remained so only at the master's discretion, not because the slave determined it to be. If slaves married or visited family or friends on a nearby plantation, they did so only with the master's permission. If they raised a family, they could remain together only as long as the master did not separate them by sale. Whatever slaves wanted to do, they had always to consider the response of their masters.

When power was distributed as unequally as it was between masters and slaves, every action on the part of the enslaved involved a certain calculation, conscious or unconscious. The consequences of every act, of every expression or gesture, had to be considered. In that sense, the line between freedom and slavery penetrated every corner of a slave's life, and it was an absolute and overwhelming distinction.

SLAVERY AND RACE One other stark fact reinforced the sharp line between freedom and slavery: slaves were distinguished on the basis of color. While the peculiar institution was an economic system of labor, it was also a **caste system** based on race. The color line of slavery made it much easier to brand black people as somehow different. It made it easier to defend the institution and win the support of yeoman farmers and poor white southerners, even though in many ways the system held them back. Hence slavery must be understood on many levels: not only as an economic system but also as a racial and cultural one, not only in terms of its outward conditions of life and labor but also through the inner demands it made on the soul.

Work and Discipline

The conditions slaves encountered varied widely, depending on the size of the farm or plantation, the crop being grown, the personality of the master, and whether he was an absentee owner. On small farms slaves worked in the fields with the owners and had much closer contact with whites. On plantations, in contrast, most slaves dealt primarily with the overseer, who was paid by the size of the harvest he brought in and was therefore often harsh in his approach. The largest plantations, which raised rice and sugar, also required the longest hours and the most grueling labor.

ORGANIZATION OF SLAVE LABOR House servants and the drivers, who supervised the field hands, were accorded the highest status, and skilled artisans such as carpenters and blacksmiths also received special recognition. Field hands, both men and women, did the hardest work and were sometimes divided into plowhands and hoe gangs. In the summer of 1854 Olmsted watched a group of Mississippi slaves return to work in the fields after a thunderstorm. "First came, led by an old driver carrying a whip, 40 of the largest and strongest women I ever saw together; . . . they carried themselves loftily, each having a hoe over the shoulder, and walking with a free, powerful swing like [soldiers] on the march." Behind them were the plowhands on the mules, "the cavalry, thirty strong, mostly men, but a few of them women." Bringing up the rear was "a lean and vigilant white overseer, on a brisk pony."

Some planters organized their slaves by the gang system, in which a white overseer or a black driver supervised gangs of 20 to 25 adults. Although the approach extracted long hours of hard labor, the slaves had to be constantly supervised and shirkers were difficult to detect. Other planters preferred the task system, under which each slave was given a specific daily assignment to complete, after which he or she was finished for the day. This system allowed slaves to work at their own pace, gave them an incentive to do careful work, and freed overseers from having to closely supervise the work. But, as drivers also discovered, slaves resisted vigorously if masters tried to increase the workload. The task system was most common in the rice fields, whereas the gang system predominated in the cotton districts. Many planters used a combination of the two systems.

Toil began just before sunrise and continued until dusk. During cultivation and harvest, slaves were in the field 15 to 16 hours a day, eating a noonday meal there and resting before resuming labor. Work was uncommon on Sundays, and frequently only a half day was required on Saturdays. Even so, the routine was taxing. "We . . . have everybody at work before day dawns," an Arkansas cotton planter reported. "I am never caught in bed after day light nor is any body else on the place, and we continue in the cotton fields when we can have fair weather till it is so dark we can't see to work."

Often masters gave money, additional food, gifts, and time off to slaves who worked diligently, but the threat of punishment was always present. Slaves could be denied passes; their food allowance could be reduced; and if all else failed, they could be sold. The most common instrument of punishment, however, was the whip. The frequency of its use varied from plantation to plantation, but few slaves escaped the lash entirely. "We have to rely more and more on the power of fear," the planter James Henry Hammond acknowledged. "We are determined to continue masters, and to do so we have to draw the rein tighter and tighter day by day to be assured that we hold them in complete check."

Slave Maintenance

CLOTHING AND HOUSING Planters generally bought rough, cheap cloth for slave clothing and each year gave adults at most only a couple of outfits and a pair of shoes that were worn out by the end of the year. Few had enough clothing or blankets to keep warm when the weather dipped below freezing. Some planters provided well-built housing, but more commonly slaves lived in cramped, poorly built cabins that were leaky in wet weather, drafty in cold, and furnished with only a few crude chairs, benches and a table, perhaps a mattress filled with corn husks or straw, and a few pots and dishes. To keep medical expenses down, slaveowners treated sick slaves themselves and called in a doctor only for serious cases. Conditions varied widely, but on average, a slaveowner spent less than a dollar a year on medical care for each slave.

SLAVES' LOWER LIFE EXPECTANCY Even so, the United States was the only slave society in the Americas where the slave population increased naturally—indeed, at about the same rate as the white population. Nevertheless, a deficient diet, inadequate clothing and shelter, long hours of hard toil, and poor medical care resulted in a lower life expectancy among slaves.

Resistance

SLAVE REVOLTS IN LATIN AMERICA Slaves resisted the bondage imposed on them. The most radical form of resistance was rebellion, which occurred repeatedly in slave societies in the Americas. In Latin America, slave revolts were frequent, involving hundreds and even thousands of slaves and pitched battles in which large numbers were killed. The most successful slave revolt occurred in France's sugar-rich colony Saint-Domingue (the western part of the Caribbean island of Hispaniola). There, free blacks who had fought in the American Revolution because of France's alliance with the United States brought back the ideals of freedom and equality. The brutally overworked population of half a million slaves was ready to revolt and received further encouragement from the example of the French Revolution. Under the leadership of Toussaint L'Ouverture, rebellion led to the establishment of Haiti in 1804, the second independent republic in the Western Hemisphere.

Elsewhere, Jamaica averaged one significant slave revolt every year from 1731 to 1823, while in 1823 thousands revolted in British Guiana. Jamaica, too, witnessed an uprising, of some 20,000 slaves in 1831. These revolts, and ones in 1823 and 1824 in British-controlled Demerara, were savagely suppressed. And in Brazil, which had the largest number of slaves outside the United States, the government took 50 years to suppress with military force a colony of about 20,000 slaves who had sought refuge in the mountains.

INFREQUENCY OF REVOLTS IN THE UNITED STATES

In contrast, slave revolts were rare in the United States. Whereas in Latin America, blacks outnumbered whites, the reverse was true in most of the American South. In the United States, too, the government was much more powerful, most slaves were native-born, and family life was much stronger. Slaves recognized the odds against them, and many potential leaders became fugitives instead. In a sense, what is remarkable is that American slaves revolted at all.

Early in the nineteenth century several well-organized uprisings in the United States nearly materialized. In 1800 Gabriel Prosser, a slave blacksmith, recruited perhaps a couple hundred slaves in a plan to march on Richmond and capture the governor. But a heavy thunderstorm postponed the attack and a few slaves then betrayed the plot. Prosser and other leaders were eventually captured and executed. Denmark Vesey's conspiracy in Charleston in 1822 met a similar fate (see Chapter 11).

NAT TURNER'S REBELLION The most famous slave revolt, led by a literate slave preacher named Nat Turner, was smaller and more spontaneous. Turner, who lived on a farm in southeastern Virginia, was given unusual privileges by his master, whom he described as a kind and trusting man. Spurred on by an almost fanatic mysticism, Turner became convinced that God intended to punish white people. One night in 1831 following an eclipse of the sun, he and six confederates stole out and murdered Turner's master and family. Gaining some 70 recruits as they went, Turner's band killed 57 white men, women, and children. Along the way, the members voiced their grievances against slavery and announced that they intended to confiscate their masters' wealth.

Although the uprising was put down and Turner executed, it left white southerners throughout the region with a haunting uneasiness. Nat Turner had seemed a model slave, yet who could read a slave's true emotions behind the mask of obedience?

DAY-TO-DAY RESISTANCE Beyond outright rebellion, there were other, more subtle, ways of resisting a master's authority. Running away was one. With the odds stacked heavily against them, few runaways escaped safely to freedom except from the border states. More frequently, slaves fled to nearby woods or swamps to avoid punishment or protest their treatment. Some runaways stayed out only a few days; others held out for months.

Many slaves resisted by abusing their masters' property. They mishandled animals, broke tools and machinery, misplaced items, and worked carelessly in the fields. Slaves also sought to trick the master by feigning illness or injury and by hiding rocks in the cotton they picked. Slaves complained directly to the owner about an overseer's mistreatment, thereby attempting to drive a wedge between the two.

The most common form of resistance, and a persistent annoyance to slaveowners, was theft. Slaves took produce from the garden, raided the master's smokehouse, secretly slaughtered his stock, and killed his poultry. "They always told us it was wrong to lie and steal," recalled Josephine Howard, a former slave in Texas, "but why did the white folks steal my mammy and her mammy? They lived over in Africa. . . . That's the sinfullest stealing there is."

SLAVES' HIDDEN FEELINGS Slaves learned to outwit their masters by wearing an "impenetrable mask" around

| Slaves resisted their masters by fleeing to nearby swamps or forests. Masters often used specially trained dogs to track them. Those shown here were imported from Cuba, and Zachary Taylor, who was elected president of the United States in 1848, was among the planters who imported them.
©Walker Art Gallery/National Museums Liverpool/ Bridgeman Images

whites, one bondsman recalled. "How much of joy, of sorrow, of misery and anguish have they hidden from their tormentors." Frederick Douglass, the most famous fugitive slave, explained that "as the master studies to keep the slave ignorant, the slave is cunning enough to make the master think he succeeds."

✓ REVIEW
In what ways did slaves resist their oppression?

SLAVE CULTURE

TRAPPED IN BONDAGE, FACED WITH the futility of revolt, slaves could at least forge a culture of their own. By the nineteenth century, American slaves had been separated from much of their traditional African heritage, but that did not mean they had fully accepted the dominant white culture. Instead, slaves combined strands from their African past with customs that evolved from their life in America. This slave culture was most distinct on big plantations, where the slave population was large and slaves had more opportunity to live apart from white scrutiny.

The Slave Family

BREAKUP OF FAMILIES Maintaining a sense of family was one of the most remarkable achievements of African Americans in bondage, given the obstacles that faced them. Southern law did not recognize slave marriages as legally binding, nor did it allow slave parents complete authority over their children. Black women faced the possibility of rape by the master or overseer without legal recourse, and husbands, wives, and children had to live with the fear of being sold and separated. From 1820 to 1860 more than 2 million slaves were sold in the domestic slave trade. Such sales separated perhaps 600,000 husbands and wives.

FAMILY TIES IN SLAVERY Despite their vulnerability, family ties remained strong, as slave culture demonstrated. The marriage ceremony among slaves varied from a formal religious service to jumping over a broomstick in front of the slave community to nothing more than the master giving verbal approval. Whatever the ceremony, slaves viewed the ritual as a public affirmation of the couple's commitment to their new responsibilities. Rather than adopting white norms, slaves developed their own moral code concerning sexual relations and marriage. Although young slaves often engaged in premarital sex, they were expected to choose a partner and become part of a stable family. It has been estimated that at least one in five slave women had one or more children before marriage, but most of these mothers eventually married. "The negroes had their own ideas of morality, and they held them very strictly," the daughter of a Georgia planter recalled. Black churches played a leading role in condemning adultery.

GENDER ROLES The traditional nuclear family of father, mother, and children was the rule, not the exception, among slaves. Within the marriage the father was viewed as the traditional head of the family; wives were to be submissive and obey their husbands. Labor in the quarters was divided according to sex. Women did the indoor work, such as cooking, washing, and sewing, and men performed outdoor chores, such as gathering firewood, hauling water, and tend-

Students of this painting speculate that the participants in this Kitchen Ball at White Sulphur Springs included both free blacks and slaves who had accompanied their masters to this resort in present-day West Virginia (then part of Virginia). Note the individuality of the faces and figures represented here—a striking contrast to the minstrelsy caricatures of blacks in many paintings of the period.

©De Agostini Picture Library/Bridgeman Images

ing the animals and garden plots. The men also hunted and fished to supplement the spare weekly rations.

Beyond the nuclear family, slaves developed strong kinship networks that promoted a sense of community. Aunts and uncles looked after children who lost their parents through death or sale. When children were sold to a new plantation, a family in the slave quarters took them in. Thus all members of the slave society drew together in an extended network of mutual obligation.

Slave Songs and Stories

PROTEST AND CELEBRATION   In the songs they sang, slaves expressed some of their deepest feelings about love and work and the joys and pain of life. "The songs of the slave represent the sorrows of his heart," commented Frederick Douglass. Surely there was bitterness as well as sorrow when slaves sang:

> We raise the wheat
> They give us the corn
> We bake the bread
> They give us the crust
> We sift the meal
> They give us the husk
> We peel the meat
> They give us the skin
> And that's the way
> They take us in

Yet songs were also central to the celebrations held in the slave quarters: for marriages, Christmas revels, and after harvest time. And a slave on the way to the fields might sing:

> Saturday night and Sunday too
> Young gals on my mind.
> Monday morning 'way 'fore day,
> Old master's got me gwine.
> Peggy does you love me now?

FOLKTALES   Slaves expressed themselves through stories as well as song. Most often these folktales used animals as symbolic models for the predicaments in which slaves found themselves. In the best known of these, the cunning Brer Rabbit was a weak fellow who defeated larger animals like Brer Fox and Brer Bear by using his wits. Other stories were less symbolic and contained more overt hostility to white people; slaves usually told them only among themselves. But the message, whether direct or symbolic, was much the same: to laugh at the master's shortcomings and teach the young how to survive in a hostile world.

Steal Away to Jesus

At the center of slave culture was religion. The Second Great Awakening, which had begun on the southern frontier, converted many slaves, most of whom joined the Methodist and Baptist churches. Slaves constituted more than a quarter of the members of both of these southern churches.

Some slaveowners encouraged religion among slaves as one means of social control. Masters provided slaves with a minister (often white), set the time and place of services, and usually insisted that a white person be present. "Church was what they called it," one former slave protested, "but all that preacher talked about was for us slaves to obey our masters and not to lie and steal." In response, some slaves rejected all religion, while others continued to believe in conjuring, voodoo, and various practices derived from African religion.

SLAVE RELIGION   But most slaves sought a Christianity firmly their own, beyond the control of the master. On many plantations they met secretly at night, in the quarters or at "hush harbors" in the safety of the woods, where they broke into rhythmic singing and dancing, modeled on the ring shout of African religion. Even regular services generated intense enthusiasm. "The way in which we worshiped is almost indescribable," one slave preacher recalled. "The singing was accompanied by a certain ecstasy of motion, clapping of hands, tossing of heads. . . ." In an environment where slaves,

Source: National Gallery of Art, Washington

| *Slave or free? In 1863 artist Eastman Johnson sketched this confident black man, whose high boots, high-buttoned shirt, and jacket suggest he might have driven a carriage or perhaps was a freedman who worked in the army during the Civil War. We don't know the man's identity, and the boundary line between slave and free was sometimes stretched, especially for slaves whose job required them to travel unsupervised.*

for most of the day, were prevented from expressing their deepest feelings, such meetings served as a satisfying emotional release.

Religion also provided slaves with values and gave them a sense of self-worth. Slaves learned that God would redeem the poor and downtrodden and raise them one day to honor and glory. Rejecting the teaching of some white ministers that slavery was punishment, slave preachers assured their congregations that they were the chosen people of God. "This is one reason why I believe in hell," a former slave declared. "I don't believe a just God is going to take no such man as my former master into His Kingdom."

SLAVE SPIRITUALS Again, song played a central role. Slaves sang religious "spirituals" at work and at play as well as in religious services. Seemingly meek and otherworldly, the songs often contained a hidden element of protest. Frederick Douglass disclosed that when slaves sang longingly of "Canaan, sweet Canaan," they were thinking not only of the Bible's Promised Land but also of the North and freedom. When slaves heard "Steal Away to Jesus" sung in the fields, they knew that a secret devotional meeting was scheduled that evening. Songs became one of the few ways that slaves could openly express, in the approved language of Christianity, their yearning for freedom.

The Slave Community

HIERARCHY Although slaves managed with remarkable success to preserve a sense of self-worth in a religion and a culture of their own, the hard reality of slavery made it impossible to escape fully from white control. Even the social hierarchy within the slave quarters never was entirely free from the white world. Slave preachers, conjurers, and herb doctors held status that no white conferred, but the prestige of a slave driver rested ultimately on the authority of the white master. Similarly, skilled slaves and house servants often felt superior to other slaves, an attitude masters consciously promoted. "We house slaves thought we was better'n the others what worked in the field," one personal servant confessed. Light-skinned slaves sometimes deemed their color a badge of superiority. Fanny Kemble, a British actress married to a wealthy planter, recorded that one woman begged to be relieved of field labor, which she considered degrading, "on 'account of her color.' "

Lucy Skipworth, who was the daughter of a driver and had been educated by her mistress, was a member of the slave elite on both counts. At Hopewell plantation in Alabama, she was in full charge of the main residence during her master's frequent absences. She ran a plantation school (despite white opposition) and, as a devout Baptist, supervised her fellow slaves' religious life. Eager for her master's approval, Skipworth on several occasions reported slave disobedience, which temporarily estranged her from the slave community. Yet in the end she was always welcomed back. While Skipworth never rebelled or apparently never considered running away, she was far from submissive. She defied white

authority, protected her family, and used her influence to get rid of an overseer the slaves disliked. Like many house servants, she lived between two worlds—her master's and the slave quarters—and was never entirely comfortable in either.

But the realities of slavery and white racism inevitably drove black people closer together in a common bond. Walled in from the individualistic white society beyond, slaves out of necessity created a community of their own.

Free Black Southerners

Of the 4 million African Americans living in the South in 1860, only 260,000—about 7 percent—were free. More than 85 percent of them lived in the Upper South, with almost 200,000 in Maryland, Virginia, and North Carolina alone. Free black southerners were also much more urban than the southern white and slave populations. As a rule, free African Americans were more literate than slaves, and they were disproportionately female and much more likely to be of mixed ancestry.

Most free black southerners lived in rural areas, although usually not near plantations. A majority eked out a living farming or in low-paying unskilled jobs, but some did well enough to own slaves themselves. In 1830 about 3,600 did, although commonly their "property" was their wives or children, purchased because they could not be emancipated under state laws. Only a few were full-blown slaveowners.

BETWEEN FREEDOM AND SLAVERY The boundary sometimes blurred between free and enslaved African Americans. Sally Thomas of Nashville was technically a slave, but in the 1830s and 1840s her owner allowed her to ply her trade as a laundress and keep some of her wages. (She saved some $350, which she used to purchase the freedom of one of her sons.) The boundary stretched especially for African Americans working along rivers and the seashore in the fishing trades, as pilots or seamen, or as "watermen" ferrying supplies and stores in small boats. Under such conditions, laborers preserved more freedom and initiative than did most agricultural workers.

Along Albemarle Sound in North Carolina, free blacks and slaves flocked from miles around to "fisherman's courts," a kind of annual hiring fair. Amid drinking, carousing, cockfighting, and boxing, men who ran commercial fishing operations signed up workers. The crews would then go down to the shore in late February or early March to net vast schools of fish, hauling up onto the beach over 100,000 herring in four to seven hours. Women and children then headed, gutted, cleaned, and salted the fish. A good "cutter" might head tens of thousands of herring a day. In such settings African Americans, both free and slave, could share news with folk they did not regularly see.

Following Nat Turner's Rebellion of 1831, southern legislatures increased the restrictions on free African Americans. They were forbidden to enter a different state, had to carry papers certifying their freedom, could not assemble when they wished, were subject to a curfew, often had to post a

©Afro American Newspapers/Gado/Getty Images

| This painting shows a free African American news vendor in Baltimore. Urban blacks in the South, including slaves, enjoyed greater personal freedom and access to more social opportunities but had only limited economic opportunity.

bond and be licensed to work, and could not vote, hold office, or testify in court against white people.

Free African Americans occupied an uncertain position in southern society, well above black slaves but distinctly beneath even poorer white southerners. They were victims of a society that had no place for them.

 REVIEW

In what ways did the culture and communities created by blacks help to sustain them in slavery?

SOUTHERN SOCIETY AND THE DEFENSE OF SLAVERY

FROM WEALTHY PLANTERS TO YEOMAN farmers, from free black slaveholders to white mountaineers, from cotton field hands to urban craftworkers, the South was a remarkably diverse region. Yet it was united by its dependence on staple crops and above all by the institution of slavery. As the South's economy became more and more dependent on slave-produced staples, slavery became more central to the life of the South, to its culture and its identity.

The Virginia Debate of 1832

At the time of the Revolution, the leading critics of slavery had been southerners—Jefferson, Washington, Madison, and Patrick Henry among them. But beginning in the 1820s, in the wake of the controversy over admitting Missouri as a slave state (see Chapter 9), southern leaders became less apologetic about slavery and more aggressive in defending it. The turning point occurred in the early 1830s, when the South found itself increasingly under attack. It was in 1831 that William Lloyd Garrison began publishing his abolitionist newspaper, *The Liberator.* In that year, too, Nat Turner launched the revolt that frightened so many white southerners.

SIGNIFICANCE OF THE VIRGINIA DEBATE In response to the Turner insurrection, a number of Virginia's western counties, where there were few slaves, petitioned the legislature to adopt a program for gradual emancipation. Between January 16 and 25, 1832, the House of Delegates engaged in a remarkable debate over the merits of slavery. In the end, however, the legislature refused, by a vote of 73 to 58, to consider legislation to end slavery. The debate marked the last significant attempt of white southerners to challenge the peculiar institution.

In its aftermath most of them felt that the subject was no longer open to debate. Instead, during the 1830s and 1840s, southern leaders defended slavery as a positive good, not just for white people but for black people as well. As South Carolina Senator John C. Calhoun proclaimed in 1837, "I hold that in the present state of civilization, where two races . . . distinguished by color and other physical differences, as well as intellectual, are brought together, the relation now existing in the slaveholding states between the two is, instead of an evil, a good—a positive good."

The Proslavery Argument

RELIGIOUS, SOCIAL, AND RACIAL ARGUMENTS Politicians like Calhoun were not alone. White southern leaders justified slavery in a variety of ways. Ministers argued that none of the biblical prophets or Christ himself had ever condemned slavery. They also pointed out that classical Greece and Rome depended on slavery. They even cited John Locke, that giant of the Enlightenment, who had recognized slavery in the constitution he drafted for the colony of Carolina. African Americans belonged to an intellectually and emotionally inferior race, slavery's defenders argued, and therefore lacked the ability to care for themselves and required white guardianship.

Proslavery writers sometimes argued that slaves in the South lived better than factory workers in the North. Masters cared for slaves for life, whereas northern workers had no claim on their employer when they were unemployed, old, or no longer able to work. In advancing this argument, white southerners exaggerated the material comforts of slavery and minimized the average worker's standard of living—to say nothing of the psychological value of freedom. Still, to many white southerners, slavery seemed a more humane system of labor relations.

Defenders of slavery did not really expect to influence public opinion in the North. Their target was more often the slaveowners. As one southern editor explained: "We must satisfy the consciences, we must allay the fears of our own people.

George Washington, Slaveholder

This image is a lithograph of a painting. What's a lithograph? (Well worth it to Google "lithograph.")

Washington himself. Why so formally dressed for the hay field?

Source: Library of Congress, Prints and Photographs Division [LC-DIG-pga-02419]

Washington's two step-grandchildren

A young neighbor, perhaps Washington's overseer or a yeoman or tenant farmer

Advocates of the proslavery argument made strategic use of anecdotes and images portraying George Washington as the master of Mount Vernon, his plantation—without mentioning that upon his death, his will freed all his slaves. Based on a painting of 1851, this 1853 lithograph and others conveying a similar proslavery message found their way into thousands of southern parlors and libraries before the Civil War. (Historians of technology tell us that lithography came into widespread use in the early nineteenth century, allowing for the cheap mass production of images as well as print.) Such stories and pictures portrayed Washington as a benevolent patriarch—a father to his slaves as well as to his country—and depicted slavery as a benevolent institution. At the center of this scene, a group of hale, neatly outfitted black men refresh themselves with water brought by a slave woman, demurely dressed right up to her head covering. Judging by the riding crop in his hand and the horse (far left), Washington has just dismounted, perhaps to give some instructions to his overseer, a young man who holds not a whip but a rake—to help the slaves with the hay-gathering.

THINKING CRITICALLY

What is the significance of placing whites in the foreground of the painting? What point was the artist making by drawing Washington's two step-grandchildren happily at play in the left corner? What was the artist implying by portraying Washington and the young man (who is plainly of lesser status), talking with easy familiarity?

We must satisfy them that slavery is of itself right—that it is not a sin against God—that it is not an evil, moral or political. In this way only," he went on, "can we prepare our own people to defend their institutions."

Closing Ranks

Not all white southerners could quell their doubts. Still, a striking change in southern opinion seems to have occurred in the three decades before the Civil War. Outside the border states, few white southerners after 1840 would admit even in private that slavery was wrong. Those who continued to oppose slavery found themselves harassed, assaulted, and driven into exile. Southern mobs destroyed the presses of antislavery papers and threatened the editors into either keeping silent or leaving the state. Southern mails were forcibly closed to abolitionist propaganda, and defenders of the South's institutions carefully scrutinized textbooks and faculty members in southern schools.

Pivotal Moments for the Old South

THE SPREAD OF COTTON AND SLAVERY		POLITICAL FLASHPOINTS	
1793	Cotton gin sparks spread of crop	1820	Missouri Compromise
1815–1830s	Land rush into Alabama, Mississippi	1831	Garrison publishes *The Liberator*; Nat Turner Rebellion
1830–1838	Indian removal accelerates the rush	1832	Virginia Debate over slavery and emancipation
1840s	Spread to Red River, Arkansas, and east Texas	1836	Abolitionist mailing campaign; southerners pass "gag rule" on antislavery petition
1860	U.S. produces 75% of the world's cotton	1840s	Methodist and Baptist churches split into northern and southern organizations

Source: USDA Natural Resources Conservation Service

Increasingly, too, the debate over slavery spread to the national political arena. Before 1836 Andrew Jackson's enormous popularity in the South blocked the formation of a competitive two-party system there. The rise of the abolitionist movement in the 1830s, however, left many southerners uneasy, and when the Democrats nominated the northerner Martin Van Buren in 1836, southern Whigs seized on the issue of the security of slavery and charged that Van Buren could not be counted on to meet the abolitionist threat. The Whigs made impressive gains in the South in 1836, carrying several states and significantly narrowing the margin between the two parties.

During the Jacksonian era, most southern political battles did not revolve around slavery. Even so, southern politicians in both parties had to be careful to avoid the stigma of antislavery, since they were under mounting pressure from John Calhoun and his followers. Frustrated in his presidential hopes by the nullification crisis in 1832–1833 (Chapter 11), Calhoun sought to unite the South behind his leadership by agitating the slavery issue, introducing inflammatory resolutions in Congress, seizing on the abolitionist mailing campaign to demand censorship of the mails, and insisting on a gag rule to block antislavery petitions. During the 1830s and early 1840s few southern politicians followed his lead, but they did become extremely careful about being in the least critical of southern institutions. They knew quite well that even if their constituents were not as fanatical as Calhoun, southern voters overwhelmingly supported slavery.

> ✓ **REVIEW**
>
> How did southern whites defend slavery as a positive good?

PUTTING HISTORY IN GLOBAL CONTEXT

TWO REMARKABLE TRANSFORMATIONS were sweeping the world in the first half of the nineteenth century. The first was a series of political upheavals leading to increased democratic participation in many nation-states. The second, the Industrial Revolution, applied machine labor and technological innovation to commercial and agricultural economies.

Although it is common to identify the Industrial Revolution with New England's factories and the North's cities, that revolution transformed the rural South too. Cotton could not have become king without the demand created by textile factories or without the ability to "gin" the seeds out of cotton by Eli Whitney's invention. Nor could cotton production flourish without industrial advances in transportation, which allowed raw materials to be shipped worldwide. As for democratic change, the suffrage was extended in Britain by the Reform Bill of 1832, and popular uprisings spread across Europe in 1830 and 1848. In the United States, white southerners and northerners participated in the democratic reforms of the 1820s and 1830s.

The industrial and democratic revolutions thus transformed the South as well as the North, though in different ways. Increasingly, slavery became the focus of disputes between the two sections. The Industrial Revolution's demand for cotton increased the demand for slave labor and the profits to be gained from it. Yet the spread of democratic ideology worldwide increased pressure to abolish slavery. France and Britain had already done so. In eastern Europe the near-slavery of feudal serfdom was being eliminated as well: in 1848 within the Hapsburg empire; in 1861 in Russia; in 1864 in Romania.

In the mid-1840s the contradictory pressures of the industrial and democratic revolutions would begin to sharpen, as the United States embarked on a new program of westward expansion that thrust the slavery issue into the center of politics. Americans were forced to debate how much of the newly won territory should be open to slavery; and in doing so, some citizens began to question whether the Union could permanently endure, half slave and half free.

CHAPTER SUMMARY

The old south was a complex, biracial society that increasingly diverged from the rest of the United States in the years before 1860.

- Southerners placed heavy emphasis on agriculture. Given this rural way of life, few cities and towns developed.

  ► Southern commercial agriculture produced staple crops for sale in northern and European markets: tobacco, sugar, rice, and, above all, cotton.

  ► As southern agriculture expanded into the fresh lands of the Deep South, the slave population moved steadily westward and southward, and the Upper South became more diversified agriculturally.

- Slavery played a major role in shaping the class structure of the Old South.

  ► Ownership of slaves brought privilege and status.

  ► Planters on the older Eastern Seaboard enjoyed a more refined lifestyle than those on the new cotton frontier.

- Most slaveowners, however, owned only a few slaves, and the majority of southern whites were non-slaveowning yeoman farmers.

- The institution of slavery was both a labor system and a social system, regulating relations between the races.

  ► Slaves resisted bondage in many ways. Slave revolts, however, were rare.

  ► Slaves developed their own culture in which family, religion, and songs all helped cope with the pressures of bondage.

- As slavery came under mounting attack, white southerners developed a set of arguments defending slavery as a positive good.

Digging Deeper

The reports of Frederick Law Olmsted, who traveled through the South in the 1850s, make a fascinating jumping-off point for a first look at the region. Much of Olmsted's material is conveniently collected in Lawrence Powell, ed., *The Cotton Kingdom* (1984). A contrasting approach to traveling about is to stay at one plantation, as Erskine Clarke does in his brilliant *Dwelling Place: A Plantation Epic* (2005). Based on meticulous research, this upstairs/downstairs saga profiles the intertwined lives of masters and slaves on a Georgia coastal plantation from 1805 to 1869. James Oakes, *Slavery and Freedom* (1990), and William W. Freehling, *The Road to Disunion* (1990), are good syntheses that analyze the diversity and the contradictions of the antebellum South. For a global perspective on the cotton South, see Sven Beckert, *Empire of Cotton* (2014).

Frank Owsley's *Plain Folk of the Old South* (1949), about southern yeoman farmers, is still useful and can be supplemented by Samuel C. Hyde Jr., ed., *Plain Folk of the South Revisited* (1997); and Jeff Forret, *Race Relations at the Margins* (2006), a study of poor whites and blacks. The lives of upper-class southern white women and their servants are analyzed in Elizabeth Fox-Genovese, *Within the Plantation Household* (1988); Victoria E. Bynum, *Unruly Women* (1992), deals with white and black women of lower status.

The best exploration of slavery as a labor system remains Kenneth M. Stampp, *The Peculiar Institution* (1956). For a perceptive treatment of slave culture, see Eugene D. Genovese, *Roll, Jordan, Roll* (1974). Charles Joyner, *Down by the Riverside* (1984), sensitively re-creates slave culture in the rice districts; and Steven Hahn, *A Nation under Our Feet* (2003), illuminates black political struggles in the rural South throughout the nineteenth century. John Hope Franklin and Loren Schweninger, *Runaway Slaves* (1999), details an important aspect of slave resistance. Walter Johnson, *Soul by Soul: Life Inside the Antebellum Slave Market* (1999), provides a concrete and chilling view of the trade that helped sustain the "peculiar institution." His more recent *River of Dark Dreams* (2013) vividly portrays slavery in the cotton South. Ira Berlin, *Slaves without Masters* (1974), offers an excellent account of free black southerners, as does Melvin Patrick Ely, *Israel on the Appomattox* (2004). For the proslavery argument, see Lacy K. Ford's, *Deliver Us from Evil* (2009); and James Oakes's *The Ruling Race* (1982).

14 Western Expansion and the Rise of the Slavery Issue

1820–1850

The Hidatsa Indians retreated to these well-insulated earth lodges in the forested and more sheltered river bottoms to escape the fierce winter storms of the Plains. The Hidatsa survived on stores of dried beans, corn, squash, and meat. The man with the spear at left is playing chunkey, a traditional hoop and pole game whose origin dates back 600 years. (For more information, see a similar illustration in Chapter 1.)

©Historical Picture Archive/Corbis/Getty Images

>> **An American Story**

STRANGERS ON THE GREAT PLAINS

At first the Indians of the Great Plains paid little attention to the new people moving out from the forests far to the east. After all, for as long as they could remember, nations such as the Crow had called the plains their own. But the new arrivals came armed with superior weapons and brought a great many women and children. And they seemed to have an unlimited appetite for land. They attacked the villages of the Plains Indians, massacred women and children, and forced defeated enemies to live on reservations. In little more than a century and a half—from the first days when only a handful of their hunters had come into the land—they had become the masters of the northern plains.

The invaders who established this political and military dominance were *not* the strange "white men," who also came from the forest. During the 1830s and early 1840s whites were still few in number. The more dangerous people—the ones who truly worried the Plains tribes—were the Sioux.

Westward expansion is often told as a one-dimensional tale, centering on the wagon trains pressing toward the Pacific. But frontiers are the transition lines between different cultures or environments, and during the nineteenth century those frontiers were constantly shifting. They moved not only east to west, as with the white and the Sioux migrations, but also south to north, as Spanish culture diffused, and west to east, as Asian emigrants came to California. Furthermore, frontiers marked not only human but also animal boundaries. Horses, cattle, and pigs, all species imported from Europe, moved across the continent, usually in advance of European settlers. Frontiers could be technological, as in the case of trade goods like firearms. Moreover, disease frontiers created disastrous consequences for natives who had not acquired immunity to European microorganisms.

Three frontiers revolutionized the lives of the Sioux: those of the horse, the gun, and disease. Horses spread from the southwest, ahead of the Spanish who had originally brought them. Unlike English and French traders, however, Spanish colonists generally refused to sell firearms to Indians, so the gun frontier moved in the opposite direction, from northeast to southwest. The two waves crossed along the upper Missouri during the first half of the eighteenth century. Horses provided Indians with greater mobility, both for hunting

bison and for fighting. Guns, too, conferred obvious advantages, and the arrival of these new elements sparked an extremely unsettled era for Plains Indian cultures.

The Sioux were first lured from the forest onto the Minnesota prairie during the early 1700s to hunt beaver, whose pelts could be exchanged with white traders for guns and other manufactured goods. The Sioux then drove the Omahas, Otos, Cheyennes, and Missouris (who had not yet acquired guns) south and west. But by the 1770s any further advance was blocked by the powerful Mandan, Hidatsa, and Arikara peoples. They were primarily horticultural, raising corn, beans, and squash and living in well-fortified towns. They also owned more horses than the Sioux; thus it was easier for them to resist attacks.

But the third frontier, disease, threw the balance of power toward the Sioux after 1779. That year, a continental smallpox pandemic struck the plains via Louisiana. Those who raised crops were hit especially hard because they lived in densely populated villages, where the epidemic spread more easily. By the time Lewis and Clark came through in 1804, the Sioux controlled much of the upper Missouri, for their nomadic life, centered on the buffalo hunt, enabled them to avoid the worst ravages of disease, especially the smallpox epidemic of 1837, which ravaged Plains Indian populations. And as white Americans moved westward, their own frontier lines produced similar disruptions, not only between white settlers and Indians but also between Anglo-American and Hispanic cultures. The relations between Indian peoples and the diverse inhabitants of Mexico were

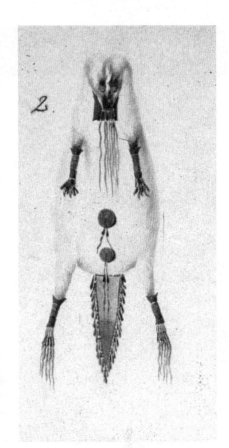

©MPI/Getty Images

| *Pouch made from a white skunk skin. The skin, plus the decorative beads, were obtained from a white trapper. The pouch probably held tobacco, also a trade good.*

also in flux, as many tribes across the plains began attacking Mexicans during the 1830s. There would even be a frontier moving west to east, as thousands of Chinese were drawn, as were other immigrants from North and South America, Australia, and Hawaii, to gold fields discovered after 1849.

Ironically, perhaps the greatest instability created by the moving frontiers occurred in established American society. As the political system of the United States struggled to incorporate territories, the North and South engaged in a fierce debate over whether the new lands should become slave or free. Just as the Sioux's cultural identity was brought into question by moving frontiers, so too was the identity of the American Republic. <<

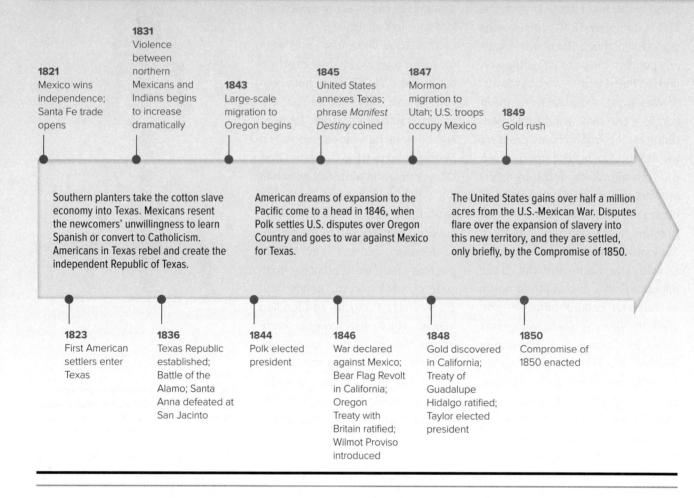

1821
Mexico wins independence; Santa Fe trade opens

1831
Violence between northern Mexicans and Indians begins to increase dramatically

1843
Large-scale migration to Oregon begins

1845
United States annexes Texas; phrase *Manifest Destiny* coined

1847
Mormon migration to Utah; U.S. troops occupy Mexico

1849
Gold rush

Southern planters take the cotton slave economy into Texas. Mexicans resent the newcomers' unwillingness to learn Spanish or convert to Catholicism. Americans in Texas rebel and create the independent Republic of Texas.

American dreams of expansion to the Pacific come to a head in 1846, when Polk settles U.S. disputes over Oregon Country and goes to war against Mexico for Texas.

The United States gains over half a million acres from the U.S.-Mexican War. Disputes flare over the expansion of slavery into this new territory, and they are settled, only briefly, by the Compromise of 1850.

1823
First American settlers enter Texas

1836
Texas Republic established; Battle of the Alamo; Santa Anna defeated at San Jacinto

1844
Polk elected president

1846
War declared against Mexico; Bear Flag Revolt in California; Oregon Treaty with Britain ratified; Wilmot Proviso introduced

1848
Gold discovered in California; Treaty of Guadalupe Hidalgo ratified; Taylor elected president

1850
Compromise of 1850 enacted

Manifest (and Not so Manifest) Destiny

MANIFEST DESTINY "Make way . . . for the young American Buffalo—he has not yet got land enough," roared one American politician in 1844. In the space of a few years, the United States acquired Texas, New Mexico, California, the lower half of the Oregon Territory, and the lands between the Rockies and California: nearly 1.5 million square miles in all. John L. O'Sullivan, a prominent Democratic editor in New York, struck a responsive chord when he declared that it had become the United States' "manifest destiny to overspread the continent allotted by Providence for the free development of our yearly multiplying millions." The cry of **Manifest Destiny** soon echoed in other editorial pages and in the halls of Congress.

The Roots of the Doctrine

Many Americans had long believed that their country had a special, even divine, mission, which could be traced back

to the Puritans' attempt to build a "city on a hill." Manifest Destiny also contained a political component, inherited from the ideology of the Revolution. In the mid-nineteenth century, Americans spoke of extending democracy, with widespread suffrage among white males, no king or aristocracy, and no established church, "over the whole North American continent."

Americans believed that their social and economic system, too, should spread around the globe. They pointed to its broad ownership of land, individualism, and free play of economic opportunity as superior features of American life. More importantly, Manifest Destiny was about power, especially economic power. American business interests recognized the value of the fine harbors along the Pacific coast, which promised a lucrative trade with Asia, and they hoped to make those harbors American.

RACISM Finally, underlying the doctrine of Manifest Destiny was a widespread racism. The same belief in racial superiority that was used to justify Indian removal under Jackson, to uphold slavery in the South, and to excuse

| The idea that the United States could expand to become a continental republic seemed far-fetched to most Americans of the early Republic. But the coming of the telegraph, whose wires allowed for instant communication over long distances, helped convince many that expansion to the Pacific might indeed be the nation's "Manifest Destiny."

©Science History Images/ Alamy

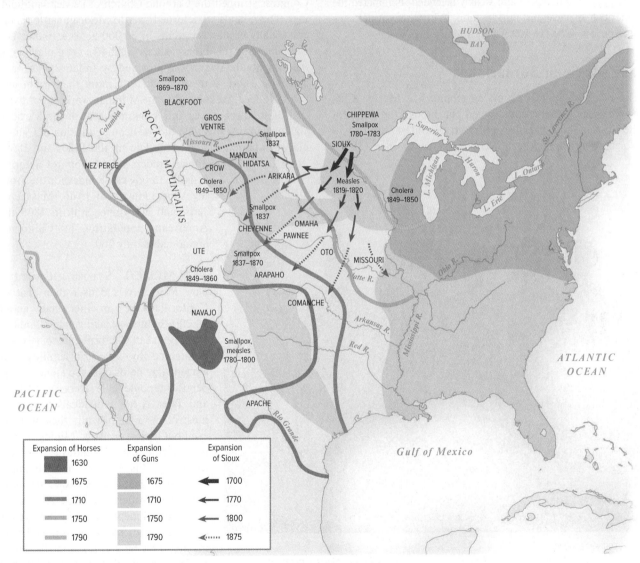

SIOUX EXPANSION AND THE HORSE AND GUN FRONTIERS

In 1710 the horse and gun frontiers had not yet crossed, but by 1750 the two waves began to overlap. The Sioux pushed west during the early eighteenth century thanks to firearms; they were checked from further expansion until the 1770s, when smallpox epidemics again turned the balance in their favor. **Why did the Sioux population survive better than the Mandan, Hidatsa, and Arikara peoples?**

segregation in the North also proved handy to defend expansion westward. The United States had a duty to regenerate the backward peoples of America, declared politicians and propagandists. Their reference was not so much to Indians: the forced expulsion of assimilated Cherokees during Indian removal made clear what most American policy makers thought about Indian "regeneration." By the 1840s it was rather the Mexicans who had caught the attention of Manifest Destiny's prophets of progress. The Mexican race "must amalgamate and be lost, in the superior vigor of the Anglo-Saxon race," proclaimed O'Sullivan's *Democratic Review,* "or they must utterly perish."

Before 1845 most Americans assumed that expansion would be achieved without international war. American settlement would expand westward, and when the time was right, neighboring provinces, like ripe fruit, would fall naturally into American hands. Texas, New Mexico, Oregon, and California—areas that were sparsely populated and weakly defended—dominated the American expansionist imagination. With time, Americans became less willing to wait patiently for the fruit to fall.

The Mexican Borderlands

The heart of Spain's American empire was Mexico City, where spacious boulevards spread out through the center of the city and the University of Mexico, the oldest university in North America, had been accepting students since 1553, a full 85 years earlier than Harvard. From the Mexican point of view, the frontier was 1,000 miles to the north, a four-week journey to Texas, another two weeks to New Mexico, and three months by land and sea to the missions of California. Being so isolated, these Mexican provinces developed largely free from royal supervision.

CALIFORNIO SOCIETY California's settlements were anchored by four coastal *presidios,* or forts, at San Diego, Santa Barbara, Monterey, and San Francisco. Between them lay 21 Catholic missions run by a handful of Franciscans (there were only 36 in 1821). The missions controlled enormous tracts of land on which grazed gigantic herds of cattle, sheep, and horses. The animals and irrigated fields were tended by about 20,000 Indians, who in certain regards lived and worked like slaves.

When Mexico won its independence from Spain in 1821, California at first was little affected. But in 1833 the Mexican Congress stripped the Catholic Church of its vast landholdings. These lands were turned over to Mexican cattle ranchers, usually in massive grants of 50,000 acres or more. The new *rancheros* ruled their estates much like great planters of the Old South. Labor was provided by Indians, who once again were forced to work for little more than room and board. Indeed, the mortality rate of Indian workers was twice that of southern slaves and four times that of the Mexican Californians. At this time the Mexican population of California was approximately 4,000. During the 1820s and 1830s Yankee traders set up shop in California in order to buy cattle hides for the growing shoe industry at Lynn, Massachusetts, and elsewhere. Still, in 1845 the American population in California amounted to only 700.

NEW MEXICO Spanish settlement of New Mexico was denser than that of California: the province had about 44,000 Spanish-speaking inhabitants in 1827. But as in California, its society was dominated by *ranchero* families that grazed large herds of sheep along the upper Rio Grande valley between El Paso and Taos. A few individuals controlled most of the wealth, while their workers eked out a meager living. Mining of copper and gold was a side industry, and here too the profits enriched a small upper class. Spain had long outlawed any commerce with Americans, but after Mexico declared its independence in 1821, yearly caravans from the United States began making the long journey along the Santa Fe Trail. Although this trade flourished over the next two decades, developments in the third Mexican borderland, neighboring Texas, worsened relations between Mexico and the United States.

©Florilegius/SSPL/Getty Images

| *In addition to baptism and an education in certain crafts and skills, Christian missions in California and elsewhere offered native people food, clothing, and sanctuary in a rapidly changing world. Often missions were also places of harsh discipline, physical coercion, and rampant disease. The Ohlone, or Costanoan, people pictured here are native to northern California and were drawn or coerced into missions starting in the 1760s.*

The Texas Revolution

AMERICAN EMIGRATION TO TEXAS   At first, the new government in Mexico encouraged American emigration to Texas, where only about 3,000 Mexicans, mostly ranchers, lived. In 1821 Moses Austin, an American, received a grant from the Spanish government to establish a colony. After his death, his son Stephen took over the project, laying out the little town of San Felipe de Austin along the Brazos River and offering large grants of land at almost no cost. By 1824 the colony's population exceeded 2,000. Stephen Austin was only the first of a new wave of American land agents, or *empresarios,* that obtained permission from Mexican authorities to settle families in Texas. Ninety percent of the new arrivals came from the South. Many, intending to grow cotton, brought slaves.

ILLEGAL IMMIGRATION IN TEXAS   Tensions between Mexicans and American immigrants grew with the Texas economy. Most settlers from the States were Protestant. Although the Mexican government did not insist that all new citizens become Catholic, it did officially bar Protestant churches. In 1829 Mexico abolished slavery, then looked the other way when Texas slaveholders evaded the law. In the early 1830s the Mexican government began to have second thoughts about American settlement and passed laws prohibiting any new immigration. Austin likened the new anti-immigration laws to "trying to stop the Mississippi with a dam of straw." It was an apt metaphor: between 1830 and 1833, illegal American emigrants and their slaves flooded into Mexican Texas, nearly doubling its colonial population.

GROWING TENSIONS   Admitting that the new regulations had served only to inflame Texans, Mexico repealed them in 1833. But by then colonial ill-will had ballooned along with the population. By mid-decade the American white population of 40,000 was nearly 10 times the number of Mexicans in the territory. Once again Mexico's government talked of abolishing slavery in Texas. Even more disturbing to the American newcomers, in 1834 President Antonio López de Santa Anna and his allies in the Mexican Congress began passing legislation that took power away from the states and concentrated it in Mexico City. Texans had been struggling for more autonomy, not less. When Santa Anna brutally suppressed an uprising against the central government in the state of Zacatecas, Texans grew all the more nervous. Finally, when conflicts over taxes led Santa Anna to march an army north and enforce his new regime, a ragtag Texas army drove back the advance party and then captured Mexican troops in nearby San Antonio. A full-scale rebellion was under way.

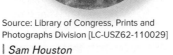

Source: Library of Congress, Prints and Photographs Division [LC-USZ62-110029]

| Sam Houston

The Texas Republic

THE ALAMO   As Santa Anna massed his forces, a provisional government on March 2, 1836, proclaimed Texan independence. The document was signed by a number of prominent **Tejanos,** Mexican residents of Texas. The constitution of the new Texas Republic borrowed heavily from the U.S. Constitution, except that it explicitly prohibited the new Texas Congress from interfering with slavery. Meanwhile, Santa Anna's troops overran a Texan garrison at an old mission in San Antonio, known as the Alamo, and killed all of its 187 defenders—including the famous backwoodsman and U.S. congressman, Davy Crockett. The Mexicans, however, paid dearly for the victory, losing more than 1,500 men. The massacre of another force at Goliad after it surrendered further inflamed American resistance.

SAM HOUSTON   But anger was one thing; organized resistance was another. The commander of the Texas forces was Sam Houston, a former governor of Tennessee. Physically gifted and something of an eccentric, Houston had a flair for wearing colorful clothing to attract attention. His political career in Tennessee might have continued, except that the failure of his marriage led him to resign abruptly as governor and go to live with the Cherokees. Eventually he made his way to Texas, where his intellectual ability and unexcelled talent as a stump speaker propelled him to the forefront of the independence movement. Steadily retreating eastward, Houston tried to discipline his fighting force and wait for an opportunity to counterattack.

That opportunity came in late April. Reinforced by eager volunteers from the United States, Houston's army surprised Santa Anna's force when spies revealed that they were resting unaware near the San Jacinto River. Admonished to "remember the Alamo," Houston's men burst upon the stunned Mexican force, killing dozens in a brief battle. Driven by revenge, the Texans then pursued the fleeing Mexican soldiers and massacred hundreds. By day's end 630 Mexicans lay dead on the field (compared to only nine Texans), and a humiliated Santa Anna had been taken into custody.

TEXAN INDEPENDENCE   Threatened with execution, the Mexican commander signed treaties recognizing Texan independence and ordering his remaining troops south of the Rio Grande. Texans would later claim that Santa Anna thereby acknowledged the Rio Grande to be Texas's southern boundary. The Mexican Congress repudiated the agreement, especially the claim to the Rio Grande. Over the next decade both sides engaged in low-level border conflict, but neither had the power to mount a successful invasion. In the meantime, Houston assumed office in October 1836 as president of the new republic, determined to bring Texas into the American Union as quickly as possible.

The Mexican Borderlands

Source: Library of Congress, Prints and Photographs Division [LC-USZC4-2133]

"If I owned Texas and Hell, I would rent out Texas and live in Hell."
—Philip Henry Sheridan

Context

What had been a portion of Spain's sprawling colonial American empire—Texas and the rest of the southwestern United States today—came into the possession of Mexico after that country waged its successful war for colonial independence in 1821.

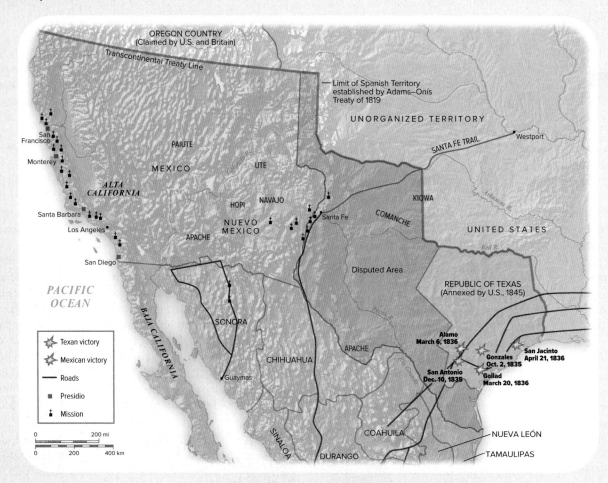

Map Reading

1. Identify the Indian nations that occupied the Mexican borderlands.
2. What areas had the largest concentration of missions and presidios?
3. Identify the sites of Texan and Mexican victories during the Texans' campaign for independence.
4. Which nations claimed the Oregon Country?

Map Interpretation

1. Which parties contended over the "Disputed Area" west of what became the Republic of Texas? Which wielded the greatest power in that region?
2. Why did Mexico resist the Texans' campaign for independence? What purpose had the Mexican government hoped that the settlement of Texas would serve?
3. What made settlement in Texas attractive to migrants from the United States?
4. What groups in the United States might have opposed the annexation of Texas and why?

As an old Tennessee protégé of Andrew Jackson, Houston assumed that the United States would quickly annex such a vast and inviting territory. But Jackson worried that any such move would revive sectional tensions and hurt Martin Van Buren's chances in the 1836 presidential election. Only on his last day in office did he extend formal diplomatic recognition to the Texas Republic. Van Buren, distracted by the economic panic that broke out shortly after he entered office, took no action during his term.

Rebuffed, Texans decided to go their own way. In the 10 years following independence, the Lone Star Republic attracted more than 100,000 immigrants by offering free land to settlers. Mexico refused to recognize Texan independence, and the vast majority of its citizens still wished to join the United States, where most of them, after all, had been born. There matters stood when the Whigs and William Henry Harrison won the presidency in 1840.

 REVIEW

What regions made up the Spanish borderlands; and why did Mexico lose Texas?

THE TREK WEST

AS THOUSANDS OF WHITE AMERICANS were moving into Texas, and increasingly bringing slaves with them, a much smaller trickle headed toward the Oregon Country. Since 1818 the United States and Great Britain had occupied that territory jointly, as far north as latitude 54°40′. Although white settlement remained sparse, by 1836 American settlers outnumbered the British in the Willamette valley.

Pushed by the Panic of 1837 and six years of depression and pulled by tales of Oregon's lush, fertile valleys and the healthy, frost-free climate along California's Sacramento River, many American farmers struck out for the West Coast. Missouri was "cleaned" out of money, worried farmer Daniel Waldo, and his wife was even more adamant about heading west: "If you want to stay here another summer and shake your liver out with the fever and ague, you can do it," she announced to her husband, "but in the spring I am going to take the children and go to Oregon, Indians or no Indians." The wagon trains began rolling west.

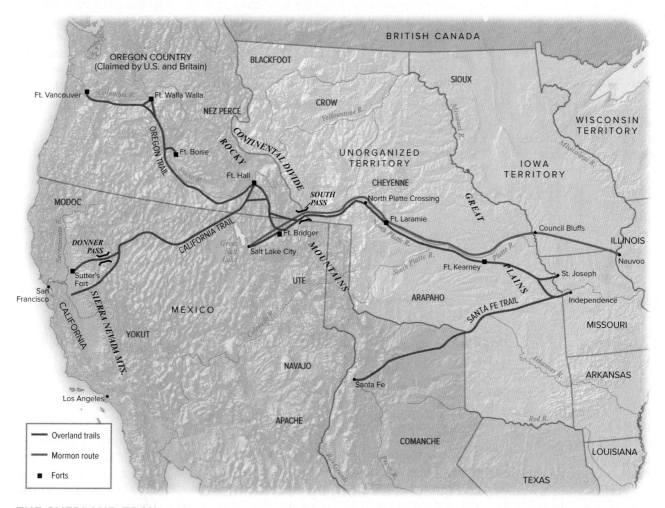

THE OVERLAND TRAIL

Beginning at several different points, the Overland Trail followed the Platte and Sweetwater Rivers across the plains to South Pass, where it crossed the Continental Divide. The trail split again near Fort Hall. Between 1840 and 1860 more than a quarter of a million emigrants made the trek. Following news of the gold strikes in 1848, the flow of westward emigrants increased and shifted toward California.

The Overland Trail

MIGRATION WEST   Only a few hundred emigrants reached the West in 1841 and 1842, but in 1843 more than 800 followed the Overland Trail across the mountains to Oregon. From then on, they came by the thousands. Every spring brought a new rush of families to Independence or later to St. Joseph, Missouri, or to Council Bluffs, Iowa, where they waited for the spring rains to end and the trails to become passable. The migration was primarily a family enterprise, and many couples had only recently married. Most adults were between 20 and 50 years old; the hard journey discouraged the elderly. Furthermore, a family of four needed about $600 to outfit its journey, an amount that excluded the poor.

Caravans of 20 to 30 wagons were not uncommon the first few years, but after 1845 parties traveled in smaller trains of 8 to 10 wagons. The trip itself lasted about 6 months, since the wagons normally covered only 15 miles a day, and the weather, repairs, deaths, and other eventualities necessitated occasional halts. Breakdowns were frequent, and increasing traffic meant that migrants' cattle, horses, and mules quickly devoured grass along the trail. Scarcity made disagreements more likely and created desperate problems for Indian peoples trying to keep their own herds alive in winter.

Women on the Overland Trail

The journey west often placed a special strain on women. Few wives were as eager as Daniel Waldo's to undertake the journey. "Poor Ma said only this morning, 'Oh I wish we never had started,'" one daughter reported, "and she looks so sorrowful and dejected." In one study of Oregon-bound parties, three-fourths of the women did not want to make the move.

BREAKDOWN OF WOMEN'S TRADITIONAL ROLE   At first, parties divided work by gender, as had been done back home. Women cooked, washed, sewed, and took care of the children, while men drove the wagons, cared for the stock, stood guard, and did the heavy labor. Necessity placed new demands on women, however, and eventually altered their roles. Within a few weeks, they found themselves helping to repair wagons and construct bridges. When men became exhausted, sick, or injured, women stood guard and drove the oxen. The change in work assignments proceeded only in one direction, however, for few men undertook "women's work."

As women strove to maintain a semblance of home on the trail, they often experienced a profound sense of loss. Trains often worked or traveled on the Sabbath, which back home had long been a day for worship and rest and an emblem of women's moral authority. Women also felt the lack of close companions to whom they could turn for comfort. One woman, whose husband separated their wagon from the train after a dispute, sadly watched the other wagons pull away: "I felt that indeed I had left all my friends to journey over the dreaded plains without one female acquaintance even for a companion—of course I wept and grieved about it but to no purpose."

Indians and the Trail Experience

PRESSURES ON PLAINS INDIANS   The nations whose lands were crossed by white wagon trains reacted in a number of ways to the westward tide. The Sioux, who had long been trading with whites, were among the peoples who regularly visited overlanders to trade for blankets, clothes, cows, rifles, and knives. But the white migrants took a heavy toll on the Plains Indians' way of life: emigrant parties scared off game and reduced buffalo herds, overgrazed the grass, and depleted the supply of wood. Having petitioned unsuccessfully in 1846 for government compensation, some Sioux decided to demand payment from the wagon trains crossing their lands. Whether parties paid or not depended on the relative strength of the two groups, but whites complained bitterly of what seemed to them outright robbery.

Their fears aroused by sensational stories, overland parties were wary of Indians, but this menace was greatly exaggerated, especially on the plains. Few wagon trains were attacked by Indians, and less than 4 percent of deaths on the trail were caused by Indians. In truth, emigrants killed more Indians than Indians killed emigrants. For overlanders the most aggravating problem posed by native peoples was theft of stock. Many companies received valuable assistance from Indians, who acted as guides, directed them to grass and water, and transported stock and wagons across rivers.

As trail congestion and conflict increased, the government constructed a string of protective forts and in 1851 summoned Plains Indians to a conference at Fort Laramie. The U.S. government agreed to make an annual payment as compensation for the damages caused by the wagon trains but also required tribes to confine themselves to areas north or south of a corridor through which the Overland Trail ran. Some tribes were unwilling to surrender their freedom of movement and refused to agree. The Sioux, the most powerful people on the plains, signed and then ignored the terms.

 REVIEW

What motivated men and women from the United States to migrate on overland trails?

THE POLITICAL ORIGINS OF EXPANSION

PRESIDENT WILLIAM HENRY HARRISON MADE the gravest mistake of his brief presidential career when he ventured out one raw spring day, bareheaded and without an overcoat, to buy groceries at the Washington markets. He developed pneumonia and died only one month after his inauguration.

TYLER BECOMES PRESIDENT   For the first time in the nation's history, a vice president succeeded to the nation's highest office on the death of the president. John Tyler of

| *An emigrant wagon train. Note the women at left.*

Virginia had been a Democrat who supported states' rights so strongly that, during the nullification crisis, he was the only senator to vote against the Force Bill. After that, Jackson and the Democrats would have nothing to do with him, so Tyler joined the Whigs despite his strict constructionist principles. In 1840 the Whigs put him on the ticket with Harrison in order to balance the ticket sectionally. In the rollicking 1840 campaign, the Whigs sang all too accurately: "And we'll vote for Tyler, therefore, / Without a why or wherefore."

Tyler's Texas Ploy

TYLER BREAKS WITH THE WHIGS   Tyler's courteous manner and personal warmth masked a rigid mind. Repeatedly, when his mentor Henry Clay and the Whigs in Congress passed a major bill, Tyler opposed it. After Tyler twice vetoed bills to charter a new national bank, disgusted congressional Whigs formally expelled their president from the party. Most Democrats, too, avoided him as an untrustworthy "renegade." A man without a party, Tyler decided that he could revive his reputation with a great accomplishment—the annexation of Texas.

He found support from Democrats disgruntled with their former leader, Martin Van Buren. Jackson's successor was, in their eyes, an ineffective leader who had stumbled through a depression and in 1840 gone down in ignominious defeat. "They mean to throw Van overboard," reported one delighted Whig, who caught wind of the plans. Meanwhile, Tyler's allies launched rumors designed to frighten southerners into pushing for annexation. Britain was ready to offer economic aid if Texas would abolish slavery, they claimed. (The rumor was false.) In April 1844 Tyler sent to the Senate for ratification a treaty he had secretly negotiated to bring Texas into the Union.

Van Overboard

The front-runners for the Whig and Democratic presidential nominations were Clay and Van Buren. Although rivals, they were

| *James K. Polk*

both moderates who feared the slavery issue. Apparently by prearrangement, both men issued letters opposing annexation on the grounds that it threatened the Union and would provoke war with Mexico.

POLK'S NOMINATION   As expected, the Whigs unanimously nominated Clay on a platform that ignored the expansion issue entirely. The Democrats, however, had a more difficult time. Those who opposed Van Buren persuaded the Democratic convention to adopt a rule requiring a two-thirds vote to nominate a candidate. That blocked Van Buren's nomination. On the ninth ballot the delegates finally turned to James K. Polk of Tennessee, who was pro-Texas. The 1844 Democratic platform called for the "reannexation" of Texas (under the dubious claim it had been part of the Louisiana Purchase) and the "reoccupation" of Oregon, all the way to its northernmost boundary at 54°40′.

Angered by the convention's outcome, Van Buren's supporters in the Senate joined the Whigs in decisively defeating Tyler's treaty of annexation. Tyler eventually withdrew from the race as an independent candidate, but the Texas issue would not go away. Henry Clay found many southerners slipping out of his camp because he opposed annexation; backtracking, he announced that he would be glad to see Texas annexed if it could be done without war or dishonor and without threatening the Union. And in the North, a few antislavery Whigs turned to James G. Birney, running on the Liberty Party ticket.

ELECTION OF 1844   In the end, Polk squeaked through by about 38,000 votes out of nearly 3 million cast. If just half of Birney's 15,000 ballots in New York had gone to Clay, he would have carried the state and been narrowly elected president by the Electoral College. Indignant Whigs charged that by refusing to support Clay, political abolitionists had made the annexation of Texas, and hence the addition of slave territory to the Union, inevitable. And indeed, Tyler again asked Congress to annex Texas—this time by a joint resolution, which required only a majority in both houses rather than a two-thirds vote for a treaty in the Senate. In the new atmosphere following Polk's victory, the resolution narrowly passed, and on March 3, 1845, his last day in office, Tyler invited Texas to enter the Union.

To the Pacific

Polk pursued his objectives as president with a dogged determination. Humorless, calculating, and often deceitful, he was not particularly brilliant in his maneuvering. But the life of politics consumed him, he knew his mind, and he could take the political pounding by his opponents. Embracing a continental vision of the United States, Polk not only endorsed Tyler's offer of annexation but also looked beyond, hoping to gain the three best harbors on the Pacific: San Diego, San Francisco, and Puget Sound. That meant wresting Oregon from Britain and California from Mexico.

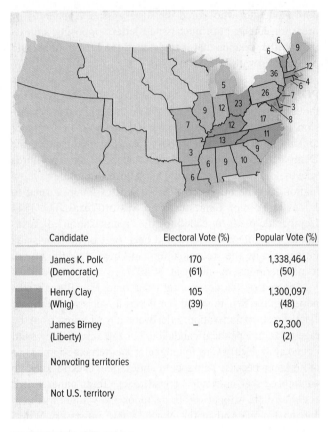

Candidate	Electoral Vote (%)	Popular Vote (%)
James K. Polk (Democratic)	170 (61)	1,338,464 (50)
Henry Clay (Whig)	105 (39)	1,300,097 (48)
James Birney (Liberty)	–	62,300 (2)
Nonvoting territories		
Not U.S. territory		

ELECTION OF 1844

Claiming that the American title was "clear and unquestionable," the new president brushed aside any notion of continuing joint occupation of Oregon with Britain. To pressure the British, he induced Congress to give the required one-year notice terminating the joint occupation of Oregon. His blustering was reinforced by the knowledge that American settlers in Oregon outnumbered the British 5,000 to 750. On the other hand, Polk hardly wanted war with a nation as powerful as Great Britain. So when the British offered, in June 1846, to divide the Oregon Territory along the 49th parallel, he readily agreed (see map, Territorial Growth and the Compromise of 1850). Britain retained Vancouver Island, where the Hudson's Bay Company's headquarters was located. But the arrangement gave the United States Puget Sound, which had been the president's objective all along.

Provoking a War

DISPUTED BOUNDARY OF TEXAS The Oregon settlement left Polk free to deal with Mexico. In 1845 Congress had admitted Texas to the Union as a slave state, but Mexico had never formally recognized Texas's independence. Mexico insisted, moreover, that Texas's southern boundary was the Nueces River, not the Rio Grande, 130 miles to the south, as claimed by Texas. In reality, Texas had never controlled the disputed region; the Nueces had always been Texas's boundary when it was a Mexican province; and if taken literally, the Rio Grande border incorporated most of New Mexico,

including Santa Fe, Albuquerque, Taos, and other major towns. Few Texans had ever even been to these places. Indeed, the one time Texas tried to exert authority in the region, New Mexicans had to ride out onto the plains to save the lost and starving expedition, and ultimately sent the men to Mexico City in chains. Nonetheless, Polk was already looking toward the Pacific and thus supported the Rio Grande boundary.

As soon as the Texans entered the Union, Mexico broke off diplomatic relations with the United States, and Polk sent American troops under General Zachary Taylor into the newly acquired state. At the same time, knowing that the unstable Mexican government desperately needed money, he attempted to buy territory to the Pacific. Sending John Slidell of Louisiana to Mexico as his special minister, Polk was prepared to offer $2 million in return for clear title to the Rio Grande boundary, $5 million for the remaining part of New Mexico, and up to $25 million for California. But the Mexican public overwhelmingly opposed ceding any more territory to the land-hungry "Yankees" from the United States, and the government refused to receive Slidell. "Depend upon it," reported Slidell, as he departed from Mexico in March 1846, "we can never get along well with them, until we have given them a good drubbing."

Blocked on the diplomatic front, Polk ordered Taylor, who had already crossed the Nueces with 4,000 troops, to proceed south to the Rio Grande. From the Mexican standpoint, the Americans had invaded their country and occupied their territory. For his part, Polk wanted to be in position to defend the disputed region if the two countries went to war. More importantly, once he realized that Mexico would not cave in to bullying diplomacy, Polk hoped that Taylor's position on the Rio Grande would provoke the Mexican army into starting a war.

By May 9 Polk and his cabinet had lost patience with the plan and decided to submit a war message to Congress without Mexican action. But on that day word arrived that two weeks earlier Mexican forces had crossed the Rio Grande and attacked some of Taylor's troops, killing 11 Americans. The president quickly rewrote his war message, placing the entire blame for the war on Mexico. "Mexico has passed the boundary of the United States, has invaded our territory, and shed American blood upon American soil," he told Congress on May 11. "War exists, and notwithstanding all our efforts to avoid it, exists by the act of Mexico herself." The administration sent a bill to Congress calling for volunteers and requesting money to supply American troops.

Indians and Mexicans

Mexican forces would often outnumber their American enemies in battle, but Mexico nonetheless suffered from critical disadvantages in the war. Chronic instability in its central government left the nation divided against itself in its moment of crisis. An empty national treasury fueled this instability and made it difficult to mobilize an effective response to the U.S. invasion. Mexico was also at a disadvantage in terms of military technology. While Mexican forces had to rely on bulky, fixed cannons, the U.S. Army employed new light artillery that could be repositioned quickly as battles progressed. Light artillery would tip the balance in several crucial engagements.

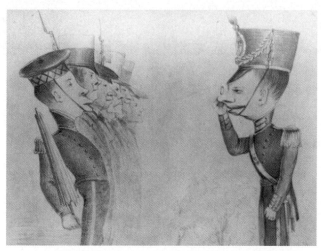

Source: Library of Congress, Prints and Photographs Division [LC-USZ62-1272]

| *The U.S.-Mexican War divided Americans, as this cartoon shows by mocking early recruits. One soldier holds a parasol instead of a rifle while his prissy commander squints through a monocle.*

Finally, much of Mexico had to fight two wars at once. While Mexico enjoyed formal diplomatic title to most of the present-day American West, Indians still controlled the vast majority of that territory, and Mexico had seen its relations with these Indians collapse in the 15 years before the U.S. invasion. During the late eighteenth century, Comanches, Navajos, Utes, and several different tribes of Apaches had made peace with Spanish authorities, ending decades of destructive war. Spaniards provided Indian leaders with gifts, guaranteed fair trade, and even handed out rations to minimize the animal thefts that could spark conflict.

THE END OF A FRAGILE PEACE This expensive and delicate system began to falter once Mexico achieved independence in 1821. Lacking the finances, the political unity, the stability, and the diplomatic resources of their Spanish predecessors, Mexican authorities watched the peace with northern Indians slip away. By the early 1830s, Native men were traveling hundreds of miles to raid Mexican ranches, haciendas, and towns, killing or capturing the people they found there, and stealing or destroying animals and other property. Whenever they were able, Mexicans did the same things to their Indian enemies. American markets helped drive the increasing violence, as Indian or white traders from the United States eagerly purchased horses and mules stolen from Mexico and supplied the raiders' arms and ammunition in return. By the eve of the U.S. invasion of Mexico, the violence encompassed all or parts of nine Mexican states and had claimed thousands of Mexican and Indian lives.

THE U.S.-MEXICAN WAR Thus, when American troops invaded northern Mexico they were literally marching in the footsteps of Comanches and Apaches, traversing territory that had already endured more than a decade of war. As Indian peoples pursued their own political, strategic,

and economic goals, they made it far easier for the United States to achieve its goals. Impoverished, exhausted, and divided, and facing ongoing Indian raids, few northern Mexicans were willing or able to resist the U.S. conquest and occupation.

Opposition to the War

The war with Mexico posed a dilemma for Whigs. They were convinced (correctly) that Polk had provoked the conflict in order to acquire more territory from Mexico, and many northern Whigs accused the president of seeking to extend slavery. But they remembered, too, that the Federalist Party had doomed itself to extinction by opposing the War of 1812. Throughout the conflict, they strenuously attacked the conduct of "Mr. Polk's War." But they could not bring themselves to cut off funding for the war.

Pro-war sentiment was strongest in the Old Southwest and most of the Old Northwest. It was much weaker in the East, where antislavery "Conscience Whigs" were prominent. "If I were a Mexican," Senator Thomas Corwin of Ohio affirmed in the Senate, "I would tell you, . . . 'we will greet you with bloody hands and welcome you to hospitable graves.'" With their party deeply divided over the issue of the expansion of slavery, Whigs opposed the acquisition of any territory from Mexico.

The Price of Victory

Even before any word of hostilities arrived in California, a group of impetuous American settlers around Sacramento launched the "Bear Flag Revolt." In June 1846 they proclaimed California an independent republic. American forces in the area soon put down any Mexican resistance, and by the following January California was safely in American hands.

CONQUEST OF MEXICO Meanwhile, Taylor moved south from the Rio Grande and won several battles. At each town conquered or surrendered, he read statements provided in advance by President Polk and the War Department, promising to respect private property and protect the long-suffering residents from Indian attack. Taylor's campaign culminated in a narrow victory over General Antonio López de Santa Anna at Buena Vista in southern Coahuila. Polk had gained the territory he sought to reach the Pacific and wanted an end to the war. But Mexico refused to surrender, so Polk ordered an invasion into the heart of the country.

TREATY OF GUADALUPE HIDALGO After an American army commanded by General Winfield Scott captured Mexico City on September 14, 1847, Mexico agreed to come to terms. The two nations ratified a peace treaty in 1848. Including Texas, which Mexico had continued to lay claim to, the Treaty of Guadalupe Hidalgo transferred half of Mexico's territory—more than half a million square miles—to the

IN WHAT COUNTRY DID THE U.S.-MEXICAN WAR BEGIN?

When President Polk insisted that Mexico had "shed American blood upon American soil," his critics demanded proof. Everyone acknowledged that the initial clash occurred just north of the Rio Grande. But did the boundary of Texas (and hence the boundary of the United States) extend to the Rio Grande, as Polk insisted, or only to the Nueces River, as had been internationally recognized before the Texas rebellion? Nearly all Mexicans believed that the fighting happened in Mexico, and some prominent Americans agreed. Among their number was a freshman member of Congress, Abraham Lincoln, whose "spot resolutions" took Polk to task. The dispute was motivated partly by politics: Lincoln, a Whig, happily criticized the Democratic Polk. Still, Lincoln's resolutions reflected genuine doubts about the war's legitimacy.

DOCUMENT 1
The War Began in the United States: President James K. Polk

The existing state of the relations between the United States and Mexico renders it proper that I should bring the subject to the consideration of Congress. . . . An envoy of the United States repaired to Mexico with full powers to adjust every existing difference. But though present on Mexican soil by agreement between the two Governments, invested with full powers, and bearing evidence of the most friendly dispositions, his mission has been unavailing. The Mexican Government not only refused to receive him or listen to his propositions, but after a long-continued series of menaces have at last invaded our territory and shed the blood of our fellow-citizens on our own soil. . . . In my message at the commencement of the present session I informed you that upon the earnest appeal both of the Congress and convention of Texas I had ordered an efficient military force to take a position "between the Nueces and Del Norte." This had become necessary to meet a threatened invasion of Texas by the Mexican forces, for which extensive military preparations had been made. The invasion was threatened solely because Texas had determined, in accordance with a solemn resolution of the Congress of the United States, to annex herself to our Union, and under these circumstances it was plainly our duty to extend our protection over her citizens and soil. . . . Meantime Texas, by the final act of our Congress, had become an integral part of our Union. The Congress of Texas, by its act of December 19, 1836, had declared the Rio del Norte to be the boundary of that Republic. Its jurisdiction had been extended and exercised beyond the Nueces. The country between that river and the Del Norte had been represented in the Congress and in the convention of Texas, had thus taken part in the act of annexation itself, and is now included within one of our Congressional districts. Our own Congress had, moreover, with great unanimity, by the act approved December 31, 1845, recognized the country beyond the Nueces as a part of our territory by including it within our own revenue system, and a revenue officer to reside within that district had been appointed by and with the advice and consent of the Senate. It became, therefore, of urgent necessity to provide for the defense of that portion of our country. . . . But no open act of hostility was committed until the 24th of April. On that day General [Mariano] Arista, who had succeeded to the command of the Mexican forces, communicated to General Taylor that "he considered hostilities commenced and should prosecute them." A party of dragoons of 63 men and officers were on the same day dispatched from the American camp up the Rio del Norte, on its left bank, to ascertain whether the Mexican troops had crossed or were preparing to cross the river, "became engaged with a large body of these troops, and after a short affair, in which some 16 were killed and wounded, appear to have been surrounded and compelled to surrender."

Source: Message to Congress, Washington, May 11, 1846, in Richardson, James D., ed., *A Compilation of the Messages and Papers of the Presidents, Vol. 4.* New York, NY: Bureau of National Literature and Art, 1908, 437–443.

DOCUMENT 2
The "Spot" Was beyond the U.S. Borders: Representative Abraham Lincoln

Whereas the President of the United States, in his message of May 11, 1846, has declared that "the Mexican Government not only refused to receive him, [the envoy of the United States,] or listen to his propositions, but, after a long-continued series of menaces, has at last invaded *our territory* and shed the blood of our fellow-citizens on our *own soil:*"

And again, in his message of December 8, 1846, that "we had ample cause of war against Mexico long before the breaking out of hostilities; but even then we forbore to take redress into our own hands until Mexico herself became the aggressor, by invading *our soil* in hostile array, and shedding the blood of our citizens:"

And yet again, in his message of December 7, 1847, that "the Mexican Government refused even to hear the terms of adjustment which he [our minister of peace] was authorized to propose, and, finally, under wholly unjustifiable pretexts, involved the two countries in war, by invading the territory of the State of Texas, striking the first blow, and shedding the blood of our citizens on *our own soil.*"

And whereas this House is desirous to obtain a full knowledge of all the facts which go to establish whether the particular spot on which the blood of our citizens was so shed was or was not at that time *our own soil:* Therefore,

Resolved By the House of Representatives, That the President of the United

States be respectfully requested to inform this House—

1st. Whether the spot on which the blood of our citizens was shed, as in his messages declared, was or was not within the territory of Spain, at least after the treaty of 1819, until the Mexican revolution.

2d. Whether that spot is or is not within the territory which was wrested from Spain by the revolutionary Government of Mexico.

3d. Whether that spot is or is not within a settlement of people, which settlement has existed ever since long before the Texas revolution, and until its inhabitants fled before the approach of the United States army.

4th. Whether that settlement is or is not isolated from any and all other settlements by the Gulf and the Rio Grande on the south and west, and by wide uninhabited regions on the north and east.

5th. Whether the people of that settlement, or a majority of them, or any of them, have ever submitted themselves to the government or laws of Texas or the United States, by consent or compulsion, either by accepting office, or voting at elections, or paying tax, or serving on juries, or having process served upon them, or in any other way.

6th. Whether the people of that settlement did or did not flee from the approach of the United States army, leaving unprotected their homes and their growing crops, *before* the blood was shed, as in the messages stated; and whether the first blood, so shed, was or was not shed within the enclosure of one of the people who had thus fled from it.

7th. Whether our *citizens,* whose blood was shed, as in his message declared, were or were not, at that time, armed officers and soldiers, sent into that

settlement by the military order of the President, through the Secretary of War.

8th. Whether the military force of the United States was or was not sent into that settlement after General Taylor had more than once intimated to the War Department that, in his opinion, no such movement was necessary to the defence or protection of Texas.

Resolutions introduced into the House of Representatives Dec. 22, 1847. Available at http://teachingamericanhistory.org/library/index.asp?document=2463.

THINKING CRITICALLY

How does Polk justify Taylor's presence on the Rio Grande? How does Lincoln critique Taylor's presence on the Rio Grande? Do they disagree over facts, or over which facts matter? What more information would you need to decide who makes the more persuasive case?

United States. In return the United States recalled its army and ended its aggressive war. It also assumed all the outstanding claims that U.S. citizens had against Mexico and gave the Mexicans 15 million dollars.

The war had cost the United States $97 million and 13,000 American lives, mostly as a result of disease. Yet the real cost was even higher. By bringing vast new territories into the Union, the war forced the explosive slavery issue to the center of national politics and threatened to upset the balance of power between North and South. Ralph Waldo Emerson had been prophetic: "The United States will conquer Mexico," he wrote when the U.S.-Mexican War began, "but it will be as the man who swallows the arsenic which brings him down in turn. Mexico will poison us."

The Rise of the Slavery Issue

When the second party system emerged during the 1820s, Martin Van Buren had championed political parties as one way to forge links between North and South that would strengthen the Union. But the Texas movement increased sectional suspicions, and President Polk did nothing to ease this problem.

NORTHERN DISCONTENT   Polk was a politician to his bones: constantly maneuvering, promising one thing, doing another, making a pledge, taking it back—using any means to accomplish his ends. Discontent over his double-dealing finally erupted in August 1846, when Polk requested $2 million from Congress, as he vaguely explained, to "facilitate negotiations" with Mexico. It was widely understood that the money was to be used to

bribe the Mexican government to cede territory to the United States.

WILMOT PROVISO   On August 8 David Wilmot, an obscure Pennsylvania congressman, startled Democratic leaders by introducing an amendment to the bill that barred slavery from any territory acquired from Mexico. The Wilmot Proviso, as the amendment became known, passed the northern-controlled House of Representatives several times, only to be rejected in the Senate, where the South had more power. As such, it revealed mounting sectional tensions.

Wilmot himself was hardly an abolitionist. Indeed, he hoped to keep not only slaves but all black people out of the territories. Denying any "morbid sympathy for the slave," he declared, "I would preserve for white free labor a fair country . . . where the sons of toil, of my own race and color, can live without the disgrace which association with negro slavery brings upon free labor." The Wilmot Proviso aimed not to destroy slavery in the South but to confine the institution to those states where it already existed. Still, abolitionists had long contended that southern slaveholders—the "Slave Power"—were plotting to extend their sway over the rest of the country. The political maneuverings of slaveholders such as Tyler, and especially Polk, convinced growing numbers of northerners that the Slave Power did indeed exist and that it was aggressively looking to expand its influence.

NEW LANDS, NEW TENSIONS   The status of slavery in the territories became more than an abstract question once

Settan Annual Calendar of the Kiowa

The black bars represent trees without leaves, indicating winter.

Winter of 1839–1840: what might this pictograph of a man covered in red spots represent?

 "Hide-quiver expedition winter"

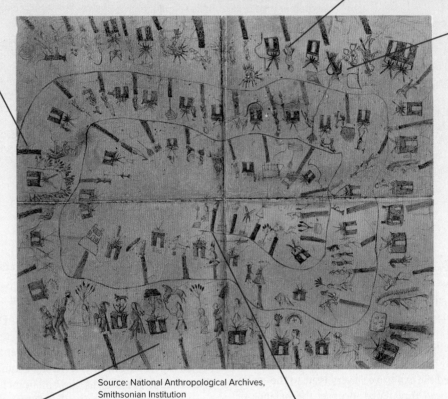

Source: National Anthropological Archives, Smithsonian Institution

The recurring pictograph of a medicine bundle atop a lodge represents the Sun Dance, a sacred ceremony Kiowas held in summer.

What year is the last winter represented on the calendar?

Kiowas kept pictographic calendars painted on hides. The pictographs memorialized two key events each year, one for summer and one for winter. A Kiowa named Settan (Little Bear) produced the one above, which proceeds in a spiral beginning with the summer of 1832 in the upper-left corner. The calendar marks the winter of 1840–1841 as "Hide-quiver expedition winter." What does that signify? By the 1840s young Kiowa warriors preferred quivers made from sleek leather or panther skin to those made from rougher buffalo hide, which only old men used. "Hide-quiver war expedition winter" refers to a campaign made up of older men who headed south into Mexico. Traditionally, Kiowas and Comanches would leave older men behind to protect women and children and guard their herds of horses and mules. But in 1840 a peace agreement with their traditional Cheyenne and Arapaho enemies left the Kiowas and Comanches feeling more secure. When winter came, even aged warriors rode off with their hide quivers to steal horses and mules from Mexicans hundreds of miles below the Rio Grande. Indirectly, attacks such as these helped the United States win its own war against Mexico.

Source: www.texasbeyondhistory.net/plateaus/peoples/images/calendar-full.html.

THINKING CRITICALLY

Kiowas passed on their history through spoken word. How could a calendar such as this enhance oral tradition? Does the selection of events in the calendar indicate a very different approach to historical memory than the one in this textbook? How would a historian use a document such as this? What other kinds of evidence could historians put this calendar in conversation with?

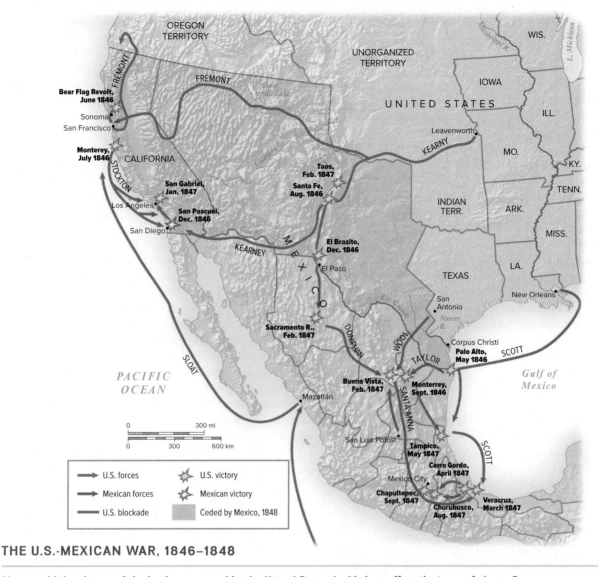

THE U.S.-MEXICAN WAR, 1846–1848

How would the climate of the lands conquered by the United States be likely to affect the issue of slavery?

the peace with Mexico had been finalized. The United States gained title to an immense territory, including all of what would become the states of California, Nevada, and Utah, nearly all of New Mexico, most of Arizona and Colorado, and parts of Wyoming, Kansas, and Oklahoma. These territories included some of the finest natural harbors in the world, regions of immense agricultural potential, and vast, still-hidden riches in oil, gas, and mineral wealth. With the United States in control of the Pacific Coast from San Diego to Puget Sound, Polk's continental vision had become a reality. But slavery would once again dominate national politics.

 **REVIEW**

How did Indians affect the U.S.-Mexican War?

NEW SOCIETIES IN THE WEST

AS HISPANIC, INDIAN, ASIAN, AND Anglo-American cultures interacted, the patterns of development along the frontier varied widely. Some newcomers re-created the farm economies and small towns of the Anglo-American East; others continued the cattle-ranching life of the Hispanic West. In California the new settlements were overwhelmingly shaped by the rush for gold after 1848. And in the Great Basin around Salt Lake the Mormons established a society whose sense of religious mission was as strong as that of the Puritans.

Farming in the West

The overlanders expected to replicate the societies they had left behind. When a wagon train arrived at its destination, members had usually exhausted their resources and thus quickly scattered in search of employment or a good farm site. "Friday, October 27.—Arrived at Oregon City at the falls of the Willamette," read one pioneer diary. "Saturday, October 28.—Went to work."

NEW SOCIETIES IN THE WEST In a process repeated over and over, settlers in a new area set up the machinery of government. Although violence was common on the frontier, farming communities tended to resolve problems by traditional means. Churches took time to establish, for ministers were hard to recruit and congregations were often not large enough to support a church. As the population grew, however, a more conventional society evolved. Towns and a middle class developed, the proportion of women increased, schools were established, and the residents became less mobile.

Although opportunity was greater on the frontier and early arrivals had a special advantage, more and more the agricultural frontier of the West resembled the older society of the East. With the development of markets and transportation, wealth became concentrated, some families fell to the lower rungs of society, and those who were less successful left, seeking yet another fresh start.

The Gold Rush

In January 1848, while constructing a sawmill along the American River, James Marshall noticed gold flecks in the millrace. More discoveries followed, and when the news

©Hulton Archive/Getty Images

With their distinctive clothing and bamboo hats, Chinese miners could be seen throughout the diggings. Chinese immigration reached a peak in 1852, when 20,000 arrived in California. In the heyday of the mining camps, perhaps 20 percent of the miners were Chinese. Confronted with intense hostility from other miners, they worked abandoned claims and unpromising sites with primitive and less expensive equipment.

reached the East, it spread like wildfire. The following spring the Overland Trail was jammed with eager "forty-niners." Some 80,000 emigrants journeyed to California that year, about 55,000 of whom took the overland route. In only two years, from 1848 to the end of 1849, California's population jumped from 14,000 to 100,000. By 1860 it stood at 380,000.

LIFE IN THE MINING CAMPS Among those who went to California was William Swain, a 27-year-old farmer in western New York. Deciding that he had had enough of the hard work of farming, he bid good-bye to his wife and daughter in 1849 and set off for the gold fields to make his fortune. On his arrival in November he entered a partnership and staked a claim along the Feather River, but after several months of backbreaking work in icy waters, he and his partners discovered that their claim was "worth nothing." He sold out and joined another company, but early rains soon forced them to stop work. In October 1850, after less than a year in the diggings, Swain decided to return home. With only a few hundred dollars to show for his labor, he counted himself one of the vast majority of miners who had seen "their bright daydreams of golden wealth vanish like the dreams of night." He arrived home the following February and resumed farming.

Predictably, "mining" the miners offered a more reliable road to prosperity. Perhaps half the inhabitants of a mining town were shopkeepers, businesspeople, and professionals who provided services for prospectors. Also conspicuous were gamblers, card sharks, and other outcasts, all bent on separating the miner from his riches.

NATIVIST AND RACIAL PREJUDICES More than 80 percent of the prospectors who poured into the gold country were Americans, including free blacks. Mexicans, Australians, Argentinians, Hawaiians, Chinese, French, English, and Irish also came. Observers praised the diggings' democratic spirit. Yet such assertions overlooked strongly held nativist prejudices: when frustrated by a lack of success, American miners directed their hostility toward foreigners. Mob violence drove Mexicans out of nearly every camp, and the Chinese were confined to claims abandoned by Americans as unprofitable. The state eventually enacted a foreign miners' tax that fell largely on the Chinese. Free African Americans felt the sting of discrimination as well, both in the camps and in state law. White American miners proclaimed that "colored men were not privileged to work in a country intended only for American citizens."

WOMEN IN THE CAMPS Only about 5 percent of gold rush emigrants were women or children; given this relative scarcity, men were willing to pay top dollar for women's domestic skills. Women supported themselves by cooking, sewing, and washing, as well as by running hotels and boardinghouses. "A smart woman can do very well in this country," one woman informed a friend in the East. "It is the only country I ever was in where a woman received anything like a just compensation for work." Women went to the mining frontier to be with their husbands, to make money, or to find adventure. But the class most frequently seen in the diggings was prostitutes, who numbered perhaps 20 percent of female Californians in 1850.

MINING'S ENVIRONMENTAL LEGACY Before long, the most easily worked claims had been played out and large corporations moved in heavy equipment to get at hidden ore. Shafts were dug deep into the ground, high-pressure water jets tore away ore-bearing gravel, and veins of quartz rock were blasted out and crushed in large stamping mills. This type of mining left a lasting environmental legacy. Abandoned prospect holes and diggings pockmarked the gold fields and created piles of debris that heavy rains would wash down the valley, choking streams and ruining lands below. Excavation of hillsides, construction of dams to divert rivers, and the destruction of the forest cover to meet the heavy demand for lumber and firewood caused serious erosion of the soil and severe flooding in the spring.

Instant City: San Francisco

When the United States assumed control of California, San Francisco had a population of perhaps 200. But thousands of emigrants took the water route west, passing through San Francisco's harbor on their way to the diggings. By 1856 the city's population had jumped to an astonishing 50,000. In a mere 8 years the city had attained the size New York City had taken 190 years to reach.

SAN FRANCISCO'S CHAOTIC GROWTH The product of economic self-interest, San Francisco developed in helter-skelter fashion. Land prices soared, speculation was rampant, and commercial forces became paramount. Residents lived in tents or poorly constructed, half-finished buildings. To enlarge the commercial district, hills began to be leveled, with the dirt used to fill in the bay (thereby creating more usable land). Since the city government took virtually no role in directing development, almost no land was reserved for public use. Property owners defeated a proposal to widen the streets, prompting the city's leading newspaper to complain, "To sell a few more feet of lots, the streets were compressed like a cheese, into half their width."

The Migration from China

The gold rush that swelled San Francisco's streets was a global phenomenon. Americans predominated in the mining population, but Latin Americans, Europeans, Australians, and Chinese swarmed into California. An amazing assortment of languages could be heard on the city's streets: indeed, in 1860 San Francisco's inhabitants were 50 percent foreign-born.

CONDITIONS IN CHINA The most distinctive ethnic group was the Chinese. They had come to Gum San, the land of the golden mountain. Those who arrived in California overwhelmingly hailed from the area of southern China around Canton—and not by accident. Although other provinces of China also suffered from economic distress, population pressures, social unrest, and political upheaval, Canton had a large European presence, since it was the only port open to outsiders. That situation changed after the first Opium War (1839–1842), when Britain forced China to open other ports to trade. For Cantonese, the sudden loss of their

Source: Library of Congress, Prints and Photographs Division [LC-USZC4-7421]

San Francisco in 1850. In this daguerreotype, the masts of hundreds of sailing ships along the wharves appear like a forest, hemming in the chaos and overcrowding of a city thrown up over a space of months.

trade monopoly produced widespread economic hardship. At the same time, a series of religious and political revolts in the region led to severe fighting that devastated the countryside. A growing number of residents concluded that emigration was the only way to survive, and the presence of Western ships in the harbors of Canton and nearby Hong Kong (a British possession since 1842) made it easier to migrate to California rather than to southeast Asia.

Between 1849 and 1854, some 45,000 Chinese flocked to California. Among those who went was 16-year-old Lee Chew, who left for California after a man from his village returned with great wealth from the "country of the American wizards." Like the other gold seekers, these Chinese immigrants were overwhelmingly young and male, and they wanted only to accumulate savings and return home to their families. (Indeed, only 16 Chinese women arrived before 1854.) Generally poor, Chinese emigrants arrived already in debt, having borrowed the price of their steamship ticket; they fell further into debt to Chinese merchants in San Francisco, who loaned them money to purchase needed supplies.

OCCUPATIONS When the Chinese were harassed in the mines, many opened laundries in San Francisco and elsewhere, since little capital was required—soap, scrub board, iron, and ironing board. The going rate at the time for washing, ironing, and starching shirts was an exorbitant $8 per dozen. Many early San Franciscans actually found it cheaper to send their dirty laundry to Canton or Honolulu, to be returned several months later. Other Chinese around San Francisco set up restaurants or worked in the fishing industry. In these early years they found Americans less hostile, as long as they stayed away from the gold fields. As immigration and the competition for jobs increased, however, anti-Chinese sentiment intensified.

Gradually, San Francisco took on the trappings of a more orderly community. The city government established a public school system, erected streetlights, created a municipal water system, and halted further filling in of the bay. Industry was confined to the area south of the city; several new working-class neighborhoods grew up near the downtown section. Fashionable neighborhoods sprouted on several hills, as high rents drove many residents from the developing commercial center, and churches and families became more common. By 1856, the city of the gold rush had been replaced by a new city whose stone and brick buildings gave it a new sense of permanence.

California Genocide

Eager to possess native land, resources, and even Indian slaves; determined to avenge Indian thefts or attacks (real or imagined); or anxious about purported Indian conspiracies, many white Californians attempted to exterminate the state's indigenous population.

GOVERNMENT SUPPORT In 1859 California's governor hired notorious Indian killer Walter S. Jarboe to kill or capture any Yuki Indians found outside their newly established reservation. After four months Jarboe boasted that he and his men had killed or captured nearly 500 Yuki. "However cruel it may be," Jarboe candidly explained, "nothing short of extermination will suffice to rid the Country of them." Some white Californians protested Jarboe's "deliberate, cowardly, brutal massacre of defenseless men, women, and children." But others celebrated, and the state legislature reimbursed Jarboe and men like him for their expenses. Washington encouraged extermination by rejecting treaties that might have provided Indians some land and security, ignoring the pleas of dismayed federal Indian agents. The federal government reimbursed California nearly $1.5 million for the costs of its ongoing Indian campaigns.

LAW AND CATASTROPHE Survivors lived to see the seizure of their historic territories, the destruction of the animals they relied upon, profound ecological transformation through overgrazing and hydraulic mining, and the dissolution of families through kidnapping and enslavement. In 1850 the California legislature passed the "Act for the Government and Protection of Indians." The measure legalized the seizure and forced labor of Indian children, as well as the capture of native men and women for loitering, begging, or leading "an immoral or profligate course of life." People seized on these counts were leased out to the highest bidder, for a four-month term of forced labor. By the late 1850s white observers reported Indian villages comprised almost totally of adults, most of the children "doubtless having been stolen and sold."

Though population estimates are imprecise, few historians doubt that California's Indians experienced a demographic, social, and spiritual catastrophe in the mid-nineteenth century. In the twenty years following the U.S.-Mexican War, homicide, displacement, captivity, forced labor, malnutrition, disease, and social trauma reduced the state's native population from perhaps 150,000 to some 30,000. That said, men like Jarboe and their patrons in state and national government failed to "exterminate" California's Indians. Native men, women, and children employed a host of tactics to protect their families and preserve their cultures and values. Today hundreds of thousands of Californians self-identify as Native American, many of them descended from survivors of the California genocide.

The Mormons in Utah

The makeshift, often chaotic society spawned by the gold rush was a product of largely uncontrolled economic forces. In contrast, the society evolving in the Great Basin of Utah exhibited an entirely different but equally remarkable growth. Salt Lake City became the center of a religious kingdom established by the Church of Jesus Christ of Latter-Day Saints.

STATE OF DESERET After Joseph Smith's death in 1844 (see Chapter 12), the Mormon Church was led by Brigham Young, who lacked Smith's religious mysticism but was a brilliant organizer. Young decided to move his followers to the

IRRIGATION AND COMMUNITY The Mormons connected control of water to their sense of mission and respect for hierarchy. The Valley of the Great Salt Lake, where the Mormons established their holy community, lacked significant rivers or abundant sources of water. Thus success depended on irrigating the region, something never before attempted. When the first Mormons arrived from the East, they began constructing a coordinated series of dams, aqueducts, and ditches, bringing life-giving water to the valleys of the region. Fanning out from their original settlement, they founded a series of colonies throughout the West, all tied to Salt Lake City and joined by ribbons of water. Mormon farmers grew corn, wheat, hay, and an assortment of fruits and vegetables. By 1850 there were more than 16,000 irrigated acres in what would eventually become the state of Utah. The Mormons were the first Anglos to extensively use irrigation in North America.

Control of water reinforced the Mormons' sense of hierarchy and group discipline. Centralization of authority in the hands of church officials made possible an overall plan of development, allowed for maximum exploitation of resources, and freed communities from the disputes over water rights that plagued many settlements in the arid West. In a radical departure from American ideals, church leaders insisted that water belonged to the community, not individuals, and vested this authority in the hands of the local bishop. Control of water resources, which were vital for survival in the desert, reinforced the power of the church hierarchy over not just the faithful but dissidents as well. Community needs, as interpreted by church leaders, took precedence over individual rights. Thus irrigation did more than make the desert bloom. By checking the Jeffersonian ideal of an independent, self-sufficient farmer, it also made possible a centralized, well-regulated society under the firm control of the church.

Mexican-American Rights and Property

At the conclusion of the U.S.-Mexican War, some 100,000 Mexican citizens suddenly found themselves living inside the newly expanded United States. The Treaty of Guadalupe Hidalgo guaranteed them "the free enjoyment of their liberty and property." Mexican negotiators understood how critical that was: without land, their former citizens would enjoy neither economic security nor political influence in their new country. But the treaty said little about how Mexican Americans would prove their ownership of land. They rarely had the sort of

CROSSING THE PLAINS WITH A HAND-CART.

©North Wind Picture Archives/Alamy

In 1847 about a thousand Mormons trekked across the Great Plains to the Great Salt Lake. Thousands more soon followed, many of them hauling their belongings using only handcarts.

Great Basin, an isolated area a thousand miles from the settled parts of the United States. In 1847 the first thousand settlers arrived, the vanguard of thousands more who extended Mormon settlement throughout the Valley of the Great Salt Lake and the West. Church officials also held the government positions, and Young had supreme power in legislative, executive, and judicial matters as well as religious affairs. In 1849 the state of Deseret was officially established, with Brigham Young as governor. It applied for admission to the Union.

POLYGAMY The most controversial church teaching was the doctrine of polygamy, or plural marriage, which Young finally sanctioned publicly in 1852. Visitors reported with surprise that few Mormon wives seemed to rebel against the practice. Some plural wives developed close friendships; indeed, in one sample almost a third of plural marriages included at least two sisters. Moreover, because polygamy distinguished Mormonism from other religions, plural wives saw it as an expression of their religious faith. "I want to be assured of *position in God's estimation,*" one such wife explained. "If polygamy is the Lord's order, we must carry it out."

Source: Library of Congress, Prints and Photographs Division
[LC-USZ62-119579]

Juan Cortina, the leader of a guerrilla war against settlers from the United States who took over land owned earlier by Mexicans. Cortina condemned American lawyers as "vampires, in the guise of men," who used the new, unfamiliar American legal system to rob Mexicans of their property.

documentation that American courts expected. Differences in legal culture, combined with racism and pervasive fraud, led to the dispossession and impoverishment of most Spanish-speaking property holders in the Southwest.

LEGAL FEES AND LAND LOSS California's Land Act of 1851 required everyone with Spanish or Mexican era claims to document them within two years. Hundreds failed to file claims in the time allotted, and by the terms of the Land Act all their territories passed into the public domain. The board eventually confirmed three-quarters of the claims it did receive. But resolution often took years and proved to be enormously expensive. Property owners had to mortgage their lands to pay legal fees, and in the end the great majority were ruined. Claimants in New Mexico likewise lost vast tracts of lands to Anglo ranchers and, especially, to lawyers. The lengthy and expensive review process left Mexican and Pueblo Indian claimants holding only about 6 percent of the lands they had possessed before the U.S. Invasion.

TEJANO RESISTANCE Tejanos faced similar pressures. Stigmatized and despised by whites as racial inferiors, they were the poorest group in free society. One response to this dislocation, an option commonly taken by persecuted minorities, was social banditry. An example was the folk hero Juan Cortina. A member of a displaced landed family in southern Texas, Cortina was driven into resistance in the 1850s by American harassment. He began stealing from wealthy Anglos to aid poor Mexicans, proclaiming, "To me is

entrusted the breaking of the chains of your slavery." Cortina continued to raid Texas border settlements until finally he was imprisoned by Mexican authorities. While failing to produce any lasting change, Cortina demonstrated the depth of frustration and resentment among Hispanics over their abuse at the hands of the new Anglo majority.

 REVIEW
Who were the winners and losers in the California gold rush?

ESCAPE FROM CRISIS

ISSUE OF SLAVERY'S EXTENSION WITH THE RETURN OF PEACE, Congress confronted the problem of whether to allow slavery in the newly acquired territories. David Wilmot, in his controversial proviso, had already proposed to outlaw slavery throughout the Mexican cession. John C. Calhoun, representing the extreme southern position, countered that slavery was legal in all territories. The federal government had acted as the agent of all the states in acquiring the land, he argued, and southerners had a right to take their property there, including slaves. Only when the residents of a territory drafted a state constitution could they decide the question of slavery.

Between these extremes were two moderate positions. One proposed extending the Missouri Compromise line of 36°30′ to the Pacific, which would have continued the earlier policy of dividing the national domain between the North and the South. The other proposal, championed by Senator Lewis Cass of Michigan and Senator Stephen A. Douglas of Illinois, was to allow the people of the territory rather than Congress to decide the status of slavery. This solution, which became known as **popular sovereignty**, was deliberately ambiguous, since its supporters refused to specify whether the residents could make this decision at any time or only when drafting a state constitution, as Calhoun insisted.

When Congress organized the Oregon Territory in 1848, it prohibited slavery there, since even southerners admitted that the region was too far north to grow the South's staple crops. But this seemingly straightforward decision made it impossible to apply the Missouri Compromise line to the other territories. Without Oregon as a part of the package, the bulk of the remaining land would be open to slavery, something at which the North balked. Almost inadvertently, one of the two moderate solutions had been discarded by the summer of 1848.

A Two-Faced Campaign

In the election of 1848 both major parties tried to avoid the slavery issue. The Democrats nominated Lewis Cass, a supporter of popular sovereignty, while the Whigs bypassed all their prominent leaders and selected General Zachary Taylor, who had taken no position on any public issue and who remained silent throughout the campaign. The Whigs adopted no platform and planned instead to emphasize the general's war record.

©IanDagnall Computing/Alamy

Nicknamed "Old Rough and Ready," General Zachary Taylor was indifferent to fancy dress uniforms and blunt in speech and manner. But Whig party leaders managed to keep the war hero from saying much during the election campaign of 1848. Many southern voters assumed that Taylor, a slaveholder from Louisiana, would wish to extend slavery into the newly annexed territories. They were in for a surprise.

FREE SOIL PARTY But the slavery issue would not be ignored. A new antislavery coalition, the **Free Soil Party** helped force the issue. Alienated by Polk's policies and still angry over the 1844 convention, northern Democrats loyal to Van Buren spearheaded its creation. They were joined by "Conscience Whigs," who disavowed Taylor's nomination because he was a slaveholder. Furthermore, political abolitionists like Salmon P. Chase left the Liberty party in favor of this broader coalition. To widen its appeal, the Free Soil platform focused on the dangers of extending slavery rather than on the evil of slavery itself. Ironically, the party's convention named as its candidate Martin Van Buren—the man who for years had struggled to keep the slavery issue out of politics.

ELECTION OF 1848 With the Free Soilers strongly supporting the Wilmot Proviso, the Whigs and Democrats could not ignore the slavery question. The two major parties responded by running different campaigns in the North and the South. To southern audiences, each party promised that it would protect slavery in the territories; to northern voters, each claimed that it would keep the territories free. In this two-faced, sectional campaign, the Whigs won their second national victory. Taylor held on to the core of Whig voters in both sections (Van Buren and Cass, after all, had long been Democrats). But in the South, where the contest pitted a southern slaveholder

against two northerners, Taylor won many more votes than Clay had in 1844. As one southern Democrat complained, "We have lost hundreds of votes, solely on the ground that General Cass was a Northerner and General Taylor a Southern man." Furthermore, Van Buren polled five times as many votes as the Liberty Party had four years earlier. It seemed that the national system of political parties was being gradually pulled apart.

The Compromise of 1850

Once he became president, Taylor could no longer remain silent. The territories gained from Mexico had to be organized; furthermore, by 1849 California had gained enough residents to be admitted as a state. In the Senate the balance of power between North and South stood at 15 states each. California's admission would break the sectional balance.

TAYLOR'S PLAN Called "Old Rough and Ready" by his troops, Taylor was a forthright man of action, but he was politically inexperienced and he oversimplified complex problems. Since even Calhoun conceded that entering states had the right to ban slavery, Taylor proposed that the way to end the sectional crisis was to skip the territorial stage by combining all the Mexican cession into two very large states, New Mexico and California. So the president sent agents to California and New Mexico with instructions to set the machinery in motion for both territories to draft constitutions and apply for statehood directly. Even more shocking to southern Whigs, he proposed to apply the Wilmot Proviso to the entire area, since he was convinced that slavery would never flourish there. By the time Congress convened in December 1849, California had drafted a constitution and applied for admission as a free state. Taylor reported that New Mexico (which included most of Arizona, Utah, and Colorado) would soon do the same and recommended that both be admitted as free states. The president's plan touched off the most serious sectional crisis the Union had yet confronted.

Into this turmoil stepped Henry Clay, now 73 years old and nearing the end of his career. A savvy card player all his life, Clay loved politics: the bargaining, the wheeling and dealing, the late-night trade-offs eased along by a bottle of bourbon. Thirty years earlier he had engineered the Missouri Compromise, and in 1833 he had helped defuse the nullification crisis. Clay decided that a grand compromise was needed to save the Union. Already, Mississippi had summoned other southern states to meet in a convention at Nashville to discuss the crisis, and southern extremists were pushing for secession. The points of disagreement went beyond the question of the western territories. Many northerners considered it disgraceful that slaves were bought and sold in the nation's capital, where slavery was still permitted. Southerners complained bitterly that northern states ignored the 1793 Fugitive Slave Law and prevented them from reclaiming runaway slaves.

Territorial Transformations in the American West, 1819–1850

DATE	EVENT	SIGNIFICANCE
1819	Transcontinental Treaty (Adams-Onís Treaty)	Establishes the boundary between northern New Spain and the western U.S.; gives U.S. formal access to the Pacific (see map, Chapter 9).
1821	Mexican independence	Independent Mexico assumes rights to all North American territory formerly claimed by Spain.
1820s and 1830s	Indian removal	Responding to threats, incentives, and, finally, military coercion, tens of thousands of eastern Indians relocate to present-day Oklahoma. Change fuels conflict and eventually accommodation with western Indians.
1836	Texan independence	Republic of Texas claims sovereignty over what had been Mexican Texas and insists on the Rio Grande from source to mouth as its western and southern border.
1840	"Great Peace" on the Arkansas	Peace between Comanches and Kiowas on the Southern Plains and Southern Cheyennes and Arapahos on the Central Plains puts an end to struggle in the Arkansas Valley; resulting security and trade opportunities encourage Indian raids into Mexico.
1845	Texas annexed to United States	Federal government under Polk pledges to uphold Texas's claims to the Rio Grande; Mexico severs diplomatic relations.
1846	Oregon Treaty	Settles dispute between Great Britain and U.S. over Oregon territory; fixes boundary at 49th parallel, but Britain retains all of Vancouver Island. Oregon organized as a territory in 1848.
1847	Mormon migration to Great Basin	Beginning of migration that would involve many thousands into the Valley of the Great Salt Lake; state of Deseret proclaimed in 1849.
1848	Treaty of Guadalupe Hidalgo	At the close of the U.S.-Mexican War, Republic of Mexico surrenders more than 750,000 square miles of land to the United States (including Texas), amounting to more than half of Mexico's national territory.
1850	Compromise of 1850	Texas relinquishes claim to Rio Grande as western boundary but is given El Paso; California admitted as state; New Mexico and Utah organized as territories.

CLAY'S COMPROMISE Clay's compromise, submitted in January 1850, addressed all these concerns. California, he proposed, should be admitted as a free state, which represented the clear wishes of most settlers there. The rest of the Mexican cession would be organized as two territories, New Mexico and Utah, under the doctrine of popular sovereignty. Thus slavery would not be prohibited from these regions. Clay also proposed that Congress abolish the slave trade but not slavery itself in the District of Columbia and that a new, more rigorous fugitive slave law be passed to enable southerners to reclaim runaway slaves. To reinforce the idea that both North and South were yielding ground, Clay combined those provisions that dealt with the former Mexican territory and several others adjusting the Texas–New Mexico boundary into a larger package known as the Omnibus Bill.

With the stakes so high, the Senate debated the bill for six months. Daniel Webster of Massachusetts, always deep-voiced, seemed more somber than usual when he delivered a pro-Compromise speech on the seventh of March. "I wish to speak today not as a Massachusetts man, not as a Northern man, but as an American. . . . I speak today for the preservation of the Union. Hear me for my cause." Calhoun, whose aged, crevassed face mirrored the lines that had been drawn so deeply between the two sections, was near death and too ill to deliver his final speech to the Senate, which a colleague read for him as he listened silently. The "cords of Union," he warned—those ties of interest and affection that held the nation together—were snapping one by one. Only equal rights for the South and an end to the agitation against slavery could preserve the Union.

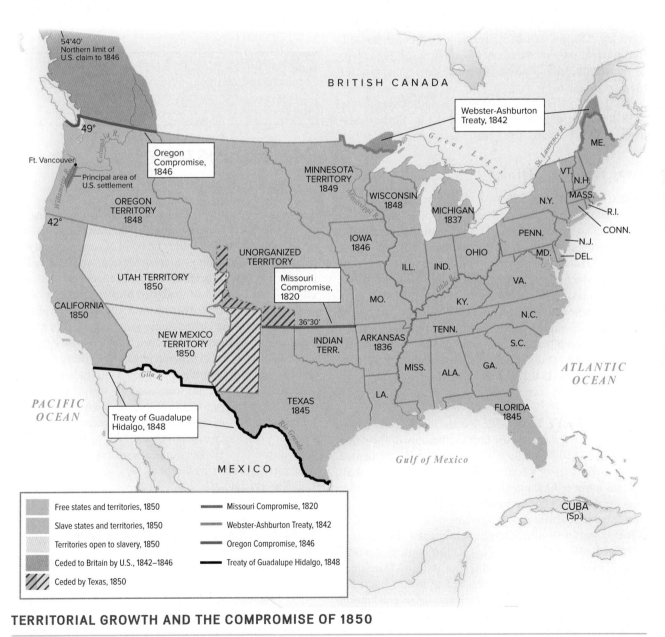

TERRITORIAL GROWTH AND THE COMPROMISE OF 1850

The Webster-Ashburton Treaty established Maine's northern boundary as well as the American-Canadian boundary west of the Great Lakes.

Clay, wracked by a hacking cough, spent long hours trying to line up the needed votes. But for once, the great card enthusiast had misplayed his hand. The Omnibus Bill required that the components of the compromise be approved as a package. Extremists in Congress from both regions, however, combined against the moderates and rejected the bill.

PASSAGE OF THE COMPROMISE OF 1850 With Clay exhausted and his strategy in shambles, Democrat Stephen A. Douglas assumed leadership of the pro-Compromise forces. The sudden death in July of President Taylor, who had threatened to veto Clay's plan, aided the compromise movement. One by one, Douglas submitted the individual measures for a vote. Northern representatives provided the necessary votes to admit California and abolish the slave trade in the District of Columbia, while southern representatives supplied the edge needed to organize the Utah and New Mexico territories and pass the new fugitive slave law. On the face of it, everyone had compromised. But in truth, only 61 members of Congress, or 21 percent of the membership, had not voted against some part of the Compromise.

By September 17 all the separate parts of the Compromise of 1850 had passed and been signed into law by the new president, Millard Fillmore. The Union, it seemed, was safe.

Away from the Brink

REJECTION OF SECESSION The general public, both North and South, rallied to the Compromise. At the convention of southern states in Nashville, the fire-eaters—the radical proponents of states' rights and secession—found themselves voted down by more moderate voices. Even in the Deep South, coalitions of pro-Compromise Whigs and Democrats soundly defeated secessionists in the state elections that followed. Still, most southerners felt that a firm line had been drawn. With California's admission, they were now outnumbered in the Senate, so it was critical that slaveholders be granted equal legal access to the territories. They announced that any breach of the Compromise of 1850 would justify secession.

FUGITIVE SLAVE LAW The North, for its part, found the new fugitive slave law the hardest measure of the Compromise of 1850 to swallow. The controversial law denied an accused runaway a trial by jury, and it required that all citizens assist federal marshals in its enforcement. Harriet Beecher Stowe's popular novel *Uncle Tom's Cabin* (1852) presented a powerful moral indictment of the law—and of slavery as an institution. Despite sentimental characters, a contrived plot, and clumsy dialect, the book profoundly moved its readers. Emphasizing the duty of Christians toward the downtrodden, it reached a greater audience than any previous abolitionist work and heightened moral opposition to the institution.

In reality, however, fewer than 1,000 slaves a year ran away to the North, many of whom did not succeed. Despite some cases of well-publicized resistance, the 1850 Fugitive Slave Law was generally enforced in the free states. Many northerners did not like the law, but they were unwilling to tamper with the Compromise. Stephen Douglas spoke accurately enough when he boasted in 1851, "The whole country is acquiescing in the compromise measures—everywhere, North and South. Nobody proposes to repeal or disturb them."

And so calm returned. In the lackluster 1852 presidential campaign, both the Whigs and the Democrats endorsed the Compromise. Franklin Pierce, a little-known New Hampshire Democrat, soundly defeated the Whig candidate, Winfield Scott. Even more significant, the antislavery Free Soil candidate received only about half as many votes as Van Buren had four years before. With the slavery issue seemingly losing political force, it appeared that the Republic had weathered the storm unleashed by the Wilmot Proviso.

> ✓ **REVIEW**
>
> How did the U.S.-Mexican War reignite the sectional controversy, and what did the Compromise of 1850 do to ease it?

PUTTING HISTORY IN GLOBAL CONTEXT

THE MOVING FRONTIER had worked many changes during the 1830s and 1840s; and many more upheavals awaited the decade ahead. From a continental point of view, political relations among the United States, Mexico, and the Indian peoples had shifted significantly. Indian attacks on Mexico in the 1820s and 1830s had weakened Mexico's ability to repel an invasion by the United States. And with the Treaty of Guadalupe Hidalgo, the United States gained over half a million square miles. Its frontier had leaped from the Mississippi valley to the Pacific, but in between remained territory still unorganized and still controlled by formidable Indian peoples. And as the North became increasingly industrialized and the South more firmly committed to an economy based on cotton and slavery, the movement of Americans into those territories would revive growing conflict between the two sections over slavery. The disputes would shatter the Jacksonian party system, reignite the slavery issue, and shake the Union to its foundation.

CHAPTER SUMMARY

In the 1840s the United States expanded to the Pacific, a development that required an aggressive war and that led to the rise of the slavery issue in national politics.

- In the 1840s Americans proclaimed that it was the United States' Manifest Destiny to expand across the North American continent.

- Americans in Texas increasingly clashed with Mexican authorities, and in 1836 Texans revolted and established an independent republic.

- Americans headed for Oregon and California on the Overland Trail.

  - The journey put special pressures on women as the traditional division of labor by gender broke down.

  - White migration also put pressure on Plains Indians' grazing lands, forests, and freedom of movement.

  - The gold rush spawned a unique society that was overwhelmingly male, highly mobile, and strongly nativist and racist. There was Indian genocide in California.

  - Led by Brigham Young, the Mormons established a tightly organized, centrally controlled society in the Great Basin of Utah.

  - Throughout the Southwest the Hispanic population suffered at the hands of the new Anglo majority, as did the Chinese emigrants who flocked to California.

- President James K. Polk entered office with a vision of the United States as a continental nation.

  - He upheld President John Tyler's annexation of Texas and agreed to divide the Oregon country with Britain.

  - Polk instigated a war with Mexico in order to obtain that country's northern territories.

  - Divided, impoverished, and distracted by ongoing wars with Indians, Mexico was forced to surrender more than half a million square miles of territory in the aftermath of the war.

- The U.S.-Mexican War reinjected the slavery issue into American national politics.

  - The Wilmot Proviso sought to prohibit slavery from any territory acquired from Mexico.

  - The struggle over the Proviso eventually disrupted both major parties.

  - Congress momentarily stilled the sectional crisis with the Compromise of 1850.

Digging Deeper

For the Sioux, see Richard White, "The Winning of the West: The Expansion of the Western Sioux in the Eighteenth and Nineteenth Centuries," *Journal of American History* (1978), 319–343; and Jeffrey Ostler, *The Lakotas and the Black Hills* (2011). For the traumas and challenges facing one Plains Indian community, see Elizabeth A. Fenn's haunting *Encounters at the Heart of the World* (2015). Western trading families are the focus of Anne F. Hyde's sweeping *Empires, Nations and Families* (2002). David J. Weber, *The Mexican Frontier, 1821–1846* (1982), is a superb study of the Southwest prior to American control. For a more recent account, with a transnational interpretation of the Texas Rebellion, see Andrés Reséndez, *Changing National Identities at the Frontier* (2005). For the Overland Trail, see John Mack Faragher, *Women and Men on the Overland Trail* (1979). *Mormonism: A Very Short Introduction* (2008), by Richard Bushman, is an elegant primer. For California's missions, see Steven W. Hackel's *Children of Coyote, Missionaries of Saint Francis* (2005). Susan Lee Johnson's *Roaring Camp* (2001) explores social interaction during the California gold rush. For the environmental consequences of mining, see Andrew C. Isenberg's *Mining California* (2005).

The fullest treatment of American life in this period is Daniel Walker Howe's magisterial book *What Hath God Wrought* (2007). Thomas R. Hietala offers a stimulating analysis of the social roots of expansionism in *Manifest Design* (1985). For Indians and the geopolitics of the era, see Brian DeLay, *War of a Thousand Deserts: Indian Raids and the U.S.-Mexican War* (2008). Andrew J. Torget's *Seeds of Empire* (2015) excavates the centrality of cotton to turning points in Texas's nineteenth-century history. The best discussion of Polk's handling of the Oregon and Texas issues remains David M. Pletcher, *The Diplomacy of Annexation* (1973). Michael F. Holt presents a powerful analysis of the Whig Party's difficulties in this decade in *The Rise and Fall of the American Whig Party* (1999). For the California Indian genocide, see Brendan C. Lindsay, *Murder State* (2012); and Benjamin Madley, *An American Genocide* (2016). Howard R. Lamar's classic account *The Far Southwest* (1966) explores political and economic power in the territories after conquest. Holman Hamilton, *Prologue to Conflict* (new ed., 2005), is an excellent study of the Compromise of 1850.

15 The Union Broken

1850–1861

"Imagine a man standing in a pair of long boots, covered with dust and mud . . . the handle of a large bowie-knife projecting from one or both boot-tops; a leathern belt buckled around his waist, on each side of which is fastened a large revolver . . . an old slouched hat . . . an unshaved face and unwashed hands. Imagine such a picture of humanity, who can swear any given number of oaths in any specified time, drink any quantity of bad whiskey without getting drunk, and boast of having stolen a half dozen horses and killed one or more abolitionists—and you will have a pretty fair conception of a Border Ruffian, as he appears in Missouri and in Kansas." So wrote a northerner who arrived in Kansas Territory at a time when it became a fierce battleground over whether slavery would expand into new regions of the United States.

Source: Library of Congress, Prints and Photographs Division [LC-DIG-ppmsca-40662]

>> An American Story

THE SACKING OF A TOWN IN KANSAS

Into town they rode, several hundred strong, their faces flushed with excitement. They were unshaven, rough-talking men, "armed . . . to the teeth with rifles and revolvers, cutlasses and bowie-knives." At the head of the procession an American flag flapped softly in the warm May breeze. Alongside it was another with a crouching tiger emblazoned on black and white stripes, followed by other banners proclaiming "Southern Rights" and "The Superiority of the White Race." At the rear rolled five artillery pieces, which were quickly dragged into range of the town's main street. Watching intently from a window in his office, Josiah Miller, the editor of the Lawrence *Kansas Free State,* predicted, "Well, boys, we're in for it."

Startling News!
OUR BORDER IN DANGER!!
Missouri to be Invaded!

We have authority which will not admit of doubt, for stating that Lane, with 3000 lawless abolitionists, and 10 pieces of artillery, is about to march into Missouri, and sack the border towns of Lexington, Independence, Westport, and New Santa Fe. This is no idle rumor; and there can be no doubt of it. These desperadoes swear they wil carry everything before them, and spare nothing.

©Kansas State Historical Society

A proslavery newspaper. Missouri was never invaded.

For the residents of Lawrence, Kansas, the worst seemed at hand. The town had been founded by the New England Emigrant Aid Company, a Yankee association that recruited settlers in an effort to keep Kansas Territory from becoming a slave state. Accepting Stephen Douglas's idea that the people should decide the status of slavery, the town's residents intended to see to it that under this doctrine of **popular sovereignty** Kansas entered the Union as a free state. Immigrants from the neighboring slave state of Missouri were equally determined that no "abolition tyrants" or "negro thieves" would control the territory. There had been conflict in Kansas almost immediately: land disputes, horse thievery, shootings on both sides.

In the ensuing turmoil, the federal government seemed to back the proslavery forces. In the spring of 1856 a U.S. district court indicted several of Lawrence's leading citizens for treason, and federal marshal Israel Donaldson led a posse, swelled by volunteers from across the Missouri border, to Lawrence on May 20 to make the arrests.

Meanwhile, Lawrence's "committee of safety" had agreed on a policy of nonresistance. Most of those indicted had fled, but Donaldson arrested two men without incident. Then he dismissed his posse.

The posse, however, was not ready to go home. Already thoroughly liquored up, it marched into town cheering. Ignoring the pleas of some leaders, its members smashed the presses of two newspapers, the *Herald of Freedom* and the *Kansas Free State*. Then the horde unleashed its wrath on the now-deserted Free State Hotel, which more closely resembled a fort. The invaders unsuccessfully attempted to batter it down with cannon fire and blow it up with gunpowder; finally they put a torch to the building. When the mob finally rode off, it left the residents of Lawrence unharmed but thoroughly terrified.

Retaliation by free-state partisans was not long in coming. Hurrying north along a different road to Lawrence, an older man with a grim face and steely eyes heard the news the next morning that the town had been attacked. "Old Man Brown," as everyone called him, was on his way with several of his sons to provide reinforcements. A severe, God-fearing Calvinist, John Brown was also a staunch abolitionist who had once remarked to a friend that he believed "God had raised him up on purpose to break the jaws of the wicked." Brooding over the failure of the free-staters to resist the "slave hounds" from Missouri, Brown headed toward Pottawatomie Creek in Franklin County, Kansas, on the night of May 24, 1856, with half a dozen others, including his sons. Announcing that they were "the Northern Army" come to serve justice, they burst into the cabin of James Doyle, a proslavery man from Tennessee, with cutlasses drawn. As Brown marched off Doyle and his three sons, Doyle's terrified wife, Mahala, begged him to spare her youngest, and the old man relented. The others were led no more than 100 yards down the road before Owen and Salmon Brown hacked them to death with broadswords. Old Man Brown then walked up to James Doyle's body and put a bullet through his forehead. Before the night was done, two more cabins had been visited and two more proslavery settlers brutally executed. Not one of the five murdered men owned a single slave or had any connection with the raid on Lawrence.

Brown's action precipitated a new wave of fighting in Kansas and controversy throughout the nation. "Everybody here feels as if we are upon a volcano," remarked one congressman in Washington.

The country was indeed atop a smoldering volcano that would finally erupt in the spring of 1861, showering civil war, death, and destruction across the land. Popular sovereignty, the last remaining moderate solution to the controversy over the expansion of slavery, had failed dismally in Kansas. The violence and disorder in the territory provided a stark reply to Stephen Douglas's proposition: What could be more peaceable, more fair than the notion of popular sovereignty? <<

341

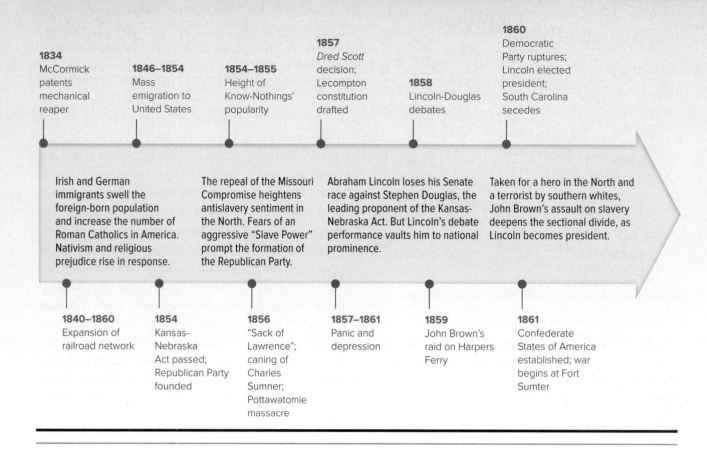

1834
McCormick patents mechanical reaper

1846–1854
Mass emigration to United States

1854–1855
Height of Know-Nothings' popularity

1857
Dred Scott decision; Lecompton constitution drafted

1858
Lincoln-Douglas debates

1860
Democratic Party ruptures; Lincoln elected president; South Carolina secedes

Irish and German immigrants swell the foreign-born population and increase the number of Roman Catholics in America. Nativism and religious prejudice rise in response.

The repeal of the Missouri Compromise heightens antislavery sentiment in the North. Fears of an aggressive "Slave Power" prompt the formation of the Republican Party.

Abraham Lincoln loses his Senate race against Stephen Douglas, the leading proponent of the Kansas-Nebraska Act. But Lincoln's debate performance vaults him to national prominence.

Taken for a hero in the North and a terrorist by southern whites, John Brown's assault on slavery deepens the sectional divide, as Lincoln becomes president.

1840–1860
Expansion of railroad network

1854
Kansas-Nebraska Act passed; Republican Party founded

1856
"Sack of Lawrence"; caning of Charles Sumner; Pottawatomie massacre

1857–1861
Panic and depression

1859
John Brown's raid on Harpers Ferry

1861
Confederate States of America established; war begins at Fort Sumter

SECTIONAL CHANGES IN AMERICAN SOCIETY

THE ROAD TO WAR WAS not a straight or short one. Six years elapsed between the Compromise of 1850 and the crisis in "Bleeding Kansas." Another five years would pass before the first shot was fired. And the process of separation involved more than ineffective politicians and an unwillingness to compromise. As we have seen, Americans were bound by a growing transportation network, by national markets, and by a national political system. These social and political ties—the "cords of Union," the powerful South Carolina senator John C. Calhoun called them—could not be severed all at once. Increasingly, however, the changes occurring in American society heightened sectional tensions. As the North continued to industrialize, its society came into conflict with that of the South. The Old Northwest, which had long been a political ally of the South, became more closely linked to the East. The coming of civil war, in other words, involved social and economic changes as well as political ones.

The Growth of a Railroad Economy

By the time the Compromise of 1850 produced a lull in the tensions between North and South, the American economy had left behind the depression of the early 1840s and was roaring again. Its basic structure, however, was changing. Cotton remained the nation's major export, but it was no longer the driving force for American economic growth. After 1839 this role was taken over by the construction of a vast railroad network covering the eastern half of the continent. By 1850 the United States possessed more than 9,000 miles of track; 10 years later it had over 30,000 miles, more than the rest of the world combined. Much of the new construction during the 1850s occurred west of the Appalachian Mountains.

Because western railroads ran through less settled areas, they were especially dependent on public aid. State and local governments made loans to rail companies and sometimes exempted them temporarily from taxes. About a quarter of the cost of railroad construction came from state and local governments, but federal land grants were crucial, too. By mortgaging or selling the land to farmers, the rail companies raised construction capital and also stimulated settlement, which increased its business and profits.

On a national map, the rail network in place by 1860 looked impressive, but these lines were not fully integrated. A few trunk-line roads such as the New York Central had combined a number of smaller lines to facilitate the shipment of freight. But roadbeds had not yet been standardized, so that no fewer than 12 different gauges, or track widths, were in use. Moreover, cities at the end of rail lines jealously strove to maintain their commercial advantages, not wanting to connect with competing port cities for fear that freight would pass through to the next city down the line.

RAILROADS' IMPACT ON THE ECONOMY The effect of the new lines rippled outward through the economy. Farmers along the tracks began to specialize in cash crops and market them in distant locations. With their profits they purchased manufactured goods that earlier they might have made at home. Before the railroad reached Athens, Tennessee, the surrounding counties produced about 25,000 bushels of wheat, which sold for less than 50 cents a bushel. Once the railroad came, farmers in these same counties grew 400,000 bushels and sold their crop at a dollar a bushel. Railroads also stimulated other areas of the economy, notably the mining and iron industries.

REORIENTATION OF WESTERN TRADE The new rail networks shifted the direction of western trade. In 1840 most northwestern grain was shipped down the Mississippi River to the bustling port of New Orleans. But low water made steamboat travel risky in summer, and ice shut down traffic in winter. Products such as lard, tallow, and cheese quickly spoiled if stored in New Orleans's sweltering warehouses. Increasingly, traffic from the Midwest flowed west to east, over the new rail lines. Chicago became the region's hub, linking the farms of the upper Midwest to New York and other eastern cities by more than 2,000 miles of track in 1855. Thus, while the value of goods shipped by river to New Orleans continued to increase, the South's overall share of western trade dropped dramatically.

These new patterns of commerce and agriculture weakened the traditional political alliance between the South and the West, which had been based on shared economic interests. "The power of cotton over the financial affairs of the Union has in the last few years rapidly diminished," one pundit remarked in 1849, "and breadstuffs will now become the governing power."

Railroads and the Prairie Environment

As railroad lines fanned out from Chicago, farmers began to acquire open prairie land in Illinois and then Iowa, putting its deep black soil into production. Commercial agriculture transformed this remarkable treeless environment.

To settlers accustomed to woodlands, the thousands of square miles of tall grass were an awesome sight. Indian grass, Canadian wild rye, and native big bluestem all grew higher than a person. In 1838 Edmund Flagg gazed upon "the tall grasstops waving in . . . billowy beauty in the breeze; the narrow pathway winding off like a serpent over the rolling surface, disappearing and reappearing till lost in the luxuriant herbage." Long-grass prairies had their perils too: summer or winter storms sent travelers searching for the shelter of trees along river valleys. Dewitt Smith recalled the fierce green-headed flies awaiting the unsuspecting. "A journey across the big praries was, in the summer time, undertaken only at night," he recalled, "because on a hot summer day horses would be literally stung and worried to death."

IMPACT OF TECHNOLOGY Because eastern plows could not penetrate the densely tangled roots of prairie grass, the earliest settlers erected farms along the boundary separating the forest from the prairie. In 1837, however, John Deere patented a sharp-cutting steel plow that sliced through the sod without soil sticking to the blade. In addition, Cyrus McCormick refined a mechanical reaper that harvested 14 times more wheat with the same amount of labor. By the 1850s McCormick was selling 1,000 reapers a year and could not keep up with demand, while Deere turned out 10,000 plows annually.

CHANGES IN THE LANDSCAPE The new commercial farming fundamentally altered the landscape and the environment. Indians had grown corn in the region for years, but never in such large fields as did white farmers, whose surpluses were shipped east. Prairie farmers also introduced new crops that were not part of

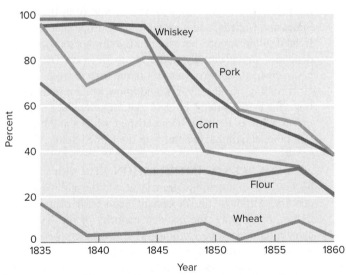

Proportion of Western Exports Shipped via New Orleans, 1835–1860

In 1835 nearly 100 percent of western exports of corn, pork, and whiskey were being shipped via New Orleans. By 1860 only about 40 percent of pork and whiskey and 20 percent of flour and corn were. The change in shipping patterns weakened the political ties between the South and the Old Northwest.

the earlier ecological system, notably wheat, along with fruits and vegetables. Native grasses were replaced by a small number of plants cultivated as commodities.

Western farmers also altered the landscape by reducing the annual fires, often set by Indians, that had kept the prairie free from trees. In the fires' absence, trees reappeared on land not in cultivation and, if undisturbed, eventually formed woodlots. The earlier unbroken landscape gave way to independent farms, each fenced in the precise checkerboard pattern established by the Northwest Ordinance. It was an artificial ecosystem of animals, woodlots, and crops whose large, uniform layout made western farms more efficient than the irregular farms in the East.

Railroads and the Urban Environment

INFLUENCE ON LOCATION OF TOWNS Railroads transformed the urban environment as well. Communities soon recognized that their economic survival depended on creating adequate rail links to the countryside and to major urban markets. Large cities feared they would be left behind in the struggle to be the dominant city in the region. Smaller communities saw their very survival at stake in the battle for rail connections. When the new railroad line bypassed the prairie village of Auburn, Illinois, its fate was sealed, and residents quickly abandoned it for more promising locations.

Even communities that obtained rail links found the presence of this new technology difficult to adjust to. When a railroad began serving nearby Jacksonville, Illinois, merchants complained about the noise, dirt, and billowing smoke when locomotives hissed through the business district. "Many of the people were as much scared as the horses at the steaming monster," recalled one resident. After a few years, the tracks were relocated on the outskirts of town. Jacksonville's experience became the norm: increasingly, communities kept railroads away from fashionable neighborhoods and shopping areas. As the tracks became a physical manifestation of social and economic divisions, the notion of living "on the wrong side of the tracks" became crucial to defining the urban landscape.

Rising Industrialization

On the eve of the Civil War, 60 percent of American laborers worked on farms. In 1860, for the first time, that figure dropped below 50 percent in the North. The expansion of commercial agriculture spurred the growth of industry. Of the 10 leading American industries, 8 processed raw materials produced by agriculture, including flour milling and the manufacture of textiles, shoes, and woolens. (The only exceptions were iron and machinery.) Industrial growth also spurted during the 1850s as water power was increasingly replaced by steam, since there were only a fixed number of water-power sites.

Most important, the factory system of organizing labor and the technology of interchangeable parts spread to other areas of the economy. Many industries during the 1850s adopted interchangeable parts. Isaac Singer began using them in 1851 to mass-produce sewing machines, which made possible the ready-made clothing industry, while workers who assembled farm implements performed a single step in the process over and over again. By 1860 the United States had nearly a billion dollars invested in manufacturing, almost twice as much as in 1849.

Immigration

The surge of industry required a large factory labor force. Natural increase helped swell the population to more than 30 million by 1860, but only in part, since the birthrate had begun to decline. On the eve of the Civil War the average white mother bore five children, compared to seven at the turn of the century. It was the beginning of mass emigration to America during the mid-1840s that kept population growth soaring.

INFLUX FROM ABROAD In the 20 years from 1820 to 1840, about 700,000 newcomers had entered the United States. That figure jumped to 1.7 million in the 1840s, then to 2.6 million in the 1850s. Though even greater numbers arrived after the Civil War, as a percentage of the nation's total population, the wave from 1845 to 1854 was the largest influx of immigrants in American history. Most newcomers were young people in the prime of life: out of 224,000 arrivals in 1856, only 31,000 were under 10 and only 20,000 were over 40.

Certainly the booming economy and the lure of freedom drew immigrants, but they were also pushed by deteriorating conditions in Europe. In Ireland, a potato blight created *an Gorta Mór*—the "Great Famine"—leaving potatoes rotting in the fields. The blight may well have spread from the United States and Canada, and it also infected Europe generally. But Ireland suffered more, because nearly a third of its population depended almost entirely on the potato for food. "They are all gone—clean gone," wrote a priest in the Irish town of Galway. "If travelling by night, you would know when a potato field was near by the smell." In 1846 and for several years following, as many as a million Irish perished, while a million and a half more emigrated, two-thirds to the United States.

NEW SOURCES OF IMMIGRATION The Irish tended to be poorer than other immigrant groups in the mid nineteenth century. Although the Protestant Scots-Irish continued as before to emigrate, the decided majority of the Irish who came after 1845 were Catholic. The newcomers were generally mostly unmarried younger sons and daughters of hard-pressed rural families. Because they were poor and unskilled, the Irish congregated in the cities, where the women performed domestic service and took factory jobs and the men did manual labor.

Germans and Scandinavians also had economic reasons for leaving Europe. They included small farmers whose lands had become marginal or who had been displaced by landlords, and skilled workers thrown out of work by

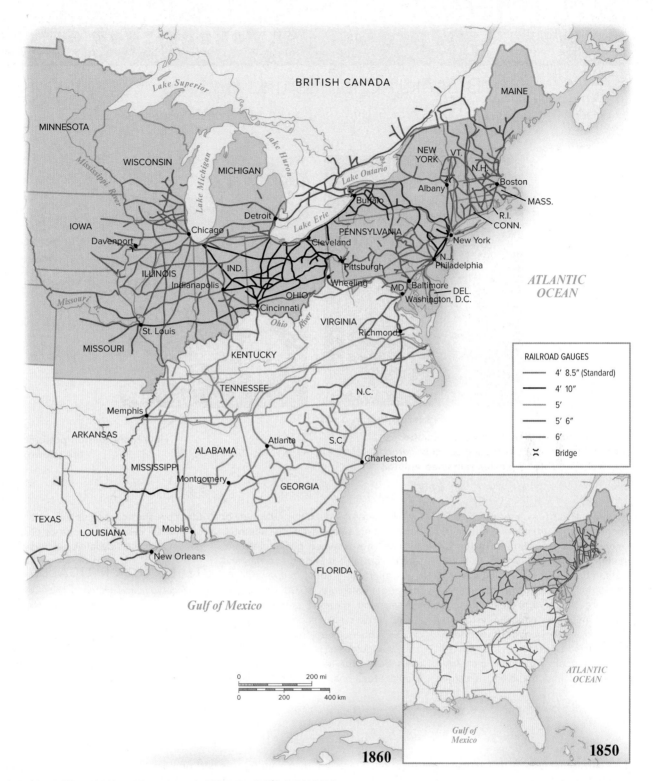

RAILROADS, 1850 AND 1860, WITH TRACK GAUGES

During the 1850s a significant amount of railroad track was laid, but total track mileage is misleading because the United States lacked a fully integrated rail network in 1860. A few trunk-line roads had combined a number of smaller lines into a single system to facilitate shipment. The Pennsylvania Railroad, for example, connected Philadelphia and Pittsburgh. But the existence of five major track gauges as well as minor ones meant that passengers and freight often had to be transferred from one line to the next. And north-south traffic was further disrupted by the lack of bridges over the Ohio River. How many changes in railroad cars does the map indicate would have to be made for freight to ship from Chicago to New York City? from St. Louis to New Orleans?

Brandied Cherries and Buttons

Brandied cherries
from France

©David Hawley/Arabia Steamboat Museum, Kansas City, MO

The brandy, the tight seal, and the steamboat's location in cold, wet silt preserved most cargo well. A bottle of pickles remained edible.

Buttons matched patterns on
calico print dresses.

**How many button patterns
are shown?**

Although railroads reshaped the U.S. economy, steamboats continued to play a major role—as demonstrated by the remarkable case of the *Arabia*. In 1856 the steamboat sank in shallows along the Missouri River, its hull punctured by a sunken tree. Over 130 years later, a group of ambitious amateur historians located the wreck, buried 35 feet deep in a Kansas cornfield (the river's course having changed). Excavators painstakingly restored and preserved a cargo that illustrates the quantity and variety of goods being shipped up the Missouri: not only the expected guns, axes, and saddles but also brandied cherries and sardines from France, preserved pie fruits from Baltimore, 35,000 buttons to be sewn on dresses, perfumes (their scents preserved), shoes and boots (5,000), rubbers, bleeding knives (used for medicinal purposes), and some 5 million glass beads for trade to Indians. The Arabia Steamboat Museum in Kansas City now showcases this treasure trove of material culture, a snapshot of antebellum America's dynamic economy.

THINKING CRITICALLY

How could historians use such evidence as an old bottle of brandied cherries or a pair of shoes to understand life in the western territories during this period? How might it help to know the relative numbers of various goods being shipped? their origins?

---

industrialization. Others fled religious persecution. Some, particularly among the Germans, left after the liberal revolutions of 1848 failed, in order to live under the free institutions of the United States. Since coming to America, wrote a Swede who settled in Iowa in 1850, "I have not been compelled to pay a penny for the privilege of living. Neither is my cap worn out from lifting it in the presence of gentlemen."

THE REVOLUTIONS OF 1848 Unprecedented unrest and upheaval prevailed in Europe in 1848, the so-called year of revolutions. The famine that had driven so many Irish out of their country was part of a larger food shortage caused by a series of poor harvests. Mounting unemployment and overburdened relief programs increased suffering. In this situation middle-class reformers, who wanted civil liberty and a more representative government, joined forces with lower-class workers to overthrow several regimes, sometimes by also appealing to nationalist feelings. France, Austria, Hungary, Italy, and Prussia all witnessed major popular uprisings. Although these revolts succeeded at first, they were all crushed by the forces of the old order. Liberal hopes for a more open, democratic society suffered a severe setback.

©The Metropolitan Museum of Art/Art Resource, NY

| *German emigrants enjoyed gathering for music and conversation in beer gardens. One of the most elegant and spacious of its day was New York City's German Winter-Garden in the Bowery neighborhood, shown in this watercolor by Fritz Meyer. "These are immense buildings," wrote one American, "fitted up in imitation of a garden. . . . Germans carry their families there to spend a day, or an evening."*

In the aftermath of this failure, a number of hard-pressed German workers and farmers, as well as disillusioned radicals and reformers, emigrated to the United States, the symbol of democratic liberalism in the world. They were joined by the first significant migration from Asia, as thousands of Chinese headed to the gold rush in California and other strikes (see Chapter 14). This migration was simply part of a century-long phenomenon, as approximately 50 million Europeans, largely from rural areas, would migrate to the Western Hemisphere.

IMMIGRANTS AND INDUSTRIALIZATION Factories came more and more to depend on immigrant labor, including children, since newcomers would work for lower wages and were less prone to protest harsh working conditions. The shift to an immigrant workforce could be seen most clearly in the textile industry, where by 1860 more than half the workers in New England mills were foreign-born. Tensions between native- and foreign-born workers, as well as among immigrants of various nationalities, made it difficult for workers to unite.

URBAN RESOURCES STRAINED The sizable foreign-born population in many American cities severely strained urban resources. Immigrants who could barely make ends meet were forced to live in overcrowded, unheated tenement houses, damp cellars, and even shacks—"the hall was dark and reeking with the worst filth," reported one New York journalist; the house was "filled with little narrow rooms, each one having five

or six occupants; all very filthy." Urban slums became notorious for crime and drinking, which took a heavy toll on families and the poor. In the eyes of many native-born Americans, immigrants were to blame for driving down factory wages and pushing American workers out of jobs. Overshadowing these complaints was a fear that America might not be able to **assimilate** the new groups, with their unfamiliar social customs, strange languages, and national pride. These fears sparked an outburst of political **nativism** in the mid-1850s.

Southern Complaints

With British and northern factories buying cotton in unprecedented quantities, southern planters prospered in the 1850s. Their operations, like those of northern commercial farmers, became more highly capitalized to keep up with the demand. But instead of machinery, white southerners invested in slaves. During the 1850s the price of prime field hands reached record levels.

Nonetheless, a number of southern nationalists, who advocated that the South should become a separate nation, pressed for greater industrialization to make the region more independent. "At present, the North fattens and grows rich upon the South," one Alabama newspaper complained in 1851, noting that "we purchase all our luxuries and necessities from the North," including clothing, shoes, implements and machinery, saddles and carriages, and even books. But most southerners ignored such pleas. As long as investments

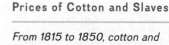

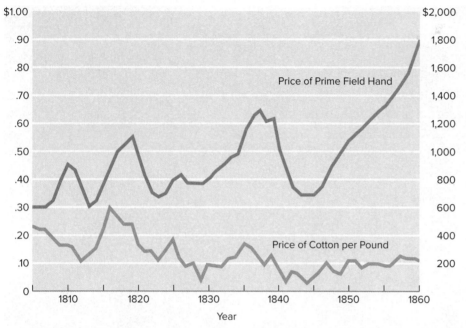

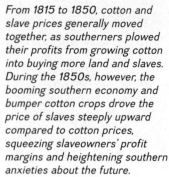

From 1815 to 1850, cotton and slave prices generally moved together, as southerners plowed their profits from growing cotton into buying more land and slaves. During the 1850s, however, the booming southern economy and bumper cotton crops drove the price of slaves steeply upward compared to cotton prices, squeezing slaveowners' profit margins and heightening southern anxieties about the future.

in cotton and slaves absorbed most of the South's capital, efforts to promote southern industry made little headway.

SOUTHERN ECONOMIC DEPENDENCE Despite southern prosperity, the section's leaders complained that the North used its power over banking and commerce to convert the South into a colony. In the absence of any significant southern shipping, northern intermediaries controlled the South's commodities through a complex series of transfers from planter to manufacturer. Storage and shipping charges, insurance, port fees, and commissions together added an estimated 20 percent to the cost of cotton and other commodities. These revenues went into the pockets of northern merchants, shippers, and bankers. The idea that the South was a colony of the North was inaccurate, but southern whites found it a convincing explanation of the North's growing wealth. More important, it reinforced their resistance to federal aid for economic development, which they were convinced would inevitably enrich the North at southern expense. This attitude further weakened the South's political alliance with the West, which needed federal aid for transportation.

White southerners also feared that the new tide of immigration would shift the sectional balance of power. Some immigrants did settle in the South's few cities, but most shunned the region, because they did not want to compete with cheap slave labor. The lack of industry and the limited demand for skilled labor also shunted immigrants northward. As a result, the North surged even further ahead of the South in population, thereby strengthening its control of the House of Representatives and heightening southern concern that the North would rapidly settle the western territories.

 **REVIEW**

How did the new railroads affect urban and prairie environments? How did they increase sectional tensions?

THE POLITICAL REALIGNMENT OF THE 1850S

WHEN FRANKLIN PIERCE (he pronounced it "Purse") assumed the presidency in 1853, he was only 48 years old, the youngest man yet to be elected president. He was also a supporter of the "Young America" movement of the Democratic Party, which eagerly looked to spread democracy across the globe by annexing additional territory to the United States.

GADSDEN PURCHASE The believers in Young America felt it idle to argue about slavery when the nation could be developing new resources. But they failed to appreciate how each new plan for expansion would stir up the slavery issue. In 1853 Pierce did manage to conclude the Gadsden Purchase, thereby gaining control of about 45,000 square miles of Mexican desert that contained the most practical southern route for a transcontinental railroad (see Mapping the Past).

OSTEND MANIFESTO Pierce had no success, however, with his major goal, the acquisition of Cuba. Spain rebuffed all efforts to purchase the rich sugar-producing region in which slavery had once been strong and still existed. Then, in 1854, the American ministers meeting at Ostend in Belgium confidentially recommended that if Spain would not sell Cuba, the island should be seized. The contents of the "Ostend Manifesto" soon leaked, and Pierce was forced to renounce any notion of acquiring Cuba by force. In any case the president soon had his hands full with the proposals of another Democrat of the Young America stamp, Senator Stephen A. Douglas of Illinois.

The Kansas-Nebraska Act

Known as the Little Giant, Douglas was ambitious, bursting with energy, and impatient to get things done. As chairman of

>> MAPPING THE PAST <<

THE KANSAS-NEBRASKA ACT

Source: Library of Congress, Prints and Photographs Division [LC-DIG-pga-08982]

"... part and parcel of an atrocious plot to exclude from a vast unoccupied region immigrants from the Old World and free laborers from our own States, and convert it into a dreary region of despotism, inhabited by masters and slaves."—Salmon Chase and Charles Sumner on the repeal of the Missouri Compromise

CONTEXT

When the Kansas-Nebraska Act of 1854 opened the remaining portion of the Louisiana Purchase to slavery under the doctrine of popular sovereignty, conflict between the two sections focused on the control of Kansas, directly west of the slave state of Missouri.

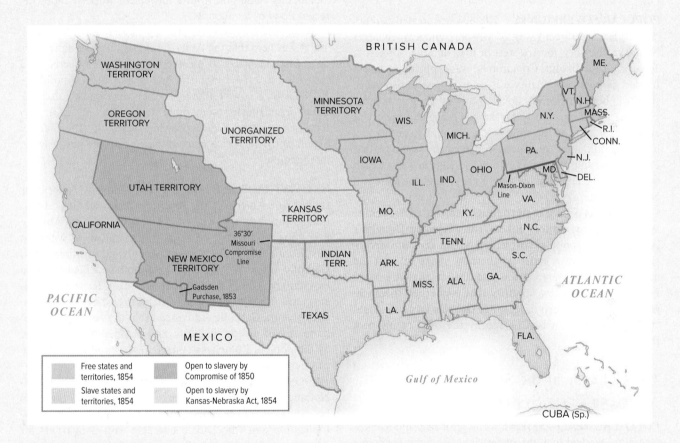

Legend:
- Free states and territories, 1854
- Slave states and territories, 1854
- Open to slavery by Compromise of 1850
- Open to slavery by Kansas-Nebraska Act, 1854

MAP READING

1. Which part of the map indicates the unorganized portion of the Louisiana Purchase?
2. What was the situation of the Utah and New Mexico Territories with respect to slavery?
3. How did the number of slave states compare with the number of free states in 1854?

MAP INTERPRETATION

1. How did the doctrine of popular sovereignty, in effect, repeal the Missouri Compromise?
2. Why would southern slaveholders in neighboring Missouri have welcomed the opportunity for slave states to emerge from Kansas Territory?
3. What opportunities would enslaved blacks in Missouri have envisaged if free states emerged from Kansas Territory?

the Senate's Committee on Territories, he was eager to organize federal lands west of Missouri as part of his program for economic development. And as a citizen of Illinois, he wanted Chicago selected as the eastern terminus of the transcontinental railroad to California. Chicago would never be chosen over St. Louis and New Orleans, however, unless the rest of the Louisiana Purchase was organized, for any northern rail route would have to run through that region.

REPEAL OF THE MISSOURI COMPROMISE Under the terms of the Missouri Compromise of 1820, slavery was prohibited in this portion of the Louisiana Purchase. Douglas had already tried in 1853 to organize the area while keeping a ban on slavery—only to have his bill voted down by southern opposition in the Senate. Bowing to southern pressure, the Illinois leader removed the prohibition on slavery that had been in effect for 34 years. The Kansas-Nebraska Act was passed in May 1854.

POPULAR SOVEREIGNTY The new act created two territories: Kansas, directly west of Missouri, and a much larger Nebraska Territory, located west of Iowa and the Minnesota Territory. The Missouri Compromise was explicitly repealed. Instead, popular sovereignty was to determine the status of slavery in both territories, though it was left unclear whether residents of Kansas and Nebraska could prohibit slavery at any time or only at the time of statehood, as southerners insisted. Still, most members of Congress assumed that Douglas had split the region into two territories so that each section could claim another state: Kansas would be slave and Nebraska free.

The Kansas-Nebraska Act outraged northern Democrats, Whigs, and Free Soilers alike. Critics rejected Douglas's contention that popular sovereignty would keep the territories free. As always, most northerners spoke little of the moral evils of slavery; it was the chance that the Slave Power might gain new territory that concerned them. So great was the northern outcry that Douglas joked he could "travel from Boston to Chicago by the light of my own [burning] effigy."

The Collapse of the Second American Party System

POLITICAL REALIGNMENT The furor over the Kansas-Nebraska Act laid bare the underlying social and economic tensions that had developed between the North and the South. These tensions put mounting pressure on the political parties, and in the 1850s the Jacksonian party system collapsed. Voters who had been loyal to one party for years, even decades, began switching allegiances, while new voters were mobilized. By the time the process of realignment was completed, a new party system had emerged, divided this time along clearly sectional lines.

DISILLUSIONMENT WITH THE PARTIES In part, the old party system decayed because new problems had replaced the traditional economic issues of both Whigs and Democrats. The Whigs alienated many of their traditional Protestant supporters by openly seeking the support of Catholics and recent immigrants. Then, too, the growing agitation by Protestant reformers for the prohibition of alcohol divided both parties, especially the Whigs. But the Kansas-Nebraska Act provided the final blow, dividing the two major parties along sectional lines. Northern congressional Whigs, who unanimously opposed the bill, found themselves deserted by virtually all their southern colleagues. And fully half the northern Democratic representatives in the House voted against Douglas's bill.

The Know-Nothings

In such an unstable atmosphere, independent parties flourished. The most dramatic challenge to the Whigs and Democrats came first from a movement worried about the recent flood of immigrants.

New York City was the primary gateway for immigrants, and it was here that the American Party, a secret nativist society, first organized. Its members were sworn to secrecy and instructed to answer inquiries by replying "I know nothing." In 1853 the Know-Nothings, as they were quickly dubbed, began organizing in several other states; after only a year they had become the fastest-growing party in the nation. Significantly, 1854 also marked the peak of the new wave of immigration.

NATIVIST IMPULSE Taking as its slogan "Americans should rule America," the American Party advocated that immigrants be forced to wait not 5 but 21 years before becoming naturalized citizens. It also called on voters to oust from office politicians who openly bid for foreign and Catholic votes. Know-Nothings denounced illegal voting by immigrants, the rising crime and disorder in urban areas, and immigrants' heavy drinking. They were also strongly anti-Catholic, convinced that the "undemocratic" hierarchy of priests, bishops, and archbishops controlled by the pope in Rome was conspiring to undermine American democracy.

To young native-born American workers, the Know-Nothing message was particularly appealing. It was they who bore the brunt of the economic dislocations caused by industrialization and who had to compete with immigrants for jobs. In the 1854 elections the Know-Nothings won a series of remarkable victories, as former Whigs flocked to the new party in droves. Fueled by its success the American Party turned its attention south, and in a few months it had organized in every state of the Union. With perhaps a million voters enrolled in its lodges in 1855, Know-Nothing leaders confidently predicted that they would elect the next president.

KNOW-NOTHINGS' DECLINE Yet only a year later the party had collapsed as quickly as it had risen. Many Know-Nothing officeholders proved woefully incompetent. Voters

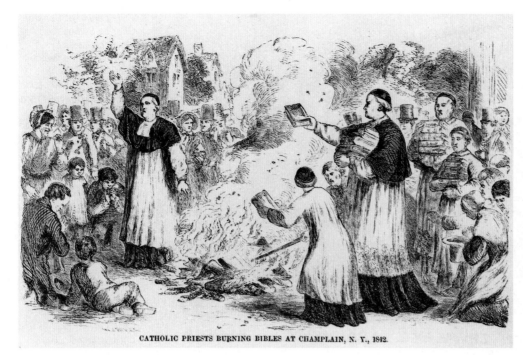

| Edward Beecher, one of Lyman Beecher's sons, in 1854 published the inflammatory Papal Conspiracy Exposed. Protestant Bibles had been widely distributed and in northern New York, not far from heavily Catholic Quebec, a renegade friar gathered up a handful of copies and burned them. The story, magnified in the retelling, fanned anti-Catholic and nativist sentiment.

©American Antiquarian Society, Worcester, Massachusetts, USA/ Bridgeman Images

CATHOLIC PRIESTS BURNING BIBLES AT CHAMPLAIN, N. Y., 1842.

deserted them when the party failed to enact its program. But the death knell of the party was rising sectional tensions. In 1856 most northern delegates walked out of the American Party's national convention when it adopted a proslavery platform. Significantly, they deserted to the other new party, the Republicans. This party, unlike the Know-Nothings, had no base in the South. It intended to elect a president by sweeping the free states, which controlled a majority of the electoral votes.

The Republicans and Bleeding Kansas

Initially, the Republican Party made little headway in the North. Many moderate Whigs and Democrats viewed it as too radical. A Democratic newspaper expressed the prevailing view when it declared, "Nobody believes that this Republican movement can prove the basis of a permanent party."

Such predictions, however, did not reckon with the emotions stirred up by developments in Kansas. Most early settlers migrated to Kansas for the same reasons other white Americans headed west—the chance to prosper in a new land. But Douglas's idea of popular sovereignty transformed the process of settlement into a referendum on slavery in the territories. A race soon developed between northerners and southerners to settle Kansas first. To the proslavery residents of neighboring Missouri, free-state communities such as Lawrence seemed ominous threats. "We are playing for a mighty stake," former senator David Rice Atchison insisted. "If we win, we carry slavery to the Pacific Ocean; if we fail, we lose Missouri, Arkansas and Texas and all the territories; the game must be played boldly."

TURMOIL IN KANSAS When the first Kansas elections were held in 1854 and 1855, Missourians poured over the border, seized the polls, and stuffed the ballot boxes. This massive fraud tarnished popular sovereignty at the outset and greatly aroused public opinion in the North. It also provided proslavery forces with a commanding majority in the Kansas legislature, where they promptly expelled the legally elected free-state members and enacted a strict legal code limiting such time-honored rights as freedom of speech, impartial juries, and fair elections. Mobilized into action, the free-staters in the fall of 1855 organized a separate government, drafted a state constitution prohibiting slavery, and asked Congress to admit Kansas as a free state. In such a polarized situation, violence quickly broke out between the two factions, leading to the proslavery attack on Lawrence and to John Brown's reprisals.

The Caning of Charles Sumner

In May 1856, only a few days before the proslavery attack on Lawrence, Republican Senator Charles Sumner of Massachusetts delivered a scathing speech, "The Crime against Kansas." Sumner not only condemned slavery, but he also deliberately insulted the state of South Carolina and one of its senators, Andrew Butler. Preston S. Brooks, a South Carolina congressman who was related to Butler, was outraged that Sumner had insulted his relative and mocked his state.

Several days later, Brooks strode into the Senate after it had adjourned, went up to Sumner, who was seated at his desk, and proceeded to beat the Massachusetts leader over the head with his cane. The cane shattered from the violence of the attack, but Brooks, swept up in the emotion of the moment, continued hitting Sumner until the senator collapsed to the floor, drenched in blood.

SIGNIFICANCE OF THE CANING Northerners were shocked to learn that a senator of the United States had been

SOUTHERN CHIVALRY — ARGUMENT versus CLUB'S.

The caning of Senator Charles Sumner of Massachusetts by Representative Preston S. Brooks of South Carolina inflamed public opinion. In this northern drawing, the fallen Sumner, a martyr to free speech, raises his pen against Brooks's club. In the background, several prominent Democrats look on in amusement. Printmakers, rushing to capitalize on the furor, did not know what the obscure Brooks looked like and thus had to devise ingenious ways of portraying the incident. In this print, Brooks's face is hidden by his raised arm.
©Bettmann/Getty Images

beaten unconscious in the Senate chamber. But what caused them even greater consternation was southern reaction to Sumner's caning—for in his own region, Preston Brooks was lionized as a hero. Instantly, the Sumner caning breathed life into the fledgling Republican Party. Its claims about "Bleeding Kansas" and the Slave Power now seemed credible. Sumner, reelected in 1857 by the Massachusetts legislature, was unable to return to the Senate until 1860, his chair left vacant as a symbol of southern brutality.

The Election of 1856

Given the storm that had arisen over Kansas, Democrats concluded that no candidate associated with the repeal of the Missouri Compromise had a chance to win. So the Democrats turned to James Buchanan of Pennsylvania as their presidential nominee. Buchanan's supreme qualification was having the good fortune to have been out of the country when the Kansas-Nebraska Act was passed. The American Party, split badly by the Kansas issue, nominated former president Millard Fillmore. The Republicans chose John C. Frémont, a western explorer who had helped liberate California during the Mexican War. The party's platform denounced slavery as a "relic of barbarism" and demanded that Kansas be admitted as a free state. Throughout the summer the party hammered away on Bleeding Sumner and Bleeding Kansas.

IDEOLOGY OF THE REPUBLICAN PARTY
A number of principles guided the Republican

©David J. & Janice L. Frent/ The Frent Collection/Getty Images

| *A campaign badge supporting John C. Frémont*

Party, including the ideal of free labor. Slavery degraded labor, Republicans argued, and would inevitably drive free labor out of the territories. Condemning the South as stagnant, hierarchical, and economically backward, Republicans praised the North as a society of opportunity where enterprising individuals could rise through hard work and self-discipline. Stopping the expansion of slavery, they argued, would preserve this heritage of economic independence for white Americans. Republicans by and large remained blind to ways in which industrialization was closing off avenues of social mobility for poor workers.

Also important was the moral opposition to slavery, which such works as Harriet Beecher Stowe's *Uncle Tom's Cabin* had strengthened. Republican speakers and editors stressed that slavery was a moral wrong, that it was incompatible with the ideals of the Republic and Christianity. "Never forget," Republican leader Abraham Lincoln declared on one occasion, "that we have before us this whole matter of the right and wrong of slavery in this Union, though the immediate question is as to its spreading out into new Territories and States."

CONCEPT OF THE SLAVE POWER More negatively, Republicans gained support by shifting their attacks from slavery itself to the Slave Power, or the political influence of the planter class. Pointing to the Sumner assault and the incidents in Kansas, Republicans contended that the Slave Power had set out to destroy the liberties of northern whites. "The question has passed on from that of slavery for negro servants, to that of tyranny over free white men," one Republican insisted in the 1856 campaign.

HERITAGE OF REPUBLICANISM All these fears played on a strong northern attachment to the heritage of the American Revolution. Just as the nation's founders had battled against slavery, tyranny, aristocracy, and minority rule, so the North faced the unrepublican Slave Power. "The liberties of our country are in tenfold the danger that they were at the commencement of the American Revolution," warned one Republican paper. "We then had a distant foe to contend with. Now the enemy is within our borders."

In the election, Buchanan all but swept the South (losing only Maryland to Fillmore) and won enough free states to push him over the top, with 174 electoral votes to Frémont's 114 and Fillmore's 8. Still, the violence in Kansas and Sumner's caning nearly carried Frémont into the presidency. He ran ahead of both Buchanan and Fillmore in the North and won 11 free states out of 16. Had he carried Pennsylvania plus one more state, he would have been elected. For the first time in American history, an antislavery party based entirely in the North threatened to elect a president and snap the bonds of union.

> ✓ **REVIEW**
>
> What events led the political realignment of the 1850s to at first favor the Know-Nothings? What events led the Republicans to emerge as a powerful party?

THE WORSENING CRISIS

BUCHANAN'S CHARACTER James Buchanan had spent much of his life in public service: more than 20 years in the House and the Senate, secretary of state under Polk, and minister to Russia and to Great Britain. A tall, heavyset man with flowing white hair, he struck White House visitors as exceptionally courteous: an eye defect caused him to tilt his head slightly forward and to one side, which reinforced the impression of deference and attentiveness. A dutiful party member, he had over the years carefully cultivated wide personal support, yet he was a cautious and uninspiring leader who had a strong stubborn streak and deeply resented opposition to his policies.

Moderates in both sections hoped that the new president would thwart Republican radicals and secessionists of the Deep South, popularly known as "fire-eaters." Throughout his career, however, Buchanan had taken the southern position on sectional matters. Moreover, on March 6, 1857, only two days after Buchanan's inauguration, the Supreme Court gave the new administration an unintended jolt with one of the most controversial decisions in its history.

The *Dred Scott* Decision

The owner of a Missouri slave named Dred Scott had taken him to live for several years in Illinois, a free state, and in the Wisconsin Territory, in what is now Minnesota, where slavery had been banned by the Missouri Compromise. Scott had returned to Missouri with his owner, only to sue eventually for his freedom on the grounds that his residence in a free state and a free territory had made him free. His case ultimately went to the Supreme Court. Two northern justices joined all five southern members of the Court in ruling 7 to 2 that Scott remained a slave. The majority opinion was written by Chief Justice Roger Taney of Maryland, who argued that under Missouri law, which took precedence, Scott was still a slave.

PROTECTION OF SLAVERY Had the Court stopped there, the public outcry would have been minimal. But the Court majority believed that they had a responsibility to deal with the larger controversy between the two sections. In particular, Chief Justice Taney wanted to strengthen the judicial protection of slavery. Taney, a former Maryland slaveowner who had freed his slaves, ruled that African Americans could not be and never had been citizens of the United States. Instead, he insisted that at the time the Constitution was adopted, they were "regarded as beings of an inferior order, so far inferior that they had no rights which the white man was bound to respect." In addition, the Court ruled that the Missouri Compromise was unconstitutional. Congress, it declared, had no power to ban slavery from *any* territory of the United States.

REACTION TO THE DECISION While southerners rejoiced at this outcome, Republicans denounced the Court. Their platform declared, after all, that Congress ought to prohibit slavery in all territories. "We know the court . . . has often over-ruled its own decisions," Abraham Lincoln observed, "and we shall do what we can to have it over-rule this." But the decision was sobering. If all territories were now open to slavery, how long would it be before a move was made to reintroduce slavery in the free states? For Republicans, the Court's decision foreshadowed the spread of slavery throughout the West and even throughout the nation.

(detail) Source: Missouri Historical Society (1897.9.1)

| *Dred Scott*

Source: Library of Congress, Prints and Photographs Division [LC-DIG-cwpbh-00788]

| *Chief Justice Roger Taney*

But the decision also threatened Douglas's more moderate solution of popular sovereignty. If Congress had no power to prohibit slavery in a territory, how could it authorize a territorial legislature to do so? Although the Court did not rule on this point, the clear implication of the *Dred Scott* decision was that popular sovereignty was also unconstitutional. The Court, in effect, had endorsed John C. Calhoun's radical view that slavery was legal in all the territories. It had intended to settle the question of slavery in the territories once and for all. Instead, the Court succeeded only in strengthening the forces of extremism in American politics.

The Panic of 1857

ECONOMIC ISSUES INCREASE SECTIONAL TENSIONS As the nation grappled with the *Dred Scott* decision, an economic depression aggravated sectional conflict. Once again, boom gave way to bust as falling wheat prices and contracted credit hurt commercial farmers and overextended railroad investors. The Panic of 1857 was nowhere near as severe as the depression of 1837–1843. But the psychological results were far-reaching, for the South remained relatively untouched. With the price of cotton and other southern commodities still high, southern secessionists hailed the panic as proof that an independent southern nation was economically workable. Insisting that cotton sustained the international economy, James Henry Hammond, a senator from South Carolina, boasted: "What would happen if no cotton was furnished for three years? England would topple headlong and carry the whole civilized world with her save the South. No, you dare not make war on cotton. No power on earth dares to make war on it. Cotton is king."

For their part, northerners urged federal action to spur the economy. Southerners defeated an attempt to increase the tariff duties, at their lowest level since 1815, and Buchanan, under southern pressure, vetoed bills to improve navigation on the Great Lakes and to give free farms to western settlers. Many businesspeople and conservative ex-Whigs condemned these southern actions and now endorsed the Republican Party.

The Lecompton Constitution

ATTEMPT TO MAKE KANSAS A SLAVE STATE Although the *Dred Scott* decision and economic depression weakened the bonds of the Union, Kansas remained at the center of the political stage. In June 1857, when the territory elected delegates to draft a state constitution, free-state voters boycotted the election, thereby giving proslavery forces control of the convention that met in Lecompton. The delegates drafted a constitution that made slavery legal. Even more boldly, they scheduled a referendum in which voters could choose only whether to admit additional slaves into the territory. They could not vote against the constitution, and they could not vote to get rid of slavery entirely. Once again, free-staters boycotted the election, and the Lecompton constitution was approved.

DEFEAT OF THE LECOMPTON CONSTITUTION As a supporter of popular sovereignty, President Buchanan had pledged a free and fair vote on the Lecompton constitution. But the outcome offered him the unexpected opportunity to satisfy his southern supporters by pushing the Lecompton constitution through Congress. This action was too much for Douglas, who broke party ranks and denounced the Lecompton constitution as a fraud. Nevertheless, the administration prevailed in the Senate. Buchanan now pulled out all the stops to gain the necessary votes in the House to admit Kansas as a slave state. But the House, where northern representation was much stronger, rejected the constitution. In a compromise, Congress, using indirect language, returned the constitution to Kansas for another vote. This time it was decisively defeated, 11,300 to 1,788. No doubt remained that as soon as Kansas had sufficient population, it would come into the Union as a free state.

The attempt to force slavery on the people of Kansas drove many conservative northerners into the Republican Party. And Douglas, once the Democrats' strongest potential candidate in 1860, now found himself assailed by the southern wing of his party. On top of that, in the summer of 1858, Douglas faced a desperate fight in his race for reelection to the Senate against Republican Abraham Lincoln.

The Lincoln-Douglas Debates

LINCOLN'S VIEW OF THE CRISIS "He is the strong man of his party . . . and the best stump speaker, with his droll ways and dry jokes, in the West," Douglas commented when he learned of Lincoln's nomination to oppose him. "He is as honest as he is shrewd, and if I beat him my victory will be hardly won." Tall (6 feet 4 inches) and gangly, Lincoln had a gaunt face, high cheekbones, deep-socketed gray eyes, and a shock of unruly hair. He appeared awkward as he spoke, never knowing quite what to do with his large, muscular hands. Yet his finely honed logic, his simple, eloquent language, and his sincerity carried the audience with him. His sentences, as spare as the man himself, had none of the oratorical flourishes common in that day. "If we could first know *where* we are, and *whither* we are tending, we could then better judge *what* to do, and *how* to do it," Lincoln began, in accepting his party's nomination for senator from Illinois in 1858. He quoted a proverb from the Bible:

> A house divided against itself cannot stand.
>
> I believe this government cannot endure, permanently half *slave* and half *free.*
>
> I do not expect the Union to be *dissolved*—I do not expect the house to *fall*—but I *do* expect it will cease to be divided.
>
> It will become *all* one thing, or *all* the other.
>
> Either the *opponents* of slavery, will arrest the further spread of it, and place it where the public mind shall rest in the belief that it is in course of ultimate extinction; or its *advocates* will push it forward, till it shall become alike lawful in all the States, *old* as well as new—*North* as well as *South.*

The message echoed through the hall and across the pages of the national press.

Superb debaters, Douglas and Lincoln nevertheless had very different speaking styles. The deep-voiced Douglas was constantly on the attack, drawing on his remarkable memory and showering points like buckshot in all directions. Employing sarcasm and ridicule rather than humor, he never tried to crack a joke. Lincoln, who had a high-pitched voice and a rather awkward platform manner, developed his arguments more carefully and methodically, and he relied on his sense of humor and unmatched ability as a storyteller to drive his points home to the audience.

(*left*) Source: Library of Congress, Prints and Photographs Division [LC-USZ61-2039]; (*right*) Source: Library of Congress, Prints and Photographs Division [LC-USZ62-7992]

LINCOLN'S CHARACTER Born in the slave state of Kentucky, Lincoln had grown up mostly in southern Indiana and central Illinois. He could split rails with the best frontier farmer, loved telling stories, and was at home mixing with ordinary folk. Yet his intense ambition had lifted him above the backwoods from which he came. He compensated for a lack of formal schooling through disciplined self-education, and he became a shrewd courtroom lawyer of respectable social standing. Known for his sense of humor, he was nonetheless subject to chronic depression, and his eyes often mirrored a deep melancholy.

DOUGLAS AND LINCOLN ON THE SLAVERY ISSUE At the age of 25 Lincoln entered the state legislature and soon became an important Whig strategist. After the party's decline he joined the Republicans and became one of their key leaders in Illinois. In a series of seven joint debates Lincoln challenged Douglas to discuss the issues of slavery and the sectional controversy. Douglas joined the debate by portraying Lincoln as a radical whose "House Divided" speech preached sectional warfare. The nation *could* endure half slave and half free, Douglas declared, as long as states and territories were left alone to regulate their own affairs. Accusing Lincoln of believing that blacks were his equal, Douglas countered that the American government had been "made by the white man, for the white man, to be administered by the white man."

Lincoln responded by denying any intention to interfere with slavery in the South, but he insisted that the spread of slavery to the territories was a blight on the Republic. Douglas could not be counted on to oppose slavery's expansion, Lincoln warned, for he had already admitted that he didn't care whether slavery was voted "down or up." For his part, Lincoln denied any "perfect equality between the negroes and white people" and opposed allowing blacks to vote, hold office, or intermarry with whites. But, he concluded,

> notwithstanding all this, there is no reason in the world why the negro is not entitled to all the natural rights enumerated in the Declaration of Independence, the right to life, liberty and the pursuit of happiness. . . . I agree with Judge Douglas [that the negro] is not my equal in many respects—certainly not in color, perhaps not in moral or intellectual endowment. But in the right to eat the bread, without leave of anybody else, which his own hand earns, *he is my equal and the equal of Judge Douglas, and the equal of every living man.*

FREEPORT DOCTRINE At the debate held at Freeport, Illinois, Lincoln asked Douglas how under the *Dred Scott* decision the people of a territory could lawfully exclude slavery before statehood. Douglas answered, with what became known as the Freeport Doctrine, that slavery could exist only with the protection of law and that slaveowners would never bring their slaves into an area that did not have a slave code. Therefore, Douglas explained, if the people of a territory refused to pass a slave code, slavery would never be established there.

In a close race, the legislature elected Douglas to another term in the Senate.* But Democrats from the South angrily repudiated him and condemned the Freeport

---

*State legislatures elected senators until 1913, when the Seventeenth Amendment was adopted. While Lincoln and Douglas both campaigned for the office, Illinois voters actually voted for candidates for the legislature who were pledged to one of the senatorial candidates.

Doctrine. Although Lincoln lost, Republicans thought his performance marked him as a presidential contender for 1860.

The Beleaguered South

While northerners increasingly feared that the Slave Power was conspiring to extend slavery into the free states, southerners worried that the "Black Republicans" would hem them in and undermine their political power. The very factors that brought prosperity during the 1850s stimulated the South's sense of crisis. As the price of slaves rose sharply, the proportion of southerners who owned slaves had dropped almost a third since 1830. Land also was being consolidated into larger holdings, evidence of declining opportunity for ordinary white southerners. Furthermore, California and Kansas had been closed to southern slaveholders—unfairly, in their eyes. Finally, Douglas's clever claim that a territory could effectively outlaw slavery using the Freeport Doctrine seemed to negate the *Dred Scott* decision that slavery was legal in all the territories.

FAILED SOLUTIONS The South's growing sense of moral and political isolation made this crisis more acute. By the 1850s slavery had been abolished throughout most of the Americas, and in the United States the South's

political power was steadily shrinking. Only the expansion of slavery held out any promise of new slave states needed to preserve the South's political power and protect its way of life. "The truth is," fumed one Alabama politician, ". . . the South is excluded from the common territories of the Union. The right of expansion claimed to be a necessity of her continued existence, is practically and effectively denied the South."

✓ **REVIEW**

How did the Lecompton constitution and the Lincoln-Douglas debates affect the debate over slavery in the territories?

THE ROAD TO WAR

JOHN BROWN'S RAID In 1857 JOHN BROWN—THE abolitionist firebrand—had returned to the East from Kansas, consumed with the idea of attacking slavery in the South itself. With financing from a number of prominent northern reformers, Brown gathered 21 followers, including 5 free blacks, in hope of fomenting a slave insurrection. On the night of October 16, 1859, the group seized the unguarded federal armory at Harpers Ferry in Virginia. But no slaves rallied to Brown's standard: few even lived in the area to begin with. Before long the raiders found themselves holed up in the armory's engine house with hostile townspeople taking

(*left*) Source: Library of Congress, Prints and Photographs Division [LC-USZ62-79479]; (*center*) ©FPG/Getty Images; (*right*) Source: Library of Congress, Prints and Photographs Division [LC-USZ62-8908]

| John Brown was paraded to his execution sitting in his own coffin. His raid heightened the tensions that brought on civil war, and some of the war's major figures were present. Robert E. Lee, then a colonel in the U.S. Army, led the attack that captured Brown and also viewed the execution. The scaffold was surrounded by cadets from Virginia Military Institute under the command of Thomas Jackson, who later became a Confederate officer and quickly earned the nickname "Stonewall." The photograph (right) shows a group of Virginia militia, dressed in their "grays." But one man (upper left with the moustache) was not a member of the guard. He had borrowed a uniform in order to witness the hanging. Recent research indicates he was the actor John Wilkes Booth, who assassinated Abraham Lincoln at war's end. Though he was not present, the poet Walt Whitman vividly recreated Brown's final moments:

Year of meteors! Brooding year!
I would bind in words retrospective some of your deeds and signs . . .
I would sing how an old man, tall, with white hair, mounted the scaffold in Virginia,
(I was at hand, silent I stood with teeth shut close, I watch'd,
I stood very near you old man when cool and indifferent but trembling with age
and your unheal'd wounds you mounted the scaffold;) . . .

potshots at them. Charging with bayonets fixed, federal troops commanded by Colonel Robert E. Lee soon captured Brown and his band.

Brown's raid at Harpers Ferry was yet another blow weakening the forces of compromise and moderation at the nation's political center. The invasion itself was a dismal failure, as were most of the enterprises Brown undertook in his troubled life. But the old man knew how to bear himself with a martyr's dignity. "Had I so interfered in behalf of the rich, the powerful, the intelligent, the so-called great," he declared at his trial, ". . . it would have been all right. . . . [T]o have interfered as I have done in behalf of [God's] despised poor, is no wrong, but a right." On December 2, 1859, the state of Virginia hanged Brown for treason.

REACTION TO THE RAID Republicans made haste to denounce Brown's raid, lest they be tarred as radicals, but other northerners were less cautious. Ralph Waldo Emerson described Brown as a "saint, whose martyrdom will make the gallows as glorious as the cross," and on the day of his execution, church bells tolled in many northern cities. Only a minority of northerners endorsed Brown, but southerners were shocked by such public displays of sympathy. And they were firmly convinced that the Republican Party was secretly connected to the raid.

A Sectional Election

When Congress convened in December, there were ominous signs everywhere of the growing sectional rift. Intent on destroying Douglas's Freeport Doctrine, southern radicals demanded a congressional slave code to protect slavery in the territories. To northern Democrats, such a platform spelled political death. As one Indiana Democrat put it, "We cannot carry a single congressional district on that doctrine in the state."

DISRUPTION OF THE DEMOCRATIC PARTY At the Democratic Convention in April in Charleston, South Carolina, southern radicals boldly pressed their demand for a federal slave code. After a heated debate, however, the convention adopted the Douglas platform upholding popular sovereignty, whereupon the delegations from eight southern states walked out. Unable to agree on a candidate, the convention finally reassembled two months later in Baltimore and nominated Douglas. At this point most of the remaining southern Democrats left in disgust. Joining with the Charleston seceders, they nominated their own candidate, Vice President John C. Breckinridge of Kentucky, on a platform supporting a federal slave code. The last major national party had shattered.

In May the Republicans met in Chicago, where they turned to Abraham Lincoln, a moderate on the slavery issue who was strong in Illinois and the other northern states the party had lost in 1856. The election that followed was really two contests in one. In the North, which had a majority of the electoral votes, only Lincoln and Douglas had any chance of carrying a state. In the South the race pitted Breckinridge against John Bell of Tennessee, the candidate of the new conservative Constitutional Union Party. Although Lincoln received less than 40 percent of the popular vote and had virtually no support in the South, he won 180 electoral votes, 27 more than needed for election. For the first time, the nation had elected a president who headed a completely sectional party and who was committed to stopping the expansion of slavery.

Secession

SOUTHERN FEARS Although the Republicans had not won control of either house of Congress, Lincoln's election struck many southerners as a blow of terrible finality. Lincoln had been lifted into office on the strength of the free states alone. With Republicans opposed to slavery's expansion, the South's power base could only shrink. It was not unrealistic, many fire-eaters argued, to believe that Lincoln would use federal aid to induce the border states to voluntarily free their slaves. Once slavery disappeared there, and new states were added, the necessary three-fourths majority would exist to approve a constitutional amendment abolishing slavery.

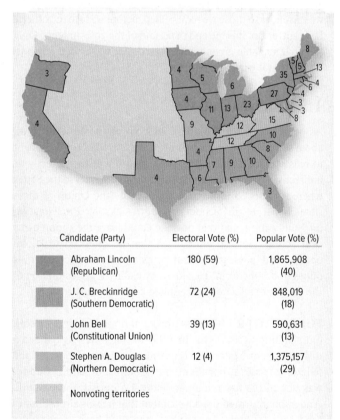

Candidate (Party)	Electoral Vote (%)	Popular Vote (%)
Abraham Lincoln (Republican)	180 (59)	1,865,908 (40)
J. C. Breckinridge (Southern Democratic)	72 (24)	848,019 (18)
John Bell (Constitutional Union)	39 (13)	590,631 (13)
Stephen A. Douglas (Northern Democratic)	12 (4)	1,375,157 (29)
Nonvoting territories		

ELECTION OF 1860

Although Lincoln did not win a majority of the popular vote, he still would have been elected even if the votes for all three of his opponents had been combined, because he won a clear majority in every state he carried except California, Oregon, and New Jersey (whose electoral votes he split with Douglas).

A torchlight parade in New York City staged by the Republican Wide-Awake Club, 1860. Most members were young white men in their late teens and early twenties. For their parades they carried torches and wore black capes and military-style caps. In remarkably few years, the Republicans' new sectional party sensed victory within its reach in the presidential election.

Source: Library of Congress, Prints and Photographs Division [LC-USZ62-59401]

Or perhaps Lincoln might send other John Browns into the South to stir up more slave insurrections. The Montgomery (Alabama) *Mail* accused Republicans of intending "to free the negroes and force amalgamation between them and the children of the poor men of the South."

CONFEDERATE STATES OF AMERICA Secession seemed the only alternative left to protect southern equality and liberty. South Carolina, which had challenged federal authority in the nullification crisis, was determined to force the other southern states to act. On December 20, 1860, a popular convention unanimously passed a resolution seceding from the Union. The rest of the Deep South followed, and on February 7, 1861, the states stretching from South Carolina to Texas organized the Confederate States of America and elected Jefferson Davis president.

But the Upper South and the border states declined to secede, hoping that once again Congress could patch together a settlement. Senator John Crittenden of Kentucky proposed a constitutional amendment extending to California the old Missouri Compromise line of 36°30′. Slavery would be prohibited north of this line and given federal protection south of it in all territories, including any acquired in the future. Furthermore, Crittenden proposed an "unamendable amendment" to the Constitution, forever preserving slavery in states where it already existed.

CRITTENDEN COMPROMISE FAILS But the Crittenden Compromise was doomed for the simple reason that the two groups who were required to make concessions—Republicans and secessionists—had no interest in doing so. "The argument is exhausted," representatives from the Deep South announced, even before Crittenden had introduced his legislative package. "We have just carried an election on principles fairly stated to

the people," Lincoln wrote in opposing compromise. "Now we are told in advance, the government shall be broken up, unless we surrender to those we have beaten, before we take the offices. If we surrender, it is the end of us, and of the government." Only the unamendable amendment passed, but war ended any possibility that it would be ratified.

The Outbreak of War

As he prepared to take office, Lincoln pondered what to do about secession. In his inaugural address on March 4, he sought to reassure southerners that he had no intention, "directly or indirectly, to interfere with the institution of slavery in the States where it exists." But he maintained that "the Union of these states is perpetual," echoing Andrew Jackson's Proclamation on Nullification, and that no state could leave the Union by its own action. He also announced that he intended to "hold, occupy and possess" federal property and collect customs duties under the tariff. He closed by calling for a restoration of the "bonds of affection" that united all Americans.

FORT SUMTER The new president hoped for time to work out a solution, but on his first day in office he was handed a dispatch from Major Robert Anderson, commander of the federal garrison at Fort Sumter in Charleston harbor. Sumter was one of the few remaining federal outposts in the South. Anderson informed the government that he was almost out of food and that, unless resupplied, he would have to surrender in six weeks. For a month Lincoln looked for a peaceful resolution, but he finally felt compelled to send a relief expedition. As a conciliatory gesture, he notified the governor of South Carolina that supplies were being sent and that if the fleet were allowed to pass, only food, and not men, arms, or ammunition, would be landed.

SLAVERY AND SECESSION

The two highest officials of the Confederacy provide contrasting opinions on slavery's relation to the Civil War. The first, Alexander Stephens, delivered his remarks (which came to be known as the "Cornerstone Speech") in Savannah, Georgia, shortly after being elected vice president of the new government. Jefferson Davis, president of the Confederacy, published his reflections after the war.

DOCUMENT 1
Slavery Is the Cornerstone: Alexander Stephens

The new Constitution [of the Confederate States of America] has put at rest *forever* all the agitating questions relating to our peculiar institutions—African slavery as it exists among us—the proper *status* of the negro in our form of civilization. *This was the immediate cause of the late rupture and present revolution.* JEFFERSON, in his forecast, had anticipated this, as the "rock upon which the old Union would split." He was right. What was conjecture with him, is now a realized fact. But whether he fully comprehended the great truth upon which that rock *stood* and *stands,* may be doubted. *The prevailing ideas entertained by him and most of the leading statesmen at the time of the formation of the Old Constitution were, that the enslavement of the African was in violation of the laws of nature; that it was wrong in principle, socially, morally and politically. It* was an evil they knew not well how to deal

with; but the general opinion of the men of that day was, that, somehow or other, in the order of Providence, the institution would be evanescent and pass away. This idea, though not incorporated in the Constitution, was the prevailing idea at the time. . . . *Those ideas, however, were fundamentally wrong. They rested upon the assumption of the equality of races. This was an error. It* was a sandy foundation, and the idea of a Government built upon it—when the "storm came and the wind blew, it fell."

Our new Government is founded upon exactly the opposite ideas; its foundations are laid, its cornerstone rests, upon the great truth that the negro is not equal to the white man; that slavery, subordination to the superior race, is his natural and moral condition. This, our new Government, is the first, in the history of the world, based upon this great physical philosophical and moral truth. . . .

It is the first Government ever instituted upon principles in strict conformity to nature, and the ordination of Providence, in furnishing the materials of human society. Many Governments have been founded upon the principles of certain classes; but the classes thus enslaved, were of the same race, and in violation of the laws of nature. Our system commits no such violation of nature's laws. The negro by nature, or by the curse against Canaan, is fitted for that condition which he occupies in our system. . . . The substratum of our society is made of the material fitted by nature for it, and by experience we know that it is the best, not only for the superior but for the inferior race, that it should be so.

Source: Alexander Stephens, speech delivered March 21, 1861, Savannah, Georgia, in Moore, Frank, ed., *The Rebellion Record, Vol. 1.* New York, 1861–1868, 45–46.

DOCUMENT 2
Slavery Did Not Cause the Civil War: Jefferson Davis

The reader of many of the treatises on these events, which have been put forth as historical . . . might naturally enough be led to the conclusion that the controversies which arose between the States, and the war in which they culminated, were caused by efforts on the one side to extend and perpetuate human slavery, and on the other to resist it and establish human liberty. The Southern States and Southern people have been sedulously represented as "propagandists" of slavery, and the Northern as the defenders and champions of universal freedom. . . .

I have not attempted, and shall not permit myself to be drawn into any discussion of the merits or demerits of slavery as an ethical or even as a political question. It would be foreign to my purpose, irrelevant to my subject, and would only serve—as it has invariably served in the hands of its agitators—to "darken counsel" and divert attention from the genuine issues involved. . . .

As a mere historical fact, we have seen that African servitude among us—confessedly the mildest and most humane of all institutions to which the name "slavery" has ever been applied—existed in all the original States, and that it was recognized and protected in the fourth article of the

Constitution. Subsequently, for climatic, industrial, and economical—not moral or sentimental—reasons, it was abolished in the Northern, while it continued to exist in the Southern States. . . . Eleven years after the agitation on the Missouri [Compromise of 1820], when the subject first took a sectional shape, the abolition of slavery was proposed and earnestly debated in the Virginia Legislature, and its advocates were so near the accomplishment of their purpose, that a declaration in its favor was defeated only by a small majority. . . . At a still later period, abolitionist lecturers and teachers were mobbed, assaulted, and threatened with tar and feather in New York, Pennsylvania, Massachusetts, New Hampshire, Connecticut, and other States. . . .

These facts prove incontestably that the sectional hostility which exhibited itself in 1820, on the application of Missouri for admission into the Union, which again broke out on the proposition for the annexation of Texas in 1844, and which reappeared after the Mexican war . . . was not the consequence of any difference on the abstract question of slavery. It was the offspring of sectional rivalry and political ambition. It would have manifested itself just as certainly if slavery had existed in all the

States, or if there had not been a negro in America. . . . It was not slavery that threatened a rupture in 1832 [during the Nullification crisis], but the unjust and unequal operation of a protective tariff. . . .

The truth remains intact and incontrovertible, that the existence of African servitude was in no wise the cause of the conflict, but only an incident. In the later controversies that arose, however, its effect in operating as a lever upon the passions, prejudices, or sympathies of mankind, was so potent that it has been spread, like a thick cloud, over the whole horizon of historical truth.

Source: Davis, Jefferson, *The Rise and Fall of the Confederate Government, Vol. 1.* New York, 1881, 77–80.

THINKING CRITICALLY

What does Stephens mean by "the curse against Canaan"? How do Davis and Stephens differ in discussing the underlying causes of the Civil War? Does the date when each man delivered his opinion suggest a reason for the attitudes toward slavery and the reasons for secession? What evidence would you seek to decide the question of whether the dispute over slavery was the primary motivation for seceding?

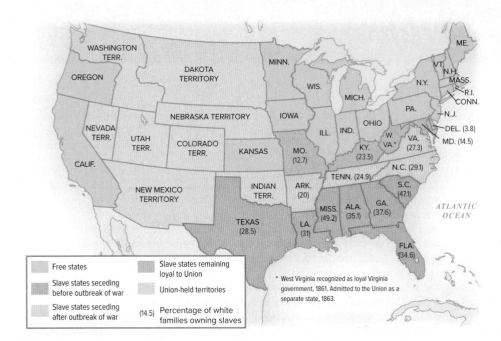

Led by South Carolina, the Deep South seceded between Lincoln's election in November and his inauguration in March. The Upper South did not secede until after the firing on Fort Sumter. The four border slave states never seceded and remained in the Union throughout the war. As the map indicates, secession sentiment was strongest in states where the highest percentage of white families owned slaves.

Free states

Slave states seceding before outbreak of war

Slave states seceding after outbreak of war

Slave states remaining loyal to Union

Union-held territories

(14.5) Percentage of white families owning slaves

* West Virginia recognized as loyal Virginia government, 1861. Admitted to the Union as a separate state, 1863.

UPPER SOUTH SECEDES The burden of decision now shifted to Jefferson Davis. From his point of view, secession was a constitutional right and the Confederacy was a legitimate government. To allow the United States to hold property and maintain military forces within the Confederacy would destroy its claim of independence. Davis therefore instructed the Confederate commander at Charleston to demand the immediate surrender of Fort Sumter and, if refused, to open fire. When Anderson declined the ultimatum, Confederate batteries began shelling the fort on April 12 at 4:30 a.m. Some 33 hours later Anderson surrendered. When in response Lincoln called for 75,000 volunteers to put down the rebellion, four states in the Upper South, led by Virginia, also seceded. Matters had passed beyond compromise.

The Roots of a Divided Society

And so the Union was broken. After 70 years, the forces of sectionalism and separatism had finally outpulled the ties binding "these United States." Why did affairs come to such a pass?

In some ways, as we have seen, the revolution in markets that transformed the nation during these years served to link together northerners and southerners. The cotton planter in Chapter 10 who rode the steamship *Fashion* along the Alabama River ("Time's money! Time's money!") was wearing ready-made clothes manufactured in New York from southern cotton. Chauncey Jerome's clocks from Connecticut were keeping time not only for commercial planters but also for Lowell mill workers like Mary Paul, who learned to measure her lunch break in minutes. Farmers in both Tennessee and Iowa were interested in the price of wheat in New York, for it affected the profits that could be made shipping their grain by the new railroad lines. American society had become far more specialized, and therefore far more interdependent, since the days of Hector St. John de Crèvecoeur's idealized self-sufficient farmer of the 1780s.

DIVERGING ECONOMIES But a specialized economy had not brought unity. For the North, specialization meant more factories, a higher percentage of urban workers, and a greater number of cities and towns. Industry affected midwestern farmers as well, for their steel plows and McCormick reapers allowed them to farm larger holdings and required greater capital investment in the new machinery. For its part, the South was transformed by the Industrial Revolution, too, as textile factories made cotton the booming mainstay of its economy. But for all its growth, the region remained largely a rural society. Its prosperity stemmed from expansion westward into new areas of cotton production, not new forms of production or technology. The dominant planter class reinforced its traditional concepts of honor, hierarchy, and deference.

Above all, the intensive labor required to produce cotton, rice, and sugar made slavery an inseparable part of the southern way of life—"so intimately mingled with our social conditions," as one Georgian admitted, "that it would be impossible to eradicate it." An increasing number of northerners viewed slavery as evil, not so much out of high-minded sympathy toward slaves but as a labor system that threatened the republican ideals of white American society.

WEAKNESSES OF THE POLITICAL SYSTEM It fell to the political system to try to resolve sectional conflict through a system of national parties that represented various interest groups and promoted democratic debate. But the political system had critical weaknesses. The American process of electing a president gave the winning candidate a state's entire electoral vote, regardless of the margin of victory. That procedure made a northern sectional party possible, since

The Road to Disunion

1854	1855	1856	1857
Kansas-Nebraska Act opens debate over status of new territories; Missouri Compromise repealed	Proslavery forces stuff ballot boxes in Kansas elections, expel free-state members of legislature; free-staters organize separate government	Lawrence, Kansas, sacked by proslavery forces; John Brown's Pottawatomie Massacre; Charles Sumner beaten unconscious on Senate floor	*Dred Scott* decision; Court rules that Congress cannot ban slavery in any territory; Missouri Compromise unconstitutional

1858	1859	1860	1861
Lincoln and Douglas debate slavery; Douglas suggests "Freeport Doctrine" as a way to block slavery, angering southern Democrats	John Brown launches raid on Harpers Ferry; Brown caught, tried, and executed	Republican Abraham Lincoln wins presidency without support of any southern states; South Carolina secedes	Confederate States of America organized; Fort Sumter attacked; war commences

Longer-Term Factors for Disunion

- Slavery gradually extinguished in the North (**1770s–1840s**); abolitionist movement expands (**1830s–1850s**)
- Railroads link Northwest more closely to Northeast (**1840s–1850s**)
- Second party system (Whigs vs. Democrats) disintegrates over slavery disputes (**1840s–1850s**)
- Electoral College system makes a northern sectional party possible (**1850s**)

(*top right*) Source: Library of Congress, Prints and Photographs Division [LC-USZ62-33407]; (*bottom left*) Source: Library of Congress, Prints and Photographs Division [LC-USZC2-3767]; (*bottom right*) Source: Library of Congress, Prints and Photographs Division [LC-USZC2-2991]

the Republicans could never have carried an election on the basis of a popular vote alone. In addition, the four-year fixed presidential term allowed Presidents Pierce and Buchanan to remain in office, pursuing disruptive policies on Kansas even after the voters had rejected those policies in the midterm congressional elections in 1854 and 1858. Finally, since 1844 the Democratic Party had required a two-thirds vote to nominate its presidential candidate. Unintentionally, this requirement made it difficult to pick any truly forceful leader and gave the South a veto over the party's candidate. Yet the South, by itself, could not elect a president.

BELIEF IN CONSPIRACIES AGAINST LIBERTY The nation's republican heritage also contributed to the political system's vulnerability. Ever since the Revolution, when Americans accused the king and Parliament of deliberately plotting to deprive them of their liberties, Americans were on the watch for political conspiracies. Such an outlook often stimulated exaggerated fears, unreasonable conclusions, and excessive reactions. For their part, Republicans emphasized

the existence of the Slave Power bent on eradicating northern rights. Southerners, on the other hand, accused the Black Republicans of conspiring to destroy southern equality. Each side viewed itself as defending the country's republican tradition from an internal threat.

> ✓ **REVIEW**
>
> Why did Lincoln's election cause the southern states to secede from the Union?

PUTTING HISTORY IN GLOBAL CONTEXT

BUT IN THE END, THE threat to the Union came not from within but from beyond its borders. As the nation expanded in the 1840s, it incorporated vast new territories, becoming a truly continental republic. And that forced the Union, in absorbing new lands, to define itself anew. If the American frontier had not swept so quickly toward the Pacific, the nation might have been able to postpone the day of reckoning on slavery until some form of gradual emancipation could be adopted. But the luxury of time was not available. The new territories became the battlegrounds for two contrasting ways of life, with slavery at the center of the debate. Elsewhere in the world the push toward abolition grew louder, whether of serfdom in eastern Europe or of slavery across the globe. Americans who saw the issue in moral terms joined that chorus. They saw no reason why the abolition of slavery should be postponed.

In 1850, supporters and opponents of slavery were still willing to compromise on how "the peculiar institution" could expand into the new territories. But a decade later, many Americans both North and South had come to accept the idea of an irrepressible conflict between two societies, one based on freedom, the other on slavery, in which only one side could ultimately prevail. At stake, it seemed, was control of the nation's future. Four years later, as a weary Abraham Lincoln looked back to the beginning of the conflict, he noted, "Both parties deprecated war, but one of them would *make* war rather than let the nation survive, and the other would *accept* war rather than let it perish, and the war came."

CHAPTER SUMMARY

In the 1850s the slavery issue reemerged in national politics and increasingly disrupted the party system, leading to the outbreak of war in 1861.

- Fundamental economic changes heightened sectional tensions in the 1850s.

  - The construction of a vast railroad network reoriented western trade from the South to the East.

  - A tide of new immigrants swelled the North's population (and hence its political power) at the expense of the South, thereby stimulating southern fears.

- The old Jacksonian party system was shattered by the nativist movement and by a renewed controversy of the expansion of slavery.

  - In the Kansas-Nebraska Act, Senator Stephen A. Douglas tried to defuse the slavery debate by incorporating popular sovereignty (the idea that the people of a territory should decide the status of slavery there). This act effectively repealed the Missouri Compromise.

  - Popular sovereignty failed in the Kansas Territory, where fighting broke out between proslavery and antislavery partisans.

  - Sectional violence reached a climax in May 1856 with the attack on Lawrence, Kansas, and the caning of Senator Charles Sumner of Massachusetts by Representative Preston S. Brooks of South Carolina.

- Sectional tensions sparked the formation of a new antislavery Republican party, and the party system realigned along sectional lines.

- The Supreme Court's *Dred Scott* decision, the Panic of 1857, the congressional struggle over the proslavery Lecompton constitution, and John Brown's attack on Harpers Ferry in 1859 strengthened the two sectional extremes.

- In 1860 Abraham Lincoln became the first Republican to be elected president.

  - Following Lincoln's triumph, the seven states of the Deep South seceded.

  - When Lincoln sent supplies to the Union garrison in Fort Sumter in Charleston harbor, Confederate batteries bombarded the fort into submission.

  - The North rallied to Lincoln's decision to use force to restore the Union, and in response the four states of the Upper South seceded.

Digging Deeper

The problem of the coming of the Civil War has attracted considerable historical attention over the years. John Ashworth, *The Republic in Crisis* (2012), is a lucid interpretation. The political aspects of the conflict also take center stage in Michael F. Holt's brief and incisive work, *The Fate of Their Country: Politicians, Slavery Extension, and the Coming of the Civil War* (2004). Holt stresses the self-interest of the political leaders and plays down the larger structural economic and social factors. A contrasting and similarly brief study can be found in Don E. Fehrenbacher, *Sectional Crisis and Southern Constitutionalism* (1995).

The heavy immigration during these years is explored in Raymond L. Cohn, *Mass Migration under Sail* (2009). For slavery's mounting implications for American politics, see Eric Foner, *The Fiery Trial* (2011).

Paul Quigley's *Shifting Grounds* (2012) puts the idea of southern nationalism in a broad spatial context. The most thorough examination of the blend of factors that produced the Republican Party is William E. Gienapp, *The Origins of the Republican Party, 1852-1856* (1987). Eric Foner's classic *Free Soil, Free Labor, Free Men* (1970), focuses on the ideas of Republican Party leaders. For the turbulent history of Kansas in this period, see Nicole Etcheson, *Bleeding Kansas* (2006). The critical events of 1857 are the focal point of Kenneth M. Stampp's *America in 1857* (1990). William W. Freehling's two-volume work *The Road to Disunion* (1991, 2007) offers a broad perspective on the secessionist project, and Charles B. Dew provides a regional view by examining the role of the secession commissioners appointed by the Confederacy to persuade wavering southerners in *Apostles of Secession* (2001). Adam Goodheart's *1861: The Civil War Awakening* (2011) presents a rich portrait of the war's beginnings. For a discussion of the broader issue of why the South chose secession and fought the Civil War, see Gary W. Gallagher and Alan T. Nolan, eds., *The Myth of the Lost Cause and Civil War History* (2000); and James L. Huston, *The British Gentry, the Southern Planter, and the Northern Family Farmer* (2015).

16 The Civil War and the Republic

1861–1865

Thousands of volunteers answered President Lincoln's call to preserve the Union, as this march in New York City on April 19, 1865, attests. Few of them thought the war would last long and engulf the nation in a struggle that transformed it. The First Battle of Bull Run three months later was the first sign that the struggle would be grueling.

©The Granger Collection, New York

>> An American Story

ROUT AT BULL RUN

"The war won't last sixty days!" Of that Jim Tinkham was confident when he quit his job as a grocery store clerk and enlisted for three months in a Massachusetts regiment. Soon he was transferred to Washington as part of the Union army being assembled under General Irvin McDowell to crush the rebellion. Tinkham was elated when in mid-July the army was finally ordered to march toward the Confederates concentrated at Manassas Junction, 25 miles away. On the way, Tinkham passed carriages carrying members of Congress and other jaunty

Source: Library of Congress, Prints and Photographs Division
[LC-DIG-pga-00335]

| *The retreat at Bull Run*

sightseers, their picnic baskets filled with provisions and fine wines. They, too, had come to witness the battle that would crush the rebellion.*

The battle began at dawn on July 21, with McDowell commanding 30,000 troops against General Pierre Beauregard's 22,000. Tinkham did not arrive on the field until early afternoon. As his regiment pushed toward the front, he felt faint at his first sight of the dead and wounded, some mangled horribly. But the Massachusetts troops were caught up in the excitement of battle as they charged up Henry Hill. Suddenly the Confederate ranks broke, and exuberant Union troops shouted, "The war is over!"

The arrival of fresh Confederate troops, however, enabled the rebels to regroup. Among the reinforcements who rushed to Henry Hill was 19-year-old Randolph McKim of Baltimore. A student at the University of Virginia, McKim joined the First Maryland Infantry as a private when Abraham Lincoln imposed martial law in his home state. "The cause of the South had become identified with liberty itself," he explained. The arrival of the First Maryland and other reinforcements in the late afternoon turned the tide of battle. The faltering Confederate line held, then charged, giving full throat for the first time to the famous "rebel yell." "There is nothing like [the yell] this side of the infernal region," explained one Union soldier. "The peculiar sensation that it sends down your backbone under these circumstances can never be told."

But with retreat came confusion. Discipline dissolved and the army quickly degenerated into a stampeding mob. Terrified troops threw away their equipment, shoved aside officers who tried to stop them, and raced frantically past the wagons, artillery pieces, and civilian carriages that clogged the road. Joining the stampede was Jim Tinkham, who confessed he would have continued on to Boston if he had not been stopped by a guard after crossing the Long Bridge into Washington. All the next day in a drizzling rain, mud-spattered troops straggled into the capital in complete disorder.

The rout at Bull Run sobered the North. Gone were dreams of ending the war with one glorious battle. Gone was the illusion that 75,000 volunteers serving three months could crush the rebellion. As one observer noted, "We have undertaken to make war without in the least knowing how." Having cast off his earlier illusions, a newly determined Jim Tinkham reenlisted for a three-year hitch.

Still, it was not surprising that both sides underestimated the magnitude of the conflict. Warfare as it had evolved in Europe consisted largely of maneuverings that took relatively few lives, generally respected private property, and left the majority of civilians unharmed. The Civil War, however, was the first war whose major battles routinely involved more than 100,000 troops. So many combatants could be equipped only through the use of factory-produced weaponry, they could be moved and supplied only with the help of railroads, and they could be sustained only through the concerted efforts of civilian society as a whole. The morale of the population, the quality of political leadership, and the utilization of industrial and economic might were all critical to the outcome. <<

---

*The Union and the Confederacy often gave different names to a battle. The Confederates called the first battle Manassas; the Union, Bull Run.

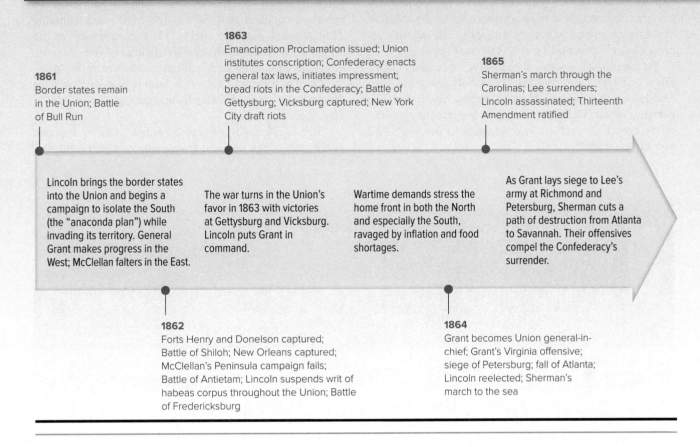

1861
Border states remain in the Union; Battle of Bull Run

Lincoln brings the border states into the Union and begins a campaign to isolate the South (the "anaconda plan") while invading its territory. General Grant makes progress in the West; McClellan falters in the East.

1862
Forts Henry and Donelson captured; Battle of Shiloh; New Orleans captured; McClellan's Peninsula campaign fails; Battle of Antietam; Lincoln suspends writ of habeas corpus throughout the Union; Battle of Fredericksburg

1863
Emancipation Proclamation issued; Union institutes conscription; Confederacy enacts general tax laws, initiates impressment; bread riots in the Confederacy; Battle of Gettysburg; Vicksburg captured; New York City draft riots

The war turns in the Union's favor in 1863 with victories at Gettysburg and Vicksburg. Lincoln puts Grant in command.

Wartime demands stress the home front in both the North and especially the South, ravaged by inflation and food shortages.

1864
Grant becomes Union general-in-chief; Grant's Virginia offensive; siege of Petersburg; fall of Atlanta; Lincoln reelected; Sherman's march to the sea

1865
Sherman's march through the Carolinas; Lee surrenders; Lincoln assassinated; Thirteenth Amendment ratified

As Grant lays siege to Lee's army at Richmond and Petersburg, Sherman cuts a path of destruction from Atlanta to Savannah. Their offensives compel the Confederacy's surrender.

OPENING MOVES

WHEN THE WAR BEGAN, THE North had an enormous advantage in manpower and industrial capacity. The Union's population was 2.5 times larger, and its advantage in white men of military age even greater. The North had a much larger merchant marine; produced more iron, firearms, and textiles; contained more railroad track and rolling stock; and possessed more than 10 times the industrial capacity.

SOUTHERN ADVANTAGES From a modern perspective, the South's attempt to defend its independence against such odds seems a hopeless cause. Yet this view indicates how much the conception of war has changed. European observers, who knew the strength and resources of the two sides, believed that the Confederacy, with its large area, poor roads, and rugged terrain, could never be conquered. Indeed, the South enjoyed definite strategic advantages. To be victorious, it did not need to invade the North—only to defend its own land and prevent the North from destroying its armies. Southern soldiers knew the topography of their home country better, and a friendly population regularly supplied them with intelligence about Union troop movements.

The North, in contrast, had to invade and conquer the Confederacy and destroy the southern will to resist. To do so it would have to deploy thousands of soldiers to defend long supply lines in enemy territory, a situation that significantly reduced the northern advantage in manpower. Yet in the end the Confederacy was not only invaded and conquered but also utterly destroyed. By 1865 the Union forces had penetrated virtually every part of the 500,000 square miles of the Confederacy and were able to move almost at will. The Civil War demonstrated the capacity of a modern society to overcome the problems of distance and terrain with technology.

Political Leadership

To sustain a commitment to war required effective political leadership. This task fell on Abraham Lincoln and Jefferson Davis, presidents of the rival governments.

Jefferson Davis grew up in Mississippi accustomed to life's advantages. Educated at West Point, he fought in the U.S.-Mexican War, served as Franklin Pierce's secretary of war, and became one of the South's leading advocates in the Senate. Although he was hardworking and committed to the cause he led, his temperament was not well suited to his new post. He quarreled tactlessly with generals and politicians and refused to work with those he disliked. "He cannot brook opposition or criticism," one member of the Confederate Congress testified, "and those who do not bow down before him have no chance of success with him." His legalistic approach to problems hurt his efforts to rouse the South.

Yet for all Davis's personal handicaps, he faced an institutional one even more daunting. The Confederacy had been founded on the ideology of states' rights. Yet to meet the demands of war, Davis would need to increase the authority of the central government beyond anything the South had ever experienced.

LINCOLN'S LEADERSHIP When Lincoln took the oath of office in 1861, his national experience consisted of one term in the House of Representatives. But Lincoln was a shrewd judge of character and a superb politician. To achieve a common goal, he willingly overlooked withering criticism and personal slights. (The commander of the Union army, General George McClellan, for one, continually snubbed the president and referred to him as "the original Gorilla.") He was not easily humbugged, overawed, or flattered and never allowed personal feelings to blind him to his larger objectives.

"This is essentially a People's contest," Lincoln asserted at the start of the war, and few presidents have been better

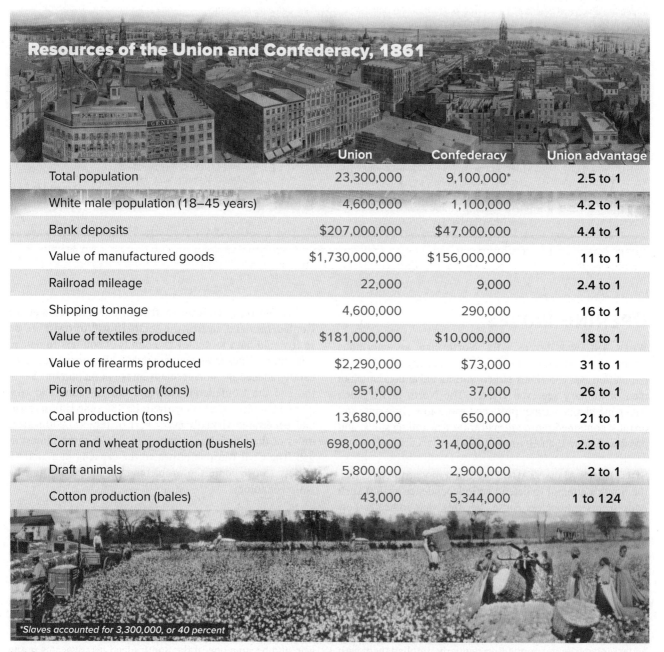

Resources of the Union and Confederacy, 1861

	Union	Confederacy	Union advantage
Total population	23,300,000	9,100,000*	2.5 to 1
White male population (18–45 years)	4,600,000	1,100,000	4.2 to 1
Bank deposits	$207,000,000	$47,000,000	4.4 to 1
Value of manufactured goods	$1,730,000,000	$156,000,000	11 to 1
Railroad mileage	22,000	9,000	2.4 to 1
Shipping tonnage	4,600,000	290,000	16 to 1
Value of textiles produced	$181,000,000	$10,000,000	18 to 1
Value of firearms produced	$2,290,000	$73,000	31 to 1
Pig iron production (tons)	951,000	37,000	26 to 1
Coal production (tons)	13,680,000	650,000	21 to 1
Corn and wheat production (bushels)	698,000,000	314,000,000	2.2 to 1
Draft animals	5,800,000	2,900,000	2 to 1
Cotton production (bales)	43,000	5,344,000	1 to 124

*Slaves accounted for 3,300,000, or 40 percent

(top): Source: Library of Congress, Prints and Photographs Division [LC-DIG-ppmsca-09854]; (bottom): Source: Library of Congress, Prints and Photographs Division [LC-USZ62-120480] ; (table): Sources: U.S. Census 1860; Lon, E. B., The Civil War Day by Day. New York, NY: Doubleday, 1971, 723.

able to communicate with the average citizen. He regularly visited Union troops in camp, in the field, and in army hospitals. "The boys liked him," wrote Joseph Twichell, from a Connecticut regiment. "[I]n fact his popularity with the army is and has been universal." Always Lincoln reminded the public that the war was being fought for the ideals of the Revolution and the Republic. It was a test, he remarked in his famous address at Gettysburg, of whether a nation "conceived in Liberty, and dedicated to the proposition that all men are created equal," could "long endure."

Lincoln also proved the more effective military leader. Jefferson Davis took his title of commander-in-chief literally, interfering with his generals even on the smallest matters. But he failed to formulate an effective overarching strategy. In contrast, Lincoln had a clear grasp of the challenge confronting the Union. He accepted General Winfield Scott's proposal to blockade and surround the Confederacy, cut off its supplies, and slowly strangle it into submission, just as the anaconda snake squeezes its prey. But unlike Scott he realized that an "anaconda plan" was not enough. The South would also have to be invaded and defeated, not only on an eastern front in Virginia but also in the West, where Union control of the Mississippi would divide the Confederacy fatally. Lincoln understood that the Union's superior manpower and matériel would become decisive only when the Confederacy was simultaneously threatened along a broad front. The Union forces could then break through at the weak points. It took time before the president found generals able to execute this novel strategy.

©Historical/Corbis/Getty Images

| Jefferson Davis

The Border States

When the war began, only Delaware of the border slave states was certain to remain in the Union. Lincoln's immediate political challenge was to retain the loyalty of Maryland, Kentucky, and Missouri. Maryland especially was crucial, for if it were lost, Washington itself would have to be abandoned.

SUPPRESSION IN MARYLAND The danger became immediately apparent when pro-Confederate forces destroyed the railroad bridges near Baltimore and isolated Washington. Only with difficulty was the administration able to move troops to the city. Once the capital was safe, Lincoln moved vigorously—even ruthlessly—to secure Maryland. He suspended the writ of **habeas corpus,** the right under the Constitution of an arrested person either to be charged with a specific crime or to be released. That done, he held without trial prominent Confederate sympathizers and suppressed pro-Confederate newspapers. Intervention by the army ensured that Unionists won a complete victory in the fall state election. The election ended any possibility that Maryland would join the Confederacy.

KENTUCKY'S NEUTRALITY At the beginning of the conflict, Kentucky officially declared its neutrality. "I think to lose Kentucky is nearly to lose the whole game," Lincoln wrote with concern. "Kentucky gone, we can not hold Missouri, nor, as I think, Maryland. These all against us, and the job on our hands is too large for us." Union generals requested permission to occupy the state, but the president refused, preferring to act cautiously and wait for Unionist sentiment to assert itself. After Unionists won control of the legislature in the summer election, a Confederate army entered the state, giving Lincoln the opening he needed. He quickly sent in troops, and Kentucky stayed in the Union.

In Missouri, Union forces secured the state only after the Union victory at the Battle of Pea Ridge in March 1862. Even so, guerrilla warfare continued throughout the remainder of the war. In Virginia, internal divisions led to the creation of a new border state, as the hilly western counties, where slavery was not strong, refused to support the Confederacy. West Virginia was formally admitted to the Union in June 1863.

IMPORTANCE OF THE BORDER STATES The Union scored an important triumph in holding the border states. The population of all five equaled that of the four states of the Upper South that had joined the Confederacy, and their production of military supplies—food, animals, and minerals—was greater. Furthermore, Maryland and West Virginia contained key railroad lines and were critical to the defense of Washington, while Kentucky and Missouri gave the Union army access to the major river systems of the western theater, down which it launched the first successful invasions of the Confederacy.

Source: Library of Congress, Prints and Photographs Division [LC-DIG-ppmsca-19211]

| Lincoln at the time of the Gettysburg Address

Blockade and Isolate

As with so many Civil War battles, the Confederate victory at Bull Run achieved no decisive military results. But a sobered Congress authorized the enlistment of half a million volunteers to serve for three years. Lincoln named 34-year-old George McClellan, a West Point graduate, to be the new commander of the Union army. Energetic and ambitious, McClellan had been working as a railroad executive when the war began. For the next eight months he appeared the very model of businesslike efficiency as he settled into the much-needed task of organizing and drilling the Army of the Potomac.

But the Union developed a strategy on water as well as on land. The U.S. Navy began the war with only 42 ships available to blockade 3,550 miles of Confederate coastline. In April 1862 Flag Officer David G. Farragut ran a gauntlet of Confederate shore batteries to capture New Orleans, the Confederacy's largest city and most important port. Memphis, another important river city, fell to Union forces in June.

IRONCLADS The blockade was hardly leakproof, and Confederates as well as smugglers working on their own slipped through using small, fast ships. "Blockade Runners" sped hundreds of thousands of guns and tons of ammunition through to Confederate agents on the coast. Still, southern trade suffered badly. In hopes of lifting the blockade, the Confederacy converted the wooden U.S.S. *Merrimack,* which was rechristened the *Virginia,* into an ironclad gunboat. In March 1862 a Union ironclad, the *Monitor,* battled it to a standoff, and the Confederates were forced to scuttle the *Virginia* when they evacuated Norfolk in May. After that, the Union's naval supremacy was secure—though smuggling would continue and remain critical to the Confederate cause throughout the war.

KING COTTON DIPLOMACY The South looked to diplomacy as another means to lift the blockade. With cotton so vital to European economies, especially Great Britain's, southerners believed that Europe would formally recognize the Confederacy and come to its aid. The North, for its part, claimed that it was merely putting down a domestic insurrection, but European countries allowed the Confederacy to purchase supplies abroad. More worrisome, leaders in France and England seemed certain that the Confederacy would inevitably go its own way. They believed the Union lacked the will and probably the power to force southerners back into the Union. From the perspective of many in Europe, the increasingly savage Civil War was a grotesque and futile mistake—one that could perhaps be rectified only by European intervention. Lincoln might have hoped for support from European abolitionists, but his own repeated and very public insistence that the war was about Union—not slavery—left many in Europe arguing that Confederate independence would actually leave southern planters in a weaker position than before the war, and would thus hasten the decline of slavery. Most fundamentally, with southern ports closed and talk of a global "cotton famine" everywhere, Europeans actively debated recognizing the Confederacy or even intervening in the war. Before the fighting broke out, Great Britain relied upon the South for 77 percent of its cotton and France 90 percent. As cotton reserves ran low,

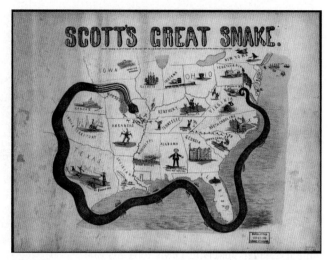

Source: Library of Congress, Geography and Map Division [G3701.S5 1861. E4 CW 11]

General Winfield Scott's "anaconda plan" called for a naval blockade of the Confederacy. Ships are sketched next to a snake in this cartoon from 1861. But Lincoln realized that the war would have to be taken to the interior of the Confederate States, in the eastern theater of battle (Virginia, the Carolinas, and Georgia) as well as in the western theater, beyond the Appalachian Mountains.

factories laid off workers, and British and French industrialists became increasingly alarmed, the two governments edged toward recognizing the Confederacy.

Grant in the West

In the western war theater the first decisive Union victory was won by a short, shabbily dressed, cigar-chomping general named Ulysses S. Grant. An undistinguished student at West Point, Grant eventually resigned his commission. He failed at everything he tried in civilian life, and when the war broke out he was a store clerk in Galena, Illinois. Almost 39, he promptly volunteered, and two months later he became a brigadier general.

GRANT'S CHARACTER Grant's quiet, self-effacing manner gave little indication of his military ability or iron determination. Alert to seize any opening, he remained extraordinarily calm and clear-headed in battle. He absorbed details on a map almost photographically, and in battles that spread out over miles, he was superb at coordinating an attack. He would "try all sorts of cross-cuts," recalled one staff officer, "ford streams and jump any number of fences to reach another road rather than go back and take a fresh start." Grant also took full advantage of the telegraph to track troop movements, stringing new lines as he advanced. (Some of his Union telegraphers were so adept that they could receive messages before a station was set up by touching the end of the wire to their tongues to pick up Morse code.) Most important, Grant grasped that hard fighting, not fancy maneuvering, would bring victory. "The art of war is simple," he once explained. "Find out where your enemy is, get at him as soon as you can and strike him as hard as you can, and keep moving on."

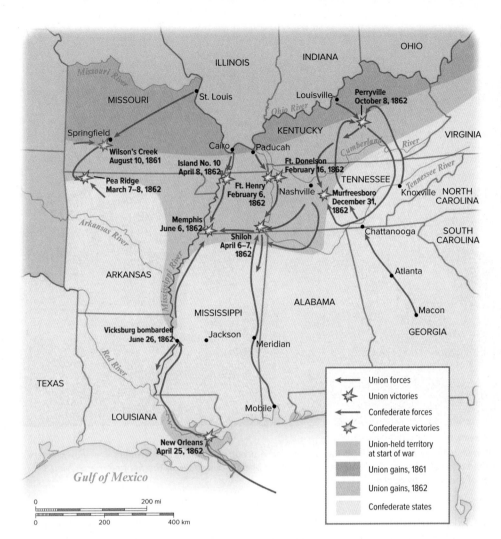

*Grant's push southward stalled
after his costly victory at Shiloh;
nevertheless, by the end of 1862
the Union had secured Kentucky
and Missouri, as well as most of
Confederate Tennessee and the
upper and lower stretches of the
Mississippi River.* **How did Grant
use the geography of the South
to plan his campaign in the West?**

SHILOH Grant realized that rivers were avenues into the interior of the Confederacy. In February 1862, supported by Union gunboats, he captured Fort Henry on the Tennessee River and Fort Donelson on the Cumberland. These victories forced the Confederates to withdraw from Kentucky and middle Tennessee. Grant continued south with 40,000 men, but he was surprised on April 6 by General Albert Sidney Johnston at Shiloh, just north of the Tennessee-Mississippi border. Johnston was killed in the day's fierce fighting, but by nightfall his army had driven the Union troops back to the Tennessee River, where they huddled numbly as a cold rain fell. William Tecumseh Sherman, one of Grant's subordinates, found the general standing under a dripping tree, his coat collar drawn up against the damp, puffing on a cigar. Sherman was about to suggest retreat, but something in Grant's eyes, lighted by the glow of his cigar, made him hesitate. So he said only, "Well, Grant, we've had the devil's own day, haven't we?" "Yes," the Union commander quietly replied. "Lick 'em tomorrow, though." And he did. With the aid of reinforcements, which he methodically ferried across the river all night, Grant counterattacked the next morning and drove the Confederates from the field.

Victory came at a high price: Shiloh inflicted more than 23,000 casualties. "The scenes on this field would have cured anyone of war," Sherman testified. Grant, who had doubted the commitment of Confederate troops, after Shiloh "gave up all idea of saving the Union except by complete conquest."

Eastern Stalemate

Grant's victories did not silence his critics, who charged he drank too much. But Lincoln was unmoved. "I can't spare this man. He fights." That was a quality in short supply in the East, where General McClellan directed operations.

LINCOLN FEARS "McCLELLAN HAS THE SLOWS" The short, handsome McClellan looked like a general, but beneath his arrogance and bravado lay a self-doubt that rendered him excessively cautious. As the months dragged on and McClellan did nothing but train and plan, Lincoln's frustration grew. "If General McClellan does not want to use the army I would like to *borrow* it," he remarked sarcastically. In the spring of 1862 the general finally transported his 130,000 troops to the Virginia coast and began inching toward Richmond, the

Source: Library of Congress, Prints and Photographs Division [LC-DIG-cwpb-01097]

With almost 23,000 casualties, Antietam was the bloodiest single day of the war. A group of Confederate soldiers are shown where they fell along the Hagerstown Pike, the scene of some of the heaviest fighting. Said one Union officer of the fighting there: "Men, I cannot say fell; they were knocked out of the ranks by dozens."

Confederate capital. In May, when McClellan was within 5 miles of Richmond, General Joseph Johnston suddenly attacked him near Fair Oaks, from which he barely escaped. Worse for McClellan, when Johnston was badly wounded, the formidable Robert E. Lee took command of the Army of Northern Virginia.

LEE'S GENERALSHIP   Where McClellan was cautious and defensive, the aristocratic Lee was daring and ever alert to assume the offensive. His first name, one of his colleagues commented, should have been Audacity: "He will take more chances, and take them quicker than any other general in this country." Joining Lee was Thomas "Stonewall" Jackson, a deeply religious Calvinist whose rigorous discipline honed his troops to a hard edge. In the Seven Days' battles, McClellan maneuvered brilliantly to parry the attacks of Lee and Jackson; still, he always stayed on the defensive, finally retreating until he was under the protection of the Union gunboats. Frustrated, Lincoln ordered the Peninsula campaign abandoned and formed a new army under John Pope. After Lee badly mauled Pope at the second Battle of Bull Run, Lincoln restored McClellan to command.

LEE'S INVASION FAILS   Realizing that the Confederacy needed a decisive victory, Lee convinced Davis to allow him to invade the North, hoping to detach Maryland and isolate Washington. But as the army crossed into Maryland, Union soldiers discovered a copy of Lee's orders, accidentally left

behind at a campsite by a Confederate officer. From this document McClellan learned that his forces vastly outnumbered Lee's—yet still he hesitated before launching a series of badly coordinated assaults near Antietam Creek on September 17 that Lee barely repulsed. The bloody exchanges horrified both sides for their sheer carnage. Within the space of seven hours nearly 5,000 soldiers were killed and another 18,000 wounded, making it the bloodiest single day in American history. Two months after McClellan allowed the Confederate army to escape back into Virginia, the president permanently relieved him of command.

The winter of 1862 was the North's Valley Forge, as morale sank to an all-time low. It took General Ambrose Burnside, who assumed McClellan's place, little more than a month to demonstrate his utter incompetence. In December, at the Battle of Fredericksburg, he suffered a disastrous defeat, which prompted Lincoln to put "Fighting Joe" Hooker in charge. In the West, Grant had emerged as the dominant figure, but the Army of the Potomac still lacked a capable commander, the deaths kept mounting, and no end to the war was in sight.

> ✔ **REVIEW**
>
> How did Lincoln mobilize for war more successfully than Jefferson Davis, and what were the opening strategies in the eastern and western theaters of war?

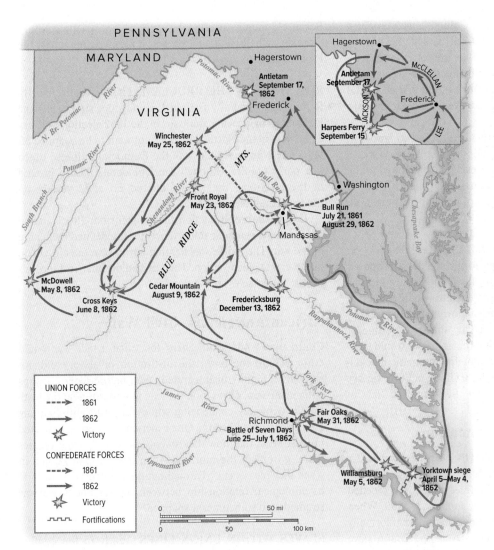

THE WAR IN THE EAST, 1861–1862

McClellan's campaign against Richmond failed when Joseph Johnston surprised him at Fair Oaks. Taking command of the Army of Northern Virginia, Lee drove back McClellan in the Seven Days' battles and then won a resounding victory in the second Battle of Bull Run. He followed this up by invading Maryland, dividing his forces to take advantage of McClellan's caution, and capturing Harpers Ferry. McClellan checked his advance at Antietam. The Army of the Potomac's devastating defeat at Fredericksburg ended a year of frustration and failure for the Union in the eastern theater. Which battles showed the steepest losses for Grant?

EMANCIPATION

In 1858 LINCOLN HAD PROCLAIMED that an American "house divided" could not stand and that the United States would eventually become either all slave or all free. When the house divided, however, Lincoln hesitated to strike at slavery. He perceived, accurately, that most white northerners were not deeply committed to emancipation. He feared the social upheaval that such a revolutionary step would cause, and he did not want to alarm the wavering border states.

LINCOLN GIVES PRIORITY TO THE UNION Still, Republican radicals such as Senator Charles Sumner and Horace Greeley pressed Lincoln to adopt a policy of emancipation. Slavery had caused the war, they argued; its destruction would hasten the war's end. Lincoln, however, placed first priority on saving the Union. "My paramount object in this struggle *is* to save the Union, and is *not* either to save or to destroy slavery," he told Greeley in 1862. "If I could save the Union without freeing *any* slave I would do it, and if I could save it by freeing *all* the slaves I would do it, and if I could save it by freeing some and leaving others alone, I would also do that." This statement summarized Lincoln's policy during the first year of the war.

The Logic of Events

CONGRESSIONAL ATTACK ON SLAVERY As the Union army began to occupy Confederate territory, slaves flocked to the Union camps. In May 1861 the army adopted the policy of declaring runaway slaves **contraband** of war and refused to return them to their rebel owners. In the Confiscation Act of August 1861, Congress provided that slaves used for military purposes by the Confederacy would become free if they fell into Union hands. For a year Lincoln accepted that position but would go no further. When two of his generals, acting on their own authority, abolished slavery in their districts, he countermanded their orders.

By the time Congress reconvened in December 1861, opinion was beginning to shift. Congress prohibited federal troops from capturing or returning fugitive slaves and freed the

2,000 slaves living in the District of Columbia with compensation to their owners. In July 1862 it passed the Second Confiscation Act, which declared that the slaves of anyone who supported the rebellion would be freed if they came into federal custody. Unlike the stipulations of the first act, it did not matter whether the slaves had been used for military purposes.

Lincoln signed this bill and then proceeded to ignore it. Instead, he emphasized state action, since slavery was a domestic institution. Twice the president summoned white representatives from the border states and prodded them to support a state-sponsored program of gradual emancipation. Both times they rejected his plea.

LINCOLN'S DECISION FOR EMANCIPATION So on July 22, 1862, Lincoln presented to his cabinet a proposed proclamation freeing the slaves in the Confederacy. He was increasingly confident that the border states would remain in the Union, and he wanted to strike a blow that would weaken the Confederacy militarily. By making the struggle one of freedom versus slavery, such a proclamation would also undermine Confederate efforts to obtain diplomatic recognition. But Lincoln decided to wait for a Union military victory so that the act would not appear one of desperation.

The Emancipation Proclamation

TERMS OF THE PROCLAMATION On September 22, following the victory at Antietam, Lincoln announced that all slaves within rebel lines would be freed unless the seceded states returned to their allegiance by January 1, 1863. When that day came, the Emancipation Proclamation went formally into effect. Excluded from its terms were the Union slave states, all of Tennessee, and the other areas of the Confederacy that were under Union control. In all, about 830,000 of the nation's 4 million slaves were not covered by its provisions.

Source: Library of Congress, Prints and Photographs Division [LC-USZC4-6160]

| Many African American churches held "watch night meetings" every New Year's Eve to welcome in the new year. With the Emancipation Proclamation set to go into effect January first, these sessions took on special significance in December 1862.

Because Lincoln justified his actions on strictly military grounds, he believed that there was no legal right to apply the Proclamation to areas not in rebellion.

REACTION TO THE PROCLAMATION In the North, Republicans generally favored Lincoln's decision, while the Democrats made it a major issue in the 1862 elections. "Every white man in the North, who does not want to be swapped off for a free Nigger, should vote the Democratic ticket," urged one party orator. Although the Democrats gained ground in the elections, the results offered no clear verdict on the Proclamation.

Despite the mixed reaction, the Emancipation Proclamation had immense symbolic importance, for it redefined the nature of the war. The North was fighting not to save the old Union but to create a new nation. The war had become, in Lincoln's words, "remorseless revolution."

African Americans' Civil War

Contrary to white southerners' fears that a race war would erupt behind the lines, the institution of slavery did not explode: it simply disintegrated. Well before federal troops entered an area, slaves took the lead in undermining the institution by openly challenging white authority and claiming greater personal freedom. One experienced overseer reported in frustration that now the "slaves will do only what pleases them, go out in the morning when it suits them, come in when they please, etc." Throughout the Confederacy the vital psychological relationship between master and slave was strained, and sometimes it snapped.

SLAVES WITHIN UNION LINES Early in the conflict slaves concluded that emancipation would be one consequence of a Union victory. Perhaps as many as half a million— one-seventh of the total slave population of the Confederacy— fled to Union lines, where they faced an uncertain reception since northern troops manifested a deep-seated racism and were often hostile. The ex-slaves, called **freedmen**, ended up living in refugee or contraband camps that were overcrowded and disease-ridden and provided only rudimentary shelter and food. Death rates in these camps approached 25 percent. "The poor Negroes die as fast as ever," one northern missionary reported. "The children are all emaciated to the last degree and have such violent coughs and dysenteries that few survive."

Convinced that freed slaves would not work on their own initiative, the U.S. government put some contrabands to work assisting the army as cooks, teamsters, woodchoppers, and other unskilled laborers. Their wages were well below those paid white citizens for the same

©Historical/Corbis/Getty Images

| African American recruits to the Union army

work. In the Mississippi valley, where two-thirds of the freed-people under Union control were located, most were forced to work on plantations leased or owned by loyal planters. This policy was officially adopted in the summer of 1863 as a way to free the army from the cost of supporting former slaves and strengthen Unionism in the South. Freedpeople had no say in the contracts negotiated between military authorities and planters, found themselves strictly disciplined, and had so many deductions taken from their wages that in the end most received only room and board. In short, the conditions often approximated slavery.

Black Soldiers

BLACKS IN COMBAT In adopting the policy of emancipation, Lincoln also announced that African Americans would be accepted in the navy and, more controversially, the army. (Throughout its history, the navy had been hard-pressed to get enough recruits, and as a result that service had always included some black sailors.) Resistance to accepting black volunteers in the army remained especially strong in the Midwest. Even black northerners were divided over whether to enlist, but Frederick Douglass spoke for the vast majority when he argued that once a black man had served in the army, there was "no power on earth which can deny that he has earned the right of citizenship in the United States."

In the end nearly 200,000 African Americans served in the Union forces, constituting about 10 percent of the Union's total military manpower. Some, including two of Douglass's sons, were free, but most were former slaves who enlisted after escaping to the Union lines. As a concession to the racism of white troops, blacks served in segregated units under white officers. They were paid only $10 a month, with $3 deducted for clothing. White soldiers, in contrast, received $13 a month plus a $3.50 clothing allowance. Not until June 1864 did Congress finally grant equal pay to black soldiers.

At first given undesirable duties such as heavy labor and burial details, black soldiers successfully lobbied for the chance to fight. They impressed white troops with their courage under fire. "I have been one of those men, who never had much confidence in colored troops fighting," one Union officer admitted, "but these doubts are now all removed, for they fought as bravely as any troops in the Fort." In the end 37,000 African American servicemen gave their lives, a rate of loss significantly higher than among white soldiers. So dismal were conditions in their camps that, compared with whites, three times the number of black soldiers died from disease. Yet black recruits had good reason to fight fiercely. They knew that the freedom of their race hung in the balance, they hoped to win civil rights at home by their performance on the battlefield, they resented racist sneers about their loyalty and ability, and they knew that capture might mean death.

> ✓ **REVIEW**
> What steps took the North along the path from a war to save the Union to a war in which emancipation became a central goal?

THE CONFEDERATE HOME FRONT

"HOW SHALL WE SUBSIST THIS winter?" John Jones wondered in the fall of 1862. A clerk in the War Department in Richmond, Jones found it increasingly difficult to make ends meet on his salary. Prices kept going up, essential items were in short supply, and the signs of hardship were everywhere: in the darned and patched clothing, the absence of meat from the market, the desperation on people's faces. Some of the residents of Richmond "look like vagabonds," Jones noted in his diary.

Nowhere were the profound effects of war more complete than within the Confederacy. These changes were especially ironic because the southern states had seceded in order to preserve their traditional ways. Not only did the war send hundreds of thousands of "Johnny Rebs" off to the front; it also put extreme burdens on the women and families at home. It fundamentally transformed the southern economy and forced the Confederate government to become more centralized. And, of course, it ended by destroying the institution of slavery, which the South had gone to war to preserve.

The New Economy

With the Union blockade tightening, the production of foodstuffs became crucial to the South's economy. Many men who normally worked in the fields had gone into the army, and with the lessening of discipline, slaves became increasingly assertive and independent. More and more plantations switched from growing cotton to raising grain and livestock. As a result, cotton production dropped from 4.5 million bales in 1861 to 300,000 in 1864. Even so, food production declined. By the last two years of the war, the shortage was serious.

ATTEMPTS TO INDUSTRIALIZE The Union blockade also made it impossible to rely on European manufactured goods. So the Confederate War Department built and ran factories, took over the region's mines, and regulated private manufacturers so as to increase the production of war goods. Although the Confederacy never became industrially self-sufficient, it sustained itself far better in industrial goods than it did in agricultural produce. It was symbolic that when Lee surrendered, his troops had sufficient guns and ammunition to continue, but they had not eaten in two days.

New Opportunities for Southern Women

Southern white women took an active role in the war. Some gained notoriety as spies; others smuggled military supplies into the South. Women also spent a good deal of time knitting and sewing clothes for soldiers. "We never went out to pay

a visit without taking our knitting along," recalled a South Carolina woman. Perhaps most important, with so many men fighting, women took charge of agricultural production. On a plantation the mistress often supervised the slaves as well as the wrenching shift from cotton to foodstuffs.

One such woman was 33-year-old Emily Lyles Harris, the wife of a small slaveowner and farmer in upcountry South Carolina. When her husband joined the army in 1862, she was left to care for their seven children as well as supervise the slaves and manage the farm. Despite the disruptions of wartime, she succeeded remarkably, one year producing the largest crop of oats in the neighborhood and always making enough money for her family to live decently. She took little pride, however, in her achievements. "I shall never get used to being left as the head of affairs at home," she wrote on one occasion. "The burden is very heavy, and there is no one to smile on me as I trudge wearily along in the dark with it.... I am not an independent woman nor ever shall be." Self-doubt, lack of privacy, and the burdens of responsibility left her depressed, and while she persevered, by 1865 she openly hoped for defeat.

The war also opened up new jobs for women off the farm. Given the manpower shortage, "government girls" became essential to fill the growing Confederate bureaucracy. At first women were paid half the wages of male coworkers, but by the end of the war they had won equal pay. White women also staffed the new factories springing up in southern cities and towns, undertaking even dangerous work that normally would have been considered off-limits. A majority of the workers in the South's munitions factories were women, some of whom lost their lives in accidental explosions.

Source: Library of Congress, Prints and Photographs Division [LC-DIG-ppmsca-37270]

| Southern women aided the war effort in a variety of ways, but in addition to the often-unexpected jobs they performed, the shadow of death was never far away. This Confederate woman wears a black mourning dress and a brooch showing a Confederate soldier (her dead husband?) and holds her son in her lap.

Confederate Finance and Government

The most serious domestic problem the Confederate government faced was finance, for which officials at Richmond never developed a satisfactory program. The South had few banks and only $27 million in specie when the war began. European governments refused to float major loans, which left taxation as the unappealing alternative. Only in 1863 did the government begin levying a **graduated income tax** (from 1 to 15 percent) and a series of excise taxes. Most controversial, the government resorted to a tax-in-kind on farmers that, after exempting a certain portion, took one-tenth of their agricultural crops. Even more unpopular was the policy of impressment, which allowed the army to seize private property for its own use, often with little or no compensation.

Face Value?

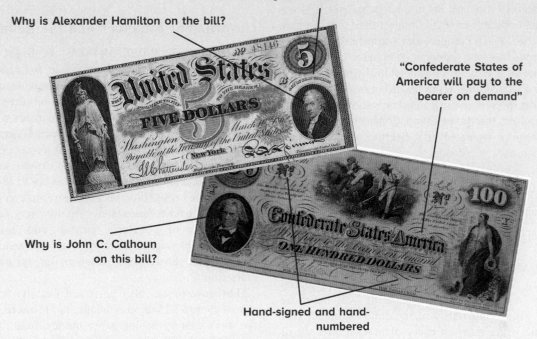

"Act of Feby 25, 1862"

Why is Alexander Hamilton on the bill?

"Confederate States of America will pay to the bearer on demand"

Why is John C. Calhoun on this bill?

Hand-signed and hand-numbered

(*top*): ©American Numismatic Association, Edward C. Rochette Money Museum (Fr-61 [face]); (*bottom*): Source: Library of Congress, Prints and Photographs Division [LC-USZ62-125842]

A government at war can survive only if it maintains its credit—not only with its bankers but with its citizens as well. Both the Union and the Confederacy issued paper money to finance the war, and by examining the bills' designs, historians can appreciate the issuers' efforts to appear creditworthy. The Union note uses Alexander Hamilton to vouch for its reliability—the Republic's first treasury secretary, who during the 1790s stabilized the nation's shaky finances. It announces the act of Congress that allows the government to issue the notes: the Legal Tender Act, passed February 25, 1862. And the intricate engraving and red treasury seal made the bill harder to counterfeit. The Confederacy had more difficulty issuing bills because few skilled engravers lived in the South. To help prevent counterfeiting, the Confederacy followed the older tradition of signing each bill individually, employing as many as 200 secretaries to do the tedious work. (The Union's signatures were printed.) But by war's end, so many Confederate notes had been issued that they were carted about in wheelbarrows to pay the hugely inflated prices for goods. In the end, mere symbols of credit could not obliterate the realities on the ground.

THINKING CRITICALLY

The fine print located above the Confederate promise to "pay on demand" reads "Six months after a ratification of a Treaty of Peace between The Confederate States & The United States of America." What effect does this condition have? Who are the people portrayed at the center of the Confederate bill? Why choose to include them?

SOARING INFLATION Above all, the Confederacy financed the war effort simply by printing paper money not backed by specie, some $1.5 billion, which amounted to three times more than the federal government issued. The result was runaway inflation, so that by 1865 a Confederate dollar was worth only 1.7 cents in gold and prices had soared to 92 times their prewar base. Prices were highest in Richmond, where flour sold for $275 a barrel by early 1864 and coats for $350. By the end of the war, flour had reached an astronomical $1,000 a barrel. Inflation that ate away at their standard of living was one of the great wartime hardships borne by southerners.

CENTRALIZATION OF POWER In politics even more than in finance the Confederacy exercised far greater powers than those of the federal government before 1861. Indeed, Jefferson Davis strove to meet the demands of war by transforming the South into a centralized, national state. He sought to limit state authority over military units, and in April 1862 the Confederacy passed the first national **conscription** law in American history, drafting all white males between 18 and 35 unless exempted. As conditions worsened, those age limits widened to 17 and 50, mobilizing virtually the entire military-age white population. Civilians, too, felt the effects of government control, for in 1862 the Congress authorized Davis to invoke martial law and suspend the writ of habeas corpus.

OPPOSITION TO DAVIS   Critics protested that Davis was destroying states' rights, the cardinal principle of the Confederacy. Concerned foremost about their states' safety, governors wanted to be able to recall troops if their own territory was threatened. When President Davis suspended the writ of habeas corpus, his vice president, Alexander H. Stephens, accused him of aiming at a dictatorship. Davis used those powers for a limited time, yet in practice it made little difference whether the writ was suspended or not. With disloyalty a greater problem than in the Union, Confederate authorities more stringently regulated civil liberties, and the army arrested thousands of civilians.

HOSTILITY TO CONSCRIPTION   But the Confederate draft, more than any other measure, produced an outcry. The law allowed the rich to provide substitutes. On the open market, the price for recruiting such a substitute eventually rose to $6,000. The Confederacy eventually abolished this privilege, but as one Georgia leader complained, "It's a notorious fact if a man has influential friends—or a little money to spare he will never be enrolled." Most controversially, the draft exempted from service one white man on every plantation with 20 or more slaves (later reduced to 15). This law was designed to preserve control of the slave population, but more and more non-slaveholders complained that it was a rich man's war and a poor man's fight. "All they want is to git you pumped up and go to fight for their infernal negroes and after you do their fighting you may kiss their hind parts for all they care," one Alabama farmer complained. In some counties where the draft was unenforceable, conscription officers ventured only at risk to their own safety.

Hardship and Suffering

By the last year of the conflict, food shortages had become so severe that ingenious southerners concocted various substitutes: parched corn in place of coffee, strained blackberries in place of vinegar. One scarce item for which there was no substitute was salt, which was essential for curing meat. The high prices and food shortages led to riots in several cities, most seriously in Richmond early in April 1863. There, about 300 women and children chanting "Bread!" looted a number of stores.

> ✔ **REVIEW**
> In what ways did the Confederacy, which championed states' rights, become a more centralized, national government?

THE UNION HOME FRONT

BECAUSE THE WAR WAS FOUGHT mostly on southern soil, northern civilians rarely felt its effects directly. Yet to be effective, the North's economic resources had to be organized and mobilized.

Government Finances and the Economy

MEASURES TO RAISE MONEY   To begin with, the North required a comprehensive system to finance its massive campaign. Taxing the populace was an obvious means, and taxes paid for 21 percent of Union war expenses, compared with only 1 percent of the Confederacy's. In August 1861 Congress passed the first federal income tax, 3 percent on all incomes over $800 a year. When that, along with increased tariff duties, proved insufficient, Congress enacted a comprehensive tax law in 1862 that for the first time brought the tax collector into every northern household. Excise fees taxed virtually every occupation, commodity, or service; income and inheritances were taxed, as were corporations and consumers. A new bureaucracy, the Internal Revenue Bureau, oversaw the collection process.

The government also borrowed heavily, through the sale of some $2.2 billion in **bonds**, and financed the rest of the war's cost by issuing paper money. In all, the Union printed $431 million in greenbacks (so named because of their color on one side). Although legal for the payment of debts, they could not be redeemed in specie, and therefore their value fluctuated. Also, by taxing state banknotes out of circulation, Congress for the first time created a uniform national currency, as well as a national banking system.

WESTERN DEVELOPMENT   During the war the Republican-controlled Congress encouraged economic development. Tariffs to protect industry from foreign competition rose to an average rate of 47 percent, compared to 19 percent in 1860. To encourage development of the West, the Homestead Act of 1862 granted 160 acres of public land—the size of the traditional American family farm—to anyone (including women) who settled and improved the land for five years. Over a million acres were distributed during the war years alone. In addition, the Land Grant College Act of 1862 donated the proceeds from certain land sales to finance public colleges and universities, creating 69 in all, many in the West.

A Rich Man's War

Over the course of the war the government purchased more than $1 billion worth of goods and services. In response to this heavy demand, the economy boomed and business and agriculture prospered. Wages increased 42 percent between 1860 and 1864, but because prices

©SuperStock/Alamy

| *The superiority of northern industry was an important factor in the war's eventual outcome. Here molten ore is cast into cannons at a foundry in West Point, New York. This factory produced 3,000 cannons during the war.*

horses, and guns that would not fire. At least 20 percent of government expenditures involved fraud.

Stocks and dividends rose with the economy as investors scrambled after profitable new opportunities. An illegal cotton trade flourished in the Mississippi valley, where northern agents bribed military authorities for passes to go through the lines in order to purchase cotton bales from southern planters. The Confederate government quietly traded cotton for contraband such as food, medicine, and enough arms and equipment to maintain an army of 50,000 men.

Women and the Workforce

Even more than in the South, the war opened new opportunities for northern women. Countless wives ran farms while their husbands were away at war. One traveler in Iowa reported, "I met more women driving teams on the road and saw more at work in the fields than men." The war also stimulated the shift to mechanization, which made the northern labor shortage less severe. By 1865 three times as many reapers and harvesters were in use as in 1861.

Beyond the farm women increasingly found work in industry, filling approximately 100,000 new jobs during the war. Like women in the South, they worked as clerks in the expanding government bureaucracy. The work was tedious and the workload heavy, but the new jobs offered good wages, a sense of economic independence, and a pride in having aided the war effort.

rose faster than wages, workers' real income dropped almost 30 percent, from $363 in 1860 to $261 in 1865. That meant the working class paid a disproportionate share of the war's costs.

CORRUPTION AND FRAUD The Republican belief that government should play a major role in the economy also fostered a cozy relationship between business and politics, inviting corruption. In the rush to profit from government contracts, some suppliers sold inferior goods at inflated prices. Uniforms made of "shoddy"—bits of unused thread and recycled cloth—were fobbed off in such numbers that the word became an adjective describing inferior quality. Unscrupulous dealers sold clothing that dissolved in the rain, shoes that fell apart, spoiled meat, broken-down

WOMEN AND MEDICINE The war also allowed women to enter and eventually dominate the profession of nursing. "Our women appear to have become almost wild on the subject of hospital nursing," protested one army physician, who like many others opposed the presence of women in military hospitals. Led by Drs. Emily and Elizabeth Blackwell, Dorothea Dix, and Mary Ann Bickerdyke, women fought the bureaucratic inefficiency of the army medical corps. Their service in the wards of the maimed and dying reduced the hostility to women in medicine.

Clara Barton, like so many other nurses, often found herself in battlefield hospitals, amid massive death and suffering. During the Battle of Fredericksburg she wiped the brows of the wounded and dying, bandaged wounds, and applied tourniquets to stop the flow of blood. She later

Source: Library of Congress, Prints and Photographs Division
[LC-USZ62-46779]

| *Field hospitals were often makeshift, like this house where the surgeon operates in front on a table. The only anesthetic is to the right of the patient's head: a bottle of whiskey. Often, wounded soldiers lay untended or waited so long for help that their open wounds teemed with maggots "as though a swarm of bees had settled" on them. Confederate Walter Lenoir had his wounded leg sawed off below the knee and then endured a 20-mile ride in a crude farm wagon, every jolt causing "a pang which felt as if my stump was thrust into liquid fire."*

recalled that as she rose from the side of one soldier, "I wrung the blood from the bottom of my clothing, before I could step, for the weight about my feet." She steeled herself at the sight of amputated arms and legs casually tossed in piles outside the front door as the surgeons cut away, yet she found the extent of suffering overwhelming. She was jolted by the occasional familiar face among the tangled mass of bodies: the sexton of the church in her hometown, his face caked in blood, or a wayward boy she had befriended years ago. Sleeping in a tent nearby, she drove herself to the brink of exhaustion until the last patients were transferred to permanent hospitals. She then returned to her home in Washington, D.C., where she broke down and wept.

WOMEN AND TEACHING   Before 1861 teaching, too, had been dominated by males, but the shortage of men forced school boards in both sections to turn to women, who were paid half to two-thirds of what men received. After the war teaching increasingly became a female profession, as many women came to see it as a career and not just a temporary occupation. Women also contributed to the war effort through volunteer work. The United States Sanitary Commission was established in 1861 to provide medical supplies and care. Much of its work was performed by women volunteers, who raised funds, collected supplies, and toiled in hospitals alongside paid nurses.

Civil Liberties and Dissent

SUSPENSION OF THE WRIT OF HABEAS CORPUS   In order to mobilize northern society, Lincoln did not hesitate to curb dissenters. Shortly after the firing on Fort Sumter, he suspended the writ of habeas corpus in specified areas, which allowed the indefinite detention of anyone suspected of disloyalty or activity against the war. Although the Constitution permitted such suspension in time of rebellion or invasion, Lincoln did so without consulting Congress (unlike President Davis), and he used his power far more broadly, expanding it in 1862 to cover the entire North for cases involving antiwar activities. Lincoln also decreed that those arrested under its provisions could be tried under the stricter rules of martial law by a military court. Eventually more than 20,000 individuals were arrested, most of whom were never charged with a specific crime or brought to trial.

Democrats attacked Lincoln as a tyrant bent on destroying the Constitution. Among those arrested was Clement Vallandigham, a Democratic member of Congress from Ohio who called for an armistice in May 1963. He was convicted by a military commission and banished to the Confederacy (in 1864 he returned to the North). The Supreme Court refused to review the case, but once the war was over, it ruled in *Ex parte Milligan* (1866) that as long as the regular courts were open, civilians could not be tried by military tribunals.

THE COPPERHEADS   Republicans labeled those who opposed the war **Copperheads**, conjuring up the image of a venomous snake waiting to strike the Union. Copperheads constituted the extreme peace wing of the Democratic Party. Often they had been hurt by the economic changes of the war, but more crucial was their bitter opposition to emancipation and also the draft, which they condemned as a violation of individual freedom and an instrument of special privilege. According to the provisions enacted in 1863, a person would be exempt from the present (but not any future) draft by paying a commutation fee of $300, about a year's wages for a worker or a typical farmer. Or those drafted could hire a substitute, the cost of which was beyond the reach of all but the wealthy. Despite this criticism, in reality poor men also bought their way out of the draft, often by pooling their resources; in addition, the government of some communities paid the commutation fee for any resident who was drafted. In all, approximately 118,000 men provided substitutes, and another 87,000 paid the commutation fee. Perhaps another 160,000 northerners illegally evaded the draft. Only 46,000 men were actually drafted into the Union army, out of more than 2 million who served.

NEW YORK CITY DRAFT RIOT   In July 1863, when the first draftees' names were drawn in New York City, workers in the Irish quarter rose in anger. Rampaging through the streets, the mob attacked draft officials and prominent Republicans, ransacked African American neighborhoods, and lynched black residents who fell into its hands. By the

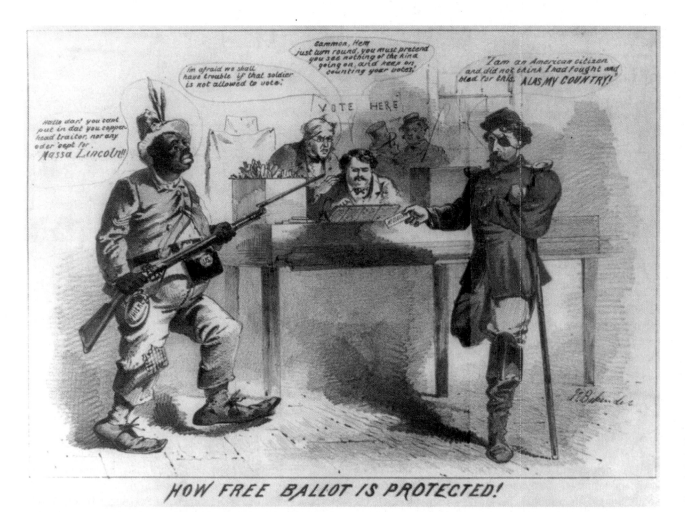

Source: Library of Congress, Prints and Photographs Division [LC-USZ62-89606]

| This anti-Republican cartoon from Philadelphia expresses the fears of many Copperhead Democrats that the war for Union had been subverted by becoming a war on slavery. A caricatured black soldier tries to prevent a legless Union veteran from voting for General George McClellan, Lincoln's opponent in the election of 1864. The election clerk beside the stuffed ballot box is told to "pretend you see nothing" of the ballot stuffing.

time order was restored four days later, at least 105 people had been killed, the worst loss of life from any riot in all of American history. (See After the Fact at the end of the chapter.)

 REVIEW

How did the war affect women in the workforce? How were civil liberties compromised?

GONE TO BE A SOLDIER

MARCUS SPIEGEL CAME TO THE United States after the revolution of 1848 failed in Germany. The son of a rabbi, Spiegel married an American woman, became a naturalized citizen, and was trying to make it in the warehouse business in Ohio when the war began. As an immigrant, he considered it his duty to preserve the Union for his children, and the regular pay of an officer was also enticing, so he enlisted in November 1861. Eventually he became one of the few Jewish colonels in the army. A loyal Democrat, Spiegel did not go to war to end slavery and flatly proclaimed that black people were not "worth fighting for." By early 1864, however, his views had changed. He had "learned and seen more of what the horrors of Slavery was than I ever knew before," and though he still doubted African Americans' capabilities, he now was "in favor of doing away with the institution of Slavery." He assured his wife that "this is no hasty conclusion but a deep conviction." A few weeks later, Marcus Spiegel died of wounds he received while fighting in Louisiana.

Soldiering and Suffering

Fervently committed or not, by war's end about 2 million men had served the Union cause and another million, the Confederate. They were mostly young; almost 40 percent of entering soldiers were age 21 or younger. They were not drawn disproportionately from the poor, and in both the North and the South, farmers and farm laborers accounted

(*left*): Source: Library of Congress, Prints and Photographs Division [LC-DIG-ppmsca-33455]; (*right*): Source: Library of Congress, Prints and Photographs Division [LC-DIG-ppmsca-27046]

| *Soldiers leaving for war often had their pictures taken with their loved ones. Such photographs are reminders of how much the war and its mounting death toll touched civilians as well as soldiers on both sides.*

for the largest group of soldiers. Unskilled workers, who were poorer than other groups, were actually underrepresented in the ranks. It is also a myth that the North hired an army of foreign-born mercenaries. The overwhelming majority of those who wore the blue and the gray were native-born, and the proportion of immigrants in both armies was roughly the same as in the eligible military population.

Most soldiers, like Marcus Spiegel, took patriotism seriously, although officers tended to be more ideological. Enlisted men usually expressed their motivation for fighting in general terms, either to defend the Union or to protect the South. But as Union soldiers personally witnessed the effects of slavery, the majority of them, like Spiegel, came to endorse ending slavery as a war aim.

DISEASE AND MEDICAL CARE   On average, soldiers spent 50 days in camp for every day in battle. Camp life was often unhealthy as well as unpleasant. Poor sanitation, miserable food, exposure to the elements, and primitive medical care contributed to widespread sickness. Officers and men alike regarded army doctors as quacks and tried to avoid them. It was a common belief that if a fellow went to the hospital, "you might as well say good bye." Conditions were even worse in the Confederate hospitals, for the Union blockade produced a shortage of medical supplies. Twice as many soldiers died from dysentery, typhoid, and other diseases as from wounds.

Treatment at field hospitals was a chilling experience. Ignorance was responsible for the existing conditions and practices, because nothing was known about germs or how wounds became infected. Years later an appalled federal surgeon recounted:

> We operated in old blood-stained and often pus-stained coats. . . . We used undisinfected instruments . . . and still worse, used marine sponges which had been used in prior pus cases and had been only washed in tap water. . . . Our silk to tie blood vessels was undisinfected. . . . We dressed the wounds with clean but undisinfected sheets, shirts, tablecloths, or other old soft linen rescued from the family ragbag. . . . We knew nothing about antiseptics and therefore used none.

DECLINE OF MORALITY   The boredom of camp life, the horrors of battle, and the influence of an all-male society all corrupted morals. Swearing and heavy drinking were common, and one Mississippian reported that after payday games of chance were "running night and day, with eager and excited crowds standing around with their hands full of money." Prostitutes flooded the camps of both armies, and an Illinois private stationed in Pulaski, Tennessee, wrote home that the price schedule in each of the brothels in town was quite reasonable. "You may think I am a hard case," he conceded, "but I am as pious as you can find in the army."

With death so near, some soldiers sought solace in religion. Religious fervor was greater in the Confederate camps, and a wave of revivals swept the ranks during the last two winters of the war, producing between 100,000 and 200,000 conversions. Significantly, the first major revivals occurred after the South's twin defeats at Vicksburg and Gettysburg. Then, too, as battle after battle thinned Confederate ranks, death became much more likely.

Death on the Field and at Home

The Civil War compelled the divided nation to confront death as never before. North and South, battle front and home front, slave and free, men and women, rich and poor: nearly all Americans living through the Civil War found themselves surrounded by the immediate reality of death or its profound and multiplying consequences at every turn.

CARNAGE AT THE FRONT   Most obviously, Americans at the front produced death and bore witness to it on a staggering scale. Upward of three-quarters of a million men died in the war. The conflict lasted 1,458 days, claiming more than 500 lives each day on average. But of course the war's carnage did not unfold gradually. The scale of the violence increased as the conflict ground on, and much of the dying came in staggering, appalling surges at places thereafter synonymous with death—places like Bull Run, Shiloh, Antietam, Gettysburg.

| Trenches like this Confederate fortification at the Battle of Petersburg disrupted both the land and the forests that supplied the wood.
Source: National Archives & Records Administration (NWDNS-111-B-372)

Technological advances in the tools of destruction helped account for staggering losses. Smoothbore muskets, which at first served as the basic infantry weapon, gave way to the rifle, so named because of the grooves etched into the barrel to give a bullet spin. A new bullet, the minié ball, allowed the rifle to be easily loaded, and the invention of the percussion cap rendered it serviceable in wet weather. More important, the new weapon had an effective range of 400 yards—four times greater than that of the old musket. As a result, soldiers fought each other from greater distances and hit their targets far more frequently. Battles took much longer to fight and produced vastly more casualties. Under such conditions, the defense became a good deal stronger than the offense. The larger artillery pieces also adopted rifled barrels, but they lacked good fuses and accurate sighting devices and could not effectively support attacking troops. Artillery remained a deadly defensive weapon, however, one that devastated advancing infantry at close range. More than 100 regiments on both sides suffered in excess of 50 percent casualties in a single battle.

As the haze of gunfire covered the land and the constant spray of bullets mimicked rain pattering through the treetops, soldiers discovered that their romantic notions about war had no place on the battlefield. Men witnessed horrors they had never envisioned as civilians and choked from the stench of decaying flesh and mortal slaughter. They realized that their efforts to convey to those back home the gruesome truth of combat were inadequate. "No tongue can tell, no mind can conceive, no pen portray the horrible sights I witnessed this morning," a Union soldier wrote after Antietam. And still they tried.

An Indiana soldier at Perryville (7,600 casualties): "It was an awful sight to see there men torn all to pieces with cannon balls and bom shells[.] [T]he dead and wounded lay thick in all directions." An Ohio soldier at Antietam (23,000 casualties), two days after the fighting: "The smell was offul . . . there was about 5 or 6,000 dead bodes decaying over the field. . . . I could have walked on the boddees all most from one end too the other." A Georgian, the day after Chancellorsville (30,000 casualties): "It looked more like a slaughter pen than anything else. . . . The shrieks and groans of the wounded . . . was heart rending beyond all description." A Maine soldier who fought at Gettysburg (50,000 casualties): "I have Seen . . . men rolling in their own blood, Some Shot in one place, Some another . . . our dead lay in the road and the Rebels in their hast to leave dragged both their baggage wagons and artillery over them and they lay mangled and torn to pieces so that Even friends could not tell them. You can form no idea of a battlefield."

Surrounded by the wreckage of war, amid the sounds and smells and sight of thousands of dead or dying men, soldiers who fell on the battlefield struggled to die as they thought they should. If they made it to a camp hospital, they might look to exhausted nurses, doctors, or aides to stay with them in their final moments. They might give comrades or outright strangers messages for kin—parents, wives, siblings, and children they knew they would never see again. Many tens of thousands simply died where they fell; some immediately, others more slowly, and some others granted final moments with treasured photographs or with letters from people they loved. Survivors became hardened through horror. "The daily sight of blood and mangled bodies," observed a Rhode Island soldier, "so blunted their finer sensibilities as almost to blot out all love, all sympathy from the heart."

THE BUSINESS OF GRIEF This multitude of war dead forced immense tasks upon the living. Millions of people across the country would spend years and lifetimes grieving as a

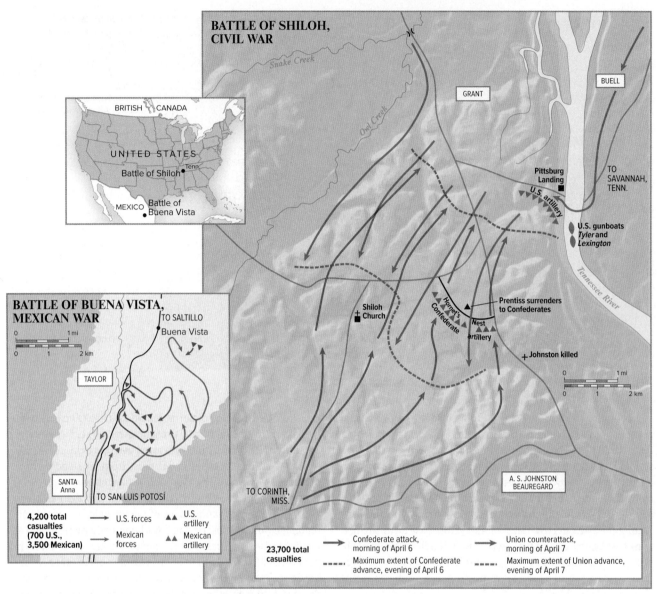

BATTLE OF SHILOH, CIVIL WAR

BRITISH CANADA

UNITED STATES

Battle of Shiloh • Tenn.

MEXICO • Battle of Buena Vista

GRANT

BUELL

Snake Creek

Owl Creek

Pittsburg Landing

TO SAVANNAH, TENN.

U.S. artillery

U.S. gunboats *Tyler* and *Lexington*

Tennessee River

Hornet's Confederate

Prentiss surrenders to Confederates

Nest artillery

Shiloh Church

+ Johnston killed

A. S. JOHNSTON BEAUREGARD

TO CORINTH, MISS.

0   1 mi
0   1   2 km

23,700 total casualties

→ Confederate attack, morning of April 6
---- Maximum extent of Confederate advance, evening of April 6
→ Union counterattack, morning of April 7
---- Maximum extent of Union advance, evening of April 7

BATTLE OF BUENA VISTA, MEXICAN WAR

TO SALTILLO
Buena Vista

0   1 mi
0   1   2 km

TAYLOR

SANTA Anna

TO SAN LUIS POTOSÍ

4,200 total casualties (700 U.S., 3,500 Mexican)

→ U.S. forces
→ Mexican forces
▲▲ U.S. artillery
▲▲ Mexican artillery

A NEW MAGNITUDE OF BATTLE

During the U.S.-Mexican War at Buena Vista (February 22–23, 1847), the American army of 4,800 men was overextended trying to defend a 2-mile line against 15,000 Mexicans. At Shiloh (April 6–7, 1862), in contrast, battle lines stretched almost 6 miles. (The maps are drawn to the same scale.) Against 40,000 Confederates, Grant galloped back and forth, rallying some 35,000 troops organized under five subordinates and coordinating the overnight reinforcement of 25,000 troops. The size of the armies, the complexity of their organization, the length of battle lines, and the number of casualties all demonstrate the extent to which the magnitude of battle had changed.

consequence of the war. They wanted to know how their loved ones died, wanted to know where their bodies were, and, increasingly, wanted to retrieve those bodies and bury them closer to home. The railroad network and the new practice of embalming made this heartfelt desire possible for the first time in the history of warfare. Volunteers like Clara Barton organized to help grieving families locate the bodies of their fallen soldiers. A feverish alliance of shipping agents and undertakers emerged to meet demand. Embalmers propped up the preserved corpses of unknown dead in shop windows to advertise their services. Responding to popular pressure, the U.S. government pledged to help in the task of identification and recovery—eventually

spending $4 million to identify the resting places of half the Union's fallen soldiers and to rebury most of them. Not until 1906 would the national government assume the same responsibilities for Confederate dead. Instead, such tasks fell to state governments and, after the war, to civic organizations like the Daughters of the Confederacy.

 REVIEW

How did the massive and constant presence of death change Civil War Americans?

THE UNION'S TRIUMPH

WHILE TALKING TO A NEIGHBOR in Covington, Georgia, Dolly Lunt suddenly saw the bluecoats coming down the road. Thinking to herself, "Oh God, the time of trial has come!" she ran home as fast as she could. William Tecumseh Sherman's dreaded army had arrived at her gate. As the Union troops swarmed over the yard, they cleaned out the smokehouse and dairy, stripped the kitchen and cellar of their contents, and killed her fowl and hogs. They broke open locks, smashed down doors, seized items of no military value such as kitchen utensils and even a doll, and marched off some of the male slaves. Not content with plundering the main house, the troops entered the slave cabins and rifled them of every valuable, even the money some of the slaves had made by doing extra work. Lunt spent a supperless night huddled in the house with her remaining slaves, who were clutching their meager possessions. As darkness descended, she reported, "the heavens from every point were lit up with flames from burning buildings." The war had come to Dolly Lunt's doorstep.

Confederate High Tide

In the spring of 1863 matters still looked promising for Lee. At the Battle of Chancellorsville, he brilliantly defeated Lincoln's latest commander, Joseph Hooker. But during the fighting the ingenious and relentless General Stonewall Jackson was accidentally shot by his own men, and he died a few days later—a grievous setback for the Confederacy. Determined to take the offensive, Lee made a characteristically audacious decision and invaded Pennsylvania in June with an army of 75,000. Lincoln's newest general, George Gordon Meade, warily shadowed the Confederates. On the first of July, advance parties from the two armies accidentally collided at the town of Gettysburg, and the war's greatest battle ensued.

THE BATTLE OF GETTYSBURG The iconic battle unfolded over the course of three bloody days. Confederate forces enjoyed some successes at first, before either side had all its troops in position, and these successes left Lee emboldened. He instructed General Richard Ewell, in command of Stonewall Jackson's corps, to seize a critical Union position called Cemetery Ridge, "if practicable." Jackson would have taken this for an order and charged his men up the hill. But Ewell, far more cautious, took Lee's wording as a suggestion rather than a command and decided against an attack. Some historians have speculated whether this inaction was the critical missed opportunity in the battle.

By the second day most Union and Confederate troops had reached Gettysburg. Northern forces arrayed themselves in a formidable defensive line—so formidable that Lee's top subordinate urged him to withdraw and find a more defensible position somewhere to the east. Lee refused, and desperate fighting raged for a second day. The rebels won some close-fought engagements, but failed to consolidate them for lack of coordination. By dusk both sides had endured great casualties, but the robust Union lines held. Again Lee was urged to withdraw. Again he refused. Convinced that he had left Union men bloodied and demoralized, he decided to mass his forces for a coordinated attack on Meade's center the following day. It would prove to be the costliest mistake of his military career.

The third day opened with some surprising Union victories, including one led by a dashing 23-year-old General named George Armstrong Custer. Not until early afternoon did Lee's plan become clear. Around 1 p.m. he gave the order and the sky exploded as massed Confederate artillery blasted away at the Union center. Meade responded in kind, and for an hour Gettysburg was a deafening furnace of explosions and shattering bodies. Then, one by one, the Union guns fell silent. Convinced that he had disabled Meade's artillery and believing victory was at hand, Lee ordered three Confederate divisions to take the Union positions. Remembered as "Pickett's Charge," after General George Pickett, the effort started off confidently with some 12,500 Confederate soldiers marching up to Cemetery Ridge. But the silencing of artillery had been a ruse; once the Confederate infantrymen were well advanced, union cannons roared back to life and began blasting them to pieces. Meade's soldiers poured musket and rifle fire into the cratering Confederate charge, with horrible results. "Pickett's division just seemed to melt away in the blue musketry smoke which now covered the hill," one Confederate officer wrote. "Nothing but stragglers came back."

Indeed, only half of the men in the charge returned to Lee's lines, leaving the great general distraught. "It's all my fault," he exclaimed. "You must help me. All good men must rally." But there would be no rally. Lee managed to get most of his surviving men back across the Potomac, barely. Lincoln implored Meade to throw his army at the retreating Confederates and finish it. But Meade's men were battered, bloody, and exhausted; and their general would do little more than harry Lee's retreat. "We had only to stretch forth our hands and they were ours," Lincoln wrote, inconsolably. "And nothing I could say or do could make the Army move." Gettysburg did not end the war. But it did rob Lee of more than 25,000 men—a third of his force. Never again would he be in a position to take the fight to the North.

Gettysburg dealt a hard blow to Confederate foreign policy as well. Soon after the battle, France's minister in Washington paid a visit to Secretary of State William Seward and acknowledged that southern defeat was now inevitable. He promised to convey his views to Emperor Napoléon III. During the first years of the war, the Confederacy had worked tirelessly to secure European recognition. England and especially France expressed sympathy in return, but after Gettysburg, recognition seemed all but impossible and the southern cause all the more desperate.

Lincoln Finds His General

CAPTURE OF VICKSBURG To the west, Grant had been trying for months to capture Vicksburg, a Rebel stronghold on the Mississippi. In a daring maneuver, he left behind his supply lines and marched inland, calculating that he could feed his

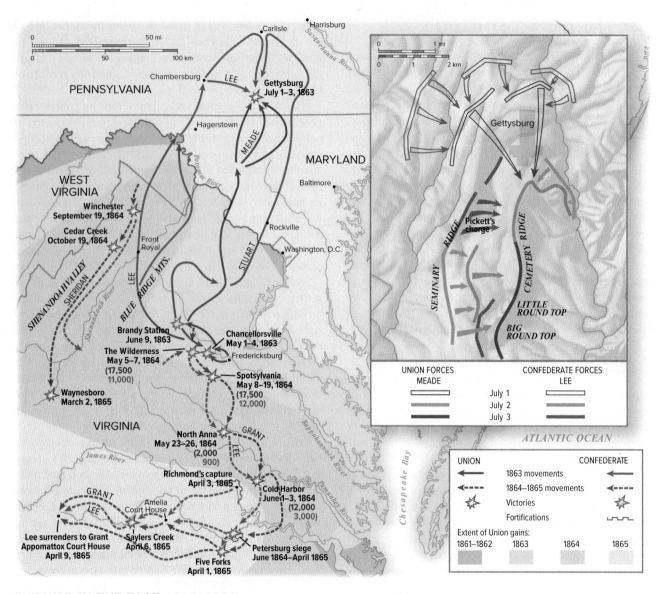

THE WAR IN THE EAST, 1863-1865

Lee won his most brilliant victory at Chancellorsville, then launched a second invasion of the North, hoping to score a decisive victory. When the two armies accidentally collided at Gettysburg on July 1, 1863, the Union's Army of the Potomac took up a strong defensive position, shaped like a fishhook and anchored by a hill at each end (see map inset). On July 2 the Confederate attack drove back the Union's left flank but failed to dislodge the right. Lee's assault on the center of the Union line on July 3 ended in a shattering defeat, and the Army of Northern Virginia retreated to Virginia. In 1864 Grant delivered a series of heavy blows against Lee's outnumbered forces in Virginia. Despite staggering losses, Grant relentlessly pressed on. Note the casualties listed for the spring and summer of 1864; from mid-May to mid-June, Grant lost nearly 60,000 men, equal to Lee's strength (listed in parentheses). Sheridan's raids against the civilian farms of the Shenandoah Valley helped deprive Lee of desperately needed supplies. On April 9, 1865, too weak to defend Richmond any longer, Lee surrendered at the Appomattox Court House.

army from the produce of Confederate farms, weakening southern resistance in the process. Few before Grant had tried these tactics. His troops drove the defenders of Vicksburg back into the city and starved them into submission. On July 4, the city surrendered. With the fall of Port Hudson, Louisiana, four days later, the Mississippi was completely in Union hands. Grant had divided the Confederacy and isolated Arkansas, Texas, and part of Louisiana from the rest of the South.

He followed up this victory by rescuing Union forces holed up in Chattanooga. His performance confirmed Lincoln's earlier judgment that "Grant is my man, and I am his the rest of the war." Congress now revived the rank of lieutenant general, held before only by George Washington, which Lincoln bestowed on Grant. In March 1864 Lincoln brought him east and put him in command of all the Union armies.

GRANT IN COMMAND   Grant recognized that the Union possessed the resources to wear down the Confederacy but that its larger armies had "acted independently and without concert, like a balky team, no two ever pulling together." He intended to change that. While he launched a major offensive against Lee in Virginia, William Tecumseh Sherman, who replaced Grant as commander of the western army, would drive a diagonal wedge through the Confederacy from Tennessee across Georgia. Grant's orders to Sherman were as blunt as his response had been that rainy night when the two had conferred at Shiloh: "Get into the interior of the enemy's country so far as you can, inflicting all the damage you can against their war resources."

UNION'S SUMMER OFFENSIVE   In May and June 1864 Grant tried to maneuver Lee out of the trenches and into an open battle. But Lee was too weak to win head-on, so he opted for a strategy of attrition, hoping to inflict such heavy losses that the northern will to continue fighting would break. It was a strategy that nearly worked, for Union casualties were staggering. In a month of fierce fighting, the Army of the Potomac lost 60,000 men—the size of Lee's entire army at the beginning of the campaign. Yet at the end of the campaign Grant's reinforced army was larger than when it started, whereas Lee's was significantly weaker.

After especially bloody losses at the Battle of Cold Harbor, Grant changed tactics. He marched his army around Richmond and settled into a siege of Petersburg, which guarded Richmond's last remaining rail link to the south. A siege would be agonizingly slow, but he counted on his numerical superiority to eventually stretch Lee's line to the breaking point. In the west, meanwhile, the gaunt and grizzled Sherman fought his way by July to the outskirts of Atlanta, which was heavily defended. "Our all depends on that army at Atlanta," wrote Mary Chesnut in August, based on her conversations with Confederate leaders. "If that fails us, the game is up."

War in the Balance

The game was nearly up for Lincoln as the 1864 election approached. In 1863 the victories at Gettysburg and Vicksburg sparked Republican victories, indicating that public opinion seemed to be swinging toward emancipation. But as the Union war machine swept more and more northerners south to their deaths and as Grant and Sherman bogged down on the Virginia and Georgia fronts, even leaders in Lincoln's own party began to mutter out loud that Lincoln was not equal to the task.

1864 ELECTION   Perhaps the most remarkable thing about the 1864 election is that it was held at all. Indeed, before World War II, the United States was the only democratic government in history to carry out a general election in wartime. But Lincoln firmly believed that to postpone it would be to lose the priceless heritage of republicanism itself: "We cannot have free government without elections, and if the rebellion could force us to forego or postpone a national election, it might fairly claim to have already conquered and ruined us." Exploiting his control of the party machinery, Lincoln easily won the Republican nomination, and he made certain that the Republican platform called for the adoption of a constitutional amendment abolishing slavery. To balance the ticket, the convention selected Andrew Johnson, the military governor of Tennessee and a pro-war Democrat, as his running mate. The two men ran under the label of the "Union" Party.

The Democrats nominated George McClellan, the former Union commander. Their platform pronounced the war a failure and called for an armistice and a peace conference. Warned that a cessation of fighting would lead to disunion, McClellan partially repudiated this position, insisting that "the Union is the one condition of peace—we ask no more." In private he made it clear that if elected he intended to restore slavery. Late in August, Lincoln was still gloomy about his prospects as well as those of the Union itself. But Admiral David Farragut won a dramatic victory at Mobile Bay, and a few weeks later, in early September, Sherman finally captured Atlanta. As Secretary of State Seward gleefully noted, "Sherman and Farragut have knocked the bottom out of the Chicago [Democratic] nominations."

SIGNIFICANCE OF LINCOLN'S REELECTION   Polling an impressive 55 percent of the popular vote, Lincoln won 212 electoral votes to McClellan's 21. Eighteen states allowed soldiers to vote in the field, and Lincoln received nearly 80 percent of their ballots. One lifelong Democrat described the sentiment in the army: "We all want peace, but none any but

Source: Library of Congress, Prints and Photographs Division [LC-DIG-ppmsca-21710]

| *Union soldiers vote in the election of 1864, in a camp near Petersburg, Virginia. The troops gave strong support to Lincoln—nearly 80 percent, compared to 55 percent of the popular vote.*

INVADERS AND DEFENDERS

William Christie from Minnesota was one of the Union soldiers under Grant's army as it besieged and then occupied Vicksburg. His letter shows the mixture of hardship, boredom, horror, and hilarity that were the lot of ordinary soldiers. Nancy Emerson lived in Augusta County, Virginia, in the Shenandoah Valley. She was a fervent Confederate who found Union raiders at her doorstep.

DOCUMENT 1
A Union View of Occupying Vicksburg: William Christie

July 19th Dear Brother I once more resume my pen, to scrible a few lines to you. We are much Pleased here with the Prospects in Tenn: and Penn, and are well satisfied with our own achievements. . . . The Mississippi River is oppen and the Southern Confederacy is cut in twain, it will be out of the question to think that the Pesky critter can live without the tail, and if Meade only gives the Head a scrunch with his heel we will soon make away with the Body.

This city is very nicely situated, and has been very handsome Before the war. I have been over the whole Place and I have changed my mind in regard to its appearance. Tis very filthy and although large gangs of Negroes have been employed in cleaning the streets, there has been But little, apparently, (comparitivly speaking) done the Rebels have been very filthy [during the siege], and it has just been here as every where else. We have been driven to a great Deal of work for healths sake. There are waggon loads of old rags of clothing, full of vermin and

disgusting to Behold, there are one or two Rebel hospitals in town, and you can tell long before you come near them By the odorous stench, where they are, and let me assure you that they as a general thing have a Peculiar odor, belong[ing] to their camps and hospitals, and you can tell when Passing through a country, where troops of Both sides have been camped. the difference, between each camp By the smell even before you see a scrap of clothing or anything else to tell the difference by. . . .

You complain of having nothing to write about, what do you suppose we Poor Devils have to write about, nothing only drumming here: and drumming there, drumming everywhere, and fiffing for the same. . . . Next we might tell of transport hot weather, then of the daily arrivals of Contraband, from the cane brakes, where they have been hid away by there masters, untill so near dead with exposure and want, poisoned by vines of various kinds, and in such horrid Plight, that numbers drop Dead in the streets, or

lie down in some unoccupied house, and die. Is this war too much for the Nation, that has had such a system in it that bears such fruits. No, and untill this accursed thing is Put from among us there will be no end to the war. . . .

My letters are wearisome, I know. But there is only one excuse for me writing and that is it lets you know I am well, I am also light in weight, (not to say or imply anything else) Being, only 140 lbs. By the scales so you see I am But a bunch of Bones: But lively and well. . . . Be Patient in all things, is my advice to you and if I had only written so at the head of this letter you would have been profittably warned and spared you self the trouble of reading such a jumble of nonsense, Read and forgive, and Remember me to all,

Believe me your affecttionate Brother

Wm G. Christie

Source: Letter of William G. Christie, July 16 [and 19], 1862. Minnesota Historical Society, facsimile text at www.mnhs.org/library/Christie/letters/0716631.html.

DOCUMENT 2
A Confederate View of Union Raiders: Nancy Emerson

Our friends at the North have probably been thinking some about us of late, hearing that the Yankees have taken Staunton, though *what* they have thought is beyond my power to divine, ignorant as we are of each others feelings. Sister C. & I very often talk of them, wonder how they fare & what they think of us, whether they set us down for incorrigible rebels against "the best government in the world," always winding up however by arguing that we do not & cannot believe they favor this unjust & abominable war, though such strange things happen these days that nothing ought to astonish us. . . .

The first day, they came in from the West, across the mountain. A party of 40

or 50 perhaps, came riding up, dismounted & rushed in. "Have you got any whiskey" said they, "got any flour? got any bacon?" with plenty of oaths "Come on boys," says one, "we'll find it all" With that, they pushed rudely by Sister C. who was terribly alarmed, & had been from the first news of their coming, & spread them selves nearly all over the house. Finding their way to a fine barrel of flour which a neighbor had given us, they proceeded to fill their sacks & pillow cases, scattering a large percent on the floor, till it was nearly exhausted. . . . Some went upstairs, opened every trunk & drawer & tossed things upside down or on the floor, even my nice bonnets, pretending to be looking for arms. . . . We did not say anything to

provoke them, but did not disguise our sentiments. They went peeping under the beds, looking for rebels as they said. Baxter told them there were no rebels here (meaning rebel soldiers) Cate spoke & said *We are all rebels.* Ellen spoke & said "Yes Baxter, I am a rebel." The Yankee looked up from her drawer, which he was searching just then, & said "That's right." Cate then said, "I am a rebel too & I *glory* in it." . . .

At one of our neighbors, they took every thing they had to eat, all the pillow cases & sheets but what were on the beds, & the towels & some of the ladies stockings. . . . At another neighbors, they took all of their meat (some 30 pieces of bacon) & nearly everything else they had to eat, all their horses (4) & persuaded off their two negro men. One of these was afterwards seen by one of our men crying to come back, but was watched so closely that he could not escape. No wonder he cried. He has been twice on the brink of the grave with pneumonia, & was nursed by his mistress as tenderly as if he had been a brother, & she was always kind to him, his master also. He will not find such treatment anywhere else. . . .

Some hid their things & had them discovered but we were more fortunate. (Some were betrayed by their servants) Some hid nothing, thinking they would not be disturbed but found themselves woefully mistaken. Others thought they might be worse dealt with if they hid anything. A lady near Staunton a little time since had two Yankee officers come to take tea with her. She was strong "secesh," but she got them a good supper. It was served up in very plain dishes. They perceived that she was wealthy, & inquired if she had not hid her plate &c. She told them she had. They asked *where*. She told them in the ash heap. They said "That is not a good place. It is the first place searched." They then very kindly & politely showed her a good place (in their opinion). She followed their advice & saved her things. In another instance, some Yankee officers politely showed a lady where to hide her silver &c. The soldiers came & searched in vain. Just as they were going away, a little black chap who had followed them around says to them in a tone of triumph, "Ah you did not find Missis things hid inside the _____."

Source: The Diary of Nancy Emerson, Albert and Shirley Small Special Collections Library, University of Virginia, Charlottesville, Virginia. Available online at http://valley.lib. virginia.edu/papers/EmeDiar#n5.

THINKING CRITICALLY

What is the "Pesky critter" in William Christie's first paragraph? What does he mean by "this accursed thing" in the second to last paragraph? Nancy Emerson indicates that she is strongly "secesh." But in what ways is she ambivalent about Northerners? What range of experiences do these documents reveal in the behavior of slaves?

an honorable one. I had rather stay out here a lifetime (much as I dislike it) than consent to a division of our country." Jefferson Davis remained defiant, but the last hope of a Confederate victory was gone.

THIRTEENTH AMENDMENT Equally important, the election of 1864 ended any doubt that slavery would be abolished in the reconstructed Union. The Emancipation Proclamation had not put an end to the question, for its legal status remained unclear. Lincoln and the Republicans insisted that a constitutional amendment was necessary to secure emancipation. After the election, the president threw all his influence behind the drive to round up the necessary votes, and the measure passed the House on January 31, 1865. By December enough states had ratified the Thirteenth Amendment to make it part of the Constitution.

ABOLITION AS A GLOBAL MOVEMENT The abolition of slavery in the United States was part of a worldwide trend. The antislavery movement was spearheaded in Britain, where Parliament abolished slavery in the empire in 1833. The other colonial powers were much slower to act. Portugal did not end slavery in its New World colonies until 1836, Sweden in 1847, Denmark and France in 1848, Holland in 1863, and Spain not until 1886. Most of the Latin American republics had ended slavery when they threw off Spanish or Portuguese control, but the institution remained important in Cuba and Brazil; Spain abolished slavery in Cuba in 1886, and Brazil ended the institution in 1888. European reformers also crusaded against slavery in Africa and Asia, and indeed the antislavery movement increased European presence in Africa. At the same time, European nations ended the medieval institution of serfdom. In Russia, where serfdom had most closely approximated slavery, Czar Alexander II emancipated the serfs in 1861, an act that led him to strongly favor the Union in the American Civil War.

The Twilight of the Confederacy

CONFEDERACY'S ABANDONMENT OF SLAVERY For the Confederacy the outcome of the 1864 election had a terrible finality. At the beginning of the war, Vice President Stephens had proclaimed slavery the cornerstone of the Confederacy, but in March 1865 the Confederate Congress authorized recruiting 300,000 slaves for military service. When signing the bill, Davis announced that freedom would be given to those who volunteered and to their families. That same month he offered through a special envoy to abolish slavery in exchange for British diplomatic recognition. A Mississippi paper denounced this proposal as "a total abandonment of the chief object of this war." The British rejected the offer, and the war ended before any slaves were mustered into the Confederate army, but the abandonment of slavery surely completed the Confederacy's internal revolution. The demands of war had forced Confederate leaders to forsake the Old South's fundamental values and institutions.

In the wake of Lincoln's reelection the Confederate will to resist rapidly disintegrated. White southerners had never fully united behind the war effort, but the large majority had endured great suffering to uphold it. As Sherman pushed deeper into the Confederacy and General Philip Sheridan mounted his devastating raid on the Shenandoah Valley, the war came home to southern civilians as never before. "We haven't got nothing in the house to eat but a little bit o meal," wrote the wife of one Alabama soldier in December 1864. "Try to get off and come home and fix us all up some and then you can go back. . . . If you put off a-coming, 'twont be no use to come, for we'll all . . . [be] in the grave yard." He deserted. In the last months of the fighting, more than half the Confederacy's soldiers were absent without leave.

MARCH TO THE SEA After the fall of Atlanta, Sherman imitated Grant's strategy by abandoning his supply lines for an audicious 300-mile march to the sea. Sherman intended to deprive Lee's army of the supplies it desperately needed to continue and to break the southern will to resist. Or as he bluntly put it, "to whip the Rebels, to humble their pride, to follow them to their recesses, and make them fear and dread us."

Moving in four columns, Sherman's army covered about 10 miles a day, cutting a path of destruction 50 miles wide. "We had a gay old campaign," one of his soldiers wrote. "Destroyed all we could not eat, stole their niggers, burned their cotton and gins, spilled their sorghum, burned and twisted their railroads and raised Hell generally." Sherman estimated that his men did $100 million in damage, of which $20 million was necessary to supply his army and the rest was wanton destruction. After he captured Savannah in late December, he turned north and wreaked even greater havoc in South Carolina, which Union troops considered the seedbed of the rebellion.

By December the interior of the Confederacy was essentially conquered. Only Lee's army remained, entrenched around Petersburg, Virginia, as Grant relentlessly extended his lines, stretching the Confederates thinner and thinner. On April 2 Confederate forces evacuated Richmond.

LEE'S SURRENDER Grant doggedly pursued the Army of Northern Virginia westward for another hundred miles. After Union forces captured supplies waiting for Lee at Appomattox Court House, the weary gentleman from Virginia asked to see Grant. Lee surrendered on April 9, 1865. As the vanquished foe mounted his horse, Grant saluted by raising his hat; Lee raised his respectfully and rode off at a slow trot. "On our part," one federal officer wrote, there was "not a sound of trumpet . . . nor roll of drum; not a cheer . . . but an awed stillness rather." The guns were quiet.

With Lee's army gone, resistance throughout the Confederacy collapsed within a matter of weeks. Visiting the captured city of Richmond on April 4, Lincoln was enthusiastically greeted by the black population. He looked "pale, haggard, utterly worn out," noted one observer. The lines in his face showed how much the war had aged him in only four years. Often his friends had counseled rest, but Lincoln had observed that "the tired part of me is *inside* and out of reach." Day after day, the grim telegrams had arrived at the War Department, or mothers had come to see him, begging him to spare their youngest son because the other two had died in battle. The burden, he confessed, was almost too much to bear.

LINCOLN'S ASSASSINATION Back in Washington the president received news of Lee's surrender with relief. The evening of April 14, Lincoln, seeking a welcome escape, went to see a comedy at Ford's Theater. In the midst of the performance John Wilkes Booth, a mentally unstable actor and Confederate sympathizer, slipped into the presidential box

Pivot Points along the Union's Road to Victory

	MILITARY	POLITICAL	SOCIAL/ECONOMIC
1861	Naval blockade set up	Lincoln secures border states for Union; First Confiscation Act frees slaves used for Confederate military purposes	Wartime demand sparks economic boom in industry and agriculture
1862	Grant succeeds in his western campaigns	Legal Tender Act; first federal income tax	Northern factories turn out military supplies; railroad construction
1863	Stonewall Jackson dies; Battles of Gettysburg and Vicksburg	Emancipation Proclamation issued	African Americans increasingly defect from southern plantations, join Union forces
1864	Grant given command of Union armies; Sherman marches through Georgia, captures Atlanta	Lincoln wins election in middle of war	Broader public support as military victories buoy North
1865	Sherman drives through Carolinas; Lee surrenders to Grant at Appomattox Court House		

THE WAR IN THE WEST, 1863–1865

Source: Library of Congress, Prints and Photographs Division [LC-USZC4-4166]

"It would cause me more sadness than satisfaction to be ordered to the command of the Army of the Potomac. Here [in the West] I know the officers and men and what each Gen. is capable of as a separate commander. There I would have all to learn.—Ulysses S. Grant, after the fall of Vicksburg, August 5, 1863

CONTEXT

The Union continued its war of mobility in the western theater, bringing more Confederate territory under its control. After Grant captured Vicksburg, the entire Mississippi lay in Union hands. His victories at Lookout Mountain and Missionary Ridge, near Chattanooga, ended the Confederate threat to Tennessee. In 1864 Sherman divided the Confederacy by seizing Atlanta and marching across Georgia; then he turned north. When Joseph Johnston surrendered several weeks after Lee's capitulation at Appomattox, the war was effectively over.

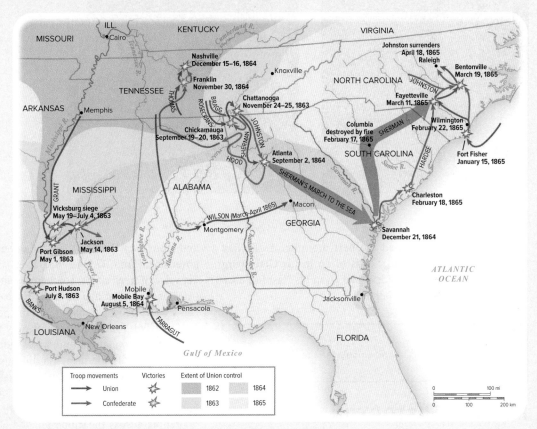

MAP READING

1. Trace the Union's drive up and down the Mississippi.
2. Trace the progress of Sherman's army.
3. Trace the engagements in and around Tennessee after the fall of Vicksburg.

MAP INTERPRETATION

1. Why was control of the Mississippi River so crucial to Union military strategy?
2. What made Sherman's march a particularly risky and daring strategy?
3. Why did Tennessee and the surrounding territory become the focus of so much of the fighting?
4. What was Sherman's purpose in heading north after the destruction of Columbia, South Carolina?

| The war's greatest generals, Ulysses S. Grant (left) and Robert E. Lee (right), confronted each other in the eastern theater during the last year of the war. A member of a distinguished Virginia family, the tall, impeccably dressed Lee was every inch the aristocratic gentleman. Grant, a short, slouched figure with a stubby beard, dressed indifferently, often wearing a private's uniform with only the stars on his shoulders to indicate his rank. But his determination is readily apparent in this picture, taken at his field headquarters in 1864.

(left): ©Library of Congress/Corbis/Getty Images; (right): Source: Library of Congress, Prints and Photographs Division [LC-USZ61-903]

and shot him. Lincoln died the next morning. As he had called upon his fellow Americans to do in his Gettysburg Address, the sixteenth president had given his "last full measure of devotion" to the Republic.

 REVIEW
What decisions by Grant and Lincoln led the Union to victory?

PUTTING HISTORY IN GLOBAL CONTEXT

THE ASSASSINATION, WHICH CAPPED four years of bloody war, left a tiredness in the nation's bones—a tiredness "inside" and not easily within reach. In every way the conflict had produced fundamental, often devastating changes. There was, of course, the carnage. Hundreds of thousands of men on both sides lost their lives, almost as many as in all the other wars the nation has fought from the Revolution through Vietnam combined. In material terms, the conflict cost an estimated $20 billion, or about 10 times the value of all slaves in the country in 1860

and more than 11 times the total amount spent by the federal government from 1789 to 1861. Even without adding the market value of freed slaves, southern wealth declined 43 percent, transforming what had been the richest section in the nation (on a white per-capita basis) into the poorest.

The Civil War reordered not only the national economy but also economic relations worldwide. Manufacturers were forced to supply the army on an unprecedented scale over great distances. One consequence was the creation of truly national industries in flour milling, meat packing, clothing and shoe manufacture, and machinery making.

People across the globe felt the effects of the war, particularly due to changes in the cotton trade. By 1860 the South was supplying more than three-quarters of all cotton imported by Britain, France, Germany, and Russia. When the war cut off that supply, manufacturers scrambled to find new sources. India, Egypt, and Brazil all improved their railroad facilities and ports in order to encourage planters to open new cotton fields. The effect of the trade on Egypt was so great, historians of that nation rank the American Civil War along with the construction of the Suez Canal as the most crucial events in its nineteenth-century history.

Politically, the war dramatically changed the balance of power. The South lost its substantial influence, as did the Democratic Party, while the Republicans emerged in a dominant position. The Union's military victory also signaled the triumph of nationalism. The war destroyed the idea that the Union was a voluntary confederacy of sovereign states. The Union was perpetual, as Andrew Jackson had first suggested—truly an indivisible nation.

In the short run the price was disillusionment and bitterness. The war's corrosive effect on morals corrupted American politics, destroyed idealism, and crippled humanitarian reform. Millennialism and perfectionism were victims of the war's appalling slaughter, forsaken for a new emphasis on practicality, order, materialism, and science.

George Ticknor, a prominent critic of the day, reflected on the changes that had shaken the nation. The war, it seemed to him, had left "a great gulf between what happened before it in our century and what has happened since. . . . It does not seem to me as if I were living in the country in which I was born."

CHAPTER SUMMARY

The Civil War's outcome depended not just on armies but also on the mobilization of each society's human, economic, and intellectual resources.

- Confederate president Jefferson Davis's policy of concentrating power in the government at Richmond, along with the resort to a draft and impressment of private property, provoked strong protests from many southerners.

- Abraham Lincoln's suspension of habeas corpus and interference with civil liberties were equally controversial.

- But Lincoln skillfully kept the border states in the Union.

- Lincoln at first resisted pressure to make emancipation a Union war aim, but he eventually issued the Emancipation Proclamation, which transformed the meaning of the war.

- African Americans helped undermine slavery and contributed vitally to the Union's military victory.

- On the home front, women confronted new responsibilities and enjoyed new occupational opportunities.

- Confederate financial and tax policies and the tightening Union blockade increased hardships within the Confederacy.

- Technology, particularly the use of rifles and rifled artillery, revolutionized the tactics of warfare, bringing the war home to the South's civilian population.

- The Union victory at Gettysburg and Lincoln's choice of Grant to lead Union forces marked the turning point of the war. Union success relied in part on the strategy of attacking the civilian population of the South.

Digging Deeper

A good single-volume history of the Civil War remains James M. McPherson's *Battle Cry of Freedom*. (1988); also see Mark E. Neely's *The Civil War and the Limits of Destruction* (2007). For the evolution of the Union's strategy toward southern civilians, see Mark Grimsley, *The Hard Hand of War* (1995).

The best biography of Lincoln is David Herbert Donald, *Lincoln* (1995). William E. Gienapp, *Abraham Lincoln and Civil War America* (2002), is concise and focuses on the presidential years. The president's complex thinking on slavery is the subject of Eric Foner's masterful book *The Fiery Trial* (2011). For the contradictions of the southern project, see Stephanie McCurry, *Confederate Reckoning* (2010). Drew Gilpin Faust, *Mothers of Invention* (1996), is an imaginative study of slaveholding women; Edward L. Ayers, *In the Presence of Mine Enemies* (2003), examines the consequences of war in Virginia and Pennsylvania. For the northern home front, see J. Matthew Gallman, *The North Fights the Civil War* (1994). Chandra Manning, in *What This Cruel War Was Over* (2007), argues that Union rank-and-file widely believed in emancipation as early as the end of 1861. Drew Gilpin Faust, *This Republic of Suffering* (2008), brilliantly explores how death, grieving, and belief were changed by this most deadly of wars; and Martha Hodes, *Mourning Lincoln* (2015), delves into the ways that ordinary people, North and South, responded to the president's assassination. For Britain's critical role in the diplomacy of the Civil War, see Amanda Foreman's *A World on Fire* (2011); and for that conflict's global significance, read Don H. Doyle's *The Cause of All Nations* (2015).

After the Fact

| Historians Reconstruct the Past |

What Caused the New York City Draft Riots?

Making sense out of the chaos of war surely presents one of the greatest challenges for historians. Yet amid the carnage of attack and counterattack, at least officers are working to coordinate troop movements and lines of battle. Civil disturbances, rebellions, and riots are even more chaotic, leaving a greater puzzle to decode. How does a historian make sense of the "draft riots" that shook New York City in the summer of 1863?

Observers could hardly have predicted the outburst from the opening day of the Union draft, on Saturday, July 11, 1863. Atop a platform, with a small crowd looking on, a blindfolded man stood beside a cylinder as an attendant cranked it around. When the cylinder stopped, the blindfolded man reached in and pulled out a rolled-up slip of paper with a name on it. In similar fashion the day's selections were made one by one, all without incident.

Monday, however, was another story. Bright and early, hundreds of laborers streamed up Eighth and Ninth Avenues. Waving "No Draft" placards, they rousted other workers from the stores and factories they passed, stopping at last outside the draft office. Someone fired a pistol. Then members of the mob burst in, destroyed the selection cylinder, and set the building afire. Firefighters tried to stop the blaze from spreading, but another angry mob arrived in time to prevent them. All over the city the chaos spread. "Men left their various pursuits,"

CHARGE OF THE POLICE ON THE RIOTERS AT THE "TRIBUNE" OFFICE.

Source: Library of Congress, Prints and Photographs Division [LC-USZ62-47037]

wrote one reporter; store owners "put up their shutters; factories were emptied, conductors or drivers left their cars" until a "concourse of over twelve thousand" men, women, and children were roaming the streets.

Over the next several days, the riots became even more violent. Fires burned out of control, telegraph wires were cut, railroad tracks were torn up, and crowds staged pitched battles with police and troops. Targets of the mob's wrath included both high officials and ordinary citizens. Homes of the wealthy were looted and set afire, but so was the Colored Orphan Asylum. Policemen caught by the rioters were stripped of their clothes, and their faces were beaten to bloody pulps. Abraham Franklin, a crippled black coachman, was dragged from his rooms and hung while onlookers cheered for Jefferson Davis. By Friday order was at last restored by troops that had been rushed back from their recent victory at Gettysburg. At least 105 people, mostly rioters, lost their lives, and more than a million dollars in property had been destroyed. It was the highest loss of life in any civil disturbance in all of American history. A month later, the draft resumed in New York City.

WERE THE DRAFT RIOTS ABOUT THE DRAFT?

WHAT WAS THE CAUSE OF such an immense tumult? "Absolute disloyalty," huffed the Republican *New York Tribune*. "It is absurd . . . to attribute this ruffianism to anything else than sympathy with the Rebels." The Democratic *New York World*, which had condemned the draft beforehand, offered an equally straightforward answer: the riot was a spontaneous protest against Lincoln's "wanton exercise of arbitrary powers." Having perverted the war into a struggle to destroy slavery, the paper complained, the administration was now determined to enforce an unconstitutional conscription law that allowed the rich to escape while sweeping the poor into the army's ranks.

At first glance, the *World*'s emphasis on the draft seems sufficient. Rioters, after all, carried "No Draft" placards. They attacked draft officials and, by direct intimidation, forced the government to suspend the draft. Eyewitnesses agreed, moreover, that the rioters were overwhelmingly workers and mostly immigrants. These men certainly could not afford to pay the $300 commutation fee to avoid the draft. For them, $300 represented a year's wages or more.

Still, a closer look at the evidence suggests that there was more to these riots than a simple protest of the Union draft. Historians look to put the protest in a broader context by asking questions about the rioters involved: Just who were they? What were their motives for rioting? Do the obvious explanations hold up? To begin with, the draft did not apply to immigrants unless they were naturalized citizens or had declared their intention to be naturalized. Thus many foreign-born rioters were not even eligible. In addition, observers noted that rioters, including some of the most violent, were remarkably young. Dismissing talk of an oppressive conscription law, the *New York Times* asserted that "three-fourths of those who have been actively engaged in violence have been boys and young men under twenty years of age and not at all subject to Conscription." And if the $300 clause was what most angered the mobs, why did they attack free blacks, who were also subject to the draft and almost all of whom were too poor to pay the fee?

Historians who have examined Union conscription records cast further doubt on this explanation. Despite complaints by Democrats that the $300 fee was an instrument of class privilege, in reality poor men as well as wealthy ones bought their way out of the draft. In New York City, the rate of commutation was as high in poorer wards as in wealthy ones. In fact, over the course of the war 98 percent of the men drafted in the Irish districts of the city either paid the fee or provided substitutes. For as little as $10, workers could buy the equivalent of draft insurance by joining commutation clubs, in which members pooled their money to pay the fee for any contributor who was drafted.

If the draft was not the sole cause of the riots, what else was behind the mob's anger? For historians, evidence is not easy to come by. Members of rioting crowds rarely leave written records. More often, descriptions are the work of unsympathetic observers. Still, for historians actions can speak as loudly as words. Look closely at what the mobs did. Whom did they choose as the targets of their violence? Did different mobs express their anger in different ways? By examining the riots as they evolved over several days, it is possible to discover vital evidence concerning motivation. In the New York City disturbances, the makeup of the crowds changed dramatically from one day to the next, and the targets the rioters attacked also varied.

On Monday morning, industrial laborers and skilled workers, especially from the building trades, took a leading role. They were joined by some of the city's fire companies. Although some native-born workers participated, the protesters were largely immigrants, Germans as well as Irish. As they marched to the draft office, they announced a one-day strike in protest against the draft. By noon this throng of workers had halted the selection process.

Other rioters, however, began to attack the police and free blacks. As the mayhem escalated, some members of the morning demonstration, including those from several fire companies, now aided the authorities in trying to restore order. For those who switched sides, opposition to the draft had been paramount, and they were unwilling to sanction looting or murder.

SACKING A DRUG STORE IN SECOND AVENUE.

Source: Library of Congress, Prints and Photographs Division [LC-USZ62-89865]

Observers noted that many rioters were boys.

WHO WERE THE MOB'S TARGETS?

WHEN THE RIOTS CONTINUED ON Tuesday and Wednesday, the crowds became much more heavily Irish. German Americans, some of whom were Republicans, no longer joined in. In fact, on several occasions they stepped in to protect free blacks. Skilled workers such as bricklayers, painters, and stonecutters for the most part also held back. Instead, rioters were largely industrial workers and common laborers and included many women and children. Their anger was directed no longer against the draft but against the Republican government and all its policies, including emancipation. Thus they vandalized homes of prominent Republicans, chanted pro-Confederate slogans, and fought pitched battles with the police and soldiers. The offices of Horace Greeley's pro-Republican *New York Tribune* were attacked several times, and Greeley was forced to hide in a nearby restaurant to escape a beating.

For common laborers—longshoremen, street pavers, cartmen—African Americans increasingly became the target of vengeance. Mobs assaulted blacks and lynched at least 12, ransacked businesses that catered to black customers, and destroyed tenements in which African Americans lived. These attacks were designed to purge neighborhoods of any black presence, especially in areas where black workers had been used to break strikes. These common laborers sought to restore the traditional racial order threatened by Republican policies, most notably emancipation.

In contrast, attacks on blacks and black residences were not common in wards where large numbers of industrial workers lived. While heavily Irish, industrial laborers in iron foundries and railroad shops did not work alongside African Americans. Although hostile to blacks, they aimed their anger more directly at the Republican Party. Rather than roaming throughout the city as many common laborers did, industrial workers concentrated on their own neighborhoods, from which they tried to remove all reminders of Republican authority, particularly draft officials, policemen, and soldiers. Although many policemen were not Republicans, the Metropolitan Police had been created by the Republican Party in 1857, and its members had been particularly zealous in arresting individuals suspected of disloyalty.

In the end, no single grievance can explain New York City's draft riots. Hostility to Republican employers, Protestant reformers, and authorities merged with anti-black racism, fears of job competition, and economic marginality. By itself, opposition to the draft did not produce the escalating violence and extraordinary destruction. But when that inflammatory issue sparked an avalanche of protest, it provided an outlet for more deeply rooted grievances. The result was the most serious civil disturbance of the war.

Source: Library of Congress, Prints and Photographs Division [LC-USZ62-89865]

Common laborers in particular vented their anger on African Americans. As with colonial mob actions, such protests exhibited ritualistic overtones. The victim here not only is being hanged and burned but is being shot as well.

17 Reconstructing the Union

1865–1877

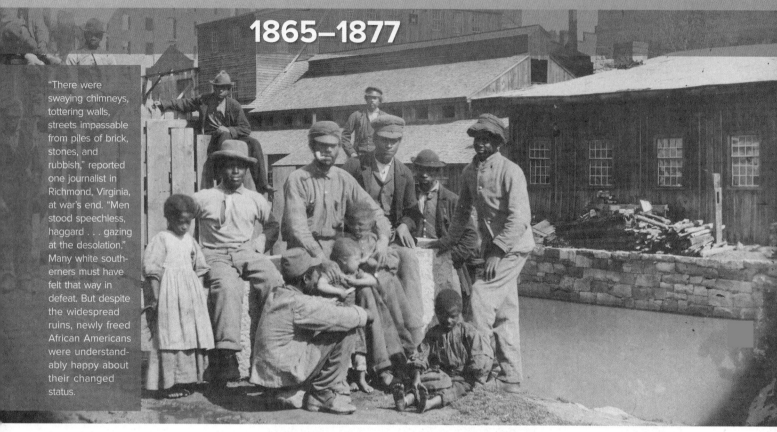

"There were swaying chimneys, tottering walls, streets impassable from piles of brick, stones, and rubbish," reported one journalist in Richmond, Virginia, at war's end. "Men stood speechless, haggard . . . gazing at the desolation." Many white southerners must have felt that way in defeat. But despite the widespread ruins, newly freed African Americans were understandably happy about their changed status.

Source: Library of Congress, Prints and Photographs Division [LC-DIG-cwpb-00468]

>> An American Story

THE SECRET SALE AT DAVIS BEND

Joseph Davis had had enough. Well on in years and financially ruined by the war, he decided to quit farming. In November 1866 he sold his Mississippi plantations Hurricane and Brierfield to Benjamin Montgomery and his sons. The sale of southern plantations was common enough after the war, but this transaction was bound to attract attention, since Joseph Davis was the elder brother of Jefferson Davis. Indeed, before the war the Confederate president had operated Brierfield as his own plantation, although his brother retained legal title to it. In truth, the sale was so unusual that the parties involved agreed to keep it secret, since the Montgomerys were black, and Mississippi law prohibited African Americans from owning land.

©Fotosearch/Stringer/Getty Images
| *Benjamin Montgomery*

Though a slave, Montgomery had been the business manager of the two Davis plantations before the war. He had also operated a store on Hurricane Plantation for white as well as black customers with his own line of credit in New Orleans. In 1863 Montgomery fled to the North, but when the war was over, he returned to Davis Bend, where the federal government was leasing plots of the land on confiscated plantations, including Hurricane and Brierfield, to black farmers. Montgomery quickly emerged as the leader of the African American community at the Bend.

Then, in 1866, President Andrew Johnson pardoned Joseph Davis and restored his lands. By then Davis was over 80 years old and lacked the will and stamina to rebuild. Yet unlike many ex-slaveholders, he still felt bound by obligations to his former slaves. He was convinced that with proper encouragement African Americans could succeed economically in freedom. Only when the law prohibiting African Americans from owning land was overturned in 1867 did Davis publicly confirm the sale to his former slave.

For his part, Montgomery undertook to create a model society at Davis Bend based on mutual cooperation. He rented land to black farmers, hired others to work his own fields, sold supplies on credit, and ginned and marketed the crops. To the growing African American community, he preached the gospel of hard work, self-reliance, and education.

Various difficulties dogged these black farmers, including the destruction caused by the war, several disastrous floods, insects, droughts, and declining cotton prices. Yet before long, cotton production exceeded that of the prewar years, and in 1870 the black families at Davis Bend produced 2,500 bales. The Montgomerys eventually acquired another plantation and owned 5,500 acres, which made them reputedly the third-largest planters in the state. They won national and international awards for the quality of their cotton. Their success demonstrated what African Americans, given a fair chance, might accomplish.

The experiences of Benjamin Montgomery during the years after 1865 were not those of most black southerners, who did not own land or have a powerful white benefactor. Yet Montgomery's dream of economic independence was shared by all African Americans. As one black veteran noted, "Every colored man will be a slave, and feel himself a slave until he can raise him own bale of cotton and put him own mark upon it and say dis is mine!" Blacks could not gain effective freedom simply through a proclamation of emancipation. They needed economic power, including their own land that no one could unfairly take away.

For nearly two centuries the laws had prevented slaves from possessing such economic power. If those conditions were to be overturned, black Americans needed political power too. Thus the Republic would have to be reconstructed to give African Americans political power that they had been previously denied.

War, in its blunt way, had roughed out the contours of a solution, but only in broad terms. Clearly, African Americans would no longer be enslaved. The North, with its industrial might, would be the driving force in the nation's economy and retain the dominant political voice. But, beyond that, the outlines of a reconstructed Republic remained vague. Would African Americans receive effective power? How would the North and the South readjust their economic and political relations? These questions lay at the heart of the problem of Reconstruction. <<

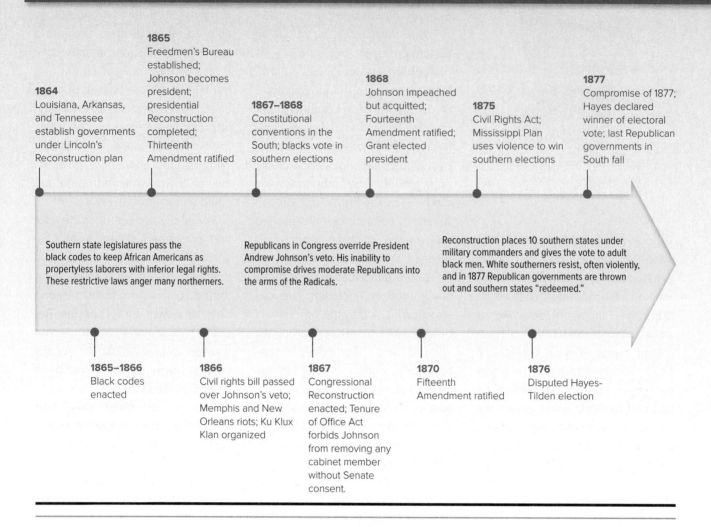

1864
Louisiana, Arkansas, and Tennessee establish governments under Lincoln's Reconstruction plan

1865
Freedmen's Bureau established; Johnson becomes president; presidential Reconstruction completed; Thirteenth Amendment ratified

1867–1868
Constitutional conventions in the South; blacks vote in southern elections

1868
Johnson impeached but acquitted; Fourteenth Amendment ratified; Grant elected president

1875
Civil Rights Act; Mississippi Plan uses violence to win southern elections

1877
Compromise of 1877; Hayes declared winner of electoral vote; last Republican governments in South fall

Southern state legislatures pass the black codes to keep African Americans as propertyless laborers with inferior legal rights. These restrictive laws anger many northerners.

Republicans in Congress override President Andrew Johnson's veto. His inability to compromise drives moderate Republicans into the arms of the Radicals.

Reconstruction places 10 southern states under military commanders and gives the vote to adult black men. White southerners resist, often violently, and in 1877 Republican governments are thrown out and southern states "redeemed."

1865–1866
Black codes enacted

1866
Civil rights bill passed over Johnson's veto; Memphis and New Orleans riots; Ku Klux Klan organized

1867
Congressional Reconstruction enacted; Tenure of Office Act forbids Johnson from removing any cabinet member without Senate consent.

1870
Fifteenth Amendment ratified

1876
Disputed Hayes-Tilden election

PRESIDENTIAL RECONSTRUCTION

THROUGHOUT THE WAR ABRAHAM LINCOLN had considered Reconstruction his responsibility. Elected with less than 40 percent of the popular vote in 1860, he was acutely aware that once the states of the Confederacy were restored to the Union, the Republicans would be weakened unless they ceased to be a sectional party. By a generous peace, Lincoln hoped to attract former Whigs in the South, who supported many of the Republicans' economic policies, and build up a southern wing of the party.

Lincoln's 10 Percent Plan

Lincoln outlined his program in a Proclamation of **Amnesty** and Reconstruction issued in December 1863. When a minimum of 10 percent of the qualified voters from 1860

took a **loyalty oath** to the Union, they could organize a state government. The new state constitution had to be republican in form, abolish slavery, and provide for black education, but Lincoln did not insist that high-ranking Confederate leaders be barred from public life.

Lincoln indicated that he would be generous in granting pardons and did not rule out compensation for slave property. Moreover, while he privately suggested permitting some black men to vote in the disloyal states, "as for instance, the very intelligent and especially those who have fought gallantly in our ranks," he did not demand social or political equality for black Americans, and he recognized pro-Union governments in Louisiana, Arkansas, and Tennessee that allowed only white men to vote.

RADICAL REPUBLICANS   The Radical Republicans found Lincoln's approach much too lenient. Strongly antislavery, Radical members of Congress had led the struggle to make emancipation a war aim. Now they were in the forefront in advocating rights for the freed people. Lincoln argued that the executive branch should bear the responsibility for restoring proper relations with the former Confederate states. The Radicals, on the other hand, believed that it was the duty of Congress to set the terms under which states would regain their rights in the Union. Though the Radicals often disagreed on other matters, they were united in a determination to readmit southern states only after slavery had been ended, black rights protected, and the power of the planter class destroyed.

WADE-DAVIS BILL Under the direction of Senator Benjamin Wade of Ohio and Representative Henry Winter Davis of Maryland, Congress formulated a much stricter plan of Reconstruction. It proposed that Confederate states be ruled temporarily by a military governor, required half the white adult males to take an oath of allegiance before drafting a new state constitution, and restricted political power to the hard-core Unionists in each state. When the Wade-Davis bill passed on the final day of the 1864 congressional session, Lincoln exercised his right of a **pocket veto.** Still, his own program could not succeed without the assistance of Congress, which refused to seat Unionist representatives who had been elected from Louisiana or Arkansas. As the war drew to a close, Lincoln appeared ready to make concessions to the Radicals. At his final cabinet meeting, he approved placing the defeated South temporarily under military rule. But only a few days later Booth's bullet found its mark, and Lincoln's final approach to Reconstruction would never be known.

The Mood of the South

In the wake of defeat, the immediate reaction among white southerners was one of shock, despair, and hopelessness. Some former Confederates, of course, were openly antagonistic. A North Carolina innkeeper remarked bitterly that Yankees had stolen his slaves, burned his house, and killed all his sons, leaving him only one privilege: "To hate 'em. I git up at half-past four in the morning, and sit up till twelve at night, to hate 'em." Most Confederate soldiers were less defiant, having had their fill of war. Even among hostile civilians the feeling was widespread that the South must accept northern terms.

| The mood of white southerners at the end of the war was mixed. Many, like the veteran caricatured here by northern cartoonist Thomas Nast, remained hostile. Others, like Texas captain Samuel Foster, came to believe that the institution of slavery "had been abused" and that men "who actually owned and held slaves up to this time,—have now changed in their opinions regarding slavery . . . to see that for a man to have property in man was wrong, and that the 'Declaration of Independence' meant more than they had ever been able to see before."

Source: Library of Congress, Prints and Photographs Division [LC-USZ62-131562]

This psychological moment was critical. To prevent a resurgence of resistance, the president needed to lay out clearly what white southerners had to do to regain their old status in the Union. Any wavering on the peace terms could only increase the likelihood of resistance. Perhaps even a clear and firm policy would not have been enough. But with Lincoln's death, the executive power had come to rest in far less capable hands.

Johnson's Program of Reconstruction

JOHNSON'S CHARACTER AND VALUES Andrew Johnson, the new president, had been born in North Carolina and eventually moved to Tennessee, where he worked as a tailor. Barely able to read and write when he married, he rose to political power by portraying himself as the champion of the people against the wealthy planter class. "Some day I will show the stuck-up aristocrats who is running the country," he vowed as he began his political career. He had not opposed slavery before the war—in fact, he hoped to disperse slave ownership more widely in southern society. Although he accepted emancipation as one consequence of the war, Johnson remained a confirmed racist. "Damn the negroes," he said during the war, "I am fighting these traitorous aristocrats, their masters."

Because Johnson disliked the planter class, Republican Radicals in Congress expected him to uphold their views on Reconstruction. In fact, the new president did speak of trying Confederate leaders and breaking up planters' estates. Unlike most Republicans, however, Johnson strongly supported states' rights. Furthermore, his prickly personality made conflict between the president and Congress inevitable. Scarred by his humble origins, Johnson remained an outsider throughout his life. When challenged or criticized he became tactless and inflexible, alienating even those who sought to work with him.

JOHNSON'S PROGRAM Johnson moved quickly to return the southern states to their place in the Union. He prescribed a loyalty oath that white southerners would have to take to regain their civil and political rights and to have their property, except for slaves, restored. Excluded were high Confederate officials and those with property worth over $20,000, who had to apply for individual pardons. Johnson announced that once a state had drafted a new constitution and elected state officers and members of Congress, he would revoke martial law and recognize the new state government. Suffrage was limited to white citizens who had taken the loyalty oath. This plan was similar to Lincoln's, though more lenient. Only informally did Johnson ask that the southern states renounce their ordinances of secession, repudiate the Confederate debt, and ratify the proposed Thirteenth Amendment abolishing slavery.

The Failure of Johnson's Program

SOUTHERN DEFIANCE The southern delegates who met to construct new governments were in no frame of mind to follow Johnson's recommendations. Several states

merely repealed instead of repudiating their ordinances of secession, rejected the Thirteenth Amendment, or refused to repudiate the Confederate debt.

BLACK CODES Nor did the new governments allow African Americans any political rights or make any effective provisions for black education. In addition, each state passed a series of laws, often modeled on its old slave code, that applied only to African Americans. These **black codes** did grant African Americans some rights that had not been enjoyed by slaves. They legalized marriages performed under slavery and allowed black southerners to hold and sell property and to sue and be sued in state courts. Yet their primary purpose was to keep African Americans as propertyless agricultural laborers with inferior legal rights. The new freedmen, or freedpeople, could not serve on juries, testify against whites, or work as they pleased. South Carolina forbade blacks to engage in anything other than agricultural labor without a special license; Mississippi prohibited them from buying or renting farmland. Most states ominously provided that black people who were vagrants could be arrested and hired out to landowners. Many northerners were incensed by the restrictive black codes.

ELECTIONS IN THE SOUTH Southern voters under Johnson's plan also defiantly elected prominent Confederate military and political leaders to office, headed by Alexander Stephens, the vice president of the Confederacy, who was elected senator from Georgia. At this point, Johnson could have called for new elections or admitted that a different program of Reconstruction was needed. Instead, he caved in. For all his harsh rhetoric, he shrank from the prospect

Source: Library of Congress, Prints and Photographs Division [LC-DIG-cwpbh-00460]

| *Thaddeus Stevens, Radical leader in the House*

of social upheaval, and he found it enormously gratifying when upper-class planters praised his conduct and requested pardons. As the lines of ex-Confederates waiting to see him lengthened, he began issuing special pardons almost as fast as they could be printed. In the next two years he pardoned some 13,500 former rebels.

In private, Johnson warned southerners against a reckless course. Publicly he put on a bold face, announcing that Reconstruction had been successfully completed. But many members of Congress were deeply alarmed.

Johnson's Break with Congress

The new Congress was by no means of one mind. A small number of Democrats and a few conservative Republicans backed the president's program. At the other end of the spectrum, a larger group of Radical Republicans, led by Thaddeus Stevens, Charles Sumner, Benjamin Wade, and others, was bent on remaking southern society in the image of the North. Reconstruction must "revolutionize Southern institutions, habits, and manners," insisted Representative Stevens, ". . . or all our blood and treasure have been spent in vain." Unlike Johnson, Radicals championed civil and political rights for African Americans and believed that the only way to maintain loyal governments and develop a Republican Party in the South was to give black men the ballot.

As a minority, the Radicals could accomplish nothing without the aid of the moderate Republicans, the largest bloc in Congress. Led by William Pitt Fessenden and Lyman Trumbull, the moderates hoped to avoid a lash with the president, and they had no esire to foster social revolution or promote racial equality in the South. But they wanted to keep Confederate leaders from reassuming power, and they were convinced that the former slaves needed federal protection. Otherwise, Trumbull declared, the freedpeople would "be tyrannized over, abused, and virtually reenslaved."

Moderates agreed that the new southern governments were too harsh toward African Americans, but they feared that too great an emphasis on black civil rights would alienate northern voters.

In December 1865, when southern representatives to Congress appeared in Washington, a majority in Congress voted to exclude them. Congress also appointed a joint committee, chaired by Senator Fessenden, to look into how to implement Reconstruction. The split with the president became clearer when Congress passed a bill extending the life of the Freedmen's Bureau. Created in March 1865, the bureau provided emergency food, clothing, and medical care to war refugees (including white southerners) and took charge of settling freedpeople on abandoned lands. The new bill gave the bureau the added responsibilities of supervising special courts to resolve disputes involving freedpeople and establishing schools for black southerners. Although this bill passed with near-unanimous Republican support, Johnson vetoed it. Congress failed to override his veto.

JOHNSON'S VETOES   Johnson also vetoed a civil rights bill designed to overturn the most severe provisions of the black codes. The law made African Americans citizens of the United States and granted them the right to own property, make contracts, and have access to courts as parties and witnesses. For most Republicans Johnson's action was the last straw, and in April 1866 Congress overrode his veto, the first major legislation in American history to be enacted over a presidential veto. Congress then approved a slightly revised Freedmen's Bureau bill in July and promptly overrode the president's veto. Johnson's refusal to compromise drove the moderates into the arms of the Radicals.

The Fourteenth Amendment

To prevent unrepentant Confederates from taking over the reconstructed state governments and denying African Americans basic freedoms, the Joint Committee on Reconstruction proposed an amendment to the Constitution, which passed both houses of Congress with the necessary two-thirds vote in June 1866. The amendment, coupled with the Freedmen's Bureau and civil rights bills, represented the moderates' terms for Reconstruction.

PROVISIONS OF THE AMENDMENT   The Fourteenth Amendment put a number of matters beyond the control of the president. The amendment guaranteed repayment of the national war debt and prohibited repayment of the Confederate debt. To counteract the president's wholesale pardons, it disqualified prominent Confederates from holding office and provided that only Congress by a two-thirds vote could remove this penalty. Because moderates, fearful of the reaction of white

northerners, balked at giving the vote to African Americans, the amendment merely gave Congress the right to reduce the representation of any state that did not have impartial male suffrage. The practical effect of this provision, which Radicals labeled a "swindle," was to allow northern states to restrict suffrage to whites if they wished, since unlike southern states they had few African Americans and thus would not be penalized.

The amendment's most important provision, Section 1, defined an American citizen as anyone born in the United States or naturalized, thereby automatically making African Americans citizens. Section 1 also prohibited states from abridging "the privileges or immunities" of citizens, depriving "any person of life, liberty, or property, without due process of law," or denying "any person . . . equal protection of the laws." The framers of the amendment probably intended to prohibit laws that applied to one race only, such as the black codes, or that made certain acts felonies when committed by black but not white people, or that decreed different penalties for the same crime when committed by white and black lawbreakers. The framers probably did not intend to prevent African Americans from being excluded from juries or to forbid segregation (the legal separation of the races) in schools and public places.

Nevertheless, Johnson denounced the proposed amendment and urged southern states not to ratify it. Ironically, of the seceded states only the president's own state ratified the amendment, and Congress readmitted Tennessee with no further restrictions. The telegram sent to Congress by a longtime foe of Johnson announcing Tennessee's approval ended, "Give my respects to the dead dog in the White House." The amendment was ratified in 1868.

The Elections of 1866

ANTIBLACK RIOTS   When Congress blocked his policies, Johnson undertook a speaking tour of the East and Midwest in the fall of 1866 to drum up popular support. But the president found it difficult to convince northern audiences that white southerners were fully repentant. News that summer of major race riots in Memphis and New Orleans heightened northern concern. Forty-six African Americans died when white mobs invaded the black section of Memphis, burning homes, churches, and schoolhouses. About the same number were killed in New Orleans when whites attacked both black and white delegates to a convention supporting black suffrage. "The negroes now know, to their sorrow, that it is best not to arouse the fury of the white man," boasted one Memphis newspaper. When the president encountered hostile audiences during his northern campaign, he made matters only worse by trading insults and ranting that the Radicals were traitors. Even supporters found his performance humiliating.

Not to be outdone, the Radicals vilified Johnson as a traitor aiming to turn the country over to rebels and Copperheads. Resorting to the tactic of "waving the **bloody shirt,**" they appealed to voters by reviving bitter memories of the war. In a classic example of such rhetoric, Governor Oliver Morton of Indiana proclaimed that "every bounty jumper, every deserter, every sneak who ran away from the draft calls himself a

EQUALITY AND THE VOTE IN RECONSTRUCTION

Debate swirled around not only the conditions southern states needed to fulfill to return to the Union but also the rights of citizenship granted to former slaves. At war's end, African Americans held a number of conventions to set forth their views (Document 1). President Andrew Johnson privately conveyed to white southern leaders his idea of how they should act (Document 2). And Representative Thaddeus Stevens of Pennsylvania spoke for Radical Republicans (Document 3).

DOCUMENT 1
African Americans Seek the Vote

We, the delegates of the colored people of the State of Virginia . . . solemnly [declare] that we desire to live upon the most friendly and agreeable terms with all men; we feel no ill-will or prejudice towards our former oppressors . . . and that we believe that in this State we have still many warm and solid friends among the white people. . . .

We must, on the other hand, be allowed to aver and assert that we believe that we have among the white people of this State, many who are our most inveterate enemies . . . who despise us simply because we are black, and more especially, because we have been made free by the power of the United States Government; and that they—the class last mentioned—will not, in our estimation, be willing to accord to us, as freemen, that protection which all freemen must contend for, if they would be worthy of freedom. . . .

We claim, then, as citizens of this State, the laws of the Commonwealth shall give to all men equal protection; that each and every man may appeal to the law for his equal rights without regard to the color of his skin; and we believe this can only be done by extending to us the elective franchise, which we believe to be our inalienable right as freemen, and which the Declaration of Independence guarantees to all free citizens of this Government and which is the privilege of the nation.

Source: Proceedings of the Convention of the Colored People of Virginia in Foner, Philip S., & Walker, George E., eds., Proceedings of the Black State Conventions, 1840–1865, Volume 2. Philadelphia, PA: Temple University Press, 1980, 262–264.

DOCUMENT 2
President Johnson Advises Southern Leaders

I hope that without delay your convention will amend your State constitution . . . [to] adopt the amendment to the Constitution of the United States abolishing slavery. If you could extend the elective franchise to all persons of color who can read the Constitution of the United States in English and write their names, and to all persons of color who own real estate valued at not less than two hundred and fifty dollars and pay taxes thereon, you would completely disarm the adversary and set an example the other States will follow. This you can do with perfect safety, and you would thus place Southern States in reference to the free persons of color upon the same basis with the free States. . . . And as a consequence the radicals, who are wild upon negro franchise, will be completely foiled in their attempts to keep the Southern States from renewing their relations to the Union by not accepting their Senators and Representatives.

Source: Fleming, Walter L., ed., Documentary History of Reconstruction, Volume 1. Cleveland, OH: A. H. Clark Co., 1906, 177.

DOCUMENT 3
Representative Stevens on Equal Privileges

But this is not all that we ought to do before these inveterate rebels are invited to participate in our legislation. We have turned, or are about to turn, loose four million slaves without a hut to shelter them or a cent in their pockets. The infernal laws of slavery have prevented them from acquiring an education, understanding the commonest laws of contract, or of managing the ordinary business of life. This Congress is bound to provide for them until they can take care of themselves. If we do not furnish them with homesteads, and hedge them around with protective laws; if we leave them to the legislation of their late masters, we had better have left them in bondage . . . equal rights to all the privileges of the Government is innate to every immortal being, no matter what the shape or color of the tabernacle which it inhabits. . . .

If equal privileges were granted to all, I should not expect to any but white men to be elected to office for long ages to come. . . . But it would still be beneficial to the weaker races. In a country where political divisions will always exist, their power, joined with just white men, would greatly modify, if it did not entirely prevent, the injustice of majorities. Without the right of suffrage in the late slave States, (I do not speak of the free States,) I believe the slaves had far better been left in bondage. . . .

[Men of influence] proclaim, "This is a white man's Government," and the whole coil of copperheads echo the same sentiment, and upstart, jealous Republicans join the cry. Is it any wonder ignorant foreigners and illiterate natives should learn this doctrine, and be led to despise and maltreat a whole race of their fellow men?

Source: Congressional Globe, 39th Congress, 1st Session, 1865, 72–73

THINKING CRITICALLY

Each of the writers recommends that African Americans receive the vote in some way. Which document is the most radical? Which the least so? Who does President Johnson refer to as "the adversary"? How does he intend to "foil" the Radicals? And what does Thaddeus Stevens not speak about? Why?

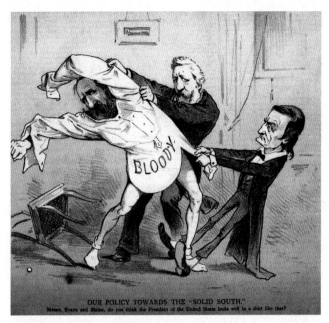

©The Granger Collection, New York

| *These rival politicians are trying to clothe Rutherford B. Hayes with a "bloody shirt," a tactic usually reserved for discrediting Democrats.*

Democrat. . . . Every 'Son of Liberty' who conspired to murder, burn, rob arsenals and release rebel prisoners calls himself a Democrat. . . . In short, the Democratic Party may be described as a common sewer."

REPUDIATION OF JOHNSON   Voters soundly repudiated Johnson, as the Republicans won more than a two-thirds majority in both houses of Congress, every northern gubernatorial contest, and control of every northern legislature. The Radicals had reached the height of their power.

> ✔ **REVIEW**
>
> What were Lincoln's and Andrew Johnson's approaches to Reconstruction, and why did Congress reject Johnson's approach?

CONGRESSIONAL RECONSTRUCTION

WITH A CLEAR MANDATE IN hand, congressional Republicans passed their own program of Reconstruction, beginning with the first Reconstruction Act in March 1867. Like all later pieces of Reconstruction legislation, it was repassed over Johnson's veto.

Placing the 10 unreconstructed states under military commanders, the act directed officials to include black adult males as voters but not former Confederates barred from holding office under the Fourteenth Amendment. State conventions would frame constitutions that provided for black suffrage and that disqualified prominent ex-Confederates from office. The first state legislatures to meet under the new constitution were required to ratify the Fourteenth Amendment. Once these steps were completed and Congress approved the new state constitution, a state could send representatives to Congress.

RESISTANCE OF SOUTHERN WHITES   White southerners found these requirements so insulting that officials took no steps to register voters. Congress then enacted a second Reconstruction Act, also in March, ordering the local military commanders to put the machinery of Reconstruction into motion. Johnson's efforts to limit the power of military commanders produced a third act, passed in July, that upheld their superiority in all matters. When elections were held to ratify the new state constitutions, white southerners boycotted them in large numbers. Undaunted, Congress passed the fourth Reconstruction Act (March 1868), which required ratification of the constitution by only a majority of those voting rather than those who were registered.

By June 1868 Congress had readmitted the representatives of seven states. Georgia's state legislature expelled its black members once it had been readmitted, granting seats to those barred by Congress from holding office. Congress ordered the military commander to reverse these actions, and Georgia was then admitted a second time in July 1870. Texas, Virginia, and Mississippi did not complete the process until 1869.

Post-Emancipation Societies in the Americas

With the exception of Haiti's revolution (1791–1804), the United States was the only society in the Americas in which the destruction of slavery was accomplished by violence. But the United States, uniquely among these societies, enfranchised former slaves almost immediately after the emancipation. Thus in the United States former masters and slaves battled for control of the state in ways that did not occur in other post-emancipation societies. In most of the Caribbean, property requirements for voting left the planters in political control. Jamaica, for example, with a population of 500,000 in the 1860s, had only 3,000 voters.

Moreover, in reaction to political efforts to mobilize **disenfranchised** black peasants, Jamaican planters dissolved the assembly and reverted to being a Crown colony governed from London. Of the sugar islands, all but Barbados adopted the same policy, thereby blocking the potential for any future black peasant democracy. Nor did any of these societies have the counterparts of the Radical Republicans, a group of outsiders with political power that promoted the fundamental transformation of the post-emancipation South. These comparisons highlight the radicalism of Reconstruction in the United States, which alone saw an effort to forge an interracial democracy.

The Land Issue

BLACKS' DESIRE FOR LAND   While the political process of Reconstruction proceeded, Congress confronted the question of whether land should be given to former slaves to foster economic independence. At a meeting with Secretary of War Edwin Stanton near the end of the war, African American

Map legend:
- Former Confederate states
- Military district boundaries
- 1870 Date of readmission to the Union
- 1871 Date of "redemption"

leaders declared, "The way we can best take care of ourselves is to have land, and till it by our own labor." During the war, the Second Confiscation Act of 1862 had authorized the government to seize and sell the property, including land, of supporters of the rebellion. In June 1866, however, President Johnson ruled that confiscation laws applied only to wartime.

Congress debated land confiscation off and on from December 1865 until early 1867. Thaddeus Stevens, a leading Radical in the House, advocated confiscating 394 million acres of land from about 70,000 of what he termed the "chief rebels" in the South, who made up less than 5 percent of the South's white families. He proposed to give 40 acres to every adult male freedperson and then sell the remaining land, which would amount to nine-tenths of the total, to pay off the public debt, compensate loyal southerners for losses they suffered during the war, and fund Union veterans' pensions. Land, he insisted, would be far more valuable to African Americans than the right to vote.

FAILURE OF LAND REDISTRIBUTION But in the end Congress rejected all proposals. Given Americans' strong belief in self-reliance, little sympathy existed for the idea that government should support any group. In addition, land redistribution represented an attack on property rights, another cherished American value. By 1867 land reform was dead.

Few freedpeople acquired land after the war, a development that severely limited African Americans' economic independence and left them vulnerable to white coercion. It is doubtful, however, that this decision was the basic cause of the failure of Reconstruction. In the face of white hostility and institutionalized racism, African Americans probably would have been no more successful in protecting their property than they were in maintaining the right to vote.

Impeachment

TENURE OF OFFICE ACT Throughout 1867 Congress routinely overrode Johnson's vetoes. Still, the president had other ways of undercutting congressional Reconstruction. He interpreted the new laws as narrowly as possible and removed military commanders who vigorously enforced them.

Congress responded by restricting Johnson's power to issue orders to military commanders in the South. It also passed the Tenure of Office Act, which forbade Johnson to remove any member of the cabinet without the Senate's consent. The intention of this law was to prevent him from firing Secretary of War Edwin Stanton, the only Radical in the cabinet.

JOHNSON ACQUITTED When Johnson tried to dismiss Stanton in February 1868, the determined secretary of war barricaded himself in his office (where he remained night and day for about two months). Angrily, the House of Representatives approved articles of impeachment. The articles focused on the violation of the Tenure of Office Act, but the charge with the most substance was that Johnson had conspired to systematically obstruct Reconstruction legislation. In the trial before the Senate, his lawyers argued that a president could be impeached only for an indictable crime, which Johnson clearly had not committed. The Radicals countered that impeachment applied to political offenses, not merely criminal acts. In May 1868 the Senate voted 36 to 19 to convict, one vote short of the two-thirds majority needed. The seven Republicans who joined the Democrats in voting for acquittal were uneasy about using impeachment as a political weapon.

 REVIEW

What was Congress's approach to Reconstruction, and why did it not include a provision for giving land to former slaves?

RECONSTRUCTION IN THE SOUTH

THE REFUSAL OF CONGRESS to convict Johnson sent a clear signal: the power of the Radicals in Congress was waning. Increasingly the success or failure of Reconstruction hinged on developments not in Congress but in the southern states themselves. Power there rested with the new Republican parties, representing a coalition of black and white southerners and transplanted northerners.

Black Officeholding

Almost from the beginning of Reconstruction, African Americans had lobbied for the right to vote. After they received the **franchise,** black men constituted as much as 80 percent of the Republican voters in the South. They steadfastly opposed the Democratic Party with its appeal to white supremacy.

Throughout Reconstruction, African Americans never held office in proportion to their voting strength. No African American was ever elected governor, and only in South Carolina, where more than 60 percent of the population was black, did they control even one house of the legislature. During Reconstruction between 15 and 20 percent of the state officers and 6 percent of members of Congress (2 senators and 15 representatives) were black. Only in South Carolina did black officeholders approach their proportion of the population.

BACKGROUND OF BLACK POLITICAL LEADERS Blacks who held office generally came from the top levels of African American society. Among state and federal officeholders, perhaps four-fifths were literate, and more than a quarter had been free before the war, both marks of distinction in the black community. Their occupations also set them apart: two-fifths were professionals (mostly clergy), and of the third who were farmers, nearly all owned land. Among black members of Congress, all but three had a secondary school education, and four had gone to college. In their political and social values, African American leaders were more conservative than the rural black population was, and they showed little interest in land reform.

White Republicans in the South

Black citizens were a majority of the voters only in South Carolina, Mississippi, and Louisiana. Thus in most of the South the Republican Party had to secure white votes to stay in power. Opponents scornfully labeled white southerners who allied with the Republican Party **scalawags,** yet an estimated quarter of white southerners at one time voted Republican. Although the party appealed to some wealthy planters, they were outnumbered by Unionists from the upland counties and hill areas who were largely yeoman farmers. Such voters were attracted by Republican promises to rebuild the South, restore prosperity, create public schools, and open isolated areas to the market with railroads.

The other group of white Republicans in the South was known as **carpetbaggers.** Originally from the North, they allegedly had arrived with all their worldly possessions stuffed in a carpetbag, ready to plunder the defeated South. Some did, but northerners moved south for a variety of reasons. Those in political office were especially well educated. Though carpetbaggers made up only a small percentage of Republican voters, they controlled almost a third of the

©Sarin Images/The Granger Collection, New York

| Harper's Illustrated Weekly *celebrated African Americans who voted for the first time in 1867. First in line is a skilled craftworker, his tools in his pocket; then an urban resident of some sophistication, followed by a veteran. Why would the artist choose these men as examples?*

offices in the South. More than half of all southern Republican governors and nearly half of Republican members of Congress were originally northerners.

DIVISIONS AMONG SOUTHERN REPUBLICANS The Republican Party in the South had difficulty maintaining unity. Scalawags were especially susceptible to the race issue and social pressure. "Even my own kinspeople have turned the cold shoulder to me because I hold office under a Republican administration," testified a Mississippi white Republican. As black southerners pressed for greater recognition and a greater share of the offices, white southerners increasingly defected to the Democrats. Carpetbaggers were less sensitive to race, although most felt that their black allies should be content with minor offices. The friction between scalawags and carpetbaggers, which grew out of their rivalry for party honors, was particularly intense.

The New State Governments

NEW STATE CONSTITUTIONS The new southern state constitutions enacted several reforms. They put in place fairer systems of legislative representation, allowed voters to elect many officials who before had been appointed, and abolished property requirements for officeholding. In South

Carolina, for the first time, voters were allowed to vote for the president, governor, and other state officers. (Previously, presidential electors as well as the governor had been chosen by the South Carolina legislature.) The Radical state governments also assumed some responsibility for social welfare and established the first statewide systems of public schools in the South.

RACE AND SOCIAL EQUALITY All the new constitutions proclaimed the principle of equality and granted black adult males the right to vote. On social relations they were much more cautious. No state outlawed segregation, and South Carolina and Louisiana were the only states that required integration in public schools (a mandate that was almost universally ignored).

Economic Issues and Corruption

The war left the southern economy in ruins, and problems of economic reconstruction were as difficult as those of politics. The new Republican governments encouraged industrial development by providing subsidies, loans, and even temporary exemptions from taxes. These governments also largely rebuilt the southern railroad system, often offering lavish aid to railroad corporations. The investments in the South helped double its manufacturing establishments in the two decades after 1860. Yet the harsh reality was that the South steadily slipped further behind the booming industrial economy of the North. Between 1854 and 1879, 7,000 miles of railroad track were laid in the South, but in the same period 45,000 miles were constructed in the rest of the nation.

CORRUPTION The expansion of government services offered temptations for corruption. In many southern states, officials regularly received bribes and kickbacks for their award of railroad charters, franchises, and other contracts. By 1872 the debts of the 11 states of the Confederacy had increased by $132 million, largely because of railroad grants and new social services such as schools. The tax rate grew as expenditures went up; by the 1870s it was four times the rate of 1860.

Corruption, however, was not only a problem in the South: the decline in morality affected the entire nation. During these years in New York City alone, the Democratic Tweed Ring stole more money than all the Radical Republican governments in the South combined. Moreover, corruption in the South was hardly limited to Republicans. Many Democrats and white business leaders participated in the looting. "Everybody is demoralizing down here. Corruption is the fashion," reported Louisiana governor Henry Warmoth.

Corruption in Radical governments existed, but southern whites exaggerated its extent for partisan purposes. Conservatives just as bitterly opposed honest Radical regimes as they did corrupt ones. In the eyes of most white southerners the real crime of the Radical governments was

that they allowed black citizens to hold some offices and tried to protect the civil rights of African Americans. Race was the conservatives' greatest weapon. And it would prove the most effective means to undermine Republican power in the South.

> **✓ REVIEW**
>
> What roles did African Americans, southern whites, and northern whites play in the Reconstruction governments of the South?

BLACK ASPIRATIONS

EMANCIPATION CAME TO SLAVES IN different ways and at different times. For some it arrived during the war when Union soldiers entered an area; for others it came some time after the Confederacy's collapse, when Union troops or officials announced that they were free. Whatever the timing, freedom meant a host of precious blessings to people who had been in bondage all their lives.

Experiencing Freedom

The first impulse was to think of freedom as a contrast to slavery. Emancipation immediately released slaves from the most oppressive aspects of bondage—the whippings, the breakup of families, the sexual exploitation. Freedom also meant movement, the right to travel without a pass or white permission. Above all, freedom meant that African Americans' labor would be for their own benefit. One Arkansas freedman, who earned his first dollar working on a railroad, recalled that when he was paid, "I felt like the richest man in the world."

CHANGING EMPLOYMENT Freedom included finding a new place to work. Changing jobs was one concrete way to break the psychological ties of slavery. Even planters with reputations for kindness sometimes saw their former hands depart. The cook who left a South Carolina family even though they offered her higher wages than her new job explained, "I must go. If I stays here I'll never know I'm free."

IMPORTANCE OF NAMES Symbolically, freedom meant having a full name, and African Americans now adopted last names. More than a few took the last name of some prominent individual; more common was to take the name of the first master in the family's oral history as far back as it could be recalled. Most, however, retained their first name, especially if the name had been given to them by their parents (as most often had been the case among slaves). It had been their form of identity in bondage, and for those separated from their family it was the only link with their parents. Whatever name they took, it was important to black Americans that they make the decision themselves without white interference.

The Black Family

UPHOLDING THE FAMILY African Americans also sought to strengthen the family in freedom. Because slave marriages had not been recognized as legal, thousands of former slaves insisted on being married again by proper authorities, even though a ceremony was not required by law. Blacks who had been forcibly separated in slavery and later remarried confronted the dilemma of which spouse to take. Laura Spicer, whose husband had been sold away in slavery, received a series of wrenching letters from him after the war. He had thought her dead, had remarried, and had a new family. "You know it never was our wishes to be separated from each other, and it never was our fault. I had rather anything to had happened to me most than ever have been parted from you and the children," he wrote. "As I am, I do not know which I love best, you or Anna." Declining to return, he closed, "Laura, truly, I have got another wife, and I am very sorry. . . ."

Like white husbands, black husbands deemed themselves the head of the family and acted legally for their wives. They often insisted that their wives would not work in the fields as they had in slavery, a decision that had major economic repercussions for agricultural labor. In negotiating contracts, a father also demanded the right to control his children and their labor. All these changes were designed to insulate the black family from white control.

Source: Library of Congress, Prints and Photographs Division [LC-DIG-cwpbh-03275]

| *Hiram Revels, a minister and educator, became the first African American to serve in the U.S. Senate, representing Mississippi. Later he served as president of Alcorn University.*

The Schoolhouse and the Church

BLACK EDUCATION In freedom, the schoolhouse and the black church became essential institutions in the black community. Next to ownership of land, African Americans saw education as the best hope for advancement. At first, northern churches and missionaries, working with the Freedmen's Bureau, set up black schools in the South. Tuition represented 10 percent or more of a laborer's monthly wages. Yet these schools were full. Many parents sent their children by day and attended classes themselves at night. Eventually, the Bureau schools were replaced by the new public school systems, which by 1876 enrolled 40 percent of African American children.

Black adults had good reasons for seeking literacy. They wanted to be able to read the Bible, to defend their newly gained civil and political rights, and to protect themselves from being cheated. One elderly Louisiana freedman explained that giving children an education was better than giving them a fortune, "because if you left them even $500, some man having more education than they had would come along and cheat them out of it all."

TEACHERS IN BLACK SCHOOLS Teachers in the Freedmen's Bureau schools were primarily northern middle-class white women sent south by northern missionary societies. "I feel that it is a precious privilege," Esther Douglass wrote, "to be allowed to do something for these poor people." Many saw themselves as peacetime soldiers, struggling to make emancipation a reality. Indeed, on more than one occasion, hostile white southerners destroyed black schools and threatened and even murdered white teachers. Then there were the everyday challenges: low pay, dilapidated buildings, lack of sufficient books, classes of 100 or more children, and irregular attendance. Meanwhile, the Freedmen's Bureau undertook to train black teachers, and by 1869 most of the 3,000 teachers in freedmen's schools were black.

INDEPENDENT BLACK CHURCHES Before the war, most slaves had attended white churches or services supervised by whites. Once free, African Americans quickly established their own congregations led by black preachers. In the first year of freedom, the Methodist Church South lost fully half of its black members. By 1870 the Negro Baptist Church had increased its membership threefold when compared to the membership in 1850, and the African Methodist Episcopal Church expanded at an even greater rate.

Black churches were so important because they were the only major organizations in the African American community controlled by blacks. Black ministers were respected leaders, and many of the black men elected to political office during Reconstruction were preachers. As it had in slavery, religion offered African Americans a place of refuge in a hostile white world and provided them with hope, comfort, and a means of self-identification.

New Working Conditions

As a largely propertyless class, blacks in the postwar South had no choice but to work for white landowners. Except for paying

After living for years in a society where teaching slaves to read and write was usually illegal, freedpeople viewed literacy as a key to securing their newfound freedom. African Americans were not merely "anxious to learn," a school official in Virginia reported, they were "crazy to learn."

©Bettmann/Getty Images

wages, whites wanted to retain the old system of labor, including close supervision, gang labor, and physical punishment. Determined to remove all emblems of servitude, African Americans refused to work under these conditions, and they demanded time off to devote to their own interests. Convinced that working at one's own pace was part of freedom, they simply would not work as long or as hard as they had in slavery. Because of shorter hours and the withdrawal of children and women from the fields, work output declined by an estimated 35 percent in freedom. Blacks also refused to live in the old slave quarters located near the master's house. Instead, they erected cabins on distant parts of the plantation. Wages at first were $5 or $6 a month plus provisions and a cabin; by 1867, they had risen to an average of $10 a month.

SHARECROPPING These changes eventually led to the rise of sharecropping. Under this arrangement, African American families farmed discrete plots of land and then at the end of the year split the crop with the white landowner. Sharecropping had higher status and offered greater personal freedom than being a wage laborer. "I am not working for wages," one black farmer declared in defending his right to leave the plantation at will, "but am part owner of the crop and as [such,] I have all the rights that you or any other man has." Although black per-capita agricultural income increased 40 percent in freedom, sharecropping was a harshly exploitative system in which black families often sank into perpetual debt.

The Freedmen's Bureau

The task of supervising the transition from slavery to freedom on southern plantations fell to the Freedmen's Bureau, a unique experiment in social policy supported by the federal government. Assigned the task of protecting freedpeople's economic rights, approximately 550 local agents supervised and regulated working conditions in southern agriculture after the war. The racial attitudes of Bureau agents varied widely, as did their commitment and competence. Then, too, they had to depend on the army to enforce their decisions.

BUREAU'S MIXED RECORD Most agents encouraged or required written contracts between white planters and black laborers, specifying not only wages but also the conditions of employment. Although agents sometimes intervened to protect freedpeople from unfair treatment, they also provided important help to planters. They insisted that black laborers not desert at harvest time; they arrested those who violated their contracts or refused to sign new ones at the beginning of the year; and they preached the gospel of work and the need to be orderly and respectful. Given such attitudes, freedpeople increasingly complained that Bureau agents were mere tools of the planter class. "They are, in fact, the planters' guards, and nothing else," claimed the *New Orleans Tribune,* a black newspaper.

END OF THE BUREAU The primary means of enforcing working conditions were the Freedmen's Courts, which Congress created in 1866 to avoid the discrimination African Americans received in state courts. These new courts functioned as military tribunals, and often the agent was the entire court. The sympathy black laborers received varied from state to state.

But in 1869, with the Bureau's work scarcely under way, Congress decided to shut it down, and by 1872 it had gone out of business. Despite its mixed record, it was the most effective agency in protecting blacks' civil and political rights.

>> MAPPING THE PAST <<

A Georgia Plantation after the War

Source: Library of Congress, Prints and Photographs Division [LC-DIG-ppmsca-20632]

"We made crops on shares for three years after freedom, and then we commenced to rent. They [the white landlords] didn't pay everything they promised. They [have] taken a lot of it away from us. They said figures don't lie. You know how it was. You dassent [dare not] dispute a man's word then."—Richard Crump, an ex-slave

CONTEXT

After emancipation, sharecropping became the dominant form of agricultural labor in the South. Black families no longer lived in the old slave quarters but dispersed to separate plots of land that they farmed for themselves. At the end of the year, each sharecropper turned over part of the crop to the white landowner.

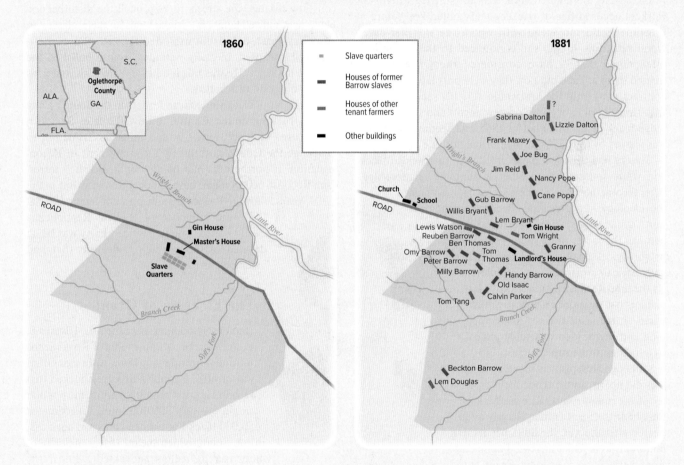

MAP READING

1. Compare the location of the master's house in relationship to the slave quarters with the location of the landlord's house and the houses of former slaves and other tenant farmers.
2. What buildings appear on the 1881 map but not on the 1860s map?
3. Describe the location of the houses of other tenant farmers in relationship to the houses of former slaves.

MAP INTERPRETATION

1. What might explain the positioning of the master's house between the slave quarters and the gin house on the 1860 map?
2. What does the location of houses on the 1881 map suggest about relations between former slaves and other tenant farmers? Between all tenant farmers and the landlord?
3. What do the names and colors of the tenant farmer homes suggest about the mobility of families during Reconstruction?

Its disbanding signaled the beginning of the northern retreat from Reconstruction.

Planters and a New Way of Life

PLANTERS' NEW VALUES Planters and other white southerners faced emancipation with dread. "All the traditions and habits of both races had been suddenly overthrown," a Tennessee planter recalled, "and neither knew just what to do, or how to accommodate themselves to the new situation."

The old ideal of a paternalistic planter, which required a facade of black subservience and affection, gave way to an emphasis on strictly economic relationships. Mary Jones, a Georgia slaveholder before the war who did more for her workers than the law required, lost all patience when two workers accused her of trickery and hauled her before a Freedmen's Bureau agent, with whom she won her case. Upon returning home, she announced to the assembled freedpeople that "I have considered them friends and treated them as such but now they were only laborers under contract, and only the law would rule between us." Only with time did planters develop new norms and standards to judge black behavior. What in 1865 had seemed insolence was viewed by the 1870s as the normal attitude of freedom.

Slavery had been a complex institution that welded black and white southerners together in intimate relationships. After the war, however, planters increasingly embraced the ideology of segregation. Because emancipation significantly reduced the social distance between the races, white southerners sought psychological separation and kept dealings with African Americans to a minimum. By the time Reconstruction ended, white planters had developed a new way of life based on the institutions of sharecropping and segregation and undergirded by a militant white supremacy.

Although most planters kept their land, they did not regain the economic prosperity of the prewar years. Rice plantations, unsuitable to tenant farming, largely disappeared after the war. In addition, southern cotton growers faced increased competition from new areas such as India, Egypt, and Brazil. Cotton prices began a long decline, and by 1880 the value of southern farms had slid 33 percent below the level of 1860.

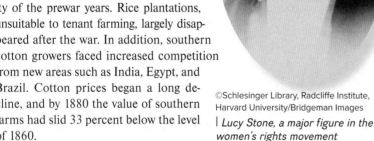

©Schlesinger Library, Radcliffe Institute, Harvard University/Bridgeman Images

| *Lucy Stone, a major figure in the women's rights movement*

✓ **REVIEW**

Why were the church and the school central to African American hopes after the Civil War? To what degree did working conditions for African Americans change?

THE ABANDONMENT OF RECONSTRUCTION

ON CHRISTMAS DAY 1875, A white acquaintance approached Charles Caldwell on the streets of Clinton, Mississippi, and invited him into Chilton's store to have a drink to celebrate the holiday. A former slave, Caldwell was a state senator and the leader of the Republican Party in Hinds County, Mississippi. But the black leader's fearlessness made him a marked man. Only two months earlier, he had been forced to flee the county to escape a white mob angry about a Republican barbecue he and his fellow Republicans had organized. For four days the mob hunted down and killed nearly 40 Republican leaders for presuming to hold a political meeting. Despite that hostility, Caldwell had returned to vote in the November state election. Even more boldly, he had led a black militia company through the streets to help quell the disturbances. Now, as Caldwell and his "friend" raised their glasses in a holiday toast, a gunshot exploded through the window. Caldwell collapsed, mortally wounded from a bullet to the back of his head. He was taken outside, where his assassins riddled his body with bullets.

A number of black Republican leaders in the South during Reconstruction shared Charles Caldwell's fate. Southern whites used violence, terror, and political assassination to challenge the federal government's commitment to Reconstruction. If northerners had boldly countered such terrorism, Reconstruction might have ended differently. But in the years following President Johnson's impeachment trial in 1868, the influence of Radical Republicans steadily waned. The Republican Party was being drained of the crusading idealism that had stamped its early years.

The Election of Grant

Immensely popular after the war, Ulysses S. Grant was the natural choice of Republicans to run for president in 1868. Although Grant was elected, Republicans were shocked that despite his great military stature, his popular margin was only 300,000 votes. An estimated 450,000 black Republican votes had been cast in the South, which meant that a majority of whites casting ballots had voted Democratic. The 1868 election helped convince Republican leaders that an amendment securing black suffrage throughout the nation was necessary.

FIFTEENTH AMENDMENT In February 1869 Congress sent the Fifteenth Amendment to the states for ratification. It forbade any state to deny the right to vote on grounds of race, color, or previous condition of servitude. Some Radicals had hoped to forbid literacy or property requirements to protect blacks further. Others wanted a simple

Source: Library of Congress, Prints and Photographs Division [LC-USZC4-2399]

| *From the beginning of Reconstruction, African Americans demanded the right to vote as free citizens. The Fifteenth Amendment, ratified in 1870, secured that right for black males. In New York City, black citizens paraded in support of Ulysses S. Grant for president. Parades played a central role in campaigning: this parade exhibits the usual banners, flags, costumes, and a band. Blacks in both the North and the South voted solidly for the Republican Party as the party of Lincoln and emancipation, although white violence in the South increasingly reduced black turnout.*

declaration that all adult male citizens had the right to vote. But the moderates in the party were aware that many northerners were increasingly worried about the number of emigrants who were again entering the country and wanted to be able to restrict their voting. As a result, the final amendment left loopholes that eventually allowed southern states to disenfranchise African Americans. The amendment was ratified in March 1870, aided by the votes of the four southern states that had not completed the process of Reconstruction and thus were also required to endorse this amendment before being readmitted to Congress.

WOMEN'S SUFFRAGE REJECTED Proponents of women's suffrage were gravely disappointed when Congress refused to prohibit voting discrimination on the basis of sex

as well as race. The Women's Loyal League, led by Elizabeth Cady Stanton and Susan B. Anthony, had pressed for first the Fourteenth and then the Fifteenth Amendment to recognize women's public role. But even most Radicals, contending that black rights had to be ensured first, were unwilling to back women's suffrage. The Fifteenth Amendment ruptured the feminist movement. Although disappointed that women were not included in its provisions, Lucy Stone and the American Woman Suffrage Association urged ratification. Stanton and Anthony, however, broke with their former allies among the Radicals, denounced the amendment, and organized the National Woman Suffrage Association to work for passage of a new amendment giving women the ballot. The division hampered the women's rights movement for decades to come.

The Grant Administration

Ulysses Grant was ill at ease with the political process. His simple, quiet manner, while superb for commanding armies, did not serve him as well in public life, and his well-known resolution withered when he was uncertain of his goal. Also, he lacked the moral commitment to make Reconstruction succeed.

CORRUPTION UNDER GRANT A series of scandals wracked Grant's presidency. Although Grant did not profit personally, he remained loyal to his friends and displayed little zeal to root out wrongdoing. His relatives were implicated in a scheme to corner the gold market, and his private secretary escaped conviction for stealing federal whiskey revenues only because Grant interceded on his behalf. His secretary of war resigned to avoid impeachment.

Nor was Congress immune from the lowered tone of public life. In such a climate ruthless state machines, led by men who favored the status quo, came to dominate the party. Office and power became ends in themselves, and party leaders worked in close cooperation with northern industrial interests. The few Radicals still active in public life increasingly repudiated Grant and the Republican governments in the South. Congress in 1872 passed an amnesty act, removing the restrictions of the Fourteenth Amendment on officeholding except for about 200 to 300 ex-Confederate leaders.

As corruption in both the North and the South worsened, reformers became more interested in cleaning up government than in protecting blacks' rights. These liberal Republicans opposed the continued presence of the army in the South, denounced the corruption of southern governments as well as the national government, and advocated free trade and civil service reform. In 1872 they broke with the Republican Party and nominated for president Horace Greeley, the editor of the *New York Tribune.* A onetime Radical, Greeley had become disillusioned with Reconstruction and urged a restoration of home rule in the South as well as adoption of civil service reform. Democrats decided to back the Liberal Republican ticket. The Republicans renominated Grant, who, despite the defection of a number of prominent Radicals, won an easy victory with 56 percent of the popular vote.

As president, Ulysses Grant's gratitude toward friends led him to appoint a number of officials who betrayed his trust. But the president acted firmly to prosecute terrorism pursued by the Ku Klux Klan, and he appointed a record number of African Americans to government positions. Frederick Douglass approvingly noted that one federal department he visited included 249 black officials and there were "many more holding important [government] positions . . . in different parts of the country."

Source: Library of Congress, Prints and Photographs Division [LC-DIG-pga-07644]

OUR TICKET.

for President Vice President.

SEYMOUR. BLAIR.

OUR MOTTO:
THIS IS A WHITE MAN'S COUNTRY:
LET WHITE MEN RULE.

©The Frent Collection/Getty Images

| *This campaign badge from 1868 made the sentiments of white Democrats clear.*

Growing Northern Disillusionment

CIVIL RIGHTS ACT OF 1875 During Grant's second term, Congress passed the Civil Rights Act of 1875, the last major piece of Reconstruction legislation. This law prohibited racial discrimination in all public accommodations, transportation, places of amusement, and juries. At the same time, Congress rejected a ban on segregation in public schools, which was almost universally practiced in the North as well as the South. Although some railroads, streetcars, and public accommodations in both sections were desegregated after the bill passed, the federal government made little attempt to enforce the law, and it was ignored throughout most of the South. In 1883 the Supreme Court struck down its provisions except the one relating to juries.

Despite passage of the Civil Rights Act, many northerners were growing disillusioned with Reconstruction. They were repelled by the corruption of the southern governments, they were tired of the violence and disorder in the South, and they had little faith in black Americans. "We have tried this long enough," remarked one influential northern Republican of Reconstruction. "Now let the South alone."

DEPRESSION AND DEMOCRATIC RESURGENCE As the agony of the war became more distant, the Panic of 1873 diverted public attention from Reconstruction to economic issues. In the severe depression that followed over the next four years, some 3 million people found themselves out of work. Congress became caught up in the question of whether printing greenbacks would help the economy prosper. Battered by the panic and the corruption issue, the Republicans lost a shocking 77 seats in Congress in the 1874 elections and, along with them, control of the House of Representatives for the first time

Major Players in Reconstruction

Radical Republicans	Advocated rights for freedpeople; believed Congress should set terms of Reconstruction
Moderate Republicans	Looked to bar Confederates from regaining power and to give slaves federal protection, but did not favor racial equality
African American officials	15–20 percent of state officeholders, 6 percent of members of Congress; generally more conservative than rural southern blacks
Scalawags	White southern Republicans; mostly yeoman farmers from upland counties; looked to restore prosperity, build railroads and schools
Carpetbaggers	White northerners in the South; made up a small percentage of Republican voters but held disproportionate number of political offices
Teachers, Freedmen's Bureau Schools	At first, northern middle-class white women sent by missionary societies; by 1869 black teachers made up a majority
Ministers, African American churches	Community leaders; black churches spread widely in the South after the war
White planters	Most did not regain prewar prosperity; developed a new way of life based on sharecropping and segregation
Redeemers	White Democrats who ousted Reconstruction governments; KKK and other paramilitary organizations used force to achieve their goals

(*all photos*) Source: Library of Congress, Prints and Photographs Division [LC-USZC4-2399]

since 1861. "The truth is our people are tired out with the worn out cry of 'Southern outrages'!!" one Republican concluded. "Hard times and heavy taxes make them wish the 'ever lasting nigger' were in hell or Africa." Republicans spoke more and more about cutting loose the unpopular southern governments.

The Triumph of White Supremacy

As northern commitment to Reconstruction waned, southern Democrats set out to overthrow the remaining Radical governments. White Republicans already in the South felt heavy pressure to desert their party. In Mississippi one party member justified his decision to leave on the grounds that otherwise he would have "to live a life of social oblivion" and his children would have no future.

RACISM To poor white southerners who lacked social standing, the Democratic appeal to racial solidarity offered great comfort. As one explained, "I may be poor and my manners may be crude, but . . . because I am a white man, I have a right to be treated with respect by Negroes. . . . That I am poor is not

as important as that I am a white man; and no Negro is ever going to forget that he is not a white man." The large landowners and other wealthy groups that led southern Democrats objected less to black southerners voting. These well-to-do leaders did not face social and economic competition from African Americans, and in any case, they were confident that if outside influences were removed, they could control the black vote.

Democrats also resorted to economic pressure to undermine Republican power. In heavily black counties, white observers at the polls took down the names of black residents who cast Republican ballots and published them in local newspapers. Planters were urged to discharge black tenants who persisted in voting Republican. But terror and violence provided the most effective means to overthrow the Radical regimes. A number of paramilitary organizations broke up Republican meetings, terrorized white and black Republicans, assassinated Republican leaders, and prevented black citizens from voting. The most famous was the Ku Klux Klan, or KKK, founded in 1866 in Tennessee. It and similar groups functioned as unofficial arms of the Democratic Party.

CONTESTING THE NIGHT In the war for supremacy, contesting control of the night was of paramount concern to both southern whites and blacks. Before emancipation, masters attempted to control the nighttime hours, with a system of passes and patrols that chased slaves who went hunting or tried to sneak a visit to a family member at a neighboring plantation. For slaves the night provided precious hours not devoted to work: time to read, to meet for worship, school, or dancing. During Reconstruction, African Americans actively took back the night for a host of activities, including a custom that white Americans had enjoyed since the beginning of the republic: torchlight political parades. In Holly Springs, Mississippi, hundreds, even thousands of black citizens filled the streets during campaigns, holding aloft torches and "transparencies"–pictures painted on thin cloth, 10 to 12 feet long–the entire scene lit in an eerie, flickering glow.

Part of the Klan's mission was to recoup this contested ground and to limit the ability of African Americans to use the night as they pleased. Sometimes the Klan's threat of violence was indirect: one or two riders galloping through black neighborhoods rattling fences with lances. Other times several "dens" of the KKK might gather to ride from plantation to plantation over the course of a night, stopping in every black home they could reach and demanding all firearms. Other times the violence was direct: beatings and executions–again, heightened by the dark of night.

Congress finally moved to break the power of the Klan with the Force Act of 1870 and the Ku Klux Klan Act of 1871. These laws made it a felony to interfere with the right to vote; they also authorized use of the army and suspension of the writ of habeas corpus. The Grant administration eventually suspended the writ of habeas corpus in nine South Carolina counties and arrested hundreds of suspected Klan members throughout the South. Although these actions weakened the Klan, terrorist organizations continued to operate underground.

MISSISSIPPI PLAN Then in 1875 Democrats inaugurated what became known as the Mississippi Plan, the decision to use as much violence as necessary to carry the state election. Several local papers trumpeted, "Carry the election peaceably if we can, forcibly if we must." When Republican governor Adelbert Ames requested federal troops to stop the violence, Grant's advisors warned that sending troops to Mississippi would cost the party the Ohio election. In the end the administration told Ames to depend on his own forces. Bolstered by terrorism, the Democrats swept the election in Mississippi. Violence and intimidation prevented as many as 60,000 black and white Republicans from voting, converting the normal Republican majority into a Democratic majority of 30,000. Mississippi had been "redeemed."

The Disputed Election of 1876

With Republicans on the defensive across the nation, the 1876 presidential election was crucial to the final overthrow of Reconstruction. The Republicans nominated Ohio governor Rutherford B. Hayes to oppose Samuel Tilden, governor of

New York. Once again, violence prevented many Republican votes, this time an estimated quarter of a million, from being cast in the South. Tilden had a clear majority of 250,000 in the popular vote, but the outcome in the Electoral College was in doubt because both parties claimed South Carolina, Florida, and Louisiana, the only reconstructed states still in Republican hands. Hayes needed all three states to be elected, for even without them, Tilden had amassed 184 electoral votes, one short of a majority. Republican canvassing boards in power disqualified enough Democratic votes to give each state to Hayes.

To arbitrate the disputed returns, Congress established a 15-member electoral commission: 5 members each from the Senate, the House, and the Supreme Court. By a straight party vote of 8 to 7, the commission awarded the disputed electoral votes–and the presidency–to Hayes.

COMPROMISE OF 1877 When angry Democrats threatened a filibuster to prevent the electoral votes from being counted, key Republicans met with southern Democrats on February 26 at the Wormley Hotel in Washington. There they reached an informal understanding, later known as the Compromise of 1877. Hayes's supporters agreed to withdraw federal troops from the South and not oppose the new Democratic state governments. For their part, southern Democrats dropped their opposition to Hayes's election and pledged to respect the rights of African Americans.

REDEEMERS TAKE CONTROL Without federal support, the Republican governments in South Carolina and Louisiana promptly collapsed, and Democrats took control of the remaining states of the Confederacy. By 1877, the entire South was in the hands of the **Redeemers,** as they called themselves. Reconstruction and Republican rule had come to an end.

The Failure of Reconstruction

Reconstruction failed for a multitude of reasons. The reforming impulse that had created the Republican Party in the 1850s had been battered and worn down by the war. The new materialism of industrial America inspired in many Americans a jaded cynicism about the corruption of the age and a desire to forget uncomfortable issues. In the South, African American voters and leaders inevitably lacked a certain amount of education and experience; elsewhere, Republicans were divided over policies and options.

Yet beyond these obstacles, the sad fact remains that the ideals of Reconstruction were most clearly defeated by the deep-seated racism that permeated American life. Racism was why the white South so unrelentingly resisted Reconstruction. Racism was why most white northerners had little interest in black rights except as a means to preserve the Union or to safeguard the Republic. Racism was why northerners were willing to write off Reconstruction and with it the welfare of African Americans. While Congress might pass a constitutional amendment abolishing slavery, it could not overturn at a stroke the social habits of two centuries.

Dressed to Kill

Klan members drawn for *Harper's Weekly* magazine, 1868

Advertisement for a minstrel show, 1864

(*right & left*) Source: Library of Congress, Prints and Photographs Division [LC-USZ62-119565]; (*center*) ©The New York Public Library/Art Resource, NY

Why wear a hooded mask? Does the advertisement suggest more than one reason?

The costumes of Ku Klux Klan night riders—pointed hoods and white sheets—have become a staple of history books. But why use such outlandish disguises? To hide the identity of members, according to some accounts, or to terrorize freedpeople into thinking they were being menaced by Confederate ghosts. Historian Elaine F. Parsons has suggested that KKK performances took their cues from American popular culture: the costumes of Mardi Gras and similar carnivals, as well as minstrel shows. In behaving like carnival revelers, KKK members may have hoped to lull northern authorities into viewing the night rides as humorous pranks, not a threat to Radical rule. For southern white Democrats the theatrical night rides helped overturn the social order of Reconstruction, just as carousers at carnivals disrupted the night. The ritual garb provided seemingly innocent cover for what was truly a campaign of terror and intimidation that often turned deadly.

THINKING CRITICALLY

In what ways does the advertisement speak of experiences both frightening and humorous? In terms of popular culture, do modern horror films sometimes combine both terror and humor? Assess how this dynamic of horror and jest might have worked in terms of the different groups perceiving the Klan's activities: white northerners, white southerners, and African Americans. If this theory of why the Klan dressed as they did is true, does it make them more effective or less so as a terrorist organization?

Certainly the political equations of power, in the long term, had been changed. The North had fought fiercely during the war to preserve the Union. In doing so, it had secured the power to dominate the economic and political destiny of the nation. With the overthrow of Reconstruction, the white South had won back some of the power it had lost in 1865. But even with white supremacy triumphant, African Americans did not return to the social position they had occupied before the war. They were no longer slaves, and black southerners who walked dusty roads in search of family members, sent their children to school, or

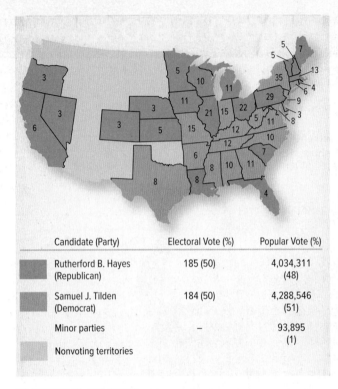

Candidate (Party)	Electoral Vote (%)	Popular Vote (%)
Rutherford B. Hayes (Republican)	185 (50)	4,034,311 (48)
Samuel J. Tilden (Democrat)	184 (50)	4,288,546 (51)
Minor parties	–	93,895 (1)
Nonvoting territories		

ELECTION OF 1876

worshiped in churches they controlled knew what a momentous change emancipation was. Even under the exploitative share-cropping system, black income rose significantly in freedom. Then, too, the Fourteenth Amendment principles of "equal protection" and "due process of law" had been written into the Constitution. These guarantees would be available for later generations to use in championing once again the Radicals' goal of racial equality.

END OF THE DAVIS BEND EXPERIMENT   But this was a struggle left to future reformers. For the time being, the clear trend was away from change or hope—especially for former slaves like Benjamin Montgomery and his sons, the owners of the old Davis plantations in Mississippi. In the 1870s bad crops, lower cotton prices, and falling land values undermined the Montgomerys' financial position, and in 1875 Jefferson Davis sued to have the sale of Brierfield invalidated. A lower court ruled against him, since he had never received legal title to the plantation. Davis appealed to the state supreme court, which, following the overthrow of Mississippi's Radical government, had a white conservative majority. In a politically motivated decision, the court awarded Brierfield to Davis in 1878, and the Montgomerys lost Hurricane as well. Reconstruction was over and done, along with the hopes that came with it.

 REVIEW

What factors in the North and the South led the federal government to abandon Reconstruction in the South?

THE WANING DAYS OF RECONSTRUCTION were filled with such ironies: of governments "redeemed" by violence and Supreme Court decisions using Fourteenth Amendment rights to protect giant corporations rather than individual African Americans. Increasingly, the industrial North focused on the economic task of integrating the South and the West into the Union. Northern factories sought southern and western raw materials (cotton, timber, cattle, and minerals) to produce goods to sell in national and international markets.

This trend was global in scope. During the coming decades European nations also scrambled to acquire natural resources and markets. In the onrushing age of imperialism, Western nations would seek to dominate newly acquired colonies in Africa and Asia. There would be gold rushes in South Africa as well as in the United States, vast cattle ranches in Argentina and Canada as well as across the American Great Plains. Farmers would open up lands in New Zealand and Australia as well as in Oklahoma and Wyoming. And just as racism replaced slavery as the central justification for white supremacy in the South, it promoted the campaigns against Indians and Hispanics in the West and in a belief in "inferior races" to be swept aside by imperialists all across the world. The ideal of a truly diverse and democratic society remained largely unsought and unfulfilled.

CHAPTER SUMMARY

Presidents Abraham Lincoln and Andrew Johnson and the Republican-dominated Congress each developed a program of Reconstruction to restore the Confederate states to the Union.

- Lincoln's 10 percent plan required that 10 percent of qualified voters from 1860 swear an oath of loyalty to begin organizing state government.

- Following Lincoln's assassination, Andrew Johnson changed Lincoln's terms and lessened Reconstruction's requirements.

- The more-radical Congress repudiated Johnson's state governments and enacted its own program of Reconstruction, which included the principle of black suffrage.

  ► Congress passed the Fourteenth and Fifteenth Amendments and also extended the life of the Freedmen's Bureau, a unique experiment in social welfare.

  ► Congress rejected land reform, however, which would have provided the freedpeople with a greater economic stake.

  ► The effort to remove Johnson from office through impeachment failed.

- The Radical governments in the South, led by black and white southerners and transplanted northerners, compiled a mixed record on matters such as racial equality, education, economic issues, and corruption.

- Reconstruction was a time of both joy and frustration for former slaves.
  - ▶ Former slaves took steps to reunite their families and establish black-controlled churches.
  - ▶ They evidenced a widespread desire for land and education.
  - ▶ Black resistance to the old system of labor led to the adoption of sharecropping.
  - ▶ The Freedmen's Bureau fostered these new working arrangements and also the beginnings of black education in the South.

- Northern public opinion became disillusioned with Reconstruction during the presidency of Ulysses S. Grant.

- Southern whites used violence, economic coercion, and racism to overthrow the Republican state governments.

- In 1877 Republican leaders agreed to end Reconstruction in exchange for Rutherford B. Hayes's election as president.

- Racism played a key role in the eventual failure of Reconstruction.

Digging Deeper

Historians' views of reconstruction have dramatically changed over the past half century. Modern studies offer a more sympathetic assessment of Reconstruction and the experience of African Americans. Indicative of this trend is Eric Foner, *Reconstruction* (2014), and his briefer treatment (with photographic essays by Joshua Brown) *Forever Free: The Story of Emancipation and Reconstruction* (2005). Michael Les Benedict treats the clash between Andrew Johnson and Congress in *The Impeachment and Trial of Andrew Johnson* (1973). Political affairs in the South during Reconstruction are examined in Dan T. Carter, *When the War Was Over* (1985), and Thomas Holt, *Black Over White* (1977), an imaginative study of black political leadership in South Carolina. Hans L. Trefousse, *Thaddeus Stevens: Nineteenth-Century Egalitarian* (1997), provides a sympathetic reassessment of the influential Radical Republican. Mark Wahlgren Summers, *A Dangerous Stir* (2009), deftly examines the ways in which fear and paranoia shaped Reconstruction. Ron Chernow, *Grant* (2017) highlights the man's commitment to fair treatment for African Americans, both through vigorous prosecution of the KKK and by the inclusion of African Americans in executive departments.

Leon F. Litwack's Pulitzer Prize-winning *Been in the Storm So Long* (1979) sensitively analyzes the transition of enslaved African Americans to freedom. Heather Andrea Williams, *Self-Taught: African American Education in Slavery and Freedom* (2005), illustrates the black drive for literacy and education. The dialectic of black-white relations is charted from the antebellum years through Reconstruction and beyond in Steven Hahn, *A Nation under Our Feet: Black Political Struggles in the Rural South from Slavery to the Great Migration* (2003). Excellent studies of changing labor relations in southern agriculture include Amy Dru Stanley's *From Bondage to Contract* (1998), Julie Saville's *The Work of Reconstruction* (1995), and John C. Rodrigue's *Reconstruction in the Cane Fields* (2001). For contrasting views of the Freedmen's Bureau, see George R. Bentley, *A History of the Freedmen's Bureau* (1955)—favorable—and Donald G. Nieman, *To Set the Law in Motion* (1979)—critical. Heather Cox Richardson explores the postwar context in the North in *The Death of Reconstruction* (2004) and considers Reconstruction in the West in *West from Appomattox* (2008).

18 The New South and the Trans-Mississippi West

1870–1914

African American migrants, known as Exodusters, hold a religious service in 1879 at Floral Hall on the Topeka, Kansas, fairgrounds. The Exodusters' journey was uncertain, as they often traveled with few resources; maintaining their faith gave them strength in their search for a better place to live in the West.

RELIGIOUS SERVICES IN THE NORTH WING OF FLORAL HALL.

>> An American Story

"COME WEST"

The news spread across the South during the late 1870s. Perhaps a man came around with a handbill telling of cheap land, or a letter might arrive from friends or relatives and be read aloud at church. The news spread in different ways, but in the end, it always spelled Kansas.

Few black farmers had been that far west themselves. More than a few knew that the abolitionist Old John Brown had made his home in Kansas before coming east to raid Harpers Ferry and set off a chain of events that led to the Civil War. After the war, it seemed that black folks might live more freely in Kansas. "You can buy land at from a dollar and a half to two dollars an acre," wrote one black settler to a friend in Louisiana. There was another advantage, he added: "They do not kill Negroes here for voting."

In 1878 such prospects excited hundreds of black families already stretched to their limits by hardship, even bloodshed. With Rutherford Hayes president, Reconstruction was at an end. Conservative whites had "redeemed" southern state governments from black and white Republicans. The future seemed uncertain.

"COME WEST," concluded *The Colored Citizen,* a newspaper in Topeka. "COME TO KANSAS." St. Louis learned of these rumblings in the first raw days of March 1879, as steamers from downriver began unloading freedpeople in large numbers. Some came with belongings and money; others, with only the clothes on their backs. By the end of 1879 more than 20,000 had arrived. With the weather still cold, they sought shelter beneath tarpaulins along the river levee, built fires, and got out frying pans to cook meals.

When the crowds overwhelmed the wharves and temporary shelters, the city's black churches banded together to house the "refugees," feed them and help them on to Kansas. Rumors that rail passage would not be free failed to shake their hopes. "We's like de chilun ob Israel when dey was led from out o' bondage by Moses," one explained, referring to the Bible's tale of the exodus of Jews from Egypt. So the "Exodusters," as they became known, pressed westward. In the end, black emigrants settled in growing towns such as Topeka and Kansas City. Men worked as hired hands; women took in laundry. With luck, couples made $350 a year, saved a bit for a home, and put down roots.

The host of Exodusters who poured into Kansas was part of a human flood westward. It had many sources—played-out farms of New England and the South, crowded cities, virtually all of Europe. In 1879, as African Americans traveled up the Mississippi to St. Louis, 1,000 white emigrants also arrived in Kansas every week. Special trains brought settlers to the plains, all eager to start anew. During the 1880s the number of Kansans jumped by 50 percent—from a million to a million and a half. Other western states experienced similar booms.

The optimism of boomers black and white could not mask the strains in the South and the Trans-Mississippi West. Largely agricultural, they struggled to find their place in the new age of industry. In the South, despite a strong push to industrialize, the continuing dominance of white supremacy helped to undercut economic growth, encouraging the scourge of sharecropping and farm tenancy and spawning a system of racial violence and caste to replace slavery. For their part, citizens of the booming West began to realize at least some of the dreams of antebellum reformers: free homesteads in Kansas and beyond, a railroad that spanned the continent, land-grant colleges to educate its people. Despite those differences, the West also built a society based on racial violence and hierarchy.

Much as the national markets emerging after the War of 1812 drew the lands beyond the Appalachian Mountains into their spheres, the industrial economy emerging after the Civil War incorporated the South and the Trans-Mississippi West in their domains. By the end of the nineteenth century, the South and the West had assumed their places as suppliers of raw materials, providers of foodstuffs, and consumers of finished goods. A nation of "regional nations" was thus knit together in the last third of the nineteenth century. Not all southerners and westerners were happy with the result. As we shall see in Chapter 21, their frustrations mounted as the Northeast enriched itself at their expense and the powers in Washington ignored their plight. <<

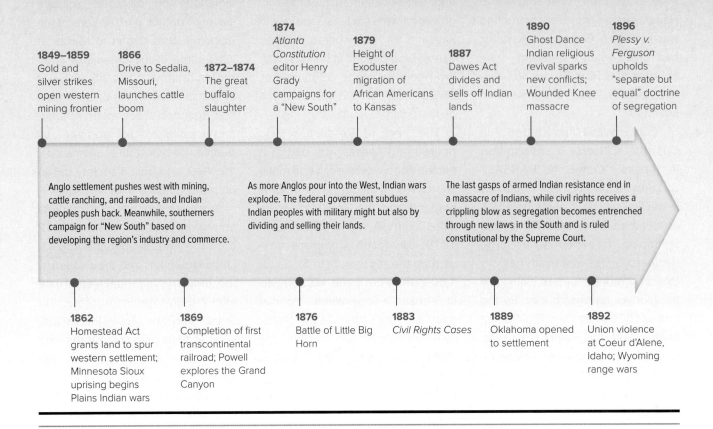

1849–1859 Gold and silver strikes open western mining frontier

1866 Drive to Sedalia, Missouri, launches cattle boom

1872–1874 The great buffalo slaughter

1874 *Atlanta Constitution* editor Henry Grady campaigns for a "New South"

1879 Height of Exoduster migration of African Americans to Kansas

1887 Dawes Act divides and sells off Indian lands

1890 Ghost Dance Indian religious revival sparks new conflicts; Wounded Knee massacre

1896 *Plessy v. Ferguson* upholds "separate but equal" doctrine of segregation

Anglo settlement pushes west with mining, cattle ranching, and railroads, and Indian peoples push back. Meanwhile, southerners campaign for "New South" based on developing the region's industry and commerce.

As more Anglos pour into the West, Indian wars explode. The federal government subdues Indian peoples with military might but also by dividing and selling their lands.

The last gasps of armed Indian resistance end in a massacre of Indians, while civil rights receives a crippling blow as segregation becomes entrenched through new laws in the South and is ruled constitutional by the Supreme Court.

1862 Homestead Act grants land to spur western settlement; Minnesota Sioux uprising begins Plains Indian wars

1869 Completion of first transcontinental railroad; Powell explores the Grand Canyon

1876 Battle of Little Big Horn

1883 *Civil Rights Cases*

1889 Oklahoma opened to settlement

1892 Union violence at Coeur d'Alene, Idaho; Wyoming range wars

THE SOUTHERN BURDEN

INEQUITIES BETWEEN THE AGRICULTURAL SOUTH and the industrial North infuriated Henry Grady, the editor of the *Atlanta Constitution*. Grady often told the story of the poor cotton farmer buried in a pine coffin in the piney woods of Georgia. Except the coffin hadn't been made in Georgia but in Cincinnati. The coffin nails had been forged in Pittsburgh, though an iron mine lay nearby. Even the farmer's cotton coat was made in New York and his trousers in Chicago. The "South didn't furnish a thing on earth for that funeral but the corpse and the hole in the ground!" fumed Grady. The irony of the story was the tragedy of the South. The region had human and natural resources aplenty but few factories to manufacture the goods it needed and none of the profits more of them would surely bring.

THE GOSPEL OF A "NEW SOUTH" In the 1880s Grady campaigned to bring about a frothy "New South" of bustling industry, cities, and commerce. According to his gospel, the business class would displace the old planter class as southerners raced "to out-Yankee the Yankee." Grady and other publicists recognized the South's potential. Extending from Delaware south to Florida and west to Texas, the region

took in a third of the nation's total area. It held a third of its arable farmlands, vast tracts of lumber, and rich deposits of coal, iron, oil, and fertilizers.

To overcome the destruction of the Civil War and the loss of slaveholding wealth, apostles of the New South campaigned to catch up with the industrial North. Yet well into the twentieth century, Grady's New South remained the poorest section of the country. Worse still, the South suffered the burden of an unwieldy labor system that was often unskilled, usually underpaid, and always divided by race.

Agriculture in the New South

A COTTON-DOMINATED ECONOMY For all the hopeful talk of industrialization, the economy of the postwar South remained agricultural, tied to cash crops like tobacco, rice, sugar, and especially cotton. By using fertilizers, planters were able to introduce cotton into areas once considered marginal. The number of acres planted with cotton more than doubled between 1870 and 1900. Some southern farmers sought prosperity in crops other than cotton. George Washington Carver, of Alabama's Tuskegee Institute (see Chapter 21), persuaded many poor black farmers to plant peanuts. But most southern soils were too acidic and the spring rains too heavy for other legumes and grains to flourish. Parasites and diseases plagued cattle herds. Work animals like mules were raised more cheaply in other regions. Try as southerners might to diversify, cotton still dominated their economy.

From 1880 to 1900 world demand for cotton grew slowly, and prices fell. As farms in other parts of the country became larger and more efficient and tended by fewer workers per acre, southern farms decreased in size, the result of old plantations splintering and new births mushrooming. Across the country, the number of children born per mother was dropping, but in the South, large families remained common because more children meant more farmhands. Each year, fewer acres of land were available for each person to cultivate. Even though the southern economy kept pace with national growth, **per capita income** fell behind.

Tenancy and Sharecropping

The end of slavery brought hopes of economic independence to newly freed slaves across the South. John Solomon Lewis rented land to grow cotton in Tensas Parish, Louisiana, after

©The Metropolitan Museum of Art/Art Resource, NY

After the Civil War, African Americans marked their freedom by ending field labor for most women and children. The women instead played a vital role in the domestic economy. Home garden plots supplemented the family food supply.

the Civil War. A depression in the 1870s dashed his dreams. "I was in debt," Lewis explained, "and the man I rented land from said every year I must rent again to pay the other year, and so I rents and rents and each year I gets deeper and deeper in debt."

AGRICULTURAL LADDER The dream of economic independence rested on a theory of landholding called the "agricultural ladder." According to this theory, any poor man willing to work hard and pinch pennies could eventually become a landowner, moving rung by rung up an imaginary ladder, first as a paid hand, then as a sharecropper reimbursed with a portion of the crop, then as a tenant who rented the land he worked, and finally emerging as an independent, landowning farmer.

In practice, harsh realities overwhelmed theory, as John Solomon Lewis and other poor farmers—black and white—learned. The South's best land remained in the hands of large plantation owners. Few freedpeople or poor whites ever had enough money to acquire property. The problem lay in a ruinous system of credit. The harvest, whether produced by croppers or tenants or even small, independent farmers, was rarely enough for the worker to make ends meet, let alone to pay off debts and move up the agricultural ladder. Most farmers borrowed money in the spring just to buy seeds, tools, or necessities such as food and clothing. Usually the only source of supplies and credit was the country store.

When John Solomon Lewis and other tenants entered the store, they saw two prices: one for cash and one for credit. The credit price might be as much as 60 percent higher. Creditors justified the difference on the grounds that high interest rates protected them against unpaid loans. As security for the loan, independent farmers mortgaged their land and soon slipped into tenancy as debts mounted and creditors foreclosed on their farms. The only asset tenants had was the crop they owned or the share they received. So they put up a mortgage, or **lien,** on the crop. The lien gave the shopkeeper first claim on the crop until the debt was paid.

Across the South, sharecropping and crop liens reduced many farmers to virtual slavery by shackling them to perpetual debt. Year after year, they rented or worked the land and borrowed against their future returns until they found themselves so deeply in debt that they could never escape. This economic dependence, known as **debt peonage,** turned the agricultural ladder into an agricultural slide, robbing small farmers of their land and sending them to the bottom rungs of tenancy, sharecropping, and migrant-farm work. By the 1880s three of every four African American farmers in the Black Belt states of Mississippi, Alabama, and Georgia were croppers. Twenty years later a majority of southern white farmers had fallen into sharecropping. Few moved up. The landlord or shopkeeper (often the same person) could insist that tenants grow only cash crops such as cotton rather than things they could eat. Most landlords also required that cotton be ginned, baled, and marketed through their mills—at rates they controlled.

>> MAPPING THE PAST <<

TENANT FARMING, 1900

Source: Library of Congress, Prints and Photographs Division [LC-DIG-stereo-1s03961]

> "You get off. I don't need you no more." —Unnamed landlord to tenant farmer Walter Ballard on the day Ballard was let go

CONTEXT

Tenant farming dominated southern agriculture after the Civil War. It spread rapidly across the states of the former Confederacy and replaced slavery as the principal source of farm labor. By 1900, it had moved west of the Mississippi River, where low crop prices, high costs, and a harsh environment forced many independent farmers into tenancy.

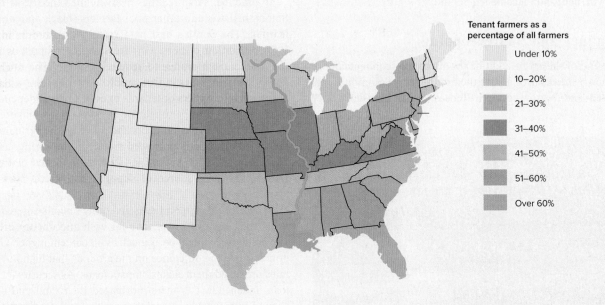

Tenant farmers as a percentage of all farmers

- Under 10%
- 10–20%
- 21–30%
- 31–40%
- 41–50%
- 51–60%
- Over 60%

MAP READING

For some questions, information on the map later in this chapter, "Natural Environment of the West," may prove useful.

1. In what region is farm tenancy most heavily concentrated?
2. Which states have the lowest concentrations of tenant farmers?
3. Where is the Mississippi River? In what states west of the Mississippi do we find tenant farmers? Where do they form more than 30 percent of all farmers?

MAP INTERPRETATION

1. What geographic factors help account for the low percentage of tenant farmers in the band of states extending south from Montana and Idaho? In the Northeast?
2. The information above suggests that a harsh environment helped push independent farmers into tenancy. Yet in the Black Belt areas of the South and in South Carolina, conditions are good for raising crops. What other factors lead these states to have such high rates of tenancy?

DEBT PEONAGE IN INDIA, EGYPT, AND BRAZIL The slide of sharecroppers and tenants into debt peonage occurred elsewhere in the cotton-growing world. In India, Egypt, and Brazil agricultural laborers gave up **subsistence farming** to raise cotton as a cash crop during the American Civil War, when the North prevented southern cotton from being exported. New railroad and telegraph lines built in these growing regions helped make the export of cotton more efficient and profitable. But when prices fell, growers borrowed to make ends meet, as in the American South. In India, moneylenders charged interest as high as 24 percent annually on such debts; in Egypt, sometimes as high as 60 percent. In the mid-1870s, the pressures on cotton growers led them to revolt in India and Brazil, attacking moneylenders, destroying land records, and refusing to pay taxes. As we shall see in Chapter 21, in the 1890s, American farmers rose up too.

Southern Industry

The crusade for a New South did bring change. One of the most important adjustments began on May 30, 1886. The wider gauge or track width of southern railroads had presented endless difficulties for moving freight and passengers between North and South. In a single day 8,000 workers narrowed the gauge on 2,000 miles of the Lackawanna & Northern Railroad's southern line. Within three days thousands more workers converted the space between tracks across the South to the smaller standard of the North. For the first time trains moved easily from one region to another. Coupled with a railroad building boom starting in 1879, the South began knitting itself into a national transportation network and an industrialized economy. From 1869 to 1909, industrial production in the South grew faster than the national rate. So did productivity for southern workers.

BOOM IN TEXTILES   Among the booming industries of the South, cotton remained king. With cotton fiber and cheap labor close at hand, 400 cotton mills were humming by 1900. They employed almost 100,000 workers. Most new textile workers were poor white southerners escaping competition from black farm laborers or fleeing the hardscrabble life of the mountains. Entire families worked in the mills. Older men had the most trouble adjusting. They lacked the experience, temperament, and dexterity to tend spindles and looms in cramped mills. Only over time, as farm folk adapted to the tedious rhythm of factories, did southerners become competitive with workers from other regions of the United States and western Europe.

TOBACCO AND CIGARETTES   The tobacco industry also thrived in the New South. Before the Civil War, American tastes had run to cigars, snuff (powdered tobacco that is inhaled), and chewing tobacco. In 1876 James Bonsack, an 18-year-old Virginian, invented a machine to roll cigarettes. That was just the device Washington Duke and his son James needed to boost the fortunes of their growing tobacco business. Cigarettes suited the new urban market in the North, "clean, quick, and potent" according to one observer.

Between 1860 and 1900 the annual rate of tobacco consumption nearly quadrupled. Americans spent more money on tobacco than on clothes or shoes. The sudden interest in smoking offered southerners a rare opportunity to control a national market. But its factories were so hot, the stench of tobacco so strong, and the work so exhausting that native-born white southerners generally refused the jobs. Duke solved the labor problem by hiring Jewish immigrants, experts in making cigars, to train black southerners in the techniques of tobacco work. He promoted cigarettes in a national advertising campaign, using gimmicks, such as collectible picture cards. By the 1890s his American Tobacco Company led the industry.

Timber and Steel

The realities of southern economic life were more accurately reflected in lumber and steel than in tobacco and textiles. After the Civil War, the South possessed more than 60 percent of the nation's timber resources. With growing demand from towns and cities across the nation, lumber and turpentine became the South's chief industries and employers.

| This girl had been working in a cotton mill in Whitnel, North Carolina, for about a year, sometimes on the night shift. She made 48 cents a day. When asked how old she was, she hesitated, then said, "I don't remember." But then she added, confidentially, "I'm not old enough to work, but do just the same."
Source: National Archives & Records Administration (NWDNS-102-LH-462)

Source: Library of Congress, Prints and Photographs Division [LC-USZ62-79320]

| *Tobacco and sex became entwined in the nineteenth century, as this label for B. H. Watson's "Gentlemen's Delight" tobacco reveals. A bare-shouldered woman, her dark hair tumbling behind her, beckons buyers to purchase the product that promises nothing but the delight on the label's title.*

If anything, however, aggressive lumbering left the South poorer. Corruption of state officials and a relaxed federal timber policy allowed northerners and foreigners to acquire huge forest tracts at artificially low prices. The timber was then sold as raw lumber rather than as more profitable finished products such as cedar shingles or the coffins Henry Grady liked to mention. Overcutting added little to local economies. Logging camps were isolated and temporary. Visitors described the lumberjacks as "single, homeless, and possessionless." Once loggers leveled the forests around their camps, they moved on to other sites. Most sawmills operated for only a few years before the owners followed the loggers to a new area.

ENVIRONMENTAL COSTS The environmental costs were high. In the South, as elsewhere, overcutting and other logging practices stripped hillsides bare. As spring rains eroded soil and unleashed floods, forests lost their capacity for self-renewal. By 1901 a Georgian complained that "from most of the visible land the timber is entirely gone." With it went the golden eagles, the peregrine falcons, and other native species.

Turpentine mills, logging, and lumber milling provided young black southerners with their greatest source of employment. Occasionally an African American rose to be a supervisor, though most supervisors were white. Southerners often blamed these workers, not the operators or the dreadful working conditions and low pay, for the industry's high turnover rates and low morale among workers. As one critic complained, "The sawmill negro is rather shiftless and is not

inclined to stay in any one location." In fact, most black workers left the mills in search of higher wages or to sharecrop in order to marry and support families.

BIRMINGHAM STEEL The iron and steel industry most disappointed promoters of the New South. The availability of coke as a fuel made Chattanooga, Tennessee, and Birmingham, Alabama, major centers for foundries. By the 1890s the Tennessee Coal, Iron, and Railway Company (TCI) of Birmingham was turning out iron pipe for gas, water, and sewer lines vital to cities. Unfortunately Birmingham's iron deposits were ill-suited for the kinds of steel in demand. In 1907 the financially strapped TCI was sold to the giant U.S. Steel Corporation, controlled by northern interests.

The pattern of lost opportunity was repeated in other southern industries—mining, chemical fertilizers, cottonseed oil, and railroads. Under the campaign for a New South, all grew dramatically in employment and value, but not enough to end poverty or industrialize the region.

The Sources of Southern Poverty

Why did poverty persist in the New South? Surely, as many southerners claimed, the South became a colonial economy controlled by northern business interests. Raw materials such as minerals, timber, and cotton were shipped to other regions, which earned larger profits by turning them into finished goods.

LATE START IN INDUSTRIALIZING Three other factors also contributed to the region's poverty. First, the South began to industrialize later than the Northeast. Northern workers produced more not because they were more energetic or disciplined but because they were more experienced.

Second, the South contained only a small technological community to guide its industrial development. Northern engineers and mechanics seldom followed northern capital into the region. Few people were available to adapt modern technology to southern conditions or to teach southerners how to do it themselves, however much they wanted to learn.

UNDEREDUCATED LABOR Education might have overcome the problem by upgrading the region's workforce. But no region in the nation spent less on schooling than did the South. Southern leaders, drawn from the ranks of the upper class, cared little about educating ordinary white residents and openly resisted educating black southerners. And the region's low wages encouraged educated workers to leave the South for higher pay. Few southern states invested much in technical colleges and engineering schools. As a result, none could match those of the North.

THE ISOLATED SOUTHERN LABOR MARKET Lack of education aggravated the third and most important source of southern poverty: the isolation of its labor force. In 1900 agriculture still dominated the southern economy. It required unskilled, low-paid sharecroppers and wage laborers.

| The booming timber industry often left the South poorer due to the harsh methods of extracting lumber. Here logs that have been floated down Lost Creek, Tennessee, are loaded onto a train. Getting the logs out was a messy affair: skidding them down crude paths to a creek and leaving behind open fields piled with rotting branches and leaves or needles, where once a forest stood. Rains eroded the newly bare hillsides, polluting streams. Downriver, tanneries, pulp mills, and sawmills emptied waste and sewage into the water, making many streams into little more than open sewers.
©Corbis via Getty Images

Southerners feared that outsiders, with their new ways, might spread discontent among workers. So southern states discouraged social services and opportunities that might have attracted human and financial resources. Educated, skilled workers often left for higher-paying jobs in the more hospitable North. The South remained poor because it received too little, not too much, outside investment.

> ✓ **REVIEW**
>
> What factors explain the failure of the campaign for a "New South" and which, in your view, is the most important?

LIFE IN THE NEW SOUTH

LIFE IN THE NEW SOUTH was a constant struggle to balance love of hell-raising with the equally powerful pull of Christian piety. Divided in its soul, the South was also divided by race. Even after the Civil War ended slavery, 90 percent of African Americans continued to live in the rural South. Without slavery, however, southerners lost the system of social control that had defined race relations. Over time they substituted a new system of **segregation,** or racial separation, that eased but never eliminated white fear that African Americans might overturn the racial hierarchy.

Rural Life

Pleasure, piety, race—all divided southern life, in town and country alike. Life separated along lines of gender as well, especially in the rural areas where most southerners lived.

HUNTING Southern males found one source of pleasure in hunting. Hunting offered men welcome relief from heavy farmwork. For rural people a successful hunt could also add meat and fish to a scanty diet. And through hunting many boys found a path to manhood. Seeing his father and

brothers return with wild turkeys, young Edward McIlhenny longed for "the time when I would be old enough to hunt this bird."

The thrill of illicit pleasure also drew many southern men to events of violence and chance, including cockfighting. They valued combative birds and were convinced that their champions fought more boldly than did northern bantams. Gambling doubtless heightened the thrills. Such sport offended churchgoing southerners by its cruelty and wantonness. They condemned as sinful "the beer garden, the base ball, the low theater, the dog fight and cock fight and the ring for the pugilist and brute."

FARM ENTERTAINMENTS Many southern customs involved no such disorderly behavior. Work-sharing festivals such as house raisings, log rollings, quiltings, and roadwork gave isolated farm folk the chance to break their daily routine, to socialize, and to work for a common good. These events, too, generally segregated along gender lines. Men did the heavy chores and competed in contests of physical prowess. Women shared domestic tasks such as cooking, quilting, and sewing. Community gatherings also offered young southerners a relaxed place for courtship. In one courting game, the young man who found a rare red ear of corn could have the rare treat of kissing "the lady of his choice."

TOWN For rural folk a trip to town brought special excitement, along with a bit of danger. Saturdays, court days, and holidays drew throngs of people. Court week, when a district judge arrived to mete out justice, drew the biggest crowds. As ever, there were male and female domains. For men the saloon, the blacksmith shop, or the storefront was a place to do business and to let off steam. Few men went to town without participating in social drinking in the local saloon, but when men who had had one too many took to the streets, the threat of brawling and violence drove most women away.

©Bayard Wooten/Library of Congress/Corbis/Getty Images

For Baptists in the South, both white and black, the ceremony of adult baptism included total immersion, often in a nearby river. The ritual symbolized the waters of newfound faith washing away sins. Virginia's James River was the site of this occasion.

The Church

At the center of southern life stood (and beyond its leadership very much the domain of women) the church as a great stabilizer and custodian of social order. "When one joined the Methodist church," a southern woman remembered, "he was expected to give up all such things as cards, dancing, theatres, in fact all so called worldly amusements." Many devout southerners pursued these ideals, although such restraint asked more of people than many could muster, except perhaps on Sunday.

RURAL RELIGION Congregations were often so small and isolated that they could attract a preacher only once or twice a month. The pious counted on the Sunday sermon to steer them from sin. In town, a sermon might last 30 to 45 minutes, but in the slower-paced countryside, a preacher could go on for two hours or more, whipping up worshipers until "even the little children wept."

By 1870 southern churches were segregated by race. Indeed, the black church was the only institution controlled by African Americans after slavery and thus a principal source of leadership and identity as well as comfort (see Chapter 17). Within churches both black and white

congregations were segregated by gender, too. As a boy entered manhood, he moved from the female to the male section. Yet churches were, at base, female domains. Considered guardians of virtue, more women than men were members, attended services, and ran church activities.

Church was a place to socialize as well as worship. Many of the young went simply to meet those of the opposite sex. Church picnics and all-day sings brought as many as 30 or 40 young people together for hours of eating, talk, services, and hymn singing. Still, these occasions could not match the fervor of a weeklong camp meeting. In the late summer or early fall, town and countryside emptied as folks set up tents in shady groves and listened to two or three ministers preach day and night in the largest event of the year. The camp meeting refired faith while celebrating traditional values of home and family.

Segregation

Nothing challenged tradition in the South more than race. With the abolition of slavery and the end of Reconstruction, white northerners and southerners achieved sectional harmony by sacrificing the rights of black citizens. During the 1880s Redeemer governments moved to formalize a system of segregation or racial separation. Redeemers were Democratic politicians who came to power in southern states to end the Republican rule established during Reconstruction. They were eager to reap the benefits of economic expansion and to attract the business classes—bankers, railroad promoters, industrial operators. As their part of the bargain, the Redeemers assured anxious northerners that Redeemer rule would not mean political disenfranchisement of the freedpeople. That part of the bargain they would not keep.

Pressure to reach a new racial accommodation in the South increased as more African Americans moved into southern towns and cities, competing for jobs with poor whites and sharing public space, especially on railroads and other public conveyances. One way to preserve the social and economic superiority of white southerners, poor as well as rich, was to separate blacks as an inferior caste. The first step came even before the end of Reconstruction. Starting in 1870, Tennessee—where whites outnumbered blacks by a ratio of nearly 3 to 1—outlawed racial intermarriage. Soon every southern state enacted similar laws. Over the next 20 years the white South began to construct a legal wall separating the races almost everywhere.

Federal laws designed to enforce the Civil Rights Act of 1866 and the Fourteenth Amendment, which promised equal protection for all under law, stood in the way. In effect, these laws established social equality for all races in public places such as hotels, theaters, and railroads. But in 1883 the Supreme Court ruled (in the *Civil Rights Cases*) that hotels and railroads were not "public" institutions, because private individuals owned them. The Fourteenth Amendment was thus limited to protecting citizens from violations of their civil rights by states, not by private individuals. The national policy of **laissez faire** in race relations could not have been made any clearer.

JIM CROW LAWS Within 20 years every southern state had enacted segregation as law. The earliest laws legalized segregation in trains and other such public conveyances where blacks and whites were likely to mingle. Soon a complex web of "Jim Crow" statutes drew an indelible color line in prisons, parks, hotels, restaurants, hospitals, and virtually all public gathering places except streets and stores. (The term *Jim Crow*, used to denote a policy of segregation, originated in a song of the same name sung in minstrel shows of the day.)

In 1892 Homer Adolph Plessy, an African American, agreed to test a Louisiana law requiring segregated railroad facilities by sitting in the all-white section of a local train. Even though he was only 1/8 black, he was still considered African American. Having warned railroad authorities that he intended to test the law, he was promptly arrested. Slowly the case of *Plessy v. Ferguson* worked its way up to the Supreme Court. In 1896 the Court ruled that segregation did not constitute discrimination as long as accommodations for both races were "separate but equal." Justice John Marshall Harlan (ironically from a

former slaveholding family) issued the lone dissent: separate, whether equal or not, was always a "badge of servitude" and a violation of the "color-blind" Constitution. The doctrine of **separate but equal** nonetheless became part of the fabric of American law and governed race relations for more than half a century to come. When coupled with a growing campaign in the 1890s to disenfranchise black voters across the South (see Chapter 21), segregation provided a formidable barrier to African American progress.

By the turn of the century segregation was firmly in place, stifling economic competition between the races and reducing African Americans to second-class citizenship. Many kinds of employment, such as work in the textile mills, went largely to whites. Skilled and professional black workers generally served black clients. African Americans were barred from juries and usually received far stiffer penalties than whites for the same crimes.

Segregation, lynching, and disenfranchisement (see Chapter 17) were not the only means by which southern state governments sought to control African Americans and replace the labor lost with the abolition of slavery. Among the harsher and more corrupt practices was the convict leasing system. Southern states leased convicts, predominantly African Americans who were often imprisoned for vagrancy and other minor offenses, to plantations and private industry. Employers received cheap labor and state governments large revenues. The convicts were worked mercilessly, poorly fed, housed in dilapidated buildings, and beaten, sometimes to death. It was, wrote one historian, "slavery by another name."

As Jim Crow laws became entrenched, so did stifling social custom. Black southerners always addressed white southerners as "Mister," "Miss," and "Ma'am"—even those of lower status. But white southerners called black southerners by their first names or more simply "Sister" or "Boy," no matter their age or profession. Any African American who crossed the color line risked violence. Some were tarred and feathered, others whipped and beaten, and many lynched. Of the 187 lynchings averaged each year of the 1890s, some 80 percent occurred in the South. The victims were almost always African Americans.

COST OF JIM CROW The cost of Jim Crow segregation and other discriminatory practices to southerners black and white was incalculable. The race question trumped all other issues and produced a one-party region, where fear of black political participation hamstrung any opposition to all-white Redeemer Democrats. Because Democratic Party regulars controlled nominations and thus elections, politics sparked little public interest and fell into the hands of professionals who helped few ordinary southerners. Supporting a two-tiered system of public services drained money from southern treasuries no matter how inferior black institutions were. All suffered under the rule of racial separation, whether they realized it or not.

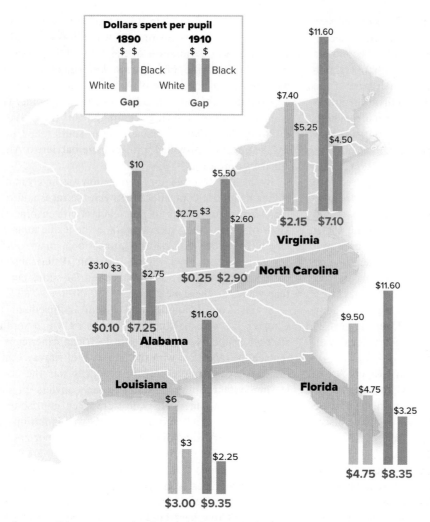

Dollars spent per pupil

1890	1910
White / Black — Gap	White / Black — Gap

$11.60

$7.40

$5.25

$4.50

$10

$5.50

$2.75 $3

$2.60

$2.15 $7.10

Virginia

$3.10 $3

$2.75

$0.25 $2.90

North Carolina

$11.60

$9.50

$0.10 $7.25

Alabama

$11.60

Louisiana

$6

Florida

$4.75

$3.25

$3

$2.25

$4.75 $8.35

$3.00 $9.35

Spending on Education in the South before and after Disenfranchisement

With disenfranchisement and segregation, education was separate but hardly equal, for blacks and whites. In these states, after blacks were disenfranchised, spending on white students rose while spending on black students decreased. **Why were differences between expenditures on black and white students smaller in 1890 than by 1910?**

Source: Margo, Robert A., *Disenfranchisement, School Finance, and the Economics of Segregated Schools in the U.S. South, 1890–1910.* New York, NY: Garland Press, 1985, Table 1-1.

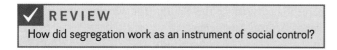

✓ **REVIEW**

How did segregation work as an instrument of social control?

WESTERN FRONTIERS

THE BLACK EXODUSTERS FLOODING INTO Kansas in the 1870s and 1880s were only part of the vast migration west. Looking beyond the Mississippi in the 1840s and 1850s, white "overlanders"—those traveling over land instead of by sea—had set their sights on California and Oregon and the promise of land. They headed across the Mississippi River, pushing the frontier of Anglo settlement to the edge of the continent.

The overlanders went west in search of opportunity and "free" land. They found opportunity elusive to those without money or power. They also found Indians—perhaps as many as 360,000—and "Hispanos," settlers of Spanish descent, who hardly considered the land free for use by Anglos.

MOVING FRONTIERS The overlanders discovered as well that the West was not one region but many, each governed by a different ecology. And its frontiers moved in many directions, not just from east to west. Before the Civil War, the frontier for easterners had moved beyond the Mississippi to the timberlands of Missouri but skipped over the Great Plains, as the overlanders settled in California and Oregon. But another frontier then pushed east from the Pacific coast, following miners into the Sierra Nevada. For Texans the frontier moved from south to north as cattle ranchers sought new grazing land, as had the ancestors of the Spanish rancheros of the Southwest. For American Indians, these constantly shifting frontiers shaped and reshaped their ways of life.

Western Landscapes

DRY TERRITORY WEST OF THE 98TH MERIDIAN Early travelers from the United States labeled the vast region beyond the Mississippi the "Great American Desert." Most of the land between the 98th meridian and the lush lowlands of the West Coast receives fewer than 20 inches of rain a year, making what came to be known as the Great Plains a treeless expanse of prairie grass and dunes. Rare stands of timber cluster along river bottoms. Wood for housing and fences is scarce. Overlanders of the 1840s and 1850s compared its vast windy spaces to the oceans: a "sea of grass" and crossed by wagons called "prairie schooners."

The plains are only part of the Trans-Mississippi West. And even they can be divided. In the northern Plains, bitterly cold winters made survival a struggle for animals and humans alike. In the south, native peoples such as the Cheyenne enjoyed milder winters and access to the horses of ranches in northern Mexico. The Great Plains west of the 98th meridian are semiarid, but the eastern Prairie Plains have good soil and abundant rain.

Beyond the plains the jagged peaks of the Rocky Mountains stretch from Alaska to New Mexico. West of the mountains lies the Great Basin of Utah, Nevada, and eastern California, where temperatures climb above 100 degrees. Near the coast rise the towering Sierra Nevada and Cascade Mountains, rich in minerals and lumber and sloping to the temperate shores and fertile valleys of the Pacific.

Easterners who watched the wagons roll west liked to conjure up the image of a "trackless wilderness." In truth, even in the 1840s, the Great Plains and mountain frontier constituted a complex web of cultures and environments in which Spanish, Anglo-American, and Indian cultures penetrated one another and often produced dramatic changes.

One example is the horse, introduced into North America by the colonial Spanish. By the eighteenth century horses were grazing on prairie grass across the Great Plains. By the nineteenth century the Comanche, Cheyenne, Apache, and other tribes had become master riders and hunters who could shoot their arrows with deadly accuracy at a full gallop. The new mobility of the Plains Indians far extended the area in which they could hunt buffalo, which soon became a staple of their existence. Their lives shifted from settled, village-centered agriculture to nomadic hunting, seminomadic foraging, and even cultivation of the staple crops.

Indian Peoples and the Western Environment

Some whites embraced the myth of the Indian as "noble savage" who lived in perfect harmony with the natural world. To be sure, Plains Indians were inventive in using scarce resources. Cottonwood bark fed horses in winter, and the buffalo supplied not only meat but also bones for tools, fat for cosmetics, sinews for thread, even dung for fuel. Yet Indians could not help but shape and even damage their ecosystems. Plains Indians hunted buffalo by stampeding herds over cliffs, which often led to waste. They irrigated crops and set fires not easily controlled to improve vegetation and game. By the mid-nineteenth century some tribes had become so enmeshed in trade with whites that they overtrapped their own hunting grounds.

VARIETY OF INDIAN CULTURES   Ecosystems, in turn, shaped Indian cultures. Although big-game hunting was common among many western tribes, the mobile buffalo culture of the Great Plains Indians was hardly representative. In the lush forests and mountain ranges of the Pacific Northwest, Yurok, Chinook, and other tribes hunted bear, moose, elk, and deer. Along the rocky coast they took whales, seals, and a variety of fish from the ocean. The early Hohokam and later the Pima and other tribes in New Mexico and Arizona developed irrigation to allow farming of beans, squash, and corn in the arid climate.

Ecological diversity produced a stunning variety of smaller bands, larger tribes, and Indian peoples who nonetheless shared experiences and values. Most bands, components of tribes, were small kinship groups of 300 to 500 people in which the well-being of all outweighed the needs of each member. Although some bands were materially better off than others, the gap between rich and poor within them was seldom large and among Plains peoples often revolved around the possession of horses and mules. Such small material differences frequently promoted communal decision making. The Cheyenne, for example, employed a council of 44 to advise the chief.

Indians also shared a reverence for nature, whatever their actual impact on the natural world. They believed human

©The Metropolitan Museum of Art/Art Resource, NY

| *The Navajo blanket shown here is an "eyedazzler," popular in the second half of the nineteenth century when the market for such blankets was shifting from natives to tourists. Navajo weavers redesigned their blankets for non-Indian consumers, employing the brightly colored threads of European dye makers with the geometric designs of Mexican serapes (patterns themselves derived from the Moorish artisans of Spain).*

beings were part of an interconnected world of animals, plants, and other natural elements. All had souls of their own but were bound together, as if by contract, to live in balance through the ceremonial life of the tribe and the customs related to plants and animals. Whites were mystified by the explanation of one chief for why his people refused to farm: "You ask me to cut grass and make hay and sell it, and be rich like white men! But how dare I cut off my mother's hair?"

Regard for the land endowed special places with religious meaning often indecipherable to whites. Where the Sioux saw in the Black Hills the sacred home of Wakan Tanka—the burial place of the dead and the site of their vision quests—whites saw grass for grazing and gold for the taking.

Whites and the Western Environment: Competing Visions

WILLIAM GILPIN, A WESTERN BOOSTER   As discoveries of gold and silver lured whites into Indian territory, many whites adopted the decidedly un-Indian outlook of

Missouri politician William Gilpin. Only a lack of vision prevented the opening of the West for exploitation, Gilpin told a Missouri audience in 1849. What was most needed were cheap lands and a railroad linking the two coasts "like ears on a human head." Distance, climate, topography, and the Indians were mere obstacles.

By 1868 a generous Congress had granted western settlers their two greatest wishes: free land under the Homestead Act of 1862 and a transcontinental railroad.

As the new governor of Colorado, Gilpin crowed about the region's limitless resources. One day, he believed, the West would support more than a billion people. Scarce rainfall and water did not daunt him, for in his eyes the West was no "Great American Desert" but an Eden-like garden, awaiting only the plow and the rain that would follow it.

Gilpin subscribed to the popular notion that "rain follows the plow." The idea was as simple as it was widely held—and wrong.

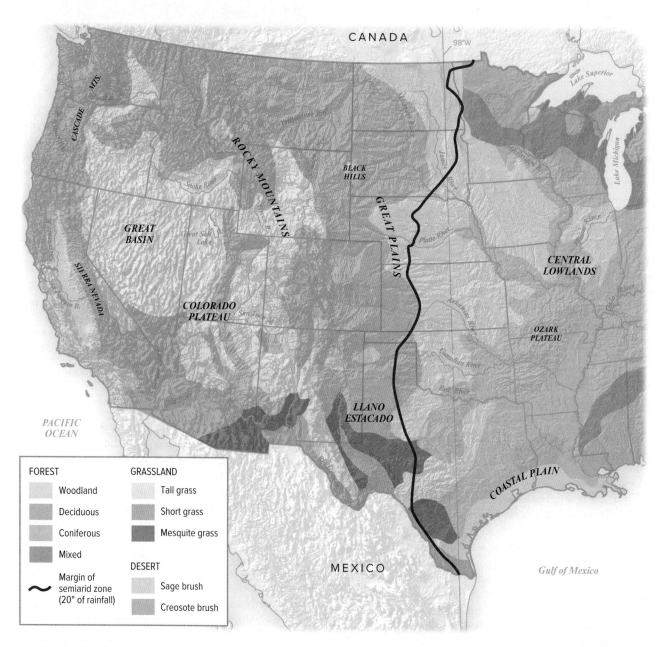

NATURAL ENVIRONMENT OF THE WEST

With the exception of Oregon and Washington in the Pacific Northwest, few areas west of the 20-inch rainfall line receive enough annual precipitation to support agriculture without irrigation. Consequently, water has been the key to growth and development in the area west of the 98th meridian, which encompasses more than half the land area of the continental United States. The dominance of short grasses and coniferous (evergreen) trees reflects the rainfall patterns. **Which two western states have the largest proportion of land that receives enough annual rainfall to support agriculture without irrigation?**

Settling dry lands and plowing fields would release moisture into the air, the theory maintained, thereby increasing cloud cover and rain. Early climatologist Cyrus Thomas and amateur scientist Charles Dana Wilbur helped popularize the notion. Whites settling the West and speculators profiting from developing it justified their actions as transforming "desert into a farm or garden." An unusually wet cycle from 1878 to 1886 helped to sustain the myth. The fact that such human activity did increase precipitation locally by drawing rain from nearby areas only undermined the few skeptics who rightly argued that the plow produced no change in climate over large regions.

JOHN WESLEY POWELL   Unlike the visionary Gilpin, John Wesley Powell knew something about water and farming. After losing an arm in the Civil War, geologist Powell went west. In 1869 and 1871 he led scientific expeditions down the Green and Colorado Rivers through the Grand Canyon. He returned to warn Congress that developing the West required more scientific planning. Much of the region had yet to be mapped or its resources identified.

WATER AS A KEY RESOURCE   In 1880 Powell became director of the recently formed U.S. Geological Survey. He, too, had a vision of the West, but one based on the limits of its environment. Water, not land, was the key. In the water-rich East, whoever owned the banks of a river or stream controlled as much water as they might take, regardless of the consequences for those downstream. The same practice in the water-starved West, Powell recognized, would enrich the small number with access while spelling ruin for the rest.

The alternative was to treat water as community property. The practice would benefit many rather than a privileged few. Powell suggested that the federal government establish political boundaries defined by watersheds and regulate the distribution of the scarce resource. Such scientific realism could not overcome the popular vision of the West as an American Eden. Powerful interests ensured that development occurred with the same helter-skelter, laissez-faire credo that was shaping the East.

REVIEW

How did Indian conceptions of the environment compare and contrast with white conceptions?

THE WAR FOR THE WEST

SO MARGINAL DID FEDERAL OFFICIALS consider the Great Plains that they left the lands to the Indians. By the end of the Civil War some two-thirds of all Indian peoples lived on the Great Plains. Even before the war a series of gold and silver discoveries beginning in 1848 signaled the first serious interest by white settlers in the arid and semiarid lands beyond the Mississippi. White prospectors, settlers, merchants, and developers soon flooded the Trans-Mississippi West. The first to feel the effects of this unrestrained expansion were the Indians and Latinos of the region.

Those effects ripped the Navajo people from their land like a tornado. In January 1864, to solve the "Navajo problem," the army started rounding up thousands of the tribe. Over the next several months—in the dead of winter and the blazing heat of summer—armed guards marched them along seven trails from present-day Arizona and western New Mexico to an encampment called *Bosque Redondo* near Fort Sumner. Some walked as many as 450 miles. More than 200 died, among them stragglers shot for failing to keep up on the "Long Walk." Those who survived soon found themselves packed into a 40-square-mile stretch of short prairie grass and scorched desert that straddled the Pecos River. The encampment was originally designed to hold 5,000 people. By the spring of 1865, over 9,000 squeezed into ramshackle dwellings made of twigs and grimy canvas.

POLICY OF CONCENTRATION   The Long Walk was part of an experiment. To open more land to whites and to provide Indians a safe haven, federal officials had introduced a policy of "concentration" in 1851. They pressed tribes to sign treaties limiting the boundaries of their hunting grounds to "reservations"—the Sioux to the Dakotas, the Cheyenne to the foothills of Colorado. Some tribes like the Navajo were

Source: Library of Congress, Prints and Photographs Division [LC-USZC4-8292]

John Wesley Powell's second expedition into the Grand Canyon launching on the Green River in 1871. Despite near drownings as well as the loss of boats and supplies, Powell successfully explored the wild Colorado River at a time when Indian legends suggested the river might disappear underground in some spots.

moved at rifle point. And for them, the experiment ended tragically. Conditions at *Bosco Redondo* were so horrid that nearly one in three Navajo died. In 1868, the government finally closed down the camp. The Navajo returned to their territory in one of the earliest instances of forced relocation home.

Despite treaty claims that their provisions would last "as long as waters run," land-hungry pioneers broke the promises of their government time after time by squatting on Indian territory and demanding federal protection. The government, in turn, forced more restrictive agreements on the western tribes. This cycle of promises made and broken continued, until a full-scale war for the West raged between whites and Indians.

Contact and Conflict

The policy of concentration began in the Pacific Northwest and produced some of the earliest clashes between whites and Indians. In an oft-repeated pattern Indian resistance led to war and war to Indian defeat. In the 1850s, as territorial governor Isaac Stevens was browbeating local tribes into giving up millions of acres in Washington Territory, a gold strike flooded the Indian homelands with miners. The tribes fought them off, only to be crushed and forced onto reservations.

In similar fashion, by 1862 the lands of the Santee Sioux had been whittled down to a strip 10 miles wide and 150 miles long along the Minnesota River. Lashing out in frustration, the tribe attacked several undefended white settlements on the Minnesota frontier. In response, General John Pope arrived in St. Paul declaring his intention to wipe out the Sioux. "They are to be treated as maniacs or wild beasts and by no means as people," he instructed his officers. When Pope's forces captured 1,800 Sioux, white Minnesotans were outraged that President Lincoln ordered only 38 hanged. It was, nonetheless, the largest mass execution in U.S. history.

CHIVINGTON MASSACRE   The campaign under General Pope was the opening of a guerrilla war that continued on and off for 30 years. The conflict gained momentum in 1864, when Governor John Evans of Colorado sought to end all land treaties with Indian peoples in eastern Colorado. In November a force of 700 Colorado volunteers under Colonel John Chivington, a former Methodist pastor, fell on a band of friendly Cheyenne gathered at Sand Creek under army protection. Chief Black Kettle raised an American flag to signal friendship, but Chivington would have none of it. "Kill and scalp all, big and little," he told his men. The troops massacred at least 150, including children holding white flags of truce and mothers with babies in their arms. A joint congressional investigation later condemned Chivington. A year later, in 1865, virtually all Plains Indians joined in the First Sioux War to drive whites from their lands.

BUFFALO SOLDIERS   Among the soldiers who fought the Plains Indians were African American veterans of the Civil War. In 1866 two regiments of black soldiers formed the Ninth and Tenth Cavalry under the command of white officers. Their Indian foes dubbed them "buffalo soldiers," reflecting the similarity they saw between African American hair and buffalo hair. It was also a sign of hard-won respect. The buffalo soldiers fought Indians across the West for more than 20 years. They also served as agents of white settlement, subduing bandits, cattle thieves, and gunmen for the safety of local businesses; locating water, wood, and grasslands for eager homesteaders; and laying the foundations for posts such as Fort Sill in Oklahoma.

White settlement undermined tribal cultures. Diseases introduced by settlers, including smallpox, measles, and cholera, killed more Indians than combat. Liquor furnished by white traders entrapped many a brave in a deadly cycle of alcoholism. Trading posts altered traditional ways of life with metal pots and pans, traps, coffee, and sugar but furnished no employment and thus few ways for their Indian customers to pay for these goods. Mines, crops, grazing herds, and fences disturbed native hunting and farming lands across the West.

On the Great Plains white incursions wreaked havoc with Indian life. The railroad disrupted the migratory patterns of the buffalo and thus the hunt on which Plains Indians depended for survival. Demand for buffalo products nearly destroyed the herds. When buffalo robes became popular in the East in the 1870s and hides a source of leather for industrial belts, commercial companies hired professional hunters, who could kill as many as 100 bison an hour. Even Indians were caught up in the whirl of commercial trading, killing bison for profit rather than provisions. By 1883 the great herds had nearly disappeared from the Plains (see Historians Reconstruct the Past, "Where Have All the Bison Gone?" in After the Fact at the end of the chapter). With them went a way of life that left Plains Indians more vulnerable to white expansion.

Custer's "Last Stand"—and the Indians'

In 1868 the Treaty of Fort Laramie capped four bloody years of fighting between whites and Indians, including the Santee and Lakota Sioux. The treaty established two large Indian reservations, one in Oklahoma and the other in the Dakota Badlands. Only six years later, Colonel George Armstrong Custer broke the treaty by leading an expedition into *Paha Sapa,* the sacred Black Hills of the Sioux. Custer, a Civil War veteran, already had a reputation for cruelty as a "squaw killer" from his days fighting Indians in western Kansas. To open the Black Hills to whites, his expedition spread rumors of gold "from the grass roots down." Prospectors poured into Indian country. When negotiations for a new treaty failed, President Grant ordered all "hostiles" in the area driven onto the reservations.

BATTLE OF LITTLE BIG HORN   In the summer of 1876 several army columns, among them Custer's Seventh Cavalry of over 600 troops, marched against the Sioux. Eager for glory, Custer arrived at the Little Big Horn River a day

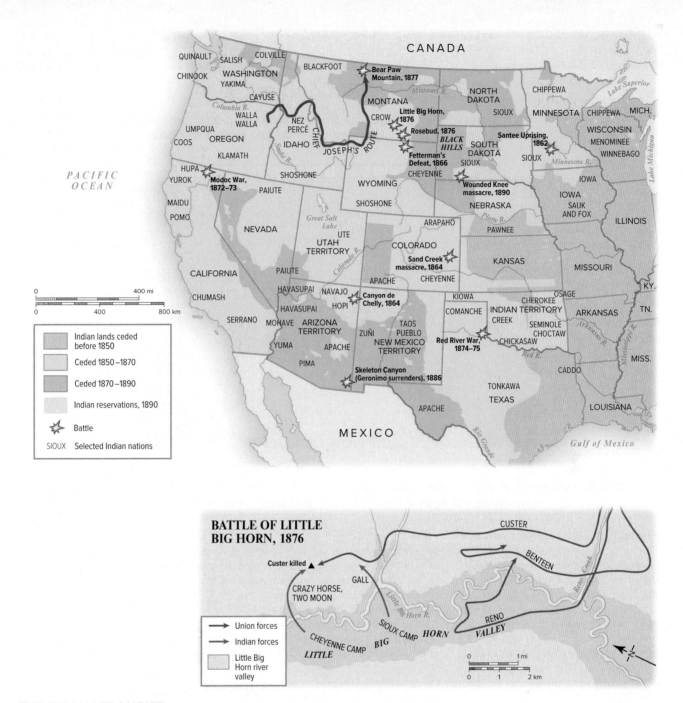

BATTLE OF LITTLE BIG HORN, 1876

- → Union forces
- → Indian forces
- Little Big Horn river valley

THE INDIAN FRONTIER

*As conflict erupted between Indian and white cultures in the West, the government sought increasingly to concentrate tribes on reservations. Resistance to the reservation concept helped unite the Sioux and Cheyenne, traditionally enemies, in the Dakotas during the 1870s. In the Battle of Little Big Horn (known among Indians as "the Battle of the Greasy Grass"), the impetuous Custer underestimated the strength of his Indian opponents and attacked before supporting troops were in a position to help. **Based on the dates of land cessions, which Indian groups held out against white expansion the longest?***

earlier than the other columns. Hearing of a native village nearby, he attacked, only to discover that he had stumbled onto an encampment of more than 7,000 Sioux and Cheyenne allied for the first time. From a deep ravine Sioux leader Crazy Horse charged Custer, killing him and 267 soldiers.

As he led the attack Crazy Horse yelled "It is a good day to die!"—the traditional war cry. He spoke more truth than he knew. Although Custer had been killed, railroads stood ready to extend their lines, prospectors to make fortunes, settlers to lay down roots, and soldiers to protect them all. By late summer the Sioux were forced to split into small bands to evade

Custer's Defeat, Indian Style

What kinds of weapons are the Sioux warriors using? What does this tell us about the nature of warfare in the late nineteenth century?

©The Granger Collection, New York

Upside-down American flags are both carried by a cavalryman and lie on the ground.

Some of the soldiers' heads are scalped. How can we tell? Why would Indians want the scalps of the dead?

Firsthand historical accounts come in a variety of forms. Some are spoken and recorded, others written, and still others drawn. In 1881, five years after George Armstrong Custer's defeat at the Battle of Little Big Horn, a Minneconjou Lakota Sioux warrior named Red Horse composed 42 drawings of the battle at the behest of army physician Charles E. McChesney at the Cheyenne River Agency, an Indian reservation in South Dakota where Red Horse lived. He had fought at Little Big Horn and surrendered a year later. The result was a series of

stunning colored-pencil-and-ink drawings that depict the horror of war from an Indian point of view. Cavalrymen flee charging braves, while the bloody and beheaded bodies of soldiers litter the bottom of the drawing, some of them with their hair scalped. Among the dead at the lower right side is a man wearing what appears to be a plaid shirt and pants without the typical stripe of an army uniform. Red Horse mentioned the presence of civilians among the American force when using sign language to tell his story. The body may be either Custer's youngest brother,

Boston Custer, or his nephew, Henry Armstrong Reed. This is hardly the image most white Americans have of Custer's heroic "last stand."

THINKING CRITICALLY

At the center and foot of the illustration, American flags have been drawn upside down, surely not the way soldiers carried them. Why would Red Horse have depicted them this way? Recall that he was, in effect, a prisoner of war with only the power of his pens and pencils to express himself.

the army. Sioux holy man Sitting Bull barely escaped to Canada; Crazy Horse and 800 other Cheyennes and Sioux surrendered in 1876 after a winter of suffering and starvation. Custer's "last stand" marked the beginning of the end of Indian military successes.

These battles did not end the war between whites and Indians, but never again would it reach such proportions nor would Indians win many victories like that of the Little Big Horn. Even the peaceful Nez Percé of Idaho found no security

once whites looked to their lands. The Nez Percé had become breeders of livestock, rich in horses and cattle that they grazed in the meadows west of the Snake River canyon. Their livestock business did not prevent the government from trying to force them onto a small reservation in 1877.

Rather than see his people humiliated, Chief Joseph led almost 600 Nez Percé toward Canada with the U.S. Army in hot pursuit. In just 75 days they traveled more than 1,300 miles. Every time the army closed to attack, Chief

Joseph and his warriors drove them off. But before the Nez Percé could reach the border, they were forced to surrender. Chief Joseph's words still ring with eloquence: "Hear me, my chiefs, I am tired; my heart is sick and sad. From where the sun now stands I will fight no more forever." The government then shipped the defeated tribe to the bleak Indian country of Oklahoma. There, disease and starvation finished what the army began.

Killing with Kindness

Over these same years Indians saw their legal sovereignty being whittled away, sometimes even with the best intentions. Originally, federal authorities regarded various tribes as autonomous nations within the United States, with whom treaties could be made. That tribal status began shrinking in 1831, when the Supreme Court declared Indians "domestic dependent nations." Although the United States continued to negotiate treaties with the tribes, government officials began treating Indians as wards of the state who should be treated like inept children and raised with Christian values and white styles of living. Finally, in 1871, Congress abandoned the treaty system altogether and with it the legal core of Indian autonomy.

LA FLESCHE AND JACKSON Some whites and Indians spoke out against the tragedy taking place on the Great Plains. In the 1870s Susan La Flesche, daughter of an Omaha chief and the first Indian woman in the United States to become a physician, lectured eastern audiences about the mistreatment of Indian peoples and inspired reformers to action. Similarly moved, the poet Helen Hunt Jackson lobbied for Indian rights and against government policy. In 1881 she published *A Century of Dishonor*, a best-selling exposé that detailed government fraud and corruption in Indian affairs, as well as the many treaties broken by the United States.

Reformers began pressing for assimilation of Indians into white society, ironically as the only means of preserving Indians in a society that seemed bent on destroying them. The Women's National Indian Association, created in 1874, and the later Indian Rights Association, joined by Helen Hunt Jackson, sought to end the Indian way of life by suppressing communal activities, reeducating Indian children, and establishing individual homesteads.

DAWES ACT Reformers also recognized that the policy of concentrating Indians on reservations had failed. Deprived of their traditional lands and culture, reservation tribes became dependent on government aid. In any case, whites who coveted Indian lands were quick to violate treaty terms. With a mix of good intentions and unbridled greed, Congress adopted the Dawes Severalty Act in 1887. It sought to eliminate reservations, which were collectively owned by tribal members, and replace them with plots of land owned by individuals—160 acres to the head of a family and 80 acres to single adults or orphans. Senator Henry Laurens Dawes of Massachusetts and other backers of the law believed that tribes stood in the way of "civilizing" Indians and that doing away with collective property would eventually do away with tribes.

In practice, the Dawes Act was more destructive than any blow struck by the army. It undermined the communal structure of tribal culture. Lands held by tribes were parceled out to individuals. Those who took the land and "adopted the habits of civilized life" received American citizenship. But as John Wesley Powell had warned, small homestead farms in the West could not support a family—white or Indian—unless the farms were irrigated. Most Indians, moreover, had no experience with farming, managing money, or other white ways. Perhaps worst of all, reservation lands not allocated to Indians were opened to non-Indian homesteaders. In 1881 Indians held more than 155 million acres of land. By 1900 the figure had dropped to just under 78 million.

Source: Library of Congress, Prints and Photographs Division [LC-USZ62-26786]

| *The all-male Carlisle Indian School Band was formed in 1881, two years after this Indian boarding school was founded in Pennsylvania. School authorities saw music as one way to "civilize" their charges. Writing a wealthy donor, the school's superintendent suggested, "If you will give me a set of brass band instruments, I will give them to the 'tom tom' boys and they can toot on them and this will stop the 'tom tom.'" Pianos were also donated for the girls.*

WOUNDED KNEE Against such a dismal future some Indians assimilated, cutting their hair, abandoning the old ways, and adopting the ways of the white man. Others, like the women of the Southern Utes, had more complex responses. They assimilated when it served their interests, resisted when it did not, in one instance openly opposing schools for their children outside of the reservation.

Still other tribes turned to cults and movements to revive Indian culture. In 1890 a religious revival swept the Indian nations when word came from the Nevada desert that a humble Paiute named Wovoka had received revelations from the Great Spirit. Wovoka preached that if his followers adopted his mystical rituals and lived together in love and harmony, the Indian dead would come back to life, whites would be driven from the land, and game would be plentiful again. As the rituals spread, alarmed settlers referred to their ritualized shuffling and chanting as the "Ghost Dance." The army moved to stamp out the Ghost Dance for fear of another uprising. At Wounded Knee in South Dakota the cavalry fell on a band of followers. As the soldiers were disarming the Indians, a shot rang out, setting off a blaze of army machine-gun fire. When the smoke cleared, some 300 Sioux men, women, and children and 25 soldiers lay dead.

Wounded Knee was yet another blow against Indian life. But after 1890 the battle was over assimilation, not extinction. The system of markets, rail networks, and extractive industries was linking the Far West with the rest of the nation. Free-roaming bison were being replaced by herded cattle and sheep, nomadic tribes by prairie sodbusters, and sacred hunting grounds by gold fields. Reformers relied on education, citizenship, and allotments to move Indians into white society. Many Indians were equally determined to preserve their tribal ways and separateness as a people.

Borderlands

The coming of the railroad in the 1880s and 1890s brought wrenching changes to the Southwest as well, especially to the states and territories along the old border with Mexico. But here there was a twist. As new markets and industries sprang up, new settlers poured in not only from the east but also from the south, across the Mexican border. Indians such as the Navajo and the Apache thus faced the hostility of newcomers—Anglos and Mexicans alike—as well as of Hispanos, those settlers of Spanish descent long in the region. Before the Mexican War of 1846, the Spanish governors of northern Mexico had offered bounties for Indian scalps.

JUAN JOSÉ HERRERA AND THE WHITE CAPS Like Indians, Hispanos discovered that they had either to accommodate or to resist the flood of new Anglos. The elite, or Ricos, often aligned themselves with Anglos against their countryfolk to protect their status and property. Others, like Juan José Herrera, resisted the newcomers. When Anglo cattle ranchers began forcing Hispanos off their lands near Las Vegas, New Mexico, Herrera assembled a band of masked night riders known as *Las Gorras Blancas* (The White Caps). In 1889 and 1890 as many as 700 White Caps burned Anglo fences, haystacks, and occasionally barns and houses. In one fiery turn, Herrera's followers set thousands of railroad ties ablaze when the Atchison, Topeka and Santa Fe Railroad refused to raise the low wages of its Hispano workers.

New Anglos frequently fought Hispanos. But it was western lawyers and politicians, using legal tactics, who deprived Hispanos of most of their property. Thomas Catron, an ambitious New Mexico lawyer, squeezed out many Hispanos by contesting land titles so aggressively that his holdings grew to 3 million acres. Still, in those areas of New Mexico and California where they remained a majority, Hispanos continued to play a role in public life. During the early 1890s Herrera and his allies formed a "People's Party," swept local elections, and managed to defeat a bid by Catron to represent the territory in Congress.

MEXICAN IMMIGRANTS With the railroads came more white settlers as well as Mexican laborers. Just as the southern economy depended on African American labor, the economy of the Southwest rested on the backs of Mexicans. Mexican immigrants served mostly as contract and seasonal workers for railroads and large farms. Many of them settled in the growing cities along the rail lines: El Paso, Albuquerque, Tucson, Phoenix, and Los Angeles. They lived in segregated barrios, Spanish towns where their cultural traditions persisted. What little power they had lay in the hands of political bosses (see Chapter 20), some Latino, some Anglo.

FORMATION OF REGIONAL COMMUNITIES To focus on cities alone would distort the experience of most southwesterners of Spanish descent, especially those who lived in the small villages of northern New Mexico and southern Colorado. There a pattern of adaptation and resistance to Anglo penetration emerged. As the market economy advanced, Hispanic villagers turned to migratory labor to adapt. Women continued to work in the old villages; men traveled from wage job to wage job in mining, in farming, and on the railroads. A new culture developed rooted in the web of villages and migrant workers that furnished a base from which Hispanics could seek employment and a safe haven to which they could return. The resulting "regional community" served a dual purpose: preservation of the communal life of the old Hispanic village and transition into the new world of market capitalism that was transforming the West.

Ethno-Racial Identity in the New West

The New West met the Old South in the diamond-shaped Blackland Prairie of central Texas. Before the Civil War, King Cotton thrived in its rich soil. Afterward, Texas became the leading cotton-producing state in the country. Having embraced the slave system of the Old South, Texas also adopted the New South's system of race management, with its racial separation, restrictions on black voting, and biracial labor force of African Americans and poor whites. Yet Texas was part of the borderlands of the American West, where the Anglo culture of European Americans also confronted the Latino culture of Mexicans and Mexican Americans.

The War for the West

WAR/BATTLE	DATE	DESCRIPTION
Sioux Wars	1854–1890	Under Crazy Horse and Sitting Bull, Sioux resist whites streaming into their hunting grounds in Minnesota, South Dakota, and Wyoming.
Apache Attacks	1861	Led by Geronimo and Cochise, bands of Apaches escape reservations and begin to attack white outposts in New Mexico, Arizona, and Texas.
Santee Uprising	1862	Clashes between whites and Santee Sioux in southwestern Minnesota; 38 Indians are hanged in the largest-scale execution in U.S. history.
Battle of Canyon de Chelly	1864	Final battle between the Navajo and U.S. forces under Kit Carson. Survivors forced on "Long Walk" 400 miles from Arizona to Fort Sumner, New Mexico.
Sand Creek	1864	At Sand Creek, Colorado, white militia slaughter some 160 Cheyenne Indians.
Fort Kearny	1866	Near Fort Kearny, Wyoming, Cheyenne and Sioux kill Captain William J. Fetterman and his 80 men.
Modoc War	1872–1873	In the only Indian war in California, Captain Jack and 60 Modoc followers flee reservation to Tule Lake, where they fight until 1873.
Red River Wars	1874–1875	In northwestern Texas, General William T. Sherman leads an army force against the Arapaho, Cheyenne, Comanche, and Kiowa; final defeat of Plains Indians.
Battle of Little Big Horn	1876	Under Sitting Bull and Crazy Horse, Cheyenne and Sioux crush Custer's Seventh Cavalry.
Nez Percé War	1877	In Oregon, Chief Joseph and the Nez Percé resist white encroachment and then flee into Montana, surrendering 40 miles short of the Canadian border.
Battle of Skeleton Canyon	1886	Geronimo surrenders in southeastern Arizona, ending Apache Wars.
Wounded Knee	1890	At Wounded Knee, South Dakota, cavalry killed some 300 Lakota Sioux in what is regarded as the last engagement of U.S. soldiers and American Indians.

(*left*) Source: Library of Congress, Prints and Photographs Division [LC-DIG-ppmsc-02515]; (*right*) Source: Library of Congress, Prints and Photographs Division [LC-DIG-ppmsc-02552]

"AMERICANIZING" THE INDIAN

The federal government began a program to "Americanize" Indians in 1887, by force if necessary. Children were separated from parents and sent to boarding schools such as the one at the Carlisle Barracks in Pennsylvania. Its founder, Captain Richard Pratt, explains the rationale for the schools in the first document below. In the second document, Zitkala-Sa (later known as Gertrude Simmons Bonnin) describes the experience from an Indian point of view.

DOCUMENT 1
Advantages of "Americanizing" Indians

A great general has said that the only good Indian is a dead one, and that high sanction of his destruction has been an enormous factor in promoting Indian massacres. In a sense, I agree with the sentiment, but only in this: that all the Indian there is in the race should be dead. Kill the Indian in him, and save the man. . . .

It is a sad day for the Indians when they fall under the assaults of our troops, as in the Piegan massacre, the massacre of Old Black Kettle and his Cheyennes at what is termed "the battle of the Washita," and hundreds of other like places in the history of our dealings with them; but a far sadder day is it for them when they fall under the baneful influences of a treaty agreement with the United States whereby they are to receive large annuities, and to be protected on reservations, and held apart from all association with the best of our civilization. The destruction is not so speedy, but it is far more general. . . .

The Indians under our care remained savage, because forced back upon themselves and away from association with English-speaking and civilized people, and because of our savage example and treatment of them. . . .

We make our greatest mistake in feeding our civilization to the Indians instead of feeding the Indians to our civilization. America has different customs and civilizations from Germany. What would be the result of an attempt to plant American customs and civilization among the Germans in Germany, demanding that they shall become thoroughly American before we admit them to the country? Now, what we have all along attempted to do for and with the Indians is just exactly that, and nothing else. We invite the Germans to come into our country and communities, and share our customs, our civilization, to be of it; and the result is immediate success. Why not try it on the Indians? Why not invite them into experiences in our communities? Why always invite and compel them to remain a people unto themselves? . . .

The school at Carlisle is an attempt on the part of the government to do this. Carlisle has always planted treason to the tribe and loyalty to the nation at large. It has preached against colonizing Indians, and in favor of individualizing them. It has demanded for them the same multiplicity of chances which all others in the country enjoy. Carlisle fills young Indians with the spirit of loyalty to the stars and stripes, and then moves them out into our communities to show by their conduct and ability that the Indian is no different from the white or the colored, that he has the inalienable right to liberty and opportunity that the white and the negro have. Carlisle does not dictate to him what line of life he should fill, so it is an honest one. It says to him that, if he gets his living by the sweat of his brow, and demonstrates to the nation that he is a man, he does more good for his race than hundreds of his fellows who cling to their tribal communistic surroundings.

Source: Official Report of the Nineteenth Annual Conference of Charities and Correction, 1892, 46–59, as reprinted in Pratt, Richard H., "The Advantages of Mingling Indians with Whites," Americanizing Indians: Writings by the "Friends of the Indian" 1880–1900. Cambridge, MA: 1973, 260–271.

DOCUMENT 2
An Indian Girl's Experience

Late in the morning, my friend Judewin gave me a terrible warning. . . . She heard the paleface woman talk about cutting our long, heavy hair. Our mothers had taught us that only unskilled warriors who were captured had their hair shingled by the enemy. Among our people, short hair was worn by mourners, and shingled hair by cowards! We discussed our fate some moments, and when Judewin said, "We have to submit, because they are strong," I rebelled.

"No, I will not submit! I will struggle first!" I answered. . . .

I watched for my chance, and when no one noticed I disappeared, I crept up the stairs as quietly as I could in my squeaking shoes—my moccasins had been exchanged for shoes. . . . On my hands and knees I crawled under [a] bed, and cuddled myself in the dark corner. . . .

What caused them to stoop and look under the bed I do not know. I remember being dragged out, though I resisted by kicking and scratching wildly. In spite of myself, I was carried downstairs and tied fast in a chair.

I cried aloud, shaking my head all the while until I felt the cold blades on the scissors, against my neck, and heard them gnaw off one of my thick braids. Then I lost my spirit. Since the day I was taken from my mother I had suffered extreme indignities. People had stared at me. I had been tossed about in the air like a wooden puppet. And now my long hair was shingled like a coward's! In my anguish I moaned for my mother, but no one came to comfort me.

Not a soul reasoned quietly with me, as my own mother used to do; for now I was only one of many little animals driven by a herder.

Source: Zitkala-Sa (Gertrude Simmons Bonnin), "The School Days of an Indian Girl," Atlantic Monthly, vol. 89, January-March 1900, 45–47, 190, 192–194.

THINKING CRITICALLY

What does Captain Richard Pratt mean by "kill the Indian . . . and save the man"? How does he justify the Americanization program at Carlisle, and why might some whites at the time consider his reasoning to be "enlightened"? What effect do efforts at Americanization, in particular haircutting, have on Zitkala-Sa? In your view, who is more "civilized," Pratt or Zitkala-Sa?

Western cities attracted ethnically diverse populations. This market in San Antonio, Texas, known as Military Plaza, served the city's large Latino population in 1887.
Source: Library of Congress, Prints and Photographs Division [LC-USZ62-24772]

A NEW RACIAL TRIAD Between 1890 and 1910 the Spanish-speaking population of the Southwest nearly doubled. In central Texas the presence of this large and growing force of Mexicano laborers complicated racial matters. The black-and-white poles of European and African Americans that had defined identity in the Old South were now replaced by a new racial triad of black, white, and brown that negotiated identity and status among themselves.

Like African Americans, Mexican Americans and Mexican emigrants in Texas were separated from Anglos by a color line. Most whites considered them inferior and justified their prejudice on the grounds that Mexicans were shiftless, ignorant, and weak-minded, like all "darker races." But unlike African Americans, Texans of Mexican descent sometimes found themselves part of a three-cornered racial dynamic that left them swinging between the white world of privilege and the black world of disadvantage. In 1914, for example, Mexicans gained status by joining Anglos in the Land League, a radical organization of Texas renters dedicated to land reform. Its white secretary, frustrated over the reluctance of other whites to sign on, extolled the courage and steadfastness of Mexican members, claiming that they would "starve before they will submit to a higher rent than the League and the law says is just."

In this fluid dynamic, whites could lose status, as had the many Texans who sank into landlessness and poverty on the eve of World War I. White landowners disdained them as "white trash" and a "white scourge," found them to be more expensive tenants, and thus were more likely to rent to what they now regarded as "hardworking" Mexican Americans and Mexican immigrants. As small white operators lost their farms and ranches to large corporations, they saw the social distance shrink between themselves and black and brown laborers, sharecroppers, and tenants. By the 1920s a multiracial labor force of landless wage earners worked on giant ranches and farms across the Southwest. In Texas the labor force was triracial, but in California it also included Asian Americans and, elsewhere, American Indians.

Source: Library of Congress, Prints and Photographs Division [4a03262]

In the Far West, ethno-racial identity added other categories to the mix, including Chinese. These workers stop for refreshments at a stand with signs in English.

> ✓ **REVIEW**
> Through what means did American Indians lose their independence and land?

BOOM AND BUST IN THE WEST

OPPORTUNITY IN THE NEW WEST lay in land and resources, but wealth also accumulated in towns and cities. Each time speculative fever struck, new communities sprouted to serve those who rushed in to grab riches. The western boom began in mining with the California gold rush of 1849 and the rise of San Francisco (see Chapter 14). In the decades that followed, new hordes threw up towns in Park City, Utah, Tombstone, Arizona, and other promising sites. All too often, busts followed booms and boom towns became ghost towns.

Mining Sets a Pattern

The gold and silver strikes of the 1840s and 1850s set a pattern followed by other booms. Stories of easy riches attracted single prospectors with their shovels and wash pans. Muddy mining camps sprang up in which a prospector could register a claim, get provisions, bathe, and buy a drink or a companion. Almost all the prospectors were male, and nearly half were born abroad. In local saloons English, Irish brogues, German, French, Spanish, Chinese, Italian, Hawaiian, and various Indian dialects collided noisily.

PROSTITUTION Prostitution flourished openly in mining towns (as it did in cattle towns). Such makeshift communities provided ideal conditions: large numbers of rootless men, few women, and money to purchase any favor. In the booming towns of Gold Hill and Virginia City near the Comstock Lode of Nevada, men outnumbered women 2 to 1 in 1875. Almost 1 woman in 12 was a prostitute. Usually prostitutes were young, in their teens and 20s. They walked the streets and plied their trade in one-room shacks called "cribs." If young and in demand, they worked in dance halls, saloons, and brothels. Pay varied by race, with Anglos at the top, followed by African Americans, Mexicans, and Indians. A far more profitable source of revenue came from outfitting these boom societies with the equipment they needed. Sales siphoned riches into the pockets of store owners and other suppliers, all with a stake in the town's survival. Once the quick profits were gone, a period of consolidation brought more order to towns destined to remain. Police departments replaced vigilantes. Brothels, saloons, and gambling dens were limited to "red-light" districts. Larger scale came to regional businesses.

ENVIRONMENTAL COSTS OF MINING In the mine fields, that meant corporations with the capital for hydraulic water jets to blast ore loose and for the heavy equipment needed to crush rock and extract silver and gold from deeper veins. Their quest for profit often led to environmental disaster. With each snow melt and rain the gravel from hydraulic mining worked its way down into river systems. The resulting floods, mudslides, and dirty streams threatened the livelihood of farmers in the valleys below. Outside Sacramento 39,000 acres of farmland lay under the debris by the 1890s, and another 14,000 acres were nearly ruined. In Butte, Montana, smoke from sulfur-belching smelters turned the air so black that by the 1880s townsfolk had trouble seeing even in daylight.

| Blasting away with pressurized water jets, miners loosen gold-bearing gravel. Such techniques damaged the environment in the rush to exploit western resources. These miners are working in Nevada County, California.
Source: Library of Congress, Prints and Photographs Division [LC-USZ62-9889]

In a common cycle, the rowdy mining frontier of small-scale prospectors was integrated into the industrial system of wage labor, large-scale resource extraction, and high-finance capital. Large corporations managed operations from afar. Paid laborers replaced the independent prospectors of earlier days. As these miners sought better wages and working conditions, shorter hours, and the right to unionize, management fought back. In Coeur d'Alene, Idaho, troops crushed a strike in 1892, killing seven miners. The miners then created the Western Federation of Miners, a union in which, in the decade after 1893, ttracted some 50,000 members and gained a reputation for militancy.

The Transcontinental Railroad

As William Gilpin predicted in 1849, the development of the West awaited the railroads. Before the Central and

Union Pacific railroads were joined to span the continent in 1869, travel was slow and dusty. Daunting distances and sparse population gave entrepreneurs little chance to follow the eastern practice of building local railroads from city to city.

RAILROAD LAND GRANTS Vision and greed overcame those problems, and the federal government helped, too, often at the expense of other interests. In 1862 Congress granted the Central Pacific Railroad the right to build the western link of the transcontinental railroad eastward from Sacramento. To the Union Pacific Corporation fell responsibility for the section from Omaha westward. Generous loans and gifts of federal and state lands made the venture wildly profitable. For every mile of track completed, the rail companies received between 200 and 400 square miles of land, eventually totaling some 45 million acres. Fraudulent stock practices, corrupt accounting, and wholesale bribery

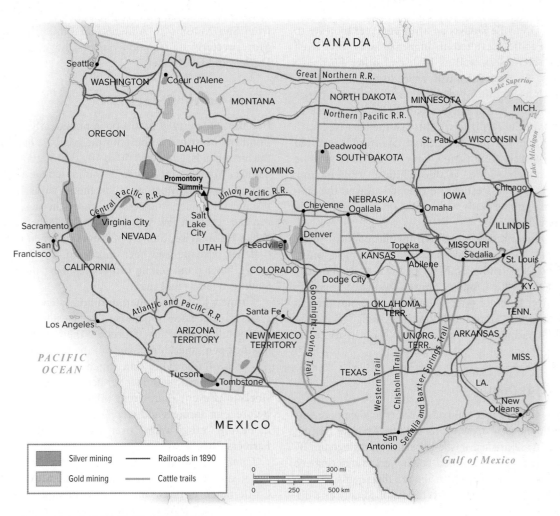

THE MINING AND CATTLE FRONTIERS

In the vast spaces of the West, railroads, cattle trails, and mining for gold, silver, and other precious metals and minerals usually preceded the arrival of enough settlers to establish towns and cities. The railroads forged a crucial link between the region's natural resources and urban markets in the East and in Europe, but by transecting the plains they also disrupted the migratory patterns of the buffalo herds, undermining Plains Indian cultures while opening the land to cattle grazing and farming. They also lured settlers to sometimes barely habitable areas of the country. What reasons might railroad barons have had for choosing the routes their lines took?

(involving a vice president of the United States and at least two members of Congress) swelled profits even more. "Our method of doing business is founded upon lying, cheating and stealing—all bad things," one railroad baron observed. Over 75 western railroads eventually benefited from such government generosity.

Millions of ordinary Americans eventually benefited, too, as did the national economy, but at the time the railroads were the chief beneficiaries. With legislators in their pockets and investors clamoring for a piece of the action, the companies ran seven lines across hundreds of miles of arid, empty grasslands containing few people or businesses to justify the often-inflated price tag. Then they enticed farmers with splashy handbills and posters to places along their lines in western Nebraska and Kansas, where sparse rainfall doomed them to failure. Ruthless profiteering spawned incompetence, inefficiency, and waste. Even railroad boosters had to admit that, as one of them put it, "empty railroad trains ran across deserted prairies to vacant towns."

General Grenville Dodge, an army engineer on leave to the Union Pacific, recruited his immense labor force from Civil War veterans as well as Irish and other European immigrants. He drove them with army discipline, completing as much as 10 miles of track in a single day. Charles Crocker of the Central Pacific had no similar source of cheap labor in California to cut through the massive Sierra Nevada. When his partner Leland Stanford suggested importing workers from China, Crocker laughed, until he ran the numbers. Soon, 10,000 Chinese were inching eastward. They built trestles and chipped away at the Sierras' looming granite walls with picks, shovels, and deadly kegs of dynamite.

Once Chinese crews broke into the flat country of the desert basin, the two railroads raced to claim as much federal land as possible. On May 10, 1869, at Promontory Summit, Utah, with Chinese laborers banished from the scene, a silver hammer pounded a gold spike into the last tie. East and West were finally linked by rail. Travel time across the continent was slashed from months to barely a week.

Cattle Kingdom

Westerners realized that railroads were crucial components of the cattle industry. Cow towns such as Abilene, Denver, and Cheyenne flourished in the growing cattle kingdom. By 1860 some 5 million longhorn cattle were wandering the grassy plains of Texas. Ranchers allowed their herds to roam the unbroken or "open" range freely, identified only by a distinctive brand on their hides.

Cattle ranching in the United States already had a long history in Texas and California, developed largely by Tejanos and Californios of Spanish descent. Anglo-Americans who came to Texas readily adopted the equipment of Tejanos: the tough mustangs and broncos (horses suited to managing mean-spirited longhorns), the branding iron for marking the herds, the corral for holding cattle, and the riata, or lariat, for roping. The cowboys also wore Mexican chaps, spurs, and broad-brimmed sombreros, or "hats that provide shade." In Texas at least a third of all cowboys were Mexicans and black freedmen after the Civil War, the rest largely Confederate veterans. Rivalries sometimes developed among them. One Mexican *corrido,* or ballad, boasted of a herd of 500 steers that could not be corralled by 30 Anglo cowboys, when suddenly five Mexican *vaqueros* arrived: *"Esos cinco mexicanos al momento los echaron / y los trienta americanos se quedaron azorados."* ("Those five Mexicans in a moment put in the steers / and the thirty Americans were left astonished.")

In 1866, as rail lines swept west, Texas ranchers began driving their herds north to railheads for shipment to market. These "long drives" lasted two to three months and sometimes covered more than 1,000 miles. When early routes to Sedalia, Missouri, proved unfriendly, ranchers scouted alternative paths. The Chisholm Trail led from San Antonio to Abilene and Ellsworth in Kansas. More westerly routes soon ran to Dodge City and even Denver and Cheyenne.

Home on the Range

Because cattle grazed on the open range, early ranches were primitive. Most had a house for the family, a bunkhouse for the hired hands, and about 30 to 40 acres of grazing land per animal. Women were scarce in the masculine world of the cattle kingdom. Most were ranchers' wives, strong and resourceful women who cooked, nursed the sick, and helped run the ranch. A few stalwart women ranched themselves. When Helen Wiser Stewart of Nevada learned in July 1884 that her husband had been murdered, she took over the ranch, buying and selling cattle, managing the hands, and tending to family and crops.

Farmers looking for their own homesteads soon became rivals to the cattle ranchers. The "nesters," as ranchers disdainfully called them, fenced off their lands, thus shrinking the open range. Vast grants to the railroads also limited the area of free land, and ranchers intent on breeding heavier cattle with more-tender beef began to fence in their stock to prevent them from mixing with inferior strays. Before long, farmers and ranchers found themselves locked in deadly "range wars" over grazing and water rights. Farmers usually won.

Conflicts also arose between cattle ranchers and herders of another animal introduced by the Mexicans—sheep. Cattle ranchers had nothing but contempt for sheep raisers and their "woolies." Sheep cropped grasses so short that cattle could not graze. To protect the range they saw as their own from the "hooved locust," cattle ranchers attacked shepherds and their flocks. The feuds often burst into range wars, some more violent than those between farmers and ranchers.

Source: Dallas Museum of Art, Ted Dealey Purchase Prize, Seventeenth Annual Dallas Allied Arts Exhibition, 1946

| *Clara Williamson painted this herd on the long drive north from Texas, here crossing a river. At upper left, one cowboy corners a calf that has escaped. So strenuous was the work that each cowboy brought with him about eight horses so that fresh mounts would always be available.*

A Boom-and-Bust Cycle

The cattle boom that began with the first long drive of 1866 reached its peak from 1880 to 1885. Ranchers came to expect profits of 25 to 40 percent a year. Millions of dollars poured into the West from eastern and foreign interests eager to cash in on rocketing cattle prices.

INCREASING EROSION As in most booms, a bust often followed. High profits soon swelled the size of the herds and led to overproduction. Increased competition from cattle producers in Canada and Argentina caused beef prices to fall. And nature imposed its own limits. On the plains, nutritious buffalo and gamma grasses were eaten to the nub, only to be replaced by unpalatable species. When overgrazing combined with drought, as in New Mexico in the 1880s and 1890s, the results could be disastrous. In all these regions, as vegetation changed, erosion increased, further weakening the ecosystem. In 1870, 5 acres of plains land could feed a steer. By the mid-1880s, it took 50 acres.

By the 1890s cattle ranching was changing. The open range and long drives had virtually vanished. What prevailed were the larger cattle corporations such as the King Ranch of Texas. Only these businesses had enough capital to acquire and fence vast grazing lands, hire foremen to manage herds, and pay for feed during winter months. Most cowboys became wage laborers employed by the ranching corporations. Like mining, cattle ranching was turning into a corporate industrial enterprise, succumbing to the eastern pattern of economic concentration and labor specialization.

 REVIEW
How were mining and cattle ranching changed into large-scale operations in the decades after the Civil War?

THE FINAL FRONTIER

IN THE 1860s THEY HAD come in a trickle; in the 1870s they came in a torrent—farmers from the East and Midwest, black freedpeople from the rural South, and peasant-born immigrants from Europe. What bound them together was a craving for land. They had read railroad and steamship advertisements and heard stories from friends about millions of free acres west of the 98th meridian. Hardier strands of wheat like the "Turkey Red" from Russia, improved machinery, and new farming methods made it possible to raise crops in what once had been the "Great American Desert." The number of farms in the United States jumped from some 2 million on the eve of the Civil War to almost 6 million in 1900.

A Rush for Land

BOOMERS AND SOONERS The desire for land was so intense that in the spring of 1889 nearly 100,000 people made their way by wagon, horseback, carriage, mule, even on bicycles and on foot to a line near present-day Oklahoma City, in the center of land once reserved for the Indians. These were "Boomers," gathered for the last great land rush in the Trans-Mississippi West. At noon on April 22, 1889, the Boomers raced across the line to claim some 2 million acres of Indian territory just opened for settlement. Beyond the line lay the "Sooners"—those who had jumped the gun and hidden in gullies and thickets, ready to leap out an instant after noon to claim their stake in prosperity.

Even as the hopefuls lined up in Oklahoma, thousands of other settlers were abandoning their farms to escape mounting debts. The dream of the West as a garden paradise was already being shaken by harsh weather, overproduction, and competition from abroad. Wheat sold for $1.60 a bushel during the Civil War. It fell to 49 cents in the 1890s.

Farming on the Plains

HOMESTEAD ACT Farmers looking to plow the plains faced a daunting task. Under the Homestead Act (1862), government land could be bought for $1.25 an acre or claimed free if a homesteader worked it for 5 years. But the best parcels—near a railroad line, with access to eastern markets—were owned by the railroads or speculators and sold for much more, around $25 an acre.

Once land was acquired, expenses mounted. Sturdy steel-tipped plows and spring-toothed harrows, which turned over sunbaked prairie soil and left a blanket of dust to reduce evaporation, were needed for **dry farming** in parched climates. Newly developed threshers, combines, and harvesters brought in the crop, and powerful steam tractors pulled the heavy equipment. For such machinery, along with horses, seed, and other farm tools, the average farmer spent $1,200, a small fortune in 1880. (Bigger operators invested 10 or 20 times that total.) If their land abutted a ranch, farmers also had to erect fences to keep cattle from trampling fields. Lacking wood, they found the answer in barbed wire, first marketed by Illinois farmer Joseph Glidden in 1874. Crop yields of wheat increased tenfold as a result of these innovations.

BONANZA FARMS Tracts of 160 acres granted under the Homestead Act might be enough for eastern farms, but in the drier West more land was needed to produce the same harvest. Farms of more than 1,000 acres, known as "bonanza farms," were most common in the wheat lands of the northern plains. A steam tractor working a bonanza farm could plow, harrow, and seed up to 50 acres a day—20 times more than a single person could do without machinery. Against such competition, small-scale farmers could scarcely survive. Like the southerners, many westerners became tenants on land owned by someone else, often in return for room, board, and 50 cents a day in wages.

A Plains Existence

For poor farm families, life on the plains meant sod houses or dugouts carved from hillsides for protection against the wind. Tough, root-bound sod was cut into bricks a foot wide and three feet long and laid edgewise to create walls. The average house was seldom more than 18 by 24 feet. In severe weather it had to accommodate animals as well as people. The thick walls kept the house warm in winter and cool in summer, but a heavy, soaking rain or snow could bring the roof down or drip mud and water into the living area. Armies of flies, gnats, mosquitoes, and fleas attacked inhabitants as soon as they moved in. Heavy burdens fell to women. With stores and supplies

Source: Library of Congress, American Memory Collection [rbpe.13401300]

| *Land advertisements like this one were distributed widely in the East. Sellers promised credit at low interest rates as well as the inducement of "free rooms" for those interested in seeing what they might buy. The land in this ad is being offered by the Burlington and Missouri River Railroad Company. Railroads stood to profit not only from the sale of the land but also from the commodities that homesteaders might raise when they were ready to ship them to market.*

©Nebraska State Historical Society (RG2608 PH3535)

| *Even out on the plains in sod huts, farmers cherished the culture they could bring from distant places. Here, family members proudly display the pump organ they imported from the East.*

scarce, they spent countless hours over hot tubs preparing tallow wax for candles or soaking ashes and boiling lye with grease and pork rinds to make soap. In the early years of settlement, wool was in such short supply that resourceful women used hair from wolves and other wild animals to make cloth. Buttons had to be fashioned from old wooden spoons.

Nature added its hardships. In summer, searing winds blasted the plains for weeks. Grasses grew so dry that a single spark could ignite wildfires that engulfed thousands of acres. From Missouri to Oregon nothing spelled disaster like locusts. They descended without warning in swarms 100 miles long. Beating against houses like hailstones, they stripped all vegetation, including the bark of trees. Winter held special horrors. Blizzards swept the plains, piling snow to the rooftops and halting all travel. Settlers might awaken to find their food frozen and snow on their beds. Weeks would pass before farm families saw an outsider.

THE COMFORT OF RELIGION   In the face of such hardships many westerners found comfort in religion. Indians turned to traditional spiritualism and Hispanics to the Catholic Church to cope with nature and hardship. Though Catholics and Jews came west, evangelical Protestants dominated the Anglo frontier in the mining towns and in other western communities. Worship offered an emotional outlet and intellectual stimulation as well as a means of preserving old values and sustaining hope. In the West, as in the rural South, circuit riders compensated for the shortage of preachers, while large-scale camp meetings offered the chance to socialize. Both brought contact with a world beyond the prairie. In many communities it was the churches that first instilled order on public life, addressing problems such as the need for schools or charity for the poor.

The Urban Frontier

Not all westerners lived in isolation. By 1890 the percentage of those in cities of 10,000 or more was greater than in any other section of the country except the Northeast. Unruly, chaotic, and unplanned, western cities were usually the products of history, geography, technology, and commerce.

Some western cities—San Antonio, El Paso, and Los Angeles—were old Spanish towns whose growth had been sparked by Anglo migrants, Mexican immigrants, and the spread of railroad lines. Other cities profited from their location near commercial routes, such as Portland near the Columbia River in western Oregon. Still others, such as Wichita, Kansas, arose to serve the cattle and mining booms. As technology freed people from the need to produce their own food and clothing, westerners turned to the business of supplying goods and services, enterprises that required the labor of more densely populated cities.

Most newer cities had wide streets and large blocks. Whereas the streets of eastern cities measured 30 to 60 feet across, street widths of 80 feet or more were common in the West, where thoroughfares had to be broad enough to allow ox-drawn wagons to turn. The dimensions also reflected the big plans of promoters for the future. "Every town in the West," marveled one European, "is laid out on a plan as vast as though it were destined, at no distant future, to contain a million of inhabitants."

DENVER Denver, Colorado, was typical. Founded in 1859, Denver flourished with the discovery of gold at the mouth of Cherry Creek. The town catered largely to miners with a mix of supply stores, saloons, gambling parlors, and brothels. As it grew, so did its reputation for violence. "A man's life is of no more worth than a dog's," complained one disgusted visitor. Until the early 1860s, when the city hired its first police force, vigilante committees kept the peace with "the rope and the revolver."

In the 1870s Denver embarked on a new phase of growth. The completion of the Denver Pacific and Kansas Pacific Railroads made it the leading city on the eastern slope of the Rocky Mountains. Its economy diversified, and its population soared from about 5,000 in 1870 to more than 100,000 by 1890, when its population ranked behind only Los Angeles and Omaha among western cities.

Development was so rapid that Denver struggled to keep up with itself. By 1900 the city contained over 130,000 residents and 800 miles of streets, but only 24 miles of them were paved. A British observer marveled at "how [Denver's] future vast proportions seem to exist already in the minds of its

projectors." So, too, with the rest of the urban West, where human imagination began to transform the natural landscape into man-made metropolises.

The West and the World Economy

The ceaseless search for resources led all manner of people—and their money—west, including foreign investors. As raw materials flowed out of the region, capital flowed in, mostly from the East and from Europe.

Foreign investments varied from industry to industry but generally came in two forms: direct stock purchases and loans to western corporations and individuals. The great open-range cattle boom of the 1870s and 1880s brought an estimated $45 million into the western livestock industry from Great Britain alone. The Scottish-owned Prairie Cattle Company snapped up nearly 8,000 square miles of western cattle land in three huge tracts. By 1887 Congress had become so alarmed at foreign ownership that it enacted the Alien Land Law, which prohibited the purchase of any land in western territories by foreign corporations or by individuals who did not intend to become citizens. Capital-hungry westerners ignored it.

Like southerners, westerners rarely consumed what they took from the ground. In most instances, they located the resources, extracted them, and sent them outside the region to be turned into finished products. Only when manufactured goods returned to the West did westerners finally consume them, not simply as westerners but as part of a worldwide network of production and trade. Between 1865 and 1915, world population increased by more than 50 percent, and demand mushroomed. Better and cheaper transportation allowed westerners to supply raw materials and agricultural goods to places they knew only as exotic names on a map.

Global reach came at a cost. Decisions made elsewhere—in London and Paris, in Tokyo and Buenos Aires—now determined what westerners charged and how much they

Source: Library of Congress, Prints and Photographs Division [LC-DIG-ppmsca-09570]

| *Denver, Colorado, was one of the growing urban centres of the American West by the end of the nineteenth century. This photograph by William Henry Jackson shows the Rocky Mountains in the background, but makes clear the city was no longer a frontier town.*

| *This photograph of Buffalo Bill Cody (standing in front with his hand resting on a rope) and the cast of his Wild West was taken on a cross-Atlantic voyage to England in 1887. The troupe played to audiences as far away as Outer Mongolia.*

made. A bumper crop in Europe could drive down grain prices so sharply that debt-ridden farmers lost their land. And the effect in Europe was just as devastating, squeezing peasant farmers out and sending many of them to the Great Plains, where they increased the rivalry for land and profits.

No one linked the West to the wider world and shaped perceptions of the region more than William F. ("Buffalo Bill") Cody. Already a well-known scout for the frontier army and a buffalo hunter for hungry railroad crews, Cody garnered added fame when Edward Judson, writing under the pen name "Ned Buntline," published a series of novels in the 1870s based loosely on Cody's life. In them the dashing Buffalo Bill fought desperadoes and Indians, saved distressed damsels, and brought order to the wild frontier. He became an icon of a mythic West: where opportunity was there for the taking, where good always triumphed over evil, where all Indians hunted bison and lived in tepees, and where romance and adventure obscured the realities of Anglo conquest, unchecked exploitation, and growing corporate control.

BUFFALO BILL CODY'S WILD WEST SHOW Trading on his fame and a flair for showmanship, Cody packaged the West in 1883, when he created the "Wild West, Rocky Mountain, and Prairie Exhibition" and took it on tour. Rope-twirling, gun-slinging cowboys, Indians, portrayed as savages, and Annie Oakley, as celebrated for her beauty as for her pinpoint aim, entertained audiences as large as 40,000 or more in giant, open-air theaters. They reenacted famous frontier events, including Custer's Last Stand, and performed daring feats of marksmanship, horseback riding, and calf-roping. Cody even hired Sitting Bull, the most famous Indian in America, to stare glumly at gawking ticket holders.

Marginalized as a people, Indians were now typecast and commercialized as a commodity and packaged along with other stereotypes of the American West, including the sturdy, brave cowboy of legend. Yet the show also broke stereotypes that spoke to Cody's own reformist impulses—for women's rights in the graceful, gun-toting Annie Oakley and for the preservation of Indian life in its remnant representatives whooping and galloping across the arena.

The popularity of Buffalo Bill's Wild West show soon extended overseas. Cody's troupe, animals and all, circled the globe by steamship, train, and wagon. The photograph shows them embarking for London from New York in 1887, but they played to audiences as far away as Outer Mongolia. Queen Victoria saw them twice. For many Europeans the "Wild West" of Buffalo Bill Cody was America.

The South and the West in Sum

Examining the periodic population count taken in 1890, the superintendent of the census noted that landed settlements stretched so far that "there can hardly be said to be a frontier line." He might have added that in the process, the territories that had composed it were vanishing. One after another, they were becoming states: Nebraska in 1867; Colorado in 1876; North Dakota, South Dakota, Montana, and Washington in 1889; Wyoming in 1890;

Utah in 1896; Oklahoma in 1907; and New Mexico and Arizona in 1912. A new West was emerging as a mosaic of ethnicities, races, cultures, and climates, but with the shared identity of a single region.

That sense of a regional identity was heightened for both westerners and southerners because so many of them felt isolated from the mainstream of industrial America. Ironically, it was not their isolation from northern industry but their links to it that marginalized them. The campaign for a New South to out-Yankee the industrial Yankee could not overcome the low wages and high fertility rates of an older South. The promoters of the West had greater success in adapting large-scale industry and investment to mining, cattle ranching, and farming. Still, they, too, confronted the limits of their region, whose resources were not endless and whose rainfall did not follow the plow. Like easterners, westerners found that large corporations with near-monopoly control over markets and transportation bred inequality, corrupt politics, and resentment.

 REVIEW
What problems did the environment of the West present for farmers and ranchers?

PUTTING HISTORY IN GLOBAL CONTEXT

IN THE END, IT WAS NOT simply the disappearance of the American "frontier" within the United States that was at work. Across the globe boundaries between peoples were being breached as the industrialized world scrambled for colonies rich in natural resources and potential for markets. Miners combed the hills of California for gold in 1849, as they did two years later in Victoria, Australia. In South Africa the rush was for diamonds discovered along the Vaal and Orange Rivers and gold near present-day Johannesburg. In Canada, Argentina, Australia, and New Zealand, farmers and cattle ranchers moved steadily toward establishing thelarger commercial farms seen in the American West.

In cities and on farms, deep in mineshafts, and atop towering forests, southerners and westerners were thus being linked to the world economy. Cotton picked by sharecroppers in the Mississippi delta might end up in the petticoats of royalty. Longhorn cattle that grazed on the prairies of Texas fed the cities of Europe. Timber from the piney woods of Georgia or the redwood forests of the Pacific Northwest could find its way into the coffins of Mexico City's dead or the hulls of British schooners.

Racialism—the era's widely accepted practice of categorizing people according to race—justified exploitation elsewhere in the world just as it was used to thwart southern black sharecroppers or Indians driven from their land by prospectors, cowhands, and sodbusters. Coolie laborers died by the thousands in India clearing jungles for tea plantations owned by British firms, while black miners labored in South Africa for Dutch diamond companies and Chinese workers in Australia for European investors, only to be excluded from mainstream society wherever they worked.

The small cotton growers in India, Egypt, and Brazil who faced plummeting prices were just as baffled by market economics as cotton farmers in the American South who found themselves deep in debt to merchants. One British official, traveling into a remote corner of India, reported that cotton growers there found "some difficulty in realizing . . . that, by means of the Electric Telegraph, the throbbings of the pulse of the Home markets communicate themselves instantly to Hingunghat and other trade centres throughout the country." Throughout the world, he might have added. Indeed, it was the "pulse of Home markets" worldwide that controlled the fortunes of those in the cotton fields of both India and the United States. A global industrial system increasingly determined interest rates, prices, and wages in ways that affected ordinary folk everywhere.

CHAPTER SUMMARY

In the years after the Civil War, both the South and the West became more closely linked to the industrial Northeast.

- Despite differences in geography and history, the South and the West shared many features.

  ▶ Both became sources of agricultural goods and raw materials that fed urban and industrial growth.

  ▶ Both were racially divided societies in which whites often used violence to assert their dominance.

  ▶ Both looked beyond their regions for the human and financial resources needed to boost their economies.

  ▶ Southerners embraced the philosophy of the "New South" that industrialization would bring prosperity.

- The South nonetheless remained wedded to agriculture, especially cotton, and to a system of labor that exploited poor whites and blacks.

  ▶ Important in the South were the *crop-lien system*, which shackled poor southerners to the land through debt, and *Jim Crow segregation*, which kept blacks and whites apart.

- White westerners, too, exploited people of other races and ethnicities through settlement, conquest, and capture.

  ▶ By 1890 the emergence of the Ghost Dance and the closing of the frontier signaled that Indians must adapt to life within the boundaries set by white culture despite their efforts at resistance.

  ▶ Latinos were increasingly subjected to similar exploitation but resisted and adapted more effectively to the intrusions of white culture and market economy.

  ▶ In a pattern that became typical for western mining, ranching, and agriculture, small operators first grabbed quick profits and then were followed by large corporations that increased both the scale and the wealth of these industries.

Digging Deeper

The themes of change and continuity have characterized interpretations of southern history after Reconstruction. C. Vann Woodward's classic *Origins of the New South* (1951) dominated thinking about the region for years. Edward L. Ayers, *The Promise of the New South* (1992), offers a comprehensive synthesis that sees both change and continuity. Ted Ownby, *Subduing Satan* (1990), provides a valuable discussion of southern social life, especially the role of religion. On race relations see Joel Williamson, *The Crucible of Race: Black-White Relations in the South since Emancipation* (1984), and on black migrations west, Nell Irvin Painter, *Exodusters: Black Migration to Kansas after Reconstruction* (1976). For the convict leasing system, see Douglas A. Blackmon, *Slavery by Another Name: The Re-Enslavement of Black Americans from the Civil War to World War II* (2008).

The contours of western history were first mapped by Frederick Jackson Turner in his famous address "The Significance of the Frontier in American History" (1893) but have been substantially reshaped by Richard White, *"It's Your Own Misfortune and None of My Own": A New History of the American West* (1992); Patricia Limerick, *A Legacy of Conquest: The Unbroken Past of the American West* (1987); and Gregory H. Nobles, *American Frontier: Cultural Encounters and Continental Conquest* (1997). Each describes the history of the West less as a saga of triumphs than as an analysis of how the region and its resources have been exploited by various peoples and cultures. White adds to his critique of western development in *Railroaded: The Transcontinentals and the Making of Modern* America (2011).

For a well-written and superbly researched study of the Great Plains as a contested zone among environment, animals, and people, see Elliott West's *The Contested Plains: Indians, Goldseekers, and the Rush to Colorado* (1998). Studies of the environment are growing. Among the best are Shepherd Krech III, *The Ecological Indian: Myth and History* (1999); Karl Jacoby, *Crimes against Nature: Squatters, Poachers, Thieves, and the Hidden History of American Conservation* (2001); and Dan Flores, *The Natural West: Environmental History in the Great Plains and Rocky Mountains* (2001). Donald Worster, *A River Running West: The Life of John Wesley Powell* (2002), chronicles that naturalist's feats. Sarah Deutsch, *No Separate Refuge: Culture, Class, and Gender on an Anglo-Hispanic Frontier in the American Southwest, 1880-1940* (1987), develops the concept of regional community in New Mexico and Colorado. On the growing literature of ethno-racial identity in the West, see Neil Foley, *The White Scourge: Mexicans, Blacks, and Poor Whites in Texas Cotton Culture* (1997); and David G. Gutiérrez, *Walls and Mirrors: Mexican Americans, Mexican Immigrants, and the Politics of Ethnicity* (1995). John Weber's *From South Texas to the Nation: The Exploitation of Mexican Labor in the Twentieth Century* (2015) builds on their work to examine mobility and immobility as devices for exploiting Mexican workers. Robert M. Utley expertly surveys *The Indian Frontier of the American West, 1846-1890* (1984). Ari Kelman's award-winning *A Misplaced Massacre: Struggling Over the Memory of Sand Creek* (2013) looks at the contested terrain of memory, while Jeffrey Ostler's *The Lakotas and the Black Hills: The Struggle for Sacred Ground* (2010) carefully examines the Indian point of view of "sacred ground." S. C. Gwynne's *Empire of the Summer Moon: Quanah Parker and the Rise and Fall of the Comanches, the Most Powerful Indian Tribe in American History* (2011) tells the story of a mixed-race Comanche chief and the Indian nation that dominated the southern plains. Margaret D. Jacobs brings a comparative dimension to Indian boarding schools in *White Mother to a Dark Race: Settler Colonialism, Materialism, and the Removal of Indigenous Children in the American West and Australia, 1880-1940* (2009). For the African American experience, see Quintard Taylor, *In Search of the Racial Frontier: African Americans in the American West, 1528-1990* (1998).

After the Fact

| Historians Reconstruct the Past |

Where Have All the Bison Gone?

Between 1872 and 1874 the great American bison—staple of Plains Indian life and an increasingly profitable source of commercial coats and robes—nearly became extinct in the American West. For years people believed that the steep decline was the result of white hunters decimating the herds. But by combining tools from various disciplines—meteorology, ecology, dendrology, animal husbandry, and old-fashioned history—historians offer a more complex and intriguing answer to the important question of where all the bison have gone. Why does that question matter for understanding the history of the Great Plains and its people?

HUNTING BISON

IN LATE SUMMER OF 1875 a herd of great American bison—the largest animals in North America—grazed lazily along a shallow creek bed. Summering on the highlands of the southern plains, they fed on the mid and tall grasses of early spring and the late-sprouting short grasses of summer. They groomed, played, and mated before beginning their slow trek down to the river bottoms, where naturally cured short grasses and cottonwood bark nourished them during the winter months.

Source: Library of Congress, Prints and Photographs Division [LC-DIG-ppmsca-08974]

Source: Library of Congress Prints and Photographs Division [LC-USZ62-133890]

Hunters firing away from a train on the Kansas-Pacific Railroad.

So the cycle had spun for thousands of years. But on this day in 1875 the bison of this herd began mysteriously to die. One by one, they dropped to the ground as if swatted by a huge, invisible hand. Those at the herd's edges went first. Occasionally the animals gathered about a carcass and sniffed at the warm blood. Or they raised their heads to scent the wind for trouble. With the poorest eyesight on the plains, the bison could see little—certainly not the puff of smoke that appeared downwind as each new bison staggered and fell.

The hunter lay perfectly still. No need to move—his powerful .50-caliber Sharps rifle could drop a "shaggy" at 600 feet. No need for horses—they would only spook the herd. The man lay quietly downwind, ideally firing one, maybe two rounds a minute, keeping the pace of killing slow and steady. With care, a good hunter might bag as many as a hundred bison a day. And Tom Nixon was a good hunter, a professional in it for profit.

On this day in 1875, legend has it, Nixon killed 120 bison in 40 minutes. The barrel of his Sharps grew so hot that his bullets wobbled in flight. He forgot about the slow and steady kill, forgot even about his rifle, which was ruined in the hunt. That day he was out for a record, and he got it. The season was as profitable as the day. From September 15 to October 20, Nixon killed 2,127 bison.

Other hunters fared well, too. A buffalo robe fetched as much as $5 in the East. Operating in bands of three or four—a shooter, two skinners, and a cook—professional hunters wreaked havoc with the southern herd of the Great Plains in the 1870s. And within a decade, the northern herd had nearly vanished. By some counts the 30 million bison that roamed the plains in the early nineteenth century shrank to 5,000 by the mid-1880s.

THE QUESTIONS

WHERE HAD ALL THE BISON GONE? Popular historical accounts have focused almost entirely on the gun-toting white hunters of legend and the smoke-belching railroad: symbols of a market economy penetrating the West. Without doubt, the market economy played a role in eliminating the vast herds. As far back as the 1830s and 1840s, fur trappers and traders were eating buffalo meat; so, too, were the railroad crews who extended tracks west. More to the point, the new rail lines provided easy transport of bulky robes and skins to the East. Railroad companies also brought whole trainloads of tourists to shoot at the herd from open windows or atop the cars. In all, the great hunts brought about 10 million bison hides to market.

Ten million is an immense number. But even conservative estimates have suggested that 30 million buffalo had been roaming the plains. What other factors can account for the precipitous drop?

Understanding the fate of the bison herds has required historians to analyze the entire ecology of the plains, of which the bison were an integral part. In many ways, the decades of the 1870s and 1880s represent the end of a process begun much earlier. In reconstructing that process, historians have assembled evidence ranging from traditional accounts of traders and trappers to Indian oral traditions, agricultural census data for livestock, and meteorology reports. They have even found ingenious ways to evaluate the rings of trees and pollen sediment.

One piece of the bison puzzle appears in the 1850s, nearly 20 years before the great white hunts. Starving Indians began to appear across the central and southern plains. Traders reported that the Cheyenne were eating their treasured horses, and other tribes were raiding Mexico for stock. Historians are also able to catch a glimpse of these hard times in the painted-robe calendars of the Kiowa. The calendars show the sign for "few or no bison" for four successive years beginning in 1849.

©MPI/Stringer/Getty Images

The buffalo robe of a Hidatsa warrior. Kiowa Indians kept calendars on buffalo-skin robes, which historians have used to help estimate bison populations.

Contemporaries blamed white emigrants headed overland to the Pacific coast. But the pressures of overland migration alone were not enough to bring the Indians to starvation. From accounts in their diaries and letters, overlanders themselves admitted to being poor hunters of bison. Few recorded ever killing more than a handful at a time. More puzzling, many overlanders reported seeing the "blanched skulls and bones" of bison in the early 1840s, *before* the height of the overland migration. Most puzzling, bison were disappearing first from the western portion of the central plains, where whites were most scarce.

Here, in the western plains, was precisely where Indians were plentiful. Since the seventeenth century, Indian peoples had been lured to the bison-rich plains. The bison became a staple of Indian life, providing a "grocery store on the hoof," hides for clothing and shelter, and a source of powerful religious symbols. Most Plains Indians followed the herds for their subsistence, but as the commercial trade in buffalo robes grew in the 1870s, tribes such as the Blackfeet were being drawn into the hunt for profit. In the first half of the nineteenth century, moreover, new Indian peoples had come to the plains, pushed by the westward advance of European Americans and by hostile tribes from the Great Lakes region. The Indian population in the central plains grew from perhaps 8,000 in 1820 to as many as 20,000 in the 1850s.

For a time the competition between tribes actually helped protect the bison. Warring groups created buffer zones between them. These contested spaces served as refuges for bison, because hunting could be conducted only sporadically for fear of enemy attack. But after 1840, Indian diplomacy brought peace among many rival tribes. The bison began to disappear as Indians stepped up the hunt across the former buffer zones of the western range. They especially favored two- to five-year-old bison cows for their tender meat and their thinner, more easily processed hides. The death of these cows, the most fertile members of the herd, sharply reduced the number of new births.

BIOTIC INVASIONS AND CLIMATE CHANGES

YET MORE WAS AT WORK on the plains than the onslaught of hunters, white or Indian. A broader biotic invasion was under way. Incoming whites and Indians carried animals with them. Indians brought tens of thousands of horses, while the Pacific-bound overlanders brought oxen, cattle, mules, and sheep. These ungulates carried diseases new to the plains—brucellosis, tuberculosis, and a variety of parasites. Later in the century, bison in refuges were found to be riddled with these deadly ailments. The new species also competed for grazing land. So overlanders and Indians were weakening the herds less through slaughter than by occupying the *habitats* of the bison and consuming their food.

Then, beginning in the late 1840s, two decades of unusually heavy rainfall were followed by years of drought. Scientists can deduce these conditions using the science of dendrochronology, which focuses on reading tree rings to provide clues about the weather of a particular era. Around 1850 tree rings began to shrink, indicating the onset of a cycle with more frequent droughts. As highland springs and creeks dried up and summer short grasses grew poorly, more bison began to disappear.

Earlier cycles of drought had led to the virtual disappearance of bison from the plains. No bison bones appear, for example, at archaeological levels that match pollen data indicating droughts between 5,000 and 2,500 BCE and between 500 and 1,300 CE. Thereafter a cycle of above-average rainfall and cooler weather created a more hospitable climate for bison. Unusually abundant rains in the early nineteenth century allowed the herds to grow much larger than normal, as Indian calendars also noted. When drought set in, the herds started to shrink.

In the end the bison were brought low not by one factor but by many. Drought, Indian population increases, and Indian market hunting weakened the great herds. The disturbances created by overlanders and their animals, the appearance of new bovine diseases, and the increased competition for grazing land only made matters worse. By the time the great white hunts began, the bison, though still numerous, were already in crisis.

By comparing the rings from this pine tree taken from the Grand Canyon, historians can date the years of its growth. The widest ring, indicating the wettest year, was 1767.

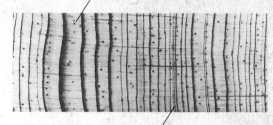

In contrast, 1754 was extremely dry.
Courtesy of American Forests

19

The New Industrial Order

1870–1914

The magnificent steel arches of the Eads Bridge awed T. S. Hudson in his train travel across the continent. When it opened in 1874, it was the longest bridge in the world and the first to cross the Mississippi and to carry railroad tracks. It could not have been built without the newly achieved industrial systems of transportation, mining, finance, and, above all, the manufacture of steel.

Source: Library of Congress, Prints and Photographs Division [LC-USZC4-4899]

>> An American Story

"WAITING FOR THEIR BRAINS"

It was so dark, Robert Ferguson could not see his own feet. Inching along the railroad tracks, he suddenly pitched forward and felt his breath taken away as the ground vanished beneath him. To his dismay, he found himself wedged between two railroad ties, his legs dangling high in the air. Scrambling back to solid ground, he retreated along the tracks to the railroad car, where he sat meekly until dawn.

Ferguson, a Scot visiting America in 1866, had been in Memphis only two days earlier, ready to take the "Great Southern Mail Route" east some 850 miles to Washington. Things had gone badly from the start. About 50 miles outside of town, a broken river bridge forced him to take a ferry, then a mule-drawn truck before learning that the rail line did not resume for another 40 miles. Disheartened, he returned to Memphis to try again.

The train to Memphis arrived six hours late, dawdled its way home, and then, barely three miles from the city, derailed in the middle of the night. When a few passengers decided to hike the remaining distance into town, Ferguson tagged along. It was then that he fell between the tracks onto a flimsy river bridge. Before he finally reached Washington, the Scot faced six more days of difficult travel. One line ended, and passengers and freight would be forced onto another because rail gauges—the width of the track—differed from line to line. Or a bridge was out, or there was no bridge at all. Trains had no meals "on board" or any sleeping cars. "It was certainly what the Americans would call 'hard travelling,'" Ferguson huffed.

Cross-country travel proved so rough that it inspired fantasy. In 1859, the *Southern Literary Messenger* carried the first of several installments of a futuristic "science romance" describing Miss Jane Delaware Peyton's trip to Washington, D.C., from Rasselas, Oregon, in 2029. Elegant trains whisked her across the country in only eight days at the "immense velocity" of 60 miles an hour. Like all train riders, Miss Peyton had to guard against "Tourbilliere," a common mental disorder of the future. After 10 hours on a speeding train, passengers found perception accelerating but memory lapsing. "The mind loses an idea almost as soon as it has been formed," Miss Peyton reported. The only cure was to stop and let the mind catch up to its changing surroundings. So every few days Miss Peyton and her fellow travelers sat quietly at a train station until their symptoms subsided. Such persons were said to be "waiting for their brains."

By the 1880s some of our writer's fantasies had come true, as British tourist T. S. Hudson discovered in 1882 when he launched a self-proclaimed "Scamper through America." Hudson did not cross the continent in quite 8 days, but it took him just 60 to go from England to San Francisco and back. He rode in Pullman "Palace" cars with luxury sleeping quarters and a full breakfast. Newly installed air brakes made trains safer and their stops smoother. Bridges appeared where none had been before, including a "magnificent" span over the Mississippi at St. Louis. Hudson also found himself in the midst of a communications revolution. Traveling across the plains he was struck by the number of telephone poles along the route.

What made America in the 1880s so different from just a few decades earlier was not simply the speed and comfort of travel or the wonders of new technologies. The true marvel was the emerging industrial order that underlay those technologies. Because this order was essentially in place by the beginning of the twentieth century, we tend to take its existence for granted. Yet its growth was at first slow and

haphazard and required innovations in many different areas of society. The transformation brought pain along with progress. The demand for natural resources led to virgin forests being cut down and

Source: Library of Congress, Prints and Photographs Division [LC-USZC4-611]
| *The Pullman "Palace" fantasy*

open-pit mines spewing hazardous runoffs. Factory-lined rivers of the Northeast were left toxic with industrial wastes. In 1882, the year Hudson scampered by rail across America, an average of 675 people were killed on the job every week. Like most people, workers scrambled—sometimes literally—to adjust. Few Americans anywhere had time to "wait for their brains" to catch up to the dizzying pace of change. <<

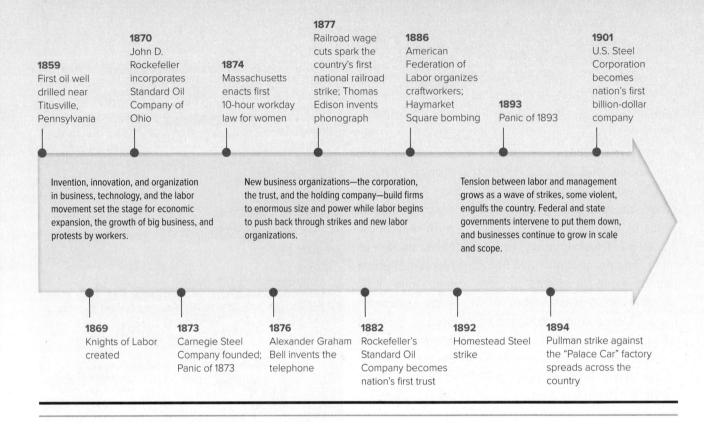

1859
First oil well drilled near Titusville, Pennsylvania

1870
John D. Rockefeller incorporates Standard Oil Company of Ohio

1874
Massachusetts enacts first 10-hour workday law for women

1877
Railroad wage cuts spark the country's first national railroad strike; Thomas Edison invents phonograph

1886
American Federation of Labor organizes craftworkers; Haymarket Square bombing

1893
Panic of 1893

1901
U.S. Steel Corporation becomes nation's first billion-dollar company

Invention, innovation, and organization in business, technology, and the labor movement set the stage for economic expansion, the growth of big business, and protests by workers.

New business organizations—the corporation, the trust, and the holding company—build firms to enormous size and power while labor begins to push back through strikes and new labor organizations.

Tension between labor and management grows as a wave of strikes, some violent, engulfs the country. Federal and state governments intervene to put them down, and businesses continue to grow in scale and scope.

1869
Knights of Labor created

1873
Carnegie Steel Company founded; Panic of 1873

1876
Alexander Graham Bell invents the telephone

1882
Rockefeller's Standard Oil Company becomes nation's first trust

1892
Homestead Steel strike

1894
Pullman strike against the "Palace Car" factory spreads across the country

The Development of Industrial Systems

THE PROCESS OF INDUSTRIALIZATION BEGAN in the United States at least three decades before the Civil War, with small factories producing light consumer goods such as clothing, shoes, and furniture. Much of the economy remained local. Only after the 1850s did the industrial economy develop a set of interlocking systems that allowed larger factories, using more and bigger machines, to produce goods with greater efficiency and market them on a national and international scale in a new industrial order of unprecedented scope.

The new order can best be understood as a web of complex industrial systems woven together in the second half of the nineteenth century. By "industrial system," historians mean a set of arrangements or processes—whether of extraction, production, transportation, distribution, or finance—organized to make the whole industrial order function smoothly. Look, for example, at the industrial systems required to build the bridge across the Mississippi that T. S. Hudson so admired. When James B. Eads

constructed its soaring arches in 1874, he needed steel, probably from iron ore mined in northern Michigan. Giant steam shovels scooped up the ore and loaded whole freight cars in a few strokes. A transportation system—railroads, boats, and other carriers—moved the ore to Pittsburgh, where factories furnished the labor and machinery to finish the steel. The capital to create such factories came from a system of finance that linked investment banks and stock markets to entrepreneurs in need of money. Only with a national network of industrial systems could the Eads bridge be built and a new age of industry dawn.

Natural Resources and Industrial Technology

The earliest European settlers marveled at the "merchantable commodities" of America, from the glittering silver mines of the Spanish Empire to the continent's hardwood forests. What set the new industrial economy apart from that older America was the scale and efficiency of using such natural resources. New technologies made it possible to exploit them in ways undreamed of only decades earlier.

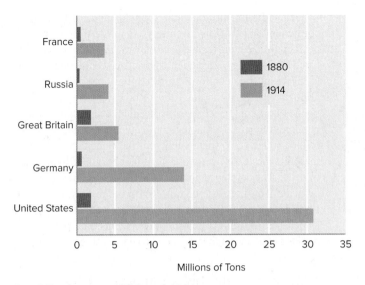

Steel Production, 1880 and 1914

While steel production jumped in Western industrial nations from 1880 to 1914, it skyrocketed in the United States because of rich resources, cheap labor, and aggressive management.

BESSEMER PROCESS Steel, for example, had been made from iron and carbon alloyed with other metals and forged into fine swords as far back as the Middle Ages. In the 1850s inventors in England and America discovered a cheaper way—called the Bessemer process after its British developer, Henry Bessemer—to convert large quantities of iron into stronger, more durable steel. By the late 1870s the price of steel had dropped by more than half. Steel tracks soon carried most rail traffic; steel girders replaced old cast-iron building frames; steel cables supported new suspension bridges.

PETROLEUM INDUSTRY Industrial technology made some natural resources more valuable. New distilling methods transformed a thick, smelly liquid called petroleum into kerosene for lighting lamps, oil for lubricating machinery, and paraffin for making candles. Beginning in 1859, new drilling techniques began to tap vast pools of petroleum belowground. About the same time, Frenchman Etienne Lenoir constructed the first practical internal combustion engine. After 1900 new vehicles, such as the gasoline-powered carriage, turned the oil business into a major industry.

ENVIRONMENTAL CONSEQUENCES The scale of these operations used vast amounts of resources and produced huge quantities of waste. Coal mining, logging, and the industrial toxins of factories led to the most obvious forms of environmental degradation—scarred land, vanishing forests, contaminated waters. As giant water cannons blasted away hillsides in search of gold in California, rock and gravel washed into rivers, raising their beds and threatening populations downstream with floods. Some industrialists limited pollution, often to turn a profit as much as to protect the environment.

Chicago meat packers used every conceivable part of the animals that came into their plants. Straight-length bones were turned into cutlery, hoofs and feet into glue and oil, fat into oleomargarine.

Systematic Invention

Industrial technology rested on invention. For sheer inventiveness, the 40 years following the Civil War have rarely been matched in American history. Between 1790 and 1860, 36,000 **patents** on new inventions were registered with the government. Over the next three decades the U.S. Patent Office granted more than half a million, as the process of invention became systematized. Orderly "invention factories"—forerunners of expensive research labs—replaced small-scale inventors.

EDISON'S CONTRIBUTIONS No one did more to bring system, order, and profitability to invention than Thomas Alva Edison. In 1868, at the age of 21, Edison went to work for a New York brokerage house and promptly improved the design of the company's stock tickers. A $40,000 bonus (worth a little over $952,000 in current dollars) allowed him to become an independent inventor. For the next five years, Edison patented a new invention almost every five months.

| *Thomas Edison, unkempt and wrinkled, in his research lab*
©Bettmann/Getty Images

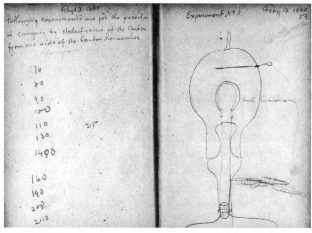

©Fotosearch/Getty Images

| *This page from one of Thomas Edison's notebooks shows sketches of and notes on some of his early experiments with an incandescent lamp—what we know as an electric lightbulb. Edison was not only the most celebrated inventor of his day but by the early twentieth century also one of the greatest popular heroes in American life in a time when scientific and technological progress was considered the defining feature of the age.*

Edison was determined to bring system and order to the process of invention. Only then could breakthroughs come in a steady and profitable stream. He moved 15 of his workers to Menlo Park, New Jersey, where in 1876 he created perhaps his greatest invention—an "invention factory." Like a manufacturer, Edison subdivided the work among gifted inventors, engineers, toolmakers, and others.

THE SPREAD OF AN ELECTRICAL POWER SYSTEM
This orderly bureaucracy soon evolved into the Edison Electric Light Company. Its ambitious owner aimed at more than perfecting his new electric lightbulb. Edison wanted to create a unified electrical power system—central stations to generate electric current, wired to users, all powering millions of small bulbs in homes and businesses. To launch his enterprise, Edison won the backing of several large banking houses by lighting up the Wall Street district in 1882. It was like "writing by daylight," recorded one reporter. Soon Edison power plants sprang up in major cities across the country.

Electricity was more flexible than earlier sources of energy. Factories no longer had to be built near rivers and falls to make use of water power. Before the end of the century, electricity was running automatic looms, trolley cars, subways, and factory machinery. Electricity not only revolutionized industry; it also worked in the homes of ordinary citizens. The electric motor, developed commercially by George Westinghouse and Nikola Tesla in 1886, powered everything from sewing machines to Edison's "gramophone," later known as the record player.

George Eastman revolutionized photography by making the consumer a part of his inventive system. In the process, he democratized picture taking, once the province of the skilled professional, by inventing a camera that anyone could use at a price ($25) many could afford. In 1888 Eastman marketed the "Kodak" camera. The small black box weighed just over 2 pounds and contained a strip of celluloid film that replaced hundreds of pounds of photography equipment. After 100 snaps of the shutter, the owner simply sent the camera back to Eastman's Rochester, New York, factory, along with a $10 fee, then waited for the developed photos and a reloaded camera to return by mail. "You press the button—we do the rest" was Eastman Kodak's apt slogan. So successful was Eastman that competitors launched legal wars for control of his patents. In a pattern that has held ever since, other inventors faced similar court battles.

Transportation and Communication

THE PROBLEM OF SCALE Abundant resources and new inventions remained worthless to industry until they could be moved to processing plants, factories, and offices. But distance was daunting. Where 100 miles of railroad track would do for shipping goods in Germany and England, 1,000 miles was necessary in America.

Nonetheless, by 1870 an efficient transportation system created an integrated national market and tied the United States into an emerging international economy. By the 1870s railroads crisscrossed the country, and steam-powered ships (introduced before the Civil War) were pushing barges down rivers and carrying passengers and freight across the oceans. The time of transatlantic travel was cut in half, to about 10 days. Eventually the rail and water transportation systems fused. By 1900 railroad companies owned nearly all the country's domestic steamship lines.

TELEGRAPH A thriving industrial nation also required effective communication. Information was a precious commodity, as essential to industry as were resources or technology. In the early 1840s, it took newspapers as many as 10 days to reach Indiana from New York and 3 months to arrive by ship in San Francisco. In 1844 Samuel Morse succeeded in testing his new invention, the "telegraph," by tapping out the first message over an electrical wire between cities. By 1861 the Western Union Company had strung 76,000 miles of telegraph lines across the country. If a bank collapsed in Chicago, bankers in Dallas knew of it that day. Railroads could keep traffic unsnarled through the dots and dashes of Morse's code. By the turn of the century a million miles of telegraph wire handled 63 million messages annually, not to mention those flashing across underwater cables to China, Japan, Africa, and South America.

TELEPHONE A second innovation in communication, the telephone, vastly improved on the telegraph. Alexander Graham Bell, a Scottish immigrant, was teaching the deaf when he began experimenting with ways to transmit speech electrically. In 1876 he transmitted his famous first words to a young assistant: "Mr. Watson, come here! I want you." No

| A young Alexander Graham Bell with an early version of his "speaking telegraph."
©The Granger Collection, New York

©Comstock Images/Alamy
| Telegraph key

longer did messages require a telegraph office, the unwieldy Morse code, and couriers to deliver them.

President Rutherford B. Hayes installed the first telephone in the White House in 1878, when the instrument was still a curiosity. The same year, the city of New Haven, Connecticut, opened the first telephone exchange in America. By 1900 there were 1.5 million of Bell's machines in America. The telephone patent proved to be the most valuable ever granted. In the scramble for profits, the Bell Telephone Company battled challenges from competitors and suits from rivals who claimed that their contributions were worth a share of the rights.

Along with other innovations in communication, telephones modernized offices and eased business transactions. In 1915 the American Telephone and Telegraph Company opened the first transcontinental line. When commercial rates dropped after the turn of the century, the telephone became part of a social revolution. Like the railroad and the telegraph, it compressed distances and reduced differences across the country, tying the nation together through another network of communication.

Finance Capital

As industry grew so did the demand for investment capital—the money spent on land, buildings, and machinery. The scale of industry required more funds than ever. Between 1870 and 1900 the number of workers in an average iron and steel firm grew from 100 to 400, and the capital invested jumped to nearly $1 million, about seven times what it had been in 1870.

SOURCES OF CAPITAL Where did the money come from? For the first three-quarters of the nineteenth century, investment capital came mostly from the savings of firms. In the second half of the century, "capital deepening"—a process essential for industrialization—took place. Simply put, as national wealth increased, people began to save and invest more of their money, which meant that more funds could be loaned out. Capital deepening was the key to financing the new industrial order.

Savings and investment grew more attractive with the development of a complex network of financial institutions. Commercial and savings banks, investment houses, and insurance companies gave savers new opportunities to channel money to industry. The New York Stock Exchange, in existence since 1792, linked eager investors with money-hungry firms. By the end of the nineteenth century, the stock market had established itself as the basic means of making capital available to industry.

The Corporation

For those business leaders with the skill to knit the industrial pieces together, large profits awaited. This was the era of the "robber barons," entrepreneurs who bullied their way to success at the expense of competitors and employees. To be sure, sheer ruthlessness went a long way in the fortune-building game. "Law? Who cares about law!" railroad magnate Cornelius Vanderbilt once boasted. "Hain't I got the power?"

To survive in the long term, business leaders could not depend on ruthlessness alone. They also needed ingenuity, an eye for detail, and the gift of foresight. The growing scale of enterprise and capital led them to adapt an old device, the corporation, to the new industrial order. Corporations had existed since colonial times, when governments granted charters of incorporation to organizations that ran facilities for public use such as turnpikes, canals, and banks. After the Civil War the modern corporation came into use for raising money and protecting business holdings.

ADVANTAGES OF THE CORPORATION Colonial governments limited grants of incorporation only to those companies operating in the public interest, such as banks and canal companies, because of the many advantages corporations enjoyed over traditional forms of ownership: the single owner and the partnership. A corporation could raise large sums quickly by selling "stock certificates," or shares in its business. It could also outlive its owners or stockholders, requiring no legal reorganization if one of them died. It limited liability by relieving owners of personal responsibility for business debts. And it separated owners from day-to-day management of the company. A growing corps of highly skilled professional managers could now operate complex businesses. So clear were these advantages that before the turn of the century, corporations were making two-thirds of all manufactured products in the United States.

An International Pool of Labor

Last, but hardly least important for the new industrial order, was a pool of labor. In the United States the demand for workers far outstripped what native-born citizens could supply. In 1860 it took about 4.3 million workers to run all the factories, mills, and shops in the United States. By 1900 there were approximately 20 million workers in industrial and associated enterprises.

GLOBAL LABOR NETWORK In part, the United States relied on a vast global network to fill its need for workers. From the edges of the industrialized world in southern and eastern Europe as well as Latin America, Asia, Africa, and the Middle East, seasonal migrations provided a rich source of workers for many nations, including the United States. Beginning in the 1870s, for example, rural laborers and tenant farmers from the Mezzogiorno in Italy traveled throughout Europe seeking wage work in construction during the building season from spring through early fall. Mechanization, poverty, oppression, and ambition pushed many of these rural laborers from farms into industrial cities and soon to other continents once steamships cut cross-Atlantic travel to under a week in the 1880s.

To draw these workers to the United States, industrialists advertised in newspapers, distributed pamphlets, and sent agents fanning out across the globe. Between 1870 and 1890, more than 8 million immigrants arrived in the United States, another 14 million by 1914. Some came from Asia and Latin America, but most came from Europe and settled in industrial cities. Like migratory laborers elsewhere, they hoped to find work, fatten their purses, and go home. According to one estimate, between 25 and 60 percent of all immigrants returned to their homelands from the United States during these years.

MIGRATION CHAINS In the United States as in other countries, immigrants relied on well-defined migration chains of family and friends to get jobs. A brother might find work with other Slavs in the mines of Pennsylvania; or the daughter of Greek parents, in a New England textile mill filled with relatives. Labor contractors also served as a funnel to industry. Tough and savvy immigrants themselves, they met newcomers at the docks and train stations with contracts

Source: Library of Congress, Prints and Photographs Division [LC-USZ62-5422]

| *Chicago laborer*

to work in local factories, mines, and other industries. For their trouble they took a fee or a slice of the new workers' wages. Among Italians they were known as *padrones;* among Mexicans, as *enganchistas.* By the end of the nineteenth century such contractors controlled two-thirds of the labor in New York City.

Mexicans, too, formed part of this transnational labor pool, streaming across the border especially after the Mexican Revolution in 1910. Even earlier, seasonal migration of Mexican laborers to plant and pick crops from Texas to California was common enough to spawn cross-border family networks. "Come! Come! Come over," a Mexican migrant remembered being told by family friends north of the Rio Grande. Along with Chinese immigrants, Mexican laborers also helped build the transcontinental railroad and, after the turn of the century, moved farther north to tanneries, meatpacking plants, foundries, and rail yards in Chicago, St. Louis, and other centers of industry.

DOMESTIC SOURCES Rural Americans—some 11 million between 1865 and 1920—provided a homegrown source of labor, similar to immigrants in the roots and patterns of their movements. Driven from the farm by machines and bad times or the desire for a new life, most lacked the skills for high-paying jobs. But unlike their foreign counterparts, they spoke English. Many could read and write, and few thought of returning home. In iron and steel cities as well as in coal-mining towns, the better industrial jobs and supervisory positions often went to them. Other rural migrants found work in retail stores or offices and slowly entered the new urban middle class of white-collar workers.

Most African Americans continued to work the fields of the South. About 300,000 moved to northern cities between 1870 and 1910, perhaps more to southern cities. Between 1880 and 1910 the black urban population across the South jumped, more than doubling in industrial cities such as Birmingham. In some instances black migrants were escaping domineering fathers; in others, seeking the excitement of the city; and in still others, following a husband or fleeing the prejudices of the Old South. These migrants, too, relied on family migration chains in their journey, sometimes traveling in groups, sometimes alone. On occasion they brought siblings or spouses and children, often one by one, after they had found work.

Like immigrants and other migrants, African Americans came in search of opportunity, and all faced the burden of continued discrimination when they arrived. Newer industries such as textile manufacturing and railroad shop work refused to hire African Americans, but some businesses, such as Andrew Carnegie's steel mills in Pittsburgh, employed blacks as janitors and wage laborers. Women found jobs as domestic servants and laundresses. Still, by 1890 less than 10 percent of black laborers worked in industry.

> ✓ **REVIEW**
> What factors led to the development of industrial systems?

RAILROADS: AMERICA'S FIRST BIG BUSINESS

RAILROAD TIME THE SYSTEM WAS A MESS: any good railroad executive knew as much. Along the tracks that spanned the country, each town—sometimes each rail station—set its clocks separately by the sun. In 1882, the year T. S. Hudson scampered across America, New York City and Boston were 11 minutes 45 seconds apart. Stations often had several clocks showing the time on different rail lines, along with one displaying "local mean time." In 1883, without consulting anyone, the railroad companies solved the problem by dividing the country into four zones, each an hour apart. Congress did not make the division official until 1918.

At the center of the new industrial systems lay the railroads, moving people and freight, spreading communications, reinventing time, ultimately binding the nation together. Railroads also stimulated economic growth, simply because building them required so many resources—coal, wood, glass, rubber, brass, and by the 1880s 75 percent of all U.S. steel. By lowering transportation costs, railroads allowed manufacturers to reduce prices, attract more buyers, and increase business. Perhaps most important, as America's first truly big business—spanning the country; employing hundreds of thousands; serving millions—railroads created modern management, soon adopted by other industries.

A Managerial Revolution

To the men who ran them, railroads provided a challenge in organization and finance. In the 1850s the Pepperell textile mills of Maine, one of the largest industrial enterprises in America, employed about 800 workers. By the early 1880s the Pennsylvania Railroad had nearly 50,000 people on its payroll. From setting schedules and rates to determining costs and profits, such size required a level of coordination unknown in earlier businesses.

PIONEERING TRUNK LINES The so-called trunk lines pioneered new systems of management. Scores of early companies serviced local networks of cities and communities, often with less than 50 miles of track. During the 1850s longer trunk lines emerged east of the Mississippi to connect the shorter branches, or "feeder" lines. By the outbreak of the Civil War, four great trunk lines linked the Eastern Seaboard with the Great Lakes and western rivers. After the war, trunk lines grew in the South and West.

THE NEW MANAGERS The operations of large lines gave rise to a new managerial elite, beneath owners but with complete authority over daily operations. Cautious by nature they preferred to negotiate and administer rather than compete. In the 1850s Daniel McCallum, superintendent of the New York and Erie Railroad, laid the foundation for this system by drawing up the first table of organization for an American company. A tree trunk with roots represented the president and board of directors; five branches constituted the main operating divisions; leaves stood for the local agents, train crews, and other workers. Information moved up and down the trunk so that managers could get daily reports to and from the separate parts.

By the turn of the century these managerial techniques had spread to other industries. Local superintendents were responsible for daily activities. Central offices served as corporate nerve centers, housing divisions for purchases, production, transportation, sales, and accounting. As a new class of middle managers imposed new order on business operations, executives, managers, and workers operated in increasingly precise and coordinated ways. This represented a revolution in management and became the most important contribution of the railroads to the rise of big business.

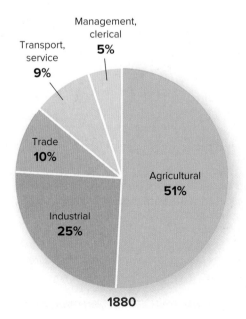

1880

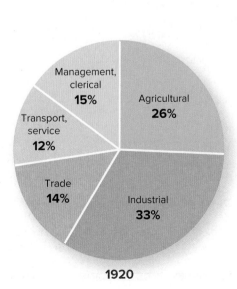

1920

Occupational Distribution, 1880 and 1920

Between 1880 and 1920, management and industrial work—employing white- and blue-collar workers—grew at the expense of farmwork.

>> MAPPING THE PAST <<

RAILROADS TIE THE NATION TOGETHER

©DEA/Biblioteca Ambrosiana/Getty Images

"A railroad is like a lie, you have to keep building it to make it stand."
—Mark Twain.

CONTEXT

In just a few decades, railroad companies built a web of lines that tied the nation together as never before. As this map reveals, by 1890 the railroad network stretched from one end of the country to the other, with more miles of track than in all of Europe. New York City and Chicago, linked by the New York Central "trunk" line, became the new commercial axes. Beyond the Mississippi River a less dense network of trunk lines snaked their way to the West Coast. Note the cities they serviced along their lines.

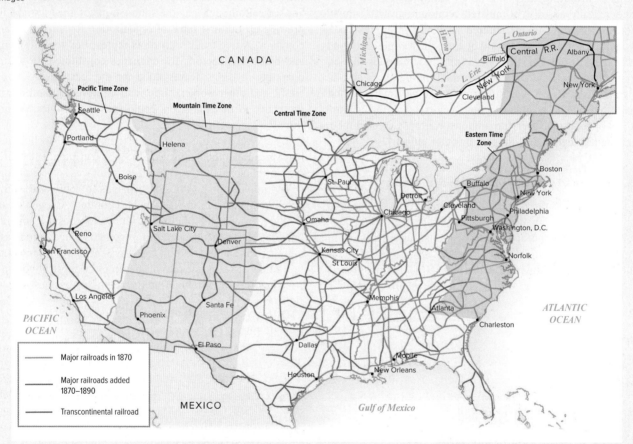

MAP READING

1. Which regions of the country had their railroad lines built earliest?
2. Which regions had the most major lines added between 1870 and 1890?
3. What cities are the terminal points of the Transcontinental Railroad?
4. Which cities are the terminal points of the New York Central Railroad?

MAP INTERPRETATION

1. Why are the earliest rail lines built in the East? What geographic factors caused the railroad network in other regions to be less dense than in the East?
2. Why is the New York Central trunk line so important? Which cities did it most benefit?
3. What role did railroads play in the settlement of the West?
4. What role did cities play in mapping the national railroad network?

Competition and Consolidation

Although managers made operations more systematic, the struggle among railroad companies to dominate the industry was anything but precise and rational. In the 1870s and 1880s the pain of railroad expansion began to tell.

In addition to large start-up costs, railroads were saddled with enormous fixed costs—payrolls, equipment, debts. These remained constant regardless of the volume of traffic. Beginning in the 1860s railroads constructed more lines in hopes of increasing traffic and thereby revenues. Soon the railroads had overbuilt. With so much extra capacity, railroad owners schemed to win new accounts. They gave free passes to favored shippers, promised them free sidings at their plants, offered free land to lure businesses to their territory.

The most savage and costly competition came over the rates charged for shipping goods. Managers lowered rates for freight that was shipped in bulk, on long hauls, or on return routes (since the cars were empty anyway). They used "rebates"—secret discounts to preferred customers—to drop prices below the posted rates of competitors (and then recouped the losses by overcharging small shippers like farmers). When the economy plunged or a weak line sought to improve its position, rate wars broke out. By 1880, 65 lines had declared bankruptcy.

POOLING Cooperation worked better than competition. During the 1870s railroad managers created regional federations to combine traffic, set prices, and divide profits among members. Pooling—informal agreements among competing companies to act together—was designed to remove the competition that led to rate wars. Initially, pools achieved their goal of reducing these rate wars, but because they lacked the force of law, they ultimately failed. Members broke ranks by cutting prices for quick gain. In the end, rate wars died down only when weaker lines failed or stronger ones bought up competitors.

The Challenge of Finance

Earlier in the nineteenth century many railroads relied on state governments for financial backing. They also looked to counties, cities, and towns for bonds and other forms of aid. People living near the ends of rail lines, who stood to gain from construction, were persuaded to take railroad stock in exchange for land or labor. In the 1850s and 1860s western promoters went to Washington for help and returned with $65 million in loans to six western railroads and some 131 million acres of land.

NEW WAYS OF RAISING MONEY Federal aid helped to build only part of the nation's railroads. Most of the money came from private investors. The New York **Stock Exchange** expanded rapidly as railroad corporations began to trade their stocks and bonds. Large investment banks developed financial networks to track down money at home and abroad. By 1898 a third of the assets of American life insurance companies had gone into railroads, while Europeans owned nearly a third of all American railroad stocks.

Because investment bankers played such large roles in funding railroads, they found themselves advising companies about their business affairs. If a company fell into bankruptcy, bankers sometimes served as the "receivers" who oversaw the property until financial health returned. By absorbing smaller lines into larger ones, eliminating rebates, and stabilizing rates, the bankers helped reduce competition and impose order and centralization. In the process, they often came to control the companies they counseled.

By 1900 the new industrial systems had transformed American railroads. Nearly 200,000 miles of track were in operation, 80 percent of it owned by only six groups of railroads. Time zones coordinated schedules; standardized track made cross-country freighting easier. Soon passengers were traveling 16 billion miles a year. To that traffic could be added farm goods, raw materials, and factory-finished products. Everything moved with a new regularity that allowed businesses to plan and prosper.

> ✓ **REVIEW**
> How did the railroads contribute to the rise of big business?

THE GROWTH OF BIG BUSINESS

IN 1865, 26-YEAR-OLD John D. Rockefeller sat stone-faced in the office of his Cleveland oil refinery, about to conclude the biggest deal of his life. Rockefeller's business was flourishing, but not his partnership with Maurice Clark. The two had fallen out over how quickly to expand. Rockefeller was eager to grow fast; the cautious Clark was not. They dissolved their partnership and agreed to bid for the company. Bidding opened at $500, rocketed to $72,500, and abruptly stopped. "The business is yours," said Clark. The men shook hands and a thin smile crept across Rockefeller's face.

Twenty years later Rockefeller's Standard Oil Company controlled 90 percent of the nation's refining capacity and an oil empire that stretched well beyond Cleveland. Around the clock, trains sped Standard executives to New York, Philadelphia, and other eastern cities. The railroads were a fitting form of transportation for Rockefeller's company; in many ways they were the key to his oil empire. They carried his oil products and discounted his rates, giving him the edge to squeeze out rivals. And they pioneered the business systems on which Rockefeller was building. As we shall see with other American firms, Standard Oil was improving on the practices of the railroads to do bigger and bigger business.

Strategies of Growth

First a great riddle had to be solved: how to grow and avoid the ravages of competition? In Michigan in the 1860s salt producers found themselves fighting for their existence. The

The Structures and Strategies of Big Business

STRUCTURE	DESCRIPTION	ADVANTAGES
Corporation	Company owned by stockholders	Separation of ownership and management; limited liability of owners; expert managers; access to capital
Pool	Informal horizontal combination	Stifling competition
Trust	Shares of business held "in trust" by board of directors	Consolidation and control of several businesses; domination of markets
Holding Company	Company that only owns shares in other companies	Controlling management and operations of many companies

STRATEGY	DESCRIPTION	ADVANTAGES
Horizontal Combination	Combining with competitors	Stifling competition
Vertical Integration	Acquiring stages of business operation	Control of costs
Merger	Uniting two or more companies through purchase or mutual consent|	Administrative centralization

Source: Library of Congress, Prints and Photographs Division
[LC-USZ62-63122]

presence of too many salt makers had begun an endless round of price-cutting that was driving them all out of business. In 1869, seeing salvation in combination, they drew together in the nation's first pool called the Michigan Salt Association. Pools voluntarily divided production, assigned markets, and set prices—in Michigan, at double the previous rate.

HORIZONTAL GROWTH Competition often plagued salt processing and other manufacturers of **consumer goods** because their start-up costs were low. **Horizontal combination**—joining loosely together with rivals that produced the same goods or services—had saved Michigan salt

producers. The railroads were among the first big businesses to employ pools. By the 1880s there was a whiskey pool, a cordage pool, and countless others. Such informal arrangements ultimately proved unenforceable and therefore unsatisfactory. (After 1890 they were also considered illegal restraints on trade.) But other forms of horizontal growth, such as formal mergers, spread in the wake of an economic panic in the 1890s.

VERTICAL INTEGRATION Some makers of consumer products worried less about direct competition and concentrated on boosting efficiency and sales. They adopted a growth strategy called **vertical integration,** in which one company gained control of two or more stages of a business operation. A fully integrated manufacturing company, for example, possessed its own raw materials, transportation facilities, factories, and marketing outlets.

Gustavus Swift, a New England butcher, saw the advantages of such integration when he arrived in Chicago in the mid-1870s. Aware of the demand for fresh beef in the East, he acquired new refrigerated railcars to ship meat from western slaughterhouses and a network of ice-cooled warehouses in eastern cities to store it. By 1885 he had created the first national meatpacking enterprise, Swift and Company. Swift moved upward, closer to consumers, by putting together a fleet of wagons to distribute his beef to retailers. He moved down toward raw materials, extending and coordinating the purchase of cattle at the Chicago stockyards. By the 1890s Swift and Company was a fully integrated, vertically organized corporation operating on a nationwide scale. Soon Swift, Armour and Company, and three other integrated giants—together called the "Big Five"—controlled 90 percent of the beef shipped across state lines.

Vertical growth generally brought producers of consumer goods closer to the marketplace. For them, profit came from high-volume sales. The Singer Sewing Machine Company and the McCormick Harvester Company created their own retail sales arms. Manufacturers began furnishing ordinary consumers with technical information, credit, and repair services in an effort to expand sales. Advertising expenditures grew to some $90 million by 1900, identifying markets, shaping buying habits, and drumming up business.

Carnegie Integrates Steel

Industrialization encouraged vertical integration in heavy industry but more often downward, toward reliable sources of raw materials. These firms made machinery and materials—called **producer goods**—for big users such as railroads and factory builders. Their markets changed little. For them, profits lay in securing limited raw materials and holding down costs.

Andrew Carnegie led the way in steel. A Scottish immigrant, he worked his way up from bobbin boy in a textile factory to expert telegrapher to superintendent of the western division of the Pennsylvania Railroad at the age of 24. A string of wise investments paid off handsomely. He owned a share of the first sleeping car, the first iron railroad bridge, a locomotive factory, and finally an iron factory that became the nucleus of his steel empire.

BESSEMER PROCESS In 1872, on a trip to England, Carnegie chanced to see the new Bessemer process for making steel. Awestruck by its fiery display, he rushed home to build the biggest steel mill in the world. The J. Edgar Thomson Steel Works (shrewdly named in honor of the president of the Pennsylvania Railroad) opened in 1875, in the midst of a severe depression. Over the next 25 years, Carnegie added mills at Homestead and elsewhere in Pennsylvania and moved from railroad building to city building. He supplied steel for the Brooklyn Bridge, New York City's elevated railway, and the Washington Monument.

KEYS TO CARNEGIE'S SUCCESS Carnegie succeeded, in part, by taking advantage of the boom-and-bust business cycle. He jumped in during hard times, building and buying when equipment and businesses were cheap. He also found skilled managers who employed the administrative techniques of the railroads. And Carnegie knew how to compete. He scrapped machinery, workers, even a new mill to undersell competitors.

| *Joseph Pennell's forbidding drawing,* In the Works, Homestead, *portrays the grimy reality of Andrew Carnegie's steel mills. While smoke dominated the outside landscape, fire prevailed inside. The blast furnaces were "giant caldrons," as writer Upton Sinclair put it, "big enough for all the devils of hell to brew their broth in, full of something white and blinding, bubbling and splashing, roaring as if volcanoes were blowing through it—one had to shout to be heard."*

Source: Library of Congress, Prints and Photographs Division [LC-DIG-ds-07144]

The final key to Carnegie's success was expansion. His empire spread horizontally by purchasing rival steel mills and constructing new ones. It spread vertically, buying up sources of supply, transportation, and eventually sales. Controlling such an integrated system, Carnegie could ensure a steady flow of materials from mine to mill and market as well as a steady stream of profits. In 1900 his company turned out more steel than Great Britain and netted him $40 million.

Integration of the kind Carnegie employed expressed the logic of the new industrial age. More and more, the industrial activities of society were being linked in one giant, interconnected process.

Rockefeller and the Great Standard Oil Trust

John D. Rockefeller accomplished in oil what Carnegie achieved in steel. And he went further, developing an innovative business structure—the **trust**—that promised greater control than even Carnegie's integrated system. At first Rockefeller, who specialized in refining petroleum, grew horizontally by buying out or joining competing oil refiners. To cut costs, he expanded vertically, with oil pipelines, warehouses, and barrel factories. By 1870, when he and five partners formed the Standard Oil Company of Ohio, his high-caliber, low-cost products could compete with any other.

ROCKEFELLER'S METHODS OF EXPANSION Because the oil-refining business was a jungle of competitive firms, Rockefeller proceeded to twist arms. He bribed rivals, spied on them, created phony companies, and slashed prices. His decisive edge came from the railroads. Desperate for business, they granted Standard Oil not only rebates on shipping rates but also "drawbacks," fees that railroaders paid Standard for petroleum products shipped by a rival. Within a decade Standard Oil dominated the oil business with a vertically integrated empire that stretched from drilling to selling.

Throughout the 1870s Rockefeller kept his empire stitched together through informal pools and other business combinations. But they were weak and afforded him too little control. He could try to expand further, except that corporations were restricted by state law. In Rockefeller's home state of Ohio, for example, corporations could not own plants in other states or own stock in out-of-state companies.

THE TRUST In 1879 Samuel C. T. Dodd, chief counsel of Standard Oil, came up with a solution, the "trust." Under the trust, the stockholders of corporations surrendered their shares "in trust" to a central board of directors with the power to control all property. In exchange, stockholders received certificates of trust that paid hefty dividends. Because it did not literally own other companies, the trust violated no state law.

In 1882 the Standard Oil Company of Ohio formed the country's first great trust. It brought Rockefeller what he

sought so fiercely—centralized management of the oil industry. Other businesses soon created trusts of their own—in meatpacking, wiremaking, and farm machinery, for example. Just as quickly, trusts became notorious for crushing rivals, fixing prices, and dominating markets.

The Mergers of J. Pierpont Morgan

The trust was only a stepping-stone to an even more effective means of avoiding competition, managing people, and controlling business: the corporate merger. The idea of two corporations merging—one buying out or pooling with another—remained impossible until 1889, when New Jersey began to permit corporations to own other corporations.

THE HOLDING COMPANY In 1890 the need to find a substitute for the trust grew urgent. Congress outlawed trusts under the Sherman Antitrust Act, which specifically banned business from "restraining trade" by setting prices, dividing markets, or engaging in other unfair practices. The ever-inventive Samuel Dodd came up with a new idea, the "holding company," a corporation of corporations that had the power to hold shares of other companies. Many industries converted their trusts into holding companies, including Standard Oil, which moved to New Jersey in 1899.

Two years later came the biggest corporate merger of the era, created by financial wizard J. Pierpont Morgan. His orderly mind detested the chaotic competition that threatened his profits. "I like a little competition," Morgan used to say, "but I like combination more." After the Civil War he had taken over his father's powerful investment bank. For the next 50 years the House of Morgan played a part in consolidating almost every major industry in the country.

Morgan's greatest triumph came in steel, where for years Carnegie had refused to combine with rivals. In January 1901, with the threat of a colossal steel war looming, Morgan convinced Carnegie to put a price tag on his company. When a messenger brought back the scrawled reply—more than $400 million—Morgan merely nodded and said, "I accept this price." He then bought Carnegie's eight largest competitors and announced the formation of the United States Steel Corporation.

U.S. Steel gobbled up more than 200 manufacturing and transportation companies, 1,000 miles of railways, and the whole Mesabi iron range of Minnesota. The mammoth holding company produced nearly two-thirds of all American steel. Its value of $1.4 billion exceeded the national debt and made it the country's first billion-dollar corporation, in 1901.

THE MERGER MOVEMENT What Morgan helped to create in steel was rapidly coming to pass in other industries. A wave of mergers swept through American business after the depression of 1893. As the economy plunged, cutthroat competition bled businesses until they were eager to sell out. Giants sprouted almost overnight. By 1904 in each of 50 industries one firm came to account for 60 percent or more of the total output.

©Hulton Archive/Getty Images

| *Andrew Carnegie around 1868. A decade later, a world tour he took tempered his attitude toward the Social Darwinist view that evolution had produced the superiority of Western technology and ideas. "Go and see for yourselves how greatly we are bound by prejudices, how checkered and uncertain are many of our own advances," he told friends. "No nation has all that is best . . ."*

Corporate Defenders

THE GOSPEL OF WEALTH   As Andrew Carnegie's empire grew, his conscience took command. Preaching a "gospel of wealth," he urged the rich to act as stewards for the poor, "doing for them better than they would or could do for themselves." He devoted his time to philanthropy by creating foundations and endowing libraries and universities with some $350 million in contributions. "The man who dies rich," he declared, "dies disgraced."

Defenders of the new corporate order were less troubled than Carnegie about the rough-and-tumble world of big business. They justified the system by stressing the opportunity created for individuals by economic growth. Through frugality, acquisitiveness, and discipline—the sources of cherished American individualism—they believed anyone could rise, as did Andrew Carnegie.

"SOCIAL DARWINISM"   When most ordinary citizens failed to follow in Carnegie's footsteps, defenders blamed the individual. Financial failures were lazy, ignorant, or morally depraved, they said. British philosopher Herbert Spencer added the weight of science by applying Charles Darwin's theories of evolution where naturalist Darwin had never intended—to society. Spencer maintained that in society, as in biology, only the "fittest" survived. The competitive social jungle doomed the unfit to poverty and rewarded the most fit with property and privilege. Such "social Darwinism" found strong support among turn-of-the-century business leaders. The philosophy of ruthless competition certified their success even as they worked to destroy the very competition it celebrated.

Corporate Critics

Andrew Carnegie invoked the gospel of wealth to justify his millions, but a group of radical critics looked on his libraries and foundations as desperate attempts to buy peace of mind. For all the contemporary celebrations of wealth and big business, they saw the new industrial order as exploitative, divisive, and immoral. It was built on the backs of ordinary "toilers," whose labors profited the few Carnegies of the world.

Henry George, a journalist and self-taught economist, began his critique with a simple question: How could poverty exist when industrial progress had created such wealth? George pointed to greedy landowners who bought property when it was cheap and then held it until the forces of society—labor, technology, and speculation on nearby sites—increased its value. They reaped most of the rewards, despite the hard work of others. In his best-selling book *Progress and Poverty* (1879), George proposed a single tax on these "unearned" profits. With all other taxes abolished, income would be slowly redistributed. "Single-tax" clubs sprang up throughout the country, and George nearly won the race for mayor of New York City in 1886.

The journalist Edward Bellamy tapped the same popular resentment against the inequalities of industrial capitalism. In his best-selling novel *Looking Backward* (1888), Julian West, a fictional Bostonian, falls asleep in 1887 and awakens Rip Van Winkle–like in the year 2000. In place of the competitive, class-ridden society of the nineteenth century is an orderly utopia managed by a benevolent government trust. "Fraternal cooperation," shared abundance, and "nationalism," which puts the interests of the community above those of the individual, are the guiding principles. By 1892 Bellamy's philosophy had spawned over 160 clubs in 27 states with followers demanding redistribution of wealth, civil service reform, and nationalization of railroads and utilities.

SOCIALIST LABOR PARTY   Less popular but equally hostile to capitalism was the Socialist Labor Party, formed in 1877. Under Daniel De Leon, a West Indian immigrant, it stressed class consciousness and conflict. De Leon called for a revolution to give workers control over production. Refusing to compromise their radical beliefs, advocates of **socialism** ended up attracting more intellectuals than workers. Some immigrants found its class consciousness appealing, but most rejected its radicalism and rigidity. A few party members, bent on gaining greater support, revolted and in 1901 founded the more successful Socialist Party of America. Workers were beginning to organize their own responses to industrialism.

By the mid-1880s, in response to the growing criticism of big business, government acted. Several states in the South and West enacted laws limiting the size of corporations. But these laws proved all too easy to evade when states such as New Jersey and Delaware eased their rules to allow corporations to grow nationwide.

SHERMAN ANTITRUST ACT In 1890 the public clamor against trusts that operated across states lines finally forced Congress to adopt pioneering legislation. The Sherman Antitrust Act relied on the only constitutional authority the federal government had over business: its right to regulate interstate commerce. The act outlawed "every contract, combination in the form of trust or otherwise, or conspiracy, in restraint of trade or commerce." The United States stood practically alone among industrialized nations in regulating such business combinations.

UNITED STATES v. E. C. KNIGHT Co. Its language was purposefully vague, but the Sherman Antitrust Act did give the government the power to break up trusts and other big businesses. So high was the regard for the rights of private property, however, that few in Congress expected the government to exercise that power or the courts to uphold it. They were right. Before 1901, the Justice Department filed only 14 antitrust suits against big businesses, virtually none of them successful. In 1895 the Supreme Court dealt the law a major blow by severely limiting antitrust when it ruled against the government in its suit against the E. C. Knight Company, which controlled over 90 percent of sugar refining in the country. In *United States v. E. C. Knight Co.,* the Court held that businesses involved in manufacturing (as opposed to "trade or commerce") lay outside the authority of the Sherman Act. The ruling thus excluded most firms other than transportation companies that carried goods across state lines. Not until after the turn of the century would the law be used to bust a trust.

| *In 1901 Spindletop Hill, just south of Beaumont, Texas, yielded a gusher that began the modern oil industry. Known as "black gold," oil became one of the most profitable businesses in the world, but drilling for it was dangerous. Wells could ignite, producing a deadly blast and then a fire that might last for days.*

©Texas Energy Museum, Beaumont, Texas

©The Granger Collection, New York

| *This drawing is from a 1905 edition of* Collier's *magazine, famous for exposing corporate abuses. Here it mocks John D. Rockefeller, head of the Standard Oil Company, as the new god of the industrial age by parodying the Protestant doxology of thanks: "Praise God from whom all blessings flow, Praise him all creatures here below!"*

Short- and Long-Term Costs of Doing Business

The heated debates between the critics and defenders of industrial capitalism made clear that the changes in American society were two-edged. Big businesses helped to order or rationalize production, increase national wealth, and tie the country together. Yet they also concentrated power, corrupted politics, and made the gap between rich and poor more apparent than ever. In 1890 the richest 9 percent of Americans held nearly three-quarters of all wealth in the United States. Meanwhile, by 1900 one American in eight (nearly 10 million people) lived below the poverty line.

THE BOOM-AND-BUST CYCLE The practices of big business subjected the economy to enormous disruptions. The banking system could not always keep pace with the demand for capital, and businesses failed to distribute enough profits to sustain the purchasing power of workers. The supply of goods periodically outstripped the appetite for them, and then the wrenching cycle of boom and bust set in. Three severe depressions—1873–1879, 1882–1885, and 1893–1897—rocked the economy in the last third of the nineteenth century. With hard times came fierce competition as managers searched frantically for ways to cut costs, and the industrial barons earned their reputations for ruthlessness.

The environmental costs were often steep and plain to see. In Pittsburgh, some 14,000 smokestacks spewed so much coal dust into the air that the city was permanently covered in haze. Sulfur, cyanide, ammonia, acid fumes, and other toxic gases filled the air around chemical factories. Lead paint was the norm on many buildings, even though authorities knew it could damage muscles, nerves, and the brain. Equally normal was dumping chemical wastes into nearby rivers and streams. Hardly anyone worried, assuming that it promoted public health by killing infectious bacteria in the water.

THE STUDY OF GLOBAL WARMING: FIRST STIRRINGS Not all of the costs were clear at the time. Although anyone could see the environmental impact of mining, logging, and smokestack industries on scarred hillsides, fouled rivers, and soot-filled air, the long-term effects were less apparent. In the nineteenth century most people, scientists included, assumed that Nature would maintain its own balance, largely unaffected by human action. And for the handful of observers

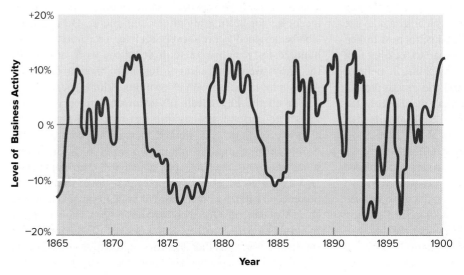

Boom-and-Bust Business Cycle, 1865–1900

Between 1865 and 1900 industrialization produced great economic growth but also wild swings of prosperity and depression. During booms productivity soared and near-full employment existed. But the rising number of industrial workers meant high unemployment during deep busts.

interested in such things as climate change only the most basic calculations were possible. Still, step by small step, scientists around the globe began to address a question that would obsess future generations: What controlled the temperature of the planet?

For eons, temperatures had ebbed and flowed in cycles stretching across vast intervals of time. Early in the nineteenth century, French scientist Joseph Fourier wondered why the Earth did not burn to a cinder given the power of solar energy. His answer: the Earth was venting heat into space. When he tallied the figures, he discovered an anomaly. On average the earth should be colder, not warmer, than he assumed. He concluded that the atmosphere must be trapping heat and radiating it back to the surface.

A Brit and a Swede, both consumed with discovering the cause of the prehistoric Ice Age, worked out the climatic ramifications. In 1859 British scientist John Tyndall posed the question of causality backward: Precisely what in the atmosphere *prevented* the Earth from freezing? By testing the gas emitted by burning coal from a jet in his laboratory, he found that methane and carbon dioxide thereby released captured heat. Historically such gases had come from volcanic eruptions and other natural occurrences, but growing amounts were now being thrown aloft by industry. In Sweden, Svante Arrhenius carried the idea one step further in 1896. If heat-trapping gases raised global temperatures even slightly, warmer air would absorb more of the biggest heat trapper of all—water vapor—raising temperatures still higher. With the age of industry in its infancy, few people paid attention to the implications for what would later be called "global warming."

 REVIEW

What strategies and structures did businesses use to grow and at what costs?

THE WORKERS' WORLD

AT SEVEN IN THE MORNING Sadie Frowne sat at her sewing machine in a Brooklyn garment factory. The boss, a man she barely knew, dropped a pile of unfinished skirts next to her. She pushed one under the needle and began to rock her foot quickly on the pedal that powered her machine. Sometimes Sadie pushed the fabric too hastily, and the needle pierced her finger. "The machines go like mad all day because the faster you work the more money you get," Sadie explained of the world of industrial work in 1902.

The cramped sweatshops, the vast steel mills, the dank tunnels of the coalfields—all demanded workers and required them to work in new ways. Farmers or peasants who had once timed themselves by the movement of the sun now lived by the clock and labored in the twilight of gaslit factories. Instead of being self-employed, they were under the thumb of a supervisor and were paid by the piece or hour. Not the seasons but the relentless cycle of machines set their pace.

Industrial Work

In 1881 the Pittsburgh Bessemer Steel Company opened its new mill in Homestead, Pennsylvania. Nearly 400 men and boys went to work in its 60 acres of sheds. They kept the mill going around the clock by working in two shifts: 12 hours a day the first week, 12 hours a night the next. In the furnace room, some men fainted from the heat, while the vibration and screeching of machinery deafened others. There were no breaks, even for lunch.

PATTERN OF INDUSTRIAL WORK Few industrial workers labored under such extreme conditions, but the Homestead mill reflected the common characteristics of industrial work: the use of machines for mass production; the division of labor into intricately organized, menial tasks; and the dictatorship of the clock. At the turn of the century two-thirds of all industrial work came from large-scale mills.

Under such conditions labor paid dearly for industrial progress. By 1900 most of those earning wages in industry worked 6 days a week, 10 hours a day. They held jobs that required more machines and fewer skills. Repetition of small chores replaced fine craftwork. In the 1880s, for example, almost all the 40 different steps that had gone into making a pair of shoes by hand could be performed by a novice, or "green hand," with a few days of instruction at a simple machine.

INDUSTRIAL ACCIDENTS With machines also came danger. Tending furnaces in a steel mill or plucking tobacco from cigarette-rolling machines was tedious. If a worker became bored or tired, disaster could strike. From 1880 to 1900 industrial mishaps killed an average of 35,000 workers a year and injured over 536,000. Workers could expect no payment from employers or the government for death or injury. The law operated under the presumption that such accidents were the worker's fault.

TAYLORISM Higher productivity and profits were the chief ends of business, and for Frederick W. Taylor, efficiency was the means. During the 1870s and 1880s Taylor undertook careful time-and-motion studies of workers' movements in the steel industry. He set up standard procedures and offered pay incentives for beating his production quotas. On one occasion he designed 15 ore shovels, each for a separate task. One hundred forty men were soon doing the work of 600. By the early twentieth century "Taylorism" was a full-blown philosophy, complete with its own professional society.

For all the high ideals of Taylorism, ordinary laborers refused to perform as cogs in a vast industrial machine. In a variety of ways, they worked to maintain control. Many European immigrants continued to observe the numerous saints' days and other religious holidays of their homelands, regardless of factory rules. When the pressure of six-day weeks became too stifling, workers resisted by taking an unauthorized "blue Monday" off. Or they slowed down production to reduce the grueling pace. Or they simply walked off the job. Come spring and warm weather, factories reported turnover rates of 100 percent or more as workers looked for new jobs elsewhere.

| This machine tool shop in West Lynn, Massachusetts, photographed in the mid-1890s, suggests something of the growing scale of factory enterprise in the late nineteenth century—and also of the extraordinary dangers workers in these early manufacturing shops faced.
©Brown Brothers

WORKER CITIZENS For some laborers, seizing control of work was more than a matter of survival or self-respect. Many workers regarded themselves as citizens of a democratic republic. They expected to earn a "competence"—enough money to support and educate their families and enough time to stay abreast of current affairs. Few but highly skilled workers could realize such democratic dreams. More and more, labor was being managed as another part of an integrated system of industry.

Children, Women, and African Americans at Work

The needs of industry for workers were so great that groups traditionally left out of the industrial ambit—children, women, African Americans—found themselves drawn into it. In the mines of Pennsylvania nimble-fingered eight- and nine-year-olds snatched bits of slate from amid the chunks of coal. In Illinois glass factories, quick-footed "dog boys" dashed with trays of red-hot bottles to the cooling ovens. By 1900 the industrial labor force included some 1.7 million children, more than double the number 30 years earlier. Parents often had no choice. As one union leader observed, "Absolute necessity compels the father . . . to take the child into the mine to assist him in winning bread for the family." On average, children worked 60 hours a week and carried home paychecks a third the size of those of adult males.

Women had always labored on family farms, but by 1870 one in four nonagricultural workers was female. In general they earned one-half of what men did. Nearly all were single and young, anywhere from their mid-teens to their mid-20s. Most lived in boardinghouses or at home with their parents. Usually they contributed their wages to the family kitty. Once married they took on a life of full-time housework and child rearing.

Only 5 percent of married women held jobs outside the home in 1900. Married black women (in need of income because of the low wages paid to their husbands) were four times more likely than married whites to work away from home. Domestic service was by far the most common occupation for these women. But industrialization inevitably pushed women into new jobs. Mainly they worked in industries considered extensions of housework: food processing, textiles and clothing, and cigar making. Many women actually preferred factory labor, with its long hours and dirty conditions, to being a live-in servant, where they were at work seven days a week and on call 24 hours a day.

New methods of management and marketing opened positions for white-collar women as "typewriters," "telephone girls," bookkeepers, and secretaries. On rare occasions women entered the professions, though law and medical schools still regarded them as unwelcome invaders. Such discrimination drove ambitious, educated women into nursing, teaching, and library work, all considered forms of feminine nurturance. Their growing presence soon "feminized" these professions, pushing men upward into managerial slots or out entirely.

Even more than women, African American men faced discrimination in the workplace. They were paid less than whites and given menial jobs. Their greatest opportunities in industry often came as strikebreakers to replace white workers, which reduced the effectiveness of strikes. Once a strike ended, however, black workers were replaced and hated by the white regulars whose jobs they had taken. The service trades furnished the largest single source of employment for African Americans. Waiting on whites in restaurants or on railroads lay within the boundaries set by prevailing prejudice. Craftworkers and a sprinkling of black professionals could usually be found in cities. After the turn of the century, black-owned businesses catering to African American patrons thrived in the growing black neighborhoods of the North and the South.

Historian's TOOLBOX

Detecting Industrial Accidents

Eastport, Maine: what adjectives would you use to describe the scene?

At first the view looks somewhat rural, but at least three elements in the photograph suggest otherwise. What are they?

What strikes you about this digitally enlarged portion of the photo?

Source: Library of Congress, Prints and Photographs Division [LC-DIG-nclc-00966]

Photographs can be both revealing and deceptive, but technology can help historians detect what the camera lens actually captured. This print (upper left) of a photo by Lewis Hine, a turn-of-the-century photographer, shows 8-year-old Phoebe Thomas returning to her house in Eastport, Maine. The scene seems to be nothing more than a little girl making her way home up a set of stairs. Hine tells us that the young Syrian worked all day in a cannery, shearing the heads off sardines with a butcher's knife. When the Library of Congress scanned the image nearly a century later, a portion of the photo could be digitally enlarged to reveal much more than meets the unaided eye. What appears to be an ordinary homecoming is, in fact, something much worse, as Hine's notes reveal. Phoebe was "running home from the factory all alone, her hand and arm bathed with blood, crying at the top of her voice. She had cut the end of her thumb nearly off, cutting sardines in the factory, and was sent home alone, her mother being busy."

THINKING CRITICALLY

How does the close-up of Phoebe Thomas change the nature of the photograph? What would we make of the photograph without Hine's explanatory notes? Google "Lewis Hine" to learn what he photographed and why.

The American Dream of Success

RISING REAL WAGES Whatever their separate experiences, working-class Americans did improve their overall lot. Though the gap between the very rich and the poor widened, most wage earners made some gains. Between 1860 and 1890 real daily wages—pay in terms of buying power—climbed some 50 percent, more the result of gradually falling prices than of increases in pay. And after 1890, the number of hours on the job began a slow decline.

Most unskilled and semiskilled workers in factories continued to receive low pay. In 1890 an unskilled laborer could

Source: (*left*) Library of Congress, Prints and Photographs Division [LC-USZ62-61588]; (*right*) ©Buyenlarge/Getty Images

| *Horatio Alger, a minister and school-teacher-turned-children's book author, achieved wide success with his dime-novel tales of down-and-out youngsters who worked hard and, through "luck and pluck," got ahead in life. Early novels, such as* The Western Boy *(1878) were printed with black-and-white covers, but the presses kept turning out the books even after Alger died in 1899. His novel* Do and Dare *appeared in this early twentieth-century edition with a color cover and characters whose style of dress was updated to reflect more current tastes.*

expect about $1.50 for a 10-hour day; a skilled one, perhaps twice that amount. It took about $600 to make ends meet, but most manufacturing workers made under $500 a year. Native-born white Americans tended to earn more than immigrants, those who spoke English more than those who did not, men more than women, and all others more than African Americans, Latinos, and Asians.

SOCIAL MOBILITY   Few workers repeated the rags-to-riches rise of Andrew Carnegie. But some did rise despite periodic unemployment and ruthless wage cuts. About one-quarter of the manual laborers in one study entered the lower middle class in their own lifetimes. More often such unskilled workers climbed in financial status within their own class. Most workers, seeing some improvement, believed in the American dream of success, even if they did not fully share in it.

HORATIO ALGER   Anyone with doubts could turn to Horatio Alger to learn how to make the dream real. The son of a minister, Alger wrote over 100 books for boys between 1864 and 1899. His young heroes bore different names—Ragged Dick, Julius the Street Boy, Tony the Tramp—but their story was always the same. A chance encounter presents a poor young boy with an opportunity. In one book it's a

runaway carriage with the daughter of a wealthy industrialist inside, in another a rich man's lost wallet. Through courage, honesty, hard work, and thrift, the boy makes the most of chance and lives a life of fame and fortune. With titles such as *Luck and Pluck, Strong and Steady, Slow and Sure,* and *Strive and Succeed,* Alger touted his simple keys for rising from what he called "rags to respectability." By the time he died at the turn of the century, his books had sold over a million copies and taught a generation how to succeed in business and life. Whether Alger's widely held virtues produced the same results in the real world was another matter.

 **REVIEW**
How did industrialization change the lives of workers?

THE SYSTEMS OF LABOR

Putting in more hours to save a few pennies, walking out in exhaustion or disgust, slowing down on the job—in these ways individual workers coped with industrial America. Sporadic and unorganized, such actions stood little chance of bringing the new industrial order under the control of labor. For ordinary workers to begin to shape industrialization they had to combine, as businesses did. They needed to combine horizontally—organizing not just locally but on a national scale. They needed to integrate vertically by coordinating action across a wide range of jobs and skills, as Andrew Carnegie coordinated the production of steel. Unions were the workers' systematic response to industrialization.

Early Unions

In the United States, **unions** began forming before the Civil War. Skilled craftworkers—carpenters, iron molders, cigar makers—joined together to protect themselves against the growing power of management. Railroad "brotherhoods" also furnished insurance for those hurt or killed on the accident-plagued lines. Largely local and exclusively male, these early craft unions remained weak and unconnected to each other as well as to the growing mass of unskilled workers.

NATIONAL LABOR UNION After the Civil War a group of craft unions, brotherhoods, and reformers united skilled and unskilled workers in a nationwide organization. The National Labor Union (NLU) hailed the virtues of a simpler America, when workers controlled their workday, earned a decent living, and had time to be good citizens. NLU leaders attacked the wage system as unfair and enslaving and urged workers to manage their own factories. By the early 1870s NLU ranks had swelled to more than 600,000.

The NLU pressed energetically for the eight-hour workday, the most popular labor demand of the era. Workers saw it as a way not merely of limiting their time on the job but of limiting the power of employers over their lives. "Eight hours for work; eight hours for rest; eight hours for what we will!" proclaimed a banner at one labor rally. Despite the popularity of the issue, the NLU wilted during the depression of 1873.

The Knights of Labor

More successful was a national union born in secrecy. In 1869 Uriah Stephens and nine Philadelphia garment cutters founded the Noble and Holy Order of the Knights of Labor. They draped themselves in ritual and regalia to deepen their sense of solidarity and met in secret to evade hostile owners. Their strongly Protestant tone repelled Catholics, who made up almost half the workforce in many industries.

©Bettmann/Getty Images

| *Clerks' jobs, traditionally held by men, came to be filled by women as growing industrial networks created more managerial jobs for men. Here a factory floor full of neatly dressed female clerks bang away at their "Type-Writers," patented first in 1868.*

Source: Library of Congress, Prints and Photographs Division

| In this painting by Robert Koehler, titled The Strike *(1886)*, labor confronts management in a strike that may soon turn bloody. One worker reaches for a stone as an anxious mother and her children look on.

TERENCE POWDERLY In 1879 the Knights elected Terence V. Powderly as their Grand Master Workman. Handsome, dynamic, Irish, and Catholic, Powderly threw off the Knights' secrecy, dropped their rituals, and opened their ranks. He called for "one big union" to embrace the "toiling millions"—skilled and unskilled, men and women, natives and immigrants, all religions, all races. By 1886 membership had leaped to over 700,000, including nearly 30,000 African Americans and 3,000 women.

Like the NLU, the radical Knights of Labor looked to abolish the wage system. In its place they wanted to construct a cooperative economy of worker-owned mines, factories, and railroads. The Knights set up more than 140 "cooperative workshops," where workers shared decisions and profits, and sponsored some 200 political candidates. To tame the new industrial order, they supported the eight-hour workday and the regulation of trusts. Underlying this program was a moral vision of society. If people only renounced greed, laziness, and dishonesty, Powderly argued, corruption and class division would disappear, and democracy would flourish. To reform citizens inside and outside of the workplace, the Knights promoted the prohibition of child and convict labor and the abolition of liquor.

It was one thing to proclaim a national union, quite another to coordinate the activities of so many members. Powderly soon found locals resorting to strikes and violence, actions he condemned. In the mid-1880s such stoppages wrung concessions from the western railroads, but the organization soon became associated with unsuccessful strikes and violent extremists. Even its impressive gains against railroads were wiped out when the Texas and Pacific Railroad broke a strike by local Knights. By 1890 the Knights of Labor, symbol of organized labor's resistance to industrial capitalism, teetered near extinction.

The American Federation of Labor

SAMUEL GOMPERS The American Federation of Labor (AFL) soon took up the Knights' position as the premier union in the nation. The AFL reflected the practicality of its leader, Samuel Gompers. Born in a London tenement, the son of a Jewish cigar maker, Gompers had emigrated in 1863 with his family to New York's Lower East Side. Unlike the visionary Powderly, Gompers preached accommodation, not resistance. He urged his followers to accept capitalism and the wage system. What he wanted was "pure and simple unionism"—a worker organization that accepted the idea of a fixed, wage-earning class and bargained for higher pay, fewer hours, improved safety, more benefits.

Gompers chose to organize highly skilled craftworkers, because they were difficult to replace. He bargained with employers and used strikes and boycotts only as last resorts. With the Cigar Makers' Union as his base, Gompers helped create the first national federation of craft unions in 1881. In 1886, it became the American Federation of Labor. Twenty-five labor groups joined, representing nearly 150,000 skilled workers. Stressing gradual, concrete gains, he made the AFL the most powerful union in the country. By 1901 it had more than a million members, almost a third of all skilled workers in America.

FAILURE OF ORGANIZED LABOR Despite the success of the AFL the laboring classes did not organize themselves as systematically as did the barons of industry. For one thing, Gompers and the AFL were less interested in vertical integration that combined skilled and unskilled workers or included women and African Americans. For another, workers themselves were separated by language and culture, divided along lines of race and gender, and fearful of retaliation by management. A strong strain of individualism made many workers regard any collective action as un-American. In 1900 union membership made up less than 10 percent of industrial workers.

The Limits of Industrial Systems

As managers increased their control over the workplace, workers often found themselves at the mercy of the new industrial order. Even in boom times, one in three workers was out of a job at least three or four months a year. The word *unemployment* dates from the late nineteenth century.

SPONTANEOUS PROTESTS   In hard times, when a worker's pay dropped and frustration mounted, when a mother worked all night and fell asleep during the day while caring for her children, when food prices suddenly jumped—anger might boil over into protest. "A mob of 1,000 people, with women in the lead, marched through the Jewish quarter of Williamsburg last evening and wrecked half a dozen butcher shops," reported the *New York Times* in 1902.

In the late nineteenth century a wave of labor activism swept the nation. More often than mobs, it was strikes and boycotts that challenged the authority of employers and gave evidence of working-class identity and discontent. Most strikes broke out spontaneously, organized by informal leaders in a factory. Thousands of rallies and organized strikes were staged as well, often on behalf of the eight-hour workday, in good times and bad, by union and nonunion workers alike.

MOLLY MAGUIRES   Some workers resorted to terrorism to resist the new industrial order. In the coalfields of Pennsylvania, Irish miners organized a secret society called the Molly Maguires, named for an earlier group of protesters in Ireland who had disguised themselves as women and roamed the Irish countryside beating and sometimes killing tyrannical landlords. The American Mollys founded their society in 1866. For the next decade the small but dedicated band resorted to intimidation, arson, and murder to combat the horrid working conditions of coal miners. They saw it as "retributive justice" imported from Ireland and employed against a new set of oppressors. In 1876, 20 Mollys were brought to trial and a year later executed for 16 murders. For most Americans justice was served, despite the questionable legality of the trial. In its wake the secret society vanished.

GREAT RAILROAD STRIKE   In 1877, in the midst of a deep depression, the country's first nationwide strike opened an era of confrontation between labor and management. When the Baltimore and Ohio Railroad cut wages by 20 percent, a crew in Martinsburg, West Virginia, seized the local depot and blocked the line. President Hayes sent federal troops to enforce a court order ending the strike, but instead two-thirds of the nation's tracks shut down in sympathy. The novel tactic suggested a growing sense of solidarity among workers. The country ground to a halt.

When owners brought in strikebreakers, workers torched rail yards, smashed engines and cars, and tore up track. Local police, state militia, and federal troops finally quashed the strike after 12 bloody days. The "Great Railroad Strike" of 1877 left 100 people dead and more than $10 million worth of railroad property in rubble. It signaled the rising power and unity of labor and sparked fears, as one newspaper warned, that "this may be the beginning of a great civil war in this country, between labor and capital."

LAUNDRESSES STRIKE   The Civil War between North and South was still fresh in the minds of Atlantans when 3,000 laundresses struck for higher wages in 1881. Over 98 percent of the city's domestic workers were black women, just a decade and a half out of slavery. Pitiful wages already had led many of them to employ informal strategies to protest. They took unauthorized breaks, pretended to be sick, or "pantoted" (stole) leftovers from the kitchens of their white employers. Washerwomen were among the most privileged domestics, because they neither worked nor lived with their employers. Instead, they labored together in common spaces in their neighborhoods, where they built social and political networks. In 1881 they formed the Washing Society and threatened to leave much of the city without clean clothes unless their demands for higher wages were met. Though little resulted from the strike, it nonetheless showed the appeal of organized protest against economic inequality and laid the groundwork for later civil rights protests.

©Everett Historical/Shutterstock

| *In 1874,* Harper's Weekly *published this illustration, "The Strike in the Coal Mines— Meeting of the 'Molly Maguire' Men." It portrays the Mollys more respectably than they were in real life. Indeed, the composition of the scene, as one historian has pointed out, rather resembles Jesus' Sermon on the Mount, given to his disciples.*

TWO SIDES OF HAYMARKET

The Haymarket Square Affair on May 4, 1886, led to the arrest and conviction of eight people for the murder of police officer Mathias J. Degan. Degan died as a result of the explosion of a pipe bomb at a labor rally organized by anarchists in the Haymarket Square in Chicago. In the first document one of the convicted defendants—an anarchist named August Spies—explains how he became a radical and what he did at Haymarket. The second document is part of Judge Joseph E. Gary's address to the convicted men.

DOCUMENT 1
A Radical Explains His Beliefs

The factory: the ignominious regulations, the surveillance, the spy system, the servility and lack of manhood among the workers and the arrogant arbitrary behavior of the boss and mamelukes—all this made an impression upon me that I have never been able to divest myself of. At first I could not understand why the workers, among them many old men with bent backs, silently and without a sign of protest bore every insult the caprice of the foreman or boss would heap upon them. I was not then aware of the fact that the opportunity to work was a privilege, a favor, and that it was in the power of those who were in the possession of the factories and instruments of labor to deny or grant this privilege. I did not then understand how difficult it was to find a purchaser for one's labor, I did not know then that there were thousands and thousands of idle human bodies in the market, ready to hire out upon most any conditions, actually begging for employment. I became conscious of this, very soon, however, and I knew then why these people were so servile, whey [sic] suffered the humiliating dictates and capricious whims of their employers. . . .

My connection with the meeting on the Haymarket on May 4th 86 did not go beyond that of an invited speaker. I had been invited to address the meeting in German, but no German speakers being present I spoke in English. The meeting had been called by the representatives of a number of Trades Union. Those present were workingmen of all beliefs and views; they were not Anarchists. Nor were the speeches anarchistic, they treated on the Eight Hour question. Anarchism was not even referred to by anyone. . . . But Anarchism was good enough to serve as a scapegoat for Bonfield. This fiend, in order to justify his murderous attack upon that meeting, said "They were Anarchists".— "Anarchists! Oh, Horror!" The stupid mass imagined that "Anarchists" must be something very bad and they joined in the chorus with their enemies and fleecers: "Crucify, Crucify!"

Source: Spies, August, Autobiography, 1886, 18-20, 31-33, as reprinted by the Chicago Historical Society, Haymarket Affair Digital Collection, www.chicagohistory.org/hadc/manuscripts/M06/M06.htm, accessed February 27, 2013.

DOCUMENT 2
The Judge Speaks of Murder and Free Speech

. . . the law is common sense. It holds each man responsible for the natural and probable consequences of his own acts. It holds that whoever advises murder, is himself guilty of the murder that is committed in pursuance of his advice, and that if men band together for a forcible resistance to the execution of the law, and advise murder, as a means to make such resistance effectual, whether such advice is to one man to murder another, or to a numerous class to murder men of another class, all who are so banded together, are guilty of any murder that may be committed in pursuance of such advice.

The People of this country love their institutions, love their homes, love their property. They will never consent that by violence and murder, those institutions shall be broken down, their houses despoiled, and their property destroyed.

And the People are strong enough to protect and sustain their institutions, and to punish all offenders against their laws. And those who threaten danger to civil society, if the law is enforced, are leading to destruction whoever shall attempt to execute such threats.

The existing order of society can be changed only by the will of the majority.

Each man has a full right to entertain and advocate, by speech and print, such opinions as suit himself, and the great body of the People will usually care little what he says, but if he proposes murder as a means of enforcing his opinions, he puts his own life at stake. And no clamor about free speech, or evils to be cured, or wrongs to be redressed, will shield him from the consequences of his crime.

His liberty is not a license to destroy. The toleration that he enjoys, he must extend to others, and not arrogantly assume that the great majority are wrong, and may rightfully be coerced by terror, or removed by dynamite.

Source: Address by Judge Joseph E. Gary, Cook County, IL Criminal Court, October 8, 1886, as reprinted by the Chicago Historical Society, Haymarket Affair Digital Collection, www.chicagohistory.org/hadc/manuscripts/M05/M05.htm, accessed February 27, 2013.

THINKING CRITICALLY

What about "the factory" so disturbed August Spies and led to his becoming a radical? On what grounds does Judge Gary explain the conviction and the sentence? (At the time, those who advocated violence were legally responsible for violent consequences.) How, if at all, does knowing that Illinois Governor John Peter Altgeld pardoned the three surviving defendants as innocent only a few years later change your view of these two documents?

HAYMARKET SQUARE RIOT In 1886 tension between labor and capital exploded in the "Great Upheaval"—a series of strikes, boycotts, and rallies that strengthened bonds among workers but turned national sympathies against labor. One of the most violent episodes occurred at Haymarket Square in Chicago. A group of anarchists was protesting the recent killing of workers by police at the McCormick Harvester Company. As rain drenched the small crowd, police armed with billy clubs and pistols ordered everyone out of the square. Suddenly a bomb was thrown into the procession of police. One officer was killed; 5 others were mortally wounded. The police opened fire, and the crowd fired back. Before the melee ended, nearly 70 policemen were injured, and at least 4 civilians died.

Conservatives charged that radicals were responsible for the "Haymarket Massacre." Though the bomb thrower was never identified, a jury found seven of eight anarchists guilty of conspiracy to commit murder and sentenced them to death. The eighth defendant received a 15-year prison sentence. Four were hanged, one killed himself, and three remained in jail until they were pardoned by Illinois Governor John Peter Altgeld in 1893. He considered their conviction a miscarriage of justice, but ordinary citizens who once had supported labor grew frightened of what newspapers called its "Samson-like power." Haymarket became a turning point in labor history. It ignited the nation's first "red scare," touching off years of official attacks on radicals for fear they were fomenting violence and revolution. (Red was the color often associated with radicals and revolutionaries.) Cities enlarged their police forces, and states built more National Guard armories on the borders of working-class neighborhoods to contain future violence. A succession of legal decisions hamstrung the union movement for decades, which in any case turned in more conservative directions.

Management Strikes Back

The strikes, rallies, and boycotts of 1886 were followed by a second surge of labor activism in 1892. In the remote silver mines of Coeur d'Alene, Idaho, and the coal mines near Tracy City, Tennessee, strikes flared, only to be crushed by management. In July, at Andrew Carnegie's steel mill in Homestead, Pennsylvania, workers literally fought back when manager Henry Clay Frick announced that no union members could work there any longer, despite having negotiated a contract with the Amalgamated Association of Iron and Steel Workers. The workers struck, and Frick called in the Pinkerton Detective Agency. Three hundred armed Pinkertons waged a fierce battle with the strikers and lost, but not before three Pinkertons and seven workers had been killed. After an appeal from Frick, the governor of Pennsylvania sent 8,000 state militiamen to restore order. The strike was broken, the mill reopened, and the Amalgamated Association was crushed.

PULLMAN STRIKE The broadest confrontation between labor and management took place two years later. A terrible depression had shaken the economy for almost a year when George Pullman, owner of the Palace Car factory and inventor of the plush railroad car, laid off workers and cut wages but kept rents high on company-owned housing. He refused to discuss any grievances. In 1894 workers struck and managed to convince the new American Railway Union to support them by boycotting all trains that used Pullman cars. Quickly the strike spread to 27 states and territories.

Anxious railroad owners appealed to President Grover Cleveland for federal help. On the slim pretext that the strike obstructed mail delivery (strikers had actually been willing to handle mail trains without Pullman cars), Cleveland secured a court order halting the strike. He then called several

"GIVING THE BUTT"—THE WAY THE "REGULAR" INFANTRY TACKLES A MOB.

Government troops were often called in to help management quell strikes. In the Pullman Strike of 1894, U.S. Regulars "give the butt" to angry laborers in this drawing by Frederick Remington.

Source: Library of Congress, Prints and Photographs Division [LC-USZ62-96502]

thousand special deputies into Chicago to enforce it. In the rioting that followed, 12 people died and scores were arrested. But the strike was crushed.

MANAGEMENT WEAPONS In all the labor disputes of this era, the central issue was the power to shape the new industrial systems. Employers always enjoyed the advantage. They hired and fired workers, set the terms of employment, and ruled the workplace. They fought unions with "yellow dog" contracts that forced workers to refuse to join. Blacklists circulated the names of labor agitators. Lockouts kept protesting workers from plants, and company spies infiltrated their organizations. With a growing pool of labor and the support of government, employers could replace strikers and break strikes.

Management could also count on local, state, and federal authorities for troops to break strikes. In addition, businesses used a powerful new legal weapon, the **injunction.** These court orders prohibited certain actions, including strikes, by barring workers from interfering with their employer's business.

It was just such an order that had brought federal deputies into the Pullman strike and put Eugene Debs, head of the American Railway Union, behind bars. The Indiana-born Debs, a former locomotive fireman and early labor organizer, received a six-month jail sentence for violating the court injunction. After his release, he abandoned the Democratic Party to become the foremost Socialist leader in America.

REVIEW

How did workers respond to industrialization?

PUTTING HISTORY IN GLOBAL CONTEXT

IN A MATTER OF only 30 or 40 years, the new industrial order transformed the landscape of America and left its mark on the world at large. British railroad tracks covered some 20,000 miles by the 1870s, while Germany and France built even larger systems and Japan began constructing its own network with the help of hundreds of engineers from the United States and Great Britain. South Africa, Mexico, Argentina, and Egypt, all rich in raw materials and agricultural commodities, followed. None outstripped the United States. By 1915 its rail network was longer than the next seven largest systems combined.

With remarkable speed, networks of communication and transportation spread across the globe. Underwater telegraph cables were laid from the United States to Europe in 1866, to Australia in 1871 and 1872, to Latin America in 1872 and 1873, and to West Africa by 1886. The completion of the Suez Canal in 1869 (the same year a golden spike connected the last link in the U.S. transcontinental railroad) hastened the switch from sail-powered to steam-driven ships by slicing thousands of miles from the journey between Europe and Asia. Wheat from the United States and India, wool from Australia, and beef from Argentina poured into Europe, while Europe sent textiles, railroad equipment, coal, and machinery to Asia and the Americas.

As these networks tied together national economies, swings in the business cycle produced global consequences. When an Austrian bank failed in 1873, depression soon reached the United States. In the mid-1880s and again in the mid-1890s, recessions drove prices down and unemployment up across the industrialized world. Industrial workers bore the brunt of the burden, but in Europe they had greater success in unionizing, especially after anticombination laws forbidding strikes were abolished in the decades following 1850. By 1900 British unions had signed up 2 million workers, twice the number of members in either the United States or Germany. As strikes became more common and labor unions more powerful, industrializing nations passed social legislation that included the first social security systems and health insurance. Despite such laws, in the new industrial order material progress walked hand in hand with social pain and upheaval.

CHAPTER SUMMARY

In the last third of the nineteenth century a new industrial order reshaped the United States.

- New systems—of resource development, technology, invention, transportation, communications, finance, corporate management, and labor—boosted industrial growth and productivity.

- Pioneered by the railroads, businesses grew big, expanding vertically and horizontally to curb costs and competition and to increase control and efficiency.

- Industrialization came at a price.
  - ► Workers found their power, job satisfaction, and free time reduced as their numbers in factories mushroomed.
  - ► The environment was degraded.
  - ► A vicious cycle of boom and bust afflicted the economy.

- Workers both resisted and accommodated the new industrial order.
  - ► Some resisted through informal mechanisms such as slowdowns, absenteeism, and quitting and through spontaneous and more-formal ones, including radical unions like the Knights of Labor.
  - ► Other workers were more accommodating, accepting low-paying jobs and layoffs and creating "pure and simple" unions, such as the American Federation of Labor, that accepted the prevailing system of private ownership and wage labor while bargaining for better wages and working conditions.

- The benefits of industrialization were equally undeniable.
  - ► Life improved materially for many Americans.
  - ► The real wages of even industrial workers climbed.

- The United States rocketed from fourth place among industrial nations in 1860 to first by 1890.

Digging Deeper

For a useful introduction to the period, see Edward C. Kirkland, *Industry Comes of Age: Business, Labor, and Public Policy, 1860–1897* (1967). Mechanization and its impact are the focus of Siegfried Giedion's classic *Mechanization Takes Command* (1948). Thomas Piketty's sweeping *Capital in the Twenty-First Century* (2013) examines wealth and income inequality across three centuries in Europe and the United States. The best overview of American labor is American Social History Project, *Who Built America? Working People and the Nation's Economy, Politics, Culture, & Society*, Volume Two: *From the Gilded Age to the Present* (1992). Herbert Gutman, *Work, Culture, and Society in Industrializing America: Essays in American Working-Class History* (1976), explores the development of working-class communities in the nineteenth century, especially the role of ethnicity in creating a working-class culture. On wage earners, see Joshua L. Rosenbloom, *Looking for Work, Searching for Workers: American Labor Markets during Industrialization* (2002). David Montgomery offers a broad look at the impact of industrialization on American labor in *The Fall of the House of Labor: The Workplace, the State, and American Labor Activism, 1865–1925* (1987); and Leon Fink, *Workingmen's Democracy: The Knights of Labor and American Politics* (1983) examines early efforts of the Knights of Labor to challenge corporate capitalism by organizing workers and socializing them into a labor culture. Alice Kessler-Harris, *Out to Work: A History of Wage-Earning Women in the United States* (1982), surveys female wage earners and their effect on American culture, family life, and values. Paul Avrich's rich *The Haymarket Tragedy* (1984) sees the whole affair as a tragic miscarriage of justice. After looking at the actual trial transcript and a host of other original materials, Timothy Messer-Kruse concludes the trial followed common legal procedure and fairly convicted the eight anarchists, however tragic their deaths, in *The Trial of the Haymarket Anarchists: Terrorism and Justice in the Gilded Age* (2011).

No book did more to set the idea of big business as ruthless robber barons than Matthew Josephson, *The Robber Barons: The Great American Capitalists, 1861–1901* (1934). T. J. Stiles's *Tycoon: The Epic Life of Cornelius Vanderbilt* (2009) offers a detailed account of the public and personal life of the first great railroad baron. Ron Chernow's *Titan: The Life of John D. Rockefeller, Sr.* (1998) helps to debunk the image of business leaders as "robber barons," without minimizing their ruthlessness. Legal, social, and communal effects of the rise of railroads are addressed in Barbara Young Welke, *Recasting American Liberty: Gender, Race, Law, and the Railroad Revolution, 1865–1920* (2001). Richard White's *Railroaded: The Transcontinentals and the Making of Modern America* (2012) makes a powerful case for the profligacy of the transcontinental railroad lines in a revisionist retelling of the epic story. Business historian Alfred D. Chandler Jr.'s *Strategy and Structure: Chapters in the History of American Industrial Enterprise* (1962) and *The Visible Hand: The Managerial Revolution in American Business* (1977) are seminal accounts of business organization and management that stress the adaptations of business structures and the emergence of a new class of managers. For a comparative view of the rise of big business in the United States, Great Britain, and Germany, see his *Scale and Scope* (1988). On the problem of climate change, see Spencer R. Weart, *The Discovery of Global Warming* (2003).

20

The Rise of an Urban Order

1870–1914

Fires broke out often enough in nineteenth-century cities. There were several the week before the Great Chicago Fire of 1871. But the environment worked against the city that Sunday night, with a stiff wind out of the southwest that sent flaming brands swirling into the air, spreading the blaze quickly. "Nature had withheld her accustomed measure of prevention," commented one historian at the time. But environmental factors also ensured that the city would be rebuilt, since Chicago was located at the center of a new urban-industrial complex.

©Chicago History Museum/Archive Photos/Getty Images

>> An American Story

"THE DOGS OF HELL"

"The dogs of hell were upon the housetops . . . bounding from one to another," gasped Horace White, a Chicago reporter, as he described the fire consuming his city on a hot October day in 1871. Whipped by dry prairie winds, tornadoes of flame were whirling through Chicago, at times faster than fleeing residents. Locals called the flaming twisters "fire devils." Flames leapt from building to building, block to block, spinning and spewing fiery debris that fed the inferno. The heat was so intense that stone walls collapsed with a force that shook the earth. A burning ember set the roof of the Waterworks ablaze, leaving the city without enough water to fight the fire. Even the Chicago River burst into flame as industrial grease and oil floating on its surface ignited.

| *Chicago's Masonic Temple building was a skyscraper in the new style: tall, sleek, without ornamentation.*

The Great Chicago Fire was the worst disaster in the city's history. When the flames finally burned out more than a day later, a smoldering scar of cinders and rubble four miles long and three-quarters of a mile wide cut through the city. The fire destroyed the business district and left a third of the city's 300,000 residents homeless. As many as 300 people died. Could the city—any city—recover from such a calamity?

Unitarian minister Robert Collyer had the answer. "We have not lost, first, our geography," he told his congregation; for he believed that geography was destiny. "Nature called the lakes, the forests, the prairies together in convention long before we were born, and they decided that on this spot a great city would be built." Linking eastern railroads and the Great Lakes with the West, Chicago's prime location at the crossroads of continental commerce had not moved one inch.

More than geography favored recovery. An astounding assortment of assets survived the fire. The city's stockyards and packinghouses, the center of a meat industry that made Chicago "Hog Butcher of the World," lay untouched. Along the wharfs on the Chicago River, lumberyards and mills miraculously survived. To the west, two-thirds of the city's grain elevators still stood, their giant silos holding corn, wheat, and other grains for processing and shipment. And the rails that connected Chicago to the rest of the country remained largely intact.

Opportunity beckoned, and people poured into the city. Chicago grew vertically, attracting a whole school of young architects whose soaring structures created a new cityscape. It grew horizontally, with new rail and telephone lines spreading onto empty prairie. As its commerce and industry radiated outward, the city transformed the landscape and ecosystems around it. By 1900, Chicago was the fastest-growing city in the world with a population that topped a million and a half people.

Chicago was not the only American city to flourish. In 1898, New York's five boroughs merged into one giant metropolis. Like Chicago, it was knitted together by a series of bridges and rail lines that allowed it and other industrial cities to function with new precision and efficiency on a scale never before dreamed of. The industrial city reshaped the environment, remade the urban landscape, and gave rise to a new kind of politician drawn from the ranks of ordinary people, many of them immigrants or their children. They came from the streets and saloons, the slums and tenements, the firehouses and funeral homes. Many of their families had only recently arrived in America. While the Irish of Tammany Hall ran New York City, Germans governed St. Louis, Scandinavians Minneapolis, and Jews San Francisco.

In an earlier age political leadership had been drawn from the ranks of the wealthy and native-born. America had been an agrarian republic where personal relationships were grounded in small communities. By the late nineteenth century, the country was in the midst of an urban explosion. Industrial cities of unparalleled size and diversity were remaking American life. They lured people from all over the globe, created tensions between natives and newcomers, refashioned the social order in a more fluid urban world. A new urban age was dawning. The golden door of opportunity opened onto the city. <<

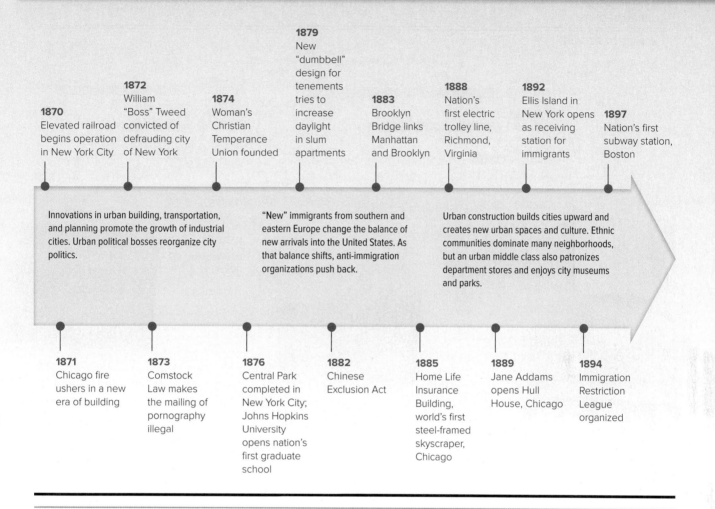

1870 Elevated railroad begins operation in New York City

1872 William "Boss" Tweed convicted of defrauding city of New York

1874 Woman's Christian Temperance Union founded

1879 New "dumbbell" design for tenements tries to increase daylight in slum apartments

1883 Brooklyn Bridge links Manhattan and Brooklyn

1888 Nation's first electric trolley line, Richmond, Virginia

1892 Ellis Island in New York opens as receiving station for immigrants

1897 Nation's first subway station, Boston

Innovations in urban building, transportation, and planning promote the growth of industrial cities. Urban political bosses reorganize city politics.

"New" immigrants from southern and eastern Europe change the balance of new arrivals into the United States. As that balance shifts, anti-immigration organizations push back.

Urban construction builds cities upward and creates new urban spaces and culture. Ethnic communities dominate many neighborhoods, but an urban middle class also patronizes department stores and enjoys city museums and parks.

1871 Chicago fire ushers in a new era of building

1873 Comstock Law makes the mailing of pornography illegal

1876 Central Park completed in New York City; Johns Hopkins University opens nation's first graduate school

1882 Chinese Exclusion Act

1885 Home Life Insurance Building, world's first steel-framed skyscraper, Chicago

1889 Jane Addams opens Hull House, Chicago

1894 Immigration Restriction League organized

A NEW URBAN AGE

THE MODERN CITY WAS THE product of industrialization. Cities contained the great investment banks, the smoky mills and dingy sweatshops, the spreading railroad yards, the grimy tenements and sparkling mansions, the new department stores and skyscrapers. People came from places as near as the countryside and as far as Russia, Armenia, China, and Japan. By the end of the nineteenth century America had entered a new urban age, with tens of millions of "urbanites," an urban landscape, and a growing urban culture.

The Urban Explosion

During the 50 years after the Civil War the population of the United States nearly tripled—from roughly 33 million to 92 million. Yet the number of people living in American cities increased nearly sevenfold. In 1860 only one American in six lived in a city with a population of 8,000 or more; in 1900 one in three did. By 1910 nearly half the nation lived in cities large and small.

Cities grew in every region of the country, some faster than others. In the Northeast and upper Midwest, early industrialization created more cities than in the West and the South, although those regions contained big cities as well. Atlanta, Nashville, and later Dallas and Houston boomed under the influence of railroads. Los Angeles had barely 6,000 people in 1870; by 1900, with a population of 100,000, it trailed only San Francisco among large cities on the Pacific coast.

Large urban centers dominated whole regions and tied the country together in a complex urban network. New York City, the nation's banker, printer, and chief marketplace, ruled the East. Smaller cities operated within narrower spheres of influence and often specialized. Milwaukee was famous for its

The Growth of Cities (1900)

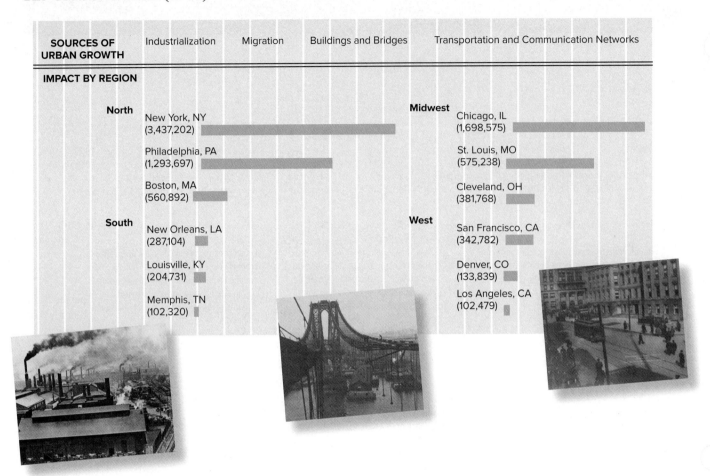

SOURCES OF URBAN GROWTH	Industrialization	Migration	Buildings and Bridges	Transportation and Communication Networks

IMPACT BY REGION

North

New York, NY (3,437,202)

Philadelphia, PA (1,293,697)

Boston, MA (560,892)

South

New Orleans, LA (287,104)

Louisville, KY (204,731)

Memphis, TN (102,320)

Midwest

Chicago, IL (1,698,575)

St. Louis, MO (575,238)

Cleveland, OH (381,768)

West

San Francisco, CA (342,782)

Denver, CO (133,839)

Los Angeles, CA (102,479)

(*left*) ©Welgos/Stringer/Getty Images; (*center*) Source: Library of Congress, Prints and Photographs Division [LC-USZ62-79052]; (*right*) Source: Library of Congress, Prints and Photographs Division [LC-USZ62-92622]

beer, Tulsa for oil, and Hershey, Pennsylvania, for chocolate. Such specialization prevented competition between cities in the same region.

ECOLOGICAL IMPACT ON THE REGIONS AROUND THEM Cities even shaped the natural environment hundreds of miles beyond their limits. Chicago became not only the gateway to the West but also a powerful agent of ecological change. As its lines of commerce and industry radiated outward, the city transformed the ecosystems of the West. Wheat to feed Chicago's millions replaced sheltering prairie grasses. Great stands of white pine in Wisconsin vanished, only to reappear in the furniture and frames of Chicago houses or as fence rails shipped to prairie farms.

The Great Global Migration

Between 1820 and 1920 some 60 million people left farms and villages for cities across the globe. They formed part of a migrating pool of labor, moving from country to country in search of work. Beginning in the 1870s the use of oceangoing, steam-powered ships extended the reach of migrating laborers across continents and created a labor exchange that spanned the globe.

PUSH AND PULL FACTORS Several factors pushed people from Europe. Mushrooming populations, aided by scientific breakthroughs and advances in technology, gave emigrants a powerful shove out. The end of the Napoleonic Wars in 1815 launched a cycle of baby booms that continued at 20-year intervals for the rest of the century. Improved diet and sanitation, aided by Louis Pasteur's discovery that bacteria cause infection and disease, reduced deaths. Meanwhile, machinery cut the need for farmworkers. In 1896 one man in a wheat field could do what had taken 18 men just 60 years earlier. Surplus farmworkers formed a ragtag army of migrants both in America and in Europe.

Other factors pulled emigrants to industrialized countries, including the United States. The prospect of factory work for better pay and fewer hours lured young emigrants to cities. So did labor agents, who combed Europe, pulling emigrants to the United States often with false promises of high-paying jobs and unimagined riches. "They told me that in America the streets were paved with gold," reported one immigrant.

"When I got here, I found the streets were not paved with gold, they were not paved at all, and they expected me to pave them." Unlike these immigrants who were mostly young men, migrants from countryside to city inside the United States were largely made up of young farm women. Mechanization and the rise of commercial agriculture made them less valuable in the fields, while mass-produced goods from mail-order houses made them less useful at home.

CHINESE IMMIGRANTS Asia sent comparatively fewer newcomers to the United States, Canada, and other industrializing nations hungry for workers, but Asian immigrants followed migration patterns similar to those of the workers leaving Europe and for similar reasons. In China, for example, rising taxes and rents on land and declining markets drove some 370,000 people across the Pacific to the United States and Hawaii between 1850 and 1882. In Japan and other Asian nations similar forces of push and pull sparked migration into the United States, including some 400,000 Japanese between 1885 and 1924.

THE "NEW" IMMIGRATION Immigration from Europe dwarfed all others, drawing people from new regions of the continent. Earlier in the century European immigrants had come to the United States from northern and western Europe. In the 1880s, however, **"new" immigrants** from southern and eastern Europe began to arrive. Some, like Russian and

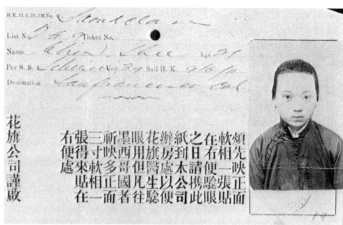

Source: National Archives & Records Administration (595309)

| *Chin Shee was 21 years old and bound for San Francisco at the time this boarding pass was issued in Hong Kong in 1911.*

Polish Jews, were fleeing religious and political persecution. Others left to evade famine or diseases such as cholera, which swept across southern Italy in 1887. But most came for the same reasons as migrants from the American countryside—a job, more money, a fresh start.

Ambitious, hardy, and resourceful, immigrants found themselves tested every step of the way to America. They left behind the comfort of family, friends, and old ways. The price of one-way passage by steamship—about $50 in 1904—was far too expensive for most to bring relatives, at least at first. And

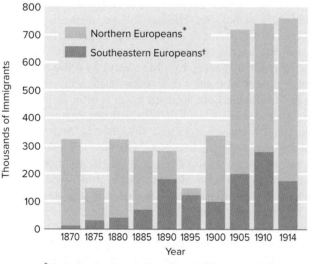

* Includes immigrants from Great Britain, Ireland, Germany, and the Scandinavian countries.

† Includes immigrants from Poland, Russia, Italy, and other Baltic and Eastern European countries.

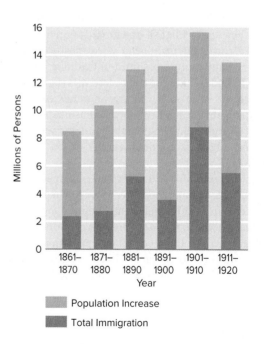

Immigration and Population, 1860–1920

Between 1860 and 1920 immigration increased dramatically as the sources of immigrants shifted from northern Europe to southeastern Europe. Despite fears to the contrary the proportion of newcomers as a percentage of population increases did not show nearly the same jump. In which year was the proportion of southeastern Europeans highest? About what percentage of the total did they comprise in that year?

the trip was dangerous even before immigrants stepped on board a ship. They traveled for weeks, stealing across heavily guarded borders, just to reach a port such as Le Havre in France.

It took one to two weeks to cross the Atlantic aboard steam-powered ships. Immigrants spent most of the time belowdecks in cramped, filthy compartments called **steerage.** Most arrived at New York City's Castle Garden until the newer facility on nearby Ellis Island opened in 1892. Other entry ports attracted growing numbers. New Orleans drew so many immigrants from Italy that it contained more Italians than any other city in the country between 1850 and 1870. By 1900, 8 of 10 residents of the city's famous French Quarter were Italian. If from Asia, newcomers landed at Angel Island in San Francisco Bay. Sometimes they were held in the facility for weeks. As one Chinese newcomer gazed out on San Francisco Bay, he scribbled a poem on the gray walls in despair:

> Why do I have to languish in this jail?
> It is because my country is weak and my family poor.
> My parents wait in vain for news;
> My wife and child, wrapped in their quilt, sigh with loneliness.

Immigrants then had to pass a medical examination, have their names recorded by customs officials, and pay an entry tax. At any point, they could be detained or shipped home.

IMMIGRANT PROFILE   Newcomers arrived in staggering numbers—over 6 million between 1877 and 1890, some 30 million by 1920. By 1900 they made up nearly 15 percent of the population. Most were young, between the ages of 15 and 40. Few spoke English or had skills or much education. Unlike earlier arrivals, who were mostly Protestant, these new immigrants worshiped in Catholic, Greek, or Russian Orthodox churches and Jewish synagogues. Almost two-thirds were men. A large number came to make money for buying land or starting businesses back home. Some changed their minds and sent for relatives, but those returning were common enough to be labeled "birds of passage."

Jews were an exception. Russian Jews escaped from Europe by the tens of thousands after the assassination of Czar Alexander II in 1881 rekindled anti-Semitic "pogroms," or riots. Between 1880 and 1914 a third of eastern Europe's Jews left. They made up 10 percent of all emigration to the United States during those years. Almost all stayed and brought their families, often one by one. They had few choices.

Holding the City Together

PATTERNS OF SETTLEMENT   In colonial days Benjamin Franklin could walk from one end of Boston to the other in an hour. Only Franklin's adopted home, Philadelphia, spilled into suburbs. Over the years these colonial "walking cities" developed ringed patterns of settlement. Merchants,

professionals, and the upper classes lived near their shops and offices in the city center. As one walked outward, the income and status of the residents declined. Cities of the late nineteenth century still exhibited this ringed pattern, except that industrialization had reversed the order of settlement and increased urban sprawl. The wealthy now lived at the outskirts of the city and the poor and working poor at the industrial center.

For all their differences, the circles of settlement held together as a part of a massive and interdependent whole. One reason was an evolving system of urban transportation. By the mid-nineteenth century, horse-drawn railways were conveying some 35 million passengers a year in New York City alone. With railcars pulled along tracks by horses, their problems were legendary: so slow, a person could walk faster; so dirty, tons of manure were left in the streets every day; so crowded (according to Mark Twain), you "had to hang on by your eyelashes and toenails."

Civic leaders came to understand that the modern city could not survive, much less grow, without improved transportation. San Francisco installed trolley cars pulled by steam-driven cables. It worked so well in San Francisco that Chicago, Seattle, and other hilly cities installed cable systems in the 1880s. Some cities experimented with elevated trestles to carry steam locomotives; others, with cable lines high above crowded streets. But none of the breakthroughs quite did the trick. Cables remained slow and unreliable; the elevated railways, or "els," were dirty, ugly, and noisy.

ROLE OF ELECTRICITY   Electricity rescued city travelers. In 1888 Frank Julian Sprague, a naval engineer who had once worked for Thomas Edison, installed the first electric trolley line in Richmond, Virginia. Electrified streetcars were soon speeding along at 12 miles an hour, twice as fast as horses. By 1902 electricity drove nearly all city railways. Sprague's innovations also meant that "subways" could be built beneath ground without having to worry about tunnels filled with a steam engine's smoke and soot. Between 1895 and 1897 Boston built the first underground electric line. New York followed in 1904 with a subway that ran from city hall on the southern tip of Manhattan north to Harlem. Once considered too far afield, Harlem soon became dotted with new apartments and tenements. When the white middle class refused to move so far uptown, Philip A. Payton convinced landlords to allow his Afro-American Realty Company to handle the properties. Within a decade Harlem became the black capital of America.

The rich had long been able to keep homes outside city limits, traveling to and fro in private carriages. New systems of mass transit freed the middle class and even the poor to live miles from work. For a nickel or two, anyone could ride from central shopping and business districts to the suburban fringes and back. A network of moving vehicles held the segmented and sprawling city together and widened its reach out to "streetcar suburbs."

>> MAPPING THE PAST <<

RIDING THE CHICAGO LOOP

Source: Library of Congress, Prints and Photographs Division [LC-USZC4-2652]

CONTEXT

Railroads shaped travel across the nation but also within cities, first on city streets, then elevated above them, and finally in subterranean tunnels below them. This map shows one of Chicago's earliest elevated railway systems. "Els" first appeared in Chicago in 1892 as a way of providing mass transit across the city without disrupting street traffic. The earliest lines did not extend downtown, but by 1897 elevated railways were whisking passengers from the outskirts to the center of the city. The circular elevated line downtown was known as "the Loop."

Source: Library of Congress, Geography and Map Division [G4104.C6P33 1897.P6]

MAP READING

1. Chicago is located along the shore of Lake Michigan. Where is the lake on the map? Where is the Chicago River?
2. Locate "the Loop" on the map.
3. Where is the Chicago Rock Island and Pacific Railway Station? Chicago is nowhere near the Pacific Ocean. Why does the railroad have "Pacific" as a part of its name?

MAP INTERPRETATION

1. This map shows the location of the El's tracks and its stations, but also those for the Rock Island and Pacific Railway (marked in red as A, B and C). Is the map promoting the El or the Rock Island Railway? How can you tell?
2. The drawing at lower-left is labeled "Elevated Station of the 'Rock Island' Van Buren St. Station" and shows a large flag proclaiming "Rock Island Route." Where is the station on the map? Why draw the station larger-than-life?
3. In this new industrial age, why is it significant that the local and national rail systems are shown on this city map?

Bridges and Skyscrapers

Because cities often grew along rivers and harbors, their separate parts sometimes had to be joined over water. The principles of building large river bridges had already been worked out by the railroads. It remained for a German immigrant and his son, John and Washington Roebling, to make the bridge a symbol of urban growth.

The Brooklyn Bridge, linking Manhattan with Brooklyn, took 13 years to complete. It cost $15 million and 20 lives, including that of designer John Roebling. When it opened in 1883 it stretched more than a mile across the East River, with passage broad enough for a footpath, two double carriage lanes, and two railroad lines. Its arches were cut like giant cathedral windows, and its supporting cables hung, said an awestruck observer, "like divine messages from above." Soon other suspension bridges were spanning the railroad yards in St. Louis and the bay at Galveston, Texas.

Source: Library of Congress, Prints and Photographs Division [LC-DIG-det-4a21395]

| *Designed by Chicago architect Daniel Burnham and completed in 1902, the Fuller Building quickly became known as the "Flatiron Building" for its uniquely triangular shape. With a steel frame, it soared to a height of 22 stories, making it one of the tallest structures in New York City. "I found myself agape," wrote science fiction novelist H. G. Wells when he saw the building, "admiring a sky-scraper, the prow of the Flat-iron Building, to be particular, ploughing up through the traffic of Broadway and Fifth Avenue in the afternoon light."*

Even as late as 1880 church steeples dominated the urban landscape. They towered over squat factories and office buildings. But growing congestion and the increasing value of land pushed architects to search for ways to make buildings taller. In place of thick walls of brick that restricted factory floor space, builders used cast-iron columns. The new "cloudscrapers" were strong, durable, and fire-resistant. Their open floors were ideal for warehouses and also for office buildings and department stores.

Steel, with greater flexibility and strength than iron, turned cloudscrapers into skyscrapers. William LeBaron Jenney first used steel in his 10-story Home Insurance Building (1885) in Chicago. By the end of the century steel frames and girders raised buildings to 30 stories or more. New York City's triangular Flatiron building, named for its shape, used the new technology to project an angular yet remarkably delicate elegance. In Chicago, Daniel Burnham's Reliance Building (1890) relied so heavily on new plate glass windows that contemporaries called it "a glass tower fifteen stories high."

It was no accident that many of the new skyscrapers arose in Chicago. The Great Fire of 1871 engulfed more than 3 square miles of downtown and turned it into an architect's playground. John Root, aware that the decorative trim of buildings had fueled the blaze, designed new office towers that were sleek, simple, and immense. The young maverick Louis H. Sullivan promised a new urban profile in which the skyscraper would be "every inch a proud and soaring thing." In the Wainwright Building (1890) in St. Louis and the Carson, Pirie, and Scott department store (1889–1904) in Chicago, Sullivan produced sky-high structures that symbolized the modern industrial city and gave rise to what people were soon calling the "Chicago School of Architecture."

Architects did not create the towering landscapes of modern industrial cities without help. Reinforced concrete that could tolerate the weight and height of new buildings and plate glass that permitted people to see outside made the structures strong and supple. But soaring skyscrapers were of little value without an efficient, safe means of transporting people aloft. In 1861 Elisha Graves Otis developed a trustworthy, fast elevator. By the 1890s new electric elevators driven by hydraulic pumps were whisking people to the tops of skyscrapers in seconds. The elevator extended the city upward, just as the streetcar extended it outward, and in the process both knitted the physical and social fabric of urban America more tightly together.

The Urban Environment: Slum and Tenement

Far below the skyscrapers lay the slums and tenements of the inner city. In cramped rooms and sunless hallways, along narrow alleys and in flooded basements, lived the city's poor. They often worked there, too, in "sweaters' shops" where as many as 18 people labored and slept in foul two-room flats.

PERILS OF THE SLUM NEIGHBORHOOD In New York City, whose slums were the nation's worst, crime thrived in places called "Bandit's Roost" and "Hell's Kitchen." Bands of young toughs with such names as the "Sewer Rats" and the "Rock Gang" stalked the streets in search of thrills and easy money. Gambling, prostitution, and alcoholism all claimed their victims most readily in the slums. The poor usually turned to such crime in despair. A 20-year-old prostitute supporting a sickly mother and four brothers and sisters made no apologies: "Let God Almighty judge who's to blame most, I that was driven, or them that drove me to the pass I'm in."

The poor diets of slum dwellers left them vulnerable to disease, but it was their close quarters and often filthy surroundings that raised their rates of infection to epidemic levels. Cholera, typhoid, and an outbreak of yellow fever in Memphis in the 1870s killed tens of thousands. Tuberculosis was deadlier still. As late as 1900, among infectious diseases it ranked behind only influenza and pneumonia *combined* as a killer. Slum children—all city children—were most vulnerable. Almost a quarter of children born in American cities in 1890 never lived to see their first birthday.

The installation of new sewage and water purification systems helped. The modern flush toilet came into use only after the turn of the century. Until then people relied on water closets and communal privies, some of the latter catering to as many as 800. All too often cities dumped waste into old private vaults or rivers used for drinking water. In 1881 an exasperated mayor of Cleveland called the Cuyahoga River "an open sewer through the center of the city."

Slum housing was often more dangerous than the water. The bacteria that spawned the deadly lung disease tuberculosis flourished in musty, windowless tenements. In 1879 New York City enacted a new housing law requiring a window in all bedrooms of new **tenements.** Architect James E. Ware won a competition with a design that contained an indentation on both sides of the building. When two tenements abutted each other, the indentations formed a narrow shaft for air and light. From above, the buildings looked like giant dumbbells. Up to 16 families lived on a floor, with only two toilets in the hall.

Originally hailed as an innovation, Ware's dumbbell tenement spread across such cities as Cleveland, Cincinnati, and Boston "like a scab," said an unhappy reformer. Ordinary blocks contained 10 such tenements and housed as many as 4,000 people. The airshafts became giant silos for trash. They blocked what little light had entered and, worse still, carried fires from one story to the next. When the New York

 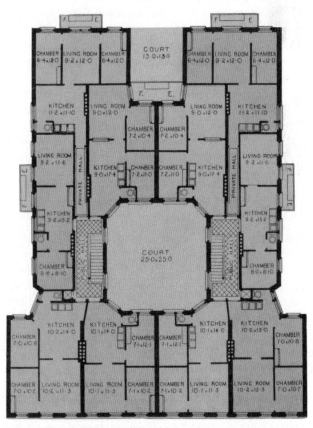

Source: Irma and Paul Milstein Division of United States History, Local History and Genealogy/The New York Public Library

| *"Dumbbell" tenements were designed to use every inch of available space in the standard 25-by-200-foot city lot while providing ventilation and reducing the spread of disease.*

City housing commission met in 1900, it concluded that conditions were worse than when reformers had started 33 years earlier.

 REVIEW
How did industrial cities grow and at what costs?

RUNNING AND REFORMING THE CITY

EVERY NEW ARRIVAL TO THE city brought dreams and altogether too many needs. Schools and houses had to be built, streets paved, garbage collected, sewers dug, fires fought, utility lines laid. Running the city became a full-time job, and a new breed of professional politician rose to the task. So, too, did a new breed of reformer, determined to help the needy cope with the ravages of urban life.

WEAKNESSES OF CITY GOVERNMENTS The need for change was clear. Many city charters dating from the eighteenth century included a paralyzing system of checks and balances. Mayors vetoed city councils; councils ignored mayors. Jealous state legislatures allowed cities only the most limited and unpopular taxes, such as those on property. But to the cities more than the states fell responsibility for providing services. Municipal governments were often decentralized—fragmented, scattered branches at odds with one another. By 1890 Chicago had 11 branches of government, each with its own regulations and taxing authority. Just as such decentralization paralyzed city governments, the traditional sources of political leadership evaporated. The middle and upper classes were being drawn into business and moving to the suburbs. With cities mushrooming in size and population, the structures of urban government strained to adapt.

Boss Rule

"Why must there be a boss," journalist Lincoln Steffens asked Boss Richard Croker of New York, "when we've got a mayor—and a city council?" "That's why," Croker broke in. "It's because we've got a mayor and a council and judges—and—a hundred other men to deal with." The boss was right. Cities were so decentralized that they could not provide the leadership required to run them. Boss rule supplied cities with the centralization, authority, and services they sorely needed.

Bosses ruled through the **political machine**. Often, like New York City's Tammany Hall, machines dated back to the late eighteenth and early nineteenth centuries. They began as fraternal and charitable organizations. Over the years they became centers of political power. In New York City the machine was Democratic; in Philadelphia, Republican. Some

were less centralized, as in Chicago; some less ethnically mixed, such as Detroit's. Machines could be found even in rural areas. In Duval County, Texas, for instance, the Spanish-speaking Anglo boss Archie Parr molded a powerful alliance with Mexican American landowners.

In an age of enterprise, the boss operated his political machine like a business corporation. His office might be a saloon, a funeral home, or, like New York's George Washington Plunkitt's, a shoe-shine stand. His managers were party activists, connected in a corporate-style chain of command. Local committeemen reported to district captains, captains to district leaders, district leaders to the boss or bosses who directed the machine.

A CRUDE WELFARE SYSTEM The goods and services of the machine were basic: a Christmas turkey, coal for the winter, jobs for the unemployed, English language classes for newcomers, flowers for the ill and deceased. Bosses sponsored fun, too—sports teams, glee clubs, balls and barbecues with bands playing and drink flowing. This system, rough and uneven as it was, served as a form of public welfare at a time when private charity could not cope with the crush of demand. To the unskilled, the boss doled out jobs in public construction. For bright, ambitious young men, he had places in city offices or in the party. These positions represented the first steps into the middle class, a concrete (if limited) example of social mobility for the masses.

In return, citizens were expected to show their gratitude at the ballot box by voting to keep bosses and their machines in power. Sometimes the votes of grateful constituents were not enough, so bosses turned elsewhere. "Little Bob" Davies of Jersey City mobilized the "graveyard vote." He drew names from tombstones to pad lists of registered voters and hired "repeaters" to vote under the phony names. When reformers introduced the Australian (secret) ballot in the 1880s to prevent fraud, bosses pulled the "Tasmanian dodge" by pre-marking ballots for voters. Failing that, they dumped whole ballot boxes into the river or drove unpersuaded voters from the polls with hired thugs.

Rewards, Costs, and Accomplishments

Why did bosses go to such lengths? Some simply loved politics. More often bosses loved money and power. Their success was limited only by their ingenuity or the occasional victories of reformers. The record for sheer brassiness probably goes to Boss William Tweed. During his reign in the 1860s and 1870s Tweed swindled the city of New York out of a fortune. His masterpiece was a chunky three-story courthouse in lower Manhattan originally budgeted at $250,000. When Boss Tweed was through, the city had spent more than $13 million, over 60 percent of which ended up in the pockets of Tweed and his cronies. Tweed died in prison, but with such profits to be made, it was small wonder that bosses rivaled the pharaohs of Egypt as builders.

Machine-Age Voting

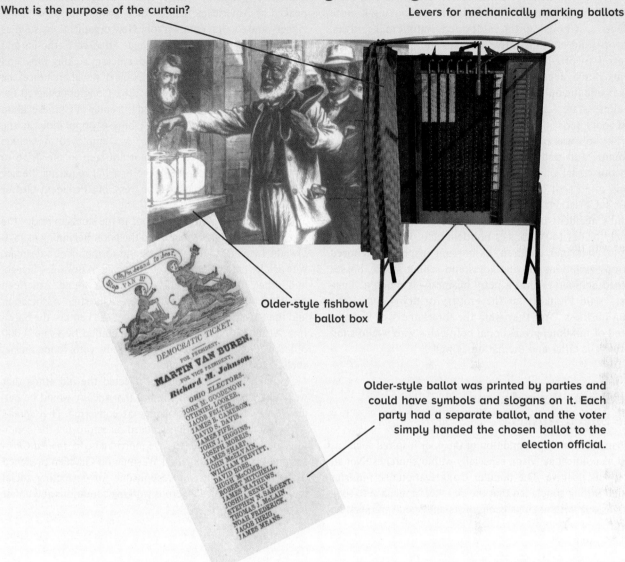

What is the purpose of the curtain?

Levers for mechanically marking ballots

Older-style fishbowl ballot box

Older-style ballot was printed by parties and could have symbols and slogans on it. Each party had a separate ballot, and the voter simply handed the chosen ballot to the election official.

(*top left*) Source: Library of Congress, Prints and Photographs Division [LC-USZ62-47205]; (*top right*) ©Randy Duchaine/Alamy; (*bottom*) Source: Library of Congress, Prints and Photographs Division [LC-USZ61-1654]

In the late nineteenth century, political corruption often began with voting. Pre-marking ballots, stuffing ballot boxes, paying "repeaters" to vote more than once were all ways to fix the outcome of elections. Reformers fought back. The "Australian," or secret, ballot (first used in Victoria, Australia, in 1858 and in the United States in 1888) employed standardized paper ballots, distributed one to a voter at poll places and marked in a booth in secret. Each ballot had the names of candidates printed on it at government expense, as opposed to earlier ballots, which political parties printed and handed out, often with pictures or symbols on them. Transparent "fishbowl" ballot boxes made it difficult to stuff the boxes beforehand. Taking the process one step further, Jacob A. Myers tested his new "gear-and-lever" voting machine in Lockport, New York, in 1892. He devised the machine, he said, to "protect mechanically the voter from rascaldom, and make the process of casting the ballot perfectly plain, simple and secret." Some called it "the inventive triumph of its age." The voter simply pulled a lever that closed a curtain around him for privacy. Other levers allowed him to vote for individual candidates or straight-party tickets. The machine recorded and tallied the votes.

THINKING CRITICALLY

What advantages did the voting machine offer over the Australian paper ballot? Over the older-style ballots provided by parties? What were the disadvantages of voting machines? Which system was better if voters could not read? What potential for voting fraud exists with today's electronic or optical-scan voting machines?

In their fashion, bosses played a vital role in the industrial city. Rising from the bottom ranks, they guided immigrants into American life and helped some of the underprivileged up from poverty. They changed the urban landscape with massive construction programs and modernized city government by uniting it and making it more effective. Choosing the aldermen, municipal judges, mayors, and administrative officials, bosses exerted new control to provide the contracts and franchises to run cities. Such accomplishments fostered the notion that government could be called on to help the needy. The "welfare state," as yet unnamed and still decades away, had roots here.

The toll was often outrageous. Inflated taxes, extorted revenue, and unpunished vice and crime were only the obvious costs. Unsafe working and unhealthy living conditions often cost lives. A woman whose family enjoyed a boss's Christmas turkey might be widowed by her husband's accident in a dangerous sweatshop kept open by timely bribes to the boss's political club. Filthy buildings might claim her children, as corrupt inspectors ignored serious violations. Buying votes and selling favors, bosses turned democracy into a petty business—as much a "business," said Plunkitt, "as the grocery or dry-goods or the drug business." Yet they were the forerunners of the new breed of full-time, professional politicians who would soon govern the cities and the nation as well.

Nativism, Revivals, and the Social Gospel

Urban blight and the condition of the poor inspired social as well as political activism, especially within churches. Not all of it was positive. The popular Congregationalist minister Josiah Strong concluded that the city was "a menace to society." Along with anxious economists and social workers, he held immigrants responsible for everything from corruption to unemployment and urged restrictions on their entry into the country.

In the 1880s and 1890s two depressions sharpened such anxieties. Nativism, a defensive and fearful nationalism, peaked as Americans blamed their economic woes on foreigners and foreign competition. New organizations such as the Immigration Restriction League attacked Catholics and the foreign-born for subverting democracy, taking jobs, and polarizing society. Already the victims of racial prejudice, the Chinese were an easy target. In 1882 Congress enacted the Chinese Exclusion Act. It banned the entry of Chinese laborers, stranding a mostly male Chinese population in the States. It was the first time race was employed to exclude people and represented an important step in the drive to restrict immigration. In 1897 the first bill requiring literacy tests for immigrants passed Congress, but President Grover Cleveland vetoed it.

Some clergy took their missions to the slums to bridge the gap between the middle class and the poor. Beginning in 1870 Dwight Lyman Moody, a 300-pound former shoe salesman, won armies of lowly converts with revivals in Boston, Chicago, and other cities. Evangelists helped to found American branches of the British Young Men's Christian Association and the Salvation Army. By the end of the century the Salvation Army had grown to 700 corps staffed by some 3,000 officers. They ministered to the needy with food, music, shelter, and simple good fellowship.

A small group of ministers rejected the old ethos that weak character explained sin and that society would be perfected only as individual sinners were converted. They spread a new "Social Gospel" that focused on improving the conditions of society in order to save individuals. In *Applied Christianity* (1886), the influential Washington Gladden preached that the church must be responsible for correcting social injustices, including dangerous working conditions and unfair labor practices.

| By the 1890s a flood of southern and eastern European immigrants were streaming into the new receiving center of Ellis Island in New York harbor, while the relatively fewer Asian immigrants who arrived (most were barred from entry by the Chinese Exclusion Act of 1882) came through Angel Island in San Francisco Bay. The rapid rise in immigration ignited nativist fears that immigrants were taking over the country. In the 1870s cartoon pictured here, Irish and Chinese immigrants in their native dress literally gobble up Uncle Sam.

Source: Library of Congress, Prints and Photographs Division [LC-DIG-pga-03047]

THE GREAT FEAR OF THE PERIOD
THAT *UNCLE SAM* MAY BE SWALLOWED BY FOREIGNERS.

The Social Settlement Movement

Church-sponsored programs sometimes repelled the immigrant poor when they saw them as thinly disguised missionary efforts. Not all were. Many urban church programs, such as A. B. Simpson's in New York City, served body and soul successfully without relying on heavy-handed evangelizing.

THE SETTLEMENT HOUSE Immigrants and other slum dwellers were more receptive to a bold experiment called the **settlement house**. Often situated in the worst slums, these early community centers were run by middle-class women and men to help the poor and foreign-born. At the turn of the century there were more than 100 of them, the most famous being Jane Addams's Hull House in Chicago. When Hull House opened in 1889 it occupied a crumbling mansion on South Halstead Street. Slowly it grew to a dozen buildings over more than a city block. In 1898 the Catholic Church sponsored its first settlement house in New York City, and in 1900 Bronson House opened its doors to the Latino community in Los Angeles.

High purposes inspired settlement workers. They left comfortable middle-class homes to live in settlement houses and dedicated themselves (like the "early Christians," said one) to service and sacrifice. Teaching immigrants American ways and creating a community spirit would foster "right living through social relations." But immigrants were also urged to preserve their heritages through festivals, parades, and museums. Like political bosses settlement reformers furnished help, from day nurseries to English language and cooking classes to playgrounds and libraries. Armed with statistics and personal experiences, they also lobbied for social legislation to improve housing, women's working conditions, and public schools.

> **REVIEW**
>
> In what ways did boss rule represent "reform" of city government, and at whose expense did such reform come?

City Life

URBAN SOCIAL STRATIFICATION Every city had its grimy tenements and slums but also its fashionable avenues for the rich, who constituted barely 1 percent of the population but owned a fourth of all wealth. In between tenement and mansion lived the broad middle of urban society—educated professionals, white-collar clerks and salespeople, shopkeepers, corporate managers and executives, public employees, and their families. They composed nearly a third of the population and owned about half the nation's wealth. With more money and more leisure time, their power and influence were growing.

City life reflected the stratified nature of American society in the late nineteenth century. Class distinctions continued to be based not on lineage as in Europe but on wealth and income. No longer were dress and manners enough to distinguish one class from another in the United States. What told such differences was more often where people lived, what they bought, which organizations they joined, and how they spent their time.

The Immigrant in the City

When the ship put into port, the first thing an immigrant was likely to see was a city. Perhaps it was Boston or New York City or Galveston, Texas, where an overflow of Jewish immigrants was directed after the turn of the century. Enough of the newcomers traveled inland so that by 1900 three-quarters of the residents of Minnesota and Wisconsin and nearly two-thirds in Utah had at least one foreign-born parent.* But some 70 percent of all immigrants, exhausted physically and financially, settled in cities.

ETHNIC NEIGHBORHOODS Cities developed well-defined mosaics of ethnic communities, because immigrants usually clustered on the basis of Old World families, villages, or provinces. These neighborhoods were constantly changing. As many as half the residents moved out every 10 years, often because of better-paying jobs or more family members who worked. Though one nationality usually dominated a neighborhood, there were always others.

ADAPTING TO AMERICA Ethnic communities served as havens from an unfamiliar culture and as springboards to a new life. From the moment they stepped off the boat newcomers felt pressed to learn English, don American clothes, and drop their "greenhorn" ways. Yet in their neighborhoods they also found comrades who spoke their language, theaters that performed their plays and music, restaurants that served their food. Houses of worship were always at the center of neighborhood life, often reflecting the practices of individual towns or provinces. Foreign-language newspapers reported events from both the Old World and the New in a native tongue first-generation immigrants could understand. Meanwhile, immigrant aid societies furnished assistance with housing and jobs and sponsored insurance programs, English classes, and even baseball teams.

Sometimes immigrants combined the old and new in creative adaptations. Italians developed a pidgin dialect called "Italglish." The Fourth of July became "Il Forte Gelato" (literally "The Great Freeze"), a play on the sound of the words. The phrases permitted them to communicate quickly with Americans and to absorb American customs. Other immigrant groups invented similar idioms, like Chuco, a dialect that developed among border Mexicans in El Paso.

Where they came from often influenced the jobs immigrants took. Because Chinese men did not scorn washing or ironing, more than 7,500 of them could be found in San Francisco laundries by 1880. Sewing ladies' garments seemed

---

*Mormons serving as missionaries in Europe and Great Britain especially swelled Utah's population with converts.

Source: Library of Congress, Prints and Photographs Division [LC-USZ62-51301]

| *Hester Street, Lower East Side, New York City*

unmanly to many native-born Americans but not to Russian and Italian tailors. Slavs tended to be physically robust and valued steady income over education. They often worked in the mines for better pay than in factories and pulled their children from school to earn a living.

FAMILY LIFE   On the whole, immigrants married later and had more children than the native-born. Greeks and eastern European Jews prearranged marriages according to tradition. They imported "picture brides," betrothed by mail with a photograph. After marriage men ruled the household, but women managed it. Although child-rearing practices varied, immigrants resisted the relative permissiveness of American parents. Youngsters were expected to contribute like "little adults" to the welfare of the family.

In these "family economies" of working-class immigrants, key decisions—over whether and whom to marry, over work and education, over when to leave home—were made on the basis of collective rather than individual needs. But customs differed among different immigrant groups. While many valued the ideal of women staying home,

financial reality sometimes meant that women worked outside as well as inside the home. Italian women were more likely to stay home, taking in boarders or doing sewing, laundry, and other forms of piecework to earn money. Jewish women could often be found working alongside their husbands in a family-owned business. Though boys were more likely to be employed outside the home than girls, daughters in immigrant families went to work at an early age so that sons could continue their education. For others, education for daughters was seen as the only path to well-paying jobs. Among still others, it was customary for one daughter to remain unmarried so that she could care for younger siblings or aged parents.

SPECIAL SITUATION OF THE CHINESE   The Chinese were an exception to the pattern. The ban on the immigration of Chinese laborers in the 1880s had frozen the sex ratio of Chinese communities into a curious imbalance. Like other immigrants, most Chinese newcomers had been single men. In the wake of the ban those in the United States could not bring over their wives and families. Nor by law in 13 states

could they marry whites. With few women, Chinese communities suffered from high rates of prostitution, large numbers of gangs and secret societies, and low birth totals. When the San Francisco earthquake and fire destroyed birth records in 1906, resourceful Chinese immigrants created "paper sons" (and less often "paper daughters") by forging American birth certificates and claiming their China-born children as American citizens.

ACCULTURATION   Caught between past and present, immigrants from all countries clung to tradition and acculturated slowly. Their children adjusted more quickly. They soon spoke English like natives, married whomever they pleased, and worked their way out of old neighborhoods. Rapid as it was for some children, the process was not always easy. Children sometimes faced heartrending clashes with parents and rejection from peers. Sara Smolinsky, the immigrant heroine of Anzia Yezierska's novel *Bread Givers* (1925), broke away from her tyrannical family, only to discover a terrible isolation: "I can't live in the old world and I'm yet too green for the new."

Urban Middle-Class Life

THE HOME AS STATUS SYMBOL AND HAVEN   Life and leisure for the urban middle class revolved around home and family. By the turn of the century just over a third of middle-class urbanites owned their homes. Often two or three stories, made of brick or brownstone, these houses were a measure of their owners' social standing. The plush furniture, heavy drapes, antiques, and curios all signaled status and refinement.

Such homes, usually on their own lots, served as sanctuaries from the chaos of the industrial city. Seventeenth-century notions of children as inherently sinful had given way to modern theories about the shaping influence of environment. Calm and orderly households with nurturing mothers would launch children on the right course and encourage sobriety, self-restraint, and communal commitment as the foundations of a civil society. "A clean, fresh, and well-ordered house," stipulated a domestic advisor in 1883, "exercises over its inmates a moral, no less than physical influence, and has a direct tendency to make members

Source: The Winterthur Library (RBR NK2740 R32 PF tc)

Newly developed "electroplating," which deposited a thin layer of silver or gold over less expensive material, allowed manufacturers to sell wares previously reserved for the wealthy to middle-class consumers. Pictured here are a silver- and gold-plated card receiver and a calling card, once part of the courtly culture of elites and by the 1880s found in more and more middle-class homes. This "downward mobility" of manners and material culture allowed the middle class to ape the conventions of their social superiors, in this case by using calling cards to reinforce social networks and to serve as social barriers should personal contact be unwanted.

of the family sober, peaceable, and considerate of the feelings and happiness of each other."

A woman was judged by the state of her home. The typical homemaker prepared elaborate meals, cleaned, laundered, and sewed. Each task took time. Baking bread alone required several hours, and in 1890 four of five loaves were still made at home. Perhaps 25 percent of urban households had live-in servants to help with the work. They were on call about 100 hours a week, were off just one evening and part of Sunday, and averaged $2 to $5 a week in wages.

By the 1890s a host of new consumer products eased the burdens of housework. Brand names trumpeted a new age of commercially prepared food—Campbell's soup, Quaker oats, Pillsbury flour, Jell-O, and Cracker Jacks, to name a few. New appliances such as "self-working" washers offered mechanical assistance, but shredded shirts and aching arms testified to how far short mechanization still fell.

Toward the end of the century Saturday became less of a workday and more of a family day. Sunday mornings remained a time for church, still an important center of family life. Afternoons had a more secular flavor. There were

shopping trips (city stores often stayed open) and visits to lakes, zoos, and amusement parks (usually built at the end of trolley lines to attract more riders). Outside institutions of all kinds—fraternal organizations, inspirational groups, athletic teams, and church groups—were becoming part of middle-class urban family life.

Victorianism and the Pursuit of Virtue

Middle-class life reflected a code of behavior called Victorianism, named for Britain's long-reigning Queen Victoria (1837–1901). It emerged in the 1830s and 1840s as part of an effort to tame the turbulent urban-industrial society developing in Europe.

Victorianism dictated that personal conduct be based on orderly behavior and disciplined moralism. It stressed sobriety, industriousness, self-control, and sexual modesty and taught that demeanor, particularly proper manners, was the backbone of society. It strictly divided the gender roles of men and women, especially in the realm of sexuality. According to its rules, women were "pure vessels" devoid of sexual desire, men wild beasts unable to tame their lust. A woman's job was to control the "lower natures" of her husband by withholding sex except for procreation.

The values of the Victorians migrated across the Atlantic and embedded themselves in the "Gilded Age" of late-nineteenth-century America—so named for its material extravagance. In the United States, even women's fashions mirrored them. Strenuously laced corsets ("an instrument of torture," one woman called them) pushed breasts up, stomachs in, and rear ends out. Internal organs pressed unnaturally against one another; ribs occasionally cracked; uteruses sagged. Fainting spells and headaches were common. But the resulting wasplike figure accentuated the image of women as child bearers. Ankle-length skirts were draped over bustles, hoops, and petticoats to make hips look larger and suggest fertility. Such elegant dress symbolized wealth, status, and modesty. It also set off middle- and upper-class women from those below, whose plain clothes signaled lives less luxurious.

WOMAN'S CHRISTIAN TEMPERANCE UNION When working-class Americans failed to follow these social guidelines, reformers helped them pursue virtue. It seemed natural to Frances Willard that women, who cared for the moral and physical well-being of their families, should lead the charge, despite the fact that she remained single and childless for her entire life. She resigned her position as dean of women at Northwestern University and in 1879 became the second president of the newly founded Woman's Christian Temperance Union (WCTU, organized in 1874). The very title of the organization, stressing the singular "woman," spoke for the unity of all women. Under Willard's leadership, the organization grew by the 1890s to 150,000 members, all of them women and most of them middle-class and white. By the turn of the century it was the largest women's organization in the world.

Initially the WCTU focused on **temperance**—the movement, begun in the 1820s, to stamp out the sale of alcoholic beverages

CITY SCENES

In the late nineteenth and early twentieth centuries, city scenes of daily life were the subject of count-less renderings, from pen-and-ink drawings to lithographs and paintings to photographs beginning in the mid-nineteenth century. Each brought a different perspective to the bustling life of industrial cities, and all reflected the point of view of the artist creating them. Two street scenes appear below, both from turn-of-the-century New York but in very different forms. Both offer panoramic views of busy New York streets. The first is a photograph taken in 1900 of an Easter Day parade on Fifth Avenue. The second is a crowded New York intersection, titled simply New York, *and painted in 1911 by the realist painter George Bellows.*

DOCUMENT 1

Source: National Archives & Records Administration (513360)

THINKING CRITICALLY

How many different types of urban transport can you see in each image? (Note, for example, an early automo-bile driving toward the camera on the left side of Fifth Avenue in the photo-graph.) What can these various forms of transportation tell us about the speed and nature of technological change? Which rendering captures the vibrancy of the city best? Why? What is each artist—photographer and painter—trying to say about city life? How, if at all, does each medium shape the message?

DOCUMENT 2

Source: National Gallery of Art, Washington (1986.72.1)

Source: Library of Congress, Prints and Photographs Division [LC-USZ61-790]

Frances Willard, reformer and educator, took up the cause of temperance, but her efforts went beyond combating the abuses of alcohol. She also wanted to give the vote to women over 21, to give women political power. "God sets male and female side by side throughout his realm of law," she argued.

and to end drunkenness. For these women, the campaign seemed not merely a way to reform society but also a way to protect their homes and families from abuse at the hands of drunken husbands and fathers. In attacking the saloon, Willard also sought to spread democracy by storming these all-male bastions, where political bosses conducted so much political business and where women were refused entry. Soon, under the slogan "Do Everything," the WCTU was promoting suffrage for women, prison reform, better working conditions, and an end to prostitution. Just as important, it offered talented, committed women an opportunity to move out of their homes and churches and into the public arena of lobbying and politics.

COMSTOCK LAW Anthony Comstock crusaded with equal vigor against what he saw as moral pollution, ranging from pornography and gambling to the use of nude art models. In 1873 President Ulysses S. Grant signed the so-called Comstock Law, a statute banning from the mails all materials "designed to incite lust." Two days later Comstock went to work as a special agent for the Postal Service. In his 41-year career he claimed to have made more than 3,000 arrests and destroyed 160 tons of vice-ridden books and photographs.

Victorian crusaders like Comstock were not simply missionaries of a stuffy morality. They were apostles of a middle-class creed of social control and discipline who responded to growing alcoholism, venereal disease, gambling debts, prostitution, and unwanted pregnancies. No doubt they overreacted in warning that the road to ruin lay behind the door of every saloon, pool hall, or bedroom. Yet the new urban environment did indeed reflect the disorder of a rapidly industrializing society.

CONTRACEPTIVES AND ABORTION The insistence with which moralists warned against "impropriety" suggests that many people did not heed their advice. Three-quarters of women surveyed toward the turn of the century reported that they enjoyed sex. The growing variety of contraceptives—including spermicidal douches, sheaths made of animal intestines, rubber condoms, and forerunners of the diaphragm—testified to the desire for pregnancy-free intercourse. Abortion, too, was prevalent. According to one estimate, a third of all pregnancies were aborted, usually with the aid of a midwife. (By the 1880s abortion had been made illegal in most states, following the lead of the first antiabortion statute in England in 1803.) Despite Victorian marriage manuals, middle-class Americans became more conscious of sexuality as an emotional dimension of a satisfying union.

City Life and the Crisis of "Manliness"

The corrupting influence of city life on manhood troubled some onlookers as much as political or moral corruption distressed reformers. The components of traditional "manliness"—physical vigor, honor and integrity, courage and independence—seemed under assault by life in the industrial city, particularly among white middle- and upper-class men who found themselves working at desks and living in cushy comfort. As early as the 1850s Oliver Wendell Holmes Sr. (father of the famous Supreme Court justice) lamented that "such a set of stiff-jointed, —soft-muscled, paste-complexioned youth as we can boast in our Atlantic cities never before sprang from the loins of Anglo-Saxon lineage."

The dangers of this decline in "Anglo-Saxon" manliness risked catastrophe according to anxious observers. Soft, listless white men lacked vitality but also the manly discipline and character that came from living what Theodore Roosevelt called "The Strenuous Life" of action and struggle. Debased by the seamy pursuit of business, Roosevelt warned, such "weaklings" left the nation "[trembling] on the brink of doom," its future imperiled by laziness, timidity, and dishonesty. The "virile qualities" essential for achievement and leadership would vanish. Roosevelt, frail and asthmatic as a boy, turned himself into a strapping man through backbreaking workouts. He commanded desk-bound, "civilized" white men to follow his lead, even to reinvigorate their intellects with the "barbarian virtues" of physical strength he saw in darker-hued "primitives." Gender and race were being blended into a heady brew of white supremacy.

A frenzy of fitness spread across the nation. Bicycling, rowing, boxing, and what one historian called a college "cult of sports" promised to return middle- and upper-class men to "vigorous and unsullied manhood." Austrian bodybuilder Eugen Sandow ignited a weightlifting craze when he toured the country in the 1890s with feats of strength and poses he dubbed "muscle display performances." In a show of manly courage a young Theodore Roosevelt lit out for the Dakota Badlands, writer Richard Harding Davis for Cuba in the middle of the Spanish-American War, and explorers Robert Peary and Matthew Henson for the North Pole in 1898. (In their last attempt to find the Pole in 1908–1909, they were carried partway on a ship called the *Roosevelt* in an homage to the rugged president.) Exploration became more than a journey of discovery; it turned into an exercise in undaunted manliness.

Challenges to Convention

VICTORIA WOODHULL   A few intrepid men and women openly challenged conventions of gender and propriety. Victoria Woodhull, publisher of *Woodhull & Claflin's Weekly,* divorced her husband, ran for president in 1872 on the Equal Rights Party ticket, and pressed the case for sexual freedom. "I am a free lover!" she shouted to a riotous audience in New York. Although Woodhull made a strong public case for sexual freedom, in private she believed in strict monogamy and romantic love for herself.

URBAN HOMOSEXUAL COMMUNITIES   The same cosmopolitan conditions that provided protection for Woodhull's unorthodox beliefs also made possible the growth of self-conscious communities of homosexual men and women. Earlier in the century Americans had idealized romantic friendships among members of the same sex, without necessarily attributing sexual overtones to them.

For friendships with an explicitly sexual dimension, the anonymity of large cities provided new meeting

©Rischgitz/Stringer/Getty Images

| *Strongman and bodybuilder, Eugen Sandow*

grounds. Single factory workers and clerks, living in furnished rooms rather than with their families in small towns and on farms, were freer to be themselves and seek others who shared their sexual orientation. Homosexual men and women began forming social networks: on the streets where they regularly met or at specific restaurants and clubs, which, to avoid controversy, sometimes passed themselves off as athletic associations or chess groups.

Only toward the end of the century did physicians begin to notice homosexual behavior, usually to condemn it as a disease or an inherited infirmity. Indeed, not until the turn of the century did the term *homosexual* come into existence. Certainly homosexual love itself was not new. But for the first time in the United States, the conditions of urban life allowed gay men and lesbians to define themselves in terms of a larger, self-aware community, even if they were stoutly condemned by contemporary standards of morality.

✓ **REVIEW**
How did class and ethnicity determine life for city dwellers?

CITY CULTURE

"WE CANNOT ALL LIVE IN cities," reformer Horace Greeley lamented just after the Civil War, "yet nearly all seemed determined to do so." Economic opportunity drew people to the teeming industrial city. So, too, did a vibrant urban culture, boasting temples of entertainment, electrified trolleys and lights, the best schools, stores and restaurants, the biggest newspapers, and virtually every museum, library, art gallery, bookshop, and orchestra in America.

Public parks followed the model of New York's Central Park. When it opened in 1858 Central Park was meant to serve as a pastoral retreat from the turbulent industrial city. Its rustic paths, leafy glades, and tranquil lakes, said designer Frederick Law Olmsted, would have "a distinctly harmonizing and refining influence" on even the rudest fellow. Bustling industrial cities looked to be modern, but public parks reflected the age-old human need to connect to the tranquility of the natural world.

Public Education in an Urban Industrial World

Those at the bottom and in the middle ranks of city life found one path to success in public education. Although the campaign for public education began in the Jacksonian era, it did not make real headway until after the Civil War, when industrial cities began to mushroom. As late as 1870 half the children in the country received no formal education, and one American in five over the age of 14 could not read. A century later, in 1970, more than 99 of every 100 Americans were literate.

Between 1870 and 1900 an educational awakening occurred. As more and more businesses required workers who could read, write, and figure sums, attendance in public schools more than doubled. The length of the school term rose from 132 to 144 days. Illiteracy fell by half. At the turn of the century nearly all the states outside the South had enacted mandatory education laws. Almost three of every four school-age children were enrolled. Even so, the average American adult still attended school for only about five years, and less than 10 percent of those eligible ever went to high school.

The school day started early. By noon most girls were released under the assumption that they needed less formal education. Curricula stressed the fundamentals of reading, writing, and arithmetic. Courses in manual training, science, and physical education were added as the demand for technical knowledge grew and opportunities to exercise shrank. Students learned by memorization, sitting in silent study with hands clasped or standing erect while they repeated phrases and sums. Few schools encouraged creative thinking. "Don't stop to think," barked a Chicago teacher to a class of terrified youngsters in the 1890s, "tell me what you know!"

EDUCATIONAL VALUES AND CONFORMITY A rigid social philosophy underlay the harsh routine. In an age of industrialization, massive immigration, and rapid change, schools taught conformity and values as much as facts and figures. Teachers acted as drillmasters, shaping their charges for the sake of society. "Teachers and books are better security than handcuffs and policemen," wrote a New Jersey college professor in 1879. In *McGuffey's Reader,* a standard textbook used in grammar schools, students learned not only how to read but also how to behave. Hard work, Christian ethics, and obedience to authority would lead boys to heroic command, girls to blissful motherhood, and society to harmonious progress.

As much as anyone, urban middle-class young women profited from education. Liberated from household chores, many attended school and some went on to high school. They walked city streets, met their peers beyond the watchful eyes of parents, and extended childhood into the new, intermediate stage of "adolescence." Through education, prim and sheltered "young ladies" were becoming "school girls," with newfound freedom to be who and what they wanted.

EDUCATIONAL DISCRIMINATION As Reconstruction faded, so did the impressive start made in black education. Most of the first generation of former slaves had been illiterate. So eager were they to learn that by the end of the century more than half of all African Americans over 14 could read. But discrimination soon took its toll. For nearly 100 years after the Civil War the doctrine of "separate but equal," upheld by the Supreme Court in *Plessy v. Ferguson* (1896), kept black and white students apart but scarcely equal (see Chapter 18). By 1882 public schools in a half-dozen southern states were segregated by law, the rest by practice. Underfunded and ill-equipped, black schools served dirt-poor families whose every member had to work. In fact, only about a third of the South's black children attended and rarely for the entire school year.

Like African Americans, immigrants saw education as a way of getting ahead. Some educators saw it as a means of Americanizing newcomers. They assumed that immigrant and native-born children would learn the same lessons in the same language and turn out the same way. Only toward the end of the century, as immigration mounted, did eastern cities begin to offer night classes that taught English, along with civics lessons for foreigners. When public education proved inadequate, immigrants established their own schools. Catholics, for example, started an elaborate expansion of their parochial schools in 1884.

EDUCATIONAL REFORMS By the 1880s educational reforms were helping schools respond to the needs of an urban society. Opened first in St. Louis in 1873, American versions

Source: National Gallery of Art, Washington (1990.60.1./DR)

| *Educational reformers in the 1870s pushed elementary schools to include drawing as a required subject. Their goal was not to turn out gifted artists but to train students in the practical skills needed in an industrial society. Winslow Homer's portrait of a teacher by her blackboard shows the geometric shapes behind practical design.*

of innovative German "kindergartens" put four- to six-year-olds in orderly classrooms while parents went off to work. **Normal schools** multiplied to provide teachers with more professional training. By 1900 almost one teacher in five had a professional degree. In the new industrial age, science and manual training supplemented more conventional subjects in order to supply industry with better-educated workers. And vocational education reduced the influence of organized labor. Now less dependent on a system of apprenticeship controlled by labor, new workers were also less subject to being recruited into unions.

Higher Learning and the Rise of the Professional

HIGHER EDUCATION As American society grew more organized, mechanized, and complex, the need for managerial, technical, and literary skills brought greater respect for college education. The Morrill Act of 1862 generated a dozen new state colleges and universities, eight mechanical and agricultural colleges, and six black colleges. Private charity added more. Railroad barons like Johns Hopkins and Leland Stanford used parts of their fortunes to found colleges named after them (Hopkins in 1873, Stanford in 1890). The number of colleges and universities nearly doubled between 1870 and 1910, though less than 5 percent of college-age Americans enrolled in them.

BLACK COLLEGES A practical impulse inspired the founding of several black colleges. In the late nineteenth century, few institutions mixed races. Church groups and private foundations, including the Peabody and Slater funds (supported by white donors from the North), underwrote black colleges such as Fisk and Howard Universities during Reconstruction and, later, colleges such as Livingstone and Spelman. By 1900, a total of 700 black students were enrolled. About 2,000 had graduated. Through hard work and persistence, some even received degrees from institutions normally reserved for whites.

PROFESSIONAL SCHOOLS In keeping with the new emphasis on practical training, professional schools multiplied to provide training beyond a college degree. American universities adopted the German model requiring young scholars to perform research as part of their training. The number of law and medical schools more than doubled between 1870 and 1900; the number of medical students almost tripled. Ten percent of medical students were women, though their numbers shrank as the male-dominated medical profession became more organized and exclusive.

Source: *Harpers New Monthly Magazine*, May 1893, Cornell University Library

| *American Impressionist Mary Cassatt painted this mural panel of women picking apples for the Gallery of Honor in the Women's Building at the Chicago World's Columbian Exposition. Titled Young Women Plucking the Fruits of Knowledge or Science, it played on the biblical story of Eve and the apple. Traditionally, the apple had always been identified as the fruit on the tree of knowledge in the Garden of Eden. That fruit was forbidden: when it was eaten by Eve, who shared it with Adam, the result was original sin. Cassatt stood the story of Eve on its head. In doing so, she suggested that the place of women in society was changing. No longer bound by cultural conventions against the dangers of educated and potentially "uppity" women, a new generation of educated females would be justly celebrated for its achievements in science, the arts, and the professions.*

Professionals of all kinds—in law, medicine, engineering, business, academics—swelled the ranks of the middle class. Slowly they were becoming a new force in urban America, replacing the ministers and gentleman freeholders of an earlier day as community leaders.

Higher Education for Women

Before the Civil War women could attend only three private colleges. After the war they had new ones all their own, among them Smith (1871), Wellesley (1875), and Bryn Mawr (1885). Many land-grant colleges, chartered to serve all people, admitted women from the start. By 1910 some 40 percent of college students were women, almost double the 1870 figure. Only one college in five refused to accept women.

Potent myths continued to make college life hard for women. As Dr. Edward Clarke of the Harvard Medical School told thousands of students in *Sex in Education* (1873), the rigors of a college education could lead the "weaker sex" to physical or mental collapse, infertility, and early death. Women's colleges therefore included a strict program of physical activity to keep students healthy. Many also offered an array of courses in "domestic science"—cooking, sewing, and other such skills—to counter the claim that higher education would be of no value to women, who were more likely to be making homes than business deals.

College students, together with office workers and female athletes, became role models for ambitious young women. These "new women," impatient with custom, cast off Victorian restrictions. Fewer of them married, and more were self-supporting. They shed their corsets and bustles and donned lighter, more comfortable clothing, including "shirtwaist" blouses (styled after men's shirts) and lower-heeled shoes. Robust and active, they could be found ice-skating in the winter, riding bicycles in the fall and spring, playing golf and tennis in the summer.

A Culture of Consumption

The city spawned a new material culture built around consumption. As standards of living rose, American industries began providing "ready-made" clothing to replace garments that had once been made at home. Similarly, food and furniture were mass-produced in greater quantities. The city became a giant marketplace for these goods, where new patterns of mass consumption took hold. Radiating outward to more rural areas, this urban consumer culture helped to level American society. Increasingly, city businesses sold the same goods to farmer and clerk, rich and poor, native-born and immigrant.

DEPARTMENT STORES Well-made, inexpensive merchandise in standard sizes and shapes found outlets in new palaces of consumption called "department stores" because they displayed their goods in separate sections or departments. The idea was imported from France, where shopping arcades had been built as early as the 1860s. Unlike the small exclusive shops of Europe, department stores were palatial, public, and filled with inviting displays of furniture, housewares, and clothing.

The French writer Émile Zola claimed that department stores "democratized luxury." Anyone could enter free of charge, handle the most elegant and expensive goods, and buy whatever they could afford. When consumers found goods too pricey, department stores pioneered layaway plans with deferred payments. Free delivery and free returns or

| "Wheelman clubs" formed in many cities to take advantage of the popularity of bicycling as a leisure-time activity. This illustration of cyclists returning from a ride along Manhattan's Riverside Drive in 1897 indicates that women eagerly undertook the sport, though debates raged over its suitability for them. In 1893 the New York Times *pronounced the use of "bicycles by the weaker sex" a question that had been "decisively settled in the affirmative."*
©Lebrecht Music and Arts Photo Library/Alamy

exchanges were available to all, not just the favored customers of exclusive fashion makers. The department store also educated people by displaying what "proper" families owned and the correct names for things like women's wear and parlor furniture. In all these ways, department stores socialized people into a culture of consumption by showing them what they needed and what they might want. This process of socialization was taking place not only in cities but also in towns and villages across America. Mass consumption was giving rise to a mass culture.

CHAIN STORES AND MAIL-ORDER HOUSES "Chain stores" (a term coined in America) spread the culture of consumption without frills. They catered to the working class, who could not afford department stores and operated on a cash-and-carry basis. Owners kept their costs down by buying in volume to fill the small stores in growing neighborhood chains. Founded in 1859 the Great Atlantic and Pacific Tea Company was the first of the chain stores. By 1876 its 76 branch stores had added groceries to its original line of teas.

Far from department and chain stores, rural Americans joined the community of consumers by mail. In 1872 Aaron Montgomery Ward sent his first price sheet to farmers from a livery stable loft in Chicago. Ward eliminated the intermediary and promised savings of 40 percent on fans, needles, trunks, harnesses, and scores of other goods. By 1884 his catalog boasted 10,000 items, each illustrated by a woodcut. Similarly, Richard W. Sears and Alvah C. Roebuck built a 500-million-dollar mail-order business by 1907. Schoolrooms that had no encyclopedia used a Ward's or Sears' catalog instead. Children were drilled in reading and spelling from them. When asked the source of the Ten Commandments, one farm boy replied that they came from Sears, Roebuck. Countrywide mass consumption was producing a mass material culture.

Leisure

As mechanization slowly reduced the number of hours on the job, factory workers found themselves with more free time. So did the middle class, with free weekends, evenings, and vacations. A new, stricter division between work and leisure developed. City dwellers turned their free time into a consumer item that often reflected differences in class, gender, and ethnicity.

SPORTS AND CLASS DISTINCTIONS Sports, for example, had been a traditional form of recreation for the rich. They continued to play polo, golf, and the newly imported English game of tennis. Croquet had more middle-class appeal because it required less skill and special equipment. Perhaps as important, croquet could be enjoyed in mixed company, like the new craze of bicycling. Bicycles evolved from unstable contraptions with large front wheels into "safety" bikes with equal-sized wheels, a dropped middle bar,

pneumatic tires, and coaster brakes. A good one cost about $100, far beyond the reach of a factory worker but within the grasp of a mechanic or a well-paid clerk. On Sunday afternoons city parks became crowded with cyclists. Women also rode the new safety bikes, although social convention forbade them to ride alone. But cycling broke down conventions too. It required looser garments, freeing women from corsets. Lady cyclists demonstrated that they were definitely not too frail for physical exertion.

SPECTATOR SPORTS FOR THE URBAN MASSES Organized spectator sports attracted crowds from every walk of life. Baseball overshadowed all others. For city dwellers with dull work, tight quarters, and isolated lives, baseball offered the chance to join thousands of others for an exciting outdoor spectacle. Nostalgia for pastoral days gone-by mixed with dynamism of the game to make it irresistible to many city dwellers already familiar with the quickened pace of urban life. By 1900, nearly 2 million Americans a year were crowding into stadiums across the country.

Baseball began to take its modern form in 1869, when the first professional team, the Cincinnati Red Stockings, appeared. Slowly the game evolved: umpires began to call balls and strikes, the overhand replaced the underhand pitch, and fielders put on gloves. Teams from eight cities formed the National League of Professional Baseball Clubs in 1876, followed by the American League in 1901. League players were distinctly working class. At first teams featured a few black players. When African Americans were barred in the 1880s, black professionals formed their own team, the Cuban Giants of Long Island, New York, looking to play anyone they could. Their name was chosen with care. In an age of racial separation, the all-black team hoped to increase its chances of playing white teams by calling itself "Cuban."

Horse racing, bicycle tournaments, and other sports of speed and violence helped to break the monotony, frustration, and routine of the industrial city. They also helped to address the "crisis of manliness" by allowing men to display their strength and courage—their "masculinity"—on a playing field rather than a battlefield. In 1869, without pads or helmets, Rutgers beat Princeton in the first intercollegiate football match. By the 1890s the service academies and state universities fielded teams. Despite protests against rising death tolls (18 players died in 1905), football soon attracted crowds of 50,000 or more. Beginning in 1891 when Dr. James Naismith nailed a peach basket to the gymnasium wall at the YMCA Training School in Springfield, Massachusetts, "basketball" filled the indoor winter interval between the outdoor sports of spring and fall.

BOXING Bare-knuckled prizefighting, illegal in some states, took place secretly in saloons and commercial gyms. In the rough-and-tumble world of the industrial city, the ring gave young men from the streets the chance to stand out from the crowd and to prove their masculinity. "Sporting clubs" of German, Irish, and African American boxers sprouted up in cities along the East Coast. *The National Police Gazette* and other magazines followed the bouts with sensational stories chronicling matches in detail. When the sport adopted the Marquis of Queensbury rules in the 1880s, including the use of gloves, boxing gained new respectability and appeal. Soon boxing, like other sports, was being commercialized with professional bouts, large purses, and championship titles.

City Entertainment at Home and on the Road

City entertainment, like city life, divided along lines of class. For the wealthy and upper-middle class there were symphonies, operas, and theater. Highbrow productions of Shakespearean plays catered to the aspirations of American upper classes for culture and European refinement. Popular melodramas gave their largely middle-class audiences the chance to ignore the ambiguities of modern life, if only for an evening. They hissed at villains and applauded heroes, all the while catching their breath as actors floated upward or jumped from one fake ice floe to another. Around the turn of the century, people started bringing their entertainment home, snapping up new phonograph recordings at the rate of 3 million a year.

Workingmen discovered a haven from the drudgery of factory, mill, and mine in the saloon. It was an all-male preserve—a workingmen's club—where drink and talk were free from Victorian finger-wagging. Rougher saloons offered fulfillment of still more illicit desires in the form of prostitutes, gambling, and drugs. Young working women sought escape alone or on dates at vaudeville shows, dance halls, and the new amusement parks with their mechanical "thrill rides." In the all-black gaming houses and honky-tonks of St. Louis and

Source: Library of Congress, Prints and Photographs Division [LC-DIG-ppmsca-54811]

| This lithograph is from an 1894 poster for the Barnum & Bailey Circus. It depicts a menagerie tent in which exotic animals are displayed side by side with "Strange and Savage Tribes," thus collapsing the boundaries between animals and human beings. Much smaller than the Big Top, menagerie tents allowed Euro-American patrons to examine animals and humans up close. The Barnum show presented its first "Ethnological Congress" of "native" peoples in 1886, as the United States began its drive for empire abroad. The human specimens were meant to give Americans a glimpse of foreign cultures and to be instructive. "Even the best informed and most intellectual had something to learn," boasted a circus route book.

New Orleans, the syncopated rhythms of African American composer Scott Joplin's "Maple Leaf Rag" (1899) and other ragtime tunes heralded the coming of jazz.

TRAVELING CIRCUSES As much as any form of entertainment, the traveling circus embodied the changes of the new urban, industrial world. From their urban bases, circuses rode the new rail system across the country, making their first transcontinental tour in 1869, the same year the transcontinental railroad was completed. With the advent of steamships, they crisscrossed the globe. The mammoth New York–based Barnum & Bailey Circus carried dozens of gilded show wagons, hundreds of animals, tons of equipment, and sometimes thousands of performers, work hands, and animal tenders. With factory-like precision, circus workers erected and dismantled small tent cities in hours, moved them across vast spaces in days or weeks, and performed as many as three shows daily.

Circuses were popular entertainment and big businesses, but they also were disseminators of culture that both supported and subverted social conventions. When in 1886 Barnum & Bailey displayed exotic peoples and animals in the first "Ethnological Congress" ever to accompany a traveling circus, patrons saw living embodiments of "strange and savage tribes" from Africa, the Middle East, and Asia. These displays opened American eyes to a wider world while reinforcing prevailing notions of white supremacy.

As the United States was embarking on a quest for empire (see Chapter 21), circuses trumpeted national expansion with celebrations of American might and exceptionalism. To audiences at home, reenactments of famous battles abroad brought faraway places near and made abstract principles of foreign policy real. To foreign audiences, those same reenactments trumpeted the rise of a new world power.

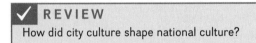

✔ REVIEW
How did city culture shape national culture?

PUTTING HISTORY IN GLOBAL CONTEXT

INDUSTRIALIZATION IGNITED THE GROWTH of cities not just in the United States but all over the world as well. In 1851 Great Britain, the birthplace of the Industrial Revolution, became the world's first country to have over half its people living in towns and cities. By 1914, on the eve of World War I, eight of every ten Britons lived in cities, as did six of ten Germans and nearly five of ten French. Growing cities spilled over into nearby towns and villages, obliterating the open spaces between them whether in the English Midlands, the Ruhr valley of Germany, or the environs of Tokyo.

Just as European emigrants poured into cities across the United States, newcomers from Europe, Asia, and the Middle East flowed into South America, Australia, and the Caribbean. Before 1900 two of every three emigrating Italians booked passage not for the United States but for Brazil or Argentina. Chinese immigrants harvested sugarcane in Cuba, built railroads and opened restaurants in Peru, and launched businesses in Trinidad. By 1920 São Paulo, the largest city in Brazil, was exploding with Asian immigrants, and Brazil boasted the world's largest Japanese population outside Japan itself.

The hubbub, the overcrowding, and the corruption of American cities were reflected elsewhere in the world. Before the arrival of mass transit, British urban workers were forced to live within walking distance of factories, in dingy row houses inundated with the overflow from privies and garbage. A deadly cholera epidemic in 1848 spurred a campaign to install iron pipes and drains to provide running water and sewers throughout major cities. About the same time, Paris underwent a radical renovation: workers tore down the city's medieval fortress walls, widened major streets into boulevards, and set aside land for green parks. Borrowing innovations from the United States, Europeans adopted horse-drawn streetcars and, later, electric trolleys. With an intracity transportation network in place, the old "walking cities" of Europe, like those in the United States, added suburbs, partially easing the crush of earlier crowding.

The world over, industrial cities transformed both the urban landscape and the daily lives of city dwellers. Critics damned the city's crime and corruption; defenders celebrated its vibrancy and diversity. No matter how they felt, Americans had to find ways to make the new industrial order something they could live with.

CHAPTER SUMMARY

The modern city was the product of industrialization, lying at the center of the new integrated systems of transportation, communications, manufacturing, marketing, and finance.

- Fed by a great global migration of laborers, cities began to grow and to assume their modern shape of ringed residential patterns around central business districts and strict divisions among different classes, races, and ethnic groups.

- The challenge for the political system was to find within its democratic traditions a way to bring order out of the seeming chaos of unchecked urban growth.

- The urban boss and the urban political machine met the needs of cities for centralized authority but at a terrible cost in corruption, while social settlement houses, the Salvation Army, and the Social Gospel churches represented only a start at coping with the problems of poverty and urban blight.

- As cities grew, the middle-class code of behavior—called Victorianism—spread, teaching the values of sobriety, hard work, self-control, and modesty that served the needs of new industrial society for efficiency and order and the middle-class need for protection against the turbulence of city life.

- Yet for all the emphasis on skills, discipline, and order, the vibrancy of city culture remained attractive, drawing millions in search of education, entertainment, and opportunity and radiating outward to almost every corner of the country.

Digging Deeper

The best treatment of the rise of cities is Howard B. Chudacoff, *The Evolution of American Urban Society* (rev. ed., 1981). John R. Stilgoe, *Borderland: Origins of the American Suburb, 1820–1939* (1988), chronicles the growth of suburban America. William Cronon, *Nature's Metropolis: Chicago and the Great West* (1991), looks at Chicago as part of the ecological landscape. In *Boss Cox's Cincinnati: Urban Politics in the Progressive Era* (1968), Zane Miller reassesses the urban political machine, and Paul Boyer explores efforts at controlling city life in *Urban Masses and Moral Order in America, 1820–1920* (1978). The best book on everyday life in nineteenth-century cities remains Gunther Barth's *City People: The Rise of Modern City Culture in Nineteenth-Century America* (1982). John F. Kasson, *Rudeness & Civility: Manners in Nineteenth-Century Urban America* (1990); and Lawrence Levine, *Highbrow/Lowbrow: The Emergence of Cultural Hierarchy in America* (1988), investigate the emerging urban culture. For a penetrating examination of traveling circuses as conduits for cultural exchanges, see Janet M. Davis's *The Circus Age: Culture and Society under the American Big Top* (2002). On the origins of baseball, see David Block's *Baseball Before We Knew It: A Search for the Roots of the Game* (2004).

Marcus Lee Hansen's classic *The Atlantic Migration, 1607–1860* (1940) began the shift in immigration history away from the national and toward a more global perspective. See also Roger Daniels's richly detailed *Coming to America: A History of Immigration and Ethnicity in American Life* (1990); and Ronald Takaki, *A Different Mirror: A History of Multicultural America* (1993). Susan A. Glenn, *Daughters of the Shtetl: Life and Labor in the Immigrant Generation* (1990), probes the gendered lives and labor of immigrant women, with particular attention to the shaping effect of Old World Jewish culture. Madeline Y. Hsu examines Chinese immigrants in her award-winning *The Good Immigrants: How the Yellow Peril Became the Model Minority* (2015). Virginia Yans-McLaughlin, ed., *Immigration Reconsidered: History, Sociology, and Politics* (1990), places American immigration in its international context. Vincent J. Cannato presents a sweeping portrait of the premier port of entry for waves of "new" immigrants in *American Passage: The History of Ellis Island* (2009). In *New Spirits: Americans in the Gilded Age, 1865–1905* (2006), Rebecca Edwards's take on the "Gilded Age" emphasizes the anxieties and optimism of ordinary people, in what she characterizes as the birth of modern America. Helen Lefkowitz Horowitz's *Rereading Sex: Battles over Sexual Knowledge and Suppression in Nineteenth-Century America* (2002) explores the contradictions of Victorian thinking about all manner of sexual matters, including contraception, abortion, pornography, and free speech. Jane H. Hunter's *How Young Ladies Became Girls: The Victorian Origins of American Girlhood* (2003) surveys the liberating experiences of female adolescents in Victorian America.

21 Realignment at Home and Empire Abroad

1877–1900

The Statue of the Republic, by sculptor Daniel Chester French, stood 65 feet tall and dominated the Court of Honor at the World's Columbian Exposition in 1893. The fair's exotic buildings, with their domes, minarets, and flags from all nations, showed how conscious Americans were becoming of the wider world.

©Bettmann/Getty Images

>> An American Story

"THE WORLD UNITED AT CHICAGO"

On May 1, 1893, nearly half a million people jostled into a dramatic plaza fronted on either side by gleaming white buildings overlooking a sparkling lagoon. Named the Court of Honor, the plaza was the center of a strange ornamental city that was at once awesome and entirely imaginary. At one end stood the Administration Building, whose magnificent white dome exceeded even the height of the Capitol in Washington, D.C. Unlike the marble-built Capitol, however, this building was all surface: a stucco shell plastered onto a steel frame and then sprayed with white oil paint to make it glisten. Beyond the Court of Honor stretched thoroughfares encompassing over 200 colonnaded buildings, piers, islands, and watercourses.

Located five miles south of Chicago's central business district, this city of the imagination proclaimed itself the "World's Columbian Exposition" in honor of the 400th anniversary of Columbus's voyage to America and to herald the country's aspirations for a place among the great industrialized powers of the globe.

Source: Library of Congress, Prints and Photographs Division [LC-USZC4-3270]

| *The fair was opened by President Grover Cleveland, lower right.*

President Grover Cleveland opened the world's fair in a way that symbolized the nation's industrial transformation. He pressed a telegrapher's key. Instantly, electric current set 7,000 feet of shafting into motion, unfurling flags, setting fountains pumping, and lighting 10,000 electric bulbs. The lights played over an array of exhibition buildings soon known as the "White City."

One English visitor dismissed the displays within as little more than "the contents of a great dry goods store mixed up with the contents of museums." In a sense he was right. Visitors paraded by an unending collection of typewriters, pins, watches, agricultural machinery, cedar canoes, and refrigerators, to say nothing of a map of the United States made entirely of pickles. But this riot of mechanical marvels, gewgaws, and bric-a-brac was symbolic too of the nation's industrial transformation. The fair resembled nothing so much as a tangible version of the new mail-order catalogs whose pages were introducing the goods of the city to the hinterlands.

The connections made by the fair were international as well. This event was the *World's* Columbian Exposition, with exhibits from 36 nations. Germany's famous arms manufacturer, Krupp, had its own separate building. It housed a 120-ton rifled gun. Easily within the range of its gunsights was a replica of the U.S. battleship *Illinois,* whose own bristling turrets stood just offshore of the exposition on Lake Michigan. At the fair's amusement park visitors encountered exotic cultures—not just temples, huts, and totems, but exhibits in the flesh. The Arabian village featured Saharan camels, veiled ladies, and elders in turbans. Nearby, Irish peasants boiled potatoes over turf fires while Samoan men threw axes.

Like all such fairs, the Columbian Exposition created a fantasy. Beyond its boundaries the real world was showing signs of strain. Early in 1893 the Philadelphia and Reading Railroad had gone bankrupt, setting off a financial panic. By the end of the year, nearly 500 banks and 15,000 businesses had failed. Although millions of tourists continued to marvel at the fair's wonders, crowds of worried and unemployed workers also gathered elsewhere in Chicago. On Labor Day, Governor John Altgeld of Illinois told a crowd that the government was powerless to soften the "suffering and distress" brought by this latest economic downturn.

In truth, the political system was ill-equipped to cope with the economic and social revolutions reshaping America. The executive branch remained weak, while members of Congress and the courts found themselves easily swayed by the financial interests of the industrial class. The crises of the 1890s strained the political order and forced it to confront such inequities.

The political system also had to take into account developments abroad. Industrialization had sent American businesses scurrying around the world in search of raw materials and markets. As that search intensified, many influential Americans argued that the United States needed to compete with European nations in acquiring territory overseas. By the end of the century the nation's political system had taken its first steps toward modernization, including a major political realignment at home and a growing empire abroad. The changes launched the United States into the twentieth century and an era of prosperity and global power. <<

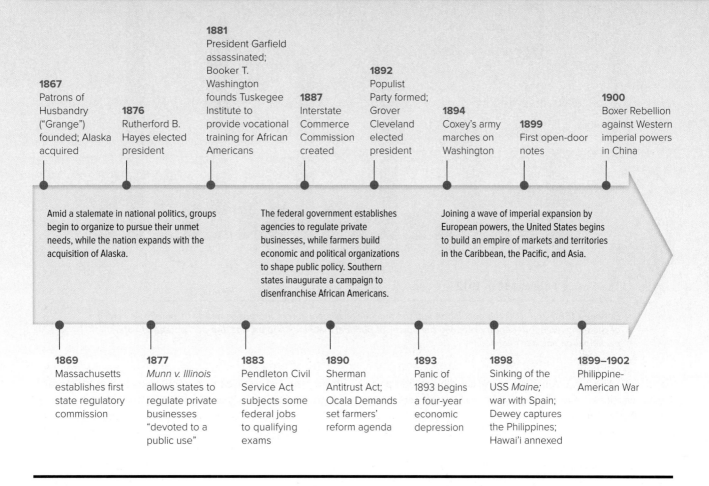

1867
Patrons of Husbandry ("Grange") founded; Alaska acquired

1876
Rutherford B. Hayes elected president

1881
President Garfield assassinated; Booker T. Washington founds Tuskegee Institute to provide vocational training for African Americans

1887
Interstate Commerce Commission created

1892
Populist Party formed; Grover Cleveland elected president

1894
Coxey's army marches on Washington

1899
First open-door notes

1900
Boxer Rebellion against Western imperial powers in China

Amid a stalemate in national politics, groups begin to organize to pursue their unmet needs, while the nation expands with the acquisition of Alaska.

The federal government establishes agencies to regulate private businesses, while farmers build economic and political organizations to shape public policy. Southern states inaugurate a campaign to disenfranchise African Americans.

Joining a wave of imperial expansion by European powers, the United States begins to build an empire of markets and territories in the Caribbean, the Pacific, and Asia.

1869
Massachusetts establishes first state regulatory commission

1877
Munn v. Illinois allows states to regulate private businesses "devoted to a public use"

1883
Pendleton Civil Service Act subjects some federal jobs to qualifying exams

1890
Sherman Antitrust Act; Ocala Demands set farmers' reform agenda

1893
Panic of 1893 begins a four-year economic depression

1898
Sinking of the USS *Maine;* war with Spain; Dewey captures the Philippines; Hawai'i annexed

1899–1902
Philippine-American War

THE POLITICS OF PARALYSIS

DURING THE 1880s AND 1890s, as the American political system came under strain, Moisei Ostrogorski was traveling across the United States. Part of a flood of foreign observers, the Russian political scientist had come to see the new democratic experiment in action. His verdict was as blunt as it was widely shared: "the constituted authorities are unequal to their duty." It seemed that the glorious experiment had fallen victim to greed, indifference, and political mediocrity.

In fact, there were deeper problems: a great gulf between rich and poor; a wrenching cycle of boom and bust; the unmet needs of African Americans, Indians, women and other "others." Politics was the traditional medium of resolution, but it was grinding into a dangerous stalemate.

Political Stalemate

From 1877 to 1897 American politics rested on a delicate balance of power that left neither Republicans nor Democrats in control. Republicans inhabited the White House for 12 years; Democrats, for 8. Margins of victory in presidential elections were paper thin. No president could count on having a majority of his party in both houses of Congress for his entire term. Usually Republicans controlled the Senate and Democrats the House of Representatives.

With elections tight, both parties worked hard to turn out voters. Brass bands, parades, cheering crowds of flag-wavers were "the order of the day and night from end to end of the country," reported a British visitor. When Election Day arrived, stores and businesses shut down. At political clubs and corner saloons men lined up for voting orders (along with free drinks) from ward bosses. Fields went untended as farmers took their families to town, cast their ballots, and bet on the outcome.

VOTER TURNOUT An average of nearly 80 percent of eligible voters turned out for presidential elections between 1860 and 1900, a figure higher than at any time since. New party discipline and organization helped to account for the turnout, but it is also true that the electorate made up a smaller percentage of the

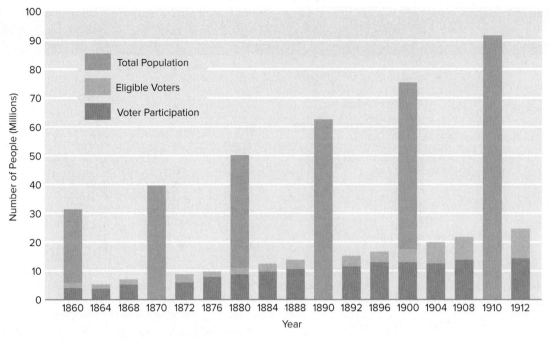

The Voting Public, 1860–1912

Between 1860 and 1910 the population and the number of eligible voters increased nearly threefold. As reforms of the early twentieth century reduced the power of political machines and parties, the percentage of voter participation actually declined.

population. About one American in five actually voted in presidential elections from 1876 to 1892. Most voters were white males. Women could vote in national elections only in a few western states, and beginning in the 1880s, the South erected barriers that eventually disenfranchised many African Americans.

Party loyalty rarely wavered and was the key to electoral success. In every election 16 states could be counted on to vote Republican and 14 Democratic (the latter mainly in the South). In only six states—the most important being New York and Ohio—were the results in doubt.

The Parties

What inspired such loyalty? While Republicans and Democrats shared broad values, they also had major differences. Both parties supported business and condemned radicalism; neither offered embattled workers or farmers much help. Democrats believed in states' rights and limited government, while Republicans favored federal activism to foster economic growth. Their strength was in the industrial North. The stronghold of Democrats lay in the South, where they reminded voters that they had led the states of the Old Confederacy, "redeemed" them from Republican Reconstruction, and championed white supremacy. Republicans dominated the North with strong support from industry and business. They, too, invoked memories of the Civil War to secure votes, black as well as white. "Not every Democrat was a rebel," they chanted, "but every rebel was a Democrat."

ETHNIC AND RELIGIOUS FACTORS Ethnicity and religion cemented voter loyalty. Republicans relied on old-stock

Protestants, who feared new immigrants and put their faith in promoting pious behavior throughout society. In the Republican Party they found support for immigration restriction, prohibition, and English-only schools. In the North the Democratic Party attracted urban political machines, their immigrant voters, and the working poor. Often Catholic, these voters saw salvation in following their own religious rituals, not in dictating the conduct of others.

Outside the two-party system, reformers often fashioned political organizations of their own. Some groups aligned themselves behind issues rather than parties. Opponents of alcohol created the Woman's Christian Temperance Union (1874) and the Anti-Saloon League (1893). Champions of women's rights joined the National Woman Suffrage Association (1890), a reunion of two branches of the women's suffrage movement that had split in 1869.

Like these political organizations, third political parties also crystallized around an issue or a group. Advocates of temperance rallied to the Prohibition Party (1869). Those who sought inflation of the currency formed the Greenback Party (1874). Angry farmers in the West and the South created the Populist, or People's, Party (1892). All drew supporters from both conventional parties, but as largely single-interest groups they mobilized minorities, not majorities.

The Issues

In Congress attention focused on well-worn issues: veterans' benefits, appointments, tariffs, and money. The presidency had been weakened by the impeachment of Andrew Johnson, the scandals of Ulysses S. Grant, and the contested victory of Rutherford B. Hayes in 1876. So Congress enjoyed the initiative in making policy as the founders intended. Time after time legislators squandered it amid electioneering and party infighting or simply were swamped by the ever-increasing flood of proposed legislation.

Some divisive issues were the bitter legacy of the Civil War. Republicans and Democrats waved the symbolic "bloody shirt," each tarring the other with responsibility for the war. The politics of the Civil War also surfaced in the lobbying efforts of veterans. The Grand Army of the Republic, an organization of more than 400,000 Union soldiers, petitioned Congress for pensions to make up for poor wartime pay and to support the widows and orphans of fallen comrades. By the turn of the century Union army veterans and their families were receiving $157 million annually. It was one of the largest public assistance programs in American history. Unintentionally, it turned out to be one of the first government programs to offer benefits to African Americans and laid the foundations of the modern welfare state.

More important than veterans' benefits was the campaign for a new method of staffing federal offices. From barely 53,000 employees at the end of the Civil War, the federal government had grown to 166,000 by the early 1890s. Far more of these new jobs required special skills. Dismantling the reigning **spoils system** proved difficult for politicians who had rewarded faithful supporters with government jobs regardless of their qualifications. American politics rested on such patronage. Without it, politicians—from presidents to lowly ward captains—feared they could attract neither workers nor money.

PENDLETON ACT   It took the assassination of President James Garfield by a frustrated office seeker in 1881 to break the log jam. In 1883 the Civil Service Act, or Pendleton Act, created a bipartisan civil service commission to administer competitive examinations for some federal jobs. Later

presidents expanded the number of positions covered by the system. By 1896 almost half of all federal workers came under civil service jurisdiction based on examination and merit.

The protective tariff also split Congress. As promoters of economic growth, Republicans usually championed this tax on imported goods to protect industries at home. Democrats, with their strength in the agrarian South, opposed such protectionism and generally sought to reduce tariffs in order to encourage freer trade, lower prices on manufactured goods, and cut the growing federal surplus. In 1890, when Republicans controlled the House of Representatives, Congress enacted the McKinley Tariff. It raised tariff rates to new highs and contained a novel twist called "reciprocity." To promote less-restricted trade, the president could lower rates if other countries did the same.

GOLD, SILVER, AND GREENBACKS   Just as divisive was the issue of currency. For most of the nineteenth century, currency was redeemable in both gold and silver. The need for more money during the Civil War had led Congress to issue "greenbacks"—currency printed on paper with a green back and not convertible to gold or silver. For the next decade and a half, Americans argued over whether to print more such paper money or take it out of circulation. Farmers and other debtors favored printing greenbacks as a way of inflating prices and thus reducing their debts. For the opposite reasons, bankers and creditors stood for "sound money" backed by the limited supply of gold to keep prices stable and interest rates (from which they drew their profits) high. Fear of **inflation** led Congress first to reduce the number of greenbacks and then in 1879 to make all remaining paper money convertible to gold.

CRIME OF '73   A more heated battle was developing over silver-backed money. By the early 1870s so little silver was being used that Congress officially stopped coining it in 1873, touching off a steep economic slide as the supply of money contracted and interest rates rose. With them came charges that a conspiracy of bankers had been responsible for "demonetizing" silver and wrecking the economy in what was widely referred to as the "Crime of '73."

BLAND-ALLISON ACT   In truth the money supply was inadequate to meet demand for the swelling number of manufactured goods. Interest rates—the charge for borrowing money—rose as consumers demanded more cash. Prices fell as too little money chased too many goods. All added to economic instability and increased calls for enlarging the supply of money. In 1878 the Bland-Allison Act inaugurated a limited form of silver coinage. But pressure for unlimited coinage of silver—coining all silver presented at U.S. mints—mounted as silver production quadrupled between 1870 and 1890. In 1890 the Sherman Silver Purchase Act obligated the government to buy 4.5 million ounces of silver every month. Paper tender called "treasury notes," redeemable in gold or silver, paid for the purchases. The compromise satisfied both sides only temporarily. The price of silver fell, pushing less money into the economy than silver enthusiasts wanted but more than the advocates of gold liked.

| New Yorkers gather to see the election returns in Manhattan's Madison Square for the presidential election of 1888 between Democrat Grover Cleveland and Republican Benjamin Harrison. The New York Herald *newspaper electrically projected the results on a large screen, proclaiming, "Harrison carries the State by 12000." The narrow victory in New York gave Harrison enough electoral votes to win the presidency, despite losing the popular vote.*
©North Wind Picture Archives/Alamy

| This cartoon, "The Tariff Tots," portrays various trusts as ill-tempered children playing roughly with dolls representing the public, consumers, and small producers. Whenever reformers tried to reduce tariffs, political support for protection made the task nearly impossible. In 1882 Congress created a commission to consider lowering tariffs, but it was quickly captured by the interests who stood to gain most from high tariffs. Complained one senator: "There was a representative of the wool growers on the commission; . . . of the iron interest . . . of the sugar interest. . . . And those interests were very carefully looked out for."

Source: Library of Congress, Prints and Photographs Division [LC-DIG-ppmsca-25984]

The White House from Hayes to Harrison

From the 1870s through the 1890s a string of nearly anonymous presidents presided over the country. Not all were mere caretakers. Some tried to energize the office, but Congress continued to curb the president and control policy.

Republican Rutherford B. Hayes was the first of the "Ohio dynasty," which included three presidents from 1876 to 1900. He moved quickly to end Reconstruction, but his pursuit of civil service reform ended only in splitting his party. Hayes left office after a single term, happy to be "out of a scrape." In 1880 Republican James Garfield, another Ohioan, spent his first hundred days in the White House besieged by office hunters. After Garfield's assassination only six months into his term, Chester A. Arthur, the "spoilsman's spoilsman," became president. To everyone's surprise, the dapper Arthur turned out to be an honest president. He broke with machine politicians, worked to lower the tariff, warmly endorsed the new Civil Service Act, and reduced the federal surplus by beginning construction of a modern navy. Such evenhandedness left him little chance for renomination from divided party leaders in 1884.

THE DIRTY ELECTION OF 1884 The election of 1884 was one of the dirtiest ever recorded. Senator James G. Blaine fought off charges of corrupt dealings with the railroads, while Democrat Grover Cleveland, the former governor of New York, admitted to fathering an illegitimate child. In the last week of the race a New York minister labeled the Democrats the party of "Rum, Romanism, and Rebellion" (alcohol, Catholicism, and the Civil War). In reaction the Irish Catholic vote swung to Cleveland and with it New York and the election.

Cleveland was the first Democrat elected to the White House since James Buchanan in 1856 and was more active than many of his predecessors. He pleased reformers by expanding the civil service. His devotion to gold-backed currency, economy, and efficiency earned him praise from business. He supported the growth of federal power by endorsing a new federal regulatory agency created by the Interstate Commerce Act (1887), new agricultural research, and federal arbitration of labor disputes.

Cleveland's presidential activism nonetheless remained limited. He vetoed two of every three bills brought to him, more than twice the number of all his predecessors. Toward the end of his term, embarrassed by the large federal surplus, Cleveland finally reasserted himself by attacking the tariff, but to no avail. The Republican-controlled Senate blocked his attempt to lower it.

In 1888 Republicans nominated a sturdy defender of tariffs, Benjamin Harrison, the grandson of President William Henry Harrison. President Cleveland won a **plurality** of the popular vote but lost in the Electoral College. The "human iceberg" (as Harrison's colleagues called him) worked hard and reasonably well with Congress, rarely delegated management, and turned the White House into a well-regulated office. He helped to shape the Sherman Silver Purchase Act (1890), kept up with the McKinley Tariff (1890), and accepted the Sherman Antitrust Act (1890) to limit the power and size of big businesses. At the end of Harrison's term in 1893, Congress completed its most productive session of the era and enacted the nation's first billion-dollar peacetime budget.

Ferment in the States and Cities

Despite its growing expenditures and more legislation, most people expected little from the federal government. Few newspapers even bothered to send correspondents to Washington. Public pressure to curb the excesses of the new industrial order mounted closer to home, in state and city governments. Experimental and often effective, state programs began to grapple with the problems of corporate power, discriminatory shipping rates, political corruption, and urban decay.

| A Chinese laborer, holding his queue of long hair in hand, proudly displays patches in support of the 1888 Democratic presidential candidate, Grover Cleveland, and his running mate, Allen G. Thurman. Cleveland and Thurman lost to Benjamin Harrison and Levi P. Morton, a wealthy New York banker. After his victory Harrison, a pious Presbyterian, grabbed the hand of Senator Matthew Quay and crowed, "Providence has given us the victory." "Providence hadn't a damn thing to do with it," Quay said later, irked that Harrison seemed to have no idea how many Republicans "were compelled to approach the gates of the penitentiary to make him President."

STATE COMMISSIONS Starting in 1869 with Massachusetts, states established commissions to investigate and regulate industry, especially railroads, America's first big business. By the turn of the century almost two-thirds of the states had them. These weak commissions gathered and publicized information on shipping rates and business practices and furnished advice about public policy. On the West Coast and in the Midwest, state legislatures empowered commissions to end rebates and monitor freight rates. Illinois in 1870 became the first of several states to define railroads as public highways subject to regulation, including setting maximum rates.

NATIONAL MUNICIPAL LEAGUE Concern over political corruption and urban blight led reformers to hold state municipal conventions to address urban problems. Iowa convened the first one in 1877. Philadelphia sponsored a national conference on good city government in 1894. A year later reformers founded the National Municipal League. It soon had more than 200 branches. Its model city charter advanced such farsighted reforms as separate city and state elections, limited contracts for utilities, and more authority for mayors. Meanwhile, cities and states in the Midwest enacted laws closing stores on Sundays, prohibiting the sale of alcohol, and making English the language of public schools—all in an effort to standardize social behavior and control the habits of new immigrants.

> ✓ **REVIEW**
> What factors led to the paralysis in the late nineteenth century?

THE REVOLT OF THE FARMERS

IN 1890 THE POLITICS OF stalemate cracked as the patience of farmers across the South and the western plains reached an end. Beginning in the 1880s a sharp depression drove down agricultural prices and forced thousands from their land. But farmers suffered from a great deal more, including heavy mortgages, widespread poverty, and railroad rates that sometimes discriminated against them. In 1890 their resentment boiled over. An agrarian revolt—called **Populism**—swept across the political landscape and helped break the political stalemate of the previous 20 years.

| Mary Shelley's novel of a man-made monster who turns against its creator strikes the theme for this 1874 cartoon titled "The American Frankenstein." Here, the railroad is a monstrous creation that crushes the common people in its path. It carries the symbols of wealth and might—a cloak of ermine and a club of capital. "Agriculture, commerce, and manufacture are all in my power," the monster bellows in the caption. Figures of authority, like the policeman at the lower right, can only snap to attention and salute.

The Harvest of Discontent

TARGETS OF FARM ANGER The revolt of the farmers stirred first on the southern frontier, spreading eastward from Texas through the rest of the Old Confederacy, then west across the plains. Farmers blamed their troubles on obvious inequalities: manufacturers protected by the tariff, railroads with sky-high shipping rates, wealthy bankers who held their mounting debts, expensive intermediaries who stored and processed their commodities. All seemed to profit at the expense of farmers.

The true picture was more complex. The tariff protected industrial goods but also supported some farm commodities such as wool and sugar. Railroad rates, however high, actually fell from 1865 to 1890. Although mortgages were heavy, most were short, no more than four years. Farmers often refinanced them and used the money to buy more land and machinery, thus increasing their debts. Millers and operators of grain elevators or storage silos earned handsome profits, yet every year more of them came under state regulation.

In hard times, when debts mounted and children went hungry, complexity mattered little. And in the South many poor farmers seemed condemned forever to hard times. Credit lay at the root of their problem, because most southern farmers had to borrow money to plant and harvest their crops. The inequities of sharecropping and the crop-lien system (Chapter 18) forced them into debt. When the prices for their crops fell they borrowed still more, stretching the financial resources of the South beyond their meager limits. Within a few years after the Civil War, Massachusetts's banks had five times as much money as all the banks of the Old Confederacy.

Beginning in the 1870s nearly 100,000 debt-ridden farmers a year picked up stakes across the Deep South and fled to Texas to escape this ruinous system of credit, only to find it waiting for them. Others stood and fought, as one pamphlet exhorted in 1889, "not with glittering musket, flaming sword and deadly cannon, but with the silent, potent and all-powerful ballot."

The Origins of the Farmers' Alliance

PATRONS OF HUSBANDRY Before farmers could vote together, they had to get together. Life on the farm was harsh, drab, and isolated. Such conditions shocked Oliver Hudson Kelley as he traveled across the South after the Civil War. In 1867 the young government clerk founded the Patrons of Husbandry to brighten the lives of isolated farmers and broaden their horizons. Local chapters, called "granges," brought a dozen or so farmers and their families together to pray, sing, and learn new farming techniques. The Grangers sponsored fairs, picnics, dances, lectures—anything to break the bleakness of farm life. By 1875 there were 800,000 members in 20,000 locals, most in the Midwest, South, and Southwest.

At first Grangers swore off politics. But in a pattern often repeated, socializing led to economic and then political action. Pooling their money to buy supplies and equipment to store and market their crops, Grangers could avoid the high charges of intermediaries. By the early 1870s they also were lobbying midwestern legislatures to adopt "Granger laws" regulating rates charged by railroads, grain elevator operators, and other middlemen.

GRANGER CASES Eight "Granger cases" came before the Supreme Court in the 1870s to test the new regulatory measures. *Munn v. Illinois* (1877) upheld the right of Illinois to regulate private property (in this case, the giant silos for storing grain) as long as it was "devoted to a public use." Later decisions allowed state regulation of railroads, but only within state lines. Congress responded in 1887 by creating the Interstate Commerce Commission, a federal agency that could regulate commerce across state boundaries. In practice it had little power, but it was a key step toward establishing the public right to oversee private companies.

SOUTHERN ALLIANCE Slumping prices in the 1870s and 1880s bred new farm organizations. Slowly they blended into what the press called the "Alliance movement." The Southern Alliance, formed in Texas in 1875, spread rapidly after Dr. Charles W. Macune took command in 1886. A doctor and lawyer as well as a farmer, Macune planned to expand the state's network of local chapters, or suballiances, into a national network of state Alliance Exchanges. Like the Grangers the exchanges pooled their resources in jointly owned enterprises for buying and selling, milling and storing, banking and manufacturing.

For a brief period, between 1886 and 1892, the Alliance cooperatives grew to more than a million members throughout the South and challenged accepted ways of doing business. Macune claimed that his new Texas Exchange saved members 40 percent on plows and 30 percent on wagons. But most Alliance cooperatives were managed by farmers without the time or experience to succeed. Usually opposed by irate local merchants, the ventures eventually failed.

COLORED FARMERS' ALLIANCE Although the Southern Alliance admitted no African Americans, it encouraged them to organize. A small group of black and white Texans founded the Colored Farmers' National Alliance and Cooperative Union in 1886. By 1891 a quarter of a million farmers had joined. Its operations were largely secret, because public action often brought swift retaliation from white supremacists. When the Colored Farmers' Alliance organized a strike of black cotton pickers near Memphis in 1891, white mobs hunted down and lynched 15 strikers. The murders went unpunished, and the Colored Alliance began to founder.

The Alliance Peaks

The key to Alliance success was not organization but leadership, both at the top and in the middle. Alliance

| *The political and social turbulence of the era is reflected in this cartoon of a businessman being tossed and buffeted by agrarian Populists and "Silverites" as well as Republicans and Democrats.*

lecturers fanned out across the South and the Great Plains, organizing suballiances and teaching new members about finance and cooperative businesses. At least one-quarter of Alliance members were women. The Alliance movement continued the old Grange practice of sponsoring family-oriented activities, such as songfests, parades, picnics, and even burial services. Although the Alliance remained sharply divided over woman suffrage, more than a few women became speakers and organizers. "Wimmin is everywhere," noted one observer. The comment seemed to apply literally to Alliance member Mary Elizabeth Lease, who in the summer of 1890 alone gave 160 speeches.

OCALA DEMANDS In 1890 members of the Alliance met in Ocala, Florida, and issued the "Ocala Demands." The manifesto reflected their deep distrust of "the money power"—large corporations and banks whose financial clout gave them the ability to manipulate markets. The Ocala Demands called on government to correct such abuses by reducing tariffs, abolishing national banks, regulating railroads, and coining silver money freely. The platform also demanded a federal income tax to bring down high

property taxes and the popular election of senators to make government more responsive to the public.

The most innovative feature of the platform came from Charles Macune. His "subtreasury system" would have required the federal government to furnish warehouses for harvested crops and low-interest loans to tide farmers over until prices rose. Under such a system farmers would no longer have had to sell in a glutted market, as they did under the crop-lien system. And they could have exerted control over the money supply, expanding it simply by borrowing at harvest time.

In the elections of 1890 the old parties faced hostile farmers across the nation. In the South the Alliance continued to work within the Democratic Party and elected 4 governors, won 8 legislatures, and sent 44 members of Congress and 3 senators to Washington. In the Great

| *This illustration by artist W. W. Denslow, titled "You Ought to Be Ashamed of Yourself," is from* The Wonderful Wizard of OZ, *published in 1900 by L. Frank Baum. It was the first of 14 best-selling books on the mythical land. Although Baum claimed only to be telling children's stories, some readers have found a symbolic resemblance to the Populist politics of the day. The "yellow brick road" is the gold standard, they say, leading to a place of false promises (the Emerald City of Oz) under the spell of a bellowing politician (the Wizard), who is exposed by the Scarecrow (farmers), the Tin Man (laborers), and the Lion (the Populists).*

Plains, Alliance candidates drew farmers from the Republican Party. Newly created farmer parties elected 5 representatives and 2 senators in Kansas and South Dakota and took over both houses of the Nebraska legislature.

In the West especially, Alliance organizers began to dream of a national third party that would be free from the corporate influence, sectionalism, and racial tensions that split Republicans and Democrats. In their minds it would be a party not just of farmers but also of the downtrodden and the "toilers," including industrial workers.

THE PEOPLE'S PARTY   In February 1892, as the presidential election year began, a convention of 900 labor, feminist, farm, and other reform delegates (100 of them black) met in St. Louis. They founded the People's, or Populist, Party and called for another convention to nominate a presidential ticket. Initially southern Populists held back, clinging to their strategy of working within the Democratic Party. But when newly elected Democrats failed to support Alliance programs, southern leaders such as Tom Watson of Georgia abandoned the Democrats and began recruiting black and white farmers for the Populists. Although he was a wealthy farmer, Watson sympathized with the poor of both races.

The national convention of Populists met in Omaha, Nebraska, on Independence Day, 1892. Their impassioned platform promised to return government "to the hands of 'the plain people.'" More-conservative southern Populists succeeded in blocking a plank for woman suffrage, though western Populists joined the campaign that would win women the right to vote in Colorado in 1893. Planks advocated the subtreasury plan, unlimited coinage of silver and expansion of the money supply, direct election of senators, an income tax, as well as government ownership of railroads, telegraph, and telephone. To attract wage earners the party endorsed the eight-hour workday, restriction of immigration, and a ban on the use of Pinkerton detectives in labor disputes—for the Pinkertons had engaged in a savage gun battle with strikers that year at Andrew Carnegie's Homestead steel plant. Delegates rallied behind the old greenbacker and Union general James B. Weaver, carefully balancing their presidential nomination with a one-legged Confederate veteran as his running mate.

The Election of 1892

The Populists enlivened the otherwise dull campaign of 1892, as Democrat Grover Cleveland and Republican incumbent Benjamin Harrison refought the election of 1888. This time Cleveland won, and for the first session since the Civil War, Democrats gained control of both houses of Congress. The Populists, too, enjoyed success. Weaver became the first third-party candidate to poll over 1 million votes in a presidential contest. Populists elected 3 governors, 5 senators, 10 representatives, and nearly 1,500 members of state legislatures.

LONG-TERM WEAKNESSES OF THE POPULISTS
Despite these short-term strengths, the election revealed dangerous longer-term weaknesses in the People's Party. Across the nation thousands of voters did change political affiliations, but most often from the Republicans to the Democrats, not to the Populists. No doubt a Democratic Party campaign of intimidation and repression hurt the People's Party in the South, where white conservatives had been appalled by Tom Watson's open courtship of black southerners. ("You are kept apart that you may be separately fleeced of your earnings," Watson had told his racially mixed audiences.) In the North, Populists failed to win over labor and most city dwellers. Both parties were more concerned with family budgets than with the problems of farmers and the downtrodden.

The darker side of Populism also put off many Americans. Its rhetoric was often violent; it spoke ominously of conspiracies and stridently in favor of immigration restriction. In fact, in 1892 the Alliance lost members, an omen of defeats to come. But for the present the People's Party had demonstrated two conflicting truths: it showed how far from the needs of many ordinary Americans the two parties had drifted and how difficult it would be to break their power.

 REVIEW

How did the Farmers' Alliance and the People's Party attempt to resolve the problems faced by farmers?

THE NEW REALIGNMENT

ON MAY 5, 1893, ONLY four days after President Grover Cleveland opened the World's Columbian Exposition in Chicago, a wave of bankruptcies swamped the economy. Overexpansion led to a massive economic contraction and once again set in motion the boom-and-bust business cycle that ruined major firms and drove stock prices to all-time lows. By the time the exposition's gleaming White City shut its doors in October, nearly 200,000 workers had lost their jobs in Chicago alone. Millions more across the nation shared that fate in what became the worst depression the Republic had ever experienced.

The sharp contrast between the White City and the nation's economic misery demonstrated the inability of the political system to smooth out the economy's cycle of boom and bust. The new industrial order that had linked Americans economically had brought prosperity in the 1880s. But in 1893 the price of interdependence became obvious, as a downturn in one sector of the economy quickly affected others. With no way to control the swings in the business cycle, depression came on a scale as large as that of the booming prosperity. Out of it emerged a new political realignment that left the Republican Party in control of national politics for decades to come.

Many HISTORIES

WHAT SHOULD THE GOVERNMENT DO?

In 1887 President Grover Cleveland vetoed the "Texas Seed Bill," legislation designed to aid drought-stricken Texas farmers through the natural disaster (Document 1). Four years later, Nebraska farmer W. M. Taylor made a desperate plea for help in the face of natural and man-made disasters (Document 2).

DOCUMENT 1
Government Should Not Help Individuals: President Grover Cleveland

It is represented that a long-continued and extensive drought has existed in certain portions of the State of Texas, resulting in a failure of crops and consequent distress and destitution. Though there has been some difference in statements concerning the extent of the people's needs in the localities thus affected, there seems to be no doubt that there has existed a condition calling for relief; and I am willing to believe that, notwithstanding the aid already furnished, a donation of seed grain to the farmers located in this region, to enable them to put in new crops, would serve to avert a continuance or return of an unfortunate blight.

And yet I feel obliged to withhold my approval of the plan as proposed by this bill, to indulge a benevolent and charitable sentiment through the appropriation of public funds for that purpose.

I can find no warrant for such an appropriation in the Constitution, and I do not believe that the power and duty of the general government ought to be extended to the relief of individual suffering which is in no manner properly related to the public service or benefit. A prevalent tendency to disregard the limited mission of this power and

duty should, I think, be steadfastly resisted, to the end that the lesson should be constantly enforced that, though the people support the government, the government should not support the people.

The friendliness and charity of our countrymen can always be relied upon to relieve their fellow citizens in misfortune. This has been repeatedly and quite lately demonstrated. Federal aid in such cases encourages the expectation of paternal care on the part of the government and weakens the sturdiness of our national character, while it prevents the indulgence among our people of that kindly sentiment and conduct which strengthens the bonds of a common brotherhood.

It is within my personal knowledge that individual aid has, to some extent, already been extended to the sufferers mentioned in this bill. The failure of the proposed appropriation of $10,000 additional, to meet their remaining wants, will not necessarily result in continued distress if the emergency is fully made known to the people of the country.

It is here suggested that the Commissioner of Agriculture is annually directed to expend a large sum of money for the purchase, propagation, and distribution of

seeds and other things of this description, two-thirds of which are, upon the request of senators, representatives, and delegates in Congress, supplied to them for distribution among their constituents.

The appropriation of the current year for this purpose is $100,000, and it will probably be no less in the appropriation for the ensuing year. I understand that a large quantity of grain is furnished for such distribution, and it is supposed that this free apportionment among their neighbors is a privilege which may be waived by our senators and representatives.

If sufficient of them should request the Commissioner of Agriculture to send their shares of the grain thus allowed them, to the suffering farmers of Texas, they might be enabled to sow their crops; the constituents, for whom in theory this grain is intended, could well bear the temporary deprivation, and the donors would experience the satisfaction attending deeds of charity.

Source: President Grover Cleveland Vetoes Disaster Relief Legislation, February 16, 1887, as reprinted in Watts, J. F. & Israel, Fred, eds., *Presidential Documents: The Speeches, Proclamations, and Policies That Have Shaped the Nation from Washington to Clinton.* New York, NY: Routledge, 2000, 164–165.

DOCUMENT 2
Farmers' Problems Are Beyond Their Control: W. M. Taylor

This season is without a parallel in this part of the country. The hot winds burned up the entire crop, leaving thousands of families wholly destitute, many of whom might have been able to run through this crisis had it not been for the galling yoke put on them by the money loaners and sharks—not by charging 7 per cent per annum, which is the lawful rate of interest of even 10 per cent, but the unlawful and inhuman country destroying rate of 3 per cent a month, some going still farther and charging 50 per cent per annum. We are cursed, many of us financially, beyond redemption, not by the hot winds so much as by the swindling game of the bankers and money loaners, who have taken the money and now are after the property, leaving the farmer moneyless and homeless. . . .

I have borrowed for example $1,000. I pay $25 besides to the commission man. I give my note and second mortgage of 3 per cent of the $1,000, which is $30 more. Then I pay 7 per cent on the $1,000 to the actual loaner. Then besides all this I pay for appraising the land, abstract, recording, etc., so when I have secured my loan I am out the first year $150. Yet I am told by the agent who loans me the money, he can't stand to loan at such low rates. This is on the farm, but now come the chattel loan. I must have $50 to save myself. I get the money; my note is made payable in thirty or sixty days for $35, secured by chattel of two horses, harness and wagon, about five times the value of the note. The time comes to pay, I ask for a few days. No I can't wait; must have

the money. If I can't get the money, I have the extreme pleasure of seeing my property taken and sold by this iron handed money loaner while my family and I suffer.

Source: W. M. Taylor Letter to Editor, *Farmer's Alliance* (Lincoln), January 10, 1891, Nebraska Historical Society, reprinted in Marcus, Robert D. & Burner, David, eds., *America Firsthand,* Vol. II. New York, NY: St. Martin's Press, 1992, 90.

THINKING CRITICALLY

How does President Cleveland justify his veto of the "Texas Seed Bill"? What, in his view, is the role of the federal government in times of disaster? What problems does the farmer face? How would President Cleveland have responded to the farmer's letter?

©Buyenlarge/SuperStock

Charles Dana Gibson, the Massachusetts-born illustrator famous for his portraits of well-bred young women in the 1890s, tackles a different subject in this ink drawing, a bread line of mixed classes during the depression of 1893.

The Depression of 1893

Railroad baron and descendant of two presidents Charles Francis Adams Jr. called the depression a "convulsion," but the country experienced it as crushing idleness. In August 1893 unemployment stood at 1 million; by the middle of 1894 it was 3 million. At the end of the year nearly one worker in five was out of a job.

Working- and middle-class families took in boarders, laundry, and sewing to make ends meet. With so many fathers and husbands unemployed, more wives and children left home to work. In the 1890s the number of laboring women increased, from 4 million to 5.3 million, but mainly in the exploitative fields of domestic and clerical work. In the South, where half the nation's working children were employed, child labor rose by 160 percent in textile mills during the decade. Concern for the young became so acute that middle-class women created the League for the Protection of the Family in 1896. Among other things it advocated compulsory education to keep children out of factories and mines.

The federal government had no program to combat the effects of the depression. "While the people should patriotically and cheerfully support their Government," President Cleveland had said at his inauguration, "its functions do not include the support of the people." The states offered little more. Relief, like poverty, was considered a private matter. The burden fell on local charities, benevolent societies, churches, labor unions, and ward bosses. In city after city citizens organized relief committees to distribute bread and clothing until their meager resources gave out.

Others were less charitable. As the popular preacher Henry Ward Beecher told his congregation, "No man in this land suffers from poverty unless it be more than his fault—unless it be his sin." But the scale of hardship was so great, its targets so random, that anyone could be thrown out of work—an industrious neighbor, a factory foreman with 20 years on the

job, a bank president. Older attitudes about personal guilt and responsibility for poverty began to give way to new ideas about its social origins and the obligation of public agencies to help.

The Rumblings of Unrest

Even before the depression, rumblings of unrest had begun to roll across the country. The Great Railroad Strike of 1877 ignited nearly two decades of labor strife (Chapter 19). After 1893 discontent mounted as employers cut wages, laid off employees, and closed factories. During the first year of the depression 1,400 strikes sent more than half a million workers from their jobs. It was the closest the country had ever come to class warfare.

COXEY'S ARMY Uneasy business executives and politicians saw radicalism and the possibility of revolution in every strike. But the depression of 1893 had unleashed a more elemental force: popular discontent. In the spring of 1894, it focused on government inaction. On Easter Sunday, "General" Jacob Coxey, a 39-year-old Populist and factory owner, launched the "Tramps' March on Washington" from Massillon, Ohio. His "Commonweal Army of Christ"—some 500 men, women, and children—descended on Washington to offer "a petition with boots on" for a federal program of public works. On May 1, Coxey's troops, armed with "clubs of peace," massed at the foot of the Capitol. When Coxey entered the Capitol grounds, 100 mounted police routed the protesters and arrested the general for trespassing on the grass. Nothing significant came of the protest, other than to signal a growing demand for federal aid.

Federal help was not to be found. President Cleveland had barely moved into the White House when the depression struck. The country blamed him; he blamed silver. In his view the Sherman Silver Purchase Act (1890) had shaken business confidence by forcing the government to use its shrinking reserves of gold to purchase (though not to coin) silver. Repeal of the act, Cleveland believed, was the way to build gold reserves and restore confidence. After bitter debates Congress complied. The economic tinkering only strengthened the resolve of "silverites" in the Democratic Party to overwhelm Cleveland's conservative "gold" wing.

Worse for the president, repeal of silver purchases brought no economic revival and cost the Democrats seats in Congress. In the short run, abandoning silver hurt the economy by shrinking the money supply just when expansion might have stimulated it by providing needed credit. As panic and unemployment spread, Cleveland's popularity wilted. Democrats were buried in the congressional elections of 1894. Dropping moralistic reforms and stressing national activism, Republicans won control of both the House and the Senate. With the Democrats now confined to the South, the politics of stalemate was over. All that remained for the Republican Party was to capture the White House in 1896.

The Battle of the Standards

The campaign of 1896 quickly became known as the "battle of the standards"—a reference to the burning question of whether gold alone or gold and silver should be the monetary standard. Most Republicans saw gold as the stable base for building business confidence and economic prosperity. They adopted a platform calling for "sound money" supported by gold alone. Their candidate, Governor William McKinley of Ohio, cautiously supported the gold plank and firmly believed in high tariffs to protect American industry.

FREE SILVER Silverites campaigned for "free and independent" coinage of silver, in which the Treasury freely minted all the silver presented to it, independent of other nations. The supply of money would increase, prices would rise, and the economy would revive—or so the silverites' theory held. But the free silver movement was more than a monetary theory. It was a symbolic protest of region and class—of the agricultural South and West against the commercial Northeast, of debt-ridden farm folk against industrialists and financiers.

"CROSS OF GOLD" SPEECH Silverites controlled the Democratic National Convention from the start. They paraded with silver banners, wore silver buttons, and wrote a plank into the platform calling for free and unlimited coinage of the metal. The high point came when William Jennings Bryan of Nebraska stepped to the lectern, threw back his head, and offered himself to "a cause as holy as the cause of liberty—the cause of humanity." The crowd was in a near frenzy as he reached the dramatic climax and spread his arms in mock crucifixion: "You shall not crucify mankind upon a cross of gold." No condemnation of a single gold standard could have been stronger. The next day the convention nominated him for the presidency.

Populists were in a quandary. They expected the Democrats to stick with the pro-gold Cleveland and send unhappy silverites headlong into their camp. Instead, the Democrats stole their thunder. "If we fuse [with the Democrats] we are sunk," complained one Populist. "If we don't fuse, all the silver men we have will leave us for the more powerful Democrats." At a bitter convention, fusionists nominated Bryan for president. The best antifusionists could do was drop the Democrats' vice presidential candidate in favor of the fiery agrarian rebel from Georgia, Tom Watson.

Bryan knew he faced an uphill battle. Adopting a more active style that would be imitated in future campaigns, he traveled 18,000 miles by train, gave as many as 30 speeches a day, and reached perhaps 3 million people in 27 states. The nomination of the People's Party actually did more harm than good by labeling Bryan a Populist (which he was not) and a radical (which he definitely was not). Devoted to the "plain people," the Great Commoner spoke for rural America and Jeffersonian values: small farmers, small towns, small government.

McKinley knew he could not compete with Bryan's barnstorming, so he contented himself with sedate speeches from his front porch in Canton, Ohio. There thousands of his supporters flocked regularly to hear him promise a "full dinner pail" for everyone. The folksy appearance of the campaign belied its reality. From the beginning it had been engineered by Marcus Alonzo Hanna, a talented Ohio industrialist. Hanna relied on modern techniques of organization and marketing. He advertised McKinley, said Theodore Roosevelt, "as if he were patent medicine." Hanna also saturated the country with

millions of leaflets, along with 1,400 speakers attacking free trade and free silver. McKinley won in a walk, the first president since Ulysses Grant to win a majority of the popular vote.

REPUBLICAN COALITION The election proved to be one of the most critical in the Republic's history.* Over the previous three decades political life had been characterized by vibrant campaigns, slim party margins, high voter turnout, and low-profile presidents. The election of 1896 signaled a new era of dwindling party loyalties, stronger presidents, and Republican rule. McKinley's victory broke the political stalemate and forged a powerful coalition that dominated politics for the next 30 years. It rested on the industrial cities of the Northeast and Midwest and combined old support from business, farmers, and Union army veterans with broader backing from industrial wage earners. The Democrats controlled little but the South. And the Populists vanished, but not before leaving a compound legacy: as a catalyst for political realignment, a cry for federal action from the South and the West, and a prelude to a new age of reform.

The Rise of Jim Crow Politics

In 1892, despite the stumping of such Populists as Tom Watson, African Americans cast their ballots for Republicans, when they were permitted to vote freely. But increasingly, their voting rights were being curtailed across the South.

As the nineteenth century drew to a close, a long-standing racialism—categorizing people on the basis of race—deepened. The arrival of "new" immigrants from eastern and southern Europe and the acquisition of new overseas colonies highlighted differences among races and helped encourage prejudices that stridently justified segregation and other forms of racial control. In the South racialism was enlisted into a political purpose: preventing an alliance of poor blacks and whites that might topple white conservative Democrats. The white supremacy campaign, on the face of it directed at African Americans, also had a broader target in the world of politics: rebellion from below, whether black or white.

DISENFRANCHISEMENT Mississippi, whose Democrats had led the move to "redeem" their state from Republican Reconstruction, in 1890 took the lead in disenfranchising or depriving African Americans of the right to vote. A new state constitution required voters to pay a poll tax and pass a literacy test, requirements that eliminated the great majority of black voters. Conservative Democrats favored the plan because it also reduced voting among poor whites, who were most likely to join opposition parties. Before the new constitution went into effect, Mississippi contained more than 250,000 eligible voters, black and white. By 1892, after its adoption, there were fewer than 77,000.

---

*Five elections, in addition to the contest of 1896, are often cited as critical shifts in voter allegiance and party alignments: the Federalist defeat of 1800, Andrew Jackson's rise in 1828, Lincoln's Republican triumph of 1860, Al Smith's Democratic loss in 1928, and—perhaps—Ronald Reagan's conservative tide of 1980.

Pinning the Winning Ticket

A lunch box (or "dinner pail") used by workmen

What are the advantages of this transparent plastic (celluloid) button?

McKINLEY AND ROOSEVELT — FOUR YEARS MORE OF THE FULL DINNER PAIL

The back of the button includes a metal pin, allowing the button to be easily affixed to clothing

©The Frent Collection/Getty Images

Sometimes even the smallest objects yield a wealth of information to historians. This button from the presidential election of 1900 displays the names of running mates William McKinley (for president) and Theodore Roosevelt (for vice president), along with their campaign slogan, a repetition of the promise McKinley made in his first successful bid for the presidency four years earlier. Celluloid buttons first appeared in the presidential election of 1896. Cheap and easy to produce, they quickly turned into electioneering staples and signaled a shift from big political rallies and emotional appeals to promotional campaigns based on education and advertising. The Ohio industrialist Mark Hanna pioneered many of these practices, including the use of short newsreel films of the candidate, when he managed McKinley's run for the White House in 1896. In 1900 McKinley's running mate Theodore Roosevelt at first deplored the unvarnished marketing of candidates. Still, the techniques worked. Celluloid buttons became the fastest-growing article in the history of American political campaigns.

THINKING CRITICALLY

What slogan does the pin contain and to which voting groups might it appeal? What visual cue reinforces the slogan? What does the pin tell us about turn-of-the-century politics? Why did political campaigns turn to advertising techniques, and what were the long-term effects of the shift?

Soon an all-white combination of conservatives and "reformers"–those disgusted by frequent election-stealing with blocs of black votes–passed disenfranchisement laws across the South. In 1898 the Supreme Court upheld these laws in *Williams v. Mississippi,* ruling that they were valid because they did not discriminate solely against African Americans. The decision dealt a mortal blow to the Republican Party in the South for generations because much of its support in the region came from African Americans. By 1908 white-supremacy and disenfranchisement campaigns had won in every southern state, barring many poor whites as well as blacks from voting.

The disenfranchisement campaign succeeded in achieving its broad aim of splitting rebellious whites from blacks, as the tragic fate of Tom Watson demonstrated. Only a dozen years after his biracial campaign of 1892, Watson was promoting black disenfranchisement and white supremacy in Georgia. Like other southern Populists, Watson returned to the Democratic Party still hoping to help poor whites. But under the increased atmosphere of intolerance, only by playing a powerful race card could he hope to win election. "What does civilization owe the negro?" he asked bitterly. "Nothing! Nothing!! NOTHING!!!"

To mount a successful campaign for disenfranchisement, white conservatives inflamed racial passions. They staged "White Supremacy Jubilees" and peppered newspaper editorials with complaints of "bumptious" and "impudent" African Americans. The lynchings of blacks peaked during the 1890s, averaging over a hundred a year for the decade. Most took place in the South.

The African American Response

IDA B. WELLS African Americans worked out their own responses to the climate of intolerance. Ida B. Wells, a black woman born into slavery, turned her talents into a nationwide campaign against lynching when a friend, Thomas Moss, and two of his partners in the People's Grocery were brutally murdered in Memphis after a fight with a white competitor in 1892. Wells meticulously documented the murders of African Americans across the South, demonstrating an astounding 200 percent increase between 1882 and 1892. Wells turned antilynching into a personal crusade. She spent much of her time educating Americans about the use of lynching and other forms of mob violence as devices for terrorizing African Americans in the absence of slavery. Black men like Thomas Moss, who might want to start black-owned businesses or alter race relations in the South, were particular targets because they threatened the prevailing racial and economic hierarchy in the South. Though her lobbying failed to produce a federal antilynching law, Wells did help organize black women, eventually into the National Association of Colored Women in 1896. It supported wide-ranging reforms, including in education, housing, and health care, and, of course, antilynching.

Wells's campaign focused on mob violence, but another former slave, Booker T. Washington, emphasized the need for accepting the framework for race relations and working within it. "I love the South," Washington reassured an audience of white and black southerners in Atlanta in 1895. He conceded that white prejudice against blacks existed throughout the region but nonetheless counseled African Americans to accept what was offered them and work for their economic betterment through manual labor. Every laborer who learned a trade, every farmer who tilled the land could increase his or her savings. And those earnings amounted to "a little green ballot" that "no one will throw out or refuse to count." Toward that end Washington organized the Tuskegee Institute in 1881 and created a curriculum stressing vocational skills for farming, manual trades, and industrial work.

ATLANTA COMPROMISE Many white Americans hailed what one black critic called the "Atlanta Compromise" because it struck the note of patient humility they were eager to hear. For African Americans it made the best of a bad situation. Washington, an astute politician, discovered that philanthropists across the nation hoped to make Tuskegee an example of their generosity. He was the honored guest of Andrew Carnegie at his imposing Skibo Castle in Scotland. California railroad magnate Collis Huntington became his friend, as did other business executives eager to discuss "public and social questions."

Washington always preached accommodation to the racial caste system. He accepted segregation (as long as separate

(*left*) Source: Library of Congress, Prints and Photographs Division [LC-DIG-ds-07456]; (*right*) ©Everett Collection Inc/Alamy

| *Booker T. Washington and Ida B. Wells reflected two different responses to the drive by southern whites for a comprehensive system of segregation and white supremacy. Washington called for hard work and patient humility on the part of African Americans as a way to achieve gradual progress. Wells viewed the rise in lynchings as clear evidence that African Americans were being walled off because they had achieved success through hard work. Only publicity, protest, and political action on a national scale, she argued, could overturn the campaign to enforce the increasingly strict "color line" of segregation.*

facilities were equal) and qualifications on voting (if they applied to white citizens as well). Above all, Washington sought economic self-improvement for common black folk in fields and factories. In 1900 he organized the National Negro Business League to help establish African Americans in business as the leaders of their people. The rapid growth of local chapters (320 by 1907) extended his influence across the country.

In the "Solid South" (as well as an openly racist North), it was Washington's restrained approach that set the agenda for most African Americans. An all-white Democratic Party split the biracial coalition of the early 1890s between black and white Populists and dominated the region, but remained a minority on the national level.

McKinley in the White House

In William McKinley, Republicans found a skillful chief with a national agenda and personal charm. He cultivated news reporters, openly walked the streets of Washington, and courted the public with handshakes and flowers from his own lapel. Firmly but carefully, he curbed the power of old-time state bosses. When necessary, he even prodded Congress to action. In all these ways he foreshadowed "modern" presidents, who would act as party leaders rather than as executive caretakers.

Fortune at first smiled on McKinley. When he entered the White House, the economy had already begun its recovery. Factory orders were slowly increasing, and unemployment dropped. Farm prices climbed. New discoveries of gold in Alaska and South Africa expanded the supply of money without causing "gold bugs" to panic that currency was being destabilized by silver.

Freed from the burdens of the economic crisis, McKinley called a special session of Congress to revise the tariff. In

An 1896 Republican campaign poster features presidential hopeful William McKinley atop a giant gold coin engraved with the words "sound money" and supported by workers and businessmen alike. The poster promises domestic prosperity and respect overseas. The links between prosperity and empire as well as commerce and civilization were made not only in McKinley's campaign but also by later presidents.
Source: Library of Congress, Prints and Photographs Division [LC-USZC4-1329]

1897 the Dingley Tariff raised protective rates still higher but allowed tariffs to come down if other nations lowered theirs. McKinley also sought a solution for resolving railroad strikes, like the earlier Pullman conflict, before they turned violent. The Erdman Act of 1898 set up machinery for government arbitration of labor disputes with railroads. McKinley even began laying plans for stronger regulation of trusts.

The same expansiveness that pushed the United States across the continent and shipped grain and cotton abroad was also drawing the country into a race for empire and a war with Spain. Regulation—and a true age of reform—would await the next century.

> ✓ **REVIEW**
>
> How did the election of 1896 resolve the politics of stalemate of the late nineteenth century?

VISIONS OF EMPIRE

THE CRISIS WITH SPAIN WAS only the affair of the moment that turned American attention abroad. Underlying the conflict were larger forces linking the future of the United States with international events. By the 1890s southern farmers were exporting half their cotton crop to factories worldwide, while western wheat farmers earned some 30 to 40 percent of their income from markets abroad. John D. Rockefeller's Standard Oil Company shipped about two-thirds of its refined products overseas, and Cyrus McCormick supplied Russian farmers with his famous reaper for harvesting crops.

More than these growing commercial ties turned American heads overseas. Since the 1840s, expansionists had spoken of a Manifest Destiny to overspread the North American continent from the Atlantic to the Pacific. Between 1880 and 1914

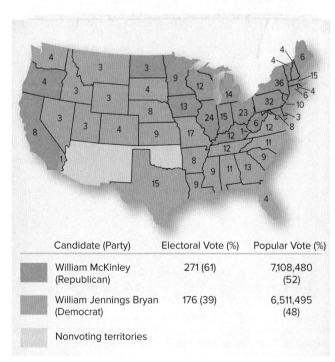

Candidate (Party)	Electoral Vote (%)	Popular Vote (%)
William McKinley (Republican)	271 (61)	7,108,480 (52)
William Jennings Bryan (Democrat)	176 (39)	6,511,495 (48)
Nonvoting territories		

ELECTION OF 1896

they watched enviously as Western nations gobbled up large chunks of the rest of the world. In 1878 less than 10 percent of Africa lay under European rule. By 1900 nearly the entire continent was controlled by Europeans. In Asia, British influence radiated outward from its stronghold in India, while France ruled Indochina (present-day Vietnam, Cambodia, and Laos). Armed with new, rapid-firing machine guns and the drug quinine to control deadly malaria, Western soldiers, merchants, and missionaries established a new age of imperialism, sometimes through outright conquest and occupation, as in India and Indochina, sometimes by forging strong ties of trade and commerce, as in Latin America.

European technology could be devastating for native populations. In 1898, at the Battle of Omdurman, a small Anglo-Egyptian contingent under the command of British general Horatio Kitchener faced 40,000 Sudanese. The Anglo-Egyptian force was armed with machine guns and artillery, the Sudanese with muskets and spears. When the smoke cleared hours later, 11,000 Sudanese had been shredded to pieces; only 48 British lay dead.

Imperialism—European versus American Style

The scramble for empire was well under way by the time the Americans, Germans, and Japanese entered the race in the late nineteenth century. Spain and Portugal still clung to the remnants of their seventeenth-century colonial empires. In the early nineteenth century England, France, and Russia accelerated their drive to control foreign peoples and lands. By the late nineteenth century a new age of **imperialism** had dawned. For the first time, powerful new arms and intersecting networks of communication, transportation, and commerce brought truly global empires within reach.

The speed and efficiency with which Europeans expanded prompted many Americans to argue for this European-style imperialism of conquest and possession. But other Americans preferred a more indirect imperialism: one that exported products, ideas, and influence. To them, this American imperialism seemed somehow purer, for without naked conquest Americans could be portrayed as bearers of long-cherished values: democracy, free-enterprise capitalism, and Protestant Christianity.

While Americans tried to justify imperial control in the name of such values, social, economic, and political forces were drawing them rapidly into the hard-knuckled race for empire. The growth of industrial networks linked them to international markets as never before, whether they were Arkansas sharecroppers dependent on world cotton prices or Pittsburgh steelworkers whose jobs were made possible by orders for Singer sewing machines for Europe, China, and the Hawaiian Islands.

The Shapers of American Imperialism

Although the climate for expansion and imperialism was present at the end of the nineteenth century, the small farmer or steelworker was little concerned with how the United States advanced its goals abroad. An elite group—Christian missionaries, intellectuals, business leaders, and commercial farmers—joined navy careerists to shape a more active American imperialism.

Without a strong navy, imperialism of any sort was out of the question. By 1880 the once-proud Civil War fleet of more than 600 warships was rotting from neglect. The U.S. Navy ranked twelfth in the world, behind Denmark and Chile. The United States had a coastal fleet but no functional fleet to protect its interests overseas. Discontented navy officers now combined with trade-hungry business leaders to lobby Congress for a modern navy.

MAHAN CALLS FOR A STRONG NAVY Alfred Thayer Mahan, a U.S. Navy captain and later admiral, formulated their ideas into a widely accepted theory of **navalism.** In *The Influence of Sea Power upon History* (1890), Mahan argued that great nations were seafaring powers that relied on foreign trade for wealth and might. In times of overproduction and depression, as had occurred repeatedly in the United States after the Civil War, overseas markets assumed even greater importance. The only way to protect foreign markets, Mahan reasoned, was with large cruisers and battleships. Operating far from American shores, these ships would need coaling stations and other resupply facilities throughout the world.

Mahan's logic was so persuasive and the profits to be reaped from foreign trade were so great that in the 1880s Congress launched a program to rebuild the old wood-and-sail navy with steam vessels of steel. By 1900 the U.S. Navy ranked third in the world. With a modern navy, the country had the means to become an imperial power.

MISSIONARIES Protestant missionaries provided a spiritual rationale for imperialism that complemented Mahan's military and economic arguments. Because missionaries often encountered people whose cultural differences often made them unreceptive to the Christian message, many of them believed that natives first had to become Western in culture before turning Christian in belief. Missionaries introduced Western goods, schools, and systems of government administration—any "civilizing medium," as one minister remarked. They eagerly took up what they called the "white man's burden" of introducing Western civilization to the "colored" races of the world but opposed outright military or political intervention.

"SOCIAL DARWINISM" From scholars, academics, and scientists came racial theories to justify European and American expansion. Charles Darwin's *On the Origin of Species* (1859) had popularized the notion that among animal species, the fittest survived througha process of natural selection. "Social Darwinists" argued that the same laws of survival governed the social order. When applied aggressively, imperialists used social Darwinism to justify theories of white supremacy as well as the slaughter and enslavement of nonwhite native peoples who resisted conquest. When combined with the somewhat more humane "white man's burden" professed by Christian missionaries, American imperialism included uplifting natives by spreading Western ideas, religion, and government.

COMMERCIAL FACTORS Perhaps more compelling than either religious or racial motives for American expansion was the

>> **MAPPING THE PAST** <<

IMPERIALIST EXPANSION, 1900

Source: Library of Congress, Prints and Photographs Division [LC-USZC4-5409]

"We cannot retreat from any soil where Providence has unfurled our banner; it is ours to save that soil for liberty and civilization."—Senator Albert Beveridge on American imperialist expansion.

CONTEXT

The race for colonies accelerated in the late nineteenth century as European nations scrambled for empire. New world powers—in particular Germany, Italy, Japan, and the United States—expanded their holdings. A comparison of Africa in 1878 (inset) and 1900 shows how quickly Europeans extended their colonial empires. Often resource-poor countries like Japan and England saw colonies as a way to acquire raw materials: diamonds from South Africa or tin from Southeast Asia. A closer look reveals that four of the most rapidly industrializing countries—Germany, Japan, Russia, and the United States—had few if any overseas possessions, even in 1900. And while China appears to be undivided, all the major powers had established spheres of influence there.

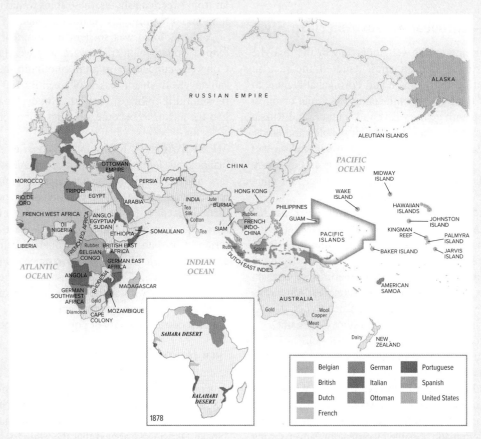

MAP READING

1. What is the biggest U.S. possession on the map? The next biggest?
2. What raw materials were imperial nations seeking in Africa? In India and Southeast Asia? In Australia and New Zealand?
3. Which European nation appears to possess the most geographically widespread empire?

MAP INTERPRETATION

1. Which countries were winning the race for empire by 1900? On what grounds should we make that judgment?
2. What geographic factors explain the location of U.S. possessions?
3. Why did rapidly industrializing nations such as Germany, Japan, Russia, and the United States have so few overseas possessions?

When Thomas Edison invented the phonograph in 1877, few people would have thought of it as a weapon of conquest. But when Americans and Europeans brought the machine to less technologically advanced societies, native peoples were awestruck by the sounds it made and sometimes cowed by those who controlled it. These white men, it appeared, had the power to conjure up the voices of invisible speakers and summon music from the air.
©Comstock Images/Alamy

need for trade. The business cycle of boom and bust reminded Americans of the unpredictability of their economy. In hard times, people sought salvation wherever they could, and one obvious road to recovery lay in markets abroad. Entrepreneurs such as Minor Keith and his Tropical Fruit Company (later the mammoth United Fruit Company) had already constructed a railroad in Costa Rica and begun importing bananas from Central America. In Cuba and Hawaii, American planters were reaping

harvests of sugarcane, pineapples, and other commercial crops to be processed and sold in domestic and foreign markets. By 1900 the Singer Sewing Machine Company was sending some 60,000 sales agents across the globe to hawk the virtues of their "iron tailor." It is no wonder, then, that as American companies extended their investments abroad and the depression of 1893 deepened at home, the National Association of Manufacturers insisted that the "expansion of our foreign trade is [the] only promise of relief."

Dreams of a Commercial Empire

WILLIAM HENRY SEWARD No one had done more to initiate the idea of a "new empire" for the United States than William Henry Seward, secretary of state (1861–1869) under Lincoln and Andrew Johnson. Seward believed that "empire has . . . made its way constantly westward . . . until the tides of the renewed and decaying civilizations of the world meet on the shores of the Pacific Ocean." The United States

Source: Library of Congress, Prints and Photographs Division [LC-USZC2-1029]

Missionaries often viewed the Chinese as uncivilized "heathen" whose souls needed saving and whose culture needed civilizing. This cartoon, published around 1900, pokes fun at the common stereotype by suggesting what the Chinese must think of American "heathen." "Contributions Received Here to Save the Foreign Devils," reads the sign of the Chinese "preacher," who laments the uncivilized behavior of corrupt American city governments, feuding backwoodsmen, rioting laborers, and mobs tormenting Chinese and black Americans.

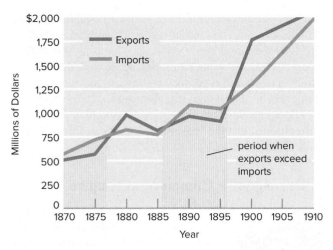

Balance of U.S. Imports and Exports, 1870–1910

After the depression of 1893 both imports and exports rose sharply, suggesting one reason why the age of imperialism was so closely linked with the emerging global industrial economy.

Source: Library of Congress, Prints and Photographs Division [LC-DIG-ggbain-13386]

| *Sisal, a form of agave, produced a strong fiber that was used for rope and twine. Native to Mexico, the plant was exported to Hawaii in the late nineteenth century as a way of diversifying the Hawaiian economy. It quickly multiplied, becoming an invasive species. The backbreaking work of harvesting the leaves was often done by workers recruited from Japan, such as those pictured here.*

must thus be prepared to win supremacy in the Far East—not by planting colonies or sending troops but by pursuing trade. The idea that a commercial empire could be gained by demanding equal access to foreign markets made Seward's strategy revolutionary.

ACQUISITION OF MIDWAY AND ALASKA While he pursued ties to Japan, Korea, and China, Seward promoted a transcontinental railroad at home and a canal across Central America. Link by link, he was trying to connect eastern factories to western ports in the United States and, from there, to markets and resources in Asia. In pursuit of these goals Seward made two acquisitions in 1867: Midway Island in the Pacific and Alaska. Unimportant by itself, the value of Midway lay as a way station to Asia not far from Hawaii, where missionary planters were already establishing an American presence. Critics called Alaska "Seward's Folly," but he paid only about 2 cents an acre for a mineral-rich territory twice the size of Texas.

Seward's conviction that the future of the United States lay in the Pacific and Asia produced little in his lifetime. But it flourished in the 1890s, when Mahan provided the naval theory necessary to make the leap and the vanishing American frontier supplied an economic rationale for extending Manifest Destiny beyond the nation's continental borders. In the 1880s Secretary of State James G. Blaine had already began to look southward for ways to expand American trade and influence to Central and South America, where Great Britain had interests of its own to protect.

BLAINE'S PAN-AMERICAN UNION Blaine launched a campaign to cancel the Clayton-Bulwer Treaty (1850), which shared with Great Britain rights to any canal built in Central America. Only in 1901, when the two nations signed the Hay-Pauncefote Treaty (named for the American Secretary of State John Hay and British ambassador Julian Pauncefote), did Blaine's efforts have the desired results. Great Britain ceded its

interest in building a canal across the Central American isthmus in return for a U.S. promise to leave such a canal open to ships of all nations. Blaine also tried to shift Central American imports from British to U.S. goods by proposing the creation of a "customs union" to reduce trade barriers in the Americas. His plan resulted in only a weak Pan-American Union to foster peaceful understanding in the region. Latin American nations balked at his more important aim of lowering their tariffs.

If American expansionists wanted to extend trade across the Pacific to China, Hawaii was the crucial link. It afforded a fine naval base and a refueling station along the route to Asia. In 1893 American sugar planters overthrew the recently enthroned Queen Liliuokalani, a Hawaiian nationalist eager to rid the island of American influence. Their success was ensured when a contingent of U.S. marines arrived ashore on the pretext of protecting American lives.

Eager to avoid the McKinley Tariff's new tax on sugar imported into the United States, planters lobbied for the annexation of Hawaii, but President Cleveland refused. He was no foe of expansion but was, as his secretary of state noted, "unalterably opposed to stealing territory, or of annexing people against their consent, and the people of Hawaii do not favor annexation." The idea of incorporating the nonwhite population also troubled Cleveland. For a time, matters stood at a stalemate.

 REVIEW

What social, economic, and cultural factors drew the United States into the race for empire?

THE IMPERIAL MOMENT

CUBA IN REVOLT IN 1895, AFTER ALMOST 15 years of planning from exile in the United States, José Martí returned to Cuba to renew the colony's struggle for independence from Spain. With cries of "Cuba libre," Martí and his rebels cut railroad lines, destroyed sugar mills, and set fire to the cane fields. Within a year, rebel forces controlled more than half the island. But even as they fought the Spanish, the rebels worried about the United States. Their island, just 90 miles off the coast of Florida, had long been a target of American expansionists and business interests. Martí had no illusions. "I have lived in the bowels of the monster," he explained of his exile in the United States, "and I know it."

The Spanish struck back at Martí and his followers with brutal force. Governor-General Valeriano Weyler herded half a million Cubans from their homes into fortified camps where filth, disease, and starvation killed perhaps 200,000. Outside these "reconcentration" camps, Weyler chased the rebels across the countryside, polluting drinking water, killing farm animals, burning crops.

The revolt in Cuba was only the first round in a struggle that would eventually end in a war between the United States and Spain. By the time it was over the Spanish-American War left Spain defeated and banished from the Western Hemisphere, Cuba free of Spanish rule, and the United States with new colonial possessions in the Pacific and the Caribbean. The knotty problem of what to do with them soon became the subject of a national debate. For better or worse, America's imperial moment had arrived.

Mounting Tensions

President Cleveland had little sympathy for the Cuban revolt, but Republican expansionists such as Theodore Roosevelt and Massachusetts senator Henry Cabot Lodge wanted to recognize Cuban independence—a step that if taken would likely provoke war with Spain. William McKinley, however, was only a moderate expansionist. As president, he lobbied Spain privately to stop cracking down on the rebels and destroying American-owned property. With over $50 million invested in Cuban sugar and an annual trade of over $100 million, American business interests had much to lose in a war with Spain.

In October 1897 Spain promised to remove the much-despised Weyler, end the reconcentration policy, and offer Cuba greater autonomy. The shift encouraged McKinley to resist pressure at home for more hostile action. But leaders of the Spanish army in Cuba had no desire to compromise. Although Weyler was removed, the military renewed efforts to quash the rebellion. Early in 1898, McKinley dispatched the battleship *Maine* to show that the United States meant to protect its interests and its citizens.

Then in February 1898 the State Department received a stolen copy of a letter to Cuba sent by the Spanish minister in Washington, Enrique Dupuy de Lôme. So did newspaper publisher William Randolph Hearst, a pioneer of sensationalist, or **yellow**, **journalism**, who was eager for war with Spain. "WORST INSULT TO THE UNITED STATES IN ITS HISTORY," screamed the headline of Hearst's *New York Journal.* What had de Lôme actually written? After referring to McKinley as a "would-be politician," the letter admitted that Spain had no intention of changing policy in Cuba. The Spanish planned to crush the rebels. Red-faced Spanish officials recalled de Lôme, but most Americans now believed that Spain had deceived the United States.

SINKING OF THE *MAINE* On February 15, 1898, as the USS *Maine* lay peacefully at anchor in the Havana harbor, explosions ripped through its hull. Within minutes the ship sank to the bottom, killing some 260 American sailors. Much later, an official investigation concluded that the explosion was the result of spontaneous combustion in a coal bunker aboard ship. Most Americans at the time, inflamed by hysterical news accounts, concluded that Spanish agents had sabotaged the ship. McKinley sought a diplomatic solution but also a $50 million appropriation "to get ready for war."

TELLER AMENDMENT Pressures for war proved too great to resist, and on April 11, McKinley asked Congress to authorize "forceful intervention" in Cuba. Nine days later

An investigation years later concluded that the sinking of the Maine resulted from a spontaneous explosion aboard ship, but at the time fervent patriots turned the event into a call for war and, as can be seen in the lower-right corner, memorabilia, here in the form of a button carrying the famous rallying cry, "Remember the Maine." The peaceful arrival of the Maine in Havana harbor is depicted in the upper-left corner of the painting, the grisly aftermath of the explosion in the large painting.

(*left*) ©The Frent Collection/ Getty Images; (*right*) ©Glass-house Images/Alamy

Congress recognized Cuban independence, insisted on the withdrawal of Spanish forces, and gave the president authority to use military force. In a flush of idealism, legislators also adopted the Teller Amendment, renouncing any aim to annex Cuba. Certainly both idealism and moral outrage led many Americans down the path to war. But in the end, what Secretary of State John Hay called the "splendid little war" resulted from less lofty ambitions—empire, trade, glory.

The Imperial War

For the 5,462 men who died there was little splendid about the Spanish-American War. Only 379 gave their lives in battle. The rest suffered from accidents, disease, and the mismanagement of an unprepared army. As war began, the American force totaled only 30,000, none of whom had been trained for fighting in tropical climates. The sudden expansion to 60,000 troops and 200,000 volunteers overtaxed the army's graft-ridden supply system. Rather than tropical uniforms, some troops were issued winter woolens, and some fed on rations that were diseased, rotten, or even lethally spoiled. Others found themselves fighting with weapons from the Civil War.

DEWEY AT MANILA The navy fared better. Decisions in the 1880s to modernize the fleet now paid off handsomely. Naval battles largely determined the outcome of the war. As soon as war was declared, Admiral George Dewey ordered his Asiatic battle squadron from China to the Philippines. Just before dawn on May 1, he began shelling the Spanish ships in Manila Bay. Five hours later the entire Spanish squadron lay at the bottom of the bay. Three hundred eighty-one Spaniards were killed, but only one American died, a ship's engineer who succumbed to a heart attack. Dewey had no plans to follow up his stunning victory with an invasion. His fleet carried no marines with which to take the city of Manila. So ill-prepared was President McKinley for war, let alone victory, that only after learning of Dewey's success did he order 11,000 American troops to the Philippines.

Halfway around the globe, another Spanish fleet had slipped into Santiago harbor in Cuba just before the arrival of the U.S. Navy. Under Admiral William Sampson, the navy blockaded the island, expecting the Spanish to flee under the cover of darkness. Instead, on July 3, the Spanish fleet made a desperate daylight dash for the open seas. So startled were the Americans that several of their ships nearly collided as they rushed to attack their exposed foes. All seven Spanish ships were sunk, with 474 casualties. Only one American was killed and one wounded. With Cuba now cut off from Spain, the war was virtually won.

War in Cuba

Few Americans had heard of the Philippine Islands; fewer still could locate them on a globe. But most Americans knew that Cuba lay barely 90 miles off the Florida coast.

RACIAL TENSIONS Before the outbreak of hostilities, Tampa, Florida, was a sleepy coastal town with a single railroad line. When it became the port of embarkation for the Cuban expeditionary force, the town exploded. Some 17,000 troops arrived in the spring of 1898 alone. Tampa's overtaxed facilities soon broke down, spawning disease, tension, and finally racial violence. President McKinley had authorized the army to raise five volunteer regiments of black soldiers. By the time war was declared over 8,000 African Americans had signed up, half of them stationed around segregated Tampa. They found that although they could sail off to die freeing the peasants of Cuba, they were forbidden from buying a soda at the local drugstore. "Is America any better than Spain?" one dismayed black chaplain wondered. After drunken white troops shot at a black child, black troops in Tampa rioted. Three white and 27 black Americans were wounded in the melee.

Matters were scarcely less chaotic as 17,000 disorganized troops and hundreds of reporters finally scrambled aboard ship early in June 1898. There they sat for a week, until sailing on June 14 for Santiago and battle. By June 30 the Americans had landed to challenge some 24,000 Spanish, many equipped with modern rifles. The following day 7,000 Americans—including the black soldiers of the Ninth and Tenth Cavalry regiments—stormed up heavily fortified San Juan Hill and nearby Kettle Hill.

THE ROUGH RIDERS Among them Lieutenant Colonel Theodore Roosevelt thrilled at the experience of battle. He had raised a cavalry troop of cowboys and college polo players, originally called "Teddy's Texas Tarantulas." By the time they arrived in Cuba, the volunteers were answering to the

Black veterans of the Indian Wars of the American West along with volunteers, segregated and commanded by white officers, made up almost a quarter of the U.S. force that invaded Cuba. Members of the Tenth Cavalry, shown here, were clearly in no mood to be subjected to the harassment they and other black troops encountered around Tampa. Later the Tenth Cavalry supported a charge by Colonel Teddy Roosevelt's Rough Riders at the battle of San Juan Hill.

Courtesy of HMCPL Special Collections: http://digitalarchives.hmcpl.org

nickname "Rough Riders." As they charged toward the high ground, Roosevelt yelled: "Gentlemen, the Almighty God and the just cause are with you. Gentlemen, charge!" The withering fire drowned out his shrill, squeaky voice, so he repeated the call to his troops. Charge they did and conquer the enemy, though the battle cost more than 1,500 American casualties. (See After the Fact, at the end of the chapter.)

Without a fleet for cover or way to escape, the Spanish garrison surrendered on July 17. In the Philippines a similar brief battle preceded the American capture of Manila on August 13. The "splendid little war" was over in less than four months.

Peace and the Debate over Empire

Conquering Cuba and the Philippines proved easier than deciding what to do with the islands. The Teller Amendment had renounced any American claim to Cuba. But clearly the United States had not freed the island to see chaos reign or American business and military interests excluded. And what of the Philippines—and Spanish Puerto Rico, which American forces had taken without a struggle? Powerful public and congressional sentiment pushed McKinley to claim empire as the fruits of victory.

ANNEXING HAWAII   The president himself favored such a course. The battle in the Pacific highlighted the need for naval bases and coaling stations. "To maintain our flag in the Philippines,

we must raise our flag in Hawaii," New York's *The Sun* insisted. On July 7, 1898, McKinley signed a joint congressional resolution annexing Hawaii, as planters wanted for nearly a decade. The Philippines presented a more difficult problem. Filipinos greeted the American forces as liberators, not new colonizers.

AGUINALDO   The popular leader of the rebel forces fighting Spain, Emilio Aguinaldo, had returned to the islands from exile in Hong Kong on an American ship. To the rebels' dismay, McKinley insisted that the islands were under American authority until the peace treaty settled matters. Such a settlement, McKinley knew, would have to include American control of the Philippines. He had no intention of leaving Spain in charge or of seeing the islands fall to other European rivals. American military advisers warned that without control of the entire island of Luzon, its capital, Manila, would be indefensible as the naval base McKinley wanted. Nor, McKinley felt certain, were the Filipinos capable of self-government. Aguinaldo and his rebels thought otherwise, and in June Aguinaldo declared himself president of a new Philippine republic.

ANTI-IMPERIALISTS   Many influential Americans—former president Grover Cleveland, steel baron Andrew Carnegie, novelist Mark Twain—opposed annexation of the Philippines. Yet even these anti-imperialists favored expansion, if only in the form of trade that would benefit the nation

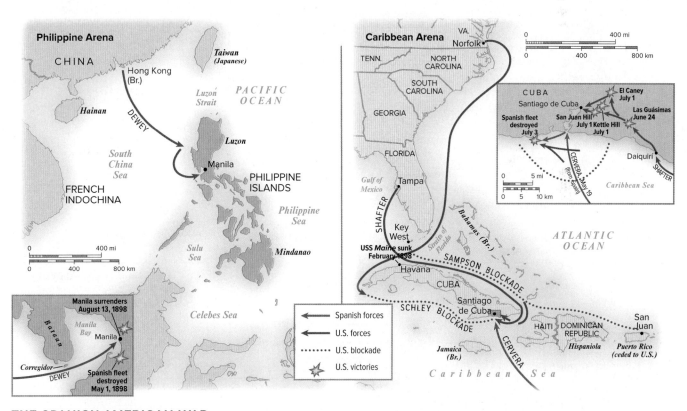

THE SPANISH-AMERICAN WAR

*Had the Spanish-American War depended largely on ground forces, the ill-prepared U.S. Army might have fared poorly. But the key to success, in both Cuba and the Philippines, was naval warfare, in which the recently modernized American fleet had a critical edge. Proximity to Cuba also gave the United States an advantage in delivering troops and supplies and in maintaining a naval blockade that isolated Spanish forces. **How did the geographic location of the United States help and hinder it in the Spanish-American War?***

without the costs of maintaining the Philippines as a colony. Annexation would mire the United States too deeply in the quicksands of Asian politics, many business leaders argued. More important, a large, costly fleet would be necessary to defend the islands. To the imperialists that was precisely the point: a large fleet was crucial to the interests of a powerful commercial nation.

THE ROLE OF RACE   Racial ideas shaped both sides of the argument. Imperialists believed that the racial inferiority of nonwhites made occupation of the Philippines necessary, and they were ready to assume the "white man's burden" by governing the islands. Filipinos, they said, would gradually be taught the virtues of Western civilization, Christianity, democracy, and self-rule. (In fact, most Filipinos were already Catholic after many years under Spanish rule.) Anti-imperialists feared racial intermixing and the possibility of Filipino and other Asian workers flooding the American labor market. They also maintained that dark-skinned people would never develop the capacity for self-government. An American government in the Philippines could

be sustained only at the point of bayonets—yet the U.S. Constitution made no provision for governing people without representation or equal rights. Such a precedent abroad, the anti-imperialists warned, might one day threaten American liberties at home.

Still, when the Senate debated the Treaty of Paris ending the Spanish-American War in 1898, the imperialists had the support of the president, most of Congress, and the majority of public opinion. Even a sturdy anti-imperialist such as William Jennings Bryan, defeated by McKinley in 1896, endorsed the treaty. In it Spain surrendered title to Cuba, ceded Puerto Rico and Guam to the United States, and in return for $20 million turned over the Philippines as well.

From Colonial War to Colonial Rule

PHILIPPINE-AMERICAN WAR   Managing an empire turned out to be even more devilish than acquiring one. As the Senate debated annexation of the Philippines in Washington, rebels fought with an American patrol outside of Manila. The few Americans who paid attention to the ensuing clash called

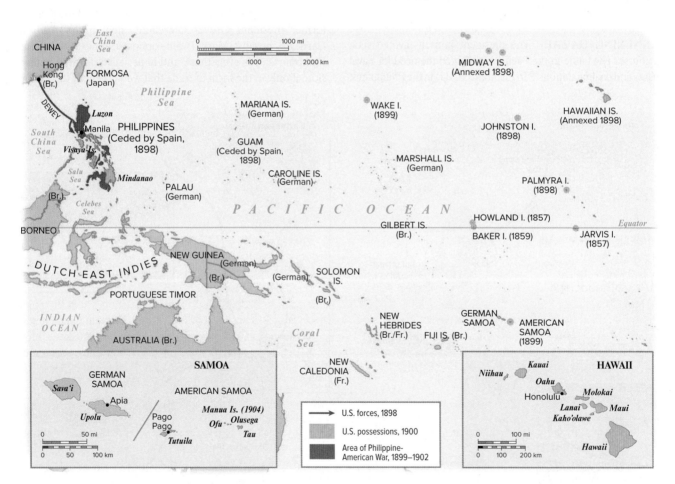

THE UNITED STATES IN THE PACIFIC

*In the late nineteenth century both Germany and the United States emerged as major naval powers and as contestants for influence and commerce in China. The island groups of the central and southwest Pacific, though of little economic value, had potential strategic significance as bases and coaling stations along the routes to Asia. Rivalry (as in the case of Samoa) sometimes threatened to erupt into open conflict. Control of Hawaii, Midway, Samoa, Guam, and the Philippines gave the United States a string of strategic stepping-stones to Asia. **Which islands seem best suited as stepping stones for empires stretching across the Pacific? What were the weaknesses of such stepping stones?***

it the "Filipino insurrection," but to those who fought, it was the brutal Philippine-American War. When it ended more than three years later, nearly 5,000 Americans, 25,000 rebels, and perhaps as many as 200,000 civilians lay dead.

Environment shaped the conduct of the war. After a series of conventional battles ended in their defeat, Filipino *insurrectos* quickly learned to take advantage of the mountainous, jungle terrain of the Philippine archipelago. From his hideaway in Bayombong, Aguinaldo ordered his men to employ "guerrilla" (literally "little war" in Spanish) tactics. Hit-and-run ambushes by lightly armed rebels perfectly suited the dense landscape. As *insurrectos* melted into tropical forests and friendly villages, Americans could barely distinguish between enemies and friends. It was the first instance of jungle warfare the United States had ever encountered.

Jungle warfare aggravated racial antagonisms and spurred savage fighting on both sides. Rebel resistance to foreign occupation was accompanied by reports of *insurrectos* treating American prisoners in "fiendish fashion," burying some alive, dismembering others, and slaughtering even Filipinos who opposed them. For their part American soldiers dismissed Filipinos as nearly subhuman in ways that evoked the Indian Wars of the American West. "The only good Filipino is a dead one," declared one U.S. soldier, echoing the infamous anti-Indian cry. Indeed, many Americans in the Philippines had fought Indians in the Dakota Badlands and northern New Mexico.

In such a climate the frustrations of ordinary troops sometimes boiled over into brutality, torture, and executions. To avenge a rebel attack, one officer promised to turn the countryside into a "howling wilderness." Another, later court-martialed for the order, exhorted his troops to shoot any Filipino over the age of 10. To combat the insurgents, General Arthur MacArthur—father of Douglas MacArthur—imposed a brutal campaign of "pacification" late in 1899. Filipinos were herded into concentration camps for their protection, while food and crops in the nearby countryside were seized or torched to starve the rebels into surrender. The strategy was embarrassingly reminiscent of the actions of "Butcher" Weyler in Cuba. Only after the capture of Aguinaldo himself and the last gasps of rebel resistance did the war finally come to a close in 1902. It marked the end of the westward march of American empire that began nearly a century earlier with the Louisiana Purchase in 1803.

In contrast to the bitter guerrilla war, the United States ruled the Philippines with relative benevolence. Under William Howard Taft, the first civilian governor, the Americans built schools, roads, sewers, and factories and instituted modern farming techniques. The aim, said Taft, was to prepare the island territory for independence, and in keeping with it, he granted great authority to local officials. These advances—social, economic, and political—benefited the Filipino elite and thus earned their support. Decades later, on July 4, 1946, the Philippines were finally granted independence.

PUERTO RICO The United States played a similar role in Puerto Rico. As in the Philippines, executive authority resided in a governor appointed by the U.S. president. Under the Foraker Act of 1900, Puerto Ricans received a voice in their

Source: P. Fremont Rockett/*Our boys in the Philippines*, scanned by Library of Congress

| *The American decision to occupy the Philippines rather than give it independence compelled Filipino nationalists to fight U.S. troops, as they had already been fighting the Spanish since 1896. Filipino forces such as these were tenacious enough to require more than 70,000 Americans to put down the rebellion. Sporadic, bloody guerrilla fighting continued until 1902, and other incidents persisted until 1906.*

government as well as a nonvoting representative in the U.S. House of Representatives. All the same, many Puerto Ricans chafed at the idea of such second-class citizenship. Some favored eventual admission to the United States as a state; others advocated independence. The division of opinion persists even today.

An Open Door in China

Like a reciprocal equation, interest in Asia drove the United States to annex the Philippines, and annexation of the Philippines only whetted American interest in Asia. The possibility of markets in China—whether for Christian souls or consumer goods—proved irresistible.

Both the British, who dominated China's export trade, and the Americans, who wanted to, worried that China might soon be carved up by other powers. Japan had defeated China in 1895, encouraging Russia, Germany, and France to join in demanding trade concessions. Each nation sought to establish an Asian **sphere of influence** in which its commercial and military interests reigned. Often such spheres resulted in restrictions against rival powers. Since Britain and the United States wanted the benefits of trade rather than actual colonies, they tried to limit foreign demands while leaving China open to all commerce.

THE OPEN-DOOR NOTES In 1899, at the urging of the British, Secretary of State John Hay circulated the first of two "open-door" notes among the imperial powers. He did not ask them to give up their spheres of influence in China, only to keep them open to free trade with other nations. The United States could hardly have enforced even so modest a proposal,

Acquiring an Empire, 1860–1900

MAJOR ACQUISITIONS	DATE	MEANS	STATUS
Alaska	1867	Purchased from Russia	Territory*
Hawaiian Islands	1898	Annexed	Territory*
Midway Island	1898	Annexed	Territory
Guam	1898	Ceded by Spain	Territory
Philippines	1898	Ceded by Spain	Territory**
Puerto Rico	1898	Ceded by Spain	Territory
American Samoa	1899	Annexed	Territory
Wake Island	1899	Annexed	Territory

*Granted statehood in 1959.
**Granted independence in 1946.

(*left*) Source: Library of Congress, Prints and Photographs Division [LC-USZC4-2678]; (*right*) Source: Library of Congress, Prints and Photographs Division [LC-DIG-ppmsca-25453]

because it lacked the military might to prevent the partitioning of China. Still, Japan and most of the European powers agreed in broad outline with Hay's policy out of fear that the Americans might tip the delicate balance by siding with a rival. Hay seized on the tepid response and brashly announced that the open door in China was international policy.

BOXER REBELLION   Unrest soon threatened to close the door. Chinese nationalists, known to Westerners as Boxers for their clenched-fist symbol, formed secret societies to drive out the *fon kwei,* or "foreign devils." Encouraged by the Chinese empress, Boxers murdered hundreds of Christian missionaries and their followers and set siege to foreign diplomats and citizens at the British Embassy in Beijing. European nations quickly dispatched troops to quell the uprising and free the diplomats, while President McKinley sent 2,500 Americans to join the march to the capital city. Along the way, the angry foreign armies plundered the countryside and killed civilians before reaching Beijing and breaking the siege.

Hay feared that once in control of Beijing the conquerors might never leave. So he sent a second open-door note in 1900, this time asking foreign powers to respect China's territorial and administrative integrity. They endorsed the proposal in principle only. In fact, the open-door notes together amounted to little more than an announcement of American desires to maintain political stability and commercial trade in Asia. Yet they reflected a fundamental purpose to which the United States dedicated itself across the globe: to open closed markets and to keep open those markets that other empires had yet to close. The new American empire would have its share of colonies, but in Asia as elsewhere it would be built primarily on trade.

SENSE OF MISSION   To expansionists such as Alfred Thayer Mahan, Theodore Roosevelt, and John Hay, American interests would be secure only when they had been established worldwide, a course of action they believed to be blessed by divine providence. Americans were "trustees under God of the civilization of the world," declared Senator Albert Beveridge of Indiana. But to one French diplomat, more accustomed to wheeling and dealing in the corridors of international power, it seemed that the Americans were tempting fate. With a whiff of Old World cynicism or perhaps a prophet's eye, he remarked, "The United States is seated at the table where the great game is played, and it cannot leave it."

The United States chose to stay at the table. In the coming century, the "great game" of global power would pay handsomely for those who envisioned the country as a world leader. The game had already settled one account. The divisive shadow of the Civil War finally faded. Despite the concerns of critics, the Spanish-American War and the quest for empire united the North and South and revitalized a generation of Americans who longed to demonstrate their prowess in an age of imperialism.

✓ REVIEW

Why did imperialists launch their quest for empire, and why did anti-imperialists oppose them?

PUTTING HISTORY IN GLOBAL CONTEXT

IN THE END, THE CHICAGO World's Fair of 1893 proved an apt reflection of the world at home and abroad. Though the fair showed off its exhibits within gleaming white buildings the political system was cracking under the strain of a depression. As the fair gathered exhibits from all over the globe, the scramble for resources and markets culminated in an age of imperialism. It seemed that national greatness went hand in hand with empire. Employing the gendered language of the day, the German historian Heinrich von Treitschke proclaimed, "Every virile people has established colonial power."

As in the United States, European imperialists sometimes justified their rule over nonwhite peoples in Darwinian fashion. "The path of progress is strewn with the wreck . . . of inferior races," proclaimed one English professor in 1900. British poet Rudyard Kipling even suggested that Europeans were making a noble sacrifice on behalf of their colonial subjects. "Take up the White Man's Burden," he exhorted his fellow Britons in 1899. "Send forth the best ye breed—/ Go bind your sons to exile/To serve your captives' need."

European critics, like those in the United States, rejected imperialism on the grounds that it delivered few economic benefits, compromised the moral standing of the colonizers, and distracted the public from undertaking much-needed reforms at home. Just as Populists in the United States called on "toilers" to band together and on government to play a more active role in managing the excesses of the new industrial order, radicals in Europe such as the German-born Karl Marx exhorted "workers of the world" to unite and "throw off your chains" by abandoning capitalism and embracing socialism.

CHAPTER SUMMARY

The end of the nineteenth century witnessed a crisis arising from political stalemate at home and the drive for empire abroad.

- Republicans and Democrats ground politics into near-gridlock over the well-worn issues of regional conflict, tariff, and monetary reform.

- Discontented Americans often fashioned political instruments of their own, whether for women's suffrage, temperance, monetary change, antilynching and civil rights, or farm issues.

- The political deadlock finally came to an end in the turbulent 1890s, when depression-spawned labor strife and a revolt of farmers produced the People's, or Populist, Party and a political realignment that left the Republicans in control of national politics.

- By the 1890s, too, the tradition of Manifest Destiny combined powerfully with the needs of the new industrial order for raw materials and markets and the closing of the American frontier to produce a powerful drive toward empire, which rested on these two principles of American foreign policy:

  ▶ The old Monroe Doctrine (1823), which warned European powers to stay out of the Americas.

  ▶ The newer open-door notes of Secretary of State John Hay (1899–1900), which stressed the importance of equal commercial access to the markets of Asia.

- Most Americans favored an overseas empire for the United States but disagreed over whether it should be territorial or commercial.

- In the end America's overseas empire was both territorial and commercial. A victory in the Spanish-American War (1898) capped an era of territorial and commercial expansion by furnishing colonial possessions in the Caribbean and the Pacific and at the same time providing more stepping-stones to the markets of Asia.

Digging Deeper

Sean Dennis Cashman, *America in the Gilded Age* (1984); and Heather Cox Richardson, *West from Appomattox: The Reconstruction of America after the Civil War* (2007), are good overviews of the era. H. W. Brands focuses on the economy of the Gilded Age in his highly readable *American Colossus: The Triumph of Capitalism, 1865–1900* (2010). In *Rebirth of a Nation: The Making of Modern America, 1877–1920* (2009), Jackson Lears offers a sweeping revision, stressing the legacy of Civil War brutality and the growing importance of race in shaping modern America. For presidential politics, see H. Wayne Morgan, *From Hayes to McKinley: National Party Politics, 1877–1896* (1969), but for the importance of ethnicity and religion, consult Paul Kleppner, *The Cross of Culture* (1970). The traditional view of the rise of the welfare state is set forth in Harold Wilensky and Charles N. Lebeaux, *Industrial Society and Social Welfare* (1958). Revising that approach, Theda Skocpol, *Protecting Soldiers and Mothers* (1994), stresses nineteenth-century origins and the interplay between the state and nongovernmental political groups.

For Populism, John D. Hicks's classic *The Populist Revolt* (1931) stresses poverty as a motivating force, and Lawrence Goodwyn's *Democratic Promise* (1976) highlights the movement's push for radical democratic change. Also useful are Robert C. McMath Jr., *American Populism* (1993); and Charles Postel, *The Populist Vision* (2007). The latter sees Populists as democratic modernizers who crossed lines of color and gender, reaching not only farmers but miners and railroad workers as well. On the issue of race in the South before and after slavery, Steven Hahn's *Under Our Feet* (2003) provides a broad and detailed panorama. On the spread of segregation after Reconstruction, see C. Vann Woodward's classic *The Strange Career of Jim Crow* (3rd rev. ed., 1974); and John W. Cell's *The Highest Stage of White Supremacy* (1982). Contrasting approaches to race relations can be seen in Louis R. Harlan's two-volume biography, *Booker T. Washington* (1972 and 1983), and David Levering Lewis, *W. E. B. DuBois: Biography of a Race* (1993). James West Davidson uses Ida B. Wells to provide a cultural portrait of the first generation of freed African Americans during these years in *"They Say": Ida B. Wells and the Reconstruction of Race* (2007).

Walter Nugent's *Habits of Empire* (2008) offers a schematic study of the creation of an American empire in the nineteenth and twentieth centuries. For other broad views of American foreign policy, see Michael H. Hunt, *Ideology and U.S Foreign Policy* (1984); John M. Dobson, *America's Ascent* (1978); and Walter LaFeber, *The American Age* (1989). LaFeber's *Inevitable Revolutions* (3rd ed., 1993) is good on Central America. For Sino-American relations, consult Michael H. Hunt, *The Making of a Special Relationship* (1983); and for the role of missionaries, especially women, see Jane Hunter, *The Gospel of Gentility* (1984). For the Spanish-American War, see Ivan Musicant, *Empire by Default* (1998). Kristin L. Hoganson's *Fighting for American Manhood* (1998) offers the best account of how gender helped to shape the Spanish-American and Philippine-American Wars. Brian McAllister Linn, *The Philippine War* (2000), presents a well-researched account, as does David J. Silbey's briefer *A War of Frontier and Empire* (2007).

After the Fact

En–Gendering the Spanish-American War

For many years historians have examined foreign policy through the traditional lenses of diplomacy, commerce, imperial ambition, national mission, and national security. Such perspectives are not likely to go out of fashion, but recently cultural historians have begun to use new categories of analysis, particularly race and gender, to understand how foreign policy is made and carried out. Though gender may seem far-fetched in penetrating the complexities of diplomacy and military action, it can add new insights into the reasons why the United States declared war against Spain in 1898.

THE SAN JUAN CHARGE

"WHAT, ARE YOU COWARDS?" The shrill voice could barely be heard above the gunfire, but for the man who possessed it, the only sounds that mattered would be the cries of Spanish troops surrendering on the San Juan Heights. For the second time, Lieutenant Colonel Theodore Roosevelt was assaulting a hill during the soggy Cuban summer of 1898. The first attack had only just ended, with Roosevelt and his "Texas Tarantulas" (recently dubbed the "Rough Riders") helping to overrun what the Americans called Kettle Hill. The colonel had been easy to spot: he was the only man on horseback. But Roosevelt had his reasons for the daring display, as he explained later: "It is always hard to get men to start when they can not see whether their comrades are going." And perhaps there was another reason: it showed manly grit to defy death.

The second charge was aimed at nearby San Juan Hill, this time on foot. With a pistol recovered from the sunken battleship *Maine* and a pair of eyeglasses in each of his ten custom-made pockets, Roosevelt stormed the Spanish entrenchment— practically alone, as it turned out. Bubbling with excitement, he had neglected to give the order to attack. A hundred yards into the assault he realized what had happened and returned to rally his men. Finally they charged and, this time, conquered.

Courtesy Frederic Remington Art Museum, Ogdensburg, New York

Artist Frederic Remington painted a fairly accurate version of the charge up Kettle Hill. Only Roosevelt was on horseback, with the other Rough Riders running uphill on foot—literally for their lives—to avoid being hit by rifle fire.

Roosevelt's triumph during the Spanish-American War gave him a legendary, career-launching victory and the manly glory he had pursued since childhood. The sickly, bespectacled boy became a man, proving his courage, honor, and character in the way he thought best, in war. "San Juan," he recalled years later, "was the great day of my life."

WHY WAR?

FOR MANY AMERICANS, ESPECIALLY THOSE born after the Civil War or too young to have fought in it, the Spanish-American War was the grand moment when their country became a great power and they a new generation of war heroes. But why did the United States go to war with Spain in 1898?

Historians have offered many explanations. Some stress the commercial rewards expected from newly acquired markets overseas. Others view the war as the global extension of the nation's Manifest Destiny to overspread the continent. Still others emphasize a geostrategic push for coaling stations in the Pacific to fuel a growing navy and for the islands in the Caribbean to block European imperialism. Humanitarian concern for the Cubans, a mission of Christian uplift for "lesser breeds," the glory of empire, political advantage at home and the spread of democracy abroad, revenge for the sinking of the *Maine,* frantic war cries from overheated journalists—all these factors enter into the historical calculus, depending on which historian is doing the math.

Yet the motives are so varied, the drums of war beating from so many quarters, historians have had difficulty tying the multiple causes into a coherent purpose. Is there a common thread among those who wanted war with Spain? Recent work has pointed to the broad-based political culture of shared values, institutions, and assumptions as the source of American belligerency. Within that political culture, some historians such as Kristin Hoganson have highlighted gender as key.

It may seem implausible to look for the sources of the Spanish-American War in the cultural roles assigned to men and women. Gender, after all, deals with the identity of individuals, whereas the study of international relations lies in the realm of sovereign nations. But the evidence pointing toward the role of gender in this war is intriguing, to say the least.

GENDERED CARTOONS AND WORDS

POLITICAL CARTOONS OFFER A GRAPHIC clue. William Randolph Hearst's *New York Journal* took the lead in howling for war. A surprising number of cartoons in Hearst's papers, and later in others, relied on then-popular images of masculinity and femininity to make their case. In one drawing, a determined Uncle Sam spoils for a fight as he rips his jacket from his chest. "Off comes his coat—now look out!" reads the caption. In another, Sam looks down from behind a cannon at an aristocrat labeled "Spain." The Spaniard holds a bloody sword and a burning torch. At his feet lie a ravaged mother ("Cuba") and her child. "Peace—But Quit That!" says Sam. In yet another cartoon, President McKinley, who had his doubts about fighting the Spanish, is depicted as an "Old Woman" trying to "Sweep Back the Sea" of congressional support for war. Finally, Secretary of State John Sherman wags his finger in disapproval at a diminutive Alfonso XIII, the boy-king of Spain, who stands

Source: Theodore Roosevelt
Collection, Harvard College Library

"Off comes his coat—now look out!"

near a shackled prisoner, a beheaded statuette, and a cage filled with Americans.

In these and other political cartoons, we find notions of masculinity and femininity at the center of the message. Resolute males stand ready to fight or to rebuke those who break the codes of chivalry. Men opposing war or indecisive about it, such as McKinley, are dressed as women. The Spanish are reduced to puny figures, like the petulant Alfonso, or are made out to be bloodthirsty violators of helpless womanhood.

True men, the cartoons seem to be saying, go to war to protect the principles of chivalry and the women who embody them; dishonorable, cowardly men ravage women or become them.

Words, too—in the halls of Congress, in boardrooms, on street corners, on the pages of newspapers—furnish more evidence. The country must take up arms, thundered Representative James R. Mann of Illinois—not because of some "fancied slight" or "commercial wrong" or lust for empire but "because it has become necessary to fight if we would uphold our manhood." When the *Maine* was sunk, Senator Richard R. Kenny of Delaware exploded over the insult: "American manhood and American chivalry give back the answer that innocent blood shall be avenged." Some urged arbitration to resolve the matter, but Senator George Perkins rejected it as unmanly: "Men do not arbitrate questions of honor," he insisted.

Such language, some historians have concluded, reflected a larger "crisis of manhood" imperiling American politics at the end of the nineteenth century. More than one observer of the political scene, they point out, worried that the creature comforts of the industrial age were making men "sluggish" and "soft," particularly upper- and middle-class men who were the source of political leadership. Worse still, the hot pursuit of money and things was corroding the manly sense of honor, integrity, and valor that contemporaries believed to be essential for good government and the basis of leadership in politics.

THREATS TO MASCULINITY

©New York Public Library/Art Resource, NY

"Another Old Woman Tries to Sweep Back the Sea."

AS IF THESE DANGERS WERE not enough, the rise of the "New Woman" threatened to emasculate men as women charged into the all-male preserve of politics. Woman activists laid claim to the right to vote and asserted the superiority of feminine virtue, which was needed to temper the corrupt "male" influence dominating the political system. Alice Stone Blackwell, editor of the prosuffrage *Woman's Journal,* put it bluntly: "Assuming for the sake of argument that this

war is . . . utterly inexcusable . . . it is a
Congress of men that has declared it."
Morality and intelligence rather than manliness, these women maintained, should be
the touchstones of politics.

The depression of 1893 only aggravated
this sense of crisis. Men lost their jobs,
their self-respect, and with them their
independence and vitality. In a Darwinian
world of killing competition—in other
words, the world as Americans of the late
nineteenth century conceived it—the loss
of male vigor could spell disaster at home
and abroad.

©New York Public Library/Art Resource, NY
"Peace—But Quit That."

RESOLUTION

WHATEVER ELSE IT DID, THE Spanish-American War offered a resolution to this crisis of
manhood. The war furnished an opportunity for action in the tradition of the legendary father
figures who fought in the American Revolution and the Civil War and thereby set the mold for
political leadership. The war would toughen American men for survival in the realm of domestic politics as well as in the rough-and-tumble world of great imperial powers. At the same
time, rescuing the Cubans from Spanish oppression would restore the heroic sense of honor
believed to be so vital to leadership. In the process, the "New Woman" would be defanged.
Women would resume their "proper" roles as nurturers who respected their men and raised
their sons to be the next generation of brave, honorable males.

Undoubtedly, such gendered rhetoric is arresting. Whether it serves to tie together the
various explanations for war and empire is another matter. Establishing the identity of a single
individual is complicated enough, for character is
shaped by many factors, including gender, race,
ethnicity, religion, class, and education. National
identity and the actions that derive from it are more
complex still, and the actions of real people in the
real world are perhaps thorniest of all. Even a
staunch booster of war and manly vigor such as
Theodore Roosevelt was capable as president of
pursuing the "unmanly" path of arbitration to end
the Russo-Japanese War in 1905.

To say that gender shaped policy is different from
saying that gender created policy. Even so, construc-
tions of gender did play a role in the Spanish-
American War, if only in their widespread use by
those who sold the country on war and by those
who fought it.

©New York Public Library/Art Resource, NY
"Secretary Sherman Talks to the Boy-King."

22 The Progressive Era

1890–1920

Artist John Sloan drew this bitter cartoon lamenting the loss of lives inflicted by the Triangle Shirtwaist fire of 1911. Sloan titled his illustration "The Real Triangle." The tragedy sparked a renewed determination of Progressive reformers to enact laws protecting workers in the new industrial order.

©Sarin Images/The Granger Collection, New York

>> An American Story

BURNED ALIVE IN THE CITY

Quitting time, March 25, 1911. The long day was about to end at the Triangle Shirtwaist Company near the lower end of Manhattan. The deafening whir of some 1,500 sewing machines soon fell silent as hundreds of workers—mostly young immigrant women—were set free.

To some, quitting time seemed like an emancipation. Twelve-hour days in stifling, crowded workrooms, weekly paychecks of only $3 to $15, fines for the tiniest mistakes, deductions for needle and thread, even for electricity, made the young seamstresses angry. Two years earlier, their frustration boiled over into an industrywide strike for better wages and working conditions. Despite a union victory, the only change visible at Triangle was that every morning the doors were locked to keep workers in and union organizers out.

The fire broke out in the lofts as the workers were leaving for home. In minutes the top stories were ablaze. Terrified seamstresses groped through the black smoke, only to find exits locked or clogged with bodies. All but one of the few working fire escapes collapsed. When the fire trucks arrived, horrified firefighters discovered that their ladders could not reach the top stories. "Spectators saw again and again pitiable companionships formed in the instant of death—girls who placed their arms around each other as they leaped," read one news story. Their bodies hit the sidewalk with a sickening thud or were spiked on the iron guard rails. One hundred forty-six people died.

A few days later 80,000 New Yorkers joined the silent funeral procession snaking slowly up Fifth Avenue in mourning in the rain. A quarter of a million watched. At the Metropolitan Opera House, union leader Rose Schneiderman told a rally, "This is not the first time that girls have been burned alive in the city. Every year thousands of us are maimed." A special state commission investigated the tragedy. Over the next four years its recommendations produced 56 state laws regulating fire safety, hours, machinery, and home work. They amounted to the most far-reaching labor code in the country.

The Triangle fire shocked the nation and underscored a widespread fear: modern industrial society had created profound strains, widespread misery, and deep class divisions. Men, women, and children worked around the clock in unsafe factories for barely enough to support themselves. Corporations grew to unimagined size, bought and sold legislators, dictated the terms of their own profit. In cities across America, tenement-bred diseases took innocent lives. Criminals threatened people and property, while saloons tied the working poor to dishonest political bosses. In the 1890s, workers and managers fought pitched battles that threatened to break the country apart. Inflation shrank middle-class wallets at the rate of 3 percent a year. "It was a world of greed," concluded one garment worker; "the human being didn't mean anything."

Human beings did mean something to followers of a reform movement sweeping the country. Progressivism emerged as a political force in the mid-1890s and continued to shape politics through World War I. The movement sprang from many impulses, mixing a liberal concern for the poor and working class with conservative efforts to stabilize business and avoid class warfare. Above all, progressives shared a desire to soften the harsher aspects of industrialization, urbanization, and immigration.

Progressivism began in the cities, where those forces converged. It was organized by an angry, idealistic middle class and percolated up from neighborhoods to city halls, state capitals, and, finally, Washington. Though usually pursued through

©Brown Brothers

Rose Schneiderman, a union activist, protested "the firetrap structures that will destroy us the minute they catch on fire. This is not the first time girls have been burned alive in the city."

politics, the goals of progressives were broadly social—to create a "good society" where people could live decently, harmoniously, and prosperously, along middle-class lines.

Unlike past reformers, progressives saw government as a protector, not an oppressor. Only government possessed the resources for the broad-based reforms they sought. Progressivism spawned the modern activist state, with its capacity to regulate the economy and manage society. And because American society had become so interdependent, progressivism became the first nationwide reform movement. It flowered in the presidencies of Republican Theodore Roosevelt and Democrat Woodrow Wilson. In 1912 it even gave birth to its own party, the Progressive, or "Bull Moose," Party. By then progressivism had filtered well beyond politics into every realm of American life. <<

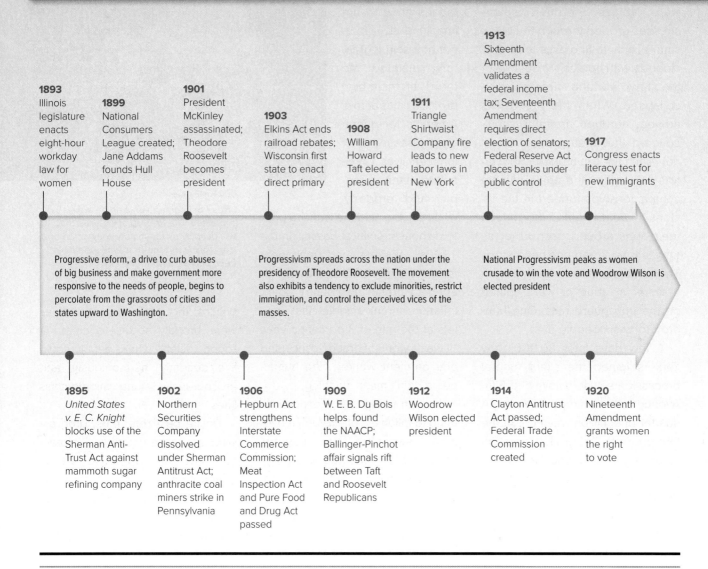

1893
Illinois legislature enacts eight-hour workday law for women

1899
National Consumers League created; Jane Addams founds Hull House

1901
President McKinley assassinated; Theodore Roosevelt becomes president

1903
Elkins Act ends railroad rebates; Wisconsin first state to enact direct primary

1908
William Howard Taft elected president

1911
Triangle Shirtwaist Company fire leads to new labor laws in New York

1913
Sixteenth Amendment validates a federal income tax; Seventeenth Amendment requires direct election of senators; Federal Reserve Act places banks under public control

1917
Congress enacts literacy test for new immigrants

Progressive reform, a drive to curb abuses of big business and make government more responsive to the needs of people, begins to percolate from the grassroots of cities and states upward to Washington.

Progressivism spreads across the nation under the presidency of Theodore Roosevelt. The movement also exhibits a tendency to exclude minorities, restrict immigration, and control the perceived vices of the masses.

National Progressivism peaks as women crusade to win the vote and Woodrow Wilson is elected president

1895
United States v. E. C. Knight blocks use of the Sherman Anti-Trust Act against mammoth sugar refining company

1902
Northern Securities Company dissolved under Sherman Antitrust Act; anthracite coal miners strike in Pennsylvania

1906
Hepburn Act strengthens Interstate Commerce Commission; Meat Inspection Act and Pure Food and Drug Act passed

1909
W. E. B. Du Bois helps found the NAACP; Ballinger-Pinchot affair signals rift between Taft and Roosevelt Republicans

1912
Woodrow Wilson elected president

1914
Clayton Antitrust Act passed; Federal Trade Commission created

1920
Nineteenth Amendment grants women the right to vote

THE ROOTS OF PROGRESSIVE REFORM

FAMILIES TURNED FROM THEIR HOMES; an army of unemployed on the roads; hunger, strikes, and bloody violence across the country—the wrenching depression of 1893 forced Americans to take a hard look at their new industrial order. They saw a society increasingly divided by class, race, and ethnicity. They also found common complaints that cut across those same lines. If streetcar companies raised fares while service deteriorated, if food processors doctored their canned goods with harmful additives, if politicians skimmed money from the public till, everyone suffered.

AIMS OF PROGRESSIVES The result was not a coherent progressive movement but a set of loosely connected goals based on clear themes: efficient government and honest politics; greater regulation of business and a more orderly economy; social justice for the urban poor and social welfare to protect children, women, workers, and consumers. Some progressives looked to purify society by outlawing alcohol and drugs, stamping out prostitution and slums, and restricting the flood of new immigrants. All tried to make business and government more responsive to the will of the people.

Paternalistic by nature, progressives often imposed their solutions, no matter what the less "enlightened" poor or oppressed saw as their own best interests. Reformers also acted out of nostalgia. In a rapidly changing world, they wanted to redeem such traditional American values as democracy, opportunity, and the spirit of public service. And finally progressives sought to save the nation from a second civil war born of class conflict that had erupted in the 1890s. Yet if the ends of progressives were traditional, their means were distinctly modern. They used the systems and methods of the new industrial order—the latest techniques of organization, management, and science—to fight its excesses and soften its impact.

The Progressive System of Beliefs

Progressives were moderate modernizers—reformers, not revolutionaries. They accepted the American system as sound, only in need of improvement. Many drew on the increasingly popular Darwinian theories of evolution to buttress this gradual approach to change. With its notion of mutation and slowly changing species, evolution undermined the acceptance of a set of unchangeable principles that had guided most social thought in the Gilded Age. Progressives saw an evolving landscape and ever-shifting values. They denied the old Calvinist doctrine of inborn sinfulness and instead saw people as having a greater potential for good than for evil.

Progressives had seen the mean side of industrialism and somehow had to explain the existence of evil and wrongdoing. Most agreed that human beings were, as one of them put it, "largely, if not wholly, products of society or environment." People went wrong, another wrote, because of "what happens to them." By changing what happened, the human potential for good could be released. As reformer Jane Addams explained, "what has been called 'the extraordinary pliability of human nature'" made it "impossible to set any bounds to the moral capabilities which might unfold under ideal civic and educational conditions."

PRAGMATISM   With an eye to results, progressives asked not "Is it true?" but "Does it work?" Philosopher Charles Peirce called this new way of thinking **pragmatism.** William James, a Harvard psychologist, became its most famous popularizer. For James, pragmatism meant "looking towards last things, fruits, consequences, facts." What mattered most were results.

The Pragmatic Approach

Pragmatism led educators, social scientists, and lawyers to adopt new approaches to reform. John Dewey, the master educator of the Progressive Era, believed that environment shaped the patterns of human thought. Instead of demanding mindless memorization of abstract and unconnected facts, Dewey tried to "make each one of our schools an embryonic community life." At his School of Pedagogy, founded in 1896 with his wife, Alice, he let students unbolt their desks from the floor, move about, and learn by doing so they could train for real life.

Psychologist John B. Watson believed that human behavior could be shaped at will. "Give me a dozen healthy infants," he wrote, ". . . and my own specified world to bring them up in,

and I'll guarantee to take any one at random and train him to become any specialist I might select, doctor, lawyer, artist, merchant, chief, and yes, even beggarman and thief." **Behaviorism** swept the social sciences and later advertising, the field where Watson himself eventually landed.

Lawyers and legal theorists applied their own blend of pragmatism and behaviorism. Justice Oliver Wendell Holmes Jr., appointed to the Supreme Court in 1902, rejected the idea that the traditions of law were constant and universal. "Long ago I decided I was not God," said Holmes. Law was a living organism to be interpreted according to experience and the needs of a changing society.

SOCIOLOGICAL JURISPRUDENCE   This environmental view of the law, known as **sociological jurisprudence**, found a skilled practitioner in Louis Brandeis. Shaken by the brutal suppression of the Homestead steel strike of 1892, Brandeis quit his corporate practice and proclaimed himself the "people's lawyer." The law must "guide by the light of reason," he wrote, by which he meant bringing everyday life to bear in any court case. Older court opinions had been based largely on legal precedent. Progressives asked courts to look at the world around them and realize society had undergone changes so fundamental that many precedents of the past no longer applied. Past and present must stand on equal footing in interpreting the law.

BRANDEIS BRIEF   Brandeis had a chance to test his practical principles when laundry owner Curt Muller challenged an Oregon law that limited his laundresses to working 10 hours a day. Brandeis defended the statute before the Supreme Court in 1908. His famous legal brief in *Muller v. Oregon* contained 102 pages describing the damaging effects of long hours on working women and only 15 pages of legal precedents. The Supreme Court upheld Oregon's right to limit the working hours of women and thus legitimized the "Brandeis Brief."

The Progressive Method

Seeing the nation riven by conflict, progressives tried to restore a sense of community through the ideal of a single public interest. Christian ethics were their guide, to be applied after using the latest scientific methods to gather and analyze data about a social problem. The modern corporation furnished an appealing model for organization. Like corporate executives, progressives relied on careful management, coordinated systems, and specialized bureaucracies to carry out reforms.

Between 1902 and 1912 a new breed of journalists investigated wrongdoers, named them in print, and described their misdeeds in vivid detail. Most of their exposés began as articles in mass-circulation magazines. *McClure's* magazine stirred controversy and boosted circulation when it sent reporter Lincoln Steffens to uncover the crooked ties between business and politics. Steffens's "Tweed Days in St. Louis" appeared in the October 1902 issue of *McClure's* and was followed in the November issue by Ida M. Tarbell's *History of the Standard Oil Company,* another stinging, well-researched indictment. Soon a full-blown literature of exposure was covering every ill from unsafe food to child labor.

MUCKRAKERS   A disgusted Theodore Roosevelt called the new reporters "muckrakers," after the man who raked up filth in the seventeenth-century classic *Pilgrim's Progress.* Still, by documenting dishonesty and blight, muckrakers not only aroused people but also educated them. No broad reform movement of American institutions would have taken place without them.

VOLUNTARY ORGANIZATIONS   To solve the problems that muckrakers exposed, progressives stressed volunteerism, civic responsibility, and collective action. They drew on the organizational impulse that seemed everywhere to be bringing people together in new interest groups. Between 1890 and 1920 nearly 400 organizations were founded, many to combat the ills of industrial society. Some, such as the National Consumers League, grew out of efforts to promote general causes—in this case protecting consumers and workers from exploitation. Others, such as the National Tuberculosis Association, aimed at a specific problem.

When voluntary action failed, progressives looked to government to protect the public welfare. They mistrusted legislators, who might be controlled by corporate interests or political machines. So they strengthened the executive branch by increasing the power of individual mayors, governors, and presidents. Then they watched those executives carefully.

PROFESSIONALS   Progressives also drew on the expertise of the newly professionalized middle class. Confident, cosmopolitan professionals—doctors, engineers, psychiatrists, city planners—mounted campaigns to stamp out sexually transmitted disease and dysentery, reform prisons and asylums, and beautify cities. At all levels—local, state, federal—new agencies and commissions staffed by impartial experts began to investigate and regulate lobbyists, insurance and railroad companies, public health, even government itself.

REVIEW
What ills did progressives see in society, what solutions did they propose, and what ideas shaped those solutions?

THE SEARCH FOR THE GOOD SOCIETY

IF PROGRESSIVISM ENDED IN POLITICS, it began with social reform: the need to reach out, to do something to bring the "good society" a step closer. Ellen Richards had just such ends in mind in 1890 when she opened the New England Kitchen in downtown Boston. Richards, a chemist and home economist, designed the Kitchen to sell cheap, wholesome food to the working poor.

The New England Kitchen promoted social as well as nutritional reform. Women freed from the drudgery of cooking could seek gainful employment. And as a "household experiment station" and center for dietary information, the Kitchen tried to educate the poor and Americanize immigrants by showing them how the middle class prepared meals. According to philanthropist Pauline Shaw, it was also a "rival to the saloon." A common belief was that poor diets fostered drinking, especially among the poor and working classes. Assumed to be wiser and more efficient, women would be freed from the drudgery of housework to seek employment outside of the home and thus help their families move up in the world.

PATTERN OF REFORM   In the end, the New England Kitchen enjoyed more success as an inexpensive eatery for middle-class working women and students than as a resource for the poor or an agency of Americanization. Still, Ellen Richards's experiment reflected a pattern typical of progressive social reform: the mix of professionalism with uplift of the needy, socially conscious women entering the public arena, the hope of creating a better world along middle-class lines.

Poverty in a New Light

During the 1890s crime reporter and photographer Jacob Riis launched a campaign to introduce middle-class audiences to urban poverty. Writing in rich detail in *How the Other Half Lives* (1890), Riis brought readers into the teeming tenement. Accompanying the text were shocking photos of poverty-stricken Americans—the "Other Half." He also publicized their plight with slide shows of his photographs. His pictures of slum life appeared artless, merely recording the desperate poverty before the camera. But Riis used them to tell a moralistic story, much the way the earlier English novelist Charles Dickens had employed his melodramatic tales to attack the abuses of industrialism in England. People began to see poverty in a new, more sympathetic light, the result less of flawed individuals than unwholesome environments.

A haunting naturalism in fiction and painting followed Riis's gritty photographic essays. In *McTeague* (1899) and *Sister Carrie* (1900), novelists Frank Norris and Theodore Dreiser spun dark tales of city dwellers struggling to keep body and soul intact. The "Ashcan school" painted urban life in grimy realistic hues. Photographer Alfred Stieglitz and painters John Sloan and George Bellows chose slums, tenements, and dirty streets as subjects. Poverty began to look less ominous and more heartrending.

SOCIAL WORK   A new profession—social work—proceeded from this new view of poverty. Social work developed out of the old settlement house movement (Chapter 20). Like the physicians from whom they drew inspiration, social workers studied hard data to diagnose the problems of their "clients." Unlike nineteenth-century philanthropists, they refused to do things to or for people. Instead, they worked with their "clients," enlisting their help to solve their own problems.

| Jacob Riis, a Danish-born reporter and photographer, stalked the streets of New York, meticulously recording the squalor in which many slum dwellers lived. Here we have a Riis photograph of a cramped tenement on Bayard Street, where for "5 cents a spot" a lodger could find a place to sleep for the night. The room, Riis wrote in How the Other Half Lives, was "not thirteen feet either way" and housed "twelve men and women, two or three in bunks in a sort of alcove, the rest on the floor." What originally had been a lifeless engraving in the first edition of the book appeared as this sharp photograph in later editions, adding detail and poignancy to its sleepy-eyed subjects.
©Bettmann/Getty Images

A social worker's "differential casework" attempted to treat individuals case by case, each according to the way the client had been shaped by environment.

In reality, poverty was only one symptom of many personal and social ills. Most progressives continued to see it as a by-product of political and corporate greed, slum neighborhoods, and "institutions of vice" such as the saloon. Less clear to them was how complex and deeply rooted poverty had become.

Expanding the "Woman's Sphere"

Progressive social reform attracted a great many women seeking what Jane Addams called "the larger life" of public affairs. In the late nineteenth century, women found that protecting their traditional sphere of home and family forced them to move beyond it. Bringing up children, making meals, keeping house, and caring for the sick now involved community decisions about schools, public health, and countless other matters.

WOMEN'S ORGANIZATIONS In the nineteenth century, many middle- and upper-middle-class women received their first taste of public life from women's organizations, including mothers' clubs, temperance societies, and church groups. By the turn of the century some 500 women's clubs boasted over 160,000 members. Through the General Federation of Women's Clubs, they funded libraries and hospitals and supported schools, settlement houses, compulsory education,

and child labor laws. Eventually they moved beyond the concerns of home and family to endorse such controversial causes as woman suffrage, unionization, and the fight against the lynching of African Americans.

NEW WOMAN The dawn of the century saw the rise of a new generation of women. Longer lived, better educated, and less often married than their mothers, they were also willing to pursue careers for fulfillment. Usually they turned to professions that involved their traditional role of nurturers—nursing, library work, teaching, and settlement house work. Professionalism joined with a concern for the less fortunate and for equal rights to put women at the forefront of social and political reform.

Custom and prejudice still restricted women. The faculty at the Massachusetts Institute of Technology refused to allow Ellen Richards to pursue a doctorate. Instead, they hired her to run the gender-segregated "Woman's Laboratory" for training public school teachers. At the turn of the century only about 1,500 women practiced law, and in 1910 women made up barely 6 percent of licensed physicians. That figure rapidly declined as male-dominated medical associations grew in power and discouraged the entry of women.

MARGARET SANGER AND BIRTH CONTROL Margaret Sanger took on one medical problem as a personal crusade: freeing women from the bonds of chronic pregnancy. Sanger, a visiting nurse on the Lower East Side of New York City, had

Source: Library of Congress, Prints and Photographs Division [LC-USZ62-22260]

| *Two women post bills promoting "Votes for Women" in Cincinnati, Ohio, in 1912.*

Social Welfare

In the "bigger family of the city," as one woman reformer called it, settlement house workers soon concluded that private acts of charity would have to be supplemented by government action to make progress. Laws had to be passed and agencies created to promote social welfare, including improved housing, workplaces, parks, and playgrounds; the abolition of child labor; and the enactment of eight-hour-day laws for working women. Women, especially those from social settlement houses, led the way.

KEATING-OWEN ACT By 1910 the more than 400 settlement houses across the nation had organized into a loose affiliation, with settlement workers ready to help shape government policy. Often it was women who led the way. Julia Lathrop, a Vassar College graduate, spent 20 years at Jane Addams's Hull House before becoming the first head of the new federal Children's Bureau in 1912. By then two-thirds of the states had adopted some legislation limiting child labor, although loopholes exempted countless youngsters from coverage. Under Lathrop's leadership, Congress was persuaded to pass the Keating-Owen Act (1916), forbidding goods manufactured by children from crossing state lines.*

Florence Kelley, who had also worked at Hull House, spearheaded a similar campaign in Illinois to protect women workers by limiting their workday to eight hours. As general secretary of the National Consumers League, she also organized boycotts of companies that treated employees inhumanely. Eventually most states enacted laws restricting the number of hours women could work.

Women's Suffrage

No one had ever seen pickets in front of the White House before, let alone picketing women. But starting on January 10, 1917, from ten in the morning until half past five in the evening, there they stood, stiff and silent at the front gates, six days a week, rain or shine. The "Silent Sentinels," as they called themselves, let their banners speak for them. One quoted the words of Inez Milholland, who had collapsed at a suffrage rally in Los Angeles. "Mr. President," she had said with her dying breath, "how long must women wait for liberty?"

Ever since the conference for women's rights held at Seneca Falls in 1848, women reformers had pressed for the right to vote on the grounds of equal opportunity and simple justice. They adopted the label "woman suffrage" to emphasize the solidarity of women in pursuit of the vote. Progressives embraced women's suffrage by stressing what they saw as the practical results: reducing political corruption, protecting the home, and increasing the voting power of native-born whites. The "purer sensibilities" of

seen too many poor women overburdened with children, pregnant year after year, with no hope of escaping the cycle. The consequences were often crippling and sometimes deadly. "Women cannot be on equal footing with men until they have complete control over their reproductive functions," she argued.

The insight came as a revelation one summer evening in 1912 when Sanger was called to the home of a distraught immigrant family on Grand Street. Sadie Sachs, mother of three, had accidentally killed herself while trying to terminate yet another pregnancy. Sanger vowed that night "to do something to change the destiny of mothers whose miseries were as vast as the sky." Her own mother had had 18 pregnancies in 22 years. Sanger became a champion of what she called "birth control." By distributing information on contraception, she hoped to free women from unwanted pregnancies and illegal "back alley" abortions that claimed lives. In 1916 she founded the first family planning and birth control clinic in the country. Nine days later, she was arrested and later convicted of distributing contraceptive information, then considered a crime.

Single or married, militant or moderate, professional or nonprofessional, white or black, more and more middle-class urban women thus became "social housekeepers." From their own homes they turned to the homes of their neighbors and from there to all of society.

*The Supreme Court struck down the law in 1918 as an improper regulation of local labor; nonetheless, the law focused greater attention on the abuses of child labor.

>> MAPPING THE PAST <<

WOMAN SUFFRAGE, 1915

TO ASK FREEDOM FOR WOMEN IS NOT A CRIME

SUFFRAGE PRISONERS SHOULD NOT BE TREATED AS CRIMINALS

Source: Library of Congress, Prints and Photographs Division [LC-DIG-hec-11942]

"Look forward women always; utterly cast away/The memory of hate and struggle and bitterness."
—Suffragist Alice Duer Miller, *Are Women People?*

CONTEXT

The drive to establish the vote for women received new life from Progressive reformers. This 1915 cartoon map, entitled "The Awakening," offers a graphic and emotion-laden map of women's suffrage. Here, a torch-bearing woman in classical dress carries the franchise from western states, where women's suffrage has already been enacted, to the eastern states, where desperate women eagerly reach out. The lines of poetry quoted above are from Miller's, *Are Women People?* The poem's title became a slogan for the women's suffrage movement. The full poem appears below the map.

THE AWAKENING

Source: Library of Congress, Prints and Photographs Division [LC-USZC2-1206]

MAP READING

Consult the "Women's Suffrage" map in the chapter for additional data.

1. Which region and what states led the way in the women's suffrage movement?
2. Among the western states, which two states were the first to grant women the vote?
3. Comparing the two suffrage maps, which state granted women the vote in 1915 after "The Awakening" map was created?

MAP INTERPRETATION

1. Why was Utah the second state to grant women the vote? Why were western states in general more receptive to women's suffrage?
2. Can you suggest why this map uses a classical image of a woman to symbolize the vote for females?
3. In what was does the artistic treatment of "The Awakening" change the purpose of the map, compared with a more straightforward geographic presentation?

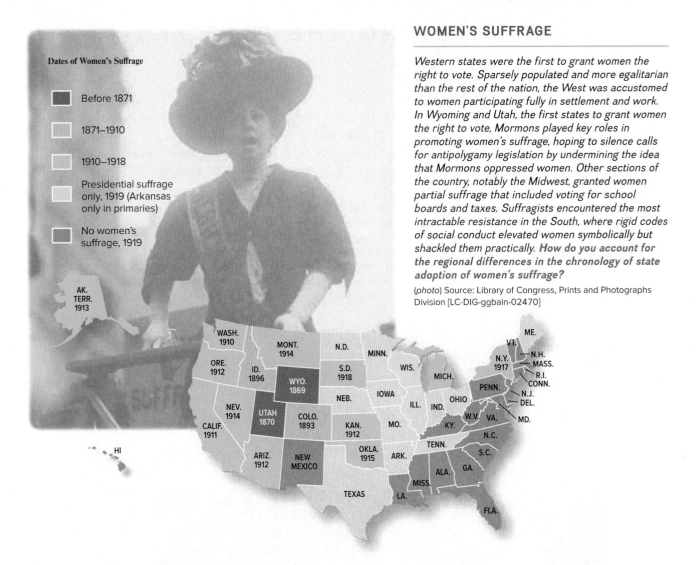

WOMEN'S SUFFRAGE

*Western states were the first to grant women the right to vote. Sparsely populated and more egalitarian than the rest of the nation, the West was accustomed to women participating fully in settlement and work. In Wyoming and Utah, the first states to grant women the right to vote, Mormons played key roles in promoting women's suffrage, hoping to silence calls for antipolygamy legislation by undermining the idea that Mormons oppressed women. Other sections of the country, notably the Midwest, granted women partial suffrage that included voting for school boards and taxes. Suffragists encountered the most intractable resistance in the South, where rigid codes of social conduct elevated women symbolically but shackled them practically. **How do you account for the regional differences in the chronology of state adoption of women's suffrage?***

(*photo*) Source: Library of Congress, Prints and Photographs Division [LC-DIG-ggbain-02470]

Dates of Women's Suffrage

- Before 1871
- 1871–1910
- 1910–1918
- Presidential suffrage only, 1919 (Arkansas only in primaries)
- No women's suffrage, 1919

women—an ideal held by conservatives and progressives alike—would help cleanse the political process of selfishness and corruption, while their sheer numbers would keep the political balance tilted away from immigrant newcomers.

The suffrage movement benefited, too, from new leadership. In 1900 Carrie Chapman Catt became president of the National American Woman Suffrage Association, founded by Susan B. Anthony in 1890. Politically astute and a skilled organizer, Catt mapped a grassroots strategy of education and persuasion from state to state. She called it "the winning plan." As the Mapping the Past feature shows, victories came first in the West, where women had already forged a more equal partnership with men to overcome the hardships of frontier life. By 1914, 10 western states (and Kansas) had granted women the vote in state elections, as Illinois had in presidential elections.

MILITANT SUFFRAGISTS The slow pace of progress drove some suffragists to militancy. The shift began in England after 1900, when Emmeline Pankhurst, her daughters, and several of their followers chained themselves to the visitors' gallery in the House of Commons. They smashed department-store windows and broke up political meetings, even burned the houses of members of Parliament. British

authorities threw many of the protesters in jail, Emmeline Pankhurst included. When the women went on hunger strikes, wardens tied them down and fed them by force.

Among the British suffragists was a small American with large, determined eyes. In 1907, barely out of her teens, Alice Paul had gone to England to join the suffrage crusade. When asked why she had enlisted, she recalled her Quaker upbringing. "One of their principles . . . is equality of the sexes," she explained. Paul marched arm-in-arm with British suffragists and more than once was imprisoned and refused to eat. In 1910 she returned to the United States and brought this more militant brand of protest with her. Three years later, in 1913, Paul organized 5,000 women to parade in protest at the inauguration of President Woodrow Wilson, who favored a state-by-state approach to women's suffrage. Half a million people watched as a near-riot ensued. Paul and other suffragists were hauled to jail, stripped naked, and thrown into cells with prostitutes.

In 1914 Paul broke with the moderate National American Woman Suffrage Association and formed the Congressional Union, dedicated to enacting national women's suffrage at any cost through a constitutional amendment. She allied her organization with western women voters in the more combative National Woman's Party in 1917. It was Paul who organized

Source: Library of Congress, Prints and Photographs Division [LC-DIG-ppm-sca-27955]

❘ Puck, *the American humor magazine, takes a wry swipe at the eugenics movement in this cover from June 1913. A physician spins the globe on his feet with his bag of medical instruments beside him, demonstrating that science has taken command of the world, even human reproduction. Cupid, whose now useless arrows fall from his quiver, cries uncontrollably as he realizes that "Eugenics" and not love "Makes the World go 'round."*

the Silent Sentinels at the White House, when President Wilson refused to see any more delegations of women urging a constitutional amendment. She was arrested at the gates of the White House and dragged off to a cellblock in the Washington jail, where she and others refused to eat. Prison officials declared her insane, but a public outcry soon led to her release.

NINETEENTH AMENDMENT Such repression only widened public support for women's suffrage. So did the contributions of women to World War I (see Chapter 23). In the wake of the war, Great Britain granted women over age 30 the right to vote in 1918, Germany and Austria in 1919, and the United States in 1920 through the Nineteenth Amendment. Overnight the number of eligible voters in the country doubled.

 REVIEW

Why were women so deeply involved in the "search for the good society," and what were some of their chief accomplishments?

CONTROLLING THE MASSES

"OBSERVE IMMIGRANTS," WROTE ONE AMERICAN in 1912. "You are struck by the fact that from ten to twenty percent are hirsute, low-browed, big-faced persons of obviously low mentality. . . . They clearly belong in skins, in wattled huts at the close of the Ice Age." The writer was neither an uneducated fanatic nor a stern opponent of change. He was Professor Edward A. Ross, a progressive from Madison, Wisconsin, who prided himself on his scientific study of sociology.

Faced with the chaos and corruption of urban life, more than a few progressives feared they were losing control of their country. Saloons and dance halls lured youngsters and impoverished laborers; prostitutes walked the streets; vulgar amusements pandered to the uneducated. Strange Old World cultures clashed with "all-American" customs, and immigrant groups jostled uneasily. The city challenged middle-class reformers to convert this riot of diversity into a more uniform society. To maintain control, progressives sometimes moved beyond education and regulation and sought to define and eradicate "social vices" of these new masses.

Stemming the Immigrant Tide

A rising tide of immigrants from southern and eastern Europe especially troubled some native-born Americans, including reformers anxious over the changing ethnic complexion of the country. In northern cities, progressives often succeeded in reducing immigrant voting power by increasing residency requirements.

EUGENICS A new science called "eugenics" lent respectability to the idea that newcomers were biologically inferior. Eugenicists believed that heredity largely shaped human behavior, and they therefore advocated selectively breeding human beings (literally choosing their mates or sterilizing those deemed unworthy) to improve the species or rid it of unwanted traits. By 1914 more magazine articles discussed eugenics than slums, tenements, and living standards combined. In *The Passing of the Great Race* (1916), upper-crust New Yorker and amateur zoologist Madison Grant helped popularize the notion that the "lesser breeds" threatened to "mongrelize" America by weakening its gene pool. So powerful was the pull of eugenics that it captured the support of some progressives. Margaret Sanger, for one, saw contraception as a way of reducing birthrates among those deemed physically and mentally "unfit." The eugenics movement also helped to promote the passage of forced sterilization laws in 30 states, the first in Indiana in 1907. The practice was affirmed by the Supreme Court in *Buck v. Bell* (1927).

AMERICANIZATION Most progressives, however, believed in the shaping impact of environment and so favored either assimilating immigrants into American society or restricting their entry into the country. Jane Addams, for one, stressed the cultural "gifts" immigrants brought with them: folk rituals, dances, music, and handicrafts. With characteristic paternalism, she and other reformers hoped to "Americanize" the foreign-born (the term was newly coined) by teaching them middle-class ways. Education was one key. Progressive educator Peter Roberts, for example, developed a lesson plan for the Young Men's Christian Association that taught immigrants to dress, tip, buy groceries, and vote.

LITERACY TEST Less-tolerant citizens sought to restrict immigration as a way of reasserting control and achieving social harmony. Though white, Protestant, and American-born, these nativists were only occasionally progressives themselves, but they did employ progressive methods of organization, investigation, education, and legislation. The first solid victory for restrictionists came in 1882, when they succeeded in barring the entry of Chinese laborers into the country. After the turn of the century, restrictionists gained strength as the tidal wave of eastern and southern European immigrants crested. Active since the 1890s the Immigration Restriction League pressed Congress in 1907 to require a literacy test for admission into the United States. Presidents Taft and Wilson vetoed it in 1913 and 1915, but Congress overrode Wilson's second veto in 1917, when war fever raised defensive nationalism to a new peak.

The Curse of Demon Rum

Tied closely to concern over immigrants was an attack on saloons. Part of a broader crusade to clean up cities, the anti-saloon campaign drew strength from the century-old drive to lessen the consumption of alcohol. Women made up a disproportionate number of alcohol reformers. The temperance movement reflected their growing campaign to storm male domains—in this case the saloon—and to contain male violence, particularly wife and child abuse associated with drinking. The "Demon Rum," as some reformers called liquor, had to be exorcised from the home as well as the street corner.

By 1900 the dangers of an alcoholic republic seemed all too real. Alcohol consumption had risen to an annual rate of more than two gallons per person. Often political bosses owned saloons or conducted their business there. To alcohol reformers, taverns and saloons seemed at the center of many social problems—gambling and prostitution, political corruption, drug trafficking, unemployment, and poverty. Few reformers recognized the complex cycle of social decay that produced such problems, fewer still the role of saloons as "workingmen's clubs." The saloon was often the only place to cash a check, find out about jobs, eat a cheap meal, or take a bath.

ANTI-SALOON LEAGUE Reformers considered a national ban on drinking unrealistic and intrusive. They concentrated on prohibiting the sale of alcohol at local and state levels and attacked businesses that profited from it. Led by the Anti-Saloon League (1893), a massive publicity campaign bombarded citizens with pamphlets and advertisements. Doctors cited scientific evidence linking alcohol to cirrhosis, heart disease, and insanity. Social workers connected alcohol consumption with the deterioration of the family; employers, to accidents on the job and lost efficiency.

By 1917 three out of four Americans lived in "dry" counties, which had taken the local option of barring the sale of alcohol.

Source: Library of Congress, Prints and Photographs Division [LC-USZC4-2714]

| *The "Inebriate's Express," loaded with drunken riders, is heading straight for hell. This detail from a chromolithograph, published around 1900, was typical of Victorian-era responses to the problems posed by alcohol. To the all-seeing eye of the omnipotent God, faith, hope, charity, and the Bible are sufficient to cure the problems of drinking.*

Nearly two-thirds of the states had adopted laws outlawing the manufacture and sale of alcohol. Not all progressives were prohibitionists, but the many who were sighed with relief at having taken the profit out of human pain and corruption. They mounted a broader, ultimately successful movement for a constitutional amendment prohibiting the manufacture, sale, transportation, and importation of alcohol.

Prostitution

Immigration restriction and prohibition calmed fears about the newcomers by promising to contain their numbers and eradicate their vices, but no vice worried reformers more than prostitution. In their eyes it was a "social evil" that threatened some of the most vulnerable members of society: young women. In 1910 the Chicago Vice Commission estimated that 5,000 full-time and 10,000 occasional prostitutes plied their trade in the city. Other cities, small and large, reported similar numbers. An unlikely group of reformers united to fight this vice: feminists who wanted husbands to be as faithful as their wives, public health officials worried about the spread of sexually transmitted disease, and immigration restrictionists who regarded the growth of prostitution as yet another sign of corrupt newcomers. Progressives condemned prostitution but saw the problem in economic

Mementos of Murder

Jesse Washington

Men face the camera without making any effort to mask their faces.

Young boys are present.

Source: Library of Congress, Prints and Photographs Division [LC-USZC4-4647]

Not all historians are professionals but even amateurs can help us see the past in a new light. James Allen described himself as a "picker," rummaging through other people's junk for things he might sell. Post-cards hadn't much interested him until he came on one that bore the photograph of a lynching. "It wasn't the corpse that bewildered me but the canine-thin faces of pack," he recalled. Collected and later published by Allen, such postcards memorializing lynchings were one segment of a larger industry that flourished in the late nineteenth and early twentieth centuries. For a penny in postage the cards might be of hotels or city streets or even just photos of individuals taken by photographers, which could be sent to friends and relatives as souvenirs. But the cards Allen came across over the years were of a different order: grisly mementos of a ritualized murder. The one above—of the lynching and burning of an African American named Jesse Washington in 1916—appears not to have been mailed.

THINKING CRITICALLY

Why might people have their photographs taken for postcards at a lynching and then send the cards to parents and other relatives? What does that practice tell us about the racial environment in which such events occurred?

and environmental terms. "Poverty causes prostitution," concluded the Illinois Vice Commission in 1916. On average, prostitutes earned five times the income of factory workers.

Some reformers saw more active agents at work. Rumors spread of a vast and profitable "white slave trade." Men armed with hypodermic needles and drinks filled with "knockout drops" were said to be lurking about streetcars, amusement parks, and dance halls in search of young women. Although the average female rider of the streetcar was hardly in danger of abduction, in every city women were held captive and forced into prostitution. By conservative estimates, such women made up some 10 percent of all prostitutes.

As real abuses blended with sensationalism, Congress passed the Mann Act (1910), prohibiting the interstate transport of women for immoral purposes. By 1918 reformers succeeded in banning previously tolerated **red-light districts** in most cities. Once again, progressives went after those businesses that, like the liquor trade, made money from misery.

"For Whites Only"

Most progressives paid little attention to the misery suffered by African Americans. The 1890s had been a low point for black citizens, most of whom still lived in the South. Across the region, the lynching of African Americans increased dramatically, as did restrictions on black voting and the use of segregated facilities to separate the races. Signs decreeing "For Whites Only" appeared on drinking fountains and restrooms and in other public places.

A few progressives, such as muckraker Ray Stannard Baker and settlement-house worker Lillian Wald, decried racial discrimination, but most ignored it—or used it to their political advantage. Throughout the South, white progressives and even old-guard politicians, including Senator Ben Tillman of South Carolina and Governor James K. Vardaman of Mississippi, used the rhetoric of reform to support white supremacy. Such "reformers" won office by promising to disenfranchise

| *Black boxing champion Jack Johnson's performance in and out of the ring exposed cultural fault lines. In a segregated society, not only did he beat—and taunt—white opponents, Johnson used his celebrity to violate racial conventions. He paraded his sexuality. He consorted with white women. He drank hard and drove fast. "I always take a chance on my pleasures," he boasted. Trespassing boundaries was one way of declaring independence, not merely in pursuit of equality but defiant superiority as well.*

African Americans in order to break the power of corrupt political machines that rested on the black vote, much as northern machines marshaled the immigrant vote.

W. E. B. DU BOIS   In the face of such discrimination African Americans fought back. After the turn of the century, black critics in the North rejected the cautious accommodation of Booker T. Washington's "Atlanta Compromise," which counseled African Americans to accept segregation and work their way up the economic ladder. W. E. B. Du Bois, a professor at Atlanta University, leveled the most stinging attack in *The Souls of Black Folk* (1903). Du Bois saw no benefit for African Americans in sacrificing intellectual growth for narrow vocational training. Nor would he accept the South's discriminatory caste system. A better future would come only if black citizens struggled politically to end segregation and achieve suffrage and equal rights.

NAACP   Instead of exhorting African Americans to pull themselves up slowly from the bottom, Du Bois called on the "talented tenth," a cultured black vanguard, to blaze a trail of protest against segregation, **disenfranchisement,** and discrimination. In 1905 he founded the Niagara Movement for political and economic equality. In 1909 a coalition of blacks and

white reformers transformed the Niagara Movement into the National Association for the Advancement of Colored People (NAACP) after an ugly race riot rocked Springfield, the capital of Illinois, in the summer of 1908. At least seven people died as whites and blacks fought pitched battles after marauding white mobs torched black homes and businesses. For the first time, however, more whites than blacks perished.

The resulting civil rights organization was biracial, drawing members from both the white and black communities. At first predominantly white, the group included Lincoln Steffens, Jane Addams, and John Dewey as well as African Americans W. E. B. Du Bois and Ida B. Wells-Barnett. As with other progressive organizations, NAACP membership was largely limited to the middle class. It worked to extend the principles of tolerance and equal opportunity in a color-blind fashion by publicizing discrimination through its journal, *The Crisis,* and mounting legal challenges to segregation and bigotry. In *Buchanan v. Worley* (1917), for example, NAACP lawyers persuaded the Supreme Court to outlaw residential segregation sponsored by state and local governments. By 1919 the NAACP boasted some 90,000 members in 300 local branches. Accommodation was giving way to new combative organizations and new forms of protest.

> ✓ **REVIEW**
>
> Which "masses" did progressives want to control, why did they want to control them, and what instruments did they employ?

THE POLITICS OF MUNICIPAL AND STATE REFORM

REFORM THE SYSTEM. IN THE end, so many urban problems seemed to return to the premise that government had to be overhauled. Jane Addams learned as much outside the doors of her beloved Hull House in Chicago. For months during the

| *Jane Addams founded her settlement at Hull House in Chicago because she was convinced, like many progressives, that reform must be practical, arising out of the needs of individuals within a community. As Addams continued her campaigns, she also looked beyond the local neighborhood to reform political structures of municipal and state governments.*

early 1890s, garbage piled up in the streets. In Chicago, as elsewhere, a corrupt band of city bosses made garbage collection a profitable plum for the company that paid the most for a contract to haul it away. Service was always spotty and often required a payoff to individual carters. The filth and stench drove Addams and her fellow workers to city hall in protest—700 times in one summer—but to no avail. In Chicago, as elsewhere, corrupt city bosses had made garbage collection a plum awarded to the company that paid them the most for it.

In desperation Addams herself submitted a bid for garbage removal in her neighborhood. When it was thrown out on a technicality, she won an appointment as garbage inspector. For almost a year she dogged collection carts, but boss politics kept things dirty. So Addams ran candidates in 1896 and 1898 against the local ward boss. They lost, but Addams kept up the fight for honest government and social reform—at city hall, in the Illinois legislature, and finally in Washington, D.C. Politics turned out to be the only way to clean things up.

The Reformation of the Cities

In the smokestack cities of the Midwest, where the frustrations of industrial and agricultural America fed each other, the urban battleground furnished the middle class with its first test of political reform. A series of colorful and independent mayors demonstrated that cities could be run humanely without changing the structure of government.

In Detroit, shoe magnate Hazen Pingree became one of the first mayors to enact a reform program when elected in 1889. By the end of Pingree's fourth term, Detroit had new parks and public baths, fairer taxes, ownership of the local light plant, and a work-relief program for victims of the depression of 1893. In 1901 Cleveland mayor Tom Johnson launched a similar reform campaign. Before the end of his campaign, municipal franchises had been limited to a fraction of their previous 99-year terms and the city ran the utility company. By 1915 nearly two out of three cities in the nation had copied some form of this "gas and water socialism" to control the runaway prices of utility companies.

| *Detroit's Hazen S. Pingree was a reforming mayor who, during the hard times of 1893, hired unemployed laborers for public works projects that, among other things, turned the city's Belle Isle into a popular island park along the Detroit River. "Old Ping," as the mayor was known, was plump, short, bald, bearded, and determined. During the depression, he mobilized vacant land in the city as "potato patches," where food was grown to tide over the urban poor during the depression.*

Tragedy dramatized the need to alter the very structure of government. On a hot summer night in 1900 a hurricane storm surge from the Gulf of Mexico smashed the port city of Galveston, Texas. Floods killed one of every six residents. The municipal government sank into confusion and political wrangling. In reaction, business leaders won approval of a new charter that replaced the mayor and city council with a powerful commission. Each of five commissioners controlled a municipal department, and together they ran the city. By 1920 nearly 400 cities had adopted the plan. Expert commissioners enhanced efficiency and helped to check party rule in municipal government.

CITY-MANAGER PLAN In other cities elected officials appointed an outside expert, or "city manager," to run things. The first was hired in Staunton, Virginia, in 1908. Within a decade, 45 cities had them. At lower levels experts took charge of services: engineers oversaw utilities; accountants, finances; doctors and nurses, public health; specially trained firefighters and police, the safety of citizens. Broad civic reforms attempted to break the corrupt alliance between companies doing business with the city and the bosses who controlled the wards. Citywide elections replaced the old ward system, and civil service laws helped create a nonpartisan bureaucracy based on merit. Political machines and ethnic voters lost power, while city government gained efficiency.

Progressivism in the States

WEAKNESSES OF CITY GOVERNMENT "Whenever we try to do anything, we run up against the charter," complained the reform mayor of Schenectady, New York. Charters granted by state governments defined the powers of cities. The rural farm interests that generally dominated state legislatures rarely gave cities adequate authority to levy taxes, set voting requirements, draw up budgets, or legislate reforms. State legislatures found themselves under the influence of business interests, party machines, and county courthouse rings. Reformers therefore tried to place their candidates where they could do some good—in governors' mansions.

State progressivism, like urban reform, enjoyed its greatest success in the Midwest, under the leadership of Robert La Follette of Wisconsin. A mainstream Republican until a party boss offered him a bribe in a railroad case, La Follette turned about and pledged to break "the power of this corrupt influence." In 1900 he won the governorship of Wisconsin as an uncommonly independent Republican.

Over the next six years "Battle Bob" La Follette made Wisconsin, in the words of Theodore Roosevelt, "the laboratory of democracy." La Follette's **Wisconsin idea** produced the most comprehensive set of state reforms in American history. There were new laws regulating railroads, controlling corruption, and expanding the civil service. His direct primary weakened the hold of party bosses by transferring nominations from the backrooms of party conventions and caucuses to the voters at large. Among La Follette's notable "firsts" were a state income tax, a state commission to oversee factory safety and sanitation, and a Legislative Reference Bureau at the University of Wisconsin. University-trained experts poured into state government.

Other states copied the Wisconsin idea or hatched their own programs of reform. All but three had direct primary laws enacted by 1916. No reform gave voters more power in choosing candidates in the West, with its scanty population, strong, independent women had the opportunity to play a larger role in shaping politics, and progressivism thrived. Western states were the nation's first to grant women the right to vote beginning with Wyoming in 1869. In Oregon the legislature limited the number of hours women could work to protect their health from harm. The middle class of heavily urban California supported progressive Hiram Johnson's drive to oust political machines from cities and the statehouse. Colorado governor John Shafroth fought the local political machine and pressed a balky legislature to regulate railroad rates, insure commercial bank deposits, and create a public service commission. Like other progressives, he supported the direct primary.

To cut the power of party organizations and make officeholders directly responsible to the public, Shafroth and other progressives worked for three additional reforms: initiative (voter introduction of legislation), referendum (voter enactment or repeal of laws), and recall (voter-initiated removal of elected officials). By 1912 a dozen states had adopted initiative and referendum, and seven, recall. A year later the Seventeenth Amendment to the Constitution permitted the direct election of senators, previously selected by state legislatures.

Almost every state established regulatory commissions with the power to hold public hearings and to examine company books and question officials. Some could set maximum prices and rates. Yet it was not always easy to define, let alone serve, the "public good." All too often commissioners found themselves refereeing battles within industries—between carriers and shippers, for example—rather than between what progressives called "the (bad) interests" and "the (good) people." Regulators had to rely on the advice of experts drawn from the business community itself. Many commissions thus became "captured" by the industries they regulated. These "captures," much more than corporate corruption, lessened the impact of regulation for industries under scrutiny.

Social welfare received special attention from the states. The lack of workers' compensation for injury, illness, or death on the job had long drawn fire from reformers and labor leaders. American courts still operated on the common-law assumption that employees accepted the risks of work. Workers or their families could collect damages only if they proved employer negligence. Most accident victims received nothing. In 1902 Maryland finally adopted the first workers' compensation act. By 1916 most states required insurance for factory accidents and over half had employer liability laws. Thirteen states also provided pensions for widows with dependent children.

SEEDS OF THE WELFARE STATE   Despite the progressive attack on machine politics, political bosses survived, in part by adapting the climate of reform to the needs of their working-class constituents. After the Triangle fire of 1911, for example, it was Tammany Democrats Robert F. Wagner and Alfred E. Smith who led the fight for a new labor code to govern conditions in the workplace. This working-class "urban liberalism" also found advocates among women's associations, especially those concerned with mothers, children, and working women. The Federation of Women's Clubs led the fight for mothers' pensions (a forerunner of aid to dependent children). When in 1912 the National Consumers League and other women's groups succeeded in establishing the Children's Bureau, it was the first federal welfare agency and the only female-run national bureau in the world. At a time when most women lacked the vote, they nonetheless sowed the seeds of the welfare state as they helped to make urban liberalism a powerful instrument of social reform.

> ✓ **REVIEW**
> What reforms did cities and states enact, and how did those reforms address the problems they faced?

PROGRESSIVISM GOES TO WASHINGTON

ON SEPTEMBER 6, 1901, AT the Pan-American Exposition in Buffalo, New York, Leon Czolgosz stood nervously in line. He was waiting to meet President William McKinley. Unemployed and bent on murder, Czolgosz shuffled toward McKinley. As the president reached out, Czolgosz fired two bullets into his chest. McKinley slumped into a chair. Eight days later the president was dead. The mantle of leadership passed to Theodore Roosevelt. At 42 he was the youngest president ever to hold office.

Roosevelt's entry into the White House was a political accident. Party leaders had seen the weak office of vice president as a way of removing him from power, but the tragedy in Buffalo foiled their plans. Surely progressivism would have come to Washington without Theodore Roosevelt, and while there he was never its most daring advocate. In many ways he was quite conservative. He saw reform as a way to avoid radical change, but he ended up ushering in an era of dramatic change for both Washington and the presidency.

TR

TR, as so many Americans called him, was the scion of seven generations of wealthy, aristocratic New Yorkers. A sickly boy, he built his body through rigorous exercise, sharpened his mind through constant study, and pursued a life so strenuous that few could keep up. He learned to ride and shoot, roped cattle in the Dakota Badlands and later climbed the Matterhorn, hunted African game, and explored the Amazon.

In 1880, driven by an urge to lead and serve, Roosevelt won election to the New York State Assembly. In rapid succession he became a civil service commissioner in Washington, New York City police commissioner, assistant secretary of the navy, and the Rough Rider hero of the Spanish-American War. At the age of 40 he won election as reform governor of New York and two years later as vice president. Through it all, TR remained a solid Republican, personally flamboyant but committed to moderate change only.

As president, Roosevelt brought to the Executive Mansion (he formally renamed it the "White House") a passion for order, a commitment to the public, and a sense of presidential possibilities. Most presidents believed the Constitution set limits on their power. Roosevelt thought that the president could do anything not expressly forbidden in the document. Recognizing the value of publicity, he gave reporters the first press room in the White House and favored them with all the stories they wanted. He was the first president to ride in an automobile, fly in an airplane, and dive in a submarine—and everyone knew it.

To dramatize racial injustice, Roosevelt invited black educator Booker T. Washington to lunch at the White House in 1901. White southern journalists called such race mingling treason, but for Roosevelt the gesture served both principle and politics. His lunch with Washington was part of a "black and tan" strategy to build a biracial coalition among southern Republicans. He denounced lynching and appointed black southerners to important federal offices in Mississippi and South Carolina.

BROWNSVILLE INCIDENT   Sensing the limits of political feasibility, Roosevelt went no further. Perhaps his own narrowness on race also stopped him. In 1906, when Atlanta exploded in a race riot that left 12 people dead, Roosevelt said nothing. Later that year he discharged "without honor" three entire companies of African American troops, because some of the soldiers were (unjustly) charged with having "shot up" Brownsville, Texas. All lost their pensions, including six winners of the Medal of Honor. The act stained Roosevelt's record. (Congress acknowledged the wrong in 1972 by granting the soldiers honorable discharges.)

A Square Deal

PHILOSOPHY OF THE SQUARE DEAL   Roosevelt could not long follow McKinley's cautious course. He had more energetic actions in mind. He accepted growth—whether of business, labor, or government—as natural. In the pluralistic system he envisioned, big labor would counterbalance big capital, big farm organizations would offset big food processors, and so on. Standing astride them all, mediating when needed, was a big government that could ensure fair results for all. Later, as he campaigned for a second term in 1904, Roosevelt named this program the "Square Deal."

ANTHRACITE COAL STRIKE   In a startling display of presidential initiative, Roosevelt in 1902 intervened in a strike that idled 140,000 miners and paralyzed the anthracite (hard) coal industry. As winter approached, public frustration with the mine owners mounted. They refused even to recognize the miners' union, let alone negotiate worker demands for higher wages and fewer hours. Roosevelt summoned both sides to the White House. When management refused, Roosevelt leaked word to Wall Street that the army would take over the mines if the owners did not yield.

Seldom had a president acted so boldly and never on behalf of strikers. In late October 1902 the owners settled by granting miners a 10 percent wage hike and a nine-hour day in return for increases in coal prices and no union recognition. Roosevelt was equally prepared to intervene on the side of management, as he did when he sent federal troops to end strikes in Arizona in 1903 and Colorado in 1904. His aim was to establish a vigorous presidency ready to deal squarely with all sides.

U.S. v. E. C. KNIGHT Roosevelt especially needed to confront the issue of economic concentration. Financial power had become consolidated in giant trusts following a wave of mergers at the end of the century. Government investigations revealed a rash of corporate abuses—rebates, collusion, **"watered" stock**, payoffs to government officials. The conservative courts showed little willingness to break up the giants or blunt their power. In *United States v.*

E. C. Knight (1895), the Supreme Court had crippled the Sherman Antitrust Act by ruling that the federal law applied only to **interstate commerce** and not to manufacturing. The decision left the American Sugar Refining Company in control of 98 percent of the nation's sugar-making factories.

In his first State of the Union message in 1901, Roosevelt told Congress that he did not oppose trusts. As he saw it, large corporations were not only inevitable but also capable of producing more goods at lower prices. He wanted to regulate, not destroy, them, to make them fairer and more efficient. Only then would the economic order be humanized, its victims protected, and class violence avoided. Like individuals, trusts had to be held to strict standards of morality. Conduct, not size, was the yardstick TR used to measure "good" and "bad" trusts.

With a progressive's faith in the power of publicity and a regulator's need for the facts, Roosevelt moved immediately to strengthen the federal power of investigation. He called for the creation of a Department of Commerce with a Bureau of Corporations that could force companies to hand over their records. Congressional conservatives shuddered at the prospect of putting corporate books on display. Finally, in 1903, after Roosevelt charged that John D. Rockefeller was orchestrating the opposition, Congress enacted the legislation and provided the Justice Department with additional staff to prosecute antitrust cases.

NORTHERN SECURITIES In 1902, to demonstrate the power of government, Roosevelt had Attorney General Philander Knox file an antitrust suit against the Northern Securities Company. The mammoth holding company virtually monopolized railroads in the Northwest. Worse still, it bloated its stock with worthless certificates and gouged consumers. Here, clearly, was a "bad trust." J. P. Morgan, one of the company's founders, rushed to the White House. "Send your man [the attorney general] to my man [Morgan's lawyer] and they can fix it up," he told Roosevelt and Knox. "We don't want to fix it up," replied the attorney general. "We want to

| Bullnecked and barrel-chested, Theodore Roosevelt was "pure act," said Henry Adams. TR may have had the attention span of a golden retriever, as one critic charged, but he also embodied the great virtues of his day—honesty, hard work, constancy, courage, and, while in power, self-control.

(*top left*) Source: Library of Congress, Prints and Photographs Division [LC-DIG-ppmsca-37306]; (*bottom left*) Source: Library of Congress, Prints and Photographs Division [LC-DIG-ppm-sca-36679]; (*bottom right*) Source: Theodore Roosevelt Digital Library, Dickinson State University

stop it." In the end the Supreme Court ordered the company to dissolve in 1904. Ultimately the Roosevelt administration brought suit against 44 giants.

RAILROAD REGULATION Despite his reputation for trust-busting, Roosevelt always preferred continuous regulation. The problems of the railroads, for example, were newly underscored by a recent round of mergers and acquisitions that contributed to higher freight rates. Roosevelt pressed Congress to strengthen the weak Interstate Commerce Commission (ICC), created in 1887. In 1903 Congress enacted the Elkins Act, which gave the ICC power to end rebates. Even the railroads supported the act because it saved them from the costly practice of granting special fee reductions to large shippers.

By the election of 1904 the president's Square Deal had won him broad popular support. He trounced his two rivals, Democrat Alton B. Parker, a jurist from New York, and Eugene V. Debs of the Socialist Party.

Conservatives in his own party opposed Roosevelt's meddling in the private sector. But progressives, goaded by Robert La Follette, demanded still more regulation of the railroads, in particular a controversial proposal for making public the value of all rail property. In 1906 the president finally reached a compromise typical of his restrained approach to reform. The Hepburn Railway Act allowed the ICC to set ceilings on rates and regulate sleeping-car companies, ferries, bridges, and terminals. La Follette did not obtain the provision to disclose company value he wanted, but the Hepburn Act drew Roosevelt nearer to his goal of continuous regulation of business.

Bad Food and Pristine Wilds

Extending the umbrella of federal protection to consumers, Roosevelt belatedly threw his weight behind two campaigns for healthy foods and drugs. In 1905 Samuel Hopkins Adams of *Collier's Weekly* wrote that "Gullible America" was buying over-the-counter patent medicines loaded with "huge quantities of alcohol, an appalling amount of opiates and narcotics," and worse—axle grease, acid, glue. Adams sent the samples he had collected to Harvey Wiley, chief chemist at the Agriculture Department. Wiley's "Poison Squad" produced scientific evidence of Adams's charges.

The appearance of Upton Sinclair's best-selling novel *The Jungle* in 1906 spurred Congress to act. Sinclair intended to recruit people to socialism by exposing the plight of workers in the meatpacking industry. (It was first published as a serial in the socialist newspaper *Appeal to Reason*.) *The Jungle* contained a brief but vivid description of the slaughter of cattle infected with tuberculosis, of meat covered with rat dung, and of men falling into cooking vats. Readers paid scant attention to the workers, but their stomachs turned at what they might be eating for breakfast. The Pure Food and Drug Act of 1906 sailed through Congress, and the Meat Inspection Act soon followed.

CONSERVATION THROUGH PLANNED MANAGEMENT Roosevelt was a latecomer to consumer protection, but on conservation he led the nation. An outdoors enthusiast, he galvanized public concern over the reckless use of natural resources. His chief forester, Gifford Pinchot, persuaded him

Patent medicines made wild curative claims. These promised to restore hair and end dandruff with extracts from the yucca plant, long used by Indians of the Southwest for medicinal and nonmedicinal purposes.

that planned management under federal guidance was needed to protect the natural domain. Cutting trees must be synchronized with tree plantings, for example, and oil pumped from the ground under controlled conditions.

CONSERVATION VERSUS PRESERVATION In the western states water was the problem, as U.S. Geological Survey director John Welsey Powell had noted years earlier (Chapter 18). Economic growth, even survival, depended on it. Two visions of what to do about Powell's water-starved West emerged. One emphasized the conservation of water (and other scarce resources) through planned use; the other, preservation of resources in a pristine state. Supporters of conservation pointed to the economic benefits flowing from planned water use: bringing marginal land into production, luring settlers into a region that was land-rich and people-poor, implanting agriculture and industry on an unimagined scale. Advocates of preservation pointed to the ecological costs of developing a region whose scarce water could be drained or contaminated and whose natural environment was thus unsuitable for agriculture and industry.

As fragmented local and state water policies sparked controversy, violence, and waste, many progressives campaigned for a federal program to replace the tangled web of rules. Democratic senator Frederick Newlands of Nevada introduced the Reclamation Act of 1902 to set aside proceeds from the sale of public lands for irrigation projects. The Reclamation Act signaled a progressive step toward the conservationist goal of rational resource development.

JOHN MUIR AND PRESERVATION Conservation, the form of environmental protection most appealing to progressives, often conflicted with the more radical vision of preservationists. As early as 1864 naturalist George Perkins Marsh sounded an alarm. In *Man and Nature; or Physical Geography as Modified by Human Action,* Marsh warned that human activity enhanced by technology could damage the planet. Already, he wrote, the agricultural and industrial revolutions had begun to erode soil, deforest timberland, dry up watersheds, and endanger plants and animals.

Another naturalist, the wilderness philosopher John Muir, took Marsh's call a step further. The Scottish-born Muir had emigrated to the United States with his family as a boy. Trained as an engineer, he nearly lost his sight when a sharp file punctured his right eye. His sight miraculously returned, and he vowed to be "true to myself" by following his passion: the study of the wild world. Study turned to activism in 1892 when Muir cofounded the Sierra Club. He hoped to maintain such natural wonders as California's Hetch Hetchy Valley in his beloved Yosemite National Park in a state of "forever wild" to benefit future generations. Many conservationists saw such valleys only as sites for dams and reservoirs to manage and control water. "When we try to pick out anything by itself," Muir wrote, "we find it hitched to everything else in the universe."

Controversy flared after 1900, when San Francisco announced plans to create a city reservoir by flooding the Hetch Hetchy Valley. Could a dam be built in a national park? For 13 years Muir waged a publicity campaign against the reservoir and its "devotees of ravaging commercialism." Pinchot enthusiastically backed San Francisco's claim. Roosevelt, torn by his friendship with Muir, did so less loudly. Not until 1913 did President Woodrow Wilson finally decide the issue in favor of San Francisco by authorizing the construction of the O'Shaughnessy Dam. Construction had trumped preservation.

Roosevelt nonetheless advanced many of Muir's goals. Over the protests of cattle and timber interests, he added nearly 200 million acres to government forest reserves; placed coal and mineral lands, oil reserves, and water-power sites in the public domain; and enlarged the national park system. When Congress balked, he reserved another 17 million acres of forest before the legislators could pass a bill limiting him. Like a good progressive, he sent hundreds of experts to work applying science, education, and technology to environmental problems.

Roosevelt's reform record was still modest when he announced in 1908 that he would not run for another term. Yet by reinvigorating the presidency and the executive branch, TR opened the way to even more reforms. The conservative business community was well aware of that possibility, as was Roosevelt, when he turned the presidency over to his successor, William Howard Taft.

The Troubled Taft

On March 4, 1909, as snow swirled outside the White House, William Howard Taft readied himself for his inauguration. Over breakfast with Roosevelt, he warmed in the glow of recent Republican victories. Taft had beaten Democrat William Jennings Bryan in the "Great Commoner's" third and last bid for the presidency. Republicans had retained control of Congress, as well as a host of northern legislatures. Reform was at high tide, and Taft was eager to continue the Roosevelt program.

"Will," as Roosevelt called Taft, was his handpicked successor. A distinguished jurist and public servant, the first American governor-general of the Philippines, and Roosevelt's secretary of war, Taft had great administrative skill and personal charm. But he disliked the political maneuvering of Washington and preferred conciliation to confrontation, judicious reasoning to emotional eruptions, discussion to decision. Even Roosevelt had doubts. "He's all right," TR had told a reporter on inauguration day. "But he's weak."

Trouble began early when progressives in the House moved to curb the near-dictatorial power of the conservative Speaker, Joseph Cannon. Taft waffled, first supporting them and then abandoning them to preserve the tariff reductions he was seeking. When progressives later broke Cannon's power without Taft's help, they scorned the president. And Taft's compromise was wasted. Senate

| *The Sierra Club, founded by naturalist John Muir* (center, with beard), *believed in the importance of preserving wilderness in its natural state. "In God's wildness," Muir wrote in 1890, "lies the hope of the world—the great fresh unlighted, unredeemed wilderness." In front of this giant redwood tree, Theodore Roosevelt stands to the left of Muir, who persuaded the president to double the number of national parks.*

protectionists peppered the tariff bill with so many amendments that rates jumped nearly to their old levels.

Late in 1909 the rift between Taft and the progressives reached the breaking point in a dispute over conservation. Taft had appointed Richard Ballinger secretary of the interior over the objections of Roosevelt's old friend and mentor Chief Forester Pinchot. When Ballinger opened a million acres of public lands for sale, Pinchot charged that shady dealings had led Ballinger to transfer Alaskan public coal lands to a syndicate that included J. P. Morgan. Early in 1910, Taft fired Pinchot for insubordination. Angry progressives saw the Ballinger-Pinchot controversy as another betrayal by Taft. They began to look longingly across the Atlantic, where TR was stalking big game in Africa.

TAFT'S ACCOMPLISHMENTS Despite his failures Taft was no conservative pawn. He ended up protecting more land than Roosevelt, and he pressured Congress to enact a progressive program regulating safety standards for mines

| *William Howard Taft* (on the far right) *was big, good-natured, modest, and reluctant to run for the presidency in 1908. At the outset of the campaign President Roosevelt sent him pointed advice: "Photographs on horseback, yes, tennis, no, and golf is fatal." But Taft played anyway. He loved golf despite its reputation as a "dude's game."*

PRESERVATION VERSUS CONSERVATION

No president is more closely associated with protecting the environment than Theodore Roosevelt. His lifelong love of nature and wilderness only deepened in 1903, when Sierra Club cofounder John Muir took him traipsing through the snow in what became, thanks to Roosevelt and Muir, Yosemite National Park in 1906. Despite their friendship, however, the two men differed on what should be done with wilderness. Muir proposed preservation of the natural world in its most pristine form, whereas Roosevelt favored conservation for a multitude of uses in the public interest.

DOCUMENT 1
Wilderness Should Be "Unspoiled": Muir

No dogma taught by the present civilization seems to form so insuperable an obstacle in the way of a right understanding of the relations which culture sustains to wildness as that which regards the world as made especially for the uses of man. Every animal, plant, and crystal controverts it in the plainest terms. Yet it is taught from century to century as something ever new and precious, and in the resulting darkness the enormous conceit is allowed to go unchallenged. . . .

The great wilds of our country, once held to be boundless and inexhaustible, are being rapidly invaded and overrun in every direction, and everything destructible in them is being destroyed. How far destruction may go it is not easy to guess. Every landscape, low and high, seems doomed to be trampled and harried. Even the sky is not safe from scath—blurred and blackened whole summers together with the smoke of fires that devour the woods.

The Shasta region [part of the Cascade Mountains in California] is still a fresh unspoiled wilderness, accessible and available for travelers of every kind and degree. Would it not then be a fine thing to set it apart like the Yellowstone and Yosemite as a National Park for the welfare and benefit of all mankind, preserving its fountains and forests and all its glad life in primeval beauty? Very little of the region can ever be more valuable for any other use—certainly not for gold nor for grain. No private right or interest need suffer, and thousands yet unborn would come from far and near and bless the country for its wise and benevolent forethought.

Source: Muir, John, *Steep Trails*, edited by William Frederic Badé. Boston, MA: Houghton Mifflin Company, September 1918, 11–12, 104.

DOCUMENT 2
Forest Land Has Multiple Uses: Roosevelt

Lands in the forest reserves that are more valuable for agriculture than for fewest purposes are being opened to settlement and entry as fast as their agricultural character can be ascertained. There is therefore no longer excuse for saying that the reserves retard the legitimate settlement and development of the country. On the contrary, they promote and sustain that development, and they do so in no way more powerful than through their direct contributions to the schools and roads. Ten per cent of all the money received from the forest reserves goes to the States for the use of the counties in which the reserves lie, to be used for schools and roads. . . .

The forest policy of the Government in the West has now become what the West desired it to be. It is a national policy, wider than the boundaries of any State, and larger than the interests of any single industry. Of course it cannot give any set of men exactly what they would choose. Undoubtedly the irrigator would often like to have less stock on his watersheds, while the stockman wants more. The lumberman would like to cut more timber, the settler and the miner would often like him to cut less. The county authorities want to see more money coming in for schools and roads, while the lumberman and stockman object to the rise in value of timber and grass. . . .

By keeping the public forests in the public hands our forest policy substitutes the good of the whole people for the profits of the privileged few. With that result none will quarrel except the men who are losing the chance of personal profit at public expense.

Our western forest policy is based upon meeting the wishes of the best public sentiment of the whole West. It proposes to create new reserves wherever forest lands still vacant are found in the public domain, and to give the reserves already made the highest possible usefulness to all the people.

Source: Theodore Roosevelt Letter to Gifford Pinchot, August 24, 1906, as reprinted in Brands, H. W., ed., *The Selected Letters of Theodore Roosevelt*. New York, NY: Cooper Square Press, 2001, 432–433.

THINKING CRITICALLY

What does wilderness mean to John Muir? What are its benefits? What does Theodore Roosevelt have in mind for "forest reserves," and what does he mean by "the good of the whole people"? How do their different positions help to shape their points of view?

and railroads, creating a federal children's bureau, and setting an eight-hour workday for federal employees. Taft's support of a **graduated income tax**—sometimes staunch, sometimes mild—was finally decisive. Early in 1913 it became the Sixteenth Amendment. Historians view it as one of the most important reforms of the century, for it eventually generated the revenue for many new social programs.

Yet no matter what Taft did, he managed to alienate conservatives and progressives alike. That spelled trouble for the Republicans as the presidential election of 1912 approached.

The Election of 1912

In June 1910 Roosevelt came home from Africa laden with hunting trophies and exuberant as ever. He found Taft unhappy and progressive Republicans threatening to defect. Party loyalty kept Roosevelt quiet through most of 1911, but in October Taft pricked him personally on the sensitive matter of busting trusts. Like TR, Taft accepted trusts as natural but demanded, more impartially, that all trusts—"good" or "bad" ones—be prevented from restraining trade. In four years as president, Taft brought nearly twice the antitrust suits Roosevelt had in seven years.

NEW NATIONALISM   Already, in a speech at Osawatomie, Kansas, in 1910, Roosevelt had sharpened his differences with Taft by outlining a program of sweeping reform. His "New Nationalism" stressed the interests of the nation as a whole and the value of government as an agent of reform. It accepted consolidation in the economy—whether in the growth of big business or big labor—but insisted on protecting the interests of individuals through big government. The New Nationalism promised government planning and efficiency under a powerful executive, "a steward of the public welfare." It promoted taxes on incomes and inheritances and greater regulation of industry. And it embraced social justice, specifically workers' compensation for accidents, minimum wages and maximum hours, child labor laws, and "equal suffrage"—a nod to women and loyal black Republicans. Roosevelt, a cautious reformer as president, grew daring as he campaigned for the White House.

PROGRESSIVE, OR "BULL MOOSE," PARTY   "My hat is in the ring!" Roosevelt announced in February 1912. The enormously popular Roosevelt won most of the primaries, but by the time Republicans met in Chicago in June 1912, Taft had used presidential patronage and promises to secure his renomination. A frustrated Roosevelt bolted and took progressive Republicans with him. Two months later, amid choruses of "Onward Christian Soldiers," delegates to the newly formed Progressive Party nominated Roosevelt for the presidency. "I'm feeling like a bull moose!" he bellowed. Progressives suddenly had a symbol for their breakaway party.

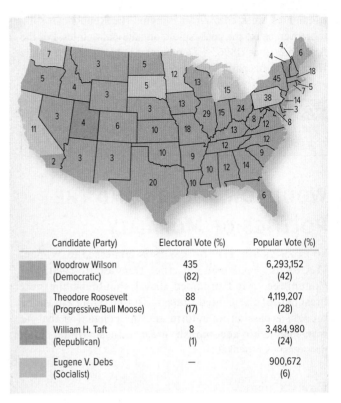

Candidate (Party)	Electoral Vote (%)	Popular Vote (%)
Woodrow Wilson (Democratic)	435 (82)	6,293,152 (42)
Theodore Roosevelt (Progressive/Bull Moose)	88 (17)	4,119,207 (28)
William H. Taft (Republican)	8 (1)	3,484,980 (24)
Eugene V. Debs (Socialist)	—	900,672 (6)

ELECTION OF 1912

WOODROW WILSON'S NEW FREEDOM   The Democrats chose as their candidate Woodrow Wilson, the progressive governor of New Jersey. Wilson wisely concentrated his fire on Roosevelt. He countered the New Nationalism with his "New Freedom." It rejected the economic consolidation that Roosevelt embraced. Bigness itself was a sin, no matter how big corporations acted, because they crowded out competition, thereby promoting inefficiency and reducing economic opportunity. Only by strictly limiting the size of business enterprises could the free market be preserved and Americans be released from the control of the wealthy and powerful. And only by keeping government small could individual liberty be protected. "Liberty," Wilson cautioned, "has never come from government," only from the "limitation of governmental power."

Increasingly, voters found the Republican Taft beside the point. In an age of reform even the Socialists looked good. Better led, financed, and more organized than ever, the Socialist Party had enlarged its membership to nearly 135,000 by 1912. Socialist mayors ran 32 cities. The party also had an appealing candidate in Eugene V. Debs, a homegrown Indiana radical. He had won over 400,000 votes in the last of his three previous bids for president in 1908. Now, in 1912, he summoned voters to make "the working class the ruling class."

On Election Day, voters gave progressive reform a resounding endorsement. Wilson won 6.3 million votes, Roosevelt 4.1 million, Taft just 3.6 million. Debs received almost a million votes. Together the two progressive candidates amassed a 3-to-1 margin. The Republican split, moreover, broke the party's hold on national politics. For the first time since 1896, a Democrat would sit in the White House with his party in control of Congress.

✓ REVIEW
How did President Roosevelt's reform agenda reflect his promise of a "Square Deal" for Americans?

WOODROW WILSON AND THE POLITICS OF MORALITY

SOON AFTER THE ELECTION WILSON confessed to William McCombs, chairman of the Democratic National Committee: "God ordained that I should be the next President of the United States." To the White House he brought a passion for reform and the conviction that he was meant to accomplish great things. Under him, progressivism peaked.

Early Career

From the moment of his birth in 1856, Thomas Woodrow Wilson could not escape a sense of destiny. In the family's Presbyterian faith, in the sermons of his minister father, in dinnertime talk ran the unbending belief in a world predetermined by God and ruled by saved souls, the "elect." Wilson ached to be one of them and behaved as if he were.

Like most southerners, he grew up loving the Democratic Party and small government, hating the tariff, and accepting racial segregation. (Under his presidency, segregation returned to Washington for the first time since Reconstruction.) An early career in law bored him, so he turned to political science and became a professor. His studies persuaded him that a modern president must act as a "prime minister," directing and uniting his party, shaping legislation and public opinion, exerting continuous leadership. In 1910, after a stormy tenure as head of Princeton University, Wilson was helped by Democratic Party bosses to win the governorship of New Jersey. In 1912 they helped him again, this time to the presidency of the country.

The Reforms of the New Freedom

As governor Wilson led New Jersey on the path of progressive reform. As president he was a model of executive leadership. More than Theodore Roosevelt he shaped policy and legislation. He went to Congress to let members know he intended to work personally with them. He kept party discipline tight and mobilized public opinion when Congress refused to act.

Lowering the high tariff was Wilson's first order of business. Progressives had long attacked the tariff as another example of the power of trusts. By protecting American manufacturers, Wilson argued, such barriers weakened the competition he cherished. When the Senate threatened to raise rates, the new president appealed directly to the public. "Industrious" and "insidious" lobbyists were blocking reform, he cried to reporters. A "brick couldn't be thrown without hitting one of them."

UNDERWOOD-SIMMONS TARIFF The Underwood-Simmons Tariff of 1913 marked the first downward revision of the tariff in 19 years and the biggest since before

| Woodrow Wilson came to the White House with promises to reform government. In this 1913 cartoon titled "A New Captain in the District," the newly elected president strides through corrupt Washington, ready to police such abuses as easy land grants and pork barreling, the much-criticized congressional practice of voting for projects that benefit home districts and constituents.

Source: Library of Congress, Prints and Photographs Division [LC-DIG-ppmsca-27931]

the Civil War. To compensate for lost revenue, Congress enacted a graduated income tax under the newly adopted Sixteenth Amendment. It applied solely to corporations and the tiny fraction of Americans who earned more than $4,000 a year. It nonetheless began a momentous shift in government revenue from its nineteenth-century base—public lands, alcohol taxes, and customs duties—to its twentieth-century base—personal and corporate incomes.

Wilson turned next to the perennial problems of money and banking. Early in 1913 a congressional committee revealed that a few powerful banks controlled the nation's credit system. They could choke Wilson's free market by raising interest rates or reducing the supply of money. As a banking reform bill moved through Congress in 1913, Wall Street conservatives lobbied for a privately controlled, centralized banking system that could issue currency and set interest rates. Rural Democrats favored a decentralized system of regional banks run by local bankers. Populists and progressives—including William Jennings Bryan and Robert La Follette—wanted government control.

FEDERAL RESERVE ACT   Wilson split their differences in the Federal Reserve Act of 1913. The new Federal Reserve System contained 12 regional banks scattered across the country. It also created a central Federal Reserve Board in Washington, appointed by the president, to supervise the system. The board could regulate credit and the money supply by setting interest rates charged member banks, by buying or selling government bonds, and by issuing paper currency called Federal Reserve notes.

FEDERAL TRADE COMMISSION   When Wilson finally took on the trusts, he moved closer to the New Nationalism of Theodore Roosevelt. The Federal Trade Commission Act of 1914 created a bipartisan executive agency to oversee business activity. The end—to enforce orderly competition—was distinctly Wilsonian, but the means—an executive commission to regulate commerce—were pure Roosevelt.

CLAYTON ANTITRUST ACT   Roosevelt would have stopped there, but Wilson made good on his campaign pledge to attack trusts. The Clayton Antitrust Act (1914) barred some of the worst corporate practices—price discrimination, holding companies, and interlocking directorates (directors of one corporate board sitting on others). Despite Wilson's bias against size, the advantages of large-scale production and distribution were inescapable. In practice his administration chose to regulate rather than break

PRESIDENT'S SIGNATURE ENACTS CURRENCY LAW

Wilson Declares It the First of Series of Constructive Acts to Aid Business.

Makes Speech to Group of Democratic Leaders.

Conference Report Adopted in Senate by Vote of 43 to 25.

Banks All Over the Country Hasten to Enter Federal Reserve System.

Gov.-Elect Walsh Calls Passage of Bill A Fine Christmas Present.

WILSON SEES DAWN OF NEW ERA IN BUSINESS

HOME VIEWS OF FOUR PENS USED CURRENCY ACT BY PRESIDENT

Aims to Make Prosperity Free to Have Unimpeded Momentum.

Source: Federal Reserve

up bigness. Wilson's Justice Department filed fewer antitrust suits than under the Taft administration and negotiated more "gentlemen's agreements" (voluntary agreements by companies to change practices) than under Roosevelt.

Labor and Social Reform

For all of Wilson's impressive accomplishments, voters turned lukewarm toward the New Freedom. In the elections of 1914, Republicans cut Democratic majorities in the House and won important industrial and farm states. To strengthen his hand in the presidential election of 1916, Wilson began edging toward the social reforms of the New Nationalism he had once criticized as paternalistic and unconstitutional. Early in 1916 he signaled the change when he nominated his close adviser Louis D. Brandeis to the Supreme Court. The progressive Brandeis had fought for the social reforms

Source: Library of Congress, Prints and Photographs Division [LC-DIG-ppmsca-06024]

Justice Louis Brandeis, who dropped his corporate law practice to become "the people's lawyer," continued to apply progressive principles after Wilson appointed him to the Supreme Court in 1916.

The Progressive Amendments

AMENDMENT	YEAR ADOPTED	WHAT IT DID	WHAT IT ADDRESSED
16th Amendment	1913	Income tax	Tax inequities
17th Amendment	1913	Direct election of U.S. senators	Political corruption through elections by state legislatures
18th Amendment	1918	Prohibition of manufacture, sale, transportation, and importation of alcohol	Reduced consumption of alcohol; liquor business profiting from "human misery"; alcoholism
19th Amendment	1920	Vote to all citizens	Women barred from voting in most elections

TO ASK FREEDOM FOR WOMEN IS NOT A CRIME SUFFRAGE PRISONERS SHOULD NOT BE TREATED AS CRIMINALS

(*left*) Source: Library of Congress, Prints and Photographs Division [LC-DIG-hec-11942]; (*right*) Source: Library of Congress, Prints and Photographs Division [LC-USZ62-123257]

lacking on Wilson's legislative agenda. His appointment also broke the anti-Semitic tradition of keeping Jews off the Court.

In other ways Wilson revealed his willingness to pursue progressive reforms for workers and farmers previously absent from his plans. He helped pass laws improving the working conditions of merchant seamen and setting an eight-hour day for workers on interstate railroads. He endorsed the Keating-Owen Child Labor Act that barred the sale of items made by children and sold across state lines, and threw his support to legislation providing farmers with low-interest loans. Just before the election Wilson intervened to avert a nationwide strike of rail workers. All reflected a turn toward the progressive goals of social justice and social welfare.

Woodrow Wilson's first administration capped a decade and a half of heady reform. Seeing chaos in the industrial city, progressives worked to reduce the damage of poverty and the hazards of factory work, control the rising tide of immigration, and spread a middle-class ideal of morality. In city halls and state legislatures they tried to break the power of corporate interests and political machines. In Washington they enlarged government and broadened its mission from caretaker to promoter of public welfare.

Inevitably they fell short. Progressive reform was a patchwork affair, uneven and incomplete. Reformers sometimes betrayed their high ideals by denying equality to African

Americans, Asians, Latinos, and other minorities. Too often government commissions designed as watchdogs found themselves captured by the interests they were supposed to oversee. Well-meaning but cumbersome regulation crippled businesses such as the railroads, while other reforms weakened political machines and corruption without fully eliminating bosses and dishonesty. Still, under progressivism the modern state—active and interventionist—was born. Public policy began to address the inequities of the age. A sense of mastery replaced the disheartening feeling of drift. The results, however mixed, set the agenda of reform for the remainder of the twentieth century.

> ✓ **REVIEW**
>
> Compare and contrast Theodore Roosevelt's approach to reform with that of Woodrow Wilson.

PUTTING HISTORY IN A GLOBAL CONTEXT

THE UNITED STATES WAS hardly first among reformers. The Machine Age triggered a wave of reform across the industrialized world. Movements for social justice and social welfare sprang up first in Great Britain, where the Industrial Revolution began. The Factory Act of 1833 outlawed child labor in textile mills for those under the age of nine. The Mines Act of 1842 made it illegal to employ all women as well as children younger than ten in work underground. In comparison, the United States failed even to enact a law prohibiting child labor until 1916. In 1884 Toynbee Hall, the world's first social settlement house, opened in London's East End to minister to the needs of the poor. It became the model for Jane Addams's Hull House in Chicago.

In political reforms the world sometimes lagged behind the United States. Except in Scandinavia, most European women did not receive the vote until after World War I. And despite the democratic revolutions that swept across Latin America in the nineteenth century, national women's suffrage was opposed by the Catholic Church and did not come to Ecuador until 1929, Brazil until 1932, and El Salvador until 1939. Asia was slower still, often because colonial rulers denied or limited suffrage or because patriarchal Asian societies looked on women as subordinate to men. Only in 1950, for example, after India achieved independence, did women receive the right to vote. In Japan, although Japanese suffragists founded the *Fusen Kakutoku Domei* (Women's Suffrage League) in 1924, Japanese militarists crushed the fledgling Japanese democracy in the 1930s, as well as any women's suffrage until 1946.

CHAPTER SUMMARY

Progressivism was a broad-based reform movement, the first truly national reform movement in American history, that attempted to address problems arising from industrialization, urbanization, and immigration.

- Progressive reform sprang from many impulses:
  - ▸ Desires to curb the advancing power of big business and to end political corruption.
  - ▸ Efforts to bring order and efficiency to economic and political life.
  - ▸ Attempts by new interest groups to make business and government more responsive to the needs of ordinary citizens.
  - ▸ Moralistic urges to rid society of industries such as the liquor trade that profited from human misery, to bridge the gap between immigrants and native-born Americans, and to soften the consequences of industrialization through social justice and social welfare.

- Led by members of the urban middle class, progressives were moderate modernizers, supporting traditional American values such as democracy, Judeo-Christian ethics, and the spirit of volunteerism and public service while employing the new techniques of management and planning, coordinated systems, and bureaucracies of experts.

- Progressive women extended their traditional sphere of home and family to become "social housekeepers" and crusaders for women's rights, especially the right to vote.

- Increasingly, progressivism animated politics, first at the local and state levels, then in the presidencies of Theodore Roosevelt and Woodrow Wilson.

- In the end, the weaknesses of progressivism—the fuzziness of its conception of the public interest, the exclusion of African Americans and other minorities, the ease with which its regulatory mechanisms were "captured" by those being regulated—were matched by its accomplishments in establishing the modern, activist state.

Digging Deeper

The long interpretive debate over what progressivism was and who the progressives were has several benchmarks, among them Arthur Link and Richard L. McCormick, *Progressivism* (1985). Benchmarks in that debate include George E. Mowry, *The California Progressives* (1951); and Richard Hofstadter, *The Age of Reform* (1955), both of which see progressives as a small elite seeking to recapture its fading status and influence. Gabriel Kolko, *The Triumph of Conservatism* (1963), makes the controversial case that business "captured" reform to control competition and stave off stricter federal regulation. Michael McGerr's *A Fierce Discontent: The Rise and Fall of the Progressive Movement* (2003) sees progressivism as a daring middle-class movement to transform society in four classically progressive ways: "to change other people; to end class conflict; to control big business; and to segregate society." David Traxel examines the reforming spirit of the Progressive Era and the First World War he sees it spawning in *Crusader Nation* (2006). Jackson Lears, *Rebirth of a Nation: The Making of Modern America, 1877-1920* (2009), places progressivism in the longer context of what Lears sees as a search for regeneration in the decades after the Civil War.

The social history of progressivism is the focus of Steven J. Diner's *A Very Different Age: Americans of the Progressive Era* (1998). Eric Rauchway's *Murdering McKinley: The Making of Theodore Roosevelt's America* (2003) presents a revisionist account of American politics and society ranging from criminal psychology to nativism, tariff and currency reform, and ideological conflict. James Chace provides a deft narrative in *1912: Wilson, Roosevelt, Taft, and Debs and the Election That Changed the Country* (2004).

John M. Blum, *The Republican Roosevelt* (1954), remains the most incisive rendering of TR; and Lewis L. Gould, *The Presidency of Theodore Roosevelt* (1991), is the best single-volume study of the White House years. Ian Tyrrell's *The Crisis of the Wasteful Nation: Conservation and Empire in Theodore Roosevelt's America* (2015) places the progressive conservation movement in a global context. Unsurpassed for its detail and depth is Arthur Link, *Woodrow Wilson*, 5 vols. (1947-1965). Robert M. Crunden's *Ministers of Reform* (1982) emphasizes the cultural origins and impact of progressivism, and Ellen Chesler's *Woman of Valor* (1992) looks through a feminist lens at the life and times of social reformer Margaret Sanger. Melvin I. Urofsky's *Louis D. Brandeis: A Life* (2009) is an admiring and authoritative biography of "the people's lawyer." In *Triangle: The Fire That Changed America* (2004), David Von Drehle offers the fullest account yet of that calamity.

23 The United States and the Collapse of the Old World Order

1901–1920

The construction of the Panama Canal was a massive feat of engineering. The volume of concrete poured to make just one of the three main locks was enough to build a wall 8 feet high, 12 feet thick, and 133 miles long. The Culebra Cut, shown here, provided what was perhaps the biggest challenge in slicing through the Continental Divide. Steam drills bored holes into the rock, which were filled with dynamite to blow open a path. Then gigantic steam shovels helped move the dirt and rock away—over 100 million cubic yards by the time the cut was completed.

©Niday Picture Library/Alamy

>> An American Story

"A PATH BETWEEN THE SEAS"

"War! War! WAR!" The news had flashed across the country in the spring of 1898. As tens of thousands of eager young Americans signed up to fight the Spanish in Cuba, the USS *Oregon* left San Francisco Bay on a roundabout route toward its battle station in the Caribbean. It headed south through the Pacific, passing Central America and leaving it thousands of miles behind. Then, in the Strait of Magellan at South America's tip, the ship encountered a gale so ferocious that the shore disappeared from sight. All communication ceased, and Americans at home feared the worst. But the *Oregon* survived and steamed north into the Atlantic. Finally, after 68 days and 13,000 miles at sea, it reached Cuba and helped win the Battle of Santiago Bay.

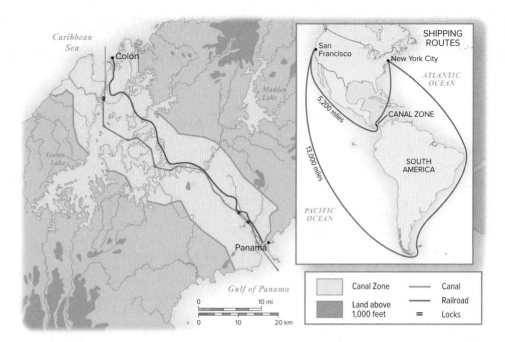

SHIPPING
ROUTES

San Francisco

New York City

ATLANTIC
OCEAN

5,200 miles

CANAL ZONE

13,000 miles

SOUTH
AMERICA

PACIFIC
OCEAN

Caribbean Sea

Colón

Madden Lake

Gatun Lake

Panamá

Gulf of Panama

0   10 mi
0   10   20 km

	Canal Zone		Canal
	Land above 1,000 feet		Railroad
		=	Locks

The daring voyage electrified the nation but worried its leaders. Since the defeat of Mexico in 1848, the United States had stretched from the Atlantic to the Pacific without enough navy to go around. As an emerging world power, the country needed a "path between the seas"—a canal across the narrow isthmus of Colombia's Panamanian province in Central America—to defend itself and promote its growing trade.

"I took the isthmus," Theodore Roosevelt later told a cheering crowd. In a way he did. As president, in 1903 he negotiated an agreement with Colombia to lease the needed strip of land. Holding out for more money and greater control over the canal, the Colombian senate refused to ratify the pact.

Privately TR talked of seizing Panama. But when he learned of a budding independence movement in Panama, he welcomed a revolt. On schedule and without bloodshed, the Panamanians rebelled late in 1903. The next day a U.S. cruiser dropped anchor offshore to prevent Colombia from landing troops. The United States quickly recognized the new Republic of Panama and signed a treaty for a renewable lease on a canal zone 10 miles wide. Panama received $10 million plus an annual rent of $250,000 (the same terms offered to Colombia).

Critics called the treaty "a rough-riding assault upon another republic" but TR never blinked. Arriving in Panama in 1906 he spent three days traveling the canal site in the pouring rain, his panama hat and white suit sagging about his body. He sloshed through the labor camps, asked workers for their complaints, and took the helm of a giant steam shovel. He never apologized for his nation's conduct, although in 1921, after oil had been discovered in the Canal Zone, Congress voted $25 million to Colombia.

The Panama Canal embodied Roosevelt's muscular foreign policy of respect through strength. He modernized the army and tripled its size, enlarged the navy, created a general staff for planning and mobilization, and established the Army War College. As a pivot point between the two hemispheres, his canal allowed the United States to flex its strength across the globe.

These expanding horizons came about largely as an outgrowth of American commercial and industrial expansion, just as the imperialist empires of England, France, Germany, Russia, and Japan were expanding, too. Americans, steeped in democratic ideals, frequently seemed uncomfortable with the naked ambitions of European empire-builders. Roosevelt's embrace of the canal, however, showed how far some progressives had come in being willing to shape the world when they believed American interests required it.

Expansionist diplomats assured each other that global order could be maintained by balancing power through carefully crafted military alliances. But that system did not hold. In 1914, the year the Panama Canal opened, this old world order collapsed in a terrible war. <<

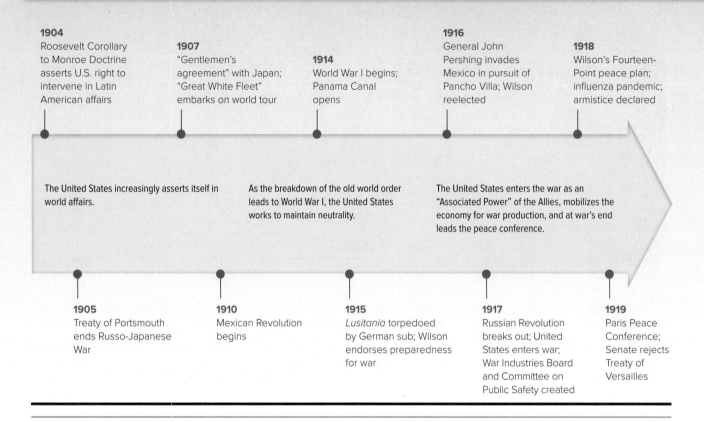

1904
Roosevelt Corollary to Monroe Doctrine asserts U.S. right to intervene in Latin American affairs

1907
"Gentlemen's agreement" with Japan; "Great White Fleet" embarks on world tour

1914
World War I begins; Panama Canal opens

1916
General John Pershing invades Mexico in pursuit of Pancho Villa; Wilson reelected

1918
Wilson's Fourteen-Point peace plan; influenza pandemic; armistice declared

The United States increasingly asserts itself in world affairs.

As the breakdown of the old world order leads to World War I, the United States works to maintain neutrality.

The United States enters the war as an "Associated Power" of the Allies, mobilizes the economy for war production, and at war's end leads the peace conference.

1905
Treaty of Portsmouth ends Russo-Japanese War

1910
Mexican Revolution begins

1915
Lusitania torpedoed by German sub; Wilson endorses preparedness for war

1917
Russian Revolution breaks out; United States enters war; War Industries Board and Committee on Public Safety created

1919
Paris Peace Conference; Senate rejects Treaty of Versailles

PROGRESSIVE DIPLOMACY

FOUNDATIONS OF PROGRESSIVE DIPLOMACY As THE PANAMA CANAL WAS being built, progressive diplomacy was taking shape. Like progressive politics, it stressed moralism and order as it stretched presidential power to new limits in an effort to mold and remake the international environment. It rested on faith in the superiority of Anglo-American values and institutions. "Of all our race, [God] has marked the American people as His chosen nation to finally lead in the redemption of the world," said one senator in 1900. In this global vision of Manifest Destiny, few progressives questioned the need to uplift and "civilize" the "darker peoples" of the tropical zones.

Economic expansion underlay the commitment to a "civilizing" mission. The depression of 1893 had encouraged American manufacturers and farmers to look overseas for markets, and that expansion continued after 1900. Every administration committed itself to opening doors of trade and keeping them open. By 1918, at the end of World War I, the United States had become the largest creditor in the world. Whatever "civilizing mission" Americans touted, the desire to expand markets for manufacturers and farmers was always at the bottom of things.

Big Stick in the Caribbean

PLATT AMENDMENT Theodore Roosevelt liked to invoke the old African proverb "Walk softly and carry a big stick." In the Caribbean he nonetheless moved loudly and mightily. The Panama Canal gave the United States a commanding position in the Western Hemisphere. Its importance required the country to "police the surrounding premises," explained Secretary of State Elihu Root. Before granting Cuba its independence in 1902, the United States reorganized its finances and attached the Platt Amendment to the Cuban constitution. The amendment gave American authorities the right to intervene in Cuba if the independence or internal order of the country were threatened. Claiming that power, U.S. troops occupied the island twice between 1906 and 1923.

In looking to enforce a favorable environment for trade in the Caribbean, Roosevelt worried about European intentions. The Monroe Doctrine of 1823 declared against further European colonization of the Western Hemisphere, but in the early twentieth century the rising debts of Latin Americans to Europeans invited intrusion. "If we intend to say hands off to the power of Europe, then sooner or later we must keep order ourselves," Roosevelt warned. In his balance-of-power system it was the obligation of great powers to avoid the spheres of others while keeping order in their own. Across the globe, great powers would thus check each other, much as big government held big business in check at home.

ROOSEVELT COROLLARY TO THE MONROE DOCTRINE

Going well beyond Monroe's concept of resisting foreign intrusions into the Western Hemisphere, Roosevelt tightened his grip on the region more like an imperialist than a protector of Latin American independence. In 1904, when the Dominican Republic defaulted on its debts, he added the "Roosevelt Corollary" to the Monroe Doctrine by claiming the right to intervene directly if Latin American countries failed to keep their finances in order. Invoking its sweeping and self-proclaimed power, the United States assumed responsibility for several Caribbean states, including the Dominican Republic, Cuba, and Panama.

A "Diplomatist of the Highest Rank"

In the Far East, Roosevelt exercised ingenuity rather than force. He realized that few Americans would support armed intervention half a world away. Like President McKinley, TR committed himself only to maintaining an "open door" of equal access to trade in China and to protecting the Philippines, which he saw as "our heel of Achilles."

TREATY OF PORTSMOUTH

The key to success lay in offsetting or counterbalancing Russian and Japanese ambitions in the region. When Japan attacked Russian holdings in the Chinese province of Manchuria in 1904, Roosevelt offered to mediate. He worried that if unchecked, Japan might threaten American interests in China and the Philippines. At the U.S. Naval Base near Portsmouth, New Hampshire, Roosevelt guided the Russians and the Japanese to the Treaty of Portsmouth in 1905. It recognized the Japanese victory, the first by an Asian power over a European country, and ceded to Japan Port Arthur, the southern half of Sakhalin Island, and, in effect, control of Korea. Japan promised to leave Manchuria as part of China and keep trade open to all foreign nations. The balance of power in Asia and the open door in China thus had been preserved. For his contributions, Roosevelt received the Nobel Peace Prize in 1906.

GENTLEMEN'S AGREEMENT

Japanese nationalists resented the peace treaty for curbing Japan's ambitions in China. Their anger surfaced in a protest lodged, of all places, against the San Francisco school board. In 1906 rising Japanese immigration led San Francisco school authorities to place the city's 93 Asian students in a separate school. In Japan citizens talked of war over the insult. Roosevelt, furious at the "infernal fools in California," summoned the mayor of San Francisco and seven school board members to the White House. In exchange for an end to the segregation

Source: Library of Congress, Prints and Photographs Division [LC-DIG-jpd-02531]

| *Sailors from the Japanese torpedo boat,* Sazanami, *board a Russian torpedo boat during a heated sea battle off Port Arthur during the Russo-Japanese War. Japan's victory, the first of an Asian over a European power, signaled Japan's new status as a great world power, as well as the country's success in "modernizing" along Western lines.*

order, Roosevelt offered to arrange a mutual restriction of immigration between Japan and the United States. In 1907 all sides accepted his "gentlemen's agreement," and each country restricted immigration to the other.

GREAT WHITE FLEET

The San Francisco school crisis sparked wild rumors that Japan was bent on taking Hawaii, or the Philippines, or the Panama Canal. In case Japan or any other nation thought of upsetting the Pacific balance, Roosevelt sent 16 gleaming white battleships on a world tour. "By George, isn't it magnificent!" he crowed as the "Great White Fleet" steamed out of Hampton Roads, Virginia, in 1907 (see Chapter 21). The fleet made its most conspicuous stop in Japan, where a group of Japanese children stood on the docks of Yokohama and sang "The Star-Spangled Banner" in English. The show of force heralded a new age of American naval might but had an unintended consequence that haunted Americans for decades: it spurred Japanese admirals to expand their own navy.

Watching Roosevelt in his second term, an amazed London's *The Morning Post* honored him as a "diplomatist of the highest rank." Abroad as at home, his brand of progressivism was grounded in an enthusiastic nationalism that mixed force with finesse to achieve balance and order.

Dollar Diplomacy

Instead of force or finesse, Roosevelt's successor in the White House turned to money to advance U.S. interests abroad. William Howard Taft stressed private investment to promote economic stability, keep peace, and tie debt-ridden nations to the United States. "Dollar diplomacy" simply amounted to "substituting dollars for bullets," Taft explained. He and Philander Knox, his prickly secretary of state, treated the restless nations of Latin America like ailing corporations, injecting capital and reorganizing management. By the time Taft left office in 1913, half of all American investments abroad were in Latin America, often relying on Roosevelt's Corollary to the Monroe Doctrine as a foundation.

Failure dogged Taft overseas as it did at home. In the Caribbean his dollar diplomacy was linked so closely with unpopular governments, corporations, and banks that his successor, Woodrow Wilson, scrapped it when he entered the White House. Taft's efforts to strengthen China with investments and trade only intensified rivalry with Japan and made China more suspicious of all foreigners, including Americans. In 1911 the southern Chinese provinces rebelled against foreign intrusion and overthrew the monarchy. Only persistent pressure from the White House kept dollar diplomacy alive in Asia. In the end, no brand of progressive diplomacy could achieve long-lasting balance and order in the face of global competition for empire.

REVIEW

How did Theodore Roosevelt's policies in Latin America and Asia differ from William Howard Taft's?

WOODROW WILSON AND MORAL DIPLOMACY

THE LIGHTFOOT CLUB HAD BEEN meeting in the Reverend Wilson's hayloft for months when the question of whether the pen was mightier than the sword came up. Young Tommy Wilson, who had organized the debating society, jumped at the chance to argue that written words were more powerful than armies. But when the boys drew lots, Tommy ended up on the other side. "I can't argue that side," he protested. "I can't argue for something I don't believe in."

Thomas Woodrow Wilson eventually dropped his first name, but he never gave up his boyhood conviction that morality, at least as he defined it, should guide all conduct. To the diplomacy of order, force, and finance, Wilson added a missionary's commitment to spreading what he saw as the American system of beliefs—justice, democracy, and the Judeo-Christian values of harmony and cooperation.

Missionary Diplomacy

Although Wilson's missionary diplomacy was deeply idealistic, it had a practical side. In the twentieth century, foreign markets would serve as America's new frontier. American industries "will burst their jackets if they cannot find free outlets in the markets of the world," Wilson

cautioned in 1912. His special genius lay in reconciling this commercial self-interest with a global idealism. In his eyes, exporting American democracy and capitalism would promote peace, prosperity, and human advancement throughout the world.

Solitary and self-assured, Wilson conducted foreign policy on his own. Bypassing the State Department, he sent personal emissaries to foreign leaders and often typed his own dispatches. Sometimes Secretary of State William Jennings Bryan had no idea of what was happening. In rare moments of doubt Wilson turned to his trusted friend, Edward M. House. The honorary "Colonel" House had yoked himself to Wilson in the early days of his political career and wielded power behind the scenes.

TWENTY-ONE DEMANDS In Asia and the Pacific, Wilson moved to put "moral and public considerations" ahead of the "material interests of individuals." He pulled American bankers out of a railroad project in China backed by President Taft. The scheme encouraged foreign intervention and undermined Chinese independence, said Wilson. The United States became the first major power to recognize the new Republic of China in 1911 when nationalists overthrew the last Manchu emperor. And in 1915 Wilson strongly opposed Japan's "Twenty-One Demands" for control of China. At the end of his first administration, the Philippines gained limited self-government, the first step toward independence finally granted in 1946.

In the Caribbean and Latin America, Wilson discovered that interests closer to home could not be pursued through high-minded words alone. In August 1914 he convinced Nicaragua, already occupied by American troops, to yield control of a naval base and grant the United States an alternate canal route. Upheavals in Haiti and the Dominican Republic brought in the U.S. Marines. By the end of his administration, American troops were still stationed there and also in Cuba. All four nations were economically dependent on the United States and were virtual protectorates. Missionary diplomacy, it turned out, could spread its gospel with steel as well as cash.

Intervention in Mexico

MEXICAN REVOLUTION A lingering crisis in Mexico turned Wilson's "moral diplomacy" into a mockery. A common border, 400 years of shared history, and millions of dollars in investments made what happened in Mexico of urgent importance to the United States.

In 1910 a revolution overthrew the aged dictator Porfirio Díaz and plunged the country into turmoil. Just as Wilson was entering the White House in 1913, the ruthless general Victoriano Huerta emerged as head of the government. Wealthy landowners and foreign investors endorsed Huerta, a conservative likely to protect their holdings. Soon a bloody civil war was raging between Huerta and his rivals.

AMERICAN INTERVENTIONS IN THE CARIBBEAN, 1898–1930

In the first three decades of the twentieth century, U.S. diplomacy transformed the Caribbean into an American lake as armed and unarmed intervention became part of the country's diplomatic arsenal. **On what grounds did the United States intervene in the region, and in which nations did the U.S. stay for the longest time?**

Most European nations recognized the Huerta regime immediately, but Wilson refused to accept the "government of butchers." Huerta had murdered the popular leader Francisco Madera with the approval of the Taft administration. When Huerta proclaimed himself dictator, Wilson banned arms shipments to Mexico. He threw his support to rebel leader Venustiano Carranza, on the condition that Carranza participate in American-sponsored elections. No Mexican was ready to tolerate such foreign interference. Carranza and his "constitutionalists" rejected the offer. With few options, Wilson armed the rebels anyway.

Wilson's distaste for Huerta was so great that he used a minor incident as a pretext for an invasion. In April 1914 the crew of the USS *Dolphin* landed without permission in the Mexican port city of Tampico. Local police arrested the sailors, only to release them with an apology. Unappeased, their squadron commander demanded a 21-gun salute to the American flag. Agreed, replied the Mexicans, but only if American guns returned the salute to Mexico. Learning of a German shipload of weapons about to land at Veracruz, Wilson broke the impasse by ordering American troops to take the city. Instead of the bloodless occupation they

expected, U.S. marines encountered stiff resistance as they stormed ashore; 126 Mexicans and 19 Americans were killed before the city fell. The intervention accomplished little except the unlikely feat of uniting the rival Mexican factions against the United States.

PANCHO VILLA Only the combined diplomacy of Argentina, Brazil, and Chile (the "ABC powers") staved off war between Mexico and the United States. When a bankrupt Huerta resigned in 1914, Carranza formed a new constitutionalist government but refused to follow Wilson's guidelines. Wilson turned to Francisco "Pancho" Villa, a wily, peasant-born general who had broken from Carranza. Together with Emiliano Zapata, another peasant leader, Villa kept a rebellion flickering.

A year later, Wilson finally recognized the Carranza regime. Villa turned against the United States in protest. In January 1916 Villa abducted 18 Americans from a train in Mexico and slaughtered them. In March he galloped into Columbus, New Mexico, killed 19 people, and left the town in flames. Wilson ordered 6,000 troops into Mexico to capture Villa "dead or alive." In the aftermath, a reluctant Carranza agreed to yet another American invasion.

Source: Library of Congress, Prints and Photographs Division [LC-DIG-ppm-sca-35144]

General John J. "Black Jack" Pershing led U.S. forces into Mexico to catch rebel leader Pancho Villa "dead or alive." Villa (pictured here with his wife, María Luz Corral) eluded the Americans for several months before they abandoned the expedition. Audacious and ruthless, he was worshiped by Mexican peasants, who extolled his exploits in folktales and ballads after his assassination in 1923 by Mexican political rivals.

For nearly two years General John Pershing chased Villa on horseback, by automobile, and in airplanes. There were bloody skirmishes with government troops but not a single one with Villa and his rebels. As the chase grew wilder and wilder, Carranza withdrew his consent for U.S. troops on Mexican soil. Early in 1917 Wilson pulled Pershing home. The "punitive expedition," as the president called it, poisoned Mexican-American relations for the next 30 years.

✓ REVIEW

What was "missionary" about Woodrow Wilson's diplomacy, and how successful was it?

THE ROAD TO WAR

IN EARLY 1917, AROUND THE time Wilson recalled Pershing, the British liner *Laconia* was making its way across the Atlantic. As the ship steamed through the inky night, passengers belowdecks talked almost casually of the war raging in Europe since 1914. "What do you think are our chances of being torpedoed?" asked Floyd Gibbons, an American reporter. Since Germany had stepped up its submarine attacks, the question was unavoidable. "I should put our chances at 250 to 1 that we don't meet a sub," replied a British diplomat.

"At that minute," recalled Gibbons, "the torpedo hit us." Whistle blasts echoed through the corridors and the passengers abandoned ship. They watched in horror from lifeboats as a second torpedo struck its target, and the *Laconia* slid silently beneath icy waters. After a miserable night bobbing in the waves, Gibbons was rescued. But by 1917 other neutral Americans had already lost their lives at sea. And in April, despite Woodrow Wilson's best efforts at peace, the United States found itself at war.

The Guns of August

CAUSES OF WORLD WAR I For a century profound strains had pushed Europe toward war. Its population tripled; its middle and working classes swelled; discontent with industrial society grew. The United States had experienced many of the same strains, of course, yet in Europe these pressures played out on a field that was at once more stratified socially and more divided ethnically and culturally. As European nations competed for empire, nationalism helped paper over these internal divisions by directing ambitions and rivalries toward other nations. By 1914 empires jostled uneasily against one another across the globe.

Europe responded to the increased competition with an arms race and a set of military alliances. Great Britain became convinced that its mastery of the seas depended on maintaining a navy equal in power to the combined navies of its closest two rivals, France and Germany. Both doubled the size of their standing armies between 1870 and 1914. Led by Kaiser Wilhelm II, Germany aligned itself with Turkey and Austria-Hungary. The established imperial powers of England and France looked to contain Germany by supporting its foe, Russia. Soon Europe bristled with weapons, troops, and armor-plated navies. These war machines were linked to one another through a web of diplomatic alliances—all of them committed to war the moment someone or something set them in motion.

ASSASSINATION OF ARCHDUKE FRANZ FERDINAND That moment came in 1914, in the Slavic province of Bosnia in southwestern Austria-Hungary. Since the 1870s the Ottoman, or Turkish, Empire had been slowly disintegrating, allowing a host of smaller, ethnically based states to emerge. Serbia was one of them. Many Serbs dreamed of uniting other Slavic peoples in a "Pan-Slavic" nation. Their ambitions had been blocked in 1908, when Austria-Hungary annexed neighboring Bosnia. Tensions in the region were high when

the Archduke Franz Ferdinand, heir to the Austro-Hungarian throne, visited Sarajevo, Bosnia's capital. On June 28, 1914, the archduke and his wife were gunned down by a Serbian nationalist as they drove through the streets of the city. The young assassin belonged to the Black Hand, a terrorist group that had vowed to reunite Bosnia with Serbia to create another Slavic nation on Austria-Hungary's border.

Austria-Hungary mobilized to punish Serbia. In response, rival Russia called up its army to help the Serbs. Germany joined with Austria-Hungary, France with Russia. On July 28, after a month of insincere demands for apologies, Austria-Hungary declared war on Serbia. On August 1 Germany issued a similar declaration against Russia and, two days later, against France. Following a battle plan drawn up well in advance, German generals pounded neutral Belgium with siege cannons the size of freight cars. Within days five German columns were slicing west through the Belgian countryside, determined to overrun France before Russia could position its slow-moving army on the eastern front.

The guns of August heralded the first global war. Like so many dominoes, the industrialized nations fell into place: Britain, Japan, Romania, and later Italy to the side of "Allies" France and Russia; Bulgaria and Turkey to the "Central Powers" of Germany and Austria-Hungary. Armies fought from the deserts of North Africa to the plains of Flanders in Belgium. Fleets battled off the coasts of Chile and Sumatra. Soldiers came from as far away as Australia and India. Nearly 8 million never returned.

THE COURSE OF WAR IN EUROPE, 1914–1917

*When World War I erupted between the Central and Allied Powers in 1914, few countries in Europe remained neutral. The armies of the Central Powers penetrated as far west as France and as far east as Russia, but by 1917, the European war had settled into a hideous standoff along the deadly line of trenches on the western front that stretched from the North Sea to the border of Switzerland. **What does the map tell us about why the British blockade of Germany was so effective?***

Neutral but Not Impartial

The outbreak of war shocked most Americans. Few knew Serbia as anything but a tiny splotch on the map of Europe. Fewer still were prepared to go to war in its defense. President Wilson issued an immediate declaration of neutrality and approved a plan for evacuating Americans stranded in Belgium.

WILSON'S NEUTRAL IDEALS Wilson came to see the calamity as an opportunity. In his mind, neutral America could take the moral high ground and lead warring nations to a new world order. Selfish nationalism would give way to cooperative internationalism, power politics to collective security and Christian charity. Progressive faith in reason would triumph over irrational violence. Only if the United States remained neutral could it lead the way to this higher peace and thus extend Wilson's moral diplomacy to a world at war. Americans must be "impartial in thought as well as action," Wilson insisted in 1914.

In a country as diverse as the United States, true impartiality was impossible. Americans of German and Austrian descent naturally sympathized with the Central Powers, as did Irish Americans, on the grounds of England's centuries-old domination of Ireland. The bonds of language, culture, and history tied most Americans to Great Britain. And gratitude for French aid during the American Revolution still lived. When the first American division marched through Paris, its commander stopped to salute the tomb of the Marquis de Lafayette, who served as a general in the Continental army: "Nous voilà, Lafayette!"—"Lafayette, we are here!"

Long-standing American economic ties to Britain and France also created a financial investment in Allied victory. The American economy boomed with the flood of war orders. The commanding British navy ensured that the Atlantic trade went mostly to the Allies. Between 1914 and 1916, business with the Allies rocketed from $800 million to $3 billion. The Allies eventually borrowed more than $2 billion from American banks to finance their purchases. In contrast, a British naval blockade reduced American **contraband** commerce with the Central Powers to a trickle.

Few Americans cared. Although some progressives admired German social reforms, Americans generally saw

Germany as an iron military power bent on conquest. Americans read British propaganda about spike-helmeted "Huns" raping Belgian women, bayoneting their children, pillaging their towns. Some of the stories were true, some embellished, some utterly false, but all worked to antagonize Americans against Germany.

The Diplomacy of Neutrality

Though Wilson insisted that all warring powers respect the right of neutrals to trade with any nation, he hesitated to retaliate against Great Britain's blockade of Germany. He recognized that the key to strangling Germany, a land power, was Britain's powerful navy and its iron blockade. Breaking it would cripple the Allied war effort. Meanwhile, Great Britain tightened its noose around Germany with caution where the Americans were concerned. When Britain forbade the sale of cotton to the Central Powers in 1915, the British government bought American surpluses. It also agreed to compensate American firms for their losses when the war was over. By the end of 1915 the United States had all but accepted the British blockade of Germany, while American supplies continued to flow to England. True neutrality was dead.

SUBMARINE WARFARE Early in 1915 Germany turned to a dreadful new weapon to even the odds at sea. It mounted a counterblockade of Great Britain with two dozen submarines, or *Unterseeboote,* called U-boats. Before submarines, sea raiders usually gave crews and passengers the chance to escape. But if thin-skinned U-boats surfaced to obey these conventions, they risked being rammed or blown from the water. So submarines attacked without warning and spared no lives. Invoking international law and national honor, President Wilson threatened to hold Germany to "strict accountability" for any American losses. Germany promised not to sink any American ships, but soon a new issue grabbed the headlines: the safety of American passengers on belligerent vessels.

LUSITANIA On the morning of May 7, 1915, the British passenger liner *Lusitania* appeared out of a fog bank off the coast of Ireland on its way from New York to England. The commander of the German U-20 could hardly believe his eyes: the giant ship filled the viewfinder of his periscope. He fired a single torpedo. A tremendous roar followed as one of the *Lusitania*'s boilers exploded. The ship stopped dead in the water and listed so badly that lifeboats could barely be launched before the vessel sank. Nearly 1,200 men, women, and children perished, including 128 Americans.

Wilson, horrified at this "murder on the high seas," did little more than send notes of protest to Germany. Secretary of State William Jennings Bryan advocated an even more measured response, what he called "real neutrality," with equal protests lodged against both German submarines and British blockaders. He suspected that the *Lusitania* carried munitions as well as passengers and was thus a legitimate target. (Much later, evidence proved him right.) Relying on

©Science History Images/Alamy

| *"It sounded like a million-ton hammer hitting a steam boiler a hundred feet high," one passenger on the* Lusitania *recalled. Within four minutes, the ship's electrical power failed, plunging the interior of the ship into darkness. With the vessel rapidly sinking, many lifeboats proved impossible to launch; others overturned in the process, spilling passengers into the water. Within 18 minutes, the vast ocean liner had plunged toward the bottom of the sea, 300 feet below. Nearly 1,200 men, women, and children perished.*

passengers for protection against attack, Bryan argued, was "like putting women and children in front of an army." Rather than endorse Wilson's policy, Bryan resigned.

Battling on two fronts in Europe, Germany wanted to keep the United States out of the war. But in February 1916 a desperate Germany declared submarine warfare on all *armed* vessels, belligerent or neutral. A month later a U-boat commander mistook the French steamer *Sussex* for a mine layer and torpedoed the unarmed vessel as it ferried passengers and freight across the English Channel. Several Americans were injured.

SUSSEX **PLEDGE** In mid-April Wilson issued an ultimatum in the aftermath of the *Sussex* sinking. If Germany refused to stop sinking nonmilitary vessels, the United States would break off diplomatic relations. War would surely follow. Without enough U-boats to control the seas, Germany agreed to Wilson's terms, all but abandoning its counterblockade. This *Sussex* pledge gave Wilson a diplomatic victory but carried a grave risk. If German submarines resumed unrestricted attacks, the United States would have to go to war. "Any little German [U-boat] commander can put us into the war at any time," the president admitted.

Peace, Preparedness, and the Election of 1916

While hundreds of young Yanks slipped across the border to enlist in the Canadian army, most Americans agreed neutrality was the wisest course. Before the war a peace movement had taken seed in the United States, nourished in 1910 by a gift of $10 million from Andrew Carnegie. In 1914 social reformers Jane Addams, Charlotte Perkins Gilman, and Lillian Wald founded the Women's International League for Peace and Freedom and the American

Union Against Militarism. Calling on Wilson to convene a peace conference, they lobbied for open diplomacy, disarmament, an end to colonial empires, and an international organization to settle disputes. In time these aims became the core of Wilson's peace plan.

Pacifists might condemn the war, but Republicans and corporate leaders argued that the nation was woefully unprepared to keep peace. The army numbered only 80,000 men in 1914, the navy just 37 battleships and a handful of new "dreadnoughts," or supercruisers. Advocates of "preparedness" called for a navy larger than Great Britain's, an army of millions of reservists, and universal military training.

By the end of 1915, frustration with German submarines led Wilson to join the preparedness cause. He toured the country promoting preparedness and promised a "navy second to none." In Washington, he pressed Congress to double the army, increase the National Guard, and begin construction of the largest navy in the world. To foot the bill, progressives pushed through new graduated taxes on higher incomes and on estates as well as additional levies on corporate profits.

"HE KEPT US OUT OF WAR"   Whoever paid for it, most Americans in 1916 were thinking of preparedness for peace, not war. The Democrats discovered the political power of peace early in the presidential campaign. As their convention opened in St. Louis in June, the keynote speaker began what he expected to be a dull description of Wilson's recent diplomatic maneuvers—only to have the crowd roar back in each case, "What did we do? What did we do?" The speaker knew the answer and shouted it back: "We didn't go to war! We didn't go to war!" The next day Wilson was renominated by acclamation. "He Kept Us Out of War" became his campaign slogan.

The Republicans had already nominated Charles Evans Hughes, the former governor of New York. Like Wilson, he endorsed "straight and honest" neutrality and peace. Despite that moderate stand, Democrats succeeded in painting Hughes as a warmonger, partly because Republican Theodore Roosevelt had rattled his own sabers so loudly. As the election approached, Democrats took out full-page advertisements in newspapers across the country: "If You Want WAR, Vote for HUGHES! If You Want Peace with Honor VOTE FOR WILSON!"

As the polls closed on Election Day, Wilson squeaked out a victory. He carried the South and key states in the Midwest and West on a tide of prosperity, progressive reform, and, most of all, promises of peace.

Wilson's Final Peace Offensive

Twice since 1915 Wilson had sent his trusted adviser Edward House to Europe to negotiate a peace among the warring powers, and twice House had failed. With the election over, Wilson opened his final peace offensive. When he asked the belligerents to state their terms for a cease-fire, neither side responded. Frustrated, fearful, and genuinely agonized,

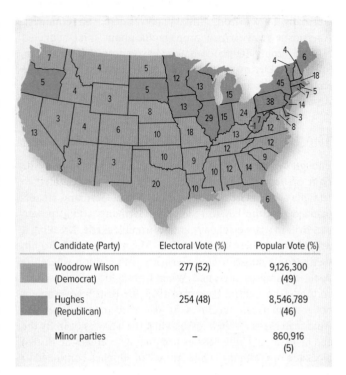

Candidate (Party)	Electoral Vote (%)	Popular Vote (%)
Woodrow Wilson (Democrat)	277 (52)	9,126,300 (49)
Hughes (Republican)	254 (48)	8,546,789 (46)
Minor parties	–	860,916 (5)

ELECTION OF 1916

Wilson called for "peace without victory": no victor, no vanquished, no embittering division of the spoils of war, only "a peace among equals," he said in January 1917.

As Wilson spoke, a fleet of U-boats was cruising toward the British Isles. Weeks earlier German military leaders had persuaded the Kaiser to take one last desperate gamble to starve the Allies into submission. On January 31, 1917, the German ambassador in Washington announced that unrestricted submarine warfare would resume the next day.

ZIMMERMANN TELEGRAM   Wilson's dream of neutrality collapsed. He asked Congress for authority to arm merchant ships and early in February severed relations with Germany. Then British authorities handed him a bombshell—an intercepted telegram from the German foreign secretary, Arthur Zimmermann, to the Kaiser's ambassador in Mexico. In the event of war with the United States, the ambassador was instructed to offer Mexico guns, money, and its "lost territory in Texas, New Mexico, and Arizona" to attack the United States. Already frustrated by Pancho Villa's raids across the U.S.-Mexican border, Wilson angrily released the Zimmermann telegram to the press. Soon after, he ordered gun crews aboard merchant ships and directed them to shoot U-boats "on sight."

Those policies now combined with events abroad to propel a reluctant United States toward war. On March 12 U-boats torpedoed the American merchant vessel *Algonquin*. On March 15 a revolution in Russia toppled Czar Nicholas II, crippling a key ally from within. By the end of the month U-boats had sunk nearly 600,000 tons of

Allied and neutral shipping. For the first time Washington received reports of cracking morale in the Allied ranks.

On April 2, 1917, accompanied by armed cavalry, Wilson rode down Pennsylvania Avenue and trudged up the steps of the Capitol. He delivered to Congress a stirring war message, full of idealistic purpose. "We shall fight for the things we have always carried nearest our hearts—for democracy, for the right of those who submit to authority to have a voice in their own governments, for the rights and liberties of small nations."

Pacifists blocked the war resolution until it finally passed on April 6, Good Friday. Six senators and 50 House members opposed it, including the first woman to be elected to Congress, Jeannette Rankin of Montana. Cultural, economic, and historical ties to the Allies, along with the German campaign of submarine warfare, had tipped the country toward war. Wilson had not wanted it, but now the battlefield seemed the only path to the higher peace Wilson sought.

> ✔ **REVIEW**
>
> What steps did Woodrow Wilson take to avoid World War I, and why did they fail?

WAR AND SOCIETY

IN 1915 THE GERMAN ZEPPELIN LZ-38, hovering at 8,000 feet, dropped a load of bombs that killed seven Londoners. For the first time in history, civilians died in an air attack. Few such aerial bombardments occurred during World War I, but they signaled the growing importance of the home front in modern combat. Governments not only fielded armies but also mobilized industry, controlled labor, even rationed food. In the United States traditions of cooperation and volunteerism helped government to organize the home front and the battle front, often in ways that were peculiarly progressive.

The Slaughter of Stalemat

TRENCH WARFARE   While the United States debated entry into the Great War, the Allies were close to losing it. Following the German assault in 1914, the war had settled into a grisly stalemate. A continuous, immovable front stretched from Flanders in the north to the border of Switzerland in the south. Troops dug ditches, 6 to 8 feet deep and 4 to 5 feet wide, to escape bullets, grenades, and artillery. Twenty-five thousand miles of these "trenches"—enough to circle the globe—cut a muddy scar across Europe. Men lived in them for years, prey to disease, lice, and a plague of rats.

War in the machine age gave the advantage to the defense. When soldiers bravely charged "over the top" of the trenches, they were shredded by machine guns that fired 600 rounds a minute. Poison gas choked them in their tracks. Giant howitzers lobbed shells on them from positions too distant to see. In the Battle of the Somme River in 1916 a million men were killed in just four months of fighting, all to enable the British

army to advance barely 7 miles. Only late in the war did new armored "landships"—code-named "tanks"—return the advantage to the offense by surmounting the trench barriers with their caterpillar treads.

By then Vladimir Lenin was speeding home to Russia aboard a special train provided by the Germans. Lenin had been exiled to Switzerland during the early stages of the Russian Revolution but returned to lead his Bolshevik ("majority" in Russian) party to power in November 1917. Soon the Bolshevik-controlled government negotiated a separate peace with Germany, which promptly transferred a million of its soldiers to the western front for the coming spring offensive.

"You're in the Army Now"

The Allies' plight forced the U.S. Army into a crash program to send a million soldiers to Europe by the spring of 1918. The United States had barely 180,000 men in uniform. Volunteers rushed to recruitment offices, especially in ethnic communities, where Mexican Americans enlisted in numbers proportionally higher than any other group.

They were not enough. To raise the necessary force, Congress passed the Selective Service Act in May 1917.

©Hulton-Deutsch Collection/Corbis/Getty Images

| *Trench warfare, wrote one general, was "marked by uniform formations, the regulation of space and time by higher commands down to the smallest details . . . fixed distances between units and individuals." The reality was something else again.*

Men between the ages of 20 and 30 would be conscripted into the armed forces. Feelings over forced military service ran high. "There is precious little difference between a conscript [draftee] and a convict," protested the Speaker of the House in 1917. Progressives disagreed. They saw military service as an opportunity to unite America and promote democracy by breaking down differences among classes and ethnicities through common military service. "Universal [military] training will jumble the boys of America all together," exclaimed progressive journalist George Creel, ". . . smashing all the petty class distinctions that now divide, and prompting a brand of real democracy."

At ten in the morning on July 20, 1917, Secretary of War Newton Baker tied a blindfold over his eyes, reached into a huge glass bowl, and drew the first number in the new draft lottery. Some 24 million men were already registered. Almost 3 million were drafted; another 2 million volunteered. Most were white and young, between the ages of 21 and 31. Some 20,000 women served as clerks, telephone operators, and nurses. In a nation of immigrants, nearly one draftee in five had been born abroad. Training often aimed at educating and Americanizing ethnic recruits. In special units called "development battalions," drill sergeants barked out orders while volunteers from the YMCA taught American history and English.

With hostility remaining high between Mexico and the United States after President Wilson sent U.S. troops into Mexico, many Mexican laborers returned to Mexico rather than be drafted into a foreign army whose goals they did not share. However, Mexican Americans, especially those whose families had long lived in the United States, enlisted in the U.S. Army.

Like Mexican Americans, African Americans volunteered in disproportionately high numbers. They quickly filled the four all-black Army and eight National Guard units already in existence. They were also granted fewer exemptions from the draft than white Americans were. Only 10 percent of the population, blacks made up 13 percent of all draftees. Overseas, where 200,000 black troops served in France, just one in five was permitted in combat compared with two of three whites. Southern Democrats in Congress had opposed training African Americans to arms, fearful of the prospect of putting "arrogant, strutting representatives of black soldiery in every community." But four regiments of the all-black 93rd Division, brigaded with the French army, were among the first Americans in the trenches and the most decorated units in the U.S. Army.

HOUSTON RIOT Racial violence sometimes flared among the troops. In the summer of 1917 it turned deadly in Houston, Texas. Harassed by white soldiers and by the city's Jim Crow laws, seasoned black regulars fought back and killed 17 white civilians. Their whole battalion was arrested and sent to New Mexico. Thirteen troopers were condemned to death and hanged within days, too quickly for appeals even to be filed.

©PJF Military Collection/ Alamy

| *Marcelino Serna, a Mexian American recruit from Texas.*

Bias also surfaced as progressive reformers enlisted the social sciences in army testing. Most recruits had fewer than seven years of education, yet they had to be classified and assigned quickly to units. Psychologists saw the chance to use new intelligence tests to help the army and prove their own theories about the value of "IQ" (intelligence quotient) in measuring the mind. In fact, these new "scientific" IQ tests often measured little more than class and cultural origins. Questions such as "Who wrote 'The Raven'?" exposed background rather than intelligence. More than half the Russian, Italian, and Polish draftees and almost 80 percent of blacks showed up as "inferior." The army stopped IQ testing in January 1919, but schools across the country adopted it after the war, reinforcing many ethnic and racial prejudices.

On the home front moral crusaders waged a war against sin, often pursuing old reforms through the prism of patriotism. Temperance leaders pressured the War Department to prohibit the sale of liquor to anyone in uniform in the vicinity of training camps. Alcohol would only impair a soldier's ability to fight. The army also declared war on venereal disease. "A Soldier who gets a dose is a Traitor!" warned one poster. The drive against sexually transmitted diseases constituted the first serious sex education many young Americans had ever received.

Mobilizing the Economy

To equip, feed, and transport an army of nearly 5 million demanded a national effort. The production of even a single ammunition shell brought components from every section of the country, in addition to vital nitrates from Chile, to assembly plants in New Jersey, Virginia, and Pennsylvania and from there to military installations or Atlantic ports.

WAR COSTS At the Treasury Department, Secretary William Gibbs McAdoo fretted over how to finance the war, which cost, finally, $32 billion. New taxes paid about a third of all war costs. The rest came from the sale of "Liberty" and "Victory" bonds and war savings certificates. At huge bond drives, movie stars Douglas Fairbanks, Mary Pickford, and other celebrities exhorted Americans to buy bonds. Boy Scouts sold them under the slogan "Every Scout to Save a Soldier." More than money was at stake. The fund-raising campaign was also designed to raise patriotism. "Every person who refuses to subscribe," McAdoo warned, "is a friend of Germany." The **national debt**, which had stood at $2 billion in 1917, soared to $20 billion only three years later.

With sweeping grants of authority provided by Congress, President Wilson constructed a massive bureaucracy to direct the home front. What emerged was a more **managed economy** than had existed before the war, one ironically similar to the federal management of Theodore Roosevelt's New Nationalism. No industries were actually nationalized. Instead, a web of nearly 5,000 new executive agencies regulated and supervised

"Over There"

William J. Reilly was a popular sailor who performed this song and others.

What language is this? Why include this version of the lyrics?

Source: Rubenstein Rare Book, Manuscript, and Special Collections Library, Duke University (n967)

Leo Feist paid the original publisher of the music $25,000 for the rights to the song, a record amount at that time. What other ways does the sheet music show that Feist was hoping to make money?

Music has always sounded the times and given historians a feel for the emotional temper of the moment. When George M. Cohan set out to put the martial spirit of the country to music in 1917, the United States had just entered the First World War. Cohan, the son of Irish Catholics, claimed to have written the song on a train ride from New Rochelle to New York City. "I read those war headlines," he later recalled, "and I got to thinking and humming to myself and for a minute, I thought I was going to dance." The song became a popular hit, a powerful recruiting tool for the armed services, and a measure of the innocence of Americans who blithely marched "over there" to save war-torn Europe, only to enter the inferno of industrialized warfare. The song begins with a rhythmic drumbeat and a call to arms: "Johnnie get your gun/Get your gun, get your gun," and builds to its famous chorus, "Over there, over there/Send the word, send the word, over there/That the Yanks are coming/The Yanks are coming/The drums rum-tumming/Ev'rywhere." (To read the entire text of the song and to hear recordings from 1917, see www.firstworldwar.com/audio/overthere.htm.)

The preceding image and text come from the Duke University Library. (Accessed on February 11, 2013, at http://scriptorium.lib.duke.edu/sheetmusic/n/n09/n0967/.)

THINKING CRITICALLY

What is the message of the lyrics of the song? How does the music affect the message? How does it help to have so many of the lines repeated? During the Second World War, songs of nostalgia for the home front such as "White Christmas" replaced martial songs such as "Over There." Why might that have been the case?

the private sector by rewarding businesses rather than punishing them. The new agencies employed business leaders from mammoth machinery makers John Deere and Evinrude to other corporate giants, the readiest source of expert managers. For a nominal "dollar a year," these executives served their country and built a partnership between big business and government. Industrial and **trade associations** as well as professional organizations of engineers and scientists tied industry and science to a network of federal agencies. Antitrust suits, recalled one official, were simply put "to sleep until the war was over."

WAR INDUSTRIES BOARD   Under the leadership of Wall Street wizard Bernard Baruch, a War Industries Board (WIB) coordinated production through industrial and trade associations. Though it had the authority to force compliance, the WIB relied instead on persuasion through publicity and "cost-plus" contracts that covered all company expenses, plus a guaranteed profit. When businesses balked—as when Henry Ford refused to accept government curbs on manufacturing automobiles—Baruch could twist arms. In this case, he threatened to have the army run Ford's factories. Ford quickly reversed himself. Overall, corporate profits tripled and production skyrocketed during the war years.

The Food Administration encouraged farmers to grow more and citizens to eat less wastefully. Herbert Hoover, who had saved starving refugees as chairman of the Commission for Relief in Belgium in 1914, was appointed administrator. Like the WIB, the Food Administration mobilized what Hoover called "the spirit of self-sacrifice." Huge publicity campaigns promoted "wheatless" and "meatless" days each week and encouraged families to plant "victory" gardens. Stirred by high commodity prices, farmers brought more marginal lands into cultivation. Their real income and thus their purchasing power jumped 25 percent.

A Fuel Administration met the army's energy needs by increasing production and limiting domestic consumption. Transportation snarls required more drastic action. In December 1917 the U.S. Railroad Administration took over rail lines for the duration of the war. Government coordination, together with a new system of permits, got freight moving and kept workers happy. Federally imposed "daylight saving time" stretched the workday and saved fuel as well. Rail workers saw their wages grow overall by $300 million. Railroad unions won recognition, an eight-hour day, and a grievance procedure. For the first time in decades, labor unrest subsided and the trains ran on schedule.

BUREAUCRATIC STATE   The modern **bureaucratic state** received a powerful boost during the 18 months of American participation in the war. Accelerating trends already under way, hundreds of federal agencies centralized authority as they cooperated with business and labor to mount an unprecedented war effort. The number of federal employees more than doubled between 1916 and 1918, to over 850,000. The wartime bureaucracy was quickly dismantled at the end of the war, but it set an important precedent for the growth of government.

Source: Library of Congress, Prints and Photographs Division [LC-USZC4-10234]

| *During World War I, the federal government became involved in the everyday lives of citizens. In this poster produced by the National War Garden Commission, Lady Liberty sows "seeds of victory," showing every citizen how to transform their gardens into "a Munitions Plant." How would planting vegetables help to win the war?*

War Work

The war benefited working men and women, though not as much as their employers, who benefited most. Government contracts guaranteed high wages, an eight-hour day, and equal pay for comparable work. To encourage people to stay on the job, federal contracting agencies set up special classes to teach employers the new science of personnel management, which sought to supervise workers more efficiently and humanely. American industry moved one step closer to the **welfare capitalism** of the 1920s, with its promises of profit sharing, company unions, and personnel departments to forestall worker discontent.

NATIONAL WAR LABOR BOARD   Personnel management was not always enough to guarantee industrial peace. In 1917 American workers called over 4,000 strikes, the largest annual outbreak in American history. To keep factories running, President Wilson created the National War Labor Board (NWLB) early in 1918. The NWLB arbitrated more than 1,000 labor disputes, helped to increase wages, established overtime pay, and supported the principle of equal pay for women. In return for no-strike pledges, the board guaranteed the rights of unions to organize and bargain collectively. Membership in the American Federation of Labor jumped from 2.7 million in 1914 to nearly 4 million by 1919.

WOMEN IN THE WORKFORCE The war brought nearly a million more women into the labor force to make up for men in service. Most were young and single. Sometimes they took over jobs once held by men as railroad engineers, drill press operators, and electric lift truck drivers. Here, too, government tried to mediate between labor and management. In 1917 the Labor Department opened the Women in Industry Service (WIS) to recommend guidelines for using female labor. Among its most important proposals were an eight-hour day, rest periods and breaks for meals, and equal pay for equal work. Most women never worked under such conditions, but for the first time, the federal government tried to upgrade their working conditions.

The prewar trend toward higher-paying jobs for women intensified. Most still earned less than the men they replaced as they moved into clerical and light industrial work. And some of the most spectacular gains in defense and government work evaporated after the war as male veterans returned. Tens of thousands of army nurses, defense workers, and war administrators lost their jobs. Agencies such as the Women's Service Section of the Railroad Administration, which fought sexual harassment and discrimination, simply closed down.

War work nonetheless helped to energize a number of women's causes and organizations. Radical suffragist Alice Paul and others who had protested against the war now argued for women's rights, including the right to vote, on the basis of it. As women worked side by side with men in wartime factories and offices, in nursing stations at home or at the front, they could argue more convincingly for both economic and political equality. One step in that direction came after the war with the ratification of the Nineteenth Amendment in 1920 granting women the right to vote (see Chapter 22).

Great Migrations

LATINO MIGRATIONS War work sparked massive migrations of laborers. As the fighting abroad choked off immigration and the draft depleted the workforce, factory owners and large-scale farmers scoured the country and beyond for willing workers. Congress waived immigration requirements in 1917 for agricultural workers from Mexico and in 1918 for workers on railroads, in mines, and on government construction projects.

Industrial cities soon swelled with newcomers, many of them Mexican and Mexican American. Between 1917 and 1920 some 50,000 Mexicans legally crossed the border into Texas, California, New Mexico, and Arizona. At least another 100,000 entered illegally. Some Mexican Americans left the

©Bettmann/Getty Images

| *Movie idol Douglas Fairbanks, brandishing a megaphone, works a huge crowd during this rally in New York City to sell war bonds. When bond sales slacked, the Treasury created a publicity campaign to promote the idea that buying the bonds was a citizen's patriotic duty.*

segregated barrios and farmlands of the West, pushed out by this cheaper labor from Mexico, and migrated to Chicago, Omaha, and other midwestern cities. Mexican *colonias,* or communities, sprang up across the industrial heartland. But most Mexicans and Mexican Americans continued to work on the farms and ranches of the Southwest, where they were freed from military service by the deferment granted to all agricultural labor.

AFRICAN AMERICANS Northern labor agents fanned out across the rural South to recruit young African Americans, while black newspapers such as *The Chicago Defender* summoned them north to the "Land of Hope." Over the war years more than 400,000 moved to the booming industrial centers of the North. Largely unskilled and semiskilled, they worked in the steel mills of Pennsylvania, the war plants of Massachusetts, the brickyards of New Jersey. Southern towns were decimated by the drain of workers. Finally, under pressure from southern politicians, the U.S. Employment Service suspended its program to assist blacks moving north.

These migrations—of African Americans into the army as well as into the city—aggravated racial tensions. Lynching parties murdered 38 black southerners in 1917 and 58 in 1918. In 1919, after the war ended, more than 70 African Americans were hanged, some still in uniform. Housing shortages and job competition helped spark race riots across the North.

In almost every city black citizens, stirred by war rhetoric of freedom and democracy, showed new militancy by fighting back. In mid-1917 some 40 black and 9 white Americans died when East St. Louis erupted in racial violence. During the "red summer" of 1919, blood flowed in the streets of Washington, D.C., Omaha, Nebraska, New York City, and

Chicago, where thousands of African Americans were burned out of their homes and hundreds injured. "The Washington riot gave me the *thrill that comes once in a life time,*" wrote a young black woman in 1919. "At last our men had stood like men, struck back, were no longer dumb driven cattle."

Propaganda and Civil Liberties

COMMITTEE ON PUBLIC INFORMATION "Once lead this people into war," President Wilson warned before American entry into World War I, "and they'll forget there ever was such a thing as tolerance." Americans succumbed to war hysteria, but they had help. Wilson knew how reluctant Americans had been to enter the war, and he created the Committee on Public Information (CPI) to boost their commitment to the war.

Under George Creel, a California journalist, the CPI launched "a fight for the *minds* of men, for the conquest of their convictions." A zealous publicity campaign produced 75 million pamphlets, patriotic "war expositions" attended by 10 million people in two dozen cities, and colorful war posters, including James Flagg's famous "I Want *You* for the U.S. Army." Seventy-five thousand fast-talking "Four-Minute Men" invaded movie theaters, lodge halls, schools, and churches to keep patriotism at "white heat" with four minutes of war tirades. The CPI organized "Loyalty Leagues" in ethnic communities and sponsored parades and rallies, among them a much-publicized immigrant "pilgrimage" to the birthplace of George Washington.

100 PERCENT AMERICANISM The line between patriotism and intolerance proved all too easy to cross. As war fever rose, voluntary patriotism blossomed into an enforced "100 percent Americanism" that bred distrust of aliens, radicals, pacifists, and dissenters. German Americans became special targets. In Iowa the governor made it a crime to speak German in public. Hamburgers were renamed "Salisbury steak"; German measles, "liberty measles." When a mob outside St. Louis lynched a naturalized German American who had tried to enlist in the navy, a jury found the leaders not guilty.

ESPIONAGE AND SEDITION ACTS Congress gave concern about espionage and **sedition** more legal bite by passing the Espionage and Sedition Acts of 1917 and 1918. Both set out harsh penalties for any actions that hindered the war effort or that could be viewed as even remotely unpatriotic. Following their passage, 1,500 citizens were arrested for offenses that included denouncing the draft, criticizing the Red Cross, and complaining about wartime taxes.

Radical groups received especially severe treatment. The Industrial Workers of the World (IWW), a militant labor union centered in western states, saw the war as a battle among capitalists and fought by workers. They threatened to strike mining and lumber companies in protest. Federal agents raided the Chicago headquarters of the IWW—familiarly known as the "Wobblies"—and arrested 113 of its leaders in September 1917. The crusade destroyed the union.

Similarly, the Socialist Party opposed the "capitalist" war. In response, the postmaster general banned a dozen Socialist publications from the mail, though the party was a legal organization that had elected mayors, municipal officials, and members of Congress. In June 1918 government agents arrested Eugene V. Debs, the Socialist candidate in the presidential election of 1912, for attacking the draft. A jury found him guilty of sedition and sentenced him to 10 years in jail. Running for the presidency from his jail cell in 1920, Debs received nearly 1 million votes.

SCHENCK v. UNITED STATES The Supreme Court endorsed such actions. In *Schenck v. United States* (1919) the Court unanimously affirmed the use of the Espionage Act to convict a Socialist Party officer who had mailed pamphlets urging resistance to the draft. Free speech had limits, wrote Justice Oliver Wendell Holmes, and the pamphlets created "a clear and present danger" to a nation at war.

Over There

The first American doughboys landed in France in June 1917, but General John Pershing held back his raw troops for nearly six months, until they received more training. He also separated them in a distinct American Expeditionary Force to preserve their identity and avoid Allied disagreements over strategy.

In the spring of 1918, as the Germans pushed within 50 miles of Paris, Pershing rushed 70,000 American troops to the front. American units helped block the Germans both at the town of Château-Thierry and a month later, in June, at Belleau Wood. At Belleau, it cost the Americans half their force to drive the enemy from the woods. Two more German attacks, one at Amiens, the other just east of the Marne River, ended in disastrous German retreats. On September 12, 1918, half a million American soldiers and a smaller number of French troops overran the German stronghold at Saint-Mihiel in four days.

"HELLO GIRLS" Some 223 Americans were often close to the trenches in France but never took up arms. They were the women who served in the U.S. Army Signal Corps. Called "Hello Girls" for the greeting they gave callers, they operated telephone switchboards and relayed vital information from headquarters and supply depots to the front lines for the first time in the history of warfare. General Pershing recruited them for their patience, eye for detail, composure, and efficiency, working phones at rates five times faster than men. They spoke both French and English and handled as many as 150,000 communications a day, even in the heat of battle.

After the war, the operators were denied the status and benefits of veterans, despite having been sworn into the military and subjected to all of its regulations. Not until 1978 did they receive the recognition and rewards they deserved as the first servicewomen of the U.S. Army. Still, the "Hello Girls" played a vital role in winning the war and later in helping women gain the vote by breaking down fallacious stereotypes of female weakness and incompetence under pressure.

THE LIMITS OF FREE SPEECH

When the Socialist Party printed and distributed 15,000 leaflets attacking the Conscription Act (1917), authorities charged the party's Secretary General Charles Schenck with having violated the newly enacted Espionage Act by opposing conscription (drafting men into military service). In ruling against Schenck, Justice Oliver Wendell Holmes, writing for the majority of the Supreme Court, outlined the limits of free speech in wartime.

DOCUMENT 1
Flyer Distributed by Socialist Party

ASSERT YOUR RIGHTS!
The Constitution of the United States is one of the greatest bulwarks of political liberty. It was born after a long, stubborn battle between king-rule and democracy. . . . In this battle the people of the United States established the principle that freedom of the individual and personal liberty are the most sacred things in life. Without them we become slaves. . . .

The Thirteenth Amendment of the Constitution of the United States . . . embodies this sacred idea. The Socialist Party says this idea is violated by the Conscription Act. When you conscript a man and compel him to go abroad to fight against his will, you violate the most sacred right of personal liberty, and substitute for it what Daniel Webster called "despotism of the worst form."

A conscript is little better than a convict. He is deprived of his liberty and of his right to think and act as a free man. A conscripted citizen is forced to surrender his right as a citizen and become a subject. He is forced into involuntary servitude. He is deprived of the protection given him by the Constitution of the United States. He is deprived of all freedom of conscience in being forced to kill against his will. . . .

In a democratic country each man must have the right to say whether he is willing to join the army. Only in countries where uncontrolled power rules can a despot force his subjects to fight. Such a man or men have no place in a democratic republic. This is tyrannical power in its worst form. It gives control over the life and death of the individual to a few men. There is no man good enough to be given such power.

Conscription laws belong to a bygone age. Even the people of Germany, long suffering under the yoke of militarism, are beginning to demand the abolition of conscription. Do you think it has a place in the United States? Do you want to see unlimited power handed over to Wall Street's chosen few in America? If you do not, join the Socialist Party in its campaign for the repeal of the Conscription Act. Write to your congressman and tell him you want the law repealed. Do not submit to intimidation. You have a right to demand the repeal of any law. Exercise your rights of free speech, peaceful assemblage and petitioning the government for a redress of grievances. Come to the headquarters of the Socialist Party . . . and sign a petition for the repeal of the Conscription Act. Help us wipe out this stain upon the Constitution!

> Help us re-establish democracy in America. Remember, "eternal vigilance is the price of liberty."
> Down with autocracy!
> Long live the Constitution of the United States!
> Long live the Republic!

Source: Flyer distributed by the Socialist Party attacking the Conscription Act, 1917, as reprinted in Cornwell, Nancy, *Freedom of the Press: Rights and Liberties under the Law.* Santa Barbara, CA: ABC-CLIO, November 2004, 261–265.

DOCUMENT 2
Justice Holmes on Free Speech in Wartime

We admit that, in many places and in ordinary times, the defendants, in saying all that was said in the circular, would have been within their constitutional rights. But the character of every act depends upon the circumstances in which it is done. The most stringent protection of free speech would not protect a man in falsely shouting fire in a theatre and causing a panic. It does not even protect a man from an injunction against uttering words that may have all the effect of force. The question in every case is whether the words used are used in such circumstances and are of such a nature as to create a clear and present danger that they will bring about the substantive evils that Congress has a right to prevent. It is a question of proximity and degree. When a nation is at war, many things that might be said in time of peace are such a hindrance to its effort that their utterance will not be endured so long as men fight, and that no Court could regard them as protected by any constitutional right. It seems to be admitted that, if an actual obstruction of the recruiting service were proved, liability for words that produced that effect might be enforced. The statute of 1917, in §4, punishes conspiracies to obstruct, as well as actual obstruction. If the act (speaking, or circulating a paper), its tendency, and the intent with which it is done are the same, we perceive no ground for saying that success alone warrants making the act a crime. Indeed, that case might be said to dispose of the present contention if the precedent covers all *media concludendi*. But, as the right to free speech was not referred to specially, we have thought fit to add a few words.

It was not argued that a conspiracy to obstruct the draft was not within the words of the [Conscription] Act of 1917. The words are "obstruct the recruiting or enlistment service," and it might be suggested that they refer only to making it hard to get volunteers. Recruiting heretofore usually having been accomplished by getting volunteers, the word is apt to call up that method only in our minds. But recruiting is gaining fresh supplies for the forces, as well by draft as otherwise. It is put as an alternative to enlistment or voluntary enrollment in this act.

Source: Schenck v. United States, 249 U.S. 47, 1919.

THINKING CRITICALLY

What actions does the leaflet call for and on what grounds? According to Justice Holmes, what are the limits of free speech in peacetime and wartime? Why are they different? Do you think that there are ever instances in war when citizen protest is permissible under the Constitution?

WILSON'S FOURTEEN POINTS By 1918, with their army in retreat and civilian morale low, Germany's leaders sought an **armistice.** They hoped to negotiate terms along the lines laid out by Woodrow Wilson in a speech to Congress in January 1918. Wilson's bright vision of peace encompassed his "Fourteen Points." The key provisions called for open diplomacy, free seas and free trade, disarmament, democratic self-rule, and an "association of nations" to guarantee collective security. It was nothing less than a new world order to end selfish nationalism, imperialism, and war.

Allied leaders were not impressed. "President Wilson and his Fourteen Points bore me," French prime minister premier Georges Clemenceau said. "Even God Almighty has only ten!" But Wilson's idealistic platform was also designed to save the Allies embarrassment. Almost as soon as it came to power in 1917, the new Bolshevik government in Moscow began publishing secret treaties from the czar's archives. They revealed that the Allies had gone to war for territory and colonies, not the high principles they claimed. Wilson's Fourteen Points now gave their cause a nobler purpose.

Wilson's ideals also stirred German liberals. On October 6, 1918, the liberals gave him the chance to put his principles into action when a telegram arrived from Berlin requesting an immediate truce on the basis of the Fourteen Points. Within a month Turkey and Austria surrendered. Early in November the Kaiser was overthrown and fled to neutral Holland. On November 11, 1918, just before dawn, German officers filed into Allied headquarters in a converted railroad car near Compiègne, France, and signed the armistice.

Of the 2 million Americans who served in France, some 116,500 died. Over 200,000 were wounded. By comparison, the war claimed 1.8 million Germans, 1.7 million Russians, 1.4 million French, 1.2 million Austro-Hungarians, and nearly a million Britons. The American contribution had nonetheless been crucial, providing vital convoys at sea and fresh, confident troops on land. The United States emerged from the war stronger than ever. Europe, in contrast, looked forward—as one newspaper put it—to "Disaster . . . Exhaustion . . . Revolution."

The Influenza Pandemic of 1918–1919

In the months before the armistice a scourge more lethal than war began to engulf the globe. It started innocently enough. At Fort Riley, Kansas, on the morning of March 11, 1918, company cook Albert Mitchell reported to the infirmary on sick call. His head and muscles ached, his throat was sore, and he had a low-grade fever.

It was influenza, a virus dangerous for infants and the old but ordinarily no threat for robust young men like Mitchell. By noon 107 soldiers had reported symptoms. Within a week, the number jumped to over 500. Cases of the flu were being reported in virtually every state, even on the isolated island of Alcatraz in San Francisco Bay. And healthy young adults Mitchell's age were dying from it.

THE FINAL GERMAN OFFENSIVE AND ALLIED COUNTERATTACK, 1918

On the morning of March 21, 1918, the Germans launched a spring offensive designed to cripple the Allies. Sixty-three German divisions sliced through Allied lines for the first time since 1914 and plunged to within 50 miles of Paris. The tide turned in July, when the Germans were stopped at the Marne. The Allied counterattack, with notable American successes at Château-Thierry, Belleau Wood, Saint-Mihiel, and Meuse-Argonne, broke the German war effort. How far into France did the Central Powers penetrate? How might that have affected Allied soldiers fighting there?

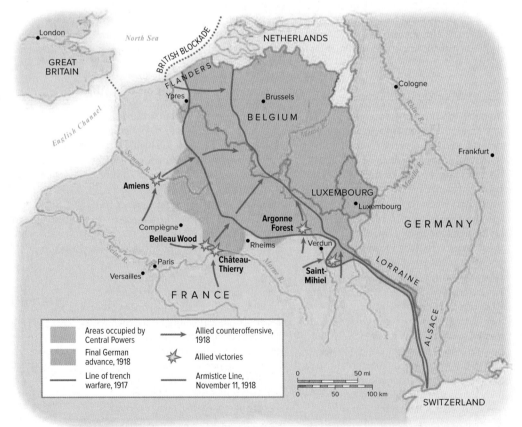

THE FLU PANDEMIC OF 1918–1919

Source: Cartoon by D.C. Boonzaier in "Die Burger," October 16, 1918

"There was no escape. Death stalked by your side incessantly, you looked into its face wherever you turned."—Artist D. C. Boonzaier of South Africa, who drew this cartoon in 1918.

CONTEXT

Maps have long charted the progress of battles and wars, portraying strategies and troop movements. But tracking the progress of an influenza pandemic also provides revealing information to historians. This map depicts the spread of the second stage of the virus, when a more virulent strain began spreading, first from France in August 1918. Study the movements of the disease and the statistics that accompany the map.

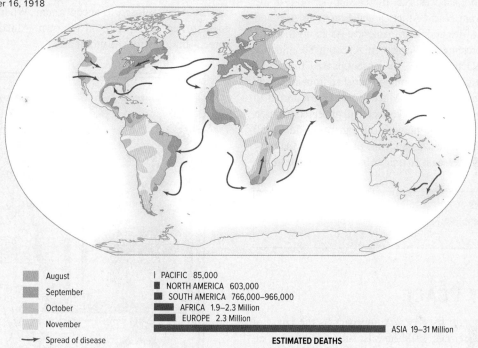

August
September
October
November
→ Spread of disease

| PACIFIC 85,000
■ NORTH AMERICA 603,000
■ SOUTH AMERICA 766,000–966,000
■ AFRICA 1.9–2.3 Million
■ EUROPE 2.3 Million
■ ASIA 19–31 Million

ESTIMATED DEATHS

MAP READING

1. *How many months does the map cover? In what year?*
2. *Which continent experienced the greatest number of deaths?*
3. *Rearrange the list of continents below in the rough order in which cases of the flu spread from one continent to the next. (The new strain appears first in France.)* **Africa Antarctica Asia Australia Europe North America South America**
4. *Which of the seven continents had no significant number of cases? Why?*

MAP INTERPRETATION

1. *How did the pandemic spread geographically within continents?*
2. *Can you suggest reasons it did not spread in certain areas, such as northwestern Canada and many parts of Russia? Why are there no deaths shown for Antarctica?*
3. *What reasons might explain the much higher number of deaths in Asia?*

The first wave of flu produced few deaths in the United States. As the virus mutated over the next year, its victims experienced more distressing symptoms: vomiting, dizziness, labored breathing, incessant sweating. Eventually sufferers drowned in their own bodily fluids from the pneumonia that accompanied the infection.

Soldiers and others living in close quarters were especially vulnerable, and for reasons that are still uncertain, so were young adults 20 to 34 years old, precisely the ages of most in the services. For every 50 people infected, 1 died. In the United States alone, the death toll rose to at least 600,000, more than the American battle deaths in World War I, World War II, the Korean War, and the war in Vietnam combined.

GLOBAL SPREAD OF THE PANDEMIC Ironically, the United States was the country least affected by this world-wide epidemic, called a **pandemic**. American soldiers seem to have carried the disease to Europe, where it jumped from one country to another in the spring and summer of 1918. French troops and civilians soon were suffering from it, then British and Germans. General Eric von Ludendorf counted the flu as one of the causes of the failure of the final German offensive in July 1918, which almost won the war for Germany.

With steamships and railroads moving people all over the globe, virtually no place was safe. By the summer of 1918 the virus had leapt from North America and Europe to Asia and Japan; by fall, to Africa and South America. As far north as the Russian city of Archangel, officials were reporting 30 influenza deaths a day by October 1918. In densely packed India, one account claimed that at least 12 million perished from influenza.

Sixteen months after Albert Mitchell had first reported to sick call, the flu vanished as quickly as it had appeared. Conservative estimates placed the number of dead worldwide at 50 million, making the influenza pandemic of 1918–1919 the most lethal outbreak of disease on an annual basis in human history.

 REVIEW
How did progressivism shape the home front during World War I?

THE LOST PEACE

AS THE USS *GEORGE WASHINGTON* approached the coast of France in mid-December 1918 the mist suddenly lifted in an omen of good hope. Woodrow Wilson had come to represent the United States at the Paris peace conference at Versailles, once the glittering palace of Louis XIV. He was the first sitting president to meet foreign heads of state on foreign soil. A world of problems awaited. Europe had been shelled into ruin and scarred with the debris of war. Some 40 million people lay dead or maimed from the fighting. Millions more had been displaced from their homelands. Throughout the Balkans and the old Turkish Empire, ethnic rivalries, social chaos, and revolution loomed.

With the old world order in shambles, Wilson felt the need for vigorous action. The president handpicked the peace commission of experts that accompanied him. Called "The Inquiry," it included economists, historians, geographers, and political scientists—but not a single member of the Republican-controlled Senate. What promised to make peace negotiations easier, in France, however, created a crippling liability in Washington, where Republicans cast a hostile eye on the mirrored halls of Versailles.

The Treaty of Versailles

Everywhere he went, cheers greeted the president. In Paris 2 million people showered him with flowers and called him "Wilson, le Juste" (the Just). In Italy they hailed him as the "peacemaker from America." And Wilson believed them, unaware of how determined the victors were to punish the vanquished Germans. David Lloyd George of England, Georges Clemenceau of France, Vittorio Orlando of Italy, and Wilson made up the Big Four at the conference that included some 27 nations. War had united them; now peacemaking threatened to divide them to compensate the winners for the costs of war.

Wilson's sweeping call for reform had taken Allied leaders by surprise. Hungry for new colonies, eager to see Germany crushed and disarmed, they had already drawn up secret treaties dividing the territories of the Central Powers. Germany offered to surrender on the basis of Wilson's Fourteen Points, but the Allies refused to accept them. When Wilson threatened to negotiate peace on his own, Allied leaders finally agreed—but only for the moment.

GOD: Woodrow Wilson, where are your 14 points?
WILSON: Don't get excited, Lord, we didn't keep your Ten Commandments either!

Source: Gene Anderson, *Simplicissimus*

| *Woodrow Wilson's famous Fourteen Points for establishing a new world order struck some observers, including this cartoonist, as being as idealistic as the Ten Commandments. For Wilson, the Fourteen Points, with their call for a peace based on national self-determination and a League of Nations, had practical political ends. The president hoped to counter the propaganda of Russian revolutionaries about the self-interested aims of the Allies and to bolster German liberals who wanted an end to the war. He also meant to boost sagging morale among the Allies with the promise of peace. Although the Fourteen Points, like the Ten Commandments, set a lofty standard of ideals, Wilson had down-to-earth results in mind.*

EUROPE AND THE MIDDLE EAST AFTER WORLD WAR I

The Treaty of Versailles changed the face of Europe and the Middle East. Compare, for example, the map "The Course of War in Europe, 1914–1917," earlier in the chapter with the one above. What European countries have been created that did not exist at the start of the war? What Middle Eastern countries? Which reflected the influence of Wilson's Fourteen Points?

Noticeably absent when the peace conference convened in January 1919 were the Russians. None of the Western democracies had recognized the Bolshevik regime in Moscow out of fear that the communist revolution might spread. Instead, France and Britain were helping to finance a civil war to overthrow the Bolsheviks. Even Wilson was persuaded to send a small number of American troops to join the Allied occupation of Murmansk in northern Russia and Vladivostok on the Sea of Japan. The Soviets neither forgot nor forgave this invasion of their soil.

Grueling peace negotiations forced Wilson to yield several of his Fourteen Points. Britain, with its powerful navy, refused even to discuss the issues of free trade and freedom of the seas. Wilson's promised "open diplomacy" was conducted behind closed doors by the Big Four. The only mention of disarmament involved Germany, which was permanently barred from rearming. Wilson's call for "peace without victory" gave way to a "guilt clause" that saddled Germany with responsibility for the war. Worse still, the victors imposed an impoverishing debt of $33 billion in reparations on the vanquished to compensate the winners for the costs of war.

Wilson did achieve some successes. His pleas for national self-determination led to the creation of a dozen new states in Europe, including Yugoslavia, Hungary, and Austria. (Newly created Poland and Czechoslovakia, however, contained millions of ethnic Germans.) Former colonies gained new status as "mandates" of the victors, who were obligated to prepare them for independence. The old German and Turkish Empires in the Middle East and Africa became the responsibility of France and England, while Japan took over virtually all German possessions in the Pacific north of the equator.

LEAGUE OF NATIONS   Wilson never lost sight of his main goal, his Fourteenth Point calling for a "general association of nations." He had given so much ground precisely because he believed this new world organization would correct any mistakes in the peace settlement. As

The Fate of Woodrow Wilson's Fourteen Points

POINT	FATE
1. End to secret treaties	rejected
2. Free navigation of seas "alike in peace and in war"	rejected
3. Free trade among nations	rejected
4. Arms reduction "consistent with domestic safety"	rejected
5. Impartial decisions about future of colonies	rejected
6. German army removed from Russia; Russia accepted internationally	rejected
7. Belgium "evacuated and restored" to prewar independence	**accepted**
8. German army removed from France; Alsace-Lorraine returned to France	**accepted**
9. Restoration of Italy's borders "along clearly recognizable lines of nationality"	modified
10. Self-government for peoples of the former Austro-Hungarian Empire	modified
11. Self-government and independence for Balkan states	modified
12. Self-government for peoples of the former Ottoman Empire; sovereignty for Turkey	modified
13. Creation of an independent Poland with access to sea	**accepted**
14. Establishment of a "general association of nations" to guarantee independence and territorial integrity of all members	modified

(*photo*) Source: Library of Congress, Prints and Photographs Division [LC-DIG-ppmsca-07634]

constituted, what came to be called the "League of Nations" comprised a general Body of Delegates, a select Executive Council, and a Court of International Justice. Members vowed to submit all war-provoking disagreements to arbitration and to isolate aggressors by cutting off commercial and military trade. Article X (Wilson called it "the heart of the covenant") bound members to respect one another's independence and territory and to join together against attack. "It is definitely a guarantee of peace," the president told the delegates in February 1919. Future wars, he hoped, would now be avoided through negotiation and arbitration.

The Battle for the Treaty

Wilson left immediately for home to address growing opposition in Congress. In the off-year elections of 1918, voters unhappy with wartime controls, new taxes, and attacks on civil liberties had given both houses to the Republicans. A slim Republican majority in the Senate put Wilson's archrival, Henry Cabot Lodge of Massachusetts, in the chairman's seat of the all-important Foreign Relations Committee. "I never expected to hate anyone in politics with the hatred I feel toward Wilson," Lodge confessed.

While most of the country favored the treaty, Lodge abhorred it, in part because he feared that the general association of nations—called the "League of Nations"—would hamstring American foreign-policy makers. He worried that the League would force Americans to subject themselves to "the will of other nations," surrendering even the war-making powers of Congress when the international body saw fit. And he certainly did not want Democrats to win votes by taking credit for the treaty. Securing the signatures of enough senators to block any treaty, Lodge rose in the Senate just before midnight on March 3, 1919, to read a "round robin" resolution against the League. "Woodrow Wilson's League of Nations died in the Senate tonight," concluded New York's *The Sun*.

Wilson formally presented the treaty in July. "Dare we reject it and break the heart of the world?" he asked the senators. His only hope of winning the necessary two-thirds majority for passage of the treaty lay in compromise, but temperamentally he could not abide it. Worn out by the concessions already wrung from him in Paris, afflicted by numbing headaches and a twitch in his left eye, he resisted any more changes. Despite his doctor's warnings, Wilson took his case to the people in a month-long stump across the nation to rally public opinion and bend the Senate to his will.

WILSON'S STROKE In Pueblo, Colorado, a crowd of 10,000 heard perhaps the greatest oration of Wilson's career. He spoke that evening, utterly exhausted, and collapsed in a spasm of pain. On October 2, four days after being rushed to the White House, the president fell to the bathroom floor, knocked unconscious by a stroke.

For six weeks Wilson could do no work at all and for months after worked little more than an hour a day. His second wife, Edith Bolling Wilson, handled the routine business of government along with the president's secretary and his doctor. The country knew nothing of the seriousness of his condition. Wilson recovered slowly but never fully. More and more the battle for the treaty consumed his fading energies.

In November 1919 Lodge finally reported the treaty out of committee with 14 reservations to match Wilson's Fourteen Points, limiting American responsibilities and defending American rights under the treaty. The most important asserted that the United States assumed no obligation to come to the aid of League members unless Congress consented. Wilson believed Lodge had delivered a "knife thrust at the heart of the treaty" and refused to compromise. Whatever ill will Lodge bore Wilson, his objections did not destroy the treaty but only weakened it by protecting the congressional prerogative to declare war.

Under orders from the president, Democrats joined Republicans to defeat the treaty with Lodge's reservations. An attempt to pass the unamended treaty failed. Although four-fifths of the senators favored it in some form, Wilson and Lodge refused to compromise. The Treaty of Versailles was dead, and loyal Democrats were forced to deliver the killing blow. Not until July 1921 did Congress enact a joint resolution ending the war. The United States, which had fought separately from the Allies, made a separate peace as well.

Source: Library of Congress, Prints and Photographs Division [LC-USZ62-85742]

"If we were in the League of Nations," warns this cartoon ominously, the United States would see more wounded and dead soldiers coming home by the boatload. Uncle Sam watches silently as the remnants of the American army return, including a flag-draped coffin in the background, while "J[ohn] Bull" (symbol of Great Britain) shouts: "Send over a new army!"

In September 1919 some 300,000 steelworkers struck for higher wages, recognition of their union, and a reduction in the 70-hour workweek. In Gary, Indiana, women in sympathy with the strike prepare to picket the plant.

Source: Library of Congress, Prints and Photographs Division [LC-USZ62-77535]

Red Scare

Peace abroad did not bring peace at home. On May Day 1919, six months after the war ended, mobs in a dozen cities broke up Socialist parades, injured hundreds, and killed three people. On the floor of the Senate, Kenneth McKellar of Tennessee advocated sending citizens with radical beliefs to a penal colony on the Pacific island of Guam.

RADICALS AND LABOR UNREST The spontaneous violence and extremism occurred because Americans believed they were under attack. The millions of soldiers who had returned home were now unemployed and looking for work. With prices rising and war regulations lifted, laborers were demanding higher wages and striking when they failed to get them. In Boston even the police walked off their jobs. When a strike by conservative trade unionists paralyzed Seattle for five days in January, Mayor Ole Hanson draped his car in an American flag and led troops through the streets in a show of force. Hanson blamed radicals, while Congress ascribed the national ills to Bolshevik agents inspired by the revolution in Russia.

The menace of radicalism was overblown. With Socialist Eugene Debs in prison, his dwindling party numbered only about 30,000. Radicals at first hoped that the success of

Source: Library of Congress, Prints and Photographs Division [LC-USZ62-36869]

A. Mitchell Palmer, a Quaker and a progressive, was shocked by the anarchist bombings and took a hard line against the terrorist campaign.

the Russian Revolution would help reverse their fortunes in the United States. But most Americans found the prospect of Russian agitators threatening, especially after March 1919, when the new Russian government formed the Comintern to spread revolution abroad. Furthermore, the Left itself splintered. In 1919 dissidents deserted the Socialists to form the more radical Communist Labor Party. About the same time, a group of mainly Slavic radicals created a separate Communist Party in the United States. Both organizations together counted no more than 40,000 members.

Terrorism stoked the flames of fear. On April 28, Mayor Hanson received a small brown parcel at his office, apparently another present from an admirer of his tough patriotism. It was a homemade bomb. Within days 20 such packages were discovered, including ones sent to John D. Rockefeller, Supreme Court Justice Oliver Wendell Holmes, and Postmaster General Albert Burleson. On June 2 bombs exploded simultaneously in eight different cities. One of them demolished the front porch of A. Mitchell Palmer, the attorney general of the United States. The bomb thrower was blown to bits, but enough remained to identify him as an Italian anarchist from Philadelphia. Already edgy over Bolshevism and labor militancy, many Americans assumed that an organized conspiracy of radicals was at the bottom of the bombings and aimed to overthrow the government.

PALMER RAIDS Palmer, a Quaker and a staunch progressive, hardened in the wake of the bombings. In November 1919 and again in January 1920, he launched raids in cities across the United States. In a single night in January, government agents invaded private homes, meeting halls, and pool parlors in 33 cities. They took 4,000 people into custody without warrants, sometimes beating those who resisted. Many were Russians, some were communists, but most were victims of suspicion run amok. Prisoners were marched through streets in chains, crammed into dilapidated jails, and held incommunicado without hearings. Over 200 aliens, most of whom had no criminal records, were deported to the Soviet Union. Arrests continued at the rate of 200 a week through March.

Such abuses of civil liberties finally provoked a backlash. After the New York legislature expelled five elected Socialists in 1919, responsible politicians—from former presidential candidate Charles Evans Hughes to Ohio senator Warren Harding—began to denounce the action. Assistant Secretary of Labor Louis Post refused to issue more deportation orders, and the "deportation delirium" ended early in 1920.

Palmer finally overreached himself by predicting a revolutionary uprising for May 1, 1920. Buildings were put under guard and state militia called to readiness. Nothing happened. Four months later, when a wagonload of bombs exploded on Wall Street, Palmer blamed a conspiracy fostered by Russian plotters. Despite over 30 deaths and more than 200 injuries, Americans saw it as the work of a few demented radicals (which it probably was) and went about business as usual. The Red Scare was over.

>  **REVIEW**
> What were the results of the Paris Peace Conference and the Treaty of Versailles?

PUTTING HISTORY IN GLOBAL CONTEXT

IN EARLY AUGUST 1914 the Panama Canal opened without fanfare, but no one could miss its significance: the new American empire now spanned the globe, stretching from the Caribbean to the Pacific and linked by a waterway between the seas. There were plans for a tremendous celebration in which the battleship *Oregon,* whose 1898 "race around the Horn" had inspired the idea of an American-owned canal, would lead a flotilla of ships through the locks. But the plans were scrapped, for in that fateful month of August, the old world order collapsed into a world war.

World War I was rightly named "the Great War" by Europeans, because it transformed the continent and left a bitter legacy that shaped the rest of the twentieth century. In Europe, France and Great Britain triumphed, only to find their economies enfeebled, their people dispirited and fearful, their empires near collapse. Two other empires—of

vanquished Austria-Hungary and Turkey—were dismembered. Revolution toppled the once-mighty czars of Russia, bringing an end to the Russian Empire and the beginning of the Soviet Union under Joseph Stalin. Germany suffered defeat, humiliation, and a crushing burden of debt, which together paved the way for Adolf Hitler and the Nazis.

Elsewhere, a victorious Japan left the Paris peace table shamed by what it regarded as paltry spoils of war and determined to rise to global greatness that equaled the West. Japan's flickering democracy soon crumbled as a cult of militarism and emperor worship took hold. In the Middle East, in Africa, and on the Indian subcontinent, the unfulfilled promises of a world made "safe for democracy" sparked a growing number of nationalist and anticolonialist movements. The twentieth century, a century of global change and violence, was forged in the crucible of the Great War.

CHAPTER SUMMARY

World War I marked the beginning of the end of the old world order of colonial imperialism, military alliances, and balances of power; it also marked a failed effort to establish a new world order based on the progressive ideals of international cooperation and collective security.

- Progressive diplomacy—whether through Theodore Roosevelt's big stick diplomacy, William Taft's dollar diplomacy, or Woodrow Wilson's missionary diplomacy—stressed moralism and order, championed "uplifting" nonwhites, and stretched presidential authority to its limits.

- With the outbreak of World War I in 1914, Woodrow Wilson saw an opportunity for the United States to lead the world to a higher peace of international cooperation and collective security by remaining neutral and brokering the peace settlement.

- However, American sympathy for the Allies, heavy American investments in the Allies, and the German campaign of unrestricted submarine warfare finally drew the United States into the war in 1917.

- Progressive faith in government, planning, efficiency, and publicity produced a greatly expanded bureaucratic state that managed the war effort on the home front.

  ► The darker side of progressivism also flourished as the war transformed progressive impulses for assimilation and social control into campaigns for superpatriotism and conformity that helped to produce a postwar Red Scare in 1919 and 1920.

  ► Meanwhile, changes were already under way, including more women in the labor force and migrations of African Americans and Mexican Americans from rural to urban America, vastly accelerated with the expansion of opportunities for war work.

- When the war ended, Wilson's hopes for "peace without victory" and a new world order, embodied in his Fourteen Points, were dashed when his European allies imposed a harsh settlement on Germany and the U.S. Senate failed to ratify the Treaty of Versailles.

Digging Deeper

For progressive diplomacy, see Howard K. Beale, *Theodore Roosevelt and the Rise of America to World Power* (1956); and Arthur Link, *Woodrow Wilson: Revolution, War, and Peace* (1968). Walter LaFeber's *Inevitable Revolutions* (rev. ed., 1993) presents an incisive account of American foreign policy in Honduras, El Salvador, Guatemala, Nicaragua, and Costa Rica. Julie Greene studies the workers who built the Panama Canal and their families, many of them blacks from the Caribbean, and sees the canal as America's springboard to empire in *The Canal Builders: Making America's Empire at the Panama Canal* (2009). Ernest R. May examines American prewar diplomacy and the policies of the Great Powers, especially Germany's U-boat campaign, in *The World War and American Isolation, 1914-1917* (1957).

The debate over American entry into World War I has a long history. Early revisionist accounts emphasizing a financial conspiracy include Charles Beard, *The Open Door to War* (1934); and Charles C. Tansill, *America Goes to War* (1938). A good account from the school of realism, critical of Wilson's moral motives, is George F. Kennan, *American Diplomacy, 1900-1950* (rev. ed., 1971). Christopher Clark's *The Sleepwalkers: How Europe Went to War in 1914* (2014) sees the war in Europe as the result of human foibles. David M. Kennedy, *Over Here: The First World War and American Society* (1980), is the definitive account of mobilization and the home front, but see also Maurine W. Greenwald's *Women, War, and Work* (1980); Susan Zeiger's *In Uncle Sam's Service: Women Workers with the American Expeditionary Force, 1917-1919* (1999); and Lynn Dumenil's *The Second Line of Defense: American Women and World War I* (2017), on the status and role of women during the war. Elizabeth Cobb tells the story of *The Hello Girls: America's First Women Soldiers* (2017). Joe William Trotter Jr., *The Great Migration in Historical Perspective* (1991), is a fine collection of essays that stresses gender and class in the wartime experience of African Americans. Mark Ellis, *Race, War, and Surveillance* (2001); and Mark Robert Schneider, *"We Return Fighting": The Civil Rights Movement in the Jazz Age* (2001), look at the effects of the war on African American civil rights. Isabel Wilkerson provides a riveting portrait of the Great Migration in *The Warmth of Other Suns* (2010) that upsets many stereotypes of those who journeyed north. Frank Freidel re-creates the horrors of trench warfare in *Over There* (1964), while Jennifer D. Keene, *Doughboys, the Great War, and the Remaking of America* (2001), looks at the impact of the war on soldiers and on the country. For African Americans on the battle front, see Chad L. Williams, *Torchbearers of Democracy: African American Soldiers in the World War I Era* (2013). Robert H. Ferrell, *Woodrow Wilson and World War I* (1985), analyzes Wilson's wartime diplomacy and the fate of the Treaty of Versailles. For the influenza pandemic, see Alfred W. Crosby, *America's Forgotten Pandemic: The Influenza of 1918* (1989); and Dorothy A. Pettit, *A Cruel Wind: Pandemic Flu in America, 1918-1920* (2008). For a colorful account of the Paris Peace Conference, see Margaret MacMillan and Richard Holbrooke, *Paris, 1919: Six Months That Changed the World* (2001). Beverly Gage's *The Day Wall Street Exploded: A Story of America in Its First Age of Terror* (2009) revisits the unsolved Wall Street bombing of 1920 within the context of class warfare and labor radicalism.

1920–1929

The Twenties seemed like a "New Era" for many reasons: new ways of dressing (including shorter skirts and the lack of bulky petticoats for women and patent leather dance shoes for men). New styles of dancing included the "Charleston," a jazz tune created by two African Americans, Jimmy Johnson and Cecil Mack, whose sheet music for the song is shown here. The tune (by Johnson) was inspired by the music of South Carolina dockworkers, and first premiered in a Broadway musical comedy, *Runnin' Wild* (1923). More traditional Americans agreed with that title, condemning the "wriggling movement and sensuous stimulation of the abominable jazz orchestra."

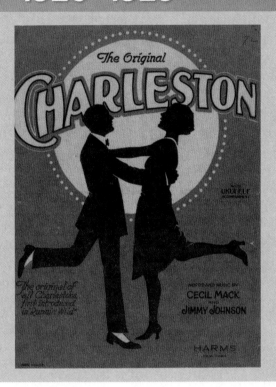

©The Advertising Archives/Alamy

>> An American Story

YESTERDAY MEETS TODAY IN THE NEW ERA

Just before Christmas 1918 the "Gospel Car" pulled into Los Angeles. Bold letters on the side announced: "JESUS IS COMING—GET READY." Aimee Semple McPherson, the ravishing red-headed driver, had completed a cross-country drive to seek her destiny as an evangelist in the West. With only "ten dollars and a tambourine," Sister Aimee at first found destiny elusive. After wandering the state for three years, she landed in San Diego. With the highest rates of illness and suicide in California, the city was perfect for the healing message of her "Foursquare Gospel." Her revival there attracted 30,000 people, who witnessed her first proclaimed miracle: a paralytic walked.

After the miracle in San Diego, her fame spread. She returned triumphantly to Los Angeles, where nearly three-quarters of a million people, many from the nation's heartland, had migrated in search of opportunity, sun, and perhaps salvation. In heading west, most had lost touch with the traditional Protestant denominations at home. Sister Aimee put her traveling gospel tent away.

To the blare of trumpets on New Year's Day, 1923, she unveiled the $1.5 million Angelus Temple, graced by a 75-foot, rotating electrified cross. It was visible at night from 50 miles away. Inside was a 5,000-seat auditorium, radio station KFSG (Kall Four Square Gospel), a "Cradle Roll Chapel" for babies, and a "Miracle Room" filled with crutches and canes discarded by the cured faithful. Services were not simply a matter of hymns, prayers, and sermons. Sister added pageants, Holy Land slide shows, and healing sessions.

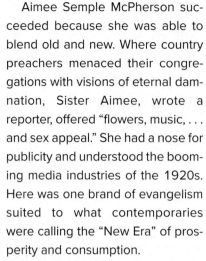

| *Sister Aimee*
©Bettmann/Getty Images

Aimee Semple McPherson succeeded because she was able to blend old and new. Where country preachers menaced their congregations with visions of eternal damnation, Sister Aimee, wrote a reporter, offered "flowers, music, . . . and sex appeal." She had a nose for publicity and understood the booming media industries of the 1920s. Here was one brand of evangelism suited to what contemporaries were calling the "New Era" of prosperity and consumption.

Modernizing the gospel was just one change ushered in by what people were calling the "New Era." Writing in 1931, journalist Frederick Lewis Allen found the changes of the preceding decade so dizzying that he could hardly believe 1919 was *Only Yesterday,* as he titled his best-selling book. To give a sense of the transformation, Allen followed an average American couple, the fictitious "Mr. and Mrs. Smith," through the 1920s. The same revolution in industry and technology that allowed sweet-voiced Sister Aimee to save souls had also transformed the Smiths' home with radios, canned foods, and new electrical gadgets like vacuum cleaners.

Perhaps the most visible changes involved women. By the end of the decade, Mrs. Smith's corset vanished and her hemline jumped from her ankle to her knee. Mimicking stylish young flappers, she bobbed, or cut, her long hair to the popular, near-boyish length. With Prohibition in force, she and other women walked into illegal speakeasy saloons as readily as men. In the trendy hotels she and her husband danced to jazz. But the most striking difference

about these "average" Americans was that they lived in the city. The census of 1920 showed that for the first time just over half the population were urbanites.

Yet the city-dwelling Smiths of Frederick Allen's imagination were scarcely average. Nearly as many Americans still lived on isolated farms, in villages, and in small towns as in cities. In fact, many "city" dwellers lived there, too. By defining cities as incorporated municipalities with 2,500 people or more, the Census Bureau had created hundreds of statistical illusions. New York with its millions of inhabitants ranked in the census tables alongside tiny Hyden, located on the Cumberland plateau of eastern Kentucky. In Hyden, Main Street remained unpaved, and God-fearing Baptists still repaired to the Middle Fork of the Kentucky River for an open-air baptism when they declared their new birth in Christ. They would have nothing to do with flapper girls or the showy miracles of Aimee McPherson.

Whether Americans embraced the New Era or condemned it, change came nonetheless, in the form of a mass-produced consumer economy, a culture shaped by mass media, and a more materialistic society. Most Americans believed the New Era of prosperity would last forever and ripple across the globe. Little did they realize that their roaring economy was honeycombed with weaknesses and that those who promised to save them turned out to be false saviors. Even Sister Aimee failed: barely three years after her glowing tower lit the skies of Los Angeles, her career had sunk as low as her reputation following her mysterious disappearance (and reappearance) amid charges that she had run away with a married man. <<

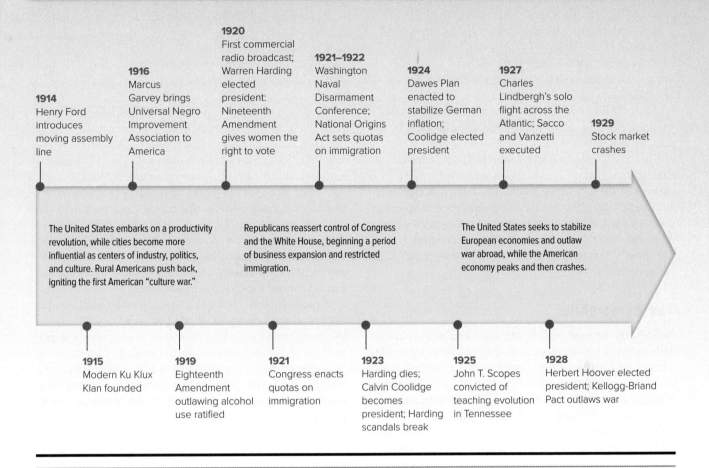

1914 Henry Ford introduces moving assembly line

1916 Marcus Garvey brings Universal Negro Improvement Association to America

1920 First commercial radio broadcast; Warren Harding elected president: Nineteenth Amendment gives women the right to vote

1921–1922 Washington Naval Disarmament Conference; National Origins Act sets quotas on immigration

1924 Dawes Plan enacted to stabilize German inflation; Coolidge elected president

1927 Charles Lindbergh's solo flight across the Atlantic; Sacco and Vanzetti executed

1929 Stock market crashes

The United States embarks on a productivity revolution, while cities become more influential as centers of industry, politics, and culture. Rural Americans push back, igniting the first American "culture war."

Republicans reassert control of Congress and the White House, beginning a period of business expansion and restricted immigration.

The United States seeks to stabilize European economies and outlaw war abroad, while the American economy peaks and then crashes.

1915 Modern Ku Klux Klan founded

1919 Eighteenth Amendment outlawing alcohol use ratified

1921 Congress enacts quotas on immigration

1923 Harding dies; Calvin Coolidge becomes president; Harding scandals break

1925 John T. Scopes convicted of teaching evolution in Tennessee

1928 Herbert Hoover elected president; Kellogg-Briand Pact outlaws war

THE ROARING ECONOMY

IN THE 1920S THE UNITED States was in the midst of a production boom. Not only did manufacturing increase sharply—by 64 percent over the decade—but so did productivity. Output per worker jumped 40 percent. Between 1922 and 1927 the economy grew by 7 percent a year—the largest peacetime growth rate ever. If anything roared in the "Roaring Twenties," it was the economy.

Technology and Consumer Spending

Technology was partly responsible. Steam turbines and shovels, electric motors, belt and bucket conveyors, and countless other new machines became common at work sites. Rising demand, especially for new consumer goods, kept the labor force growing at a faster rate than the population, even though machines replaced 200,000 workers annually. Pay improved: between 1919 and 1927, average income climbed nearly $150 for each industrial worker.

Consumer goods, the product of a maturing industrial economy, fueled rising demand. Cigarette lighters, wristwatches, radios, and other new products disappeared from store shelves almost as quickly as they were stocked. As demand grew, productivity gains helped keep prices down. The cost of a tire and an inner tube, for example, dropped by half between 1914 and 1929. Meanwhile, the purchasing power of wages climbed by 20 percent. Americans enjoyed the highest standard of living any people had ever known.

Yet for all the prosperity, a dangerous imbalance was developing. Most Americans saved little in the mistaken belief that prosperity was here to stay. Falling prices made many items seem cheap, and the rapid expansion of credit allowed consumers to put off paying for what they purchased. As a result, personal debt rose two and a half times faster than personal income, an unhealthy sign of consumers scrambling to spend.

The Booming Construction Industry

Along with technology and consumer spending, new "boom industries" promoted economic growth. Construction, both residential and commercial, was one of the most important. In a rebound after the war years, even midsize cities such as Beaumont, Texas, and Memphis, Tennessee, were erecting buildings of 20 stories or more. New York City got a new skyline of tall towers, topped in 1931 when the Empire State Building rose to the world-record height of 86 stories.

Residential construction doubled as people moved from cities to suburbs. Suburban Grosse Point, near Detroit, grew by 700 percent, and Beverly Hills, on the outskirts of Los Angeles, by 2,500 percent. Road construction made suburban life possible and pumped millions of dollars into the economy. In 1919 Oregon, New Mexico, and Colorado hit on a novel idea for financing roads—a tax on gasoline. Within a decade every state had one.

Construction stimulated other businesses: steel, concrete, lumber, home mortgages, and insurance. It even helped change the nation's eating habits. The limited storage space of small "kitchenettes" in new apartments boosted supermarket chains and the canning industry. As shipments of fresh fruits and vegetables sped across new roads, interest in nutrition grew. Vitamins, publicized with new zeal, appeared on breakfast tables.

The Automobile

No industry boomed more than automobile manufacturing. Although cars had first appeared on streets at the turn of the century, for many years they remained little more than expensive toys. By 1929 there were 26 million of them, 1 for every 5 people (compared to 1 for every 43 in Britain and 1 for every 7,000 in Russia). Automakers bought one-seventh of the nation's steel and more rubber, plate glass, nickel, and lead than any other industry. One American in four somehow earned a living from automobiles.

HENRY FORD   Henry Ford helped to make the boom possible by pushing standardization and mass production to such ruthless extremes that the automobiles became affordable. Trading on his fame as a race-car manufacturer, he founded the Ford Motor Company in 1903 with the dream of building a "motor car for the multitude." He believed that the way to succeed was to drive down costs by making all the cars alike, "just like one pin is like another pin." In 1908 Ford perfected the Model T. It had a 20-horsepower engine and a body of steel. It was high enough to ride the worst roads, and it came in only one color: black.

Priced at $845, the Model T was inexpensive by industry standards but still too costly and time-consuming to build. Two Ford engineers suggested copying a practice of Chicago meatpacking houses, where beef carcasses were carried on moving chains past meat dressers. In 1914 Ford introduced the moving assembly line. A conveyor belt, positioned waist high to eliminate bending or walking, propelled the chassis at 6 feet per minute as stationary workers put the cars together. The process cut assembly time in half. In 1925 new Model Ts were rolling off Ford's lines every 10 seconds. At $290, almost anybody could buy one. Within three years, Ford had sold 15 million of his "tin lizzies."

DOCTRINE OF HIGH WAGES   Ford was also a social prophet. Breaking with other manufacturers, he preached a "doctrine of high wages." According to it, workers with extra money in their pockets would buy enough to sustain a booming prosperity. In 1915 Ford's plants in Dearborn established the "Five-Dollar Day," twice the wage rate in Detroit. He reduced working hours from 48 to 40 a week and cut the workweek to five days. By 1926 he also employed 10,000 African Americans, many of whom had advanced far enough to hire and fire their white subordinates.

Yet Ford workers were not happy. Ford admitted that the repetitive operations on his assembly line made it scarcely possible "that any man would care to continue long at the same job." The Five-Dollar Day was designed, in part, to reduce the turnover rate of 300 percent a year at Ford plants. And Ford recouped his profits by speeding up the assembly line and enforcing ruthless efficiencies. Ford workers could not talk, whistle, smoke, or sit on the job. A Sociological Department spied on workers in their homes, and the Education Department taught plant procedures but also Americanization classes where immigrant workers learned English, proper dress, and even etiquette.

General Motors copied Ford's production techniques but not his business strategies. While Ford tried to sell everyone the same car, GM created "a car for every purse and purpose." There were Cadillacs for the wealthy, Chevrolets for the modest. GM cars were painted in a rainbow of colors, and every year the style changed. In a standardized society, such details made automobiles symbols of distinction as well as prestige.

A CAR CULTURE   By making automobiles available to nearly everyone, the industry changed the face of America. The spreading web of paved roads fueled urban sprawl, real estate booms in California and Florida, and a new roadside culture of restaurants, service stations, and motels. Thousands of "auto camps" opened to provide tourists with tents and crude toilets. Automobile travel had cultural and social consequences. It broke down the isolation and provincialism of Americans and helped to standardize dialects and manners.

Across the country the automobile gave the young unprecedented freedom from parental authority. After hearing 30 cases of "sex crimes" (19 had occurred in cars), an exasperated juvenile court judge declared that the automobile was "a house of prostitution on wheels." It was, of course, much more. The automobile was to the 1920s what the railroad had been to the nineteenth century: the catalyst for economic growth, a transportation revolution, and a cultural symbol.

The Future of Energy

The automobile had initially been seen as a clean machine, a more hygienic alternative to horse-drawn vehicles that left mounds of manure on roads and city streets and created breeding grounds for killers such as tuberculosis. The automobile also helped to ensure that the future of energy would be anything but clean. During the 1920s, the consumption of fuel oils more than doubled. But the shift to power based on hydrocarbons such as coal and petroleum was never foreordained. It was the result of several factors—some natural, others economic, still others corporate-made—all converging on the automobile.

One was abundance. Beginning with the great oil strike at Titusville, Pennsylvania, in 1859, drillers tapped into huge pools of petroleum beneath the earth's surface in Ohio, Indiana, Illinois, and other states in the South and the West. The biggest boom came in southeast Texas in 1901 at Spindletop. The first six wells drilled in a field just over a quarter of a square mile produced more oil than all the other wells in the world put together. Crude or unrefined oil from Spindletop retailed at 3 cents a barrel. Coal-driven railroad and steamship companies jumped at the chance to buy new energy at cut-rate costs.

Chemistry abetted abundance. Over the next 20 years, refiners vastly improved the process of turning crude into the light fuel oil needed for automobile engines. With intense pressure and heat, chemists could "crack" or break the string of carbon molecules in oil, more than doubling the gasoline squeezed from unrefined petroleum. In the early 1920s engineers at General Motors discovered that adding certain compounds, including tetraethyl lead, could raise the energy level of new "high-octane" gasoline. The new Ethyl Corporation, the result of a partnership between GM and Standard Oil of New Jersey, manufactured the additive and promoted it as the most economical and efficient means of increasing power.

Among other additives was alcohol. Alcohol from fermented plants was also capable of powering gasoline engines. Peanut oil drove the first diesel engines. By 1925 Henry Ford was calling alcohol "the fuel of the future." Ford was particularly impressed with the availability of fuel alcohol. It could be manufactured, he said, "from fruit like that sumac out by the road, or from apples, weeds, sawdust—almost anything . . . that can be fermented." Hydrocarbons were bound to run out, leaving the United States dependent on foreign oil in the short run and eventually the planet without its most precious source of fuel. But as long as plants grew, alcohol was endlessly renewable. To Ford, it was the energy of tomorrow.

For a time in the 1920s other automobile manufacturers as well as engineers and chemists agreed, but in the end alcohol lost out. For one thing, alcohol provided 30 percent less energy than gasoline. For another, it cost significantly more energy to produce, when growing, harvesting, distilling, and transporting were taken into account. As important, new oil discoveries on the eve of the Great Depression drove down the price of crude to 2 cents a barrel by 1931. Finally, GM and its Ethyl Corporation, which stood to profit from leaded gasoline, waged a relentless campaign against alcohol as a

©North Wind Picture Archives/Alamy
| *Henry Ford*

fuel or an additive. Facing such obstacles, alcohol enthusiasts lost out.

The long-term price paid for energy dependence on oil and leaded gasoline was high. Half a century later, long lines at local gas stations and high prices at the pump testified to the power of foreign petroleum producers to vex American consumers and threaten national security by reducing the flow of oil into the country. Even earlier, minute flecks of lead in factories poisoned workers, while lead-laden emissions from automobiles contaminated soil and water. Smog thickened by car exhausts engulfed some cities in a dangerous haze, prompting "smog alerts" and air-quality warnings for residents with respiratory ailments. Pioneered by California, new state and federal laws set limits on harmful auto emissions in the 1960s and 1970s and banned lead in gasoline and other products.

The Business of America

In business, said Henry Ford, the "fundamentals are all summed up in the single word, 'service.'" President Calvin Coolidge echoed the theme of service to society in 1925: "The business of America is business. The man who builds a factory builds a temple. The man who works there worships there." A generation earlier, progressives had criticized business for its social irresponsibility. The wartime contributions of business managers and the return of prosperity in 1922 gained them renewed respect.

CORPORATE CONSOLIDATION   Encouraged by federal permissiveness, a wave of mergers swept the country. Between 1919 and 1930 some 8,000 firms disappeared as large gobbled small. Oligopolies (a few firms that dominate whole industries) flourished in steel, meatpacking, cigarettes, and other businesses. National chains began to replace local "mom-and-pop" stores. By 1929 one bag of groceries in ten came from the 15,000 red-and-gold supermarkets of the Great Atlantic and Pacific Tea Company, commonly known as A&P.

MANAGERIAL ELITE   This expansion and consolidation meant that the wealth was being controlled not by individuals but by corporations. The model of modern business was the large, bureaucratic corporation, in which those who actually managed the company had little to do with the shareholders who owned it. A salaried bureaucracy of executives and plant managers formed a new elite. They learned the techniques of **scientific management** taught at Harvard and other new schools of business through journals, professional societies, and consulting firms. They channeled earnings back into their companies to expand factories, carry on research, and grow in size and profitability. By the end of the decade, half of all industrial income was concentrated in 100 corporations.

| The East Coryell Company marketed ethyl alcohol gasoline as an alternative to hydrocarbon-based fuels. In Lincoln, Nebraska, this gas station touted the virtue of "corn alcohol gasoline" using an eye-catching pump with an ear of corn painted on each of its four sides.
©Nebraska State Historical Society (RG2183-1933-0411-1)

Welfare Capitalism

The new "scientific management" also stressed smooth relations between managers and employees. The rash of postwar strikes had left business leaders as suspicious as ever of labor unions and determined to find ways to limit their influence.

THE AMERICAN PLAN Some tactics were more strong-armed than scientific. In 1921 the National Association of Manufacturers, the Chamber of Commerce, and other employer groups launched the "American Plan," aimed at opening "closed shops," factories where only union members could work. Employers made workers sign agreements disavowing union membership. Labor organizers called them "yellow-dog contracts" because they reduced workers to the "level of a yellow dog." Companies infiltrated unions with spies, locked union members out of factories if they protested, and boycotted firms that hired union labor.

The gentler side of the American Plan involved a social innovation called "welfare capitalism." Companies such as General Electric and Bethlehem Steel pledged to care for their employees and give them incentives for working hard.

They built clean, safe factories, installed cafeterias, hired trained dietitians, formed baseball teams and glee clubs. Several hundred firms encouraged perhaps a million workers to buy company stock. Millions more enrolled in company unions. Called "Kiss-Me Clubs" for their lack of power, they offered what few independent unions could match: health and safety insurance; a grievance procedure; and representation for African Americans, women, and immigrants.

As it turned out, welfare capitalism affected barely 5 percent of the workforce and often gave benefits only to skilled laborers, the hardest to replace. Most workers lost ground. In the 1920s a family of four could live in "minimum health and decency" on $2,000 a year. The average industrial wage was $1,304. Thus working-class families often needed more than one wage earner just to get by.

By the end of the decade, labor grievances burst into massive strikes. In 1927, in the most famous strike of the decade, 2,500 mill hands in the textile town of Gastonia, North Carolina, walked off their jobs. Even strikebreakers quit. Eventually, authorities broke the strike, foreshadowing a national trend. A year later there were only 629 strikes, a record low for the nation. Union membership shrank from almost 5 million in 1921 to less than 3.5 million in 1929.

Instant Beauty

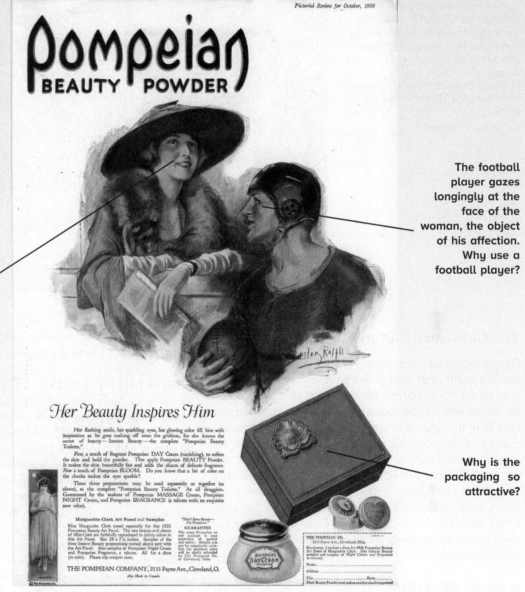

The flawless skin of the woman pictured here suggests the effectiveness of the beauty powder in producing "beauty" that "inspires him" to love her. What does her clothing tell us about the audience at which this advertisement is aimed?

The football player gazes longingly at the face of the woman, the object of his affection. Why use a football player?

Why is the packaging so attractive?

©The Advertising Archives/Alamy

Historians of popular culture find their sources in the materials of everyday life, including advertisements such as this one for Pompeian Beauty Powder. In the 1920s, as mass advertising reached new heights, promoters of products such as this "Pompeian Beauty Toilette" shifted strategies from simply listing the advantages of their wares to meeting primary demands for health, love, and in this case youth with splashy advertisements in full color. More and more they targeted women. All reflected the new emphasis on gaining personal contentment not through hard work, achievement, or even religion but through consumption. How might modern psychology, then a new social science, have played a role in creating this ad?

THINKING CRITICALLY

What other primary demands do advertisers seek to stimulate? Through what products might these demands be satisfied then and now? Why were women a growing target of advertisers in the 1920s?

| This pen-and-ink drawing depicts a cavernous street in New York City awash in advertising. Its title, *Picturesque America, is a play on the growing use of signs to sell products. Already by 1909, when the graphic artist Harry Grant Dart drew the piece, advertising and the consumer culture were overtaking the country—in this case, transforming buildings into billboards for hawking everything from foreign-language courses to cigars, furs, and automobiles. "Electric signs,"* promises one electrified sign, *"make night beautiful."* The artist did not agree.

Source: Dover Publications

The Consumer Culture

During the late nineteenth century the economy had boomed, too, but much of its growth had gone into producer goods: huge steel factories and rail, telephone, and electric networks. By World War I these industrial networks had penetrated enough of the country to create mass markets for consumer goods such as refrigerators, bicycles, and other products for average Americans. As an increasing percentage of the nation's industries turned out consumer goods, prosperity hinged on consumption. If ordinary buyers purchased more goods, production would increase at the same time that costs would decrease. Lower production costs would allow for lower prices, which would lift sales, production, and employment still higher.

ROLE OF ADVERTISING   Consumption was the key, and increased consumption rested on two innovations: advertising to help people buy and credit to help them pay. Around the turn of the century, advertisers began a critical shift from emphasizing *products* to stressing a consumer's *desires:* health, popularity, social status. Albert Lasker, the owner of Chicago's largest advertising firm, Lord and Thomas, created modern advertising in America. His eye-catching ads were hard-hitting, positive, and often preposterous. To expand the sales of Lucky Strike cigarettes, Lord and Thomas claimed smoking made people slimmer and more courageous. "Luckies" became one of the most popular brands in America. Bogus doctors and dentists lent an air of authority to ad campaigns by endorsing

all kinds of products, including toothpaste containing potassium chloride—8 grams of which was lethal.

INSTALLMENT BUYING AS CREDIT   Advertisers encouraged Americans to borrow against tomorrow to purchase what advertising convinced them they wanted today. Installment buying had once been confined to sewing machines and pianos. In the 1920s it grew into the tenth biggest business in the United States. In 1919 Alfred Sloan created millions of new customers by establishing the General Motors Acceptance Corporation, the nation's first consumer credit organization. By 1929 Americans were buying most of their cars, radios, and furniture on the installment plan. Such credit purchases had an unfortunate result. Across the decade, consumer debt jumped 250 percent to $7 billion, almost twice the federal budget.

 REVIEW

What factors produced unprecedented economic growth in the 1920s?

A MASS SOCIETY

IN THE EVENING AFTER A day's work in the fields—perhaps in front of an adobe house built by one of the western sugar-beet companies—Mexican American workers might gather to chat or sing a *corrido* or two. The *corrido* was a traditional Mexican folk ballad whose lyrics chronicled daily life, good and bad. One *corrido,* written during the 1920s, told of a field laborer distressed that his family had rejected old Mexican customs in favor of new American fashions. His wife, he sang, now had "a bob-tailed dress of silk" and, wearing makeup, went about "painted like a *piñata.*" It was enough to make him long for Mexico.

For Americans from all backgrounds the New Era was witness to "a vast dissolution of ancient habits," commented columnist Walter Lippmann. Mass marketing and mass distribution led not simply to a higher standard of living but also to a life less regional and diverse. In the place of moral standards set by local communities and churches came "modern" fashions and attitudes, spread by the new mass media of movies, radio, and magazines. In the place of "ancient habits" came the forces of mass society: independent women, freer love, standardized culture, urban energy and impersonality, and sometimes alienation.

A "New Woman"

In the tumultuous 1890s a "New Woman" appeared, one who was more assertive, athletic, and independent than her Victorian peers. By the 1920s more-modern versions of this New Woman were being charged with nothing less than leading what Frederick Lewis Allen called the "revolution in manners and morals." The most flamboyant of them wore close-fitting felt hats and makeup, long-waisted dresses and few undergarments, strings of beads, and unbuckled galoshes (which earned them the nickname "flappers"). Dripping with cocktails, footloose and economically free, the New Woman became a symbol of liberation and sexuality to some, of decadence and decline to others.

World War I served as a social catalyst, continuing the prewar trend of an increase in the female percentage of the workforce and changing many attitudes. Before the war, women were arrested for smoking cigarettes openly, using profanity, and driving automobiles without men beside them. With women bagging explosives, running locomotives, and drilling with rifles during the war, the old taboos often seemed silly.

MARGARET SANGER Disseminating birth control information by mail had also been a crime before the war and still was after it. But by the armistice there was a birth control clinic in Brooklyn, a National Birth Control League, and later an American Birth Control League led by Margaret Sanger. Sanger's crusade had begun as an attempt to save poor women from the burdens of unwanted pregnancies (see Chapter 22,) and, less nobly, to reduce births among those considered "unfit," including many of the immigrants flooding the country. In the 1920s her message found a receptive middle-class audience. Surveys showed that by the 1930s nearly 90 percent of college-educated couples practiced contraception.

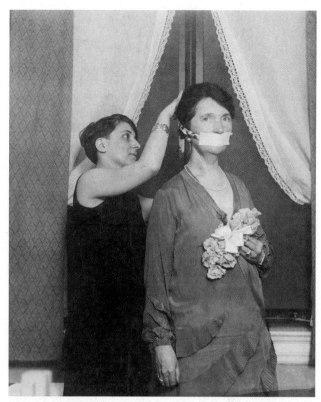

©Bettmann/Getty Images

| *According to the* Brooklyn Daily Eagle, *April 17, 1929: "A feature at the meeting will be the attendance of Mrs. Margaret Sanger, fresh from [the] raid on her New York clinic. Adhesive tape will seal her lips that they may not preach birth control while in Boston, Mass., but she will be permitted to write on the blackboard." Sanger had been threatened with arrest by Mayor James Curley of Boston, which she put to good use to publicize her appearance. As she stood, her speech was read by a Harvard historian at the meeting, Arthur Schlesinger Sr.*

Being able to control pregnancy to a degree, women felt less guilt about enjoying sex and less fear over the consequences. In 1909 Sigmund Freud had come to America to lecture on his theories of coping with the unconscious and overcoming harmful repressions. Some of Freud's ideas, specifically his emphasis on childhood sexuality, shocked Americans, while most of his complex theories sailed blissfully over their heads. As popularized in the 1920s, however, Freudian psychology stamped sexuality as a key to health.

Sexuality became more important in the new model of marriage emerging during the decade. No longer were couples duty-bound to marry for procreation alone and, once married, to keep to separate male and female spheres. As old conventions crumbled and women became more assertive, love replaced duty as the bond holding a couple together. Companionship—spending time with each other and sharing interests (including sex)—became the key to marital bliss. This new "companionate" marriage afforded women greater freedom and equality by breaking down gendered spheres and strengthening ties between husbands and wives. It also gave well-heeled Americans another way to feel superior. Without the money and leisure often needed for companionate marriages, the working class and working poor continued to play traditional married roles.

Such changes in the social climate were real enough, but the life of a flapper girl, as free and independent as a man, hardly mirrored the lives of most American women. Relatively few worked outside of their homes, and pay for those who did never equaled a man's. Over the decade the female labor force grew but only by 1 or 2 percent, slowing the prewar and wartime trends toward greater employment of women. The paltry gain did little to change the profile of working women. As late as 1930 nearly 60 percent were African American or foreign-born and generally held low-paying jobs in domestic service or the garment industry.

The New Era did spawn new careers for women. The consumer culture capitalized on a preoccupation with appearance and led to the opening of some 40,000 beauty parlors staffed by hairdressers, manicurists, and cosmeticians. Progressive reformers expanded opportunities in education, libraries, and social welfare, all within the bounds of nurturing "women's fields." Women earned a higher percentage of doctoral degrees (from 1 percent in 1910 to 15.4 percent in 1930) and held more college teaching posts than ever (32 percent). But in most areas, professional men resisted the "feminization" of the workforce. The number of female doctors dropped by half as medical schools imposed restrictive quotas and hospitals rejected female interns.

In 1924 two women—Nellie Ross in Wyoming and Miriam ("Ma") Ferguson in Texas—were elected governors, the first female chief executives. But most women continued to be marginalized in party politics, though still involved in educational and welfare programs. Operating outside male-dominated political parties, women activists succeeded in winning passage of the Sheppard-Towner Federal Maternity and Infancy Act in 1921 to fight infant mortality with rural prenatal and baby-care centers. It was the first federal welfare statute. Yet by the end of the decade the Sheppard-Towner Act had lapsed.

EQUAL RIGHTS AMENDMENT In the wake of their greatest success, the hard-won vote for women, feminists splintered. The National Woman Suffrage Association disbanded in 1920. In its place the new League of Women Voters encouraged informed voting with nonpartisan publicity. For the more militant Alice Paul and her allies, that was not enough. Their National Woman's Party pressed for a constitutional Equal Rights Amendment (ERA). Social workers and others familiar with the conditions under which women labored opposed it. Death and injury rates for women were nearly double those for men. To them the ERA meant losing the protection as well as the benefits women derived from mothers' pensions and maternity insurance. Joined by most men and a majority of Congress, they fought the amendment to a standstill.

Mass Media

MOTION PICTURES In sunny Southern California, where movies could be made year-round, Hollywood helped give the New Woman notoriety as a temptress and trendsetter. When sexy Theda Bara appeared in *The Blue Flame* in 1920, crowds mobbed theaters. And just as Hollywood dictated standards of physical attraction, it became the judge of taste and fashion in countless other ways because motion pictures were a near-universal medium. The black-and-white images parading across the screen required nothing of viewers but their eyesight. It didn't matter whether audiences could speak English, let alone read it. The power of the moving picture alone was enough to tell a story.

Motion pictures, invented in 1889, had first been shown in tiny neighborhood theaters called "nickelodeons." For a nickel, patrons watched a silent screen flicker with moving images as an accompanist played music on a tinny piano. The audience was anything but silent. The theater reverberated with the cracking of Indian nuts, the day's equivalent of popcorn, while young cowboys shot off their Kilgore repeating cap pistols during dramatic scenes. Often children read the subtitles aloud to their immigrant parents, translating into Italian, Yiddish, and German.

After the first feature-length film, *The Great Train Robbery* (1903), productions became rich in spectacle, attracted middle-class audiences, and turned into America's favorite form of entertainment. By 1926 more than 20,000 movie houses offered customers lavish theaters with overstuffed seats, live music, and a celluloid dream world—all for 50 cents or less. At the end of the decade, these picture palaces were drawing in over 100 million people a week, roughly the equivalent of the national population.

In the spring of 1920 Frank Conrad of the Westinghouse Company in East Pittsburgh rigged up a research station in his barn and started transmitting phonograph music and baseball scores to local, mostly male, wireless operators. Local stores began selling equipment to "be used by those who listen to Dr. Conrad's programs." Six months later Westinghouse Broadcast Company opened the first licensed radio station in history, KDKA, to stimulate sales of its supplies. By 1922 the number of licensed stations had jumped to 430. By the end of the decade nearly one home in three had a radio ("furniture that talks," comedian Fred Allen called it).

At first radio was seen as a civilizing force. "The air is your theater, your college, your newspaper, your library," exalted one ad in 1924. But with the growing number of sets came commercial broadcasting, catering to common tastes. The money poured in. By 1931 advertisers were paying $10,000 an hour for a national hookup, and the most popular show on radio was *Amos 'n' Andy,* a comedy about African Americans created by two white vaudevillians in 1926. It borrowed its style from black comedians Aubrey Lyles and Flournoy Miller, who occasionally wrote dialogue for the show. A slice of black culture, usually stereotyped, entered mainstream American life.

As movies became more popular, theater owners rushed to outdo one another in making the viewing experience extraordinary. In Hollywood, film capital of the world, Grauman's Chinese Theater opened in 1927, complete with ushers in exotic costumes to show patrons to their seats. Such lavish movie houses sought to attract more prosperous middle-class audiences with pomp and splendor.

©hollywoodphotographs.com

At night families gathered around the radio instead of the hearth, perhaps listening to a concert or a comedian rather than going out. Ticket sales at vaudeville theaters collapsed as a vast national audience emerged, linked by nothing but airwaves.

NEWSPAPER CHAINS   Print journalism also broadened its reach during the 1920s. In 1923 Yale classmates Henry R. Luce and Briton Hadden rewrote news stories in a snappy style, mixed them with photographs, and created the country's first national weekly, *Time* magazine. By 1927, 55 giant newspaper chains distributed 230 newspapers with a combined circulation of 13 million. Though they controlled less than 10 percent of all papers, the chains pioneered modern mass news techniques. Editors relied on central offices and syndicates to prepare editorials, sports, gossip, and Sunday features for a national readership.

The Cult of Celebrity

In a world in which Americans were rapidly being reduced to anonymous parts of mass, industrialized society, media offered them a chance to identify with the achievements of individuals by creating a world of celebrities and heroes. Sports figures such as home-run king "Babe" Ruth, business executives like Henry Ford, and movie stars led by the "Latin lover" Rudolph Valentino found their exploits splashed across the front pages of newspapers and magazines and followed on radio by millions hungry for excitement and eager to project their own dreams onto others.

CHARLES LINDBERGH   No hero attracted more attention than a shy, reed-thin 25-year-old named Charles Lindbergh. Early on the morning of May 20, 1927, "Lucky Lindy" streaked into the skies above Long Island in a silver-winged monoplane called the *Spirit of St. Louis,* headed east, and 33 hours 30 minutes later, landed just outside Paris. Lindbergh was the first flier to cross the Atlantic alone; eight others had died trying. An ecstatic mob swamped him and nearly tore his plane to pieces in search of souvenirs.

Lindbergh, dubbed by reporters the "Lone Eagle," returned with his plane aboard the warship USS *Memphis.* In New York City alone, he was greeted by nearly 4 million cheering fans. Lindbergh had "fired the imagination of mankind," observed one newspaper. Never had one person mastered a machine so completely or conquered nature so courageously. To Americans ambivalent over mass society and worried about being overwhelmed by technology and bureaucracy, Lindbergh's accomplishment signaled salvation. Perhaps they could control the New Era without losing their cherished individualism.

"Ain't We Got Fun?"

SPECTATOR SPORTS   "Ev'ry morning, ev'ry evening, ain't we got fun?" ran the 1921 hit song. As the average hours on the job each week decreased from 47.2 in 1920 to 42 by 1930, spending on amusement and recreation tripled. Spectator sports came of age. In 1921 some 60,000 fans paid $1.8 million to see Jack Dempsey, the "Manassas Mauler," knock out French champion Georges Carpentier. Millions more listened as radio took them ringside for the first time in sports history. Universities constructed huge stadiums for football—a 60,000-seater at Berkeley, a 64,000-seater at Ohio State. By the end of the decade, college football games were outdrawing major league baseball.

Baseball remained the national pastime but became a bigger business. An ugly World Series scandal in 1919 led owners to appoint Judge Kenesaw Mountain Landis as "czar" of the sport to avoid the possibility of more stringent government regulation. His iron-fisted rule reformed the game enough to ward off federal intervention. In 1920 the grandson of German immigrants revolutionized it. George Herman "Babe" Ruth hit 54 home runs and made the New York Yankees the first club to attract a million fans in one season. A heroic producer in an era of consumption, Ruth was also baseball's bad boy: he smoked, drank, cursed, and chased every skirt in sight. Under the guidance of the first modern sports agent, Christy Walsh, Ruth became the highest-paid player in the game and made a fortune endorsing everything from clothing to candy bars.

At parties old diversions—charades, card tricks, recitations—faded in popularity as dancing took over. The ungainly camel walk, the sultry tango, and in 1924 the frantic Charleston were the urban standards. A cultural counterweight to what some regarded as such unseemingly displays, square dancing enjoyed a revival with music provided by Detroit's WBZ, courtesy of Henry Ford.

JAZZ   The new energy could not be contained. From the turn-of-the-century brothels and gaming houses of New Orleans, Memphis, and St. Louis came a rhythmic, compelling music that swept into nightclubs and over the airwaves: jazz. Jazz was a remarkably complex blend of several older African American musical traditions, combining the soulfulness of the blues with the brighter syncopated rhythms of ragtime music. The distinctive style of jazz bands came from a marvelous improvising as the musicians embellished melodies and played off one another.

The style spread when the all-white "Original Dixieland Jazz Band" recorded several pieces for the phonograph. The music business, dominated by white publishers, recording studios, and radio stations, seized on the sound. The music became a sensation in New York in 1917 and spread across the country. Black New Orleans stalwarts like Joe "King" Oliver's Creole Jazz Band began touring. In 1924 Paul Whiteman inaugurated respectable "white" jazz in a concert at Carnegie Hall. When self-appointed guardians of good taste denounced such music as "intellectual and spiritual

debauchery," Whiteman disagreed: "Jazz is the folk music of the machine age."

The Art of Alienation

EXPATRIATES   Before World War I a generation of young writers had begun to rebel against Victorian purity. The savagery of the war drove many of them even farther from any faith in reason or progress. Instead, they embraced a "nihilism" that denied all meaning in life. When the war ended, they turned their resentment against American life, especially its small towns and big businesses, its conformity, technology, and materialism. Some led unconventional lives in New York City's Greenwich Village. Others, called **expatriates,** left the country for the artistic freedom of London and Paris. Their alienation helped produce a literary outpouring unmatched in American history.

On the eve of World War I the poet Ezra Pound had predicted an "American *Risorgimento*" that would "make the Italian Renaissance look like a tempest in a teapot." From Europe the expatriate Pound began to make it happen. Abandoning rhyme and meter in his poetry, he decried the "botched civilization" that had produced the war. Another voluntary exile, T. S. Eliot, bemoaned the emptiness of modern life in his epic poem *The Waste Land* (1922). Ernest Hemingway captured the disillusionment of the age in *The Sun Also Rises* (1926) and *A Farewell to Arms* (1929), novels in which resolution came as it had in war—by death.

At home Minnesota-born Sinclair Lewis, the first American to win a Nobel Prize in literature, sketched a scathing vision of midwestern small-town life in *Main Street* (1920). The book described "savorless people . . . saying mechanical things about the excellence of Ford automobiles, and viewing themselves as the greatest race in the world." His next novel, *Babbitt* (1922), dissected small-town businessman George Follansbee Babbitt, a peppy realtor from the fictional city of Zenith. Faintly absurd and supremely dull, Babbitt was the epitome of average.

The novels of another Minnesotan, F. Scott Fitzgerald, glorified youth and romantic individualism but found redemption nowhere. Fitzgerald's heroes, like Amory Blaine in *This Side of Paradise* (1920), spoke for a generation "grown up to find all Gods dead, all wars fought, all faiths in man shaken." Like most writers of the decade, Fitzgerald saw life largely as a personal affair—opulent, self-absorbing, and ultimately tragic.

A "New Negro"

MARCUS GARVEY   As World War I seared white intellectuals, so, too, did it galvanize black Americans. Wartime labor shortages had spurred a migration of over

| Blues, *painted in 1929 by African American artist Archibald Motley Jr., evokes the improvised rhythms of the Jazz Age. New Orleans–born Motley was one of a group of black genre painters in the 1920s who became part of the Harlem Renaissance.*

a million African Americans out of the rural South into northern industrial cities. But postwar unemployment and racial violence quickly dashed black hopes for equality and thwarted their progress. Common folk in these urban enclaves found an outlet for their alienation in a charismatic black nationalist from Jamaica named Marcus Garvey.

Garvey brought his organization, the Universal Negro Improvement Association (UNIA), to America in 1916 in hopes of restoring black pride by returning African Americans to Africa and Africa to Africans. Whereas Booker T. Washington had counseled accommodation of segregated America and W. E. B. Du Bois and the NAACP had pursued racial integration, Garvey urged separation of the races. Yet he stood not entirely apart from these other activists. Garvey relied, like Washington, on a message of self-help and demanded, like Du Bois, an end to colonialism.

"Up you mighty race," Garvey told his followers, "you can accomplish what you will." When Garvey spoke at the first national UNIA convention in 1920, over 25,000 supporters jammed Madison Square Garden in New York City to listen. Even his harshest critics admitted there were at least half a million UNIA members in more than 30 branches of his organization. It was the first mass movement of African Americans in history. But in 1925 Garvey was convicted of mail fraud and sentenced to prison for having oversold stock in his Black Star Line, the steamship company founded to return African Americans to Africa. His dream shattered, but not the image of a proud black man standing up against racial bigotry and intolerance. The memory of Garvey and his movement nurtured budding black nationalism for decades to come.

HARLEM RENAISSANCE As Garvey rose to prominence an outpouring of black literature, painting, and sculpture was brewing in Harlem at the northern end of Manhattan. Since the completion of Manhattan's subway system in 1904, Harlem had grown black after eagerly expected white renters

THE PROBLEM OF RACE

"The problem of the twentieth century," wrote African American scholar and activist W. E. B. Du Bois, "is the problem of the color-line." For Du Bois, segregation and the prejudice from which it sprang defined the racial problem of the twentieth century. For Claude McKay, the radical poet and novelist, the solution is clear.

DOCUMENT 1
W. E. B. Du Bois Defines the Problem of Race

Between me and the other world there is ever an unasked question: unasked by some through feelings of delicacy; by others through the difficulty of rightly framing it. All, nevertheless, flutter round it. They approach me in a half-hesitant sort of way, eye me curiously or compassionately, and then, instead of saying directly, How does it feel to be a problem? they say, I know an excellent colored man in my town; or, I fought at Mechanicsville; or, Do not these Southern outrages make your blood boil?

At these I smile, or am interested, or reduce the boiling to a simmer, as the occasion may require. To the real question, How does it feel to be a problem? I answer seldom a word. . . .

The history of the American Negro is the history of this strife—this longing to attain self-conscious manhood, to merge his double self into a better and truer self. In this merging he wishes neither of the older selves to be lost. He would not Africanize America, for America has too

much to teach the world and Africa. He would not bleach his Negro soul in a flood of white Americanism, for he knows that Negro blood has a message for the world. He simply wishes to make it possible for a man to be both a Negro and an American, without being cursed and spit upon by his fellows, without having the doors of Opportunity closed roughly in his face.

Source: Du Bois, W. E. B., *The Souls of Black Folk: Essays and Sketches.* Chicago, IL: A.C. McClurg & Co., 1903.

DOCUMENT 2
A Militant's Solution

If we must die, let it not be like hogs
Hunted and penned in an inglorious spot,
While round us bark the mad and hungry dogs,
Making their mock at our accursèd lot.
If we must die, O let us nobly die,
So that our precious blood may not be shed
In vain; then even the monsters we defy
Shall be constrained to honor us though dead!
O kinsmen! we must meet the common foe!
Though far outnumbered let us show us brave,
And for their thousand blows deal one death-blow!

What though before us lies the open grave?
Like men we'll face the murderous, cowardly pack,
Pressed to the wall, dying, but fighting back!

Claude McKay, originally published in *The Liberator* (July 1922) and reprinted in Claude McKay, *Harlem Shadows* (1922)

Source: McKay, Claude. "If We Must Die." *The Liberator,* July 1919.

THINKING CRITICALLY

What is the "other world" that DuBois points to? Why are African Americans a "problem" that whites are afraid to ask about directly? How do you think Du Bois would answer the question if it were asked directly? How would Claude McKay respond? What is McKay's solution?

failed to appear. By the end of World War I, Harlem had become the cultural capital of black America.

The first inklings of what came to be called the Harlem Renaissance struck a strident tone. In 1922 Claude McKay, another Jamaican immigrant, published a book of poems titled *White Shadows.* His most famous poem, "If We Must Die," called for defiance and dignity: "Like men we'll face the murderous, cowardly pack / Pressed to the wall, dying but fighting back!" Often supported by white patrons, or "angels," the young black writers and artists of Harlem found their subjects in the street life of cities, the folkways of the rural South, and the primitivism of preindustrial cultures. They wrote without embarrassment of prostitution and pimping, celebrated sex and alcohol, and reveled in the joys of life and love on the streets of Harlem.

Source: Library of Congress, Prints and Photographs Division [LC-USZ62-62394]

| *Zora Neale Hurston*

Middle-class reformers such as Du Bois shuddered at such frank depictions, bent as they were on demonstrating the moral equivalency of the races. McKay's colorful descriptions of "brown lips full and pouted for sweet kissing" and "brown breasts throbbing with love" seemed only to reinforce the stereotypes of unbridled black sexuality and made Du Bois, for one, feel "like taking a bath." Renaissance writers did not care. For them, vitality and instinct were among the hallmarks of the New Negro. So, too, were these hallmarks for painters such as Aaron Douglas. His vibrant murals and illustrations fused geometric designs with African myth and everyday African American life and religion. Poet Langston Hughes reminded his readers of the ancient heritage of African Americans in "The Negro Speaks of Rivers," while Zora

The Culture Wars of the 1920s

OPPONENTS	WHAT THEY BELIEVED IN	WEAPONS THEY USED
TRADITIONALISTS 	Small-town life; small government; small business; local control; superiority of white Anglo-Saxons; traditional, home-centered roles for women; traditional Protestantism	Immigration restriction; prohibition of alcohol; antievolution legislation; Ku Klux Klan
MODERNISTS 	Urban life; big government; big business; racial, ethnic, and religious diversity; liberated women	Opposition to restrictions of traditionalists through court cases, legislation, and public media

Source: Library of Congress, Prints and Photographs Division [LC-USZ62-115130]

Neale Hurston collected folktales, songs, and prayers of black southerners.

Though generally not a racial protest, the Harlem Renaissance drew on the new assertiveness of African Americans as well as on the alienation of white intellectuals. In 1925 Alain Locke, a black professor from Howard University, collected a sampling of African American works in *The New Negro*. The New Negro, Locke wrote, was "not a cultural foundling without his own inheritance" but "a conscious contributor . . . collaborator and participant in American civilization." The title of the book reflected not only a distinctively black artistic movement but also a new racial consciousness: militant, uncompromising, and self-consciously proud.

 REVIEW

How did mass media and mass culture reshape American life in the 1920s?

DEFENDERS OF THE FAITH

AS MASS SOCIETY PUSHED THE country into a future of machines, organization, middle-class living, ethnic diversity, and cosmopolitan culture, not everyone approved. Dr. and Mrs. Wilbur Crafts, the authors of *Intoxicating Drinks and Drugs in All Lands and Times*, set forth a litany of sins that tempted young people in this modern "age of cities." "Foul pictures, corrupt literature, leprous shows, gambling slot machines, saloons, and Sabbath breaking. . . . *We are trying to raise saints in hell.*"

The changing values of the New Era seemed especially threatening to traditionalists like the Crafts. Their deeply held beliefs reflected the rural roots of so many Americans: an ethic that valued neighborliness; small communities; a sameness of race, religion, and ethnicity; and a reliance on localities rather than federal or state government. Improvements in mass media—radio, movies, magazines—made it impossible for isolated communities to avoid national trends, even when they disapproved of them. Such "traditionalists" could be found among countryfolk and rural migrants to cities as well as an embattled Protestant elite, who felt as if they were drowning in a sea of modern ways and new immigrants. All were determined to defend their older faiths against the modern age of urban anonymity, moral fluidity, diverse races and ethnicities, and religious pluralism. In the 1920s a full-scale culture war erupted pitting these traditionalists against the forces of change and the "modernists" who applauded them.

Nativism and Immigration Restriction

In 1921 two Italian immigrants, who freely admitted to being radical anarchists, presented a dramatic challenge to those older faiths. Nicola Sacco and Bartolomeo Vanzetti were sentenced to death—on the face of it, for a shoe company robbery and murder in South Braintree, Massachusetts, committed a year earlier. The evidence against them was controversial, and critics charged that Sacco and Vanzetti were convicted primarily because they were foreign-born radicals. During the trial the presiding judge had scorned them in private as "anarchist bastards" and later refused all motions for a retrial, in spite of a confession to the robbery by a well-known gang member. For protesters around the world, Sacco and Vanzetti's execution in 1927 was a symbol of American bigotry and prejudice.

By then nativism—a rabid hostility to foreigners—had produced the most restrictive immigration laws in American history. In the aftermath of World War I immigration was running close to 1 million a year, almost as high as prewar levels. Most immigrants came from eastern and southern Europe and from Mexico; most were Catholics and Jews. Alarmed white native-born Protestants warned that if the flood

continued, Americans might become "a hybrid race of people as worthless and futile as the good-for-nothing mongrels of Central America and Southeastern Europe." Appreciating the potential for higher wages in a shrunken labor pool, the American Federation of Labor supported restriction.

MEXICAN AMERICANS In the Southwest, Mexicans and Mexican Americans became a target of concern. The Spanish had inhabited the region for nearly 400 years, producing a rich blend of European and Indian cultures. By 1900 about 300,000 Mexican Americans lived in the United States. In the following decade Mexicans fleeing poverty and a revolution in 1910 almost doubled the Latino population of Texas and New Mexico. In California it quadrupled. During World War I labor shortages led authorities to relax immigration laws, and in the 1920s American farmers opened a campaign to attract Mexican farmworkers.

Thousands of single young men, known as *solos,* also crossed the border to catch trains for northern industrial cities. By the end of the 1920s thriving communities of Mexicans could be found in the "barrios"—Mexican neighborhoods—of Kansas City, Detroit, and elsewhere. Spanish-speaking newcomers settled into an immigrant life of family and festivals, churchgoing, hard work, and slow adaptation. As with other immigrants, some returned home, but some brought their families. The census of 1930 listed nearly 1.5 million Mexicans living in the United States, not including an untold number who had entered the country illegally.

NATIONAL ORIGINS ACTS Mexicans were just one target of the first National Origins Act, passed in 1921. It capped all immigration at 350,000 and parceled out entry by admitting up to 3 percent of each nationality living in the United States as of 1910. The new system of quotas privileged "races" commonly believed to be superior—"Nordics" (from northern and western Europe)—over those considered inferior—"Alpines" and "Mediterraneans" (from southern and eastern Europe). Asian immigration was virtually banned. In 1924 immigration restrictionists went further. A second National Origins Act cut the quota to 150,000, reduced the percentage to 2, and pushed the base year back to 1890, before the bulk of southern and eastern Europeans had arrived. These were the very groups that many native-born Americans feared. To control the flow of illegal aliens, Congress also created the Border Patrol. Its tiny force of 450 agents, stationed along the boundaries with Canada and Mexico, constituted nothing more than a symbolic statement of restrictionist sentiment.

The National Origins Act fixed the pattern of immigration for the next four decades. Immigration from southern and eastern Europe was reduced to a trickle. The free

| Sacco and Vanzetti

POPULATION GROWTH AND AFRICAN AMERICAN MIGRATION, 1920s

Source: Library of Congress, Prints and Photographs Division, FSA/OWI Collection [LC-DIG-fsa-8b32371]

"They left as though they were fleeing some curse. They were willing to make almost any sacrifice . . . and they left with the intention of staying."
—Emmett J. Scott, a scholar studying black migration, 1920.

CONTEXT

In the 1920s the population of urban America grew by some 15 million people, at the time the greatest 10-year jump in American history. For the first time, more people lived in urban than rural areas. Spurred first by the industrial demands of World War I and then by declining farm income, cities grew largely by depopulating farms and small towns. In the most dramatic manifestation of the overall trend, more than a million African Americans migrated from the rural South to the urban North.

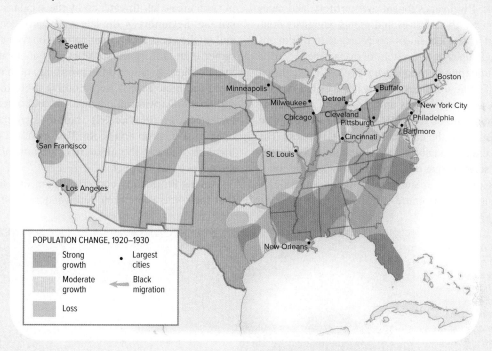

POPULATION CHANGE, 1920–1930

- Strong growth
- Moderate growth
- Loss
- Largest cities
- Black migration

MAP READING

1. Which regions of the country experienced the biggest gains in population? Which regions experienced the biggest declines?
2. From which region of the country did African Americans depart? To what sort of areas did they migrate?
3. Which cities were located in the areas of greatest growth?

MAP INTERPRETATION

1. What economic and social factors might have prompted people to leave their homes and move to other parts of the country?
2. What might have led African Americans to move from farms and towns in the South to cities in the North?
3. How would the popularity of the automobile have affected social mobility and migration?

---

movement of Europeans to America, a migration of classes and nationalities unimpeded for 300 years, came to an end.

The "Noble Experiment"

EIGHTEENTH AMENDMENT For nearly a hundred years reformers had tried—with sporadic success—to reduce the consumption of alcohol. In the heated atmosphere of the 1920s, when fear of immigrants from drinking cultures peaked, their most ambitious campaign climaxed. In January 1920 the Eighteenth Amendment went into effect, sanctioning the prohibition of liquor. Prohibition was not total: private citizens could still drink. They simply could not make, sell, transport, or import any "intoxicating beverage" containing

0.5 percent alcohol or more. The aim was to take the profit out of the liquor trade and reduce alcohol consumption without trampling too heavily on the rights of individuals. By some estimates, the consumption of liquor was cut in half.

CONSEQUENCES OF PROHIBITION The consequences of so vast a social experiment were significant and often unexpected. Prohibition reversed the prewar trend toward beer and wine, because hard liquor brought greater profits to bootleggers. Prohibition also advanced women's rights. Whereas saloons had discriminated against "ladies," either barring any but prostitutes or having them enter by a separate door, speakeasies—taverns operating under cover—welcomed them and inadvertently helped to level the playing field between the sexes. Prohibition lined the pockets and boosted the fame of gangsters, including "Scarface" Al Capone. Like Capone, thousands of poor immigrants looked to illegal **bootlegging** to move them out of the slums. Rival gangs fought over territory, and cities erupted in violence. To save lives and profits, gangsters organized crime as if it were a business by dividing their operations and territory and imposing a hierarchy of management.

For all its unhappy consequences, Prohibition enjoyed wide backing. The liquor industry hurt itself with a terrible record of corrupting legislatures and, worse still, corrupting minors, who were one target of its aggressive campaign to recruit new drinkers in the competitive saloon business. The best science of the day taught that alcohol was bad for health; the best social science, that it corroded family life and weakened society. Corporate executives and labor leaders supported Prohibition to promote an efficient and healthy workforce. So did many Catholics, who saw the road to perdition lined with liquor bottles.

Prohibition can best be understood as cultural and class legislation. Support had always run deepest in Protestant churches, especially among the evangelical Baptists and Methodists. And there had always been a strong antiurban and anti-immigrant bias among reformers. As it turned out, the steepest decline in drinking occurred among working-class ethnics. Only the well-to-do had enough money to drink regularly without risking death or blindness, the common effects of cheap, tainted liquor. Traditionalists might celebrate the triumph of the "noble experiment," but modern urbanites either ignored or resented it.

Fundamentalism versus Darwinism

Although Aimee Semple McPherson embraced the fashions and technology of the New Era, many Protestants, especially in rural areas, felt threatened by the secular aspects of modern life. Beginning in the late nineteenth century, scientists and intellectuals began treating religion as a subject of study rather than faith. They spoke openly about the relativity of moral values, questioned the possibility of miracles, and analyzed the Bible as if it were nothing more than a historical document. Darwinism, pragmatism, and other philosophical and scientific theories left traditional religious teachings open to skepticism and scorn. Pastors noted that despite an increase of nearly 13 million in church membership, church attendance was slipping.

Among Protestants, conservatives of various sects worried that their liberal brethren had wandered too far from their

| The artist, John Steuart Curry, recalled: "This baptism was on the farm of our neighbor, Will McBride. . . . [Immersion baptisms] were usually held in the creeks, but at this particular time the creeks were dry and the only available water suitable was in the [farm watering] tanks. It was not considered a strange procedure. . . . At that time, the setting, the ceremony, the flying pigeons, the emotional crowd affected me, and years later I put down what my poor abilities permitted me." But like many in the New Era, Curry began to question his devout faith, especially after his brother died while still in college.

©akg-images

faith. As early as the 1870s, liberal Protestants had sought to make Christianity more relevant to contemporary life. Their movement became known as "Modernism," defined by one leader as "the use of scientific, historical and social methods in understanding and applying evangelical Christianity to the needs of living persons."

THE FUNDAMENTALS Conservatives disagreed with this updating of orthodoxy, nowhere more publicly than in a series of pamphlets called *The Fundamentals* published between 1910 and 1915 and subsidized by two wealthy oilmen from Los Angeles, Lyman and Milton Stewart. The 3 million copies distributed nationwide called for a return to what they considered to be the fundamentals of belief, among them the virgin birth and resurrection of Jesus, a literal reading of the Creation account in Genesis, and the divinely inspired authorship of the Bible. Whereas liberal theologians saw the Bible as the product of human beings observing and interpreting godly action within their historical and cultural context, conservatives insisted the Bible was the timeless, revealed word of God. After 1920 a wide variety of conservative Protestants began calling themselves "Fundamentalists."

The Fundamentalist movement grew dramatically in the first two decades of the twentieth century. It fed on fears of Protestant Modernism but also of the Catholic and Jewish immigrants flooding into the country. Fundamentalists maintained effective ministries nationwide but especially among Southern Baptists. Nothing disturbed them more than Darwinian theories of evolution that called into question the divine origins of humankind. In 1925 what began as an in-house fight among Protestants became a national brawl when the Tennessee legislature made it illegal to teach that "man has descended from a lower order of animals." Oklahoma, Florida, Mississippi, and Arkansas passed similar statutes.

SCOPES TRIAL Encouraged by the newly formed American Civil Liberties Union, a number of skeptics in the town of Dayton, Tennessee, decided to test the law by arresting a bespectacled biology teacher named John T. Scopes for teaching evolution. Behind the scenes, Scopes's sponsors were as much preoccupied with boosting their town's commercial fortunes as with the defense of academic freedom.

When the Scopes trial opened in July, millions listened over the radio to the first court case ever broadcast. Clarence Darrow, the renowned defense lawyer from Chicago and a professed agnostic, acted as co-counsel for Scopes. Serving as a co-prosecutor was William Jennings Bryan, the three-time presidential candidate who had recently joined the antievolution crusade. It was urban Darrow against rural Bryan in what Bryan described as a "duel to the death" between Christianity and evolution.

As Bryan saw it, nonbelievers as well as believers had a stake in the trial's outcome, at least if they lived in small-town America. The Industrial Revolution, he argued, had brought unprecedented organization to society and had concentrated power in big business and big government. The result was the erosion of community control and personal autonomy. Thus, for Bryan, the teaching of evolution became another battlefield in the struggle between localities and centralized authority, whether in business or government or even science, that was far removed from ordinary citizens.

The presiding judge ruled that scientists could not be used to defend evolution. He considered their testimony "hearsay" because they had not been present at the Creation. The defense virtually collapsed until Darrow called Bryan to the stand as an "expert on the Bible." Under withering cross-examination Bryan admitted, to the horror of his followers, that the Earth might not have been made "in six days of 24-hours." Even so, the Dayton jury took only eight minutes to find Scopes guilty of violating the law and fine him $100. Scopes never paid the fine after a later court ruling overturned the verdict on a technicality.

By then the excesses of the Scopes trial had transformed it into more of a national joke than a confrontation between darkness and light. Yet the debate over evolution raised a larger issue that continues to reverberate. As scientific,

©Heritage Image Partnership Ltd/Alamy

| *Clarence Darrow* (left), *the lawyer who defended John T. Scopes in the trial over the teaching of evolution, poses with William Jennings Bryan, the former presidential candidate and a devout Presbyterian who had joined the prosecution. Darrow cross-examined Bryan, a Fundamentalist, on the witness stand in order to prove that the Bible could not be taken as a scientific narrative of creation. Bryan holds a fan because the courtroom was scorchingly hot.*

religious, and cultural standards clash, how much should religious beliefs and local standards influence public education?

In the wake of the Scopes trial, the question was resolved in favor of secular over religious instruction, at least in public schools. Before the trial, public education had always contained explicitly religious—indeed, Protestant—components. Now it became increasingly nonreligious. Fundamentalism collapsed into the single image of the Bible-thumping southern redneck clinging to outmoded beliefs. The faith of these true believers never wavered, however. They spent the next two decades spreading their word over the radio and through Bible study and other parachurch groups outside of traditional denominations, biding their time and growing in numbers.

KKK

On Thanksgiving Day 1915, just outside Atlanta, 16 men trudged up a rocky trail to the crest of Stone Mountain. There, as night fell, they set ablaze a large wooden cross and swore allegiance to the Invisible Empire, Knights of the Ku Klux Klan. The KKK was reborn.

NEW KLAN The modern Klan, a throwback to the hooded order of Reconstruction days, had clear differences as well. While the Klan of old directed its anger against African Americans, the new Klan reflected the insecurities of many traditionalists. Klansmen worried about the changes and conflicts in American society, which they attributed to the rising tide of new immigrants, newly independent "uppity women," African Americans who refused to "recognize their place," and Jews. While any white man could join the old Klan, the new one admitted only "native born, white, gentile [Protestant] Americans." And the reborn Klan was not confined to the rural South, like the hooded nightriders of Reconstruction. In Texas, Klansmen fed off hatred of Mexicans; in California, of Japanese; in New York, of Jews and other immigrants. By the 1920s the capital of the Klan was Indianapolis, Indiana. More than half of its leadership and over a third of its members came from cities of more than 100,000 people.

The new Klan drew on the culture of small-town America and responded to some of its anxieties about lost personal independence and waning community control. It was patriotic, gave to local charities, and boasted the kind of outfits and rituals adopted by many fraternal lodges. Klansmen (and Klanswomen) wore white hoods and satin robes. A typical gathering brought the whole family to a barbecue with fireworks and hymn singing, capped by the burning of a giant cross. Members came mostly from the middle and working classes: small businesspeople, clerical workers, independent professionals, farmers, and laborers with few skills. The Klan offered them status, security, and the promise of restoring an older America where white supremacy, chastity, and virtuous Protestantism reigned. When boycotts and whispering campaigns failed to cleanse communities of Jews, Mexicans, Japanese, "uppity women," or others who offended their social code, the Klan resorted to floggings, kidnappings, acid mutilations, and murder.

Using modern methods of promotion, the Klan enrolled perhaps 3 million dues-paying members by the early 1920s. Moving into politics, Klan candidates won control of legislatures in Indiana, Texas, Oklahoma, and Oregon. The organization was instrumental in electing six governors, three

| As the Ku Klux Klan grew in influence after World War I, race riots erupted in over 25 cities beginning in 1919, including Chicago; Longview, Texas; Knoxville, Tennessee; and Omaha, Nebraska. More than 70 African Americans were lynched in the first year after the end of the war, and 11 were burned alive. Many blacks fought back, their experience in World War I having made them determined to resist repression. In June 1921 rioting in Tulsa left 21 African Americans as well as 11 whites dead. As the billowing smoke in this photograph indicates, white mobs burned down entire neighborhoods belonging to the black community. The National Guard was called out to reestablish order.
©Research Division of the Oklahoma Historical Society (OHS#16936)

senators, and thousands of local officials. In the end, like Aimee Semple McPherson, the Klan was undone by the personal excesses of its leaders that shattered its claim to righteous virtue. In November 1925, amid charges of financial corruption, Grand Dragon David Stephenson of the Indiana Klan and the most powerful leader in the Midwest was sentenced to life imprisonment for rape and second-degree murder. The KKK never fully recovered.

✓ REVIEW

Along what fronts did traditionalists fight the culture war of the 1920s, and with what weapons?

REPUBLICANS ASCENDANT

"THE CHANGE IS AMAZING," WROTE a Washington reporter shortly after the inauguration of Warren G. Harding on March 4, 1921. Sentries disappeared from the gates of the White House, tourists again walked the halls, and reporters freely questioned the president. The reign of "normalcy," a word Harding coined, had begun. "By 'normalcy,'" he explained, ". . . I mean normal procedure, the natural way, without excess."

The Politics of "Normalcy"

"Normalcy," according to Harding, turned out to be anything but normality. After eight years of Democratic rule, Republicans controlled the White House from 1921 to 1933 and both houses of Congress from 1918 to 1930. Fifteen years of bold reform gave way to eight years of cautious pro-business governing. A strengthened executive fell into weaker hands. The cabinet and the Congress set the course of the nation.

WARREN G. HARDING Harding and his successor, Calvin Coolidge, were content with delegating power. Harding appointed to the cabinet some men of quality, what he called the "best minds": jurist Charles Evans Hughes as secretary of state; farm leader Henry C. Wallace as secretary of agriculture; and Herbert Hoover, savior of Belgian war refugees and former head of the Food Administration, as secretary of commerce. He also made, as one critic put it, some "unspeakably bad appointments": his old crony Harry Daugherty as attorney general and New Mexico senator Albert Fall as interior secretary. Daugherty sold influence for cash and resigned in 1923. Only a divided jury saved him from jail. In 1929 Albert Fall became the first cabinet member to be convicted of a felony. In 1922 he had accepted bribes of more than $400,000 for secretly leasing naval oil reserves at Elk Hills, California, and Teapot Dome, Wyoming, to private oil companies.

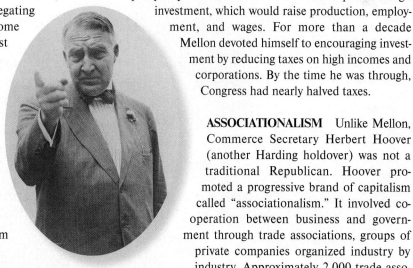

Source: Library of Congress, Prints and Photographs Division [LC-USZ62-130973]

| *Warren G. Harding*

Harding died suddenly in August 1923, before most of the scandals came to light. Though he would be remembered as lackluster, his tolerance and moderation had a calming influence on the strife-ridden nation. Slowly he had even begun to lead. In 1921 he created a new Bureau of the Budget, which brought modern accounting techniques to the management of federal revenues. Toward the end of his administration he cleared an early scandal from the Veterans' Bureau and set an agenda for Congress that included expanding the merchant marine.

CALVIN COOLIDGE To his credit Calvin Coolidge handled Harding's unfavorable legacy with skill and dispatch. He created a special investigatory commission, prosecuted the wrongdoers, and restored public confidence. Decisiveness, when he chose to exercise it, was one of Coolidge's hallmarks. He believed in small-town democracy and minimalist government. "One of the most important accomplishments of my administration has been minding my own business," he boasted. Above all Coolidge worshiped wealth. "Civilization and profits," he once said, "go hand in hand."

Coolidge had been in office barely a year when voters returned him to the White House by a margin of nearly 2 to 1 in the election in 1924. It was another sign that Americans had wearied of reform and delighted in surging prosperity. Whether the business-dominated policies served the economy or the nation well in the long term is open to question.

The Policies of Mellon and Hoover

Coolidge retained most of Harding's cabinet, including his powerful Treasury secretary, Andrew Mellon. The former president of aluminum giant Alcoa, Mellon believed that prosperity "trickled down" from rich to poor through investment, which would raise production, employment, and wages. For more than a decade Mellon devoted himself to encouraging investment by reducing taxes on high incomes and corporations. By the time he was through, Congress had nearly halved taxes.

ASSOCIATIONALISM Unlike Mellon, Commerce Secretary Herbert Hoover (another Harding holdover) was not a traditional Republican. Hoover promoted a progressive brand of capitalism called "associationalism." It involved cooperation between business and government through trade associations, groups of private companies organized industry by industry. Approximately 2,000 trade associations had come into being by 1929, many of them nurtured in the heyday of business-government cooperation during World War I. The role of government, as Hoover saw it, was to promote cooperation among businesses, to advise them on how best to act in the public interest, and to ensure that everyone obeyed the rules. Through associationalism, Hoover married the individualism of the past with what progressives had seen as the efficiency, organization, and cooperation of the future.

In these ways, Hoover hoped to eliminate waste, cut costs, and end the boom-and-bust business cycle of ruthless competition. Lower costs would be passed on to consumers in the form of lower prices and so would serve the public interest, as would the principles of welfare capitalism. Hoover promoted these ideals by prodding firms to sponsor company unions, pay workers decent wages, and protect them from factory hazards and unemployment. Meanwhile, his Commerce Department worked to expand foreign markets and fight international cartels. As such, Hoover represented the best of the New Era, at least in theory.

In practice, both Hoover and Mellon ended up placing government in service of business. Mellon's tax policies helped concentrate wealth in the hands of fewer individuals and corporations, while Hoover's associationalism, for all its faith in the ability of businesses to act for public good, helped them consolidate their power at the expense of the public. By the end of the decade, 200 giant corporations controlled almost half the corporate wealth and nearly a fifth of national wealth. In keeping with this government-sponsored trend, the Antitrust Division of the Justice Department offered few objections and brought few antitrust suits, while the Supreme Court affirmed the constitutionality of trade associations. Competition among businesses decreased, while consumer groups were largely ignored. And for all the talk of limiting government, its role in the economy grew. So did its size, by more than 40,000 employees between 1921 and 1930. Building on their wartime partnership, government and business dropped all pretense of a laissez-faire economy. "Never before, here or elsewhere, has a government been so completely fused with business," noted the *Wall Street Journal.*

| Andrew Mellon, secretary of the Treasury and the millionaire head of an aluminum monopoly, is flanked by Grace and Calvin Coolidge on the lawn of the White House. A disciple of business, President Coolidge believed that what was of "real importance to wage-earners was not how they might conduct a quarrel with their employers but how the business of the country might be so organized as to insure steady employment at a fair rate of pay. If that were done there would be no occasion for a quarrel, and if it were not done a quarrel would do no good."
©Bettmann/Getty Images

Problems and Some Solutions at Home and Abroad

Some economic groups remained outside the magic circle of Republican prosperity. Ironically, they included those people who made up the biggest business in America: farmers.

In 1920 farming still had an investment value greater than manufacturing, all utilities, and all railroads combined. A third of the population relied on farming for a living. Yet the farmers' portion of the national income shrank by almost half during the 1920s.

The reasons were as complex as they were devastating. The government withdrew wartime price supports for wheat and ended its practice of feeding refugees with American surpluses. As European farms began producing again, the demand for American exports dropped. New dietary habits meant that average Americans of 1920 ate 75 fewer pounds of food annually than they had 10 years earlier. New synthetic fibers drove down demand for natural wool and cotton fibers.

In 1921 a group of southern and western senators organized the "farm bloc" in Congress to coordinate relief for farmers. Over the next two years they succeeded in bringing stockyards, packers, and grain exchanges under federal supervision. Other legislation exempted farm cooperatives from antitrust actions and created a dozen banks for low-interest farm loans. But regulation and credit were not enough, and over the decade the purchasing power of farmers continued to slide. Over the decade farm foreclosures mounted, eventually exceeding even those during the Great Depression.

For the five years that Coolidge ran a "businessman's government," workers reaped few gains in wages, purchasing power, and bargaining rights. Although welfare capitalism promised workers profit-sharing and other benefits, only a handful of companies put it into practice. Those that did often used it to weaken independent unions. As dangerous imbalances in the economy developed, Coolidge ignored them.

THE GREAT FLOOD OF 1927   One problem no one could ignore: the great Mississippi flood of 1927. After years of deforestation and months of heavy rain, the Mississippi River burst through its levees, rampaging across an area roughly the size of New England from southern Missouri to Louisiana. Floodwaters reached 100 feet in some places and did not recede for three months.

A network of private agencies was quickly knit together and placed under the control of Secretary of Commerce Herbert Hoover. An army of local citizens, many of them black and some conscripted at gunpoint, erected a series of refugee camps to cope with the 700,000 people displaced by the flood, but relief efforts were hardly equal to the task. Nearly 250 people died, and 130,000 homes were destroyed. Property damage ran to $350 million ($5 billion in today's dollars). Before the end of 1928 half the African American population of the Mississippi delta's Black Belt had fled the region. For the rest of the decade commerce throughout the central United States suffered. Still, federal legislation had been passed—for the first time—giving the government responsibility for controlling such disasters along the Mississippi.

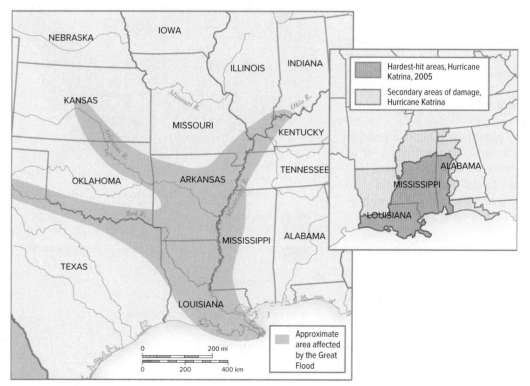

THE GREAT FLOOD OF 1927

Hurricane Katrina scarred the Gulf Coast at the start of the twenty-first century, but the Great Flood of 1927 actually stretched across more states as the map to the left indicates. **How do regional natural disasters affect government policy?**

If Americans paid little attention to many of the problems at home, most completely disregarded economic unrest abroad. At the end of World War I, Europe's victors had forced Germany to take on $33 billion in war costs or reparations, partly to repay their own war debts to the United States. When Germany defaulted in 1923, French forces occupied the Ruhr valley, the center of German industry. Germany struck back by printing more money to cope with the crushing burden of debt. Runaway inflation soon wiped out the savings of the German middle class, shook confidence in the new democratic Weimar Republic, and eventually threatened the economic structure of all Europe.

THE DAWES PLAN In 1924 American business leader Charles G. Dawes took a stab at solving the problem by persuading victorious Europeans to scale down reparations. In return the United States promised to help stabilize the German economy. Encouraged by the State Department, American bankers made large loans to Germany, with which the Germans paid their reparations. The European victors then used those funds to repay *their* war debts to the United States. It amounted to taking money out of one American vault and depositing it in another. In 1926 the United States also reduced European war debts. Canceling them altogether would have made more sense, but few Americans were so forgiving.

KELLOGG-BRIAND PACT Two grand, if finally futile, gestures reflected the twin desires for peace and prudent budgeting in a world chastened by war, arms races, and military spending. In 1921, in a conference held in Washington, the sea powers of the world agreed to freeze battleship construction for 10 years and to set ratios on the tonnage of each navy. The Five-Power Agreement was the first disarmament treaty in modern history. A more extravagant gesture came in 1928, when the major nations of the world (except the Soviet Union) signed the Kellogg-Briand Pact outlawing war. "Peace is proclaimed," announced Secretary of State Frank Kellogg as he signed the document with a foot-long pen of gold.

What seemed so bold on paper proved timid in practice. The French and Japanese resented the lower limits set on their battleships under the Five-Power Agreement and touched off a new arms race by building smaller warships such as submarines, cruisers, and destroyers. And with no means of enforcement, the Kellogg-Briand Pact remained a hollow proclamation.

The Election of 1928

On August 2, 1927, in a small classroom in Rapid City, South Dakota, Calvin Coolidge handed a terse, typewritten message to reporters: "I do not choose to run for President in nineteen twenty-eight." Republicans honored the request and nominated Herbert Hoover. Hoover was not a politician but an administrator who had never once campaigned for public office. It did not matter. Republican prosperity made it difficult for any Democrat to win. Hoover, perhaps the most admired public official in America, made it impossible.

The Democratic Party continued to fracture between its rural supporters in the South and West and ethnic laborers in the urban Northeast. The two factions had clashed during the 1924 convention, scuttling the presidential candidacy of New York governor Al Smith. By 1928 the shift in population toward cities had given an edge to the party's urban wing. Al Smith won the nomination on the first ballot, even though his handicaps were evident. When the New York City–bred Smith spoke "poysonally" on the "rha-dio," his accent made voters across America wince. Though he pledged to enforce Prohibition, he campaigned against it and even took an occasional drink (which produced the false rumor that he was a hopeless alcoholic). Most damaging of all, Smith was Catholic at a time when anti-Catholicism remained strong in many areas of the country.

In the election of 1928 nearly 60 percent of the eligible voters turned out to give all but eight states to Hoover. The solidly Democratic South cracked for the first time. Still, the stirrings of a major political realignment lay buried in the returns. The 12 largest cities in the country had gone to the Republicans in 1924; in 1928 the Democrats won them. Western farmers, ignored by Republicans for a decade, also voted for Smith.

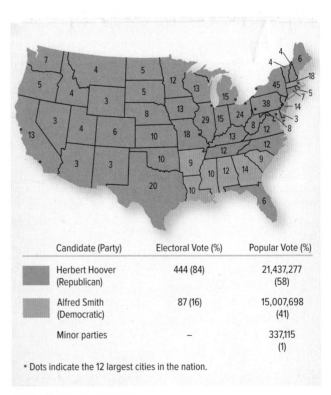

Candidate (Party)	Electoral Vote (%)	Popular Vote (%)
Herbert Hoover (Republican)	444 (84)	21,437,277 (58)
Alfred Smith (Democratic)	87 (16)	15,007,698 (41)
Minor parties	–	337,115 (1)

• Dots indicate the 12 largest cities in the nation.

ELECTION OF 1928

The stirrings of a major political realignment were under way. The Democrats were becoming the party of the cities, of immigrants, and of the long-ignored. Around this core, they would build the most powerful vote-getting coalition of the twentieth century.

As important, a new kind of electorate was emerging. No longer were voters part of a vast partisan army whose loyalties were tied to the same party year in and year out by barbecues, rallies, and torchlight parades. The reforms of the Progressive Era had restricted the power of political machines and the discipline they could exert over voters. The culture of consumption that shaped American life in the 1920s also shaped politics. Increasingly, parties courted voters with newspaper advertisements and radio "spots." In 1929 the Democrats created the first public relations department in American politics. The twentieth century would witness a deterioration of party loyalty and election voting as the growing reliance on the media to communicate with "consumer/voters" weakened traditional party networks.

 REVIEW

What public policies did Presidents Harding and Coolidge pursue during the 1920s and why did they pursue them?

THE GREAT BULL MARKET

STROLLING ACROSS THE FELT-PADDED FLOOR of the New York Stock Exchange, Superintendent William Crawford greeted the New Year with swaggering confidence. Nineteen twenty-eight had broken all stock-buying records. The rampaging "bulls," or buyers of stock, had routed the hibernating "bears," those who sell. It was the greatest bull market in history as eager purchasers drove prices to new highs. At the end of the last business day, Crawford surveyed the floor and declared flatly, "The millennium's arrived."

Veteran financial analyst Alexander Noyes had his doubts. Speculation—buying and selling purely on the expectation that rising prices will yield quick gains—had taken over the stock market. "Something has to give," said Noyes in September 1929. Less than a month later, the Great Bull Market fell in a heap.

The Rampaging Bull

NEW BREED   No one knows exactly what caused the wave of speculation that boosted the stock market to dizzying heights. Driven alternately by greed and fear, the market succumbed to greed in a decade that considered it a virtue.

NEW MONEY   Money and credit to fuel the market became plentiful. From 1922 to 1929 some $900 million worth of gold flowed into the country. The money supply expanded by

$6 billion. Over the decade corporate profits grew by 80 percent. At interest rates as high as 25 percent, more could be made from lending money to brokers (who then made "brokers' loans" to clients for stock purchase) than from constructing new factories. By 1929 brokers' loans had almost tripled from two years earlier.

"Margin requirements," the cash actually put down to purchase stock, hovered around 50 percent for most of the decade. Thus buyers had to come up with only half the price of a share. The rest came from credit furnished by brokers' loans. As trading reached record heights in August 1929, the Federal Reserve Board tried to dampen speculation by raising the interest rates. Higher interest rates made borrowing of all kinds more expensive and, authorities hoped, would rein in the galloping bull market. They were wrong. It was already too late.

The Great Crash

At the opening bell on Thursday, October 24, 1929, a torrent of sell orders flooded the New York Stock Exchange, triggered by nervous speculators who had been selling for the past week. Prices plunged as panic set in. By the end of "Black Thursday" nearly 13 million shares had been traded—a record. Losses stood at $3 billion, another record.

Prices rallied for the rest of the week, buoyed by a bankers' buying pool organized at the House of Morgan. The following Tuesday, October 29, 1929, the bubble burst. Stockholders lost $10 billion in a single day. At their peak in 1929, stocks had been worth $87 billion. In 1933 they bottomed out at $18 billion. In other words, the downward slide of stock prices continued for almost four years.

ROLE OF THE CRASH   The Great Crash did not cause the Great Depression, but it did damage the economy. And as a symbol of weakening financial confidence, it also helped to break the unbounded optimism on which the New Era rested. Although only about 500,000 people were actually trading stocks by the end of the decade, their investments had helped to sustain prosperity as well as faith in the economy. Thousands of wealthy investors saw their fortunes disappear. The hard-earned savings of middle-class stockholders vanished too, and with them their futures. Commercial banks—some loaded with corporate stocks, others financing brokers' loans—reeled in the wake of the crash and struggled to survive.

The Sickening Slide in Global Perspective

The Great Crash signaled the start of the greatest depression in the history of the modern world. In the United States, the gains of the 1920s were wiped out in a few years. In the first three years after the crash, national income fell by half, factory wages by almost half. By some estimates 85,000 businesses failed.

Source: Library of Congress, Prints and Photographs Division [LC-USZ62-123429]

| *Anxious investors swarmed around the New York Stock Exchange on Wall Street when stock prices began to crash in 1929.*

Although the Great Depression was less prolonged in other countries, the shock waves from the United States rippled across the globe, helping to topple already fragile economies in Europe. American loans, investments, and purchases had propped up Europe since the end of World War I. When American resources dried up, European governments defaulted on war debts. More European banks failed; more businesses collapsed; unemployment surged to at least 30 million worldwide by 1932. Workers in industrialized European nations experienced jobless rates between 20 and nearly 40 percent.

Europeans scrambled to protect themselves. Led by Great Britain in 1931, 41 nations abandoned the gold standard. Foreign governments hoped to devalue their currencies by expanding their supplies of money. Exports would be cheaper and foreign trade would increase. But several countries did so at once, while each country raised tariffs to protect itself from foreign competition. Devaluation failed, and the resulting trade barriers only deepened the

crisis. Between 1929 and 1933 world exports declined by two-thirds, from a high of nearly $3 billion to less than $1 billion. (See the chart.)

In Latin America and other regions where countries depended on exporting raw materials, the slide varied. Shrinking sales of metallic minerals, timber, and hides crippled Chile, Bolivia, Peru, and Malaya, while exports of fuel oils still needed to warm homes and run factories shielded Venezuela. Only the Soviet Union escaped catastrophe, with its limited exports and a command economy that had launched a breakneck campaign of industrialization. Even in the Soviet Union, however, bumper crops of Russian wheat forced onto the world market at deflated prices led millions of peasants to starve to death in 1932–1933. Virtually everywhere else economies cracked under the weight of slackening demand and contracting world trade.

In the United States declining sales abroad sent crop prices to new lows. Farm income dropped by more than half.

The epidemic of rural bank failures spread to the cities. Nervous depositors rushed to withdraw their cash. Even healthy banks could not bear the strain. In August 1930 every bank in Toledo but one closed its doors. Between 1929 and 1933, collapsing banks took more than $20 billion in assets with them. The economy was spiraling downward, and no one could stop it.

The Causes of the Great Depression

What, then, caused the Great Depression in the United States? In the months before the crash, with national attention riveted on the booming stock market, hardly anyone paid attention to existing defects in the American economy. But by 1928 the booming construction and automobile industries began to lose vitality as demand sagged. In fact, increases in consumer spending for all goods and services slowed to a lethargic 1.5 percent for 1928–1929. Warehouses began to fill as business inventories climbed, from $500 million in 1928 to $1.8 billion in 1929.

OVEREXPANSION AND RELATIVE DECLINE IN PURCHASING POWER
In one sense, businesses had done all too well. Corporations had boosted their profits by some 80 percent during the 1920s by keeping the cost of labor and raw materials low as well as by increasing productivity. Businesses used the profits to expand factories rather than to pay workers higher wages. Without strong labor unions or government support, real wages increased

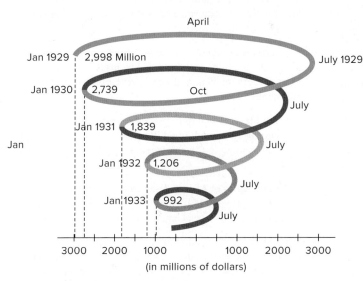

Declining World Trade, 1929–1933

As the Great Depression deepened, world trade spiraled downward. Here the imports of 75 countries are tracked from 1929 to 1933. (The amounts are measured in millions of U.S. gold dollars.) The greatest annual decline occurred between 1930 and 1931 as production plummeted and nation after nation began to erect high tariff barriers to protect their domestic markets from cheaper imports. Over the four-year period, world import trade fell by almost two-thirds, only underscoring the growing interdependence of the global economy.

(largely because of falling prices) but never kept pace with productivity, which led to a paradox. As consumers, workers did not have enough money to buy the products they were making more efficiently and at lower cost.

CONSUMER DEBT AND UNEVEN DISTRIBUTION OF WEALTH
People made up the difference between earnings and purchases by borrowing. Consumers bought "on time," paying for merchandise a little each month. During the decade, consumer debt rose by 250 percent. Few could afford to keep spending at that rate. Nor could the distribution of wealth sustain prosperity. By 1929, 1 percent of the population owned 36 percent of all personal wealth. The wealthy had more money than they could possibly spend and saved too much. The working and middle classes had not nearly enough to keep the economy growing, spend though they might.

BANKING SYSTEM
Another problem lay with the banking system. Mismanagement, greed, and the emergence of a new type of executive—half banker, half broker—led banks to divert more funds into speculative investments. The uniquely decentralized American banking system left no way to set things right if a bank failed. At the end of the decade, half of the 25,000 banks in America lay outside the Federal Reserve System. Its controls even over member banks were weak, and during the decade, 6,000 banks failed.

CORPORATE STRUCTURE AND PUBLIC POLICY
A shaky corporate structure only made matters worse. No government agency monitored the stock exchanges, while big business operated largely free from government regulation. Insider stock trading, shady stock deals, and outright stock fraud ran rampant. Meanwhile, public policy encouraged corporate consolidation and control because the government filed few antitrust suits. High profits and the Mellon tax program helped make many corporations wealthy enough to avoid borrowing. Thus changes in interest rates—over which the Federal Reserve exercised some control—had little influence on such corporations. Free from government regulation, fluctuating prices, and the need for loans, big businesses ruled the economy. And they ruled badly.

"SICK" INDUSTRIES
Unemployment began to increase as early as 1927, a sign of growing softness in the economy. By the fall of 1929 some 2 million people were out of work. Many of them were in textiles, coal mining, lumbering, and railroads. All were "sick" industries during the decade because they suffered from overexpansion, killing competition, reduced demand, and weak management. Farmers were in trouble too. As European agriculture revived after World War I, farm prices tumbled. American farmers earned 16 percent of the national income in 1919 but only 9 percent in 1929. As more

farmers went bust, so did many of the rural banks that had lent them money.

ECONOMIC IGNORANCE   Finally, plain economic ignorance contributed to the calamity. High tariffs protected American industries but discouraged European business from selling to the world's most profitable market. Because Europeans weren't profiting, they lacked the money for American goods being shipped to Europe. Only American loans and investments supported demand abroad. When the American economy collapsed, those vanished and with them went American foreign trade. Furthermore, the Federal Reserve had been stimulating the economy both by expanding the money supply and by lowering interest rates. Those moves only fed the speculative fever by furnishing investors with more money at lower costs. A decision finally to raise interest rates in 1929 to stem speculation ended up speeding the slide by making it more expensive to borrow when investments with borrowed money would have slowed the decline.

REVIEW
What caused the Great Depression?

PUTTING HISTORY IN GLOBAL CONTEXT

"EVERYONE OUGHT TO BE RICH," proclaimed one enthusiastic investment advisor in *Ladies' Home Journal*—at a time when the economy was still bubbling and the stock market was setting new highs. Americans like him had nothing but faith in their New Era: in its capacity to produce abundance and spread wealth, in its promise of technological freedom from toil and want, in its ability to blend the vast differences among Americans into a mass culture in which individuals would nonetheless retain their identities. They put their money, some quite literally, on this modernism. Others objected to the price being paid in lost community and independence. They wanted to resurrect a world less organized, less bureaucratized, less complex and varied—a world less modern. In the 1920s, the tensions between these contrasting ideals sparked the first culture wars of the twentieth century.

The mix of exuberance, hedonism, and anxiety was mirrored in other nations. As the postwar recession lifted, many of the world's political systems seemed to sustain Woodrow Wilson's dream of a world made safe for democracy. A Germany ruled by Hohenzollern monarchs transformed itself into the Weimar Republic, whose constitution provided universal suffrage and a bill of rights. The new nations carved out of the old Russian and Austro-Hungarian Empires attempted to create similarly democratic governments, while in Turkey, Kemal Ataturk abolished the sultanate and established the Turkish Republic. In India,

the Congress Party formed by Mohandas K. Gandhi united socialists and powerful industrial capitalists and pushed the British to grant them greater political representation. Even where the political mix was more volatile, as in China and Indochina (Vietnam), nationalism mixed with communism as a means of liberating colonial peoples from imperialist rule.

The Great Crash and the Great Depression rocked these fragile beginnings. Fledgling democracies in Japan and Germany gave way to authoritarian states, while dire economic straits strengthened the hands of dictators in Italy and the Soviet Union. Japan, too, departed from its peaceful path of trade and foreign investment toward aggressive militarism and expansion. No one—not the brokers of Wall Street, not the captains of industry, not the diplomats at the League of Nations—could predict the future in such an unstable world.

CHAPTER SUMMARY

The new era of the 1920s brought a booming economy and modern times to America, vastly accelerating the forces of change—bureaucracy, productivity, technology, advertising and consumerism, mass media, peer culture, and suburbanization. Urban-rural tensions peaked with shifts in population that gave cities new power. But as the decade wore on, weaknesses in the economy and a new ethos of getting and spending, too much of it on credit, proved to be the New Era's undoing.

- Technology, advertising and consumer spending, and such boom industries as automobile manufacturing and construction fueled the largest peacetime economic growth in American history.

- Key features of modern life—mass society, mass culture, and mass consumption—took hold, fed by mass media in the form of radio, movies, and mass-circulation newspapers and magazines.

- Modern life unsettled old ways and eroded social conventions that had limited life especially for women and children, leading to the emergence of a New Woman and a youth culture.

- Great migrations of African Americans from the rural South to the urban North and of Latinos from Mexico to the United States reshaped the social landscape.

- Traditional culture, centered in rural America, hardened and defended itself against change through immigration restriction, Prohibition, Fundamentalism, and a reborn Ku Klux Klan.

- A galloping bull market in stocks reflected the commitment of government to big business and economic growth.

- When the stock market crashed in 1929, weaknesses in the economy—overexpansion, declining purchasing power, uneven distribution of wealth, weak banking and corporate structures, "sick" industries, and economic ignorance—finally brought the economy down, and with it the New Era came to a close.

Digging Deeper

For years, Frederick Lewis Allen, *Only Yesterday: An Informal History of the 1920s* (1931), shaped the stereotyped view of the decade as a frivolous interlude between World War I and the Great Depression. William E. Leuchtenburg, *The Perils of Prosperity, 1914-1932* (1958), began an important reconsideration by stressing the serious conflict between urban and rural America and the emergence of modern mass society. Lynn Dumenil updates Leuchtenburg in her excellent *The Modern Temper: American Culture and Society in the 1920s* (1995). Ann Douglas, *Terrible Honesty: Mongrel Manhattan in the 1920s* (1995), puts Manhattan at the core of the cultural transformation, especially its success at bringing African American folk and popular art into the mainstream. On immigration restriction beginning in 1882 and ending with debates sparked by 9/11, see Roger Daniels, *Guarding the Golden Door* (2004). Paul Avrich, *Sacco and Vanzetti* (1991), covers the two men, as both victims and militant anarchists. For another sympathetic treatment, see Bruce Watson, *Sacco and Vanzetti: The Men, the Murders, and the Judgment of Mankind* (2007). On the Scopes trial, see Edward J. Larson, *Summer for the Gods* (1997). Michael Lienesch's *In the Beginning* (2007) focuses on the rise of Fundamentalism and its continuing role in the battle over "creationism." Matthew Avery Sutton, *Aimee Semple McPherson and the Resurrection of Christian America* (2009), places McPherson and her International Church of the Foursquare Gospel at the center of the religious movement that eventually moved Pentecostals and Evangelicals into the cultural limelight. Lisa McGirr's *The War on Alcohol: Prohibition and the Rise of the American State* (2015) takes a new look at the anti-alcohol crusade as a means of growing the penal power of government.

Roland Marchand, *Advertising the American Dream* (1985), analyzes the role of advertising in shaping mass consumption, values, and culture; and Ellis W. Hawley, *The Great War and the Search for a Modern Order* (1979), emphasizes economic institutions. For women in the 1920s, see Kathleen M. Blee, *Women of the Klan* (1991); Virginia Scharff, *Taking the Wheel: Women and the Coming of the Motor Age* (1991); and Jacqueline Jones, *Labor of Love, Labor of Sorrow: Black Women, Work, and Family, from Slavery to the Present* (1985). In a penetrating and gendered discussion of Garveyism and of the Harlem Renaissance, Martin Summers profiles evolving notions of what it meant to be a black man in the early years of the twentieth century in *Manliness and Its Discontents* (2004).

The most readable examination of the stock market and its relation to the economy and public policy is still Robert Sobel, *The Great Bull Market: Wall Street in the 1920s* (1968). See also Maury Klein's colorful *Rainbow's End: The Crash of 1929* (2001). The best books on the disintegration of the American economy remain Lester Vernon Chandler's *America's Greatest Depression, 1929-1941* (1970); and, from a global standpoint, Charles P. Kindleberger's *The World in Depression, 1929-1939* (1973). For an analysis of the Great Depression, from the perspective of Keynesian economics, see John Kenneth Galbraith, *The Great Crash, 1929* (rev. ed., 1988). For the argument of monetarists, who see the roots of the Depression in the shrinking money supply, see Milton Friedman and Anna Jacobson Schwartz, *A Monetary History of the United States, 1867-1960* (1963); and Peter Temin, *Did Monetary Forces Cause the Great Depression?* (1976). John M. Barry, *Rising Tide: The Great Mississippi Flood of 1927 and How It Changed America* (1997), is especially good in describing the fate of African Americans and the failure of government and private aid organizations.

1929–1939

Just as journalist Lorena Hickok fanned out across the country acting as the eyes and ears of Eleanor Roosevelt, photographers working for the Farm Security Administration documented the lives of ordinary Americans during the Great Depression. John Vachon, one of them, recalled how he discovered a carbon black plant while driving along the Texas panhandle. "From 5 or 10 miles [away] it's a huge black cloud out there ahead of you. Then you drive right up to it and it's just exactly like driving from a sunny day into the middle of night." The plants "make carbon which is powdery black stuff in big bags worth 3 cents a pound, used in making tires, paints, & numerous other places. . . . Anyway, in working there, I got dirtier, that is blacker, than I have ever been in my life. . . . Right through the clothes it goes. I washed carefully my face and hands, but I'm leaving the rest for a while, it's really kind of beautiful."

Source: Library of Congress, Prints and Photographs Division [LC-DIG-fsac-1a35446]

>> An American Story

LETTERS FROM THE EDGE

Winner, South Dakota, November 10, 1933. "Dammit, I don't WANT to write to you again tonight. It's been a long, long day, and I'm tired." All the days had been long since Lorena Hickok began her cross-country trek. Four months earlier Harry Hopkins, the new federal relief administrator, hired the journalist to report on the relief efforts of the New Deal. "Talk with the unemployed," he told her, ". . . and when you talk to them, don't ever forget that but for the grace of God you, I, any of our friends might be in their shoes."

In 1933 and 1934, Hickok found that President Franklin Roosevelt's relief program was falling short. Its half-billion-dollar subsidy to states, localities, and charities was still leaving out too many Americans, like the sharecropper Hickok discovered near Raleigh, North

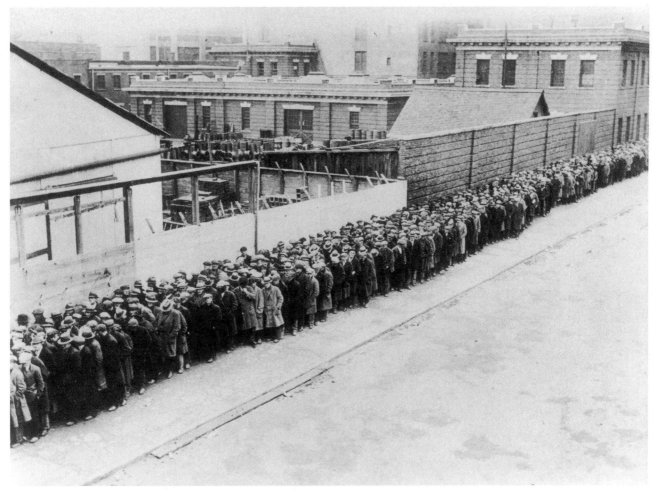

©Fotosearch/Getty Images

| *The unemployed, New York City, 1930*

Carolina. He and his daughters had been living in a tobacco barn for two weeks on little more than weeds and table scraps. "Seems like we just keep goin' lower and lower," said the 16-year-old. To Hickok's surprise, hope still flickered in her eyes. Hickok couldn't explain it until she noticed a pin on the girl's chest. It was a campaign button from the 1932 election—"a profile of the President." Hope sprang from the man in the White House.

Before Franklin D. Roosevelt and the New Deal, the White House was far removed from ordinary citizens. The only federal agency with which they had any contact was the post office. And these days it usually delivered bad news. But as Hickok traveled across the country in 1933, she detected a change. People were talking about government programs. Perhaps it was long-awaited contributions to relief or maybe reforms in securities and banking or the new recovery programs for industry and agriculture. Just as likely it was Roosevelt himself. People, she wrote, were "for the President."

The message was clear: Franklin Roosevelt and the New Deal had begun to restore national confidence. Though it never brought full recovery, the New Deal did improve economic conditions and provided relief to millions of Americans. It reformed the economic system and committed the federal government to managing its busts and booms. In doing so it extended the progressive drive to soften industrialization and translated decades of growing concern for the disadvantaged into a federal responsibility and federally funded aid programs. For the first time, Americans believed Washington would help them through a terrible crisis. The liberal state came of age: active, interventionist, and committed to social welfare. <<

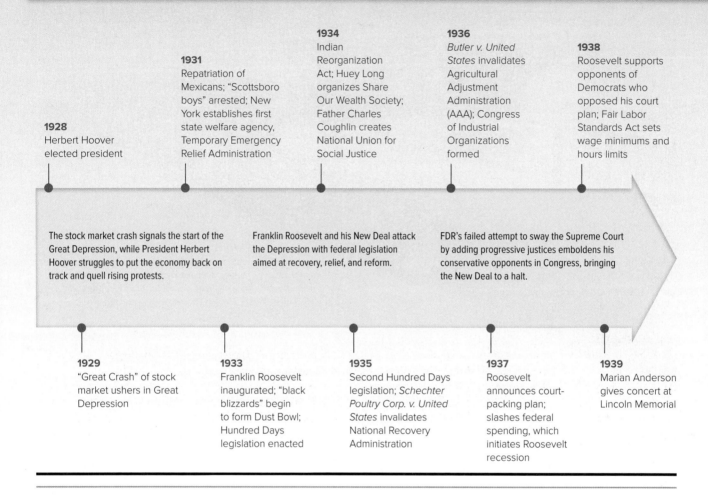

1928
Herbert Hoover elected president

1931
Repatriation of Mexicans; "Scottsboro boys" arrested; New York establishes first state welfare agency, Temporary Emergency Relief Administration

1934
Indian Reorganization Act; Huey Long organizes Share Our Wealth Society; Father Charles Coughlin creates National Union for Social Justice

1936
Butler v. United States invalidates Agricultural Adjustment Administration (AAA); Congress of Industrial Organizations formed

1938
Roosevelt supports opponents of Democrats who opposed his court plan; Fair Labor Standards Act sets wage minimums and hours limits

The stock market crash signals the start of the Great Depression, while President Herbert Hoover struggles to put the economy back on track and quell rising protests.

Franklin Roosevelt and his New Deal attack the Depression with federal legislation aimed at recovery, relief, and reform.

FDR's failed attempt to sway the Supreme Court by adding progressive justices emboldens his conservative opponents in Congress, bringing the New Deal to a halt.

1929
"Great Crash" of stock market ushers in Great Depression

1933
Franklin Roosevelt inaugurated; "black blizzards" begin to form Dust Bowl; Hundred Days legislation enacted

1935
Second Hundred Days legislation; *Schechter Poultry Corp. v. United States* invalidates National Recovery Administration

1937
Roosevelt announces court-packing plan; slashes federal spending, which initiates Roosevelt recession

1939
Marian Anderson gives concert at Lincoln Memorial

THE HUMAN IMPACT OF THE GREAT DEPRESSION

LONG BREADLINES SNAKED AROUND STREET CORNERS. Vacant-eyed apple-sellers stood shivering in the wind. A man with his hat in his hand came to the back door asking for food in exchange for work. Between 1929 and 1932 an average of 100,000 people lost their jobs every week until some 13 million Americans were jobless. At least one worker in four could find no employment. For the first time in American history, the number of people leaving the country exceeded the number entering because jobs were so scarce in the United States.

The Great Depression was a great leveler that reduced differences in the face of common want. It often provoked the same human responses regardless of different circumstances. The Baltimore laundress without enough wash to pay her rent felt the same pinch of frustration, anxiety, and anger as the UC Berkeley student whose college education was cut short when the bank let her father go. Not everyone was devastated.

Most Americans survived by cooperating with one another and scrimping to make ends meet. As one Depression victim recalled, "We lived lean."

Hard Times

Hard times lasted for a decade. Even before the Great Crash many Americans were having trouble making a living. In 1929 a family of four required $2,000 a year for bare necessities—more money than 60 percent of American families earned.

Unable to pay mortgages or rent, many families lived off the generosity of forgiving landlords. Some traded down to smaller quarters or simply lost their homes. By 1932 between 1 and 2 million Americans were homeless wanderers, among them an estimated 25,000 nomadic families. For the first time, emigration out of the country exceeded immigration into it because Americans could find no work at home. Despite official claims that no one had died of hunger, the New York City Welfare Council reported 29 victims of starvation and 110 dead of malnourishment in 1932 alone.

MARRIAGE AND THE FAMILY Marriages and births, symbols of faith in the future, plummeted. For the first time in three centuries the curve of population growth began to level, as many young couples postponed having children. Experts worried about an impending "baby crop shortage." Strong families hung together and grew closer; weak ones languished or fell apart. Although divorce declined, desertion—the "poor man's divorce"—mushroomed. Under the strain, rates of mental illness and suicide rose as well.

Many fathers, whose lives had been defined by work, suddenly had nothing to do. They grew listless and depressed. Most mothers stayed home and found their traditional roles as nurturer and household manager less disrupted than the breadwinning roles of their husbands. Between 1929 and 1933 living costs dropped 25 percent, but family incomes tumbled by an average of 40 percent.

Homemakers watched household budgets with a closer eye than ever. They canned more food and substituted less expensive fish for meat. When they earned extra money, they often did so within the confines of the "woman's sphere" by taking in boarders, laundry, and sewing; opening beauty parlors in their kitchens; and selling baked goods.

For those women who worked outside the home, prejudice still relegated them to so-called "women's work." Over half the female labor force continued to work in domestic service or the garment trades, while others found traditional employment as schoolteachers, social workers, and secretaries. Only slowly did the female proportion of the workforce reach pre-Depression levels, until it rose finally to 25 percent by 1940, largely because women were willing to take almost any job.

PSYCHOLOGICAL IMPACT Whether in the renewed importance of homemaking or the reemergence of home industries, the Great Depression sent ordinary Americans scurrying for the reassuring shelter of past practices and left many of them badly shaken. Shame, self-doubt, and pessimism became epidemic as people blamed themselves for their circumstances. "I would go stand on the relief line [and] bend my head low so nobody would recognize me," recalled one man. The lasting legacy of humiliation and fear—that you had caused your own downfall; that the bottom of the economy would drop out again—was what one writer called an "invisible scar."

The Golden Age of Radio and Film

By the end of the decade almost 9 out of 10 families owned radios. People depended on radios for nearly everything—news, sports, and weather; music and entertainment; recipes for meals or finding salvation. Some programming helped change national habits. When *The Sporting News* conducted a baseball poll in 1932, editors were surprised to discover that a "new crop of fans has been created by radio . . . the women." Many women were at home during the day when most games were played, and broadcasters went out of their way to educate these new listeners. Night games soon outran day games

Source: Library of Congress, Prints and Photographs Division, FSA/OWI Collection [LC-DIG-fsa-8a18464]

In the shantytowns or "Hoovervilles" that sprang up during the Great Depression, housing was makeshift, with the homeless living in crude tin and wood shacks or tents. This young girl in Circleville, Ohio, has a toy tractor that looks as run-down as the tire she's sitting on.

in attendance, in part because husbands began taking wives and daughters, whose interest was sparked by radio.

Radio entered a golden age of commercialism. Advertisers hawked their products on variety programs like Major Bowes's *Amateur Hour* and comedy shows with entertainers such as George Burns and Gracie Allen. Daytime melodramas (called "soap operas" because they were sponsored by soap companies) aimed at women with stories of the personal struggles of ordinary folk.

RADIO'S UNIFYING EFFECT Radio continued to bind the country together. A teenager in Splendora, Texas, could listen to the same wisecracks from Jack Benny, the same music from Guy Lombardo, as kids in New York City and Los Angeles. In 1938 Orson Welles broadcast H. G. Wells's classic science fiction tale *The War of the Worlds*. Americans everywhere listened to breathless reports of an "invasion from Mars," and many believed them. In Newark, New Jersey, cars jammed roads as families rushed to evacuate the city. The nation, bombarded with reports of impending war in Europe and accustomed to responding to radio advertising, was prepared to believe almost anything, even reports of invaders from Mars.

In Hollywood an efficient but autocratic studio system churned out a record number of feature films. Eight motion picture companies produced more than two-thirds of them. Color, first introduced to feature films in *Becky Sharp* (1935), soon complemented sound, which had debuted in the 1927 version of *The Jazz Singer*. Neither alone could keep movie theaters full. As attendance dropped early in the Depression, big studios such as Metro-Goldwyn-Mayer and Universal lured audiences back with films that shocked, titillated, and just plain entertained.

Wonder Woman, Women's Rights, and Birth Control

Peters's note to Marston complains that Wonder Woman's shoes look like "a stenographer's." How might changing her shoes—to near knee-length boots—change Wonder Woman's image?

Artist Harry G. Peters made these preliminary sketches of Wonder Woman for William M. Marston, the character's creator.

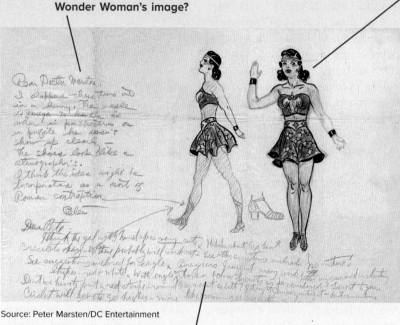

Source: Peter Marsten/DC Entertainment

Marston's reply tells Peters he thinks the woman "very cute" but wants a belt to cover her bare waist and something "more like a crown" to cover her head. Why might these be necessary?

Comic book superheroes may appear to be little more than child's play. But historians can also use them to penetrate the complexities of culture, just as they do radio programs and films. In 1941 a new superhero leapt from the pages of DC comics: "Wonder Woman," the warrior-princess of a lost tribe of man-hating Amazons. She looked like a movie star, with jet-black hair, a gold tiara, and ruby-red lipstick. Rivaling the strength of Superman, she flew an invisible plane, wore bullet-deflecting bracelets, and carried a magic lasso that forced all whom it touched to tell the truth.

Wonder Woman was the brainchild of the remarkable William Moulton Marston,

a free-thinking renegade psychologist who had gained earlier notoriety for inventing a "lie detector" machine meant to aid in the prosecution of criminals. As an advisor to DC Comics, Marston created a character designed to "set up a standard among children and young people of strong, free, courageous womanhood; to combat the idea that women are inferior to men." He took inspiration for his character not only from the powerful female figures of Greek mythology, but also from Margaret Sanger, who, as it happened, was the aunt of Marston's long-time mistress. The birth-control and women's rights advocate represented the

unflinching, independent woman Marston hoped would rule the world someday.

THINKING CRITICALLY

More than three-quarters of a century later, Wonder Woman remains the most popular female superhero ever created. Why? What does Wonder Woman tell us about the 1930s and 1940s? About our own day? Can you think of other superheroes who reflect their culture at the moment of their creation? How might their changes over time have mirrored broader changes in culture?

MASS MEDIA AT HOME AND ABROAD By the mid-1930s more than 60 percent of Americans were going to the movies at least once a week. They saw tamer films as the industry began regulating movie content in the face of growing criticism. In 1933 the Catholic Church created the Legion of Decency to monitor features. To avoid censorship and

boycotts, studios stiffened their own regulations. Producers could not depict homosexuality, abortion, drug use, or sex. (Even the word "sex" was banned, as was all profanity.) Middle-class morality reigned on the screen, and most Depression movies, like most of popular culture, preserved traditional values.

In Europe the "mass aspects" of media could cut more than one way politically and culturally. While Hollywood produced films that affirmed popular faith in democratic government, a capitalist economy, and the success ethic, totalitarian Nazi Germany broadcast the fiery rallies and speeches of Adolf Hitler, which seemed bent on encouraging racist fears and inflaming public hysteria. In *Triumph of the Will* (1935), German director Leni Riefenstahl used her cinematic gifts to combine myth, symbol, and documentary into an image of Hitler as the Führer, a national savior with the power of a pagan god and the charisma of cult leader.

©Science & Society Picture Library/Getty Images

| *Art Deco, popularized in the 1920s and 1930s, relied on geometrical patterns of machines in decorative designs. This four-valve TRF (Tuned Radio Frequency) was battery-powered and came in a case made of "Bakelite," a moldable, insulated plastic perfect for Art Deco radios.*

"Dirty Thirties": An Ecological Disaster

DUST BOWL   Each year between 1932 and 1939 an average of nearly 50 dust storms, or "black blizzards," turned 1,500 square miles between the Panhandle of western Oklahoma and western Kansas into a gigantic "Dust Bowl," whose baleful effects were felt as far north as the Dakotas and as far south as Texas. It was one of the worst ecological disasters in modern history. Nature played its part, scorching the earth with years of drought and whipping the winds into howling gales. But human beings were mostly responsible for the "dirty thirties." The semiarid lands west of the 98th meridian were unsuitable for agriculture or livestock. Sixty years of intensive farming and grazing had stripped the prairie of its natural vegetation and rendered it defenseless against the elements. When the dry winds blew, they carried away one-third of the soil of the Great Plains.

EFFECT OF COMMERCIAL FARMING   Some 3.5 million plains people abandoned their farms. Landowners or corporations forced off about half of them as large-scale commercial farming slowly spread into the heartland of America. Commercial farms were more common in California, where 10 percent of the farms grew more than 50 percent of the crops. As in industrial America, the strategy in agricultural America was to consolidate and mechanize. In most Dust Bowl counties, people owned less than half the land they farmed. American agriculture was turning from a way of life into an industry. As the economy contracted, owners followed the common industrial strategy of cutting costs by cutting workers.

Relief offices around the country reported a change in migrant families. Rather than black or brown, more and more were white and native-born, typically a young married couple with one child. Long-distance migrants from Oklahoma, Arizona, and Texas usually set their sights on California. If they were like the Joad family in John Steinbeck's classic novel *The Grapes of Wrath* (1939), they drove west along Route 66 through Arizona and New Mexico, their belongings piled high atop rickety jalopies, heading for the West Coast and the promise of jobs picking fruit and harvesting vegetables.

More than 350,000 Oklahomans migrated to California—so many that "Okie" came to mean any Dust Bowler, even though most of Oklahoma, including the home of the fictional Joads, lay outside the Dust Bowl. According to one government study, between 1935 and 1940 only a third of migrants from the Southwest to California had lived on farms before leaving. More than half had resided in cities. Unlike the Joads, most ended up in one California city or another.

Wherever they landed, only one in two or three migrants actually found work. The labor surplus allowed growers to cut wages to less than a third the subsistence level. Families that did not work formed wretched enclaves called "little Oklahomas." The worst were located in California's fertile Imperial Valley. There, at the end of the decade, relief officials discovered a family of 10 living in a 1921 Ford.

Mexican Americans and Repatriation

CÉSAR CHÁVEZ   The Chávez family lost their family farm in Arizona in 1934. César, barely six years old at the time, remembered only images of their departure: a "giant tractor" leveling the corral; the loss of his room and bed; a beat-up Chevy hauling the family west; his father promising to buy another farm. But the elder Chávez could never keep his promise. Instead, he and his family "followed the crops" in California. In eight years César went to 37 schools. When they found work, his family earned less than $10 a week. His father joined strikers in the Imperial Valley in the mid-1930s, only to have the strikes crushed. "Some people put this out of their minds," said César Chávez years later. "I don't." Thirty years later he founded the United Farm Workers of America, the first union of migrant workers in the country.

REPATRIATION   A deep ambivalence had always characterized American attitudes toward Mexicans and Mexican Americans like the Chávezes, but the Great Depression turned most Anglo communities against them. Cities such as Los Angeles, fearing the burden of relief, found it cheaper to ship Mexicans home. Some migrants left voluntarily. Frustrated officials or angry neighbors drove out others. Beginning in 1931 the federal government launched a series of deportations, or **"repatriations,"** of Mexicans back to Mexico. These deportations included the Mexicans' American-born children, who by law were citizens of the United States.

During the decade the Latino population of the Southwest dropped by 500,000. In Chicago the Mexican community shrank by almost half. Staying in the United States often turned out to be as difficult as leaving. The average income of

Source: Library of Congress, Prints and Photographs Division, FSA/OWI Collection [LC-USF34-018215-E]

| *Immigration station near U.S. border, 1938*

Mexican American families in the Rio Grande valley of Texas was $506 a year. Following the harvest made schooling particularly difficult: fewer than two Mexican American children in ten completed five years of school.

LULAC AND ETHNIC IDENTITY   For Americans of Mexican descent, the Great Depression only deepened anxiety over identity. Were they Mexicans, as many Anglos regarded them, or were they Americans, as they regarded themselves? In the 1920s such questions produced several organizations founded to assert the American identity of native-born and naturalized Mexican Americans and to pursue their civil rights. In 1929, on the eve of the Depression, many of these organizations were consolidated into the League of United Latin American Citizens (LULAC). By the early 1940s, "Flying Squadrons" of LULAC organizers had created 80 chapters nationwide, making it the largest Mexican American civil rights association in the country.

LULAC permitted only those Latinos who were American citizens to join, excluding hundreds of thousands of ethnic Mexicans who nonetheless regarded the United States as their home. It pointedly conducted meetings in English. An assimilated middle class provided its leadership and stressed desegregation of public schools, voter registration, and an end to discrimination in public facilities and on juries.

African Americans in the Depression

Hard times were nothing new to African Americans. "The Negro was born in depression," opined one black man. "It only became official when it hit the white man." Still, when the Depression struck, black unemployment surged. By 1932 it reached 50 percent, twice the national level. By 1933 several

| *"Juke joints" like this one in Belle Glade, Florida, provided a temporary haven, and sometimes living quarters, for African American migratory workers who came to drink and dance to the songs played on a jukebox.*

Source: Library of Congress, Prints and Photographs Division [LC-DIG-fsac-1a34396]

cities reported between 25 and 40 percent of their black residents with no support except relief payments.

Migration out of the rural South, up 800,000 during the 1920s, dropped by 50 percent in the 1930s. As late as 1940 three of four African Americans still lived in rural areas; yet conditions there were just as bad as in cities. In 1934 one study estimated the average income for black cotton farmers at under $200 a year.

FATHER DIVINE AND ELIJAH MUHAMMAD Like many African Americans, George Baker refused to be victimized by the Depression. Baker had moved from Georgia to Harlem in 1915. He changed his name to M. J. Divine and founded a religious cult that promised followers an afterlife of full equality. In the 1930s "Father Divine" preached economic cooperation and opened shelters, or "heavens," for regenerate "angels," black and white. In Detroit, Elijah Poole began calling himself Elijah Muhammad and in 1931 established the Black Muslims, a blend of Islamic faith and black nationalism. He exhorted African Americans to celebrate their African heritage, to live lives of self-discipline and self-help, and to strive for a separate all-black nation.

SCOTTSBORO BOYS The Depression inflamed racial prejudice. Lynchings tripled between 1932 and 1933. In 1932 the Supreme Court ordered a retrial in the most celebrated racial case of the decade. A year earlier nine black teenagers had been accused of raping two white women on a train bound for Scottsboro, Alabama. Within weeks all-white juries sentenced eight of them to death. The convictions rested on the testimony of the women, one of whom later admitted the boys had been framed. Appeals kept the case alive for almost a decade. In the end, charges against four of the "Scottsboro boys" were dropped. The other five received substantial prison sentences.

REVIEW

What were the human costs of the Great Depression for Anglos, Latinos, and African Americans?

THE TRAGEDY OF HERBERT HOOVER

THE PRESIDENCY OF HERBERT HOOVER began with great promise but soon became a nightmare both personal and professional. "I have no fears for the future of our country," he announced at his inauguration in March 1929. But within seven months a "depression" struck. (Hoover used the word instead of the traditional "panic" to downplay the emergency.) Despite more effort than any of his predecessors to restore a damaged economy, he failed to turn the economic tide. For all of Hoover's promise and innovative intelligence, he was a transitional figure, important as a break from the do-nothing policies of past depression presidents and a herald of more active presidents to come.

The Failure of Relief

By the winter of 1931–1932 the picture was bleak: relief organizations with too little money and too few resources to make much headway against the Depression. Once-mighty private charity dwindled to 6 percent of all relief funds.

Ethnic charities tried to stave off disaster for their own. Over the years Mexican Americans and Puerto Ricans turned to *mutualistas,* traditional societies that provided members with social support, life insurance, and sickness benefits. In San Francisco, the Chinese Six Companies offered food and clothing to needy Chinese Americans. But as the head of the Federation of Jewish Charities warned, private efforts were failing. The government would be "compelled, by the cruel events ahead of us, to step into the situation and bring relief on a large scale."

CITY SERVICES An estimated 30 million needy people nationwide quickly depleted city treasuries, already pressed because nearly 30 percent of city taxpayers had fallen behind in what they owed. In Philadelphia relief payments to a family of four totaled $5.50 a week, the highest in the country. Some cities gave nothing to unmarried people or childless couples, no matter how impoverished they were.

Cities clamored for help from state capitals, but after a decade of extravagant spending and sloppy bookkeeping, many states were already in debt. As businesses and property values collapsed, tax bases shrank and with them state revenues. Until New York established its Temporary Emergency Relief Administration (TERA) in 1931, no state had an agency to handle the unemployed.

The Hoover Depression Program

Beginning in 1930 President Hoover assumed leadership in combating the Depression with more vigor and compassion than any other executive. It was a mark of his character. Orphaned at nine, he became one of Stanford University's first graduates and, before the age of 40, the millionaire head of one of the most successful mine engineering firms in the world. As a good Quaker he balanced private gain with public service, saving starving Belgian refugees in 1915 after war broke out in Europe. He worked 14 hours a day, paid his own salary, and convinced private organizations and businesses to donate food, clothing, and other necessities. In his honor, Finns coined a new word: to "hoover" meant to help.

When the Depression struck, Hoover was no passive executive. Past presidents feared that any intervention by government would upset the natural workings of the economy. They saw their sole responsibility as keeping the federal budget balanced. But Hoover understood the vicious cycle in which rising unemployment drove down consumer demand and appreciated the need for stimulating investment. He set in motion an unprecedented program of government activism.

PROGRAM FAILURES Despite all his work, Hoover's program failed. At first he rallied business leaders, who pledged to maintain employment, wages, and prices—only to back down as

| Artist Don Freeman's Home Relief *portrays the often chaotic efforts of private charities to aid individuals and families desperate for food, clothing and shelter. Those asking for aid often felt humiliated by the process and stripped of their self respect.*

Source: Gift of the Works Progress Administration, Federal Art Project

the economy sputtered. He pushed a tax cut through Congress in 1930 in order to increase the purchasing power of consumers. When cuts unbalanced the federal budget, Hoover reversed course. At bottom he firmly believed that a balanced federal budget was the most important requirement to restore business confidence and prosperity. So he agreed to tax increases in 1932 to bring the federal budget into balance. But taxes only undermined the economy by soaking up money that might have been used to invest in businesses or buy what was being sold. Without investment and consumption there could be no recovery.

Equally disastrous, the president endorsed the Smoot-Hawley Tariff (1930) to protect the United States from cheap foreign goods. That bill brought a wave of retaliation from countries abroad, which choked world trade and reduced American sales overseas. Even the $1 billion that Hoover spent on **public works**—more than the total spent by all his predecessors combined—did not approach the $10 billion needed to employ only half the jobless. Spending such huge sums seemed unthinkable when the entire federal budget was only $3.2 billion.

RECONSTRUCTION FINANCE CORPORATION Under pressure from Congress, Hoover took his boldest action to save the banks. Between 1930 and 1932 some 5,100 banks failed as panicky depositors withdrew their funds. Without loans from sound banks for investment, the economy would never recover. Hoover agreed to permit the creation of the Reconstruction Finance Corporation (RFC) in 1932, an agency that could lend money to banks. Modeled on a similar agency created during World War I, the RFC had a capital stock of $500 million and the power to borrow four times that amount. Within three months bank failures dropped from 70 a week to 1 every two weeks.

In spite of this success Hoover drew criticism for rescuing banks and not people. From the start he rejected the idea of federal relief for the unemployed for fear that a "dole," or giveaway program, would damage the initiative of recipients,

perhaps even produce a permanent underclass. The bureaucracy that would be needed to police recipients, moreover, would inevitably meddle in the private lives of citizens and bring a "train of corruption and waste," Hoover said. He assumed neighborliness and cooperation would be enough.

UNEMPLOYMENT RELIEF As unemployment worsened, Hoover softened his stand on federal relief. In 1932 he allowed Congress to pass the Emergency Relief and Construction Act. It authorized the RFC to lend up to $1.5 billion for "reproductive" public works that paid for themselves—like toll bridges and slum clearance. Another $300 million went to states as loans for the unemployed. It barely mattered. Too few public works were ready to go, and too little money was ready to be handed out. When the governor of Pennsylvania requested loans to furnish the destitute with 13 cents a day for a year, the RFC sent only enough for 3 cents a day.

Stirrings of Discontent

Despite unprecedented action, Hoover could not stem rising discontent. "The word revolution is heard at every hand," one writer warned in 1932. Some wondered if capitalism itself had gone bankrupt.

In 1932 anger erupted into violence. Wisconsin dairy farmers overturned tens of thousands of milk cans in a fruitless effort to increase prices. A 48-mile-long "coal caravan" of striking miners drove through southern Illinois in protest. Three thousand marchers stormed Henry Ford's plant in Dearborn, only to have Ford police turn power water hoses and guns on them. When it was over, four marchers lay dead and over 20 more wounded.

COMMUNIST PARTY For all the stirrings of discontent, revolution was never a danger. In 1932 the Communist Party of the United States had 20,000 members—up from 6,500 only three years earlier but hardly enough to constitute a political

©The Museum of the City of New York/Art Resource, NY

‖ *In the early years of the Depression, demonstrations by the unemployed, some organized by Communists and other radicals, broke out all over the country. On March 6, 1930, a Communist-led protest at Union Square in New York City turned into an ugly riot. In 1935 Communist parties, under orders from Moscow, allied with democratic and socialist groups against fascism, proclaiming in the United States that "Communism is twentieth-century Americanism."*

force. Deeply suspicious of Marxist doctrine, most Americans rejected the Communists' calls for collectivism and an end to capitalism. Despite its strong support for civil rights, fewer than 1,000 African Americans joined the party in the early 1930s.

At first hostile to established politics, the Communists adopted a more cooperative strategy to contain Adolf Hitler when his Nazi Party won control of Germany in 1933. Two years later, the Soviet Union ordered Communist parties in Europe and the United States to join with liberal politicians in a "popular front" against Nazism. Thereafter Communist Party membership in the United States peaked in the mid-1930s at about 80,000.

The Bonus Army

Less radical was the "Bonus Army," a scruffy collection of World War I veterans who marched on Washington in the summer of 1932. They were hungry and looking to cash in the bonus certificates they had received from Congress in 1924 as a reward for wartime service. By the time they reached the Capitol in June, their numbers had swelled to nearly 20,000. It was the largest protest in the city's history. President Hoover sympathized with them but only to a point, as the veterans learned when he dismissed them as a

special-interest lobby and refused to meet with their leaders. When the Senate blocked the bonus bill, most veterans left.

About 2,000 stayed to dramatize their plight, camping with their families and parading peaceably. Despite eviction orders, the protesters refused to leave. By the end of July, the president had had enough. He called in the U.S. Army under the command of Chief of Staff General Douglas MacArthur. MacArthur arrived with four troops of saber-brandishing cavalry, six tanks, and a column of infantry with fixed bayonets. By the time the smoke cleared the next morning, only 300 wounded veterans remained.

Though he had intended that the army only assist the police, Hoover accepted responsibility for the action. But the sight of unarmed and unemployed veterans under attack by American troops soured most Americans and left Hoover looking even more unsympathetic to the plight of the needy. In Albany, New York, Governor Franklin D. Roosevelt exploded at the president's failure: "There is nothing inside the man but jelly."

The Election of 1932

In 1932 Republicans stuck with Hoover and endorsed his Depression program. Democrats countered with Franklin D. Roosevelt, the charismatic New York governor. As a sign of change, Roosevelt broke precedent by flying to Chicago and addressing the delegates in person. "I pledge you, I pledge myself to a new deal for the American people," he told them.

Without a national following, Roosevelt zigged and zagged in an effort to appeal to the broadest possible bloc of voters. One minute he called for a balanced budget, the next for costly public works and aid to the unemployed. He promised to help business, then spoke of remembering the "forgotten man" and "distributing wealth and products more equitably." For his part, Hoover denounced Roosevelt's New Deal as a "dangerous departure" from tradition that would destroy American values and institutions and "build a bureaucracy such as we have never seen in our history."

On Election Day, Roosevelt captured a thundering 58 percent of the popular vote and carried large Democratic majorities into the Congress. Just as telling as the margin of victory were its sources. Industrial workers in the North, poor farmers in the South and West, immigrants and big-city dwellers from every region were being galvanized into a broad new coalition. They had experienced firsthand the savage effects of the boom-and-bust business cycle and wanted change. They turned to Roosevelt and the Democrats, who recognized that in a modern industrial state it was not enough to rally round business and hope that capitalism would right itself, as Hoover and the Republicans wanted. With the election of 1932, over 30 years of nearly unbroken Republican rule came to an end.

> ✔ **REVIEW**
>
> In what ways did Herbert Hoover actively seek to counteract the Great Depression? What discouraged him from doing more?

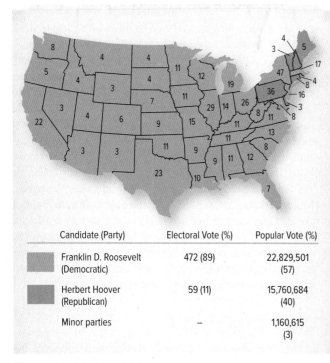

Candidate (Party)	Electoral Vote (%)	Popular Vote (%)
Franklin D. Roosevelt (Democratic)	472 (89)	22,829,501 (57)
Herbert Hoover (Republican)	59 (11)	15,760,684 (40)
Minor parties	–	1,160,615 (3)

ELECTION OF 1932

THE EARLY NEW DEAL (1933–1935)

ON MARCH 4, 1933, AS the clocks struck noon, Eleanor Roosevelt wondered if it were possible to "do anything to save America now." She looked at her husband, who had just been sworn in as thirty-second president of the United States. Franklin Roosevelt radiated confidence as he faced the audience of over 100,000. "The only thing we have to fear is fear itself," he declared. Heeding the call for "action, and action now," he promised to exercise "broad Executive power to wage a war against the emergency." The crowd cheered. Eleanor was terrified: "One has the feeling of going it blindly because we're in a tremendous stream, and none of us knows where we're going to land."

RECOVERY, RELIEF, REFORM The early New Deal unfolded in the spring of 1933 with a chaotic 100-day burst of legislation. It stressed recovery through planning and cooperation with business but also tried to provide relief for the unemployed and reform the economic system. Above all, the early New Deal broke the cycle of despair. With Roosevelt in the White House, most Americans believed that they were in good hands, wherever they landed.

The Democratic Roosevelts

From the moment they entered it in 1933, Franklin and Eleanor—the Democratic Roosevelts—transformed the White House. No more seven-course meals as Hoover had served in an effort to show that nothing was really wrong. Instead, visitors got fare fit for a boardinghouse. Roosevelt's lunches of hash and a poached egg cost 19 cents. The gesture was symbolic, but it made the president's point of ending business as usual.

Such belt-tightening was new to Franklin Roosevelt. Born of an old Dutch family in New York, he grew up rich and pampered. He idolized his Republican cousin Theodore Roosevelt and mimicked his career, except as a Democrat. Like Theodore, Franklin graduated from Harvard University (in 1904), won a seat in the New York State legislature (in 1910), secured an appointment as assistant secretary of the navy (in 1913), and ran for the vice presidency (in 1920). Then disaster struck. On vacation in the summer of 1921, Roosevelt fell ill with poliomyelitis. The disease paralyzed him from the waist down.

Roosevelt emerged from the ordeal to win the governorship of New York in 1928. When the Depression struck he created the first state relief agency in 1931, the Temporary Emergency Relief Administration. Aid to the jobless "must be extended by Government, not as a matter of charity, but as a matter of social duty," he explained. He considered himself a progressive but moved well beyond the cautious federal activism of most progressives. He adopted no single ideology. He cared little about economic principles. He wanted results. Experimentation became a hallmark of the New Deal.

Eleanor Roosevelt redefined what it meant to be First Lady. Never had a president's wife been so visible, so much of a crusader, so cool under fire. She was the first First Lady to hold weekly press conferences. Her column, "My Day," appeared in 135 newspapers, and her twice-weekly broadcasts made her a radio personality rivaling her husband. She became his eyes, ears, and legs, traveling 40,000 miles a year. Secret Service men code-named her "Rover."

Eleanor believed she was only a spur to presidential action. But she was active in her own right, as a teacher and social reformer before Franklin became president and afterward as a tireless advocate of the underdog. In the White House, she pressed him to hire more women and minorities, supported antilynching and anti-poll-tax measures when he would not, and pressed for experimental towns for the homeless. By 1939 more Americans approved of her than of her husband.

©Martin McEvilly/New York Daily News/Getty Images

| *Franklin Roosevelt contracted polio in 1921 and remained paralyzed from the waist down for the rest of his life. Out of deference to Roosevelt, photographers rarely showed him wearing heavy leg braces or sitting in a wheelchair. This photograph, snapped outside his New York City brownstone in September 1933 during his first year as president, is one of the few in which Roosevelt's braces are visible (just below the cuffs of his trousers). Note the wooden handrails constructed specifically to help him navigate the stairs.*

Saving the Banks

Before the election Roosevelt had gathered a group of economic advisors called the "Brains Trust." Out of their recommendations came the early, or "first," New Deal of government planning, intervention, and experimentation. Although Brains Trusters disagreed over the means, they agreed over ends: economic recovery, relief for the unemployed, and sweeping reform to ward off future depressions. The first step was to save the banks. By the eve of the inauguration, governors in 38 states had temporarily closed their banks to stem the withdrawal of deposits.

On March 5, the day after his inauguration, Roosevelt ordered every bank in the country closed for four days. He shrewdly called it a "bank holiday." On March 9 the president introduced emergency banking legislation. The House passed the measure, sight unseen, and the Senate endorsed it later in the day. Roosevelt signed it that night.

EMERGENCY BANKING ACT Rather than nationalizing the banks as radicals wanted, the Emergency Banking Act followed the modest course of extending federal assistance to them. Sound banks would reopen immediately with government support. Troubled banks would be handed over to federal "conservators," who would guide them to solvency. In plain and simple language, Roosevelt explained what was happening in the first of his many informal "fireside chat" radio broadcasts. When banks reopened the next day, deposits exceeded withdrawals.

FEDERAL DEPOSIT INSURANCE CORPORATION To guard against another stock crash, financial reforms gave government greater authority to manage the currency and regulate stock transactions. In April 1933 Roosevelt dropped the gold standard and began experimenting with the value of the dollar to boost prices. Later that spring the Glass-Steagall Banking Act restricted speculation by banks and, more important, created federal insurance for bank deposits of up to $2,500. Despite Roosevelt's objections that the Federal Deposit Insurance Corporation would preserve weak banks at the expense of strong ones, fewer banks failed for the rest of the decade than in the best year of the 1920s. The Securities Exchange Act (1934) established a new federal agency, the Securities and Exchange Commission, to oversee the stock market.

Relief for the Unemployed

Saving the banks and financial markets meant little if human suffering continued. Mortgage relief for the millions who had lost their homes came eventually in 1934 in the Home Owners' Loan Act. The need to alleviate starvation led Roosevelt to propose a bold new giveaway program. The Federal Emergency Relief Administration (FERA) opened its door in May 1933. Sitting amid unpacked boxes, gulping coffee and chain-smoking, former social worker Harry Hopkins spent $5 million in his first two hours as head of the new agency. In its two-year existence, FERA furnished more than $1 billion in grants of money and food to states, local areas, and private charities.

TWO VIEWS OF THE "FORGOTTEN MAN"

When President Franklin Roosevelt promised to help the "forgotten man" during the Great Depression, not everyone agreed that such poverty-stricken Americans needed it. Two views of forgotten men and women follow, one from an Indiana farmwoman critical of any form of assistance (Document 1), the other from a reporter stressing the necessity for more aid and the danger of failing to provide it (Document 2).

DOCUMENT 1
Aid Rewards the "Shiftless"

We have always had a shiftless, never-do-well class of people whose one and only aim in life is to live without work. I have been rubbing elbows with this class for nearly sixty years and have tried to help some of the most promising and have seen others try to help them, but it can't be done. We cannot help those who will not try to help themselves and if they do try, a square deal is all they need, and by the way that is all this country needs or ever has needed: a square deal for all and then, let each paddle their own canoe, or sink. . . .

The women and children around here have had to work at the fields to help save the crops and several women fainted while at work and at the same time we couldn't go up or down the road without stumbling over some of the reliefers, moping around

carrying dirt from one side of the road to the other and back again, or else asleep. I live alone on a farm and have not raised any crops for the last two years as there was no help to be had. I am feeding the stock and have been cutting the wood to keep my home fires burning. There are several reliefers around here now who have been kicked off relief, but they refuse to work unless they can get relief hours and wages, but they are so worthless no one can afford to hire them.

As for the clearance of the real slums, it can't be done as long as their inhabitants are allowed to reproduce their kind. I would like for you to see what a family of that class can do to a decent house in a short time. Such a family moved into an almost new, neat, four-room house near here last winter. They even cut down some of the shade trees for fuel,

after they had burned everything they could pry loose. . . . I will not try to describe their filth for you would not believe me. They paid no rent while there and left between two suns [sic] owing everyone from whom they could get nickels worth of anything. They are just a fair sample of the class of people on whom so much of our hard earned tax money is being squandered and on whom so much sympathy is being wasted. . . .

Is it any wonder the taxpayers are discouraged by all this penalizing of thrift and industry to reward shiftlessness, or that the whole country is on the brink of chaos?

Source: Minnie A. Harden (Columbus, Ind) to Mrs. F. D. Roosevelt, December 14, 1937, as reprinted in McElvaine, Robert, ed., *Down and Out in the Great Depression: Letters from the Forgotten Man.* Chapel Hill, NC: University of North Carolina Press, 1983, 145–147.

DOCUMENT 2
Aid Helps the Truly Needy

. . . One hears a good deal about "relief psychology" these days—that if it were all direct relief, with no work, thousands would never apply. No social worker out in the field would deny this. Through work the stigma has to some extent been removed from relief. Into every relief office in the country have come applicants, not for relief, but for jobs. More of them than you would perhaps believe have shaken their heads and turned away when informed that it was really relief. Without doubt there are many thousands of families on work relief in this country who would not have applied had they not been able to call it—to themselves at any rate—"a job." But when one hears the testimony of clinical doctors, school nurses, teachers, and social workers that the "marginal families"—those who haven't yet come on relief—are really worse off than those on relief, one wonders how long these people could have held out after all. . . . This from a doctor in a mental hygiene clinic in Providence, R. I.: "most

people we see are not on relief, but are starving. Many of these are white collar people and people in the skilled labor class who avoid relief, whose pride remains stronger than hunger. The result on the children is malnutrition and a neurotic condition produced by hearing and being constantly part of parental fear. The child grows obsessed with the material problems of the home and mentally shoulders them, and the nervous system cracks."

. . . a FERA (Federal Emergency Relief Administration) investigator a few weeks ago sent this poem from a town in Ohio. It was written by an 18-year-old boy:

Prayer of Bitter Men

We are the men who ride the swaying freights,
We are the men whom Life has beaten down,
Leaving for Death nought but the final pain
Of degradation. Men who stand in line
An hour for a bowl of watered soup,
Grudgingly given, savagely received.
We are the Ishmaels, outcasts of the earth,

Who shrink before the sordidness of Life
And cringe before the filthiness of Death.
Will there not come a great, a glittering Man,
A radiant leader with a heavier sword
To crush to earth the enemies who crush
Those who seek food and freedom on
the roads?
We care not if their flag be white or red,
Come, ruthless Savior, messenger of God,
Lenin or Christ, we follow Thy bright sword.

Source: Report Summary, Lorena Hickok to Harry Hopkins, January 1, 1935, Franklin D. Roosevelt Library, Federal Relief Agency Papers, FERA-WPA Narrative Field Reports, Surveys by Investigators, 1934–1938.

THINKING CRITICALLY

What complaints does the woman in the first letter make to the First Lady, and why does she make them? What picture emerges from the field report, including the poem of the young man appended to the end of the report? How do you account for the differences between the two views?

WORK RELIEF Hopkins persuaded Roosevelt to expand relief with an innovative shift from government giveaways to a work program to see workers through the winter of 1933–1934. Paying someone "to do something socially useful," Hopkins explained, "preserves a man's morale." The Civil Works Administration (CWA) employed 4 million Americans. Alarmed at the high cost of the program, Roosevelt disbanded the CWA in the spring of 1934. Its program of work relief nonetheless created a new weapon against unemployment and an important precedent for future aid programs.

Another work relief program established in 1933 proved even more creative. The Civilian Conservation Corps (CCC) was Roosevelt's pet project. It combined his concern for conservation with compassion for youth. The CCC took unmarried 18- to 25-year-olds from relief rolls and sent them into the woods and fields to plant trees, build parks, and fight soil erosion. During its 10 years, the CCC provided 2.5 million young men with jobs (which prompted some critics of the all-male program to chant, "Where's the she, she, she?").

TENNESSEE VALLEY AUTHORITY New Dealers intended relief programs to last only through the crisis. But the Tennessee Valley Authority (TVA)—a massive public works project created in 1933—helped to relieve unemployment but also made a continuing contribution to regional planning. For a decade planners had dreamed of transforming the flood-ridden basin of the Tennessee River, one of the poorest areas of the country, with a program of regional development and social engineering. The TVA constructed a series of dams along the seven-state basin to control flooding, improve navigation, and generate cheap hydroelectric power. In cooperation with state and local officials, it also launched social projects to stamp out malaria, provide library bookmobiles, and create recreational lakes.

Like many New Deal programs the TVA produced a mixed legacy. It saved 3 million acres from erosion, multiplied the average income in the valley tenfold, and repaid its original investment in federal taxes. Its cheap electricity helped to bring down the rates of private utility companies. But the experiment in regional planning also pushed thousands of families from their land, failed to end poverty, and created an agency that became one of the worst polluters in the country.

Planning for Industrial Recovery

Planning, not just for regions but for the whole economy, seemed to many New Dealers the key to recovery. Some held that if businesses planned and cooperated with each another, the ruthless competition that was driving down prices, wages, and employment could be controlled and the riddle of recovery solved. Business leaders had been urging such a course since 1931, and in his fashion President Hoover had tried to do as much. In June 1933, under the National Industrial Recovery Act (NIRA), Roosevelt put planning to work for industry.

PUBLIC WORKS ADMINISTRATION The legislation created two new agencies. The Public Works Administration (PWA) was designed to boost industrial activity and consumer spending with a $3.3 billion public works program. The companies put under contract and the workers they employed would help stimulate the economy through their purchases and leave a legacy of capital improvement. Harold Ickes, the prickly interior secretary who headed PWA, built the Triborough Bridge and Lincoln Tunnel in New York, the port city of Brownsville, Texas, and two aircraft carriers. But because he worried so much about waste and corruption, he never spent enough money quickly enough to jump-start the economy.

NATIONAL RECOVERY ADMINISTRATION A second federal agency, the National Recovery Administration (NRA), aimed directly at controlling competition among businesses. Under NRA chief Hugh Johnson, representatives from government and business (and also from labor and consumer groups) drew up "codes of fair practices." Industry by industry, the codes established minimum prices, minimum wages, and maximum hours. No company could seek a competitive edge by cutting prices or wages below certain levels or by working a few employees mercilessly and firing the rest. It also required business to accept key demands of labor, including union rights to organize and bargain with management (thus ensuring that if prices jumped, so, too, might wages). Each code promised improved working conditions and outlawed such practices as child labor and sweatshops.

No business was forced to comply because New Dealers feared that government coercion might be ruled unconstitutional. The NRA relied on voluntary participation. A publicity campaign of parades, posters, and public pledges exhorted businesses to join the NRA and consumers to buy only NRA-sanctioned products. More than 2 million employers eventually signed up. In store windows and on merchandise, shiny decals with blue-eagle crests alerted customers that "We Do Our Part."

For all the hoopla, the NRA failed to spark recovery. Big businesses shaped the codes to their advantage and frequently limited production to maintain or even raise prices. Not all businesses joined, and those that did often found the codes too complicated or costly to follow. Even NRA support for labor tottered, for it had no means of enforcing its guarantee of union rights. Business survived under the NRA, but without increasing production there was no incentive for the expansion and new investment needed to end hard times. The NRA soon produced little but evasion and criticism.

***SCHECTER* DECISION** On May 27, 1935, the Supreme Court struck down the floundering NRA in *Schecter Poultry Corp. v. United States.* The justices unanimously ruled that the NRA had exceeded federal power over commerce among the states by regulating the Schecter brothers' poultry business in a single state, New York. Privately, Roosevelt was relieved to be rid of the NRA. But he and other New Dealers were plainly shaken by the grounds of the decision. Their broad view of the commerce clause to fight the Depression suffered a grave blow. Distress inside the administration only grew when Justice Benjamin Cardozo added a

DISTRIBUTING UNEMPLOYMENT RELIEF

Source: Library of Congress, Prints and Photographs Division, FSA/OWI Collection [LC-USF34-018187-E]

"Aid to the unemployed must be extended by Government, not as a matter of charity, but as a matter of social duty."—Franklin D. Roosevelt

CONTEXT

Under Franklin Roosevelt's New Deal, the federal government took responsibility for providing "relief" or public assistance to the unemployed for the first time. Beginning in 1934, through the new Federal Emergency Relief Administration, states received grants of food and money to distribute as they saw fit. Different states had different needs and different resources, both public and private, on which to draw. The percentage of those receiving unemployment relief differed markedly throughout the nation.

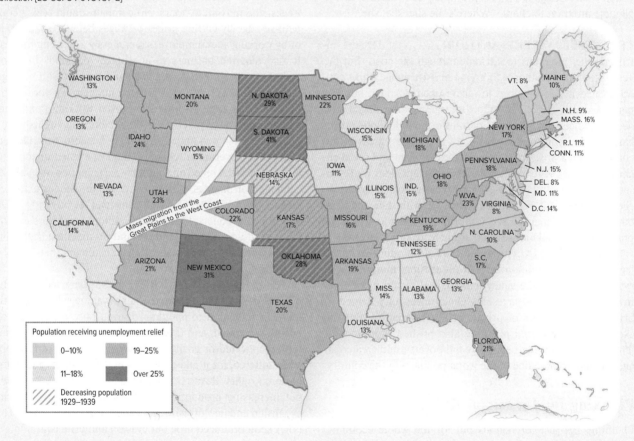

Population receiving unemployment relief
- 0–10%
- 11–18%
- 19–25%
- Over 25%
- Decreasing population 1929–1939

MAP READING

1. Which state had the highest percentage of its population receiving unemployment relief? Which states had the lowest?

2. Which states lost population from 1929 to 1939?

3. Which state does the map indicate received the most migrants from those states that lost population?

MAP INTERPRETATION

1. Which regions of the country were hardest hit by the Depression, based on these relief figures? Which regions seem to have been least hit?

2. What factors might have contributed to South Dakota having the highest percentage of those receiving unemployment relief and Vermont and Virginia being among the lowest?

3. Why might Americans have migrated to the West Coast, and what impact might the migrants have had on states receiving them? For those losing them?

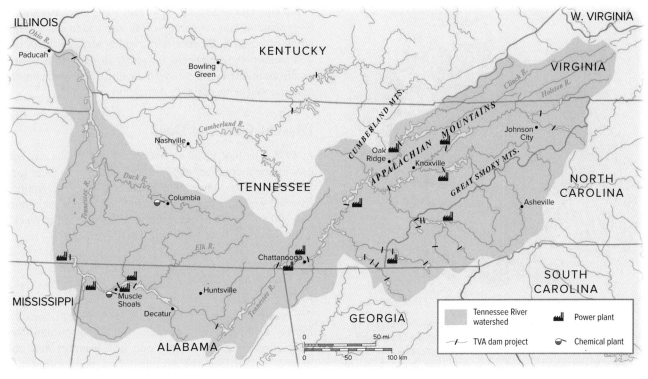

THE TENNESSEE VALLEY AUTHORITY

The Tennessee River basin encompassed parts of seven states. Rivers honeycombed the area, which received some of the heaviest rainfall in the nation. A longtime dream of Senator George Norris, the Tennessee Valley Authority, created in 1933, constructed some 20 dams and improved 5 others over the next 20 years to control chronic flooding and erosion and to produce cheap hydroelectric power and fertilizers. **Why was this project considered an exercise in regional planning?**

chilling afterthought: the NRA's code making represented "an unconstitutional delegation of legislative power" to the executive branch. Without the ability to make rules and regulations, all the executive agencies of the New Deal might flounder.

Planning for Agriculture

Like planning for industry, New Deal planning for agriculture relied on private interests—the farmers—to act as the principal planners. Under the Agricultural Adjustment Act of 1933, farmers limited their own production. The government, in turn, paid them for leaving their fields fallow, while a tax on millers, cotton ginners, and other processors financed the payments. In theory, production limits would reduce surpluses, demand for farm commodities would rise (as would prices), and agriculture would recover.

AGRICULTURE ADJUSTMENT ADMINISTRATION In practice, the Agricultural Adjustment Administration (AAA) did help to increase prices. Unlike the code-ridden NRA, the AAA wisely confined coverage to seven basic commodities. As a way to push prices even higher, the new Commodity Credit Corporation gave loans to farmers who stored their crops rather than sold them—a revival of the Populists' old

subtreasury plan (see Chapter 21). Farm income rose from $5.5 billion in 1932 to $8.7 billion in 1935.

Not all the gains in farm income were the result of government actions or free from problems. In the mid-1930s dust storms, droughts, and floods helped reduce harvests and push up prices. The AAA, moreover, failed to distribute its benefits equally. Large landowners controlled decisions over which plots would be left fallow. In the South these decisions frequently meant cutting the acreage of tenants and sharecroppers or forcing them out. Even when they reduced the acreage that they themselves plowed, big farmers could increase yields through intensive cultivation.

In 1936 the Supreme Court voided the Agricultural Adjustment Act. In *Butler v. U.S.,* the six-justice majority concluded that the government had no right to regulate agriculture, either by limiting production or by taxing processors. A hastily drawn replacement, the Soil Conservation and Domestic Allotment Act (1936), addressed the complaints. Farmers were now subsidized for practicing "conservation"— taking soil-depleting crops off the land—and paid from general revenues instead of a special tax. A second Agricultural Adjustment Act in 1938 returned production quotas.

Other agencies tried to help impoverished farmers. The Farm Credit Administration refinanced about a fifth of all farm mortgages so that farmers could keep their farms by

OF COURSE WE MAY HAVE TO CHANGE REMEDIES IF WE DONT GET RESULTS

©The Granger Collection, New York

| *Anti-Roosevelt cartoonists had a field day with the New Deal's many agencies created to provide relief during the Depression. Here the president, attended by a willing congressional nursemaid, supplies an overabundance of patent medicines, which the doctor cheerfully acknowledges may not work. How many bottles of the medicine can you decipher? Are any of the agencies still in existence today? Why is the bottle marked NRA the largest?*

making the terms of their loans more affordable. In 1935 the Resettlement Administration gave struggling farmers a fresh start by moving them to more productive land. Beginning in 1937 the Farm Security Administration furnished low-interest loans to help tenants buy family farms. In no case, however, did the rural poor have enough political clout to obtain sufficient funds from Congress. Fewer than 5,000 families of a projected 500,000 were resettled, and less than 2 percent of tenant farmers received loans.

> ✓ REVIEW
>
> What measures did the early New Deal take to relieve the Depression, and how successful were they?

A SECOND NEW DEAL (1935–1936)

"BOYS—THIS IS OUR HOUR," CROWED the president's closest advisor, Harry Hopkins, in the spring of 1935. A year earlier voters broke precedent by returning the party in power to Congress, giving the Democrats their largest majorities in decades. With the presidential election only a year away, time was short and Hopkins knew it: "We've got to get everything we want—a works program, social security, wages and hours, everything—now or never."

Hopkins calculated correctly. In 1935 politics, swept along by a torrent of protest, led to a "second hundred days" of

lawmaking and a "Second New Deal." The emphasis shifted from planning and cooperation with business to greater regulation of business, broader relief, and bolder reform. A limited welfare state emerged in which the government was finally committed, at least symbolically, to guaranteeing the material well-being of needy Americans.

Dissent from the Deal

In 1934 a mob of 6,000 stormed the Minneapolis city hall, demanding more relief and higher pay for government jobs. In San Francisco longshoremen walked off the job, igniting a citywide strike. By year's end 1.5 million workers had joined in 1,800 strikes. Conditions were improving but not quickly enough, and across the country dissent grew.

LIBERTY LEAGUE From the right came the charges of a few wealthy business executives and conservatives that Roosevelt was an enemy of private property and a dictator in the making. In August 1934 they founded the American Liberty League. Despite spending $1 million in anti–New Deal advertising, the league won little support and only helped to convince the president that cooperation with business was failing.

"END POVERTY IN CALIFORNIA" In California discontented voters took over the Democratic Party and turned sharply to the left by nominating novelist Upton Sinclair, a Socialist, for governor. Running under the slogan "End Poverty in California" (EPIC), Sinclair proposed to confiscate idle factories and land and permit the unemployed to produce for their own use. Republicans mounted a no-holds-barred counterattack, including fake newsreels depicting Sinclair as a Bolshevik, atheist, and free-lover. He lost the election but won nearly 1 million votes.

HUEY LONG Huey P. Long, the flamboyant Democratic senator from Louisiana, had ridden to power on a wave of rural discontent against banks, corporations, and political machines. As governor of Louisiana, he pushed through reforms regulating utilities, building roads and schools, even distributing free schoolbooks. Opponents called him a "dictator"; most Louisianans simply called him the "Kingfish." Breaking with Roosevelt in 1933, Long pledged to bring about recovery by making "every man a king." His "Share Our Wealth" plan was a drastic but simple program for recovery: the government would limit the size of all fortunes and confiscate the rest. Every family would be guaranteed an annual income of $2,500 and an estate of $5,000, enough to buy a house, an automobile, and a radio (over which Long had already built a national following).

By 1935, one year after its founding, Long's Share Our Wealth organization boasted 27,000 clubs with files containing nearly 8 million names. Democratic National Committee members shuddered at polls showing that Long might capture up to 4 million votes in 1936, not enough to win but enough to put a Republican in the White House. Late in 1935, in the

Source: Library of Congress, Prints and Photographs Division [LC-DIG-hec-38452]

| *Louisiana governor and one-time U.S. senator Huey Long promised to make "every man a king," but critics predicted that only Long would wear the crown. Power-hungry and charismatic, the Kingfish made no secret of his presidential aspirations and built them on promises to redistribute wealth in America.*

corridors of the Louisiana State Capitol, Long was shot to death by a disgruntled constituent whose family had been wronged by the Long political machine.

CHARLES COUGHLIN   Father Charles Coughlin was Long's urban counterpart. Where Long explained the Depression as the result of bloated fortunes, Coughlin blamed banks. In weekly broadcasts from the Shrine of the Little Flower in suburban Detroit, the "Radio Priest" told his working-class, largely Catholic audience that international bankers had toppled the world economy by manipulating gold-backed currencies.

Coughlin promised to end the Depression with simple strokes: nationalizing banks, inflating the currency with silver, spreading work. (None would have worked because each would have dampened investment, the key to recovery.) Across the urban North, 30 to 40 million Americans—the largest audience in the world—huddled around their radios to listen. In 1934 Coughlin organized the National Union for Social Justice to pressure both parties. As the election of 1936 approached, the Union loomed on the political horizon.

FRANCIS TOWNSEND   A less ominous challenge came from Dr. Francis Townsend. The 67-year-old physician had recently retired from California's public health service. Moved by the plight of elderly Americans without pensions or medical insurance, Townsend created Old Age Revolving Pensions, Limited, in 1934. He proposed to have the government pay $200 a month to those 60 years or older who quit their jobs and spent the money within 30 days. By 1936 Townsend clubs counted 3.5 million members, most of them small businesspeople and farmers at or beyond retirement age.

For all their differences, Sinclair, Long, Coughlin, Townsend, and other critics struck similar chords. Although the solutions they proposed were simplistic and unworkable, the problems they addressed were serious and real: a maldistribution of goods and wealth, inadequacies in the money supply, the plight of the elderly. They attacked the growing control of corporations, banks, and government over individuals and communities. And they created mass political movements based on social as well as economic dissatisfaction. When Sinclair supporters pledged to produce for their own use and Long's followers swore to "share our wealth," when Coughlinites damned the "monied interests" and elderly Townsendites bemoaned foul-ups in Washington, they were also trying to protect their freedom and their communities from the intrusion of big business and big government.

The Second Hundred Days

By the spring of 1935 the forces of discontent were pushing Roosevelt to more action. So was Congress. With Democrats accounting for more than two-thirds of both houses, they were prepared to outspend the president in extending the New Deal. A "second hundred days" produced a legislative barrage that moved the New Deal toward Roosevelt's ultimate destination—"a little to the left of center," where government could soften the impact of industrialism, protect the needy, and compensate for the boom-and-bust business cycle.

WORKS PROGRESS ADMINISTRATION   To help the many Americans who were still jobless, Roosevelt proposed the Emergency Relief Appropriation Act of 1935, with a record $4.8 billion for relief and employment. Some of the money went to the new National Youth Administration (NYA) for more than 4.5 million jobs for young people. The lion's share went to the new Works Progress Administration (WPA), where Harry Hopkins mounted the largest work relief program in history. Before its end in 1943, the WPA employed at least 8.5 million people.

Constrained from competing with private industry, Hopkins showed remarkable ingenuity. WPA workers pulled libraries on the backs of horses through the foothills of Kentucky and drafted a map in Braille for sightless citizens in Massachusetts. They taught art in a Cincinnati psychiatric ward and built the handcrafted Timberline Lodge near the peak of Mount Hood in Oregon. In 1938 alone the WPA put 3.3 million Americans to work. Before its demise in 1943, it spent 80 percent of its budget on wages.

The ambitious Social Security Act, passed in 1935, sought to help those who could not help themselves: the aged poor, the infirmed, dependent children. In this commitment to the destitute it laid the groundwork for the modern welfare state. Social Security also acted as an economic stabilizer by furnishing pensions for retirees and insurance for those who lost their jobs. A payroll tax on both employer and employee underwrote pensions after age 65, while an employer-financed system of insurance made possible government payments to unemployed workers.

Social Security marked a historic reversal in American political values. A new social contract between the government and the people replaced the gospel of self-help and the older policies of laissez faire. At last government acknowledged a broad responsibility to protect the social rights of citizens. The welfare state, foreshadowed in the aid given veterans and their families after the Civil War, was institutionalized, though its coverage was limited. To win the votes of southern congressmen hostile to African Americans, the legislation excluded farmworkers and domestic servants, doubtless among the neediest Americans but often black and disproportionately southern.

NATIONAL LABOR RELATIONS ACT Congress whittled down Roosevelt's plan for "cradle-to-grave" social insurance, but its labor legislation pushed the president well beyond his goal of providing paternalistic aid for workers, such as establishing pension plans and unemployment payments. New York senator Robert Wagner, the son of a

Source: Library of Congress, Prints and Photographs Division [LC-DIG-ppmsca-07216]

| *Social Security poster, 1935*

janitor, wanted workers to fight their own battles. In 1933 he had included union recognition in the NRA. When the Supreme Court killed the NRA in 1935, Wagner introduced what became the National Labor Relations Act. So important had labor support become to Roosevelt that he gave the bill his belated blessing. The "Wagner Act" created a National Labor Relations Board (NLRB) to supervise the election of unions and ensure union rights to bargain. Most vital, the NLRB had the power to enforce these policies. By 1941 the number of unionized workers had doubled.

Roosevelt responded to the growing hostility of business by turning against the wealthy and powerful in 1935. The popularity of Long's tirades against the rich and Coughlin's against banks sharpened his points of attack. The Revenue Act of 1935 (called the "Wealth Tax Act") threatened to "soak the rich." By the time it worked its way through Congress, however, it levied only moderate taxes on high incomes and inheritances. The Banking Act of 1935 centralized authority over the money market in the Board of Governors of the Federal Reserve System. By controlling interest rates and the money supply, the Board increased its ability to compensate for swings in the economy and reduced the power of banks. The Public Utilities Holding Company Act (1935) limited the size of utility empires. Long the target of progressive reformers, the giant holding companies produced nothing but higher profits for speculators and higher prices for consumers. Diluted like the wealth tax, the utility law was still a political victory for New Dealers.

The Election of 1936

In June 1936 Roosevelt traveled to Philadelphia to accept the Democratic nomination for a second term as president. "This generation of Americans has a rendezvous with destiny," he told a crowd of 100,000. Whatever destiny had in store, Roosevelt knew that the coming election would turn on a single issue: "It's myself."

Roosevelt ignored his Republican opponent, Governor Alfred Landon of Kansas. Despite a bulging campaign chest of $14 million, Landon lacked luster as well as issues. He favored the regulation of business, a balanced budget, and much of the New Deal. For his part Roosevelt turned the election into a contest between haves and have-nots. The forces of "organized money are unanimous in their hate for me," he told a roaring crowd at New York City's Madison Square Garden, "and I welcome their hatred."

The strategy deflated Republicans, discredited conservatives, and stole the thunder of the newly formed Union Party of Townsendites, Coughlinites, and old Long supporters. The election returns shocked even experienced observers. Roosevelt won the largest Electoral College victory ever—523 to 8—and a whopping 60.8 percent of the popular vote. The margin of victory came from those at the bottom of the economic ladder, grateful for help furnished by the New Deal.

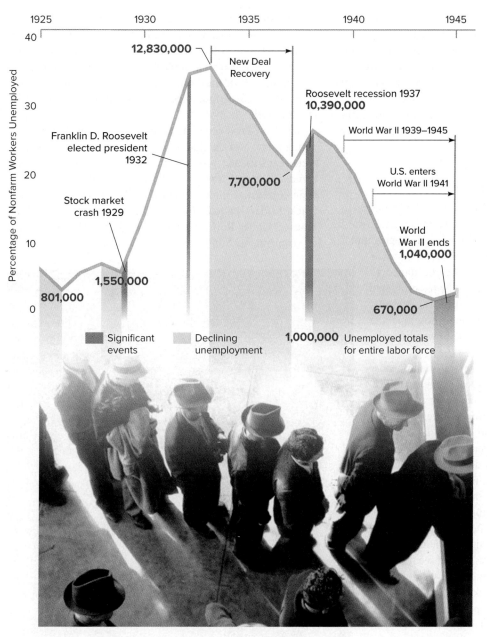

12,830,000

New Deal Recovery

Roosevelt recession 1937
10,390,000

World War II 1939–1945

Franklin D. Roosevelt elected president 1932

U.S. enters World War II 1941

Stock market crash 1929

7,700,000

World War II ends
1,040,000

1,550,000

801,000

670,000

Percentage of Nonfarm Workers Unemployed

1925　1930　1935　1940　1945

| | | |
| Significant events | Declining unemployment | **1,000,000** Unemployed totals for entire labor force |

Unemployment mushroomed in the wake of the stock market crash of 1929. It did not drop to 1929 levels until American entry into the Second World War in 1941. The yellow bands indicate periods of declining unemployment. Note that unemployment begins to rise in 1945 as the military services begin to stand down, wartime industries begin the slow shift to peacetime production, and returning veterans begin to flood the labor force.

(*photo*) Source: Library of Congress, Prints and Photographs Division [LC-USF34-018310-D]

ROOSEVELT COALITION A dramatic political realignment was now clearly in place, as important as the Republican rise to power in 1896. The Democrats reigned as the new majority party for the next 30 years. The "Roosevelt coalition" rested on three pillars: traditional Democratic support in the South; citizens of the big cities, particularly ethnics and African Americans; and labor, both organized and unorganized. The minority Republicans became the party of big business and small towns.

 REVIEW

What were the differences between the "first" and "second" New Deals?

THE NEW DEAL AND THE AMERICAN PEOPLE

BEFORE 1939, FARMERS IN THE Hill Country of Texas spent their evenings in the light of 25-watt kerosene lamps. Their wives washed eight loads of laundry a week, all by hand. Every day, they hauled home 200 gallons—about 1,500 pounds—of water from nearby wells. Farms had no milking machines, no washers, no automatic pumps or water heaters, no refrigerators, and no radios.

RURAL ELECTRIFICATION ADMINISTRATION The reason for this limited life was simple: the Hill Country had no electricity. Thus no agency of the Roosevelt administration changed the way people lived more dramatically than the Rural Electrification Administration (REA), created in 1935. At the time, less than 10 percent of American farms had electricity. Six years later 40 percent did, and by 1950, 90 percent. The New Deal did not always have such a marked impact, and its overall record was mixed. But time and again it changed the lives of ordinary people as government never had before.

The New Deal and Western Water

In September 1936, President Roosevelt pushed a button in Washington, D.C., and sent electricity pulsing westward from the towering Hoover Dam in Nevada (begun under the Hoover administration) to cities as far away as Los Angeles. The waters diverted by the dam irrigated 2.5 million acres, while its floodgates protected millions of people in Southern California, Nevada, and Arizona. In its water management programs, the New Deal further extended federal power, literally across the country.

The Hoover Dam was one of several multipurpose dams completed under the New Deal in the arid West. The aim was simple: to control whole river systems for regional use. Buchanan Dam on the lower Colorado River, the Bonneville and Grand Coulee dams on the Columbia, and many smaller versions curbed floods, generated cheap electricity, and developed river basins from Texas to Washington State. Beginning in 1938 the All-American Canal channeled the Colorado River to irrigate the Imperial Valley in California.

Environmental degradation often accompanied such human intervention. The once-mighty Columbia River, its surging waters checked by dams, flowed sedately from human-made lake to lake, but without the salmon whose spawning runs were also checked. Blocked by the All-American Canal from its path to the sea, the Colorado River slowly turned salty, until by 1950 its waters were unfit for drinking or irrigation.

The Limited Reach of the New Deal

In the spring of 1939 the Daughters of the American Revolution refused to permit the black contralto Marian Anderson to sing at Constitution Hall in Washington, D.C. Eleanor Roosevelt quit the DAR in protest, and Secretary of the Interior Harold Ickes began looking for another site. On a nippy Easter Sunday, in the shadow of the Lincoln Memorial, Anderson finally stepped to the microphone and sang to a crowd of 7,500. Lincoln himself would not have missed the irony.

AFRICAN AMERICANS In 1932 most African Americans cast their ballots as they had since Reconstruction—for Republicans, the party of Abraham

Lincoln and emancipation. But disenchantment with decades of broken promises was spreading, and by 1934 African Americans were voting for Democrats. "Let Jesus lead you and Roosevelt feed you," a black preacher told his congregation on the eve of the 1936 election. When the returns were counted, three of four black voters had cast their ballots for Roosevelt.

The New Deal accounted for this voting revolution. Sympathetic but never a champion, Roosevelt regarded African Americans as one of many groups whose interests he brokered. Even that was an improvement. Federal offices had been segregated since Woodrow Wilson's day. In the 1920s black leaders called Hoover "the man in the lily-White House." Under Roosevelt racial integration slowly returned to government. Supporters of civil rights such as Eleanor

©Spencer Grant/agefotostock/SuperStock

| *California's multiethnic workforce is captured in this detail from one of the murals that adorn Coit Tower, built in 1933 on San Francisco's Telegraph Hill. Like other American muralists, John Langley Howard drew on the work of Mexican artists such as Diego Rivera and David Alfaro Siqueiros to paint murals and frescoes with political themes. Here Howard shows resolute workers rallying on May Day, an international labor holiday commemorating, among other things, the Haymarket Square Riot of 1886.*

Roosevelt and Harold Ickes brought economist Robert C. Weaver and other African American advisors into the administration, forming a "Black Cabinet" to help design federal policy. Mary McLeod Bethune, a sharecropper's daughter and founder of Bethune-Cookman College, ran a division of the National Youth Administration.

Outside of government the Urban League continued to lobby for economic advancement, and the NAACP pressed to make lynching a federal crime. (Though publicly against lynching and privately in favor of an antilynching bill, Roosevelt refused to make it "must" legislation to avoid losing the white southern members of Congress he needed "to save America.") In New York's Harlem, the Reverend John H. Johnson organized the Citizens' League for Fair Play in 1933 to persuade white merchants to hire black clerks. After picketers blocked storefronts, hundreds of African Americans got jobs with Harlem retailers and utility companies. Racial tension over employment and housing continued to run high, and in 1935 Harlem exploded in the only race riot of the decade.

Discrimination persisted under the New Deal. Black newspapers reported hundreds of cases of NRA codes resulting in jobs lost to white workers or wages lower than white rates of pay. Disgusted editors renamed the agency "Negroes Ruined Again." Federal efforts to promote grassroots democracy often gave control of New Deal programs to local governments, where discrimination went unchallenged. New Deal showplaces such as the TVA's model town of Norris, Tennessee, and the homestead village of Arthurdale, West Virginia, were closed to African Americans.

African Americans reaped some benefits from the New Deal. The WPA hired black workers for almost 20 percent of its jobs, even though African Americans made up less than 10 percent of the population. When it was discovered that the WPA was paying black workers less than whites, Roosevelt issued an executive order to halt the practice. Public Works administrator Ickes established the first quota system for hiring black Americans. By 1941 the percentage of African Americans working for the government exceeded their proportion of the population.

MEXICAN AMERICANS   Civil rights was not a priority of the New Deal, and the nearly 1 million Mexican Americans in the United States were never a target of relief or of any efforts to support their rights as citizens. They received even less help than African Americans. Latino culture sometimes frustrated meager federal efforts to help. Mexican folk traditions of self-help inhibited some from seeking aid; others remained unfamiliar with claim procedures. Still others failed to meet residency requirements. Meanwhile, low voter turnout hampered their political influence, and discrimination limited economic advancement.

In the Southwest and California the Civilian Conservation Corps and the Works Progress Administration furnished some jobs, though fewer and for less pay on average than for whites. On Capitol Hill Dennis Chávez of New Mexico, the only Mexican American in the Senate, channeled what funds he could into Spanish-speaking communities. But like African Americans, most Latinos remained mired in poverty. The many Mexican Americans who worked the fields as migratory laborers lay outside the reach of most New Deal programs, which had virtually no impact on them.

| *During the wave of agricultural strikes in California in 1933, Mexican laborers who had been evicted from their homes settled in camps such as this one in Corcoran. The camp held well over 3,000 people, each family providing an old tent or burlap bags for habitation. Makeshift streets were named in honor of Mexican towns and heroes. By chance the field had been occupied previously by a Mexican circus, the Circo Azteca, which provided nightly entertainment.*

Source: Library of Congress, Prints and Photographs Division
[LC-USF344-007487]

Tribal Rights

The New Deal renewed federal interest in Indians. Among the most disadvantaged Americans, Indian families on reservations rarely earned more than $100 a year. Their infant mortality rate was the highest in the country; their life expectancy the shortest; their education level the lowest. Their rate of unemployment was three times the national average.

JOHN COLLIER'S INDIAN REORGANIZATION ACT In the 1930s Indians had no stronger friend in Washington, D.C., than John Collier. For years he had fought as a social worker among the Pueblos to restore tribal culture. As the new commissioner of Indian affairs, he reversed the decades-old policy of assimilation and promoted tribal life. Under the Indian Reorganization Act of 1934, elders were urged to celebrate festivals, artists to work in native styles, children to learn the old languages. A special Court of Indian Affairs removed Indians from state jurisdiction. Tribal governments ruled reservations. Perhaps most important, tribes regained control over Indian land. Since the Dawes Act of 1887 the land had been allotted to individual Indians, who were often forced by poverty to sell to whites. By the end of the 1930s, under Collier's direction, Indian landholding had increased for the first time in years.

Indians split over Collier's policies. The Pueblos, with a strong communal spirit and already functioning communal societies, favored them. The tribes of Oklahoma and the Great Plains tended to oppose them. Individualism, the profit motive, and an unwillingness to share property with other tribe members fed resistance. So did age-old suspicion of all government

programs. And some Indians such as the Navajos genuinely desired assimilation and saw tribal government as a step backward.

A New Deal for Women

As the tides of change washed across the country, a new deal for women was unfolding in Washington. The New Deal's welfare agencies offered unprecedented opportunity for social workers, teachers, and other women who had spent their lives helping the downtrodden. They were already experts on social welfare. Several were friends with professional ties, and together they formed a network of activists in the New Deal promoting women's interests and social reform. Women received federal appointments in unprecedented numbers, serving on the consumers' advisory board of the NRA, helping to administer the relief program, and winning positions on the Social Security Board.

Women also became part of the Democratic Party machinery. Under the leadership of social worker Mary W. "Molly" Dewson, the Women's Division of the Democratic National Committee played a critical role in the election of 1936. Thousands of women mounted a "mouth-to-mouth" campaign, traveling from door to door to drum up support for Roosevelt and other Democrats. When the ballots were tallied, women formed an important part of the new Roosevelt coalition.

Federal appointments and party politics broke new ground for women, but in general the New Deal abided by existing social standards. Gender equality, like racial equality, was never high on its agenda, and women never came close to achieving it. One-quarter of all NRA codes permitted women to be paid less than men, while WPA wages averaged $2 a day

Source: Amy Jones

| In 1937 artist Amy Jones painted life on an Iroquois reservation in the Adirondack Mountains. Indian rates for tuberculosis were high; a doctor and a nurse examine an Indian child for the disease (left side of the painting). On the right, Iroquois women and children weave baskets from wooden splints while Indian workers split logs to be made into splints for baskets. These themes of public health, manual labor, and Indian crafts formed powerful points of emphasis in the New Deal.

more for men. Despite some impressive appointments, the New Deal gave relatively few jobs to women, and when it did, they were often in gender-segregated trades such as sewing. Government employment patterns for women fell were less equitable than even those in the private sector. Most women in the workforce fared better during the Progressive Era.

Reflecting old conceptions of reform, New Dealers placed greater emphasis on aiding and protecting women than on employing them. The Federal Emergency Relief Administration built 17 camps for homeless women in 11 states. Social Security furnished subsidies to mothers with dependent children, and the WPA established emergency nursery schools (which also became the government's first foray into early childhood education). But even federal protection fell short. Social Security, for example, did not cover domestic servants, most of whom were women.

The Rise of Organized Labor

Although women and minorities discovered that the New Deal had limits to the changes it promoted, a powerful union movement arose in the 1930s by taking full advantage of the new climate. At the outset of the Depression barely 6 percent of the labor force belonged to unions. By the end of the decade, nearly a third were union members.

CAWIU FARM STRIKE Though the New Deal left farmworkers outside its coverage, its promise of support encouraged these workers to act on their own. In California, where large agribusinesses employed migrant laborers to pick crops, some 37 strikes involving over 50,000 workers swept the state after Roosevelt took office. The most famous strike broke out in the cotton fields of the San Joaquin Valley under the auspices of the Cannery and Agricultural Workers Industrial Union (CAWIU). Most of the strikers were Mexican, supported more by a complex network of families, friends, and coworkers than by the weak CAWIU. The government finally stepped in to arbitrate a wage

settlement. The strike ended but at a fraction of the pay the workers sought.

Such government support was not enough to embolden the cautious American Federation of Labor (AFL), the nation's premier union. Historically bound to skilled labor and organized on the basis of craft, it paid no attention to unskilled workers, who made up most of the industrial labor force, and virtually ignored women and black workers. The AFL also avoided major industries like rubber, automobiles, and steel, long hostile to unions and employing many workers with few skills.

CONGRESS OF INDUSTRIAL ORGANIZATIONS In 1935 John L. Lewis of the United Mine Workers and the heads of seven other AFL unions announced the formation of the Committee for Industrial Organization (CIO). The AFL suspended the rogue unions in 1936. The CIO, later rechristened the Congress of Industrial Organizations, turned to the unskilled. CIO representatives concentrated on the mighty steel industry, which had clung to the "open," or nonunion, shop since 1919. Unskilled and semi-skilled workers gained a powerful voice at the bargaining table.

(*left*): ©Walter P. Reuther Library/Wayne State University; (*right*): ©Bettmann/Getty Images

| *The wives of workers at a General Motors auto plant in Flint, Michigan, march past windows broken in a battle the day before. The windows were smashed not by the strikers inside the plant but by women who had established an "Emergency Brigade." Rumors had spread that the men inside were being gassed. Women played a vital role in supporting the strikes, collecting and distributing food to strikers and their families, setting up a first-aid station, and furnishing day care. Women of the Emergency Brigade wore red tams and armbands with the initials "EB" as shown here.*

In other industries the rank-and-file did not wait. Emboldened by the recent passage of the Wagner Act, a group of rubber workers in Akron, Ohio, simply sat down on the job in early 1936. Since the strikers occupied the plants, managers could not replace them with strikebreakers. Nor could the rubber companies call in the military or police without risk to their property. The leaders of the United Rubber Workers Union opposed the "sit-downs," but when the Goodyear Tire & Rubber Company laid off 70 workers, 1,400 rubber workers struck on their own. An 11-mile picket line sprang up outside. Eventually Goodyear settled by recognizing the union and accepting its demands on wages and hours.

The biggest strikes erupted in the automobile industry. A series of spontaneous strikes at General Motors plants in Atlanta, Kansas City, and Cleveland spread to Fisher Body No. 2 in Flint, Michigan, late in December 1936. Singing the unionists' anthem, "Solidarity Forever," workers took over the plant while wives, friends, and fellow union members handed food and clothing through the windows. Local police tried to break up supply lines, only to be driven off by a hail of nuts, bolts, coffee mugs, and bottles.

In the wake of this "Battle of Running Bulls" (a reference to the retreating police), Governor Frank Murphy finally called out the National Guard, not to arrest but to protect strikers. General Motors surrendered in February 1937. Less than a month later U.S. Steel capitulated without a strike. By the end of the year every automobile manufacturer except Henry Ford had negotiated with the United Auto Workers.

UNION GAINS Bloody violence accompanied some drives. On Memorial Day 1937, 10 strikers lost their lives when Chicago police fired on them as they marched peacefully toward the Republic Steel plant. And sit-down strikes often alienated an otherwise sympathetic middle class. (In 1939 the Supreme Court outlawed the tactic.) Yet a momentous transfer of power had taken place. Union membership swelled, and the unskilled now had a powerful voice in the form of the CIO. Women's membership in unions tripled between 1930 and 1940, and African Americans also made gains. Independent unions had become a significant part of industrial America.

"Art for the Millions"

No agency of the New Deal touched more Americans than Federal One, the bureaucratic umbrella of the WPA's arts program. For the first time, thousands of unemployed writers, musicians, painters, actors, and photographers went on the federal payroll. Public projects—from massive murals to tiny guidebooks—would make "art for the millions."

A Federal Writers' Project (FWP) produced about a thousand publications. Its 81 state, territorial, and city guides were so popular that commercial publishers happily printed them. Interest in American history peaked during the Depression as people looked to the past for signs of the resilience of the republic. Feeding that interest, the FWP

(*left*) Source: Library of Congress, Prints and Photographs Division [LC-DIG-fsa-8b29516]; (*right*) Source: Library of Congress, Prints and Photographs Division

| "Look in her eyes" read the caption of the photograph on the left, snapped by photojournalist Dorothea Lange in 1936. Titled Migrant Mother, the photo became an icon of the era, depicting the anxiety and desperation of so many Americans as well as the perseverance of 32-year-old peapicker Florence Thompson. Her worry-worn face is framed by her children as they turn away from the camera and lean on their mother for support. Lange took at least six photographs of Thompson and her family for the Farm Security Administration. Other poses were less haunting, as can be seen from the photo on the right where the little girl smiles almost reflexively into the camera. FSA administrators chose the more moving photograph to show the human costs of the Depression and to justify the cost of government programs to help the dispossessed.

collected folklore, studied ethnic groups, and recorded the reminiscences of 200 former slaves. Meanwhile, the Federal Music Project (FMP) employed some 15,000 out-of-work musicians. For a token charge, Americans could hear the music of Bach and Beethoven played by first-rate, previously unemployed musicians. In the Federal Art Project (FAP), artists taught sculpture, painting, and carving while watercolorists and drafters painstakingly prepared the Index of American Design with elaborate illustrations of American material culture, from skillets to cigar-store Indians.

RIVERA AND OROZCO The most notable contribution of the FAP came in the form of murals. Under the influence of Mexican muralists Diego Rivera and José Clemente Orozco, American artists covered the walls of thousands of airports, post offices, and other government buildings with wall paintings glorifying local life and work. The rare treatment of class conflict later opened the FAP to charges of communist infiltration, but most of the murals stressed the enduring qualities of American life: family, work, community.

The Federal Theatre Project (FTP) reached the greatest number of people—some 30 million—and aroused the most controversy. As its head, Hallie Flanagan made government-supported theater vital, daring, and relevant. *Living Newspapers* dramatized headlines of the day. Occasionally, frank depictions of class conflict riled congressional conservatives, and, beginning in 1938, the House Un-American Activities Committee investigated the FTP as "a branch of the Communistic organization." A year later Congress slashed its budget and brought government-sponsored theater to an end.

DOCUMENTARY REALISM The documentary impulse to record life permeated the arts in the 1930s. Novels such as Erskine Caldwell's *Tobacco Road*, feature films such as John Ford's *The Grapes of Wrath*, and such federally funded documentaries as Pare Lorentz's *The River* stirred the social conscience of the country. Photographers produced an unvarnished pictorial record of the Great Depression. Their raw, haunting photographs turned history into propaganda and art. New Dealers had practical motives for promoting documentary realism. They wanted to blunt criticism of New Deal relief measures by documenting the distress.

 REVIEW

How did the New Deal help minorities and workers?

THE END OF THE NEW DEAL (1937–1940)

"I SEE ONE-THIRD OF A nation ill-housed, ill-clad, ill-nourished," the president lamented in his second inaugural address on January 20, 1937 (the first January inauguration under a new constitutional amendment). Industrial output had doubled

since 1932; farm income had almost quadrupled. But full recovery remained elusive. Over 7 million Americans or 14 percent of the labor force were still out of work, and national income was only half again as large as it had been in 1933, when Roosevelt took office. At the height of his popularity, with bulging majorities in Congress, Roosevelt planned to expand the New Deal. Within a year, however, the New Deal was largely over, drowned in a sea of economic and political troubles—many of them Roosevelt's own doing.

Packing the Courts

As Roosevelt's second term began, only the Supreme Court clouded the political horizon. A conservative majority spearheaded a new judicial activism. It rested on a narrow view of the constitutional powers of Congress and the president. As the New Deal broadened those powers, the Supreme Court unleashed a torrent of rulings declaring important parts of Roosevelt's program unconstitutional.

In 1935 the Court wiped out the NRA on the grounds that manufacturing was not involved in interstate commerce and thus lay beyond federal regulation. In 1936 it canceled the AAA, arguing that the Constitution did not permit the government to tax one group (processors) to pay another (farmers). In *Moorehead v. Tipaldo* (1936) the Court ruled a New York minimum-wage law invalid because it interfered with the right of workers to negotiate a contract. A frustrated Roosevelt complained that the Court had created a "'no-man's land,' where no government—State or Federal" could act. The Supreme Court had become a major obstacle to the New Deal.

ROOSEVELT'S PLAN The president's frustration only grew when none of the aged justices seemed ready to resign his lifetime appointment. Roosevelt was the first president since James Monroe to serve four years without making a Supreme Court appointment. Among federal judges Republicans outnumbered Democrats by more than two to one in 1933. Roosevelt intended to redress the balance with legislation that added new judges to the federal bench, including the Supreme Court. The federal courts were overburdened and too many judges "aged or infirm," he declared in February 1937. In the interests of efficiency, he proposed to "vitalize" the judiciary with new members. When a 70-year-old judge who had served at least 10 years failed to retire, the president could add another, up to 6 to the Supreme Court and 44 to the lower federal courts.

Roosevelt badly miscalculated. He regarded courts as political, not sacred, institutions and had ample precedent for altering even the Supreme Court. As recently as 1869 Congress had increased its size to nine. But in the midst of the Depression-spawned crisis, most Americans clung to the courts as symbols of stability. Few accepted Roosevelt's efficiency argument, and no one on Capitol Hill—with its share of 70-year-olds—believed that seven decades of life necessarily made one too infirm to work. Worse still, the proposal ignited conservative-liberal antagonisms within the Democratic Party, where many conservatives abandoned him.

THE COURT REVERSES DIRECTION Suddenly the Court reversed itself. In April, *N.L.R.B. v. Jones and Laughlin Steel Corporation* upheld the Wagner Act by one vote. A month later the justices sustained the Social Security Act as a legitimate exercise of the commerce power. When Justice Willis Van Devanter, the oldest and most conservative justice, retired later that year, Roosevelt at last made his first appointment to the Supreme Court.

With Democrats deserting him, the president accepted a substitute measure that ignored his proposal to appoint new judges. Roosevelt nonetheless claimed victory. After all, the Court shifted course. And eventually he appointed nine Supreme Court justices. But victory came at a high price. The momentum of the 1936 election was squandered and the unity of the Democratic Party undermined. Opponents learned that Roosevelt could be beaten. Even more politically damaging, a conservative coalition of Republicans and rural Democrats had come together around the first of several anti–New Deal causes.

The End of the New Deal

As early as 1936 Secretary of the Treasury Henry Morgenthau began to plead for fiscal restraint. With productivity rising and unemployment falling, he argued that it was time to reduce spending, balance the budget, and permit business to lead the recovery. "Strip off the bandages, throw away the crutches," and let the economy "stand on its own feet," he said.

Morgenthau was preaching to the converted. Although the president had been willing to run budget deficits in the crisis, he was never comfortable with them. Still, some experts believed he was on the right track. In a startling new theory British economist John Maynard Keynes called on government not to balance the budget but to spend its way out of depression, even if it meant running up deficits. When prosperity returned, Keynes argued, government could pay off its debts through tax increases. This deliberate policy of "countercyclical" action (spending in bad times, taxing in good) would compensate for swings in the economy.

THE DEPRESSION ABROAD Keynes's theory was precisely the path chosen by several industrial nations in which recovery came more quickly than in the United States. Germany for one built its rapid recuperation on spending. When Adolf Hitler and his National Socialist (Nazi) Party came to power in 1933, they went on a spending spree, constructing huge highways called *Autobahns,* enormous government buildings, and other public works. Later they spent lavishly as they armed for war. Between 1933 and 1939 the German national debt almost quadrupled, while in the

United States it rose by barely 50 percent. For Germans the price in lost freedoms was incalculable, but by 1936 their depression was over.

Not all nations relied on military spending. And many of them, such as Great Britain and France, had not shared in the economic expansion of the 1920s, which meant their economies had a shorter distance to rise in order to reach pre-Depression levels. Yet spending of one kind or another helped light the path to recovery in country after country. In Great Britain, for example, low interest rates plus government assistance to the needy ignited a housing boom, while government subsidies to the automobile industry and to companies willing to build factories in depressed areas slowed the slide. By 1937 Britain had halved unemployment.

THE ROOSEVELT RECESSION In the United States, Roosevelt ordered cuts in federal spending early in 1937. Within six months the economy sputtered. At the end of the year, unemployment stood at 10.5 million as the "Roosevelt recession" deepened. Finally, with the jobless rate approaching 20 percent of the labor force, spenders convinced him to propose a $3.75 billion omnibus measure in April 1938. Facing an election, Congress happily reversed spending cuts, quadrupled farm subsidies, and embarked on a new shipbuilding program. The economy revived but never recovered. Keynesian economics was vindicated, though it would take decades before becoming widely accepted.

With Roosevelt vulnerable, conservatives in Congress struck, pressing their own agenda to cut federal authority and spending. They trimmed public housing programs and

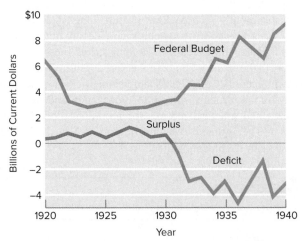

Federal Budget and Surplus/Deficit, 1920–1940

During the 1920s the federal government ran a modest surplus as spending dropped sharply after World War I. Deficits grew steadily as Franklin Roosevelt's New Deal spent boldly and as revenues from taxes and tariffs continued to shrink. In 1937 federal spending cuts to balance the budget reduced the deficit but brought on a recession that was quickly followed by renewed federal spending and increasing deficits.

minimum wage guarantees in the South. The president's few successes came where he could act alone, principally in a renewed attack on big business. At his urging the Justice Department opened investigations of corporate concentration. Even Congress responded by creating the Temporary National Economic Committee to examine corporate abuses and recommend revisions in the antitrust laws. These were small consolations. The president, wrote Interior Secretary Harold Ickes in August 1938, "is punch drunk from the punishment."

Vainly, Roosevelt fought back in the arena of campaign politics. In the off-year elections of 1938 he tried to purge Democrats who had deserted him. The five senators he targeted for defeat all won. Republicans posted gains in the House and Senate and won 13 governorships. Democrats still held majorities in both houses, but conservatives now had the votes to block new programs. The New Deal passed into history.

The Legacy of the New Deal

The New Deal lasted only five years, from 1933 to 1938, and it never spent enough to end the Depression. Though it pledged itself to the "forgotten" Americans, it failed to help the neediest among them: sharecroppers, tenant farmers, migrant workers. In many ways it was quite conservative. It left capitalism intact and overturned few cultural conventions. Even its reforms followed the old progressive formula of softening industrialism by strengthening the state.

For all its conservatism and continuities the New Deal left a legacy of change. Government assumed a broader role in the economy. To regulation was now added the complicated task of maintaining economic stability—compensating for swings in the business cycle. In its securities and banking regulations, unemployment insurance, and requirements for wages and hours, the New Deal created stabilizers to avoid future breakdowns.

What the New Deal Did . . .

	RELIEF	RECOVERY	REFORM
FOR THE FARMER	Rural electrifification Administration (1936) Farm Security Administration (1937)	Agriculture Adjustment Act (1933)	
FOR THE WORKER		National Industrial Recovery Act (1933)	National Labor Relations Act (1935) Fair Labor Standards Act (1938)
FOR THE MIDDLE CLASS	Home Owners Loan Act (1934)		Revenue ("Wealth Tax") Act (1935) Public Utilities Holding Company Act (1935)
FOR THE NEEDY	Federal Emergency Relief Act (1933) Civilian Conservation Corps (1933) Civil Works Administration (1933) National Public Housing Act (1937) Emergency Relief Appropriation Act (1935)		
FOR PROTECTION AGAINST FUTURE DEPRESSIONS			Federal Deposit Insurance Corporation (1933) Securities Exchange Act (1934) Social Security Act (1935)

Franklin Roosevelt and the New Dealers modernized the presidency. They turned the White House into the heart of government. Americans looked to the president to set the public agenda, spread new ideas, initiate legislation, and assume responsibility for fixing the nation. The power of Congress diminished, but the size and scope of government grew. In 1932 there were 605,000 federal employees; by 1939 there were nearly a million (and by 1945, after World War II, some 3.5 million). The many programs of the New Deal touched the lives of ordinary Americans as government never had done before, made them more secure, bolstered the middle class, and formed the outlines of a new welfare state.

At a time when dictators and militarists came to power in Germany, Italy, Japan, and Russia, the New Deal strengthened democracy in America. Roosevelt acted as a political broker, responding first to one group, then to another. His "broker state" embraced groups previously spurned: unions, farm organizations, ethnic minorities, women. During the 1930s the United States found a middle way to avoid the extremes of communism and fascism. The broker state had limits. The unorganized, whether in city slums or in sharecroppers' shacks, often found themselves on their own.

Under the New Deal the Democratic Party dominated politics. In a quiet revolution African Americans came into the party, joining workers and farmers. Political attention shifted to from cultural battles over Prohibition and immigration restriction to bread-and-butter issues of economic security—unemployment, labor relations, tax reform, public housing, and the TVA. Perhaps most important of all, Americans now assumed that in hard times government would help them, in Roosevelt's words, "not as a matter of charity but as a matter of social duty."

 REVIEW

What did the New Deal accomplish, and what did it fail to accomplish?

PUTTING HISTORY IN GLOBAL CONTEXT

THE DEPRESSION SHOOK BOTH the political and material pillars of democratic culture—even more turbulently around the world than at home. By 1939, on the eve of World War II, the Soviet Union, Germany, and Italy were firmly under the control of dictators bent on expanding both their powers and their nations' territory. The number of European democracies shrank from 27 to 10. Latin America was ruled by a variety of dictators and military juntas, little different from the new despots of Europe. China suffered not only from invasion by Japan's militarists but also from the corrupt and ineffectual one-party dictatorship of Chiang Kai-shek.

The New Deal attempted to combat the Depression through the methods of parliamentary democracy, expanding government to humanize industrial society and generate prosperity. New Dealers from the president down nonetheless recognized that the federal government could not do everything. But "it bought us time to think," commented Eleanor Roosevelt in 1939. Even as she spoke those words a measure of doubt crept into her voice. "Is it going to be worthwhile?" With the threat of war on the horizon, only future generations would know for certain.

CHAPTER SUMMARY

The Great Depression of the 1930s was the longest in the history of the nation; it forced virtually all Americans to live leaner lives, and it spawned Franklin Roosevelt's New Deal.

- The Great Depression acted as a great leveler that reduced differences in income and status and left many Americans with an "invisible scar" of shame, self-doubt, and lost confidence.

  ► Unemployment and suffering were especially acute among agricultural migrants, African Americans, Latinos, and American Indians.

  ► Rates of marriage and birth declined in all social classes, and many women found themselves working additional hours inside and outside the home to supplement family incomes.

  ► Popular culture rallied to reinforce basic tenets of American life: middle-class morality, family, capitalism, and democracy.

- President Herbert Hoover represented a transition from the old, do-nothing policies of the past to the interventionist policies of the future. In the end, his program of voluntary cooperation and limited government activism failed, and in 1932 he lost the presidency to Franklin Roosevelt.

- Roosevelt's New Deal attacked the Great Depression along three broad fronts: recovery for the economy, relief for the needy, and reforms to ward off future depressions.

- The New Deal failed to achieve full recovery but did result in lasting changes:

  ► The creation of economic stabilizers such as federal insurance for bank deposits, unemployment assistance, and greater control over money and banking that were designed to compensate for swings in the economy.

  ► The establishment of a limited welfare state to provide minimum standards of well-being for all Americans.

  ► The revitalization of the Democratic party and the formation of a powerful new political coalition of labor, urban ethnics, women, African Americans, and the South.

  ► The modernization of the presidency.

Digging Deeper

The best overall examination of the Great Depression and the Second World War is David M. Kennedy's *Freedom from Fear: The American People in Depression and War, 1929-1945* (1999). For a comparative look at responses to the Great Depression, see John A. Garraty, *The Great Depression* (1987); and Wolfgang Schivelbusch, *Three New Deals: Reflections on Roosevelt's America, Mussolini's Italy, and Hitler's Germany, 1933-1939* (2006). Robert S. Sobel, *The Great Bull Market: Wall Street in the 1920s* (1968), is a brief, evenhanded study. Caroline Bird, *The Invisible Scar* (1966), remains the most sensitive treatment of the human impact of the Great Depression, but see also Studs Terkel, *Hard Times: An Oral History of the Great Depression* (1970); and Robert McElvaine, *The Great Depression: America, 1929-1941* (1984). Joan Hoff Wilson, *Herbert Hoover: Forgotten Progressive* (1975), makes clear Hoover's progressive impulses.

William E. Leuchtenburg, *Franklin D. Roosevelt and the New Deal, 1932-1940* (1963), remains the best single-volume study of the New Deal and falls within the liberal tradition of New Deal scholarship that is admiringly critical of Roosevelt's use of power. Jean Edward Smith's *FDR* (2007) is the best single-volume biography of Roosevelt and offers a positive, if critical, reinterpretation with greater emphasis on his personal life. For sharp criticism of New Left historians, see Paul K. Conkin, *The New Deal* (1967). Alan Lawson's *A Commonwealth of Hope* (2006) argues that the New Deal was less a makeshift reaction to the Great Depression and more a part of a longer tradition of planning and reform. Amity Shlaes, *The Forgotten Man: A New History of the Great Depression* (New York, 2007), provides a conservative critique of the New Deal that rests on stories of "forgotten" men and women and argues that its policies actually prolonged the Great Depression. Douglas Brinkley's *Rightful Heritage: Franklin D. Roosevelt and the Land of America* (2016) explores Roosevelt's conservation efforts with a broad brush. Ira Katznelson, *Fear Itself: The New Deal and the Origins of Our Time* (2013), stresses the importance of fear in shaping the New Deal's broker state.

Eleanor Roosevelt is analyzed in rich detail and from a frankly feminist viewpoint in Blanche Wiesen Cook, *Eleanor Roosevelt*, 3 vols. (1992-2016). For a biography of the second-most powerful female New Dealer, see Kirsten Downey, *The Woman Behind the New Deal: The Life and Legacy of Frances Perkins—Social Security, Unemployment Insurance, and the Minimum Wage* (2009). Susan Ware, *Beyond Suffrage: Women in the New Deal* (1981), locates a women's political network within the New Deal. Lauren Rebecca Sklaroff's *Black Culture and the New Deal: The Quest for Civil Rights in the Roosevelt Era* (2009) looks at the New Deal's support for black writers, artists, and intellectuals. The culture and politics of working men and women during the Great Depression are the subject of Lisabeth Cohen, *Making a New Deal: Industrial Workers in Chicago, 1919-1939* (1990). Morris Dickstein's *Dancing in the Dark: A Cultural History of the Great Depression* (2009) evokes the era's pure fantasy on the one hand and its penetrating social criticism on the other. Linda Gordon, *Dorothea Lange: A Life Beyond Limits* (2009), depicts this pioneering photojournalist as a searing social critic with a camera eye for the downtrodden but no heart for revolution. For a probing analysis of New Deal liberalism and its retreat from reform, see Alan Brinkley, *The End of Reform* (1995). In Jill Lepore's *The Secret History of Wonder Woman* (2015), the most popular superheroine of all time becomes part of the women's rights movement. Food, increasingly a focus of historical scholarship, is the subject of Jane Ziegelman and Andrew Coe's *A Square Meal: A Culinary History of the Great Depression* (2016).

26 America's Rise to Globalism

1927–1945

Aircraft carriers and the planes that launched from their decks proved to be instrumental to winning the war against Japan in the vast spaces of the Pacific Ocean. Fortunately for the United States, most carriers were not anchored at Pearl Harbor when the Japanese carried out their surprise attack. As each plane lands here, handling crews are shown rushing to move it off the landing area and forward where it could be serviced. In the foreground (*right*), the Air Control Officer and Group Commander monitor operations from what was known as the "bird cage."

Source: Gift of Abbott Laboratories/Naval History and Heritage Command

>> An American Story

"OH BOY"

John Garcia, a native Hawaiian pipe fitter's apprentice at the Pearl Harbor Navy Yard in Honolulu, planned a lazy Sunday for December 7, 1941. By the time his grandmother rushed in to wake him that morning at eight, he had already missed the worst of it. "The Japanese were bombing Pearl Harbor," he recalled her yelling at him. John listened in disbelief. "I said, 'They're just practicing.'" "No," his grandmother replied. It was real. He catapulted his huge frame from the bed, ran to the front porch, and caught sight of the antiaircraft fire in the sky. "Oh boy" were his only words.

Hopping on his motorcycle, Garcia sped the 4 miles to the harbor in 10 minutes. "It was a mess," he remembered. The USS *Shaw* was in flames. The battleship *Pennsylvania,* a bomb

| *The battleship West Virginia in flames at Pearl Harbor*

nesting one deck above the powder and ammunition, was about to blow. When ordered to put out its fires, he refused. "There ain't no way I'm gonna go down there," he told the navy officer. Instead, he spent the rest of the day pulling bodies from the water. There were so many, he lost count. Surveying the wreckage the following morning, he noted that the battleship *Arizona* "was a total washout." So was the *West Virginia*. The *Oklahoma* had "turned turtle, totally upside down." It took two weeks to get all the fires out.

The World War, spreading since 1937, had largely spared the United States until December 7. Suddenly the surprise attack at Pearl Harbor transformed the Pacific into an avenue of potential assault. Dennis Keegan, a young college student at the University of San Francisco, could not believe the radio reports on Pearl Harbor. "These places were so far away from us," he remembered. "It just didn't seem possible that we were at war."

All along the West Coast panic spread. That night downtown San Francisco was "bedlam." "The United Artists Theater had a huge marquee with those dancing lights, going on and off," Keegan recalled, "People were throwing everything they could to put those lights out, screaming Blackout! Blackout!" The next day a false army report of 30 Japanese planes flying toward the coast set off triggered air-raid sirens throughout the city. Los Angeles turned trigger happy. A young police officer named Tom Bradley (who later served as mayor of the city) heard "sirens going off, aircraft guns firing." "Here we are in the middle of the night," he said; "there was no enemy in sight, but somebody thought they saw the enemy." In

January 1942 worried officials moved the Rose Bowl from Pasadena, California, to Durham, North Carolina. Though overheated, their fears were not entirely imaginary. Japanese submarines shelled an oil facility near Santa Barbara and Fort Stevens in Oregon. Balloons carrying incendiary devices caused several deaths in Oregon.

Although the Japanese would never invade the mainland, in a world with long-range bombers and submarines no place seemed safe. The global scale of this war was unprecedented. Arrayed against the Axis powers of Germany, Italy, and Japan were the Allies—Great Britain, the Soviet Union, the United States, China, and the Free French. Their armies fought from the Arctic to the southwestern Pacific, in the great cities of Europe and Asia and the small villages of North Africa and Indochina, in malarial jungles and scorching deserts, on six continents and across four oceans. Perhaps as many as 100 million people took up arms; some 40 to 50 million lost their lives.

Tragedy on such a scale taught a generation of Americans that they could no longer isolate themselves from any part of the world, no matter how remote. Manchuria, Ethiopia, and Poland had once seemed far away to many Americans, yet the road to war had led from those distant places to the United States. Retreat into isolation had not cured the worldwide depression or preserved the peace. To avoid other such disasters, the United States eventually assumed a far wider role in managing the world's geopolitical and economic systems. <<

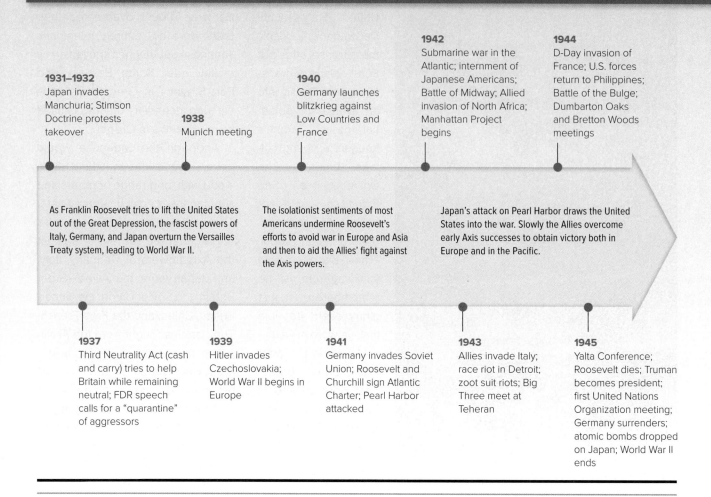

1931–1932
Japan invades Manchuria; Stimson Doctrine protests takeover

1938
Munich meeting

1940
Germany launches blitzkrieg against Low Countries and France

1942
Submarine war in the Atlantic; internment of Japanese Americans; Battle of Midway; Allied invasion of North Africa; Manhattan Project begins

1944
D-Day invasion of France; U.S. forces return to Philippines; Battle of the Bulge; Dumbarton Oaks and Bretton Woods meetings

As Franklin Roosevelt tries to lift the United States out of the Great Depression, the fascist powers of Italy, Germany, and Japan overturn the Versailles Treaty system, leading to World War II.

The isolationist sentiments of most Americans undermine Roosevelt's efforts to avoid war in Europe and Asia and then to aid the Allies' fight against the Axis powers.

Japan's attack on Pearl Harbor draws the United States into the war. Slowly the Allies overcome early Axis successes to obtain victory both in Europe and in the Pacific.

1937
Third Neutrality Act (cash and carry) tries to help Britain while remaining neutral; FDR speech calls for a "quarantine" of aggressors

1939
Hitler invades Czechoslovakia; World War II begins in Europe

1941
Germany invades Soviet Union; Roosevelt and Churchill sign Atlantic Charter; Pearl Harbor attacked

1943
Allies invade Italy; race riot in Detroit; zoot suit riots; Big Three meet at Teheran

1945
Yalta Conference; Roosevelt dies; Truman becomes president; first United Nations Organization meeting; Germany surrenders; atomic bombs dropped on Japan; World War II ends

THE UNITED STATES IN A TROUBLED WORLD

THE OUTBREAK OF WORLD WAR II had its roots in the aftermath of World War I. So vast was the devastation of the Great War that the victors suffered almost as much as the vanquished. Some of the victorious as well as most of the defeated nations were deeply dissatisfied with the peace terms adopted at Versailles. Over the next two decades Germany, the Soviet Union, Italy, Poland, and Japan all sought to achieve unilaterally what Allied leaders had denied them at Versailles. In central and eastern Europe rivalry among fascists, communists, National Socialists, and other political factions led to frequent violence and instability. Reparations imposed at Versailles shackled Germany's economy. As Germany struggled to recover, so did all of Europe. Although the United States possessed the resources to ease international tensions, it declined to lead in world affairs. It even rejected membership in the League of Nations.

Conflict in China

A preference for isolation did not mean the United States could simply ignore foreign affairs. In assuming colonial control over the Philippines, Americans acquired a major interest in the western Pacific that created a potentially dangerous rivalry with Japan. The United States had also committed itself to an open-door policy (Chapter 21) to prevent foreign powers from dividing China. That temptation seemed especially great during the 1920s, because China was wracked by civil war. In 1927 the Nationalist Party, led by Chiang Kai-shek, consolidated power by attacking their former Communist Party allies.

The Japanese had long dominated Korea, and during the 1920s they expanded their influence on the Chinese mainland. In 1931 Japanese agents staged an explosion on a rail line in Manchuria (meant to appear as if carried out by Chinese nationalists) that provided Japan with an excuse to occupy the whole province. A year later Japan converted Manchuria into a puppet state called Manchukuo.

STIMSON DOCTRINE Here was a direct threat to the Versailles system and the open door. But neither the major powers in Europe nor the United States were willing to risk a war with Japan over China. President Hoover would allow Secretary of State Henry Stimson only to protest that the United States would refuse to recognize Japan's takeover of Manchuria. The policy of "nonrecognition" became known as the Stimson Doctrine, even though Stimson himself doubted its worth. He was right to be skeptical. Three weeks later Japan's imperial navy shelled the Chinese port city of Shanghai. When the League of Nations condemned Japan in 1933, the Japanese withdrew from the League. The seeds of war in Asia had been sown.

Becoming a Good Neighbor

GOOD NEIGHBOR POLICY Trouble abroad encouraged the United States to improve relations with nations closer to home. By the late 1920s the United States had intervened in Latin America so often that the Roosevelt Corollary

©Everett Collection, Inc/Alamy

| As war broke out in Europe, Roosevelt's Good Neighbor policy became even more important in cementing alliances in South America. To that end the State Department commissioned a goodwill tour that sent movie studio head Walt Disney to several Latin American nations, some of whom had friendly relations with Nazi Germany. The end result was a documentary of the trip, Saludos Amigos, interspersed with animated films in which the popular Donald Duck created mayhem with a new Latin animated character, Joe Carioca, "the Brazilian Jitterbird."

(Chapter 22) had become an embarrassment. Slowly, Washington began to abandon some of its high-handed policies. In 1927, when Mexico confiscated American-owned properties, President Coolidge sent an ambassador, instead of the marines, to settle the dispute. In 1933, when some critics compared the American position in Nicaragua to Japan's in Manchuria, Secretary Stimson ordered U.S. troops to withdraw. In those gestures and in President Hoover's efforts to cultivate goodwill south of the border lay the roots of a "Good Neighbor" policy.

Franklin Roosevelt pushed the good neighbor idea. To Roosevelt that meant correcting the political inequities between the United States and Latin America. At the seventh Pan-American Conference in 1933, his administration accepted a resolution denying any country "the right to intervene in the internal or external affairs of another." The following year he negotiated a treaty with Cuba that renounced the American right to intervene under the Platt Amendment (Chapter 23). Moving forward, the United States would replace direct military presence with indirect (but still substantial) economic influence.

As the threat of war increased during the 1930s, the United States found that its new sense of Pan Americanism promoted cooperation in matters of common defense. In the first visit of an American president to the capital of Argentina, Roosevelt opened the Pan-American Conference in 1936 by declaring that outside aggressors "will find a Hemisphere wholly prepared to consult together for our mutual safety and our mutual good." By the end of 1940 the administration had defense agreements in place with every Latin American country but Argentina. The United States faced the threat of war with the American hemisphere largely secured.

The Quest for Neutrality

THE RISE OF FASCISM During the 1920s Benito Mussolini had appealed to Italian nationalism and fear of communism to gain power in Italy. Spinning dreams of a new Roman empire, Mussolini embodied the rising force of fascism. Mussolini's *Fasci di Combattimento,* or fascists, used terrorism and murder to create an "all-embracing" single-party state, outside which "no human or spiritual values can exist, let alone be desirable." Italian fascists rejected the liberal belief in political parties in favor of a glorified nation-state dominated by the middle class, small businesspeople, and small farmers. Then, on March 5, 1933, one day after the inauguration of Franklin Roosevelt, the German legislature gave Adolf Hitler control of Germany. Riding a wave of anti-communism and anti-Semitism, Hitler's Nazi Party promised to unite all Germans in a Greater Third Reich that would last a thousand years. Just over a week earlier, Yosuke Matsuoka had led the Japanese out of the League of Nations. Governed by militarists, Japan began to carve out its own empire, which it called the Greater East Asia Co-Prosperity Sphere. The rise of fascism and militarism in Europe and Asia brought the world to war.

As much as Roosevelt wanted the United States to play a leading role in world affairs, the nation proved unwilling to follow. "It's a terrible thing to look over your shoulder when you are trying to lead—and to find no one there," he commented during the mid-1930s. Programs to pull the economy out of the Great Depression gained broad support; efforts to resolve crises abroad provoked controversy.

NYE COMMITTEE American involvement in foreign affairs became more difficult in 1935 after Senator Gerald P. Nye of North Dakota held hearings on the role of bankers and munitions makers in World War I. These so-called **merchants of death**, Nye's committee revealed, had made enormous profits during World War I. The Nye Committee report implied, but could not prove, that business interests had even steered the United States into war. "When Americans went into the fray," declared Senator Nye, "they little thought that they were there and fighting to save the skins of American bankers who had bet too boldly on the outcome of the war and had two billions of dollars of loans to the Allies in jeopardy."

INTERNATIONALISTS VERSUS ISOLATIONISTS Such charges provoked debate over how the United States should respond to the growing threats to peace. Internationalists such as the League of Women Voters and former secretary of state Henry Stimson favored a policy of collective security—working actively with other nations. "The only certain way to keep out of a great war is to prevent war," Stimson declared. "The only hope of preventing war . . . is by the earnest, intelligent, and unselfish cooperation of the nations of the world towards that end."

On the other side stood the **isolationists**, united by their firm opposition to war and the conviction that the United States should avoid entangling alliances. Yet many strange bedfellows made up the isolationist movement. It included liberal reformers such as George W. Norris and conservatives such as Robert A. Taft of Ohio, a concentration of midwesterners as well as major leaders from both coasts, and a number of Democrats as well as leading Republicans. Pacifists added yet another element to the debate.

Neutrality Legislation

Roused by the Nye Committee hearings, Congress debated the Neutrality Act of 1935, which prohibited the sale of arms to all belligerents in time of war. Internationalists protested: the embargo should apply only to aggressor nations. Otherwise, aggressors could strike when they had an advantage over their victims. A troubled Roosevelt argued that, without the power to apply the embargo selectively, the Neutrality Act might "drag us into war rather than keeping us out."

The limitations of the Neutrality Act became immediately apparent. In October 1935 Benito Mussolini ordered Italian forces into the North African country of Ethiopia. Against tanks and planes, the troops of Emperor Haile Selassie fought with spears and flintlock rifles. Roosevelt immediately invoked the act in hopes of depriving Italy of war goods. Unfortunately for Roosevelt, Italy needed not arms but oil, steel, and copper—materials not included under the Neutrality Act. When Secretary of State Cordell Hull called for a "moral embargo" on such goods, hard-pressed American businesses shipped them anyway. With no effective opposition from the

| A flag company of Hitler Youth parades past its Führer, *Adolf Hitler (centered in the balcony doorway). Hitler's shrewd use of patriotic and party symbols, mass rallies, and marches exploited the possibilities for mass politics and propaganda.*
©Alan Band/Keystone/Getty Images

League of Nations or the United States, Mussolini quickly completed his conquest. In a second Neutrality Act, Congress added a ban on loans or credits to belligerents.

Neutrality legislation also encouraged Nazi dictator Adolf Hitler to launch military operations. In March 1936 German troops thrust into the demilitarized area west of the Rhine River. This flagrant act violated the Treaty of Versailles. As Hitler shrewdly calculated, Britain and France did nothing, while the League of Nations sputtered out a worthless condemnation. Roosevelt remained aloof. The Soviet Union's lonely call for collective action fell on deaf ears.

SPANISH CIVIL WAR Then came a rebellion against Spain's fledgling democracy. In July 1936 Generalissimo Francisco Franco, made bold by Hitler's success, sought to overthrow the newly elected Popular Front government. The civil war that followed became a staging ground for World War II. Hitler and Mussolini sent supplies, weapons, and troops to Franco's Fascists, while the Soviet Union and Mexico aided the left-leaning government. The war divided opinion in Europe and America. Catholics supported the anticommunist Franco forces. Leftists, including 3,000 Americans who called themselves the Abraham Lincoln brigade, backed the democratic government. In the face of domestic political divisions, Roosevelt refused to take sides in the conflict. Lacking vital resources, the Spanish Republic fell to Franco in 1939.

CASH-AND-CARRY Congress sought a way to allow American trade to continue (and thus to promote economic recovery at home) without drawing the nation into war. Under new "cash-and-carry" provisions in the Neutrality Act of 1937, belligerents could buy supplies other than munitions. But they would have to pay beforehand and carry the supplies on their own ships. If war spread, these terms favored the British, whose navy would ensure that supplies reached England.

AGGRESSION IN CHINA But the policy of cash-and-carry hurt China. In 1937 Japanese forces pushed into its southern regions. In order to give China continued access to American goods, Roosevelt refused to invoke the Neutrality Act, which would have cut off trade with both nations. But Japan had by far a greater volume of trade with the United States. Because the president lacked the freedom to impose a selective embargo, Japan could use American resources to support the invasion.

Inching toward War

QUARANTINE SPEECH With Italy, Germany, and Japan fully armed, war seemed inevitable in both Europe and Asia. The three militant nations signed the Anti-Comintern Pact in 1937. On the face of it, the pact was merely a pledge of mutual support against the Soviet Union. But the Rome-Berlin-Tokyo axis freed those nations for further expansion. Roosevelt groped for a way to contain the Axis powers—these "bandit nations." In his first foreign policy speech in 14 months, he called for an international "quarantine" of aggressor nations.

©Central Press/Getty Images

| *"I believe it is peace in our time," announced Prime Minister Neville Chamberlain, who flourished the agreement he and Hitler signed at Munich, promising to resolve differences peacefully. Hitler overran Czechoslovakia six months later.*

Most newspaper editorials applauded his remarks, yet the American public remained skeptical, and Roosevelt quickly retreated. When Japanese planes sank the American gunboat *Panay* on China's Yangtze River in December, only two months later, he meekly accepted an apology for the unprovoked attack.

APPEASEMENT In Europe the Nazi menace continued to grow as German troops marched into Austria in 1938. Hitler then insisted that the 3.5 million ethnic Germans in the Sudetenland of Czechoslovakia be brought into the Reich. With Germany threatening to invade Czechoslovakia, the leaders of France and Britain flew to Munich in September 1938, where they struck a deal to appease Hitler. Czechoslovakia would give up the Sudetenland in return for German pledges to seek no more territory in Europe. When British prime minister Neville Chamberlain returned to England, he told cheering crowds that the Munich Pact would bring "peace in our time." Six months later, in open contempt for the European democracies, Hitler took over the remainder of Czechoslovakia. **"Appeasement"** became synonymous with betrayal, weakness, and surrender.

Hitler's Invasion

By 1939 Hitler made little secret that he intended to recapture territory lost to Poland after World War I. Russia was the key to his success. If Soviet leader Joseph Stalin joined the Western powers, Hitler might face war on two fronts. But Stalin suspected that the West hoped to turn Hitler against the Soviet Union. On August 24, 1939, the foreign ministers of Russia and Germany signed a nonaggression pact, shocking the rest of the world. The secret protocols of the agreement freed Hitler to invade Poland without having to fight a war with enemies attacking on two fronts. Stalin could extend his western borders by bringing eastern Poland, the Baltic states (Latvia, Estonia, and Lithuania), and parts of Romania and Finland into the Soviet sphere.

GERMANY BEGINS WORLD WAR II   On the hot Saturday of September 1, 1939, German tanks and troops surged into Poland. "It's come at last," Roosevelt sighed. "God help us all." Within days France and England declared war on Germany. Stalin quickly moved into eastern Poland, where German and Russian armor took just three weeks to crush the Polish cavalry. As Hitler consolidated his hold on eastern Europe, Stalin invaded Finland.

Once spring arrived in 1940, Hitler moved to protect his sea lanes by capturing Denmark and Norway. The French retreated behind their Maginot Line, a steel and concrete fortification at the German border. Undeterred, German panzer divisions supported by air power knifed through Belgium and Holland in a blitzkrieg—a "lightning war." The Low Countries fell in 23 days, giving the Germans a route into France. By May a third of a million British and French troops had been driven back onto the Atlantic beaches of Dunkirk. Only a strenuous rescue effort, staged by the Royal Navy and a flotilla of English pleasure craft, saved them. The way was clear for the Germans to march to Paris.

On June 22, less than six weeks after the German invasion, France capitulated. Hitler insisted that the surrender come in the very railway car in which Germany had submitted in 1918. William Shirer, an American war correspondent standing 50 yards away, watched the dictator through binoculars: "He swiftly snaps his hands on his hips, arches his shoulders, plants his feet wide apart. It is a magnificent gesture of defiance, of burning contempt for this place and all that it has stood for in the twenty-two years since it witnessed the humbling of the German Empire."

Steps Short of War

Now, only Britain stood between Hitler and the United States. If the Nazis defeated the British fleet, what would prevent the Atlantic Ocean from becoming a gateway to the Americas? Isolationism suddenly seemed dangerous. By the spring of 1940 Roosevelt was openly aiding the Allied war effort. In May he requested funds to motorize the army (it had only 350 tanks) and build 50,000 airplanes a year (fewer than 3,000 existed, most outmoded). Over isolationist protests he soon persuaded Congress to adopt a bill for the first peacetime draft in history.

BATTLE OF BRITAIN   That summer thousands of German fighter planes and heavy bombers struck targets in England. In the Battle of Britain, Hitler and his air chief, Hermann Goering, sought to soften up England for a German invasion from occupied France. Radio reporters relayed graphic descriptions of London in flames and Royal Air Force pilots putting up a heroic defense. Such tales convinced a majority of Americans that the United States should help Britain win the war, though few favored military involvement.

LEND-LEASE AID   In the 1940 election campaign both Roosevelt and his Republican opponent, Wendell Willkie, favored an internationalist course short of war. In defeating Willkie, Roosevelt promised voters that "your boys are not going to be sent into any foreign wars." He portrayed the United States, instead, as "the great arsenal of democracy." Because the British no longer could pay for arms under the provisions of cash-and-carry, Roosevelt proposed a scheme to "lease, lend, or otherwise dispose of" arms and supplies to countries whose defense was vital to the United States. That meant sending supplies to England on the dubious premise that they would be returned when the war ended. Roosevelt likened "lend-lease" to lending a garden hose to a neighbor whose house was on fire. Isolationist senator Robert Taft thought a comparison to "chewing gum" more apt: after a neighbor used it, "you don't want it back." In March 1941 Congress rejected isolationism, passing the Lend-Lease Act by a large majority.

Step by step Roosevelt led the United States to the verge of war in Europe. Then, in June 1941 Hitler, ever audacious, launched a surprise invasion of the Soviet Union. The Allies expected a swift Russian collapse. Soviet armies had fought poorly in the Finnish War, and Stalin in a series of purges three years earlier had executed much of his officer corps. But when the Russians threw up a heroic resistance, Roosevelt extended lend-lease to the Soviet Union.

©Everett Collection Historical/Alamy

| *During World War II President Franklin Roosevelt and British Prime Minister Winston Churchill developed the closest relationship ever between an American president and the head of another government. These distant cousins shared a sense of the continuities of Anglo-American culture and of the global strategy for pursuing the war to a successful end. In 1943, FDR took Churchill fishing at the Maryland presidential retreat Roosevelt named "Shangri-La," today known as Camp David.*

In August 1941 Roosevelt took a secret voyage to Argentia Bay off the coast of Newfoundland. There he met Britain's new war prime minister, Winston Churchill. Almost every day since England and Germany had gone to war, the two leaders had exchanged phone calls, letters, or cables. The Argentia meetings cemented this partnership—one key to Allied victory. Roosevelt and Churchill also drew up the Atlantic Charter, a statement of principles that the two nations held in common. The charter condemned "Nazi tyranny" and embraced the "Four Freedoms"—freedom of speech and expression, freedom of worship, freedom from want, and freedom from fear. In effect, the Atlantic Charter was an unofficial statement of war aims. It put humanitarian values ahead of narrow interests.

By the time of the Argentia meetings, American destroyers in the North Atlantic were stalking German U-boats and reporting their whereabouts to British commanders. Given the harsh weather and aggressive American policy, incidents were inevitable. In October a U-boat sank the destroyer *Reuben James* with the loss of more than 100 American sailors. That attack increased public support for the Allied cause. Yet as late as September 1941, eight of ten Americans opposed entering the hostilities. Few in the United States suspected that an attack by Japan, not Germany, would bring a unified America into the war.

Disaster in the Pacific

Worried most by the prospect of a German victory in Europe, Roosevelt avoided a showdown with Japan. The navy, the president told his cabinet, had "not got enough ships to go round, and every little episode in the Pacific means fewer ships in the Atlantic." But precisely because American and European attention lay elsewhere, Japan was emboldened to expand militarily into Southeast Asia.

JAPANESE EXPANSION Japanese leaders viewed their sphere of influence—what they called the Greater East Asia Co-Prosperity Sphere—as an Asian version of the Monroe Doctrine. Japan, the preeminent power in the region, would replace the Europeans as a promoter of economic development. American leaders, however, viewed Japan's invasion of Nationalist China as a threat to the U.S. open-door policy. Even more disturbing, in 1937 and 1938, Japanese soldiers launched a murderous attack on civilians in Nanking, the Chinese capital, leaving hundreds of thousands dead. By the summer of 1941 Japanese forces controlled the Chinese coast and all major cities. When its army marched into French Indochina (present-day Vietnam) in July, Japan stood ready to conquer the entire Southeast Asian peninsula and the oil-rich Dutch East Indies.

Roosevelt believed he had to act. He embargoed trade, froze Japanese assets in American banks, and barred shipments of vital scrap iron and petroleum. Japanese leaders indicated a willingness to negotiate with the United States, but diplomats from both sides were only going through the motions. The two nations' goals were totally at odds. Japan demanded that its conquests be recognized; the United States insisted that Japan withdraw from China and renounce the alliance it had made with Germany and Italy in 1940. As negotiations sputtered on, the Japanese secretly prepared for an attack on American positions in Guam, the Philippines, and Hawaii.

PEARL HARBOR In late November American intelligence located, and then lost, a Japanese armada in Hitokappu Bay in Japan. Observing strict radio silence, the six carriers and their escorts steamed across the North Pacific toward the American base at Pearl Harbor in Hawaii. On Sunday morning, December 7, 1941, the first wave of Japanese planes roared down on the Pacific Fleet lying at anchor. For more than an hour the Japanese pounded the harbor and nearby airfields. "We were flabbergasted by the devastation," a sailor wrote. Altogether 19 ships—the heart of the Pacific Fleet—were sunk or battered. Practically all of the 200 American aircraft were damaged or destroyed. Only the aircraft carriers, sent to reinforce Midway and Wake Island, escaped the worst naval defeat in American history.

In Washington, Secretary of War Henry Stimson could not believe the news. "My God! This can't be true, this must mean the Philippines." Later that day the Japanese did attack the Philippines, along with Guam, Midway, and British forces in Hong Kong and on the Malay Peninsula. On December 8, Franklin Roosevelt told a stunned nation that "yesterday, December 7, 1941," was "a date which will live in infamy." America, the "reluctant belligerent," was in the war at last. Three days later Hitler declared war on the "half Judaized and the other half Negrified" people of the United States. Italy quickly followed suit.

> ✓ **REVIEW**
>
> What were the major turning points that pushed the United States from isolationism to intervention in World War II?

A GLOBAL WAR

PRIME MINISTER CHURCHILL GREETED THE news of Pearl Harbor with shock but, even more, relief. Great Britain would no longer stand alone in the North Atlantic and the Pacific wars. "We have won the war," he thought, and that night he slept "the sleep of the saved and thankful."

Japan's shocking triumph over U.S. forces united Americans in a way Roosevelt never could. And, as Churchill recognized, only with the Americans fully committed to war could the Allies make full use of the enormous matériel and human resources of the United States. Still, the Allies needed to secure an alliance between the Anglo-American democracies and the Soviet Communist dictatorship. And they needed to find a strategy to win both the war and the peace to follow.

Strategies for War

Within two weeks Churchill was in Washington, meeting with Roosevelt to coordinate production schedules for ships, planes, and armaments. The numbers they announced were so large that some critics openly laughed—at first. A year later combined British, Canadian, and American production boards not only met but exceeded the schedules.

DEFEAT GERMANY FIRST   Roosevelt and Churchill also planned grand strategy. Outraged by the attack on Pearl Harbor, many Americans thought Japan should be the primary target. But the two leaders agreed that Germany posed the greater threat. The Pacific war would be fought as a holding action until the Allies defeated the Nazis. In a global war, in which arms and resources had to be allocated carefully, the Allies faced a daunting future indeed.

Gloomy Prospects

U-BOAT WAR   By summer's end in 1942 the Allies faced defeat. The Nazi military, or *Wehrmacht,* had become the world's deadliest fighting force. Nazi troops were massed outside the Soviet Union's three major cities—Leningrad, Moscow, and Stalingrad. In North Africa General Erwin Rommel, the famed "Desert Fox," swept into Egypt with his Afrika Korps and stood within striking distance of the Suez Canal—a crucial link to the resources of the British Empire. German U-boats in the North Atlantic threatened to break the ocean link between the United States and Britain. U-boat sailors called the first six months of 1942 "the American hunting season" as they sank 400 Allied ships in U.S. territorial waters. So deadly were these "wolfpacks" that merchant sailors developed a grim humor about sleeping. Those on freighters carrying iron ore slept above decks because the heavily laden ships could sink in less than a minute. On flammable oil tankers, however, sailors closed their doors, undressed, and slept soundly. If a torpedo hit, no one would survive.

FALL OF THE PHILIPPINES   In the Far East the Allies fared no better. Japanese forces had invaded the Philippines, British Malaya, and the Dutch East Indies. The supposedly impregnable British bastion of Singapore fell in just one week, and at the Battle of Java Sea, the Japanese navy destroyed almost the entire remaining Allied naval force in the western Pacific. In April 1942 General Douglas MacArthur, commander of American forces in the Philippines, fled to Australia. In what appeared to be an empty pledge, he vowed, "I shall return." Left behind with scant arms and food, American and Philippine troops on Bataan and Corregidor put up a heroic but doomed struggle. By summer no significant Allied forces stood between the Japanese and India or Australia.

The chain of spectacular victories disguised fatal weaknesses within the Axis alliance. Arrogance would lead Hitler into major strategic blunders. Japan and Germany were fighting separate wars, each on two fronts. They never coordinated strategies. Vast armies in China and Russia drained them of both personnel and supplies. Brutal occupation policies made enemies of conquered populations. Axis armies had to use valuable forces to maintain control and move supplies. The Nazis were especially harsh. They launched a major campaign to exterminate Europe's Jews, Slavs, and Gypsies. Resistance movements grew as the victims of Axis aggression fought back. At the war's height 50 countries joined the Allies, who referred to themselves as the United Nations.

THE U-BOAT WAR

*In the world's first truly global war, the need to coordinate and supply troops and matériel became paramount. But as German U-boats took a heavy toll on Allied shipping, it became difficult to deliver American supplies to Europe. Avoiding the North Atlantic route forced an arduous 12,000-mile journey around Africa to the Persian Gulf and then across Iran by land. The elimination of German submarines greatly eased the shipping problem and, as much as any single battle, ensured victory. **Why did so many U-boat sinkings occur off the north coast of South America?***

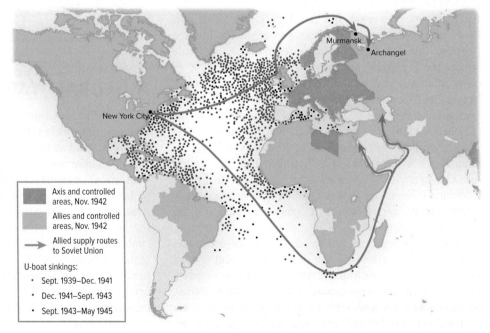

Axis and controlled areas, Nov. 1942

Allies and controlled areas, Nov. 1942

→ Allied supply routes to Soviet Union

U-boat sinkings:
- Sept. 1939–Dec. 1941
- Dec. 1941–Sept. 1943
- Sept. 1943–May 1945

A Grand Alliance

Early defeats obscured Allied strengths. Chief among these were the human resources of the Soviet Union and the industrial capacity of the United States. During World War II, Americans would develop a global economy. Safe from the fighting, American farms and factories could produce enough food and munitions to supply two separate wars at once. By the end of the war, American factories had turned out 300,000 airplanes, 87,000 ships, 400,000 artillery pieces, 102,000 tanks and self-propelled guns, and 47 million tons of ammunition.

THE BIG THREE The Allies benefited too from exceptional leadership. The "Big Three"—Joseph Stalin, Winston Churchill, and Franklin Roosevelt—all had shortcomings but were able to maintain a unity of purpose that eluded Axis leaders. All three understood the global nature of the war. To a remarkable degree, they managed to set aside their differences in pursuit of a common goal—the defeat of Nazi Germany. The staunch anticommunist Churchill pledged Britain's resources to assist the defense of the world's largest Communist state. The anti-imperialist Roosevelt poured American resources into the war effort of two of Europe's imperial powers, and the Marxist Joseph Stalin allied with two capitalist states.

To be sure, each nation had its own needs. Russian forces faced 3.5 million Axis troops along a 1,600-mile front in eastern Europe. To ease the pressure on those troops, Stalin repeatedly called on the Allies to open a second front in western Europe. So urgent were his demands that one Allied diplomat remarked that Stalin's foreign minister knew only four words in English: *yes, no,* and *second front.* But Churchill and Roosevelt felt compelled to turn Stalin down. In August 1942 the western Allies lacked the massive, well-trained force needed for a successful invasion of Europe. Churchill himself flew to Moscow to give Stalin the bad news: no second front in Europe until 1943. Postponed again until mid-1944, the second front became a source of festering Russian discontent.

OPERATION TORCH Yet, after his initial anger over the postponement, Stalin accepted Churchill's rationale for a substitute action. British and American forces would invade North Africa by the end of 1942. Code-named Operation Torch, the North African campaign could be mounted quickly. Equally important, it could bring British and American troops into direct combat with the Germans and stood an excellent chance of succeeding. Here was an example of how personal contact among the Big Three ensured Allied cooperation. The alliance sometimes bent but never broke.

The Naval War in the Pacific

Despite the decision to concentrate on defeating Germany first, the Allies' earliest successes came in the Pacific. At the Battle of Coral Sea in May 1942, planes from the aircraft carriers *Yorktown* and *Lexington* stopped a large Japanese invading force headed for Port Moresby in New Guinea (see Mapping the Past later in the chapter). For the first time in history, two fleets fought without seeing each other. The age of naval aviation had arrived. The Japanese fleet actually inflicted greater damage but decided to turn back to nurse its wounds. Had they captured Port Moresby, the Japanese could have severed Allied shipping routes to Australia.

MIDWAY To extend Japan's defenses, Admiral Isoruku Yamamoto ordered the capture of Midway, a small island guarding the approach west of Hawaii. The Americans, in possession of decoded messages, knew the Japanese were coming. On June 3, as the Japanese main fleet bore down on Midway, American aircraft sank four enemy carriers, a cruiser, and three destroyers. The Japanese sank only one American aircraft carrier, the *Yorktown.* More important, the Japanese lost many of their best carrier pilots, who were more difficult to replace than planes. The Battle of Midway broke Japanese naval supremacy in the Pacific. In August 1942 American forces launched their first offensive—on the Solomon Islands, east of New Guinea. With the landing of American marines on the key island of Guadalcanal, the Allies started on the bloody road to Japan and victory.

Turning Points in Europe

By the fall of 1942 the Allies had their first successes in the European war. At El Alamein, 75 miles from the Suez Canal, British forces under General Bernard Montgomery broke through Rommel's lines. Weeks later, the Allies launched Operation Torch, the invasion of North Africa. Under the command of General Dwight D. Eisenhower, Allied forces swept eastward through Morocco and Algeria. They were halted in February 1943 at the Kasserine Pass in Tunisia, but General George S. Patton regrouped them and masterminded an impressive string of victories. By May 1943 Rommel had fled from North Africa, leaving behind 300,000 German troops.

STALINGRAD Success in North Africa provided a stirring complement to the Russian stand at Stalingrad. From August 1942 until February 1943, Axis and Soviet armies threw into battle more than a million troops. In one of the bloodiest engagements in history, each side suffered more casualties than the Americans did during the entire war. When it was over, the Germans had lost an army and their momentum. Stalin's forces went on the offensive, moving south and west through the Ukraine toward Poland and Romania. By the fall of 1942 the Allies had also gained the edge in the war for the Atlantic. Supplies moved easily after antisubmarine forces sank 785 out of the nearly 1,200 U-boats the Germans built.

Mobilizing for a Global War

Assembling an army brought together Americans from all regions, social classes, and ethnic backgrounds. "The first time I ever heard a New England accent," recalled a midwesterner, "was at Fort Benning. The southerner was an exotic creature to me." More than any other social institution the army acted as a melting pot. It also offered educational opportunities and job skills or suggested the need for them. "I could be a technical sergeant only I haven't had enough school," reported one Navajo soldier in a letter home to New Mexico. "Make my little brother go to school even if you have to lasso him."

In waging the world's first global war, the U.S. armed forces swept millions of Americans into new worlds and new experiences. When Pearl Harbor came, the army had 1.6 million men in uniform. By 1945 it had more than 7 million; the navy, 3.9 million; the army air corps, 2.3 million; and the marines, 600,000. Nineteen-year-olds who had never left home found themselves swept off to Europe or to the South Pacific.

At basic training new recruits were subjected to forms of regimentation—the army haircut, foul-mouthed drill sergeants, and barracks life—they had seldom experienced in other areas of America's democratic culture.

In this war, as in most wars, the infantry bore the brunt of the fighting and dying. They suffered 90 percent of the battlefield casualties. In all, almost 400,000 Americans died and more than 600,000 were wounded. But service in the military did not mean constant combat. Most battles were reasonably short, followed by long periods of waiting and preparation. The army used almost 2 million soldiers just to move supplies. Yet even during the lull in battle, the soldiers' biggest enemy, disease, stalked them: malaria, dysentery, typhus, and

WORLD WAR II IN EUROPE AND NORTH AFRICA

Coordination of Allied strategy was crucial to victory. Until 1944 Soviet forces engaged the bulk of the Axis armies across a massive front. The Battle of Stalingrad prevented Hitler from reinforcing Rommel against the British in North Africa. After winning North Africa, the Allies turned north to knock Italy out of the war. The final key to defeating the Nazis was the invasion of western Europe at Normandy. D-Day would not have been possible had the Allies been unable to use England as a base to gather their forces. Stalin supported D-Day with a spring offensive in eastern Europe. **Why did the first Anglo-American ground campaigns occur in North Africa?**

even plague. In the Pacific theater, the thermometer sometimes rose to over 110 degrees Fahrenheit.

Wherever they fought, American soldiers usually lived in foxholes dug by hand with small shovels. Whenever possible they turned a hole in the ground into a home. "The American soldier is a born housewife," observed war correspondent Ernie Pyle. Between battles, movies were about the only entertainment many troops had. Each film was a tenuous link to a more comfortable world at home, a place American soldiers yearned for with special intensity. It was not a country or an idea for which they fought so much as a set of memories—a house, a car, Mom and Pop.

Minorities Go to War

AFRICAN AMERICANS Minorities enlisted in unusually large numbers because the services offered training and opportunities unavailable in civilian life. Still, prejudice against African Americans and other minorities remained high. The army was strictly segregated and generally assigned black soldiers to noncombatant roles. The navy accepted them only as cooks and servants. At first the air corps and marines would not take them at all. The American Red Cross even kept "black" and "white" blood plasma separated, as if there were a difference. (Ironically, a black physician, Charles Drew, had invented the process for storing plasma.)

Despite the persistence of prejudice more than a million black men and women served. As the war progressed, leaders of the black community pressured the military to ease segregation and allow black soldiers a more active role. The army did form some black combat units, usually led by white officers, as well as a black air corps unit. By mid-1942 black officers were being trained and graduated from integrated officer candidate schools at the rate of 200 a month. More than 80 black pilots won the Distinguished Flying Cross.

For both Mexican Americans and Asian Americans the war offered an opportunity to enter the American mainstream. Putting on a uniform was an essential act of citizenship. Mexican Americans had a higher enlistment rate than the general population. A California congressional representative observed that "as I read the casualty list from my state, I find that anywhere from one-fourth to one-third of these names are names such as Gonzales and Sanchez." Chinese Americans served at the highest rate of all population groups. As Harold Liu of New York's Chinatown recalled, "for the first time Chinese were accepted as being friends. . . . All of a sudden we became part of an American dream." Korean Americans were especially valuable in the Pacific theater because many could translate Japanese.

Like other Asian Americans, Filipinos had powerful reasons to enlist. Service offered an opportunity to fight for the liberation of their homeland from Japanese invaders. And, like other minorities, Filipino Americans realized that in fighting for freedom abroad they were fighting for freedom at home. A Filipino soldier commented that he was doing something he had never before been allowed to do: serve "as an equal with American boys." Such loyalty had its rewards. Filipinos who volunteered became citizens. The California attorney general reinterpreted laws that had once prevented Filipinos from owning land in the state. Now they could buy their own farms. Jobs opened in war factories. The status of other Asian Americans and Mexican Americans improved in similar ways. After the war, minority veterans would provide new leadership in their communities.

CHOICES FOR HOMOSEXUALS Homosexuals who wished to join the military faced a dilemma. Few Americans of the day had any knowledge of gays in their midst, and fewer had much tolerance for homosexuality. Still, many gays risked exposure. Charles Rowland, from Arizona, recalled that he and other gay friends "were not about to be deprived the privilege of serving our country in a time of great national emergency by virtue of some stupid regulation about being gay." Homosexuals who did pass the screening test found themselves in gender-segregated bases, where life in an overwhelmingly male or female environment allowed many, for the first time in their lives, to meet like-minded gay men and women. Like other servicemen and women, they served in a host of roles, fighting and dying on the battlefield or doing the unglamorous jobs that kept the army going.

Women at War

WACS World War II brought an end to the military as an exclusive male enclave that women entered only as nurses. During the prewar mobilization, Eleanor Roosevelt and

©James West Davidson

| *In the face of Japanese occupation, many Filipinos actively supported the American war effort. Valentine Untalan survived capture by the Japanese and went on to serve in the American army's elite Philippine Scouts. Like a growing number of Filipinos, he moved to the United States after the war ended.*

"Nose Art" and Gender Relations

Other subjects of
nose art included a
shark face with
gaping teeth (to
make the plane look
like a marauder) as
well as cowboys,
dragons, or kicking
mules, to name only
a few.

What is Rose doing?

Would you consider
this imagery
masculine, feminine,
or both? Why, and
in what ways?

©Tillamook Air Museum/Image Courtesy of James West Davidson

During World War I and even more in World War II, fighter planes began sporting "nose art," decorative images painted on the nose cone. The images helped to identify friendly planes but also expressed their crews' individual identities. Military regulations sometimes forbade such decorations, but commanders looked the other way, fearing protests or lowered morale. The paintings portrayed a variety of subjects, but "pin-up" art was always the favorite. It derived first from paintings of scantily clad models in *Esquire* magazine (often pinned on walls near bunks). Original designs, like "Rose's Raiders," were created by amateurs among the ground crews. Nose art made a comeback during the Persian Gulf and Iraq Wars, allowed (always unofficially) so long as the female models were clothed. How to interpret the cultural effects of this folk art? No doubt the decorations eased homesickness and brought to mind memories of female companionship for soldiers caught in the brutal world of combat. But the stereotyping and objectification also made life more difficult for women in the service.

THINKING CRITICALLY

What wartime conditions led men to create nose art? What social functions did such art perform? Do popular perceptions of what is offensive change over time? Have they here? Would it be relevant to consider the Defense Department's statement in 2012 that approximately 26,000 female and male service members had been sexually assaulted?

other female leaders had campaigned for a regular military organization for women. The War Department came up with a compromise that allowed women to join the Women's Army Auxiliary Corps (WAAC), but only with inferior status and lower pay. By 1943 the "Auxiliary" had dropped out of the title: WAACs became WACs, with full army status, equal ranks, and equal pay. (The navy had a similar force called the WAVES.)

Women could look with a mixture of pride and resentment on their wartime military service. Thousands served close to the battlefields, working as technicians, mechanics, radio operators, postal clerks, and secretaries. Although filling a vital need, these jobs were largely traditional female ones that implied a separate and inferior status. Until 1944 women were prevented by law from serving in war zones, even as noncombatants. There were female pilots, but they were restricted to shuttling planes behind the lines. At many posts WAVEs and WACs lived behind barbed wire and could move about only in groups under armed escort.

 REVIEW

What strategy did the "Big Three" adopt in fighting the war, and what were the first turning points of that strategy in Europe and in the Pacific?

MOBILIZING THE HOME FRONT

WHEN PEARL HARBOR BROUGHT THE United States into the war, Thomas Chinn sold his publishing business and devoted himself full-time to war work. Like many other Chinese Americans, he was working for the first time outside Chinatown. He served as a supervisor in the Army Quartermaster Market Center, which was responsible for supplying the armed forces with fresh food as it was harvested across California. Chinn found himself coordinating a host of cold storage warehouses all the way from the Oregon border as far south as Fresno. "At times," he recalled, "in order to catch seasonal goods such as fresh vegetables, as many as 200 or 300 railroad cars would be shuttling in and out" of the warehouses.

Food production and distribution were only two of the many areas that demanded attention from the government. After Pearl Harbor, steel, aluminum, and electric power were all in short supply, creating bottlenecks in production lines. Roosevelt saw a need for more-direct government management of the economy.

Although the conversion from peace to war came slowly at first, the president used a mix of compulsory and voluntary programs to control inflation and guarantee an ever-increasing supply of food, munitions, and equipment. In the end the United States worked a miracle of production that proved every bit as important to victory as any battle fought overseas.

Increasing Production

Roosevelt first attempted to coordinate the production effort by setting up a War Production Board (WPB). In one of its first acts the WPB ordered an end to all civilian car and truck production. The American people would have no new cars until the war ended.

©James West Davidson

| To fight inflation, the Office of Price Administration (OPA) imposed rationing on products in short supply. Consumers received coupons to trade for goods such as meat, shoes, and gasoline. The program was one of the most unpopular of the war.

In practice, the WPB was hindered by other federal agencies with their own czars in control of petroleum, rubber, and labor resources. To end the bottlenecks once and for all, the president in 1943 installed Supreme Court Justice James F. Byrnes as director of the new Office of War Mobilization (OWM). A canny politician, Byrnes became the dictator the economy needed. By assuming control over vital materials such as steel, aluminum, and copper, the OWM made the bottlenecks disappear. Such centralized planning helped ease the conversion to war production of industries both large and small. While the "Big Three" automakers—Ford, General Motors, and Chrysler—generated some 20 percent of all war goods, small business also played a vital role. A manufacturer of model trains, for example, made bomb fuses.

WEST COAST WAR INDUSTRIES   The aircraft industry transformed the industrial landscape of the West Coast. When production of aircraft factories peaked in 1944, the industry had 2.1 million workers. Most of the new factories were located around Los Angeles, San Diego, and Seattle, where large labor pools, temperate climates, and available land made the locations attractive. The demand for workers opened opportunities for many Asian workers who had been limited to jobs within their own ethnic communities. By 1943, 15 percent of all shipyard workers around San Francisco Bay were Chinese.

As the military relied on large, established firms to turn out planes, ships, and tanks, big corporations increased their dominance over the American economy. Workers in companies with more than 10,000 employees amounted to just 13 percent of the workforce in 1939; by 1944 they made up more than 30 percent. In agriculture a similar move toward bigness occurred, as small farms were consolidated into larger ones. Large commercial farming by corporations rather than individuals (later called "agribusiness") came to dominate agriculture.

Productivity increased for a less tangible but equally important reason: pride in work done for a common cause. Civilians volunteered for civil defense, hospitals, and countless scrap drives. Children became "Uncle Sam's Scrappers" and "Tin-Can Colonels" as they scoured vacant lots for valuable trash. One teenager in Maywood, Illinois, collected more than 100 tons of paper between Pearl Harbor and D-Day. Backyard "victory" gardens added 8 million tons of food to the harvest in 1943; car-pooling conserved millions of tires. Morale ran high because people believed that every contribution, no matter how small, helped defeat the Axis.

Science, the War, and the Environment

Victory gardens and recycling drives reshaped the environment at home in order to project a war reaching into every corner of the globe. The war's physical damage to the environment was obvious, of course, and vast: buildings leveled; fields and forests pockmarked by bomb craters; millions of gallons of oil, steel, and other natural resources extracted from the earth, refined and recast, and thrown into battle. But changes to the environment were not merely monumental in size, they were new in kind. And science was at the center of those alterations.

When the Japanese and American fleets met in the Coral Sea and Midway, new technology affected how the Americans fought. In both battles weather conditions and great distances prevented direct observation of the enemy. The Americans used radar gunnery and airplanes to spot and sink enemy ships. Elsewhere, improved fighter planes and long-range bombers allowed Allied air forces to take the war to the Axis homelands. As a result, the idea of a front line lost its meaning. New offensive weapons inspired better defensive weapons such as radar and sonar, which detected enemy aircraft and submarines.

Applied mathematics and game theory helped the U.S. Navy find and destroy the U-boats that preyed on Allied shipping. The electronic calculators used to designate search patterns became a basis for future computers. One of the most critical technical advances—developed with as much secrecy as the atomic bomb—produced the proximity fuse. A small radio device placed in an antiaircraft shell could detect nearby metal and then detonate the shell without having to hit the target.

METEOROLOGY AND CLIMATE CHANGE In their quest to defeat fascism, scientists began to explore some of the basic forces of nature. Because the fortunes of battle could turn on the weather, the navy and the Massachusetts Institute of Technology created a professional program in meteorology, using the principles of physics to better understand the patterns of climate. Meteorology and other fields of geophysics provided the military with information on the winds, ocean currents, and tides in far-flung theaters of the war. These efforts laid the foundation for future understanding of climate change.

No scientific quest did more to alter the relationship between humans and the natural world than the effort to build an atomic bomb. In 1938 German scientists discovered the process of nuclear **fission**. Atoms of uranium-235 when split released enormous energy. Leading American physicists, many of them refugees from fascist Europe, understood that a fast fission reaction might be used to build a bomb. In 1939 Albert Einstein, Enrico Fermi, and Leo Szilard warned President Roosevelt that the Germans might be well on the way to creating a weapon, the use of which might determine the war.

MANHATTAN PROJECT Immediately, Roosevelt authorized what became an enormous research and development effort, code named the Manhattan Project. Over 100,000 scientists, engineers, technicians, and support staff from Canada, England, and the United States worked at 39 installations in a concerted effort to build an atomic bomb. Yet even as they spent over $2 billion in their quest, leaders of the project feared the Germans might succeed before they did.

Applied science was not simply about destruction. Production of war matériel mattered as well. With so many farmers at war, increased agricultural productivity became vital. In the 1930s plant geneticists had learned to cross-pollinate corn to create new varieties. These hybrids greatly increased yields per acre. Plastics offered an alternative to natural materials such as glass, rubber, wood, steel, and copper, all in short supply. For example, commercial production of polyvinyl chloride (PVC) began modestly in 1933. Given its stability and flexibility, PVC was ideal for use in construction, plumbing, packaging, and flooring. Production jumped from 1 million pounds a year before 1941 to 120 million by 1945.

ENVIRONMENTAL BENEFITS AND RISKS Some scientific advances increased health and life expectancy. Antibiotics were first used widely during the war. Infectious diseases such as tuberculosis, syphilis, and pneumonia, once the scourge of armies, could now be contained. Pesticides such as DDT controlled insects that spread malaria and other deadly and debilitating diseases. With the use of these chemicals, the health of the nation actually improved. Life expectancy increased an average of three years over all and jumped by five years for African Americans. Infant mortality fell by a third.

The atomic bomb, DDT, PVC, and hybrid seeds symbolized for many Americans humankind's ability to improve on nature. What they did not anticipate were the environmental dangers those discoveries posed. Atomic bombs spewed clouds of radiation into the atmosphere. DDT controlled insect pests but killed beneficial insects and proved harmful to wildlife. PVC production produced carcinogens dangerous to humans. And the products existed nowhere in nature and,

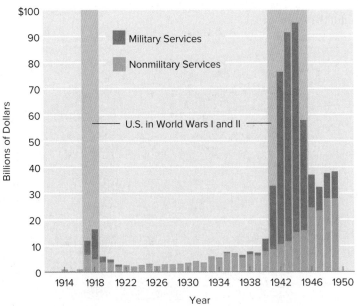

The Impact of World War II on Government Spending

As the chart shows, the war spurred government spending more than the New Deal, even on nonmilitary sectors. Note that after both world wars, nonmilitary spending was higher than in the prewar years.

once discarded, took ages to degrade. The widespread use of hybrid seeds created through artificial pollination greatly reduced genetic variety. Some scientists anticipated these dangers, but any concerns were brushed aside in the determination to win the war.

The Return of Prosperity

Not only did war production end the Depression, it revived prosperity. As late as 1940 unemployment stood at almost 7 million. By 1944 it had virtually disappeared. Jeff Davies, president of Hoboes of America, reported in 1942 that 2 million of his members were "off the road." Employers, eager to overcome the labor shortage, welcomed disabled workers. The hearing-impaired found jobs in deafening factories; very short people became aircraft inspectors because they could crawl inside wings and other cramped spaces. By the summer of 1943, nearly 3 million children aged 12 to 17 were working.

TAX REFORM Roosevelt had to find some means to pay the war's enormous cost without undermining prosperity. His approach mixed both conservative and liberal elements. The Treasury Department raised money voluntarily, by selling war bonds through advertising campaigns. To raise more funds, Secretary of the Treasury Henry Morgenthau proposed a tax structure that was highly progressive—that is, it taxed higher income at a higher rate. Conservatives in Congress balked at sweeping tax reforms. After six months of wrangling, Congress passed a compromise, the Revenue Act of 1942, which levied a flat 5 percent tax on all annual incomes over $624. That provision struck hardest at low-income workers: in 1942 almost 50 million citizens paid taxes compared with 13 million the year before.

Organized Labor

WAR LABOR BOARD Wartime prosperity did not end the tug-of-war between business and labor. In 1941 alone more than 2 million workers walked off their jobs in protest over wages and working conditions. To end labor strife, Roosevelt established the War Labor Board (WLB) in 1942. Like the agency Woodrow Wilson had created during World War I, the new WLB had authority to impose arbitration in any labor dispute. Its most far-reaching decision established a compromise between employers and unions that gave workers 15 days to leave the union after a contract was signed. Any worker who remained a member had to pay union dues for the life of the contract. That policy led to an almost 40 percent growth in union membership between 1941 and 1945, when a record 14.75 million workers belonged to unions.

Source: Library of Congress, Prints and Photographs Division [LC-DIG-hec-21637]
| *John L. Lewis*

LEWIS LEADS A COAL STRIKE Despite the efforts of the WLB, strikes did occur. Dissatisfied railroad workers tied up rail lines in a wildcat strike in 1943. General George C. Marshall cursed it as the "damnedest crime ever committed against America." To break the impasse, the government seized the railroads and then granted wage increases. That same year the pugnacious John L. Lewis allowed his United Mine Workers to go on strike. "The coal miners of America are hungry," he charged. "They are ill-fed and undernourished." Roosevelt seized the mines and ran them for a time; he even considered arresting union leaders and drafting striking miners. But as Secretary of the Interior Harold Ickes noted, a "jailed miner produces no more coal than a striking miner." In the end the government negotiated a settlement that gave miners substantial new benefits.

Most Americans were unwilling to forgive Lewis or his miners. A huge coal shortage along the East Coast had left homes dark and cold. "John L. Lewis—Damn your coal black soul," wrote the military newspaper *Stars and Stripes*. In reaction, Congress easily passed the Smith-Connolly Act of 1943. It gave the president more authority to seize vital war plants shut by strikes and required union leaders to observe a 30-day "cooling-off" period before striking. Roosevelt vetoed the bill, only to be overridden in both houses.

Despite these incidents, workers remained dedicated to the war effort. Stoppages actually accounted for only about one-tenth of 1 percent of total work time during the war. When workers did strike, it was usually in defiance of their union leadership, and they left their jobs for just a few days.

In other ways, however, the workforce was transformed by the turmoil of war. In the years after Pearl Harbor, over 15 million civilians changed their addresses. "The war dispersed the reservation people as nothing ever had," recalled Vine DeLoria, an Indian activist. "Every day, it seemed, we would be bidding farewell to families as they headed west to work in defense plants on the coast." So many African Americans left the South that cotton growers began to buy mechanical harvesters to replace their labor. So many Appalachian hill people traveled back and forth from Kentucky to Detroit that the bus company added an express service. Western states that had deported Mexican workers during the Depression now welcomed a contract labor program set up by the Department of Agriculture, which brought in several hundred thousand *braceros,* or farm laborers. Their labor was vital to the war effort.

Women Workers

WOMANPOWER FILLS THE LABOR SHORTAGE With as many as 12 million men in uniform, women (especially married women) became the nation's largest untapped source of labor. During the high-unemployment years of the Depression, both government and business had

| Viola Sievers was one of many women during the war who took jobs traditionally performed by men. Here she cleaned a locomotive using a scalding hot stream of steam.

Source: Library of Congress, Prints and Photographs Division [LC-USZCN4-94]

discouraged women from competing with men for jobs. Now, suddenly, magazines and government bulletins began trumpeting "the vast resource of womanpower." The percentage of female workers grew from around a quarter in 1940 to more than a third by 1945. These women were no longer mostly young and single, as female workers of the past had been. A majority were either married or between 55 and 64 years old.

Beyond patriotism, many women preferred the relative freedom of work and wages to the confines of home. With husbands off at war, millions of women needed additional income and had more free time. Black women in particular realized dramatic gains. Once concentrated in low-paying domestic and farm jobs with erratic hours and tedious labor, some 300,000 rushed into factories that offered higher pay and more-regular hours. Given the chance to learn skills like welding, aircraft assembly, and electronics, women shattered many stereotypes about their capabilities. The diary of a ship welder in Oregon recorded both amazement and pride at what she accomplished:

I, who hates heights, climbed stair after stair after stair till I thought I must be close to the sun. I stopped on the [tanker's] top deck. I, who hate confined spaces, went through narrow corridors, stumbling my way over rubber-coated leads. . . . I welded in the poop deck lying on the floor while another welder spattered sparks from the ceiling and chippers like giant woodpeckers shattered our eardrums. . . . I did overhead welding, horizontal, flat, vertical. . . . I made some good welds and some frightful ones. But now a door in the poop deck of an oil tanker is hanging, four feet by six of solid steel, by my welds. Pretty exciting!

Although the demand for labor improved the economic status of women, it did not alter conventional views about gender roles. Most Americans assumed that when the war ended, veterans would pick up their old jobs and women would return to the home. The birthrate, which had fallen during the Depression, began to rise in 1943 as prosperity returned. And other traditional barriers continued to limit women's opportunities, even in wartime. As women flooded into government bureaucracies, factory production lines, and corporate offices, few became managers. Supervision remained men's work. In short, the war inspired a change in economic roles for women without fomenting a revolution in attitudes about gender. That would come later.

 REVIEW

How did advances in science help the Allied war effort, and what environmental problems were overlooked in the process?

A QUESTION OF RIGHTS

FRANKLIN ROOSEVELT HAD BEEN A government official during World War I. Now, presiding over a bigger world war, he was determined to avoid many of the patriotic excesses he had witnessed then: mobs menacing immigrants, the patriotic appeals to spy on neighbors, the raids on pacifist radicals. Even so, the conflicts arising over race, ethnic background, and class differences could not be avoided. In a society in which immigration laws discriminated against Asians by race, the war with Japan made life difficult for loyal Asian Americans of all backgrounds. Black and Latino workers faced as much discrimination in shipyards and airplane factories as they had in peacetime industries.

Little Italy

Aliens from enemy countries fared far better in World War II than in World War I. When the war began, about 600,000 Italian aliens and 5 million Italian Americans lived in the United States. Most still resided in Italian neighborhoods centered around churches, fraternal organizations, and clubs. Some had been proud of Mussolini and supported *fascismo*. "Mussolini was a hero," recalled one Italian American. "A superhero. He made us feel special." Those attitudes changed abruptly after Pearl Harbor. During the war, Italian Americans pledged their loyalties to the United States.

At first the government treated Italians without citizenship (along with Japanese and Germans) as "aliens of enemy nationality." They could not travel without permission, enter strategic areas, or possess shortwave radios, guns, or maps. By 1942 few Americans believed that German Americans or Italian Americans posed any real danger. Eager to keep the support of Italian voters in the 1942 congressional elections, Roosevelt chose Columbus Day 1942 to lift restrictions on Italian aliens.

Concentration Camps

Americans were not similarly tolerant toward the 127,000 Japanese living in the United States, whether they were aliens or citizens. Ironically, tensions were least high in Hawaii, where the war with Japan had begun. Local newspapers there expressed confidence in the loyalty of Japanese Americans, who in any case were crucial to Hawaii's economy.

ISSEI On the mainland, Japanese Americans remained largely separated from the mainstream of American life. State laws and local custom threw up complex barriers to integration. In the western states, where they were concentrated around urban areas, most Japanese could not vote, own land, or live outside of designated neighborhoods. Approximately 47,000 Japanese aliens, known as **Issei**, were ineligible for citizenship under American law. Only their children could become citizens. Despite such restrictions, some Japanese achieved success in small businesses like landscaping, while many others worked on or owned farms that supplied fruits and vegetables to growing cities.

NISEI West Coast politicians pressed the Roosevelt administration to evacuate the Japanese from their communities. It did not seem to matter that about 80,000 were American citizens, called **Nisei**, and that no evidence indicated that they posed any threat. "A Jap's a Jap," commented Lieutenant General John L. DeWitt, commander of West Coast defenses. "It makes no difference whether he is an American citizen or not." In response, the War Department in February 1942 drew up Executive Order 9066, which allowed the exclusion of any person from designated military areas. Under De Witt's authority, the order was applied only on the West Coast against Japanese Americans. By late February, Roosevelt had agreed that both Issei and Nisei would be evacuated. But where would they go?

The army began to ship the entire Japanese community to "assembly centers." Most Nisei incurred heavy financial losses as they sold property at far below market value. Their distress became a windfall for people who had long resented their economic competition. "We've been charged with wanting to get rid of the Japs for selfish reasons," admitted the Grower-Shipper Vegetable Association. "We might as well be honest. We do. It's a question of whether the white man lives on the Pacific Coast or the brown man." At the assembly centers—racetracks, fairgrounds, and similar temporary locations—the army had not prepared basic sanitation, comfort, or privacy. "We lived in a horse stable," remembered one young girl. "We filled our cheesecloth with straw—for our mattress." The authorities at least had the decency to keep families together.

INTERNMENT CAMPS Most Japanese were interned in 10 camps in remote areas of seven western states. No claim of humane intent could change the reality—these were

©Eliot Elisofon/The LIFE Picture Collection/Getty Images

| *The bleak landscape of the internment camp at Manzanar, California, was typical of the sites to which the government sent Japanese Americans. In such a harsh environment, the Japanese had no real opportunity to create productive farm communities, as government officials had promised.*

"WHO DO YOU WANT TO WIN THIS WAR?"— JUSTIFYING INTERNMENT

In June 1943, Lieutenant General John L. DeWitt submitted a report on the evacuation of Japanese Americans from the West Coast, justifying his actions (Document 1). Mary Suzuki Ichino grew up in Los Angeles, California, and was interned at Camp Manzanar, about 230 miles northeast of there. Document 2 is a transcript of an interview with her, made decades later.

DOCUMENT 1
Sabotage on a Mass Scale

The Department of Justice had agreed to authorize its special field agents of the Federal Bureau of Investigation to undertake spot raids without warrant to determine the possession of arms, cameras and other contraband by Japanese. . . . In the Monterey area in California a Federal Bureau of Investigation spot raid made about February 12, 1942, found more than 60,000 rounds of ammunition and many rifles, shotguns and maps of all kinds. . . .

The combination of spot raids revealing hidden caches of contraband, the attacks on coastwise shipping, the interception of illicit radio transmissions, the nightly observation of visual signal lamps from constantly changing locations, and the success of the enemy offensive in the Pacific, had so aroused the public along the West Coast against the Japanese that it was ready to take matters into its own hands. . . .

Because of the ties of race, the intense feeling of filial piety and the strong bonds of common tradition, culture and customs, this population presented a tightly-knit racial group. It included in excess of 115,000 persons deployed along the Pacific Coast. Whether by design or accident, virtually always their communities were adjacent to very vital shore installations, war plants, etc. . . . It could not be established, of course, that the location of thousands of Japanese adjacent to strategic points verified the existence of some vast conspiracy to which all of them were parties. Some of them doubtless resided there through mere coincidence. It seems equally beyond doubt, however, that the presence of others was not mere coincidence. It was difficult to explain the situation in Santa Barbara County, for example, by coincidence alone.

Throughout the Santa Maria Valley in that County, including the cities of Santa Maria and Guadalupe, every utility, air field, bridge, telephone and power line or other facility of importance was flanked by Japanese. They even surrounded the oil fields in this area. Only a few miles south, however, in the Santa Ynez Valley, lay an area equally as productive agriculturally as the Santa Maria Valley and with lands equally available for purchase and lease, but without any strategic installations whatever. There were no Japanese in the Santa Ynez Valley. . . . It was certainly evident that the Japanese population of the Pacific Coast was, as a whole, ideally situated with reference to points of strategic importance, to carry into execution a tremendous program of sabotage on a mass scale should any considerable number of them have been inclined to do so.

Source: Lieutenant John L. Dewitt, *Final Report: Japanese Evacuation from the West Coast 1942.* Washington, D.C.: Government Printing Office, 1943, Chapter 2.

DOCUMENT 2
Interview with Mary Ichino

RP [Richard Potashin]: Tell us about what your attitude, where your attitude was at, or your opinions about this based on the rumors and the opinions that you were hearing. Did you form your own ideas about the injustice of this, the unconstitutionality of it? Was that something you were thinking about?

MI [Mary Ichino]: I think I was a little bit naïve that way. I didn't, I think, understand that depth of the, you know, the situation. You just kind of wonder, and then you follow on. I think as you mature, and I realized as I go—well, I told you about that letter I wrote to General DeWitt. It took me until I got in camp for me to realize, "What was I doing in this place?" And I go, "Why didn't that hit me before this as a question?"

RP: So your attitude changed—

MI: My attitude changed because—

RP: —when you got into camp?

MI: —I thought, it's sort of like an adventure, you know, for a teenager, when you think about it. You're moving, you're going, you know. But when I started seeing that my dad is losing his business, we're losing all our property, he lost his new car that he worked so darn hard for—What for? We're not from Japan. You know? Then when finally we went to camp is when I realized the injustice of the whole thing. And you're always taught in civics in high school that we're all equal under the law, and I said, "But how can you be equal when you haven't had a hearing as to

whether you're guilty or not guilty?" And that's when I wrote that letter to General DeWitt.

RP: There was another friend that you—

MI: Yeah, Marie Hisamune. She was my classmate at Sacred Heart. And we decided to put our—well, she and I, in order to keep busy, decided to write—first we started writing a murder mystery. And we came to a point where we couldn't figure out how to end the darn thing. And then, so then the next thing was, "You know what? We ought to write to General DeWitt." Says, "You know what, I don't know what we're doing in here." And so Marie and I put our heads together and we wrote, and we said, "We haven't gotten our constitutional hearing before we're declared guilty to be put into this place. Why is it? How is it? And how could it be?" And then we wanted an explanation. And then we're getting a little bit smarter, you know, at that age. "Okay, we better send it to General DeWitt." "Oh," somebody says, "They'll throw it out." "No they won't. We're going to make it registered directly to him." And so he must have gotten it because we never got the letter back, anything. No answer—

RP: No reply?

MI: No, never got a letter back.

RP: How long had you been in camp before you decided to take this course of action?

MI: Not quite six months, I bet. It dawned on us real quick.

RP: You just looked around and—

MI: Says, "Oh my God, can't get out of camp, you can't do this, you can't do that. The food is lousy. The physical facility's lousy. What did I do to deserve this?" You know.

RP: Right.

MI: And then it turned out to be, at that age we were realizing that it was hysteria. We figured that out.

RP: Did you have any second thoughts about writing that letter after you'd sent it? You know, like, "Are they going to, you know, are we going to be—"

MI: No.

RP: —on a blacklist or anything or—

MI: Nope.

RP: You felt—

MI: Fearless.

RP: Let's—what have you got to lose?

MI: The reason, we're only sixteen. What are they going to do with us? You know? I mean, 'cause, yeah. Mmhmm. I'd been told more that once, "Oh, you're probably on the blacklist." I said, "So?" In a way, it's sort of a compliment, you know?

RP: Right. Yeah, it took a lot of courage to do that.

MI: It's either your courage, or you're so darned innocent. If you're worried about what's going to happen or what will happen to you, you're not going to do a thing. If you think you're right and you need an explanation, it's as simple as that. That was it. So there was no gaman there. Tell it like it is.

Source: 16. Item # Acc-196 (letter to Mary Ichino): Mary Suzuki Ichino [MI], MANZ 1216A, interviewed by Richard Potashin [RP] Disc 1, Part 2 (DVD), 22:41–27:53.

THINKING CRITICALLY

What contraband items does DeWitt cite to indicate Japanese disloyalty? Do they substantiate his case? What elements Mary Ichino cites throw doubt on DeWitt's arguments? What do you think gave Ichino the courage to write directly to General DeWitt? Why might she be proud to be on a blacklist?

---

concentration camps. Internees were held in wire-enclosed compounds by armed guards. Temporary tar-papered barracks housed families or small groups in single rooms. Each room had a few cots, some blankets, and a single lightbulb. That was home.

Some Japanese within the camps protested. Especially offensive was a government loyalty questionnaire that asked Nisei if they would be willing to serve in the armed forces. "What do they take us for? Saps?" asked Dunks Oshima, a camp prisoner. "First, they . . . run me out of town, and now they want me to volunteer for a suicide squad so I could get killed for this damn democracy. That's going some, for sheer brass!" Yet thousands of Nisei did enlist, and many distinguished themselves in combat.

KOREMATSU AND HIRABAYASHI Other Japanese Americans challenged the government through the courts. Fred Korematsu in California and Gordon Hirabayashi in Washington State were arrested when they refused to report for relocation. "As an American citizen, I wanted to uphold the principles of the Constitution," recalled Hirabayashi. But the Supreme Court let stand military policies aimed specifically at Japanese Americans. The majority opinion stated that "residents having ethnic affiliations with an invading enemy may be a greater source of danger than those of different ancestry," even though the army had never demonstrated that any danger existed. And in *Korematsu v. United States* (1944), the Court upheld the government's relocation program as a wartime necessity. Three justices dissented, criticizing relocation as the "legalization of racism."

Concentration camps in America did not perpetuate the horror of Nazi death camps, but they were built on racism and fear. Worse, they violated the traditions of civil rights and liberties for which Americans believed they were fighting.

At War with Jim Crow

When World War II began, Americans lived in a society deeply segregated along racial lines. Three-quarters of the 12 million black Americans lived in the South. Hispanic Americans, then numbering around 1 million, resided largely in a belt along the U.S.-Mexican border. Though separated by geography, religion, language, and history, these two groups shared many common experiences. Both were segregated in housing and in public places. Neither had much access to health care, decent educations, or good jobs. Both found employment primarily as low-wage agricultural workers.

Hispanic and black leaders recognized the irony of a war their government fought in the name of freedom. That same government denied them basic civil rights and liberties, including the right to vote. "A jim crow army cannot fight for a free world," the NAACP declared. Several barriers stood in the way of the freedom to seek higher-wage work and improved housing. For one, many unions simply refused to allow minorities to join. For another, most employers refused to hire minorities or restricted them to unskilled jobs such as janitor. Finally, residential segregation was deeply embedded in the South by law and throughout the country by common practice.

A. PHILIP RANDOLPH These were inequities A. Philip Randolph was determined to eliminate. Randolph had developed organizing skills as a leader of the Brotherhood of Sleeping Car Porters, the most powerful black labor organization. Now, he looked to bring down the wall of discrimination that blocked minority workers from skilled jobs in defense industries and segregated them in government agencies, unions, and the armed forces. "The Administration leaders in Washington will never give the Negro justice," Randolph argued, "until they see masses—ten, twenty, fifty thousand Negroes on the White House lawn." To that end, he began in 1941 to organize a march on Washington.

FEPC President Roosevelt wished to avoid any show of racial discontent. He had the power to issue an executive order banning workplace segregation within the government and within companies receiving federal contracts, as Randolph demanded. Fearful of alienating southerners and union members, Roosevelt refused to act until confronted by the threat of the march. Only then, in June 1941, did he issue Executive Order 8802 barring discrimination in the hiring of government or defense industry workers. To enforce the order, he established the Fair Employment Practices Commission (FEPC).

While it never fulfilled Randolph's hopes, the FEPC was in some ways the boldest step toward racial justice since the era of Reconstruction. The commission opened jobs in California's shipyards and aircraft factories that had previously refused to hire Hispanics. Thousands of workers migrated to the coast from Texas, where job discrimination was the most severe. Facing acute labor shortages, the United States joined with the Mexican government to create a guest worker, or *bracero,* program. It guaranteed laborers from Mexico both better wages and improved working conditions. Despite the need for labor, opposition to the program from nativists in Texas remained severe.

Black Americans encountered similar resistance. More than half of all defense jobs were closed to minorities. In the aircraft industry, blacks held just 200 janitorial positions out of over 100,000 new jobs created. The FEPC had the authority to investigate these conditions, but when faced with powerful employers and unions the commission acted reluctantly if at all. In most sections of the country it honored "whites only" hiring practices. "Hitler has not done anything to the colored people," one worker told the president, "—it's people right here in the United States who are keeping us out of work and keeping us down." In the end, labor shortages more than government action improved the job situation. By 1944 African Americans, who made up 10 percent of the nation's population, held 8 percent of its jobs.

DETROIT RACE RIOT As blacks and Hispanics moved into urban areas, they also competed with whites for the diminishing supply of housing. The government tried to ease the problem by building new developments. In Detroit, housing authorities picked a site along the edge of a Polish neighborhood. When the first black family moved into the new development, Detroit authorities sent in the National Guard to protect the newcomers from a band of the Ku Klux Klan. As summer approached, tensions rose with the heat. Sporadic rioting broke out until, in June 1943, white mobs began beating blacks riding the trolley lines or going to movies. In retaliation, black rioters looted white stores. It took 6,000 regular army soldiers to impose a troubled calm, but not before violence claimed the lives of 24 blacks and 9 whites.

The situation in Southern California was no less volatile. There Hispanics were frustrated by the persistence of white racism, job and housing discrimination, and high unemployment even amid a booming economy. Whites, in turn, blamed the rapid growth in the Hispanic population for an increase in crime. Their particular hostility focused on pachucos, or "zoot suiters." These were young Hispanic men and boys who adopted the style of Harlem hipsters: oiled hair swept back into a ducktail; broad-shouldered, long-waisted suit coats; baggy pants pegged at the ankles, the whole outfit polished off with a knee-length, gold chain. For most "zooters" this style expressed a modest form of rebellion; for a few it was the uniform of a criminal culture; for many whites it was a racial affront. The all-white Los Angeles city council even made it a crime to wear a zoot suit.

ZOOT SUIT RIOTS In June 1943 navy shipmen stationed at the local base invaded Hispanic neighborhoods in search of zooters who had allegedly assaulted their comrades. These self-styled vigilantes grabbed any zooters they saw, ripped their clothes, shaved their heads, and beat their victims. Only when Hispanics retaliated did the Los Angeles police respond, all the while ignoring white violence. The local press added to the hysteria with irresponsible and inaccurate headlines such as "Zooters Threaten L.A. Police." An investigatory commission appointed by California governor Earl Warren rejected the press charges and placed the blame more properly on white racism and the daily indignities faced by the Hispanic community.

CORE Despite their many frustrations, minority leaders recognized the war effort as an opportunity to develop new strategies to confront old grievances. For example, the Congress of Racial Equality **(CORE)** found inspiration in the nonviolent passive resistance adopted by the leader of India's independence movement, Mohandas K. Gandhi. In northern cities CORE used sit-ins, boycotts, and picketing in an effort to desegregate movie theaters, restaurants, and other public places. In 1944 the Supreme Court indicated that it was reconsidering issues of racial inequality when, in *Smith v. Allwright,* it struck down the "all-white" primary used in southern states to disenfranchise black voters. In the one-party South the candidate who won the

©Bettmann/Getty Images

| A "zoot suiter" gets escorted by the police.

primary usually ran without major opposition in the general election. Unable to participate in the primaries, black voters had no meaningful influence. In rejecting this practice the Court indicated another way in which wartime experiences had opened new approaches to confronting racial discrimination.

The New Deal in Retreat

After Pearl Harbor, Roosevelt told reporters that "Dr. New Deal" had retired so that "Dr. Win-the-War" could get down to business. Political opposition, however, could not be eliminated even during a global conflict. The increasingly powerful anti–New Deal coalition of Republicans and rural Democrats saw in the war an opportunity to attack programs they had long resented. They quickly ended the Civilian Conservation Corps and the National Youth Administration, reduced the powers of the Farm Security Administration, and blocked moves to extend Social Security and unemployment benefits. Seeming to approve such measures, voters in the 1942 elections sent an additional 44 Republicans to the House and another 9 to the Senate. The GOP began eyeing the White House.

ROOSEVELT WINS A FOURTH TERM By the spring of 1944 no one knew whether Franklin Roosevelt would seek an unprecedented fourth term. The president's health had declined noticeably. Pallid skin, sagging shoulders, and

shaking hands seemed obvious signs that he had aged too much to run. In July, one week before the Democratic Convention, Roosevelt announced his decision: "All that is within me cries out to go back to my home on the Hudson River. . . . But as a good soldier . . . I will accept and serve." Conservative Democrats, however, made sure to remove Roosevelt's liberal vice president, Henry Wallace, from the ticket. In his place they settled on Harry S Truman of Missouri, a loyal New Dealer and party stalwart. The Republicans chose the moderate governor of New York, Thomas E. Dewey, to run against Roosevelt, but the stiff and formal Dewey never had much of a chance. At the polls, voters gave Roosevelt 25.6 million popular votes to Dewey's 22 million, a clear victory, although the election was tighter than any since 1916. Like its aging leader, the New Deal coalition was breaking down.

> ✓ REVIEW
>
> How did the war affect the rights of Italian Americans, Japanese Americans, African Americans, and Mexican Americans?

ENDING THE WAR, WINNING THE PEACE

TO IMPRESS UPON NEWLY ARRIVED officers the vastness of the war theater in the Pacific, General Douglas MacArthur laid out a map of the region. Over it he placed an outline map of the United States. Running the war from headquarters in Australia, MacArthur pointed out, the distances were about the same as if, in the Western Hemisphere, the center was located in South America. On the same scale Tokyo would lie far up in northern Canada, Iwo Jima somewhere in Hudson Bay, Singapore in Utah, Manila in North Dakota, and Hawaii off the coast of Scotland.

In a war that stretched from one end of the globe to the other, the Allies had to coordinate their strategies on a grand scale. Which war theaters would receive equipment in short supply? Who would administer conquered territories? Inevitably, the questions of fighting a war slid into discussions of the peace that would follow. What would happen to occupied territories? What peace terms would the Allies offer? If a more stable world order could not be created, the cycle of violence might never end. So, as Allied armies struggled mile by mile to defeat the Axis, Allied diplomacy concentrated winning the peace as well as the war.

The Fall of the Third Reich

After pushing the Germans out of North Africa in May 1943, Allied forces looked to drive Italy from the war. Late in July, two weeks after a quarter of a million British and American troops had landed on Sicily, Mussolini fled to German-held

D-DAY, 1944

The final key to defeating the Nazis was the invasion of western Europe at Normandy. D-Day for the invasion was June 6, 1944, and the massive undertaking would not have been possible had the Allies been unable to use England as a base to gather their forces. Stalin supported D-Day with a spring offensive in eastern Europe. Why might Hitler have assumed Calais was the Allies' likely target?

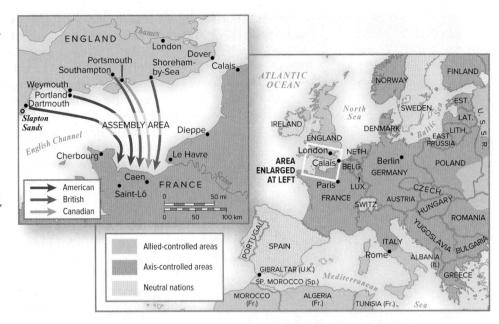

northern Italy. Although Italy surrendered early in September, Germany continued to pour in reinforcements. It took the Allies almost a year of bloody fighting to reach Rome, and at the end of the campaign they had yet to break German lines. Along the eastern front, Soviet armies steadily pushed the Germans out of Russia and back toward Berlin.

D-DAY General Dwight D. Eisenhower, fresh from battle in North Africa and the Mediterranean, took command of Allied preparations for Operation Overlord, a massive invasion of Europe striking from across the English Channel. By June 1944 all attention focused on the coast of France, for Hitler, of course, knew the Allies were preparing to invade. He suspected they would hit Calais, the French port city closest to the British Isles. Allied planners did their best to encourage this belief, even deploying fake armaments across the channel. On the morning of June 6, 1944, the invasion began—not at Calais but on the less fortified beaches of Normandy. Almost 3 million men, 11,000 aircraft, and more than 2,000 vessels took part in D-Day.

As Allied forces hit the beaches, luck and Eisenhower's meticulous planning favored their cause. Persuaded that the Allies still wanted Calais, Hitler delayed sending in two reserve divisions. His indecision allowed the Allied forces to secure a foothold. Over the next few days more than 1.5 million soldiers landed on the beaches—but they still had to move inland. The Allied advance from Normandy took almost two months, not several weeks as expected. But once Allied tanks broke through German lines, their progress was spectacular. In August Paris was liberated, and by mid-September the Allies had driven the Germans from France and Belgium.

All went well until December 1944, when Hitler threw his reserves into a last, desperate gamble. The unexpected German onslaught drove the Allied lines back along a 50-mile bulge. There the Germans trapped the 101st Airborne Division. When asked to surrender, General Tony McAuliffe

sent back a one-word reply: "Nuts!" His troops held, General George Patton raced to the rescue, and the last German offensive collapsed. Little stood between the Allies and Berlin.

Two Roads to Tokyo

In the bleak days of 1942 General Douglas MacArthur—flamboyant and jaunty with his dark sunglasses and corncob pipe—had emerged as America's only military hero. MacArthur believed that the future of America lay in the Far East. The Pacific theater, not the European, should have top priority, he argued. In March 1943 the Combined Chiefs of Staff agreed to his plan for a westward advance along the northern coast of New Guinea toward the Philippines and Tokyo. Naval forces directed by Admiral Chester Nimitz used amphibious warfare to move up the island chains of the Central Pacific (see Mapping the Past later in the chapter).

By July 1944 the navy's leapfrogging campaign had reached the Marianas, east of the Philippines. From there B-29 bombers could reach the Japanese home islands. As a result, Admiral Nimitz proposed bypassing the Philippines in favor of a direct attack on Formosa (present-day Taiwan). MacArthur insisted on keeping his promise "to eighteen million Christian Filipinos that the Americans would return." Roosevelt himself came to Hawaii to resolve the impasse, giving MacArthur the green light. Backed by more than 100 ships of the Pacific Fleet, the general splashed ashore on the island of Leyte in October 1944 to announce his return.

BATTLE OF LEYTE GULF The decision to invade the Philippines led to savage fighting and heavy American and Filipino casualties. As retreating Japanese armies left Manila, they tortured and slaughtered tens of thousands of Filipino civilians. The United States suffered 62,000 casualties redeeming MacArthur's pledge. But a spectacular U.S. Navy victory

Source: Navy Art Collection, Naval History and Heritage Command

| *During an attack as complicated as the one on D-Day 1944, communication was immensely important for successful coordination of millions of troops and thousands of landing vessels. Here, a Navy signalman uses a semaphore light to blink out Morse code to a battleship offshore. Another uses a telescope to pick up the replies from the ship.*

at the Battle of Leyte Gulf spelled the end of the Japanese Imperial Navy as a fighting force. MacArthur and Nimitz prepared to tighten the noose around Japan's home islands.

Big Three Diplomacy

While the Allies cooperated to gain military victories in both Europe and the Pacific, negotiations over the postwar peace proved knottier. Churchill believed that only a stable European balance of power, not an international agency, could preserve peace. In his view the Soviet Union was the greatest threat to upsetting that balance of power. Premier Joseph Stalin left no doubt that an expansive notion of Russian security defined his war aims. For future protection Stalin expected to annex the Baltic states, once Russian provinces, along with bits of Finland and Romania and about half of prewar Poland. In eastern Europe and other border areas such as Iran, Korea, and Turkey, he wanted "friendly" neighbors. It soon became apparent that "friendly" meant regimes dependent on Moscow.

Early on Franklin Roosevelt had promoted his own version of an international balance of power, which he called the "Four Policemen." Under its framework the Soviet Union, Great Britain, the United States, and China would guarantee peace through military cooperation. But by 1944 Roosevelt was seeking an alternative both to this scheme and to Churchill's wish to return to a balance of power that safely hemmed in the Russians. He preferred to bring the Soviet Union into a peacekeeping system based on an international organization similar to the League of Nations. This time

Roosevelt intended that the United States, as well as all the great powers, would participate. Whether Churchill and Stalin—or the American people as a whole—would accept the idea was not yet clear.

The Road to Yalta

TEHERAN CONFERENCE   The outlines—and the problems—of a postwar settlement became clearer during several summit conferences among the Allied leaders. In November 1943, with Italy's surrender in hand and the war against Germany going well, Churchill and Roosevelt agreed to make a hazardous trip to Teheran, Iran. There, the Big Three leaders had their chance to take a personal measure of each other. ("Seems very confident," Roosevelt said of Stalin, "very sure of himself, moves slowly—altogether quite impressive.") The president tried to charm the Soviet premier, teasing Churchill for Stalin's benefit, keeping it up "until Stalin was laughing with me, and it was then that I called him 'Uncle Joe.'"

Teheran was the high point of cooperation among the Big Three. There Roosevelt and Churchill committed to the D-Day invasion Stalin had so long sought, although Churchill's promise was halfhearted at best. The British hoped to delay D-Day as long as possible, largely to minimize British casualties. Stalin, for his part, promised to launch a spring offensive to keep German troops occupied on the eastern front. He also reaffirmed his earlier pledge to declare war against Japan once Germany was beaten.

THE PACIFIC CAMPAIGNS OF WORLD WAR II

Source: Gift of Abbott Laboratories/Naval History and Heritage Command

"Each phase of advance had as its objective an airfield which could serve as a steppingstone to the next advance. In addition, as this air line moved forward, naval forces under newly established air cover began to regain the sea lanes. . . . It was the practical application of this system of warfare—to avoid the frontal attack with its terrible loss of life; to by-pass Japanese strongpoints and neutralize them by cutting their lines of supply . . . to, as [baseball player] Willie Keeler used to say, 'hit 'em where they ain't'—that from this time forward guided my movements and operations."
—General Douglas MacArthur

CONTEXT

The extraordinary distances of the Pacific spurred the United States to devise a two-front strategy to defeat Japan. MacArthur's army forces used Australia as a base of operations, aiming for the Philippines and the southeast coast of China. The navy, under the command of Admiral Nimitz, set out to destroy the Japanese fleet and to conduct an "island-hopping" campaign: a series of landings on island chains in the Central Pacific.

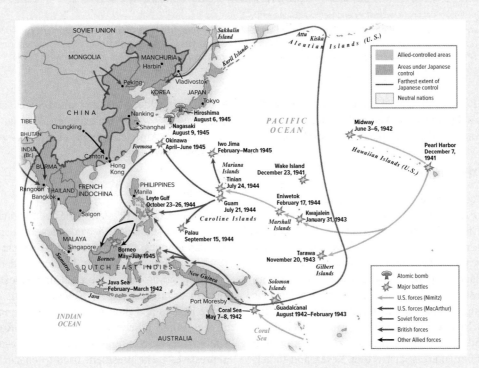

MAP READING

1. Where does Admiral Nimitz start his "island-hopping" campaign? Trace its course to the Mariana Islands.
2. Where does General MacArthur's campaign lead, moving out of Australia? What major island group does he attempt to recover?
3. Locate Manchuria. Which nation attacks Japanese positions there?
4. Locate Midway Island. How does its geographic position make it important?

MAP INTERPRETATION

1. What does MacArthur mean when he says his strategy was to "hit 'em where they ain't"?
2. Why did the success of the naval campaign in the central Pacific make it unnecessary to invade the Philippines?
3. Why might the Soviet Union's attack in Manchuria in August 1945 have affected Japan's decision to surrender?

YALTA CONFERENCE   But thorny disagreements over the postwar peace remained unresolved. That was clear in February 1945, when the Big Three met one last time, at the Russian resort city of Yalta, on the Black Sea. By then, Russian, British, and American troops were closing in on Germany. Roosevelt arrived tired, ashen. At 62, limited by his paralysis, he had visibly aged. He came to Yalta mindful that although Germany was all but beaten, Japan still held out in the Pacific. Under no circumstances did he want Stalin to withdraw his promises to enter the fight against Japan and to join a postwar international organization. Churchill remained profoundly mistrustful of Soviet intentions. As Germany and Japan disintegrated, he saw power vacuums opening up in both Europe and Asia. These the Russians appeared only too eager to fill. Most diplomats in the American State Department and a growing number of military officers and politicians shared Churchill's fears.

DISPUTE OVER POLAND   Britain entered the war, in part, to ensure that Poland survived as an independent nation. For Stalin, Poland was the historic corridor of invasion used by Russia's enemies. After Soviet troops reentered Poland, he insisted that he would recognize only the Communist-controlled government at Lublin. Stalin also demanded that Russia receive territory in eastern Poland, for which the Poles would be compensated with German lands. That was hardly the **self-determination** called for in the Atlantic Charter. Roosevelt proposed a compromise. For the time being, Poland would have a coalition government; after the war, free elections would settle the question of who should rule. The Soviets would also receive the territory they demanded in eastern Poland, and the western boundary would be established later.

Similarly, the Allies remained at odds about Germany's postwar future. Stalin was determined that the Germans would never invade Russia again. Many Americans shared his desire to have Germany punished and its war-making capacity eliminated. At the Teheran Conference, Roosevelt and Stalin had proposed that the Third Reich be drastically dismembered, split into five powerless parts. Churchill was much less eager to bring low the nation that was the most natural barrier to Russian expansion. The era after World War I, he believed, demonstrated that a healthy European economy required an industrialized Germany.

DIVIDING GERMANY   Again, the Big Three put off making a firm decision. For the time being, they agreed to divide Germany into separate occupation zones (France would receive a zone carved from British and American territory). These four powers would jointly occupy Berlin, while an Allied Control Council supervised the national government.

When the Big Three turned their attention to the Far East, Stalin held a trump card. Roosevelt believed that only a bloody invasion of Japan itself could force a surrender. He thus secured from Stalin a pledge to enter the Pacific war within three months of Germany's defeat. His price was high. Stalin wanted to reclaim territories that Russia had lost in the

Russo-Japanese War of 1904–1906, including islands north of Japan as well as control over the Chinese Eastern and South Manchurian railroads.

The agreements reached at Yalta depended on Stalin's willingness to cooperate. In public Roosevelt put the best face on matters. He argued that the new world organization (which Stalin had agreed to support) would "provide the greatest opportunity in all history" to secure a lasting peace. As if to lay to rest the isolationist sentiments that had destroyed Woodrow Wilson's dream, Roosevelt told Congress, "We shall take responsibility for world collaboration, or we shall have to bear the responsibility for another world conflict." Privately the president was less optimistic. He confessed to one friend that he doubted that, "when the chips were down, Stalin would be able to carry out and deliver what he had agreed to."

Who Is Harry Truman?

The Yalta Conference marked one of the last and most controversial chapters of Franklin Roosevelt's presidency. Critics charged that the concessions to Stalin had left American national interests unprotected. Poland had been betrayed; China sold out; the United Nations crippled at birth. Yet Roosevelt gave to Stalin little that Stalin had not liberated with Russian blood and could have taken anyway. Four out of five Nazi soldiers killed in action died on the eastern front.

What peace Roosevelt might have achieved can never be known. He returned from Yalta visibly ill. On April 12, 1945, while sitting for his portrait at his vacation home in Warm Springs, Georgia, he complained of a "terrific headache," then suddenly fell unconscious. Two hours later he was dead, the victim of a cerebral hemorrhage. Not since the assassination of Lincoln had the nation so grieved. Under Roosevelt's leadership government had become a protector, the president a father and friend, and the United States the leader in the struggle against Axis tyranny. Eleanor Roosevelt recalled how many Americans later told her that "they missed the way the President used to talk to them. . . . There was a real dialogue between Franklin and the people."

TRUMAN BECOMES PRESIDENT   Harry S Truman faced the awesome task of replacing Roosevelt. "Who the hell is Harry Truman?" the chief of staff had asked when Truman was nominated for the vice presidency in 1944. In the brief period he served as vice president, Truman had met with Roosevelt fewer than 10 times. He knew almost nothing about the president's postwar plans and promises. When a reporter now addressed him as "Mr. President," he winced. "I wish you didn't have to call me that," he said. Sensing his own inadequacies, Truman adopted a tough pose and made his mind up quickly. People welcomed the new president's decisiveness as a relief from Roosevelt's evasive style. Too often, though, Truman acted before the issues were clear. He at least knew victory in Europe was near as Allied troops swept into Germany.

The Holocaust

The horror of war in no way prepared the invading armies for the liberation of the concentration camps. Hitler, they discovered, had ordered the systematic extermination of all European Jews, as well as Gypsies, homosexuals, and others considered deviant. The SS, Hitler's security force, had constructed six extermination centers in Germany and Poland. By rail from all over Europe, the SS shipped Jews to die in the gas chambers.

No issue of World War II more starkly raised questions of human good and evil than what came to be known as the Holocaust. Tragically, the United States could have done more to save some of the 6 million Jews that were killed. Until the autumn of 1941 the Nazis permitted Jews to leave Europe, but few countries would accept them—including the United States. Americans haunted by unemployment feared that a tide of new immigrants would make competition for jobs even worse. Tales of persecution from war refugees had little effect on most citizens: opinion polls showed that more than 70 percent of Americans opposed easing quotas. After 1938 the restrictive provisions of the 1924 Immigration Act were made even tighter.

American Jews wanted to help, especially after 1942, when they learned of the death camps. But they worried that highly visible protests might only aggravate American **anti-Semitism**. They were also split over support for Zionists working to establish a Jewish homeland in Palestine. The British had blocked Jewish emigration to Palestine and, to avoid alienating the Arabs, opposed Zionism. Roosevelt and his advisors ultimately decided that the best way to save Jews was to win the war quickly, but that strategy still does not explain why the Allies did not do more. They could have bombed the rail lines to the camps, sent commando forces, or tried to destroy the death factories.

A Lasting Peace

BRETTON WOODS ECONOMIC STRATEGIES After 15 years of depression and then war, the Allies sought a new international framework for cooperation among nations. That system, many believed, needed to be economic as well as political. At a 1944 meeting at Bretton Woods, a resort in New Hampshire, Americans led the way in creating two new economic organizations: the International Monetary Fund (IMF) and the International Bank for Reconstruction and Development, later known as the World Bank. The IMF hoped to promote trade by stabilizing national currencies, and the World Bank was designed to stimulate economic growth by investing in projects worldwide.

Pivotal Events in World War II

	MILITARY/DIPLOMATIC	HOME FRONT	SOCIOECONOMIC
1941	Germany invades Russia "Four Freedoms" states war principles Japanese attack Pearl Harbor	Labor unrest Lend-Lease Act Roosevelt creates FEPC to fight discrimination	Increased war production boosts economy
1942	Battle of Midway breaks Japanese naval superiority Invasion of North Africa Battle of Stalingrad	Japanese aliens and Japanese Americans placed in internment camps New Deal in retreat	Industry converts to war production; auto manufacturing halted
1943	Allies invade Sicily and Italy Central Pacific island-hopping campaign Teheran Conference	Detroit race riot Zoot suit riots Coal miners strike	Women flood into war industries Prosperity returns
1944	D-Day: Allies invade France Battle of the Bulge MacArthur invades the Philippines	Roosevelt reelected to fourth term Supreme Court upholds Japanese internment	International Monetary Fund and World Bank created
1945	Yalta Conference Holocaust revealed Germany surrenders Potsdam Conference Atomic bombs dropped on Japan; war ends	Roosevelt dies; Harry Truman becomes president	

Source: Library of Congress, Prints and Photographs Division [LC-DIG-ppmsca-18531]

In April 1945, at the concentration camp in Buchenwald, Germany, Senator Alben Barkley of Kentucky viewed a grisly reminder of the horrors of the Nazis' "final solution." As vice president under Harry Truman, Barkley urged the administration to support an independent homeland in Israel for Jews.

Source: National Archives (292594)

DUMBARTON OAKS AND THE UNO Later that summer the Allies met at Dumbarton Oaks, a Washington, D.C., estate, to lay out the structure for the proposed United Nations Organization (UNO, later known simply as the UN). An 11-member Security Council would oversee a General Assembly composed of delegates from all member nations. By the end of the first organizational meeting, held in San Francisco in April 1945, it had become clear that the United Nations would favor the Western powers in most postwar disputes.

While the United Nations was organizing itself in San Francisco, the Axis powers were collapsing in Europe. As Mussolini attempted to escape to Germany, antifascist mobs in Italy captured and slaughtered him like a pig. Adolf Hitler committed suicide in his Berlin bunker on April 30. Two weeks later General Eisenhower accepted the German surrender.

POTSDAM SUMMIT In one final summit meeting, held in July 1945 at Potsdam (just outside Berlin), President Truman met Churchill and Stalin for the first time. Two issues dominated the meeting: Germany's political fate and how much the defeated nation would pay in reparations. The three leaders agreed that Germany should be occupied and demilitarized. Stalin insisted that Russia receive a minimum of $10 billion, regardless of how much it might hurt postwar Germany or the European economy. A complicated compromise allowed Britain and the United States to restrict reparations from their zones. But in large part Stalin had his way. For the foreseeable future, Germany would remain divided into occupation zones and without a central government of its own.

Atomic Diplomacy

In their negotiations at Potsdam, the Allies never addressed one of the most crucial issues they faced: What would be the future of atomic weapons? On July 16, 1945, the first atomic fireball rose from the desert in Alamogordo, New Mexico. Scientists at the Manhattan Project had successfully detonated their first explosive device. On receiving the news, Truman returned to the negotiations a changed man—firmer, more confident. He "told the Russians just where they got on and off and generally bossed the whole meeting," observed Churchill. Several questions loomed: Should the United States now use the bomb? Should it warn Japan before dropping it? And perhaps equally vital, should Truman inform Stalin?

SHOULD THE BOMB BE DROPPED? Some scientists recommended not using the bomb or at least attempting to convince Japan to surrender by exploding a demonstration bomb to show the Japanese the danger they faced. A high-level committee considered but then dismissed that idea, though some committee members later regretted they did so. Nor did Truman choose to tell Stalin about the bomb. He mentioned only obliquely that the United States possessed a weapon of "awesome destructiveness." Stalin, whose spies had already informed him of the bomb, showed no surprise. He remarked casually that he hoped the Americans would use their new weapon to good effect against Japan. Atomic diplomacy had failed its first test. Stalin immediately stepped up the Russian program to build an atom bomb. After Potsdam the nuclear arms race was on.

Source: Standish Backus Jr., *Hiroshima*, 1945. Navy Art Collection, Naval Historical Center, Washington, DC

| *This aerial view of Hiroshima gives stark testimony to the destructive force of the atomic blast. In one of the many bitter ironies, only the shells of the Western-style buildings survived.*

Finally, Truman and Churchill decided to drop the first bomb with only an implied warning to the Japanese. In an ultimatum issued at Potsdam, they demanded unconditional surrender and threatened Japan with "inevitable and complete destruction" using the "full application of our military power" if it did not comply. Unaware of the warning's full meaning, officials in Tokyo made no formal reply.

THE BOMB AS A THREAT TO THE SOVIETS   Truman and Churchill knew Japan was on the verge of defeat. Japan's leaders had even sent peace feelers to the Russians. Why, then, did the Allies insist on unconditional surrender? Some historians have charged that Secretary of State James Byrnes, a staunch anticommunist, wanted a dramatic combat demonstration of the bomb that would persuade Stalin to behave less aggressively in negotiations with the British and Americans. However much Byrnes had Soviet diplomacy on his mind, most evidence indicates that Truman decided to drop the bomb in order to end the war quickly.

Before leaving Potsdam, Truman ordered crews on Tinian Island in the South Pacific to proceed to their first target as soon as weather permitted. On August 6 the *Enola Gay,* a B-29 bomber, dropped a uranium bomb nicknamed "Little Boy" that leveled 4 square miles of Hiroshima, an industrial and military center. The blast immediately killed nearly 80,000 people (including 20 American prisoners of war). A German priest came upon soldiers who had looked up as the bomb exploded. Their eyeballs had melted from their sockets. Another eyewitness spoke of survivors "so broken and confused that they moved and behaved like automatons." Two days later the Soviet Union declared war on Japan, and on August 9 the United States detonated a second atomic bomb (a plutonium weapon nicknamed "Fat Man") over the port of Nagasaki. Another 60,000 people were killed instantly. In both cities many who lived through the horror began to sicken and die as radiation poisoning claimed tens of thousands of additional lives.

The two explosions left the Japanese stunned. Breaking all precedents, the emperor intervened and declared openly for peace. On September 3 a humiliated Japanese delegation boarded the battleship *Missouri* in Tokyo Bay and signed the document of surrender. World War II had ended.

 REVIEW

In what ways did Allied diplomacy deal with the postwar world in terms of Germany, international stability, and the role of atomic weapons?

PUTTING HISTORY IN A GLOBAL CONTEXT

"WORLD WAR II CHANGED everything," observed an admiral long after the war. The despair of the Depression gave way to the exhilaration of victory. Before the war Americans seldom exerted leadership in international affairs. After, the world looked to the United States to rebuild the economies of Europe and Asia and to maintain peace. World War II had not only shown the global interdependence of economic and political systems; it had also increased that interdependence. Out of the war developed a truly international economy. At home the trends toward bigness and centralization vastly accelerated. Advances in electronics, communications, and aviation brought the world closer to every home. Government grew, too. The size of the national debt alone guaranteed that Washington, D.C., would continue to dominate the economy. Americans had come to believe in a strong defense, even if that meant a large federal bureaucracy and a generous military budget.

Still, a number of fears loomed, despite the victory parades snaking down the nation's main streets. Would the inevitable cutbacks in spending bring on another depression? Would Soviet ambitions undo the new global peace, much as fascism and economic instability had undone the peace of Versailles? And then there was the shadow of the atomic bomb looming over the victorious as well as the defeated. As a sobered Robert Oppenheimer, director of the bomb project at Los Alamos, told a group of scientists: "If atomic bombs are to be added to the arsenals of warring nations . . . then the day will come when mankind will curse the names of Los Alamos and Hiroshima." With the advent of the atomic age, no one in the world, not even in the United States, was safe anymore.

CHAPTER SUMMARY

World War II deepened the global interdependence of nations and left the United States as the greatest economic and military power in the world.

- As fascism spread in Europe and as militarism spread in Asia, Franklin Roosevelt struggled to help America's allies by overcoming domestic political isolation and the fervor for neutrality.

- Despite German aggression against Poland in 1939, France and the Low Countries in 1940, and the Soviet Union in 1941, the United States did not enter the war until the Japanese surprise attack on Pearl Harbor in December 1941.

- The alliance forged among British prime minister Winston Churchill, Soviet premier Joseph Stalin, and President Franklin Roosevelt did not swerve from its decision to subdue Germany first, even though early defeats and America's lack of preparation slowed the war effort until 1943.

- At home America's factories produced enough goods to supply the domestic economy and America's allies.

  ▸ Demands for labor created opportunities for women and minorities.

  ▸ War hysteria aggravated old prejudices and led to the internment of Japanese Americans.

  ▸ New Deal reform ended as "Dr. Win-the-War" replaced "Dr. New Deal."

- Although the successful landings in France on D-Day and the island-hopping campaign in the Pacific made it clear that the Allies would win the war, issues over Poland, Germany, and postwar boundaries raised doubts about the peace.

- The war ended with the atomic bombings of Hiroshima and Nagasaki, but not soon enough to limit the horrors of the Holocaust.

Digging Deeper

A comprehensive treatment of the war years is David M. Kennedy, *The American People in World War II: Freedom from Fear: Part II* (2003). Robert A. Divine, *The Reluctant Belligerent* (2nd ed., 1979), is still excellent on the prewar diplomacy. Andrew Roberts, *Masters and Commanders: How Four Titans Won the War in the West, 1941-1945* (2009), explains the dynamics of Anglo-American relations. Perhaps the most powerful single volume on the war is Max Hastings's *Inferno: The World at War, 1939-1945* (2011), while Martin Gilbert's *The Second World War: A Complete History* (2004) captures the vast scale. Richard Lingeman, *Don't You Know There's a War On? The American Home Front, 1941-1945* (updated ed., 2003), is a classic study. Emily Yellin, *Our Mothers' War: American Women at Home and at the Front during World War II* (2005), explores the many roles women played. Tetsuden Kashima, *Judgment without Trial: Japanese American Imprisonment during World War II* (2003), examines the diverse experiences of those in the camps and reveals that planning for internment of the Japanese began well before the war.

The decision to drop two atomic bombs on Japan remains one of the most controversial legacies of the war. To better understand the racial dimension, see John W. Dower, *War without Mercy: Race and Power in the Pacific War* (1986). Richard Rhodes, *The Making of the Atomic Bomb* (1987), re-creates the history of the Manhattan Project. Gar Alperovitz, *The Decision to Use the Atomic Bomb* (1995), extends an interpretation he first advanced in *Atomic Diplomacy* (1965) that the Soviet Union was the planners' real target. Martin J. Sherwin, *A World Destroyed* (rev. ed., 1985), with Kai Bird, *American Prometheus: The Triumph and Tragedy of J. Robert Oppenheimer* (2005), discusses the process of designing and using the bomb. David Holloway, *Stalin and the Bomb: The Soviet Union and Atomic Energy, 1939-1956* (1994), uses Russian sources to trace the origins of atomic diplomacy. Students who wish to work with some of the original documents should see Michael Stoff et al., *The Manhattan Project: A Documentary Introduction to the Atomic Age* (1991).

After the Fact

Did the Atomic Bomb Save Lives?

History is littered with countless *what ifs,* especially concerning events of great moment. What if the South had won the Civil War? What if Washington's crossing of the Delaware had failed? What if the Allies had defeated Japan without dropping two atomic bombs? Historians regularly deal with such counterfactual questions, but they often find it difficult to weigh alternatives or realistically explore the roads not taken. Whether the use of the atomic bomb actually saved lives is one such question, and it was debated almost right from the moment of decision. How do we weigh the alternatives?

When news came that the United States had exploded a powerful new atomic device over Japan, the GIs in the field saw immediately that there would be no need for a massive invasion of Japan. As the

©Everett Collection Inc/Alamy

lyrics of one popular song put it, "I believe the bomb that struck Hiroshima/was the answer to a fighting boy's prayers." After the war, Winston Churchill made the same point by calling the bomb "a miracle of deliverance." To conquer Japan "yard by yard might well require the loss of a million American lives," he told Congress. President Truman's memoirs put the totals somewhat lower: he referred to military estimates of over a million *casualties* (members of the military lost to service because of injury, capture, or death), including half a million American deaths.

> made use of this newly gained power. If the test should
> fail, then it would be even more important to us to bring
> about a surrender before we had to make a physical conquest
> of Japan. General Marshall told me that it might cost half
> a million American lives to force the enemy's surrender on
> his home grounds.

Harry S Truman, Memoirs, typescript, page 804: an estimate of half a million deaths. Reprinted by permission of Margaret Truman Daniel.

To most Americans, such large numbers made sense. Japanese resistance during the Pacific campaigns had been fierce. On the island of Okinawa alone, hand-to-hand fighting claimed over 12,000 American soldiers, sailors, and marines. American troops used flamethrowers to burn Japanese out of caves and holes. In the half century following World War II, most historians assumed that dropping the bomb saved the United States from mounting a bloody invasion of the Japanese home islands.

But how did Truman, Churchill, and other participants arrive at such casualty figures? The conclusion that the United States dropped the bomb to end the war quickly and to avoid 500,000 American deaths became one of the most controversial of World War II. The debate arose, in part, because of the horror of nuclear weaponry. Critics have suggested that Japan might well have been persuaded to surrender without an atomic attack.

WOULD JAPAN SURRENDER?

THAT DEBATE—WHICH BEGAN IN earnest during the 1960s—has analyzed a host of factors affecting Truman's decision. Many navy and air corps officers believed that a naval blockade and conventional bombing were enough to force Japan's surrender without an invasion. The country, after all, was virtually without defense against bombing raids. Later critics have suggested that the Allies should have modified their demand for "unconditional surrender," instead allowing the Japanese to keep their revered institution of the emperor. (As events turned out, Japan surrendered only after such a guarantee was issued.) Others argue that the United States should have arranged for a demonstration of the bomb's power without actually detonating one over Japan.

Yet, as the debates over these alternatives swirled during the 1960s and 1970s, no one challenged the estimates of a million casualties if the Allies invaded. That number had been put forward in 1947 by Henry Stimson, the highly respected former secretary of war. In an article for *Harper's* magazine Stimson wrote, "We estimated the major fighting would not end until the latter part of 1946 at the earliest. I was informed that such operations might be expected to cost over a million casualties, to American forces alone."

SHIFTING NUMBERS

STIMSON'S ACCOUNT CAST A LONG shadow. A few years later Harry Truman provided an air force historian with a significantly lower number. Truman recalled that General George Marshall,

Source: National Archives (542192)
Hiroshima, August 6, 1945

the army chief of staff, had told him in July 1945 that in an invasion of Japan one-quarter of a million casualties would be the cost as well as an equal number of Japanese. But when a White House aide checked Truman's memory against Stimson's account, he discovered the discrepancy—one million versus only a quarter million. "The President's casualty figure [should] be changed to conform with that of Secretary Stimson," the aide advised, "because presumably Stimson got his from Gen. Marshall; the size of the casualty figures is very important."

©Brian Brake/Science Source

Remains of a wristwatch from the atomic blast site at Hiroshima. The bomb exploded at 8:16 a.m.

The last phrase is significant. Why were the numbers so important? Obviously, the higher the number of potential casualties, the stronger the case that using the bomb saved lives. So it is worth looking a bit more closely at Stimson's article.

In fact, the idea to write an article was not actually Stimson's. It came from another atomic policy maker, James Conant. Conant, the president of Harvard University, had become increasingly concerned about "the spreading accusation that it was unnecessary to use the atomic bomb at all." He complained privately in 1946 that "this type of sentimentalism . . . is bound to have a great deal of influence on the next generation. The type of person who goes into teaching, particularly school teaching, will be influenced a great deal by this type of argument." Conant believed that Stimson had the prestige to counter such criticisms. He had distinguished himself twice as secretary of war, and also as an ambassador and secretary of state.

So Stimson agreed to write an article. But where did he get his casualty estimates? During the war a memo from former president Herbert Hoover had been circulated, warning that an invasion could claim anywhere from half a million to a million American lives. At the time, in June 1945, a successful test of an atomic bomb was still a month away and the possibility of an invasion loomed larger. Stimson was convinced that the war might be ended without an invasion if the Allies would only assure the Japanese that the position of emperor would be protected. Hoover's dire warning about the costs of an invasion reinforced Stimson's argument against invading.

But unlike the aide who later helped Truman with his memoirs, Stimson did not get similarly high casualty estimates from General Marshall. Marshall's staff

©Fotosearch/Stringer/Getty Images

Japanese fighting on Okinawa and other Pacific islands produced high casualty and death rates for American forces, reinforcing the notion that an invasion of Japan would claim many American lives.

thought Hoover's estimates were way too high. They estimated that the first-stage invasion (of Kyushu Island) might produce American casualties of perhaps 31,000, including about 7,000 to 8,000 deaths. If the invasion of Japan's main island, Honshu, took place, those numbers would rise to 120,000 casualties and 25,000 deaths. Estimates by General MacArthur were slightly higher, but within the same range. For reasons that remain unclear, however, when Stimson wrote his article after the war, he chose to use the higher estimates.

Thus, intentionally or not, Stimson's article greatly overestimated the number of invasion casualties predicted by the American military. And Conant's private worries show that those who dropped the bomb were more sensitive about their decision than they wished to admit. One of the most telling illustrations of the pressure to keep the estimates high can be seen in the successive drafts of Harry

Earlier letter from Truman to an air force historian. Here, Truman's and Marshall's estimate is a quarter of a million casualties, not deaths.

Truman's own memoirs, which were finally published in 1955. The assistants who helped Truman kept revising the figure upward. Truman's recollection, in 1952, mentioned only 250,000 casualties (not deaths); that figure jumped to 500,000 casualties in the first draft; then, in the published version, to a "half-million" *lives* saved.

WEIGHING POLITICAL CALCULATIONS

DO THE LOWER FIGURES MEAN that historians should condemn Truman, Stimson, and others for preferring to use the bomb rather than invade Japan? Not necessarily. After Japan's surprise attack on Pearl Harbor and its fierce resistance in the Pacific islands, American sentiments against the Japanese ran high. The atomic bomb had cost $2 billion to develop, and officials always assumed that if the bomb were successful, it would be used. Why else develop it? Truman (and most Americans) probably believed that even an invasion costing 25,000 lives would have justified using the bomb. Historian Max Hastings observed that in August 1945 after six years of horrific carnage, "to Allied leaders the lives of their own people had come to seem very precious, those of their enemies very cheap." Certainly, as Hastings added, Japanese leaders bore "overwhelming responsibility," for if they had bowed to the inevitable and shown more concern for their own people "by quitting the war, the atomic bombs would not have been dropped."

Historians must constantly remind themselves that seemingly "impartial" accounts are influenced by the conditions under which they were created. Stimson set out not simply to tell the facts about the decision to drop the bomb. He wished to justify a decision he believed was necessary and proper. Like Conant, he understood that the record of the past is always shaped by those who do the telling. "History," he wrote in 1948, "is often not what actually happened but what is recorded as such."

1945–1954

The Honest John rocket was the first nuclear armed surface-to-surface missile manufactured by the United States in the early 1950s. It could carry either a conventional explosive or a 20-kiloton nuclear warhead. As World War II gave way to a cold war between two new superpowers, the United States and the Soviet Union, American military planners began to rely increasingly on nuclear weapons.

©Bettmann/Getty Images

>> An American Story

GLAD TO BE HOME?

The war had been over for almost five months and still troopships steamed into New York City and other ports. Timuel Black was packing his duffel belowdecks when he heard some of the white soldiers shout, "There she is! The Statue of Liberty!" Black felt a little bitter about the war. He'd been drafted in Chicago in 1943, just after race riots ripped the city. His father, a strong supporter of civil rights, was angry. "What the hell are you goin' to fight in Europe for? The fight is here." He wanted his son to go with him to demonstrate in Detroit, except the roads were blocked and the buses and trains screened to prevent more African Americans from coming in.

Instead, Black went off to fight the Nazis, serving in a segregated army. He'd gone ashore during the D-Day invasion, survived the Battle of the Bulge, and marched through one of the

German concentration camps. "The first thing you get is the stench," he recalled. "Everybody knows that's human stench. You begin to realize something terrible had happened. There's quietness. You get closer and you begin to see what's happened to these creatures. And you get—I got more passionately angry than I guess I'd ever been." He thought: if it could happen here, to the Germans, it could happen anywhere. It could happen to black folk in America. So when the white soldiers called to come up and see the Statue of Liberty, Black's reaction was, "Hell, I'm not goin' up there. Damn that." But after all, he went up. "All of a sudden, I found myself with tears, cryin' and saying the same thing [the white soldiers] were saying. Glad to be home, proud of my country, as irregular as it is. Determined that it could be better."

At the same time, Betty Basye was working across the continent as a nurse in a burn-and-blind center at Menlo Park, California. Her hospital treated soldiers shipped back from the Pacific: "Blind young men. Eyes gone, legs gone. Parts of the face. Burns—you'd land with a fire-bomb and be up in flames." She'd joke with the men, trying to keep their spirits up, talking about times to come. She liked to take Bill, one of her favorites, for walks downtown. Half of Bill's face was gone, and civilians would stare. It happened to other patients, too. "Nicely dressed women, absolutely staring, just standing there staring." Some people wrote the local paper, wondering why disfigured vets couldn't be kept on their own grounds and off the streets. Such callousness made Basye indignant. The war was over— "and we're still here." After a time,

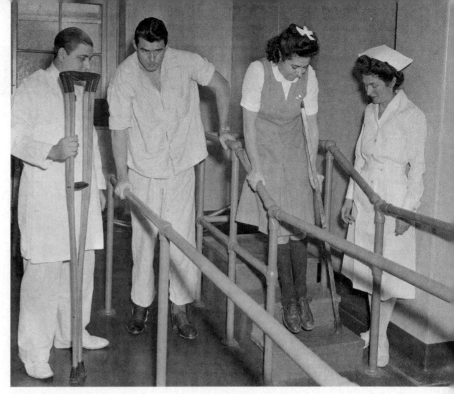

©Bettmann/Getty Images
| *A rehabilitation center*

she started dating a soldier back from the South Pacific. "I got busy after the war," she recalled, "getting married and having my four children. That's what you were supposed to do. And getting your house in suburbia."

Yet as Basye and Black soon discovered, the return to "normal" life was filled with uncertainties. The first truly global war had left a large part of Europe in ruins and the old balance of power shattered. The dramatic events occurring month after month during 1945 and 1946 made it clear that whatever new world order emerged, the United States would have a central role in building it. Isolation seemed neither practical nor desirable in an era in which the power of the Soviet Union and communism seemed on the rise.

To blunt that threat, the United States converted not so much to peace as to a "cold war" against its former Soviet ally. This undeclared war came to affect almost every

aspect of American life. Abroad, it justified a far wider military and economic role for the United States in areas like the Middle East and the Pacific Rim nations of Asia, from Korea to Indochina. At home it sent politicians scurrying across the land in a search for Communist spies and **"subversives,"** from the State Department to the movie studios of Hollywood and even into college classrooms.

Preparing for war in times of peace dramatically increased the role of the military-industrial-university complex formed during World War II. A nation that had traditionally followed an isolationist foreign policy would come to deploy military forces across the globe. A people who had once kept government intrusion into the economy at a minimum now voted to maintain programs that ensured an active federal role. That economy produced prosperity beyond anything Americans had known before. <<

685

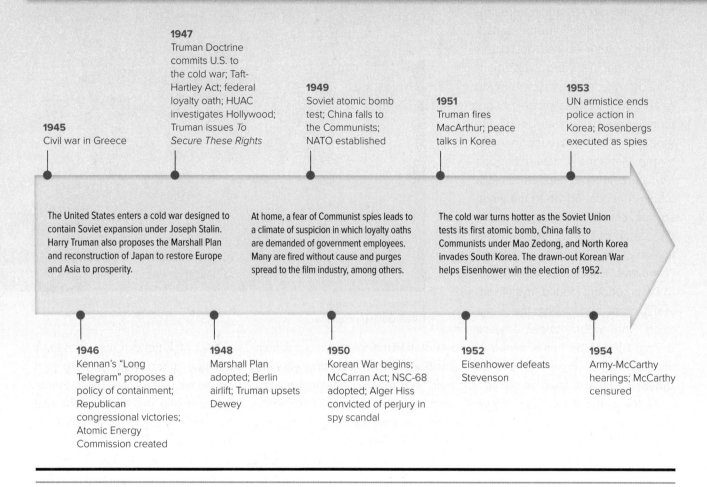

1945
Civil war in Greece

1946
Kennan's "Long Telegram" proposes a policy of containment; Republican congressional victories; Atomic Energy Commission created

1947
Truman Doctrine commits U.S. to the cold war; Taft-Hartley Act; federal loyalty oath; HUAC investigates Hollywood; Truman issues *To Secure These Rights*

1948
Marshall Plan adopted; Berlin airlift; Truman upsets Dewey

1949
Soviet atomic bomb test; China falls to the Communists; NATO established

1950
Korean War begins; McCarran Act; NSC-68 adopted; Alger Hiss convicted of perjury in spy scandal

1951
Truman fires MacArthur; peace talks in Korea

1952
Eisenhower defeats Stevenson

1953
UN armistice ends police action in Korea; Rosenbergs executed as spies

1954
Army-McCarthy hearings; McCarthy censured

The United States enters a cold war designed to contain Soviet expansion under Joseph Stalin. Harry Truman also proposes the Marshall Plan and reconstruction of Japan to restore Europe and Asia to prosperity.

At home, a fear of Communist spies leads to a climate of suspicion in which loyalty oaths are demanded of government employees. Many are fired without cause and purges spread to the film industry, among others.

The cold war turns hotter as the Soviet Union tests its first atomic bomb, China falls to Communists under Mao Zedong, and North Korea invades South Korea. The drawn-out Korean War helps Eisenhower win the election of 1952.

THE RISE OF THE COLD WAR

WORLD WAR II DEVASTATED LANDS and people almost everywhere outside the Western Hemisphere. Once the war ended, the world struggled to rebuild. Power that had once been centered in Europe shifted to nations on its periphery. In place of Germany, France, and England, the United States and the Soviet Union emerged as the world's two reigning superpowers—and as enemies. Their rivalry was not altogether an equal one. The United States ended the war with a booming economy, a massive military establishment, and the atomic bomb. In contrast, much of the Soviet Union lay in ruins.

AMERICANS FEAR SOVIET INTENTIONS But the defeat of Germany and Japan left no power in Europe or Asia to block the still-formidable Soviet army. And many Americans feared that desperate, war-weary peoples would find the appeal of communism irresistible. If Stalin intended to extend the Soviet Union's dominion, only the United States had the economic and military might to block him.

Events in the critical years of 1945 and 1946 persuaded most Americans that Stalin did have such a plan. The Truman administration concluded that "the USSR has engaged the United States in a struggle for power, or 'cold war,' in which our national security is at stake and from which we cannot withdraw short of national suicide." What had happened that led Western leaders to such a dire view of their former Soviet allies? How did such a wide breach open between the two nations?

American Suspicions

ROOTS OF THE COLD WAR Even before postwar events deepened American suspicions of the Soviets, an ideological gulf had separated the two nations. The October Revolution of 1917 shocked most Americans. They had come to view Lenin's Bolshevik revolutionaries with a mixture of fear, suspicion, and loathing. As the Communists grasped power, they had often used violence and terror to achieve their ends. As Marxists they rejected both religion and the notion of private property, two institutions central to the American way of life.

Source: United States Army Signal Corps. Harry S. Truman Library & Museum

| *Churchill, Truman, and Stalin met at Potsdam in July 1945. Their smiles masked serious disagreements about the shape of the postwar world.*

Furthermore, Soviet propagandists had made no secret that they intended to export revolution throughout the world, including the United States.

MUNICH ANALOGY   One event leading to World War II taught Western leaders to resist "appeasement." In 1938 British prime minister Neville Chamberlain's attempt to satisfy Hitler's demands on Czechoslovakia only emboldened the Nazis to expand further. After the war, Secretary of the Navy James Forrestal applied the Munich analogy to the new Europe. Appeasing Russian demands, he believed, would only seem like an attempt "to buy their understanding and sympathy. We tried that once with Hitler. . . . There are no returns on appeasement." To many of Truman's advisors, the Soviet dictator seemed as much bent on conquest as Hitler had been.

Communist Expansion

During the war Stalin did make numerous demands to control territory along the Soviet borders. And with the coming of peace, he continued to push for greater influence. He asked for a role in controlling the Dardanelles, the narrow strait linking Soviet ports on the Black Sea with the Mediterranean Sea. Soviet forces occupying northern Iran backed a rebellion against the Iranian government. In Greece, local Communists led the fighting to overturn the traditional monarchy.

Asia, too, seemed a target for Communist ambitions. Russian occupation forces in Manchuria were turning over captured Japanese arms to Chinese Communists under Mao Zedong. Russian troops controlled the northern half of Korea. In Vietnam leftist nationalists were fighting against the return of French colonial rule.

Despite Russian actions, many historians have argued, American policy makers consistently exaggerated Stalin's ambitions. At war's end, much of the farmland and industry in the Soviet Union lay in ruins. When Stalin looked outward, he saw American occupation forces in Europe and Asia ringing the Soviet Union, their military might backed by a newly developed atomic arsenal. American corporations owned or controlled vast oil fields in the Middle East. Along with the French and the British, the United States was a strong presence in Southeast Asia. Given that situation, many historians have argued, Stalin's actions after the war were primarily defensive, designed to counter what appeared to him a threatening American-European alliance.

More recent evidence from once-secret files of the Soviet Union suggests that despite the ravages of war, Stalin recognized that in 1945 the Soviet Union was emerging as a world power. With Germany and Japan defeated, Soviet borders to the east and west were secure from invasion. Only to the south did Stalin see a problem, along the border with Iran. Further, he recognized that the people of Britain and the United States were tired of war. Their leaders were not about to attack the Soviet Union, at least not in the near term. Equally significant, Soviet spies had informed Stalin in 1946 that the United States possessed only a few atomic bombs. For the time being, the nuclear threat was more symbolic than real. As a political realist, Stalin saw an opportunity to advance the interests of the Soviet state and his own regime—as long as his actions did not risk war.

The tensions arising from the conflicting Soviet and American points of view came to a head in the first months of 1946. Stalin announced in February that the Soviet Union would act vigorously to preserve its national security. In a world dominated by capitalism, he warned, future wars were inevitable. The Russian people had to ensure against "any eventuality" by undertaking a new five-year plan for economic development.

THE MOVE TO "GET TOUGH"   Although some Americans thought Stalin was merely rallying Russian support for his domestic programs, others agreed with *Time* magazine, an early voice for a "get tough" policy, when it called Stalin's speech "the most warlike pronouncement uttered by any top-rank statesman since V-J day." "I'm tired of babying the Soviets," remarked President Truman, who in any case seldom wore kid gloves. Truman's advisors spelled out the political advantages of taking this tough line toward the Soviet Union. "The worse matters get . . . ," they told him, "the more there is a sense of crisis. In times of crisis, the American citizen tends to back up his president." In March, Winston Churchill warned that the Soviets had dropped an "Iron Curtain"

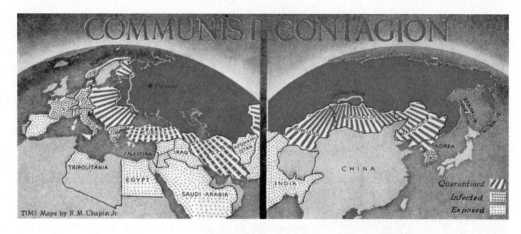

| As American fears of Soviet intentions increased, journalists often described communism as though it were a disease, an inhuman force, or a savage predator. In April 1946 Time magazine, a particularly outspoken source of anticommunist rhetoric, portrayed the spread of "infection" throughout Europe and Asia as the "Red Menace."
©AP Photo

between their satellite nations and the free world. Poland, East Germany, Romania, and Bulgaria lay behind it. Iran, Greece, Turkey, and much of Europe seemed at risk.

Containment

As policy makers groped for an effective way to deal with these developments, the State Department received a diplomatic cable, extraordinary for both its length (8,000 words) and its impact in Washington. The author was George Kennan, chargé d'affaires in Moscow and long a student of Soviet conduct. Kennan argued that Russian leaders, including Stalin, were so paranoid that it was impossible to reach any useful accommodations with them. This temperament could best be explained by "the traditional and instinctive Russian sense of insecurity." That insecurity, when combined with Marxist ideology that viewed capitalism as the enemy, created a potent force for expansion. Soviet power, Kennan explained, "moves inexorably along a prescribed path, like a toy automobile wound up and headed in a given direction, stopping only when it meets some unanswerable force."

GEORGE KENNAN DEFINES CONTAINMENT   The response Kennan recommended was "containment." The United States must apply "unalterable counterforce at every point where [the Soviets] show signs of encroaching upon the interests of a peaceful and stable world." The idea of containment was not particularly novel, but Kennan's historical analysis provided leaders in Washington with a framework for analyzing Soviet behavior. By applying firm diplomatic, economic, and military counterpressure, the United States could block Russian aggression. Truman wholeheartedly adopted the doctrine of containment.

The Truman Doctrine

At first it appeared that Iran, lying along the Soviet Union's southern border, would provide a key test. An independent Iran seemed crucial in protecting rich fields of petroleum in the Persian Gulf region. Stalin had pledged to withdraw Russian troops from Iran after the war, but did not, hoping

to force Iran to grant the Soviets economic and political concessions. In March 1946 Secretary of State James Byrnes went to the United Nations, determined to force a showdown over continued Soviet occupation of northern Iran. But before he could extract his pound of Russian flesh, the Soviets reached an agreement with Iran to withdraw.

AID TO GREECE AND TURKEY   The face-off in Iran only intensified American suspicions. In Europe severe winter storms and a depressed postwar economy threatened to encourage domestic Communist movements. A turning point in the cold war came in early 1947, when Great Britain announced that it could no longer support the governments of Greece and Turkey. Without British aid, the Communists seemed destined to win critical victories. Truman decided that the United States should provide $400 million in military and economic aid. He went before Congress in March, determined to "scare hell out of the country." The world was now divided into two hostile camps, the president warned. To preserve the American way of life the United States must now step forward and help "free people" threatened by "**totalitarian** regimes." This rationale for aid to Greece and Turkey soon became known as the Truman Doctrine.

The Truman Doctrine marked a new level of American commitment to a cold war. Just what responsibility the Soviets had for unrest in Greece and Turkey remained unclear. But Truman had linked communism with rebel movements all around the globe. That committed Americans to a relatively open-ended struggle. In the battle between communism and freedom, the president gained expanded powers to act when unrest threatened. Occasionally, Congress would regret giving the executive branch so much power, but by 1947 anticommunism had become the dominant theme in American policy, both foreign and domestic.

The Marshall Plan

For all its importance, the Truman Doctrine did not address the area of primary concern to Washington, Western Europe. Across Europe desperate people scrounged for food and coal to heat their homes. Streets stood dark at night.

National treasuries had neither capital nor credit needed to reopen idled factories. American diplomats warned that without aid to revive the European economy, Communists would seize power in Germany, Italy, and France.

In June 1947 Secretary of State George C. Marshall stepped before a Harvard commencement audience to announce a recovery plan for Europe. He invited all European nations, East and West, to request assistance to rebuild their economies. Unlike Truman, Marshall did not emphasize the Communist menace. All the same, his massive aid plan was designed to eliminate conditions that produced the discontent Communists often exploited. Humanitarian aid also had its practical benefits. As Europe recovered, so would its ability to buy American goods. The secretary did not rule out Soviet participation, but he gambled that fears of American economic domination would lead the Soviets and their allies to reject his offer.

COMMUNISM IN CZECHOSLOVAKIA At first **neo-isolationists** in Congress argued that the United States could not afford such generosity. But when Communists expelled the non-Communists from Czechoslovakia's government, the cold war seemed to spread. Congress then approved the Marshall Plan, as it became known. And as the secretary anticipated, the Soviets blocked the efforts of Czechoslovakia and Poland to participate. The blame for dividing Europe fell, as Marshall guessed it would, on the Soviet Union, not the United States.

The Fall of Eastern Europe

American efforts to stabilize Europe and the eastern Mediterranean led Stalin to take countermeasures. Most shocking to the Western nations were his steps to consolidate Soviet political and military domination over Eastern Europe. In 1947 he moved against Hungary, run since 1945 by a moderate government chosen under relatively free elections. Soviet forces imposed a Communist regime dependent on Moscow. In February 1948 Communists toppled the duly elected government of Czechoslovakia. Shortly after, news came that the popular Czech foreign minister, Jan Masaryk, had fallen to his death from a small bathroom window. Suicide was the official explanation, but many suspected murder. In response to the Marshall Plan, the Soviet foreign ministry initiated a series of trade agreements tightly linking the Soviet and Eastern European economies. It also established the Cominform, or Communist Information Bureau, to assert greater political control over foreign Communist parties.

BERLIN AIRLIFT The spring of 1948 brought another clash between the Soviets and their former allies, this time over Germany. There, the United States, Great Britain, and France decided to transform their occupation zones into an independent West German state. The Western-controlled sectors of Berlin, however, lay over 100 miles to the east, well within the Soviet zone. On June 24 the Soviets reacted by blockading land access to Berlin. Truman did not hesitate to respond. "We are going to stay, period." But he did say no when General Lucius Clay proposed to shoot his way through the blockade. Instead, the United States began a massive airlift of supplies that lasted almost a year. In May 1949 Stalin lifted the blockade, conceding that he could not prevent the creation of West Germany.

NATO FORMED Stalin's aggressive actions accelerated the American effort to use military means to contain Soviet ambitions. By 1949 the United States and Canada had joined with Britain, France, Belgium, the Netherlands, and Luxembourg to establish the North Atlantic Treaty Organization (NATO) as a mutual defense pact. For the first time since George Washington had warned against the practice in his Farewell Address of 1793, the United States during peacetime entered into entangling alliances with European nations.

ISRAEL RECOGNIZED Truman's firm handling of the Berlin crisis won him applause from both Democrats and Republicans. They were equally enthusiastic about another bold presidential action. Minutes after the Israelis announced

©Apic/Getty Images

| *Few cities suffered as severely during World War II as Dresden in Germany. The Allies subjected it to systematic firebombing that provoked Kurt Vonnegut to write* Slaughterhouse Five. *In 1946 little had been done to rebuild the city. Much of Europe suffered widespread destruction, and the Marshall Plan provided aid to rebuild.*

>> MAPPING THE PAST <<

COLD WAR EUROPE

Source: Library of Congress, Prints and Photographs Division [yan 1a37802]

"From Stettin in the Baltic to Trieste in the Adriatic an iron curtain has descended across the Continent. Behind that line lie all the capitals of the ancient states of Central and Eastern Europe. Warsaw, Berlin, Prague, Vienna, Budapest, Belgrade, Bucharest and Sofia, all these famous cities and the populations around them lie in what I must call the Soviet sphere, and all are subject in one form or another, not only to Soviet influence but to a very high and, in some cases, increasing measure of control from Moscow." —Prime Minister Winston Churchill of the United Kingdom

CONTEXT

During the first decade of the cold war, the United States fought a hot war in Korea and became involved in Vietnam. Yet the majority of Americans agreed that it was most important to contain the Soviet threat to Western Europe. To that end, the United States adopted the Truman Doctrine and Marshall Plan and created the North Atlantic Treaty Organization (NATO). The Soviets, in response, formed the Warsaw bloc and sent assistance to Egypt and Syria while pressuring Turkey and Iran.

MAP READING

1. Which four nations occupied zones in Berlin?
2. What important Western European countries had not joined NATO by 1956?
3. What feature shown in the insert reveals why the British, French, and Americans preserved their zones in Berlin during the 1948 crisis?

MAP INTERPRETATION

1. Why would Berlin's location make it a focus of East-West tensions? On the inset map, why are there airplane symbols in three of the zones but not the fourth?
2. Of the seven Western European nations that did not belong to NATO in 1956, which do you think made their choice for political reasons and which because of geography?
3. Why would the Dardanelles and Bosporus Straits be so important to both the Warsaw bloc and NATO countries?
4. Why might the Soviet Union put pressure on Iran, Turkey, and Greece, known as the "Northern Tier"?

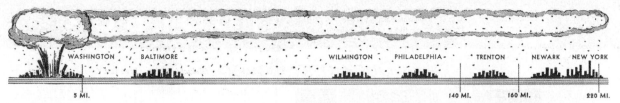

| As this diagram of a hypothetical bombing of Washington suggests, Americans began to understand that radioactive fallout was a grave danger as well.

their independence in May 1948, Truman recognized the new state of Israel. He had previously supported the emigration of Jews into Palestine despite the opposition of oil-rich Arab states and diplomats in the State Department. The president sympathized with Jewish aspirations for a homeland. He also faced a tough campaign in 1948 in which Jewish votes would be critical. As British prime minister Clement Attlee observed, "There's no Arab vote in America, but there's a heavy Jewish vote and the Americans are always having elections."

Creating an Atomic Shield

The Berlin crisis forced Truman to consider the possibility of war. If it came, would atomic weapons again be used? That dilemma raised two other difficult questions: Should the decision to use atomic weapons rest in civilian or military hands? And was it possible to create an international system to control nuclear power?

ATOMIC ENERGY COMMISSION On the question of civilian or military control of the bomb, Truman's response was firm. He was not going to have "some dashing lieutenant colonel decide when would be the proper time to drop one." In 1946 Congress seemed to have decided the issue in Truman's favor when it passed the McMahon Act. This bill established the Atomic Energy Commission (AEC), with control of all fissionable materials for both peacetime and military applications. The AEC was a civilian, not a military, agency.

But civilian control was not as complete as Truman had demanded. The wartime head of the Manhattan Project, General Leslie Groves, had been working behind the scenes to give the military a decisive voice in atomic policy. During debate over the bill, Groves had leaked information about a Canadian atomic spy ring delivering secrets to the Soviet Union. That news spread doubts that scientists and civilians could be trusted with key secrets. Thus Groves persuaded Congress to allow the military to review many civilian decisions and even severely limit their actions.

BARUCH PLAN The idea of international control of atomic energy also fell victim to cold war fears. Originally, a high-level government committee proposed to Truman that the mining and use of the world's atomic raw materials be supervised by an agency of the United Nations. The committee argued that in the long run the United States would be more secure under a system of international control than

relying on its temporary nuclear monopoly. But Truman chose Bernard Baruch, a staunch cold warrior, to draw up the recommendations to the United Nations in June 1946. Baruch's proposals ensured that the United States would dominate any international atomic agency. The Soviets countered with a plan calling for destruction of all nuclear bombs and a ban on their use. But Baruch had no intention of bargaining. It was either his plan or nothing, he announced. And so it was nothing. The Truman administration never seriously considered giving up the American nuclear monopoly. Stalin, for his part, made the Soviet atomic weapons program a top priority. Baruch's inflexibility at the UN promoted an arms race without ensuring the American nuclear monopoly.

NUCLEAR DETERRENCE As the cold war heated up, American military planners were forced to adopt a nuclear strategy in face of the overwhelming superiority of Soviet forces. The Soviet army had at its command over 260 divisions. In contrast, the United States had reduced its forces by 1947 to little more than a single division. That meant that only the prospect of a devastating atomic counterattack was likely to deter any Soviet threat.

At first, this strategy of nuclear **deterrence** was little more than a makeshift doomsday scenario to incinerate vast areas of the Soviet Union. A 1946 war plan, "Pincher," proposed obliterating 20 Soviet cities if the Soviets attacked Western Europe. But, by 1949, the Joint Chiefs of Staff had fully committed themselves to a policy of nuclear deterrence in an indefinitely extended cold war. Western Europe was on its way to economic recovery, thanks to the Marshall Plan. Soviet pressure on Iran, Greece, and Turkey had abated.

Yet these tentative successes brought little comfort. The Soviet Union was not simply a major power seeking to protect its interests and expand where opportunity permitted. In the eyes of many Americans, the Soviets were determined, if they could, to overthrow the United States from either without or within. This war was being fought not only around the globe but right in America as well, by unseen agents using subversive means. In this way, the cold war mentality soon came to shape the lives of Americans at home much as it did American policy abroad.

✓ REVIEW

What were Soviet and American strategies after World War II, and what were the hot spots where these strategies clashed?

Duck and Cover

Sound track and music: ". . . and Bert the Turtle was very alert. When danger threatened him, he never got hurt, He knew just what to do . . ."

What tone is set by using "Bert the Turtle" and a monkey for teaching students the tactic of *Duck and Cover* in an atomic attack?

Go to YouTube and search for *Duck and Cover*. Play the film. How do the sound track, animation, music, and script contribute to the impression the film gives of an atomic bomb?

Narrator: "Now, [laughs] you and I don't have shells to crawl into like Bert the Turtle, so we have to cover up in our own way. First you duck . . ."

". . . and then you cover! And very tightly, you cover the back of your neck . . ." How do you react to the idea that "ducking and covering" would protect these children in case of a nuclear attack?

Source: Office for Emergency Management. Office of Civilian Defense. 5/20/1941-6/30/1945

The Soviet Union's explosion of an atomic bomb in 1949 confronted American civil defense planners with a delicate task. On the one hand, they had to warn citizens that a nuclear attack against the United States was a distinct possibility. On the other, in order to avoid panic and hysteria, they had to reassure Americans that an atomic war did not mean certain death and destruction. The film *Duck and Cover,* a collaboration of civil defense officials and educators in 1951, was designed to convey to students the message that government had plans in place to protect them. Did the message get across? And perhaps just as interesting to consider, did the officials making the film believe what they were teaching? If not, why teach the techniques? In the end, *Time* magazine concluded that while Americans feared the bomb, they accepted "the idea they must live with it."

THINKING CRITICALLY

In what ways does the use of cartoon images and humor make the message more or less credible? Can you describe a more effective way to get across the civil defense message that to survive people need to be prepared to act immediately in a nuclear crisis? Or was there no effective defense?

POSTWAR PROSPERITY

AT WAR'S END MANY BUSINESS leaders feared that a sudden drop in government purchases would bring back the hard times of the 1930s. Instead, despite a rocky year or two adjusting to the peacetime economy, Americans entered into the longest period of prosperity in the nation's history, lasting until the 1970s. Even the fear of communism could not dampen the simple joys of getting and spending.

SOURCES OF PROSPERITY Two forces drove the postwar economic boom. One was unbridled consumer and business spending that followed 16 years of depression and war. High war wages had piled up in savings accounts and war bonds. Eager consumers set off to find the new cars, appliances, and foods unavailable during the war. Second, government expenditures at the local, state, and federal levels provided a boost to prosperity. The three major growth industries in the decades after World War II were health care, education, and government programs. Each of these spurred public spending. Equally important, the federal government poured billions of dollars into the military-industrial sector. The defense budget, which fell to $9 billion in 1947, reached $50 billion by the time Truman left office. Over the longer term, these factors promoting economic growth became clearer. In 1946, though, the road from war to peace seemed more uncertain, especially for Americans at the margins of the economy.

Energy and the Environment in Postwar America

Fighting World War II made many planners in government all too aware that modern economies depended heavily on fossil fuels, especially coal and petroleum products. Faced with decreasing oil reserves at home, Petroleum Administrator for War Harold Ickes wondered if the United States "could fuel another war." Rather than consider alternate energy sources, planners looked to the Middle East, which had cheap and seemingly unlimited supplies. But the region was also politically unstable as nationalists challenged their colonial rulers. To protect the Middle East's energy, the United States would have to influence the region's political future.

At home, manufacturers began producing automobiles and other consumer goods again, as well as taking advantage of a wide array of new materials and technologies developed during the war. Among them were pesticides such as DDT; hybrid seeds; and synthetic fertilizers for farming, plastics to replace natural products, and long-range airplanes for transportation. Chemical giant DuPont caught the spirit of the American fascination with these new wonders as it promised "Better Things for Better Living . . . through Chemistry." Since hydrocarbons from petroleum formed the basis for many fertilizers and plastics, cheap oil promoted economic growth.

But the ideal of a full-blown consumer society contained a serious flaw: it largely ignored the impact that synthetic goods and the burning of fossil fuels would have on the environment. The

For five days in October 1948, an inversion layer in the atmosphere trapped a deadly mix of pollutants in a smog over Donora, Pennsylvania. In addition to 20 people, some 800 animals died from the effects of sulfur dioxide, metal dust, and carbon monoxide.

©Bettmann/Getty Images

factories producing plastics so essential to automobiles, homes, and appliances emitted toxic substances into the air, land, and water. Because plastic did not degrade naturally, it added mountains of trash to the nation's landfills. The dangers that "miracle" chemicals posed was seen in the small industrial town of Donora, Pennsylvania, outside Pittsburgh, in 1948. During a five-day period an inversion layer over the town trapped a toxic brew of sulfur dioxide, carbon monoxide, and metal dust spewing from the metal smelters there. Some 20 people died, and half the town's 7,000 residents were hospitalized.

Industry officials viewed the accident as unfortunate but argued that the atmosphere was a "useful natural resource" to be used "for the dispersion of wastes within its capacity to do so without harm to the surroundings." A few critics charged that such ideas ignored the fundamental principles of ecology. Fairfield Osborn in *Our Plundered Planet* (1948) warned that humans had to recognize the interdependence of life and cooperate with nature, rather than dominate it. Aldo Leopold, a pioneering ecologist, proposed in *A Sand County Almanac* (1949) what he called a "land ethic." He observed that "we abuse the land because we see it as a commodity belonging to us." Instead, Leopold believed, "When we see land as a community to which we belong, we may use it with love and respect."

But most Americans in the postwar years were not ready to heed such warnings. They believed that cheap energy, new technologies, and a growing economy would keep the depression wolf from their doors.

Peacetime Adjustments

Despite these hopes the transition from wartime to the new consumer economy was far from smooth.

With millions of veterans looking for peacetime jobs, workers on the home front, especially women and minorities, found themselves out of work. As peace came, almost 75 percent of the working women in one survey indicated that they hoped to continue their jobs. But male social scientists stressed how important it was for women to accept "more than the wife's usual responsibility for her marriage" and offer "lavish—and undemanding—affection" on returning GIs. One marriage counselor urged women to let their husbands know "you are tired of living alone, that you want him now to take charge."

Congress debated over how much it should do to ease the transition to peace and bring down unemployment. Organized labor, led by the CIO, argued that "all Americans able to work and seeking work have the right to a useful and remunerative job." Congress, especially conservative Republicans, was unwilling to go so far, but the Employment Act of 1946 at least created the Council of Economic Advisers to guide the president's policies. The bill thus established the principle that the government, not the private sector, was responsible for managing unemployment.

For minorities, the end of the war brought the return of an old labor practice, "last hired, first fired." At the height of the war over 200,000 African Americans and Hispanics worked in shipbuilding. By 1946 that number had dwindled to fewer than 10,000. The influx of Mexican laborers under the *bracero* program temporarily halted. In the South, where the large majority of black Americans lived, wartime labor shortages had become surpluses, leaving few jobs available.

AMERICAN G.I. FORUM   At the same time, many Hispanic and black veterans who had fought for their country during the war resented returning to a deeply segregated society. Such GIs "have acquired a new courage, have become more vocal in protesting the restrictions and inequalities with which they are confronted," noted one white Texan. When a funeral director in Three Rivers, Texas, refused to open its segregated cemetery for the burial of Felix Longoria, a Mexican soldier killed in battle, his supporters organized. Led by Dr. Hector Garcia, a former army medical officer, the American G.I. Forum was founded in 1948 to campaign for civil rights. Longoria was finally buried in Arlington National Cemetery after the G.I. Forum convinced Congressman Lyndon Baines Johnson to intervene.

BLACK VETERANS AND CIVIL RIGHTS   Black veterans had a similar impact on the civil rights movement. Angered by violence, frustrated by the slow pace of desegregation, they breathed new energy into civil rights organizations such as the NAACP and CORE (the Congress of Racial Equality). Some voting registration drives in the South had success in urban centers such as Atlanta. Other black leaders pressed for improved education.

TO SECURE THESE RIGHTS   Out in the countryside, however, segregationists used economic intimidation, violence, and even murder, to preserve the Jim Crow system. President Truman, who saw civil rights as a key ingredient in his reform agenda, was especially disturbed when he learned that police in South Carolina had gouged out the eyes of a recently discharged black veteran. In December 1946 he appointed a Committee on Civil Rights, which published its report, *To Secure These Rights,* a year later.

Discovering inequities for minorities, the committee exposed a racial caste system that denied African Americans employment opportunities, equal education, voting rights,

| *The Liga Pro Defensa Escolar, or Pro Schools Defense League, pushed to abolish segregated schooling, which affected Latinos as well as African Americans. No doubt deliberately, the league's emblem was written in English.*

Source: Rare Books and Manuscripts, Benson Latin American Collection, University of Texas, Austin

and decent housing. But every time Truman appealed to Congress to implement the committee's recommendations, southern senators threatened to filibuster. So the president resorted to executive authority to achieve some modest results. In his most direct attack on segregation, he issued an **executive order** in July 1948 banning discrimination in the armed forces. Segregationists predicted disaster, but integrated units fought well and exhibited minimal racial tension.

ORGANIZED LABOR For organized labor, reconversion brought an abrupt drop in hours worked and overtime paid. As wages declined and inflation ate into paychecks, strikes spread. Autoworkers walked off the job in the fall of 1945; steelworkers, in January 1946; miners, in April. In 1946 some 5 million workers struck, a rate triple that of any previous year. Antiunion sentiment soared. The crisis peaked in May 1946 with a national rail strike, which temporarily paralyzed the nation's transportation network. An angry President Truman asked, "What decent American would pull a rail strike at a time like this?"

At first Truman threatened to seize the railroads and then requested from Congress the power to draft striking workers into the military. He planned a speech in which he would say, "Let's put transportation and production back to work, hang a few traitors, and make our country safe for democracy." More-temperate aides persuaded him to revise the speech, but he still insisted on congressional action to authorize drafting strikers. The strike was settled before the threat was carried out, but few people, whether conservative or liberal, approved the idea of using the draft to punish political foes.

Republicans gained control of both houses of Congress. Not since 1928 had the Democrats fared so poorly.

TAFT-HARTLEY ACT Leading the rightward swing was Senator Robert A. Taft of Ohio, son of former president William Howard Taft. Bob Taft not only wanted to halt the spread of the New Deal—he wanted to dismantle it. "We have to get over the corrupting idea we can legislate prosperity, legislate equality, legislate opportunity," he said in dismissing the liberal agenda. Taft especially wished to limit the power of the unions. In 1947 he pushed the Taft-Hartley Act through Congress, over Truman's veto. In the event of a strike, the bill allowed the president to order workers back on the job during a 90-day cooling-off period while collective bargaining continued. It also permitted states to adopt right-to-work laws, which banned the closed shop by eliminating union membership as a prerequisite for many jobs. Union leaders criticized the new law as a slave-labor act but discovered they could live with it, though it did hurt union efforts to organize, especially in the South.

A Program for GIs

THE GI BILL Despite Republican gains, most Americans still supported the New Deal's major accomplishments: Social Security, a minimum-wage law, and a more active role for government in reducing unemployment. The administration maintained its commitment to setting a minimum hourly wage, raising it again in 1950, from 45 to 75 cents. Social

Truman under Attack

In September 1945 Harry Truman had boldly claimed his intention to extend the New Deal into the postwar era. He called for legislation to guarantee full employment, subsidized public housing, national health insurance, and a peacetime version of the Fair Employment Practices Commission to fight job discrimination. Instead of promoting his liberal agenda, he found himself fighting a conservative backlash. Labor unrest was just one source of his troubles. The increased demand for consumer goods temporarily in short supply triggered a sharp inflation. For two years prices rose as much as 15 percent annually.

With Truman's political stock falling, conservative Republicans and Democrats blocked the president's attempts to extend the New Deal. As the congressional elections of 1946 neared, Republicans pointed to production shortages, the procession of strikes, the mismanagement of the economy. "To err is Truman," proclaimed the campaign buttons—or, more simply, "Had Enough?" Many voters had. The

Source: Center for Legislative Archives, US Senate Collection, National Archives (A-072_10-19-1948)

| *Everyone, including opinion pollsters, assumed Dewey would easily defeat Truman.*

Many HISTORIES

TAFT-HARTLEY: CONTAINING LABOR

Widespread strikes involving over 5 million workers sparked conservative efforts to curb union power, leading to the Taft-Hartley or Labor Management Relations Act of 1947. The act forbid wildcat strikes, solidarity or political strikes, secondary boycotts, closed shops, and donations to federal political campaigns. John L. Lewis, the outspoken president of the United Mine Workers, warned the American Federation of Labor to fight Taft-Hartley (Document 1). Lewis especially disliked a clause that required union officers, but not business officials, to sign noncommunist affidavits. Senator Robert A. Taft defended his bill (Document 2).

DOCUMENT 1
John L. Lewis Condemns the Taft-Hartley Act

The question of signing the anti-Communist affidavit, which is only one small feature of the abrogations of this act, has occupied the minds of our leaders and the columns of the public press now for more than six weeks, and at last we come to the fatal and unhappy day when men who purport to lead the mighty hosts within the American Federation of Labor cry aloud and say, "There is nothing else for us to do—nothing else for us to do!"

I will tell you what you should do at least once in your lives—you should do your duty by your membership.

I suppose it is hardly necessary for me to say that I am not a Communist. I suppose it is hardly necessary for me to say that I was fighting Communism in America, with the other members of my

organization, before many people in this country knew what Communism stood for in America and throughout the world. . . . The United Mine Workers of America has been in the vanguard of our citizenship in opposing the cast iron Oriental philosophy of Communism or any other damned kind of ism in this country. And we expect to remain in that position. We don't expect to change our principles too often; and we do expect some support from the American labor movement, because we think that our attitude reflects the attitude of the rank and file in these great organizations of labor who work for a living and who want a country tomorrow in which their children and their grandchildren can live.

The signing of the affidavit isn't the only thing that an organization has to do

to conform to this Act. This Act is a trap, a pitfall for the organizations of labor, and I am surprised that those who have been attempting to analyze it haven't looked down the road just a few months or a year to find out some of the things that are inherent in this Act. This Act was passed to oppress labor, to make difficult its current enterprises for collective bargaining, to make more difficult the securing of new members for this labor movement, without which our movement will become so possessed of inertia that there is no action and no growth, and in a labor movement where there is no growth there is no security for its existence, because deterioration sets in and unions, like men, retrograde.

Source: Lewis, John L., Speech Delivered before the AFL Convention, October 14, 1947.

DOCUMENT 2
Taft Defends His Act

In the last few weeks the air has been filled with the raucous cries of union officials that every Congressman and Senator who voted for the Taft-Hartley law, or voted against its repeal, shall be liquidated in 1950. . . . The CIO is to collect more millions and apparently Ohio [Taft's home state] is to get more than its share of these millions. Labor officials . . . accused me of opposing every interest of the working man on housing, welfare, education, wages and prices . . . [overlooking] the fact that I blocked Truman's real slave labor bill to draft railroad workers and miners into the army, that I was for continuing price control and that Truman was the one who brought it to an end. . . .

As for the Taft-Hartley law . . . for a while they called it a slave labor law but that has become so ridiculous they have dropped the epithet. It is hard to see how it could be a slave labor law when the unions have gained a million members since its enactment and enjoy the best contracts, welfare services, and pensions they have ever had. The

Taft-Hartley Act had only one purpose, to protect and strengthen collective bargaining by restoring equality between management and labor. . . . Before the passage of this act previous laws [like the Wagner Act of 1935], while giving the unions many rights to which they were entitled, completely relieved them from any responsibility to the public, to employers, or even to their own members. . . .

The Act protects the people. The number of strikes has been cut in half since the passage of the Act as compared to the period between the end of the war and the passage of the Act. . . . The Act gives equal treatment to employers and penalizes unfair labor practices on the part of the labor union officials, retaining, of course, the prohibition of unfair practices on the part of employers just as provided by the Wagner Act. . . .

In the third place, the Act protects the union member. It makes it an unfair labor practice for a union to coerce employees. It prohibits the use of the dues of union

members for political purposes, to be used perhaps against their best friends. It requires a non-communist affidavit so that they may know whether their officers are communists. It requires financial reports so they may know what their officers are doing with their money. It require written consent before their dues can be deducted from their wages. It prohibits excessive and discriminatory initiation fees.

Source: Taft, Robert A., Speech to Smaller Businessmen of America, September 7, 1949, as reprinted in Wunderlin, Clarence E., *The Papers of Robert A. Taft: 1949–1953.* Kent, OH: The Kent State University Press, 2006, 99–100.

THINKING CRITICALLY

Why would Congress call for a loyalty oath—the noncommunist affidavit—in 1947? Besides the loyalty oath provision, why did Lewis oppose Taft-Hartley? Why does Robert Taft believe his act is fair to labor? What is he referring to when he mentions Truman's "slave labor law to draft railroad workers"?

Security coverage was broadened to cover an additional 10 million workers. Furthermore, a growing list of welfare programs benefited not only the poor but also veterans, middle-income families, the elderly, and students. The most striking of these was the GI Bill of 1944, designed to reward soldiers for their service during the war.

For veterans the "GI Bill of Rights" created unparalleled opportunity. Those with more than two years of service received all tuition and fees plus living expenses for three years of college education. By 1948 the government was paying the college costs of nearly half of all male students as more than 2 million veterans took advantage of the GI Bill. Increased educational levels encouraged a shift from blue- to white-collar work and self-employment. Veterans also received low-interest loans to start businesses or farms of their own and to buy homes. The GI Bill accelerated trends that would transform American society into a prosperous, heavily middle-class suburban nation.

Less fortunately, the bill did little to help minorities and females. Few women received benefits under the bill. African Americans and Hispanics, even those eligible for veterans' benefits, were hampered by Jim Crow restrictions in segregated universities and in jobs in both the public and private sectors. The Federal Housing Administration even helped draw up "model" restrictive housing covenants. In order to "retain stability," neighborhoods were allowed to use the covenants to segregate according to "social and racial classes."

The Election of 1948

HENRY WALLACE AND THE PROGRESSIVES As the election of 1948 approached, the New Deal coalition that Franklin Roosevelt had held together for so long seemed to be coming apart. On the left Truman was challenged by Henry Wallace, a progressive who had been vice president under Roosevelt and who wanted to pursue New Deal reforms even more vigorously than Truman did. Disaffected liberals bolted the Democratic Party to support Wallace on a third-party Progressive ticket.

DIXIECRATS Within the southern conservative wing of the party, archsegregationists resented Truman's moderate civil rights proposals for a voting rights bill and an antilynching law. When the liberal wing of the party passed a civil rights plank as part of the Democratic platform, delegates from several Deep South states stalked out of the convention. They banded together to create the States' Rights, or "Dixiecrat," Party, with J. Strom Thurmond, the segregationist governor of South Carolina, as their candidate.

With the Democrats divided, Republicans smelled victory. They moved toward the political center by rejecting the conservative Taft in favor of the more moderate former New York governor Thomas Dewey. Dewey proved so aloof that he inspired scant enthusiasm. "You have to know Dewey well to really dislike him," quipped one Taft supporter. Still, most observers assumed that Dewey would walk away with the race.

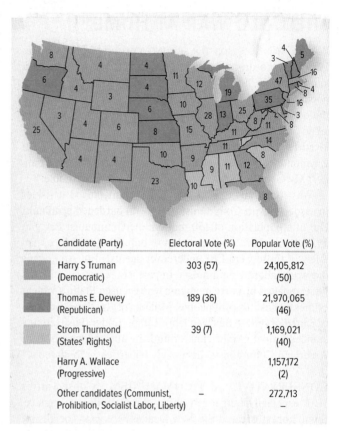

Candidate (Party)	Electoral Vote (%)	Popular Vote (%)
Harry S Truman (Democratic)	303 (57)	24,105,812 (50)
Thomas E. Dewey (Republican)	189 (36)	21,970,065 (46)
Strom Thurmond (States' Rights)	39 (7)	1,169,021 (40)
Harry A. Wallace (Progressive)		1,157,172 (2)
Other candidates (Communist, Prohibition, Socialist Labor, Liberty)	–	272,713 –

ELECTION OF 1948

TRUMAN FIGHTS BACK Truman, did not meekly roll over and play dead. He launched a stinging attack against the "reactionaries" in Congress: that "bunch of old mossbacks . . . gluttons of privilege . . . all set to do a hatchet job on the New Deal." From the rear platform of his campaign train, he made almost 400 speeches in eight weeks. Over and over he hammered away at the "do-nothing" 80th Congress, which, he told farmers, "had stuck a pitchfork" in their backs. Hours before the polls closed, the archconservative *Chicago Daily Tribune* happily headlined "Dewey Defeats Truman." But the experts were wrong. Not only did the voters return Truman by over 2 million popular votes, but they also gave the Democrats commanding majorities in the House and Senate.

THE FAIR DEAL As he began his new term, Harry Truman expressed his conviction that all Americans were entitled to a "Fair Deal" from their government. He called for a vigorous revival of New Deal programs such as national health insurance and regional TVA-style projects. Echoing an old Populist idea, Truman hoped to keep his working coalition together by forging stronger links between farmers and labor. But the conservative coalition of Democrats and Republicans in Congress blocked any significant new initiatives. On the domestic front, Truman remained largely the conservator of Franklin Roosevelt's legacy.

✓ **REVIEW**

What government policies encouraged postwar prosperity?

THE COLD WAR AT HOME

BOB RAYMONDI, A MOBSTER SERVING a prison term in the late 1940s, was no stranger to extortion, racketeering, or gangland killings. In fact, he was so feared that he dominated the inmate population at Dannemora Prison. Raymondi began to make the acquaintance of a group of Communists who had been jailed for advocating the overthrow of the government. He enjoyed talking with people who had some education. When Raymondi's sister learned about his new friends, she was frantic. "My God, Bob," she told him. "You'll get into trouble."

Was something amiss? Most Americans judged it riskier to associate with Communists than with hardened criminals. Out of a population of 150 million, the Communist Party in 1950 could claim a membership of only 43,000. (More than a few of those were FBI undercover agents.) But Americans did worry about Communists. In part, conscientious citizens were appalled by party members who excused Stalin's violent crimes against his own people. Millions of Russians had been executed or sent to Siberian labor camps; under those circumstances, most Americans found it outrageous to hear American Communists dismiss civil liberties as "bourgeois."

CONSERVATIVE ANTICOMMUNISM Conservatives were especially outspoken about the Communist menace. Some honestly feared the New Deal as "creeping socialism." The president's advisors, it seemed to them, were either Communist agents or their unwitting dupes. Leftists, they believed, controlled labor unions, Hollywood, and other interest groups sympathetic to the New Deal. Conservative outrage grew as Stalin extended Soviet control in Eastern Europe and Asia. Many conservatives charged that a conspiracy within Roosevelt's administration had sold out America to its enemies. More-cynical conservatives used "Red baiting" simply to discredit people and ideas they disliked.

The Shocks of 1949

THE H-BOMB Truman won in 1948 in large part because of his strong leadership in foreign affairs. In 1949 a series of foreign policy shocks allowed Republicans to seize the anticommunist issue. In August, American scientists reported that rainfall monitored in the Pacific contained traces of hot nuclear waste. Only one conclusion seemed possible: the Soviet Union had exploded its own atomic bomb. When Truman announced the news, Congress was debating whether to spend $1.5 billion for military aid to the newly formed NATO alliance. The House stopped debating and passed the bill, while Truman decided to accelerate research into a newer, more powerful fusion, or hydrogen, bomb. Senator Arthur Vandenberg, a Republican leader in international affairs, summed up the reaction of many officials to the end of the American nuclear monopoly: "This is now a different world."

CHINA FALLS TO COMMUNISTS Then in December came more disturbing news. The long-embattled Nationalist government of Chiang Kai-shek had fled mainland China to the offshore island of Formosa (present-day Taiwan). By January, Communist troops under Mao Zedong were swarming into Beijing, China's capital city. Chiang's defeat came as no surprise to State Department officials, who had long regarded the Nationalists as hopelessly corrupt and inefficient. Despite major American efforts to save Chiang's regime, full-scale civil war had broken out in 1947. Mao's triumph was hardly unexpected.

But Republicans, who had up until 1949 supported the president's foreign policy, now broke ranks. For some time, many conservatives had resented the administration's preoccupation with Europe. Time-Life publisher Henry Luce used his magazines to campaign for a greater concern for Asian affairs and especially more aid to defeat Mao Zedong. Luce and his associates, known as the "China Lobby," were supported in part with funds from the Chinese embassy. When Chiang at last collapsed, his American backers charged that Democrats had let the Communists win.

THE HISS CASE Worries that subversives had sold out the country were heightened when former State Department official Alger Hiss was brought to trial in 1949 for perjury. Hiss, an advisor to Roosevelt at the Yalta Conference, had been accused by former Communist Whittaker Chambers of passing secrets to the Soviet Union during the 1930s. Though the evidence in the case was far from conclusive, the jury convicted Hiss for lying about his association with Chambers. And in February 1950 the nation was further shocked to learn that a high-ranking British physicist, Klaus Fuchs, had spied for the Russians while working on the Manhattan Project. Here was clear evidence of conspiracy at work.

The Loyalty Crusade

President Truman sought to blunt Republican accusations that he was "soft" on communism. Ten days after proposing the Truman Doctrine in March 1947, the president signed an

| *The fall of China to Mao Zedong and his Communist forces were some of the chilling cold war shocks of 1949.*

executive order establishing a Federal Employee Loyalty Program designed to guard against the possible disloyalty of "Reds, phonies, and 'parlor pinks.'" Since the FBI could hardly find time to examine all of the 2 million government employees, the order required supervisors to review and certify the loyalties of those who worked below them, reporting to a system of federal loyalty review boards.

LOYALTY REVIEW BOARD The system quickly got out of hand. Seth Richardson, the conservative head of the Loyalty Review Board, argued that the government could "discharge any employee for reasons which seem sufficient to the Government, and without extending to such employee any hearing whatsoever." After several years the difficulty of proving that employees were actually disloyal became clear, and Truman allowed the boards to fire those who were "potentially" disloyal or "bad security risks," such as alcoholics, homosexuals, and debtors. Suspect employees, in other words, were assumed guilty until proven innocent. After some 5 million investigations, the program identified a few hundred employees who, though not Communists, had at one time been associated with suspect groups. Rather than calm public fears, the loyalty program gave credibility to the growing Red Scare.

HUAC, Hollywood, and Unions

About the same time Truman established the Loyalty Review Board, the House Un-American Activities Committee (HUAC) began to investigate Communist influence in the film industry. Hollywood, with its wealth, glamour, and highly visible Jewish and foreign celebrities, had long aroused a mixture of attraction and suspicion among traditional Americans. "Large numbers of moving pictures that come out of Hollywood carry the

©Warner Bros./Photofest, Inc.

| Many Hollywood films exploited anticommunist fears.

Communist line," charged committee member John Rankin of Mississippi. Indeed, during the Depression some Hollywood figures had developed ties to the Communist Party or had become sympathetic to party causes. To generate support for the Allies during the war, Hollywood (with Roosevelt's blessing) produced films with a positive view of the Soviet Union such as *Mission to Moscow* and *Song of Russia*.

HOLLYWOOD TEN HUAC called a parade of movie stars, screenwriters, and producers to sit in the glare of its public hearings. Some witnesses, such as Gary Cooper and

| The energetic and opportunistic Roy Cohn (left) *served as a key strategist in the inquisition that made Senator Joseph McCarthy a figure to fear. He and fellow staffer David Schine* (right) *helped McCarthy turn a minor Senate subcommittee into a major power center.*

©Eve Arnold/Magnum Photos

Ronald Reagan, were considered "friendly" because they supplied names of suspected leftists. Others refused to inform on their colleagues. Eventually, 10 uncooperative witnesses, known as the "Hollywood Ten," refused on First Amendment grounds to say whether they were or ever had been Communists. They served prison terms for contempt of Congress.

BLACKLISTING For all its probing, HUAC never offered convincing evidence that filmmakers were in any way subversive. About the most damning evidence presented was that one eager left-leaning extra, when asked to "whistle something" during his walk-on part, hummed a few bars of the Communist anthem the "Internationale." The investigations did, however, inspire nervous Hollywood producers to turn out films such as *I Was a Communist for the FBI* (1950). The studios also adopted a blacklist that prevented admitted or accused Communists from finding work. Because no judicial proceedings were involved, victims of false charges, rumors, or spiteful accusations found it nearly impossible to clear their names.

McCARRAN ACT Suspicion of aliens and immigrants led finally to the passage, over Truman's veto, of the McCarran Act (1950). It required all Communists to register with the attorney general, forbade the entry of anyone who had belonged to a totalitarian organization, and allowed the Justice Department to detain suspect aliens indefinitely during deportation hearings. That same year a Senate committee began an inquiry designed to root out homosexuals holding government jobs. Even one "sex pervert in a Government agency tends to have a corrosive influence upon his fellow employees," warned the committee. The campaign had effects beyond government offices: the armed forces stepped up their rates of dismissal for sexual orientation, while city police more frequently raided gay bars and social clubs.

The Ambitious Senator McCarthy

By 1950 anticommunism had created a climate of fear in which legitimate concerns mixed with irrational hysteria. Joseph R. McCarthy, a Senate nonentity from Wisconsin, saw in that fear an issue with which to build his political fortunes. To an audience in Wheeling, West Virginia, in February 1950 he waved a sheaf of papers in the air and announced that he had a list of 205—or perhaps 81, 57, or "a lot of"—Communists in the State Department. (No one, including the senator, could remember the number, which he continually changed.) In the following months McCarthy leveled charge after charge. He had penetrated the "iron curtain" of the State Department to discover "card-carrying Communists," the "top Russian espionage agent" in the United States, "egg-sucking phony liberals," and "Communists and queers" who wrote "perfumed notes."

Cold War/Red Scare: Mileposts

	FOREIGN	DOMESTIC
1945–1946	Iranian crisis	Labor unrest
1946	Kennan's "Long Telegram" Stalin: future wars inevitable Churchill: "Iron Curtain" Baruch Plan: no international nuclear control	"Red baiting" begins
1947	Truman Doctrine announced	Federal Employee Loyalty Program HUAC investigates Hollywood Taft-Hartley Act
1948	Marshall Plan Fall of governments in Czechoslovakia and Hungary Berlin blockade	Progressive Party's liberal agenda
1949	NATO created Soviets explode an atomic bomb China falls to Communists	Alger Hiss convicted of perjury Klaus Fuchs charged as atomic spy
1950	NSC-68 North Korea invades South Korea: Korean War	McCarthy's list of Communists in the State Department McCarran Act
1953	Armistice signed in Korean War	Rosenbergs executed as spies
1954		Senate censures McCarthy

(*top right*) Source: Library of Congress, Prints and Photographs Division [LC-USZ62-117876]; (*bottom right*) ©Eve Arnold/Magnum Photos

It didn't seem to matter that McCarthy never substantiated his charges. When examined, his lists contained names of people who had left the State Department long before or who had been cleared by the FBI. When forced into a corner, McCarthy simply lied and went on to another accusation. No one seemed beyond reach. In the summer of 1950 a Senate committee headed by Millard F. Tydings of Maryland concluded that McCarthy's charges were "a fraud and a hoax." Such candor among those in government did not last long, as "Jolting Joe" (one of McCarthy's favorite macho nicknames) in 1952 helped defeat Tydings and several other Senate critics.

McCarthy served as a blunt instrument that some conservative Republicans used to damage the Democrats. Without this support McCarthy would have had little credibility. Many of his accusations came from information secretly (and illegally) funneled to him by FBI director J. Edgar Hoover. But McCarthyism was also the bitter fruit Truman and the Democrats reaped from their own attempts to exploit the anticommunist mood. McCarthy, more than Truman, tapped the fears and hatreds of a broad coalition of Catholic leaders, conservatives, and neo-isolationists who harbored suspicion of things foreign, liberal, internationalist, European, or a touch too intellectual. They saw McCarthy and his allies as the protectors of a deeply felt spirit of Americanism.

By the time Truman left office in 1953, 32 states had laws requiring teachers to take loyalty oaths and government loyalty boards were asking employees what newspapers they subscribed to or phonograph records they collected. A library in Indiana had banned *Robin Hood* because the idea of stealing from the rich to give to the poor seemed too leftish. As one historian commented, "Opening the valve of anticommunist hysteria was a good deal simpler than closing it."

REVIEW

How did the Truman administration contribute to the Red Scare?

FROM COLD WAR TO HOT WAR AND BACK

AS THE COLD WAR HEATED up in 1949, the Truman administration searched for a more assertive foreign policy. Responsibility for developing that policy fell to the National Security Council (NSC), an agency created by Congress in 1947 as part of a plan to help the executive branch respond more effectively to cold war crises. Rather than merely "contain" the Soviets, as George Kennan had suggested, the National Security Council wanted the United States to "strive for victory." In April 1950 it sent Truman a document, NSC-68, which came to serve as the framework for American policy over the next 20 years.

NSC-68 NSC-68 called for an immediate increase in defense spending from $13 billion to $50 billion a year, to be paid for with a large tax increase. Most of the funds would go to rebuild

conventional forces, but the NSC urged that the hydrogen bomb be developed to offset the Soviet nuclear capacity. Efforts to carry out NSC-68 at first aroused widespread opposition as too expensive, too simplistic, and too militaristic. But all such reservations were swept away on June 25, 1950. "Korea came along and saved us," Secretary of State Dean Acheson later remarked.

Police Action

In 1950 Korea was about the last place in the world Americans might have imagined themselves fighting a war. Since World War II the country had been divided along the 38th parallel, the north controlled by the Communist government of Kim Il Sung, the south by the dictatorship of Syngman Rhee. Preoccupied with China and the rebuilding of Japan, the Truman administration's interest had dwindled steadily after the war. When Secretary of State Acheson discussed American policy in Asia before the National Press Club in January 1950, he did not even mention Korea.

NORTH KOREAN INVASION On June 24 Harry Truman was enjoying a leisurely break from politics at the family home in Independence, Missouri. In Korea it was already Sunday morning when Acheson called the president. North Korean troops had crossed the 38th parallel, Acheson reported, possibly to fulfill Kim Il Sung's proclaimed intention to "liberate" the South. A full-scale invasion was in progress. The United Nations, meeting in emergency session, had ordered a cease-fire, which the North Koreans were ignoring. Truman flew back to Washington, convinced that Stalin and his Chinese Communist allies had ordered the invasion. The threat of a third world war, this one atomic, seemed agonizingly real. The president wanted to respond firmly enough to deter aggression but without provoking a larger war with the Soviet Union or China.

Truman did not hesitate; American troops would fight the North Koreans, though the United States would not declare war. The fighting in Korea would be a "police action" supervised by the United Nations. On June 27 the Security Council passed a U.S. resolution to send United Nations forces to Korea. That move succeeded only because the Soviet delegate, who possessed veto power, had walked out six months earlier in protest over the council's refusal to seat mainland China. Stalin had secretly approved North Korea's attack, but he promised only supplies. Neither Russian troops nor prestige would be involved, he warned Kim.

Americans of almost all political persuasions supported Truman's forceful response. Congress quickly voted the huge increase in defense funds needed to carry out the recommendations of NSC-68. American allies were less committed to the action. Though 16 nations contributed to the war effort, the United States provided half of the ground troops, 86 percent of the naval units, and 93 percent of the air force. By the time the UN forces could be marshaled, North Korean forces had pinned the South Koreans within a small defensive perimeter centered on Pusan. Then Douglas MacArthur, commander of the UN forces, launched a daring amphibious attack behind North Korean lines at Inchon, near the

In their opening offensive, North Korean troops almost pushed South Korean and American forces into the sea at Pusan. After MacArthur rallied UN forces, he commanded a successful landing at Inchon behind North Korean lines and then crossed the 38th parallel into North Korea. Red Chinese troops counterattacked, inflicting one of the most humiliating defeats on U.S. troops in American military history. Fighting continued for another two years. How did Korea's geographic location increase the risk of escalating the scale of the war?

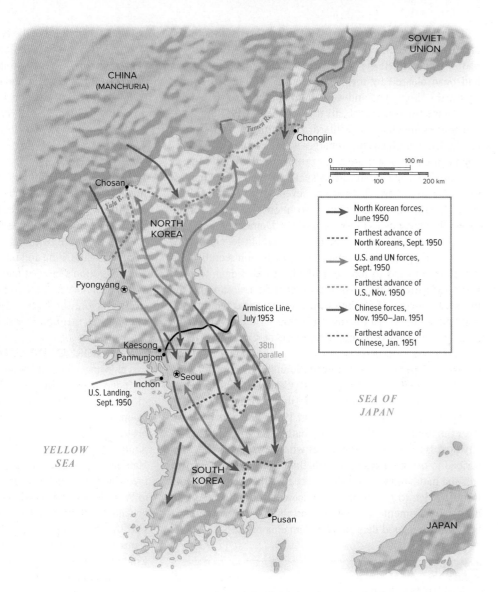

western end of the 38th parallel. Fighting eastward, MacArthur's troops threatened to trap the invaders, who fled back to the North.

The Chinese Intervene

MacArthur's success led Truman to a fateful decision. With the South liberated, he gave MacArthur permission to cross the 38th parallel, drive the Communists from the North, and reunite the country under Syngman Rhee. With Senator Joe McCarthy on the attack at home, the 1950 elections nearing, and the McCarran Act just passed, Truman welcomed the chance to vanquish the North Koreans. By Thanksgiving American troops had roundly defeated northern forces and were advancing on several fronts toward the frozen Yalu River, the boundary between Korea and China. MacArthur, emboldened by success, promised that the boys would be home by Christmas.

Throughout the fall offensive, however, Chinese premier Zhou Enlai warned that his country would not tolerate an American presence on its border. Washington officials belittled

Source: Navy Art Collection, Naval History and Heritage Command

| General Douglas MacArthur launched an amphibious attack at Inchon harbor. Because the harbor was shallow and muddy, any invasion required precise timing to take advantage of the autumn high tides. Otherwise, landing craft would run aground on the mud flats before reaching shore.

the warning. Mao Zedong, they assumed, was a Soviet puppet, and Stalin had declared the Korean conflict to be merely a "civil war" and off-limits. But after MacArthur launched his end-the-war offensive, some 400,000 Chinese troops poured across the Yalu, smashing through lightly defended UN lines. At Chosan they trapped 20,000 American and South Korean troops, inflicting one of the worst defeats in American military history. Within three weeks they had driven UN forces back behind the 38th parallel. So total was the rout that Truman wondered publicly about using the atomic bomb. That remark sent a frightened British prime minister Clement Attlee flying to Washington to dissuade the president. He readily agreed that the war must remain limited and withdrew his nuclear threat.

Truman versus MacArthur

The military stalemate in Korea brought into the open a simmering feud between MacArthur and Truman. The general had made no secret of his political ambitions or of his differences with Truman over American policy in Asia. He was eager to bomb Chinese and Russian supply bases across the Korean border, to blockade China's coast, and to "unleash" Chiang Kai-shek on mainland China. On March 23 he issued a personal ultimatum to Chinese military commanders demanding total surrender. To his Republican congressional supporters he sent a letter declaring, "We must win. There is no substitute for victory."

To Truman, MacArthur's insubordination threatened the tradition that military policy remained under clear civilian control. Equally alarming, MacArthur's strategy appeared to be an open invitation to another world war. Despite the general's popularity, Truman made plans to discipline him. When General Omar Bradley reported that MacArthur threatened to resign before Truman could act, the irate Truman replied, "The son of a bitch isn't going to resign on me. I want him fired!" Military leaders agreed. On April 11 a stunned nation learned that the celebrated military commander had been relieved of his duties. On his return home, cheering crowds gave MacArthur one of the largest ticker-tape parades in New York City's history. Truman's move seemed one of the great political mistakes of his career.

The Global Implications of the Cold War

Behind the scenes, however, Truman was winning this personal clash. At stake was not simply the issue of whether he or MacArthur would prevail. Rather, the outcome would determine the future direction of American foreign policy. The cold war crisis forced American leaders to think globally. Where in the world did the nation's interests lie? What region was most critical to the future? MacArthur believed that the Pacific basin would "determine the course of history in the next ten thousand years." To avoid being swept aside, the United States should make an all-out effort, not just to contain the Communist onslaught in Korea, but to play a major role throughout Asia. "What I advocate is that we defend every place, and I say that we have the capacity to do it," insisted MacArthur. Many conservative Republicans and groups like the China Lobby shared MacArthur's view.

Source: Library of Congress, Prints and Photographs Division [LC-USZ62-139030]

| *General Douglas MacArthur, who was lionized when Truman fired him, became a more ambiguous figure after his bid for the presidency fizzled. Here, in 1953, he is portrayed as the silent Sphinx of Egypt, unwilling to give his opinion on the Korean armistice agreement.*

EUROPE, NOT ASIA, FIRST Truman and his advisors continued to see Europe as the key to American foreign policy. Western Europe in particular, they believed, remained the center of the world's economic and military power. Political scientist Hans Morgenthau argued that "he who controls Europe is well on his way toward controlling the whole world." Further, Eurocentric Americans felt that the cultural differences between the United States and Asia were so great that the battle for Asia could not be won by military might. As theologian Reinhold Niebuhr put it, using American cold war weapons against the ideology of communism would be "like the spears of the knights when gunpowder challenged their reign."

Secretary of State Acheson agreed with the Eurocentrists. Korea was to Acheson but a small link in a global "collective security system." The wider war in Asia that MacArthur favored would threaten American interests in Europe because American resources would be stretched too thinly. Or, as General Bradley told Congress, a war in Asia would lead to "the wrong war, at the wrong place, at the wrong time, and with the wrong enemy." In this debate the Eurocentric faction prevailed. Congressional leaders agreed with Truman that the war in Korea should remain limited and that American resources should go to rebuilding Europe's defenses.

Meanwhile, the war in Korea bogged down in stalemate. As peace negotiators argued over how to reunify Korea, the United States suffered another 32,000 casualties in an ugly war of attrition. By March 1952 Truman's popularity had sunk so low that he lost the New Hampshire presidential primary to Senator Estes Kefauver of Tennessee. With that defeat, he announced he would not run for reelection in 1952.

I LIKE IKE

©Gado Images/Alamy

The Election of 1952

With Truman out of the race, the war in stalemate, and the Fair Deal agenda blunted by anticommunist crusades, the Republicans were determined to triumph in the 1952 elections. Rather than choose Senator Robert Taft from the party's conservative wing, they tapped General Dwight Eisenhower, a World War II hero. Eisenhower was less ideological: in fact, no one even knew whether he was a Republican or a Democrat until he announced he was joining the Republican Party. Although the Democratic candidate, Senator Adlai Stevenson of Illinois, was an eloquent speaker, he lacked Eisenhower's common touch. "I like Ike!" proclaimed his campaign posters. A pledge that if elected, he would go to Korea personally to help end the conflict, highlighted Eisenhower's stature as a leader.

The election outcome was never much in doubt. Eisenhower's broad smile and confident manner won him more than 55 percent of the popular vote. A carefully staged television advertising campaign revealed the power of the new media to influence political outcomes. "The great problem of America today," Eisenhower had said during the campaign, "is to take that straight road down the middle." Most Americans who voted for him were comforted to think that was just where they were headed.

EISENHOWER IN KOREA Even before taking office, Eisenhower traveled to Korea to appraise the situation firsthand. Once in office, he renewed negotiations but warned that unless the talks made speedy progress, the United States might retaliate "under circumstances of our choosing." The carrot-and-stick approach worked. On July 27, 1953, the Communists and the UN forces signed an armistice ending a "police action" in which 54,000 Americans had died. Korea remained divided, almost as it had been in 1950. Communism had been "contained," but at a high price in human lives.

The Fall of McCarthy

It was less clear, however, whether domestic anticommunism could be contained. Eisenhower boasted that he was a "modern" Republican, distinguishing himself from what he called the more "hidebound" members of the GOP. Their continuing anticommunist campaigns caused him increasing embarrassment. Senator McCarthy's reckless antics, at first directed at Democrats, began to hit Republican targets as well.

By the summer of 1953 the senator was on a rampage. He dispatched two young staff members, Roy Cohn and David Schine, to investigate the State Department's overseas information agency and the Voice of America radio stations. Behaving more like college pranksters, the two conducted a whirlwind 18-day witch hunt through Western Europe, condemning government libraries for possessing "subversive" books, including volumes by John Dewey and Foster Rhea Dulles, a conservative historian and cousin of Eisenhower's secretary of state. Some librarians, fearing for their careers, burned a number of books. That action drove President Eisenhower to denounce "book burners," though soon afterward he reassured McCarthy's supporters that he did not advocate free speech for Communists.

THE ROSENBERGS EXECUTED The administration's own behavior contributed to the hysteria on which McCarthy thrived. The president launched a loyalty campaign, which he claimed resulted in 3,000 firings and 5,000 resignations of government employees. It was a godsend to McCarthyites: What further proof was needed that subversives were lurking in the federal bureaucracy? Furthermore, a well-publicized spy trial had led to the conviction of Ethel and Julius Rosenberg, a couple accused of passing atomic secrets to the Soviets. Although the evidence against Ethel was not conclusive, the judge sentenced both Rosenbergs to the electric chair, an unusually harsh punishment even in cases of espionage. When asked to commute the death sentence to life imprisonment, Eisenhower refused, and the Rosenbergs were executed in June 1953.

McCARTHY VERSUS THE ARMY In such a climate—where Democrats remained silent for fear of being called leftists and Eisenhower cautiously refused to "get in the gutter with *that* guy"—McCarthy lost all sense of proportion. When the army denied his aide David Schine special treatment, McCarthy decided to investigate communism in the army. The new American Broadcasting Company network, eager to fill its afternoon program slots, televised the hearings. For three weeks, the public had an opportunity to see McCarthy badger witnesses and make a mockery of Senate procedures. Soon after, his popularity began to slide, and the anticommunist hysteria ebbed as well. In 1954 the Senate finally moved to censure him. He died three years later, destroyed by alcohol and the habit of throwing so many reckless punches.

> ✓ **REVIEW**
> How did differences over strategy during the Korean War lead to the firing of General MacArthur?

PUTTING HISTORY IN GLOBAL CONTEXT

WITH THE DEMOCRATS OUT OF the White House for the first time since the Depression and with right-wing McCarthyites in retreat, Eisenhower did indeed seem to be leading the nation on a course "right down the middle." Still, it is worth noting how much that sense of "middle" had changed.

Both the Great Depression and World War II made most Americans realize that the nation's economy was firmly tied to the international order. The crash in 1929, with its worldwide effects, illustrated the closeness of the links. The New Deal demonstrated that Americans were willing to give the federal government power to influence American society in major new ways. And the war led the government to intervene in the economy even more actively.

So when peace came in 1945, it became clear that the "middle road" did not mean a return to the laissez-faire economics of the 1920s or the isolationist politics of the 1930s. Supporters of the Marshall Plan recognized that the economic recovery of Europe should be an American priority for reasons of self-interest as much as of charity. Gone were the policies of the 1920s, under which the United States sternly demanded repayment of European war debts. ("They hired the money, didn't they?" President Coolidge allegedly complained in 1926.) Encompassing the liberal theories of John Maynard Keynes, the Marshall Plan assumed that American intervention in the world economy would promote not only prosperity but also international security. At home, "moderate Republicans" supported social welfare programs such as Social Security and granted that the federal government had the power to lower unemployment, control inflation, and manage the economy in a variety of ways.

Finally, the shift from war to peace demonstrated that it was no longer possible to make global war without making a global peace. Under the new balance of power in the postwar world, the United States and the Soviet Union stood alone as superpowers, with the potential capability to annihilate each other and the rest of the world.

CHAPTER SUMMARY

In the postwar period, the cold war between the Soviet Union and the United States affected every aspect of American domestic and foreign policy and overshadowed American life.

- The cold war had roots in American suspicions of Soviet communism dating back to World War I, but Stalin's aggressive posture toward Eastern Europe and the Persian Gulf region raised new fears among American policy makers.

- In response, the Truman administration applied a policy of containment through the Truman Doctrine, the Marshall Plan, and NSC-68.

- Despite a brief period of inflation, labor unrest, and shortages of goods and housing, the transition from war to peace launched the longest period of prosperity in the nation's history.

- Domestic fear of Communist subversion led the Truman administration to devise a government loyalty program and inspired the witch hunts of Senator Joseph McCarthy.

- The Soviet detonation of an atomic bomb and the fall of China to the Communists, followed one year later by the Korean War, undermined the popularity of Harry Truman and the Democrats, opening the way for Dwight Eisenhower's victory in the 1952 presidential election.

Digging Deeper

A good place to begin reading on the cold war is Fredrik Logevall and Campbell Craig, *America's Cold War* (2009). For the science and politics of the H-bomb, see Gregg Herken, *Brotherhood of the Bomb: The Tangled Lives and Loyalties of Robert Oppenheimer, Ernest Lawrence, and Edward Teller* (2003); and Kai Bird and Martin Sherwin, *American Prometheus: The Triumph and Tragedy of J. Robert Oppenheimer* (2006). On the domestic cold war, see David Halberstam's *The Fifties* (1994) and Stephen J. Whitfield's, *The Culture of the Cold War* (1991). Robert Sklar, *Movie-Made America: A Cultural History of American Movies* (rev. ed., 1994), offers insight into how the cold war affected Hollywood.

Brian Burnes, *Harry S. Truman: His Life and Times* (2003), is a lively account of a president who became more popular with the passage of time. Elizabeth Edwards Spalding, *The First Cold Warrior: Harry Truman, Containment, and the Remaking of Liberal Internationalism* (2006), measures Truman as an architect of the postwar world order. The best account of the man who gave his name to the Red Scare is David M. Oshinsky, *A Conspiracy So Immense: The World of Joe McCarthy* (2005). Two historians have shown how cold war politics and the civil rights movement intersected: Thomas Borstelmann, *The Cold War and the Color Line: American Race Relations in the Global Arena* (2003); and Mary L. Dudziak, *Cold War Civil Rights: Race and the Image of American Democracy* (2002).

28 The Suburban Era

1945–1963

To many, the growing territory of the suburbs promised the chance to own a home in a modern, almost utopian setting. This vision from 1955 imagined a not-distant future when suburbanites could get around in their own personal aircraft. The social utopia, however, remained firmly planted in the pre-feminist 1950s: it's mom, not dad, going for groceries and taking care of the kids. In addition, the suburban home below spreads out in a distinctly low-density suburb. Compare the spaciousness of these yards with the photo later in this chapter of houses going up in Levittown.

©GraphicaArtis/Getty Images

>> An American Story

DYNAMIC OBSOLESCENCE (THE WONDERFUL WORLD OF HARLEY EARL)

No company epitomized the corporate culture of the 1950s more than General Motors. GM executives sought to blend in rather than to stand out. They chose their suits in drab colors—dark blue, dark gray, or light gray—to increase their anonymity. Not head car designer Harley Earl. Earl brought a touch of Hollywood into the world of corporate bureaucrats. He had a closet filled with colorful suits. His staff would marvel as he headed off to a board meeting dressed in white linen with a dark blue shirt and *blue suede shoes,* the same shoes that Elvis Presley sang so protectively about.

©Transstock/SuperStock

| *The monstrous tail fins of the 1959 Cadillac.*

Mr. Earl—no one who worked for him ever called him Harley—could afford to be a maverick. He created the cars that brought customers into GM showrooms across the country. Before he came to Detroit, engineering sold cars. Advertising stressed the mechanical virtues of reliable brakes or power steering. Earl made style the distinctive feature. Unlike the boxy look other designers favored, an Earl car was low and sleek, suggesting motion even when the car stood still. No feature stood out more distinctively than the fins he first put on the 1948 Cadillac. By the mid-1950s jet planes inspired Earl to design ever more outrageous fins, complemented by huge, shiny chrome grills and ornaments. Critics dismissed the designs as jukeboxes on wheels.

To Earl and GM the criticism hardly mattered. Design sold cars. "It gave [customers] an extra receipt for their money in the form of visible prestige marking for an expensive car," Earl said. The "Big Three" auto manufacturers—General Motors, Ford, and Chrysler—raced one another to redesign their annual models. Earl once joked, "I'd put smokestacks right in the middle of the sons of bitches if I thought I could sell more cars." In the lingo of the Detroit stylists, these designs were "gasaroony," an adjective *Popular Mechanics* magazine translated as "terrific, overpowering, weird." The goal was not a better car but what Earl called "dynamic obsolescence," or change for change's sake. Even a successful style had to go within a year. "We would design a car to make a man unhappy with his 1957 Ford 'long about the end of 1958." Even though the mechanics of cars changed little from year to year, dynamic obsolescence persuaded Americans in the 1950s to buy new cars in record numbers.

Fins, roadside motels, "gaseterias," drive-in burger huts, interstate highways, shopping centers, and, of course, suburbs—all these were part of a culture of mobility in the 1950s. Americans continued their exodus from rural areas to cities and from the cities to the suburbs. African Americans left the South, heading for industrial centers in the Northeast, Midwest, and West Coast. Mexican Americans concentrated in southwestern cities, while Puerto Ricans came largely to New York. And for Americans in the Snow Belt, the climate of the West and South (at least when civilized by air-conditioning) made the Sun Belt irresistible to ever-larger numbers.

The mobility was social, too. As the economy continued to expand, the size of the American middle class grew. In an era of prosperity and peace, some commentators began to speak of a "**consensus**"—a general agreement in American culture, based on values of the broad middle class. In a positive light, consensus reflected the agreement among most Americans about fundamental democratic values. Most citizens embraced the material benefits of prosperity as evidence of the virtue of "the American way." And they opposed the spread of communism abroad.

But consensus had its dark side. Critics worried that it bred a mindless **conformity**. Were Americans becoming too homogenized? Was there a depressing sameness in the material goods they owned, in the places they lived, and in the values they held? Besides, wasn't any notion of consensus hollow as long as racism and segregation prevented African Americans and other minorities from fully sharing in American life?

The baby boomers born into this era seldom agonized over such issues. In the White House, President Eisenhower radiated a comforting sense that the affairs of the nation and the world were in capable hands. That left teenagers free to worry about what really mattered: a first date, a first kiss, a first job, a first choice for college, and whether or not to "go all the way" in the backseat of one of Harley Earl's fin-swept Buicks. <<

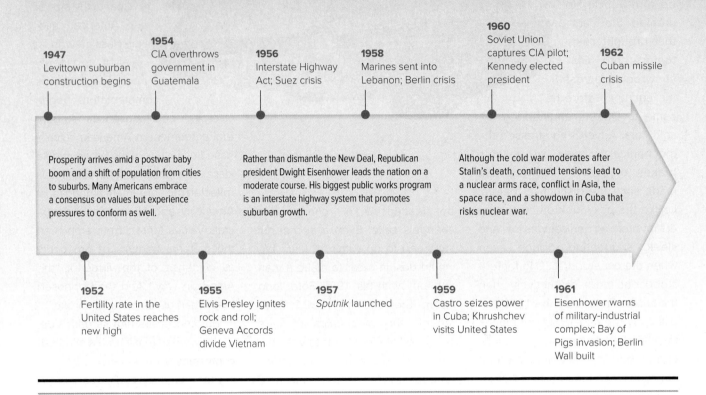

1947 Levittown suburban construction begins

1954 CIA overthrows government in Guatemala

1956 Interstate Highway Act; Suez crisis

1958 Marines sent into Lebanon; Berlin crisis

1960 Soviet Union captures CIA pilot; Kennedy elected president

1962 Cuban missile crisis

Prosperity arrives amid a postwar baby boom and a shift of population from cities to suburbs. Many Americans embrace a consensus on values but experience pressures to conform as well.

Rather than dismantle the New Deal, Republican president Dwight Eisenhower leads the nation on a moderate course. His biggest public works program is an interstate highway system that promotes suburban growth.

Although the cold war moderates after Stalin's death, continued tensions lead to a nuclear arms race, conflict in Asia, the space race, and a showdown in Cuba that risks nuclear war.

1952 Fertility rate in the United States reaches new high

1955 Elvis Presley ignites rock and roll; Geneva Accords divide Vietnam

1957 *Sputnik* launched

1959 Castro seizes power in Cuba; Khrushchev visits United States

1961 Eisenhower warns of military-industrial complex; Bay of Pigs invasion; Berlin Wall built

THE RISE OF THE SUBURBS

SUBURBAN GROWTH ACCELERATED SHARPLY AT the end of World War II. During the 1950s suburbs grew 40 times faster than cities, so that by 1960 half the American people lived in them. The return of prosperity brought a baby boom and a need for new housing. Automobiles made the suburbs accessible. But the spurt in suburban growth took its toll on the cities, which suffered as the middle class fled urban areas. And the lack of planning regulations saddled suburbanites with the pollution and congestion they hoped to escape.

A Boom in Babies and in Housing

The Depression forced many couples to delay beginning a family. In the 1930s birthrates had reached the low point of American history, about 18 to 19 per thousand. As prosperity returned during the war, birthrates began to rise. In 1946 Americans married in record numbers, twice as many as in 1932. The new brides were also younger, most in their peak years of fertility. In a 10-year period the American population increased by 30 million, giving the United States a rate of growth comparable to that of India. By 1952 the birthrate passed 25 live births per thousand, and it did not peak until 1957. Ten years later it had dropped to under 18.

THE BOOM WORLDWIDE Historians and demographers have been hard-pressed to explain this extraordinary population bulge. It was not limited to the United States. In several other industrialized nations fertility rates also soared, Australia, New Zealand, Britain, and West Germany prime among them. Yet as the chart indicates, the long-term trend in American fertility rates was downward, as it was in other industrialized nations. Fertility rates peaked in Australia and New Zealand in 1961 and, three years later, in Great Britain and West Germany. Hence the baby boom stands as an anomaly, one that remains hard to explain.

Perhaps Americans were indeed "making up for lost time" after the war. Rising income allowed more people to afford marriage and children. But Americans should have caught up by the early 1950s, whereas the baby boom continued into the 1960s. Worldwide, urbanization and higher living standards are linked to lower birthrates. In 1950 the most industrialized and urban nations had a birthrate of 21.8 live births per thousand, while in less developed and less densely settled sub-Saharan Africa the rate was 49.8. In South Asia it was 44.8.

Whatever factors contributed to the baby boom, it had both immediate and long-term consequences for American society. For one, the boom in marriages and families increased demand for housing. At war's end, 5 million

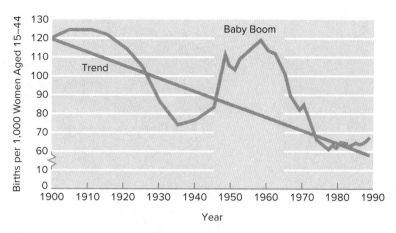

The United States Birthrate, 1900–1989

Despite periods of rapid rise and fall, the nation's birthrate has shown a steady downward trend. The Depression years showed an even sharper decline as financially strapped couples deferred childbearing. Younger marriages and postwar prosperity triggered the baby boom, but in general, affluence encourages lower birthrates.

American families were eagerly searching for housing, tired of living in doubled-up conditions with other families, in basements, or even in coal cellars. With the help of the GI Bill and the rising prosperity, the chance to own a house rather than rent became a reality for over half of American families. The suburbs also offered the residence most idealized in American culture: a detached single-family house with a lawn and garden.

LEVITTOWN, U.S.A. After World War II inexpensive, suburban housing became synonymous with William Levitt. From building houses for war workers, Levitt learned how to use mass-production techniques. In 1947 he began construction of a 17,000-house community in the New York City suburb of Hempstead. All the materials for a Levittown house were precut and assembled at a factory, then moved to the site for assembly. If all went according to schedule, a new house was erected on a cement slab every 16 minutes. Buoyed by his success in Hempstead, Levitt later built developments in Bucks County, Pennsylvania, and Willingboro, New Jersey.

The typical early Levitt house, a "Cape Codder," had a living room, kitchen, bath, and two bedrooms on the ground floor and an expansion attic, all for $7,990. None had custom features, insulation, or any amenities that complicated construction. "The reason we have it so good in this country," Levitt said, "is that we can produce lots of things at low prices through mass production." Uniformity in house style extended to behavior as well. Levitt discouraged owners from changing colors or adding distinctive features to the house or yard. Buyers promised to cut the grass each week of the summer and not to hang out wash on weekends. African Americans were expressly excluded. Other suburban communities excluded Jews and ethnic Americans through restrictive covenants that dictated who could take up residence.

In California, a state with three cars registered for every four residents, suburbs bloomed across the landscape. By 1962 it had become the nation's most populous state. Growth was greatest around Los Angeles. In 1940 city planners began building a freeway system to lure shoppers into downtown Los Angeles. Instead, white Angelinos saw the road network as an opportunity to migrate to the suburbs. Eventually one-third of the Los Angeles area was covered by highways, parking lots, and interchanges, increasing to two-thirds in the downtown areas.

Cities and Suburbs Transformed

Single-family houses on their own plots of land required plenty of open land, unlike the row houses built side by side in earlier suburban developments. That meant Levitt and other builders chose vacant areas outside major urban areas. With the new houses farther away from factories, offices, and jobs, the automobile became more indispensable than ever.

INTERSTATE HIGHWAY ACT OF 1956 As the population shifted to suburbs, traffic choked old country roads. To ease this congestion, the Eisenhower administration proposed a 20-year plan to build a massive interstate highway system of some 41,000 miles. Eisenhower addressed cold war fears to build support, arguing that the new system would ease evacuation of cities in case of nuclear attack. In 1956 Congress passed the National Interstate and Defense Highway Act, setting in motion the largest public works project in history. The federal government picked

©H. Armstrong Roberts/Retrofile/Getty Images

| *"The reason we have it so good in this country is that we can produce lots of things at low prices through mass production." So said William Levitt, who applied the principle to the construction of new suburban homes out of precut materials assembled on the fly. At its fastest, construction crews raced to complete a new house on a cement slab every 16 minutes.*

AVERAGE ANNUAL REGIONAL MIGRATION, 1947–1960

In this period, African Americans were moving in significant numbers to urban centers in the Northeast, the Midwest, and the Far West. Whites were being drawn to the increasingly diversified economy of the South as well as to the new industries, stimulated by the war, in the Far West. By the 1970s the trend had become known as the "Sun Belt" phenomenon.

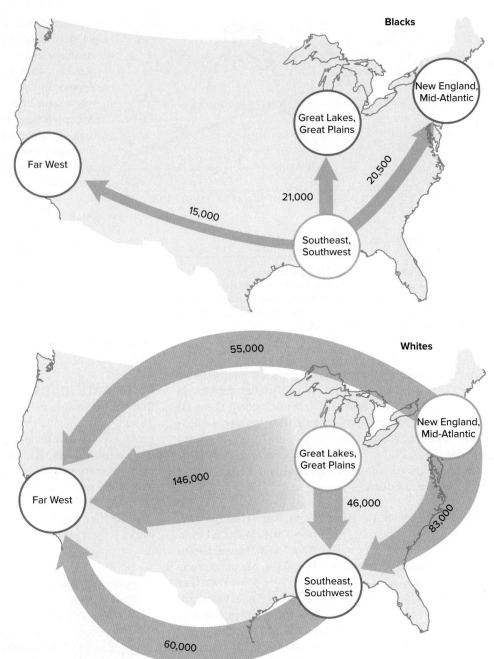

up 90 percent of the cost through a Highway Trust Fund, financed by special taxes on cars, gas, tires, lubricants, and auto parts.

The Interstate Highway Act had an enormous impact on American life. Average annual driving increased by 400 percent. Shopping centers, linked by the new roads, sprang up to provide suburbanites with an alternative to the longer trip downtown. Almost every community had at least one highway strip dotted with drive-in movies, stores, bowling alleys, gas stations, and fast-food joints.

DECLINING CITIES For cities, the interstates created other problems. The new highway system featured beltways—ring roads around major urban areas. Instead of leading traffic downtown, the beltways allowed motorists to avoid the center city altogether. As people took to their cars, intercity rail service and mass transit declined. Seventy-five percent of all government transportation dollars went to subsidize travel by car and truck; only 1 percent was earmarked for urban mass transit. At the same time that middle-class homeowners were moving to the suburbs, many low-paying, unskilled jobs disappeared from the cities, especially in old industrial centers. These trends forced the urban poor into reverse commuting, from city to suburb. All these trends made cities less attractive places to live or do business. With fewer well-to-do taxpayers to draw on, city governments lacked the tax base to finance public services. A vicious cycle ensued that proved most damaging to the urban poor, who had few means of escape.

African Americans and Hispanics replaced much of the white population that left cities for suburbs. These newcomers were part of larger migrations, especially of millions of black families leaving the South to search for work in urban centers. Most headed for the Middle Atlantic, Northeast, upper Midwest, and the Far West regions. While central cities lost 3.6 million white residents, they gained 4.5 million African Americans. Indeed, by 1960 half of all black Americans were living in central cities.

Earlier waves of European immigrants had been absorbed by the expanding urban economy. During the 1950s, however, the flight of jobs and middle-class taxpayers to the suburbs made it difficult for African Americans and Hispanics to follow the same path. In the cities fewer jobs awaited them, while declining school systems made it harder for newcomers to acculturate. In the hardest-hit urban areas, unemployment rose to over 40 percent.

MINORITIES AND SUBURBS In contrast, the suburbs remained beyond the reach of most minorities. Because few black or Hispanic families could afford the cost of suburban living, they accounted for less than 5 percent of the population there. The few black suburbs that existed dated from before the war and had little in common with the newer white "bedroom communities." Black suburbanites were poorer, held lower-status jobs, lived in more-ramshackle housing, and had less education than urban African Americans. Even minorities who could afford the suburbs discovered that most real estate agents refused to show them houses; bankers would not provide mortgages. The developers of Levittown did not sell directly to African Americans until 1960.

Suburban Blues

During the suburban boom, homebuilders seldom took the environment into account—until something happened to make residents sit up and take notice. In late summer of 1956 some residents of Portuguese Bend, California, discovered that their houses were actually on the move. By October 156 homes, along with their lawns, gardens, and swimming pools, had "gently slumped downhill as though they were so much custard pudding." Over time, the effluent from septic systems, abetted by lawn watering, slicked the underlying shale that naturally tilted toward the nearby Pacific Ocean. Gravity did the rest of the work.

During the 1950s developers in Los Angeles built two-thirds of all new houses on the region's hills. Such construction was especially popular in California. Powerful bulldozers and other earth-moving equipment made hillside building practical, while lower land prices made it cheaper. The landslides that periodically occurred after heavy rains soon provoked a move toward stricter building codes. Nor was California alone. Suburbs in Washington, D.C., Cincinnati, and Pittsburgh suffered similar disasters. Other misfortunes occurred when developers built in wetlands and on floodplains. Even on dry level ground, cheap septic systems often failed, leaving homeowners with large repair bills, sewage

stench, and the threat of infectious disease. In the following decades the federal government was forced to spend billions of dollars to replace septic systems with local sewers.

The disappearance of open space confronted many suburbanites with yet another threat to their dreams. "No more sweep of green," mourned sociologist William Whyte; "across the hills are splattered scores of random subdivisions, each laid out with the same dreary curves. Gone are the streams, brooks, woods and forests that the subdivisions signs talked about." Gone, too, were habitats for birds, small mammals, fish, and amphibians. Years later, homeowners' desire to preserve a shred of the suburban dream would contribute to the movement to protect the environment.

REVIEW

What factors pushed the growth of suburbs, and what were the environmental costs of pushing too hard?

SUBURBAN CULTURE

AT PARTIES IN SUBURBS ACROSS America, a new appetizer began appearing. Named the California Dip, it was the brainchild of the Lipton Company, which was searching for new ways to market its dehydrated onion soup. Homemakers simply mixed Lipton's soup powder with sour cream and served it up with chips. As one commentator has noted,

> Using potato chips as little shovels, you gathered up the deliciously salty but drip-prone liquid and popped it, potato chip and all, into your mouth as quickly and gracefully as possible. There was anxiety in all this—particularly the fear that a great glop of the stuff would land on your tie or the rug—but also immense satisfaction.

As much genius, perhaps, went into the naming of the dip as into the recipe. Sour cream had been a mainstay in ethnic dishes such as blintzes (thin Jewish pancakes) and borscht (an Eastern European beet soup). With the all-American name of "California Dip," sour cream's ethnic associations were left behind. The ingredient went mainstream—into the consensus.

The evolving culture of the suburbs reflected a similar process, a shucking off of ethnic associations. In many city neighborhoods, immigrant parents or grandparents lived on the same block or even in the same apartment with their children. In the suburbs, single-family dwellers often left their relatives and in-laws behind, which meant that ethnic lifestyles were less pronounced. The restrictive immigration policies of the 1920s had also reduced the number of newly arrived foreign-born Americans. Thus suburban culture reflected the tastes of the broad, mostly assimilated middle classes.

SUBURBS AND SOCIAL CLASS Class distinctions were more pronounced between suburban communities than within them. The upper middle class clustered in older developments, which often revolved around country clubs. Working-class suburbs sprouted on the outskirts of large

©Elliott Erwitt/Magnum Photos

| Baptist Billy Graham led the revival of evangelical religion in American culture. While his message emphasized the traditional Fundamentalist themes of sin, redemption, and the Second Coming of Christ, his up-to-date methods took advantage of television, advertising, radio, and paperback books to reach the widest possible audience.

manufacturing centers, where blue-collar families eagerly escaped the city. Within suburbs a more homogeneous suburban culture evolved. "We see eye to eye on most things," commented one Levittown resident, "about raising kids, doing things together with your husband . . . we have practically the same identical background."

American Civil Religion

If suburban residents retained less of their ethnic heritages, most held on to their religious beliefs. Religion continued to be a distinctive and segregating factor during the 1950s. Catholics, Protestants, and Jews generally married within their own faiths, and in the suburbs they kept their social distance as well.

THE RELIGIOUS DIVISION Communities that showed no obvious class distinctions were sometimes deeply divided along religious lines. Many Catholics attended parochial rather than public schools, formed their own clubs, and generally did not socialize with their Protestant neighbors. Protestant and Catholic members of the same country club usually did not play golf or tennis in the same foursomes. As for Jews, one historian remarked, whereas a gulf divided many Catholics and Protestants, Jews and Gentiles "seem to have lived on the opposite sides of a religious Grand Canyon." Even superficial signs of friendliness masked the persistence of old stereotypes.

Although such religious boundaries remained distinct, religion was central to American life. Church membership rose

to more than 50 percent for the first time in the twentieth century, and by 1957 the Census Bureau reported that 96 percent of the American people cited a specific affiliation when asked, "What is your religion?" The religious upswing was supported in part by the prevailing cold war mood, because communists were avowedly atheists. Cold war fervor led Congress in 1954 to add the phrase "under God" to the Pledge of Allegiance.

Patriotic and anticommunist themes were strong in the preaching of clergy who pioneered the use of television. Billy Graham, a Baptist revival preacher, first attracted national attention at a tent meeting in Los Angeles in 1949. Following in the tradition of nineteenth-century revivalists like Charles Finney and Dwight Moody, he soon achieved an even wider impact by televising his meetings. Though no revivalist, the Roman Catholic bishop Fulton J. Sheen became a popular television celebrity. In his weekly program he extolled traditional values and attacked communism.

The growing consensus among Americans was that *any* religious belief was better than none. President Eisenhower made the point quite clear: "Our government makes no sense unless it is founded on a deeply religious faith," he proclaimed, "—and I don't care what it is." Children got the message, too. Every Friday afternoon kids watching *The Howdy Doody Show* were exhorted by Buffalo Bob to worship "at the church or synagogue of your choice."

"Homemaking" Women in the Workaday World

The growth of a suburban culture revealed a contradiction in the lives of middle-class women. Never before were their traditional roles as housewives and mothers so central to American society. Yet never before did more women join the workforce outside the home.

Most housewives found that suburban homes and growing families required increasing time and energy. With relatives less likely to live nearby, mothering became full-time work. Dependence on automobiles made many a suburban housewife the chauffeur for her family. In the 1920s grocers or milkmen had commonly delivered their goods from door to door; by the 1950s delivery services were being replaced by housewives doing "errands."

WORKING WOMEN Yet between 1940 and 1960 the percentage of wives working outside the home doubled, from 15 to 30 percent. Although some women took jobs simply to help make ends meet, often more than financial necessity was involved. Middle-class married women went to work as often as lower-class wives, and women with college degrees were the most likely to get a job. Two-income families were able to spend far more on extras: gifts, education, recreation, and household appliances. In addition, women found status and self-fulfillment in their jobs, as well as a chance for increased social contacts.

More women were going to college, too, but that increased education did not translate into economic equality.

The percentage of women holding professional jobs actually dropped between 1950 and 1960. And the gap between men's and women's wages was greater than in any other industrialized nation. In the United States, the median wage for women was less than half that for men.

When women possessed leverage, they reshaped traditional work roles. Many nurses, for example, left the profession after World War II to start families. As the health care industry grew sharply, an acute nursing shortage occurred. As health administrators (almost all men) sought new recruits, professional nursing associations pressed for increased wages and part-time positions, on-site child care, and maternity leaves so that nurse mothers had flexibility in working. In heavily female jobs such as teaching, stenography, and retail clerking, where fewer shortages existed, women did not achieve comparable gains until much later.

MEDIA IMAGES OF WOMEN   Despite women's wider roles in society, the media most often portrayed women either as sex objects or as domesticated housewives and mothers. A typical article appearing in *Redbook* in 1957 made a heroine of Junior, a "little freckle-faced brunette" who had given up work. As the story closed, Junior nursed her baby at two in the morning, crooning "I'm glad, glad, glad I'm just a housewife." In 1950 Lynn White, the president of Mills College for women, advocated a curriculum that displaced traditional academic subjects with those that were "distinctly feminine," such as crafts and home economics.

A Revolution in Sexuality?

Throughout the twentieth century, a trend had been under way deemphasizing the tradition that sex within marriage was primarily for the procreation of children—a duty (especially for women) to be endured rather than enjoyed. During the 1920s reformer Ben Lindsey promoted the idea of "companionate marriage," stressing personal happiness and satisfaction as primary goals. Such a marriage included the enjoyment of sex for both wife and husband. The suburban home of the 1950s encouraged such ideals, symbolizing as it did a place of relaxation and enjoyment. Unlike city apartments, where extended families often lived in crowded conditions, the suburban single-family houses provided greater privacy and more space for intimacy.

THE KINSEY REPORTS   Social scientists noted that sexual pleasure was becoming part of successful marriages. That idea received additional attention in 1948 with the publication of an apparently dry scientific study, *Sexual Behavior in the Human Male*. Its author, Professor Alfred Kinsey, hardly expected the storm of publicity his study and its companion, *Sexual Behavior in the Human Female* (1953), provoked. Kinsey began his research career as a zoologist with a zest for classifying data. During the 1940s he turned to collecting information on sexual behavior. Based on more than 10,000 interviews, Kinsey reached conclusions that were unorthodox and even startling for his day. Masturbation and premarital petting, he reported, were widespread. Women did not just endure sex as a wifely duty; they enjoyed it in much the same way men did. Extramarital sex was common for both husbands and wives. About 10 percent of the population was homosexual.

Publicly, Kinsey maintained a posture of scientific objectivity. He argued that he had only published a report "on what people do" and wasn't concerned with "what they should do." But biographers of Kinsey have revealed that, in fact, he was as much interested in social change as in

Television's "Wasteland"

How does this television differ from today's models? Based on what you read below, was this model made after 1961?

A blackboard can be seen to the right of the woman on television. What kind of programming do these students appear to be watching? What other clues in the photograph suggest that answer?

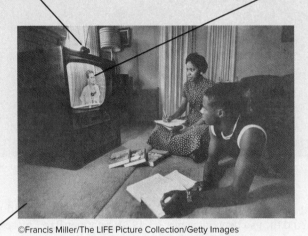

©Francis Miller/The LIFE Picture Collection/Getty Images

Was this photograph candid or staged? What elements in the picture inform your answer?

Television came to dominate popular culture in the era after World War II. In 1945, fewer than 10,000 people owned TV sets. By 1960, fully 90 percent of American families did. Some early promoters of television hoped it would enrich people's lives. Newton Minow, appointed to head the Federal Communications Commission by President Kennedy, argued that the networks had largely failed to realize that potential. Yes, he granted, occasional news, theatrical, and imaginative shows presented fine programming, but "when television is bad, nothing is worse." Minow challenged anyone to watch a single day's broadcast programs from start to finish, without concluding that television was "a vast wasteland."

Most network programs portrayed a society that was mostly white, young, middle-class, with leaders who were mostly male. Clearly, the educational program these students appear to be watching was an exception. But in 1961, Minow did succeed in getting Congress to pass an act requiring that all televisions sold in the United States be capable of receiving UHF channels. Those added frequencies made it easier for nonprofit, educational broadcasting stations to operate.

THINKING CRITICALLY

For decades, the primary television networks were CBS, NBC, and ABC. What educational networks have grown up? What clues does the picture give you about the social class of this family? Why did television networks pay so little attention to minorities and other people outside the mainstream?

scientific research, believing that many acts treated as deviant should be placed within a normal range of sexual behavior. Kinsey's views on sexuality provoked intense controversy. Social scientists objected that his sample was too narrow to produce valid norms, and his most severe critics called him "a menace to society." According to opinion polls, most Americans disagreed. The large majority took comfort (as he had hoped) that behaviors once condemned as sinful or perverse were widely practiced.

The Flickering Gray Screen

In the glow of postwar prosperity, most Americans found themselves with more leisure time and more income. In the suburbs, a yard to tend and a young family to raise determined that much of that free time would be spent around the house. The new medium of television fit perfectly into suburban lifestyles. It provided an ideal way to entertain families at home as well as to sell them consumer goods.

Television viewership boomed after World War II. By 1949 Americans had bought a million sets; by 1960 that number had jumped to 46 million, and by then more Americans had television sets than had bathrooms. Home viewing transformed American entertainment habits, cutting sharply into pastimes like movies and professional sports. In cities around the country, more than 4,000 neighborhood theaters closed. Many were replaced in the suburbs by popular drive-ins, which allowed whole families to enjoy movies in the comfort of their cars.

TELEVISION AND POLITICS In 1948 television began to affect politics, covering both the Democratic and the Republican Conventions. Two years later, it combined entertainment, politics, and news by televising a series of hearings on organized crime chaired by Senator Estes Kefauver. Some 30 million viewers watched senators grill mobster Frank Costello about his criminal organization and its ties to city governments. Millions more watched Senator Joseph McCarthy's ill-fated crusade against the army in 1954. Clearly, television demonstrated the potential to shape the political life of the nation. By the mid-1950s, however, controversy over news coverage of issues like McCarthyism led the networks to downgrade public affairs programs. As an alternative, the networks turned to Hollywood film studios, which provided them with telefilm series. By selling time to advertisers, the networks, rather than the sponsors, gained ultimate control over program content. By 1959 live television was virtually a thing of the past.

REVIEW
How were the ideals of a middle-class consensus reflected in religion, the world of the suburban home, and television?

THE POLITICS OF CALM

IN PRESIDING OVER THESE CHANGES in American society, President Dwight David Eisenhower projected an aura of paternal calm. Pursuing "modern Republicanism," the new president sought consensus, not confrontation. Eisenhower declared that he was "conservative when it comes to money and liberal when it comes to human beings."

Eisenhower's Modern Republicanism

Eisenhower had been raised in a large Kansas farm family. His parents, though poor, provided him a warm, caring home steeped in religious faith. A graduate of West Point, "Ike" was neither a scholar nor a flamboyant general like George Patton. Yet his genial ways could not hide his ambition or his ability to judge character shrewdly. In an era of organization men, Eisenhower succeeded by mastering the military's bureaucratic politics. It took a gifted organizer to coordinate the D-Day invasion and to hold together the egocentric generals

who pushed east to Berlin. Eisenhower was such a promising candidate that both parties had considered him for the 1948 presidential race.

In pursuing his pragmatic course, Eisenhower resisted conservative demands to dismantle New Deal programs. He even agreed to increases in Social Security, unemployment insurance, and the minimum wage. He accepted a small public housing program and a modest federally supported medical insurance plan for the needy. But as a conservative, Eisenhower remained uncomfortable with big government. Thus he rejected more far-reaching liberal proposals on housing and universal health care through the Social Security system.

Success for the Eisenhower administration depended most on how well it managed the economy. The Democrats of the New Deal had established a tradition of activism. When the economy faltered, deficit spending and tax cuts stimulated it. Eisenhower, in contrast, wanted to reduce federal spending and the government's role in the economy. When a recession struck in 1953–1954, the administration was concerned more with balancing the budget and holding inflation in line than with reducing unemployment through government spending.

Eisenhower was similarly pragmatic in other areas. When major projects called for federal leadership, as with the Highway Act, he supported the policy. In 1954 he signed the St. Lawrence Seaway Act, which joined the United States and Canada in an ambitious engineering project to open the Great Lakes to ocean shipping. Like the highway program, the Seaway was fiscally acceptable because the funding came from user tolls and taxes rather than from general revenues.

EISENHOWER REELECTED Despite a recession in 1953–1954, Eisenhower remained popular. Even after he suffered a major heart attack in 1955, voters gladly reelected him over Adlai Stevenson in 1956. But poor economic performance took its toll on the Republican Party. In 1958, when recession again dragged down the economy, the Democrats took a commanding 68-seat majority in the House and a 12-vote advantage in the Senate. Modern Republicanism did not put down deep roots outside Eisenhower's White House.

The Conglomerate World

Large corporations welcomed the administration's probusiness attitudes as well as the era's general prosperity. Wages for the average worker rose over 35 percent between 1950 and 1960. At the same time, the economic distress of the 1930s had led corporate executives to devise new ways to minimize the danger of economic downturns. Each of the approaches expanded the size of corporations in various ways in order to minimize shocks in specific markets.

DIVERSIFICATION One expansion strategy took the form of diversification. In the 1930s a giant General Electric had concentrated largely in one industrial area: equipment for generating electric power and light. When the Depression struck, GE found its markets evaporating. The company

©Bettmann/Getty Images

| *Eisenhower was a popular president, but his health created widespread public concern. He suffered a heart attack in September 1955, and timely surgery on a bowel obstruction the following June saved his life. Despite his age and ill health, the president was easily reelected in 1956. Here he recuperates after the 1955 heart attack, at an army hospital in Denver.*

responded by entering markets for appliances, X-ray machines, and elevators—all products developed or enhanced by the company's research labs. In the postwar era General Electric diversified even further to become a **conglomerate**, expanding into nuclear power, jet engines, and television. Diversification was most practical for large industrial firms, whose size allowed them to support extensive research and development.

Conglomeration often turned small companies into giants. Unlike earlier horizontal and vertical combinations, conglomerate mergers could join companies with seemingly unrelated products. Over a 20-year period International Telephone and Telegraph branched out from its basic communications business into baking, hotels and motels, car rental, home building, and insurance. Corporations also became multinational by expanding their overseas operations or buying out potential foreign competitors. Large integrated oil companies like Mobil and Standard Oil of New Jersey (Exxon) developed huge oil fields in the Middle East and markets around the free world.

Many large corporations also decided they could profit more from cooperating with labor unions rather than reviving the pitched battles of the 1930s. As former GM executive Lee Iacocca explained, "Because strikes were so devastating, the leaders of industry would do almost anything to avoid one." He added, "In those days we could afford to be generous. Because we had a lock on the market, we could continually spend more money on labor and simply pass the additional costs on to the consumer in the form of price increases." Unions gladly negotiated higher wages and generous benefits, while their members avoided losing wages to strikes.

One aid to managing these modern corporate giants was the advent of electronic data processing. In the early 1950s computers were virtually unknown in private industry. But banks and insurance companies saw these calculating machines as an answer to their need to manipulate huge quantities of records and statistical data. Manufacturers, especially in the petroleum, chemical, automotive, and electronics industries, began to use computers to monitor their production lines, quality control, and inventory.

Corporations that manufactured consumer goods depended on advertising to reach potential customers. "The only institution which we have for instilling new needs, for training people to act as consumers, for altering men's values, and thus for hastening their adjustment to potential abundance is advertising," historian David Potter concluded in 1954. About the same time, economist John Kenneth Galbraith agreed that advertising "creates desires—to bring into being wants that previously did not exist."

The great "cola war" dramatized Potter's point. The smaller Pepsi corporation touted itself as a David battling Goliath—Coca-Cola. In reality, while the two soft-drink companies cultivated alternative images to gain market share, they did not attack each other nor did either raise the most obvious question: "Which tastes better?" Instead, Pepsi created ads that suggested its drinkers were young, fashionable, and popular:

> Be sociable, look smart
> Keep up-to-date with Pepsi
> Drink light refreshing Pepsi
> Stay young and fair and debonair
> Be sociable, have a Pepsi!

Pepsi's decision to target the young and women transformed its corporate fortunes. From 1949 to 1959, while Coke's gross profits rose about 50 percent (albeit from a high level), Pepsi's rose 500 percent, enough to make it a formidable rival. Each product had its brand identity—Coke, the cola with a universal appeal that stood the test of time, versus Pepsi, the drink for young, upwardly mobile, suburban families.

 REVIEW

How did conglomerates fit into the scheme of Eisenhower's "modern Republicanism"?

CRACKS IN THE CONSENSUS

As CORPORATIONS MERGED IN ORDER to increase their reach, power, and stability, they saw themselves as a part of the emerging consensus over the American way. ("What's good for the country is good for General Motors.") Yet there were distinct cracks in the consensus. Intellectuals and social critics spoke out against the stifling features of a conformist corporate culture. At the fringes of American society, the "beats" rejected conformity, while the popularity of rock and roll signaled the emergence of a distinct youth culture.

Critics of Mass Culture

In Levittown, New Jersey, a woman who had invited her neighbors to a cocktail party eagerly awaited them dressed in newly fashionable Capri pants—a tight-fitting calf-length style. Alas, one early-arriving couple glimpsed the woman through a window. What on earth was the hostess wearing? *Pajamas?* Who in their right mind would entertain in pajamas? The couple sneaked home, afraid they had made a mistake about the day of the party.

Finally, they mustered enough courage to drop in. But when the hostess later learned of their misunderstanding, she put her Capri pants in the closet. Levittown was not ready for such a change in fashion.

SUBURBAN CONFORMITY   Was America turning into a vast suburban wasteland, where the neighbors' worries over Capri pants would stifle all individuality? Many intellectuals worried openly about the homogenized lifestyle created by mass consumption, conformity, and **mass media.** Critics such as Dwight Macdonald sarcastically attacked the culture of the suburban middle classes: *Reader's Digest* Condensed Books, uplifting film spectacles such as *The Ten Commandments,* television dramas that pretended to be high art but in reality were little more than simplistic pontificating. "Midcult," Macdonald called it, which was his shorthand for middlebrow culture.

DAVID RIESMAN'S *THE LONELY CROWD*   Other critics charged that the skyscrapers and factories of giant conglomerates housed an all-too-impersonal world. In large, increasingly automated workplaces, skilled laborers seemed little more than caretakers of machines. Large corporations required middle-level executives to submerge their personal goals in the processes and work routines of a large bureaucracy. David Riesman, a sociologist, condemned stifling conformity in *The Lonely Crowd* (1950). In nineteenth-century America, Riesman argued, Americans had been "inner directed." It was their own consciences that formed their values and drove them to seek success. In contrast, modern workers had developed a personality shaped not so much by inner convictions as by the opinions of their peers. The new "other-directed" society of suburbia preferred security to success. "Go along to get along" was its motto.

©Bettmann/Getty Images

| *Capri pants, 1950s. Were such fashions too radical for the conformist suburbs?*

WILLIAM WHYTE'S *THE ORGANIZATION MAN*   William Whyte carried Riesman's critique from the workplace to the suburb in *The Organization Man* (1956). Here he found rootless families, shifted from town to town by the demands of corporations. (IBM, according to one standard joke, stood for "I've Been Moved.") The typical organization man was sociable but not terribly ambitious. He sought primarily to keep up with the Joneses and the number of consumer goods they owned. He lived in a suburban "split-level trap," as one critic put it, one among millions of "haggard" men, "tense and anxious" women, and "the gimme kids," who, like the cartoon character Dennis the Menace, looked up from the litter under the Christmas tree to ask, "Is that all?"

No doubt such portraits were overdrawn. (Where, after all, did Riesman's nineteenth-century inner-directed Americans get their values, if not from the society around them?) But such critiques indicated the problems of adjustment faced by people working within large bureaucratic organizations and living in suburbs that were decentralized and self-contained.

The Rebellion of Young America

JUVENILE DELINQUENCY   Young Americans were among suburbia's sharpest critics. Dance crazes, outlandish clothing, strange jargon, rebelliousness toward parents, and sexual precociousness—all these behaviors challenged middle-class respectability. More than a few parents and public figures warned that America had spawned a generation of rebellious juvenile delinquents. Psychiatrist Fredric Wertham told a group of doctors, "You cannot understand present-day juvenile delinquency if you do not take into account the pathogenic and pathoplastic [infectious] influence of comic books." Others laid the blame on films and the lyrics of popular music.

The center of the new teen culture was the high school. Whether in consolidated rural school districts, new suburban schools, or city systems, the large, comprehensive high schools of the 1950s were often miniature melting pots in which middle-class students were exposed to, and often adopted, the style of the lower classes. Alarmed school administrators complained of juvenile delinquents who wore jeans and T-shirts, challenged authority, and defiantly smoked cigarettes, much like the motorcycle gang leader portrayed by Marlon Brando in the film *The Wild One* (1954).

In many ways the argument about juvenile delinquency was an argument about social class and, to a lesser degree, race. Adults who complained that delinquent teenagers dressed poorly, lacked ambition, and were irresponsible and sexually promiscuous were voicing the same arguments traditionally used to denigrate other outsiders—immigrants, the poor, and African Americans. Nowhere were these racial and class undertones more evident than in the hue and cry greeting the arrival of rock and roll.

THE RISE OF ROCK AND ROLL Before 1954 popular music had been divided into four major categories: pop, country and western, jazz, and rhythm and blues. A handful of record companies with almost exclusively white singers dominated the pop charts. On one fringe of the popular field was country and western, often split into cowboy musicians such as Roy Rogers and Gene Autry and the hillbilly style associated with Nashville. The music industry generally treated jazz and rhythm and blues as "race music," whose performers and audience were largely black. Each of these musical traditions grew out of regional cultures. As the West and the South merged into the national culture, so too were these musical subcultures gradually integrated into the national mainstream.

By the mid-1950s the distinctiveness of these styles began to blur. Singers on the white pop charts recorded a few songs from country and from rhythm and blues. The popularity of crossover songs such as "Sh-boom," "Tutti-Frutti," and "Earth Angel" indicated that a major shift in taste and market was under way. Lyrics still reflected the pop field's preoccupation with young love, marriage, and happiness,

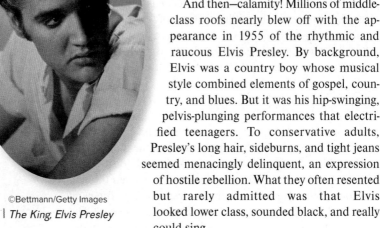

©Bettmann/Getty Images

The King, Elvis Presley

but the music now vibrated with the rawer, earthier style of rhythm and blues. Country and western singer Bill Haley brought the new blend to the fore in 1954 with "Shake, Rattle, and Roll," the first rock song to reach the top ten on the pop charts.

And then—calamity! Millions of middle-class roofs nearly blew off with the appearance in 1955 of the rhythmic and raucous Elvis Presley. By background, Elvis was a country boy whose musical style combined elements of gospel, country, and blues. But it was his hip-swinging, pelvis-plunging performances that electrified teenagers. To conservative adults, Presley's long hair, sideburns, and tight jeans seemed menacingly delinquent, an expression of hostile rebellion. What they often resented but rarely admitted was that Elvis looked lower class, sounded black, and really could sing.

The "Beat" Generation

Beyond the frenetic rhythms of rock and roll, and even farther beyond the pale of suburban culture, flourished a subculture known as the "beat" generation. In run-down urban neighborhoods and college towns this collection of artists, intellectuals, musicians, and middle-class students dropped out of mainstream society. In dress and behavior the beats self-consciously rejected what they viewed as the excessive spiritual bankruptcy of America's middle-class culture. Cool urban hipsters—especially African American jazz musicians such as John Coltrane and Sonny Rollins—were their models. They read poetry, listened to jazz, explored Asian philosophy, and experimented openly with drugs, mystical religions, and sex.

The beats viewed themselves as being driven to the margins of society, rejecting the culture of abundance, materialism, and conformity. In his 1955 poem *Howl,* Allen Ginsberg protested that the best minds of his generation were being driven by the pressures of conformity and capitalism into drugs, sex, and disillusionment. Jack Kerouac tapped the frenzied energy beneath the beats' cool facade in *On the Road* (1957), a novel based on his travels across the country with his friend Neal Cassady. Kerouac finished the novel in one frenetic three-week binge, spilling out tales of pot, jazz, crazy sex, and all-night raps undertaken in a search for "IT"—the ultimate moment when mind and experience mesh.

 REVIEW

Why did social critics worry about "conformity" in the 1950s, and what aspects of American life upset that conformity?

Consensus versus Conflict in the Suburban Era

ELEMENTS OF CONSENSUS

Suburban life: Uniform styles in suburban housing tracts

Creation of a broad middle class

Television as a homogeneous medium of middle-class taste

Civil religion and the emphasis on religiosity

Growth of a new corporate culture and the rise of the "organization man"

The feminine ideal of domesticity

Eisenhower's "modern Republicanism"

Widely accepted anticommunism and support for free-enterprise democracy

ELEMENTS OF CONFLICT

Discrimination against Jews and minorities in new suburbs

Undermining of American cities in favor of suburbs

Opposition to destruction of countryside by suburban development

Intellectual attacks on conformity, midcult, organizational behavior, and materialism

Controversy over the Kinsey Reports and the sexual revolution

New teen culture built around comic books, movies, and rock and roll

Religious issues during the 1960 election

Eisenhower's warning about the dangers of the "military-industrial complex"

Debate over the policies of "mutual assured destruction" and nuclear arms race

(*top left*) ©Bettmann/Getty Images; (*bottom center*) ©The Advertising Archives/Alamy

NATIONALISM IN AN AGE OF SUPERPOWERS

TRY AS THEY MIGHT, THE beats, like other Americans, could not ignore the atomic menace that overshadowed the world. Along the Iron Curtain of Eastern Europe and across the battle lines of northern Asia, Soviet-American rivalry had settled into a stalemate. The American public shared with most foreign policy makers a view of the globe as divided between the "free world" nations and the "Communist bloc." Thus the Eisenhower administration continued even more aggressively Truman's policy of containing the Soviets: setting up security and trade agreements, employing covert action to install governments favorable to the United States, and using the threat of nuclear war, if need be.

To the Brink?

JOHN FOSTER DULLES As a general who had fought in a global war, Eisenhower was no stranger to world politics. Still, he shared the conduct of foreign policy with his secretary of state, John Foster Dulles. Dulles approached his job with a somber enthusiasm. Coming from a family of missionaries and diplomats, he had within him a touch of both. He viewed the Soviet-American struggle in almost religious terms: a fight of good against evil between two irreconcilable superpowers. Admirers praised his global vision; detractors saw him as "the wooliest type of pontificating American." Certainly Dulles did not lack confidence. "With my understanding of the intricate relationship between the peoples of the world," he told Eisenhower, "and your sensitiveness to the political considerations, we will make the most successful team in history."

The administration was determined to make Truman's containment strategy more forceful. Dulles, the more confrontational of the two men, wanted the United States to aid in liberating the "captive peoples" of Eastern Europe and other Communist nations. On the other hand, Eisenhower was equally determined to cut back military spending in order to keep the budget balanced. The president, who understood well how the military services and defense industries competed for government money, was irked at the "fantastic programs" the Pentagon kept proposing. "If we demand too much in taxes in order to build planes and ships," he argued, "we will tend to dry up the accumulations of capital that are necessary to provide jobs for the million or more new workers that we must absorb each year."

THE NEW LOOK IN FOREIGN POLICY So Eisenhower and Dulles hit on a less costly strategy. Rather than rely on conventional forces, they would contain Soviet aggression by using the threat of massive nuclear retaliation. Dulles insisted that Americans should not shrink from the threat of nuclear war: "If you are scared to go to the brink, you are lost." As Treasury Secretary George Humphrey put it, a nuclear strategy provided "a bigger bang for the buck." Henceforth American foreign policy would have an aggressive "New Look." Behind the more militant rhetoric, however, lay an ongoing commitment to containment.

Brinkmanship in Asia

TAIWAN AND MAINLAND CHINA Moving from talk of **brinkmanship** to concrete action did not prove easy. When Dulles announced American intentions to "unleash" Chiang Kai-shek to attack mainland China from his outpost on Taiwan (formerly Formosa), China threatened to invade Taiwan. At that, Eisenhower ordered the Seventh Fleet into the area to protect rather than unleash Chiang. If the Communists attacked, he warned bluntly in 1955, "we'll have to use atomic weapons."

Nuclear weapons also figured in the American response to a crisis in Southeast Asia. There, Vietnamese forces led by Ho Chi Minh were fighting the French, who had returned to reestablish their own colonial rule. Between 1950 and 1954, the United States provided France with more than $1 billion in military aid in Vietnam. Eisenhower worried that if Vietnam fell to a communist revolutionary like Ho, other nations of Southeast Asia would soon follow. "You have a row of dominoes set up," the president warned, "you knock over the first one. . . . You could have the beginning of a disintegration that would have the most profound influences."

VIETNAMESE VICTORY AT DIEN BIEN PHU The French in 1954 tried to force a showdown with Ho's forces at Dien Bien Phu. With Vietnamese and Chinese communist troops holding the surrounding hilltops, the French garrison of 12,000 could not have chosen a worse place to do battle. A desperate French government pleaded for more American aid and the Joint Chiefs of Staff responded by volunteering to relieve the besieged French forces with a massive American air raid—including the use of tactical nuclear weapons, if necessary. Instead, Eisenhower pulled back. After Korea, the idea of American involvement in another Asian war aroused opposition from both allies and domestic political leaders.

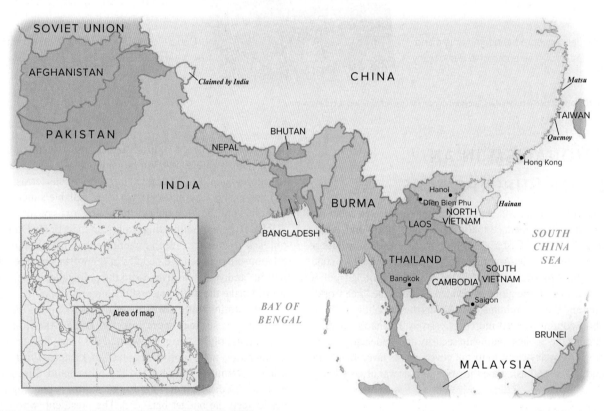

ASIAN TROUBLE SPOTS IN COLD WAR ERA

After the Geneva Accords divided Indochina into North and South Vietnam, Secretary of State Dulles organized the Southeast Asia Treaty Organization (SEATO) to resist communist aggression in Southeast Asia. Curiously, Thailand and the Philippines were the only Southeast Asian countries to join, while such trouble spots as Indonesia and Laos did not. In addition to the conflict in Vietnam, tensions were fueled by the mutual hostility between mainland Communist China and Chiang Kai-shek's Taiwan as well as the offshore islands of Quemoy and Matsu. **Why would Thailand be such a critical American ally in the region?**

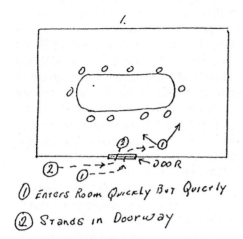

Conference Room Technique

1.

4.

① Enters Room Quickly But Quietly

② Stands in Doorway

① Finishes Burst. Commands "Shift". Props Back Thru Door. Replaces Magazine. Covers Corridor.

② On Command, "Shift" Re-enters room. Covers group. Kills Survivors with Two-Round Bursts. Leaves Propaganda.

I The CIA secretly helped overthrow the Guatemalan government in 1954. One plan, apparently never carried out, called for the assassination of 58 Guatemalan officials. But the CIA's chilling "Conference Room Technique" survived, a four-step plan showing how "a room containing as many as a dozen subjects can be 'purified' in about 20 seconds" by two assassins. Step 4 was to "leave propaganda," making it seem as if Communists had carried out the massacre.

Source: Central Intelligence Agency

UNITED STATES BACKS DIEM Collapsing under the siege, the French garrison at Dien Bien Phu surrendered in May 1954. At a peace conference held in Geneva, Switzerland, Ho Chi Minh agreed to withdraw his forces north of the 17th parallel, temporarily dividing the nation into North and South Vietnam. Because of Ho's widespread popularity, he could count on an easy victory in the elections that the peace conference agreed would be held within two years. Dulles, however, viewed any communist victory as unacceptable, even if the election was democratic. He convinced Eisenhower to support a South Vietnamese government under Ngo Dinh Diem. Diem, Dulles insisted, was not bound by the agreement signed in Geneva to hold any election. The United States took what proved to be a tragic step when it sent a military mission to help keep Diem in power.

The Covert Side of the New Look

OVERTHROWING MOSSADEQ In pursuing their aggressive New Look in foreign policy, Dulles and Eisenhower sometimes authorized the Central Intelligence Agency (CIA) to use **covert operations** against those they saw as sympathetic to Moscow. For example, in Iran in 1951 a nationalist government under Mohammed Mossadeq seized the giant British-owned Anglo-Iranian Oil Company. With the United States boycotting Iranian oil, Dulles worried that Mossadeq would turn to the neighboring Soviet Union for aid. Eisenhower approved a secret CIA

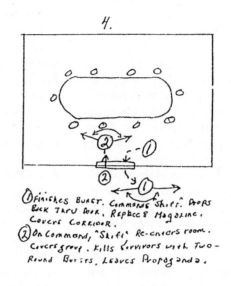

©Bettmann/Getty Images

I Nikita Khrushchev was by turns bombastic and somber, threatening and conciliatory—a style that both captivated and alarmed Americans.

operation to topple the Mossadeq government. Led by Teddy Roosevelt's grandson, Kermit, Operation Ajax ousted Mossadeq and returned Iran's monarch, Shah Mohammad Reza Pahlavi, to his throne in August 1953.

INTERVENTION IN GUATEMALA Dulles looked to use another clandestine mission in Guatemala. Unlike Iran, however, Guatemala had an elected democratic government under Colonel Jacobo Arbenz Guzmán. Arbenz was determined to reduce the poverty in his country by giving the peasants the idle farmland of large landowners. Guatemala's richest landowner was the Boston-based United Fruit Company. When Arbenz seized 400,000 acres from United Fruit, the company's agents branded him a communist. Arbenz was no communist, but as the American ambassador later explained "the man thought like a communist and talked like a communist, and if not actually one, would do until one came along." A week after a CIA-trained band of Latin American mercenaries entered the country, supported by American warplanes, the leader of the Guatemalan rebels replaced the Arbenz democracy with a military dictatorship that quickly returned the expropriated lands to United Fruit.

Success in Iran and Guatemala convinced American policy makers that covert operations could achieve dramatic results at low cost. But in overthrowing popular governments or defending unpopular ones, the United States gained a reputation in many Third World countries as a foe of national liberation, popular democracy, and social reform. In 1958 the depth of anti-American feeling became obvious when angry crowds in several Latin American countries attacked Vice President Richard Nixon's car, spat at him, and pelted him with eggs and stones.

Rising Nationalism

Korea, Indochina, Iran, Guatemala—to Dulles and Eisenhower, the crises in all these countries could be traced back to the Soviet Union. Yet American policy could not be simply anticommunist. As nationalists in the Middle East, Africa, and Southeast Asia fought to gain independence from their colonial masters, new nations like India proclaimed themselves "nonaligned," independent of the Soviet Union and the United States. As the two superpowers competed for the allegiance of emerging nations, the United States sought to counter the moves of the dynamic Soviet leader who had replaced Joseph Stalin.

NIKITA KHRUSHCHEV Stalin died in March 1953 after becoming increasingly isolated, vengeful, and perhaps simply mad. Nikita Khrushchev, a party stalwart with a formidable intellect and peasant origins in the farm country of the Ukraine, soon gained power. In some ways Khrushchev resembled another farm-belt politician, Harry Truman. Both were unsophisticated yet shrewd, earthy in their senses of humor, energetic, short-tempered, and largely inexperienced in international affairs. Khrushchev kept American diplomats off balance: at times genial and conciliatory, he would suddenly become demanding and boastful.

At home Khrushchev established a more moderate regime, gradually shifting the economy toward production of consumer goods. Internationally, he sought to ease tensions and reduce forces in Europe, hoping to make Western Europeans less dependent on the United States. Yet the growing tide of nationalism made it difficult for either superpower to pursue more-conciliatory policies.

When Khrushchev began to ease Stalin's iron ways, nationalists in Soviet-controlled Eastern Europe pushed for greater independence. Riots erupted in Poland, while in Hungary students took to the streets. When the rioting spread, Moscow accepted the new Hungarian government and began to remove Soviet tanks. But Hungary's decision to withdraw from the Warsaw Pact proved too threatening. In October 1956 Soviet tanks rolled back into Budapest to crush the uprising. The U.S. State Department issued formal protests but did nothing to help liberate the "captive nations." For all Dulles's tough talk, the New Look foreign policy recognized that the Soviets possessed a sphere of influence in which the United States would not intervene.

Eastern Europe was not the only nationalist crisis Eisenhower faced in 1956. In Egypt, the nationalist colonel Gamal Abdel Nasser was attempting to modernize his country. Dulles hoped to win Nasser's friendship by offering American aid to build the Aswan Dam, a massive power project on the Nile River. But when Nasser formed an Arab alliance against the young state of Israel and continued to pursue economic ties with the Warsaw bloc, Dulles decided to teach the Egyptian leader a lesson: he withdrew the American pledge on Aswan. Nasser angrily upped the ante by seizing the Suez Canal, through which tankers carried most of Europe's oil.

Events moved quickly. Israel, alarmed at Nasser's Arab alliance, invaded Egypt's Sinai peninsula on October 29—the same day Hungary announced it was leaving the Warsaw Pact. Three days later French and British forces seized the canal in an attempt to restore their own interests and prestige. Eisenhower saw it as colonialism reborn and joined the Soviet Union in supporting a UN resolution condemning Britain, France, and Israel. The two superpowers demanded an immediate cease-fire. By December, American pressures forced Britain and France to remove their forces.

Nationalist forces were also in ferment in Latin American countries, where only 2 percent of the people controlled 75 percent of the land. Repressive dictatorships exercised power, and foreign interests—especially American—dominated Latin American economies. Given the unequal distribution of wealth and a rapidly growing population, social tensions were rising. Cuba, only 90 miles south of American shores, was typical.

CASTRO'S REVOLUTION IN CUBA Americans owned many Cuban economic resources, including 80 percent of its utilities, and operated a naval base at Guantánamo Bay. Cuban dictator Fulgencio Batista had close ties both to the American government and to major crime figures who operated gambling, prostitution, and drug rings in Havana. A disgruntled middle-class lawyer, Fidel Castro, gained the support of impoverished peasants in Cuba's mountains and in January 1959 drove Batista from power.

At first many Americans applauded the revolution and welcomed Castro when he visited the United States. But President Eisenhower was distinctly cool to the cigar-smoking Cuban. By summer Castro had filled key positions with communists, launched a sweeping agricultural reform, and confiscated American properties. In retaliation Eisenhower placed an embargo on Cuban sugar and mobilized opposition to Castro in other Latin American countries. Cut off from American markets and aid, Castro turned to the Soviet Union.

The Shock of *Sputnik*

Castro's turn to the Soviets seemed all the more dangerous because the Soviet Union in 1957 stunned America by launching the first space satellite, dubbed *Sputnik*. By 1959 the Soviets had crash-landed a much larger payload on the moon. If the Russians could target the moon, surely they could launch nuclear missiles against America. In contrast, the American space program suffered so many delays and mishaps that rockets exploding on launch were nicknamed "flopniks" and "kaputniks."

A MISSILE GAP? How had the Soviets managed to catch up with American technology so quickly? Some analysts blamed U.S. schools, especially weak programs in science

THE KITCHEN DEBATE

On July 24, 1959, Vice President Richard Nixon and Soviet Premier Nikita Khrushchev met at an exhibition in Moscow, show-casing American technology and culture. For Nixon the consumer goods on display offered proof of the superiority of the American free-enterprise system. Khrushchev argued forcefully, though defensively, that the Soviet Union could provide equally well for its housewives. While the event appeared to be spontaneous, Nixon had been looking for an opportunity to stand up to the pugnacious Russian leader. In this primary newspaper account, the dueling is within a single document.

DOCUMENT 1
Khrushchev-Nixon Debate

Nixon: "There are some instances where you may be ahead of us, for example in the development of the thrust of your rockets for the investigation of outer space; there may be some instances in which we are ahead of you—in color television, for instance."

Khrushchev: "No, we are up with you on this, too. We have bested you in one technique and also in the other."

Nixon: "You see, you never concede anything."

Khrushchev: "I do not give up."

Nixon: "Wait till you see the picture. Let's have far more communication and exchange in this very area that we speak of. We should hear you more on our televisions. You should hear us more on yours."

Khrushchev: "That's a good idea. Let's do it like this. You appear before our people. We will appear before your people. People will see and appreciate this."

Nixon: "There is not a day in the United States when we cannot read what you say. When Kozlov was speaking in California about peace, you were talking here in somewhat different terms. This was reported extensively in the American press. Never make a statement here if you don't want it to be read in the United States. I can promise you every word you say will be translated into English."

Khrushchev: "I doubt it. I want you to give your word that this speech of mine will be heard by the American people."

Nixon: [shaking hands on it] "By the same token, everything I say will be translated and heard all over the Soviet Union?"

Khrushchev: "That's agreed."

Nixon: "You must not be afraid of ideas."

Khrushchev: "We are telling you not to be afraid of ideas. We have no reason to be afraid. We have already broken free from such a situation."

Nixon: "Well, then, let's have more exchange of them. We are all agreed on that. All right? All right?". . .

Khrushchev: [after Nixon called attention to a built-in panel-controlled washing machine]: "We have such things."

Nixon: "This is the newest model. This is the kind which is built in thousands of units for direct installation in the houses." He added that Americans were interested in making life easier for their women.

Mr. Khrushchev remarked that in the Soviet Union, they did not have "the capitalist attitude toward women."

Nixon: "I think that this attitude toward women is universal. What we want to do is make easier the life of our housewives." He explained that the house could be built for $14,000 and that most veterans had bought houses for between $10,000 and $15,000. . . .

"Let me give you an example you can appreciate. Our steelworkers, as you know, are on strike. But any steelworker could buy this house. They earn $3 an hour. This house costs about $100 a month to buy on a contract running 25 to 30 years."

Khrushchev: "We have steel workers and we have peasants who also can afford to spend $14,000 for a house." He said American houses were built to last only 20 years, so builders could sell new houses at the end of that period. "We build firmly. We build for our children and grandchildren."

Mr. Nixon said he thought American houses would last more than 20 years, but even so, after 20 years many Americans want a new home or a new kitchen, which would be obsolete then. The American system is designed to take advantage of new inventions and new techniques, he said.

Khrushchev: "This theory does not hold water." He said some things never got out of date—furniture and furnishings, perhaps, but not houses. He said he did not think houses. He said he did not think that what Americans had written about their houses was all strictly accurate.

Nixon: [pointing to television screen] "We can see here what is happening in other parts of the home."

Khrushchev: "This is probably always out of order."

Nixon: "Da [yes]."

Khrushchev: "Don't you have a machine that puts food into the mouth and pushes it down? Many things you've shown us are interesting, but they are not needed in life. They have no useful purpose. They are merely gadgets. We have a saying, if you have bedbugs you have to catch one and pour boiling water into the ear."

Nixon: "We have another saying. This is that the way to kill a fly is to make it drink whisky. But we have a better use for whisky. [Aside] I like to have this battle of wits with the Chairman. He knows his business."

Source: "The Kitchen Debate," Vice President Richard Nixon and Soviet Premier Nikita Khrushchev, July 24, 1959, Moscow, Soviet Union.

THINKING CRITICALLY

How does Khrushchev counter Nixon's explanation of "planned obsolescence"? What is Khrushchev's attitude about high-tech American consumer goods? Why was Nixon so insistent that his ideas be broadcast in the Soviet Union? In what way could women be offended by the two leaders' comments?

©Dmitri Kessel/The LIFE Picture Collection/Getty Images

| *Even before the launch of Sputnik in 1957, Americans had begun devising fallout shelters for protection from the effects of a nuclear attack. What messages about nuclear war does this photo send?*

and math. In 1958 Eisenhower joined with Congress to enact a National Defense Education Act, designed to strengthen graduate education and the teaching of science, math, and foreign languages. At the same time, the administration encouraged a crash program to build basement fallout shelters as protection in case of a nuclear attack. Democrats charged that the United States now faced an unacceptable "missile gap" (an accusation that was not borne out).

Thaws and Freezes

Throughout this series of crises, each superpower found it difficult to interpret the other's motives. The Russians exploited nationalist revolutions where they could—less successfully in Egypt, more so in Cuba. "We will bury you," Khrushchev admonished Americans, though it was unclear whether he meant through peaceful competition or military confrontation.

Rather than adopt a more belligerent course, Eisenhower determined to use the final 18 months of his presidency to improve Soviet-American relations. The shift in policy was made easier after Dulles died and the president learned from American intelligence (but could not admit publicly) that the missile gap was not real. Eisenhower chose to invite Khrushchev to visit the United States in September 1959. The Soviet premier undertook a picturesque tour across America, swapping comments about manure with Iowa farmers, reacting puritanically to movie cancan dancers, and grousing when his visit to the new capitalist marvel, Disneyland, was canceled for security reasons.

THE U-2 INCIDENT Eisenhower's plans for a return visit to the Soviet Union were abruptly canceled in 1960 after the Russians shot down a high-altitude U-2 American spy plane over Soviet territory. At first Eisenhower claimed that the plane had strayed off course while doing weather research, but Khrushchev sprang his trap: the CIA pilot, Gary Powers, had been captured alive. The president then admitted that for reasons of national security he had personally authorized the U-2 overflights.

That episode ended Eisenhower's hopes that his personal diplomacy might thaw cold war tensions. Yet a less mature president might have led the United States into more severe conflict or even war. Eisenhower was not readily impressed by the promises of new weapons systems or overheated talk about a missile gap between the United States and the Soviet Union. He left office with a warning that too much military spending would lead to "an unwarranted influence, whether sought or unsought" by the **military-industrial complex** at the expense of democratic institutions.

 REVIEW

How did Eisenhower's aggressive policy of the "New Look" play out in Asia, Iran, and Guatemala?

THE COLD WAR ON A NEW FRONTIER

THE 1960 ELECTION PROMISED TO bring the winds of change to Washington. The opponents—Vice President Richard Nixon and Senator John F. Kennedy of Massachusetts—were the first major presidential candidates born in the twentieth century. At the age of 43 Kennedy would be the youngest person ever elected to the presidency, and Nixon was only four years older. The nation needed to find new challenges and "new frontiers," Kennedy proclaimed. His rhetoric was noble, but the direction in which he would take the nation was far from clear.

The Election of 1960

THE CATHOLIC ISSUE Jack Kennedy's biggest hurdle to election was social as much as political. He was a Roman Catholic out of Irish Boston, and no Catholic had ever been elected president. Conservative Protestants, many concentrated in the heavily Democratic South, were convinced that a Catholic president would never be "free to exercise his own judgment" if the pope ordered otherwise. Kennedy chose to confront the issue head-on. In September he entered the lions' den, addressing an association of hostile Protestant ministers in Houston. The speech was the best of his campaign. "I believe in an America where the separation of church and state is absolute," he said, "—where no Catholic prelate would tell the President (should he be Catholic) how to act, and no Protestant minister would tell his parishioners how to vote." House Speaker Sam Rayburn, an old Texas pol, was astonished by Kennedy's bravura performance. "My God! . . . He's eating them blood raw."

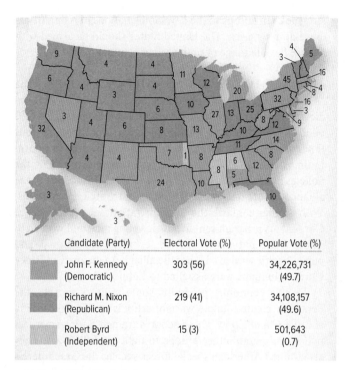

Candidate (Party)	Electoral Vote (%)	Popular Vote (%)
John F. Kennedy (Democratic)	303 (56)	34,226,731 (49.7)
Richard M. Nixon (Republican)	219 (41)	34,108,157 (49.6)
Robert Byrd (Independent)	15 (3)	501,643 (0.7)

ELECTION OF 1960

TELEVISED PRESIDENTIAL DEBATES Both candidates stressed cold war themes. Kennedy lamented the apparent "missile gap" and attacked Eisenhower and Nixon for not better managing tensions between Communist China and the nationalists on Formosa (Taiwan). Vice President Richard Nixon ran on his record as an experienced leader and staunch anticommunist, but his campaign faltered in October as unemployment rose. Nixon agreed to a series of debates with Kennedy—the first to be televised nationally. Image proved more telling than issues. According to one poll, radio listeners believed Nixon won the debate; but television viewers saw a fatigued candidate with "five o'clock shadow," because Nixon had refused to use television makeup. A relaxed Kennedy convinced many viewers that he could handle the job.

In the end religion, ethnicity, and race played decisive roles in Kennedy's triumph. One voter was asked if he voted for Kennedy because he was a Catholic. "No, because *I* am," he answered; and in key states Catholic support made a difference. "Hyphenated" Americans—Hispanic, Jewish, Irish, Italian, Polish, and German—voted Democratic in record numbers, while much of the black vote that had gone to Eisenhower in 1956 returned to the Democratic fold. Indeed, when civil rights leader Dr. Martin Luther King Jr. was imprisoned during a protest in Georgia, Kennedy attracted the support of black Americans by telephoning his sympathy to Dr. King's wife. Interest in the election ran so high that 64 percent of voters turned out, the largest percentage in 50 years. Out of 68.8 million ballots cast, Kennedy won by a margin of just 119,000.

The Hard-Nosed Idealists of Camelot

Many observers compared the Kennedy White House to Camelot, King Arthur's magical court. With youthful vigor, Kennedy brought into his administration bright, energetic advisors. He and his stylish wife, Jacqueline, invited artists, musicians, and intellectuals to the White House. Impromptu touch football games on the White House lawn displayed a rough-and-tumble playfulness, akin to Arthur's jousting tournaments of old.

In truth, Kennedy was not a liberal by temperament. Handsome and intelligent, he possessed an ironic, self-deprecating humor. In Congress he had led an undistinguished career, supported Senator Joe McCarthy, and earned a reputation as a playboy. Once Kennedy set his sights on the White House, however, he revealed a facility for political maneuvering and organization.

(*left*) ©Photofest, Inc.; (*center*) ©Bettmann/Getty Images; (*right*) ©Photofest, Inc.

| *The urbane and energetic John F. Kennedy* (center) *was associated with both King Arthur (left, played by Richard Burton in the 1960 musical) and the spy James Bond (played by Sean Connery, right). Kennedy and his advisors prided themselves on their pragmatic, hard-nosed idealism. But whereas Bond used advanced technology and covert operations to save the world, in real life such approaches had their downside, as the growing civil war in Vietnam would demonstrate.*

ROBERT MCNAMARA Robert Strange McNamara typified the pragmatic, liberal bent of the new Kennedy team. Steely and brilliant, McNamara was one of the postwar breed of young executives known as the "whiz kids." As a Harvard Business School professor and later as president of Ford Motor Company, he specialized in using quantitative tools to streamline business. As the new secretary of defense, McNamara intended to find more flexible and efficient ways of conducting the cold war.

Kennedy liked men such as McNamara—witty, bright, ambitious—because they seemed comfortable with power and not afraid to use it. The president's leisure reading reflected a similar adventurous taste: the popular James Bond spy novels. Agent 007, with his license to kill, was sophisticated, a cool womanizer (as Kennedy himself continued to be), and ready to use the latest technology to dispatch communist villains. Ironically, Bond demonstrated that there could be plenty of glamour in being hard-nosed and pragmatic. That illicit pleasure was the underside, perhaps, of Camelot's high ideals.

The (Somewhat) New Frontier at Home

Despite bold campaign promises, the president's domestic legislative achievements were modest. Once in the White House, Kennedy found himself hemmed in by a Democratic Congress dominated by conservatives. He convinced Congress to raise the minimum hourly wage to $1.25. But on key issues, including aid to education and medical insurance, Kennedy made no headway.

Always pragmatic, Kennedy hoped to work with, not against, the leaders of big business to promote growth for the whole nation. But he did believe that the government should be able to limit wages and prices for large corporations and unions; if not, an inflationary spiral might result. Wage increases would be followed by price increases followed by even higher wage demands.

SHOWDOWN WITH BIG STEEL To prevent inflation, the Council of Economic Advisers proposed to stabilize prices by tying wage increases to improved productivity. In April 1962 the United Steelworkers, like most other major unions, agreed to a contract that followed those guidelines. The large steel corporations, however, broke their part of the informal bargain by raising steel prices substantially. Incensed, Kennedy called for investigations into price fixing, mounted antitrust proceedings, and shifted Pentagon purchases to smaller steel companies that had not raised prices. The pressure caused the big companies to drop the price hikes but soured relations between Kennedy and the business community.

Kennedy's Cold War

During the 1960 race for the White House, Kennedy had pledged to fight the cold war with new vigor. Once elected, the new president was determined not to be seen as soft on communism, as Republicans so often charged the Democrats. The cold war contest, Kennedy argued, had shifted from the struggle over Europe to the developing nations in Asia, Africa, and Latin America. The United States should be armed with a more flexible range of military and economic options.

ALLIANCE FOR PROGRESS AND PEACE CORPS The "Alliance for Progress," announced in the spring of 1961, indicated the course Kennedy would follow. He promised $20 billion in foreign aid to Latin America over 10 years—four times what Truman and Eisenhower had provided. In return, Latin American nations would agree to reform unfair tax policies and begin agricultural land reforms. If successful, the alliance would discourage future Castro-style revolutions. With similar fanfare, the administration set up the Peace Corps. This program sent idealistic young men and women to Third World nations to provide technical, educational, and public health services. Under the alliance, a majority of Peace Corps volunteers were assigned to Latin America.

To give economic programs some military muscle, the Pentagon created jungle warfare schools in North Carolina and the Canal Zone. These schools trained Latin American police and paramilitary groups to fight guerrilla wars. They also trained American special forces such as the Green Berets in the arts of jungle warfare. If the Soviets or their allies promoted "wars of liberation," United States commandos would be ready to fight back.

SPACE PROGRAM Kennedy believed, too, that the Soviets had made space the final frontier of the cold war. Only a few months after the president's inauguration, a Russian cosmonaut orbited the world for the first time. In response, Kennedy challenged Congress to authorize a manned space mission to the moon that would land by the end of the decade. In February 1962 John Glenn circled the earth three times in a "fireball of a ride." The race to the moon was on.

Cold War Frustrations

In down-to-earth ways, high ideals did not translate easily into practical results. In the first five years of the alliance, nine Latin American governments were overthrown by military coups. The Peace Corps, for its part, proved a tremendous public relations success and helped thousands of Third World farmers on a people-to-people basis. But individual Peace Corps workers could do little to change corrupt policies on a national level, and more than a few worked for the CIA.

BAY OF PIGS INVASION Nor did Kennedy succeed in countering revolutionary "wars of liberation." His prime target was Fidel Castro's communist regime in Cuba. After breaking diplomatic relations in 1960, the Eisenhower administration had secretly authorized the CIA to organize an invasion of that nation. The CIA assured Kennedy that its 1,400-member army of Cuban exiles could inspire discontented Cubans to overthrow Castro. Eager to establish his own cold war credentials, the president approved an attack. But the invasion in April 1961 turned into a disaster. The poorly equipped rebel forces landed at the swampy Bay of

>> MAPPING THE PAST <<

THE WORLD OF THE SUPERPOWERS

Source: Library of Congress Prints and Photographs Division (HAER ND-9-F-10)

"The Soviet Union . . . seeks to impose its absolute authority over the rest of the world. Conflict has, therefore, become endemic and is waged, on the part of the Soviet Union, by violent or non-violent methods in accordance with the dictates of expediency. With the development of increasingly terrifying weapons of mass destruction, every individual faces the ever-present possibility of annihilation should the conflict enter the phase of total war."—NSC 68, National Security Council policy paper

CONTEXT

By the 1960s the Soviet Union and the United States were engaged in an arms race that presented the world with the threat of nuclear destruction. The two powers adopted a policy popularly known as MAD—mutually assured destruction. Each side maintained enough nuclear weapons to discourage the other from launching an attack without fear of receiving a counterattack equal in kind. Movie director Stanley Kubrick captured this situation in his 1964 film *Dr. Strangelove or: How I Learned to Stop Worrying and Love the Bomb*. The movie ends when an American B-52 bomber drops a nuclear weapon that triggers the Soviet's world-ending "Doomsday Machine."

MAP READING

1. Where are most military bases located?
2. Which European countries and which major South Asian country have no bases?
3. Where have a great many of the cold war conflicts been concentrated?
4. Where is the farthest north U.S. base?

MAP INTERPRETATION

1. What advantages does this polar projection—viewing the globe from above the North Pole—provide in understanding the cold war conflict?
2. If the Soviet Union and Communist China were allies, what explains the large number of Soviet bases along the borders of China?
3. The United States created a "triad" (land-based missiles, submarine-based missiles, and strategic bombers) to guarantee surviving a Russian first strike. How does the "triad" strategy affect the distribution of U.S. bases shown on the map?
4. In what ways does the map suggest strategic and tactical advantages each side possesses?

Pigs with no protective cover for miles. Within two days Castro's army had rounded them up. Taking responsibility for the fiasco, Kennedy suffered a bitter humiliation whose sting goaded the administration to undertake further covert operations. The CIA secretly hatched plans to destabilize the Cuban government or even murder Castro.

KENNEDY AND VIETNAM   Kennedy's advisors took a similar covert approach in South Vietnam. There, a civil war with religious overtones was under way. The unpopular dictator Ngo Dinh Diem remained in power. South Vietnamese communists, known as the Vietcong, waged a guerrilla war against Diem with support from North Vietnam. Buddhist elements also backed the rebellion against Diem, who was a Catholic. In May 1961, a month after the Bay of Pigs invasion, Kennedy secretly ordered 500 Green Berets and military advisors to Vietnam to help Diem. By 1963 the number of "military advisors" had risen to more than 16,000. Increasingly, they were being drawn into combat with the Vietcong.

DIEM FALLS   Diem's corruption, police state tactics, and ruthless campaign against his Buddhist opposition isolated the regime. As the Kennedy administration lost faith in Diem, it tacitly encouraged a military coup by South Vietnamese military officers. To the surprise of American officials, the coup plotters not only captured Diem but shot him in November 1963. Despite Kennedy's policy of pragmatic idealism, the United States found itself mired in a Vietnamese civil war, which it had no clear strategy for winning.

Confronting Khrushchev

Vietnam and Cuba were just two areas in the Third World where Kennedy sought to battle communist forces. But the conflict between the United States and the Soviet Union soon overshadowed developments in Asia, Africa, and Latin America.

THE BERLIN WALL   June 1961 was the president's first chance to take the measure of Nikita Khrushchev, at a summit meeting held in Vienna. For two long days, Khrushchev was brash and belligerent. East and West Germany must be reunited, he demanded. In the divided capital of Berlin, located deep within East Germany (see map in Chapter 27), citizens from all across East Germany were crossing from the eastern sector of Berlin into the free western zone as a way of escaping communist rule. This "problem" must be settled within six months, Khrushchev insisted. Kennedy tried to stand up to Khrushchev's bullying, but he left Vienna worried that the Soviet leader perceived him as weak and inexperienced. By August events in Berlin confirmed his fears. Under cover of night, the Soviets threw up a wall sealing off any entry into West Berlin. Despite American protests, the heavily guarded Berlin Wall stayed up.

A FLEXIBLE NUCLEAR RESPONSE   Tensions with the Soviet Union led the administration to rethink American nuclear strategy. Under the Dulles doctrine of massive retaliation, almost any incident threatened to trigger a launch of the full arsenal of nuclear missiles. Kennedy and McNamara sought to replace the policy of **mutually assured destruction (MAD)** with a "flexible response doctrine." By limiting the level of a first nuclear strike, they would leave room for negotiation. In that case, however, conventional forces in Europe would have to be built up so that they could better deter aggression. McNamara proposed equipping them with smaller tactical nuclear weapons.

But what if the Soviets launched a first-strike attack to knock out American missiles? McNamara's flexible response policy required that enough missiles survive so that the Americans could retaliate. If the Soviets knew the United States could survive a first strike, they would then be less likely to launch a surprise attack. So McNamara began a program to place missile sites underground and to develop submarine-launched missiles. The new flexible response policies resulted in a 15 percent increase in the 1961 military budget, compared with only 2 percent increases during the last two years of Eisenhower's term. Under Kennedy, the military-industrial complex thrived.

The Missiles of October

The peril of nuclear confrontation became dramatically clear in the Cuban missile crisis of October 1962. President Kennedy had emphasized repeatedly that the United States would treat any attempt to place offensive weapons in Cuba as an unacceptable threat. Khrushchev promised that the Soviet Union had no such intention but bristled privately at what he perceived as a gross inequality in the cold war. "The Americans had surrounded our country with military bases and threatened us with nuclear weapons," he told high Soviet officials in May 1962. In that month he convinced them to begin building a secret nuclear base in Cuba. "Now [the Americans] would learn just what it feels like to have enemy missiles pointing at you."

Throughout the summer the buildup went undetected by Americans. But by October 14, overflights of Cuba by U-2 spy planes had revealed the offensive missile sites. Kennedy was outraged.

For a week, American security advisors met in secret strategy sessions. Hawkish advisors urged air strikes against the missile sites, and at first Kennedy agreed. "We're certainly going to . . . take out these . . . missiles," he said. But more cautious advisors pointed out that the U-2 flights had not photographed all of Cuba. What if there were more concealed bases with missiles ready to fire? The Soviets could then launch an atomic attack on the United States despite the air strikes. Furthermore, if the United States attacked Cuba with no advance warning, the act would appear to the world uncomfortably like the Japanese surprise attack on Pearl Harbor in World War II.

A NAVAL BLOCKADE   Although the Joint Chiefs of Staff continued to press for a large air attack, Kennedy finally chose the more restrained option, a naval blockade to intercept "all offensive military equipment under shipment to Cuba." On October 22, word of the confrontation began to

MISSILE ERECTOR

THEODOLITE STATION

5 TRUCKS UNDER CAMOUFLAGE NETTING

CABLE

5 TRUCKS UNDER CAMOUFLAGE NETTING

MISSILE SHELTER TENTS

| *The discovery of Soviet offensive missile sites in Cuba, revealed by low-level American reconnaissance flights, led to the first nuclear showdown of the cold war. For several tense days in October 1962, President Kennedy met with his National Security Council to debate the proper course of action.*

©Popperfoto/Getty Images

leak out. "CAPITAL CRISIS AIR HINTS AT DEVELOPMENTS ON CUBA; KENNEDY TV TALK IS LIKELY," ran the headline in the *New York Times*. Americans were stunned that evening by the president's television address.

Over the next few days, tensions mounted as a Soviet submarine approached the line of American ships. On October 25 the navy stopped an oil tanker. Several Soviet ships reversed course. In Cuba, Soviet general Issa Pliyev felt that he had to assume the worst—that despite all the talk of a blockade, an American invasion of Cuba was being prepared. Pliyev sent a coded message to Moscow that "in the opinion of the Cuban friends [that is, the Castro government] the U.S. air strike on our installations in Cuba will occur in the night between October 26 and October 27 or at dawn on October 27." Equally ominously, he added, "We have taken measures to disperse 'techniki' [the nuclear warheads] in the zone of operations." In other words, Pliyev was making his nuclear missiles operational.

The morning of October 27, alarmed Soviet technicians detected a U-2 plane flying over Cuba. Was this the beginning of the expected attack? General Pliyev had issued strict instructions not to use force without his authorization, but when the air defense command looked to consult him, he could not be found. Soviet officers went ahead and shot it down, killing its pilot.

Meanwhile, Kennedy strove to resolve the crisis through diplomatic channels. On October 26 he had received a rambling message from Khrushchev agreeing to remove the missiles in return for an American promise not to invade Cuba. The following day a second, more troubling message arrived with a new condition, that the United States must also dismantle its missile bases in Turkey, which bordered on the Soviet Union. Then word came of the downed U-2, further

heightening tension. If the Soviets launched an attack from their Cuban bases, stated policy called for U.S. retaliation. Worried that events might spiral out of control, the president put off that decision until the following morning.

Kennedy decided to ignore Khrushchev's second letter and accept the offer in the first: removal of Soviet missiles if the Americans pledged not to invade Cuba. He also gave private assurances that the missiles in Turkey would come out within half a year. In Moscow, Khrushchev agreed reluctantly to the deal, telling his advisors somberly that there were times to advance and times to retreat; and this time, "we found ourselves face to face with the danger of war and of nuclear catastrophe, with the possible result of destroying the human race." Thus the face-off ended on terms that saved either side from overt humiliation.

NUCLEAR TEST BAN TREATY The nuclear showdown prompted Kennedy and his advisors to seek ways to control the nuclear arms race. "We all inhabit this small planet," he warned in June 1963. "We all breathe the same air. We all cherish our children's future. And we are all mortal." The administration negotiated a nuclear test ban with the Soviets, prohibiting all aboveground nuclear tests. Growing concern over radioactive fallout increased public support for the treaty. A telephone hotline was also installed, providing a direct communications link between the White House and the Kremlin for use in times of crisis. At the same time, Kennedy's prestige soared for "standing up" to the Soviets.

 REVIEW

How did Kennedy confront the Soviet Union at the Bay of Pigs, in Berlin, and during the Cuban missile crisis?

Putting History in Global Context

THE CUBAN MISSILE CRISIS WAS the closest the world had come to "destroying the human race," in Khrushchev's words, and it sobered both superpowers. It did not end the cold war, however; indeed, both nations endured long, drawn-out regional wars before scaling back their ambitions—the United States in Vietnam and the Soviet Union in Afghanistan. Yet the intensity of confrontation—with Eisenhower and Dulles's brinkmanship, Khrushchev's provocations, and Kennedy's cold war rhetoric—began to ease. The nuclear anxieties of the 1950s, so much a part of the suburban era, yielded to different concerns in the 1960s.

In large part that change came about because the supposed consensus of the 1950s masked a profound *lack* of consensus concerning the state of equality in America. While the suburbs flourished, urban areas decayed. While more white Americans went to college, more African Americans found themselves out of work on southern farms or desperate for jobs in northern ghettos, and still in segregated schools. As Mexican American migrant workers picked crops in California or followed the harvest north from Texas, they saw their employers resist every attempt to unionize and improve their wages. To all these Americans, the often-proclaimed "consensus" about opportunity in American life was no longer acceptable. The 1950s sparked a movement pursued by ordinary Americans who acted, despite the reluctance of their leaders, to bring about a civil rights revolution.

Chapter Summary

At midcentury, during an era of peace and prosperity, the United States began to build a new social and political agenda.

- Automobiles and the culture of the highways helped bind Americans to one another in a "consensus" about what it meant to be an American.
  - ▸ Highways made possible rapid suburban growth.
  - ▸ Suburbs proved popular with the growing white-collar middle class.
  - ▸ Consensus in suburbs blurred class distinctions and promoted the notion of "civil religion."
  - ▸ Suburban life nurtured the ideal of the woman who found fulfillment as a homemaker and a mother, even though more women began to work outside the home.
- President Eisenhower resisted the demands of conservatives to dismantle the New Deal and of liberals to extend it, in favor of moderate, or "middle of the road," Republicanism.
- Cracks in consensus appeared among discontented intellectuals and among teenagers who, through Elvis Presley and new teen idols, discovered the power of rock and roll.
- Efforts to contain more vigorously the Soviet Union and Communist China, through a policy of "brinkmanship," proved difficult to apply because of growing Third World nationalism.

  - ▸ Eisenhower held back from using tactical nuclear weapons during crises in Vietnam and Taiwan.
  - ▸ Successful CIA operations in Iran and Guatemala encouraged American policy makers to use covert operations more frequently.
  - ▸ Postcolonial nationalism contributed to crises in Hungary, Egypt, and Cuba, where President Kennedy was embarrassed by the failure of an invasion attempt to overthrow Fidel Castro.
- Relations between the two superpowers thawed gradually but not without recurring confrontations between the United States and the Soviet Union.
  - ▸ Under Eisenhower, the Soviet success with *Sputnik* increased fears that the United States was vulnerable to missile attacks, while the U-2 spy plane incident worsened relations.
  - ▸ John F. Kennedy proved willing to use covert operations as well as diplomatic and economic initiatives such as the Peace Corps and the Alliance for Progress.
  - ▸ The construction of Soviet missile bases 90 miles from American shores triggered the Cuban missile crisis of 1962, the closest the United States and the Soviet Union ever came to nuclear war.

Digging Deeper

David Halberstam profiles suburban America engagingly in *The Fifties* (1994); using suburban Orange County, California, as her focus, Lisa McGirr, *Suburban Warriors: The Origins of the New American Right* (2001), explores how conservatives organized at the political grassroots level. An interesting source linking suburbia to a new environmental consciousness is Adam Rome, *The Bulldozer in the Countryside: Suburban Sprawl and the Rise of American Environmentalism* (2001). Karal Ann Marling, *As Seen on TV: The Visual Culture of Everyday Life in the 1950s* (1998), gives insight into the popular aesthetics of the era. Glenn C. Altschuler, *All Shook Up: How Rock and Roll Changed America* (2003), shows how rock music reshaped American culture. As a corrective response to the view of women in the 1950s popularized by Betty Friedan, *The Feminine Mystique* (1963), see the provocative essays in Joanne Meyerowitz, ed., *Not June Cleaver: Women and Gender in Postwar America, 1945-1960* (1994).

Fred I. Greenstein, *The Hidden-Hand Presidency: Eisenhower as Leader* (rev. ed., 1994), contradicted the view of Ike as a bumbling president. Just as historians have refurbished Eisenhower's image, they have also removed some of the tarnish from Kennedy. See, for example, Graham Allison and Philip Zelikow, *Essence of Decision: Explaining the Cuban Missile Crisis* (2nd ed., 1999); and Warren Bass, *Support Any Friend: Kennedy's Middle East, and the Making of the U.S.-Israel Alliance* (2003). To do some judging on your own, look at Ernest R. May and Philip D. Zelikow, eds., *The Kennedy Tapes: Inside the White House during the Cuban Missile Crisis* (1997). Two fine books on Kennedy and Vietnam are Fredrik Logevall, *Choosing War: The Lost Chance for Peace and the Escalation of War in Vietnam* (2003); and David Kaiser, *American Tragedy: Kennedy, Johnson, and the Origins of the Vietnam War* (2002).

29 Civil Rights and Uncivil Liberties

1947–1969

On August 28, 1963, more than 250,000 demonstrators joined the great civil rights march on Washington, D.C., where Martin Luther King Jr. gave his "I Have a Dream" speech.

©Paul Schutzer/The LIFE Picture Collection/Getty Images

>> An American Story

TWO ROADS TO INTEGRATION

Six-year-old Ruby knew the drill. She was to look straight ahead—not to one side or the other—and especially not at *them*. She was to keep walking. Above all, she was not to look back once she'd passed, because that would encourage them. Despite her parents' warnings, Ruby still struggled to keep her eyes straight. Her first day of school in New Orleans, federal marshals were there along with her mother and father. So were hundreds of angry white people who came near enough to yell things like "You little nigger, we'll get you and kill you." Then she was within the building's quiet halls and alone with her teacher. She was the only person in class: none of the white students had come. As the days went by during that autumn of 1960, the marshals stopped walking with her but the hecklers still waited. And once in a while Ruby couldn't help looking back, trying to see the face of one woman in particular.

©Bettmann/Getty Images

| *Ruby, being picked up by federal marshals, who escorted her to school.*

Ruby's parents were not social activists. They signed their daughter up for the white school because "we thought it was for all the colored to do, and we never thought Ruby would be alone." Her father's white employer fired him; letters and phone calls threatened the family's lives and home. Ruby seemed to take it all in stride, though her parents worried that she was not eating the way she used to. Often she left her school lunch untouched or refused anything other than packaged food such as potato chips. It was only after a time that the problem was traced to the hecklers. "They tells me I'm going to die, and that it'll be soon. And that one lady tells me every morning I'm getting poisoned soon, when she can fix it." Ruby was convinced that the woman owned the nearby variety store and would carry out her threat by poisoning the family's food.

Over the course of a year white students gradually returned to class and life settled into a new routine. By the time Ruby was 10 she had developed a remarkably clear perception of herself. "Maybe because of all the trouble going to school in the beginning I learned more about my people. Maybe I would have anyway; because when you get older you see yourself and the white kids; and you find out the difference. You try to forget it, and say there is none; and if there is you won't say what it be. Then you say it's my own people, and so I can be proud of them instead of ashamed."

If the new ways were hard for Ruby, they were not easy for white southerners either—even those who saw the need for change. One woman, for years a dedicated teacher in Atlanta, vividly recalled a traumatic summer 10 years earlier, when she went north to New York City to take courses in education. There were black students living in the dormitory, an integrated situation that was new to her. One day as she stepped from her shower, so did a black student from the nearby stall. "When I saw her I didn't know what to do," the woman recalled. "I felt sick all over, and frightened. What I remember—I'll never forget it—is that horrible feeling of being caught in a terrible trap, and not knowing what to do about it. I thought of running out of the room and screaming, or screaming at the woman to get out, or running back into the shower. . . . My sense of propriety was with me, though—miraculously—and I didn't want to hurt the woman. It wasn't *her* that was upsetting me. I knew that, even in that moment of sickness and panic." So she ducked back into the shower until the other woman left.

Summer was almost over before she felt comfortable eating with black students at the same table. And when she returned home, she told no one about her experiences. "At that time people would have thought one of two things: I was crazy (for being so upset and ashamed) or a fool who in a summer had become a dangerous 'race mixer.'" She continued to love the South and to speak up for its traditions of dignity, neighborliness, and honor, but she saw the need for change. And so in 1961 she volunteered to teach one of the first integrated high school classes in Atlanta, even though she had her doubts. By the end of two years she concluded that she had never spent a more exciting time teaching. "I've never felt so useful, so constantly useful, not just to the children but to our whole society. American as well as Southern. Those children, all of them, have given me more than I've given them." <<

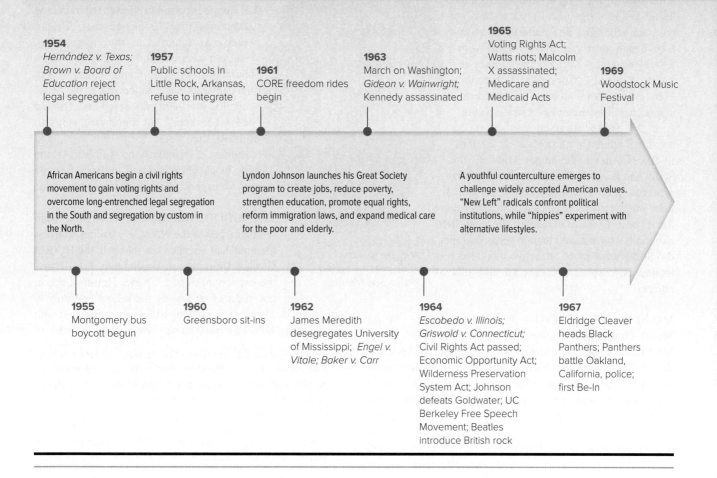

1954
Hernández v. Texas; Brown v. Board of Education reject legal segregation

1957
Public schools in Little Rock, Arkansas, refuse to integrate

1961
CORE freedom rides begin

1963
March on Washington; *Gideon v. Wainwright;* Kennedy assassinated

1965
Voting Rights Act; Watts riots; Malcolm X assassinated; Medicare and Medicaid Acts

1969
Woodstock Music Festival

African Americans begin a civil rights movement to gain voting rights and overcome long-entrenched legal segregation in the South and segregation by custom in the North.

Lyndon Johnson launches his Great Society program to create jobs, reduce poverty, strengthen education, promote equal rights, reform immigration laws, and expand medical care for the poor and elderly.

A youthful counterculture emerges to challenge widely accepted American values. "New Left" radicals confront political institutions, while "hippies" experiment with alternative lifestyles.

1955
Montgomery bus boycott begun

1960
Greensboro sit-ins

1962
James Meredith desegregates University of Mississippi; *Engel v. Vitale; Baker v. Carr*

1964
Escobedo v. Illinois; Griswold v. Connecticut; Civil Rights Act passed; Economic Opportunity Act; Wilderness Preservation System Act; Johnson defeats Goldwater; UC Berkeley Free Speech Movement; Beatles introduce British rock

1967
Eldridge Cleaver heads Black Panthers; Panthers battle Oakland, California, police; first Be-In

THE CIVIL RIGHTS MOVEMENT

FOR AMERICANS IN ALL WALKS of life, the upheavals that swept America in the 1960s were wrenching. From the schoolrooms and lunch counters of the South to the college campuses of the North, from eastern slums to western migrant-labor camps, American society was in ferment. And at the center of that ferment was a battle for civil rights.

On the face of it such agitation seemed to be a dramatic reversal of the placid 1950s. Turbulence and activism had overturned stability and consensus. Yet the events of the 1960s grew naturally out of the social conditions that preceded those years. The civil rights movement was brought about not by a group of farsighted leaders in government but by ordinary folk who sought change, often despite the reluctance or even fierce opposition of people in power. After World War II, grassroots organizations such as the NAACP for blacks and the American GI Forum for Latinos acted with a new determination to achieve the equality of opportunity promised by the American creed.

Thus the 1950s were a seedbed for the more turbulent revolutions of the 1960s. The booming postwar economy held out the possibility of better lives for minorities; yet systematic discrimination and racism, long embedded in American life by custom and law, prevented prosperity from spreading equally. Time and again, activists challenged the political system to deal with what the 1950s had done—and what had been left undone. As one friend of Martin Luther King Jr. predicted in 1958, "If the young people are aroused from their lethargy through this fight, it will affect broad circles throughout the country." And, he might have added, around the world, because a similar spirit of reform existed on a global scale.

The struggle of African Americans for equality during the postwar era is filled with ironies. By the time barriers to legal segregation in the South began to fall, millions of black families were leaving for regions where discrimination was less easily challenged. The South they left behind was in the early stages of an economic boom. The cities to which many migrated had entered a period of decline. Yet, as if to close a circle, the rise of large black voting blocs in major cities created political pressures that helped force the nation to dismantle the worst legal and institutional barriers to racial equality.

The Changing South and African Americans

After World War II the southern economy began to grow significantly faster than the national economy. The remarkable about-face began during the New Deal with federal programs such as the Tennessee Valley Authority. World War II brought even more federal dollars to build and maintain military bases and defense plants. And the South attracted new business because it offered a "clean slate." In contrast to the Northeast and upper Midwest, the South had few unions, little regulation and bureaucracy, and low wages and taxes. Finally, there was the matter of climate, which later caused the region to be nicknamed the **Sun Belt.** Especially with improvements in air-conditioning, the South grew more attractive to skilled professionals, corporate managers, and affluent retirees.

MECHANIZED COTTON FARMING Before World War II, 80 percent of African Americans lived in the South. Most raised cotton as sharecroppers and tenant farmers. But the war created a labor shortage, as millions of workers went off to fight and others labored in war industries. This shortage gave cotton growers an incentive to mechanize cotton picking. In 1950 only 5 percent of the crop was picked mechanically; by 1960 at least half was. Farmers began to consolidate land into larger holdings. Tenant farmers, sharecroppers, and hired labor of both races, no longer in short supply, left the countryside for the city.

The national level of wages also profoundly affected southern labor. When federal minimum-wage laws forced lumber or textile mills to raise their pay scales, the mills no longer expanded. In addition, steel and other industries with strong national unions and manufacturers with plants around the country set wages by national standards. Those changes brought southern wages closer to the national average by the 1960s. As the southern economy grew, what had for many years been a distinct regional economy became more diversified and more integrated into the national economy.

As wages rose and unskilled work disappeared, job opportunities for black southerners declined. Outside cotton farming, the lumber industry had provided the largest number of jobs for young black men. There, the number of black teenagers hired by lumber mills dropped 74 percent between 1950 and 1960. New high-wage jobs were reserved for white southerners, because outside industries arriving in the South made no effort to change local patterns of discrimination. So the ultimate irony arose. As per capita income rose and industrialization brought in new jobs, black laborers poured out of the region in search of work. They arrived in cities that showed scant tolerance for racial differences and little willingness or ability to hire unskilled black labor.

Source: Library of Congress, Prints and Photographs Division [LC-DIG-ppmsc-01271]

| Thurgood Marshall

The NAACP and Civil Rights

In the postwar era the NAACP decided to use the judicial system to attack Jim Crow laws. That stepped-up attack reflected the increased national political influence that African Americans achieved as they migrated in great numbers out of the South. No longer could northern politicians readily ignore the demands black leaders made for greater equality. Presidents Roosevelt and Truman had taken small but significant steps to address the worst forms of legal and economic discrimination. And across the South black churches and colleges became centers for organized resistance to segregation.

THURGOOD MARSHALL Thurgood Marshall emerged as the NAACP's leading attorney. Marshall had attended law school in the 1930s at Howard University in Washington, D.C. There, the law school's dean, Charles Houston, was in the midst of revamping the school and turning out sharp, dedicated lawyers, Marshall among them, but with a difference. "Before he came along," one observer noted,

> the principal black leaders—men like Du Bois and James Weldon Johnson and Charles Houston—didn't talk the language of the people. They were upper-class and upper-middle-class Negroes. Thurgood Marshall was *of* the people. . . . Out in Texas or Oklahoma or down the street here in Washington at the Baptist church, he would make these rousing speeches that would have 'em all jumping out of their seats. . . . "We ain't gettin' what we should," was what it came down to, and he made them see that.

During the late 1930s and early 1940s Marshall toured the South (in "a little old beat-up '29 Ford"), typing out legal briefs in the backseat, trying to get teachers to sue for equal pay, and defending blacks accused of murder in a Klan-infested county in Florida. He was friendly with whites, not shy, and black citizens who had never even considered the possibility that a member of their race might win a legal battle "would come for miles, some of them on muleback or horseback, to see 'the nigger lawyer' who stood up in white men's courtrooms."

For years NAACP lawyers had worked hard to organize local chapters, to support members of the community willing to risk their jobs, property, and lives in order to challenge segregation. But they waged a moderate, pragmatic campaign. They chose not to attack head-on the Supreme Court decision (*Plessy v. Ferguson,* 1896) that permitted "separate but equal" segregated facilities. They simply demonstrated that a black college or school might be separate, but it was hardly equal if it lacked a law school or even indoor plumbing.

The *Brown* and *Plessy* Decisions

In 1950 the NAACP determined to attack the separate but equal doctrine itself. Oliver Brown was one of the people who provided a path to the Supreme Court. Brown objected because his daughter Linda had to walk past an all-white school on her way to catch the bus to her segregated black school in Topeka, Kansas. A three-judge federal panel rejected Brown's suit because the schools in Topeka, while segregated, did meet the court's test of equality. But after two years of arguments, the NAACP convinced the Supreme Court to overturn the lower court ruling in *Brown v. Board of Education of Topeka* (1954).

OVERTURNING *PLESSY* Marshall and his colleagues succeeded in part because of a change in the Court itself. The year before, President Eisenhower had appointed Earl Warren, a liberal Republican from California, as chief justice. Warren, a forceful advocate, persuaded even the Court's segregationists that segregation as defined in *Plessy* perpetuated racial supremacy. The Court ruled unanimously that separate facilities were inherently unequal. To keep black children segregated by race, it ruled, "generates a feeling of inferiority as to their status in the community that may affect their hearts and minds in a way unlikely ever to be undone."

At the time of the *Brown* decision, 21 states and the District of Columbia operated segregated school systems. All of them had to decide, in some way, how to comply with the new ruling. The Court allowed a certain amount of leeway, handing down a second ruling in 1955 that required that desegregation be carried out "with all deliberate speed." Some border states reluctantly decided to comply, but in the Deep South, many citizens called for die-hard defiance. In 1956, 19 U.S. senators and 81 representatives issued a "Southern Manifesto," which declared their intent to use "all lawful means" to reestablish legal segregation.

Latino Civil Rights and the *Hernández* Decision

Mexican Americans also considered school desegregation as central to their campaign for civil rights. At the end of World War II, only 1 percent of children of Mexican descent in Texas graduated from high school. Both the American GI Forum and the League of United Latin American Citizens (LULAC; see Chapter 25) supported legal challenges to the system.

***DELGADO* AND SEGREGATED SCHOOLS** In a 1947 case, *Mendez et al. v. Westminster School District of Orange County,* the courts had ordered several California school districts to integrate. LULAC saw a way to apply that ruling in Texas. The superintendent in the town of Bastrop had refused a request to enroll first-grader Minerva Delgado in a nearby all-white school. Civil rights lawyer and activist Gus Garcia, an advisor to both LULAC and the GI Forum, helped bring a case on Minerva's behalf against the school district. Before *Delgado et al. v. Bastrop et al.* went to trial, a Texas judge ordered an end to segregated schools beyond the first grade (based on the assumption that the youngest Mexican American children needed special classes to learn English). *Delgado* served notice that Mexicans would no longer accept

©Carl Iwasaki/The LIFE Picture Collection/Getty Images

| *Linda Brown and her younger sister Terry Lynn. To get to her school bus stop, Linda had to dodge through a five-track switching yard—where large engines maneuvered railcars of lumber, eggs, beer, and potatoes—then cross Kansas Street, a busy thoroughfare. In freezing weather, she sometimes became so cold, she cried or turned back. Yet there was a white school located closer to her home. Linda's father, Oliver Brown, sued Topeka's Board of Education in a case that reached the Supreme Court.*

second-class citizenship. It also served as a precedent in *Brown v. Board of Education* in 1954.

Latinos faced a peculiar Jim Crow system that left them segregated in practice, but technically not by law. Throughout the Southwest the states recognized just two races: black and white. That dividing line left Mexican Americans in legal limbo. Though legally grouped with whites, they were by longstanding social custom barred from many public places, they could not serve on juries, and they faced widespread job discrimination. To remedy the situation, Mexican Americans had to establish themselves in the courts as a distinct class of people.

***HERNÁNDEZ* AND DESEGREGATION** An opportunity arose in the case of Pete Hernández, who had been convicted of murder by an all-white jury in Jackson County, Texas. Indeed, as Mexican American lawyer Gus Garcia realized, no Mexican American had served on a Jackson jury in the previous 25 years. Garcia, one of the leaders of the American GI Forum, saw in the tactics of Thurgood Marshall and the NAACP a way to use the Hernández case to extend to Mexicans the benefits of the Fourteenth Amendment's equal protection clause.

The key to the case was ingenious but direct. The state argued that because Mexicans were white, a jury without Mexicans was still a jury of peers. Yet the courthouse in which Hernández was tried had two men's rooms. One said simply, "MEN." The other, labeled with a crudely hand-lettered sign, said "COLORED MEN" and below that, in Spanish, "HOMBRES AQUI [MEN HERE]." As one of Gus Garcia's colleagues recalled, "In the jury pool, Mexicans may have been white, but when it came to nature's functions they were not." This and similar examples of discrimination persuaded the Supreme Court, in *Hernández v. Texas,* to throw out the state's argument. Latinos in south Texas, like African Americans across the South, were held to be a discrete group whose members deserved equal protection under the law. "The Fourteenth Amendment is not directed solely against discrimination due to a 'two-class theory,' that is, based on differences between 'white' and Negro," ruled Chief Justice Earl Warren. Warren's reasoning made it possible for Latinos to seek redress as a group rather than as individuals. After *Hernández,* the Mexican American community had both the legal basis and the leadership to broaden its attack against discrimination.

A New Civil Rights Strategy

ROSA PARKS   Neither the *Brown* nor the *Hernández* decision ended segregation, but they combined with political and economic forces to usher in a new era of southern race relations. In December 1955 Rosa Parks, a 43-year-old black civil rights activist, was riding the bus home in Montgomery, Alabama. When the driver ordered her to give her seat to a white man, as Alabama Jim Crow laws required, she refused. Police took her to jail and eventually fined her $14.

Determined to overturn the law, a number of women from the NAACP, friends of Parks, met secretly at midnight to draft a letter of protest.

> Another Negro woman has been arrested and thrown into jail because she refused to get up out of her seat on the bus and give it to a white person. . . . Until we do something to stop these arrests, they will continue. The next time it may be you, or you or you. This woman's case will come up Monday. We are, therefore, asking every Negro to stay off the buses on Monday in protest of the arrest and trial.

Thousands of copies of the letter circulated, and the Monday **boycott** was such a success it was extended indefinitely. Buses wheeled around the city virtually empty, losing over 30,000 fares a day. The white community, in an effort to halt the unprecedented black challenge, resorted to various forms of legal and physical intimidation. No local agent would insure cars used to carpool black workers. A bomb exploded in the house of the Reverend Martin Luther King Jr., the key boycott leader. And when that failed to provoke the violence that whites could use to justify harsh reprisals, 90 black leaders were arrested for organizing an illegal boycott. Still, the campaign continued until November 23, 1956, when the Supreme Court ruled that bus segregation was illegal.

MARTIN LUTHER KING JR.   The triumph was especially sweet for Martin Luther King Jr., whose leadership in Montgomery brought him national fame. Before becoming a minister at the Dexter Street Baptist Church, King had little personal contact with the worst forms of white racism. He had grown up in the relatively affluent middle-class black community of Atlanta, Georgia, the son of one of the city's most prominent black ministers. He attended Morehouse College, an academically respected black school in Atlanta, and Crozer Theological

Seminary in Philadelphia before entering the doctoral program in theology at Boston University. As a graduate student, King embraced the pacifism and nonviolence of the Indian leader Mohandas Gandhi and the activism of Christian reformers of the Progressive Era. King heeded the call to Dexter Street in 1954 with the idea of becoming a theologian after he served his active ministry and finished his dissertation.

NONVIOLENCE AS A STRATEGY As boycott leader, King had the responsibility to rally black support without triggering violence. Because local officials were all too eager for any excuse to use force, King's nonviolent approach was the ideal strategy. King offered his audience two visions. First, he reminded them of the many injustices they had been forced to endure. The boycott, he asserted, was a good way to seek redress. Then he counseled his followers to avoid the actions of their oppressors. There would be no cross burnings, he insisted; no mobs dragging white people from their homes to be murdered. Instead, King laid out the Christian and republican ideals that would become key themes of his civil rights crusade. Protests must be grounded in dignity, love, and nonviolence. If they were, history would record that African Americans had possessed the moral courage to stand up for their rights—and in doing so, had deepened the achievements of human civilization.

Indeed, the African Americans of Montgomery did set an example of moral courage that rewrote the pages of American race relations. Their firm stand caught the attention of the national news media. King and his colleagues were developing the tactics needed to launch a more aggressive phase of the civil rights movement.

Little Rock and the White Backlash

The civil rights spotlight moved the following year to Little Rock, Arkansas. White officials there had reluctantly adopted a plan to integrate the schools with a most deliberate lack of speed. Nine black students were scheduled to enroll in September 1957 at the all-white Central High School. Instead, the school board urged them to stay home. Governor Orval Faubus, generally a moderate on race relations, called out the Arkansas National Guard on the excuse of maintaining order. President Eisenhower tacitly supported Faubus in his defiance of court-ordered integration by remarking that "you cannot change people's hearts merely by laws."

Still, the Justice Department could not simply let Faubus defy the federal courts. It won an injunction against the governor, but when the nine blacks returned on September 23 a mob of 1,000 abusive whites greeted them. So great was national attention that President Eisenhower felt compelled to send in federal troops and take control of the National Guard. For a year the Guard preserved order until Faubus, in a last-ditch maneuver, closed the schools. Only in 1959, under pressure of another federal court ruling, did Little Rock schools reopen and resume the plan for gradual integration.

The skirmishes of Montgomery and Little Rock were a beginning, not an end. In fact, segregationist resistance

©John Bryson/The LIFE Picture Collection/Getty Images

 Governor Faubus first called out the National Guard to prevent African American students from integrating Little Rock's Central High School. Once President Eisenhower federalized the Guard, soldiers stayed at the school to protect the nine students who dared to cross the color line.

increased in the wake of King's Montgomery success. From 1955 to 1959, civil rights protesters endured over 200 acts of violence in the South. Legislatures and city councils passed scores of laws attempting to either outlaw the NAACP or prevent it from functioning. Black leaders were unable to achieve momentum on a national scale until 1960. Then, a series of demonstrations by young people changed everything.

> ✓ **REVIEW**
>
> How did African American and Latino civil rights cases spark a civil rights movement that went beyond court challenges?

A MOVEMENT BECOMES A CRUSADE

ON JANUARY 31, 1960, Joseph McNeill got off the bus in Greensboro, North Carolina, a freshman on the way back to college. When he looked for something to eat at the lunch

In May 1961 a mob in Montgomery, Alabama, surrounded the Negro First Baptist Church where Martin Luther King Jr. was leading an all-night vigil. King put in a call to Attorney General Robert Kennedy, who sent 400 federal marshals to keep order.

©Bettmann/Getty Images

counter, the waitress gave the familiar reply: "We don't serve Negroes here."

It was a refrain repeated countless times and in countless places. Yet for some reason this rebuke particularly offended McNeill. He and his roommates had read a pamphlet describing the 1955 bus boycott in Montgomery, Alabama. They decided it was time to make their own protest against segregation. Proceeding the next day to the "whites only" lunch counter at a local store, they sat politely waiting for service. "The waitress looked at me as if I were from outer space," recalled one of the protesters. Rather than serve them, the manager closed the counter. Word of the action spread. A day later—Tuesday—the four students were joined by 27 more. Wednesday, the number jumped to 63; Thursday, to over 300, including whites. Come the weekend, 1,600 students rallied to plan further action.

On Monday, February 8, **sit-ins** began in nearby Durham and Winston-Salem. Tuesday it was Charlotte; Thursday, High Point and Portsmouth, Virginia. A news broadcast reassured white residents in Raleigh that black students there would not follow Greensboro's example. In response, angry black students launched massive sit-ins at variety stores in Raleigh. By Lincoln's birthday the demonstrations had spread to Tennessee and Florida; by April to 78 different southern and border communities. By September at least 70,000 African Americans as well as whites had participated. Thousands had been arrested and jailed.

The campaign for black civil rights gained momentum not so much by the power of national movements as through a host of individual decisions by local groups, churches, and citizens. When New Orleans schools were desegregated in 1960, young Ruby's parents had not intended to make a social statement. But once involved, they refused to back down. The students at Greensboro had not been approached by the NAACP, but acted on their own initiative.

Riding to Freedom

NEWER CIVIL RIGHTS ORGANIZATIONS   Of course, organizations channeled these discontents and aspirations. But the new generation of younger activists also shaped and altered the organizations. Beginning in the 1960s, the push for desegregation moved from court actions launched by the NAACP and the Urban League to newer groups determined to take direct action. Since organizing the Montgomery boycott, Martin Luther King Jr. and his Southern Christian Leadership Conference (SCLC) had continued to advocate nonviolent protest. A second key organization, the Congress of Racial Equality (CORE), was more willing than the SCLC to force confrontations with the segregationist system. Another group, the Student Non-Violent Coordinating Committee (SNCC, pronounced "Snick"), grew out of the Greensboro sit-in. SNCC represented the more militant, younger generation of black activists who grew increasingly impatient with the slow pace of reform.

In May 1961 CORE director James Farmer led a group of black and white "freedom riders" on a bus trip into the heart of the South. They hoped their trip from Washington, D.C., to New Orleans would focus national attention on the inequality of segregated facilities. Violent southern mobs gave them the kind of attention they feared. In South Carolina, thugs beat divinity student John Lewis as he tried to enter an all-white waiting room. Mobs in Anniston and Birmingham, Alabama, assaulted the freedom riders as police ignored the violence. One of the buses was burned.

President Kennedy had sought to avoid forceful federal intervention in the South. When the freedom riders persisted in their plans, he tried to convince Alabama officials to protect the demonstrators so that he would not have to send federal forces. The mounting violence forced him to act. From a phone booth outside the bus terminal, John Doar, a Justice Department official in Montgomery, relayed the horror to Attorney General Robert Kennedy, the president's brother:

> Now the passengers are coming off. They're standing on a corner of the platform. Oh, there are fists, punching! A bunch of men led by a guy with a bleeding face are beating them. There are no cops. It's terrible! It's terrible! There's not a cop in sight. People are yelling, "There those niggers are! Get 'em, get 'em!" It's awful.

FREEDOM RIDERS ATTACKED Appalled, Robert Kennedy ordered in 400 federal marshals, who barely managed to hold off the crowd. Martin Luther King Jr., addressing a meeting in town, phoned the attorney general to say that the church had been surrounded by an angry mob of several thousand—jeering, throwing rocks, and carrying firebombs. As Kennedy later recalled, "I said that we were doing the best that we could and that he'd be as dead as Kelsey's nuts if it hadn't been for the marshals and the efforts that we made."

Both Kennedys understood that civil rights was the most divisive issue the administration faced. For liberals, civil rights measured Kennedy's credentials as a reformer. Kennedy needed black and liberal votes to win reelection. Yet an active federal role threatened to drive white southerners from the Democratic Party. It was for that reason that Kennedy had hedged on his promise to introduce major civil rights legislation. Through executive orders, he assured black leaders, he could eliminate discrimination in the government civil service and in businesses filling government contracts. He appointed several African Americans to high administrative positions and five, including Thurgood Marshall, to the federal courts. The Justice Department beefed up its civil rights enforcement procedures. But the freedom riders, by their bold actions, forced the Kennedys to do more.

Civil Rights at High Tide

By the fall of 1961 Attorney General Robert Kennedy had persuaded SNCC to shift tactics to voter registration, which he assumed would stir less violence. Voting booths, Kennedy noted, were not like schools, where people would protest, "We don't want our little blond daughter going to school with a Negro."

As SNCC and CORE workers arrived in southern towns in the spring of 1962, they discovered that voting rights was not a peaceful issue. Over two years in Mississippi they registered only 4,000 out of 394,000 black adults. Angry racists attacked with legal harassment, jailings, beatings, bombings, and murders. Terrorized workers who called for protection found it woefully lacking. FBI agents often stood by taking notes while SNCC workers were assaulted. Undaunted, SNCC workers made it clear that they intended to stay. They fanned out across the countryside to speak with farmers who had never before dared to ask for a vote.

JAMES MEREDITH Confrontation increased after a federal court ordered the segregated University of Mississippi to admit James Meredith, a black applicant. When Governor Ross Barnett personally blocked Meredith's registration in September 1962, Kennedy faced a crisis much as Eisenhower did with Little Rock in 1957. The president ordered several hundred federal marshals to escort Meredith into a university dormitory. Kennedy then announced on national television that the university had been integrated and asked students to follow the law of the land. Instead, a mob moved on campus, shooting out streetlights, commandeering a bulldozer, and throwing rocks and bottles. To save the marshals Kennedy finally sent in federal troops, but not before 2 people were killed and 375 wounded.

| Police chief Bull Connor ordered harsh tactics in attempting to break up protest marches in Birmingham, Alabama. High-pressure fire hoses used against marchers were strong enough to rip bark off trees; here a police dog rips open the pant leg of a demonstrator.

©Black Star/Alamy

"LETTER FROM BIRMINGHAM JAIL"

In Mississippi, President Kennedy had begun to lose control of the civil rights issue. The House of Representatives, influenced by television coverage of the violence, introduced a number of civil rights measures. And Martin Luther King Jr. led a group to Birmingham, Alabama, to force a showdown against segregation. From a prison cell there, he produced one of the most eloquent documents of the civil rights movement, his "Letter from Birmingham Jail." Addressed to local ministers who had counseled an end to confrontation, King defended the use of civil disobedience. The choice, he warned, was not between obeying the law and nonviolently breaking it to bring about change; it was between his way and streets "flowing with blood," as restive black citizens turned toward more-militant ideologies.

Once freed, King led new demonstrations. Television cameras were on hand that May as Birmingham police chief "Bull" Connor, a man with a short fuse, unleashed attack dogs, club-wielding police, and fire hoses powerful enough to peel the bark off trees. When segregationist bombs went off in African American neighborhoods, black mobs retaliated with their own riot, burning a number of shops and businesses owned by whites. In the following 10 weeks, more than 750 riots erupted in 186 cities and towns, both North and South. King's warning of streets "flowing with blood" no longer seemed far-fetched.

Kennedy sensed that he could no longer compromise on civil rights. In phrases that, like King's, drew heavily on Christian and republican rhetoric, he asked the nation, "If [an American with dark skin] cannot enjoy the full and free life all of us want, then who among us would be content to have the color of his skin changed and stand in his place? Who among us would then be content with counsels of patience and delay?" The president threw his support behind a strong civil rights bill to end segregation and protect black voters. When King announced a massive march on Washington for August 1963, Kennedy objected that it would undermine support for his bill. King was unmoved. He had never launched a protest, he told the president, that did not seem badly timed to someone.

THE MARCH ON WASHINGTON

On August 28 some 250,000 people gathered at the Lincoln Memorial to march and sing in support of civil rights and racial harmony. Appropriately, the day belonged to King. In the powerful tones of a southern preacher, he reminded the crowd that the Declaration of Independence was a promise that applied to all people, black and white. He had a dream, he told them, that one day black men and white, Christians, Jews, and Gentiles—all would come together to rejoice by singing the words of the traditional African American spiritual, "Free at

©AP Photo

| Malcolm X

last! Free at last! Thank God Almighty, we are free at last!" Congress began deliberation of the civil rights bill, which was reported out of the Judiciary Committee on October 23.

The Fire Next Time

TRAGEDY IN DALLAS With civil rights dividing the Democratic Party, the president scheduled a trip to Texas to recoup some southern support. On November 22, 1963, the people of Dallas lined the streets for his motorcade. Suddenly, a sniper's rifle fired several times. Kennedy slumped into his wife's arms, fatally wounded. His assassin, Lee Harvey Oswald, was caught several hours later. Oswald seemed a mysterious figure: emotionally unstable, he had spent several years in the Soviet Union. But his actions were never fully explained, because only two days after his arrest—in full view of television cameras—a disgruntled nightclub operator named Jack Ruby gunned him down.

In the face of such mounting violence, many Americans came to doubt that gradual reform could hold the nation together. A few black radicals believed that the Kennedy assassination was a payback to a system that had tolerated its own racial violence—the "chickens coming home to roost," as separatist Malcolm X put it. Many younger black leaders observed that civil rights received the greatest national coverage when white, not black, demonstrators were killed. They wondered, too, how Lyndon Johnson, a consummate southern politician, would approach the civil rights programs.

LBJ AND THE CIVIL RIGHTS ACT OF 1964 The new president, however, saw the need for action. Just as the Catholic issue had tested Kennedy's ability to lead, Johnson knew that without strong leadership on civil rights, "I'd be dead before I could ever begin." On November 23, his first day in office, he promised civil rights leaders that he would pass Kennedy's bill. Despite a southern filibuster in the Senate, the Civil Rights Act of 1964 became law the following summer. The bill marked one of the great moments in the history of American reform. It barred discrimination in public accommodations such as lunch counters, bus stations, and hotels; it authorized the attorney general to bring suit to desegregate schools, museums, and other public facilities; it outlawed discrimination in employment by race, color, religion, sex, or national origin.

VOTING RIGHTS ACT OF 1965 Still, the Civil Rights Act did not bar the techniques that southern registrars routinely used to prevent black citizens from voting. A coalition of idealistic young black and white protesters had continued the Mississippi voting drive in what they called "Freedom Summer." In 1965 Martin Luther King Jr., in the face of police violence, led a series of demonstrations. The campaign climaxed with a 54-mile walk from Selma to Montgomery, Alabama. As pressure mounted, Johnson sent Congress a strong Voting Rights Act, which was passed in August 1965. The act suspended literacy tests and authorized federal officials to supervise elections in many southern districts. With some justice, Johnson called the act "one of the most monumental laws in the entire history of American freedom." Within a five-year period, black registration in the South jumped from 35 to 65 percent.

Black Power

The civil rights laws did not strike at the **de facto segregation** found outside the South. This segregation was not codified in law but practiced through unwritten custom. In large areas of America, African Americans were locked out of suburbs, kept out of decent schools, barred from exclusive clubs, and denied all but the most menial jobs. Nor did the Voting Rights Act deal with the sources of urban black poverty. The median income for urban black residents was approximately half that for whites.

NATION OF ISLAM In such an atmosphere, militants sharply questioned the liberal goal of integration. Since the 1930s the Nation of Islam, dedicated to complete separation from white society, had attracted as many as 100,000 members, mostly young men. During the early 1960s the sect drew even wider attention through the energetic efforts of Malcolm X. This charismatic leader had learned the language of the downtrodden from his own experience as a former hustler, gambler, and prison inmate. His militancy alarmed whites, though by 1965 Malcolm was in fact moving toward a moderate position. He accepted integration but emphasized black community action. After he broke with Elijah Muhammad, leader of the Black Muslims, Malcolm was gunned down by rivals.

But by 1965–1966, even CORE and SNCC had begun to give up working for nonviolent change. If black Americans were to liberate themselves fully, militants argued, they could not merely accept rights "given" to them by whites—they had to claim them. Some members began carrying guns to defend themselves. In 1966 Stokely Carmichael of SNCC gave the militants a slogan—"Black Power"—and the defiant symbol of a gloved fist raised in the air. In its moderate form, the black power movement encouraged African Americans to recover their cultural roots, their African heritage, and a new sense of identity. African clothes and natural hairstyles became popular. On college campuses, black students pressed universities to hire black faculty, create black studies programs, and provide segregated social and residential space.

BLACK PANTHERS Among more militant factions, the Black Panther Party of Oakland called on the black community to arm. Because California law forbade carrying concealed weapons, Panther leader Huey Newton and his followers openly brandished shotguns and rifles as they patrolled the streets protecting blacks from police harassment. In February 1967 Newton forced the showdown he had been looking for. "O.K., you big fat racist pig, draw your gun," he

shouted while waving a shotgun. A gun battle with police left Newton wounded and in jail.

Eldridge Cleaver, who assumed leadership of the party, attracted the attention of whites with his searing autobiography, *Soul on Ice*. But even at the height of the Black Panthers' notoriety, the group never counted more than 2,000 members nationwide.

Violence in the Streets

No ideology shaped the reservoir of frustration and despair that existed in the ghettos. Often, a seemingly minor incident such as an arrest or an argument on the streets triggered violence. A mob would gather, and police cars and white-owned stores would be firebombed or looted. Riots broke out in Harlem and Rochester, New York, in 1964, the Watts area of Los Angeles in 1965, Chicago in 1966, and Newark and Detroit in 1967. In the riot at Watts, more than $200 million in property was destroyed and 34 people died, all of them black. It took nearly 5,000 troops to end the bloodiest rioting in Detroit, where 40 died, 2,000 were injured, and 5,000 were left homeless.

To most whites the violence was unfathomable and inexcusable. Lyndon Johnson spoke for many when he argued that "neither old wrongs nor new fears can justify arson and murder." Martin Luther King Jr., still pursuing the tactics of nonviolence, came to understand the anger behind it. Touring Watts only days after the riots, he was approached by a band of young blacks. "We won," they told him proudly. King asked them how they could say they "won" when dozens of African Americans had died during the riots, their neighborhoods had been destroyed, and the disturbances were being used by some whites as an excuse for doing nothing. The youngsters were unmoved. "We won because we made them pay attention to us."

For Johnson, ghetto violence and black militancy mocked his efforts to achieve racial progress. The Civil Rights and Voting Rights Acts were essential parts of the Great Society he hoped to

©Keystone Pictures USA/Alamy

Often, seemingly trivial events set off riots, revealing the depths of explosive rage within urban ghettos. In the riots of 1965 in Watts, Los Angeles, not only stores were burnt, but automobiles were overturned and set on fire as well.

Power to Which People?

White authorities wear coats and ties.

Despite the guns and tense atmosphere, does the black officer look generally at ease? If so, why?

©Steve Starr/AP Photo

What messages do the protesters' clothing, hairstyles, and gear convey?

News photographs provide journalists with both drama and answers to the basic reporters' questions: Who? What? When? Where? Why? How? But historians have ample time to analyze the details and the mixed messages. During Parents' Weekend at Cornell University in April 1969, a burning cross was erected late one night in front of Wari House, a cooperative run by black Cornell students. The next day student members of the Afro-American Society took over the student union, Willard Straight Hall, to protest what they viewed as long-standing racism on campus as well as the slow progress toward establishing a black studies program. During the 36-hour takeover, these armed students emerged from the building with members of the administration. Both consciously and unconsciously, the clothing as well as facial and body expressions send different messages about who has power and who does not in this particular situation.

THINKING CRITICALLY

Analyze this photo in terms of the following categories: age, race, gender. Is each category significant? Why would this image, set at a university, have been particularly shocking to many observers?

build. In that effort he had achieved a legislative record virtually unequaled by any other president in the nation's history. What Kennedy had promised, Johnson delivered. But the growing white backlash and the anger exploding in the nation's cities exposed serious flaws in the theory and practice of liberal reform.

 REVIEW

What were the different tactics, and where was each used in the civil rights campaigns led by CORE, SCLC, and SNCC?

CIVIL RIGHTS: PATTERNS OF PROTEST AND UNREST

Source: Library of Congress
Prints and Photographs Division
(LC-USZ62-123293)

"It is a call for black people in this country to unite, to recognize their heritage, to build a sense of community. It is a call for black people to define their own goals, to lead their own organizations."—Stokely Carmichael, discussing the term "Black Power"

CONTEXT

The earliest civil rights protests such as those in Montgomery, Alabama, in 1955, took place largely in the South. Martin Luther King Jr. proclaimed a doctrine of "nonviolence" would prevail. Over time, frustrations and passions rose, and new civil rights activists pressed for a more aggressive approach. Violence erupted both in the South and in the urban centers that became home to African Americans leaving the region in search of more opportunities and better lives.

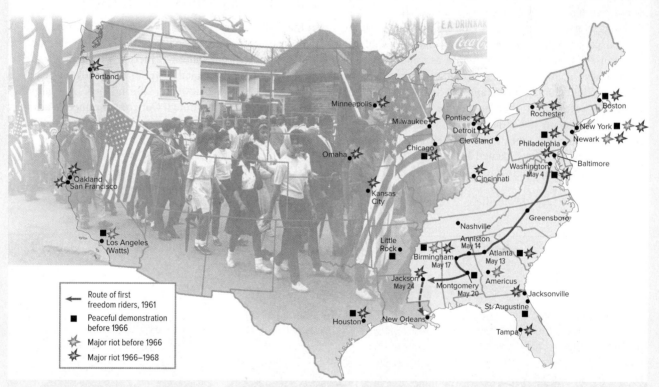

Legend:
- ← Route of first freedom riders, 1961
- ■ Peaceful demonstration before 1966
- ✦ Major riot before 1966
- ✦ Major riot 1966–1968

Source: Library of Congress, Prints and Photographs Division (LC-DIG-ppmsca-08102)

MAP READING

1. Where did the first freedom riders depart? What was their final destination? What on the map suggests they did not reach it?
2. Where were the most peaceful protests held?
3. Which cities had major riots both before and after 1966?
4. Did more riots occur before or after the passage of the Civil Rights Act in 1964 and the Voting Rights Act in 1965?

MAP INTERPRETATION

1. What characteristics did the cities that experienced major riots outside the South have in common?
2. What explains the large number of racially charged events in Georgia, Alabama, and Mississippi?
3. Type "list of riots" in your browser and go to the article of that name in Wikipedia. Look at the riots listed for the 1960s and choose one from a southern city and one from a northern or western city. Compare the two accounts for similarities and differences. Is there mention of any riots from earlier in the city's history?

Lyndon Johnson and the Great Society

Like the state he hailed from, Lyndon Baines Johnson was in all things bigger than life. His gifts were greater, his flaws more glaring. Insecurity was his Achilles' heel and the engine that drove him. If Kennedy had been good as president, Johnson would be "the greatest of them all, the whole bunch of them." If FDR won in a landslide in 1936, Johnson would produce an even larger margin in 1964. And to anyone who displeased him, he could be ruthlessly cruel. His scatological language and preoccupation with barnyard sex amused few and offended many. Yet Johnson could not understand why so few people genuinely liked him; one courageous diplomat, when pressed, found the nerve to respond, "Because, Mr. President, you are not a very likable man."

Johnson was born in Stonewall, Texas, in the Hill Country outside Austin, where the dry climate and rough terrain only grudgingly yielded up a living. He arrived in Washington in 1932 as an ardent New Dealer who loved the political game. When he became majority leader of the Senate in 1954, he cultivated an image as a moderate conservative who knew what strings to pull or levers to jog to get the job done. On an important bill, he latched onto the undecided votes until they succumbed to the famous "Johnson treatment," a combination of arguments, threats, emotional or patriotic appeals, and enticing rewards. Florida senator George Smathers likened Johnson to "a great overpowering thunderstorm that consumed you as it closed around you."

JOHNSON'S LIBERAL FAITH Despite his compulsion to control every person and situation, Johnson possessed certain bedrock strengths. No one was better at hammering out compromises among competing interest groups. To those who served him well, he could be loyal and generous. As president, he cared sincerely about society's underdogs. His support for civil rights, aid to the poor, education, and the welfare of the elderly came from genuine conviction. Like Franklin Roosevelt, whom he deeply admired, Johnson shared the liberal belief that the government should play an active role in managing the economy in order to soften the boom-and-bust swings of capitalism. Like progressives from the turn of the century, liberals looked to improve society by applying the intelligence of "experts." Liberals had confidence, at times bordering on arrogance, that poverty could be eliminated and the good society achieved. That faith might prove naive, but during the 1960s such optimism was both infectious and energizing.

The Origins of the Great Society

In the first months after the assassination, Johnson acted as the conservator of the Kennedy legacy. "Let us continue," he told a grief-stricken nation. Liberals who had dismissed Johnson as an unprincipled power broker grudgingly came to respect the energy he showed in steering the Civil Rights Act and tax-cut legislation through Congress. Kennedy's advisors believed tax cuts would create economic growth beneficial to the poor. Under Johnson, they did.

DISCOVERING POVERTY Kennedy had come to recognize that prosperity alone would not ease the plight of

©George Tames/The New York Times/Redux Pictures

Lyndon Johnson applied the "Johnson treatment" (as shown here, in 1957, to Senator Theodore Green) whenever he wanted people to see things his way. Few could say no, as he leaned in and reminded them who dominated the situation.

America's poor. In 1962 Michael Harrington's book *The Other America* brought attention to the widespread persistence of poverty despite the nation's affluence. Harrington focused attention on the hills of Appalachia that stretched from western Pennsylvania south to Alabama. In some counties a quarter of the population survived on a diet of flour and dried-milk paste supplied by federal surplus food programs. Under Kennedy, Congress had passed a new food stamp program as well as laws designed to revive the economies of poor areas, replacing urban slums with newer housing and retraining the unemployed. Robert Kennedy also headed a presidential committee to fight juvenile delinquency in urban slums by involving the poor in **community action programs.** Direct participation, they hoped, would overcome "a sense of resignation and fatalism" that sociologist Oscar Lewis had found while studying the Puerto Rican community of New York City.

It fell to Lyndon Johnson to fight Kennedy's "War on Poverty." By August 1964 this master politician had driven through Congress the most sweeping social welfare bill since the New Deal. The Economic Opportunity Act addressed almost every major cause of poverty. It included training programs such as the Job Corps, granted loans to rural families and urban small businesses as well as aid to migrant workers, and launched a domestic version of the Peace Corps, known as VISTA (Volunteers in Service to America). Even if the price tag for these programs was high, the scale of the problems dwarfed the almost $1 billion Johnson committed to Sargent Shriver, a Kennedy brother-in-law, who directed the new Office of Economic Opportunity (OEO).

The speed Johnson demanded led inevitably to confusion, conflict, and waste. Officials at OEO often found themselves battling with other cabinet departments as well as with state and local officials. For example, OEO workers organized voter registration drives in order to oust corrupt city officials. Others led rent strikes to force improvements in public housing. The director of city housing in Syracuse, New York, reacted typically: "We are experiencing a class struggle in the traditional Karl Marx style in Syracuse, and I do not like it." Such battles for power and bureaucratic turf undermined federal poverty programs.

The Election of 1964

In 1964, however, before these controversies surfaced, Johnson's political stock remained high. To an audience at the University of Michigan in May, he announced his ambition to forge a "Great Society," in which poverty and racial injustice no longer existed. The chance to fulfill his dreams seemed open to him, for the Republicans nominated Senator Barry Goldwater of Arizona as their presidential candidate. Ruggedly handsome, Goldwater was a true son of the West who held a narrow view of what government should do, for he was at heart a **libertarian.** Government, he argued, should not dispense welfare, subsidize farmers, tax incomes on a progressive basis, or aid public education. At the same time, Goldwater was so anticommunist that he championed a large defense establishment.

Goldwater's extreme views allowed Johnson to portray himself as a moderate. He chose Minnesota's liberal senator Hubert Humphrey to balance the ticket. Only the candidacy of Governor George Wallace of Alabama marred Johnson's election prospects. In Democratic primaries Wallace's segregationist appeal won nearly a third or more of the votes in Wisconsin, Indiana, and Maryland—hardly the Deep South. Wallace was persuaded, however, to drop out of the race.

The election produced the landslide Johnson craved. Carrying every state except Arizona and four in the Deep South, he received 61 percent of the vote. Democrats gained better than 2-to-1 majorities in the Senate and the House. Many observers saw the election as a repudiation of Goldwater and his conservative values. In reality, his defeat opened the way for grassroots conservatives to gain control of the Republican Party.

The Great Society

In January 1965 Johnson announced a legislative vision that would extend welfare programs on a scale beyond Franklin Roosevelt's New Deal. By the end of 1965, 50 bills had been passed, many of them major pieces of legislation, with more on the agenda for the following year.

PROGRAMS IN EDUCATION As a former teacher, Johnson made education the cornerstone of his Great Society. Stronger schools would compensate the poor for their disadvantaged homes, he believed. Under the Elementary and Secondary School Act, students in low-income school districts were to receive educational equipment, money for books, and enrichment programs such as Project Head Start for nursery-school-age children.

MEDICARE AND MEDICAID Johnson also pushed through the Medicare Act to provide the elderly with hospital

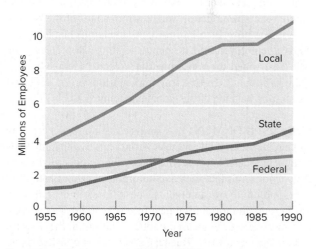

Growth of Government, 1955–1990

Government has been a major growth industry since World War II. Most people think of "big government" as federal government. But even during the Great Society, far more people worked in state and local government.

health insurance. Medicare targeted the elderly, because older people used hospitals three times more than other Americans and generally had incomes only half as large. Because Medicare made no provision for the poor who were not elderly, Congress also passed a program called Medicaid. Participating states received federal matching grants to pay the medical expenses of those on welfare or too poor to afford medical care.

IMMIGRATION REFORM The Great Society reformed immigration policy, in ways that reflected the drastic changes in global economics and culture since the last major immigration legislation was passed in 1924. Then, the National Origins Act (see Chapter 24) reflected the deeply Eurocentric orientation of American society and its prejudices against people of color. Virtually all the annual admissions quota of 154,000 went to Northern Europeans. Asians were barred almost entirely. By the 1960s American attitudes were changing, in terms of both race and region. American soldiers, after all, had fought wars to defend Korea, the Philippines, Vietnam, Taiwan, Japan, and other Asian nations. How could it justify discriminating against citizens from those countries?

By 1965, with Asian economies growing, the war in Vietnam expanding, and civil rights sentiments at a peak, the need for reform took on special urgency. The Immigration Act of 1965 abolished the national origins system. It increased annual admissions to 170,000 people and put a cap of 20,000 annually on immigrants from any single nation. The law gave marked preference to reuniting families of those immigrants already in the United States—so much so that some observers nicknamed it the "brothers and sisters act." Asians and Eastern Europeans were among its prime beneficiaries.

The act's liberalization was offset, however, by prejudice toward Central Americans, especially Mexicans. The National Origins Act of 1924 had placed no limit on immigrants from the Americas. But by the 1960s many in Congress feared a massive influx of workers from south of the border. Widespread poverty in Latin American nations had left thousands unemployed and desperate to find work. Hence the new act capped arrivals from the Western Hemisphere at 120,000 annually. In that way immigration reform reflected the shifting balance of the global economy.

THE ENVIRONMENT A mass-consumption economy took an increasing toll on the environment. By the mid-1960s many Americans had become increasingly concerned about acrid smog from factories and automobiles; about lakes and rivers polluted by detergents, pesticides, and industrial wastes; and about the disappearance of wildlife. The woman who most forcefully focused public attention on these issues was biologist and writer Rachel Carson, who published *Silent Spring* in 1962.

More than one observer compared *Silent Spring* to older American muckraking classics: Harriet Beecher Stowe's *Uncle Tom's Cabin* and Upton Sinclair's *The Jungle.* Carson warned that "the contamination of man's total environment with such substances of incredible harm"—most significantly the persistent pesticide DDT—could "alter the very material of heredity upon which the shape of the future depends." Beyond that she challenged the popular belief that humans through science and technology could "improve on nature." The "control of nature," she wrote, was "a phrase conceived in arrogance, born of the Neanderthal age of biology and philosophy when it was supposed that nature exists for the convenience of man."

Carson's critics dismissed her as hysterical, linking her to "the organic gardeners, the anti-fluoride leaguers, the worshippers of 'natural foods,' . . . and other pseudo-scientists and faddists." But a scientific panel appointed by the Kennedy administration essentially vindicated the charges *Silent Spring* made. Equally important, Carson taught Americans to think ecologically. She showed in moving and elegant language the interconnection of living things and the means by which toxic chemicals moved through the food chain. The alarm she sounded helped to inspire a broad movement to protect the environment.

In response, Congress in 1964 passed the National Wilderness Preservation System Act to set aside 9.1 million acres of wilderness as "forever wild." Lady Bird Johnson, the president's wife, campaigned to eliminate the garish billboards and junkyards along many of the nation's roads. Congress first established pollution standards for interstate waterways and a year later provided funds for sewage treatment and water purification. Legislation also tightened standards on air pollution. Environmental reform provoked opposition from such groups as mining companies, cattlegrazers, and the timber industry, who wanted to continue using the public domain for their own purposes. But the public accepted the benefits of the new regulation.

For all he had done, Johnson wanted to do more. In 1966 he pushed through bills to raise the minimum wage, improve auto safety, aid mass transit, and develop "model cities." But opposition mounted. "Doesn't matter what kind of majority you come in with," Johnson predicted early on. "You've got just one year when they treat you right, and before they start worrying about themselves." Yet as late as 1968 Johnson pushed major legislation through Congress to ban discrimination in housing (Fair Housing Act), to build public housing, to protect consumers from unfair credit practices (Truth-in-Lending Act), and to protect scenic rivers and expand the national park system.

EVALUATING THE GREAT SOCIETY Historians have difficulty measuring the Great Society's impact. It produced more legislation and more reforms than the New Deal. However, economic statistics suggested that general prosperity, accelerated by the tax-cut bill, did more to fight poverty than all the OEO programs. And the inevitable scandals began to surface.

Despite such problems the Great Society established the high-water mark of interventionist government, a trend that began in the Progressive Era and flourished during the Great Depression and in World War II. Although Americans

Convinced that pesticides such as DDT posed no threat to humans, public health and agriculture officials sprayed people and land with a reckless abandon that compelled Rachel Carson to begin efforts to curb pesticide use.
©Bettmann/Getty Images

continued to pay lip service to the notion that government should remain small and interfere little in citizens' lives, no strong movement emerged to eliminate Medicare or Medicaid. Few Americans disputed the right of the government to regulate industrial pollution, or to manage the economy, and provide citizens with a safety net of benefits in sickness and in old age. In this sense, the tradition of liberalism prevailed, whatever Johnson's failings.

The Reforms of the Warren Court

Although Lyndon Johnson and the Congress left the stamp of liberalism on federal power during the decade, the third branch of government played a role that, in the long run, proved equally significant. Supreme Court chief justice Earl Warren turned what was traditionally the least activist branch of government into a center of liberal reform. His political skills, compassion, and tact had been instrumental in bringing his colleagues to a unanimous ruling on school desegregation in *Brown v. Board of Education*. Warren continued to use these skills, until his retirement in 1969, to forge a liberal coalition of justices who handed down a series of landmark decisions in broad areas of civil liberties and civil rights.

PROTECTING DUE PROCESS In 1960 the rights of citizens accused of a crime but not yet convicted were often unclear. Those too poor to afford lawyers frequently faced trial without representation. The police and the courts seldom

I was sentenced to the state Penitentiary by The Circuit Court of Bay County, State of Florida. The present proceeding was commenced on a ☓ petition for a Writ of Habeus Corpus to The Supreme Court of The State of Florida to vacate the sentence, on the grounds that I was made to stand Trial without the aid of counsel, and, at all times of my incarceretion. The said Court refused To appoint counsel and therefore deprived me of Due process of law, and violate my rights in The Bill of Rights and the constitution of the United States.

5th day of Jan 1962 Petitioner

Clarence Earl Gideon

Laurence C Duvyca
NOTARY PUBLIC
Notary Publ...
My Comm... ... 19, 1962
Bonded by American Surety Co. of N.Y.

Gideon's Letter to the Supreme Court
John F. Davis, Clerk, Supreme Court of the United States

Clarence Earl Gideon (right) used this handwritten letter to bring his appeal to the attention of the Supreme Court. In the Gideon case, the Court ruled that even poor defendants have the right to legal counsel. Such incidents, while rare, restore faith in the idea of a government for the people.
©AP Photo

The Warren Court: Critical Decisions in an Era of Upheaval

CIVIL RIGHTS AND VOTING RIGHTS

1954 *Brown v. Board of Education of Topeka, Kansas*
Reversed *Plessy v. Ferguson* (1896) and the doctrine of "separate but equal"; ordered lower courts to admit African American students to public schools without discrimination and "with all deliberate speed."

1954 *Hernandez v. Texas*
Ruled that the Fourteenth Amendment's equal protection clause extended to other racial groups besides African Americans.

1962 *Baker v. Carr*
Declared that states must base legislative districts on the principle of "one person, one vote," forcing nearly every state to redraw district lines and increasing the political power of previously underrepresented metropolitan areas.

FREE SPEECH AND CENSORSHIP

1962 *Engel v. Vitali*
Banned school prayer: "It is no part of the business of government to compose official prayers to be recited as part of a religious program carried on by government."

1964 *New York Times v. Sullivan*
Increased protection of freedom of the press; protected newspaper reporting on civil rights campaigns in the South from the threat of libel suits by requiring a strict standard of proving "actual malice." A publisher had to know that a statement was false or had to act in reckless disregard of its truth or falsity.

1964 *Griswold v. Connecticut*
Ruled that a Connecticut law banning the use of contraceptives was unconstitutional because the Constitution protected a citizen's right to privacy.

RIGHTS OF THE ACCUSED

1963 *Gideon v. Wainwright*
Established that defendants have the right to legal counsel in cases that involve a potential jail sentence.

1964 *Escobedo v. Illinois*
Extended its decision in *Gideon* by ruling that, under the Sixth Amendment, a suspect had the right to an attorney during police questioning.

1966 *Miranda v. Arizona*
Held that statements by a defendant in police custody would be admissible at trial only if the prosecution showed that the defendant was informed of the right to consult with an attorney before and during questioning and of the right against self-incrimination but "waived," or gave up, that right.

Photos: (left) ©Comstock Images/Getty Images; *(right)* ©Hisham F. Ibrahim/Getty Images

informed those accused of a crime of their rights under the Constitution. In a series of decisions, the Court ruled that the Fourteenth Amendment provided broad guarantees of **due process** under the law. *Gideon v. Wainwright* (1963), an appeal launched by a Florida prisoner, made it clear that all citizens were entitled to legal counsel in any case involving a possible jail sentence. In *Escobedo v. Illinois* (1964) and *Miranda v. Arizona* (1966), the Court declared that individuals detained for a crime must be informed of the charges against them, of their right to remain silent, and of their right to have an attorney present during questioning. Though these decisions applied to all citizens, they were primarily intended to benefit the poor, who were most likely to be in trouble with the law and least likely to understand their rights.

BANNING SCHOOL PRAYER In *Engel v. Vitale* (1962), the Court issued a ruling that especially troubled conservative religious groups. The case involved a nonsectarian prayer written by the New York State Board of Regents that public school students were required to recite. Even if dissenting

children could be excused, the Court ruled, they faced indirect pressure to recite the prayer. That violated the constitutional separation of church and state. The following year the Court extended the ban on school prayer to cover the reading of the Bible and the Lord's Prayer.

Other decisions promoted a more liberal social climate. In *Griswold v. Connecticut* (1964), the Warren Court overturned a nineteenth-century law banning the sale of contraceptives or providing medical advice about their use. The Court demonstrated its distaste for censorship by greatly narrowing the legal definition of obscenity. A book had to be "utterly without redeeming social value" to permit censorship. The combination of decisions reforming criminal rights, prayer, free speech, and morality angered conservatives of almost all social and political backgrounds. These issues would again become a political battleground in the 1980s and beyond.

ONE PERSON, ONE VOTE   The Court's most far-reaching decision was probably one of its least controversial, though politically most sensitive. As cities and suburbs grew, few states redrew their legislative districts to reflect the change. Rural (and generally conservative) elements continued to dominate state legislatures. In *Baker v. Carr* (1962) and a series of later cases, the Court ruled that the states must apportion seats not by "land or trees or pastures" but as closely as possible by the principle of "one person, one vote."

> **REVIEW**
> What were the major legislative achievements of Johnson's Great Society agenda?

THE COUNTERCULTURE

IN 1964 SOME 800 STUDENTS from UC Berkeley, Oberlin, and other colleges met in western Ohio to train for the voter registration campaign in the South. Protest-hardened SNCC coordinators instructed middle-class students who had grown up in peaceful white suburbs on the perils of "Mississippi Freedom Summer." The lessons were sobering. When beaten by police, the SNCC staff advised, assume the fetal position—hands protecting the neck, elbows covering the temples. That minimized injuries from nightsticks. A few days later, grim news arrived. Local police in Philadelphia, Mississippi, had already arrested a volunteer who had left two days earlier. Now he and two others were "missing." Six weeks later, searchers uncovered their mangled bodies, bulldozed into the earthworks of a freshly finished dam. That did not stop other sobered volunteers from heading to Mississippi.

By the mid-1960s conservatives, civil rights groups, and the poor were not alone in rejecting liberal solutions. The students who returned to campus from the voter registration campaign that summer of 1964 were the shock troops of a much larger movement. Dissatisfied members of the middle class—especially the young—joined a revolt against the conventions of society and politics as usual.

Activists on the New Left and Right

SDS AND PORT HURON   More than a few students had become disillusioned with the slow pace of reform. Since the "establishment"—whether it was liberal or conservative—blocked meaningful change, why not overthrow it? Tom Hayden, raised in a working-class family outside Detroit, went to college at the University of Michigan, then traveled to UC Berkeley, and soon joined civil rights workers in Mississippi. Hayden, along with Al Haber, another student at the University of Michigan, was a driving force in forming the radical Students for a Democratic Society (SDS). SDS had little sympathy with an "old left" generation of radicals who grew up in the 1930s and still debated the merits of Marxism. Action was the route to change, Hayden argued: through sit-ins, protest marches, and direct confrontation. At a meeting

in Port Huron, Michigan, in 1962 the group condemned the modern bureaucratic society exemplified by the organization man of the 1950s. The Port Huron Statement called for "participatory democracy," in which large organizations run by bureaucrats would be decentralized and turned into face-to-face communities in which individual participation mattered.

THE FREE SPEECH MOVEMENT   The Free Speech Movement at the University of California, Berkeley, was a case in point. To most liberals, Berkeley seemed the gem of the California state university system. Like so many other universities, it had educated a generation of GIs following World War II. But to people like Tom Hayden and the SDS, Berkeley was a bureaucratic monster, enrolling more than 30,000 students and marching them into impersonal classrooms to hear lectures from remote professors. In the fall of 1964 Berkeley declared off-limits the one small area in which political organizations had been allowed to advertise their causes. When university police tried to remove a recruiter for CORE, thousands of angry students surrounded the police

©History collection 2016/Alamy

A handwritten poster recruiting for the Mississippi Freedom Project in the summer of 1964. Many white students from the North returned to their campuses, radicalized about the need for change in their own schools. One such student was Mario Savio, who launched the Free Speech Movement at the University of California, Berkeley.

STUDENT VOICES FOR A NEW AMERICA

In 1960 students created three organizations committed to ideals of political and moral regeneration for America. The organizations were the Student Non-Violent Coordinating Committee (SNCC), Young Americans for Freedom (YAF), and the Students for a Democratic Society (SDS). Each organization addressed the issue of justice but in different ways.

DOCUMENT 1
SNCC Statement of Purpose

We affirm the philosophical or religious ideal of nonviolence as the foundation of our purpose, the presupposition of our belief, and the manner of our action. Nonviolence as it grows from the Judaic-Christian tradition seeks a social order of justice permeated by love. Integration of human endeavor represents the crucial first step towards such a society.

Through nonviolence, courage displaces fear; love transcends hate.

Acceptance dissipates prejudice; hope ends despair. Peace dominates war; faith reconciles doubt. Mutual regards cancel enmity. Justice for all overthrows injustice. The redemptive community supersedes systems of gross immorality.

Love is the central motif of nonviolence. Love is the force by which God binds man to Himself and man to man. Such love goes to the extreme; it remains loving and forgiving even in the midst of

hostility. It matches the capacity of evil to inflict suffering with an even more enduring capacity to absorb evil, all the while persisting in love.

By appealing to conscience and standing on the moral nature of human existence, nonviolence nurtures the atmosphere in which reconciliation and justice become actual possibilities.

Adopted at Raleigh, North Carolina, April, 1960.

Source: SNCC Statement of Purpose.

DOCUMENT 2
YAF Sharon Statement

In this time of moral and political crises, it is the responsibility of the youth of America to affirm certain eternal truths.

We, as young conservatives, believe:

That foremost among the transcendent values is the individual's use of his God-given free will, whence derives his right to be free from the restrictions of arbitrary force;

That liberty is indivisible, and that political freedom cannot long exist without economic freedom;

That the purpose of government is to protect those freedoms through the

preservation of internal order, the provision of national defense, and the administration of justice;

That when government ventures beyond these rightful functions, it accumulates power, which tends to diminish order and liberty. . . .

That we will be free only so long as the national sovereignty of the United States is secure; that history shows periods of freedom are rare, and can exist only when free citizens concertedly defend their rights against all enemies;

That the forces of international Communism are, at present, the greatest single threat to these liberties;

That the United States should stress victory over, rather than coexistence with, this menace; and

That American foreign policy must be judged by this criterion: does it serve the just interests of the United States?

Adopted in conference at Sharon, Connecticut, September 11, 1960.

Source: Sharon Statement by Young Americans for Freedom, 1960. http://www.yaf.org/sharon_statement.aspx.

DOCUMENT 3
SDS Port Huron Statement

INTRODUCTION: AGENDA FOR A GENERATION
We are people of this generation, bred in at least modest comfort, housed now in universities, looking uncomfortably to the world we inherit. . . . Freedom and equality for each individual, government of, by, and for the people—these American values we found good, principles by which we could live as men. Many of us began maturing in complacency.

As we grew, however, our comfort was penetrated by events too troubling to

dismiss. First, the permeating and victimizing fact of human degradation, symbolized by the Southern struggle against racial bigotry, compelled most of us from silence to activism. Second, the enclosing fact of the Cold War, symbolized by the presence of the Bomb, brought awareness that we ourselves, and our friends, and millions of abstract "others" we knew more directly because of our common peril, might die at any time. We might deliberately ignore, or avoid, or fail

to feel all other human problems, but not these two, for these were too immediate and crushing in their impact, too challenging in the demand that we as individuals take the responsibility for encounter and resolution.

While these and other problems either directly oppressed us or rankled our consciences and became our own subjective concerns, we began to see complicated and disturbing paradoxes in our surrounding America. The declaration "all men are created equal . . ." rang hollow before the facts of Negro life in the South and the big cities of the North. The proclaimed peaceful intentions of the United States contradicted its economic and military investments in the Cold War status quo. . . .

Some would have us believe that Americans feel contentment amidst prosperity—but might it not be better called a glaze above deeply felt anxieties about their role in the new world? And if these anxieties produce a developed indifference to human affairs, do they not as well produce a yearning to believe there is an alternative to the present, that something

can be done to change circumstances in the school, the workplaces, the bureaucracies, the government? It is to this latter yearning, at once the spark and engine of change, that we direct our present appeal. The search for truly democratic alternatives to the present, and a commitment to social experimentation with them, is a worthy and fulfilling human enterprise, one which moves us and, we hope, others today. On such a basis do we offer this document of our convictions and analysis: as an effort in understanding and changing the conditions of humanity in the late twentieth century, an effort rooted in the ancient, still unfulfilled conception of man

attaining determining influence over his circumstances of life.

Adopted at Port Huron, Michigan, June 15, 1962.

Source: Hayden, Tom, The Port Huron Statement: The Visionary Call of the 1960s Revolution. New York, NY: Thunder's Mouth Press, 2005, 45–48.

THINKING CRITICALLY

How would you characterize the tone of each of these statements? What evidence in each suggests that students believed the United States faced a spiritual crisis? In what ways do they disagree about the meaning of such ideals as "freedom," "justice," and "equality"?

car for 32 hours. Out of this protest a student named Mario Savio emerged as a spokesperson and leader.

Before traveling south to Freedom Summer in 1964, Savio had been a graduate student in philosophy. Mississippi politicized him. And not just Savio. Twelve of the 21 Freedom Summer veterans at Berkeley were arrested during the protest. "In our free-speech fight," Savio proclaimed, "we have come up against what may emerge as the greatest problem of our nation—depersonalized, unresponsive bureaucracy." When the university's president, Clark Kerr, threatened to expel Savio, 6,000 students took control of the administration building, stopped classes with a strike, and convinced many faculty members to join them. Kerr backed down, placing no limits on free speech on campus except those that applied to society at large. But the rebellious spirit spread to other major universities, such as Michigan, Yale, and Columbia, and then to campuses across the nation.

YOUNG AMERICANS FOR FREEDOM Not all radicalized students on college campuses were leftists. To the conservative members of Young Americans for Freedom (YAF), those behind the Free Speech Movement at Berkeley were a motley crowd of beats, liberals, and Communists. YAF had a larger (though probably less visible) membership than leftist groups like SNCC or SDS. These clean-cut young Americans seldom marched or demonstrated. They wanted instead to limit the power of the federal government that they believed threatened true freedom and liberty. Both Eisenhower's "middle-of-the-road Republicanism" and Kennedy's liberalism, they charged, sapped the "moral and physical strength of the nation." YAF denounced the Peace Corps as "a grand exercise in—self-denial and altruism, paid for by the American taxpayers and administered by the United Nations." Barry Goldwater embodied for YAF members the values they cherished. Although Goldwater went down to defeat, the ranks of the YAF would supply a new generation of conservative activists.

Vatican II and American Catholics

Many conservatives feared that the secular trends of modern life threatened the Christian faith as well. They worried that even the traditions of the Roman Catholic Church seemed under siege when Pope John XXIII summoned church leaders to an ecumenical council, popularly known as Vatican II. It assembled in October 1962.

ECUMENISM Racing against the cancer that would soon fell him, Pope John bade the council deal with issues of social change engaging the world in the 1960s, including poverty, nuclear war, atheism, and birth control. He wished, as well, to bring the church hierarchy more closely in touch with lay members and with the modern world around it. By the time the council concluded in 1965 Pope John had died, having been succeeded by Pope Paul VI, and the acts of the council had transformed the church. At a superficial level, many changes seemed small, though they affected the everyday lives of Catholics. No longer was it a requirement to go without meat on "fish Fridays" or to say confession on Saturdays. More significant, during services priests would now face the congregation rather than the altar and conduct the mass in the vernacular rather than Latin. Lay members would also have a greater role in implementing the faith. In addition, Vatican II encouraged a spirit of **ecumenism,** in which Catholics would seek greater understanding with other Christians.

The changes of Vatican II energized many American Catholics and led them to embrace further reform within and without the church. Priests such as Fathers Daniel and Philip Berrigan were active in the antipoverty and antiwar movements of the era. Many female Catholics sought a larger role for women in religious life. Yet even those who did not take to the streets or the pulpit felt the effects of Vatican II.

The Rise of the Counterculture

Spiritual matters also aroused secular rebels, who found their culture too materialistic and shallow. These alienated students, often from conservative backgrounds, began to grope toward spiritual, nonmaterial goals. "Turn on to the scene, tune in to what is happening, and drop out of high school, college, grad school, junior executive," advised Timothy Leary, a Harvard psychology professor who dropped out himself. People who heeded Leary's call to spiritual renewal rejected politics for a lifestyle of experimentation with music, sex, and drugs. Observers labeled their movement a "counterculture."

COMMUNES The counterculture of the 1960s had much in common with earlier religious revival and utopian movements. It admired the quirky individualism of Henry David Thoreau, and like Thoreau, it turned to Zen Buddhism and other Oriental philosophies. Like Brook Farm and other nineteenth-century utopian communities, the new hippie communes sought perfection along the fringes of society. Communards built geodesic domes based on the designs of architect Buckminster Fuller; they "learned how to scrounge materials, tear down abandoned buildings, use the unusable," as one member of the Drop City commune put it. The introduction of the birth control pill in 1962 ushered in an era of increased sexual freedom. Young rebels embraced the new freedoms as a means to liberate them from the repressive inhibitions that distorted the lives of their "uptight" parents. Drugs appeared to open the inner mind to a higher state of consciousness or pleasure. No longer would people be bound by conventional relationships and the goals of a liberal, bourgeois society.

©Jeff Morgan 16/Alamy

| *LSD inspired the genre of psychedelic art that adorned this Grateful Dead phonograph album cover, with its freaked-out lettering that seemed to dazzle and dance even if the viewer had not inhaled or ingested hallucinogens. (The album is* American Beauty.*)*

The early threads of the 1960s counterculture led back to the 1950s and the subculture of the beat generation (Chapter 28). For the beats, unconventional drugs had long been a part of the scene, but now their use expanded dramatically. Professor Timothy Leary began experimenting with hallucinogenic mushrooms in Mexico and soon moved on to LSD. The drug "blew his mind," as he put it, and he became so outspoken in making converts that Harvard blew him straight out of its hallowed doors.

Whereas Leary's approach to LSD was cool and contemplative, novelist Ken Kesey *(One Flew over the Cuckoo's Nest)* embraced it with antic frenzy. His ragtag company of druggies and freaks formed the "Merry Pranksters" at Kesey's home outside San Francisco. Writer Tom Wolfe chronicled their outrageous style in *The Electric Kool-Aid Acid Test,* a book that pioneered the "New Journalism." Wolfe dropped the rules of reporting that demanded objectivity and distance by taking himself and his readers on a **psychedelic** tour with Kesey and his fellow Pranksters. Their example inspired others to drop out.

The Rock Revolution

In the 1950s rock and roll defined a teen culture preoccupied with young love, cars, and adult pressures. One exception was the Kingston Trio, which in 1958 popularized folk music that appealed to young adult and college audiences. As the interest in folk music grew, the lyrics increasingly focused on social or political issues. Joan Baez helped define the folk style by dressing simply, wearing no makeup, and rejecting the commercialism of popular music. She joined folksinger Bob Dylan in the civil rights march on Washington in 1963, singing "We Shall Overcome" and "Blowin' in the Wind." Such folksingers reflected the activist side of the counterculture as they sought to provoke their audiences to political commitment.

THE BEATLES In 1964 a new sound from England exploded on the American scene. Within a year the Beatles, four musicians from Liverpool, were driving teen audiences into frenzies as they sang "I Want to Hold Your Hand." With hair that was considered long in the 1960s, modish English clothes, fresh faces, and irreverent wit, they looked and sounded like nothing young Americans had experienced before. Their boyish enthusiasm captured the Dionysian spirit of the new counterculture. But the Beatles' enormous commercial success also reflected the creativity of their music. Along with other English groups such as the Rolling Stones, the Beatles reconnected white American audiences with the rhythm-and-blues roots of rock and roll.

DYLAN Until 1965 Bob Dylan was the quintessential folk artist, writing about nuclear weapons, pollution, and racism. He appeared at concerts with longish frizzy hair, working-class clothes, an unamplified guitar, and a harmonica suspended on a wire support. But then Dylan shocked his fans by donning a black leather jacket and shifting to a "folk-rock" style featuring an electric guitar. His new songs seemed to suggest that the old America was almost beyond redemption. The Beatles, too, transformed themselves. After a pilgrimage to India to study transcendental meditation, they returned to produce *Sergeant Pepper's Lonely Hearts Club Band,* possibly the most influential album of the decade. It blended sound effects with music, alluded to trips taken with "Lucy in the Sky with Diamonds" (LSD), and welcomed the listener into a turned-on world. In San Francisco, bands such as the Grateful Dead pioneered "acid rock" with long pieces aimed at echoing drug-induced states of mind.

SOUL MUSIC The debt of white rock musicians to rhythm and blues led to increased integration in the music world. Before the 1960s, black rhythm-and-blues bands had played primarily to black audiences, in segregated clubs, or over black radio stations. The civil rights movement and a rising black social and political consciousness gave rise to "soul" music. One black disc jockey described soul as "the last to be hired, first to be fired, brown all year round, sit-in-the-back-of-the-bus feeling." Soul was the quality that expressed black pride and separatism. Out of Detroit came the "Motown sound," which combined elements of gospel, blues, and big band jazz. Diana Ross and the Supremes, the Temptations, Stevie Wonder, and other groups under contract to Berry Gordy's Motown Record Company appealed to black and white audiences alike. Yet, although soul music promoted black consciousness, it offered little by way of social commentary. It evoked the traditional blues themes of workday woes, unhappy marriages, and the troubles between men and women.

The West Coast Scene

For all its themes of alienation, rebellion, and utopian quest, the counterculture also signaled the increasing importance of the West Coast in defining American popular culture. In the 1950s the shift of television production from the stages of New York to the film lots of Hollywood helped establish Los Angeles as a communications center. San Francisco became notorious as a home of the beat movement. And then in 1958 the unthinkable happened: the Brooklyn Dodgers and the New York Giants baseball teams fled the Big Apple for Los Angeles and San Francisco. By 1963 the "surfing sound" of West Coast rock groups such as the Beach Boys and Jan and Dean had made Southern California's preoccupation with surfing and cars into a national fad.

THE FIRST BE-IN Before 1967 Americans were only vaguely aware of another West Coast phenomenon, the hippies. But in January a loose coalition of drug freaks, Zen cultists, and political activists banded together to hold the first well-publicized Be-In. The beat poet Allen Ginsberg was on hand to offer spiritual guidance. The Grateful Dead and Jefferson Airplane, acid rock groups based in San Francisco, provided entertainment. A mysterious group

| *Some 400,000 people converged on the Woodstock Music Festival in the summer of 1969. These two came with their psychedelic VW Microbus.*

called the Diggers somehow managed to supply free food and drink, while the notorious Hell's Angels motorcycle gang policed the occasion. Drugs of all kinds were plentiful. And a crowd attired in a bizarre mix of Native American, circus, Oriental, army surplus, and other costumes came to enjoy it all.

The West Coast had long been a magnet for Americans seeking opportunity, escape, and alternative lifestyles; now the San Francisco Bay Area staked its claim as the spiritual center of the counterculture. Politically conscious dropouts gravitated toward Berkeley; the apolitical "flower children" moved into Haight-Ashbury, a run-down San Francisco neighborhood of apartments, Victorian houses, and "head shops" selling drug paraphernalia, wall posters, Indian bedspreads, and other eccentric accessories. Similar dropout communities and communes sprang up across the country. Colleges became centers of hip culture, offering alternative courses, eliminating strict requirements, and tolerating the new sexual mores of their students.

In the summer of 1969 all the positive forces of the counterculture converged on Bethel, New York, in the Catskill Mountains resort area, to celebrate the promise of peace, love, and freedom. The Woodstock Music Festival attracted 400,000 people to the largest rock concert ever organized. For one long weekend the audience and performers joined to form an ephemeral community based on sex, drugs, and rock and roll. But even then, the counterculture was dying. Violence intruded on the laid-back urban communities that hippies had formed. Organized crime and drug pushers muscled in on the lucrative trade in LSD, amphetamines, and marijuana. Bad drugs and addiction took their toll. Urban slum dwellers turned hostile to the strange middle-class dropouts who, in ways the poor could not fathom, found poverty ennobling. Free sex often became an excuse for rape, exploitation, and loveless gratification.

Much that had once seemed outrageous in the hippie world was readily absorbed into the marketplace. Advertisers were in the forefront of promoting a "hip" style. Rock groups became big business enterprises commanding huge fees. Slick concerts with expensive tickets replaced communal dances with psychedelic light shows. Yogurt, granola, and herbal teas appeared on supermarket shelves. Ironically, much of the world that hippies embraced was generated by the society they had rejected.

 REVIEW

How did the movements of the counterculture develop both politically and socially?

PUTTING HISTORY IN GLOBAL CONTEXT

BY THE LATE 1960S MOST dreams of human betterment seemed shattered—whether those dreams emanated from the promise of the march on Washington, Lyndon Johnson's Great Society, or the communal society of the hippie counterculture. Recession and inflation brought an end to the easy affluence that made liberal reform programs and alternative lifestyles seem so easily affordable. Poverty and unemployment menaced even middle-class youth who had found havens in communes, colleges, and graduate schools. Racial tensions divided black militants and the white liberals of the civil rights movement into sometimes hostile camps.

But the civil rights movement changed the United States in fundamental ways. Although de facto segregation and racism remained entwined in American life, segregation as a legal system had been overturned. No longer was it enshrined by the decisions of the highest court in the land, as it had been in *Plessy v. Ferguson*. And the rise of black power—in both its moderate and radical forms—reflected a political and cultural current that was international as well as national. Catholics in Northern Ireland, for example, discovered in the civil rights struggle a window into their own status as second-class citizens. In Africa the drive for civil rights revolved around the effort to overthrow the imperial powers of Europe. In colony after colony, African nationalists fought for their independence, with Ghana leading the way in 1957. Too often the new governments devolved into dictatorships; and in South Africa the white regime maintained a system of *apartheid* that strictly segregated the races and smothered black political and economic progress. But colonial empires continued to fall across the globe.

The United States granted independence to its principal Asian colony, the Philippines, in 1946. Yet Americans, too, found themselves ensnared by the conflicts of colonialism. More than any other single factor, a growing war in France's former colony, Vietnam, destroyed the promise of Lyndon Johnson's Great Society and distracted from the campaign for civil rights. After 1965 the nation divided sharply as the American military role in Southeast Asia grew. Radicals on the left looked to rid America of a capitalist system that promoted race and class conflict at home and imperialism and military adventurism abroad. Conservatives who supported the war called for a return to traditional values like law and order. Both the left and the right attacked the liberal center. Their combined opposition helped undermine the consensus Lyndon Johnson had worked so hard to sustain.

CHAPTER SUMMARY

Largely excluded from the prosperity of the 1950s, African Americans and Latinos undertook a series of grassroots efforts to gain the legal and social freedoms denied them by racism and, in the South, by an entrenched system of segregation.

- Early postwar campaigns focused on legal challenges to the system, culminating with victories in the Supreme Court decisions of *Brown v. Board of Education* and *Hernández v. Texas*.

- Later in the 1950s Martin Luther King Jr. and other civil rights activists used new techniques of protest, such as the boycott, to desegregate the bus system in Montgomery, Alabama.

- Continued resistance by white southerners sparked a school integration dispute in Little Rock, Arkansas.

- Beginning in 1960 widespread grassroots efforts from African American churches, students, and political groups across the South accelerated the drive for an end to segregation.

- Violence against sit-ins, freedom rides, voter registration drives, and other forms of nonviolent protest made the nation sympathetic to the civil rights cause.

- In the wake of the assassination of President Kennedy, Lyndon Johnson persuaded Congress to adopt the Civil Rights Act of 1964 and the Voting Rights Act of 1965.

- The Supreme Court under Chief Justice Earl Warren expanded civil rights and liberties through its *Gideon, Escobedo,* and *Miranda* decisions, while also easing censorship, banning school prayer, and increasing voting rights.

- Lyndon Johnson delivered on the liberal promise of his Great Society through his 1964 tax cut, aid to education, Medicare and Medicaid, wilderness preservation, and urban redevelopment, and through the many programs of his War on Poverty.

- Johnson's liberal reforms did not satisfy student radicals, minority dissidents, gays, and the counterculture whose members sought to transform America into a more just and less materialistic society.

Digging Deeper

Steven Lawson, Charles Payne, and James Patterson provide an excellent overview in *Debating the Civil Rights Movement, 1945-1968* (2006). An older, still effective survey is Robert Weisbrot, *Freedom Bound: A History of America's Civil Rights Movement* (1990). Though exhaustive in detail (nearly 3,000 pages in all), Taylor Branch's three-volume biography of Martin Luther King Jr. is superb: *Parting the Waters: America in the King Years, 1954-63* (1988); *Pillar of Fire: America in the King Years, 1963-65* (1998); and *At Canaan's Edge: America in the King Years, 1965-68* (2006). Given the importance of leaders such as King, the prominent role of women is sometimes underrepresented. As a corrective, see Bettye Collier-Thomas and V. P. Franklin, eds., *Sisters in the Struggle: African American Women in the Civil Rights-Black Power Movements* (2001). Latino civil rights movements are covered in Henry A. J. Ramos, *The American GI Forum* (1998); and F. Arturo Rosales, *Chicano! The History of the Mexican American Civil Rights Movement* (1997).

Todd Gitlin, *The Sixties* (1987), set the early tone for books that are part history and part memoir. Terry H. Anderson, *The Movement and the Sixties* (1995), offers a view that is both politically engaged and scholarly. For a narrative history of the era, see Mark Hamilton Lytle, *America's Uncivil Wars: The Sixties Era from Elvis to the Fall of Richard Nixon* (2006). Robert Dallek, *An Unfinished Life: John F. Kennedy, 1917-1963* (2003), draws a portrait that balances Kennedy's virtues and vices. The best recent biography of Lyndon Johnson is Randall B. Woods, *LBJ: Architect of American Ambition* (2006).

30 The Vietnam Era

1963–1975

In Vietnam, helicopters gave infantry unusual mobility—a critical element in a war with no real front line, because troops could be quickly carried from one battle to another. Tim Page, who snapped this photo, described the chaos of such warfare: "On the ground it's always confusion, dust, smoke, unfamiliar territory wet or dry. Everyone seems to mill around in mad ant-like patterns waiting for the seething to calm down; maybe it will, maybe it won't, and when it's hot, it's very hot."

©Tim Page/Getty Images

>> An American Story

WHO IS THE ENEMY?

Vietnam from afar: it looked like an emerald paradise. Thomas Bird, an army rifleman sent there in 1965, recalled his first impression: "A beautiful white beach with thick jungle background. The only thing missing was naked women running down the beach, waving and shouting 'Hello, hello, hello.'" Upon landing, Bird and his buddies were each issued a "Nine-Rule" card outlining proper behavior toward the Vietnamese. "Treat the women with respect, we are guests in this country and here to help these people."

But who were they helping and who were they fighting? When American troops searched out Vietcong forces, the VC generally disappeared into the jungle beyond the villages and rice fields. When rifleman John Muir walked into a hamlet, the place looked ordinary, but the Korean lieutenant with him had been in Vietnam a while. "We have a little old lady and a little old man and two very small children," he pointed out. "According to them, the rest of the family has been spirited away. . . . So there's only four of them, and they have a pot of rice that's big enough to feed 50 people. And rice, once it's cooked, will not keep. They gotta be feeding the VC." Muir watched in disbelief as the lieutenant set the house on fire. The roof "started cooking off ammunition, because all through the thatch they had ammunition stored."

GIs soon learned to walk down jungle trails with a cautious shuffle, looking for a wire or a piece of vine that seemed too straight. "We took more casualties from booby traps than we did from actual combat," recalled David Ross, a medic. "It was very frustrating because how do you fight back against a booby trap? You're just walking along and all of a sudden your buddy doesn't have a leg. Or you don't have a leg." Yet somehow the villagers would walk the same paths and never get hurt. Who was the enemy and who the friend?

The same question was being asked half a globe away, on the campus of Kent State University on May 4, 1970. By then the American phase of the Vietnam War had dragged on for more than five years, driving President Lyndon Johnson from office and embroiling

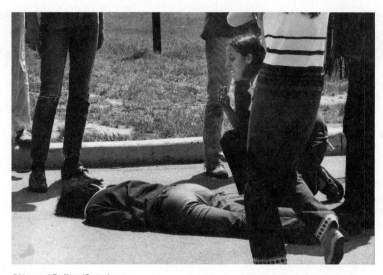

©Howard Ruffner/Getty Images

| *Death at Kent State*

his successor, Richard Nixon, in controversy. When Nixon expanded the war beyond Vietnam into Cambodia, opposition to the war had become so intense in this normally apolitical community near Akron, Ohio, that 300 angry students spilled into the nearby town, smashed shop windows, and returned to campus to burn down an old army ROTC building. Governor James Rhodes ordered in 750 of the National Guard. Student dissidents were the "worst type of people we harbor in America," he announced. "We are going to eradicate the problem."

When demonstrators assembled for a rally on the college commons, the Guard ordered them to disperse. The protesters stood their ground. So the guardsmen advanced, wearing full battle gear and armed with M-1 rifles, whose high-velocity bullets had a horizontal range of almost two miles. Some students scattered; a few picked up rocks and threw them. The guardsmen suddenly fired into the crowd, many of whom were students passing back and forth from classes. Incredulous, a

young woman knelt over Jeffrey Miller; he was dead. In addition, three other students had been killed and nine more wounded, some caught innocently by the Guard's fire.

As news of the killings swept the nation, antiwar protesters at Jackson State, a black college in Mississippi, seized a women's dormitory. State police surrounding the building opened fire without provocation, killing two more students and wounding a dozen. In both incidents the demonstrators had been unarmed. The events at Kent State and Jackson State turned sporadic protests against the American invasion of Cambodia into a nationwide student strike. Many students believed the forces of law and order sworn to protect them had betrayed the ideals of the United States.

Not since the Civil War had the nation been so deeply divided. As the war dragged on, debate moved off college campuses and into the homes of middle-class Americans, where sons went off to fight and the war came home each night on the evening news. As no other war had, Vietnam seemed to stand the nation on its head. When American soldiers shot at Vietnamese "hostiles," who could not always be separated from "friendlies," or when National Guardsmen fired on their neighbors across a college green, who were the enemies and who were the friends? <<

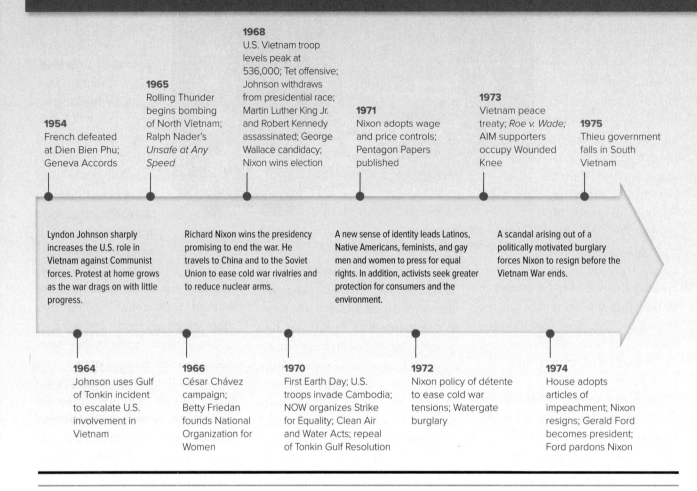

1954
French defeated at Dien Bien Phu; Geneva Accords

1965
Rolling Thunder begins bombing of North Vietnam; Ralph Nader's *Unsafe at Any Speed*

1968
U.S. Vietnam troop levels peak at 536,000; Tet offensive; Johnson withdraws from presidential race; Martin Luther King Jr. and Robert Kennedy assassinated; George Wallace candidacy; Nixon wins election

1971
Nixon adopts wage and price controls; Pentagon Papers published

1973
Vietnam peace treaty; *Roe v. Wade*; AIM supporters occupy Wounded Knee

1975
Thieu government falls in South Vietnam

Lyndon Johnson sharply increases the U.S. role in Vietnam against Communist forces. Protest at home grows as the war drags on with little progress.

Richard Nixon wins the presidency promising to end the war. He travels to China and to the Soviet Union to ease cold war rivalries and to reduce nuclear arms.

A new sense of identity leads Latinos, Native Americans, feminists, and gay men and women to press for equal rights. In addition, activists seek greater protection for consumers and the environment.

A scandal arising out of a politically motivated burglary forces Nixon to resign before the Vietnam War ends.

1964
Johnson uses Gulf of Tonkin incident to escalate U.S. involvement in Vietnam

1966
César Chávez campaign; Betty Friedan founds National Organization for Women

1970
First Earth Day; U.S. troops invade Cambodia; NOW organizes Strike for Equality; Clean Air and Water Acts; repeal of Tonkin Gulf Resolution

1972
Nixon policy of détente to ease cold war tensions; Watergate burglary

1974
House adopts articles of impeachment; Nixon resigns; Gerald Ford becomes president; Ford pardons Nixon

THE ROAD TO VIETNAM

FOR SEVERAL THOUSAND YEARS VIETNAM had struggled periodically to fight off foreign invasions. Buddhist culture had penetrated eastward from India. More often Indochina faced invasion and rule by the Chinese from the north. After 1856 the French entered as a colonial power, bringing with them a strong Catholic tradition.

HO CHI MINH   Ho Chi Minh, a Vietnamese nationalist, hoped to free his people of French as well as Chinese domination. Since the end of World War I, he had struggled to create an independent Vietnam. After World War II, he organized a guerrilla war against the French, which finally led to their defeat at Dien Bien Phu in 1954. He agreed at the Geneva Peace Conference to withdraw his forces north of the 17th parallel in return for a promise to hold free elections in both the North and the South. The Americans, having supported the French struggle against Ho, helped install Ngo Dinh Diem in South Vietnam. They then supported Diem's decision not to hold elections, which Ho's followers seemed sure to win. Frustrated South Vietnamese Communists—the

Vietcong—renewed their guerrilla war. "I think the Americans greatly underestimate the determination of the Vietnamese people," Ho remarked in 1962, as President Kennedy was committing more American advisors to South Vietnam.

Lyndon Johnson's War

THE DOMINO THEORY   For Kennedy, Vietnam had been just one of many anticommunist skirmishes his activist advisors wanted to fight. As attention focused increasingly on Vietnam, he came to discount President Eisenhower's "domino theory" that if Diem's pro-Western government fell to the Communists, the other nations of Southeast Asia would collapse one after the other. Still, he saw a Communist victory as unacceptable. But what to do? Even 16,000 American "advisors" had been unable to help the unpopular Diem, who was executed after a military coup in November 1963, which had the tacit support of the United States. When Kennedy was assassinated a few weeks later, Lyndon Johnson assumed the burden of Vietnam.

Johnson's political instincts told him to keep the Vietnam War at arm's length. He felt like a catfish, he remarked, who had "just grabbed a big juicy worm with a right sharp hook in the middle of it." Johnson's heart was in his Great Society programs. Yet the political attacks Democrats endured after the fall of China to the Communists during the Truman years and the long-stalemated Korean War taught Johnson lessons he never forgot. The political costs of defeat in Vietnam were unacceptable. That conviction led him steadily toward deeper American involvement.

Until August 1964, American advisors had focused on training and supporting the South Vietnamese army, which fought the Vietcong reluctantly. North Vietnam, for its part, infiltrated men and supplies along the Ho Chi Minh Trail, a network of jungle routes threading through Laos and Cambodia into the highlands of South Vietnam. With the Vietcong controlling some 40 percent of South Vietnam, Johnson strategists decided to relieve the South by increasing pressure on North Vietnam itself.

(*left*): ©AFP/Getty Images; (*right*): ©Bettmann/Getty Images

| *Nguyen Ai Quoc, who became Ho Chi Minh, once worked at London's posh Carlton Hotel in the pastry kitchen of the renowned chef Escoffier. But he was soon swept up in socialist and nationalist politics, appearing at the Versailles Peace Conference (left) to plead for an independent Vietnam. Ho spent a lifetime in anticolonialist and revolutionary activity and became a revered leader of his people (right). He died in 1969, six years before his dream of a united Vietnam became a reality.*

TONKIN GULF INCIDENT American ships patrolling the Gulf of Tonkin began supporting secret South Vietnamese raids against the North. On August 2, three North Vietnamese patrol boats exchanged fire with the American destroyer *Maddox*. Two nights later, in inky blackness and a heavy thunderstorm, a second incident occurred. But a follow-up investigation could not determine whether enemy ships had even been near the scene. President Johnson was not pleased. "For all I know our navy might have been shooting at whales out there," he remarked privately.

Whatever his doubts, the president publicized both incidents as "open aggression on the high sea" and ordered retaliatory air raids on North Vietnam. He did not disclose that the navy and South Vietnamese forces had been conducting secret military operations. When Johnson then asked for the authority to take "all necessary measures" to "repel any armed attack" on American forces and to "prevent future aggression," Congress overwhelmingly passed what became known as the Tonkin Gulf Resolution.

Senator Ernest Gruening of Alaska, one of only two lawmakers to vote no, objected that the resolution gave the president "a blank check" to declare war, a power the Constitution reserved to Congress. Johnson insisted that he had limited goals. But with his overwhelming victory in the 1964 election, the president felt free to exploit the powers the resolution gave him.

Rolling Thunder

ESCALATION In January 1965 Johnson received a disturbing memorandum from two top advisors. "Both of us are now pretty well convinced that our present policy can lead only to disastrous defeat," they said. The United States should either increase its attack—*escalate* was the term coined in 1965—or simply withdraw. In theory **escalation** would increase military pressure to the point at which further resistance would cost more than the enemy was willing to pay. By taking gradual steps, the United States would demonstrate its resolve to win while leaving the door open to negotiations.

Escalation hardened rather than weakened the resolve of the Vietcong and North Vietnamese. When a Vietcong mortar attack in February killed seven marines stationed at Pleiku air base, Johnson ordered U.S. planes to begin bombing North Vietnam.

AIR STRIKES Restricted air strikes did not satisfy more-hawkish leaders. Retired Air Force chief of staff Curtis LeMay complained, "We are swatting flies when we should be going after the whole manure pile." In March Johnson ordered Operation Rolling Thunder, a systematic bombing campaign aimed at bolstering confidence in South Vietnam and cutting the flow of supplies from the North. Rolling Thunder achieved none of its goals. American pilots could seldom spot the Ho Chi Minh Trail under its dense jungle canopy. Equally discouraging, South Vietnamese leaders quarreled among themselves and jockeyed for power instead of uniting against the Vietcong.

Once the Americans established bases from which to launch the new air strikes, these too became targets for guerrilla attacks. General William Westmoreland, the chief of American military operations in Vietnam, requested combat troops to defend the bases. Johnson's decision to send 3,500 marines proved to be a

>> MAPPING THE PAST <<

THE WAR IN VIETNAM

Source: National Archives and Records Administration (111-CCV-570-CC44322)

"How long would it take to succeed in Vietnam? They didn't know. How many more troops would it take? They couldn't say. Were two hundred thousand the answer? They weren't sure. Might they need more? Yes, they might need more. Could the enemy build up [their own troop strength] in exchange? Probably. So what was the plan to win the war? Well, the only plan was that attrition would wear out the Communists, and they would have had enough. Was there any indication that we've reached that point? No, there wasn't." —Defense Secretary Clark Clifford

CONTEXT

For the United States, one strategic problem was to locate and destroy the supply routes known as the Ho Chi Minh Trail. Rugged mountains and triple canopy jungles hid much of the trail from aerial observation and attack.

MAP READING

1. Locate the Gulf of Tonkin. What larger body of water is it a part of?
2. How many countries does the Ho Chi Minh Trail pass through?
3. What is the dominant terrain feature in South Vietnam?
4. How many major battles of Tet are noted on the map? Are they concentrated in any particular region of South Vietnam?

MAP INTERPRETATION

1. Why would the Gulf of Tonkin location suggest that the United States might have provoked the North Vietnamese attack on USS Turner Joy?
2. What geographic factors help explain why Richard Nixon secretly extended the war into Laos and Cambodia?
3. Despite heavy bombing, why were the Soviet Union and China able to send supplies into North Vietnam?

Vietcong guerrillas constructed elaborate tunnel systems to hide thousands of soldiers, ammunition, and medical supplies. Soldiers would hide during the day and come out at night to tend crops, look for food, or set out on missions. Despite elaborate ventilation systems and booby traps to ward off invaders, conditions below ground were harsh. Vietcong soldiers had to endure scorpions, biting ants, and poisonous centipedes. In the years after the war, this camouflaged tunnel entrance became part of a tourist attraction showing how the tunnels functioned.

©robertharding/Alamy

crucial first step toward Americanizing the war. Another 40,000 soldiers arrived in May and 50,000 more by July.

Defense Secretary McNamara ordered that the escalation be carried out in a "low-keyed manner to avoid undue concern and excitement in the Congress and in domestic public opinion." He worried also about how China and Russia might react. By 1966 almost 185,000 American troops had landed—and the call for more continued. In 1968, at the height of the war, 536,000 American troops were being supported with helicopters, jet aircraft, and other advanced military technologies. They were also supplied by a vast system that provided hot meals even in dense jungles. No more than one in nine Americans in Vietnam actually saw active combat.

 REVIEW

How did Lyndon Johnson justify escalating the war in Vietnam, and what strategies did the United States use in doing so?

SOCIAL CONSEQUENCES OF THE WAR

THE IMPACT OF THE WAR was greatest on the baby-boom generation of the 1950s. As these young people came of age, draft calls for the armed services were rising. At the same time, the civil rights movement and the growing counterculture were encouraging students to question the goals of establishment America. Whether they fought in Vietnam or protested at home, supported the government or demonstrated against it, eventually these baby boomers—as well as Americans of all ages—were forced to take a stand on Vietnam.

The Soldiers' War

EFFECTS OF THE DRAFT Most Americans sent to Vietnam were drafted. Under the Selective Service System, as it was called, privileged young people could avoid service: college students or those working in "critical" occupations, such as teachers and engineers. As the war escalated, the draft was changed so that some students were called up through a lottery system. Still, those who knew the medical requirements might produce a doctor's affidavit certifying a weak knee, flat feet, or bad eyes—all grounds for flunking the physical. Of the 1,200 men in Harvard's class of 1970, only 56 served in the military, and only 2 of them in Vietnam.

The poorest and least educated were also likely to escape service, because the Armed Forces Qualification Test and the physical often screened them out. Thus the sons of blue-collar America were most likely to accept Uncle Sam's letter of induction. Once in uniform, Hispanic and black Americans who had fewer skills were more often assigned to combat duty. The draft also made it a relatively young man's war. The average age of soldiers serving in Vietnam was 19, compared with an average of 26 for World War II.

BODY COUNTS Most American infantry came to Vietnam ready and willing to fight. But physical and psychological hardships took their toll. An American search-and-destroy mission would fight its way into a Communist-controlled hamlet, clear and burn it, and move on—only to be ordered back days or weeks later because the enemy had moved in again. Since success could not be measured in territory gained, the measure became the "body count": the number of Vietcong killed. Unable to tell who was friendly and who was hostile, GIs sometimes took out their frustrations on

©Everett Collection/Newscom

| *The use of defoliants such as Agent Orange, shown here, had a devastating effect on the Vietnamese countryside.*

innocent civilians. Officers counted those victims as Vietcong in order to inflate the numbers that suggested their tactics were working.

THE AIR WAR AND AGENT ORANGE Most Americans assumed that superior military technology could guarantee success. But technology alone could not tell friend from foe. Since the Vietcong routinely mixed with the civilian population, the chances for deadly error increased. Bombs of napalm (jellied gasoline) and white phosphorus rained liquid fire from the skies, coating everything from village huts to the flesh of fleeing humans. Since the enemy could hide in the jungle, the Americans made war on its vegetation. American planes spread more than 100 million pounds of defoliants, including Agent Orange that destroyed more than one-third of South Vietnam's timberlands—an area approximately the size of the state of Massachusetts. The long-term health and ecological effects were severe; the military benefits minimal.

The American military buildup turned Vietnam from a place once able to support a people and a culture into one designed to sustain a war. The construction in 1966 of a base at Dong Tam to house the 9th Infantry Division typified the environmental disregard with which Americans operated. The site the engineers chose for the base lay in a muddy river bottom along the Mekong River where swamps, streams, and rice paddies interlaced the area. Within a few months, engineers had pumped 2 million cubic feet of muck out of the riverine ecology to raise 90 acres 10 feet above the river. The base grew to include the largest heliport in the world, an airfield, enough barracks to house the entire division, and the water, sewage, and electric power needed to run the base. Just three years after the 9th Infantry Division arrived, in the summer of 1969, the base closed, leaving behind an uninhabited ghost town. The ecological damage it inflicted persisted for decades.

By 1967 the war cost more than $2 billion a month. To fight it, the United States dropped more bombs on Vietnam than it had during all of World War II. After one air attack on

an enemy village, American troops walked into the smoldering ruins. "We had to destroy the town in order to save it," an officer explained. As the human and material costs of the war increased, that statement stuck in the minds of many observers. What sense was there in a war that saved people by destroying their homes?

The War at Home

As the war dragged on, such questions provoked anguished debate among Americans, especially on college campuses. Faculty members held "teach-ins" to explain the issues to concerned students. Scholars familiar with Southeast Asia questioned every major assumption the president used to justify escalation. The United States and South Vietnam had brought on the war, they charged, by violating the Geneva Accords of 1954. The war was a civil war among the Vietnamese, not an effort by Soviet or Chinese Communists to conquer Southeast Asia, as Eisenhower, Kennedy, and Johnson had claimed. Moreover, the Vietcong, as an indigenous rebel force, had legitimate grievances against Saigon's corrupt government.

HAWKS AND DOVES By 1966 national leaders had divided into opposing camps of **"hawks"** and **"doves."** The hawks argued that America must win in Vietnam to save Southeast Asia from communism, to preserve the nation's prestige, and to protect the lives of American soldiers fighting the war. Most Americans supported those views. The doves were nonetheless a prominent minority. African Americans as a group were far less likely than white Americans to support the war. Some resented the diversion of resources from the cities to the war effort. Many black Americans' heightened sense of racial consciousness led them to identify with the Vietnamese people. Martin Luther King Jr., SNCC, and CORE all opposed the war. Heavyweight boxing champion Muhammad Ali, a black Muslim, refused on religious grounds to serve in the army, even though the decision cost him his title.

By 1967 crowds of college students and faculty expressed their outrage: "Hey, hey, LBJ, how many kids have you killed today?" Over 300,000 people demonstrated in April 1967 in New York City. Some college protesters burned their draft cards in defiance of federal law. In the fall more violent protests erupted as antiwar radicals stormed a draft induction center in Oakland, California. The next day 55,000 protesters ringed the Pentagon in Washington. Again, mass arrests followed.

As protests flared, key moderates became increasingly convinced the United States could not win the war. Senator William Fulbright of Arkansas was among them. Having helped President Johnson push the Tonkin Gulf Resolution through the Senate, Fulbright now held hearings sharply critical of American policy.

MCNAMARA LOSES FAITH Defense Secretary Robert McNamara became the most dramatic defector. For years the statistically minded secretary struggled to quantify the success of the war effort. By 1967 McNamara had become skeptical. If Americans had killed 300,000 Vietnamese,

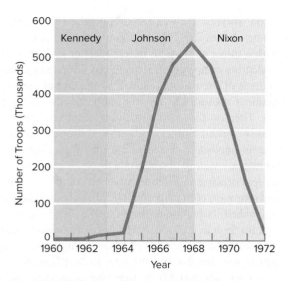

Number of U.S. Troops (Thousands) in Vietnam

The graph suggests one reason why protest against the war increased after 1964, peaked by 1968, and largely ended after 1972.

enemy forces should be shrinking. Instead, intelligence estimates indicated that North Vietnamese infiltration had risen from 35,000 a year in 1965 to 150,000 in 1967. McNamara came to have deep moral qualms about continuing the war indefinitely. "The picture of the world's greatest superpower killing or seriously injuring 1,000 noncombatants a week, while trying to pound a tiny, backward nation into submission on an issue whose merits are hotly disputed, is not a pretty one," he advised. With Johnson, who did not want to be remembered as the first American leader who lost a war, continuing to side with the hawks, McNamara resigned.

INFLATION The soaring cost of the war fueled a rising inflation. Medicare, education, housing, and other Great Society programs raised the domestic budget sharply too. Through it all Johnson refused to raise taxes, even though wages and prices rose rapidly. From 1965 to 1970, inflation jumped from about 2 percent to around 4 percent. The economy was headed for trouble.

 REVIEW

How did conditions in Vietnam make it difficult for American soldiers to fight the war, and how did conditions at home lead to dissent over the war?

THE UNRAVELING

ALMOST ALL THE FORCES DIVIDING America seemed to converge in 1968. Until January of that year, most Americans had reason to believe General Westmoreland's estimate of the war. There was, he suggested, "light at the end of the tunnel." Johnson and his advisors, whatever their private doubts, in public painted an optimistic picture. With such hope radiating from Washington, few Americans were prepared for the events of the night of January 30, 1968.

Tet Offensive

As the South Vietnamese began their celebration of Tet, the Vietnamese lunar New Year, Vietcong guerrillas launched a series of concerted attacks. They assaulted Saigon's major airport, the South Vietnamese presidential palace, and Hue, the ancient Vietnamese imperial capital. Most unnerving to Americans, 19 Vietcong commandos blasted a hole in the American embassy compound in Saigon and stormed in. They fought in the courtyard until all 19 lay dead. One reporter, stunned by the carnage, compared the courtyard to a butcher shop.

MILITARY SUCCESS AND THE "CREDIBILITY GAP" Though surprised by the Tet Offensive, American and South Vietnamese troops repulsed most of the assaults. General Westmoreland announced that the Vietcong's "well-laid plans went afoul." And in a narrow military sense, Westmoreland was right. The enemy had been driven back, sustaining perhaps 40,000 deaths. Only 1,100 American and 2,300 South Vietnamese soldiers had been killed. But Americans at home received quite another message. Tet created a "credibility gap" between the administration's optimistic reports and the war's harsh reality. The president had repeatedly claimed that the Vietcong were on their last legs. Yet as Ho Chi Minh had coolly informed the French after World War II: "You can kill ten of my men for every one I kill of yours . . . even at those odds, you will lose and I will win." Respected CBS news anchor Walter Cronkite drew a gloomy lesson of Tet for his national audience: "To say that we are mired in stalemate seems the only realistic, yet unsatisfactory, conclusion."

STALEMATE The Tet offensive sobered Lyndon Johnson as well as his new secretary of defense, Clark Clifford. Clifford was a Johnson loyalist and a believer in the war. But as he reviewed the American position in Vietnam, the Joint Chiefs of Staff, who had requested an additional 206,000 troops, offered no satisfactory answers to his questions. "How long would it take to succeed in Vietnam?" Clifford recalled asking them:

> They didn't know. How many more troops would it take? They couldn't say. Were two hundred thousand the answer? They weren't sure. Might they need more? Yes, they might need more. Could the enemy build up [their own troop strength] in exchange? Probably. So what was the plan to win the war? Well, the only plan was that attrition would wear out the Communists, and they would have had enough. Was there any indication that we've reached that point? No, there wasn't.

Clifford decided to build a case for de-escalation.

"CLEAN FOR GENE" Meanwhile, the antiwar forces had found a political champion in Senator Eugene McCarthy from Wisconsin. McCarthy was something of a maverick, who wrote poetry in his spare time. He announced that no matter how long the odds, he intended to challenge Lyndon Johnson

©Keystone Pictures USA/Alamy

| Antiwar protests spread in 1967, not only within the United States but also abroad. These protesters in Washington, D.C., call attention to the American military's use of napalm jelly, a flammable substance dumped on hamlets where Vietcong were thought to be. Civilian casualties were often the result.

in the 1968 Democratic primaries. Idealistic college students got haircuts and shaves in order to look "clean for Gene" as they campaigned for McCarthy in New Hampshire. Johnson won the primary, but his margin was so slim (300 votes) that it amounted to a defeat. To the anger of McCarthy supporters, Robert Kennedy, John Kennedy's younger brother, announced his own antiwar candidacy.

LBJ WITHDRAWS "I've got to get me a peace proposal," the beleaguered president told Clifford. White House speechwriters put together an announcement that bombing raids against North Vietnam would be halted, at least partially, in hopes that peace talks could begin. They were still trying to write an ending when Johnson told them, "Don't worry; I may have a little ending of my own." On March 31 he supplied it, announcing: "I have concluded that I should not permit the presidency to become involved in the partisan divisions that are developing in this political year. . . . Accordingly I shall not seek, and I will not accept, the nomination of my party for another term as your president."

The announcement shocked nearly everyone. The Vietnam War had pulled down one of the savviest, most effective politicians of the era. North Vietnam responded to the speech by sending delegates to a peace conference in Paris, where negotiations quickly bogged down. And American attention soon focused on the chaotic situation at home, where all the discontent and violence of the 1960s seemed to be coming together.

The Shocks of 1968

KING AND KENNEDY ASSASSINATED On April 4, Martin Luther King Jr. traveled to Memphis to support striking

sanitation workers. He was relaxing on the balcony of his motel when James Earl Ray, an escaped convict, fatally shot him with a sniper's rifle. The violent reaction to King's murder eroded his campaign of nonviolence. Riots broke out in ghetto areas of the nation's capital; by the end of the week, disturbances rocked 125 more neighborhoods across the country. Then on the evening of June 5 a disgruntled Arab nationalist, Sirhan Sirhan, assassinated Robert Kennedy. Running in opposition to the war, Kennedy had just won a crucial primary victory in California.

The loss of King and Kennedy pained Americans deeply. In their own ways both men exemplified the liberal tradition, which reached its high-water mark in the 1960s. King had retained his faith in a Christian theology of nonviolence. He sought reform for the poor of all races without resorting to the language of the fist and the gun. Robert Kennedy had come to reject the war his brother had supported, and he seemed genuinely to sympathize with the poor and minorities. At the same time, he was popular among traditional white ethnics and blue-collar workers. Would the liberal political tradition have flourished longer if these two charismatic figures had survived the turbulence of the 1960s?

Though Lyndon Johnson planned to step down, he still dominated his party and chose his loyal vice president, Hubert Humphrey, as his successor. Humphrey had begun his career as a progressive and a strong supporter of civil rights. But as vice president, he was intimately associated with the war and the old-style liberal reforms that could never satisfy radicals. The Republicans had chosen Richard Nixon, a traditional anticommunist now reborn as the "new," more moderate Nixon. As much as radicals disliked Johnson, they truly despised Nixon, "new" or old.

CONVENTION MAYHEM Chicago, where the Democrats met for their convention, was the fiefdom of Mayor Richard Daley, long a symbol of machine politics. Daley was determined that the dissatisfied radicals who poured into Chicago would not disrupt "his" Democratic convention. The radicals were equally determined that they would. For a week the police skirmished with demonstrators: police clubs, riot gear, and tear gas versus the demonstrators' eggs, rocks, and balloons filled with paint and urine. When Daley refused to allow a peaceful march past the convention site, the radicals marched anyway, and then the police, with the mayor's blessing, turned on the crowd in what a federal commission later labeled a police riot. In one pitched battle, many officers took off their badges and waded into the crowd, nightsticks swinging, chanting "Kill, kill, kill." Reporters, medics, and other innocent bystanders were injured; at 3 a.m. police invaded candidate Eugene McCarthy's hotel headquarters and pulled some of his assistants from their beds.

With feelings running so high, President Johnson did not dare appear at his own party's convention. Theodore White, a veteran journalist covering the gathering, scribbled his verdict in a notebook as police chased hippies down Michigan Avenue. "The Democrats are finished," he wrote.

Revolutionary Clashes Worldwide

The clashes in Chicago seemed homegrown, but they took place against the backdrop of a global surge in radical, often violent, student upheavals. In 1966 Chinese students were in the vanguard of Mao Zedong's Red Guards, formed to enforce a Cultural Revolution that sought to purge China of all bourgeois cultural influences. Although that revolution persecuted millions among the educated classes and left the country in economic shambles, Mao became a hero to radicals outside China. Radicals also lionized other revolutionaries who took up arms: Fidel Castro and Che Guevara in Cuba and Ho Chi Minh in Vietnam.

Radical targets varied. In Italy students denounced the official Marxism of the Soviet Union and the Italian Communist Party. French students at the Sorbonne in Paris rebelled against the university's efforts to discipline political activists. Students in Czechoslovakia launched a full-scale rebellion, known as Prague Spring, against the Soviet domination of their nation—until Soviet tanks crushed the uprising. Though the agenda varied from country to country, virtually all student revolutionaries condemned the American war in Vietnam.

Whose Silent Majority?

GEORGE WALLACE   Radicals were not the only Americans alienated from the political system in 1968. Governor George Wallace of Alabama sensed the frustration among the "average man on the street, this man in the textile mill, this man in the steel mill, this barber, this beautician, the policeman on the beat." In running for president, Wallace sought the support of blue-collar workers and the lower middle classes.

Wallace had first come to national attention in 1963, when he barred integration of the University of Alabama. Briefly, he pursued the Democratic presidential nomination in 1964. For the race in 1968 he formed his own American Independent Party. Wallace took on the "liberals, intellectuals, and long hairs [who] have run this country for too long." He did

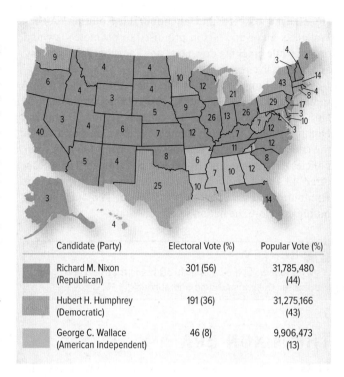

Candidate (Party)	Electoral Vote (%)	Popular Vote (%)
Richard M. Nixon (Republican)	301 (56)	31,785,480 (44)
Hubert H. Humphrey (Democratic)	191 (36)	31,275,166 (43)
George C. Wallace (American Independent)	46 (8)	9,906,473 (13)

Election of 1968

not simply appeal to law and order, militarism, and white backlash; he was too sharp for that. With roots in southern Populism, he called for federal job-training programs, stronger unemployment benefits, national health insurance, a higher minimum wage, and a further extension of union rights. Many Robert Kennedy voters shifted to Wallace. A quarter of all union members backed him.

NIXON'S "SILENT MAJORITY"   Richard Nixon, too, sought the votes of disgruntled Democrats, especially those from the once solidly Democratic South. Republicans had long been identified with big business and the money power, but Nixon himself had modest roots. He came from a middle-class family and at Duke Law School was so pinched for funds that he lived in an abandoned toolshed. His dogged hard work earned him the somewhat dubious nickname of "iron pants." And Nixon well understood the disdain ordinary laborers felt for "kids with beards from the suburbs" who seemed always to be insisting, protesting, *demanding*. Nixon believed himself a representative of the **"silent majority,"** as he later described it, not a strident minority.

He thus set two campaign goals: to distance himself from President Johnson on Vietnam and to turn Wallace's "average Americans" into a Republican majority. The Vietnam issue was delicate, because Nixon had generally supported the war. As he told one aide, "I've come to the conclusion that there's no way to win the war. But we can't say that, of course. In fact, we have to seem to say the opposite." During the campaign he hinted that he had a secret plan to end the war but steadfastly refused to disclose it.

| *Chicago police confront protesters during the 1968 Democratic National Convention. With provocation on both sides, violence inevitably erupted.*

He pledged only to find an honorable solution. As for Wallace's followers, Nixon promised to promote "law and order" while cracking down on "pot," pornography, protest, and permissiveness.

Hubert Humphrey, facing the ruins of the Chicago convention, undertook a daunting task. All through September, antiwar protesters dogged his campaign with "Dump the Hump" posters. Although Humphrey picked up steam late in the campaign (partly by cautiously criticizing Johnson's war policies), the last-minute surge was not enough. Nixon captured 43.4 percent of the popular vote to 42.7 percent for Humphrey and 13.5 percent for Wallace. The outcome did nothing to close the nation's deep divisions.

REVIEW

What four or five events in 1968 made that year a turning point for the war at home and abroad?

THE NIXON ERA

IN RICHARD NIXON, AMERICANS HAD elected two men to the presidency. The public Nixon appeared to be a traditional small-town conservative who cherished individual initiative, chamber-of-commerce capitalism, Fourth of July patriotism, and middle-class Victorian values. The private Nixon was a troubled man. His language among intimates was caustic and profane. He waxed bitter toward those he saw as enemies. Never a natural public speaker, he was physically rather awkward—a White House aide once found toothmarks on a "childproof " aspirin cap the president had been unable to pry open. The public Nixon seemed to search out challenges— "crises" to face and conquer.

Vietnamization—and Cambodia

HENRY KISSINGER A settlement of the Vietnam "crisis" thus became one of Nixon's first priorities. He found a congenial ally in National Security Advisor Henry Kissinger. Kissinger, an intensely ambitious Harvard academic, shared with the new president a global vision of foreign affairs. Like Nixon, Kissinger had a tendency to pursue his ends secretly, circumventing the traditional channels such as the State Department.

Both men wanted to end the war but insisted on "peace with honor." That meant leaving a pro-American South Vietnamese government behind. The strategy Nixon adopted was "Vietnamization," a gradual withdrawal of American troops as a way to advance peace talks in Paris. The burden of fighting would shift to the South Vietnamese army. Critics likened this strategy to little more than "changing the color of the corpses." All the same, as the media shifted their focus to the peace talks, the public had the impression the war was winding down.

At the same time, Nixon hoped to drive the North Vietnamese into negotiating peace on American terms. Quite consciously, he traded on his reputation as a cold warrior

who would stop at nothing. As he explained to his chief of staff, Robert Haldeman:

> I call it the Madman Theory, Bob. I want the North Vietnamese to believe that I've reached the point where I might do anything to stop the war. We'll just slip the word to them that, "for God's sake, you know Nixon is obsessed about Communists. We can't restrain him when he's angry—and he has his hand on the nuclear button"—and Ho Chi Minh himself will be in Paris in two days begging for peace.

INVADING CAMBODIA In the spring of 1969 the president launched a series of bombing attacks against North Vietnamese supply depots inside neighboring Cambodia. Johnson had refused to widen the war in this manner, fearing domestic reaction. Nixon simply kept the raids secret.

Ho Chi Minh's death in 1969 did not weaken the North's resolve. His successors continued to reject any offer that did not end with complete American withdrawal and an abandonment of the South Vietnamese military government. Once again Nixon turned up the heat. Over the opposition of his secretaries of defense and state, he ordered American troops into Cambodia to wipe out reported North Vietnamese bases there. On April 30, 1970, he announced the "incursion" of American troops, proclaiming that he would not allow "the world's most powerful nation" to act "like a pitiful helpless giant."

The wave of protests that followed included the fatal clashes between authorities and students at Kent State and Jackson State as well as another march on Washington by 100,000 protesters. Congress was upset enough to repeal the Tonkin Gulf Resolution, a symbolic rejection of Nixon's invasion. After two months American troops left Cambodia, having achieved little.

Fighting a No-Win War

For a time, Vietnamization seemed to work. As more American troops went home, the South Vietnamese forces improved modestly. But for American GIs still in the country, morale became a serious problem. Why were the "grunts" in the field still being asked to put their lives on the line, when it was becoming clear there would be no victory? The anger surfaced increasingly in incidents known as "fragging," in which GIs threw fragmentation grenades at officers who pursued the war too aggressively.

Nor could the army isolate itself from the trends dividing American society. Just as young Americans "turned on" to marijuana and hallucinogens, so soldiers in Vietnam used drugs. Black GIs brought with them from home the issues of black power. One white medic noticed that when Muhammad Ali refused to be drafted, African Americans in his unit began "to question why they were fighting the Honky's war against other Third World people."

The Move toward Détente

Despite Nixon's insistence on "peace with honor," Vietnam was not a war he had chosen to fight. And both Kissinger and Nixon recognized that by 1968 the United States no longer had the resources to dominate international relations around the globe. The Soviet Union remained their prime concern.

| During President Nixon's visit to China, he and his wife, Pat, were escorted to a performance of a ballet, Red Detachment of Women. *Written by a radical actress, Jiang Qing, and based on a true story, the ballet tells of a young woman who leads an uprising against an oppressive landlord and eventually joins a band of female communist revolutionaries. Nixon, Henry Kissinger, and the other Americans who attended the performance were said to have experienced a mixture of astonishment and boredom.*

©Everett Collection Inc/Alamy

Ever since Khrushchev had backed down at the Cuban missile crisis in 1962, the Soviets had steadily expanded their nuclear arsenal. The Vietnam War also diverted valuable military and economic resources making it difficult for Nixon to address instability in the Middle East and other Third World regions.

NIXON DOCTRINE In what the White House labeled the "Nixon Doctrine," the United States would remain engaged in Asia but shift some of the military burden for containment to other allies: Japan in the Pacific, the shah of Iran in the Middle East, Zaire in central Africa, and the apartheid government in South Africa. At the same time, Nixon and Kissinger looked for new ways to contain Soviet power not simply through nuclear deterrence but through negotiations to ease tensions. This policy was named, from the French, **détente**.

Kissinger and Nixon looked to ease tension by linking separate cold war issues. The arms race burdened the Soviet economy; why not offer American concessions on nuclear missiles? In return, the Soviets would be asked to put pressure on North Vietnam to negotiate an end to the war. Nixon also decided to reach out to Mao Zedong, the Communist Chinese dictator. The Soviets viewed China in some ways as more of a threat than the United States. Nixon thus calculated that they would likely cooperate in order to discourage the Americans from enlarging Chinese power. Playing this "China card" was a significant break from Nixon's conservative past. Republicans had long supported the Nationalists in Taiwan and viewed the Soviet Union and China as part of a Communist monolith. To activate this new strategy, Kissinger slipped off to China on a secret mission and then reappeared to announce the president would travel to China. During that visit in early 1972, Nixon pledged to normalize relations, a move the public enthusiastically embraced.

SALT I Later that year Nixon advanced his plan for détente. In May he traveled to the Soviet Union to join Premier Leonid Brezhnev in signing the first Strategic Arms Limitation Treaty (SALT I). In the agreement, both sides pledged to limit the number of intercontinental ballistic missiles (ICBMs) each side would deploy, as well as agreeing not to develop a new system of antiballistic missiles (ABMs).

Americans were pleased at the prospect of lower cold war tensions. But it was not clear that the linkages achieved in Moscow and Beijing would help free the United States from its war in Vietnam.

REVIEW

In what ways did Richard Nixon escalate the war even as he was working to wind it down?

THE NEW IDENTITY POLITICS

THE LIBERAL TRADITION HAD LONG embraced a belief in the common humanity of all Americans. Lyndon Johnson expressed the notion pungently, updating Shakespeare's Shylock with a Texas twang: "They cry the same tears, they feel hungry the same, they bleed the same." Differences among individuals, liberals argued, came not from race or gender but from cultural circumstances and historical experiences. Out of such beliefs, civil rights advocates committed themselves to an integrated America.

PLURALISM VERSUS ASSIMILATION But just as Vietnam weakened the liberal consensus on the need to contain communism, minority activism challenged liberal assumptions on integration. The emerging politics of the late 1960s substituted a model of **pluralism** for the unified one sought by integrationists. This model hoped to dissolve inequality not by ending divisions of social class,

Farmworkers' Altar

The crucifix suggests that the migrant worker is Catholic. Protestant Christians traditionally used the symbol of the cross without Jesus.

This is the flag of the United Farm Workers, designed at the request of César Chávez. To find out more about its symbolism on the web, what key words would you use in your search?

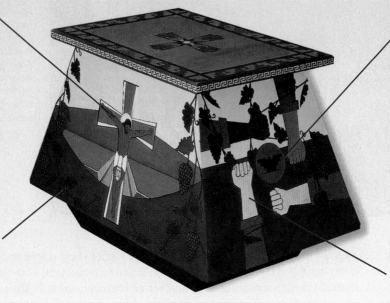

The grape leaves decorating the altar remind people of the UFW's grape boycott.

What do the different skin tones of the arms suggest?

©Smithsonian American Art Museum, Washington, DC/Art Resource, NY

Historians use artworks as a lens through which they can view the beliefs and values of an era. This altar was created by artist Emanuel Martínez at a time when the United Farm Workers were engaged in a campaign for the right to negotiate labor contracts with grape growers. In 1968 César Chávez held a 24-day hunger strike that ended successfully with the celebration of mass. This altar was used at the ceremony, which was attended by farmworkers as well as civil rights supporters, including Senator Robert F. Kennedy. The altar thus had symbolic overtones for the occasion. Most Mexican American farmworkers were devout Catholics, just as many early African American civil rights activists shared a Protestant faith. But other symbols suggest the complexity of the movement's belief system, with allegiance to union activity and political struggle, as well as the movement's connection to Aztec and mestizo traditions of Mexico.

THINKING CRITICALLY

Why would it be appropriate to end a hunger strike with a mass? What other cultural echoes in this decade resonate from the image of a raised, closed fist? In what ways do those symbols link to the "new identity politics"?

---

but by raising up the status of formerly disadvantaged groups—women, African Americans, Latinos, and other hyphenated-Americans. Traditionally, Latino civil rights activists such as LULAC and World War II veterans in the American GI Forum had looked to assimilate into American society. Now minorities began to forge identities in opposition to the prevailing culture. By 1970 black nationalists had abandoned integration for the politics of black pride. To these activists the qualities that distinguished black Americans were what made them distinct— their music, clothing, hairstyles, and religion. In similar ways radical feminists, Latinos, Native Americans, and gays demanded that the nation respect and protect their essential differences.

AFFIRMATIVE ACTION To some degree the Supreme Court had already granted that point in both the *Brown* and *Hernández* decisions of 1954 (see Chapter 29). In each case the Court declared that Latinos and African Americans had suffered not simply as individuals but as groups. To correct past injustices, identity politics called for positive steps—what the Johnson administration called **affirmative action**—to repair the damage done by past injustices.

Latino Activism

The distinct identities of minorities became more visible owing to a new wave of immigration in the 1950s and 1960s from Puerto Rico, Mexico, and Cuba. Historical and cultural ethnic differences among the three major Latino groups made it difficult to develop a common political agenda. Still, some activists did seek a greater unity.

PUERTO RICANS AND CUBANS After World War II more than a million Puerto Ricans migrated to New York City. As citizens of the United States, they could move freely to the mainland and back home again. That dual consciousness discouraged many from establishing deep roots stateside. Equally important, the newcomers were startled to discover that, whatever their status at home, on the mainland they faced racial discrimination and segregation in urban slums. Light-skinned migrants escaped those conditions by blending into the middle class as "Latin Americans." The Puerto Rican community thereby lost some of the leadership it needed to advance its political interests.

Still, during the 1960s groups such as *Aspira* adopted the strategies of civil rights activists and organizations such as the Black and Puerto Rican Caucus created links with other minority groups. The Cubans who arrived in the United States after Fidel Castro came to power in 1959—some 350,000 over the course of the decade—forged fewer ties with other Latinos. Most settled around Miami. An unusually large number came from Cuba's professional, business, and government class and were racially white and politically conservative.

Mexican Americans, however, constituted the largest segment of the Latino population. Until the 1940s most were farmers and farm laborers in Texas, New Mexico, and California. But during the 1950s the process of mechanization pushed them toward the cities—some 85 percent of the population by 1969. With urbanization came a slow improvement in the quality of jobs held. A body of skilled workers, middle-class professionals, and entrepreneurs emerged.

CÉSAR CHÁVEZ AND THE UFW Yet Mexican agricultural workers continued to face harsh working conditions and meager wages. Attempts to unionize faltered partly because workers migrated from job to job and strikebreakers were easily imported. In 1963 a soft-spoken but determined farmworker, César Chávez, recruited fellow organizers Gil Padilla and Dolores Huerta to make another attempt. Their efforts over the next several years led to the formation of the United Farm Workers labor union.

Chávez, like Martin Luther King, proclaimed an ethic of nonviolence. Also like King, he was guided by a deep religious faith (Roman Catholicism in the case of Chávez and

most Mexican American farmworkers). During a strike of Mexican and Filipino grape workers in the summer of 1966, Chávez led a 250-mile march on Sacramento. ("Dr. King had been very successful" with such marches, he noted.) Seeking additional leverage, the UFW organized a consumer boycott of grapes in supermarkets across the nation. Combined with a 24-day hunger strike—a technique Chávez borrowed from Gandhi—the boycott forced growers to negotiate contracts with the UFW beginning in 1970.

CHICANO ACTIVISTS Just as King found his nonviolent approach challenged by radical activists, Chávez saw a new generation of Mexican Americans take up an aggressive

©Arthur Schatz/The LIFE Picture Collection/Getty Images

| *Living conditions were harshest for Mexican Americans among agricultural workers. César Chávez mobilized migrant workers into the United Farm Workers union. Here he meets with Dolores Huerta, his vice president in the UFW in January 1968. Note the three iconic symbols prominently displayed in the office.*

brand of identity politics. Many began calling themselves Chicanos. Like blacks, Chicanos saw themselves as a people whose heritage had been rejected, their labor exploited, and their opportunity for advancement denied. In Denver, Rodolfo "Corky" Gonzales laid out a blueprint for a separatist Chicano society, with public housing set aside for Chicanos and the development of economically independent barrios. "We are Bronze People with a Bronze Culture," declared Gonzales. "We are a Nation. We are a union of free pueblos. We are Aztlán."

LA RAZA UNIDA   The new activism came from both college and high school students. Like others of the baby-boom generation, Mexican Americans attended college in increasing numbers. In addition, Lyndon Johnson's Educational Opportunity Programs, part of the War on Poverty, brought higher education to thousands more Latinos. By 1968 some 50 Mexican American student organizations had sprung up on college campuses. Two years later *La Raza Unida* (The Race United) launched a third-party movement to gain power in communities in which Chicanos were a majority. The more militant "Brown Berets" adopted the paramilitary tactics and radical rhetoric of the Black Panthers.

The Choices of American Indians

Ironically, the growing strength of the civil rights movement created a threat to Indian tribal identities. During the 1950s the Bureau of Indian Affairs adopted a policy called "termination." To reduce the reservation system, the bureau would cut federal services, gradually sell off tribal lands, and push the people into the "mainstream" of American life.

Although most full-blooded Indians objected to the policy, some of mixed blood and others already assimilated into white society supported the move. The relocation of some 35,000 Indians accelerated a shift from rural areas to cities. The urban Indian population, which had been barely 30,000 in 1940, reached more than 300,000 by the 1970s.

AMERICAN INDIAN MOVEMENT   Still, the activism of the 1960s inspired Indian leaders to shape their own political agenda. In 1968 urban activists in Minneapolis created AIM, the American Indian Movement. A year later like-minded Indians living around San Francisco Bay formed Indians of All Tribes. Because the Bureau of Indian Affairs refused to address the problems of urban Indians, militant members of the organization seized the abandoned federal prison on Alcatraz Island in San Francisco Bay. The Alcatraz action, though short-lived, inspired calls for a national Pan-Indian rights movement.

Then in 1973 AIM organizers Russell Means and Dennis Banks led a dramatic takeover of a trading post at Wounded Knee, on a Sioux reservation in South Dakota. In 1890 white cavalry had gunned down over a hundred Sioux (Chapter 18), at Wounded Knee. Ever since, it symbolized for Indians the betrayal of white promises and the bankruptcy of reservation policy. Even more, Wounded Knee now demonstrated how difficult it was to achieve unity when so many tribes were determined to go their own ways. Other Indians did not support the militant takeover of Wounded Knee, and federal officers soon forced its occupiers to leave. The movement splintered further as more than 100 different organizations were formed during the 1970s to pursue reform at the local, state, and federal levels.

| In 1890 the U.S. cavalry killed 146 Indians at Wounded Knee, South Dakota. In 1973 members of the American Indian Movement seized the hamlet of Wounded Knee, making it once again a symbol of conflict.
©Bettmann/Getty Images

Asian Americans

In striking down the old quota system, the 1965 Immigration Reform Act led to a sharp increase in the numbers of immigrants from Asia. Asians, who in 1960 made up less than 1 percent of the American population (about a million people), were by 1985 2 percent (about 5 million). This new wave included many middle-class professionals, a lower percentage of Japanese, and far more newcomers from Southeast and South Asia. Earlier civil rights reforms had swept away the legal barriers to full citizenship that had once stigmatized Asians.

Many Americans saw these new immigrants as "model minorities." They possessed skills in high demand, worked hard, were often Christian, and seldom protested. The 1970 census showed Japanese and Chinese Americans with incomes well above the median for white Americans. Such statistics, however, hid fault lines within communities. Although many professionals assimilated into the American mainstream, agricultural laborers and sweatshop workers remained trapped in poverty. And no matter how much Anglos praised their industry, Asian Americans still wore what one sociologist defined as a "racial uniform." They were nonwhites in a white society.

Few Americans were aware of Asian involvement in identity politics. That was in part because the large majority of Asian Americans lived in just three states—Hawaii, California, and New York. Further, Asian Americans were less likely to join the era's vocal protests. Nonetheless, Asian students did join with African Americans, Chicanos, and Native Americans to advocate a "Third World revolution" against the white establishment. Asian students, too, wanted a curriculum that recognized their histories and cultures.

Gay Rights

In 1972 Black Panther Huey Newton observed that homosexuals "might be the most oppressed people" in American society. Certainly, Newton was qualified to recognize oppression when he saw it. But by then a growing number of homosexuals had embraced liberation movements that placed them among minorities demanding equal rights.

Even during the "conformist" 1950s, gay men founded the Mattachine Society (1951) to fight antihomosexual attacks and to press for wider public acceptance. Lesbians formed a similar organization, the Daughters of Bilitis, in 1955. Beginning in the mid-1960s, more-radical gay and lesbian groups began organizing to raise individual consciousness and to establish a gay culture in which they felt free. One group called for "acceptance as full equals . . . basic rights and equality as citizens; our human dignity; . . . [our] right to love whom we wish."

STONEWALL INCIDENT The movement's defining moment came on Friday, June 27, 1969, when New York

©The Granger Collection, New York

The creation of Ms. *magazine in 1972 gave feminists a means to reach a broader audience. The cover of its first issue used the image of a many-armed Hindu goddess to satirize the many roles of the modern housewife.*

police raided the Stonewall Inn, a Greenwich Village bar. Such raids were common enough: the police regularly harassed gays and lesbians by raiding the places where they gathered. This time the patrons fought back, first with taunts and jeers, then with paving stones and parking meters. Increasingly, gay activists called on homosexuals to "come out of the closet" and publicly affirm their sexuality. In 1974 gays achieved a major symbolic victory when the American Psychiatric Association removed homosexuality from its list of mental disorders.

Feminism

Organized struggle for women's rights and equality in the United States began before the Civil War. Sustained political efforts had won women the vote in 1920. But the women's movement of the 1960s and 1970s began to push for equality in broader, deeper ways.

THE FEMININE MYSTIQUE Writer Betty Friedan was one of the earliest to voice dissatisfaction with the cultural attitudes that flourished after World War II. Even though more women were entering the job market, the media routinely glorified housewives and homemakers while

©James West Davidson

discouraging those who aspired to independent careers. In *The Feminine Mystique* (1963), Friedan identified the "problem that has no name," a dispiriting emptiness in the midst of affluent lives. "Our culture does not permit women to accept or gratify their basic need to grow and fulfill their potentialities as human beings."

The Feminine Mystique gave new life to the women's rights movement. The Commission on the Status of Women appointed by President Kennedy proposed the 1963 Equal Pay Act and helped add gender to the forms of discrimination outlawed by the 1964 Civil Rights Act. Women also assumed an important role in both the civil rights and antiwar movements. They accounted for half the students who went south for the "Freedom Summers" in 1964 and 1965. But even women who joined the protests of the 1960s often found themselves limited to providing menial services such as cooking and laundry. Casey Hayden, a veteran of SDS and SNCC, told her male comrades that the "assumptions of male superiority are as widespread . . . and every much as crippling to the woman as the assumptions of white superiority are to the Negro."

NATIONAL ORGANIZATION FOR WOMEN By 1966 activist women were less willing to remain silent. Friedan joined a group of 24 women and 2 men who formed the National Organization for Women (NOW). In arguing that "sexism" was much like racism, they persuaded President Johnson in 1967 to include women along with African Americans, Hispanics, and other minorities as a group covered by federal affirmative action programs.

Broader social trends established a receptive climate for the feminist appeal. After 1957 the birthrate began a rapid decline; improved methods of contraception, such as the birth control pill, permitted smaller families. By 1970 an unprecedented 40 percent of all women were employed outside the home. Education also spurred the shift from home to the workplace, since higher educational levels allowed women to enter an economy oriented increasingly toward white-collar service industries rather than blue-collar manufacturing.

Equal Rights and Abortion

As its influence grew, the feminist movement translated women's grievances into a political agenda. In 1967 NOW proclaimed a "bill of rights" that called for maternity leave for working mothers, federally supported day care facilities, child care tax deductions, and equal education and job training. But feminists divided on two other issues: the passage of an Equal Rights Amendment to the Constitution and a repeal of state antiabortion laws.

ROE V. WADE At first, support seemed strong for an Equal Rights Amendment that forbade all discrimination on the basis of gender. In 1972 both the House and the Senate passed the Equal Rights Amendment (ERA) virtually without opposition. Within a year, 28 of the necessary 38 states had approved the ERA. It seemed only a matter of time before 10 more state legislatures would complete its ratification. Many in the women's movement also applauded the Supreme Court's decision, in *Roe v. Wade* (1973), to strike down 46 state laws restricting a woman's access to abortion. In his opinion for the majority, Justice Harry Blackmun observed that a woman in the nineteenth century had "enjoyed a substantially broader right to terminate a pregnancy than she does in most states today." As legal abortion in the first three months of pregnancy became more readily available, the rate of maternal deaths from illegal operations, especially among minorities, declined.

But the early success of the Equal Rights Amendment and the feminist triumph in *Roe v. Wade* masked underlying divisions among women's groups. *Roe v. Wade* triggered a sharp backlash from many Catholics, Protestant evangelicals, and socially conservative women. Their opposition inspired a crusade for a "right to life" amendment to the Constitution. A similar conservative reaction breathed new life into the "STOP ERA" crusade of Phyllis Schlafly, an Illinois political organizer. Although a professional herself, Schlafly believed that women should embrace their traditional role as homemakers subordinate to their husbands. "Every change [that the ERA] requires will deprive women of a right, benefit, or exemption that they now enjoy," she argued. By 1979 supporters of ERA were forced to admit that they would not succeed in convincing the necessary three-fourths of the state legislatures to ratify the amendment.

> ✓ **REVIEW**
>
> How did each of the following groups work to change their identities and status in American society: Latinos, women, Indians, Asian Americans, and gays?

TWO VIEWS OF THE LIBERATION OF WOMEN

The publication of Betty Friedan's The Feminine Mystique in 1963 triggered a sharp debate about the role of women in society. Gloria Steinem emerged as one of the primary spokespersons for feminists who stressed economic and sexual liberation as crucial to equal standing for women. She created Ms. magazine to provide a forum for feminist ideas and interests. Efforts to pass an Equal Rights Amendment inspired Phyllis Schlafly to become an outspoken advocate for traditional family roles and an ardent opponent of feminism and the ERA. Indeed, she received much of the credit for the amendment's ultimate defeat.

DOCUMENT 1
Gloria Steinem: What Would It Be Like if Women Win?

Women do not want to change places with men. . . . That is not our goal. But we do want to change the economic system to one more based on merit. In Women's Lib Utopia, there will be free access to good jobs—and decent pay for the bad ones women have been performing all along, including housework. Increased skilled labor might lead to a four-hour workday, and higher wages would encourage further mechanization of repetitive jobs now kept alive by cheap labor. . . .

Men will have to give up ruling-class privileges, but in return they will no longer be the only ones to support the family, get drafted, bear the strain of power and responsibility. Freud to the contrary, anatomy is not destiny, at least not for more than nine months at a time. In Israel women are drafted, and some have gone to war. . . . In Sweden, both parents take care of the children. In this country, come utopia, men and women won't reverse roles; they will be free to choose according to individual talents and preferences.

If role reform sounds sexually unsettling, think how it will change the sexual hypocrisy we have now. No more sex arranged on the barter system, with women pretending interest, and men never sure whether they are loved for themselves or for the security few women can get any other way. . . . No more men who are encouraged to spend a lifetime living with inferiors; with housekeepers or dependent creatures who are still children. No more domineering wives, emasculating women, and "Jewish mothers," all of whom are simply human beings with all their normal ambition and drive confined to home. No more unequal partnerships that eventually doom sex and love.

Source: Steinem, Gloria, "What It Would Be Like if Women Win," TIME Magazine, August 31, 1970, 22- 23. Used with permission.

DOCUMENT 2
Phyllis Schlafly: What "Women's Lib" Really Means

Many women are under the mistaken impression that "women's lib" means more job employment opportunities for women, equal pay for equal work, appointments of women to high positions, admitting more women to medical schools, and other desirable objectives which all women favor. . . .

But all this is only a sweet syrup which covers the deadly poison masquerading as "women's lib." The women's libbers are radicals who are waging a total assault on the family, on marriage, and on children. Don't take my word for it—read their own literature and prove to yourself what these characters are trying to do. . . .

The women's libbers don't understand that most women want to be wife, mother and homemaker—and are happy in that role. The women's libbers actively resent the mother who stays at home with her children and likes it that way. The principal purpose of *Ms.*'s shrill tirade is to sow seeds of discontent among happy, married women so that all women can be unhappy in some new sisterhood of frustrated togetherness. . . .

It hasn't occurred to [these women's libbers] that a woman's best "escape from isolation and boredom" is . . . a husband and children who love her.

Source: From the Phyllis Schlafly Report 5, No. 7, February 1972.

THINKING CRITICALLY

In what ways do both writers deal in stereotypes and generalizations? At what class of women are their appeals aimed? On what points do they most strongly disagree? Could you describe grounds on which the two writers might agree or their views might be reconciled? Which of the two more accurately anticipates the situation in which women find themselves today?

VALUE POLITICS: THE CONSUMER AND ENVIRONMENTAL MOVEMENTS

AMONG THOSE SEEKING TO CHANGE America were reformers who defined themselves by their ideas and values rather than by personal identity. Where many participants in identity politics viewed themselves as outsiders, consumer advocates and environmentalists generally came from the social mainstream. Still, they shared with the counterculture a worry that excessive materialism wasted resources and generated pollution, while too many corporations exploited the public through misleading advertising and shoddy, even dangerous, products.

Technology and Unbridled Growth

SOURCES OF POLLUTION As early as 1962, marine biologist Rachel Carson had warned in *Silent Spring* against the widespread use of chemical pesticides, especially DDT (see Chapter 29). But pesticides were only one aspect of what environmentalists considered misguided technology. A report issued in 1965 indicated that every river near an urban area in the United States was polluted, save one (the St. Croix near St. Paul, Minnesota). Certainly, anyone with a sense of irony could not help marveling that the industrially fouled Cuyahoga River running through Cleveland, Ohio, burst into flames in 1969. Smog, radioactive fallout, lethal pesticides, and polluted rivers were the by-products of a society wedded to technology and unbridled economic growth.

To consumer advocates, rising fatality rates on American highways signaled another kind of corporate failure. Besides contributing to smog and other forms of pollution, many automobiles were inherently dangerous to their occupants. That was a conclusion announced by reformer Ralph Nader in his 1965 exposé, *Unsafe at Any Speed*. Nader's particular target was the rear-engine Chevrolet Corvair. General Motors' internal studies confirmed crash data that the Corvair tended to flip over during turns or skidded uncontrollably. Though the company fixed the problem, it also hired private investigators to try to discredit Nader.

The company picked the wrong target. Nader was the son of immigrant Lebanese parents who supported their son's success at Princeton and Harvard Law School. He lived simply and had no vices. And when he discovered GM's campaign against him, he successfully sued. GM's embarrassed president publicly apologized, but by then Nader had become a counterculture hero. In 1966 Congress passed the National Traffic and Motor Vehicle Safety Act and the Highway Safety Act. For the first time, the government required seatbelts and set safety standards for cars, tires, and roads.

NADER'S RAIDERS With the money from his lawsuit, Nader founded a consumer advocacy organization in 1969, the Center for the Study of Responsive Law. His staff of low-paid but eager lawyers, student interns, and volunteers investigated a wide range of consumer and environmental issues. "Nader's Raiders," as his staff was called, shared their leader's view that it was time for corporations "to stop stealing, stop deceiving, stop corrupting politicians with money, stop monopolizing, stop poisoning the earth, air and water, stop selling dangerous products, stop exposing workers to cruel hazards." In the tradition of progressive reform, Nader looked to an interventionist government and informed citizen-consumers to regulate corporate behavior.

FOCUS ON ECOLOGY Many environmentalists, too, had links to the Progressive Era and the idea that government action could police corporate irresponsibility and preserve scenic and natural wonders for the benefit of future generations. What made modern environmentalism distinct was a growing focus on the field of ecology. Since

©Bettmann/Getty Images

"Some river! Chocolate brown, oily, bubbling with subsurface gases, it oozes rather than flows." So Time *magazine described the Cuyahoga River when it caught fire in 1969. Newspaper photographers arrived too late to record that fire, but* Time *was able to run a photo of the blazing Cuyahoga anyway—because the river had also caught fire in 1868, 1883, 1887, 1912, 1936, 1941, 1948, and—most disastrously—in 1952, as shown here.*

the early twentieth century, this biological science had demonstrated how closely life processes throughout nature depended on one another. In condemning the abuse of pesticides, Rachel Carson had called for a **biocentric** approach to nature rather than an anthropocentric, or human-centered, one.

Barry Commoner, a politically active biologist, argued in his book *The Closing Circle* (1971) that modern society courted disaster by trying to "improve on nature." American farmers, for example, greatly increased their crop yields by switching from animal manures to artificial fertilizers. But the change consumed large quantities of energy, raised costs, often left soils sterile, and polluted nearby water. By the 1970s chemical discharges had virtually killed Lake Erie. Technology might prove profitable in the short run, Commoner argued, but in the long run modern methods were bankrupting the environment.

Political Action

ENVIRONMENTAL PROTECTION AGENCY Although he was no friend of liberal reform, President Nixon sensed that these value movements had broad popular appeal. His administration supported the passage of the National Environmental Policy Act of 1969, which required environmental impact statements for all major public projects. And in 1970 Nixon established the Environmental Protection Agency (EPA), whose first major act recognized Rachel Carson's campaign by banning most domestic uses of DDT. The president also signed a bill establishing an Occupational Safety and Health Agency (OSHA) to enforce health and safety standards in the workplace, and the Endangered Species, Clean Water, and Clean Air Acts.

EARTH DAY On April 22, 1970, millions of Americans demonstrated their commitment to a healthy environment as they celebrated the first Earth Day. Their enthusiasm reflected the movement's dual appeal: it was both practical in seeking to improve the quality of air, water, and earth and spiritual in celebrating the unity of living things. But Senator Gaylord Nelson of Wisconsin, who helped bring Earth Day about, appreciated the occasion's radical implications: "The Establishment sees this as a great big antilitter campaign. Wait until they find out what it really means . . . to clean up our earth."

The Legacy of Identity and Value Politics

Earth Day did not signal a consensus on an environmental ethic. President Nixon, for one, was unwilling to impose regulations that stifled growth, especially when facing a troubled economy. Radical activists "aren't really one damn bit interested in safety or clean air," he commented to one industry group. "What they are interested in is destroying the system." If he faced "a flat choice between jobs and smoke," nature would lose.

NIXON'S SOUTHERN STRATEGY Nixon's political instincts were shrewd. Rather than fight the popular tides, he rode them, basking, for example, in the triumphant *Apollo 11* moon landing in 1969. At the same time, he resisted those such as affirmative action that offended Republicans and traditional Democrats. Both the 1968 and 1972 presidential elections revealed a shift in political power toward the southern and western rims of the United States where traditional values flourished and where whites, in the wake of the civil rights revolution, were deserting the Democrats. These were the voters Nixon courted, in what he sometimes referred to as his "southern strategy" to replace the old New Deal coalition with a new Republican majority. By the early 1970s his silent majority worried more about job security than clean air and water. As one bumper sticker declared: "Out of work? Hungry? Eat an environmentalist."

The president sought to channel a similar backlash against identity politics. Conservatives opposed many of the era's reforms, including the Equal Rights Amendment, the integration of private clubs, and the use of racial and gender quotas for jobs and college admissions. Merit, not race or gender, should determine an individual's opportunities, they argued.

©Hulton Archive/Getty Images

| *The first Earth Day, 1970. Although President Nixon created the Environmental Protection Agency, he recognized the costs of environmental regulation did not play well with voters in the "silent majority" and the world of business. So he distanced himself from the environmental movement.*

The Making of a Quagmire: Vietnam

ENTANGLEMENT	ESCALATION	ESCAPE
1948 French name Bao Dai head of Vietnam. U.S. begins funding the French war.	**1961** President Kennedy orders 3,000 military "advisors" to Vietnam. Number rises to 16,000 by 1963.	**1968** Tet Offensive. Johnson withdraws from presidential race. Paris peace talks. Nixon claims plan to end the war.
1954 French defeated at Dien Bien Phu. Ngo Dinh Diem arrives in South Vietnam.	**1962** Military coup assassinates Diem November 2. Kennedy assassinated November 22.	**1969** Nixon bombs Cambodia; "Vietnamization." My Lai revealed. Renewed anti-war demonstrations.
1955–1956 Diem, with U.S. backing, rejects Geneva Accord provision for free elections.	**1964** Tonkin Gulf Resolution gives Johnson authority to take "all necessary measures."	**1970** Paris peace talks. U.S. invades Cambodia; Kent State and Jackson State shootings.
1959 Diem's repressive measures provoke armed resistance in the South.	**1965** Johnson escalates the U.S. role in the war.	**1971** Pentagon Papers published.
1960 National Liberation Front (NLF) created to oppose Diem.	**1966** Senate hearings on the war. U.S. troop levels reach 362,000.	**1972** "Christmas bombing" of North Vietnam.
	1967 March on Washington. U.S. troops at 535,000.	**1973** January agreement reached in Paris. Last U.S. combat troops leave South Vietnam.
		1974 Nixon resigns over Watergate. Congress rejects new military aid to South Vietnam.
		1975 Fall of Saigon. Vietnam War ends.

(top) ©Mirrorpix/The Image Works; *(bottom)* Source: National Archives & Records Administration (531457)

Ethnic identity organizations such as the Italian American Civil Rights League spoke out against affirmative action for minorities.

Most labor leaders also resisted the push for affirmative action. Rising inflation and the erosion of high-wage, union employment in major industries such as automobiles, steel, and consumer technologies left them on the defensive. They worried more about providing older members security and benefits than addressing issues that mattered to younger workers, such as job safety, working conditions, and opportunities for minorities and women. George Meany, head of the powerful AFL/CIO and an anticommunist, remained a strong supporter of the Vietnam War. And when Jock Yablonski led an insurgent movement to oust the corrupt leadership of the United Mine Workers, the union president, Tony Boyle, hired gunmen who murdered Yablonski and his wife and daughter.

Despite the backlash against reform, even critics could not deny that political and social activists had empowered people who had long seen themselves as "other" Americans who had been excluded. The reforms of the 1960s opened doors to jobs, careers, and avenues of success previously closed to all but white males. Inevitably, however, a pluralistic approach to equality tended to fragment rather than unify the nation. The road to equality—whether in the workplace, schools, or even the bedroom—remained a fault line dividing the nation.

The End of the War

Like identity politics the continuing debate over Vietnam continued to divide America. A peace settlement there eluded President Nixon because the North Vietnamese continued to reject any agreement that left the South Vietnamese government in power. Unwilling to send back American troops, in May 1972 Nixon instead mined and blockaded North Vietnam's major port, Haiphong, along with a sustained bombing campaign. In December he launched an even greater wave of

©Bill Ray/The LIFE Picture Collection/Getty Images

| Members of Nixon's "silent majority" resented antiwar and minority group protesters. This man, who lost his son in Vietnam, attacks "America's noisy scum."

attacks, as American planes dropped more bombs in 12 days than they had from 1969 to 1971.

Ironically, South Vietnamese leaders threw up the greatest obstacle to a settlement, for they were rightly convinced that General Thieu's regime would not last once the United States departed. But by January 1973, with Kissinger back in Paris, a treaty was finally arranged. Three months later the last American units were home.

> ✓ **REVIEW**
>
> How did the environmental movement attempt to change attitudes toward American habits and everyday life?

PRAGMATIC CONSERVATISM

PHILADELPHIA PLAN IN AUGUST 1969, 4,000 ANGRY white union workers marched on city hall in Pittsburgh, Pennsylvania. There, a confrontation with police turned violent, leaving 50 protesters injured and 200 under arrest. A month later the scene repeated itself in Chicago, where hundreds of construction workers "slugged it out with 400 policemen." In both cases the issue was the "Philadelphia Plan" for affirmative action. Under it, the Nixon administration adopted the rule set forth under Lyndon Johnson in 1967 that government funding would be provided only if contractors' bids had "the result of producing minority group representations in all trades and in all phases of the construction project." The building trades unions wanted to know why they had been singled out when so many other industries did not meet those goals. Race played a role as well. "Why should these guys be given special consideration, just because they happen to be black?" one angry worker asked.

By 1969 affirmative action had become a political hot potato and Richard Nixon knew it. Over the course of his first term the president charted a pragmatic course, preserving and even expanding popular entitlements such as Social Security, seeking a middle ground on civil rights and affirmative action, while following the liberal tides in areas such as environmental protection.

Nixon's New Federalism

Nixon envisioned his New Federalism as a conservative counter to liberal programs run by the federal government. Passed in 1972, a revenue-sharing act distributed $30 billion over five years in federal block grants to state and local governments. Instead of the funds being earmarked for specific purposes, localities could decide which problems needed attention and how best to attack them. A similar approach influenced aid to individuals. In the past, liberal programs from the New Deal to the Great Society often provided specific services to individuals: job retraining programs, Head Start programs for preschoolers, food supplement programs for nursing mothers. Republicans argued that such a "service strategy" too often assumed that federal bureaucrats best understood what the poor needed. Nixon favored an "income strategy," which gave recipients money to spend as they saw fit. Such grants were meant to encourage initiative and reduce government bureaucracy. Even if Nixon was determined to reverse the liberalism of the 1960s, he was hardly a deep-dyed conservative.

Stagflation

Ironically, a worsening economy forced Nixon to adopt liberal remedies. By 1970 the nation had entered its first recession in a decade. Normally a recession brought a decrease in demand for goods and a rise in unemployment as workers were laid off. Manufacturers then cut prices in order to encourage demand for their goods and cut wages in order to preserve profit margins. But in the recession of 1970, unemployment rose as economists would have expected, yet wages and prices were also rising in an inflationary spiral—a condition described as "stagflation."

Unfriendly Democrats labeled the phenomenon "Nixonomics," although in truth Lyndon Johnson had brought on inflation by refusing to raise taxes to pay for the war and for Great Society social programs. In addition, wages continued to rise partly because powerful unions had negotiated automatic cost-of-living increases into their contracts. Similarly, where a few large corporations dominated an industry, like steel and oil, prices and wages ignored market forces and continued to rise as demand and employment fell. Nixon added inflationary pressures by greatly increasing the numbers eligible for Social Security and pegging benefits to rises in the cost of living.

Mindful that his own "silent majority" were the people most pinched by the slower economy, Nixon decided that unemployment posed a greater threat than inflation. Announcing "I am now a Keynesian," he adopted a deficit budget designed to stimulate the growth of jobs. More surprising, in August 1971 he declared that to provide short-term relief, wages and prices would be frozen for 90 days. For a Republican to advocate wage and price controls was near heresy, almost as heretical as Nixon's overtures to China. For a year federal wage and price boards enforced the ground rules for any increases until the economy grew again. Controls were lifted in January 1973. As in foreign policy, Nixon had reversed long-cherished policies to achieve practical results.

Social Policies and the Court

SCHOOL BUSING Affirmative action, school prayer, contraception, criminal rights, obscenity, and school busing were all issues on which Supreme Court decisions offended the silent majority. By and large the liberal Court placed rights and liberties ahead of traditional values and law enforcement. The justices recognized, for example, that 15 years after its *Brown v. Board of Education* decision, most school districts

remained segregated. In white neighborhoods, parents opposed having their children bused to more distant, formerly all-black schools as part of a plan to achieve racial balance. Although black parents for their part worried about how their children might be treated in hostile white neighborhoods, by and large they supported busing as a means to better education.

THE NIXON COURT Under Nixon, federal policy on desegregation took a 180-degree turn. In 1969 the Justice Department supported lawyers for Mississippi who asked the Supreme Court to delay an integration plan. The Court not only rejected that proposal but two years later ruled, in *Swann v. Charlotte-Mecklenburg Board of Education* (1971), that busing, balancing ratios, and redrawing school district lines were all acceptable ways to achieve integration. Given the continuing liberal activism of the Court, the president looked to change its direction by filling vacancies with more conservative justices. He replaced Chief Justice Earl Warren in 1969 with Warren Burger, a jurist who had no wish to break new ground. When another vacancy occurred in 1969, Nixon tried twice to appoint conservative southern judges with reputations for opposing civil rights and labor unions. Congress rejected both. In the end, the president nominated Minnesotan Harry Blackmun, a moderate judge of unimpeachable integrity. Two more conservative appointments guaranteed that the Court would no longer lead the fight for minority rights. But neither would it reverse the achievements of the Warren Court.

Triumph and Revenge

MCGOVERN AND LIBERAL DEMOCRATS As the election of 1972 approached, Nixon's majority seemed to be falling into place, especially after the Democrats nominated Senator George McGovern of South Dakota. McGovern's nomination gave Nixon the split between "us" and "them" he sought. The Democratic platform embraced all the activist causes that the silent majority resented. It called for immediate withdrawal from Vietnam, abolition of the draft, amnesty for war resisters, and a minimum guaranteed income for the poor. By November the only question that remained to be settled was the size of Nixon's majority. He received almost 61 percent of the popular vote.

Yet the overwhelming victory did not relieve the president's urge to settle scores. In his political battles, Nixon exhibited a tendency to see issues in terms of a very personal "us against them." "We have not used the power in the first four years, as you know . . . ," he remarked to his chief of staff, H. R. Haldeman, "but things are going to change now." The administration began compiling an "enemies list"—everyone from television news correspondents to student activists—to be targeted for audits by the Internal Revenue Service or other forms of harassment.

THE "PLUMBERS" AND THE PENTAGON PAPERS In truth, Nixon had already begun to abuse his presidential powers. In June 1971 *The New York Times* published a secret, often highly critical military study of the Vietnam War, soon dubbed the "Pentagon Papers." Angrily the president authorized a secret group known as "the plumbers" to burglarize the office of a psychiatrist treating the disillusioned official who leaked the study. The burglars hoped to find records that were personally damaging.

Break-In

The president's fall from power began with what seemed a minor event. In June 1972 burglars entered the Democratic National Committee headquarters, located in Washington's plush Watergate apartment complex. The five burglars were an unusual lot. When they were arrested, they wore business suits and carried bugging devices, tear-gas guns, and more than $2,000 in crisp new 100-dollar bills. One had worked for the CIA. Another was carrying an address book whose phone numbers included that of a Howard Hunt at the "W. House." Nixon's press secretary dismissed the break-in as "a third-rate burglary attempt," and Nixon himself announced that "no one on the White House staff . . . was involved in this very bizarre incident. What really hurts in matters of this sort is not the fact that they occur," the president continued. "What really hurts is if you try to cover up."

In January 1973 the burglars were tried along with former White House aides E. Howard Hunt Jr. and G. Gordon Liddy. Judge John Sirica was not satisfied with the defendants' guilty plea. He wanted to know who had directed the burglars and why "these 100-dollar bills were floating around like coupons." Facing a stiff jail sentence, one of the burglars admitted that the defendants had been bribed to plead guilty and

were protecting higher government officials. Soon after, the president accepted the resignations of his two closest aides, H. R. Haldeman and John Ehrlichman. He also fired John Dean, his White House counsel, after Dean agreed to cooperate with prosecutors.

To the Oval Office

WHITE HOUSE TAPES   Over the summer of 1973 a string of officials testified at televised Senate hearings. Each witness took the trail of the burglary and its cover-up higher into White House circles. Then John Dean gave his testimony. Young, with a Boy Scout's face, Dean declared in a quiet monotone that the president had personally been involved in the cover-up. Still, it remained Dean's word against the president's until Senate committee staff discovered, almost by chance, that since 1970 Nixon had been secretly recording all conversations and phone calls in the Oval Office.

Obtaining that crucial evidence proved no easy task. Nixon agreed to appoint a special prosecutor, Harvard law professor Archibald Cox, to investigate the new disclosures, but when Cox subpoenaed the tapes of the conversations and phone calls, the president refused to turn them over. As that battle raged and the astonished public wondered if matters could possibly get worse, they did. Evidence unrelated to Watergate revealed that Vice President Spiro Agnew had systematically solicited bribes, both as governor of Maryland and while serving in Washington. He resigned the vice presidency in October. Under provisions of the Twenty-Fifth Amendment, Nixon appointed Representative Gerald R. Ford of Michigan to replace Agnew.

| Under the leadership of the folksy but razor-sharp Senator Sam Ervin of North Carolina, the Senate committee investigating the Watergate scandal attracted a large television audience. John Dean (center), the former White House legal counsel, provided the most damning evidence linking President Nixon to the cover-up—until the existence of secretly recorded White House tapes became known.
©AP Photo

Then on Saturday night, October 20, Nixon fired Special Prosecutor Cox. Reaction to this "Saturday Night Massacre" was overwhelming: 150,000 telegrams poured into Washington, and by the following Tuesday, 84 House members had sponsored 16 different bills of impeachment. The beleaguered president turned over the tapes to a new special prosecutor, Texas lawyer Leon Jaworski. Jaworski's investigations led him to request additional tapes and again the president refused, although he grudgingly supplied some 1,200 pages of typed transcripts. Littered with cynicism and profanity, even these edited documents revealed Nixon talking with his counsel John Dean about how to "take care of the jackasses who are in jail." When Dean estimated it might take a million dollars to buy their silence, Nixon replied, "We could get that. . . . You could get a million dollars. And you could get it in cash. I know where it could be gotten." Finally, Special Prosecutor Jaworski petitioned the Supreme Court to order release of the tapes he requested. In *United States v. Nixon,* the Court ruled unanimously in Jaworski's favor.

Resignation

The end came quickly. The House Judiciary Committee adopted three articles of impeachment, charging that Nixon had obstructed justice, had abused his constitutional authority in improperly using federal agencies to harass citizens, and had hindered the committee's investigation.

The tapes showed that on June 23, 1972, only a few days after the break-in, Nixon knew the burglars were tied to the White House staff and knew that Attorney General John Mitchell had acted to limit an FBI investigation. Not willing to be the first president convicted in a Senate impeachment trial, Nixon resigned on August 8, 1974. The following day Gerald Ford became president. "The Constitution works," Ford told a relieved nation. "Our long national nightmare is over."

The Road's End for Vietnam and Liberalism

As an unelected president, Gerald Ford had no popular mandate. Ford hoped to put Watergate behind the nation rather than look backward in recrimination. To that end, only a month into office and without any warning, he granted Richard Nixon a full pardon for any crimes he might have committed. But the pardon succeeded only in deepening the nation's cynicism, because Nixon would never face prosecution nor assume responsibility for his crimes.

And then there was still Vietnam, where in January 1975 North Vietnamese forces renewed their offense against the South. President Ford implored Congress to grant $1 billion in emergency aid, but the nation's political will was exhausted. "My God, we're all tired of it, we're sick to death of it," exclaimed one citizen in Oregon. "55,000 dead and $100 billion spent and for what?" In April 1975 Saigon fell, amid scenes of desperate Americans and South Vietnamese fighting to squeeze onto evacuation helicopters.

By then more than Saigon had fallen; and more than a foreign policy had failed in Vietnam. The liberalism of Lyndon Johnson's Great Society—of Franklin Roosevelt's New Deal and Harry Truman's Square Deal had reached its high-water mark and was now receding, amid the battles over the war. Like all wars, Vietnam changed more in the nation's society than anyone ever expected.

✓ **REVIEW**

In which ways did Richard Nixon's domestic policies mark a conservative turn, and in which ways take a more liberal approach to governing?

PUTTING HISTORY IN GLOBAL CONTEXT

"THE ENEMY MUST FIGHT his battles far from his home base for a long time," a Vietnamese strategist once wrote. "We must further weaken him by drawing him into protracted campaigns. Once his initial dash is broken, it will be easier to destroy him." The enemy in question was not the Americans, nor the French, but the Mongol invaders of 1284 CE. The strategy of resistance and attrition that kept the Chinese at bay for centuries also defeated the United States. Between 1961 and 1973, the war cost billions in national treasure and left some 57,000 soldiers dead and over 300,000 wounded. The cost to Southeast Asia was even more incalculable. Much of the land lay devastated, and some 6.5 million South Vietnamese had become refugees along with 3 million Laotians and Cambodians. In excess of 3 million Vietnamese soldiers and civilians died during the war.

Defeat in Vietnam marked the end of liberalism triumphant and offered a stark reminder of the limits of American power. No longer did most Americans believe that the world could be remade in their image. While the United States waged its futile war in Vietnam, power had shifted to the growing economies of Europe and the Pacific Rim and to the members of OPEC. If Richard Nixon had not overreached, he might have replaced the liberal creed with a new conservative approach to government. But Nixon had exceeded the limits of presidential power in his desire for mastery, just as liberalism exceeded its limits in the quagmire of Lyndon Johnson's war. The rise of a new conservative tide would have to wait for a new quest to restore America's power and prestige.

CHAPTER SUMMARY

Though presidents from Truman to Nixon sent American forces to Indochina, Vietnam was Lyndon Johnson's war, and the political divisions it caused ended both his presidency and the consensus on liberal reform.

- To force the North Vietnamese to negotiate, Johnson escalated the American war effort. By 1966 American soldiers were doing most of the fighting. American warplanes subjected North Vietnam to heavy bombing.

- As the nation divided into prowar hawks and antiwar doves, the Vietcong's Tet Offensive shocked Americans. Johnson almost lost the New Hampshire presidential primary to Senator Eugene McCarthy, leading the president to abandon his reelection campaign.

- In the wake of the assassinations of Martin Luther King Jr. and Robert Kennedy, Hubert Humphrey became the Democrats' presidential nominee. But riots at the Democratic National Convention in Chicago so damaged Humphrey's candidacy that Richard Nixon won the election, promising a "peace with honor" in Vietnam.

- A wide range of minorities—Latinos, Indians, Asian Americans, gays, and feminists—adopted identity politics as a way to claim their full rights and opportunities as Americans.

  ► Mexican American migrant workers led by César Chávez successfully established a farmworkers' union, the UFW, while a rising generation of Latino students adopted militant techniques for establishing a Chicano identity.

  ► Though often divided by tribal diversity, militant Native Americans called attention to the discrimination faced by Indians in urban settings as well as on reservations.

  ► Feminists campaigned for civil and political equality as well as to change deep-seated cultural attitudes of a "patriarchal" society.

  ► In addition to reform movements based on identity, the value politics of environmentalists and consumer advocates extended the spirit of reform.

- White House involvement in the Watergate break-in and the president's subsequent cover-up led to the first resignation of an American president.

- President Gerald Ford inherited an office weakened by scandal.

- The fall of Vietnam after three decades of debilitating war left liberal ideals in disarray, though Nixon's overreaching in the White House temporarily forestalled a resurgence of conservatism in the United States.

Digging Deeper

Readers interested in the Vietnam War might begin with the 10-part documentary by Ken Burns and Lynn Novick for PBS, *The Vietnam War* (2017), or consult its companion book, Geoffrey C. Ward, *The Vietnam War: An Intimate History* (2017). For the best history of American involvement, see Fredrik Logevall, *Embers of War: The Fall of an Empire and the Making of America's Vietnam* (2014). A useful comparison to another war is Robert K. Brigham, *Iraq, Vietnam, and the Limits of American Power* (2008). The disastrous ecological consequences of the war are detailed in Edwin A. Martini's *Agent Orange: History, Science, and the Politics of Uncertainty* (2012), while Meredith H. Lair's *Armed with Abundance: Consumerism and Soldiering in the Vietnam War* (2011) explores the incredible infrastructure the United States imposed on South Vietnam's preindustrial landscape.

David Kaiser, *American Tragedy: Kennedy, Johnson, and the Origins of the Vietnam War* (2000), and Fredrik Logevall, *Choosing War: The Lost Chance for Peace and the Escalation of War in Vietnam* (1999), both trace the road by which the United States escalated its military commitments in Vietnam. Among those who lay the blame with Lyndon Johnson, see Michael H. Hunt, *Lyndon Johnson's War: America's Cold War Crusade in Vietnam, 1945-1968* (1997); and Lloyd C. Gardner, *Pay Any Price: Lyndon Johnson and the Wars for Vietnam* (1997). For the soldiers' experience, look at the classic by Michael Herr, *Dispatches* (1977); and David Maraniss, *They Marched into Sunlight: War and Peace, Vietnam and America, October 1967* (2004). Maraniss looks simultaneously at soldiers on the battlefront, protest that tore apart the University of Wisconsin, and policymaking in Washington.

Keith W. Olsen's *Watergate: The Presidential Scandal That Shook America* (2003) is a lively brief account of Nixon's fall, while Stanley Kutler's *The Wars of Watergate: The Last Crisis of Richard Nixon* (1992) provides more detail. For a look at the politics of division and emergence of identity and value political movements that divided the nation, see Mark Hamilton Lytle, *America's Uncivil Wars* (2006); and for an argument that the 1970s were more significant than the 1960s, see Bruce J. Schulman, *The Seventies: The Great Shift in American Culture, Society, and Politics* (2002). Gender politics are widely explored in Ruth Rosen, *The World Split Open: How the Modern Women's Movement Changed America* (2001). Union and labor issues are explored in Jefferson Cowie, *Stayin' Alive: The 1970s and the Last Days of the Working Class* (2010). Excellent on the environmental movement is Robert Gottlieb, *Forcing the Spring: The Transformation of the American Environmental Movement* (1996). Mark Hamilton Lytle, *The Gentle Subversive: Rachel Carson,* Silent Spring, *and the Rise of the Environmental Movement* (2007), provides a brief biographical approach to the topic.

For a fresh, nonpartisan look at Richard Nixon, see Melvin Small, *The Presidency of Richard Nixon* (2003), or Richard Reeves, *President Nixon: Alone in the White House* (2002). A dissenter from the camp of Kissinger admirers is Jussi Hanhimaki, *The Flawed Architect: Henry Kissinger and American Foreign Policy* (2004).

An excellent source on the Vietnam Memorial and the controversy over its design is James Reston Jr., *A Rift in the Earth: Art, Memory and the Fight for a Vietnam War Memorial* (2017). On the broader issue of commemoration, see Harriet F. Senie, *Memorials to Shattered Myths: Vietnam to 9/11* (2016).

After the Fact

| Historians Reconstruct the Past |

The Contested Ground of Collective Memory

Perhaps the nation's most cherished commemorative space lies along the mall in Washington, D.C. As the mall makes clear, a culture defines itself by the history it elevates in public places. Such markers are hardly limited to Washington. Town squares boast statues; post office murals portray the deeds of forebears; even sports arenas hang honored jerseys from the rafters. As scholars of commemoration point out, all societies find visible ways to affirm their collective values. But the *history* of how a monument came to exist can be as revealing as the monument itself. Historians have studied such histories to discover why hallowed ground is so often contested ground. How does it happen that the building of a simple monument reveals the fault lines of an entire culture?

A SIMPLE V IN THE GROUND

FOR THE HISTORIAN THE ARRAY of monuments along the Washington mall presents an intriguing puzzle. Today the most frequently visited and publicly acclaimed site also happens to be the least epic. Unlike Washington's 555-foot obelisk, this memorial does not soar. Unlike Lincoln's Greek temple, it has no columns evoking classical grandeur. In fact, at any reasonable distance the memorial cannot even be seen. It is simply a V of highly polished black granite incised into the ground—a V whose wide arms, each 247 feet long, converge 10 feet below the surface of the boulevard. This site is the Vietnam Veterans Memorial. Amid considerable controversy, the memorial was built in the wake of what was at the time not only the nation's longest war but also a divisive one that the United States lost.

©Sandra Baker/Alamy

Why, in a mall that takes special care to burnish the nation's proudest memories, has this memorial moved so many Americans?

That question intrigues historians, who have been drawn in recent years to the study of collective memories. Their interest is not the traditional concern over whether this or that recollection is accurate. At issue instead is the *process* of memory making: "how people together searched for common memories to meet present needs, how they first recognized such a memory and then agreed, disagreed, or negotiated over its meaning." At first, the definition seems unnecessarily complex. But the process of forging a collective memory *is* complex and can take years or even decades.

CIVIL WAR MEMORIES

FOR OVER A CENTURY AFTER THE Civil War, most Americans saw no contradiction in creating statues that commemorated two former sworn enemies, Robert E. Lee and U.S. Grant. They were honoring not so much the causes, but the heroism of those who fought.

But for African Americans then and now, Confederate leaders such as Lee symbolized slavery, making this emerging collective memory difficult to endorse. Frederick Douglass, a former slave and prominent Republican, warned that monuments honoring Lee would only "reawaken the confederacy." He argued that emancipation, not martial valor, deserved the most emphasis. To that end he supported efforts of African Americans to erect the Freedmen's Memorial Monument in Washington. The nation may "shut its eyes to the past . . . ," he warned, "but the colored people of this country are bound to keep the past in lively memory till justice shall be done them." In 2017, a clash in Charlottesville, Virginia, revealed just how contested a Civil War memorial could be. White supremacists opposed a decision to remove a statue of General Lee from a public space. In their anger they protested violently, provoking one of their members to drive recklessly down a crowded street, killing one counter-protester.

The Vietnam War posed similar problems of contested memory. By the 1980s the vast majority of Americans, whether they had opposed or defended American involvement in Vietnam, agreed that the war had been a mistake. How, then, would a nation used to celebrating success find a way to remember failure?

HOW TO REMEMBER A DISPUTED WAR?

VIETNAM VETERAN JAN SCRUGGS TOOK an approach that was consciously apolitical. Rather than celebrate the war, Scruggs proposed a monument honoring the veterans themselves. From 1959 to 1975, over 3 million American men and women had served in Vietnam, of whom 75,000 returned home permanently disabled. Yet many veterans felt their sacrifices had been lost amid the debate over the war. To promote reconciliation, Congress in 1980 set aside a 2-acre site on the mall, almost equidistant from the Washington and Lincoln Memorials.

Despite his personal dislike of the statue (because the slave was kneeling rather than proudly standing), Frederick Douglass helped dedicate the Freedmen's Memorial Monument to Abraham Lincoln in 1876. Douglass believed emancipation was central to remembering the Civil War.
Source: Library of Congress, Prints and Photographs Collection [LC-USZ62-53278]

The competition to design the memorial attracted over 1,400 entries, all judged anonymously. The panel's unanimous choice came as a surprise: the entry of Maya Ying Lin, a Chinese American student at Yale University's School of Arts and Architecture. The idea for the design had occurred to her when she visited the projected site. "I thought about what death is . . . ," Lin recalled, "a sharp pain that lessens with time, but can never heal over. A scar. Take a knife and cut open the earth, and with time the grass would heal it."

To view the monument, a visitor descends a gentle incline. Because there are no steps, persons with disabilities have easy access. The memorial's polished black granite sets a somber tone, yet the open sky and reflection of the sun dispel any sense that this is a tomb or mausoleum. A person beginning the descent at first sees only a few names carved into the granite, but as the wall deepens, so does the procession of names. Altogether, 70 panels enumerate over 54,000 Americans who died in Vietnam. As Lin insisted, "you cannot ever forget that war is not just a victory or loss. It's really about individual lives."

OBJECTIONS AND COMPETING VISIONS

THE DESIGN IMMEDIATELY AROUSED CONTROVERSY. Some critics resented Lin's relative youth, her ethnicity, and her gender. Others objected to the memorial's abstract and decidedly unheroic character. Lin had rejected a traditional approach in favor of a feminine and non-Western sensibility. "I didn't set out to conquer the earth, or to overpower it the way Western man usually does," she acknowledged. Ross Perot, a major financial supporter and later a presidential candidate, called the memorial a slap in the face to veterans. Others less politely described it as a public urinal. To them the black granite seemed a mark of shame and the descent below ground level an admission of wrongdoing.

So loud were these objections that in 1982 the secretary of the interior refused a construction permit until the memorial's sponsors agreed to add to the site a realistic sculpture by Frederick Hart. Hart, one of Lin's most outspoken critics, created three soldiers with an American flag, installed in 1984. This memorial provoked a female Vietnam veteran, Diane Carlson Evans, to lead a campaign for one additional monument, to honor the women of Vietnam. This third commemorative piece (also realistic) portrays three nurses, one holding a wounded soldier.

Who captured the contested terrain of Vietnam commemoration? For the historian, the evidence lies in the crowds who flock to Maya Lin's memorial. Often, visitors seek out the name of someone they knew and make a rubbing of it to take with them. So many have left flowers, flags, and personal objects, along with messages and poems, that the National Park Service has created a museum for them. The messages vary wildly, from the hopeful and resolute to the sorrowful and disgusted:

Thank you for having the courage to fight . . .
You never would listen to anyone and you finally screwed up . . .
I am sorry Frankie, I know we left you, I hope you did not suffer too much . . .

Maya Lin
©David Bookstaver/AP Photo

©James P Blair/National Geographic Images

Given such diverse reactions, Lin's choice of polished black marble was inspired. "The point," she said, "is to see yourself reflected in the names."

For the historian who passes by—even a century from now—the site will always bear witness to Vietnam's contested ground. As on a real battlefield, the opposing sides stand arrayed: heroic, realistic figures on one side, challenged and ultimately outflanked by the wide embrace of that silent granite V. In aesthetic terms, traditional realism wars with abstract modernity. But that contrast only reflects a deeper cultural divide over the way we choose to remember war. Maya Lin's commemoration would have been unthinkable in 1946, when a triumphant United States was emerging as one of the world's superpowers. In an age of limits, when even superpowers falter, the gleam of black marble reflects faces that are less certain that martial valor can guarantee a nation's immortality.

©Sandra Baker/Alamy

31 The Conservative Challenge

1976–1992

The Reverend Jerry Falwell in 1980, outside his Thomas Road Baptist Church in Lynchburg, Virginia. By the time Ronald Reagan was making a run for the presidency, Falwell had left behind his aversion to involvement in politics, as the sign behind him makes clear: "Good Christians Make Good Voters."

>> An American Story

BORN AGAIN

When 1976 presidential candidate Jimmy Carter declared himself a "born-again Christian," many Americans were unfamiliar with the term. But Carter's outspoken devotion to his religion drew attention to the world of evangelical preachers. Many of these preachers traced their roots back to the Fundamentalist movement that flourished during the 1920s (see Chapter 25). More recently, however, their role in mainstream American life had been muted partly because many chose to separate themselves from an increasingly secular American society.

For years, the Reverend Jerry Falwell followed this path of separation. Though his father had been a bootlegger during Prohibition and his grandfather an avowed atheist, Falwell absorbed instead the faith of his devout mother and attended Baptist Bible College in Missouri. Returning to Lynchburg, Virginia, in 1956, he founded the Thomas Road Baptist Church. And following the example of popular televangelists that same year, he launched the *Old Time Gospel Hour* that aired on both TV and radio. Falwell purposely avoided politics in his preaching. "Servicing the church and letting the government take care of itself had been my lifelong policy," he recalled.

His attitude began to change during the tumult of the 1960s and 1970s. Beyond dismay at the political protests and countercultural lifestyles, Falwell and other conservative Christians had never reconciled themselves to the 1962 Supreme Court decision in *Engel v. Vitale,* which had banned prayer in public schools. And *Roe v. Wade,* handed down in 1973, made abortion legal and thus seemed, to many on the Christian right, to authorize the murder of the unborn. Falwell began to talk politics, right in church. And he told his fellow pastors they should do the same.

Traveling to Florida, he helped spearhead a fight against the Equal Rights Amendment for women. "Here's what you do," he told Florida pastors. "You tell everybody in your congregation to bring two stamped envelopes to church on Sunday. You show them a couple of sample letters. And don't assume they know who their state representative is. Show them a map of their district. Make them write those letters in church. It's all perfectly legal as long as you don't use the building for special meetings. Do it right during the service."

Falwell also rebelled against a ruling by the Internal Revenue Service denying tax exemptions to segregated Christian schools. He himself had created the all-white Lynchburg Christian Academy—not to segregate, he insisted, but to protect his students from the evils of "secular humanism." Where evangelicals saw God, the family, and the church as the moral foundation of a Christian society, humanists believed that people were capable of moral and ethical behavior without God or religion. Falwell championed homeschooling and Christian academies. "I hope to see the day when, as in the early days of our country," he said, "we won't have any public schools. The churches will take them over again and Christians will be running them."

Though Jimmy Carter was "born again," in the end he was far too sympathetic to feminism and too accepting of racial and sexual diversity for Falwell's taste. In 1979 the crusading pastor joined with other evangelicals to form the Moral Majority, an organization that campaigned openly for Ronald Reagan in the 1980 election. Ironically, Reagan was far more secular than Carter in his personal beliefs, but his conservative values better suited Falwell. The 1980 election marked a turning point for evangelicals as they joined other conservatives to challenge the liberal direction of American politics and culture. <<

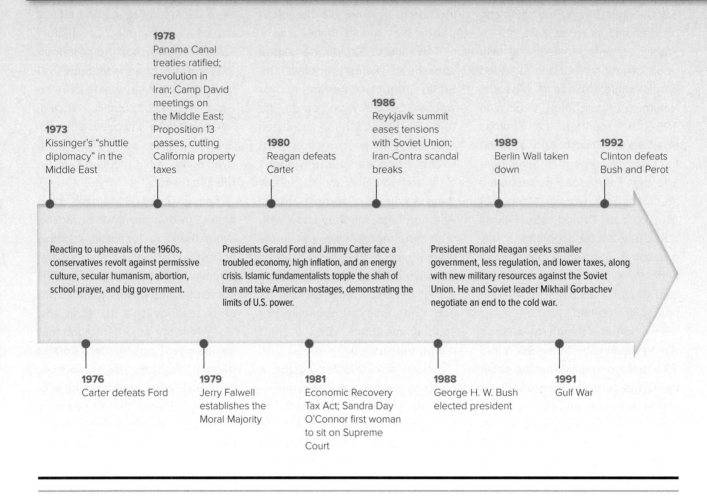

1973
Kissinger's "shuttle diplomacy" in the Middle East

1978
Panama Canal treaties ratified; revolution in Iran; Camp David meetings on the Middle East; Proposition 13 passes, cutting California property taxes

1980
Reagan defeats Carter

1986
Reykjavík summit eases tensions with Soviet Union; Iran-Contra scandal breaks

1989
Berlin Wall taken down

1992
Clinton defeats Bush and Perot

Reacting to upheavals of the 1960s, conservatives revolt against permissive culture, secular humanism, abortion, school prayer, and big government.

Presidents Gerald Ford and Jimmy Carter face a troubled economy, high inflation, and an energy crisis. Islamic fundamentalists topple the shah of Iran and take American hostages, demonstrating the limits of U.S. power.

President Ronald Reagan seeks smaller government, less regulation, and lower taxes, along with new military resources against the Soviet Union. He and Soviet leader Mikhail Gorbachev negotiate an end to the cold war.

1976
Carter defeats Ford

1979
Jerry Falwell establishes the Moral Majority

1981
Economic Recovery Tax Act; Sandra Day O'Connor first woman to sit on Supreme Court

1988
George H. W. Bush elected president

1991
Gulf War

THE CONSERVATIVE REBELLION

IN CALIFORNIA, HOWARD JARVIS, A retired Mormon businessman, regularly promoted tax-cutting referenda on the state ballot. While those measures failed to attract wide support, Jarvis's efforts to reduce property taxes did. In the case of property taxes, the issue was equity, not simply lower taxes. Small homeowners often paid taxes at much higher rates than large property owners and businesses that received breaks from friendly and often corrupt tax assessors. Hence, the extremely conservative Jarvis began to frame his antigovernment agenda in populist terms. His supporters, he claimed, were the small interests and individuals: teachers, blue-collar workers, and "a great number of Negroes." His group, the United Organizations of Taxpayers (UOT), received no money from oil companies, bankers, land speculators, or insurance companies.

Tax Revolt

PROPOSITION 13 By the late 1970s California was ripe for the Jarvis rebellion. Inflation imposed a crushing burden on middle- and lower-class homeowners. At the same time, their taxes rose steadily. One woman complained to California governor Jerry Brown that her hopes to live in a house mortgage-free were not possible, "because our government won't let this happen." An old radical and union organizer described state politicians and bureaucrats as "those leeches who must have more and more taxes." Such mounting anger helped UOT collect 1.25 million signatures to place Proposition 13 on the ballot in 1978. Opponents warned that the loss of revenue would force school closings, job losses, and reduced police and fire protection. Despite those warnings the measure passed easily.

The tax rebellion quickly spread across the nation. *The New York Times* likened it to "a modern Boston Tea Party." Over the next four years 12 states passed similar resolutions, while many legislatures cut public spending and taxes, hoping to avoid the voters' wrath. Even in Massachusetts, where government programs were generally popular, voters capped local property taxes and prevented future increases of more than 2½ percent, no matter how much inflation rose or the population grew. The only state to support the liberal George McGovern in 1972 voted narrowly for Ronald Reagan in 1980. After 1975 Americans no longer embraced the liberal consensus that professional expertise in the service of government could solve the nation's problems and promote progress.

The Diverse Evangelical World

The conservative rebellion was not merely the child of a faltering economy, stagnating wages, and a resistance to paying taxes. The social ferment of the 1960s had taken its toll on spiritual life and on the churches. During that decade mainline Protestant churches struggled over how their religious beliefs should engage with civil rights, the war in Vietnam, issues of sex and gender, and more-liberated lifestyles. As congregations embraced liberal social agendas, many worshipers found themselves yearning for a traditional religious experience. They moved in large numbers from long-established denominations such as Presbyterians and Congregationalists to evangelical churches. By the mid-1980s some 36 percent of Americans described themselves as "born again." Similar trends occurred among Catholics and Jews, many of whom also resisted the liberalization of their faith.

Among evangelicals the Southern Baptists and Assemblies of God attracted large national memberships, but their real focus was local, centered in church communities. Such congregations insisted that salvation came through a spiritual rebirth (being "born again") after a person had acknowledged sinfulness and embraced Christ's atonement. Evangelical tradition encouraged proselytizing by the faithful, often in the form of revivals and spiritual awakenings. Finally, most evangelicals anticipated the rapture, when Christ would return to transport true believers into his Father's kingdom. These shared beliefs, when combined with a commitment to piety, put evangelicals squarely at odds with modern society. They imposed a strict personal morality, often insisted on the central role of fathers in the family, and in some churches forbade such "worldly evils" as dancing, cosmetics, movies, gambling, and premarital sex.

PAT ROBERTSON Though evangelicals condemned much of modern culture, many preachers advocated a "prosperity theology" that encouraged economic success. They also used the media to spread the word, none more effectively than did Virginia-based Pat Robertson, the son of a Virginia politician. Robertson, a magnetic Southern Baptist, used cable and satellite broadcasts to expand the Christian Broadcast Network into a media empire. His *700 Club* reached an audience of millions and inspired his

colleague Jim Bakker to launch the even more popular *Praise the Lord Club*—PTL for short. Although the content featured gospel singing, fervent preaching, faith healing, and speaking in tongues, the format mirrored that of major network talk shows, opening with a Christian monologue, conversations with celebrity guests, and musical entertainment.

The Catholic Conscience

POPE JOHN PAUL II American Catholics faced their own decisions about the lines between religion and politics. In the 1960s a social activist movement had arisen out of the church council known as Vatican II (Chapter 29). Disturbed by these currents, Catholic conservatives found support for their views when the magnetic John Paul II assumed the papacy in 1979. Pope John Paul reined in the modern trends inspired by Vatican II. He ruled against a wider role for women in the church hierarchy and stiffened church policy against birth control. These edicts put him at odds with a majority of American Catholics. The American church also faced a crisis as fewer young men and women chose celibate lives as priests and nuns.

Though conservative Catholics and Protestant evangelicals were sometimes wary of one another, they shared certain views. Both groups lobbied for the government to provide federal aid to parochial schools and Fundamentalist academies. But it was the issue of abortion that attracted the greatest mutual support. Pope John Paul reaffirmed the church's teaching that all life begins at conception and that abortion amounts to murder of the unborn. Evangelicals, long skeptical of the power of secular technology and science, attacked abortion as another instance in which science had upset the moral order of life.

Religion and Politics

CONSERVATIVES AND *ROE V. WADE* Since many evangelicals believed that the apocalypse—the end-time of the world—was imminent, before the 1970s they saw little reason to reform society. Many refused even to vote. Gradually that apolitical stance weakened. A number of Supreme Court decisions, beginning with the ban on school prayer in *Engel v. Vitale* (1962), struck conservatives as an attack on their faith, but none more so than *Roe v. Wade*. If an unborn fetus was fully human, was it not necessarily endowed with both a soul and with human rights? Abortion constituted "the slaughter of the innocents." Here was a case where it seemed that the government posed a threat to faith and family. So also did the inclusion of such subjects as Darwinian evolution and sex education in school curricula.

Following Jerry Falwell's lead, many evangelicals became politically active. No longer were they content to wait for the apocalypse—the end times of the world—which many believed were fast approaching. Once the debates over legal abortion and prayer in the schools brought them into politics, they expanded their agendas. Falwell joined

During the late 1970s and the 1980s, conservatives increasingly spoke out against abortion and in favor of the right to life for an unborn fetus. Adopting the tactics of protest and civil disobedience once common to radicals in the 1960s, in this photograph they clash with pro-choice demonstrators outside Faneuil Hall in Boston.
©Bettmann/Getty Images

his fellow Baptist preacher Tim LaHaye of San Diego in a campaign to repeal a gay rights ordinance in Miami, Florida. LaHaye and his wife Beverly, a writer, had formed the Concerned Women of America (CWA), a "pro-family" organization that by the 1980s claimed more members than the National Organization for Women. The LaHayes were outspoken opponents of homosexuality and pornography. Under their leadership, CWA crusaded against abortion, no-fault divorce laws, and the Equal Rights Amendment.

THE MORAL MAJORITY   For its part, Moral Majority not only described itself as "pro-life, pro-family, pro-morality, and pro-American," it also shared the conservative opposition to labor unions, environmental reform, and most government-based social welfare programs.

The Media Battleground

Evangelicals and political conservatives believed the mass media played a central role in corrupting family values. Its permissive, even positive portrayal of unmarried women, premarital sex and drug use, profanity, homosexuality, nudity, and violence offended their moral sensibilities. The conservative determination to censor media content clashed with a liberal commitment to free speech and toleration for diversity in lifestyles.

ARCHIE BUNKER   Hollywood movies had long pushed the boundaries of acceptable content, but by the 1970s television began to introduce more controversial and politicized programming. In 1971 producer Norman Lear introduced *All in the Family,* whose main character, Archie Bunker, embodied the blue-collar backlash against liberal and permissive values. The ultimate male chauvinist, Archie treated his wife Edith like a servant, clashed with his modestly rebellious daughter Gloria, and heaped verbal abuse on his leftist Polish-American son-in-law. All things liberal or cosmopolitan—"Hebes," "Spics," and "Commie Crapola"—became targets for Archie's coarse insults. While millions watched the show, both the left and the right attacked it. Many conservatives who shared Archie's values found the language offensive, while some minority leaders charged that the show legitimized the prejudices it attacked.

SATURDAY NIGHT FEVER   If *All in the Family* defined the class anger of blue-collar Americans, the hugely popular disco movie *Saturday Night Fever* revealed their alienation. The film explores the Brooklyn world of Tony Manero, played by John Travolta, who holds a dead-end job as a hardware store clerk during the day, but at night transforms himself into a white-suited disco king. Where his loser friends walk down Brooklyn's mean streets, Tony struts. When his boss counsels him to consider his long-term prospects for getting ahead, he replies angrily, "Fuck the future." To which his boss expresses the declining prospects of blue-collar Americans: No, "the future fucks you."

The glitter of disco offers Tony a world in which he can be somebody. In the end, however, he rejects his suffocating family, loser friends, and blue-collar roots for a future across the Brooklyn Bridge in Manhattan, where his girlfriend

©Michael Ochs Archives/Getty Images

| *John Travolta, the blue-collar Brooklyn boy with aspirations, dressed to the nines and "Stayin' Alive," to the beat of the Bee Gees.*

is bent on a professional career. He embraces the notion that those with talent and dreams can escape the past and reinvent themselves. In the end, *Saturday Night Fever*, the most popular movie of the 1970s, looked to have its cake and eat it. On the one hand, it glamorized the youthful blue-collar culture with its vulgar language, violence, explicit sexuality, and drug use that so offended conservative critics of the media. But at the same time, its escapist ending offered audiences fantasy rather than a political or spiritual path to salvation.

Perhaps inevitably, the wars for the soul of prime-time entertainment spilled into the political arena. Fearful that the Moral Majority's political pressure would lead television producers to censor themselves, the creator of Archie Bunker, Norman Lear, formed People for the American Way. The organization self-consciously opposed the agenda set by LaHaye and Falwell. People for the American Way campaigned for diversity and tolerance. In turn, conservatives, particularly the religious right, advanced their pro-life and pro-family agenda.

> ✓ **REVIEW**
>
> Why did evangelicals become political in the late 1970s, and what techniques did they use to increase their influence?

THE PRESIDENCY IN TRANSITION: GERALD FORD AND JIMMY CARTER

WAR POWERS RESOLUTION THE CROSSCURRENTS IN AMERICAN CULTURE shook the political system as well. In the wake of Watergate and the Vietnam War, Congress was determined to place limits on a presidency which, under Nixon, had seemed to grow entirely too imperial. The War Powers Resolution, passed in 1973 before Gerald Ford took office, required that the president consult Congress before committing troops to the battlefield, report within two days of taking action, and withdraw troops after 60 days unless Congress voted to retain them.

Meanwhile, congressional hearings revealed that the CIA had routinely violated its charter forbidding it to spy on Americans at home. Abroad, the agency had attempted to assassinate foreign leaders in Cuba, the Congo, South Vietnam, and the Dominican Republic. The FBI had also used illegal means to infiltrate and disrupt domestic dissidents. J. Edgar Hoover had authorized an (unsuccessful) operation to drive Martin Luther King Jr. to suicide. Determined to rein in the executive branch, the Senate established committees to oversee intelligence operations.

INFLUENCE OF KISSINGER Hemmed in by a newly assertive Congress, President Gerald Ford relied on Henry Kissinger's guidance in foreign policy. The secretary of state perceived himself as a realist who offended idealists on the political left and right. Quoting the German writer Goethe, Kissinger explained, "If I had to choose between justice and disorder, on the one hand, and injustice and order, on the other, I would always choose the latter."

During the final years of Nixon's administration, Kissinger had followed that maxim (with the president's blessing) by ordering the CIA to finance a military coup in Chile in 1973. The coup overthrew the democratically elected socialist leader, Salvador Allende Gossens. Allende died, and a brutally oppressive military regime assumed power. Kissinger argued that the United States had the right to limit democratic disorder in Latin America, in order to guard against the evils of communism.

Energy and the Middle East

Kissinger also looked to manage an energy crisis brought to a head by events in the Middle East. The United States and its allies had long depended on Middle Eastern oil and, so long as the pipelines were full, low oil prices discouraged conservation or the use of alternative energy. Prime among the nation's foreign suppliers were the 13 nations making up the Organization of Petroleum Exporting Countries (OPEC)—and chief among those were seven Arab states and Iran.

THE CULTURE WARS

A series of events—including the abortion-rights case Roe v. Wade *(1973), a Miami ordinance adopted protecting the rights of homosexuals, and a move by the Internal Revenue Service to tax racially exclusive Christian schools—prompted evangelical Christian leaders Tim LaHaye and Jerry Falwell to form the Moral Majority, a political action organization. As a counterweight, Norman Lear, a liberal producer of popular TV series such as* All in the Family, Maude, *and* The Jeffersons, *created People for the American Way.*

DOCUMENT 1
Take a Stand on Moral Issues

We must reverse the trend America finds herself in today. Young people between the ages of twenty-five and forty have been born and reared in a different world than Americans of years past. The television set has been their primary baby-sitter. From the television set they have learned situation ethics and immorality—they have learned a loss of respect for human life. They have learned to disrespect the family as God has established it. They have been educated in a public-school system that is permeated with secular humanism. They have been taught that the Bible is just another book of literature. They have been taught that there are no absolutes in our world today. They have been introduced to the drug culture. They have been reared by the family and the public school in a

society that is greatly void of discipline and character-building. These same young people have been reared under the influence of a government that has taught them socialism and welfarism. They have been taught to believe that the world owes them a living whether they work or not.

It is now time to take a stand on certain moral issues, and we can only stand if we have leaders. We must stand against the Equal Rights Amendment, the feminist revolution, and the homosexual revolution. We must have a revival in this country. . . . The hope of reversing the trends of decay in our republic now lies with the Christian public in America. We cannot expect help from the liberals. They certainly are not going to call our nation back to righteousness and neither are the pornographers,

the smut peddlers, and those who are corrupting our youth. Moral Americans must be willing to put their reputations, their fortunes, and their very lives on the line for this great nation of ours. Would that we had the courage of our forefathers who knew the great responsibility that freedom carries with it. . . .

Our Founding Fathers separated church and state in function, but never intended to establish a government void of God. As is evidenced by our Constitution, good people in America must exert an influence and provide a conscience and climate of morality in which it is difficult to go wrong, not difficult for people to go right in America.

Source: Falwell, Jerry, *Listen, America!* New York, NY: Doubleday, 1980, 17–23.

DOCUMENT 2
Room for a Diversity of Voices

America and television face a new brand of monopolists, not monopolists of money or goods but of truth and values. In times of hardship, voices of stridency and division have always replaced those of reason and unity, and the results have always been a deterioration of free and open dialogue, a tension among races, classes, and religions, and the temptation to grasp at simplistic solutions to complex problems.

In our time of hardship, we find the New Right and the Religious New Right—a new breed of robber barons who have organized to corner the market on morals. . . . As communicators ourselves, it should be interesting to look at how well they are able to spread their absolutist views. There are now over 1,500 Christian radio stations blanketing the country—with approximately one new station being added each week; there are forty-some independent television stations with a full-time diet of religious programming, largely

fundamentalist; and three Christian Broadcasting Networks. . . .

There are also scores and scores of local radio and TV evangelicals, espousing the same absolutist fundamentalist points of view while attacking the integrity and character of anyone who does not stand with them. . . . Here is some of what is occurring on the local level across the country:

- In Washington and Virginia, Moral Majoritarians have attempted to secure the names of all those who borrowed books on sex education from the public library.
- Five dictionaries have been banned from use in schools throughout the state of Texas because "concerned parents" objected to such "filth" as the word "bastard" and the word "bed," when used as a verb.
- Textbooks across the country are not being bought by some school boards,

under pressure from local groups, until all liberal dogma and secular humanism has been excised by a fundamentalist couple in Texas, the Gablers.
- In North Carolina, a social studies test was found objectionable and removed because seventh graders are not emotionally or intellectually capable of dealing with such complex problems. The problems they didn't want seventh graders dealing with were food shortages, overpopulation, and ecology. . . .

Ironically, this occurs at a time when the communications industry is witnessing an explosion of new technologies, delivery systems, and satellite networks, promising as many as 100 channels to the home. With this overabundance of sources, there will be room for a diversity of voices, a place for the emergence of cultures and subcultures that have not been heard from before. . . .

The importance of that supply became clear in the autumn of 1973, when on Yom Kippur, the holiest day of the Jewish year, troops from Egypt and Syria launched a surprise attack on Israel. The seven Arab members of OPEC supported Egypt and Syria by imposing a boycott on oil exports to countries seen as friendly to the Israelis. Lasting from October 1973 to March 1974, the boycott staggered the Western nations and Japan. The price of crude oil rose from under \$2 a barrel in 1972 to over \$12 by 1976. As the price of petroleum soared, so did the cost of carbon-based plastics used in a huge range of products from phonograph records to raincoats to tires. Inflation rose to an annual rate of 14 percent. Meanwhile, with gasoline scarce, motorists found themselves waiting in line for hours at the pump, in hopes of purchasing a few gallons.

The oil crisis pushed many cities toward financial disaster. In October 1975 New York City announced it was near bankruptcy and petitioned the Ford administration for relief. When the president refused, the *New York Daily News* headline blared, "Ford to City: Drop Dead." The administration eventually extended a loan, but the political damage had been done.

To ease the crisis, Kissinger mediated the conflict between Israel and the Arab states. In negotiating he flew back and forth so often between Jerusalem in Israel and Cairo in Egypt that observers nicknamed his efforts "shuttle diplomacy." Eventually the Israelis agreed to withdraw from the west bank of the Suez Canal and to disengage from Syrian troops along the Golan Heights, which overlooked Israel. As an uncertain peace returned, OPEC lifted its boycott. The following year Congress addressed the energy crisis by ordering electric utilities to switch from expensive oil to more abundant and cheaper (though more polluting) coal. The new legislation also ordered the auto industry to improve the efficiency of its cars.

Limits across the Globe

The energy crisis was only one factor limiting American ambitions. The United States also faced mounting competition from industries in Europe and in the emerging economies of the Pacific Rim (Japan, South Korea, Taiwan, Hong Kong, Singapore, and the Philippines). Lower wages there convinced many American manufacturers to move high-wage jobs overseas. The AFL-CIO complained that as skilled union jobs disappeared, what remained would be "a nation of hamburger stands, a country stripped of its industrial capacity . . . a nation of citizens busily buying and selling hamburgers and root beer floats."

Both Ford and Henry Kissinger looked to ease America's economic burdens by further détente with the Soviet Union. The Soviet economy, like the American, was stagnating. In two summit meetings, the second held at Helsinki, Finland, in 1975, the two superpowers established the framework for a second Strategic Arms Limitation Treaty (SALT II). Conservative Republicans, led by presidential contender Ronald Reagan, strongly opposed what they saw as concessions to an untrustworthy enemy. For them, détente spelled weakness. Reagan accused Kissinger and Ford of allowing the United States "to become number two in military power in a world where it is dangerous—if not fatal—to be second best." That claim exaggerated Soviet strength and American weakness.

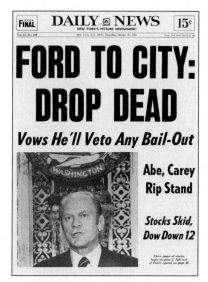

©New York Daily News/Getty Images

As the energy crisis contributed to New York City's near-bankruptcy, Gerald Ford at first opposed federal assistance. New Yorkers were not amused.

>> MAPPING THE PAST <<

OIL AND CONFLICT IN THE MIDDLE EAST, 1948–1988

Source: Library of Congress Prints and Photographs Division (LC-DIG-matpc-23032)

"Oil, enough oil within our certain grasp, seemed ardently necessary to independence and greatness in the twentieth century."—Herbert Feis, Economic Advisor for International Affairs to the Department of State (1947)

CONTEXT

After World War II the Middle East became a vital geopolitical region beset by big-power rivalry and complicated by local, tribal, ethnic, and religious divisions. Much of the world's oil reserves lie along the Persian Gulf. Proximity to the former Soviet Union and vital trade routes such as the Suez Canal have defined the region's geographic importance. Revolutions in Iran and Afghanistan, intermittent warfare between Arabs and Jews, the unresolved questions of Israel's borders and a Palestinian homeland, the disintegration of Lebanon, and a long war between Iran and Iraq were among the conflicts that unsettled the region.

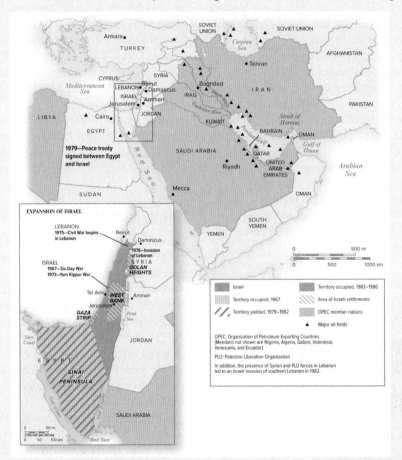

MAP READING

1. Locate the Sinai Peninsula. What is its relationship to the Suez Canal?
2. Which countries border Israel?
3. Which countries do the Tigris and Euphrates Rivers cross?
4. Which countries on the map have the most oil fields?

MAP INTERPRETATION

1. In what ways might the waters flowing in the Jordan, Tigris, and Euphrates Rivers be as much a source of conflict as the oil fields in the region?
2. A proposed "two-state solution" to the Palestinian conflict calls for an independent State of Palestine, including the West Bank, alongside the State of Israel. What does the map insert tell you about the difficulties of executing such a solution?
3. What makes the Suez Canal and the Strait of Hormuz so strategically important?
4. Why would Iraq's invasion of Kuwait in 1990 pose a threat to Saudi Arabia?

Jimmy Carter: Restoring the Faith

In the escalating war between liberal and conservative forces, James Earl "Jimmy" Carter did not fit neatly into either camp. Carter represented a new breed of Southern governors—from the Sun Belt, not the Cotton Belt; they were economic progressives, not segregationists. At the same time, Carter had credentials conservatives could appreciate. He was a former navy man and nuclear engineer; a peanut farmer from the humble town of Plains, Georgia; and had served as Georgia's governor. More unusual still, Carter openly declared his faith as a "born-again" Christian.

When he began campaigning, only 2 percent of Americans had heard of him. Carter turned his outsider's status to advantage by bringing honesty and openness to Washington. "I will not lie to you," he assured voters. President Ford, for his part, had to fight off a challenge from his party's right wing, led by Ronald Reagan. Reagan grew up as a New Deal Democrat, but as a foe of high income taxes and communism he took up conservative causes. Only by controlling the party's nominating process was Ford able to defeat Reagan at the Republican convention. In the election Carter eked out a slim victory and at his inauguration vowed to bring simplicity and directness to Washington politics. The imperial presidency, he made clear, was a thing of the past. But Congress was equally determined to rein in the executive branch in its own way. To succeed in governing, Carter and his brash Georgia outsiders would have to prove they could swim among the political sharks.

CARTER'S AGENDA Carter brought to the office a mastery of detail, disciplined work habits, and a wealth of plans to address the energy crisis, economic stagnation, the financial woes facing the nation's cities, and a host of foreign policy issues. What he and his advisors had not decided was how to set priorities. Veteran politicians warned not to try too much too soon, but Carter admitted, "it's almost impossible for me to delay something that I see needs to be done." Almost immediately he asked Congress to eliminate 19 expensive pork-barrel water projects as financially wasteful and environmentally destructive. The move stunned even Democrats, who liked bringing home funds to their communities. Their threat to bury his other legislative proposals forced Carter to restore the projects.

Energy and the Environment

The times demanded that the president address two related issues: the environment and skyrocketing energy prices. Those issues were in constant tension, since satisfying energy needs required the use of natural resources, just at the time when the need to protect them had become more evident.

Carter did make progress on a number of environmental fronts. He strengthened the Environmental Protection Agency as well as the clean air and water regulations the EPA enforced. And he championed legislation to create a Superfund that could spend $1 billion a year to clean up hazardous waste sites.

Problems arose, however, when environmental and energy policies clashed. The exceptionally harsh winter that greeted the new administration drove the price of heating oil even higher and pushed Carter to promise a comprehensive new energy policy. His preferred strategy for increasing fuel supplies was the most environmentally friendly: conservation. Americans, after all, were consuming more energy in 1977 than they had been before the OPEC oil boycott spawned gas lines during the Nixon years. But the energy industry lobbied for the opposite solution: instead of cutting back on the demand for energy, they looked to increase the supply, by deregulating the price of natural gas and oil to encourage new production.

Carter's National Energy Program was certainly comprehensive (it contained 113 separate recommendations), but it was also complicated. "Gas guzzler" taxes promoted conservation. So did new efficiency standards for buildings and appliances. Solar tax credits encouraged alternative energy. An almost incomprehensible plan targeted at oil and gas interests proposed deregulation to give energy "its true value." Citing the need to "act quickly," Carter described the fight for a comprehensive plan as "the moral equivalent of war." Unfortunately, few areas of public policy were more subject to the pressure of special interests, and after 18 months of debate Congress managed to approve only deregulation, some energy-conservation tax credits, and a new cabinet-level Department of Energy. No comprehensive policy ever emerged.

Environmentalists and energy producers clashed over climate change and nuclear energy. A 1977 report of the National Academy of Sciences warned that fossil fuel consumption raised the possibility that the world would face catastrophic warming. A *New York Times* headline announced, "Scientists Fear Heavy Use of Coal May Bring Adverse Climate Shift." Neither scientists nor energy companies were yet prepared to recommend specific policies to regulate greenhouse gases.

©Bettmann/Getty Images

Oil shortages in the 1970s increased American dependence on nuclear power as an alternative energy source. The danger became evident in 1979 when an accident closed a nuclear power plant at Three Mile Island near Harrisburg, Pennsylvania. The large towers pictured here are part of the cooling system in which the accident occurred.

THREE MILE ISLAND Some utilities favored nuclear power, since fission energy emitted no carbon dioxide. That was an option few environmentalists could abide. No permanent solution yet existed to dispose of the radioactive wastes that were a by-product of nuclear power. Then in March 1979 a plume of radioactive steam spewed from an overheated nuclear reactor at Three Mile Island in Pennsylvania. Local authorities evacuated some 100,000 panicked residents from nearby communities. Whatever support existed for nuclear energy evaporated along with the steam from the overheated reactor. While existing nuclear plants continued to operate, no new ones would be built for decades to come.

The Sagging Economy

Throughout the 1970s wages stagnated, unemployment rose, and so did inflation, spurred upward by rising energy costs, falling industrial productivity, and foreign competition. President Carter at first proposed stimulating the economy with a series of popular tax rebates. And he did win the approval of progressive politicians by finding new funding for federal programs such as food stamps, Social Security, Medicare, and Medicaid.

But the president's fiscal conservatism offset these attempts to cushion the blow of hard times. Confronted by the large deficit from the Nixon and Ford years, Carter canceled his proposed tax rebates. Government could not "eliminate poverty, or provide a bountiful economy, or reduce inflation, or save our cities, or cure illiteracy or provide energy," Carter insisted. That sentiment, spoken by a Democrat, indicated how successful conservatives had been in promoting their ideas.

Foreign Policy: Principled or Pragmatic?

In foreign policy, Jimmy Carter again gravitated between conservative and liberal impulses, between being practical and being idealistic. Like Nixon and Kissinger, he recognized that the United States had neither the strength nor the resources to police a postcolonial world. But unlike his conservative critics Carter viewed the threat of Soviet strength with greater skepticism. Too often, he believed, a knee-jerk fear of Soviet power led Americans to support right-wing dictators, no matter how brutal or corrupt, simply because they professed to be anticommunist.

HUMAN RIGHTS Instead, Carter insisted that the United States should take a moral posture by giving human rights a higher priority. He spoke out publicly on behalf of political prisoners and reduced foreign aid to some dictatorships (though strategic allies such as the Philippines under the autocratic Ferdinand Marcos were largely spared). Argentinian Nobel Peace Prize winner Adolfo Pérez Esquivel claimed he owed his life to Carter's policies. Hundreds of other journalists and dissidents, who routinely faced imprisonment, torture, and even murder, benefited as well.

PANAMA CANAL TREATIES Carter also eased decades of animosity against Yankee imperialism by negotiating a treaty to turn over to Panama control of the Canal Zone, a 10-mile-wide strip that the United States administered under a perpetual lease. For many conservatives, Carter's initiative offered further evidence of declining American power. Presidential hopeful Ronald Reagan condemned the proposed treaty as "appeasement," while Senator S. I. Hayakawa of California quipped, "It's ours; we stole it fair and square." Despite such criticisms the Senate ratified the final agreement in 1978.

For conservatives, however, the real test of Carter's mettle would come in relations with the Soviet Union. There, the president's first impulse was to continue the policy of détente scorned so long by the right wing. Soviet premier Leonid Brezhnev accepted Carter's overtures to negotiate, as his nation had been struggling with an economy saddled by inefficient industries and obligations to poor client states such as Cuba, Vietnam, and Bulgaria. The Soviets became even more willing to negotiate after the Carter administration offered diplomatic recognition to Communist China—playing "the China card" as Kissinger and Nixon once had. At a summit meeting held in Vienna in 1979, Carter and Brezhnev followed through on the strategic arms limitation agreement set in motion by President Ford. The agreement, SALT II, was seriously flawed because neither side would agree to scrap major weapon systems. Conservatives who blocked ratification of the treaty in the Senate even attacked Carter's minor concessions. To them, cooperation with the Soviet Union was not an option.

The Middle East: Hope and Hostages

Throughout the cold war, instability in the oil-rich Middle East continually threatened to set off a larger conflict. Secular dictators in Iran, Egypt, Syria, and Iraq vied with autocratic monarchies in Saudi Arabia, Kuwait, Jordan, and the United Arab Emirates. Vast inequality existed between oil-rich sheiks and impoverished peasants and nomadic tribes. Tensions simmered between rival Islamic religious sects, the Sunnis and Shi'ites, while all the Arab nations were united in their hostility toward Israel.

American policy for the region was pulled in two different directions. On the one hand, the United States wanted to ensure the free flow of Middle Eastern oil to the industrial world; on the other, it was committed to the survival of Israel. The energy crises of the 1970s heightened the tensions between these goals, as did Israel's decision to refuse Palestinian demands for a homeland in the West Bank. The diplomatic impasse eased somewhat when Egyptian president Anwar Sadat traveled to Israel to meet Israeli president Menachem Begin. Sensing an opportunity to promote peace, Carter invited the two leaders to Camp David in September 1978.

CAMP DAVID ACCORDS For 13 days the two antagonists argued, while Carter kept them at the table. Each feared the consequence of giving the other side too much. Finally, they struck a limited compromise: Sadat would recognize Israel; Israel would return the Sinai Peninsula to Egypt. On the question of a Palestinian state in the West Bank and Gaza, Begin would not yield. Even so, the discussions had been historic. Begin and Sadat shared the Nobel Peace Prize for their courageous diplomacy, but it could just as well have gone to Carter, who brokered the peace.

IRANIAN REVOLUTION Amid the turmoil of the Middle East, the shah of Iran had long seemed a stabilizing force. But in the autumn of 1978 Shi'ite fundamentalists rebelled against his dictatorship. Long dismayed by the increasing Westernization of their society, they found the presence of tens of thousands of non-Muslim American military advisors particularly offensive. When the shah's regime collapsed in February 1979, the religious leader Ayatollah Ruhollah Khomeini established an Islamic republic. Later that year the United States admitted the ailing shah to an American hospital for medical treatment, upon which several hundred Iranian students stormed the U.S. Embassy in Tehran and took 53 Americans hostage. Though this act violated every convention of Western diplomacy, the United States had no way to free the hostages.

A President Held Hostage

SOVIETS INVADE AFGHANISTAN At first, American policymakers worried that the Soviet Union might take advantage of the new Khomeini regime. In truth, the Soviets were fearful themselves that Islamic fundamentalists might spread unrest among the Muslim populations living within Soviet borders. In December 1979, the Soviet Union invaded neighboring Afghanistan, where Islamic rebels had toppled a pro-Soviet regime. President Carter condemned the invasion, but in practical terms there was little he could do to counter it. As a symbolic gesture, he announced that the United States would boycott the 1980 Olympics in Moscow.

HYPERINFLATION Once again the problems of energy dependence and the economic instability interacted to create a political crisis. Nightly newscasts aired the spectacle of "America Held Hostage" in Iran. And the turbulence in the Middle East set off another round of OPEC increases in the price of oil. Soaring energy costs soon drove up inflation to near 14 percent and some interest rates above 20 percent. Chrysler Corporation, the nation's third-leading automaker, teetered on the edge of bankruptcy and was saved only by a federally guaranteed loan.

With polls giving Carter a negative rating of 77 percent, the president once again moved to the right. He revived the cold war rhetoric of the 1950s and accelerated the development of new classes of nuclear weapons. But whereas the CIA in 1953 had successfully overthrown an Iranian government, an airborne mission launched in April 1980 to rescue the hostages ended in disaster. Eight marines died when two helicopters and a plane collided in Iran's central desert in the midst of a blinding sandstorm. Carter's secretary of state, Cyrus Vance, who had opposed the mission, resigned in protest. The United States, as even the president admitted, was mired in "a crisis of confidence."

The administration's mistakes had no doubt contributed to that malaise. Yet the obstacles to projecting American power internationally were not simply a result of Carter's mismanagement. Vietnam had demonstrated the clear limits of what U.S. forces could accomplish in distant lands; the long lines for expensive gas rose from an energy crisis decades in the making. The problems in the Middle East had proved intractable over many centuries. Finally, Carter could not be

| It was at Camp David, in private talks sponsored by President Jimmy Carter (center), that Egyptian president Anwar Sadat (left) and Israeli prime minister Menachem Begin (right) hammered out a "Framework for Peace in the Middle East" as a first step toward ending decades of war and mutual distrust.

©David Rubinger/Getty Images

blamed for the reluctance of Americans to sacrifice personal comforts for the general good. American culture had long defined wealth as having more, not wanting less. In 1980 the discouraged electorate discovered in Ronald Reagan a political leader who shared that faith.

REVIEW

In what ways did the issue of energy affect Jimmy Carter's presidency?

PRIME TIME WITH RONALD REAGAN

THE RECESSION OF THE 1970s and the accompanying runaway inflation similarly brought about a major political realignment, only the third since the Civil War. Republicans undermined the Democrats' New Deal coalition and established a conservative majority that would dominate American politics for at least three decades. In the 1980 presidential campaign Ronald Reagan asked Americans, "Are you better off now than you were four years ago?" Many thought not, as Reagan swept the election with an unexpectedly large majority. The fight against inflation and high taxes would be the cornerstone of his administration and would replace unemployment in determining federal economic policy.

THE CONSERVATIVE TIDE WORLDWIDE The United States was not the only nation to experience a resurgence of political conservatism, nationalism, and religious revival. The year before Ronald Reagan became president, Great Britain chose Margaret Thatcher as its first woman prime minister. Under her conservative leadership, "Thatcherism" became a synonym for cutting social programs, downsizing government, and privatizing state-controlled industries. Even within the Soviet bloc, rumblings could be felt as more citizens turned to religion after becoming disillusioned with the communist system. In China, the successors to revolutionary leader Mao Zedong introduced market capitalism into the economy during the 1980s.

As evangelical Christianity surged in the United States, fundamentalist religious revivals elsewhere in the world reflected a questioning of the liberal values that emerged from Europe's eighteenth-century Enlightenment. That era's faith in the rational spirit of science and technology had dominated Western thought for 200 years. Increasingly, fundamentalists demanded that traditional religion become the center of public life. The student radicals in Iran who seized the American embassy feared that Western ideas would destroy their Islamic faith. They saw the theocracy of the Ayatollah Khomeini as a way to rid Iran of Western secularism. In Israel religious conservatives became a political force as they, too, resisted secular trends in their society. And as we have seen, leadership of the Roman Catholic Church fell to Pope John Paul II, who rejected calls to liberalize doctrine on such issues as birth control, abortion, and the acceptance of female priests.

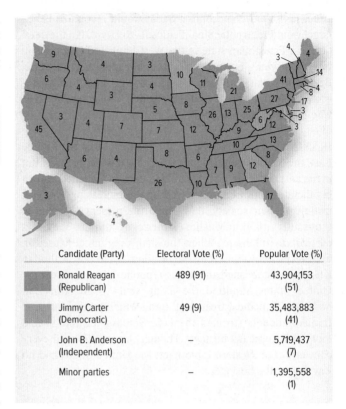

Candidate (Party)	Electoral Vote (%)	Popular Vote (%)
Ronald Reagan (Republican)	489 (91)	43,904,153 (51)
Jimmy Carter (Democratic)	49 (9)	35,483,883 (41)
John B. Anderson (Independent)	–	5,719,437 (7)
Minor parties	–	1,395,558 (1)

ELECTION OF 1980

The Great Communicator

REAGAN "REVOLUTION" Reagan's message was clear: "It is time to reawaken the industrial giant, to get government back within its means, and to lighten the punitive tax burden." To both liberals and conservatives, he signaled the onset of what came to be called "the Reagan revolution." Liberals feared—and conservatives hoped—that the revolution meant a harder line on cold war issues and an assault on a wide range of social programs and regulations at home. What both groups ignored in the early days of the administration were the moderating forces at work. As governor of California, Reagan had showed a willingness to accommodate his ideas to political realities. At times he increased both spending and taxes. As president, he appointed to his administration advisors with diverging ideas about how to fix the economy and build American prestige. *The Washington Post* commented that Reagan was not someone to allow rigid ideas to prevent flexible policies. Equally important, noted the *Post,* almost anyone who met him thought he was "a nice guy, a happy secure person who likes himself and most other people."

HANDS-OFF LEADERSHIP In other ways Reagan contradicted expectations. With his jaunty wave and jutting jaw, he projected an aura of physical vitality and movie star good looks. Yet at 69 he was the oldest person to become president, and no one, since Calvin Coolidge, slept as soundly or as much. Such serenity marked his refusal to become bogged down in the details of his job. Outsiders applauded his "hands-off" style after four years under Jimmy Carter, whose obsession with policy details led critics to say he missed the forest for the trees. Reagan set the tone and direction of his administration, leaving the rest to his advisors. Sometimes that left Reagan in the dark about major programs. Donald Regan, his first Treasury secretary, once noted, "The Presidential mind was not cluttered with facts."

The effectiveness of Reagan's message was no accident. The president had honed his public speaking skills as an actor, as a spokesperson for General Electric, and as a politician. His communications staff planned everything from the president's words to a speech's location and camera angles down to the lighting. But the elaborate preparation also depended on Reagan's discipline as a performer. The president understood as well as his staff how to use a battlefield, a classroom, or the flag to communicate a hopeful message.

HOSTAGES FREED   Luck played a role as well. Problems that handcuffed Carter seemed to ease on Reagan's watch. The day he took office, Iran announced it would release the American hostages after 444 days of captivity. Three aging Russian leaders, beginning with Leonid Brezhnev in 1982, died suddenly, thereby greatly reducing the influence of the Soviet Union. And when a disturbed gunman shot Reagan in the chest two months after his inauguration, the wounds were not life threatening. Even Reagan's critics admired his courage in the face of death.

The Reagan Agenda

In addition to luck, however, Reagan viewed the economic downturn as an opportunity to push for his revolution in government. He called for massive tax cuts, deregulation of the economy, and a reduction in spending for social programs. Only the military would be spared the budget cutters' ax, because Reagan planned a forceful foreign policy to contain Soviet power.

SUPPLY-SIDE ECONOMICS   A commitment to **supply-side economics** became the cornerstone of the Reagan revolution. Supply-side advocates argued that high taxes and government regulation stifled business. The key to revival lay in a large tax cut—a politically popular proposal, though economically controversial. Lower tax revenues would not increase the massive and growing federal budget deficits, insisted supply-side economist Arthur Laffer. His calculations suggested that lower tax rates would stimulate the economy so greatly, tax revenues would actually grow, thanks to higher profits and a renewed prosperity. Broad cuts in social programs would further reduce deficits.

TAX CUTS   After little more than half a year in office, Congress handed the president most of the cuts he requested. The Economic Recovery Tax Act (ERTA) lowered income tax rates over the following three years by 25 percent, capital gains by 40 percent, and investment income rates by 28 percent. Taxpayers

Source: Library of Congress, Prints and Photographs Division [LC-DIG-highsm-15747]

| Ronald Reagan in the Oval Office of the White House.

in the highest brackets were far and away the biggest winners. At the same time, Reagan signed the Omnibus Budget Reconciliation Act, which slashed some $35 billion in spending from government programs. *The Wall Street Journal* hailed the two measures as a "spectacular tax victory," and news commentators suggested that Reagan had ended 50 years of liberal government.

Liberal government relied on the support of big labor. Here, too, Reagan struck a decisive blow. In 1981 members of PATCO, the air traffic controllers union, struck against what they claimed were dangerous and debilitating working conditions. PATCO workers were, however, both highly paid and public service employees. Reagan declared their strike illegal and, without addressing the issues they raised, summarily fired them. Large corporations seized on the antiunion climate to wrest significant concessions on wages and work rules.

Deregulating the Environment

Many conservatives viewed environmental policies as a strategy to regulate business. They were highly skeptical of the

©Yvonne Hemsy/Getty Images

| Striking air traffic controllers protest their firing.

growing alarms over global warming. The National Climate Program Office, created by Carter, was viewed by Reaganites as "an outpost in enemy territory." As for the Environmental Protection Agency, Reagan charged its new head, Anne Gorsuch, with the task of dismantling it. During her first year the EPA filed no new enforcement cases against hazardous waste sites, though the agency knew of some 18,000 that qualified for clean-up under the "Superfund" law, passed in Carter's final year in office. That law taxed the chemical and petroleum industries in order to provide money used to help clean up sites polluted by factories and refineries.

The Occupational Safety and Health Administration (OSHA) was also severely scaled back, ending efforts to set new health and safety standards or to regulate toxic work environments. Workers were at particular risk in plants that produced polyvinyl chloride (PVC) and similar chemicals, used in a wide array of consumer products. At a chemical plant in Louisiana run by German manufacturer BASF, members of the Oil, Chemical, and Atomic Workers union (OCAW) documented chemical wastes dumped into the Mississippi River. (They constantly smelled "this chlorine all day, twenty-four hours a day, depending on what job you're working at.") When OCAW called a strike to gain improved wages and working conditions, the company locked them out for five years. OSHA showed no interest in pursuing such cases.

Other conservative activists lobbied to allow private enterprise to develop more of the vast tracts of wilderness land and forests managed by the federal government. The spokespersons for cattle, mining, and timber interests—who referred to themselves as "**Sagebrush rebels**"—led the campaign to open up such lands to logging, cattle grazing, and real estate development. Reagan appointed James Watt, one such advocate, to head the Department of the Interior. Watt's abrasive style (he once denied the Beach Boys a concert permit, because he considered their music immoral) forced him to resign in 1983. But the administration continued to attack environmental regulations as an unnecessary restraint on free enterprise.

A Halfway Revolution

"REVENUE ENHANCEMENTS" Despite Reagan's tax-cut victories in the political arena, continued recession, rising interest rates, and crippling federal deficits sent the stock market into a tailspin. At first the president refused to compromise his commitment to lower taxes. Still, the evidence was clear that supply-side predictions of booming tax revenues had failed to materialize. So Reagan reversed course and accepted the Tax Equity and Fiscal Responsibility Act of 1982, a measure including $98 billion in tax increases disguised as "revenue enhancements." A year later Social Security reform led to further tax increases. In both cases Regan allowed pragmatism to trump ideology.

After the reversal on tax cuts, the economy began a strong upturn that extended through both of the president's terms in office. Labor productivity improved, inflation subsided to 4.3 percent, unemployment fell, and the stock markets rose sharply. Falling energy costs played a major role as OPEC members exceeded their production quotas. Having sold for as much as $30 per barrel, crude prices fell as low as $10.

ECONOMIC INEQUALITY The benefits of an improved economy were distributed unevenly across economic classes and regions. For the wealthiest Americans the 1980s were the best of times. The top 1 percent commanded a greater share of wealth (37 percent) than at any time since 1929. Their earnings per year were 25 times greater than the 40 percent of Americans at the bottom of the economic ladder.

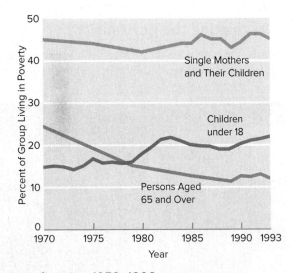

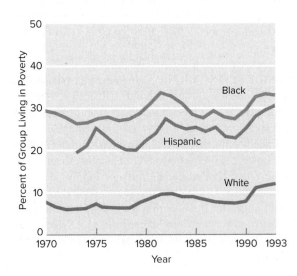

Poverty in America, 1970–1993

Social Security and other income supplements to older Americans reduced their rate of poverty. For all other traditionally impoverished groups the prosperity of the Reagan-Bush years left them slightly worse off than in 1980. The charts also indicate that poverty was most severe for single mothers and their children, and people of color.

Source: Levy, Frank, *The New Dollars and Dreams, American Incomes and Economic Change.* New York, NY: The Russell Sage Foundation, 1999.

Reagan and Bush: Conservative Revolutionaries or Pragmatic Leaders?

CONSERVATIVE GOALS	CONSERVATIVE ACTIONS/*PRAGMATIC ACTIONS*
Foreign Policy	
Restore U.S. power to the levels before the Vietnam War so that U.S. can "stand tall"	Invade Grenada and Panama Increase defense spending sharply *Withdraw U.S. forces from Lebanon after the tragic barracks bombing*
Isolate the Soviet Union as the "evil empire" and bring it down	Fail to agree to eliminate nuclear weapons *Negotiate with Soviets at Reykjavík and Moscow summits and accept sharp missile reductions under START treaty*
Proclaim the superiority of American values and American freedom	Support "authoritarian" dictators who are pro-American *Deemphasize Carter's commitment to human rights*
Fight global terrorism, insisting on no ransom for hostages	Bomb Libya *Attempt to free terrorist hostages by negotiating with Iranian "moderates"*
Oppose Castro and leftist political movements in the Americas	Attempt to overthrow the Sandinistas in Nicaragua by aiding Contras *Sell arms to Iran and use profits to buy guns for the Contras*
Domestic Policy	
Shrink the power and size of government	Restrict the role of OSHA Increase defense spending
Try to balance the federal budget by adopting "supply-side economics"	Cut income tax rates *Use "revenue enhancements" and Social Security taxes to reduce the deficit* *Agree to tax increases to close budget gap, despite "Read my lips: no new taxes"*
Reverse the liberal social agenda from the 1960s	Speak out for the Moral Majority agenda *Avoid major action on abortion rights, gay rights, and school prayer*
Create a Supreme Court hostile to such decisions as *Engle v. Vitale* and *Roe v. Wade* and opposed to the civil and criminal rights agenda of the Warren Court	Appoint Sandra Day O'Connor as first woman justice on Supreme Court *Appoint conservative justices Rehnquist, Scalia, and Thomas*
Support the Sagebrush rebels who sought reduced environmental regulation	Open public lands for development and reduce effectiveness of the EPA

(*left*) Source: National Archives & Records Administration (75853589); (*right*) ©Dirck Halstead/The LIFE Picture Collection/Getty Images

Still, good times meant new jobs—over 14.5 million of them. Three million of these were concentrated in unskilled, minimum-wage areas such as hotels, fast-food restaurants, and retail stores. High-paying jobs in financial services, real estate, insurance, and law went largely (70 percent) to white males; only 2 percent went to African Americans.

OUTSOURCING The 1980s also saw an acceleration of the trend toward **outsourcing** high-wage industrial jobs and polluting industries to areas such as Mexico and Asia. Given its commitment to free markets and free trade, the Reagan administration resisted proposals to keep jobs at home. Thus, even as the economy grew and inflation dropped below 2 percent, unemployment hovered above 6 percent, and poverty levels ranged from 11 to 15 percent. Cuts in programs such as food stamps, Medicaid, and school lunches increased the burden on the poor. The decision to classify ketchup as a vegetable and thereby meet government nutritional standards for a well-balanced diet symbolized for liberals the administration's indifference to those in need.

The Landscape of Technoburbs

THE PC REVOLUTION New technologies and an increasingly global economy accounted for changes in Americans' work and wealth distribution. During the 1980s sales soared for such new electronic goods as VCRs, cell phones, fax machines, compact disc players, and, above all, computers. In the 1970s Steve Jobs and Steve Wozniak, two techies from California, founded Apple Computer and introduced an affordable and user-friendly home computer. A few years later IBM entered the market with the PC and adopted a rival operating system, MS-DOS, designed by two software programmers, Paul Allen and Bill Gates. Success in marketing computers transformed the ways in which Americans moved, managed, and stored information.

MEDICAL TECHNOLOGIES Computer-assisted technologies were part of a larger revolution in medical technologies. The CAT scan (computed axial tomography) generated three-dimensional images of the body from flat (that is, two-dimensional) X-ray pictures. Magnetic resonance imaging and proton emission tomography (MRIs and PET scans) used different techniques to probe the human body. Neurochemistry made discoveries about brain functions that resulted in a new generation of psychotropic drugs, which modified moods and emotions. **Biogenetic engineering** was yet another dynamic technology. In 1977 Genentech Corporation used recombinant DNA research to produce a synthetic protein. Five years later, the company created a synthetic version of insulin, the first genetically engineered drug to win approval from the FDA. The health care industry in the 1980s was by far the biggest producer of new jobs.

As these technologies began to change lives, they also changed the landscape—literally. Unlike manufacturing

©Ted Thai/The LIFE Picture Collection/Getty Images

Steve Jobs poses with his Apple II computer.

industries of old, high-tech companies did not depend on transportation networks to move raw materials or ship finished products to market. They could set up shop where the quality of life was high and office rents were low or near university centers that generated new ideas, researchers, and entrepreneurs. The 1980s saw an explosion of edge cities or "technoburbs" along interstate highways where office and industrial parks housed technology companies, pharmaceutical concerns, professionals, and providers of financial services. As developers turned open meadows and farmlands into office parks, the string of technoburbs stretching between Palo Alto and San Jose came to be known as Silicon Valley—so named because of the miniature silicon wafers at the heart of microprocessor technology.

Winners and Losers in the Labor Market

YUPPIES Several characteristics distinguished workers in the new technology industries from those in older industrial sectors. In general they were much younger and better educated. Further, unlike the stuffy corporate culture of the 1950s, which stressed the idea of "go along to get along," the new businesses were far more informal. Casual clothing replaced the gray flannel suits; individualism and creativity marked the road to success, and those who flaunted authority were welcomed. The media began referring to young, upwardly mobile, urban professionals as Yuppies—part of the younger generation that repudiated the antimaterialistic values of their hippie forebears.

Access to computers marked a generational divide. To Gen-Xers, those born after 1963 (the end of the baby boom), computers and other electronic devices were second nature. Computerization and information technologies streamlined the workplace so that the time and cost of new product development and production fell sharply. Increased productivity also reduced the demand for low-skill workers. By contrast, demand for workers with education and technical skills rose (as did wages) and thereby increased the income gap between those at the top and bottom of the labor market.

WOMEN: HIGH-WAGE VS. LOW-WAGE JOBS In an economy in which brains displaced brawn, educated women were among the big winners. Not only did they find more jobs in high-tech areas and computerized offices, but they also increased their presence in law, medicine, business, and other professions. Still, many women continued to flow into lower-paying jobs in health care, education, social services, and government. The net result was that well-educated women gained far more economic independence and a more substantial political voice, while women with fewer skills and less education saw their earnings eroded. Single mothers with children, many who worked in low-wage jobs, were the nation's most impoverished group.

Job displacement in the 1980s had a devastating impact on two other groups: African American men and organized labor. Beginning in the 1970s, black males lost much of the gains they had made over the previous three decades. The decline in manufacturing industries such as steel and autos struck hardest at the older industrial cities where blacks had gained a foothold in the economy. Often lacking the education required in the technology sector, black men had difficulty finding new jobs and many simply dropped out of the labor market. Sociologists began to describe an underclass, trapped in poverty, while middle-class blacks escaped devastated urban neighborhoods.

UNION DECLINE As manufacturing declined so, too, did membership in unions. Labor organized 27 percent of all workers in 1953, 20 percent in 1980, 16 percent in 1990. Only the increase in the number of unionized government workers helped offset the shrinkage in the industrial sector. A two-tier system emerged whereby younger workers received lower pay and hence had less incentive to join unions. Smaller numbers reduced labor's political clout, weakened the Democratic Party, and spurred the conservative revolution.

 REVIEW

What were the goals of the Reagan revolution, and how did he hope to achieve them?

STANDING TALL IN A CHAOTIC WORLD

RONALD REAGAN'S VIEW OF WORLD affairs was primal. "The Soviet Union underlies all the unrest in the world," he stated in his 1980 campaign. Thus he made the defeat of the communist menace a central mission of his administration. To that end he believed Americans must put Vietnam behind them and once again stand tall in the world. Although he was pleased to see the Soviet threat dissolving by the end of his years in office, the president also discovered that firmness and military force alone were not sufficient to calm regional crises across the world.

The Military Buildup

DEFICITS Reagan described the Soviet Union as the "evil empire." His plan to defeat that enemy centered on a massive buildup of the American military. Whereas Richard Nixon had thought the United States needed enough force to fight one and one-half wars at any time, Reagan pushed for enough to fight three and one-half around the globe. That required expenditures of over $1.6 trillion in his first five years (Carter had planned for $1.2 trillion). The combination of massive defense spending and tax cuts created huge deficits. That drove up interest rates and thus the value of the dollar. The strong dollar slowed exports as the cost of American goods rose on world markets. Lower prices gave imports such as Japanese autos a large competitive advantage over American producers. The United States deficit of payments (the value of imports over exports) soared. From the end of World War I until the Reagan years, the United States had been the world's leading creditor nation. By 1986 it had become the world's largest debtor.

Debt was only one of the liabilities of the massive military buildup. Huge cost overruns and wasteful spending became widespread. Exposés of $600 toilet seats and $7,000 coffeepots symbolized spending run amok. Far more costly, however, were the multibillion-dollar weapons systems that either were unneeded or cost far more than planned. The air force, for example, persuaded Congress to fund the B-2 bomber, at a cost of $2 billion each and designed to penetrate Soviet air defenses. Only later did investigators determine that those Soviet air defenses did not exist. In general, advocates of the buildup exaggerated Soviet capabilities in order to pressure Congress to appropriate vast sums of money.

Talk of "standing tall" also spread fear. Reagan and his tough-talking defense planners spoke out about winning any nuclear exchange with the Soviet Union. Author Jonathan Schell debunked those claims in his book *Nuclear Winter.* In it, Schell described a war no one would win, in which debris in the atmosphere would create conditions fatal to all life on earth. Such warnings revived the antinuclear movement across East Asia, Europe, and America. Bishops of the American Catholic Church felt moved to announce their opposition to nuclear war.

Disaster in the Middle East

LEBANON The Middle East continued to be a flashpoint for U.S.-Soviet tensions. In 1982 Israel invaded neighboring Lebanon to destroy missiles supplied by Syria, a Soviet client state. Israeli general Ariel Sharon also used the invasion to strike a decisive blow against forces of the Palestine Liberation Organization (PLO) that were camped in Lebanon. As the Israeli offensive bogged down, however, international outrage over the massacre of Palestinians in Israeli-controlled camps forced Sharon to withdraw his troops.

Reagan then decided to send American troops to Beirut, Lebanon's capital, to protect the Palestinians and keep the peace between warring Christian and Muslim factions. Unfamiliar with the terrain or the politics, the Americans were drawn into supporting Christian militias. Muslim radicals responded first by bombing the American Embassy and then, in October 1983, a U.S. marine barracks. Some 239 troops died. Confronting a chorus of criticism from the media, Congress, and his own Defense Department, Reagan withdrew the American troops.

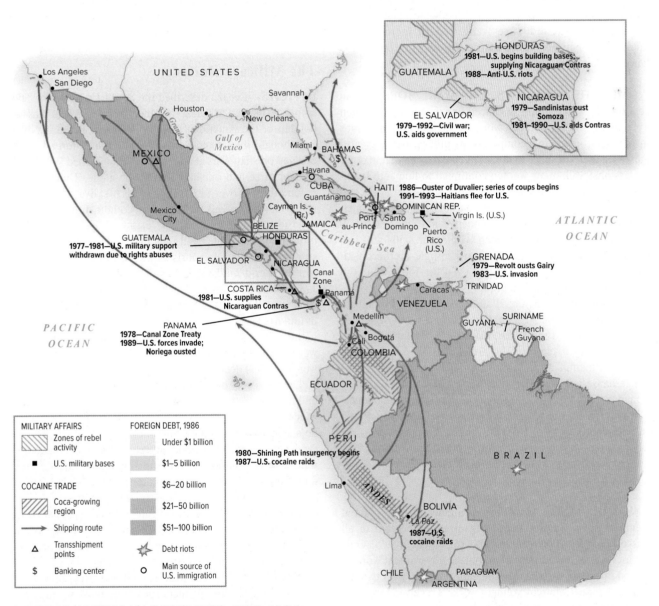

CENTRAL AMERICAN CONFLICTS, 1974–1990

President Reagan's attempts to overthrow the Sandinista government in Nicaragua and to contain communism focused American attention on Latin America. So, too, did the staggering debts Latin countries owed to banks in the United States and elsewhere. Equally distorting to the hemisphere's social and economic fabric was the sharp rise in the drug trade organized by criminal syndicates. Most notorious was the Medellín **cartel,** *which operated from a remote region in Colombia, shipping drugs through havens in Panama and the Bahamas into the United States while depositing its enormous profits in banks in Miami and offshore banking centers such as the Cayman Islands. The war on drugs led President Bush to invade Panama in December 1989 and bring its corrupt leader, Manuel Noriega, to the United States for trial.*

TERRORIST ATTACKS   The president also searched with little success for a way to respond to terrorist attacks by Islamic fundamentalists. In 1982 agents of Libya's Muammar al-Qadhafi exploded a bomb on an American airliner flying over Lockerbie, Scotland. Three years later terrorists took hostages in Lebanon, hijacked American airline flights, killed an American hostage on a Mediterranean cruise ship, and bombed a West German nightclub popular with American troops. In response to such provocations, the president was always forceful and uncompromising: "Let terrorists beware: . . . our policy will be one of swift and effective retribution."

But against whom should the United States seek retribution? American intelligence agencies had only sketchy profiles of the many terrorist factions and their political allies. In 1986 the president launched an attack against Libya, which sponsored terrorism. But so too did Syria and Iran, against whom the administration did nothing.

Frustrations in Central America

At first, Reagan found he could stand tall closer to home. On the pretext of protecting American medical students studying on the Caribbean island of Grenada, American troops crushed a band of pro-Cuban rebels and evacuated the students, who were hardly at risk. But the action in Grenada was largely symbolic.

More challenging was Reagan's campaign to overthrow the left-wing Sandinista government in Nicaragua. The president justified arming the anti-Sandinista "Contras" as "freedom fighters" battling in the spirit of America's Founding Fathers. True, the Contras included a few democrats and disillusioned Sandinistas, but the majority had served in the brutal and corrupt dictatorship of Anastasio Somoza, which the Sandinistas overthrew in 1979.

CONTRAS   Reagan had no desire to broker a settlement between the opposing forces. Instead, he allowed the CIA to help the Contras mine Nicaragua's harbor, in hopes of destabilizing the Sandinistas. When the mines damaged foreign ships—a violation of international law—conservatives and liberals alike condemned the president's actions. Congress adopted the Boland Amendment, which explicitly forbade the CIA or "any other agency or entity involved in intelligence activities" to spend money to support the Contras "directly or indirectly." Reagan reluctantly signed the measure, though he remained determined to overthrow the Sandinistas.

Neither mushrooming deficits nor frustrations in the Middle East and Central America dented Ronald Reagan's popularity. The booming economy kept his poll ratings high. In the 1984 election he easily won a second term, winning 59 percent of the popular vote against Walter Mondale of Minnesota. Mondale's choice of Geraldine Ferraro of New York as the first female running mate made the presidential campaign noteworthy. Reagan and his advisors entered his second term determined to force solutions to some of his most stubborn foreign policy problems. It was a decision that led to scandal and threatened the constitutional system of checks and balances.

The Iran-Contra Connection

By mid-1985 Reagan policy makers faced two major frustrations. First, Congress had forbidden any support of the Contras in Central America, and second, Iranian-backed terrorists continued to hold hostages in Lebanon. In the summer of 1985 a course of events was set in motion that eventually linked these two issues.

ARMS FOR HOSTAGES DEAL   The president made it increasingly clear that he wanted to find a way to free the remaining hostages. National Security Advisor Robert McFarlane suggested opening a channel to "moderate factions" in the Iranian government. If the United States sold Iran a few weapons, the grateful moderates might use their influence in Lebanon to free the hostages. But an agreement to exchange arms for hostages would violate the president's vow never to pay ransom to terrorists. Still, over the following year, four secret arms shipments went to Iran. One hostage was set free. McFarlane's successor as national security advisor, Admiral John Poindexter, had the president sign a secret intelligence "finding" that allowed him and his associates to pursue their mission without informing anyone in Congress or even the secretaries of defense and state. Because the president ignored the details of foreign policy, McFarlane, Poindexter, and their aides had assumed the power to act on their own.

OLIVER NORTH   The man most often pulling the strings was Lieutenant Colonel Oliver "Ollie" North, a junior officer under McFarlane and later Poindexter. A Vietnam veteran with a flair for the dramatic, North was impatient with bureaucratic procedures. In January 1986 he hit on the idea that the profits made selling arms to Iran could be siphoned off to buy weapons for the Contras. The Iranian arms dealer who brokered the deal thought it a great idea. "I think this is now, Ollie, the best chance, because . . . we never get such

©Lana Harris/AP Photo

Oliver North successfully took the offensive in his testimony before the congressional committee investigating the Iran-Contra scandals. Here, North delivers a pro-Contra lecture to the committee.

good money out of this," he laughed, as he was recorded on a tape North himself made. "We do everything. We do hostages free of charge; we do all terrorists free of charge; Central America free of charge." Smuggling drugs into the United States from Central America provided North with another source of funds.

Cover Blown

The secret operation was exposed in the fall of 1986, when reports of the Iranian arms deal surfaced in a Lebanese newspaper. Astonished reporters besieged the administration, demanding to know how secret arms sales to a terrorist regime benefited the president's antiterrorist campaign. As the inquiry continued, the link between the arms sales and the Contras was discovered.

IRANGATE   The press nicknamed the scandal "Irangate," comparing it to Richard Nixon's Watergate affair. But Irangate raised more troubling issues. During Watergate, President Nixon had led the cover-up to save his own political skin. But during the Iran-Contra congressional hearings, Admiral Poindexter testified that he had kept Reagan in ignorance "so that I could insulate him from the decision and provide some future deniability for the president if it ever leaked out." In that way Iran-Contra revealed a presidency out of control. An unelected segment within the government had taken upon itself the power to pursue its own policies outside legal channels.

From Cold War to *Glasnost*

Because few members of Congress wanted to impeach a popular president, the hearings came to a sputtering end. Reagan's prestige returned, in part because of substantial improvement in Soviet-American relations. By the 1980s the Soviet Union was far weaker than American experts, including the CIA, had ever recognized. The Soviet economy stagnated; the Communist Party was mired in corruption. The war in Afghanistan had become a Russian Vietnam. By accelerating the arms race, Reagan placed additional pressure on the Russians.

MIKHAIL GORBACHEV   In 1985 a fresh spirit entered the Kremlin. Unlike the aged leaders who preceded him, Mikhail Gorbachev was young and saw the need for reform within the Soviet Union. Gorbachev's fundamental restructuring, or *perestroika*, set about improving relations with the United States. He reduced military commitments and adopted a policy of openness (*glasnost*) about problems in the Soviet Union. In October, the two leaders held their second summit in Reykjavík, Iceland. Gorbachev dangled the possibility of abolishing all nuclear weapons. Reagan seemed receptive to the idea, but in the end he and his advisors backed away from such a radical proposal. A summit in Moscow two years later eliminated an entire class of nuclear missiles with ranges of 600 to 3,400 miles. Both sides agreed to allow on-site inspections of missile bases and the facilities where missiles would be destroyed.

Thus, as the election of 1988 approached, the president could claim credit for improved relations with the Soviet Union. Loyalty to Ronald Reagan made Vice President George H. W. Bush the Republican heir apparent. The Democratic challenger, Governor Michael Dukakis of Massachusetts, pointed out that poor and even many middle-class Americans had lost ground during the 1980s. But Bush put the lackluster Dukakis on the defensive. With the economy reasonably robust, Bush won by a comfortable margin. The Reagan agenda remained on track.

☑ REVIEW
How did Reagan try to overcome the legacy of Vietnam?

AN END TO THE COLD WAR

PRESIDENT GEORGE HERBERT WALKER BUSH was born to both privilege and politics. The son of a Connecticut senator, he attended an exclusive boarding school and then Ivy League Yale University. That background made him part of the East Coast establishment often scorned by more-populist Republicans. Yet once the oil business lured Bush to Texas, he moved to the right, becoming a Goldwater Republican when he ran unsuccessfully for the Senate in 1964. Foreign policy interested him far more than domestic politics. But in the end, inattention to domestic issues proved his undoing as the economy slid into recession.

A Post–Cold War Foreign Policy

To the astonishment of most Western observers, Mikhail Gorbachev's reform policies led not only to the collapse of the Soviet empire but also to the breakup of the Soviet Union itself. In December 1988, Gorbachev spoke in the United Nations of a "new world order." To that end he began liquidating the Soviet cold war legacy, as the last Russian troops began leaving Afghanistan and then Eastern Europe.

THE FALL OF COMMUNISM   Throughout 1989 Eastern Europeans began to test their newfound freedom. In Poland, Hungary, Bulgaria, Czechoslovakia, and, most violently, Romania, Communist dictators fell from power. Nothing more inspired the world than the stream of celebrating East Germans pouring through the Berlin Wall in November 1989. Within a year the wall, a symbol of Communist oppression, had been torn down and Germany reunified. Although Gorbachev struggled to keep together the 15 republics that made up the U.S.S.R., the forces of nationalism and reform pulled the Soviet Union apart. The Baltic republics—Lithuania, Latvia, and Estonia—declared their independence in 1991. Then, in December, the Slavic republics of Ukraine, Belarus, and Russia formed a new Commonwealth of Independent States. By the end of December eight more of the former Soviet republics had joined the loose federation. Boris Yeltsin, the charismatic president of Russia, became the Commonwealth's

The Berlin Wall

This platform was erected in 1969 when President Richard Nixon visited the Berlin Wall.

In what way do these paintings suggest a difference between the public cultures of East and West Berlin?

Which side of the wall is East and which is West? How can you tell?

(*top*) Source: National Archives and Records Administration (NLNP-WHPO-MOF-0388(13A)); (*bottom*) ©Owen Franken/Getty Images

No place in the world reflected cold war tensions more than the city of Berlin. And East Germany's erection of a wall there in August 1961—launched in great secrecy in the dead of night—struck many Americans as an escalation of the cold war. Suddenly, the outpouring of educated and skilled East Germans escaping to West Germany ceased. For some 28 years the Wall stood as a stark symbol of a divided Germany, and historians can use the Wall to help track the ups and downs of the long conflict between East and West. Attempted escapes, the addition of barbed wire and guard posts, espionage novels such as *The Spy Who Came in from the Cold,* the periodic scaffolding erected so that American presidents could project their messages to captive citizens. . . . By 1987 tensions had begun to ease. President Ronald Reagan, while in the city commemorating Berlin's 750th anniversary, challenged Soviet Premier Mikhail Gorbachev to "tear down this wall." Two years later the wall came down.

THINKING CRITICALLY

What geographic difficulties prompted East Germany to build the Wall? (See the map in Chapter 27.) What symbolic meanings does a wall suggest? Why did so many East Germans want to move to the West? Can you think of ways in which building a wall might have been a good thing?

dominant figure. With no Soviet Union left to preside over, Gorbachev resigned.

Although President Bush increasingly supported Gorbachev's reforms, he did so with caution. Even if he had wished to aid Eastern Europe and the new Commonwealth states, soaring deficits at home limited his options. The administration seemed to support the status quo in Communist China, too. When in June 1989 China's aging leadership crushed students rallying for democratic reform in Beijing's Tiananmen Square, Bush muted American protests.

The fall of the Soviet Union signaled the end of a cold war that, more than once, had threatened a nuclear end to human history. At a series of summits with Russian leaders, the United States and its former rivals agreed to sharp reductions

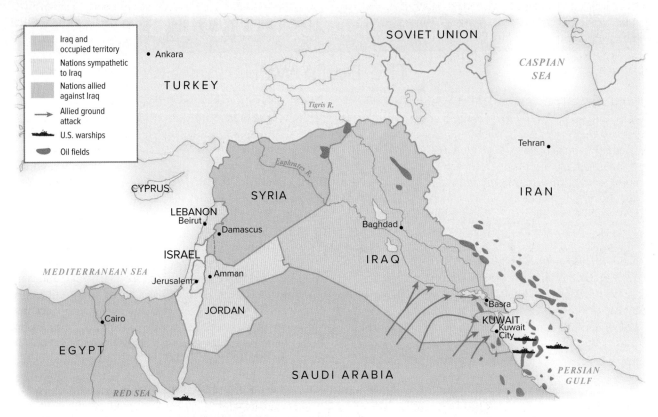

WAR WITH IRAQ: OPERATION DESERT STORM

When Saddam Hussein invaded oil-rich Kuwait on August 2, 1990, the United States formed a coalition to force out the Iraqis. (Although Turkey was not a formal member, it allowed its airfields to be used. Israel remained uninvolved to avoid antagonizing Arab coalition members.) The coalition launched Operation Desert Storm in January 1991; land forces invaded on February 24 (Operation Desert Saber), routing Iraqi troops, who left Kuwait in ruin and its oil fields aflame. **Why did Saddam Hussein's invasion of Kuwait threaten American and European interests?**

in their stockpiles of nuclear weapons. The Strategic Arms Reduction Treaty (or START), concluded in July 1991, far surpassed the limits negotiated in earlier SALT talks. By June 1992 Bush and Yeltsin had agreed to even sharper cuts.

The Gulf War

SADDAM HUSSEIN With two superpowers no longer facing off against each other, what would the "new world order" look like? If anything, regional crises loomed larger. Instability in the Middle East produced the greatest foreign policy challenge. From 1980 to 1988 Iran and Iraq had battered each other in a debilitating war. During those years the Reagan administration assisted Iraq with weapons and intelligence, until at last it won a narrow victory over Iran's fundamentalists. But Iraq's ruthless dictator, Saddam Hussein, had run up enormous debts. To ease his financial crisis, Hussein cast a covetous eye on his neighbor, the small oil-rich sheikdom of Kuwait. In August 1990, 120,000 Iraqi troops invaded and occupied Kuwait, catching the Bush administration off guard. Would Hussein stop there?

Bush compared Hussein to Hitler and was determined to free Kuwait. He successfully coordinated a United Nations–backed economic boycott. Increasing the pressure further, he deployed half a million American troops in Saudi Arabia and

the Persian Gulf. By November Bush had won a resolution from the Security Council permitting the use of military force if Hussein did not withdraw.

OPERATION DESERT STORM On January 17, 1991, air attacks by France, Italy, Britain, Saudi Arabia, and the United States launched Operation Desert Storm. After weeks of merciless pounding from the air, ground operations shattered Hussein's vaunted Republican Guards in less than 100 hours. In an act of spite, Hussein resorted to ecoterrorism. His forces set Kuwait's oil fields ablaze and dumped huge quantities of crude oil into the rich Persian Gulf ecosystem. It did him no good: by the end of February Kuwait was liberated, and nothing stood between Allied forces and Iraq's capital, Baghdad. Bush was unwilling to advance that far—and most other nations in the coalition agreed. If Hussein were toppled, it was not clear who in Iraq would fill the vacuum of power or what power could contain the ambitions of neighboring Iran.

Domestic Doldrums

Victory in the Gulf War boosted the president's popularity so high that aides brushed aside the need for any bold domestic program. "Frankly, this president doesn't need another single piece of legislation, unless it's absolutely right," asserted John Sununu, his cocky chief of staff. "In fact, if Congress wants to come together, adjourn, and leave, it's all right with us." That attitude suggested a lack of direction that proved fatal to Bush's reelection hopes.

ENVIRONMENTAL ISSUES At first Bush envisioned a "kinder, gentler" nation. Yet pressures from conservative Republicans kept the new president from straying too far from path of the Reagan revolution. When delegates from 178 nations met at an "Earth Summit" in Rio de Janeiro in 1992, the president opposed efforts to draft stricter rules to lessen the threat of global warming. Bush did sign into law the sweeping Clean Air Act passed by Congress in 1990. But soon after, Vice President Dan Quayle established a "Council on Competitiveness" to rewrite regulations that corporations found burdensome.

Similarly, the president called for reform of an educational system whose quality had declined through the 1980s. But, while he convened a well-publicized "Education Summit" in 1989, the delegates issued a modest set of goals only after the president was urged to do so by his co-chair at the summit, Governor Bill Clinton of Arkansas.

The Conservative Court

Although Presidents Reagan and Bush both spoke out against abortion, affirmative action, the banning of prayer in public schools, and other conservative social issues, neither made action a priority. Even so, both presidents shaped social policy through their appointments to the Supreme Court. Reagan placed three members on the bench, including in 1981 Sandra Day O'Connor, the first woman to sit on the high court. Bush nominated two justices. As more liberal members of the Court retired (including William Brennan and Thurgood Marshall), the decisions handed down became distinctly more conservative. The appointment of Antonin Scalia gave the Court its most outspoken conservative.

THE CLARENCE THOMAS HEARINGS In 1991 the Senate hotly debated President Bush's nomination of Clarence Thomas, an outspoken black conservative and former member of the Reagan administration. The confirmation hearings became even more contentious when Anita Hill, an attorney who had worked for Thomas, testified that he had sexually harassed her. Women's groups blasted the all-male Judiciary Committee for keeping Hill's allegations private until reporters uncovered the story. Thomas and his defenders accused his opponents of using a disgruntled woman to help conduct a latter-day lynching. In the end the Senate narrowly voted to confirm, and Thomas joined Scalia as one of the Court's most conservative members.

The Court's conservative turn affected decisions on affirmative action—those laws that gave preferred treatment to minority groups in order to remedy past discrimination.

©Dirck Halstead/The LIFE Picture Collection/Getty Images

In 1991 Justice Clarence Thomas survived a bitter Senate battle during his Supreme Court confirmation hearings. Here, he is sworn in by Chief Justice William Rehnquist as Thomas's wife and President George H. W. Bush and Barbara Bush look on. Thomas's conservative views on abortion and affirmative action were later confirmed by the votes he cast as a justice.

State and federal courts and legislatures had used techniques such as busing and the setting of quotas to overturn past injustices. As early as 1978, however, the Court began to set limits on affirmative action. In *Bakke v. Regents of the University of California* (1978), the majority ruled that college admissions staffs could not set fixed quotas, although they could still use race as a guiding factor in trying to create a more diverse student body. Increasingly, the Court made it easier for white citizens to challenge affirmative action programs. At the same time, it set higher standards for those who wished to put forward a claim of discrimination. "An amorphous claim that there has been past discrimination in a particular industry cannot justify the use of an unyielding racial quota," wrote Justice O'Connor in 1989.

Disillusionment and Anger

Ronald Reagan had given a sunny face to conservatism. He had assured voters that if taxes were cut, the economy would revive and deficits would fall. He promised that if "big government" could be scaled back, there would be a new "morning in America." Yet a decade of hands-off conservative leadership left the deficit ballooning and state and local governments larger than ever. A growing number of Americans felt that the institutions of government were seriously off track. Indeed, the attacks on big government by Reagan and Bush fueled that cynicism.

S&L CRISIS   A series of longer-term crises contributed to this sense of disillusionment. One of the most threatening centered on the nation's savings and loan institutions. By the end of the decade these thrifts were failing at the highest rate since the Great Depression. To help increase bank profits, the Carter administration and Congress had agreed to cut back federal regulations. That move allowed savings and loan institutions to invest their funds more speculatively. Few depositors noticed or cared, because their money was insured by the Federal Savings and Loan Insurance Corporation. The government, however, had to pay depositors as these banks failed in large numbers. During the Bush administration it become clear that the cost of rebuilding the failed banks and paying off huge debts might run into hundreds of billions of dollars.

The late 1980s also brought a public health crisis. Americans were spending a higher percentage of their resources on medical care than were citizens in other nations, yet they were no healthier. As medical costs soared, more than 30 million Americans had no health insurance. The crisis was worsened by a fatal disorder that physicians began diagnosing in the early 1980s: acquired immunodeficiency syndrome, or AIDS. With no cure available the disease threatened to take on epidemic proportions not only in the United States but around the globe as well. Yet because the illness at first struck hardest at the male homosexual community and intravenous drug users, many groups in American society were reluctant to address the problem.

Bank failures, skyrocketing health costs, anger over poverty and discrimination—none of these problems by themselves

©Kristoffer Tripplaar/Alamy

| *As the AIDS epidemic spread in the 1980s, quilts such as these expressed sorrow for lost friends and loved ones. The quilts also served to raise public awareness of the need for a more effective policy to help people living with AIDS and to fight the disease. The AIDS Quilt is displayed on the National Mall in Washington, D.C.*

derailed the conservative revolution. Still, the various crises demonstrated how pivotal government had become in providing social services and limiting the abuses of powerful private interests in a high-technology society.

The Election of 1992

GRAMM-RUDMAN ACT   In the end, George Bush's inability to rein in soaring government deficits damaged his reelection prospects. "Read my lips! No new taxes," he pledged to campaign audiences in 1988. But the president and Congress were at loggerheads over how to reach the holy grail of so many conservatives: a balanced budget. In 1985 Congress had passed the Gramm-Rudman Act, establishing a set of steadily increasing limits on federal spending. These limits were meant to force Congress and the president to make hard choices needed to reach a balanced budget. If they did not, automatic across-the-board cuts would go into effect. By 1990 the law's automatic procedures were threatening programs such as

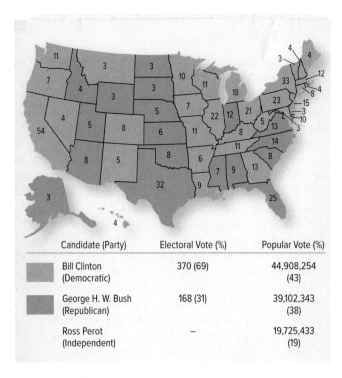

Candidate (Party)	Electoral Vote (%)	Popular Vote (%)
Bill Clinton (Democratic)	370 (69)	44,908,254 (43)
George H. W. Bush (Republican)	168 (31)	39,102,343 (38)
Ross Perot (Independent)	–	19,725,433 (19)

ELECTION OF 1992

Medicare, which Republicans and Democrats alike supported. Facing such unpopular cuts, Bush agreed to a package of new taxes along with budget cuts. Conservatives felt betrayed, and in the end, the deficit grew larger all the same.

WHITE-COLLAR UNEMPLOYMENT As the election of 1992 approached, unemployment stood at more than 8 percent, penetrating to areas of the economy not affected by most recessions. Wages for middle-class families had not increased since the early 1970s and had actually declined during Bush's presidency. Many Reagan Democrats seemed ready to return to the government activism of Franklin Roosevelt.

"IT'S THE ECONOMY . . ." Meanwhile, the Democrats nominated Governor Bill Clinton of Arkansas. During the campaign, Clinton was dogged by reports of marital infidelity, by his halfhearted admission that he had tried marijuana while a student but had not inhaled, and by his youthful opposition to the war in Vietnam. Still, he gained ground by hammering away at Bush for failing to revive the economy. "It's the economy, stupid!" read the sign tacked up at his election headquarters to remind Clinton workers of the campaign's central theme. Clinton painted himself as a new kind of Democrat: a centrist, willing to work with business, and not a creature of liberal interest groups.

At the voting booth, middle-of-the-road voters turned to Clinton and, in smaller numbers, to third-party challenger H. Ross Perot. Clinton captured 43 percent of the popular vote (to Bush's 38 and Perot's 19) in the largest turnout—55 percent—in 20 years. The election of four women to the Senate, including

the first African American woman, Carol Moseley Braun, indicated that gender had become an electoral factor.

> ✓ **REVIEW**
> How did Reagan, Bush, and Gorbachev take steps to end the cold war?

PUTTING HISTORY IN GLOBAL CONTEXT

THE 1992 ELECTION LEFT THE fate of the conservative revolution unresolved. Under Reagan and Bush the economy had grown and inflation had subsided. Yet prosperity benefited mostly those at the upper end of the income scale. The majority of Americans saw their finances stagnate or grow worse. Reagan and Bush both had supported a conservative social agenda that sought to restrict abortion rights, return prayer to the schools, and end affirmative action, but neither had done much to put that agenda into action. Both presidents significantly weakened the capacity of the federal government to implement social programs. No longer did Americans expect Washington to solve all the issues of the day. How, then, would the nation meet the future needs of the increasing numbers of poor, minority, elderly, and immigrant Americans?

Reagan and Bush had also presided over the end of the cold war. Despite a growing isolationist sentiment among Democrats and Republicans, both presidents had shown a willingness to assert American power—in Libya, in Lebanon, in Nicaragua, in Panama, in Somalia, in the Persian Gulf—though these were situations in which no major conflict threatened. What role would the United States play in the post–cold war era, when it stood as the lone superpower in the world arena? That was a question for William Jefferson Clinton as he sought to lead the United States into the twenty-first century.

CHAPTER SUMMARY

During the years of the Ford, Carter, Reagan, and Bush administrations, the nation's political and social agenda was increasingly determined by a conservative movement, including newly politicized evangelical Christians, that sought to restore traditional religious and family values, patriotism, and a limited role for government.

- An energy crisis brought on by Arab-Israeli conflict and an oil boycott by the OPEC nations worsened an already ailing American economy.

- Secretary of State Henry Kissinger used shuttle diplomacy to bring an uneasy peace to the Middle East. He and President Ford sought to preserve American power and ease diplomatic tensions by pursuing détente with the Soviet Union.

- Jimmy Carter, unable to end the recession at home, pursued a human rights policy abroad and the negotiation of the Camp David Accords between Israel and Egypt—only to have the Soviet invasion of Afghanistan and the Iranian hostage crisis undermine his foreign policy.

- Ronald Reagan led the conservative tide with a program to limit the power of labor unions, reduce government regulation, lower taxes, and sharply increase spending on the military.

- Despite a revived economy, Reagan's tax cuts had two undesirable outcomes: huge government budget deficits and a growing gap in income between the rich and poor.

- Conservative appointments to the federal judiciary and the Supreme Court led to decisions increasing limits on government intervention in the areas of civil rights, affirmative action, abortion rights, and the separation of church and state.

- Reagan's efforts to "stand tall" in foreign policy led to the Iran-Contra scandal, which revealed a broad pattern of illegal arms shipments to right-wing rebels in Nicaragua and the trading of arms to Iran in an unsuccessful attempt to win the release of hostages in Lebanon—actions for which the president was sharply criticized but not impeached.

- Both Reagan and George Bush welcomed reforms set in motion by Mikhail Gorbachev that led by 1991 to the breakup of the Soviet Union, reductions in nuclear arms, and an end to the cold war.

- In the post–cold war era, regional conflicts proved more troublesome as Iraq's invasion of Kuwait led Bush to form a UN coalition that routed the forces of Saddam Hussein in Operation Desert Storm.

- For George Bush a continuing recession, high budget deficits, and high unemployment undermined his bid for reelection.

Digging Deeper

Bruce J. Schulman, *The Seventies* (2002), follows the transition from the 1960s to the Reagan era. An intriguing new look at the same subject is Philip Jenkins, *Decade of Nightmares: The End of the Sixties and the Making of Eighties America* (2006). An evenhanded treatment of Jimmy Carter is Robert A. Strong, *Working in the World: Jimmy Carter and the Making of American Foreign Policy* (2000). Two books that do justice to Ronald Reagan and the politics of the right are John Ehrman, *The Eighties: America in the Age of Reagan* (2006); and Gil Troy, *Morning in America: How Ronald Reagan Invented the 1980s* (2005). Considering the transformation into the digital world is Fred Turner, *From Counterculture to Cyberculture: Stewart Brand, the Whole Earth Network, and the Rise of Digital Utopianism* (2006). For another view of the PC revolution, see Walter Isaacson, *Steve Jobs* (2011). Tim Wu cogently analyzes the evolution of Apple, Google, and AT&T in *The Master Switch: The Rise and Fall of Information Empires* (2010).

To understand the evangelical move into politics, see Steven P. Miller, *The Age of Evangelicalism: America's Born-Again Years* (2014). Randall Balmer, *Mine Eyes Have Seen the Glory: A Journey into the Evangelical Subculture in America* (2006), offers the perspectives of someone raised in the evangelical tradition. The issue of income inequality is well explained in Frank Levy, *The New Dollars and Dreams: American Incomes and Economic Change* (1999). Racial currents of the era are powerfully conveyed in Nicholas Lemann, *The Promised Land* (1995). The reasonably friendly treatment of George H. W. Bush by Ryan J. Barilleaux and Mark J. Rozell, *Power and Prudence: The Presidency of George H. W. Bush* (2004), can moderate the often insightful Kevin Phillips, *American Dynasty: Aristocracy, Fortune, and the Politics of Deceit in the House of Bush* (2004). On the first Gulf War, see Alberto Bin, Richard Hill, and Archer Jones, *Desert Storm: A Forgotten War* (1998).

32 The United States in a Global Community

1980–Present

These resident physicians in Orange, California, reflect the nation's growing multiracial community, as immigrants from Latin America, Asia, and Africa have joined a new wave of newcomers over the past three decades.

©Marmaduke St. John/Alamy

>> An American Story

OF GROCERY CHAINS AND MIGRATION CHAINS

Juan Chanax had never been far from San Cristobal, a village in the Guatemalan highlands where 2,000 years earlier, his Mayan ancestors had created one of the world's great civilizations. By the late 1970s, however, the San Cristobal economy offered only low-wage work at an American textile factory. Chanax, with barely enough to live on and no money to treat his son's illness, decided to go north to the United States, where "people could work and make their own lives," as he put it.

It took three months to get across the U.S.-Mexican border, evading thieves and hostile border guards. Chanax carried little more than a letter introducing him to several Guatemalans. They suggested he apply at Randall's, an upscale Houston supermarket chain, which was eager to expand as high oil prices set the Texas economy to booming. The grocery chain did not want just any low-wage workers. It specialized in high-priced goods in fancy suburban stores. Its upscale customers received valet parking, hassle-free shopping, and service from uniformed employees. Chanax was happy to do any job without complaint. Even on his minimum-wage salary, he could wire money home to his family. And when the manager said Randall's would soon need more workers, Chanax arranged for his brother-in-law and an uncle to come north. Over time Randall's began to hire Guatemalans exclusively. Shortly before a new store opened, the managers would tell Chanax how many maintenance people they needed. He would then recruit more Mayas from San Cristobal and, along with other experienced Mayas, prepare the newcomers for their jobs. That meant more than learning to clean and stack. The recruits were also told to arrive on time, work hard, and disrespect no one. When a problem arose, they did not take it to a Randall's manager but to another Guatemalan. "That way," as Chanax observed, "if a man was sick or had to leave work early or anything, we would solve it ourselves."

Within five years after Juan Chanax reached Houston, over a thousand Mayas from San Cristobal worked at Randall's. A single person had created what scholars call a migration chain. Through Chanax, Randall's had found access to a minimum-wage workforce that would perform willingly—in the company's words—as "cheerful servants." The Mayas, in turn, found opportunities unavailable in Guatemala. In the process Chanax and other early immigrants had become department managers and supervising assistants; their wives often worked as maids and servants in the homes of Houston's rapidly growing upper-income communities.

©Robert Suro/Alicia Patterson Foundation
| *Juan Chanax*

In many ways Chanax and his fellow Guatemalans mirrored the classic tale of immigrants realizing the American dream. In suburban Houston they formed their own community in an area that came to be known as Las Americas. There, various Central American immigrant groups established churches and social clubs amid some 90 apartment complexes that a decade or two earlier had housed mostly young, single office workers. On weekends and evenings, rival soccer teams played in the nearby park. (Juan, also the soccer league's president, helped new teams fill out the forms required by the parks department to use its fields.) The growth of Las Americas in the late twentieth century echoed the pattern of immigrants who had come to the United States at the century's opening.

Yet those patterns had changed too. Cities remained the mecca of most immigrants, but many newcomers of the 1980s and 1990s settled in suburban areas, particularly in the West and Southwest. Industrial factories provided the lion's share of work in the 1890s, but a century later the service industries—grocery stores, fast-food chains, janitorial companies—absorbed many more immigrants. And the faces had changed, as European immigrants found themselves outnumbered by Latinos from Mexico and Central America as well as by Asians from the Philippines, China, Korea, Southeast Asia, and the Indian subcontinent, not to mention increasing numbers of Russians, Arabs from the Middle East, and Africans. Transportation and communications networks tied immigrants to their home countries more strongly than in the past, allowing newcomers like Juan to keep regularly in touch with former neighbors and relatives. Immigrants continued to participate in home-country politics more easily; they could wire money instantly to relatives and even build homes thousands of miles away where one day they planned to retire.

With the arrival of the twenty-first century, immigration was only one factor that linked American society to the world. The interwoven strands of global finance, the blossoming connections to the new Internet, the politics of global terrorism, and above all the threat of global warming ensured that even if Americans wanted to, they could not ignore the rest of the world. <<

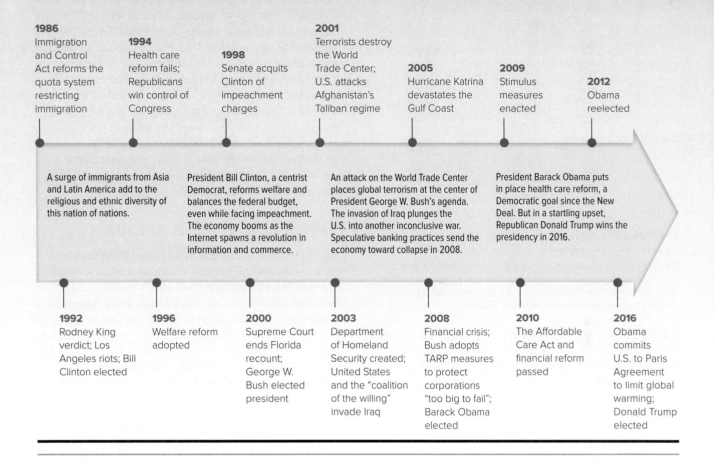

1986
Immigration and Control Act reforms the quota system restricting immigration

1994
Health care reform fails; Republicans win control of Congress

1998
Senate acquits Clinton of impeachment charges

2001
Terrorists destroy the World Trade Center; U.S. attacks Afghanistan's Taliban regime

2005
Hurricane Katrina devastates the Gulf Coast

2009
Stimulus measures enacted

2012
Obama reelected

A surge of immigrants from Asia and Latin America add to the religious and ethnic diversity of this nation of nations.

President Bill Clinton, a centrist Democrat, reforms welfare and balances the federal budget, even while facing impeachment. The economy booms as the Internet spawns a revolution in information and commerce.

An attack on the World Trade Center places global terrorism at the center of President George W. Bush's agenda. The invasion of Iraq plunges the U.S. into another inconclusive war. Speculative banking practices send the economy toward collapse in 2008.

President Barack Obama puts in place health care reform, a Democratic goal since the New Deal. But in a startling upset, Republican Donald Trump wins the presidency in 2016.

1992
Rodney King verdict; Los Angeles riots; Bill Clinton elected

1996
Welfare reform adopted

2000
Supreme Court ends Florida recount; George W. Bush elected president

2003
Department of Homeland Security created; United States and the "coalition of the willing" invade Iraq

2008
Financial crisis; Bush adopts TARP measures to protect corporations "too big to fail"; Barack Obama elected

2010
The Affordable Care Act and financial reform passed

2016
Obama commits U.S. to Paris Agreement to limit global warming; Donald Trump elected

THE NEW IMMIGRATION

THE IMMIGRATION ACT OF 1965 (see Chapter 29) altered the face of American life. The lawmakers who passed the act did not expect such far-reaching consequences, because they assumed that Europeans would continue to predominate among newcomers. Yet reform of the old quota system opened the way for a wave of immigrants unequaled since the beginning of the century.

ECONOMIC AND POLITICAL CAUSES OF IMMIGRATION Turmoil abroad pushed many immigrants toward the United States, beginning in the 1960s with Fidel Castro's revolution in Cuba and unrest in the Dominican Republic. The war in Vietnam and its aftermath produced more than 500,000 refugees in the 15 years after 1975. Revolutionary conflicts in Central America during the 1980s launched new immigration streams. Yet economic factors played as great a role as the terrors of war. Although some Filipinos fled the repressive regime of Ferdinand Marcos, many more came to the United States in a more straightforward search for jobs. When Mexico suffered an economic downturn in the 1980s, emigration there rose sharply.

In all, over 27 million immigrants arrived in the United States between 1990 and 2018. The nation's foreign-born population rose to almost 12 percent, the highest proportion since World War I. By 2009 the Latino population approached 50 million and exceeded the population of African Americans. The Asian American population grew at an even faster rate to about 16 million. Throughout the 1990s a steadily expanding economy made immigrants a welcome source of new labor. But the world economic crisis after 2007 provoked new debates over immigration and the problem of illegal aliens.

The New Look of America: Asian Americans

In 1970, 96 percent of Asian Americans were Japanese, Chinese, or Filipino. By 2000 those same three groups constituted only about half of all Asian Americans. As the diversity of Asian immigration increased, Asian Indians, Koreans, and Vietnamese came to outnumber Japanese Americans. The newcomers also varied dramatically in economic background, crowding both ends of the economic spectrum.

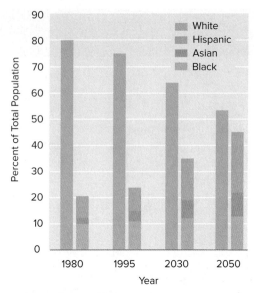

Projected Population Shifts, 1980–2050

Census figures project an increasing racial and ethnic diversity for the American people. White population is projected to drop from 80 percent in 1980 to about 53 percent in 2050, with the nation's Latino population rising most sharply.

PROSPEROUS NEWCOMERS   The higher end included many Chinese students who, beginning in the 1960s, sought out the United States for a college education, then found a job and stayed, eventually bringing in their families. "My brother-in-law left his wife in Taiwan and came here as a student to get his PhD in engineering," explained Subi Lin Felipe. "After he received his degree, he got a job in San Jose. Then he brought in a sister and his wife, who brought over one of her brothers and me. And my brother's wife then came." Asian Indians were even more acculturated on arrival because about two-thirds entered the United States speaking English and with college degrees already in hand. Indian engineers played a vital role in the computer and software industries. Similarly, Korean and Filipino professionals took skilled jobs, particularly in medical fields.

BLUE-COLLAR ASIANS   Yet Asian immigrants also included those on the lower rungs of the economic ladder. Among the new wave of Chinese immigrants, or *San Yi Man,* many blue-collar workers settled in the nation's Chinatowns, where they worked in restaurants or sewed in sweatshops. Without education and language skills, often in debt to labor contractors, most remained trapped in Chinatown's ethnic economy. Refugees from war and revolution in Southeast Asia often made harrowing journeys. Vietnamese families crowded into barely seaworthy boats, sometimes only to be terrorized by pirates, other times nearly drowned in storms before reaching poorly equipped Thai refugee camps. By 1990 almost a million refugees had arrived in the United States, three-quarters of them from Vietnam, most of the others from Laos or Cambodia. Since 2000, immigrants from China, India, and the Philippines accounted for almost half the Asian total. Thus the profile of Asian immigration resembled an hourglass, with the most newcomers either relatively affluent or extremely poor.

ASIAN DOWNWARD MOBILITY   Finally, Asian Americans experienced two forms of downward mobility. First, highly educated Asian immigrants often found it difficult to land jobs in their professions. To American observers, Korean shopkeepers seemed examples of success, when in fact such owners often enough had been former professionals forced into the risky small-business world. One Filipino doctor noted that strict state licensing standards prevented him from opening up his own medical practice. Instead, he found himself working as a restaurant meat cutter for employers who had no idea about his medical background. "They thought I was very good at separating meat from the bone," he commented ironically. Second, schools reported significant numbers of Asian American students who were failing. This "lost generation" were most often the children of families who entered the United States with little education and few job skills.

The New Look of America: Latinos

Like Asian Americans, Latinos in the United States constituted a diverse mosaic, reflecting dozens of immigrant streams. Although the groups shared a language, they usually settled in distinct urban and suburban barrios across the United States. Such enclave communities provided support to newcomers and an economic foothold for newly established businesses. Money circulated within a community; the workers and owners of an ethnic grocery, for example, spent their wages at neighboring stores, whose profits fueled other immigrant businesses in a chain reaction.

THE DOMINICANS OF WASHINGTON HEIGHTS   Washington Heights, at the northern tip of New York City, followed that path as nearly a quarter of a million Dominicans settled there during the 1970s and 1980s. A hundred blocks to the south, Manhattan's downtown skyscrapers seemed distant; shopkeepers' stereos along the major thoroughfares boomed music of trumpets and congas, while peddlers pushed heavily loaded shopping carts through busy streets, crying "¡A peso! ¡A peso!" ("For a dollar!"). In addition, Dominican social clubs planned dances or hosted political discussions. Similarly, in Miami and elsewhere in South Florida, Cuban Americans created their own self-sustaining enclaves. A large professional class and strong community leadership brought them prosperity and political influence.

EAST LOS ANGELES   Along the West Coast, Los Angeles was the urban magnet for many Latino (and Asian) immigrants. Mexican immigrants had long flocked to East Los Angeles, which facilitated access to the jobs in factories, warehouses, and railroad yards across the river. Many Mexican Americans now owned their own businesses and homes. But beginning in the mid-1980s and 1990s, the neighborhood of MacArthur Park became the focal point for the newest immigrants from Mexico and Central America. MacArthur Park was less developed as a community, and many of its residents were transient, passing quickly to other neighborhoods or jobs.

As more factories and service industries became decentralized, locating themselves beyond urban downtowns, the barrios

| *The Hmong people from Cambodia were among the many refugees fleeing Southeast Asia in the wake of the Vietnam War. While Chue and Nhia Thao Cha stayed in a refugee camp in Thailand, they stitched a traditional Hmong story cloth that, in this detail, shows refugees boarding a plane to come to the United States.*

followed as well. Las Americas near Houston, where Juan Chanax lived, was one example; but suburban barrios could be found dotted all across the nation, from Rockville, Maryland, to Pacoima, California, near Burbank. Pacoima's well-kept bungalows housed working-class Mexican Americans who had lived in California for decades. But the front lawns of many residences were often paved over to hold the cars of additional workers or families, and the garages were converted to dormitories with a sink and toilet, where four or five newcomers from Central America could rent a spot to lay a bedroll on the cement floor.

Illegal Immigration

Because Mexico and the United States share such a long common border—and an equally long history of intermingling of peoples and cultures—many Mexicans entered the United States illegally. But the number of illegal immigrants increased during the 1980s as Central Americans joined the northward flow, along with Mexicans escaping a sharp economic downturn in their own country. By 1985 the number of illegal immigrants in the United States was estimated at anywhere from 2 to 12 million.

IMMIGRATION AND CONTROL ACT OF 1986 Congress attempted to stem that flow by passing the Immigration and Control Act of 1986. Tightened border security was coupled with a new requirement that American employers bear the responsibility of certifying their workers as legal residents of the United States. At the same time, those illegal immigrants who had arrived before 1986 were granted amnesty and

| *Sikhs—seen marching here in the New York City annual Sikh Day Parade in 2003—trace their origins to India's Punjab region.*
©Jennifer Szymaszek/AP Photo

allowed to become legal residents. In the end, however, the terms of the law failed to create the clean slate Congress had hoped for. Legal immigrants continued to be intertwined with illegals in a host of different ways: as relatives helping loved ones make the transition to living in the United States, as landlords boarding newcomers until they could get on their feet, as links with communities in the home country—just as Juan Chanax continued to be after he received amnesty from the act in 1986.

Links with the Home Country

Because systems of communication and transportation drew the world closer, the new immigrants found it easier to maintain links with their points of origin and wire money back to relatives. Pacoima, the suburban barrio outside Burbank, California, boasted only a small town center. But along that half-mile stretch, 13 different currency exchanges were open for business to handle immigrant funds. By 1992 the amount of funds sent worldwide was so great that it was surpassed in volume only by the currency flows of the global oil trade.

BANDA MUSIC   And not just money traveled these routes. An immigrant entering La Curaçao, a furniture store in Los Angeles's MacArthur Park, could sign up to buy a bedroom suite on the installment plan. When the payments were completed, the furniture was released—not in Los Angeles but at a branch warehouse in El Salvador, where relatives could pick up the purchase. Cultural ties remained strong as well. Young Mexican immigrants flocked on Saturday night to popular dance halls such as the Lido in Los Angeles to hear a variety of music known as *banda.* Women wore tight tank tops and jeans or skirts, while the men's cowboy outfits were distinguished by their *cuarta,* a small riding whip at the belt, and by a kerchief hanging from the right hip pocket, with the name of the wearer's native Mexican state embroidered proudly for all to see.

Religious Diversity

The global nature of the new immigration also reshaped the religious faiths of America. During the 1950s most Americans' sense of religious diversity encompassed the mainline Protestant churches, Roman Catholicism, and Judaism. But immigrants brought with them not only their own brands of Christianity and Judaism but also Buddhist, Hindu, and Islamic beliefs. By 2001 there were perhaps a million Buddhists and a million Hindus living in the United States and anywhere from 2 to 6 million Muslims. (Precise figures are difficult to obtain.) The largest number of Muslims came from Pakistan and South Asia, but close to a million were from the Arab world, especially Lebanon, Egypt, and Syria. Mosques became common in New York City, Los Angeles, and Detroit.

Mainline Protestants and Catholics changed as well. The Presbyterian Church (U.S.A.) increased its Korean-speaking congregations from about 20 in 1970 to over 350 by 2000. In New York City, Episcopalian services were held in 14 different languages. And Catholic churches increasingly found themselves celebrating mass in both English and Spanish. Such arrangements took place not only in urban congregations such as the Church of the Nativity in South Central Los Angeles (where Latinos alternated services with African Americans) but increasingly even in rural areas like Columbus Junction, Iowa, whose Catholic church was energized by Mexican Americans working in a nearby meat-processing plant.

 REVIEW

How did the immigration populations from Asia and Latin America become more diversified during the 1980s and 1990s?

CLINTON AND THE NEW GLOBAL ORDER

IN 1993 WILLIAM JEFFERSON CLINTON became the first baby boomer to occupy the White House. His wife, Hillary Rodham Clinton, would be the most politically involved presidential wife since Eleanor Roosevelt. Like many couples of their generation, the Clintons were a two-career family. Both trained as lawyers at Yale University during the tumultuous 1960s. Bill chose politics as his career, while Hillary mixed private practice with public service. Their marriage had not been easy. Revelations of Clinton's sexual affairs as governor of Arkansas almost ruined his campaign for the presidency. The first couple seemed, however, more intent on making public policy than in defending their private lives.

Clinton envisioned himself as an activist president, not a detached leader like Reagan. Unlike the senior George Bush, he would concentrate on domestic policy. But Clinton's desire for major legislative initiatives ran up against the election results of 1992: he had received just 43 percent of the popular vote, while the Republicans had narrowed the Democratic majorities in Congress. Still, he pledged to revive the economy and rein in the federal deficit that had grown enormously during the Reagan years. Beyond that, he called for systematic reform of the welfare and health care systems.

"DON'T ASK; DON'T TELL"   As one of his first acts, the new president attempted to eliminate a rule that banned homosexuals from serving in the military. In doing so, he fulfilled a campaign pledge to the gay community. But resistance from conservatives and the military forced a compromise satisfactory to no one: "Don't ask; don't tell." As long as gay soldiers kept their sexual orientation private, they could serve their country.

Such early missteps could be set down partly to the stumbles of a newcomer learning his way around the office. But larger issues of character could not be dismissed. One observer shrewdly noted that there were two Bill Clintons—the idealistic young man from Hope, Arkansas (his hometown), and the boy from Hot Springs (his mother's home).

The latter was a resort town associated with the seamier side of Arkansas high life. With increasing frequency, the leadership mustered by the idealistic politician from Hope seemed to be undermined by the character flaws of the boy from Hot Springs.

WHITEWATER Although Clinton's conservative opponents disliked his politics, the president's moral lapses troubled them even more. Critics nicknamed him "Slick Willie" and sought continually to expose discreditable or illegal dealings from his past. Accusations arose that when Clinton was governor in the early 1980s, both he and his wife had received special treatment from a failed real estate venture known as Whitewater. Rumors also abounded about Clinton's womanizing, fanned in 1994 when a former Arkansas state employee, Paula Jones, filed a sexual harassment suit against the president. Under pressure from congressional conservatives, Attorney General Janet Reno appointed former judge Kenneth Starr as a special prosecutor to investigate Whitewater. But during Clinton's first term, Starr's investigations, as well as two Senate committees, produced no evidence that the Clintons had acted illegally.

Managing the New World Disorder

Clinton planned to concentrate on domestic rather than foreign affairs. But he could not ignore international crises. As he soon discovered, the "new world order," hailed by both Mikhail Gorbachev and George H. W. Bush, seemed more like a world of regional disorders.

In sub-Saharan Africa, brutal civil wars broke out in both Somalia and Rwanda. As president-elect, Clinton had supported President Bush's decision to send troops to aid famine relief in Somalia. But attempts to install a stable government there proved difficult. Tragically, the United States as well as European nations failed to intervene in Rwanda before more than a million people were massacred.

Closer to home, a military coup in Haiti pushed the president to act more boldly. The harsh rule by Haiti's new regime sent more than 35,000 refugees fleeing toward the United States, often in homemade boats and rafts. When a UN-sponsored economic embargo failed to oust the military regime, the Security Council in 1994 approved an invasion of Haiti by a multinational force. American troops proved crucial in convincing the military rulers to leave.

CONFLICTS IN BOSNIA AND CROATIA Europe's most difficult trouble spot proved to be Yugoslavia, a nation divided by ethnic rivalries within a number of provinces, including Serbia, Croatia, Kosovo, and Bosnia. After Bosnia became independent in 1992 both Serbs and Croats, but especially the Serbs, resorted to what was euphemistically referred to as "ethnic cleansing"—the massacre of rival populations—to secure control. The United States at first viewed the civil war in Yugoslavia as Europe's problem. But as civilian deaths mounted to a quarter million, the conflict demanded a response.

Still, many members of Congress feared the prospect of American troops bogged down in a civil war, as had happened under Lyndon Johnson in Vietnam. Over Republican objections, Clinton committed American support for NATO bombing of Serb forces and then brokered peace talks held in Dayton, Ohio. The Dayton Accords created separate Croatian, Bosnian, and Serbian nations. Some 60,000 NATO troops, including 20,000 Americans, moved into Bosnia to enforce the peace. Clinton had intervened without the loss of American lives.

MIDDLE EAST PEACE NEGOTIATIONS Clinton also worked to mediate conflict in the Middle East. Sporadic protests and rioting by Palestinians in the Israeli-occupied territories of Gaza and the West Bank gave way in the 1990s to negotiations. At a ceremony hosted by the president in 1993, Palestinian leader Yasir Arafat and Israeli prime minister Yitzhak Rabin signed a peace agreement permitting self-rule for Palestinians in the Gaza Strip and in Jericho on the West Bank. But the assassination of Prime Minister Rabin two years later by an angry Orthodox Jew launched a period of intensified suspicion on both sides, as extremists sought to derail the peace process. Clinton was unable to bring the Israelis and Palestinians together. Whether in the Middle East, Eastern Europe, Africa, or the Caribbean, regional crises demonstrated the difficulty of maintaining a new global world order.

REVIEW
How did ethnic, religious, and cultural differences play a part in regional crises in Yugoslavia and the Middle East?

THE CLINTON PRESIDENCY ON TRIAL

THROUGHOUT CLINTON'S PRESIDENCY THE NATION experienced a powerful economic expansion. Despite low unemployment, there was little inflation. Prosperity allowed the president to eliminate the budget deficits that had soared during the 1980s. But increased government revenues did not persuade Congress to support Clinton's reform agenda.

Recovery without Reform

CLINTON PROGRAM In his first speech to Congress, Clinton proposed a program that began reducing the deficit as well as providing investments to stimulate the economy and repair the nation's decaying public infrastructure. In contrast, Presidents Reagan and Bush had cut funds to rebuild schools, roads, dams, bridges, and other public structures. In August 1993 a compromise budget bill passed by only a single vote in the Senate, with Republicans blocking the stimulus portion of Clinton's program. Still, deficit reduction was a significant achievement.

| President Clinton's most ambitious attempt at reform was to overhaul the nation's health care system to provide all Americans with basic health care (along with a card to guarantee it). But medical interest groups defeated the proposal, arguing it would create yet another huge and inefficient bureaucracy.

©Ron Edmunds/AP Photo

NAFTA The victory in the budget battle gave Clinton the momentum to hammer together a bipartisan coalition that passed NAFTA, the North American Free Trade Agreement. With the promise of greater trade and more jobs, the pact linked the United States economy more closely with those of Canada and Mexico. The president also helped supporters of gun control overcome the powerful opposition of the National Rifle Association to pass the Brady Bill, which required a five-day waiting period on gun purchases.

HEALTH CARE REFORM Health care reform topped Clinton's legislative agenda. A task force led by Hillary Clinton developed a plan to provide health coverage for all Americans, including the 37 million who in 1994 remained uninsured. The plan rejected a more sweeping single-payer system, in which the government would act as the central agency reimbursing medical expenses. But a host of interest groups attacked the proposal, especially insurance companies and small businesses that worried they would bear the brunt of the system's financing. Even a compromise bill lacked the votes needed to win approval.

If the Clintons' plan had passed, the president and the Democratic majority in Congress might have staked their claim to a government that was actively responding to long-term problems. But the failure of health care reform heightened the perception of an ill-organized administration and an entrenched Congress content with the status quo. Republicans, sensing the level of public frustration, stepped up their opposition to other Democratic legislation. The 1994 midterm elections confirmed the public's anger over political gridlock, as Republicans captured majorities in both the House and the Senate.

The Conservative Revolution Revived

"THE CONTRACT WITH AMERICA" The combative new Speaker of the House, Newt Gingrich of Georgia, proclaimed himself a "genuine revolutionary" who would complete what Ronald Reagan had begun. Gingrich used the first hundred days of the new Congress to bring to a vote ten proposals from his campaign document "The Contract with America." The contract proposed a balanced budget amendment, tax cuts, and term limits for all members of Congress. To promote family values, its anticrime package included a broader death penalty and welfare restrictions aimed at reducing teen pregnancy. Although the term-limits proposal did not survive, the House passed the other nine proposals.

The whirlwind performance was impressive. "When you look back five years from now," enthused Republican governor Tommy Thompson of Wisconsin, "you're going to say 'they came, they saw, they conquered.'" But the Senate was less eager to enact the House proposals. And as Republicans assembled a more comprehensive budget, it became clear that the public was increasingly worried about the Gingrich revolution. Fiscally, the Republicans set out to balance the federal budget by scaling back Medicare expenditures and allowing premiums to double. Republicans also sought reduced protection for endangered species, relaxed pollution controls under the Clean Water Act, and greater freedom for mining, ranching, and logging interests to develop public lands.

WELFARE REFORM When President Clinton threatened to veto the Republican budget, Republicans twice forced the federal government to shut down. Most of the public viewed the self-proclaimed revolutionaries as intransigents, and,

Illustration by Anita Kunz for the *New Yorker* Magazine. Anita Kunz Limited. Reproduced by permission of the artist

| *"I am a genuine revolutionary," House Speaker Newt Gingrich proclaimed, and the newly elected Republican freshmen in Congress led the charge to complete the Reagan revolution. By clothing Newt's followers as stiff-armed, flag-waving militarists, illustrator Anita Kunz recalls Mussolini's overzealous Black Shirts. Enough of the public agreed, forcing the Republicans to backpedal.*

facing a hostile backlash, Congress backed down. At the same time, President Clinton preempted much of the Republican agenda. By 1995 he was proposing his own route toward a balanced budget by 2002. Similarly, in 1996 the president signed into law a sweeping reform of welfare. For the first time in 60 years, the social welfare policies of the liberal democratic state were being substantially reversed. The bill ended guarantees of federal aid to poor children, turning over such programs to the states. Food stamp spending was cut, and the law placed a five-year limit on payments to any family. Most adults receiving payments were required to find work within two years.

Thus, as the election of 1996 approached, the Republican revolution had been either dampened or co-opted by the president. With the economy robust, Bill Clinton became the first Democrat since Franklin Roosevelt to win a second term in the White House.

Women's Issues in the Clinton Years

Hillary Clinton used her influence to promote opportunity for women. Her husband was sympathetic. "Building up women does not diminish men," he insisted during the 1992 election campaign. In that spirit he appointed Ruth Bader Ginsburg to the Supreme Court and three women to his cabinet, including Janet Reno as his attorney general. Giving his wife, Hillary Clinton, a prominent role in the administration also underscored Clinton's interest in advancing the goals of feminists.

Both Clintons supported a woman's right to control decisions on reproduction, on which conservatives challenged them. With the Supreme Court still unwilling to overturn *Roe v. Wade,* pro-life advocates sought to limit the decision's application as much as possible. On the other hand, women continued to assume higher profiles in such formerly male-dominated professions as law, medicine, veterinary medicine, and business, though they still lagged in the areas of science, technology, engineering, and math.

Scandal

Four years into the Whitewater investigation, Special Prosecutor Kenneth Starr had spent $30 million and, despite this investment of time and money, had managed only to convict several of the president's former business partners for real estate irregularities. (The Watergate investigation during the Nixon years, in contrast, lasted only about two years.) Then in January 1998, Starr hit what looked like the jackpot. A disgruntled federal employee with links to the Bush administration produced audiotapes of phone conversations in which a 21-year-old White House intern, Monica Lewinsky, talked of an intimate relationship with the president.

Starr succeeded in preventing Clinton from learning of the tapes before the president and Lewinsky testified in depositions that they had not had "sexual relations." When word of the tapes leaked out several days later, the news media predicted ominously that the president must resign or face **impeachment**—if not for his personal conduct, at the very least for lying under oath. In September, Starr recommended that the president be impeached on the grounds of perjury, obstruction of justice, and witness tampering.

IMPEACHMENT To the astonishment of the news media, the public did not support Republican calls for impeachment. Although Clinton had clearly engaged in behavior most Americans found inappropriate or even repugnant, they seemed to draw a line between public and private actions. Furthermore, Starr's report went into such lurid detail that many questioned the special prosecutor's motives. Nonetheless, along strict party lines, a majority in the House voted three articles of impeachment for lying to the grand jury, suborning perjury, and orchestrating a cover-up. In January 1999 the matter went to the Senate for trial.

ACQUITTAL Unlike the Watergate scandals, in which Richard Nixon resigned because a bipartisan consensus determined that impeachment was necessary, Clinton's accusers and defenders divided along strongly partisan lines. The Senate voted to acquit, with 5 Republicans joining all 45 Senate Democrats in the decision.

The impeachment controversy left the president weakened, but hardly powerless. Throughout the political tempest the nation's economy had continued to grow. By 1999 the rate of unemployment had dropped to 4.1 percent, the lowest

in nearly 30 years, while the stock market reached new highs. Furthermore, as the economy expanded, federal tax receipts grew with it. By 1998 Bill Clinton faced a situation that would have seemed improbable a few years previous—a budget surplus. By balancing the budget the president had appropriated a key Republican issue.

The Cliffhanger Election of 2000

Budget surpluses, Social Security reform, and tax cuts topped the list of issues in the 2000 election. Vice President Al Gore, running for the Democrats, had served in Vietnam and the Senate, written a book on the global environmental crisis, supported the development of the Internet, and was especially active as vice president. Despite these strengths, he was a stiff and uninspiring campaigner.

By contrast, the affable Texas governor George W. Bush (son of the 41st president) had little interest in world affairs. He once asked a Saudi diplomat why people expected him to know so much about a puny country such as North Korea. "I don't have the foggiest idea about what I think about international foreign policy," he confessed. Bush's record in business was mixed at best. But Bush made character the central issue of his campaign—not his or Gore's, but Bill Clinton's. In that way, Bush deprived Gore of a vital campaign asset, because the president remained popular with voters.

The outcome of the election came down to one state—Florida, where Bush led by just 300 votes. Nationwide, Gore had a 500,000 edge in the popular vote, but without Florida's 25 electoral votes neither candidate had a majority in the Electoral College. Election irregularities, from faulty voting

machines to confusingly designed ballots, stirred controversy and led to a recount in some counties. More serious were allegations that the state had actively suppressed voting in heavily black counties. Those accusations were especially troubling since George Bush's brother, Jeb, was Florida's governor.

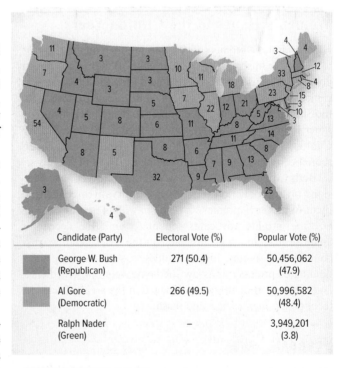

Candidate (Party)	Electoral Vote (%)	Popular Vote (%)
George W. Bush (Republican)	271 (50.4)	50,456,062 (47.9)
Al Gore (Democratic)	266 (49.5)	50,996,582 (48.4)
Ralph Nader (Green)	–	3,949,201 (3.8)

ELECTION OF 2000

BUSH V. GORE After weeks of wrangling, the U.S. Supreme Court entered the legal fray. In *Bush v. Gore,* the Court's conservative majority, all Republican appointees, ruled 5-4 that the recount must end. The majority argued that because the recount applied to only three counties, it valued some votes more than others. In the end, the Supreme Court, not the American voters, made George W. Bush the 43rd president of the United States.

REVIEW
How did partisan differences affect at least three political clashes between 1992 and 2000?

The United States in a Networked World

IN 1988 ECONOMIST LAWRENCE SUMMERS was working on the presidential campaign of Michael Dukakis. At a meeting in Chicago, the staff assigned him a car with a telephone. Summers was so impressed, he recalled, that "I used it to call my wife to tell her I was in a car with a phone." A decade later as deputy treasury secretary in the Clinton administration, he visited the Ivory Coast in Africa to help launch an American-supported health project. One village on his itinerary could be reached only by dugout canoe. As Summers stepped into the canoe for his return trip, an aide handed him a cell phone. "Washington has a question for you," the aide said. The same man who once marveled at a phone in his car in Chicago ten years later expected one in his dugout canoe in the interior of Africa.

The Internet Revolution

Like Lawrence Summers, most Americans by the beginning of the twenty-first century were linked to a global communications network. Computers, cell phones, iPads, MP3 players, and other electronic devices provided almost instant contact with a wider world.

THE WORLD WIDE WEB Early Internet pioneers shared a democratic vision, a web open and free to all. Users could communicate without restriction and find access to any form of information. Such openness was the bane of authoritarian governments, which found it difficult to control public opinion in a world in which information flowed freely. The unregulated format of the web raised substantial legal, moral, and political questions in the United States as well. By 1999 five million websites were in operation—among them sites promoting pornography, hate speech, and even instructions on how to build atomic bombs. A number of politicians and civic groups called for the censorship of the more extreme web content. Others argued that the greater danger lay in allowing the Internet to become dominated by large telecommunications companies. These advocates called for legislation protecting "Net neutrality."

E-COMMERCE Business spending on technology jumped from 3 percent in the 1960s to 45 percent by the mid-1990s, fueled by the recognition that the web's interconnectivity gave it enormous commercial potential. Businesses could now interact with their customers without respect to physical location or time zone. E-commerce practitioners began using the Internet to disseminate company or product information, generate leads, take orders, and build customer databases. Business-to-business sales went from $40 billion in 1998 to some $1.1 trillion by 2007, while retail sales approached $400 billion. Online merchandiser Amazon.com began to challenge such giant brick-and-mortar retailers as Walmart and Target.

American Workers in a Two-Tiered Economy

The benefits of the Internet revolution were not evenly distributed, however. Economists described the United States in the 1990s as a two-tiered labor market in which most increases in earning went to people at the top of the wage scale. Thus, despite the decade's prosperity, the median income of American families was barely higher in 1996 than in 1973. Indeed, the earnings of the average white male worker actually fell. Only because so many women entered the job market did the family standard of living remain the same. In the early 1970s some 37 percent of women worked outside the home; in 1999 about 57 percent did.

Education was a critical factor in determining winners in the high-tech economy. Families with college-educated parents were three times more likely to have home access to the web than were those families in which parents' education ended with high school. Because average education levels were relatively lower among African Americans and Latinos (and relatively higher among Asian Americans), the computer divide took on a racial cast as well. But the implications went beyond mere access to the web. More important, the high-wage sector of the computer economy required educated workers, and the demand for them drove up those workers' salaries.

WAGE STAGNATION Unlike computer programmers or corporate executives who were in high demand, low-skill workers were not able to increase their earnings simply by switching jobs. Some economists concluded, "the most important economic division is not between races, or genders, or economic sectors, but between the college-educated and the non-college-educated."

The prosperity of the late 1990s produced an interesting dilemma. On the one hand, it eased many social tensions that had long divided the nation. Inner-city crime rates fell; the poor began to experience a marked improvement in their finances; consumer confidence reached an all-time high. But over the longer term, the boom's statistics were not encouraging. Despite the decline in the poverty rate, it remained above the rate for any year in the 1970s. If the strongest economy in 30 years left the poverty rate higher than during the inflation-plagued years of the 1970s, what would happen if the economy faltered?

African Americans and the Persistence of the Racial Divide

In the 1990s the highest-paid celebrity in the world was an African American—basketball star Michael Jordan. Entertainer Oprah Winfrey, also an African American, was the highest-paid woman in America. Although the situation of African Americans had improved vastly compared with their position in the 1950s, race still mattered.

INNER-CITY RENEWAL By the late 1990s African Americans in increasing numbers were benefiting from a decade of economic expansion. Homeownership reached 46 percent and employment increased from around 87 percent in 1980 to nearly 92 percent in 1998. African Americans in increasing numbers rose up the ladder in corporate America. Economic success also brought new hope to the nation's inner cities. Crime and poverty decreased significantly, especially rates of murder and violence. Births to single mothers reached a postwar low. Fewer blacks lived below the poverty level and fewer were on welfare. Yet many African Americans were reserved in their reaction to such statistics. "To the extent that you proclaim your success," one community leader remarked, "people forget about you."

PROPOSITION 209 AGAINST AFFIRMATIVE ACTION Civil rights leaders were most concerned about the continued assault on affirmative action. In 1996 California voters passed a ballot initiative, Proposition 209, that eliminated racial and gender preferences in hiring and college admissions. Ironically, the leading advocate for Proposition 209 was a conservative black leader, Ward Connerly. Connerly argued that racial preferences demeaned black and other minority students by setting up a double standard that patronizingly assumed minorities could not compete on an equal basis. In any case, Proposition 209 had a striking effect. Enrollments of Latinos and blacks at the elite California university campuses and professional schools dropped sharply: at UC Berkeley, down 57 percent for black students and 34 percent for Latinos. Major state universities in Washington, Texas, and Michigan also experienced declines after passing similar laws.

The Supreme Court addressed the issue of race as a factor in college admissions in 2003, in the case of *Gratz v. Bollinger.* There, the Bush administration pressed the Court to strike down the use of any racial preference in the admissions programs of the University of Michigan. In deciding the case the justices did strike down a point system used by Michigan giving minorities preference in undergraduate

admissions. However, the Court approved, 5 to 4, a separate program used by the university's law school, which gave race some influence in the admissions process. Affirmative action had been reduced in scope but not abolished.

Global Pressures in a Multicultural America

Clearly the enormous changes wrought by immigration and the new global economy gave the United States a more multicultural flavor. Salsa rhythms became part of the pop-cultural mainstream, and Latino foods competed with Indian curries, Japanese sushi, and Pad Thai. Baseball, the national pastime, became truly all-American as major league rosters filled with stars from Japan, the Dominican Republic, Mexico, Cuba, Panama, and Venezuela.

But the mix of cultures did not occur without friction. Throughout American history, the dominant culture has reacted defensively when immigrant flows increased from new sources or when jobs were hard to find. After reforming their immigration laws in the 1960s, Americans once again debated how diverse the United States could become without losing its traditional identity.

PROPOSITION 187 In 1990, Lawrence Auster echoed earlier nativists with *The Path to National Suicide,* in which he warned of the "browning of America." Four years later opponents of immigration in California put forward a state ballot initiative that denied health, education, and welfare benefits to illegal immigrants. Despite the opposition of most major religious, ethnic, and educational organizations, the measure passed with a lopsided 59 percent majority. But the proposition never went into effect because a federal judge ruled unconstitutional the provision denying education to the children of illegal aliens.

Traditionally, nativist conflicts pit the dominant majority culture against the minority cultures of more recent arrivals. But in a multicultural society, such polar opposites often broke down. In 1998 yet another ballot initiative passed in California, mandating that schools phase out all their bilingual education programs. Students would be granted only one year of English-language immersion courses before receiving all instruction in English. In this instance both white and Latino voters approved the proposition by nearly the same margin, by nearly 62 percent. But those rules were

© *Ester Hernandez*/Library of Congress, Prints and Photographs Division [LC-USZ62-127167]

| Artist Ester Hernandez used the visual metaphor of an evolving Statue of Liberty to suggest that the nation's identity changes as immigrants continue to reach its shores and contribute to its heritage. "Although some traditional hallmarks of North American culture may be transformed," Hernandez has noted, "the transformation may create a stronger, richer, and more international culture, one that retains the best of all influences."

Mapping the Internet

Which countries in the world have a higher percentage of Internet users than the United States?

Why is the southern tip of Africa the only area of sub-equatorial Africa where more than 50 percent are Internet users?

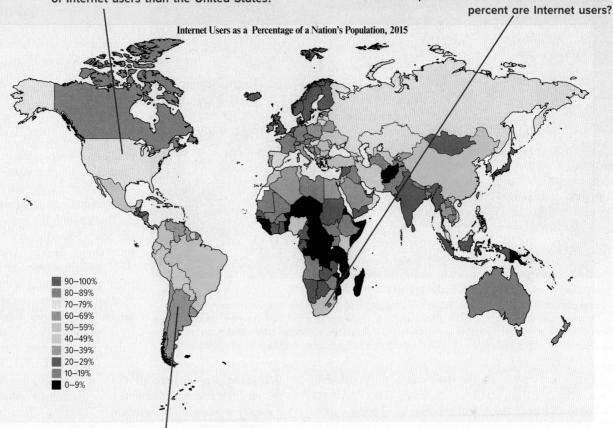

Internet Users as a Percentage of a Nation's Population, 2015

- 90–100%
- 80–89%
- 70–79%
- 60–69%
- 50–59%
- 40–49%
- 30–39%
- 20–29%
- 10–19%
- 0–9%

How does the percentage of users differ between the Northern and Southern hemispheres?

The Internet is not so much a single vast network, but a network of networks. It grew out of the efforts of the U.S. government to link major research and defense centers with a communications system that could survive a nuclear attack. The networks it joins now range from small home and office users to universities, large corporations, and national governments. Probably no phenomenon in the recent past has done more to create a truly global economy.

Experts estimate that about a quarter of the world's people (almost 2 billion) have access to the World Wide Web (www). Though many people think of the web and the Internet as the same thing, they are not. Hardware and software create the Internet (much like a railroad), while documents, sites, and other electronically accessible information make up the web.

Source: International Telecommunications Union.

THINKING CRITICALLY

How might the colors of the United States, Russia, and China on the map change if it showed variations within regions of these nations? What do the countries that have higher percentage of Internet users than the United States have in common? What explains the sharp difference of usage on the Korean Peninsula? In what ways does the Internet compare to earlier communication technologies such as telegraph, telephone, radio, and television? In what ways does it differ?

---

abolished in 2016, even as debate over immigration continued to roil the nation.

The New Debate

In 2006 immigration and especially the status of the approximately 11 million illegal immigrants were hotly debated. On the one hand, immigrant groups organized a day of marches in major cities, proclaiming their loyalty to the United States and asking Congress to make it possible for them to become citizens. On the other hand, advocates of a more restrictive policy insisted that illegal immigration imposed a heavy burden on wages and government services.

Source: U.S. Navy photo by Chief Photographer's Mate Eric J. Tilford

| *Some science fiction films of the 1950s had imagined a Manhattan like this: debris everywhere, buildings in ruin, the city shrouded in smoke and ash. On September 11, 2001, however, disaster arose not from nuclear war with another superpower but through the actions of international terrorists. In a post–cold war world, global threats could come from small groups as well as powerful nations.*

The debate revealed a split particularly among Republicans. President Bush and many in the business community hoped to keep open the flow of low-wage labor and supported a guest worker program along with a plan to legalize the status of millions of illegal aliens. Other Republicans, especially in states like Arizona with high immigrant populations, campaigned to close the borders and oust those who had entered the country illegally. All the two camps could agree on was a plan to build a 700-mile fence along the U.S.-Mexican border. Hispanics voiced their displeasure in the 2006 elections. Some 70 percent of them voted for Democrats, who tended to side with the president on the immigration debate.

 REVIEW

Did the rise of the Internet do more to unite or divide Americans? What about the rising multiculturalism of American society during the 1980s and 1990s?

TERRORISM IN A GLOBAL AGE

ALONG THE NORTHEAST COAST OF the United States, September 11, 2001, dawned bright and clear. In the World Trade Center, Francis Ledesma was sitting in his office on the sixty-fourth floor of the South Tower when a friend suggested they go for coffee. Francis seldom took early breaks, but he decided to make an

exception. In the cafeteria he heard and felt a muffled explosion: a boiler, he thought. But then he saw bricks and glass falling by the window. When he started to head back to his office for a nine o'clock meeting, his friend insisted they leave immediately. Out on the street Francis saw the smoke and gaping hole where American Airlines Flight 11 had hit the North Tower. At that moment a huge fireball erupted as United Airlines Flight 175 hit the South Tower where they worked. "We kept looking back," Francis recalled as they escaped the area, "and then all of a sudden our building, Tower 2, collapsed. I really thought that it was a mirage."

That was only the beginning of the horror. Shortly after takeoff from Dulles Airport, American Airlines Flight 77 veered from its path and crashed into the Pentagon. Several passengers on United Airlines Flight 93 from Newark to San Francisco heard the news over their cell phones before hijackers seized that plane. Rather than allow another attack, passengers stormed the cockpit. Moments later the plane crashed into a woods in western Pennsylvania.

From a secure area at Barksdale Air Force Base in Louisiana, President George W. Bush addressed a shaken nation. He called the crashes a "national tragedy" and condemned those responsible. "Freedom itself was attacked this morning by a faceless coward, and freedom will be defended," he assured the American people.

GLOBAL DIMENSIONS OF THE ATTACK In an age of instant global communications, the entire world watched as the tragedy unfolded. Three minutes after the first plane hit the World Trade Center, ABC News announced that an explosion had rocked the towers. British television was already covering the fire when the second plane reached its target at 9:03 a.m. Japanese networks were on the air with coverage of the Pentagon crash about an hour later, around midnight their time. TV Azteca in Mexico carried President Bush's statement from Barksdale Air Force Base, and China Central Television was not far behind. This was, indeed, an international tragedy. The aptly named World Trade Center was a hub for global trade and finance. Citizens of more than 50 nations had died in the attack.

ECONOMIC DOWNTURN Not since Pearl Harbor had the United States experienced such a devastating attack on its homeland. Most directly the tragedy claimed

approximately 3,000 lives. Before September 11 the booming economy of the 1990s was already showing serious signs of strain; the World Trade Center attack pushed the nation into a recession. Security fears compounded economic concerns. The attacks were not the work of an enemy nation but of an Arab terrorist group known as al Qaeda, led by a shadowy figure, Saudi national Osama bin Laden. How many of al Qaeda's terrorist cells were still undetected within the United States? After the World Trade Center attack, nations were no longer the only threat to national security. Smaller groups—subnational or international—possessed the capability of using weapons of mass destruction to make war against the most powerful nation in the world.

A Conservative Agenda at Home

Before the attacks George W. Bush's administration seemed to lack direction. Bush's claim to leadership was shaky partly because when he took office in January 2001, a majority of the electorate had voted for his opponent, Al Gore. The crisis of September 11, 2001, energized the president.

Bush in his inaugural address had promised a moderate course, but Karl Rove, the new president's trusted political advisor, urged him to govern from his base on the right. A tight group of advisors led by Rove, Vice President Dick Cheney, Defense Secretary Donald Rumsfeld, and lobbyist Grover Norquist steered the president's conservative program. Although he appointed women and minorities to his cabinet, Bush also placed evangelicals such as Attorney General John Ashcroft in key positions. Majorities in both Houses of Congress and opportunities to appoint two justices to the Supreme Court gave the Republicans control over all three branches of government.

ENERGY POLICY   The partisan tone of the administration became quickly apparent. When Vice President Cheney convened leaders of the energy industry to recommend new policies, he included no one from the environmental community. Rather than promote conservation, the gathering stressed ways to increase production: drilling in environmentally sensitive coastal areas and the Arctic National Wildlife Refuge.

TAX CUTS   Tax cuts formed the cornerstone of the Bush agenda. Many conservatives wanted lower taxes in order to limit the government's ability to initiate new policies—a strategy referred to as "starving the beast." With the threat of recession looming, Bush defended his proposals as a means to boost the economy and create more jobs. Congress supported the proposed cuts, passing first the Economic Growth and Tax Reform Reconciliation Act of 2001 (EGTRRA) and then the Job Creation and Workers Assistance Act of 2002 (JCWA). Size alone did not make these tax bills controversial. Critics objected that the cuts did little for job creation and that those in high-income brackets received most of the benefits. Citizens for Tax Justice claimed that by the end of 2010, when the Bush tax reductions were set to expire, 52 percent of the total tax relief would have gone to the richest 1 percent of Americans. Further, tax cuts turned the federal budget surpluses of the late 1990s into massive deficits.

Unilateralism in Foreign Affairs

Even before the events of September 11 the president rejected the multilateralism in foreign affairs that since World War II had guided American presidents, including his father. President Bush was determined that the United States would play a global role, but largely on its own terms.

Hallmarks of Globalization

1990–2000

Changing flows of global immigration to United States, with broader inflows from Mexico and Central America, South Asia, Africa

New **immigrants influence American culture** in religion, music, food, and sports

Sharply **increased international currency transfers**

NAFTA and outsourcing of jobs to Mexico, South America, and Asia

World regional crises affecting U.S.:

• Middle East: Palestinians and Israelis, growing terrorism

• Africa: Rwanda and Somalia

• Europe: Yugoslavia splinters into Bosnia, Croatia, and Kosovo

World Wide Web and the growth of the Internet and e-commerce

Kyoto Protocol on global warming

2000–2018

Renewed **debate over immigration** and illegal aliens

9/11 terrorist attacks and the global war on terror:

• Al Qaeda becomes global in orientation

• Invasion of Afghanistan, Taliban ousted

• Invasion of Iraq, no weapons of mass destruction found; new mission: installing stable democracy

• Taliban resurgent in Afghanistan and Pakistan, Obama increases U.S. commitment

Broader bandwidth penetration interlinking computers, cell phones, tablets, e-books

Arab Spring topples dictators in Egypt, Libya, and Yemen, while civil strife mounts in Syria

Iran and North Korea continue their efforts to develop nuclear weapons

Iran agrees to end nuclear weapons program; North Korea continues missile and nuclear programs

Paris Agreement on climate wins global support (2016); U.S. pulls out of agreement (2017)

(bottom left): ©Lourens Smak/Alamy; *(top right):* ©Damian Dovarganes/AP Photo

KYOTO PROTOCOL REJECTED The administration's unilateral approach was made clear when it rejected the 1997 Kyoto Protocol on global warming to which 178 other nations had subscribed. "We have no interest in implementing that treaty," announced Christie Whitman, head of the Environmental Protection Agency, arguing that it would unfairly burden American energy producers. Environmentalists around the globe protested. With only 4 percent of the world's population, the United States produced about 25 percent of the Earth's greenhouse gases.

After seven months in office, George Bush's conservative agenda at home and his unilateralism abroad had not stirred widespread enthusiasm. But September 11 changed perspectives around the world. "This is not only an attack on the United States but an attack on the civilized world," insisted German chancellor Gerhard Schroeder. Even normally hostile nations such as Cuba and Libya conveyed shock and regrets. At home the president was careful to distinguish between the majority of "peace-loving" Muslims and "evil-doers" such as Osama bin Laden. But he made it clear that "our enemy is a radical network of terrorists" and that

governments around the world had a simple choice: "Either you are with us or you are with the terrorists."

In a war with so many shadowy opponents, it was not easy to agree on which radical groups most threatened American security. The "radical network of terrorists" worked underground, spread across dozens of nations. Even the states most hospitable to al Qaeda proved hard to single out. Afghanistan was an obvious target. It was the seat of the Taliban, the extreme Islamic fundamentalists who ruled the country, and the haven of bin Laden. Yet 15 of the 19 hijackers in the World Trade Center attacks hailed from Saudi Arabia, long an ally of the United States.

The Roots of Terror

While booming populations and high unemployment in the Middle East fostered terrorist movements, ironically it was the cold war—and, indirectly, the United States—that provided terrorists with training and weapons. After the Soviet Union invaded Afghanistan in 1980, the Central Intelligence Agency, with help from Pakistan, Saudi Arabia, and the

(*left*): ©DMc Photography/Alamy; (*center*): ©Brian Hendler/AP Photo; (*right*): ©Ralf-Finn Hestoft/Getty Images

| *For most of the twentieth century, Americans were accustomed to thinking of terrorism as a problem encountered abroad, as in Northern Ireland, where this IRA mural was painted on a wall* (left) *or in Israel, where Palestinian terrorists used bombings to campaign for their own independent state* (center). *In 1995 terrorism at home shocked Americans, when Timothy McVeigh* (right) *was arrested for bombing a federal building in Oklahoma City.*

United Kingdom, encouraged Muslims from all over the world to join the Afghan rebels. One of the militants who journeyed to Afghanistan was Osama bin Laden, a devout Muslim and son of a Saudi business leader.

THE RISE OF OSAMA BIN LADEN During the 1980s bin Laden founded a broad-based alliance of Arab rebels, known as al Qaeda. When Iraq invaded Kuwait in 1990, bin Laden was dismayed that the Saudis allowed the United States to use their lands to invade Iraq. It was not the kind of holy war he had imagined. From his hidden camps in Afghanistan he began directing a terror network that aimed to strike back at the American infidels.

Bin Laden's organization differed from previous terrorist movements in that it had no national home, unlike the Irish Republican Army, which struggled to unify Ireland, or Palestinians, who wanted an independent state of their own. Al Qaeda's primary motivation was religious rather than nationalist.

The group's anti-American campaign began with a bombing at the World Trade Center in 1993. That attack killed six people but did only minimal damage to the building. Further attacks occurred in places far from the United States. Twice the Clinton administration retaliated against al Qaeda with missile attacks; once it narrowly missed killing bin Laden himself in one of his Afghan camps.

The War on Terror: First Phase

The military offensive against terrorism began in early October 2001. Despite American demands to deliver bin Laden "dead or alive," the Taliban rulers of Afghanistan refused. The United States then launched air attacks followed by an invasion, which quickly brought down the Taliban. The United States established a coalition government to help rebuild the nation. Although bin Laden managed to escape, this first stage of the war on terrorism went well. The president's approval ratings

remained high and Afghans celebrated the end of Taliban rule, particularly women, whose rights had been severely restricted.

USA PATRIOT ACT Domestically the war on terrorism faced a daunting task. The United States was an open society, where citizens expected to travel freely and valued their privacy. But widespread fears led the administration to propose the USA Patriot Act. Congress passed it so quickly that some members had not even read the bill before voting for it. The act broadly expanded government powers to use electronic surveillance, monitor bank transactions (to fight money laundering), and investigate suspected terrorists. To administer the Patriot Act, Bush created the cabinet-level Department of Homeland Security that brought together such diverse agencies as the Coast Guard, the Immigration and Naturalization Service (INS), and the Federal Emergency Management Agency (FEMA).

The War in Iraq

The president's focus then shifted from Osama bin Laden to Iraq's brutal dictator, Saddam Hussein. Indeed, many in the Bush administration had long wished to overthrow Hussein, even before the September 11 attacks. These "neoconservatives" argued that regime change in Iraq would promote democracy in the Middle East and protect Israel.

Steadily Bush and his administration built the case for war against Iraq. "If we know Saddam Hussein has dangerous weapons today—and we do—," he proclaimed, "does it make any sense for the world to wait . . . for the final proof, the smoking gun that could come in the form of a mushroom cloud?" The president asserted that the United States would be "ready for preemptive action when necessary to defend our liberty and to defend our lives." This **doctrine of preemption**— that the United States had the right to attack before it was itself attacked—was a major departure from the cold war policy

>> MAPPING THE PAST <<

THE WAR ON TERROR: AFGHANISTAN AND IRAQ

Source: National Archives and Records Administration (330-CFD-DF-SD-04-06253)

"Our enemy is a radical network of terrorists, and every government that supports them. Our war on terror begins with al Qaeda, but it does not end there. It will not end until every terrorist group of global reach has been found, stopped and defeated."—President George W. Bush

CONTEXT

In the wake of the attacks of September 11, 2001, President Bush declared a global war on terrorism. The first American attacks targeted the Taliban rulers of Afghanistan, who sheltered al Qaeda forces. The following year Bush extended the war into Iraq. Ethnic and religious divisions influenced allegiances in both wars. In Afghanistan, al Qaeda forces were concentrated in the mountainous region along the border with Pakistan. In Iraq the most severe resistance to American occupation occurred from around Baghdad to Fallujah in the west and Tikrit to the north.

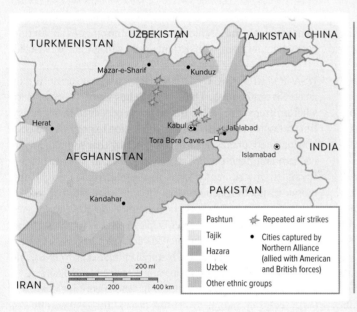

MAP READING

1. What are the three major population groups in Iraq?
2. Which major adversary of the United States borders both Afghanistan and Iraq?
3. What geographic feature does Iraq have that Afghanistan lacks?
4. From which country did the "coalition of the willing" invade Iraq?

MAP INTERPRETATION

1. In what major ways do Iraq and Afghanistan face divisions within their nations?
2. What difference makes Iran more of a threat to Iraq than to Afghanistan?
3. If ethnic and religious differences influenced allegiances in these wars, what does the pattern of airstrikes in Afghanistan suggest about the difficulty of the war?
4. What does the map show that might explain why resistance to American occupation in Iraq was strongest toward Fallujah and Tikrit?

©Pablo Martinez Monsivais/AP Photo

| *Among the leaders of the major powers, only Prime Minister Tony Blair (left) of the United Kingdom unreservedly supported President Bush's war in Iraq. The two leaders met in the Azores several days before the invasion of Iraq with the prime ministers of Spain and Portugal.*

of containment. "A preventive war, to my mind, is an impossibility," President Eisenhower had declared in 1954. In fact, much of the evidence for Iraq possessing weapons of mass destruction (WMDs) was based on what administration officials, including the president, knew was faulty intelligence.

CONTROVERSY OVER WEAPONS OF MASS DESTRUCTION Contradicting the Bush administration, UN weapons inspectors reported finding no evidence of WMDs or even programs to build them. The Security Council refused to support an American resolution giving the United States the authority to lead a UN-sponsored invasion. Only the United Kingdom, Spain, and Italy, among the major powers, were willing to join the United States. On March 19, 2003, without a UN mandate, a "coalition of the willing" consisting of 30 nations attacked Iraq in "Operation Iraqi Freedom." (The actual troops, however, were virtually all American and British.) The invasion was accomplished with amazing speed and precision. Within days U.S. forces were halfway to Baghdad. On May 1 Bush announced an end to major combat operations. Coalition casualties (135 dead and 1,511 wounded) were remarkably low.

A Messy Aftermath

The decision to invade Iraq, without adequate plans to govern or rebuild it, proved to be perhaps the greatest miscalculation an American president had made in launching a war (and most expensive, at a cost of over $2 trillion). Yet in 2003, a large majority of Americans, including many Democrats, supported the invasion. The vocal minority in opposition worried that if the United States felt free to invade a country, what was to stop other nations from launching their own "preemptive"

wars? Opponents also pointed out that no solid evidence linked the secular Saddam Hussein with the religious terrorists of al Qaeda. If the United States toppled Saddam, who would rule? And who would block Iranian fundamentalists from exporting terrorism or even invading Iran's neighbors?

ISIS The administration faced practical problems arising out of its swift victory. What, for example, should it do about those who served in Saddam's army? The decision to dissolve the army left at large a mass of bitter, as well as trained and armed, soldiers. Many of them would eventually join what would become the Islamic State of Iraq and Syria (ISIS) determined to maintain Sunni supremacy in Iraq.

As terrorists, ISIS added to the ethnic and religious factions dividing Iraq—**Shi'ite** Muslims in the southeast, **Sunni** Muslims around Baghdad, and Kurds in the north. Without Saddam's tyranny to hold the country together, the burden of peacekeeping fell to the American military. In the years to come, over 4,400 American troops died in Operation Iraqi Freedom, to say nothing of approximately half a million Iraqi deaths. In addition, the United States spent over half a billion dollars in a futile search for weapons of mass destruction. Hussein had never possessed the technology to build them.

The intangible costs of the war were also high. In the spring of 2004 Americans at home were stunned to learn that Iraqi prisoners of war being held in the Abu Ghraib prison near Baghdad had been abused and tortured by American soldiers guarding them. The Bush administration blamed a handful of "bad apples" in the military. In fact the administration had encouraged such abuses, excusing them in a Justice Department memo that argued that cruel, inhuman, or degrading acts might not be classified as torture.

Governing from the Right

ENERGIZING THE BASE Bush made the war on terror the centerpiece of his 2004 reelection campaign. His Democratic challenger, Senator John Kerry from Massachusetts, opposed the war and once again, the election's outcome came down to a single state—this time Ohio. Had 60,000 out of 5.6 million Ohio voters switched to Kerry, he would have won an electoral majority, though not the popular vote.

REFORMING SOCIAL SECURITY With Republicans in control of all three branches of government, Bush began a politically risky campaign to reform Social Security, long a conservative goal. With the baby-boom generation closing in on retirement, the federal retirement system faced insolvency if steps were not taken to fix it, the president warned. But he met stiff opposition, even from some in his own party, to his proposal to **privatize** the system by creating individual retirement accounts. Critics worried that individuals risked losing their nest eggs if they chose unwisely, whereas the existing system guaranteed a return, even if it was less dramatic than private investment.

The president pressed what proved to be a second losing issue—tax cuts. In particular, he called for the cuts scheduled to end on December 31, 2010, to be made permanent and the

©David J. Phillip/AP Photo

| *A plea from New Orleans residents threatened by Hurricane Katrina.*

With American casualties mounting in an unstable Iraq and drift in domestic affairs at home, voters voiced their displeasure in the 2006 congressional elections. Democrats also tarred Republicans with a culture of corruption, after scandals exposed a number of lobbyists and members of Congress who had traded cash, campaign contributions, and gifts for legislative favors. For the first time since 1994, Democrats took control of both the House and the Senate.

Financial Collapse

Worse was yet to come, for in the autumn of 2008 a financial crisis led the stock markets to plunge and the economy to spiral into the deepest recession since the Great Depression. Part of the crisis stemmed from the mortgage banking industry, which had been selling mortgages to prospective homeowners who possessed virtually no assets and little ability to make monthly payments. These mortgages were then packaged and sold to banks and investment firms as secure investments.

When the overheated housing market began to contract, these investments proved largely worthless. In September Lehman Brothers investment bank suddenly filed for bankruptcy, setting off a cascade of other bank failures. Seeking to end the crisis, the Bush administration rushed in to provide banks with massive government loans. The Troubled Asset Relief Program (TARP) propped up some $700 billion worth of mortgages and investments, in order to stabilize financial markets and other banks teetering at the edge of failure.

estate tax (rebranded as a "death tax") to be eliminated. Yet the issue that had worked for Republicans so well and so long seemed to be losing its appeal. With deficits soaring and no end to the Iraq War in sight, even the Republican Congress would not deliver for Bush.

Disasters Domestic and Foreign

HURRICANE KATRINA AND NEW ORLEANS FLOODING

Bush's early second-term missteps on Social Security and tax cuts proved to be no more than a headwind to his popularity—at least when compared to the gale from Hurricane Katrina. That storm slammed into the Gulf Coast in September 2005. New Orleans escaped the worst until its levees broke and the city was inundated. Most of the city's well-to-do escaped, but no one had made adequate provision to evacuate the elderly, disabled, and poor, most of whom were African American. For days desperate survivors hung to rooftops. Thousands died, while tens of thousands huddled in the damaged Superdome sports arena.

The president at first did no more than fly over the site of the disaster, and the Federal Emergency Management Agency (FEMA) floundered in trying to respond. Over two years later, residents of New Orleans still waited for a federal plan to rebuild their city. Katrina reminded Americans that there were some problems that only effective government can solve.

A DIVIDED NATION

THE 2008 ELECTION PLAYED OUT against this global financial crisis. For the Democrats, Hillary Clinton entered the presidential race as the odds-on favorite, well known and with long experience. However, Barack Obama, the junior senator from Illinois, possessed the advantages of relative youth—he was 47 when he ran—as well as discipline and an ability to inspire when he spoke. Equally striking, Obama was mixed-racial, born in Hawai'i to a white mother and a Kenyan father. In a strongly contested primary season, Obama overcame Clinton and then went on to defeat the Republican nominee, Senator John McCain of Arizona. Forty-five years after Martin Luther King Jr. shared his dreams of freedom on the Washington Mall, the United States had elected the first African American as its president.

Despite an optimistic call for "hope and change," the new president inherited serious economic and foreign policy crises. The financial system remained in free fall, millions had lost

©Doug Mills/The New York Times/Redux Pictures

| *The Obama family on election night, 2008*

mounted to redeploy troops to nearby Afghanistan, where Taliban insurgents threatened the government as well as neighboring Pakistan.

First-Term Reforms

Obama moved quickly to jump-start the collapsing economy with tax cuts and expanded unemployment benefits, as well as spending on education, health care, and infrastructure. Republicans dismissed the $787 billion stimulus package as ineffective federal spending that increased the national debt; none voted for it in the House and only three in the Senate. Liberals warned the measures were not enough—that more than a trillion dollars in spending might be needed to fully revive the economy.

AFFORDABLE CARE ACT Similar partisanship complicated Obama's pledge to reform the nation's bloated health care system. Even as costs continued to rise, the health care system did not improve basic treatment. Over 40 million people lacked health insurance, and rising unemployment threatened millions more with loss of coverage. Many Republicans had supported the idea of health care reform—indeed, as governor of Massachusetts, Mitt Romney had already established a comprehensive plan similar to Obama's. But congressional Republicans staunchly opposed any deal. After a year of bitter negotiation, the Democrats passed the Affordable Care Act (ACA) in March 2010. Among the program's many initiatives, provisions extended Medicaid to some 16 million poor people, guaranteed coverage for children, and prevented insurers from denying coverage because of preexisting conditions. The administration, however, so badly underestimated the difficulty of putting the new program into effect that its full rollout in 2013 began with many stumbles. Yet by 2017 it had extended care to over 20 million who had been uninsured.

their jobs, many others faced eviction from their homes, and major corporate icons such as General Motors and Chrysler stood on the brink of bankruptcy. Abroad, no timetable existed to bring American troops back from Iraq. Worse yet, pressure

many stumbles. Yet by 2017 it had extended care to over 20 million who had been uninsured.

With the president's support, Congress also passed the Dodd-Frank Act, perhaps the most far-reaching set of financial

| *In June 2015, White House photographer Pete Souza caught this quick succession of photos as an aide stepped in to tell President Obama that the Supreme Court had upheld a key portion of the Affordable Care Act, known informally as Obamacare. The law survived two court challenges by Republicans, though its future is in doubt after the election of 2016.*

©White House/Zuma Press/Newscom

©Pete Souza/The White House/Getty Images

| *President Obama and his security team await news of the raid on Osama bin Laden's headquarters. At far left are Vice President Joe Biden and Obama; at far right are Secretary of State Hillary Clinton and Secretary of Defense Robert Gates.*

reforms enacted since the Great Depression. The law tightened bank capital requirements and established a consumer financial protection agency to reduce credit card abuses.

TEA PARTY MOVEMENT The milestones in health care and financial reform did not translate into electoral success for the Democrats. On many issues, Obama followed a pragmatic middle course that disappointed those to both his left and right. And Republicans obstructed many of his compromise measures. (Senate Republicans threatened to filibuster the Democratic majority 256 times between 2007 and 2010, compared with 130 filibuster threats from the Democrats during the Republican-controlled Congress between 2003 and 2007.) During the midterm elections of 2010, disgruntled conservatives and independents formed a loosely coordinated alliance dubbed the Tea Party. Like Boston's original demonstrators of 1773, this modern-day version protested high taxes and called for less government in their lives, not more. The election gave Republicans a decisive majority in the House and significant gains in the Senate. And although Obama defeated his Republican opponent, Mitt Romney, in 2012, Republicans came roaring back in congressional elections of 2014, regaining control of the Senate and increasing their majority in the House. Partisan disputes placed any major legislative reforms beyond Obama's reach.

The president had more success, in the short run, with the war on terrorism. Obama withdrew American combat troops from Iraq during his first term, while sending an additional 30,000 troops into Afghanistan to fight Taliban insurgents. In Afghanistan he made effective, if controversial, use of unmanned drones and pushed his intelligence team to locate Osama bin Laden, who had gone into hiding. In the spring of 2011 the CIA tracked bin Laden to a house in Pakistan. Obama dispatched Navy SEALs on a daring nighttime

mission, where they found and killed the al Qaeda leader. But by the end of the president's second term, the situation in both Iraq and Syria had deteriorated, as a ruthless terrorist group known as the Islamic State of Iraq and Syria (ISIS) began gaining ground.

Short, Medium, Long

Every president must make choices. Short-term crises such as the financial collapse of 2008 demanded immediate attention. Health care and financial reforms could be called medium-term issues, and their success remained to be measured as they were put into effect. But long-term problems began crowding President Obama's second term. They centered on economic inequality and global warming.

A rising stock market suggested the economy was recovering. Corporate profits were strong and the number of home foreclosures and evictions declined. The job market continued its slow improvement. Yet the gap between the richest and poorest Americans continued to widen. By 2012 the chief executive officers of the 350 largest corporations earned over $14 million a year on average, 273 times more than the average worker. The average incomes of America's 400 wealthiest families exceeded $200 million a year.

GROWING ECONOMIC INEQUALITY The traditional response to such inequities was to say that in a good economy, a rising tide lifts all boats. But as one group of economists noted, "When a handful of yachts become ocean liners while the rest remain lowly canoes, something is seriously amiss." In his second inaugural address Obama acknowledged, "Our country cannot succeed when a shrinking few do very well and a growing many barely make it." As the 10-year Bush tax cuts expired, Democrats in Congress did pass a slight increase in the rates paid by taxpayers with yearly incomes of over $250,000. But the longer-term issue of inequality was never squarely addressed during Obama's second term.

Environmental Uncertainties

PARIS AGREEMENT ON CLIMATE CHANGE Global warming, however, seemed to pose the greatest threat over the long term, for both the United States and the world. Conservatives and industry leaders were frequently skeptical of the scientific evidence that the earth's warming was manmade or even a threat. Texas representative Joe Barton insisted he would "not be one of the sycophants that say climate change is the biggest problem facing the world and we need to do all these draconian things that cost jobs." But Obama sidestepped the opposition, using his executive authority to commit the United States to the Paris Agreement, a climate accord signed by 72 nations, including China and India. The agreement called signers to limit their emission of

©Andrew Lichtenstein/Getty Images

| *2016, 2012, and 2017 have been the three hottest years recorded in the contiguous United States since such records began being recorded, in 1880. One way climate change is measured involves charting the number of days in locations where record highs and lows are recorded. Until the 1970s, the number of record highs and record lows remained roughly equal each year. But that has changed over the past three decades. In 2012, 34,008 daily high records were set at weather stations that measure such data, but only 6,664 record lows were set.*

greenhouse gases enough to keep global temperatures from rising more than 2 degrees Celsius above preindustrial averages. Most climate scientists considered that to be a minimal goal.

Health care reform, economic recovery, and the Paris climate agreement were all examples of long-term problem solving. They marked the crowning achievements of Obama's presidency. But whether they would survive the election of 2016 was much in doubt. Its unexpected victor, Donald Trump, stood for virtually the polar opposite of everything Obama had championed.

DONALD TRUMP'S NATIONALIST BRAND

HILLARY RODHAM CLINTON, WHO HAD served as Obama's secretary of state, was Trump's opponent in the election. She survived a challenge from the party's left by Senator Bernie Sanders of Vermont, whose campaign centered on the issue of inequality, while Clinton was tarnished by the millions of dollars she had earned giving speeches to major banks and corporations. Clinton was also dogged by her decision as secretary of state to use a private email server, contrary to government security regulations. On the Republican side, a dog fight among 18 candidates left television celebrity and real estate mogul Donald Trump atop the party's nomination. Trump had never held political office nor possessed any deep experience in economics or world affairs. Although he touted

his business skills as proof that he could master the presidency, his past included at least four bankruptcies, fraud charges against Trump University, and dozens of lawsuits for nonpayment of debts.

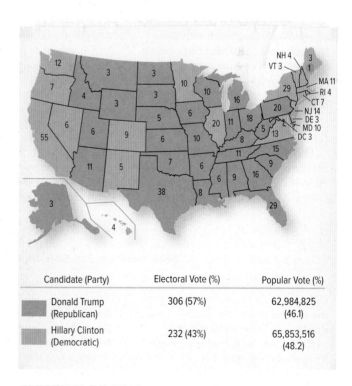

Candidate (Party)	Electoral Vote (%)	Popular Vote (%)
Donald Trump (Republican)	306 (57%)	62,984,825 (46.1)
Hillary Clinton (Democratic)	232 (43%)	65,853,516 (48.2)

ELECTION OF 2016

COLD WAR OVER GLOBAL WARMING

Over the past two decades, climatologists have reached a consensus that global warming is real and that human activities have played a part in it. But what should be done? James Inhofe, the senior Republican senator from Oklahoma, is one of the most vocal supporters of those who deny global warming is a threat. "Our Changing Climate" a report from the U.S. Global Change Research Program's 2014 National Climate Assessment stresses the human role.

DOCUMENT 1
Climate Change: "The Greatest Hoax"?

As I said on the Senate floor on July 28, 2003, "much of the debate over global warming is predicated on fear, rather than science." I called the threat of catastrophic global warming the "greatest hoax ever perpetrated on the American people," a statement that, to put it mildly, was not viewed kindly by environmental extremists and their elitist organizations. . . .

For these groups, the issue of catastrophic global warming is not just a favored fundraising tool. In truth, it's more fundamental than that. Put simply, man-induced global warming is an article of religious faith. Therefore contending that its central tenets are flawed is, to them, heresy of the most despicable kind. Furthermore, scientists who challenge its tenets are attacked, sometimes personally, for blindly ignoring the so-called "scientific consensus." But that's not all: because of their skeptical views, they are contemptuously dismissed for being "out of the mainstream." This is, it seems to me, highly ironic: aren't scientists supposed to be non-conforming and question consensus? . . .

I have insisted all along that the climate change debate should be based on fundamental principles of science, not religion. Ultimately, I hope, it will be decided by hard facts and data—and by serious scientists committed to the principles of sound science. Instead of censoring skeptical viewpoints, as my alarmist friends favor, these scientists must be heard, and I will do my part to make sure that they are heard.

Since my detailed climate change speech in 2003, the so-called "skeptics" continue to speak out. What they are saying, and what they are showing, is devastating to the alarmists. They have amassed additional scientific evidence convincingly refuting the alarmists' most cherished assumptions and beliefs. . . .

This evidence has come to light in very interesting times. Just last month, the 10th Conference of the Parties (COP-10) to the Framework Convention on Climate Change convened in Buenos Aires to discuss Kyoto's implementation and measures to pursue beyond Kyoto. As some of my colleagues know, Kyoto goes into effect on February 16th. I think the nations that ratified Kyoto and agreed to submit to its mandates are making a very serious mistake.

In addition, last month, popular author Dr. Michael Crichton, who has questioned the wisdom of those who trumpet a "scientific consensus," released a new book called "State of Fear," which is premised on the global warming debate. . . . Dr. Crichton, a medical doctor and scientist, very cleverly weaves a compelling presentation of the scientific facts of climate change—with ample footnotes and documentation throughout—into a gripping plot. From what I can gather, Dr. Crichton's book is designed to bring some sanity to the global warming debate. In the "Author's Message" at the end of the book, he refreshingly states what scientists have suspected for years: "We are also in the midst of a natural warming trend that began about 1850, as we emerged from a 400 year cold spell known as the Little Ice Age." Dr. Crichton states that, "Nobody knows how much of the present warming trend might be a natural phenomenon," and, "Nobody knows how much of the present trend might be man-made." And for those who see impending disaster in the coming century, Dr. Crichton urges calm: "I suspect that people of 2100 will be much richer than we are, consume more energy, have a smaller global population, and enjoy more wilderness than we have today. I don't think we have to worry about them."

Source: Senator James M. Inhofe, "Climate Change Update," January 4, 2005. http://inhofe.senate.gov/pressreleases/climateupdate.htm

DOCUMENT 2
"The Warming Can Only Be Explained by Human Influences"

Evidence for changes in Earth's climate can be found from the top of the atmosphere to the depths of the oceans. . . . The sum total of this evidence tells an unambiguous story: the planet is warming. . . .

In the past, climate change was driven exclusively by natural factors: explosive volcanic eruptions that injected reflective particles into the upper atmosphere, changes in energy from the sun, periodic variations in the Earth's orbit, natural cycles that transfer heat between the ocean and the atmosphere, and slowly changing natural variations in heat-trapping gases in the atmosphere. . . . Natural factors are still affecting the planet's climate today. The difference is that, since the beginning of the Industrial Revolution, humans have been increasingly affecting global climate, to the point where we are now the primary cause of recent and projected future change.

The majority of the warming at the global scale over the past 50 years can only be explained by the effects of human influences, especially the emissions from burning fossil fuels (coal, oil, and natural gas) and from deforestation. The emissions from human influences affecting climate include heat-trapping gases such as carbon dioxide (CO_2), methane, and nitrous oxide, and particles such as black carbon (soot), which has a warming influence, and sulfates, which have an overall cooling influence. . . .

Carbon dioxide has been building up in the atmosphere since the beginning of the industrial era in the mid-1700s, primarily due to burning coal, oil, and gas, and secondarily due to clearing of forests. Atmospheric levels have increased by about 40% relative to pre-industrial levels. Methane levels in the atmosphere have increased due to human activities including agriculture (with livestock producing methane in their digestive tracts and rice farming producing it via bacteria that live in the flooded fields); mining coal, extraction and transport of natural gas, and other fossil fuel-related activities; and waste disposal including sewage and decomposing garbage in landfills. Since preindustrial times, methane levels have increased by 250%.

Source: "Our Changing Climate," from *The National Climate Assessment* (2014), issued by the U.S. Global Change Research Program.

THINKING CRITICALLY

How does Inhofe's lack of training in science affect your reaction to his views on global warming? Does Michael Crichton's training as a doctor validate the claims Inhofe makes about him? Which human activities are primary contributors to global warming, according to the National Climate Assessment? How would you compare the tone of the two excerpts, and how would that affect your assessment of them?

For voters struggling to make a living and feeling ignored by traditional politicians, such considerations mattered little. They flocked to his rallies, partly because he was a Washington outsider, partly because he strongly opposed illegal immigration, and partly because he delighted in being "politically incorrect."

ELECTION OF 2016   When the election results were tallied, Clinton won the popular vote by a margin of nearly 3 million. But the Electoral College went for Trump, making 2016 one of only five presidential elections in which the popular vote had been won by the losing candidate. Class and race played a major role in shaping the results. Eighty-five percent of Trump voters were white; Clinton attracted heavy majorities among African Americans, Latinos, and Asian Americans. In the end, Republicans gained control of all three branches of the federal government along with a majority of governorships and state legislatures. What would be the consequence of one-party rule under a president with no political or government experience?

Economic Nationalism

During campaign rallies and even as president, Donald Trump often sported a red baseball camp with his signature slogan, "Make America Great Again." From the earliest days of his administration, that nationalistic goal dominated his behavior and his political agenda. But what sort of greatness was he proposing?

TRADE AND TARIFFS   Part of Trump's nationalism was economic. In matters of trade, he believed that both rivals like China as well as allies of the United States, including many European nations, were taking advantage of free trade policies to discriminate against American products.

The president renegotiated the North American Free Trade Agreement (NAFTA) with Canada and Mexico. He rejected a trade agreement with 12 nations bordering on the Pacific Ocean, known as the Trans-Pacific Partnership, which was designed to create a unified market, much as NAFTA had in North America. And he carried out his threat to raise tariffs on a host of imported goods headed by steel and aluminum. That action outraged Europeans and triggered trade wars with China and Canada. Militarily, he was suspicious of the North Atlantic Treaty Organization, complaining that Europe was not paying its fair share of NATO's expenses. Trump championed a policy of "America First," adopting a slogan that had been last used by isolationists in the 1930s.

DENYING CLIMATE CHANGE   To the dismay of environmentalists around the world, the president announced he was withdrawing the United States from the Paris Agreement on climate change. This too reflected an "America first" approach, since Trump was convinced that China and India, as developing nations, would continue to build dirty coal power plants even if the U.S. cut back. (Those two nations, in fact, have taken steps to reduce their emissions from coal-fired plants.) In addition, the administration's preference for coal over wind and solar power signaled Trump's refusal to accept that global warming was caused by human activity, as the vast majority of scientists believe. Along with many conservative groups, Trump argued that environmental regulations destroyed jobs and choked economic growth. He appointed Scott Pruitt, a determined foe of climate science, to head the Environmental Protection Agency—an agency that Pruitt, as attorney general of Oklahoma, sued 15 times. Immediately Pruitt began doing away with environmental regulations and even demanding that the EPA website stop using the term *climate change*. Revelations of Pruitt's

abuse of his office for personal gain led to his resignation, but did not change EPA efforts to promote coal through environmental deregulation.

Ethnic and Racial Nationalism

CURBING IMMIGRATION Trump's nationalism included a cultural as well as an economic dimension. From his first long ride down an escalator in Trump Tower in June 2015, when he began his campaign, the candidate called for the nation to purify itself. He denounced the flood of illegal immigrants into the United States during the 1990s and condemned even more the new wave stemming from heightened instability in the Middle East and Latin America. "They're bringing drugs," he claimed of Mexicans. "They're bringing crime. They're rapists. And some, I assume, are good people." Once in office, he issued executive orders to curb immigration through a process of "extreme vetting" and increased the detention and deportation of illegal immigrants. He continued to call for the construction of a wall along the 1,200-mile border with Mexico. Like the nationalism of nineteenth- and twentieth-century nativists, Trump's new nationalism was tinged with a suspicion of foreigners who were not Christian and immigrants who were not European.

TRUMP AND THE ALT RIGHT This nationalism was not merely anti-immigrant. At times it seemed perilously close to the views of white supremacists, who had rebranded themselves as the "alt right." For years Trump spread the false rumor that Barack Obama was born in Kenya. He carped that, as president, Obama spent "his mornings watching @ESPN. Then he plays golf, fundraises & grants amnesty to illegals." Once in office, Trump referred to African nations as "shithole" countries and African Americans and Hispanics in the United States as "living in hell . . . you're living in poverty; your schools are no good; you have no jobs." When white supremacists organized a rally to protest the removal of a statue of General Robert E. Lee in Charlottesville, Virginia, Trump refused to explicitly condemn their actions, even though the marchers paraded Klan-style with torches, chanting "Jews will not replace us." He insisted, "There were very fine people on both sides" of the dispute.

Repeal, Replace, or Reject

ATTEMPT TO REPEAL OBAMACARE In other matters of policy, Trump championed traditional Republican goals. During Obama's presidency, the House had passed dozens of measures repealing the Affordable Care Act, but these were symbolic acts, since the Senate never followed through and Obama would have vetoed the legislation in any case. With Trump in office, repeal seemed ensured. Yet Republicans failed to craft a bill fulfilling Trump's promise to replace Obamacare with "insurance for everybody" that was "a lot less expensive." When analyzed by the Congressional Budget Office, each proposed plan was projected to deprive some 20 million Americans of their health insurance. That blunt figure persuaded several Republican senators to vote no, dooming the measures. Over the next year, however, executive actions by the president chipped away at the program in significant ways.

TAX CUT The Republican Congress had more success in passing a massive tax cut of $1.5 trillion that the GOP had long favored. The Tax Cuts and Jobs Act of 2017 lowered corporate rates from 35 to 21 percent, restricted the estate

tax to inheritances above $11 million, and gave most savings to businesses and the richest Americans. Trump personally stood to reap hundreds of millions of dollars in relief. Senate Republicans wrote their version of the bill in such secrecy that most senators did not know what the bill contained until it came up for a vote. Even then, it was so rushed that it included numerous handwritten edits, some of them illegible. Not a single Democrat voted for it.

Russians and Election Meddling

Trump's combative style, more than his substance, displayed his determination to remold the presidency. With his experience in reality TV, he knew how to attract publicity, good or bad. His lavish lifestyle suggested power and success. His tweets at all hours, day or night, sent the media scurrying to write headlines.

Yet beyond the daily chaos that often enveloped the administration, a larger issue loomed, centered on an attempt by the Russian government to secretly influence the outcome of the 2016 election in favor of Trump. As a real estate developer over the previous decades, Trump received significant funding from Russian investors, although he refused to make public his tax returns and other documents that would shed light on those dealings. Throughout the campaign, he displayed a striking admiration for the Russian president, Vladimir Putin. Furthermore, over half a dozen of Trump's staff met with influential Russians or members of Russian intelligence during the campaign. That included his son Donald Jr., his son-in-law Jared Kushner, and his then-campaign manager Paul Manafort, to whom Russians promised "dirt" on Hillary Clinton obtained from Democratic emails they had hacked.

FLYNN, COMEY, AND MUELLER Less than a month after taking office, Trump was forced to fire his national security advisor, Michael T. Flynn, for lying about his contacts with the Russian ambassador to the United States. Flynn also failed to report being paid thousands of dollars for services performed for Russia and Turkey. With the FBI investigating these matters, Trump sought privately to ensure the loyalty of FBI director James B. Comey. When Comey refused to pledge it, Trump fired him, creating a firestorm over his potential obstruction of justice. ("I just fired the head of the F.B.I.," he told the Russians, in a private meeting in the Oval Office. "He was crazy, a real nut job. I faced great pressure because of Russia. That's taken off.") In May 2017, the Justice Department appointed Robert S. Mueller, a former FBI director, as special counsel with the authority to investigate Russian meddling in the election and any potential collusion with the Trump campaign.

Over the following year, Mueller's investigation continued, as well as hearings launched by both the Senate and House Intelligence Committees. Further evidence showed that Russians had planted false news accounts on social media, including Facebook, Twitter, and Instagram. Mueller indicted and obtained guilty pleas from a number of administration figures. But until he completed and released the results of his investigation, the extent of Russian influence and possible collusion remained unclear.

The unorthodox and unpredictable administration of Donald Trump raises questions about the future of the republic. Will the majority of Americans willingly accept the brand of nationalism Trump has put forward, complete with its overtones of racial and ethnic purity? Will the deep cuts in corporate and personal taxes win him more friends than enemies, and will it spur the economy to new heights? And more important, will the mounting evidence of corruption both in the Trump organization and in the presidency lead to impeachment?

There are some signs that American voters may reject Trump's unconventional revolt. Special elections in various states have shown a resurgence of Democratic voters. Beyond electoral politics, social reform movements indicate new directions. After yet another shooting rampage at a high school in Parkland, Florida, students organized marches nationwide advocating the substantial reform of gun laws. The disgrace of film producer Harvey Weinstein, accused of sexual harassment and assault by dozens of women, sparked #MeToo, a movement against similar workplace abuses. The movement sparked the exposure of numerous male leaders for sexual harassment in the news media, business, and the arts.

Donald Trump's nationalism has also threatened the multilateral nature of the post–cold war global order. Before 2017, American leaders, whether conservative or liberal, Democrat or Republican, agreed that the United States should play a central role working with other nations to address the world's problems. Additionally, the American economy exerts an enormous impact on global employment and finances. It also generates a disproportionate share of greenhouse gases and airborne and water pollutants. Yet the president, along with many in his cabinet, have sided with the climate-change deniers and economic nationalists. They have been reluctant to acknowledge that the United States cannot grow its economy or reduce global warming outside the community of nations, just as the world cannot succeed without the help of the United States.

The long-term threats humankind faces are truly global. So must be the solutions.

 REVIEW

How did terrorism become more of a global phenomenon after 9/11?

CHAPTER SUMMARY

By the twenty-first century the United States had become increasingly tied to a worldwide network of economic, financial, and demographic relationships that increased both the nation's diversity and its interdependence.

- The Immigration Act of 1965 opened the United States to a global wave of immigration in the 1980s and 1990s.

  ► Asian Americans, who had in the past come most often from Japan, China, and the Philippines, were joined by immigrants from Korea, Vietnam, and India.

  ► The diverse origins of Latino immigrants included those from the Dominican Republic and Central America, as well as Cuba and Mexico.

- Abroad, regional conflicts replaced cold war rivalries as the central challenge for President Clinton, especially in the former nation of Yugoslavia and in the Middle East.

- President Clinton's domestic agenda included rebuilding the nation's infrastructure, improving education, and reforming the health care system.

► The campaign of Republicans to impeach the president ended when the Senate failed to convict.

- The growth of the Internet, the World Wide Web, and e-commerce was part of a revolution in communications and information management.

- Battles of the 1990s over race, immigration, and multiculturalism suggest that race, ethnicity, social class, and religion continue to be sources of both strength and political conflict.

- President George W. Bush was elected president in the closely contested election of 2000.

  ► A Supreme Court ruling stopped a recount in the key state of Florida.

  ► Bush adopted a conservative agenda of major tax cuts, education reform, and promotion of private energy development.

- Arab terrorist attacks on the U.S. World Trade Center towers and the Pentagon on September 11, 2001, led President Bush to declare a global war on terrorism.

  ► A U.S. attack on Afghanistan toppled the Taliban, although Osama bin Laden escaped.

  ► In March 2003 President Bush launched a preemptive invasion of Iraq to prevent Saddam Hussein from using weapons of mass destruction against the United States. No such weapons were found.

  ► Civil war in Iraq undermined American programs for reconstruction.

  ► The slow federal response to Hurricane Katrina, growing disillusionment with the war in Iraq, and economic collapse in 2008 contributed to the election of Barack Obama in 2008.

- President Obama, the first African American president the nation had elected, looked to address the financial crisis.

  ► The Democratic Congress passed a large stimulus bill to promote jobs.

  ► Obama proposed a major reform of the health care system, the Affordable Care Act (Obamacare). After a rocky start, it extended health care coverage to some 20 million uninsured Americans.

  ► Navy SEALs located and killed Osama bin Laden. But the growth of ISIS in Iraq and Syria complicated the war on terror.

  ► Through executive action, Obama committed the United States to the Paris Agreement on climate change.

- Republican Donald Trump, a real estate developer and television celebrity, upset Hillary Clinton in the election of 2016.

  ► Trump failed to repeal Obamacare but passed large tax cuts that primarily benefited businesses and the wealthiest Americans.

  ► Special prosecutor Robert Mueller investigated possible collusion between the Trump campaign and Russians who attempted to aid Trump's election.

  ► Trump withdrew the United States from the Paris Agreement.

Digging Deeper

Accounts of the recent past often reflect the partisan spirit of those engaged in ongoing controversies. Michael I. Days, *Obama's Legacy: What He Accomplished as President* (2016), offers a thorough, if partisan, look at the politics of eight years. Sidney Blumenthal, *The Clinton Wars* (2003), is an insider's unabashed defense of the Clintons. Peter Baker's *Days of Fire: Bush and Cheney in the White House* (2013) follows Cheney's declining influence in the second term, while his *Obama: The Call of History* (2017) is remarkably even-handed. Joseph E. Stiglitz, *The Roaring Nineties: A New History of the World's Most Prosperous Decade* (2004), offers a liberal perspective on economic inequalities. On multiculturalism and the prospects for democracy, see Alan Wolfe, *Does American Democracy Still Work?* (2006). Richard Alba and Victor Nee, *Remaking the American Mainstream: Assimilation and Contemporary Immigration* (2003), argue that today's immigrants are following the same path as those in the early twentieth century.

Jacob S. Hacker and Paul Pierson, *Winner-Take-All Politics: How Washington Made the Rich Richer—and Turned Its Back on the Middle Class* (2010), trace the influence of financial markets on politics. Jeff Madrick, *Age of Greed: The Triumph of Finance and the Decline of America, 1970 to the Present* (2011), tells how the pursuit of private wealth has come to dominate economics. John Freeman, ed., *Tales of Two Americas: Stories of Inequality in a Divided Nation* (2017), presents an anthology of writings that include many leading literary voices. In a powerful memoir, J. D. Vance, *Hillbilly Elegy* (2016), explores the culture and worldview of "Blue Dog Democrats" who now vote Republican.

Lawrence Wright's *The Looming Tower: Al-Qaeda and the Road to 9/11* (2006) makes the case that Osama bin Laden purposely drew George Bush into a trap. Ron Suskind, *The One Percent Doctrine* (2006), uses CIA sources to follow the road to war in Iraq. Beth Bailey and Richard H. Immerman, *Understanding the U.S. Wars in Iraq and Afghanistan* (2015); explore the political and diplomatic sides of the conflict, while Andrew J. Bacevich, *America's War for the Greater Middle East: A Military History* (2016), covers 30 years of U.S. fighting in the region. Spencer R. Weart, *The Discovery of Global Warming* (2008), is a fascinating look at the science of climate change. Elizabeth Kolbert's *The Sixth Extinction: An Unnatural History* (2015) places the current climate crisis into the arc of natural history since the origins of life on earth.

Appendix

THE DECLARATION OF INDEPENDENCE

In Congress, July 4, 1776,

THE UNANIMOUS DECLARATION OF THE THIRTEEN UNITED STATES OF AMERICA

When, in the course of human events, it becomes necessary for one people to dissolve the political bands which have connected them with another, and to assume, among the powers of the earth, the separate and equal station to which the laws of nature and of nature's God entitle them, a decent respect to the opinions of mankind requires that they should declare the causes which impel them to the separation.

We hold these truths to be self-evident, that all men are created equal; that they are endowed by their Creator with certain unalienable rights; that among these, are life, liberty, and the pursuit of happiness. That, to secure these rights, governments are instituted among men, deriving their just powers from the consent of the governed; that, whenever any form of government becomes destructive of these ends, it is the right of the people to alter or to abolish it, and to institute a new government, laying its foundation on such principles, and organizing its powers in such form, as to them shall seem most likely to effect their safety and happiness. Prudence, indeed, will dictate that governments long established, should not be changed for light and transient causes; and, accordingly, all experience hath shown, that mankind are more disposed to suffer, while evils are sufferable, than to right themselves by abolishing the forms to which they are accustomed. But, when a long train of abuses and usurpations, pursuing invariably the same object, evinces a design to reduce them under absolute despotism, it is their right, it is their duty, to throw off such government and to provide new guards for their future security. Such has been the patient sufferance of these colonies, and such is now the necessity which constrains them to alter their former systems of government. The history of the present King of Great Britain is a history of repeated injuries and usurpations, all having, in direct object, the establishment of an absolute tyranny over these States. To prove this, let facts be submitted to a candid world:

He has refused his assent to laws the most wholesome and necessary for the public good.

He has forbidden his governors to pass laws of immediate and pressing importance, unless suspended in their operation till his assent should be obtained; and, when so suspended, he has utterly neglected to attend to them.

He has refused to pass other laws for the accommodation of large districts of people, unless those people would relinquish the right of representation in the legislature; a right inestimable to them, and formidable to tyrants only.

He has called together legislative bodies at places unusual, uncomfortable, and distant from the depository of their public records, for the sole purpose of fatiguing them into compliance with his measures.

He has dissolved representative houses repeatedly for opposing, with manly firmness, his invasions on the rights of the people.

He has refused, for a long time after such dissolutions, to cause others to be elected; whereby the legislative powers, incapable of annihilation, have returned to the people at large for their exercise; the state remaining, in the meantime, exposed to all the danger of invasion from without, and convulsions within.

He has endeavored to prevent the population of these States; for that purpose, obstructing the laws for naturalization of foreigners, refusing to pass others to encourage their migration hither, and raising the conditions of new appropriations of lands.

He has obstructed the administration of justice, by refusing his assent to laws for establishing judiciary powers.

He has made judges dependent on his will alone, for the tenure of their offices, and the amount and payment of their salaries.

He has erected a multitude of new offices, and sent hither swarms of officers to harass our people, and eat out their substance.

He has kept among us, in time of peace, standing armies, without the consent of our legislatures.

He has affected to render the military independent of, and superior to, the civil power.

He has combined, with others, to subject us to a jurisdiction foreign to our Constitution, and unacknowledged by our laws; giving his assent to their acts of pretended legislation:

For quartering large bodies of armed troops among us:

For protecting them by a mock trial, from punishment, for any murders which they should commit on the inhabitants of these States:

For cutting off our trade with all parts of the world:

For imposing taxes on us without our consent:

For depriving us, in many cases, of the benefit of trial by jury:

For transporting us beyond seas to be tried for pretended offences:

For abolishing the free system of English laws in a neighboring province, establishing therein an arbitrary government, and enlarging its boundaries, so as to render it at once an example and fit instrument for introducing the same absolute rule into these colonies:

For taking away our charters, abolishing our most valuable laws, and altering, fundamentally, the powers of our governments:

For suspending our own legislatures, and declaring themselves invested with power to legislate for us in all cases whatsoever.

He has abdicated government here, by declaring us out of his protection, and waging war against us.

He has plundered our seas, ravaged our coasts, burnt our towns, and destroyed the lives of our people.

He is, at this time, transporting large armies of foreign mercenaries to complete the works of death, desolation, and tyranny, already begun, with circumstances of cruelty and perfidy scarcely paralleled in the most barbarous ages, and totally unworthy the head of a civilized nation.

He has constrained our fellow citizens, taken captive on the high seas, to bear arms against their country, to become the executioners of their friends, and brethren, or to fall themselves by their hands.

He has excited domestic insurrections amongst us, and has endeavored to bring on the inhabitants of our frontiers, the merciless Indian savages, whose known rule of warfare is an undistinguished destruction of all ages, sexes, and conditions.

In every stage of these oppressions, we have petitioned for redress, in the most humble terms; our repeated petitions have been answered only by repeated injury. A prince, whose character is thus marked by every act which may define a tyrant, is unfit to be the ruler of a free people.

Nor have we been wanting in attention to our British brethren. We have warned them, from time to time, of attempts made by their legislature to extend an unwarrantable jurisdiction over us. We have reminded them of the circumstances of our emigration and settlement here. We have appealed to their native justice and magnanimity, and we have conjured them, by the ties of our common kindred, to disavow these usurpations, which would inevitably interrupt our connections and correspondence. They, too, have been deaf to the voice of justice and consanguinity. We must, therefore, acquiesce in the necessity which denounces our separation, and hold them as we hold the rest of mankind, enemies in war, in peace, friends.

We, therefore, the representatives of the United States of America, in general Congress assembled, appealing to the Supreme Judge of the world for the rectitude of our intentions, do, in the name, and by the authority of the good people of these colonies, solemnly publish and declare, that these united colonies are, and of right ought to be, free and independent states: that they are absolved from all allegiance to the British Crown, and that all political connection between them and the state of Great Britain is, and ought to be, totally dissolved; and that, as free and independent states, they have full power to levy war, conclude peace, contract alliances, establish commerce, and to do all other acts and things which independent states may of right do. And, for the support of this declaration, with a firm reliance on the protection of Divine Providence, we mutually pledge to each other our lives, our fortunes, and our sacred honor.

The foregoing Declaration was, by order of Congress, engrossed, and signed by the following members:

JOHN HANCOCK

NEW HAMPSHIRE	NEW YORK	PENNSYLVANIA	MARYLAND	NORTH CAROLINA
Josiah Bartlett	William Floyd	Robert Morris	Samuel Chase	William Hooper
William Whipple	Philip Livingston	Benjamin Rush	William Paca	Joseph Hewes
Matthew Thornton	Francis Lewis	Benjamin Franklin	Thomas Stone	John Penn
	Lewis Morris	John Morton	Charles Carroll, of	
MASSACHUSETTS BAY		George Clymer	Carrollton	SOUTH CAROLINA
Samuel Adams	NEW JERSEY	James Smith		Edward Rutledge
John Adams	Richard Stockton	George Taylor	VIRINIA	Thomas Heyward, Jr.
Robert Treat Paine	John Witherspoon	James Wilson	George Wythe	Thomas Lynch, Jr.
Elbridge Gerry	Francis Hopkinson	George Ross	Richard Henry Lee	Arthur Middleton
	John Hart		Thomas Jefferson	
RHODE ISLAND	Abraham Clark	DELAWARE	Benjamin Harrison	GEORGIA
Stephen Hopkins		Caesar Rodney	Thomas Nelson, Jr.	Button Gwinnett
William Ellery		George Read	Francis Lightfoot Lee	Lyman Hall
		Thomas M'Kean	Carter Braxton	George Walton
CONNECTICUT				
Roger Sherman				
Samuel Huntington				
William Williams				
Oliver Wolcott				

Resolved, That copies of the Declaration be sent to the several assemblies, conventions, and committees, or councils of safety, and to the several commanding officers of the continental troops; that it be proclaimed in each of the United States, at the head of the army.

THE CONSTITUTION OF THE UNITED STATES OF AMERICA[1]

We the People of the United States, in Order to form a more perfect Union, establish Justice, insure domestic Tranquility, provide for the common defence, promote the general Welfare, and secure the Blessings of Liberty to ourselves and our Posterity, do ordain and establish this CONSTITUTION for the United States of America.

ARTICLE I

Section 1. All legislative Powers herein granted shall be vested in a Congress of the United States, which shall consist of a Senate and House of Representatives.

Section 2. The House of Representatives shall be composed of Members chosen every second Year by the People of the several States, and the Electors in each State shall have the Qualifications requisite for Electors of the most numerous Branch of the State Legislature.

No Person shall be a Representative who shall not have attained to the Age of twenty-five Years, and been seven Years a Citizen of the United States, and who shall not, when elected, be an Inhabitant of that State in which he shall be chosen.

[Representatives and direct Taxes[2] shall be apportioned among the several States which may be included within this Union, according to their respective Numbers, which shall be determined by adding to the whole Number of free Persons, including those bound to Service for a Term of Years, and excluding Indians not taxed, three fifths of all other Persons.][3] The actual Enumeration shall be made within three Years after the first Meeting of the Congress of the United States, and within every subsequent Term of ten Years, in such Manner as they shall by Law direct. The Number of Representatives shall not exceed one for every thirty Thousand, but each State shall have at Least one Representative; and until such enumeration shall be made, the State of New Hampshire shall be entitled to chuse three, Massachusetts eight, Rhode-Island and Providence Plantations one, Connecticut five, New York six, New Jersey four, Pennsylvania eight, Delaware one, Maryland six, Virginia ten, North Carolina five, South Carolina five, and Georgia three.

When vacancies happen in the Representation from any State, the Executive Authority thereof shall issue Writs of Election to fill such Vacancies.

The House of Representatives shall chuse their Speaker and other Officers; and shall have the sole Power of Impeachment.

---

[1]This version follows the original Constitution in capitalization and spelling. It is adapted from the text published by the United States Department of the Interior, Office of Education.

[2]Altered by the Sixteenth Amendment.

[3]Negated by the Fourteenth Amendment.

Section 3. The Senate of the United States shall be composed of two Senators from each State, chosen by the Legislature thereof, for six Years; and each Senator shall have one Vote.

Immediately after they shall be assembled in Consequence of the first Election, they shall be divided as equally as may be into three Classes. The Seats of the Senators of the first Class shall be vacated at the Expiration of the second Year, of the second Class at the Expiration of the fourth Year, and of the third Class at the Expiration of the sixth Year, so that one-third may be chosen every second Year; and if Vacancies happen by Resignation, or otherwise, during the Recess of the Legislature of any State, the Executive thereof may make temporary Appointments until the next Meeting of the Legislature, which shall then fill such Vacancies.

No Person shall be a Senator who shall not have attained to the Age of thirty Years, and been nine Years a Citizen of the United States, and who shall not, when elected, be an Inhabitant of that State for which he shall be chosen.

The Vice President of the United States shall be President of the Senate, but shall have no vote, unless they be equally divided.

The Senate shall chuse their other Officers, and also a President pro tempore, in the absence of the Vice President, or when he shall exercise the Office of President of the United States.

The Senate shall have the sole Power to try all Impeachments. When sitting for that purpose they shall be on Oath or Affirmation. When the President of the United States is tried, the Chief Justice shall preside: And no person shall be convicted without the Concurrence of two thirds of the Members present.

Judgment in Cases of Impeachment shall not extend further than to removal from Office, and disqualification to hold and enjoy any Office of honor, Trust, or Profit under the United States: but the Party convicted shall nevertheless be liable and subject to Indictment, Trial, Judgment, and Punishment, according to Law.

Section 4. The Times, Places and Manner of holding Elections for Senators and Representatives, shall be prescribed in each State by the Legislature thereof; but the Congress may at any time by Law make or alter such Regulations, except as to the Places of Chusing Senators.

The Congress shall assemble at least once in every Year, and such Meeting shall be on the first Monday in December, unless they shall by Law appoint a different Day.

Section 5. Each House shall be the Judge of the Elections, Returns and Qualifications of its own Members, and a Majority of each shall constitute a Quorum to do Business; but a smaller number may adjourn from day to day, and may be authorized to compel the Attendance of absent Members, in such Manner, and under such Penalties, as each House may provide.

Each House may determine the Rules of its Proceedings, punish its Members for disorderly Behaviour, and, with the Concurrence of two thirds, expel a Member.

Each House shall keep a Journal of its Proceedings, and from time to time publish the same, excepting such Parts as may in their

Judgment require Secrecy; and the Yeas and Nays of the Members of either House on any question shall, at the Desire of one fifth of those Present, be entered on the Journal.

Neither House, during the Session of Congress, shall, without the Consent of the other, adjourn for more than three days, nor to any other Place than that in which the two Houses shall be sitting.

Section 6. The Senators and Representatives shall receive a Compensation for their Services, to be ascertained by Law, and paid out of the Treasury of the United States. They shall in all Cases, except Treason, Felony, and Breach of the Peace, be privileged from Arrest during their Attendance at the Session of their respective Houses, and in going to and returning from the same; and for any Speech or Debate in either House, they shall not be questioned in any other Place.

No Senator or Representative shall, during the Time for which he was elected, be appointed to any civil Office under the Authority of the United States, which shall have been created, or the Emoluments whereof shall have been increased, during such time; and no Person holding any Office under the United States shall be a Member of either House during his continuance in Office.

Section 7. All Bills for raising Revenue shall originate in the House of Representatives; but the Senate may propose or concur with Amendments as on other bills.

Every Bill which shall have passed the House of Representatives and the Senate, shall, before it become a Law, be presented to the President of the United States; If he approve he shall sign it, but if not he shall return it, with his Objections, to that House in which it shall have originated, who shall enter the Objections at large on their Journal, and proceed to reconsider it. If after such Reconsideration two thirds of that House shall agree to pass the bill, it shall be sent, together with the objections, to the other House, by which it shall likewise be reconsidered, and if approved by two thirds of that House, it shall become a Law. But in all such Cases the Votes of both Houses shall be determined by Yeas and Nays, and the Names of the Persons voting for and against the Bill shall be entered on the Journal of each House respectively. If any Bill shall not be returned by the President within ten Days (Sundays excepted) after it shall have been presented to him, the Same shall be a Law, in like Manner as if he had signed it, unless the Congress by their Adjournment prevent its Return, in which Case it shall not be a Law.

Every Order, Resolution, or Vote to which the Concurrence of the Senate and House of Representatives may be necessary (except on a question of Adjournment) shall be presented to the President of the United States; and before the Same shall take Effect, shall be approved by him, or being disapproved by him, shall be repassed by two thirds of the Senate and House of Representatives, according to the Rules and Limitations prescribed in the Case of a Bill.

Section 8. The Congress shall have Power To lay and collect Taxes, Duties, Imposts and Excises, to pay the Debts and provide for the common Defence and general Welfare of the United States; but all Duties, Imposts and Excises shall be uniform throughout the United States;

To borrow money on the credit of the United States;

To regulate Commerce with foreign Nations, and among the several States, and with the Indian Tribes;

To establish an uniform rule of Naturalization, and uniform Laws on the subject of Bankruptcies throughout the United States;

To coin Money, regulate the Value thereof, and of foreign Coin, and fix the Standard of Weights and Measures;

To provide for the Punishment of counterfeiting the Securities and current Coin of the United States;

To establish Post Offices and post Roads;

To promote the Progress of Science and useful Arts, by securing for limited Times to Authors and Inventors the exclusive Right to their respective Writings and Discoveries;

To constitute Tribunals inferior to the Supreme Court;

To define and punish Piracies and Felonies committed on the high Seas, and Offenses against the Law of Nations;

To declare War, grant Letters of Marque and Reprisal, and make Rules concerning Captures on Land and Water;

To raise and support Armies, but no Appropriation of Money to that Use shall be for a longer Term than two Years;

To provide and maintain a Navy;

To make Rules for the Government and Regulation of the land and naval forces;

To provide for calling forth the Militia to execute the Laws of the Union, suppress Insurrections and repel Invasions;

To provide for organizing, arming, and disciplining the Militia, and for government such Part of them as may be employed in the Service of the United States, reserving to the States respectively, the Appointment of the Officers, and the Authority of training the Militia according to the discipline prescribed by Congress;

To exercise exclusive Legislation in all Cases whatsoever, over such District (not exceeding ten Miles square) as may, by Cession of particular States, and the acceptance of Congress, become the Seat of the Government of the United States, and to exercise like Authority over all Places purchased by the Consent of the Legislature of the State in which the Same shall be, for the Erection of Forts, Magazines, Arsenals, Dock-yards, and other needful Buildings;—And

To make all Laws which shall be necessary and proper for carrying into Execution the foregoing Powers, and all other Powers vested by this Constitution in the Government of the United States, or in any Department or Officer thereof.

Section 9. The Migration or Importation of such Persons as any of the States now existing shall think proper to admit, shall not be prohibited by the Congress prior to the Year one thousand eight hundred and eight, but a tax or duty may be imposed on such Importation, not exceeding ten dollars for each Person.

The privilege of the Writ of Habeas Corpus shall not be suspended, unless when in Cases of Rebellion or Invasion the public Safety may require it.

No bill of Attainder or ex post facto Law shall be passed.

No capitation, or other direct, Tax shall be laid unless in Proportion to the Census or Enumeration herein before directed to be taken.

No Tax or Duty shall be laid on Articles exported from any State.

No Preference shall be given by any Regulation of Commerce or Revenue to the Ports of one State over those of another: nor shall Vessels bound to, or from, one State, be obliged to enter, clear, or pay Duties in another.

No Money shall be drawn from the Treasury, but in Consequence of Appropriations made by Law; and a regular Statement and Account of the Receipts and Expenditures of all public Money shall be published from time to time.

No Title of Nobility shall be granted by the United States: And no Person holding any Office of Profit or Trust under them, shall, without the Consent of the Congress, accept of any present, Emolument, Office, or Title, of any kind whatever, from any King, Prince, or foreign State.

Section 10. No State shall enter into any Treaty, Alliance, or Confederation; grant Letters of Marque and Reprisal; coin Money; emit Bills of Credit; make any Thing but gold and silver Coin a Tender in Payment of Debts; pass any Bill of Attainder, ex post facto Law, or Law impairing the Obligation of Contracts, or grant any Title of Nobility.

No State shall, without the Consent of the Congress, lay any Imposts or Duties on Imports or Exports, except what may be absolutely necessary for executing its inspection Laws; and the net Produce of all Duties and Imposts, laid by any State on Imports or Exports, shall be for the use of the Treasury of the United States; and all such Laws shall be subject to the Revision and Control of the Congress.

No state shall, without the Consent of Congress, lay any duty of Tonnage, keep Troops, or Ships of War in time of Peace, enter into any Agreement or Compact with another State, or with a foreign Power, or engage in War, unless actually invaded, or in such imminent Danger as will not admit of delay.

ARTICLE II

Section 1. The executive Power shall be vested in a President of the United States of America. He shall hold his Office during the Term of four years, and, together with the Vice President, chosen for the same Term, be elected, as follows:

Each State shall appoint, in such Manner as the Legislature thereof may direct, a Number of Electors, equal to the whole Number of Senators and Representatives to which the State may be entitled in the Congress: but no Senator or Representative, or Person holding an Office of Trust or Profit under the United States, shall be appointed an Elector.

[The Electors shall meet in their respective States, and vote by Ballot for two persons, of whom one at least shall not be an Inhabitant of the same State with themselves. And they shall make a List of all the Persons voted for, and of the Number of Votes for each; which List they shall sign and certify, and transmit sealed to the Seat of the Government of the United States, directed to the President of the Senate. The President of the Senate shall, in the Presence of the Senate and House of Representatives, open all the Certificates, and the Votes shall then be counted. The Person having the greatest Number of Votes shall be the President, if such Number be a Majority of the whole Number of Electors appointed; and if there be more than one who have such Majority, and have an equal Number of Votes, then the House of Representatives shall immediately chuse by Ballot one of them for President; and if no Person have a Majority, then from the five highest on the List the said House shall in like Manner chuse the President. But in chusing the President, the Votes shall be taken by States, the Representation from each State having one Vote; a quorum for this Purpose shall consist of a Member or Members from two-thirds of the States, and a Majority of all the States shall be necessary to a Choice. In every Case, after the Choice of the President, the Person having the greatest Number of Votes of the Electors shall be the Vice President. But if there should remain two or more who have equal votes, the Senate shall chuse from them by Ballot the Vice President.][4]

The Congress may determine the Time of chusing the Electors, and the Day on which they shall give their Votes; which Day shall be the same throughout the United States.

No person except a natural-born Citizen, or a Citizen of the United States, at the time of the Adoption of this Constitution, shall be eligible to the Office of President; neither shall any Person be eligible to that Office who shall not have attained to the Age of thirty-five years, and been fourteen Years a Resident within the United States.

In Case of the Removal of the President from Office, or of his Death, Resignation, or Inability to discharge the Powers and Duties of the said Office, the same shall devolve on the Vice President, and the Congress may by Law provide for the Case of Removal, Death, Resignation, or Inability, both of the President and Vice President, declaring what Officer shall then act as President, and such Officer shall act accordingly, until the disability be removed, or a President shall be elected.

The President shall, at stated Times, receive for his Services a Compensation, which shall neither be increased nor diminished during the Period for which he shall have been elected, and he shall not receive within that Period any other Emolument from the United States, or any of them.

Before he enter on the execution of his Office, he shall take the following Oath or Affirmation:—"I do solemnly swear (or affirm) that I will faithfully execute the Office of President of the United States, and will, to the best of my Ability, preserve, protect, and defend the Constitution of the United States."

Section 2. The President shall be Commander in Chief of the Army and Navy of the United States, and of the Militia of the several States, when called into the actual Service of the United States; he may require the Opinion, in writing, of the principal Officer in each of the executive Departments, upon any subject relating to the Duties of their respective Offices, and he shall have Power to Grant Reprieves and Pardons for Offenses against the United States, except in Cases of Impeachment.

He shall have Power, by and with the Advice and Consent of the Senate, to make Treaties, provided two-thirds of the Senators present concur; and he shall nominate, and by and with the Advice and Consent of the Senate, shall appoint Ambassadors, other public Ministers and Consuls, Judges of the supreme Court, and all other Officers of the United States, whose Appointments are not herein otherwise provided for, and which shall be established by Law: but the Congress may by Law vest the Appointment of such inferior Officers, as they think proper, in the President alone, in the Courts of Law, or in the Heads of Departments.

The President shall have Power to fill up all Vacancies that may happen during the Recess of the Senate, by granting Commissions which shall expire at the End of their next Session.

Section 3. He shall from time to time give to the Congress Information of the State of the Union, and recommend to their Consideration such Measures as he shall judge necessary and expedient; he may, on extraordinary occasions, convene both Houses, or either of them, and in Case of Disagreement between them, with respect to the Time of Adjournment, he may adjourn them to such Time as he shall think proper; he shall receive Ambassadors and other public Ministers; he shall take care that the Laws be faithfully executed, and shall Commission all the Officers of the United States.

---

[4]Revised by the Twelfth Amendment.

Section 4. The President, Vice President and all civil Officers of the United States, shall be removed from Office on Impeachment for, and Conviction of, Treason, Bribery, or other high Crimes and Misdemeanors.

ARTICLE III

Section 1. The judicial Power of the United States, shall be vested in one supreme Court, and in such inferior Courts as the Congress may from time to time ordain and establish. The Judges, both of the supreme and inferior Courts, shall hold their Offices during good Behaviour, and shall, at stated Times, receive for their Services, a Compensation, which shall not be diminished during their Continuance in Office.

Section 2. The judicial Power shall extend to all Cases, in Law and Equity, arising under this Constitution, the Laws of the United States, and Treaties made, or which shall be made, under their Authority;—to all Cases affecting ambassadors, other public ministers and consuls;—to all cases of admiralty and maritime Jurisdiction;—to Controversies to which the United States shall be a Party;—to Controversies between two or more States;—between a State and Citizens of another State;[5]—between Citizens of different States—between Citizens of the same State claiming Lands under Grants of different States, and between a State, or the Citizens thereof, and foreign States, Citizens, or Subjects.

In all Cases affecting Ambassadors, other public Ministers and Consuls, and those in which a State shall be Party, the supreme Court shall have original Jurisdiction. In all the other Cases before mentioned, the supreme Court shall have appellate Jurisdiction, both as to Law and Fact, with such Exceptions, and under such Regulations as the Congress shall make.

The trial of all Crimes, except in Cases of Impeachment, shall be by Jury; and such Trial shall be held in the State where the said Crimes shall have been committed; but when not committed within any State, the Trial shall be at such Place or Places as the Congress may by Law have directed.

Section 3. Treason against the United States, shall consist only in levying War against them, or in adhering to their Enemies, giving them Aid and Comfort. No Person shall be convicted of Treason unless on the Testimony of two Witnesses to the same overt Act, or on Confession in open Court.

The Congress shall have power to declare the Punishment of Treason, but no Attainder of Treason shall work Corruption of Blood, or Forfeiture except during the Life of the Person attainted.

ARTICLE IV

Section 1. Full Faith and Credit shall be given in each State to the public Acts, Records, and judicial Proceedings of every other State. And the Congress may by general Laws prescribe the Manner in which such Acts, Records and Proceedings shall be proved, and the Effect thereof.

Section 2. The Citizens of each State shall be entitled to all Privileges and Immunities of Citizens in the several States.

A Person charged in any State with Treason, Felony, or other Crime, who shall flee from Justice, and be found in another State,

shall on demand of the executive Authority of the State from which he fled, be delivered up, to be removed to the State having Jurisdiction of the crime.

No Person held to Service or Labour in one State, under the Laws thereof, escaping into another, shall, in Consequence of any Law or Regulation therein, be discharged from such Service or Labour, but shall be delivered up on Claim of the Party to whom such Service or Labour may be due.

Section 3. New States may be admitted by the Congress into this Union; but no new State shall be formed or erected within the Jurisdiction of any other State; nor any State be formed by the Junction of two or more States, or parts of States, without the Consent of the Legislatures of the States concerned as well as of the Congress.

The Congress shall have Power to dispose of and make all needful Rules and Regulations respecting the Territory or other Property belonging to the United States; and nothing in this Constitution shall be so construed as to Prejudice any Claims of the United States, or of any particular State.

Section 4. The United States shall guarantee to every State in this Union a Republican Form of Government, and shall protect each of them against Invasion; and on Application of the Legislature, or of the Executive (when the Legislature cannot be convened) against domestic Violence.

ARTICLE V

The Congress, whenever two-thirds of both Houses shall deem it necessary, shall propose Amendments to this Constitution, or, on the Application of the Legislatures of two-thirds of the several States, shall call a Convention for proposing Amendments, which, in either Case, shall be valid to all Intents and Purposes, as part of this Constitution, when ratified by the Legislatures of three-fourths of the several States, or by Conventions in three-fourths thereof, as the one or the other Mode of Ratification may be proposed by the Congress; Provided that no Amendment which may be made prior to the Year One thousand eight hundred and eight shall in any Manner affect the first and fourth Clauses in the Ninth Section of the first Article; and that no State, without its Consent, shall be deprived of its equal Suffrage in the Senate.

ARTICLE VI

All Debts contracted and Engagements entered into, before the Adoption of this Constitution, shall be as valid against the United States under this Constitution, as under the Confederation.

This Constitution, and the Laws of the United States which shall be made in Pursuance thereof; and all Treaties made, or which shall be made, under the Authority of the United States, shall be the supreme Law of the Land; and the Judges in every State shall be bound thereby, any Thing in the Constitution or Laws of any State to the Contrary notwithstanding.

The Senators and Representatives before mentioned, and the Members of the several State Legislatures, and all executive and judicial Officers, both of the United States and of the several States, shall be bound by Oath or Affirmation to support this Constitution; but no religious Tests shall ever be required as a qualification to any Office or public Trust under the United States.

---

[5]Qualified by the Eleventh Amendment.

ARTICLE VII

The Ratification of the Conventions of nine States shall be sufficient for the Establishment of this Constitution between the States so ratifying the same.

Done in Convention by the Unanimous Consent of the States present the Seventeenth Day of September in the Year of our Lord one thousand seven hundred and Eighty seven, and of the Independence of the United States of America the Twelfth. In Witness whereof We have hereunto subscribed our Names.[6]

GEORGE WASHINGTON
PRESIDENT AND DEPUTY FROM VIRGINIA

NEW HAMPSHIRE
John Langdon
Nicholas Gilman

MASSACHUSETTS
Nathaniel Gorham
Rufus King

CONNECTICUT
William Samuel Johnson
Roger Sherman

NEW YORK
Alexander Hamilton

NEW JERSEY
William Livingston
David Brearley
William Paterson
Jonathan Dayton

PENNSYLVANIA
Benjamin Franklin
Thomas Mifflin
Robert Morris
George Clymer
Thomas FitzSimons
Jared Ingersoll
James Wilson
Gouverneur Morris

DELAWARE
George Read
Gunning Bedford, Jr.
John Dickinson
Richard Bassett
Jacob Broom

MARYLAND
James McHenry
Daniel of St. Thomas Jenifer
Daniel Carroll

VIRGINIA
John Blair
James Madison, Jr.

NORTH CAROLINA
William Blount
Richard Dobbs Spaight
Hugh Williamson

SOUTH CAROLINA
John Rutledge
Charles Cotesworth Pinckney
Charles Pinckney
Pierce Butler

GEORGIA
William Few
Abraham Baldwin

Articles in Addition to, and Amendment of, the Constitution of the United States of America, Proposed by Congress, and Ratified by the Legislatures of the Several States, Pursuant to the Fifth Article of the Original Constitution[7]

[AMENDMENT I]

Congress shall make no law respecting an establishment of religion, or prohibiting the free exercise thereof; or abridging the freedom of speech, or of the press; or the right of the people peaceably to assemble, and to petition the Government for a redress of grievances.

[AMENDMENT II]

A well regulated Militia, being necessary to the security of a free State, the right of the people to keep and bear Arms shall not be infringed.

[AMENDMENT III]

No Soldier shall, in time of peace, be quartered in any house, without the consent of the Owner, nor in time of war, but in a manner to be prescribed by law.

[AMENDMENT IV]

The right of the people to be secure in their persons, houses, papers, and effects, against unreasonable searches and seizures, shall not be violated, and no Warrants shall issue, but upon probable cause, supported by Oath or affirmation, and particularly describing the place to be searched, and the persons or things to be seized.

[AMENDMENT V]

No person shall be held to answer for a capital or otherwise infamous crime, unless on a presentment or indictment of a Grand Jury, except in cases arising in the land or naval forces, or in the Militia, when in actual service in time of War or public danger; nor shall any person be subject for the same offence to be twice put in jeopardy of life or limb; nor shall be compelled in any criminal case to be a witness against himself, nor be deprived of life, liberty, or property, without due process of law; nor shall private property be taken for public use, without just compensation.

[AMENDMENT VI]

In all criminal prosecutions, the accused shall enjoy the right to a speedy and public trial, by an impartial jury of the State and district wherein the crime shall have been committed, which district shall have been previously ascertained by law, and to be informed of the nature and cause of the accusation; to be confronted with the witnesses against him; to have compulsory process for obtaining witnesses in his favour, and to have the Assistance of Counsel for his defence.

[AMENDMENT VII]

In suits at common law, where the value in controversy shall exceed twenty dollars, the right of trial by jury shall be preserved, and no fact tried by a jury, shall be otherwise reexamined in any Court of the United States, than according to the rules of the common law.

---

[6]These are the full names of the signers, which in some cases are not the signatures on the document.

[7]This heading appears only in the joint resolution submitting the first ten amendments, known as the Bill of Rights.

[AMENDMENT VIII]

Excessive bail shall not be required, nor excessive fines imposed, nor cruel and unusual punishments inflicted.

[AMENDMENT IX]

The enumeration of the Constitution, of certain rights, shall not be construed to deny or disparage others retained by the people.

[AMENDMENT X]

The powers not delegated to the United States by the Constitution, nor prohibited by it to the States, are reserved to the States respectively, or to the people.
[Amendments I–X, in force 1791.]

[AMENDMENT XI][8]

The Judicial power of the United States shall not be construed to extend to any suit in law or equity, commenced or prosecuted against one of the United States by Citizens of another State, or by Citizens or Subjects of any Foreign State.

[AMENDMENT XII][9]

The Electors shall meet in their respective States and vote by ballot for President and Vice-President, one of whom, at least, shall not be an inhabitant of the same State with themselves; they shall name in their ballots the person voted for as President, and in distinct ballots the person voted for as Vice-President, and they shall make distinct lists of all persons voted for as President, and of all persons voted for as Vice-President, and of the number of votes for each, which lists they shall sign and certify, and transmit sealed to the seat of the government of the United States, directed to the President of the Senate;–The President of the Senate shall, in the presence of the Senate and House of Representatives, open all the certificates and the votes shall then be counted;–The person having the greatest number of votes for President, shall be the President, if such number be a majority of the whole number of Electors appointed; and if no person have such majority, then from the persons having the highest numbers not exceeding three on the list of those voted for as President, the House of Representatives shall choose immediately, by ballot, the President. But in choosing the President, the votes shall be taken by states, the representation from each state having one vote; a quorum for this purpose shall consist of a member or members from two-thirds of the states, and a majority of all the states shall be necessary to a choice. And if the House of Representatives shall not choose a President whenever the right of choice shall devolve upon them, before the fourth day of March next following, then the Vice-President shall act as President, as in the case of the death or other constitutional disability of the President.–The person having the greatest number of votes as Vice-President, shall be the Vice-President, if such number be a majority of the whole number of Electors appointed, and if no person have a majority, then from the two highest numbers on the list, the Senate shall choose the Vice-President; a quorum for the purpose shall consist of two-thirds of the whole number of Senators, and a majority of the whole number shall be necessary

to a choice. But no person constitutionally ineligible to the office of President shall be eligible to that of Vice-President of the United States.

[AMENDMENT XIII][10]

Section 1. Neither slavery nor involuntary servitude, except as a punishment for crime whereof the party shall have been duly convicted, shall exist within the United States, or any place subject to their jurisdiction.

Section 2. Congress shall have power to enforce this article by appropriate legislation.

[AMENDMENT XIV][11]

Section 1. All persons born or naturalized in the United States, and subject to the jurisdiction thereof, are citizens of the United States and of the State wherein they reside. No State shall abridge the privileges or immunities of citizens of the United States; nor shall any State deprive any person of life, liberty, or property, without due process of law; nor deny to any person within its jurisdiction the equal protection of the laws.

Section 2. Representatives shall be apportioned among the several States according to their respective numbers, counting the whole number of persons in each State, excluding Indians not taxed. But when the right to vote at any election for the choice of electors for President and Vice-President of the United States, Representatives in Congress, the Executive and Judicial officers of a State, or the members of the Legislature thereof, is denied to any of the male inhabitants of such State, being twenty-one years of age, and citizens of the United States, or in any way abridged, except for participation in rebellion, or other crime, the basis of representation therein shall be reduced in the proportion which the number of such male citizens shall bear to the whole number of male citizens twenty-one years of age in such State.

Section 3. No person shall be a Senator or Representative in Congress, or elector of President and Vice-President, or hold any office, civil or military, under the United States, or under any State, who, having previously taken an oath, as a member of Congress, or as an officer of the United States, or as a member of any State legislature, or as an executive or judicial officer of any State, to support the Constitution of the United States, shall have engaged in insurrection or rebellion against the same, or given aid or comfort to the enemies thereof. But Congress may by a vote of two-thirds of each House, remove such disability.

Section 4. The validity of the public debt of the United States, authorized by law, including debts incurred for payment of pensions and bounties for services in suppressing insurrection or rebellion, shall not be questioned. But neither the United States nor any State shall assume or pay any debts or obligation incurred in aid of insurrection or rebellion against the United States, or any claim for the loss or emancipation of any slave; but all such debts, obligations, and claims shall be held illegal and void.

Section 5. The Congress shall have the power to enforce, by appropriate legislation, the provisions of this article.

---

[8] Adopted in 1798.
[9] Adopted in 1804.

[10] Adopted in 1865.
[11] Adopted in 1868.

[AMENDMENT XV][12]

Section 1. The right of citizens of the United States to vote shall not be denied or abridged by the United States or by any State on account of race, color, or previous condition of servitude—

Section 2. The Congress shall have power to enforce this article by appropriate legislation.

[AMENDMENT XVI][13]

The Congress shall have power to lay and collect taxes on incomes, from whatever source derived, without apportionment among the several States, and without regard to any census or enumeration.

[AMENDMENT XVII][14]

The Senate of the United States shall be composed of two Senators from each State, elected by the people thereof, for six years; and each Senator shall have one vote. The electors in each State shall have the qualifications requisite for electors of the most numerous branch of the State legislatures.

When vacancies happen in the representation of any State in the Senate, the executive authority of such State shall issue writs of election to fill such vacancies: Provided, That the legislature of any State may empower the executive thereof to make temporary appointments until the people fill the vacancies by election as the legislature may direct.

This amendment shall not be so construed as to affect the election or term of any Senator chosen before it becomes valid as part of the Constitution.

[AMENDMENT XVIII][15]

Section 1. After one year from the ratification of this article the manufacture, sale, or transportation of intoxicating liquors within, the importation thereof into, or the exportation thereof from the United States and all territory subject to the jurisdiction thereof for beverage purposes is hereby prohibited.

Section 2. The Congress and the several States shall have concurrent power to enforce this article by appropriate legislation.

Section 3. This article shall be inoperative unless it shall have been ratified as an amendment to the Constitution by the legislatures of the several States, as provided in the Constitution, within seven years from the date of the submission hereof to the States by the Congress.

[AMENDMENT XIX][16]

The right of citizens of the United States to vote shall not be denied or abridged by the United States or by any State on account of sex.

Congress shall have power to enforce this article by appropriate legislation.

[AMENDMENT XX][17]

Section 1. The terms of the President and Vice-President shall end at noon on the 20th day of January, and the terms of Senators and Representatives at noon on the 3d day of January, of the years in which such terms would have ended if this article had not been ratified; and the terms of their successors shall then begin.

Section 2. The Congress shall assemble at least once in every year, and such meeting shall begin at noon on the 3d day of January, unless they shall by law appoint a different day.

Section 3. If, at the time fixed for the beginning of the term of the President, the President elect shall have died, the Vice-President elect shall become President. If a President shall not have been chosen before the time fixed for the beginning of his term or if the President elect shall have failed to qualify, then the Vice-President elect shall act as President until a President shall have qualified; and the Congress may by law provide for the case wherein neither a President elect nor a Vice-President elect shall have qualified, declaring who shall then act as President, or the manner in which one who is to act shall be selected, and such person shall act accordingly until a President or Vice-President shall have qualified.

Section 4. The Congress may by law provide for the case of the death of any of the persons from whom the House of Representatives may choose a President whenever the right of choice shall have devolved upon them, and for the case of the death of any of the persons from whom the Senate may choose a Vice-President whenever the right of choice shall have devolved upon them.

Section 5. Sections 1 and 2 shall take effect on the 15th day of October following the ratification of this article.

Section 6. This article shall be inoperative unless it shall have been ratified as an amendment to the Constitution by the legislatures of three-fourths of the several States within seven years from the date of its submission.

[AMENDMENT XXI][18]

Section 1. The eighteenth article of amendment to the Constitution of the United States is hereby repealed.

Section 2. The transportation or importation into any State, Territory, or possession of the United States for delivery or use therein of intoxicating liquors, in violation of the laws thereof, is hereby prohibited.

Section 3. This article shall be inoperative unless it shall have been ratified as an amendment to the Constitution by conventions in the several States, as provided in the Constitution, within seven years from the date of the submission hereof to the States by the Congress.

[AMENDMENT XXII][19]

No person shall be elected to the office of the President more than twice, and no person who has held the office of President, or acted as President, for more than two years of a term to which some other person was elected President shall be elected to the office of the President more than once.

---

[12]Adopted in 1870.

[13]Adopted in 1913.

[14]Adopted in 1913.

[15]Adopted in 1918.

[16]Adopted in 1920.

---

[17]Adopted in 1933.

[18]Adopted in 1933.

[19]Adopted in 1951.

But this Article shall not apply to any person holding the office of President when this Article was proposed by the Congress, and shall not prevent any person who may be holding the office of President, or acting as President, during the term within which this Article becomes operative from holding the office of President or acting as President during the remainder of such term.

This article shall be inoperative unless it shall have been ratified as an amendment to the Constitution by the legislatures of three-fourths of the several states within seven years from the date of its submission to the states by the Congress.

[AMENDMENT XXIII][20]

Section 1. The District constituting the seat of Government of the United States shall appoint in such manner as the Congress may direct:

A number of electors of President and Vice-President equal to the whole number of Senators and Representatives in Congress to which the District would be entitled if it were a State, but in no event more than the least populous State; they shall be in addition to those appointed by the States, but they shall be considered, for the purpose of the election of President and Vice-President, to be electors appointed by a State; and they shall meet in the District and perform such duties as provided by the twelfth article of amendment.

Section 2. The Congress shall have power to enforce this article by appropriate legislation.

[AMENDMENT XXIV][21]

Section 1. The right of citizens of the United States to vote in any primary or other election for President or Vice-President, for electors for President or Vice-President, or for Senator or Representative in Congress, shall not be denied or abridged by the United States or any state by reason of failure to pay any poll tax or other tax.

Section 2. The Congress shall have the power to enforce this article by appropriate legislation.

[AMENDMENT XXV][22]

Section 1. In case of the removal of the President from office or of his death or resignation, the Vice-President shall become President.

Section 2. Whenever there is a vacancy in the office of the Vice President, the President shall nominate a Vice President who shall take office upon confirmation by a majority vote of both Houses of Congress.

Section 3. Whenever the President transmits to the President Pro Tempore of the Senate and the Speaker of the House of Representatives his written declaration that he is unable to discharge the powers and duties of his office, and until he transmits to them a written declaration to the contrary, such powers and duties shall be discharged by the Vice-President as Acting President.

Section 4. Whenever the Vice-President and a majority of either the principal officers of the executive departments or of such other body as Congress may by law provide, transmit to the President Pro Tempore of the Senate and the Speaker of the House of Representatives their written declaration that the President is unable to discharge the powers and duties of his office, the Vice President shall immediately assume the powers and duties of the office as Acting President.

Thereafter, when the President transmits to the President Pro Tempore of the Senate and the Speaker of the House of Representatives his written declaration that no inability exists, he shall resume the powers and duties of his office unless the Vice President and a majority of either the principal officers of the executive departments or of such other body as Congress may by law provide, transmit within four days to the President Pro Tempore of the Senate and the Speaker of the House of Representatives their written declaration that the President is unable to discharge the powers and duties of his office. Thereupon Congress shall decide the issue, assembling within forty-eight hours for that purpose if not in session. If the Congress, within twenty-one days after receipt of the latter written declaration, or, if Congress is not in session, within twenty-one days after Congress is required to assemble, determines by two-thirds vote of both Houses that the President is unable to discharge the powers and duties of his office, the Vice President shall continue to discharge the same as Acting President; otherwise, the President shall resume the powers and duties of his office.

[AMENDMENT XXVI][23]

Section 1. The right of citizens of the United States, who are eighteen years of age or older, to vote shall not be denied or abridged by the United States or by any State on account of age.

Section 2. The Congress shall have power to enforce this article by appropriate legislation.

[AMENDMENT XXVII][24]

No law, varying the compensation for the services of the Senators and Representatives, shall take effect, until an election of Representatives shall have intervened.

---

[20]Adopted in 1961.

[21]Adopted in 1964.

[22]Adopted in 1967.

---

[23]Adopted in 1971.

[24]Adopted in 1992.

PRESIDENTIAL ELECTIONS

YEAR	CANDIDATES	PARTIES	POPULAR VOTE	% OF POPULAR VOTE	ELECTORAL VOTE	% VOTER PARTICIPATION
1789	**George Washington**				69	
	John Adams				34	
	Other candidates				35	
1792	**George Washington**				132	
	John Adams				77	
	George Clinton				50	
	Other candidates				5	
1796	**John Adams**	Federalist			71	
	Thomas Jefferson	Dem.-Rep.			68	
	Thomas Pinckney	Federalist			59	
	Aaron Burr	Dem.-Rep.			30	
	Other candidates				48	
1800	**Thomas Jefferson**	Dem.-Rep.			73	
	Aaron Burr	Dem.-Rep.			73	
	John Adams	Federalist			65	
	Charles C. Pinckney	Federalist			64	
	John Jay	Federalist			1	
1804	**Thomas Jefferson**	Dem.-Rep.			162	
	Charles C. Pinckney	Federalist			14	
1808	**James Madison**	Dem.-Rep.			122	
	Charles C. Pinckney	Federalist			47	
	George Clinton	Dem.-Rep.			6	
1812	**James Madison**	Dem.-Rep.			128	
	DeWitt Clinton	Federalist			89	
1816	**James Monroe**	Dem.-Rep.			183	
	Rufus King	Federalist			34	
1820	**James Monroe**	Dem.-Rep.			231	
	John Quincy Adams	Indep.-Rep.			1	
1824	**John Quincy Adams**	Dem.-Rep.	113,122	31.0	84	26.9
	Andrew Jackson	Dem.-Rep.	151,271	43.0	99	
	Henry Clay	Dem.-Rep.	47,136	13.0	37	
	William H. Crawford	Dem.-Rep.	46,618	13.0	41	
1828	**Andrew Jackson**	Democratic	642,553	56.0	178	57.6
	John Quincy Adams	National Republican	500,897	44.0	83	
1832	**Andrew Jackson**	Democratic	701,780	54.5	219	55.4
	Henry Clay	National Republican	484,205	37.5	49	
	William Wirt	Anti-Masonic ⎱		8.0	7	
	John Floyd	Democratic ⎰	101,051		11	
1836	**Martin Van Buren**	Democratic	764,176	50.9	170	57.8
	William H. Harrison	Whig	550,816	49.1	73	
	Hugh L. White	Whig			26	
	Daniel Webster	Whig			14	
	W. P. Mangum	Whig			11	
1840	**William H. Harrison**	Whig	1,275,390	53.0	234	80.2
	Martin Van Buren	Democratic	1,128,854	47.0	60	

YEAR	CANDIDATES	PARTIES	POPULAR VOTE	% OF POPULAR VOTE	ELECTORAL VOTE	% VOTER PARTICIPATION
1844	**James K. Polk**	Democratic	1,339,494	49.6	170	78.9
	Henry Clay	Whig	1,300,004	48.1	105	
	James G. Birney	Liberty	62,300	2.3		
1848	**Zachary Taylor**	Whig	1,361,393	47.4	163	72.7
	Lewis Cass	Democratic	1,223,460	42.5	127	
	Martin Van Buren	Free Soil	291,263	10.1		
1852	**Franklin Pierce**	Democratic	1,607,510	50.9	254	69.6
	Winfield Scott	Whig	1,386,942	44.1	42	
	John P. Hale	Free Soil	155,825	5.0		
1856	**James Buchanan**	Democratic	1,836,072	45.3	174	78.9
	John C. Fremont	Republican	1,342,345	33.1	114	
	Millard Fillmore	American	871,731	21.6	8	
1860	**Abraham Lincoln**	Republican	1,865,908	39.8	180	81.2
	Stephen A. Douglas	Democratic	1,375,157	29.5	12	
	John C. Breckinridge	Democratic	848,019	18.1	72	
	John Bell	Constitutional Union	590,631	12.6	39	
1864	**Abraham Lincoln**	Republican	2,218,388	55.0	212	73.8
	George B. McClellan	Democratic	1,812,807	45.0	21	
1868	**Ulysses S. Grant**	Republican	3,013,650	52.7	214	78.1
	Horatio Seymour	Democratic	2,708,744	47.3	80	
1872	**Ulysses S. Grant**	Republican	3,598,235	55.6	286	71.3
	Horace Greeley	Democratic	2,834,761	43.9	66	
1876	**Rutherford B. Hayes**	Republican	4,034,311	48.0	185	81.8
	Samuel J. Tilden	Democratic	4,288,546	51.0	184	
1880	**James A. Garfield**	Republican	4,446,158	48.5	214	79.4
	Winfield S. Hancock	Democratic	4,444,260	48.1	155	
	James B. Weaver	Greenback-Labor	308,578	3.4		
1884	**Grover Cleveland**	Democratic	4,874,621	48.5	219	77.5
	James G. Blaine	Republican	4,848,936	48.2	182	
	Benjamin F. Butler	Greenback-Labor	175,370	1.8		
	John P. St. John	Prohibition	150,369	1.5		
1888	**Benjamin Harrison**	Republican	5,443,892	47.9	233	79.3
	Grover Cleveland	Democratic	5,534,488	48.6	168	
	Clinton B. Fisk	Prohibition	249,506	2.2		
	Anson J. Streeter	Union Labor	146,935	1.3		
1892	**Grover Cleveland**	Democratic	5,551,883	46.1	277	74.7
	Benjamin Harrison	Republican	5,179,244	43.0	145	
	James B. Weaver	People's	1,029,846	8.5	22	
	John Bidwell	Prohibition	264,133	2.2		
1896	**William McKinley**	Republican	7,108,480	52.0	271	79.3
	William J. Bryan	Democratic	6,511,495	48.0	176	
1900	**William McKinley**	Republican	7,218,039	51.7	292	73.2
	William J. Bryan	Democratic; Populist	6,358,345	45.5	155	
	John C. Wooley	Prohibition	208,914	1.5		
1904	**Theodore Roosevelt**	Republican	7,626,593	57.4	336	65.2
	Alton B. Parker	Democratic	5,082,898	37.6	140	
	Eugene V. Debs	Socialist	402,283	3.0		
	Silas C. Swallow	Prohibition	258,536	1.9		

YEAR	CANDIDATES	PARTIES	POPULAR VOTE	% OF POPULAR VOTE	ELECTORAL VOTE	% VOTER PARTICIPATION
1908	**William H. Taft**	Republican	7,676,258	51.6	321	65.4
	William J. Bryan	Democratic	6,406,801	43.1	162	
	Eugene V. Debs	Socialist	420,793	2.8		
	Eugene W. Chafin	Prohibition	253,840	1.7		
1912	**Woodrow Wilson**	Democratic	6,293,152	42.0	435	58.8
	Theodore Roosevelt	Progressive	4,119,207	28.0	88	
	William H. Taft	Republican	3,484,980	24.0	8	
	Eugene V. Debs	Socialist	900,672	6.0		
	Eugene W. Chafin	Prohibition	206,275	1.4		
1916	**Woodrow Wilson**	Democratic	9,126,300	49.4	277	61.6
	Charles E.. Hughes	Republican	8,546,789	46.2	254	
	A. L. Benson	Socialist	585,113	3.2		
	J. Frank Hanly	Prohibition	220,506	1.2		
1920	**Warren G. Harding**	Republican	16,153,115	60.4	404	49.2
	James M. Cox	Democratic	9,133,092	34.2	127	
	Eugene V. Debs	Socialist	919,799	3.4		
	P. P. Christensen	Farmer-Labor	265,411	1.0		
1924	**Calvin Coolidge**	Republican	15,719,921	54.0	382	48.9
	John W. Davis	Democratic	8,386,704	28.8	136	
	Robert M. La Follette	Progressive	4,831,289	16.6	13	
1928	**Herbert C. Hoover**	Republican	21,437,277	58.2	444	56.9
	Alfred E. Smith	Democratic	15,007,698	40.9	87	
1932	**Franklin D. Roosevelt**	Democratic	22,829,501	57.4	472	56.9
	Herbert C. Hoover	Republican	15,760,684	39.7	59	
	Norman Thomas	Socialist	881,951	2.2		
1936	**Franklin D. Roosevelt**	Democratic	27,757,333	60.8	523	61.0
	Alfred M. Landon	Republican	16,684,231	36.5	8	
	William Lemke	Union	882,479	1.9		
1940	**Franklin D. Roosevelt**	Democratic	27,313,041	54.8	449	62.5
	Wendell L. Wilkie	Republican	22,348,480	44.8	82	
1944	**Franklin D. Roosevelt**	Democratic	25,612,610	53.5	432	55.9
	Thomas E. Dewey	Republican	22,117,617	46.0	99	
1948	**Harry S Truman**	Democratic	24,179,345	50.0	303	53.0
	Thomas E. Dewey	Republican	21,991,291	46.0	189	
	J. Strom Thurmond	States' Rights	1,169,021	2.0	39	
	Henry A. Wallace	Progressive	1,157,172	2.0		
1952	**Dwight D. Eisenhower**	Republican	33,936,234	55.1	442	63.3
	Adlai E. Stevenson	Democratic	27,314,992	44.4	89	
1956	**Dwight D. Eisenhower**	Republican	35,590,472	57.6	457	60.6
	Adlai E. Stevenson	Democratic	26,022,752	42.1	73	
1960	**John F. Kennedy**	Democratic	34,226,731	49.7	303	62.8
	Richard M. Nixon	Republican	34,108,157	49.6	219	
	Harry F. Byrd	Independent	501,643		15	
1964	**Lyndon B. Johnson**	Democratic	43,129,566	61.1	486	61.7
	Barry M. Goldwater	Republican	27,178,188	38.5	52	
1968	**Richard M. Nixon**	Republican	31,785,480	44.0	301	60.6
	Hubert H. Humphrey	Democratic	31,275,166	42.7	191	
	George C. Wallace	American Independent	9,906,473	13.5	46	

YEAR	CANDIDATES	PARTIES	POPULAR VOTE	% OF POPULAR VOTE	ELECTORAL VOTE	% VOTER PARTICIPATION
1972	**Richard M. Nixon**	Republican	47,169,911	60.7	520	55.2
	George S. McGovern	Democratic	29,170,383	37.5	17	
	John G. Schmitz	American	1,099,482	1.4		
1976	**Jimmy Carter**	Democratic	40,830,763	50.1	297	53.5
	Gerald R. Ford	Republican	39,147,793	48.0	240	
1980	**Ronald Reagan**	Republican	43,904,153	51.0	489	52.6
	Jimmy Carter	Democratic	35,483,883	41.0	49	
	John B. Anderson	Independent	5,719,437	7.0	0	
	Ed Clark	Libertarian	920,859	1.0	0	
1984	**Ronald Reagan**	Republican	54,455,075	58.8	525	53.3
	Walter Mondale	Democratic	37,577,185	40.5	13	
1988	**George H. W. Bush**	Republican	48,886,097	53.9	426	48.6
	Michael Dukakis	Democratic	41,809,074	46.1	111	
1992	**William J. Clinton**	Democratic	44,908,254	43.0	370	55.9
	George H. W. Bush	Republican	39,102,343	37.4	168	
	H. Ross Perot	Independent	19,741,065	18.9	0	
1996	**William J. Clinton**	Democratic	45,590,703	49.3	379	49
	Robert Dole	Republican	37,816,307	40.7	159	
	H. Ross Perot	Reform	8,085,294	8.4	0	
2000	**George W. Bush**	Republican	50,456,062	47.9	271	51.2
	Al Gore	Democratic	50,996,582	48.4	266	
	Ralph Nader	Green	2,858,843	2.7	0	
2004	**George W. Bush**	Republican	62,048,610	50.7	286	60.7
	John F. Kerry	Democratic	59,028,444	48.3	251	
	Ralph Nader	Independent	465,650	0.4	0	
2008	**Barack Obama**	Democratic	65,070,487	53	365	62.2
	John McCain	Republican	57,154,810	46	173	
2012	**Barack Obama**	Democratic	65,899,660	51.0	332	58.6
	Mitt Romney	Republican	60,929,152	47.2	206	
2016	**Donald Trump**	Republican	62,984,825	46.1	306	60.2
	Hillary Clinton	Democratic	65,853,516	48.2	232	

JUSTICES OF THE SUPREME COURT

	TERM OF SERVICE	YEARS OF SERVICE	LIFE SPAN
John Jay	1789–1795	5	1745–1829
John Rutledge	1789–1791	1	1739–1800
William Cushing	1789–1810	20	1732–1810
James Wilson	1789–1798	8	1742–1798
John Blair	1789–1796	6	1732–1800
Robert H. Harrison	1789–1790	—	1745–1790
James Iredell	1790–1799	9	1751–1799
Thomas Johnson	1791–1793	1	1732–1819
William Paterson	1793–1806	13	1745–1806
*John Rutledge**	1795	—	1739–1800
Samuel Chase	1796–1811	15	1741–1811
Oliver Ellsworth	1796–1800	4	1745–1807
Bushrod Washington	1798–1829	31	1762–1829
Alfred Moore	1799–1804	4	1755–1810
John Marshall	1801–1835	34	1755–1835
William Johnson	1804–1834	30	1771–1834
H. Brockholst Livingston	1806–1823	16	1757–1823
Thomas Todd	1807–1826	18	1765–1826
Joseph Story	1811–1845	33	1779–1845
Gabriel Duval	1811–1835	24	1752–1844
Smith Thompson	1823–1843	20	1768–1843
Robert Trimble	1826–1828	2	1777–1828
John McLean	1829–1861	32	1785–1861
Henry Baldwin	1830–1844	14	1780–1844
James M. Wayne	1835–1867	32	1790–1867
Roger B. Taney	1836–1864	28	1777–1864
Philip P. Barbour	1836–1841	4	1783–1841
John Catron	1837–1865	28	1786–1865
John McKinley	1837–1852	15	1780–1852
Peter V. Daniel	1841–1860	19	1784–1860
Samuel Nelson	1845–1872	27	1792–1873
Levi Woodbury	1845–1851	5	1789–1851
Robert C. Grier	1846–1870	23	1794–1870
Benjamin R. Curtis	1851–1857	6	1809–1874
John A. Campbell	1853–1861	8	1811–1889
Nathan Clifford	1858–1881	23	1803–1881
Noah H. Swayne	1862–1881	18	1804–1884
Samuel F. Miller	1862–1890	28	1816–1890
David Davis	1862–1877	14	1815–1886
Stephen J. Field	1863–1897	34	1816–1899
Salmon P. Chase	1864–1873	8	1808–1873
William Strong	1870–1880	10	1808–1895
Joseph P. Bradley	1870–1892	22	1813–1892
Ward Hunt	1873–1882	9	1810–1886
Morrison R. Waite	1874–1888	14	1816–1888
John M. Harlan	1877–1911	34	1833–1911
William B. Woods	1880–1887	7	1824–1887
Stanley Matthews	1881–1889	7	1824–1889
Horace Gray	1882–1902	20	1828–1902
Samuel Blatchford	1882–1893	11	1820–1893
Lucius Q. C. Lamar	1888–1893	5	1825–1893
Melville W. Fuller	1888–1910	21	1833–1910
David J. Brewer	1890–1910	20	1837–1910
Henry B. Brown	1890–1906	16	1836–1913

*Appointed and served one term, but not confirmed by the Senate.
Note: Chief justices are in italics.

	TERM OF SERVICE	YEARS OF SERVICE	LIFE SPAN		TERM OF SERVICE	YEARS OF SERVICE	LIFE SPAN
George Shiras Jr.	1892–1903	10	1832–1924	Wiley B. Rutledge	1943–1949	6	1894–1949
Howell E. Jackson	1893–1895	2	1832–1895	Harold H. Burton	1945–1958	13	1888–1964
Edward D. White	1894–1910	16	1845–1921	*Fred M. Vinson*	1946–1953	7	1890–1953
Rufus W. Peckham	1895–1909	14	1838–1909	Tom C. Clark	1949–1967	18	1899–1977
Joseph McKenna	1898–1925	26	1843–1926	Sherman Minton	1949–1956	7	1890–1965
Oliver W. Holmes	1902–1932	30	1841–1935	*Earl Warren*	1953–1969	16	1891–1974
William R. Day	1903–1922	19	1849–1923	John Marshall Harlan	1955–1971	16	1899–1971
William H. Moody	1906–1910	3	1853–1917	William J. Brennan Jr.	1956–1990	33	1906–1997
Horace H. Lurton	1909–1914	4	1844–1914	Charles E. Whittaker	1957–1962	5	1901–1973
Charles E. Hughes	1910–1916	5	1862–1948	Potter Stewart	1958–1981	23	1915–1985
Edward D. White	1910–1921	11	1845–1921	Bryon R. White	1962–1993	31	1917–2002
Willis Van Devanter	1911–1937	26	1859–1941	Arthur J. Goldberg	1962–1965	3	1908–1990
Joseph R. Lamar	1911–1916	5	1857–1916	Abe Fortas	1965–1969	4	1910–1982
Mahlon Pitney	1912–1922	10	1858–1924	Thurgood Marshall	1967–1991	24	1908–1993
James C. McReynolds	1914–1941	26	1862–1946	*Warren C. Burger*	1969–1986	17	1907–1995
Louis D. Brandeis	1916–1939	22	1856–1941	Harry A. Blackmun	1970–1994	24	1908–1999
John H. Clarke	1916–1922	6	1857–1945	Lewis F. Powell Jr.	1972–1987	15	1907–1998
William H. Taft	1921–1930	8	1857–1930	William H. Rehnquist	1972–1986	14	1924–2005
George Sutherland	1922–1938	15	1862–1942	John P. Stevens III	1975–2010	35	1920–
Pierce Butler	1922–1939	16	1866–1939	Sandra Day O'Connor	1981–2006	24	1930–
Edward T. Sanford	1923–1930	7	1865–1930	*William H. Rehnquist*	1986–2005	18	1924–2005
Harlan F. Stone	1925–1941	16	1872–1946	Antonin Scalia	1986–2016	30	1936–2016
Charles E. Hughes	1930–1941	11	1862–1948	Anthony M. Kennedy	1988–2018	30	1936–
Owen J. Roberts	1930–1945	15	1875–1955	David H. Souter	1990–2009	20	1939–
Benjamin N. Cardozo	1932–1938	6	1870–1938	Clarence Thomas	1991–	—	1948–
Hugo L. Black	1937–1971	34	1886–1971	Ruth Bader Ginsburg	1993–	—	1933–
Stanley F. Reed	1938–1957	19	1884–1980	Stephen Breyer	1994–	—	1938–
Felix Frankfurter	1939–1962	23	1882–1965	*John G. Roberts Jr.*	2005–	—	1955–
William O. Douglas	1939–1975	36	1898–1980	Samuel A. Alito Jr.	2006–	—	1950–
Frank Murphy	1940–1949	9	1890–1949	Sonia Sotomayor	2009–	—	1954–
Harlan F. Stone	1941–1946	5	1872–1946	Elena Kagan	2010–	—	1960–
James F. Byrnes	1941–1942	1	1882–1972	Neil Gorsuch	2017–	—	1967–
Robert H. Jackson	1941–1954	13	1892–1954				

A SOCIAL PROFILE OF THE AMERICAN REPUBLIC

YEAR	POPULATION	PERCENT INCREASE	POPULATION PER SQUARE MILE	POPULATION PERCENT URBAN/ RURAL	PERCENT MALE/ FEMALE	PERCENT WHITE/ NONWHITE	PERSONS PER HOUSEHOLD	MEDIAN AGE
1790	3,929,214		4.5	5.1/94.9	NA/NA	80.7/19.3	5.79	NA
1800	5,308,483	35.1	6.1	6.1/93.9	NA/NA	81.1/18.9	NA	NA
1810	7,239,881	36.4	4.3	7.3/92.7	NA/NA	81.0/19.0	NA	NA
1820	9,638,453	33.1	5.5	7.2/92.8	50.8/49.2	81.6/18.4	NA	16.7
1830	12,866,020	33.5	7.4	8.8/91.2	50.8/49.2	81.9/18.1	NA	17.2
1840	17,069,453	32.7	9.8	10.8/89.2	50.9/49.1	83.2/16.8	NA	17.8
1850	23,191,876	35.9	7.9	15.3/84.7	51.0/49.0	84.3/15.7	5.55	18.9
1860	31,443,321	35.6	10.6	19.8/80.2	51.2/48.8	85.6/14.4	5.28	19.4
1870	39,818,449	26.6	13.4	25.7/74.3	50.6/49.4	86.2/13.8	5.09	20.2
1880	50,155,783	26.0	16.9	28.2/71.8	50.9/49.1	86.5/13.5	5.04	20.9
1890	62,947,714	25.5	21.2	35.1/64.9	51.2/48.8	87.5/12.5	4.93	22.0
1900	75,994,575	20.7	25.6	39.6/60.4	51.1/48.9	87.9/12.1	4.76	22.9
1910	91,972,266	21.0	31.0	45.6/54.4	51.5/48.5	88.9/11.1	4.54	24.1
1920	105,710,620	14.9	35.6	51.2/48.8	51.0/49.0	89.7/10.3	4.34	25.3
1930	122,775,046	16.1	41.2	56.1/43.9	50.6/49.4	89.8/10.2	4.11	26.4
1940	131,669,275	7.2	44.2	56.5/43.5	50.2/49.8	89.8/10.2	3.67	29.0
1950	150,697,361	14.5	50.7	64.0/36.0	49.7/50.3	89.5/10.5	3.37	30.2
1960	179,323,175	18.5	50.6	69.9/30.1	49.3/50.7	88.6/11.4	3.33	29.5
1970	203,302,031	13.4	57.4	73.5/26.5	48.7/51.3	87.6/12.4	3.14	28.0
1980	226,545,805	11.4	64.0	73.7/26.3	48.6/51.4	86.0/14.0	2.76	30.0
1990	248,709,873	9.8	70.3	75.2/24.8	48.7/51.3	80.3/19.7	2.63	32.9
2000	281,422,426	13.1	79.6	79.0/21.0	49.0/51.0	81.0/19.0	2.59	35.4
2010	308,745,538	9.7	87.4	80.7/19.3	49.2/50.8	77.1/22.9	2.58	37.2

NA = Not available.

YEAR	BIRTHS	VITAL STATISTICS (RATES PER THOUSAND)				
		YEAR	BIRTHS	DEATHS*	MARRIAGES*	DIVORCES*
1800	55.0	1900	32.3	17.2	NA	NA
1810	54.3	1910	30.1	14.7	NA	NA
1820	55.2	1920	27.7	13.0	12.0	1.6
1830	51.4	1930	21.3	11.3	9.2	1.6
1840	51.8	1940	19.4	10.8	12.1	2.0
1850	43.3	1950	24.1	9.6	11.1	2.6
1860	44.3	1960	23.7	9.5	8.5	2.2
1870	38.3	1970	18.4	9.5	10.6	3.5
1880	39.8	1980	15.9	8.8	10.6	5.2
1890	31.5	1990	16.7	8.6	9.8	4.6
		2000	14.7	8.7	8.5	4.2
		2010	13.8	8.0	6.8	3.6

NA = Not available.
*Data not available before 1900.

YEAR	TOTAL POPULATION	LIFE EXPECTANCY (IN YEARS)			
		WHITE FEMALES	NONWHITE FEMALES	WHITE MALES	NONWHITE MALES
1900	47.3	48.7	33.5	46.6	32.5
1910	50.1	52.0	37.5	48.6	33.8
1920	54.1	55.6	45.2	54.4	45.5
1930	59.7	63.5	49.2	59.7	47.3
1940	62.9	66.6	54.9	62.1	51.5
1950	68.2	72.2	62.9	66.5	59.1
1960	69.7	74.1	66.3	67.4	61.1
1970	70.9	75.6	69.4	68.0	61.3
1980	73.7	78.1	73.6	70.7	65.3
1990	75.4	79.3	75.2	72.6	67.0
2000	76.9	80.0	75.0	74.8	68.3
2010	78.3	80.8	80.3	75.7	74.5

THE CHANGING AGE STRUCTURE

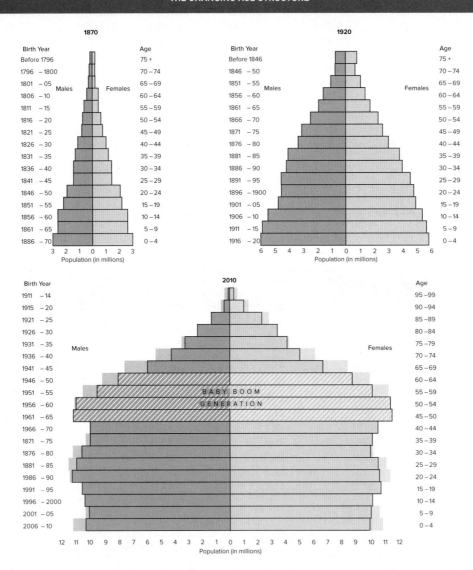

Before the twentieth century, the age distribution of Americans could be charted roughly as a pyramid, as seen in the figures for 1870 and 1920. High birthrates create a broad base at the bottom, while mortality rates winnow the population to a small tip of elderly. But by 2010, the pyramid had been transformed more nearly into a cylinder. Over the past two centuries fertility rates have undergone a steady decline, pulling in the base of the pyramid, while higher living standards have allowed Americans to live longer, broadening the top. Only the temporary bulge of the baby boom distorts the shape.

YEARS	TOTAL NUMBER OF IMMIGRANTS	REGIONAL ORIGIN OF IMMIGRANTS (PERCENT) EUROPE				WESTERN HEMISPHERE	ASIA
		TOTAL EUROPE	NORTH AND WEST	EAST AND CENTRAL	SOUTH AND OTHER		
1821–1830	143,389	69.2	67.1	—	2.1	8.4	—
1831–1840	599,125	82.8	81.8	—	1.0	5.5	—
1841–1850	1,713,251	93.8	92.9	0.1	0.3	3.6	—
1851–1860	2,598,214	94.4	93.6	0.1	0.8	2.9	1.6
1861–1870	2,314,824	89.2	87.8	0.5	0.9	7.2	2.8
1871–1880	2,812,191	80.8	73.6	4.5	2.7	14.4	4.4
1881–1890	5,246,13	90.3	72.0	11.9	6.3	8.1	1.3
1891–1900	3,687,546	96.5	44.5	32.8	19.1	1.1	1.9
1901–1910	8,795,386	92.5	21.7	44.5	6.3	4.1	2.8
1911–1920	5,735,811	76.3	17.4	33.4	25.5	19.9	3.4
1921–1930	4,107,209	60.3	31.7	14.4	14.3	36.9	2.4
1931–1940	528,431	65.9	38.8	11.0	16.1	30.3	2.8
1941–1950	1,035,039	60.1	47.5	4.6	7.9	34.3	3.1
1951–1960	2,515,479	52.8	17.7	24.3	10.8	39.6	6.0
1961–1970	3,321,677	33.8	11.7	9.4	12.9	51.7	12.9
1971–1980	4,493,300	17.8	4.3	5.6	8.4	44.3	35.2
1981–1990	7,338,000	10.4	5.9	4.8	1.1	49.3	37.3
1991–2000	9,095,417	14.9	4.8	8.6	1.6	49.3	30.7

Dash indicates less than 0.1 percent.

RECENT TRENDS IN IMMIGRATION (IN THOUSANDS)					PERCENT		
	1961–1970	1971–1980	1981–1990	1991–2000	1971–1980	1981–1990	1991–2000
All countries	3,321.7	4,493.3	7,338.1	9095.4	100.0	100.0	100.0
Europe	1,123.5	800.4	761.5	1359.7	17.8	10.4	14.9
Austria	20.6	9.5	18.3	15.5	0.2	0.3	0.2
Belgium	9.2	5.3	7.0	7.0	0.1	0.1	0.1
Czechoslovakia	3.3	6.0	7.2	9.8	0.1	0.1	0.1
Denmark	9.2	4.4	5.3	6.0	0.1	0.1	0.1
France	45.2	25.1	22.4	35.8	0.6	1.3	0.4
Germany	190.8	74.4	91.6	92.6	1.7	2.2	1.0
Greece	86.0	92.4	38.3	26.7	2.1	0.4	0.3
Hungary	5.4	6.6	6.5	9.3	0.1	0.1	0.1
Ireland	33.0	11.5	31.9	56.9	0.3	0.9	0.6
Italy	214.1	129.4	67.2	62.7	2.9	0.2	0.7
Netherlands	30.6	10.5	12.2	13.3	0.2	0.1	0.1
Norway	15.5	3.9	4.2	5.1	0.1	1.1	0.5
Poland	53.5	37.2	83.3	163.7	0.8	0.5	1.8
Portugal	76.1	101.7	40.4	22.9	2.3	0.3	0.3
Spain	44.7	39.1	20.4	17.1	0.9	0.2	0.2
Sweden	17.1	6.5	11.0	12.7	0.1	0.1	0.1
Switzerland	18.5	8.2	8.8	11.8	0.2	0.1	0.1
United Kingdom	213.8	137.4	159.2	151.8	3.1	2.2	1.7
USSR	2.5	39.0	57.7	462.8	0.9	0.3	5.1
Yugoslavia	20.4	30.5	18.8	66.5	0.7	0.5	0.7
Other Europe	9.1	18.9	8.2	57.7	0.2	0.0	0.6

| RECENT TRENDS IN IMMIGRATION (IN THOUSANDS) | | | | | PERCENT | |
| | | | | | | |
	1961–1970	1971–1980	1981–1990	1991–2000	1971–1980	1981–1990	1991–2000
Asia	427.6	1588.2	2738.1	2795.6	35.2	37.3	30.7
China	34.8	124.3	298.9	419.1	2.8	4.1	4.6
Hong Kong	75.0	113.5	98.2	109.8	2.5	1.3	1.2
India	27.2	164.1	250.7	363.1	3.7	3.4	4.0
Iran	10.3	45.1	116.0	69.0	1.0	1.6	0.8
Israel	29.6	37.7	44.2	39.4	0.8	0.6	0.4
Japan	40.0	49.8	47.0	67.9	1.1	0.6	0.7
Korea	34.5	267.6	333.8	164.2	6.0	4.5	1.8
Philippines	98.4	355.0	548.7	503.9	7.9	7.5	5.5
Turkey	10.1	13.4	23.4	38.2	0.3	0.3	0.4
Vietnam	4.3	172.8	281.0	286.1	3.8	3.8	3.1
Other Asia	36.5	176.1	631.4	735.4	3.8	8.6	8.0
America	1716.4	1982.5	3615.6	4486.8	44.3	49.3	49.3
Argentina	49.7	29.9	27.3	26.6	0.7	0.4	0.3
Canada	413.3	169.9	158.0	192.0	3.8	2.2	2.1
Colombia	72.0	77.3	122.9	128.5	1.7	1.7	1.4
Cuba	208.5	264.9	144.6	169.3	5.9	2.0	1.9
Dominican Rep.	93.3	148.1	252.0	335.3	3.3	3.4	3.7
Ecuador	36.8	50.1	56.2	76.5	1.1	0.8	0.8
El Salvador	15.0	34.4	213.5	215.7	0.8	2.9	2.4
Haiti	34.5	56.3	138.4	179.6	1.3	1.9	2.0
Jamaica	74.9	137.6	208.1	169.2	3.1	2.8	1.9
Mexico	453.9	640.3	1655.7	2249.4	14.3	22.6	24.7
Other America	264.4	373.8	639.3	744.3	8.3	8.7	8.2
Africa	29.0	80.8	176.8	355.0	1.8	2.4	3.9
Oceania	25.1	41.2	45.2	55.8	0.9	0.6	0.6

Figures may not add to total due to rounding.

NUMBER OF IMMIGRANTS AND THEIR SHARE OF THE TOTAL U.S. POPULATION, 1850–2016

The Census of 2010 was the last to collect data on international migration. Presently the American Community Survey (ACS) collects information from a more limited sample group. The graph combines that data post-2000 with earlier information to show the number of immigrants living in the United States and their percentage of the total U.S. population.

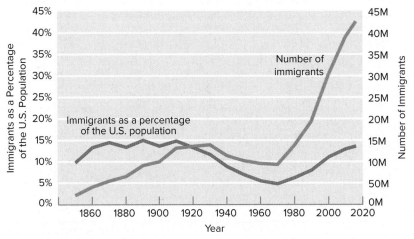

Source: Migration Policy Institute (MPI) tabulation of data from U.S. Census Bureau, 2010–2016 American Community Surveys (ACS), and 1970, 1990, and 2000 Decennial Census. All other data are from Campbell J. Gibson and Emily Lennon, "Historical Census Statistics on the Foreign-Born Population of the United States: 1850 to 1990" (Working Paper no. 29, U.S. Census Bureau, Washington, DC, 1999).

Glossary

A

actual representation view that the people can be represented only by a person whom they have actually elected to office; this understanding of representation was the consensus among colonials during the imperial crisis and the basis of their objection to the British claim that Americans were virtually represented in Parliament.

affirmative action practice of actively seeking to increase the number of racial and ethnic minorities, women, persons in a protected age category, persons with disabilities, and disabled veterans in a workplace or school. Such measures sometimes include the setting of quotas or percentages in hiring.

Alt-Right Shortened version of Alternative Right, encompassing a broad range of people and groups on the extreme right who believe that "white identity" and "white civilization" are under attack. Adherents condemn the ideal of multiculturalism and instead proclaim the doctrine of white supremacy.

amnesty general pardon granted by a government, usually for political crimes. Proposals of amnesty were made, with varying degrees of exception for high Confederate officials, by Presidents Lincoln and Johnson as well as by Congress in 1872. President Ford offered conditional amnesty in 1974 to draft evaders at the conclusion of the Vietnam War.

anti-Semitism hatred, prejudice, oppression, or discrimination against Jews or Judaism. *Semite* originally referred to the descendants of Shem, which included both Jews and Muslims in the Middle East. More recently the term has come to refer primarily to Jews.

appeasement policy of making concessions to an aggressor nation, as long as its demands appear reasonable, in order to avoid war. Hitler's full conquest of Czechoslovakia, violating his promises given at the Munich Conference in 1938, gave the term its negative connotation.

armistice mutually agreed-on truce or temporary halt in the fighting of a war so that the combatants may discuss peace.

artisan skilled craftworker, such as a blacksmith, a cooper, a miller, or a tailor. Master artisans constituted a large segment of the middle classes in American cities and towns from the beginnings of colonial settlement through the 1820s; they owned their own shops and employed a number of younger journeyman artisans, who owned only their tools, and trained even younger and less skilled apprentices in a craft.

assimilate to absorb a culturally distinct group into the dominant culture. The debate over the process of assimilation, of immigrants "becoming American," has been a persistent fault line in American politics. The debate revolves around what qualities are American and the degree to which a dominant culture should define them. The debate is extremely difficult in a society in which immigration plays a crucial role—in a "nation of nations," as Walt Whitman described the United States.

autonomy condition of being independent or, in the case of a political structure, the right to self-government.

B

balanced constitution view that England's constitution gave every part of English society some voice in the workings of its government. While the Crown represented the monarchy and the House of Lords the aristocracy, the House of Commons represented the ordinary people of England.

barter economy networks of trade based on the mutual exchange of goods and services with little or no use of coin or currency.

behaviorism school of psychology that measures human behavior, believes it can be shaped, and discounts emotion as subjective. Behaviorism was founded by psychologist John Watson and was first presented in his *Psychology as the Behaviorist Views It* (1913).

benign neglect policy also known as "salutary neglect," pursued by the British Empire in governing its American colonies until the end of the Seven Years' War.

biocentric life-centered; also a theory of moral responsibility stating that all forms of life have an inherent right to exist and that humanity is not the center of existence.

biogenetic engineering process of changing the DNA of a plant or an animal to produce desirable characteristics. Examples of desirable characteristics include fast growth and unusually large size. The health and environmental safety of genetically modified food products is a subject of debate in the scientific and lay communities.

black codes series of laws passed by southern states in 1865 and 1866, modeled on the slave codes in effect before the Civil War. The codes did grant African Americans some rights not enjoyed by slaves, but their primary purpose was to keep African Americans as propertyless agricultural laborers.

bloody shirt political campaign tactic of "waving the bloody shirt," used by Republicans against Democrats; it invoked the tremendous loss of life and casualties from the Civil War as a reason to vote for Republicans as the party of the Union and not to trust Democrats, who had often opposed the war. The tactic continued to work, with diminishing success, throughout Reconstruction.

bonds certificates of debt issued by a government or corporation promising to repay the buyers of the bonds their original investment, plus interest, by a specified date of maturity. Bonds have been traditionally used by governments as a way to raise money during wartime or for large-scale projects.

boom-and-bust economy periods of expansion and recession or depression that an economy goes through. Also referred to as *business cycle.* Major downturns in the cycle have occurred in the United States beginning in 1819, 1837, 1857, 1873, 1893, 1907, and 1929, the start of the Great Depression.

bootlegging illegal transport or sale of goods, in this case alcoholic beverages during the 1920s. The term derived from the practice of hiding a container of alcohol in the upper part of a boot.

boycott tactic used by protesters, workers, and consumers to pressure business organizations through a mass refusal to purchase their products or otherwise do business with them.

brinkmanship policy of pushing a critical situation to the edge of catastrophe by using the implicit threat of nuclear war in order to persuade an opponent to back down. The strategy was developed by Secretary of State John Foster Dulles under President Dwight Eisenhower.

bureaucratic state government run by administrative bureaus or divisions and staffed by nonelected officials.

business cycle *see* **boom-bust economy.**

C

carpetbagger white Republicans, originally from the North, who came to live in the South after the Civil War. They received their nickname from hostile southerners who claimed that the newcomers arrived carrying all that they owned stuffed into a carpetbag and eager to get rich by plundering the South.

cartel organization of private businesses that join to control production, distribution, and prices.

caste system system of social stratification separating individuals by various distinctions, among them hereditary, rank, profession, wealth, and race. Slavery as a caste system not only separated whites from blacks but also assigned value to people according to shadings of color.

cede to give up possession of, usually by treaty.

celibate abstaining from sexual intercourse; also, unmarried. Celibacy is the abstention from intercourse, a state often motivated by religious teachings.

charter document issued by a sovereign ruler, legislature, or other authority creating a public or private corporation. England's rulers issued charters setting forth the authority of corporations or joint stock companies to colonize sections of the Americas; state legislatures have issued charters to corporations; and the British (including American colonials) traced basic rights of representation to the Magna Carta (Great Charter) granted by King John in 1215 CE.

checks and balances mechanism by which each branch of government—executive, legislative, and judicial—keeps the others within the bounds of their constitutional authority; James Madison emphasized this feature of the federal constitution to assure the Anti-Federalists.

Columbian exchange transition of people, plants, insects, and microbes between the two hemispheres, initiated when Columbus reached the Americas in 1492.

commercial economy economy in which individuals are involved in a network of markets and commercial transactions. Such economies are often urban, where goods and services are exchanged for money and credit; agricultural areas are also commercial when crops and livestock are sold in markets rather than consumed by those who grew or raised them. Commercial economies are less egalitarian, because wealth can be concentrated in the hands of fewer individuals. *See also* **semisubsistence economy.**

committees of correspondence strategy devised by Samuel Adams in 1772 to rally popular support among American colonials against British imperial policies. The committees of correspondence drew up statements of American rights and grievances, distributed those documents within and among the colonies, and solicited responses from towns and counties. This committee structure formed a new communications network, one that fostered intercolonial agreement on resistance to British measures and spread the resistance from seaports into rural areas.

community action programs programs designed to identify and organize local leaders to take steps to alleviate poverty and crime in their neighborhoods. Sociologist Saul Alinsky from Chicago organized the Industrial Areas Foundation to support community action programs in the 1960s.

conformity degree to which people adjust their behavior, values, and ideas to fit into a group or society.

conglomerate corporation whose various branches or subsidiaries are either directly or indirectly spread among a variety of industries, usually unrelated to one another. The purpose of a conglomerate is generally to increase shareholder value and ensure against market cycles by spreading its risk, rather than to improve market share or production efficiency by concentrating on excelling within a single industry.

Congregationalists members of a Protestant denomination that originated in sixteenth-century Britain as part of the Puritan movement. While some early Congregationalists, known as Separatists, concluded that the Church of England was beyond reformation, most strove to reform English religion and society while remaining within the Church of England.

Early modern Congregationalists embraced Calvinist theological beliefs and held that each individual congregation should conduct its own religious affairs, answering to no higher authority. The Separatists founded Plymouth, the first northern colony, and the Non-Separating Congregationalists predominated elsewhere in seventeenth-century New England.

conscription act of compulsory enrollment for military service, as opposed to a voluntary enlistment.

consensus point of view generally shared by a group, institution, or even a culture. Scholars have analyzed and debated the institutions that contribute to the construction of a consensus viewpoint, ranging from schools and churches to the media in their various forms.

constitution framework of government establishing the contract between rulers and ruled. American revolutionaries insisted on written constitutions to protect individual rights and liberties; by contrast, Britons understood the term *constitution* to mean the existing arrangement of government— not an actual document but a collection of parliamentary laws, customs, and precedents.

consumer goods products such as food and clothing that fill the needs and wants of individuals. *Producer* or *capital goods,* in contrast, are the factory equipment and other machines used to manufacture or transport other goods or services.

Continental Army main rebel military force, created by the Second Continental Congress in July 1775 and commanded by George Washington. After the 1776 campaign, most enlistments came from the poorest and most desperate in American society, and it was they who shouldered the burden of the fighting. During the harsh winter at Valley Forge in 1778/1779, the army acquired greater discipline and expertise and thereafter scored important military victories in the mid-Atlantic and the South.

contraband goods seized by a government during wartime, when the goods were being used by an enemy nation or being shipped to an enemy nation by a neutral nation. The term was also applied during the Civil War to escaped slaves who fled behind Union lines.

Copperhead derogatory term used by Republicans to label northern Democrats who opposed the war policies of the Lincoln administration and advocated a negotiated peace.

CORE Congress of Racial Equality, an organization founded in Chicago in 1942. The group's inspiration was Krishnalal Shridharani's book *War without Violence,* which outlined Mohandas K. Gandhi's nonviolent philosophy for action. CORE believed that African Americans could use nonviolent civil disobedience to challenge racial segregation.

corporation business entity that has been granted a charter granting it legal rights, privileges, and liabilities distinct from the individual members that are a part of it. A corporation therefore may survive the death of the individuals who created and run it.

Counter-Reformation reform movement within the Roman Catholic Church in response to the Protestant Reformation, seeking to reform and reinvigorate the Church. Religious orders played a large role in the Counter-Reformation, particularly the Jesuit order, known formally as the Society of Jesus, and founded in 1534 by Ignatius of Loyola.

covert operations military or political actions carried out in secret to allow the responsible government or party to deny its role. Governments have often relied on such operations when overt military force is impractical or dangerous or when public negotiations are likely to fail.

D

de facto segregation spatial and social separation of populations brought about by social behavior rather than by laws or legal mechanisms. Segregation (especially in schools) has often existed without being sanctioned by law. When the practice is accomplished through explicit legal means, it is known as *de jure segregation.*

debt peonage paying off a debt through labor when the debtor lacks sufficient cash or other assets.

Deep South South Carolina, Georgia, Florida, Alabama, Mississippi, Louisiana, and Texas.

demographic factors relating to the characteristics of populations. Demography is the study of populations, looking at such aspects as size, growth, density, and age distribution.

depreciated decreased in value owing to market conditions. Depreciation in the value of banknotes can occur when too much paper money is put into circulation or when users doubt the ability of the government to back up the paper currency with reserves of gold or silver.

détente relaxation of strained relations between nations, especially among the United States, the Soviet Union, and China in the 1970s and late 1980s. In seeking détente, once-hostile parties begin to emphasize their common interests and reduce their points of conflict.

deterrence prevention of an action by fear of the consequences; during the cold war, the theory that war could be avoided because each side knew that the other possessed large numbers of nuclear weapons. Thus any nuclear exchange threatened the survival of both sides.

disenfranchise to deny a citizen's right to vote.

disenfranchisement denial of a citizen's right to vote.

doctrine of preemption war undertaken in anticipation of imminent attack or invasion by another nation or in hopes of gaining a strategic advantage when war seems unavoidable. In that sense the Japanese government viewed its attack on Pearl Harbor as preemptive.

domesticity devotion to home life, and a woman's place at the center of that life. The ideal of domesticity became popular during the nineteenth century as industrialization was increasingly separating work and home as individual spheres.

dove *see* **hawks and doves.**

dry farming farming system to conserve water in semiarid regions receiving less than 15 to 20 inches of rain a year. Methods include leaving some fields fallow or unplanted to reduce water use, keeping soil broken to absorb water, and growing drought-resistant crops.

due process constitutional concept, embodied in the Fifth and Fourteenth Amendments, that no person shall be deprived of life, liberty, or property without legal safeguards such as being present at a hearing, having an opportunity to be heard in court, having the opportunity to confront hostile witnesses, and being able to present evidence.

E

ecosystem a community and/or region studied as a system of functioning relationships between organisms and their environments.

ecumenism movement encouraging unity among religions, especially among Christian denominations and between Christians and Jews. Ecumenical movements promote cooperation and better understanding among different religious denominations.

egalitarian exhibiting or asserting a belief in the equality of humans in a social, political, or economic context.

elect in theology, those of the faithful chosen, or "elected," by God for eternal salvation.

elites class of people given special social, economic, or intellectual status within society. The singular noun *elite* can also be used as a plural, as in *the colonial elite.*

embargo government act prohibiting trade with a foreign country or countries, usually to exert economic pressure.

enfranchise *see* **suffrage** and **disenfranchisement.**

Enlightenment intellectual movement that flourished in Europe from the mid-1600s through the eighteenth century and stressed the power of human reason to promote social progress by discovering the laws that governed both nature and society. In the American colonies, the Enlightenment's influence encouraged scientists such as Benjamin Franklin to experiment and discover useful scientific knowledge, and it also persuaded a growing minority to accept more liberal religious views, known as "rational Christianity."

escalation process of steady intensification, rather than a sudden or marked increase, applied to the increasing American military presence in Vietnam. The term derives from an escalator, which gradually lifts its cargo to a higher level. Nuclear theorist Herman Kahn used the term geopolitically in his *On Escalation: Metaphors and Scenarios* (1968).

evangelical term that derives from a Greek word meaning the bringing of good news—in this case, the Gospel. Protestant evangelicals stressed the need for individual conversion and rebirth stemming from an awareness of sinful guilt and Christ's act of atoning, through his death, for their sins.

excise tax internal tax placed on the production or sale of a commodity, usually a luxury item or nonessential.

executive order declaration issued by the president or by a governor possessing the force of law. Executive orders are usually based on existing statutory authority and require no action by Congress or the state legislature to take effect.

expatriate one who leaves the country of one's birth or citizenship to live in another, usually out of a sense of alienation. The term is often applied to the group of writers and artists living in self-imposed exile in Paris during the 1920s and sometimes referred to as the "Lost Generation." That term was coined by the writer Gertrude Lawrence, describing the rootless generation of American expatriates who found life in the United States culturally sterile and promises of postwar freedom and democracy empty.

F

federalism governing principle established by the Constitution in which the national government and the states divide power. A stronger commitment to federalism as the basis of a national republic replaced the system established by the Articles of Confederation, which granted virtually sovereign power to individual states.

fission splitting of a nucleus of an atom into at least two other nuclei, accompanied by the release of a relatively large amount of energy. The splitting of the nucleus of the uranium isotope U-235 or its artificial cousin, plutonium, powered the atomic bomb.

Free Soil Party antislavery party formed in 1848 by northern Democrats disillusioned with southern Democratic support for slavery. The party tried to widen its appeal by focusing less on outright abolition than on opposing the spread of slavery into the territories (the need to protect "free soil" and "free labor"). The party never gained strength, however; the Republican Party in the 1850s attracted the greater number of antislavery voters.

freedmen former slaves; the term came into use during the Civil War, as greater numbers of slaves fled or were freed under the terms of the Emancipation Proclamation, and continued to be widely used during Reconstruction. More recently historians have also used the gender-neutral term, *freedpeople*.

G

graduated income tax tax based on a percentage of an individual's income, the percentage increasing as total income increases. Under such a system, wealthy individuals are taxed at a higher rate than are poorer individuals.

Great Awakening term used by some historians to describe periods of intense religious piety and commitment among Americans that fueled the expansion of Protestant churches. The First Great Awakening extended from the 1730s to the American Revolution; the Second Great Awakening includes the period from about 1790 to the 1840s; the Third Great Awakening took place during the late nineteenth and early twentieth centuries; the Fourth Great Awakening spanned the latter half of the twentieth century.

H

habeas corpus Latin phrase meaning, "you have the body." For centuries, the term referred in English law to the right of individuals to be brought before a court and informed of the crime alleged against them. The right of habeus corpus is meant to ensure that the government cannot arbitrarily arrest and imprison a citizen without giving grounds for doing so.

hawks and doves nicknames for the two opposing positions in American policy during the war in Vietnam. Hawks supported the escalation of the war and a "peace with honor." Doves, the peace faction, argued that the United States had intervened in a civil war and should withdraw its troops.

Hessians German soldiers who fought with the British Army during the American Revolution. Some Hessians taken as prisoners of war later served in the Continental Army and settled in the United States after the Revolution.

horizontal combination strategy of business growth (sometimes referred to as "horizontal integration") that attempts to stifle competition by combining more than one firm involved in the same level of production, transportation, or distribution into a single firm.

http:// abbreviation for HyperText Transfer Protocol, the set of Internet rules governing the transfer of data between a server and a computer as well as for exchanging files (text, graphic images, sound, video, and other multimedia files) on the World Wide Web.

I

impeachment under the U.S. Constitution, the process by which members of the House of Representatives bring charges against a high government official for "Treason, Bribery, or other high Crimes and Misdemeanors." Once an individual is impeached, he or she must stand trial before the Senate, where a two-thirds majority vote is required for conviction. Conviction results in removal from office.

imperialism acquisition of control over the government and the economy of another nation, usually by conquest. The United States became an imperialistic world power in the late nineteenth century by gaining control over the Hawaiian Islands and, after the Spanish American War (1898), Guam, the Philippines, Cuba, and Puerto Rico.

indemnity compensation for loss or damage.

indentures contract signed between two parties, binding one to serve the other for a specified period of time. The term originated because two copies of the agreement were made, both indented in the same way at its edges, so that each party was provided an identical record of the agreement.

inflation increase in the overall price of goods and services over an extended period of time; or a similar decrease over time of the purchasing power of money. The latter situation can be caused by an increase of the amount of currency and credit available in an economy. In such cases, when the perceived value of paper money declines (as often happens in wars, when the government tries to raise revenues by printing money), sellers raise the prices of their goods to compensate.

injunction court order requiring individuals or groups to participate in or refrain from a certain action.

interstate commerce trade in goods that crosses state lines. Regulation of interstate commerce is reserved in the Constitution for the federal government and has become the constitutional basis for much of federal regulation of business.

Iroquois League Indian confederacy, also known as the Five Nations, that exerted enormous influence throughout the region. In 1712, a sixth tribe, the Tuscaroras, joined the confederation.

isolationism belief that the United States should avoid foreign entanglements, alliances, and involvement in foreign wars. The tradition had its roots in President George Washington's farewell address, which warned in 1796, "It is our true policy to steer clear of permanent alliances with any portion of the foreign world. . . ."

Issei *see* **Nisei.**

itinerant traveling preacher attached to no settled congregation. Itinerants played an important role in the first Great Awakening, taking their inspiration from George Whitefield, who preached up and down the Atlantic Seaboard. In the early nineteenth century, many Protestant denominations—especially the Methodists and the Baptists—made strategic use of itinerants to evangelize settlers on the frontier.

J

jihad Arabic term meaning "striving or struggling in the way of God." Although broadly the term can indicate a spiritual effort on the part of a Muslim believer to come closer to Allah, the expression is also used to denote a Muslim holy war against unbelievers.

joint stock company business in which capital is held in transferable shares of stock by joint owners. The joint stock company was an innovation that allowed investors to share and spread the risks of overseas investment. Instead of only a few individuals owning a ship and its cargo—which might sink and bring ruin to its investors—joint stock allowed for smaller sums to be invested in a variety of different ventures.

journeyman person who has served an apprenticeship in a trade or craft and who is a qualified worker employed by another person.

judicial review doctrine set out by Chief Justice John Marshall in *Marbury v. Madison*. The decision established that the judicial branch of the federal government possesses the power to determine whether the laws of Congress or the actions of the executive branch violate the Constitution.

L

laissez faire a French term ("allow [people] to do [as they choose]") referring to an economic doctrine that advocates holding government interference in the economy to an absolute minimum and ideally having none at all.

landed states and landless states some of the 13 colonies that became the United States had originally been granted land whose western boundaries were vague or overlapped the land granted to other colonies. During the Confederation period, the so-called landless states had boundaries that were firmly drawn on all sides, such as Maryland, New Jersey, and Massachusetts. The so-called landed states possessed grants whose western boundaries were not fixed. (See the map in Chapter 8).

libertarian advocate of a minimalist approach to governing, in which the freedom of private individuals to do as they please ranks paramount. A libertarian philosophy contrasts with the outlook of modern liberals, in which government plays a more active role in meeting the needs of citizens or in managing social and economic life for the common good.

lien legal claim against property used to obtain a loan, which must be paid when the property is sold. Developing first in the South after the Civil War, the crop-lien system allowed merchants to claim a portion (or all) of current or future crops as payment for loans to farmers for seed, tools, and fertilizer. Merchants often insisted that indebted farmers raise a single cash crop, frequently cotton. That requirement helped to ensnare farmers in a cycle of debt as the price of such crops fell.

loyalists supporters of the king and Parliament and known to the rebels as "tories." At the outset of the American Revolution, loyalists made up about one-fifth of the white population, but their ranks diminished steadily after about 1777, as the British army alienated many civilians in every region that they occupied.

loyalty oath oath of fidelity to the state or to an organization. Plans for Reconstruction insisted that southerners returning to the Union take a loyalty oath of some sort, whether that they would be loyal henceforth to the United States or a more strict "ironclad oath" that they never had aided the Confederacy. At other times of stress—as during the Revolutionary era or during the cold war of the 1950s, loyalty oaths and loyalty investigations have been used by groups or governments to enforce obedience to the state or to a revolutionary movement.

M

managed economy economy directed by the government with power over prices, allocation of resources, and marketing of goods.

Manifest Destiny belief, as Democratic editor John L. O'Sullivan put it, that it had become the United States' "manifest destiny to overspread the continent allotted by Providence for the free development of our yearly multiplying millions." The roots of the doctrine were both religious and political. Protestant religious thinkers had long seen American settlement as setting a pious and virtuous example to the rest of the world. The political ideology of the Revolution encouraged the notion that the benefits of democracy would spread along with the political expansion of the nation. Yet Manifest Destiny was also racist in its assumption of the inferiority of other peoples and cultures; and it encompassed a purely economic desire to expand the nation's commerce and power.

"Maroon" communities collective attempts at escape typically undertaken by groups of newly arrived African slaves in the American South. Such slaves fled inland, often to the frontiers of colonial settlement, where they attempted to reconstruct the African villages from which they had been taken captive. Because of their size, such communities proved to be short-lived; they were quickly discovered by white slave patrols or by Indian tribes such as the Cherokees, who profited from returning runaways. "Maroon communities" in the Caribbean proved far more enduring and provided the bases for successful slave rebellions during the eighteenth and early nineteenth centuries.

mass media forms of communication designed to reach a vast audience, generally a nation state or larger, without personal contact between the senders and receivers. Examples would include newspapers, movies, magazines, radio, television, and—today—some sites on the Internet.

mercantilism European economic doctrine calling for strict regulation of the economy in order to ensure a balance of exports over imports and increase the amount of gold and silver in a nation's treasury.

merchants of death term popularized in the 1930s to describe American bankers and arms makers whose support for the Allied cause, some historians charged, drew the United States into World War I.

Mesoamerica the area stretching from present-day central Mexico southward through Honduras and Nicaragua, in which pre-Columbian civilizations developed.

Methodist denomination that originated as a reform movement within the Church of England during the mid-eighteenth century, much as the Puritans originated as a reform movement within the English church during the mid-sixteenth century. The distinctive features of early Methodism on both sides of the Atlantic included a strict devotional regimen, an ascetic moral discipline, and an emphasis on evangelical conversion. By the Civil War, Methodists had become the largest Protestant denomination in the United States among both whites and African Americans.

military-industrial complex combination of the U.S. armed forces, arms manufacturers, and associated political and commercial interests, which grew rapidly during the cold war era. It is another term for the mutually supportive relationship of military contractors, the Pentagon, and sympathetic members of Congress, an alliance also known as the "Iron Triangle."

militia local defense band of civilians comprising men between the ages of 16 and 65 whose military training consisted only of occasional gatherings known as musters. Militias were organized in towns and counties throughout the American colonies from the beginnings of settlement, but they played a crucial role in the war for independence by supporting the Continental Army whenever the fighting moved into their neighborhoods.

millennialism belief in the thousand-year reign of Christ predicted in the Bible's final book, the Revelation to John. The belief that dedicated Christians could help bring about this reign of holiness by converting the world to Christianity proved to be a powerful impulse to reform.

miscegenation marriage, cohabitation, or sexual relations between persons of different races. Since race is a socially constructed identifier rather than one with any scientific or genetic basis, *miscegenation* as a term is used only in its historical context.

monoculture growth of a single crop to the virtual exclusion of all others, either on a farm or more generally within a region.

mutiny refusal of rank-and-file soldiers to follow the commands of their superior officers. Mutinies plagued the Continental Army between 1779 and 1781 as resentments mounted among soldiers over spoiled food, inadequate clothing, and back pay.

mutually assured destruction (MAD) national defense strategy in which a nuclear attack by one side would inevitably trigger an equal response leading to the destruction of both the attacker and the defender. Deterrence theory suggested that when both sides possessed the capability to inflict nuclear annihilation, even after being hit by a first strike, neither side would dare use such weapons.

N

national debt cumulative total of all previous annual *federal deficits* or budget shortfalls incurred each year and owed by the federal government.

nativism outlook championing the supremacy of "native" cultural traits and political rights over those of immigrants from different backgrounds. Nativism flourished during the high immigration of the late 1840s and 1850s, evidenced by the rise of the American ("Know-Nothing") party. In the late nineteenth and early twentieth centuries, nativists pressed for the restriction of immigration and won their biggest victories when Congress enacted the National Origins Acts of 1921 and 1924. As immigrant numbers rose again in the late twentieth and early twenty-first centuries, the nativist debate again emerged.

naturalization act of granting full citizenship to someone born outside the country.

navalism theories of warfare and trade that rely on a nation's navy as a principal instrument of policy.

neo-isolationist term applied to those who after World War II believed the United States should avoid foreign entanglements. Neo-isolationists especially condemned the United Nations and its supporters, whom they contemptuously referred to as "one-worlders."

"new" immigrants called "new" because they differed substantially from earlier arrivals who had come mostly from northern and western Europe; these newcomers came to the United States between 1880 and 1920 from eastern and southern Europe. Unlike most earlier immigrants (with the exception of the Irish), these immigrants were non-Protestants: Catholics, Jews, and Russian Orthodox Christians.

Nisei American-born citizens of Japanese ancestry, contrasted with *Issei,* native-born Japanese who had moved to the United States. At the outbreak of World War II, Nisei referred specifically to Japanese Americans who lived on the West Coast (but not in Hawaii or the East Coast), who were interned during the war because of prejudice and the widespread fear that they sympathized with Japan.

nomad a member of a group of people who have no fixed home and who move about, usually seasonally, in pursuit of food, water, and other resources.

normal schools schools that trained teachers, usually for two years and mostly for teaching in the elementary grades.

Northwest Territory present-day states of Ohio, Indiana, Illinois, Michigan, and Wisconsin. The incorporation of this territory into the United States through the Northwest Ordinance of 1785 marked the major achievement of the national government under the Articles of Confederation.

O

Opposition diverse group of political thinkers and writers in Great Britain, also known as the Country Party and the Commonwealthmen, who elaborated the tradition of classical republicanism from the late seventeenth century through the eighteenth century. They warned that the executive branch of government (the king and his ministers) was conspiring to corrupt and co-opt the legislative branch of government (the House of Commons), thereby endangering popular liberties, and they called for political reforms to make Britain's government more representative of and more accountable to the people. Dismissed in England as a disaffected radical minority, the Opposition exerted a decisive influence on the political thinking of an increasing number of American colonials in the decades leading up to the Revolution.

outsourcing the contracting of goods or services from outside a company or organization in order to maintain flexibility in the size of the organization's workforce. Increasingly, outsourcing has used suppliers outside the United States in low-wage countries such as Mexico, India, and China.

P

pandemic outbreak of disease that spreads across national boundaries or across the world.

partisan warfare armed clashes among political rivals, typically involving guerrilla fighting and the violent intimidation of civilians by militias. Partisan warfare between loyalists and rebels tore apart communities everywhere in the United States during the war for independence, but the fighting was especially fierce and protracted in the South. The success of rebel insurgencies there ultimately convinced many southern whites to support the cause of independence.

patent legal document issued by the government giving the holder exclusive rights to use, make, and sell a process, product, or device for a specified period of time. The first patents in America were issued by colonial governments as early as 1641. Congress enacted the first patent law in 1790.

paternalism attitude or policy of treating individuals or groups in a fatherly manner, by providing for their needs without granting them rights or responsibilities. The relation involves both a dominant and a subordinate party. Sometimes the dominance comes from gender, as in a male patriarchy, whereby females are given subordinate roles. But paternalism can also be expressed in relations between colonial and subject peoples, masters and slaves, or culturally different groups.

pays d'en haut in the seventeenth century, the lands referred to by the French as the "upper country," the land upriver from Montreal as French fur traders passed into the Great Lakes beyond the southern shores of Lake Ontario. The trading lands stretched all the way to the Mississippi River.

peculiar institution euphemism for slavery, perhaps revealing in its use. The institution was "peculiar" to the South in that it had been abolished in the North (and other parts of the world, increasingly). *Peculiar* also suggests the contradiction with the ideals of the Declaration of Independence, that "all men are created equal."

per capita income average yearly income per person in a particular population;

it provides one statistical measure of the relative wealth of a region.

pluralism idea that identity cannot be reduced to a single shared essence. Under such a philosophy, distinct ethnic, cultural, and religious groups are tolerated and affirmed within a society. The philosophy contrasts with the belief, in American politics, that citizens should assimilate into a more uniform cultural identity of shared values. Contrasting metaphors portray an assimilationist United States as a melting pot versus a pluralist mixing bowl.

plurality in elections, a candidate who receives a plurality wins more votes than any other candidate but less than half of all votes cast. Receiving more than half of the votes cast is called a *majority*.

pocket veto means of vetoing a bill without formally doing so. Normally, if a president does not veto or sign a bill within 10 days of receiving it, the bill automatically becomes law. If it is received, however, within 10 days of Congress's adjournment, the president can simply "pocket" the bill unsigned, until Congress adjourns, and it does not go into effect.

political culture patterns, habits, institutions, and traits associated with a political system. The political culture of the Jacksonian era, for example, was marked by a number of innovations: political nominating conventions, torchlight parades, campaign songs, badges, and other souvenirs.

political machine hierarchical political organization developed in the nineteenth century that controlled the activities of a political party and was usually headed by a political boss.

popular sovereignty doctrine that a territory could decide by vote whether or not to permit slavery within its boundaries. The doctrine was devised by Senator Stephen Douglas of Illinois as a way to placate southerners who wanted slavery permitted within Kansas Territory, forbidden under the Missouri Compromise. Meant as a compromise measure, the doctrine only inflamed the situation, as both sides worked to win a vote over slavery.

Populism political outlook that supports the rights and powers of the common people in opposition to the interests of the privileged elite. The Populist Party evolved out of the economic distress of the 1890s among farmers and focused its anger against the era's large industrial corporations, railroad monopolies, and banks. But populism as an outlook and philosophy persisted long after the party had dissolved.

pragmatism philosophical movement, led by philosophers Charles S. Peirce and William James, that stressed the visible, real-world results of ideas. Pragmatism was embraced by many progressives who wanted to promote the possibilities of change by abandoning the old notion that events were predetermined and inevitable.

predestination basis of Calvinist theology and a belief that holds that God has ordained the outcome of all human history before the beginning of time, including the eternal fate of every human being. Believers in this doctrine found comfort and meaning from its assurance that God was directing the fate of nations, individuals, and all of creation toward his divine purposes.

Presbyterians members of a Protestant denomination that originated in sixteenth-century Britain as part of the Puritan movement. Like their fellow Puritan reformers, the Congregationalists, the Presbyterians embraced Calvinist theology beliefs; but unlike the Congregationalists, Presbyterians favored a more hierarchical form of church governance, a system in which individual congregations were guided by presbyteries and synods comprising both laymen and ministers.

presidio military garrison; as Spanish colonizers moved north from central Mexico in the sixteenth and seventeenth centuries, they constructed presidios to consolidate claims over new territory. Presidios often encouraged the growth of nearby towns and ranches and were probably more important as sites of diplomacy with Indians than as centers of military power. Poor funding and political instability led to the decline of the presidios after Mexican independence in 1821.

privatize transferral of an economic enterprise or public utility from the control of the government into private ownership. The Bush plan for Social Security reform sought to place retirement contributions into investment accounts managed privately, rather than into a fund managed by the Social Security Administration.

producer goods goods, such as heavy machinery, used to manufacture other goods, often consumer goods.

psychedelic characterized by or generating shifts in perception and altered states of awareness, often hallucinatory, and usually brought on by drugs such as LSD, mescaline, or psilocybin. Advocates of the psychedelic state spoke of euphoria, mystic visions, and philosophic insights produced. Critical observers pointed to the potential of inducing not only hallucinations but also sometimes psychoses.

public works government-financed construction projects, such as highways and bridges, for use by the public.

Puritans members of a reform movement within the Church of England that originated in the sixteenth century and that ultimately formed the Congregationalist and Presbyterian churches. Calvinist in their theology, the Puritans strove to reform English religion, society, and politics by restricting church membership to the pious and godly, by according the laity greater power in church governance, and by enlisting the state to enforce a strict moral code that prohibited drunkenness, gambling, swearing, and attending the theater.

Q

Quakers Protestant sect, also known as the Society of Friends, founded in mid-seventeenth-century England. The Quakers believed that the Holy Spirit dwelt within each human being and that religious conviction was the source of their egalitarian social practices, which included allowing women to speak in churches and to preach in public gatherings. Quakers settled the mid-Atlantic colonies in large numbers and founded the colony of Pennsylvania.

R

racialism *see* **racism**.

racism form of discrimination based on the belief that one race is superior to another. Racism may be expressed individually and consciously, through explicit thoughts, feelings, or acts; it can be codified into a theory that claims scientific backing for its tenets. It can also be expressed socially and unconsciously, through institutions that promote inequality between races. In the early twentieth century, when racism became much more pronounced, the term *racialism* was also coined.

reconquista military reconquest of the Iberian Peninsula from Islamic Moors of Africa by European Christian rulers. The campaign lasted on and off from 718 to 1492 CE.

Redeemers southerners who came to power in southern state governments from 1875 to 1877, claiming to have "redeemed" the South from Reconstruction. The Redeemers looked to undo many of the changes wrought by the Civil War. Their goals included minimizing the role of African Americans in government and reducing their economic independence and strengthening the "New South" through industrial development.

red-light district area in cities reserved for prostitutes. The term, first employed in the United States, resulted from the use of red lights to show that prostitutes were open for business.

repatriation act of returning people to their nation of origin. The term often refers to the act of returning soldiers or refugees to their birth country.

republican motherhood redefinition of the role of women promoted by many American reformers in the 1780s and 1790s, who believed that the success of republican government depended on educated and independent-minded mothers who would raise children to become informed and self-reliant citizens. The ideal of republican motherhood fostered improvements in educational opportunities for women and accorded them an important role in civic life, but it also reinforced the notion that women should confine the sphere of their activities to home and family.

republicanism belief that representative government safeguards popular liberties more reliably than does either monarchy or oligarchy and that all citizens must practice vigilance and self-denying virtue to prevent their rulers from succumbing to the temptations of power and becoming tyrants. This "classical republicanism" profoundly influenced the political views of many Americans from the middle of the eighteenth century to the middle of the nineteenth century.

Romanticism intellectual and artistic movement that arose in the early nineteenth century out of a rejection of the Enlightenment values of reason and balance. Romanticism emphasized the individual's expression of emotion and intuition.

S

Sagebrush rebels group of western cattlemen, loggers, miners, developers, and others who argued that federal ownership of huge tracts of land and natural resources violated the principle of states' rights. This group demanded that government transfer control to individual states, in respect of their right to make decisions about the management of both the land and the natural resources.

scalawag white southerners who supported the Republican Party. The derisive nickname was given by their opponents. Perhaps a quarter of all white southerners voted Republican at some time during Reconstruction.

scientific management system of factory production that stresses efficiency. The system was pioneered by American engineer Frederick Winslow Taylor. In *The Principles of Scientific Management* (1911), his most famous work, he emphasized time-and-motion studies to enhance productivity. The book became the bible of efficiency experts and Taylor the "Father of Scientific Management."

sedition words or actions that incite revolt against the law or duly constituted government.

segregation system, imposed through law and custom, of separating people by race; first enacted into law in Tennessee (1875) with a statute separating blacks from whites on trains, one of the most prevalent public spaces for racial mingling.

self-determination principle in international law that people have a right to determine their own form of government free from outside control. The principle contrasts with colonialism and imperialism, under which people are subject to foreign rulers.

semisubsistence economy economy in which individuals and families produce most of what they need to live on. Such economies are overwhelmingly rural and also egalitarian, in that wealth is distributed fairly broadly. During the colonial period and early republic, much of the American economy was semisubsistence. *See also* **commercial economy.**

separate but equal rationale for a policy of segregation granting equal facilities and services to African American and whites in schools, hospitals, transportation and lodging facilities, and other public places. The Supreme Court upheld such laws in *Plessy v. Ferguson* (1896). In practice such facilities were separate but seldom equal.

separation of church and state principle that religious institutions and their representatives should exercise no civil or judicial powers and that civil governments should give no official sanction, privileges, or financial support to any religious denomination or organization.

separation of powers principle that each branch of government—the legislature (Congress), the executive (the President), and the judiciary (the Supreme Court)—should wield distinct powers independent from interference or infringement by other branches of government. During the debates of the Constitutional Convention in 1797, James Madison successfully argued that this separation of powers was essential to a balanced republican government.

settlement house social reform effort that used neighborhood centers in which settlement house workers lived and worked among the poor, often in slum neighborhoods. The first settlement house, Toynbee Hall in London, was founded in 1884. The first settlement house in the United States (The Neighborhood Guild, later University Settlement House) came in 1886 in New York City and was founded by Stanton Coit.

Shi'ite and Sunni two major branches of Islam, a division not unlike the Protestant-Catholic split in Christianity. After the death of the Prophet Muhammad, followers disagreed over who should be his successor. Most believers accepted the tradition of having their leader chosen by community consensus (the Sunni branch), but a minority supported the claim of Ali, the Prophet's cousin. Over the years theological differences have separated Shi'ite and Sunni Muslims as well. Today the Shi'ites are dominant largely in Iran and southeastern Iraq.

silent majority phrase coined by President Richard Nixon in a 1969 speech, referring to the large number of Americans who supported his policies but did not express their views publicly.

sit-in form of direct action in which protesters nonviolently occupy and refuse to leave an area. Mahatma Gandhi employed the tactic during the Indian independence movement, and autoworkers used it in Flint, Michigan, in the late 1930s. Student movements around the world widely adopted the tactic in the 1960s.

social mobility movement of individuals from one social class to another. In general, the stronger the barriers of class, race, gender, or caste, the less social mobility exhibited by a society.

socialism philosophy of social and economic organization in which the means of producing and distributing goods is owned collectively or by government.

sociological jurisprudence legal theory that emphasizes the importance not merely of precedent but of contemporary social context in interpreting the law.

specie coined money of gold or silver. Also referred to as hard money or hard currency. In contrast, banknotes or notes are paper money or paper currency.

sphere of influence geographic region beyond its border over which a nation exerts political or economic control.

spoils system practice of rewarding loyal party members with jobs in government. Known more formally as "patronage," the practice drew its name from the old saying "To the victor belong the spoils," in this instance, meaning the rewards of election victories.

steerage least expensive accommodation on a passenger ship, located below decks and often used by emigrants for passage to the United States in the late nineteenth and early twentieth centuries.

stock exchange market at which shares of ownership in corporations are bought and sold. The creation of what were markets for investment capital made it easier to raise the large sums of money needed for large industrial projects.

stratified layered; in this case, according to class or social station. A highly stratified society has a greater variety of social levels, from the richest or most socially esteemed to the poorest or least socially approved. A society can be stratified according to wealth, race, religion, or a number of other social markers.

subsistence farming *see* **semisubsistence economy.**

subversive one who seeks the destruction or overthrow of a legally constituted government; also used as an adjective (for example, *subversive conduct*) to refer more generally to behavior undermining the established social order.

suffrage right to vote; also referred to as the franchise. To *disenfranchise* is to take away the right to vote.

Sun Belt areas of the southern and western parts of the United States that experienced significant economic and population growth since World War II. That growth has been a contrast to the relative decline of the *Rust Belt,* the older industrial area from New England to the mid-Atlantic region across the upper Middle West.

Sunni *see* **Shi'ite and Sunni.**

supply-side economics theory that emphasizes tax cuts and business incentives to encourage economic growth rather than deficit spending to promote demand. Businesses and individuals, the theory assumes, will use their tax savings to create new businesses and expand existing businesses, which in turn will increase productivity, employment, and general well-being.

T

tariff duty on trade, the purpose of which is primarily to regulate the flow of commerce rather than to raise a revenue. The Molasses Act of 1733, for example, imposed a hefty customs duty on molasses imported from non–British Caribbean islands to encourage American distillers to purchase molasses exclusively from the British West Indies.

task system way of organizing slave labor in the South Carolina low country during the eighteenth century. Masters and overseers of rice and indigo plantations assigned individual slaves a daily task, and after its completion, slaves could spend the rest of the day engaged in pursuits of their own choosing. Gang labor, the system practiced in the Chesapeake, afforded slaves less opportunity for freedom within slavery.

taxes duty on trade (known as external taxation) or a duty on items circulating within a nation or a colony (known as internal taxation) intended primarily to raise a revenue rather than to regulate the flow of commerce. The Sugar Act of 1764 was an external tax, whereas the Stamp Act of 1765 was an internal tax.

Tejano Texan of Hispanic descent. In the early stages of the rebellion against Santa Anna, more than a few Tejanos supported the Texan drive for independence. But as Americans continued to arrive in Texas in large numbers, many viewed Tejanos with suspicion, and they were marginalized in Texan society.

temperance movement reform movement, begun in the 1820s, to temper or restrain the sale and use of alcohol. It achieved its greatest success when the Eighteenth Amendment took effect in 1920, outlawing the manufacture, sale, transportation, and importation of alcohol. The amendment was repealed in 1933.

tenement building, often in disrepair and usually five or six stories in height, in which cheap apartments were rented to tenants. Such dilapidated housing sprang up in cities across the United States in the late nineteenth and early twentieth centuries to lodge the growing numbers of immigrants, African Americans, and other poor populations moving to urban centers.

theocracy system of government dominated by the clergy.

totalitarian government system in which the state controls all aspects of economic, political, and even social life, usually through some form of dictatorship. Nazi Germany under Adolf Hitler and the Soviet Union under Joseph Stalin are examples of totalitarian regimes.

trade association organization of individuals and firms in a given industry that provides statistical, lobbying, and other services to members.

trust business arrangement in which owners of shares in a business turn over their shares "in trust" to a board with power to control those businesses for the benefit of the trust. Following the example set by John D. Rockefeller and Standard Oil, trusts blossomed in the late nineteenth century as a means of consolidating power over production, marketing, and pricing, often crowding out other competitors.

U

union organization of workers designed to improve their economic status and working conditions. Such organizations come in two varieties: the horizontal union, in which all members share a common skill or craft, and the vertical union, composed of workers from all across the same industry.

Upper South the border states (Delaware, Maryland, Kentucky, and Missouri) and Virginia, North Carolina, Tennessee, and Arkansas.

V

vertical integration strategy of business growth that attempts to reduce costs by gaining control of the successive stages of a business operation, incorporating into a single firm several firms involved in all aspects of the manufacture of a product— from exploiting raw materials to manufacturing and distribution.

Victorianism constellation of middle-class values attributed to the proper virtues of Britain's Queen Victoria. Victorianism responded to the instabilities of an industrial age in which factory work dominated the lives of struggling workers and middle-class clerks as well as down-at-the-heels landed gentry. The culture's emphasis on "refinement" and "manners" established a social hierarchy offering some sense of stability.

virgin soil epidemic epidemic in which the populations at risk have had no previous contact with the diseases that strike them and are therefore immunologically almost defenseless.

virtual representation view that representation is not linked to election but rather to common interests; for example, during the imperial crisis the British argued that Americans were virtually represented in Parliament, even though colonials elected none of its members, because each member of Parliament stood for the interests of the whole empire. *See also* **actual representation.**

W

"watered" stock stock issued in excess of the assets of a company. The term derived from the practice of some ranchers who made their cattle drink large amounts of water before weighing them for sale.

welfare capitalism business practice of providing welfare—in the form of pension and profit-sharing programs, subsidized housing, personnel management, paid vacations, and other services and benefits—for workers. The practice was pioneered by Henry Ford under the philosophy that businesses in a capitalist economy should act for the common good of their workers. The philosophy, if not the businesswide practice, became popular in the 1920s as a way of reducing high rates of turnover among employees and integrating technological change into the workplace.

Wisconsin idea series of progressive reforms at the state level promoted by Robert La Follette during his governorship of Wisconsin (1901–1906). They included primary elections, corporate property taxes, regulation of railroads and public utilities, and supervision of public resources in the public interest. A nonpartisan civil service group, recruited mostly from faculty at the University of Wisconsin, provided a cadre of expert bureaucrats to run the new programs.

Y

yellow journalism brand of newspaper reporting that stresses excitement and shock over evenhandedness and dull fact. The term "yellow journalism" derived from the color of the ink used to print the first comic strip, which appeared in William Randolph Hearst's *New York Journal* in 1895. Hearst's newspaper specialized in yellow journalism and is often credited with igniting public passions for war with Spain in 1898.

Index

Diaz, Porfirio, 568
d'Iberville, Pierre Le Moyne, 101
Dickens, Charles, 290, 542
Dickinson, John, 114, 129–130, 142, 178
Dictatorships, 648, 721, 796
Diem, Ngo Dinh, 721, 758
Dien Bien Phu, 720–721, 758
The Diggers, 753
Dingley Tariff, 522
Diplomacy, 586, 793, 811
   atomic diplomacy, 677–678, *678*
   Big Three diplomacy, 673
   Confederate, 368
   Indian diplomacy, 452
   in Latin America, 653
   moral diplomacy, 568–570, *569m*
   pivotal events of World War II, 678
   progressive, 566–568, *569m*, 589
Disarmament, 586, 614, 767, 793, 807–808
A Discourse Concerning Westerne Planting
   (Hakluyt), 40
Discrimination, 330, 472–473, 694, 719, 810
   against African Americans, 669–671
   against Asian Americans, 666–667
   immigration laws, 492, *492*, 666
   against Latinos, 735–736, *736*
   persistence under New Deal, *640*,
     640–641
Disease, 380, 664. *See also* Epidemics; *specific*
   diseases
   biotic invasions, 453
   in colonies, 65, 78, 101
     domesticated animals and, 11–13
     land abandoned due to, 81–83
     virgin soil epidemics, 33
   environmental causes of, 296
   influenza pandemic, 582–584, *583m*
   in urban slums, 489, 539
   during World War II, 660, 664
Disease frontier, 315, *317m*
Disenfranchisement, 403, 410, 519–520, 550
   all-white primaries, 670–671
   in New South, 428, *428*
Distinguished Flying Cross, 661
District of Columbia, 337, 338
Divine, M. J. ("Father Divine"), 627
Dix, Dorothea, 280, *280*, 377
Dixiecrats, 697
Dixon, John, *137*
DNC (Democratic National Committee), 560,
   642, 779
Doar, John, 738–739
Dodd, Samuel C. T., 466
Dodd-Frank Act, 833–834
Dodge, Gen. Grenville, 442
Dollar diplomacy, 567–568
Domestic servants, 297
   strikes by, 476
   women as, 460, 471, 623, 643
Domesticity, 719
Dominican Republic, 16, 30, 567, 568, *569m*,
   815, 816
Dominion of New England, 87–88
Donaldson, Israel, 341
Donora, Pennsylvania, *693*, 694
Do-nothing Congress, 697
"Don't ask; don't tell," 818–819
Douglas, Aaron, 604

Douglas, Sen. Stephen A., 334, 357, *357m*
   Compromise of 1850 and, 335–338
   debates with Lincoln, *355*, 355–356, 361
   Freeport Doctrine, 355–356, 361
   popular sovereignty and, 341, 348, 350, 351,
    354
Douglass, Esther, 409
Douglass, Frederick, 286, *286*, 307, 309, 373,
   412, 783, *783*
Doyle, James, 341
Doyle, Mahala, 341
Draft, 375, 378
   Selective Service System, 761
   World War I, 575–576, 581
   World War II, 656
Drake, Sir Francis, *32m*, 41
Drayton, William Henry, 173
Dred Scott decision, *353*, 353–354, 361
Dreiser, Theodore, 542
Dresden, bombing of, *689*
Drew, Dr. Charles, 661
Drinker, Elizabeth, 150, 175
Drugs, 754, 766
   AIDS epidemic and, 810
   counterculture and, 752, 753, 754
   genetically engineered, 802
   psychedelics, 752, *752*, 753
Du Bois, W. E. B., 550, 603, 604
"Duck and Cover," *692*
Due process protections, *747*, 747–748
Dukakis, Gov. Michael, 806, 823
Duke, James, 423
Duke, Washington, 423
Dulles, Foster Rhea, 704
Dulles, John Foster, 719–720, *720m*,
   721, 722
Dumbarton Oaks conference, 677
Dumbbell tenements, *489*, 489–490
Dunkirk, 656
Dunmore, Lord, 143, *157*, 157–158
DuPont, 693
Durand, Asher, *252*
Dürer, Albrecht, *58*
Dust Bowl, 625
Dutch Reformed Church, 84
Dutch West India Company, 72–73, 84
Dyer, John, 105
Dylan, Bob, 752–753
Dysentery, 53, 380, 660

E

E. C. Knight Company, 468
Eads, James B., 456
Eads Bridge, 456
Earl, Harley, 706–707
Early civilizations, 1–19, *8m*
Early cultures, 15, *17m*
Early republic, 188–221
   economy of
     Hamilton's financial program, 193–196
     semisubsistence *vs.* commercial, 191–193,
      192m
   emergence of political parties in, 196–203
   French Revolution and, 197, *197*, 216, 217
   Indians in, 205, 206–208, 208–210, *209m*
   neutrality of, 197
   roles of women in, 202–203

Second Great Awakening (*See* Great
   Awakening)
second war for independence, 210–216,
   212m
   Whiskey Rebellion, 188–189, *189*
Earth Day, 775, *775*
Earth Summit, 809
Earthen mounds, 1–2
East Coryell Company, *596*
East Germany, 728, 806, 807, *807*
East India Company, 133, 135, 143, 144
Eastern Europe, 689–691, *690*, 722
Eastern woodlands cultures, 5–6, 13,
   14, 15
Eastman Kodak Company, 458
Ecology(ies), 486, 775
   disappearance of open space, 711
   Dust Bowl, 625
   of Great Plains, 428–429, *430m*, 452
   of Trans-Mississippi West, 429–431, *430m*,
    445
E-commerce, 823
Economic Growth and Tax Reform
    Reconciliation Act (EGTRRA) of
    2001, 827
Economic inequality, 833–834
Economic nationalism, 837
Economic Opportunity Act of 1964, 745
Economic policy, 172
Economic Recovery Tax Act (ERTA) of 1981,
   799
Economic stimulus package, 833
Economy, 693, 705, 796
   of 1920s, 593–598
     automobile industry, 594
     big business, 595
     construction industry, 593–594
     consumer culture, 598, *598*
     consumer economy, 592, 593
     energy from fuel oils, 594–595, *596*
     welfare capitalism, 596
   boost in, 676
   Civil War, 374, 376–377, *377*
   colonial, 126, 171–172
     53–54, 59–60
     Caribbean colonies, 64, *64*
     Chesapeake Bay colonies, *55m*
   contractions in
     bank war and, 262
     depression of 1837–1843, 354
     depressions, 516, 518, *518*, 537
     Great Depression (*See* Great Depression)
     Panic of 1819, 243–244, 249, 261, 267
     Panic of 1837, 223, 237
     Panic of 1857, 354
     Panic of 1873, 412
   of early republic
     Hamilton's financial program, 193–196
     Jefferson's policies, 204
     semisubsistence *vs.* commercial, 191–193,
      192m
   Eisenhower's policies, 715
   expansion of, 224–229, 249
     boom-and-bust cycles, 223, 243, *243*
     communications revolution, 228
     cotton cultivation, 295, *296–297*
     cotton trade, 225, *225*
     promotion of enterprise, 229

Foreign policy, 614, 688. *See also specific presidents*
   of conservative era, 796, 806–811, 812
   human rights and, 796
   in suburban era, 719–724, 726–729
Foreign Relations Committee, 587
Formosa (Taiwan), 698, 720, 720*m*, 725, 767
Forrestal, James, 687
Fort Bent, 256
Fort Caroline, 39, 50
Fort Detroit, 100
Fort Donelson, 369, *369m*
Fort Duquesne, 117
Fort Frontenac, capture of, 119*m*, 121
Fort Henry, 369, *369m*
Fort Kearny, Wyoming, 433*m*, 437
Fort Laramie, 322
Fort McHenry, 213
Fort Mims, 213
Fort Necessity, 117, 118
Fort Orange, 73
Fort Pitt, 123, 189
Fort Stevens, 651
Fort Sumner, 431, 437
Fort Sumter, 358
Forten, James, 201
Fossil fuels, 837
Foster, Capt. Samuel, *399*
Foster, Eugene A., 219–220
"Four Freedoms," 676
Fourier, Charles, 283, 290
Fourier, Joseph, 470
Fourteen Points, 582, 584, *584, 586*
Fourteenth Amendment, 416, A-8
   equal protection clause, 427, 735, 736
   ratification of, *398*
   Reconstruction and, 401–403, 411–412, 416
Fourth Amendment, A-7
Fox, Samuel, *259*
Foxe, John, 76, *76*
Foxholes, 661
Fragging, 766
Framework Convention on Climate Change, 836
France, 25, 27, 368, 386, 656, 720, 722, 765
   alliance with American rebels, 151, 199
   colonization in North America, 71–75
      maps of, 74*m*
   engaged in piracy, 39
   explorations in North America, 37
   French Revolution, 197, *197, 216, 217*
   Louisiana Purchase, 206, 207*m*
   rivalry with Britain, 102, 117
   war with Great Britain, 210
Franchise, 405
Francis I, King of France, 27
Franciscan missionaries, 49, 50–51, 94, *94*
   in California, 95, 98
   in New Mexico, 49
Franco, Generalissimo Francisco, 655
Franklin, Abraham, 393
Franklin, Benjamin, 103, 110, 111, 112, 119, 249, 486
   at Constitutional Convention, 179
   Declaration of Independence and, 143, *144*
   negotiates Treaty of Paris, 159
   negotiations with France, 151
Franquelin, Jean Baptiste Louis, 74*m*

Franz Ferdinand, Archduke of Austria-Hungary, 570–571
Fredericksburg, Battle of, 370, *371m*
Free silver movement, 518, 519
Free Soil Party, 335, 338, 350
Free Speech Movement, 749–750
Free State Hotel, 341
Freedmen, 372–373, 416–417
   black codes and, 400
   employment of, 309, 407–410
   minstrel shows, 259
   in North, 256–257, 257*m*
   in Old South, 309–310, *310*
Freedmen's Bureau, *398*, 401, 407–408, *413*
Freedmen's Bureau schools, *413*
Freedmen's Courts, 401, 408
Freedmen's Memorial Monument, 783, *783*
Freedom of speech, 581
Freedom riders, *738*, 738–739, 743*m*, 750
Freedom Summer, 741, 749, *749*, 772
Free-enterprise democracy, 719
Freeman's Farm, battle of, 150
Freemanship, 79
Freemasons, 249
Freeport Doctrine, 355–356, 357
Frémont, John C., *289*, 352, *352*, 353
French, Daniel Chester, *507*
French Revolution, 197, *197*, 216, 217
Freud, Sigmund, 599
Frick, Henry Clay, 478
Friedan, Betty, 771–772, 773
Frontier, 68
   life in backcountry, 103, *103*
   Northwest Territory, 168–170, 169*m*
   settlement of, 104*m*, *168*, 205
Frowne, Sadie, 470
FTP (Federal Theater Project), 645
Fuchs, Klaus, 698, 700
Fuel Administration, 578
Fuel oils, 594–595, *596*
Fugitive Slave Law of 1793, 335
Fugitive Slave Law of 1850, 338
Fulbright, Sen. William, 762
Fuller, Margaret, 281, 282
Fulton, Robert, 227
Fundamental Constitutions, 64
Fundamentalism, 608–610, *609*, 712, *712*
The Fundamentals (Stewart & Stewart), 609
Fur trade, 72, *242*, 243
Fusionists, 519
FWP (Federal Writers Project), 644

G

Gadsden Purchase, 348
Gage, Gen. Thomas, 135, 140–141
Galbraith, John Kenneth, 716
Galloway, Joseph, 135
Galveston hurricane of 1900, 552
Gandhi, Mohandas K. (Mahatma), 618, 670, 737
Gang system of labor, 305, 409
Garcia, Dr. Hector, 694
Garcia, Gus, 735–736, *736*
Garcia, John, 650–651
Garcia, Pedro, 52
Gardoqui, Don Diego de, 176–177
Garfield, James B., 511, 512

Garrison, William Lloyd, *285*, 285–287, 310
Garvey, Marcus, 602–603
Gary, Judge Joseph E., 477
Gaspee (ship), 133
Gaspee Commission, 133, 135
Gates, Bill, 802
Gates, Gen. Horatio, 150, 155
Gates, Robert, *834*
Gay rights, 771, *771*, 790
Gaza Strip, 819
Gender, 666, 713, 810
   crisis of masculinity and, *536*, 536–537, *537*
   in language and political cartoons, 535–536, *536, 537*
   "manliness," 498–499, *499*, 536–537
   view of Spanish-American War, 535–536
Gender segregation, 322, 425–426
Genentech Corporation, 802
General Assembly (UN), 677, 831
General Electric, 596, 715, 799
General Federation of Women's Clubs, 543
General Motors, 595, 644, 663, 833
   Nader's suit against, 774
   in Suburban era, 706–707, 716
General Motors Acceptance Corporation, 598
Geneva Accords of 1954, 762
Geneva peace conference, 721
Genocide
   ethnic cleansing in Bosnia, 819
   Holocaust, 658, 676, *677*
   of Indians, 332
Genographic Project of National Geographic Society, 23
Gentlemen's agreements, 561, 567
Gentry, 61, 112
Geographic mobility, *230*, 230–231
Geography, 482
George, David Lloyd, 584
George, Henry, 467
George II, King of England, 67
George III, King of England, 131, 135, 142, 159, *164*, 229
   appointment of Pitt, 128, 129
   criticism of, 133, 138, 143
Georgia, 36, 66, 253, 403, 421
   founding of, 67
   public schools in, 296–297
   Sherman's march through, *384m*, 388
Germain, Lord George, 142, 148, 158–159
German Americans, 667
German immigrants, 86–87, 103, 344, 346, *347*
Germantown, battle of, 149*m*, 150
Germany, 676
   Berlin airlift, 689
   Berlin Wall, 728, 806, 807, *807*
   Third Reich, 625, 653, 655, 658
      division of, 675
      fall of, 671–672
   Weimar Republic, 618
   World War I, 575, 582, 584–586, 614, 646
      Central Powers, 571–572, 572*m*, 584–586
      spring offensive of 1918, 580, 582*m*
      submarine warfare, 570, 573, *573*, 574
Geronimo, 433*m*, 437
Gerry, Elbridge, 177–178
Gettysburg, Battle of, 380, 381, 383, *384m*
Ghent, Treaty of, 214–215

Guiana, 306
Guilford Courthouse, battle of, 155, 156*m*
Gulf War, 808
Guns, 315, 317*m*, 381, 523, 805, *805*
Gypsies, extermination of, 658, 676

H

Habeas corpus, writ of, 367, 375-376, 378, 414
Haber, Al, 749
Hadden, Briton, 601
Hadley chest, 107
Haight-Ashbury, 753
Haiphong, North Vietnam, 760*m*, 777
Haiti, 16, 30, 201, 206, 216, 305, 403, 568, *569m*
Hakluyt, Richard, 40-41
Haldeman, H. R., 778
Haldeman, Robert, 766
Hall, Basil, *304*
Hamilton, Alexander, 178, 180, 189, 197, 375, *375*
  attempts to manipulate vote, 198
  doctrine of implied powers, 229
  The Federalist Papers, 180, 182
  leadership of Federalist party, 194, 198, 216
  as secretary of treasury, 193-196, *195, 196*, 199, 200, 204
Hammond, Sen. James Henry, 295, 299, 305, 354
Hancock, John, 130, *144*
Hancock, Thomas, 114
Handsome Lake, 208
Hanging chads, 822, *822*
Hanna, Marcus Alonzo, 519, 520
Hanover Street Church, 269, 270, 278
Hanson, Ole, 588
Harding, Warren G., 589, 611, *611*
Hariot, Thomas, 41
Harlan, Justice John Marshall, 427
Harlem (NYC), 486
Harlem Renaissance, *603,* 603-604, *604*
Harmar, Gen. Josiah, 205
Harper, William, 260, 261
Harpers Ferry, *356,* 356-357, *371m*
Harper's Illustrated Weekly, 406, 415
Harper's magazine, 681
Harrington, Michael, 745
Harris, Emily Lyles, 374
Harrison, Benjamin, *511,* 512, *513,* 516
Harrison, William Henry, 210, 213, 265, 265*m*, 321, 322, 512
Hart, Frederick, 784
Hartford Convention, *213,* 214
Harvard Divinity School Address, 281
Hassam, Childe, *571*
Hastings, Max, 683
Havana, Battle of, 119*m*, 121
Hawaii, 525, 530*m*, 657, 667
  annexation of, 526, 529, 532
  sugar cultivation in, 526, *526*
Hawkins, Benjamin, *166*
Hawthorne, Nathaniel, 281, 282
Hay, John, 526, 531, 532, 533
Hayakawa, Sen. S. I., 796
Hayden, Casey, 772
Hayden, Tom, 749

Hayes, Rutherford B., 414, *416,* 417
  election of 1876 and, 414, *416,* 417, 511
  presidency of, 419, 459, 476, 512
Haymarket Square Riot of 1886, *456,* 477, 478, *640*
Hayne, Sen. Robert, 260, 290
Hay-Pauncefote Treaty, 526
Hazard, Ebenezer, 112
Health care reform, 820, *820,* 833-834
Health insurance, 838
Hearst, William Randolph, 527, 535
Helsinki summit, 793
Hemings, Betty, 218, 221
Hemings, Beverly, 218
Hemings, Eston, 218, 219-220, 221
Hemings, Harriet, 218
Hemings, Madison, 218, 219, 220, 221
Hemings, Sally, 218-221, *220*
Hemingway, Ernest, 602
Hemp, 295*m*
Henry ("the Navigator"), 27-28, 30
Henry, Patrick, 127, *127,* 161, 182, 310
Henry VII, King of England, 25, 27
Henry VIII, King of England, 39-40
Henson, Matthew, 498
Hepburn Railway Act of 1906, 555
Herald of Freedom, 341
Hernandez, Ester, *824*
Hernández, Pete, 735-736, *736*
Hernández v. Texas (1954), 735-736, *736,* 748, 768
Herrera, Juan José, 436
Hessian mercenaries, 146, 149-150
Hetch Hetchy Valley, 556
Hickok, Lorena, *620,* 620-621
Hidatsa Indians, *314-315,* 315, *451*
High school shootings, 840
Higher education, 501, *501. See also specific institutions*
  black colleges, 501, 521, *521*
  GI Bill of Rights, 696-697
  for women, *501,* 502, 600
Highland Scots immigrants, 102
Highway Safety Act of 1966, 774
Highway Trust Fund, 710
Hill, Anita, 809
Hillsborough, Lord, 130
Hinds, Josiah, 302
Hine, Lewis, 472, *472*
Hirabayashi, Gordon, 669
Hiroshima, 678, *678, 681*
Hispanics. *See* Latinos
Hispaniola, 16, 30, 31, 61, 305
"Hispanos," 428, 436, 439
Hiss, Alger, 698, 700
History of the Standard Oil Company (Tarbell), 542
Hitler, Adolf, 589, 625, 629, *654,* 658, 676
  appeasement of, 655, *655,* 687
  miscalculation on D-Day, 672
  U.S. neutrality legislation and, 653-654
Hitler Youth, *654*
Hmong people, 816, *817*
Ho Chi Minh, 720, 758, *759,* 763
Ho Chi Minh Trail, 759, 760*m*
Hoe, Richard, 228
Hoe, Robert, 228
Hoganson, Kristin, 535

Hogarth, William, *110*
Hohokam culture, 5, 8*m,* 10, 14, 15, 429
Holding companies, 464, 466
Hollywood Ten, *601,* 699-700
Holmes, Justice Oliver Wendell, Jr., 498, 541, 580, 581, 588
Holmes, Oliver Wendell, Sr., 498
Holocaust, 658, 676, *677*
Home Insurance Building, 488
Home Owners' Loan Act of 1934, 631
Home Relief Station (Ribak), *628*
Homer, Winslow, *500*
Homespun, 159
Homestead Act, 376, *420,* 430, 444
Homestead Steel Strike, *456,* 541
Homestead Steel Works, 465
Homosexuals, 499, 676
  AIDS epidemic, 810, *810*
  service in military, 661, 818
Honduras, 4
Hong Kong, China, 332
Hooker, Gen. Joseph ("Fighting Joe"), 370, 383
Hooker, Isabella Beecher, 288
Hooker, Thomas, 80, 86
Hookworm, 304
Hoover, Herbert, 578, 611, 612, 627, 633, 682
  election of 1928 and, 614-615, 614*m*
  election of 1932 and, 629-630, *630*
  presidency of, 627-630, 648, 653
Hoover, J. Edgar, 701, 791
Hoover Dam, 640
Hoovervilles, *623*
Hopewell culture, 2, 6, 8*m*
Hopewell Plantation, *301,* 309
Hopkins, Harry, 620, 631, 636, 637
Hopkins, Johns, 501
Horizontal combination, 464
Horses, 442, 453, 503
  horse frontier, 315, 317*m*
  horse-drawn railways, 486
  mobility of Plains Indians and, 206, 429, *452*
Horseshoe Bend, Battle of, 213
Hostage crisis in Iran, 797, 798
Hostages, 805
House, Edward M., 568, 573
"House Divided" (Lincoln), 355
House of Burgesses (Virginia), 53, 127
House of Commons, 112, 113
House of Lords, 112, *112,* 113
House of Morgan, 615
House of Representatives, 195, 290, 348, 366
House Un-American Activities Committee (HUAC), 645, 698-699, *699,* 700
Housing market, 832
Houston, Charles, 734
Houston, Sam, 319, *319*
How the Other Half Lives (Riis), 542, *543*
Howard, John Langley, *640*
Howard, Josephine, 306
The Howdy Doody Show, 712
Howe, Adm. (Lord) Richard, 148-149
Howe, Maj. Gen. William, 141, 148-149, 151
Howe, Samuel Gridley, 280
Howl (Ginsberg), 718
HUAC (House Un-American Activities Committee), 645, 698-699, *699,* 700

Nagasaki, 678
Naismith, James, 503
Nanboa, Don Pedro, 52
Napoleon I (Bonaparte), 206, 211, 212, 213, 216, 290
Napoléon III, Emperor of France, 383
Narragansett Indians, 81, 83
Narváez, Pánfilo de, 35
Nasser, Gamal Abdel, 722
Nast, Thomas, 399
Nat Turner's Rebellion, 306, 309, 310, 312
Natchez Indians, 14, 17, 75, 101
Nation of Islam, 741
National American Woman Suffrage Association, 546-547
National Association for the Advancement of Colored People (NAACP), 550, 603, 641, 669, 694, 738
    attacks on Jim Crow laws, 734
    Montgomery bus boycott and, 736, 738
    National Association of Colored Women, 521
National Association of Manufacturers, 525, 596
National Birth Control League, 599
National Climate Program Office, 800
National Consumers' League, 542, 544, 553
National debt, 193, 204, 576, 803
National Defense Education Act of 1958, 724
National Energy Program, 795
National Environmental Policy Act of 1969, 775
National Geographic Society, 23
National Guard, 478, 574, 576, 644, 741
    at Kent State, 757
    in Little Rock, Ark., 737, 737
National Industrial Recovery Act (NIRA), 633
National Interstate and Defense Highway Act of 1956, 709, 715
National Labor Relations Act of 1935, 638, 645
National Labor Relations Board (NLRB), 638
National Labor Union (NLU), 474
National League of Professional Baseball Clubs, 503
National Municipal League, 513
National Negro Business League, 522
National Organization for Women (NOW), 772, 790
National Origins Act of 1921, 606-607
National Origins Act of 1924, 606-607, 746
National parks, 556, 784
The National Police Gazette, 504
National Recovery Administration (NRA), 633, 638, 642, 645
National Republican party, 249, 251
National Rifle Association, 820
National Security Council (NSC), 701, 729
National Socialist (Nazi) Party, 589, 629, 646, 653
National Trades' Union, 236
National Traffic and Motor Vehicle Safety Act of 1966, 774
National Tuberculosis Association, 542
National Union for Social Justice, 637
National War Garden Commission, 578
National War Labor Board (NWLB), 578-579
National Wilderness Preservation System Act of 1964, 746

National Woman Suffrage Association, 411, 510, 600
National Youth Administration (NYA), 637, 641, 671
Nationalism, 225, 571, 589, 719-724
    economic, 837
    ethnic and national, 838
Nationalist Party (China), 652, 657, 698
Native Americans. *See* Indian(s); *specific tribes*
Nativism, 330, 347, 350, 492, 492, 548, 606, 606-607
NATO (North Atlantic Treaty Organization), 691, 698, 700, 727m, 819, 837
Natural resources, 329, 416, 429, 524m, 556
    global scramble for, 416, 448
    industrial technology and, 456-457
    preservation in pristine state, 556, 557
Naturalized citizenship, 199
Nauvoo, Illinois, 284, 284-285
Navajo Indians, 14, 20, 50, 325, 429, 431-432, 437, 642
Naval blockades, 210, 212, 368, 368, 572, 728-729
Navalism, 523
Navigation Acts, 6, 55-56, 87
Navy. *See* U.S. Navy
Nazi (National Socialist) Party, 589, 629, 646, 653
Nebraska, 447
Nebraska Territory, 349m, 350
Necessary and proper clause, 196, 229
Negro Baptist Church, 409
"The Negro Speaks of Rivers" (Hughes), 604-605
Neiman, Fraser D., 220
Nelson, Sen. Gaylord, 775
Neo-isolationism, 689
Neolin (Delaware holy man), 123
Net neutrality, 823
Netherlands, 78, 104m, 386, 656
    as key economic power, 72-73
    New Netherland colony, 84
    in slave trade, 57, 64
Neutrality Act of 1935, 654
Neutrality Act of 1937, 655
Nevada, 7, 329
Neville, Gen. John, 188-189
Nevis, 60
New Amsterdam, 69, 73
"A New Captain in the District" (cartoon), 560
New Deal, 676, 698, 705
    accomplishments of, 647, 648
    early years of, 630-636
    effect on American people, 639-645
    end of, 646-647
    later years of, 636-639
New England, 87-88. *See also* Congregational Church
    colonial, 75-78, 77m
        conflict among communities, 80-81
        stability and order in, 79-83
        witchcraft in, 81, 82
        textile mills in, 232, 233, 233-234, 234
New England Emigrant Aid Company, 341
New England Kitchen, 542
New England militia, 146

New Era (1920s), 591, 591-618, 607m
    clash of values in, 605-611
    economy, 593-598
    evangelism, 591-592, 592
    rise of Republican Party, 611-615
    society of, 598-605
    stock market, 615-618
New Federalism, 777-778
New France, 71-75, 86
    in eighteenth century, 117
    maps of, 74m, 93m
New Freedom, 559-560, 560-561
New Guinea, 659, 674m
New Hampshire, 79, 86
New Harmony, Indiana, 283, 290
New Haven, 80, 259, 459
New Jersey, 84, 86, 468, 560
New Jersey Plan, 178-179
New Journalism, 752
New Mexico, 66, 316, 318, 329, 335, 337, 338, 437, 448, 606
    mesoamerican cultures, 14
    as Spanish colony (*See* New Spain)
New Nationalism, 559, 576-577
The New Negro (Locke), 605
New Netherland colony, 84, 86
New Orleans, Battle of, 214-215
New Orleans, Louisiana, 231, 296, 403, 486, 613m, 832, 832
    access to port of, 166-167
    capture of, 68, 369m
New Orleans Tribune, 409
New South, 420-422, 447-448
    daily life in, 425-427
    industry in, 423, 423, 425
    sources of poverty in, 424-425
    tenancy and sharecropping, 421-422, 422m
New Spain
    crisis in, 92-99, 93m
    Oñate's efforts, 47-49, 48
    Pueblo revolt, 50-51, 52
    siege of Acoma Pueblo, 48, 48-49
New York Central Railroad, 343, 462m
New York City, 363-364, 482, 483, 488, 579, 817
    bankruptcy crisis, 793
    colonial, 104, 105, 148-149
    population growth, 230-231
    Tammany Hall, 482, 490
New York City Draft Riots, 378-379, 392, 392-395
New York City Welfare Council, 622
New York Daily News, 793, 793
New York & Erie Railroad, 461
New York Giants, 753
New York Herald, 511
New York Journal, 527, 535
New York State, 84, 86, 589, 610, 748
New York Stock Exchange, 459, 615, 616
New York Times, 393, 729, 779, 788, 795
New York Times v. Sullivan (1964), 748
New York Tribune, 393, 395, 412
New York World, 393
Newfoundland, 18, 25
Newlands, Sen. Frederick, 556
Newton, Huey, 741, 771
Nez Percé Indians, 432-435, 433m, 437
Nez Percé War, 437

R

Rabin, Itzak, 819
Race, 96–97, 253–260, 304–305, 439, *439*, 530
"Race music," 718
Race riots, 259, 401–403, 553, 641, 670
  Houston, Texas, 576
  Ku Klux Klan and, *610*
  Springfield, Ill., 550
  Watts riots, *741,* 741–742, 743*m*
  during World War I, 579–580
  Zoot suit riots, 670, *671*
Racial nationalism, 838
Racialism, 448, 519–520
Racism, 61, 302, 373, 405, 413
  in Jacksonian era, *259,* 259–260
  Manifest Destiny and, 316, 318
  minstrel shows and, 259
Radical Republicans, 398–399, 401–404, *403,*
    407, 412, *413,* 416, 417
Radicalism, *588,* 588–589, *829*
Radicals, 477, 478, 579, 606, *606, 640*
Radio, 600–601, 602, 614, 631
  Christian broadcasting, 787, 789
  golden age of, 623–624
  Voice of America, 704
"Radio Priest," 637
Radioactivity, 678, *691, 795, 796*
RAF (Royal Air Force), 656
Ragtime music, 504–505
Raguieneau, Paul, 73
Railroad brotherhoods, 474
Railroad land grants, 441–442
Railroads, *227,* 227–228, 230, *444,* 447, 479,
    513, *513*
  cross-country rail travel, 454–455, *455*
  growth of railroad economy, 342–344, *343,*
    345*m*
  incompatible track gauges, 345*m,* 423, 455
  late 19th and early 20th century, 458,
    461–463, *462m,* 465
  near-extinction of bison and, 451–452
  regulation of, 555
  strikes, 475, 665, 695
    Great Railroad Strike of 1877, 476, 518
    Pullman Strike of 1894, *478,* 478–479,
      522
  transcontinental, 441–442, 441*m,* 479
  western land rush and, 429–430
Raleigh, Sir Walter, 25, 32*m,* 40–42, *41*
Rancheros, 318
Randall, Henry, 219
Randall's grocery stores, 814
Randolph, Ellen Coolidge, 219
Randolph, Martha Jefferson, 218
Randolph, Thomas Jefferson, 219
Range wars, 442
Rankin, Jeannette, 575
Rankin, Rep. John, 699
Ranney, William, *156*
Rape, 150, 627
Rational Christianity, 110
Rationing, *663*
Ray, James Earl, 764
Rayburn, Sam, 724
Raymondi, Bob, 698
REA (Rural Electrification Administration),
    639–640, *640*

Reader's Digest Condensed Books, 717
Reagan, Ronald, 700, 807
  election of 1980 and, 787, 789, 798, 798*m*
  election of 1984 and, 805
  opposition to Panama Canal treaty, 796
  opposition to SALT II, 793
  as president, 787, 789, 798–803, 810, 811,
    812
Reapers, 343, 360, 522
Rebates, 463
Reclamation Act of 1902, 556
"Reconcentration" camps, 527
Reconquista, 30
Reconstruction, 396–417, *413*
  abandonment of, 410–416
  African Americans (*See* African
    Americans)
  congressional plan, 403–405, *404m*
  effects on South, 405–407
  global perspective of, 416
  players in, *413*
  presidential plans, 398–403
Reconstruction Act, 403
Reconstruction Finance Corporation (RFC),
    628
Red baiting, 698, 700
Red Guards, 765
Red Horse, *434*
Red Menace, *688*
Red River Wars, 433*m,* 437
"Red scare," 478, *588,* 588–589, 699, 700
Red summer of 1919, 579
Redbook magazine, 713
Redeemers, *413,* 414, 426–427, 520
Red-light districts, 440, 549
Reed, Henry Armstrong, *434*
Reform Act of 1832 (Gr. Britain), 249
Reform Bill of 1832 (Gr. Britain), 312
Reform movements, 37–40, 290
  abolitionist (*See* Abolitionist movement)
  American Renaissance and, 281–282, *282*
  efforts at moral reform, 269–270, *270*
  party system and, 288–290, *289,* 290
  radical reform, 285–288
  Transcendentalism, 281
  Unitarian contributions, *280,* 281
Reformation, 39–40
Reformers, 236–237, 435, 510, 540–541, 542
Refugees, 676, 815, 816, *817*
Regnier, Nicolas, 29
Rehnquist, Chief Justice William, *809*
Reilly, William J., *577*
Reliance Building, 488
Relief
  for farmers in 1920s, 613
  during Great Depression, 627, 631–633
  Great flood of 1927, 613–614, 613*m*
  as private matter, 627
Religion, 429, 510, 751
  ban on school prayer, 748
  camp meetings, 445 (*See also* Camp
    meetings)
  churches (*See* Churches)
  evangelicalism (*See* Evangelicalism)
  evangelism, 492, 591–592, *592*
  as factor in 1960 election, 724–725
  Great Awakening (*See* Great Awakening)

  of immigrants, *768,* 769, 818
  missionaries (*See* Missionaries)
  in New England colonies, *80,* 80–81
  political views and, 266–267
  Protestant Reformation, 37–40
  Puritan movement, 75–76, *76*
  revivalism, 111, 492
  social programs and, 492–493
  society under control of, 332–333
  in South, 299, 308–309
  in suburban era, 712, *712*
  surge of conservatism in, 798
  utopian communities, 284
  in West, *418,* 445
  witchcraft, 27, 28, *28,* 81, 82
Religiosity, 719
Religious art, 95
Remington, Frederick, *478, 534*
Reno, Janet, 819, 821
"Repatriation," 625–626, *626*
Representation, 128–129, 179
Representative governments, 126
Republic of China, 568, *569m*
Republic of Haiti, 249
Republic of Panama, 565, *565m*
Republic of Texas, 319, 320*m,* 321,
    336, 339
Republic Steel Company, 644
Republican Guards, 808
Republican motherhood, 176
Republican National Convention, 357, 715
Republican party (Jeffersonian), 198, 200,
    203–310, 216–217
  beginnings of, 194, 197–198
  differences from Federalists, 205
  election of 1796 and, *198*
  election of 1800 and, 200*m,* 203
  election of 1808 and, 210
  Federalist repression and, 199
  War Hawks, 211–212
Republican Party (modern), *289*
  disagreement over foreign policy, 698–699
  effects of Civil War on, 391
  election of 1856 and, 352–353
  party loyalty, 509–510
  Radical Republicans, 398–399, 401–404,
    403, 407, 416, 417
  reaction to *Dred Scott* decision, 354
  reaction to Emancipation Proclamation,
    372
  during Reconstruction, 400–401, 405, *411,*
    412, *413,* 414
    Radical Republicans, *403,* 407, 412, 416,
      417
    Reconstruction Acts of, 403–405
  rise of, in 1920s, 611–615
  as target of NYC Draft Riots, 394–395
Republicanism, 126, 715, 750
  election of 1864 and, 385
  views on property, 170–171
Reservations, 431–432, 434, 435, 436, *642,*
    770
Resettlement Administration, 636
Restraint of trade, 466
Restrictive housing covenants, 697, 709
Reuben James (U.S. destroyer), 657
Revels, Hiram, *407*
Revenue Act (1764), 125